Italian Crime Filmography,
1968–1980

Italian Crime Filmography, 1968–1980

ROBERTO CURTI

McFarland & Company, Inc., Publishers
Jefferson, North Carolina, and London

All photographs are courtesy of the *Nocturno Cinema* archives except as noted.

LIBRARY OF CONGRESS CATALOGUING-IN-PUBLICATION DATA

Curti, Roberto, 1971–
Italian crime filmography, 1968–1980 / Roberto Curti.
p. cm.
Includes bibliographical references and index.

ISBN 978-0-7864-6976-5
softcover : acid free paper ♾

1. Crime films—Italy—Catalogs. 2. Motion pictures—Italy—History—20th century. I. Title.
PN1995.9.C66C87 2013
791.43'6556—dc23 2013029109

BRITISH LIBRARY CATALOGUING DATA ARE AVAILABLE

Front cover: Italian posters for *Silent Action*, 1975 (courtesy *Cinema Nocturno* archive)

Manufactured in the United States of America

McFarland & Company, Inc., Publishers
Box 611, Jefferson, North Carolina 28640
www.mcfarlandpub.com

To my wife, my one and only love, Cristina.

Table of Contents

Preface

Since the early 1960s, Italian popular cinema delivered violence, transgression and excess in ever growing doses. It was a deliberate choice on the part of producers and filmmakers, in order to make their movies palatable for an audience whom they had to re-conquer since the growing diffusion of television in the country — the first broadcasts took place in 1954 — had provoked a hemorrhage of box office takings. It was also a way to characterize their products for foreign market sales. One such example was Mario Bava's *Black Sunday* (*La maschera del demonio*, 1960), which opened with an outstandingly violent scene where a witch played by Barbara Steele is tortured and put to the stake by her captors — a scene that includes the shot of a torture device — the "Mask of Satan" — being *nailed* to Steele's face by means of a huge hammer.

The path of violence (that mixed with an emphasis on eroticism in Gothic movies and mirrored another major tendency in Italian cinema, which grew parallel to the partial loosening of censorship) was further explored by what proved to be the most popular film genre in the decade, the so-called Spaghetti Western. Since the release of Sergio Leone's *A Fistful of Dollars* (*Per un pugno di dollari*, 1964) and Sergio Corbucci's *Django* (1966) — the second becoming a reference point for violence on screen in the genre due to its insistence on a macabre mood and scenes such as the one in which Django (Franco Nero) has his hands crushed by the villains so that he can't handle a gun any longer — outrageousness became a selling point.

It couldn't last too long. To quote Karl Marx, "History repeats itself, first in tragedy, then in farce." And the Spaghetti Western, which already contained the seeds of irony in itself since Leone's "Man with No Name" walked onto the screen, couldn't help but end in laughter, as shown by the enormous success of *They Call Me Trinity* (*Lo chiamavano Trinità...*, 1970).

After the decline of the Spaghetti Western, its place as Italy's most popular and controversial genre was taken by the crime film, which monopolized much of the frustrations and rage that were dominant among moviegoers at the time. The Seventies were a tough period in Italian history. Events of 1968 paved the way for extreme political tensions, which resulted in bomb blasts, kidnappings, terrorist attacks and even an aborted attempt at a coup d'état in December 1970. Crime films put all this on screen, within the exciting and rough boundaries of genre cinema. Some of them echoed the paranoid atmosphere of a country plagued with terrorism and corrupt secret services; others portrayed infamous real events with just minimal changes. These featured tough, hard-boiled, gun-crazy cops, ruthless and sadistic criminals, brutal violence, heists, shoot-outs and spectacular car chases in city streets. Critics hated them, yet audiences queued to watch them.

Italian critics started to call this sub-genre *poliziottesco* (plural: *poliziotteschi*, to be pronounced as polittsiot-teski), a diminutive name somehow similar to Spaghetti Western in reflecting an initial contempt for the genre. The term poliziottesco was a fusion of the words *poliziotto* (cop), and the suffix *-esco*, "related to," akin to the English "-esque." It had a negative connotation, compared to *poliziesco* (from polizia, "police"), which was the commonly used term for foreign crime and action films as well as police-related dramas. It was not just used in order to distinguish Italian crime flicks from their (supposedly much better) U.S. counterparts, but it actually implied a sarcastic sneer, a biased attitude. Yet, even though the influence of films such as *Dirty Harry* (1971, Don Siegel) or *The French Connection* (1971, William Friedkin) was evident, Italian crime films were the true descendants of Westerns, set in contemporary Italy — the violent, tormented Italy of the 1970s.

The renaissance of the crime film in the '70s was predated by such respected works as Elio Petri's Oscar-winning *Investigation of a Citizen Above Suspicion* (*Indagine su un cittadino al di sopra di ogni sospetto*, 1970) and Damiano Damiani's *Confessions of a Police Captain* (*Confessione di un commissario di polizia al Procuratore della Repubblica*, 1971), which mixed social commitment and genre cinema, became huge box office hits and were praised by critics. If Petri's film won an Academy Award and assertively used a *sui generis* crime plot for a reflection on power within contemporary Italy (a famous line has the Commissioner, played by Gian Maria Volonté, state "repression is civilization" — a darkly ironic hint at the repressive role of the police force against the 1968 Student Movement), *Confessions of a Police Captain* can be seen as the true antecedent of the poliziottesco, which according to many critics began in 1972 when Stefano Vanzina's *Execution Squad* (*La polizia ringrazia*) turned out a surprise hit, launching what would be one of the most popular genres of the decade, before the economic crisis that led to the death of the Italian popular movie industry in the 1980s took hold.

After *Execution Squad*, dozens of crime films flooded the screen during the following years. They were mainly modestly budgeted works, starring popular actors — some of them, such as Franco Nero or Tomas Milian, were veterans of the Western genre while others, such as Maurizio Merli, Luc Merenda and Franco Gasparri were relative newcomers — and were helmed by capable filmmakers, including Fernando di Leo, Enzo G. Castellari, Umberto Lenzi, Stelvio Massi.

Tough cops as played by Merli (the genre's icon), Merenda, Nero and others are hard yet deeply honest men — incorruptible, often penniless and unlucky in love, with just one thing in mind: justice. They always complain that their hands are tied by unjust (read: too liberal) laws, and their enemies are not just crooks and corrupt politicians, but also magistrates and lawyers who permit criminals to stay out of jail. Happy endings were not the norm, however. In poliziottesco the tough cop most likely does not survive in the end, as he is usually shot in the back in the middle of the street, just when everyone is ready for the end credits to roll.

The sub-genre was labeled as fascist by many critics of the time, who were unable to understand that one of the keys to its success was precisely the way it cunningly exploited the viewer's dissatisfaction and demand for justice, just like Italian Westerns captured their audience by exploiting violence and sadism, without any true political colors. In the same film one could find a cop deliver an almost fascist speech and later on speak of tolerance like a left-wing activist. What's more, the hero was almost always characterized as proletarian, whereas the villains were wealthy, powerful, and right-wing. The results were more likely apolitical, if not anarchist: not an uncommon trait in genre cinema.

Most of all, however, poliziotteschi gave moviegoers the heroes they were in desperate need of, by capturing and representing their anxiety and anger in a climate of urban violence, decaying institutions and armed struggle. These films depicted exemplary characters and stories, and told sharp parables of life and death. They offered a ninety-minute trip to hell and back, a cathartic path that allowed viewers to make sense of the horror and cruelty they had to face daily in real life, and the opportunity to walk out of the theatres with their heads held high, ignoring fears and anxieties in the hope that somewhere, somehow, someone would restore justice. That's why poliziotteschi are a very important, if not essential, chapter in the history of Italian popular cinema: their study is vital to understand not only the evolution and decline of a film industry (which in the 1980s collapsed after a long-term crisis which was heightened by the rise of commercial TV networks), but also the changing moods of the country that nurtured it.

Poliziotteschi — or, as they were commonly known abroad, Italo-crime, Euro-crime or simply Italian crime films — were moderately successful in foreign markets, but didn't attain the same diffusion as the Spaghetti Western. Many were released to home video — albeit in poorly dubbed, sometimes badly cut or re-edited versions — and gradually won over a cult status, especially when younger cinephiles started getting interested in European genre cinema. A turning point came when such popular filmmakers as Quentin Tarantino started championing the films by Lenzi, Castellari, and di Leo, and talked of these directors not as mere hacks but as out-and-out *auteurs*. Meanwhile, in Italy, poliziotteschi were experiencing a critical rediscovery and reevaluation, after the biased attitude that was commonplace among Italian film critics at the time of their release. This occurred also thanks to the work of fanzines and film magazines: most notably, *Nocturno Cinema*, a mag entirely devoted to Italian exploitation and genre films which featured interviews with a number of filmmakers who had been long forgotten and provided in-depth (if sometimes overtly partisan) essays on their works. The new attention brought about the re-release of many titles for the home video market by a number of labels, most notably Alan Young, NoShame and Raro Video, allowing the younger generations to finally find out what Eurocrime was about.

This book lists all the poliziotteschi produced and released in Italy between 1968 — a key year, with the release of Carlo Lizzani's *Bandits in Milan* (*Banditi a Milano*), which proved to be a turning point for Italian crime film — and 1980 — which saw its rapid decline — based on the films' release date in their home country. Also listed are those films that, even though they cannot be considered poliziotteschi in the strictest sense, are part of threads which often crossed paths with the typical police-related dramas, since a common practice in Italian genre cinema was to mix genres and try different approaches to the subject matter. Such are the Mafia movie, which germinated after politically committed dramas such as *We Still Kill the Old Way* (*A ciascuno il suo*, 1967, Elio Petri) and *The Day of the Owl* a.k.a. *Mafia* (*Il giorno della civetta*, 1968, Damiano Damiani) and was fortified by the commercial success of Francis Ford Coppola's *The Godfather* (1972); the *film noir*, which was often akin to poliziotteschi but in most cases displayed literary origins (such as the novels by Giorgio Scerbanenco, Italy's greatest hard-boiled novelist) and had in Fernando di Leo its most important exponent; and a peculiar hybrid which mixed the poliziotteschi's flair for urban violence with a typical form of Neapolitan-based play (the so-called *sceneggiata*) which even included songs, and was immensely popular in Southern Italy in the late 1970s. Besides, I'm also briefly discussing the role and evolution of the crime film in Italian post–World War II film industry, as well as the genre's struggle for survival in the 1990s and 2000s. On the other hand, parodies and out-and-out comedies where the crime element is just a tiny pretext are not listed in the book.

Each entry has a comprehensive crew and cast list that is as complete as possible, based on the film's opening and closing credits. Uncredited extras are also listed whenever possible, as those same faces would pop up again and again in an outstanding number of Italian films. Home video releases are also listed, with preference given to DVD releases. However, even though a number of Italian crime films are available on DVD and Blu-ray, many were released only on VHS, either in Italy or in foreign markets (especially Northern Europe). When a film is mentioned in the text for the first time, its English title comes first (if there was an English language release) followed by the original Italian one and the year. For those films that circulated only in Italy, a literal translation of the Italian title is provided.

As such, this volume is the most complete work in the English language dedicated to Italian crime films so far. My aim is to make each entry stand alone and be an interesting read in itself, as well as a piece of a larger mosaic, depicting a more complex view. My hope is that, after reading this book, the casual reader has developed not just an interest in the crime genre, but also a deeper understanding of Italian post–World War II history and costume. The information provided throughout the text is the result of a thorough research from a variety of sources such as academic texts and essays on Italian history and other assorted material — interviews with filmmakers and actors, newspaper reviews, original scripts — which is listed in the bibliography.

Finally, I would like to thank from the bottom of my heart Mario and Roderick Gauci from Naxxar, Malta, and Mark Ashworth, an English gentleman in Rome, for they had the patience and dedication to read and revise the manuscript; Manlio Gomarasca, editor-in-chief of *Nocturno Cinema*, who kindly provided pictures from the magazine's archives; Carlos Aguilar, who also helped me with beautiful rare pics; Vittorio Salerno, who kindly allowed me to use stills from his own personal archive; and soundtrack expert Emanuele Leotta, for helping with OST information.

My most sincere gratitude goes also to the following, who helped in one way or the other in the making of this book: Tom Betts, José Antonio Diego Bogajo, Pino Bruni, Davide Cavaciocchi, Davide Comotti, Matteo Di Giulio, Adriano "Magou" Di Gaspero, Alessio Di Rocco, Adrián Esbilla, Giovanni Ferrari, Ernesto Gastaldi, Sergio Grmek Germani, Gabriele Giuli, Gianluca Guaitoli, Tommaso La Selva, Gabrielle Lucantonio, Antonio José Navarro, Alberto Pezzotta, Tom Prickette, Davide Pulici, Donato Totaro, Tonino Valerii.

An Overview of Italian Crime Films, 1947–1967

The history of Italian crime cinema is deeply connected to that of the country that nurtured it, even going back to the very first examples of the genre. After the restrictions and escapist dreams of the Fascist period, the immediate post-war scenario was that of a nation in ruins. Neorealism showed a side of Italy that many — including the government — thought should be best forgotten. Bandits, pimps, black market dealers made their appearance in films that recounted what was happening in the country, without sweetening the pill.

That was the case with *Tombolo* (*Tombolo paradiso nero*, 1947, Giorgio Ferroni), *Manù il contrabbandiere* (1947, Lucio De Caro), Alberto Lattuada's *The Bandit* (*Il bandito*, 1946) and *Without Pity* (*Senza pietà*, 1948), which can all be considered part of the so-called "Black Neorealism." Even Giuseppe De Santis's *Bitter Rice* (*Riso amaro*, 1949), which blended Neorealist elements with others taken from various sources, featured several sequences — such as the final shoot-out in the butcher's shop, with sides of veal and livestock hanging from the ceiling, lit in an Expressionist manner — which were the stuff of out-and-out *film noir*.

Italy's most interesting early crime films of the 1940s and '50s were Pietro Germi's *Lost Youth* (*Gioventù perduta*, 1947) and *Four Ways Out* (*La città si difende*, 1951) and Fernando Cerchio's marvelous but little-known *Il bivio* (1951). Co-scripted by Germi and, among others, future film directors Antonio Pietrangeli and Mario Monicelli, *Lost Youth* depicts the exploits of a band of robbers headed by a wealthy young man above suspicion (Jacques Sernas). The film is notable for the character of a sympathetic commissioner (Massimo Girotti) who feels inadequate in his job and bitterly regrets having left university because of the war. Stylistically, Germi moved away from Neorealism: Hollywood products were flooding Italian cinemas as a result of post-war regulations (600 American films were distributed in Italian theaters in 1946 alone), and the influence of American *film noir* is evident in the way *Lost Youth* is shot and lit, as well as in the portrayal of a town that becomes magical at night, a mysterious double of itself.

The way characters dress, move and talk in *Lost Youth* definitely shows how Hollywood imagery colonized Italian cinema: Sernas refers to Alan Ladd (his trench coat is identical to the one worn by *This Gun's for Hire*'s Philip Raven) and Robert Mitchum, and buys expensive gifts for the nightclub dancer he's in love with, just as he has seen his movie heroes do. However, Germi does not shy away from realism: Italian censors were not fond of the way *Lost Youth* depicted post–War Italy: the film was initially denied a visa for public screening, and the decision was only revoked after a letter was sent to the then Secretary of State (and president of the Censorship Commission) Giulio Andreotti, signed by Germi and 30 other directors. However, the censors demanded a couple of scenes be cut, as *Lost Youth* was judged too pessimistic and demoralizing for viewers. One such scene featured a statistic lesson in college where the focus was on the rising wave of criminality in the country on the base of graphics, statistic datas and the mention real-life recent events; while another character compared old-time criminals to the new ones (the title's "lost youth"), who would even steal their mothers' dentures — a line the censors didn't like in the least.

Germi returned to the crime film four years later with *Four Ways Out*, the story of a holdup at a stadium and its tragic aftermath. The director focused on the stories of four desperate delinquents and their tragic attempts at escape through the city: it was once again the starting point for a harsh view of early '50s Italy, a country that was laboriously rising up from the ashes but still had to face many inner contradictions and problems. The opening holdup — a silent, masterfully edited sequence — shows Germi's perfect control of the medium, and the use of real locations and several semi-documentary sequences once again hint at the director's love for American *film noir* (namely, Jules Dassin's *The Naked City* and Elia Kazan's *Panic in the Streets*). Germi resorted to the crime genre, even more so than in *Lost Youth*, as a way to make poignant social commentary.

One of *Il bivio*'s most interesting aspects is casting. In a daring move, Raf Vallone — one of Italy's most popular actors of the decade and usually typecast as the hero — plays a gang leader who infiltrates the police, becomes a vice–

Commissioner and exploits his position to commit robberies, but his ambition to control and steer other people's actions is illusory. At the heart of the film (whose title means "the crossroads") is the protagonist's growing moral dilemma: the need to face the consequences of his behavior (innocent parties arrested, ruined families, colleagues killed in the line of duty). This division between self-interest and desire to atone eventually leads the (anti)hero to his death. Both *Four Ways Out* and *Il bivio* portray a country that is trying to get back on its feet after years of disarray following World War II, but whose deep lacerations are still visible; many ideals have already collapsed — in *Il bivio* Vallone is a disillusioned war hero — and the slow economic recovery already has claimed its victims. The mirage of easy money has corrupted consciences and ruined lives. Once again the censors were not happy — this time because the film supposedly portrayed a negative image of the police force in several scenes, such as the one where the guards who are escorting a shipment of valuables by train are shown playing cards, and the one where they are disarmed and lined up, hands up and face to the wall, by a gang of robbers. Another deleted scene showed a commissioner slapping an arrested man in the face during a questioning: an image which was to become iconic in the following decades.

Germi returned once again to the genre at the end of the '50s, with a picture that he himself labeled as "the first Italian crime film." Actually, *The Facts of Murder* (*Un maledetto imbroglio*, 1959) was more of a whodunit, loosely based on one of the greatest Italian novels of the twentieth century, Carlo Emilio Gadda's experiment in language *Quer pasticciaccio brutto de via Merulana*, published in 1957. It was a bold move on Germi's part to adapt the almost impossible-to-film novel by eliminating its most recognizable element — Gadda's complex use of dialectal language and interior monologue — while retaining its thematic core. The director mixed two apparently opposite genres — police drama and comedy — but it was not his intent to make a hybrid. On the contrary, funny or naturalistic moments at times openly clash with detection and action scenes. The result is a deeply moral film that is both desperate and sarcastic at the same time. Germi himself, in the role of Inspector Ingravallo, is an ideal lead with his stern features and peculiar accent. The director would portray a similar character in Damiano Damiani's directorial debut *Lipstick* (*Il rossetto*, 1960).

In the 1960s, filmmakers who were deeply involved with social and political issues, such as Francesco Rosi, Florestano Vancini and Carlo Lizzani, once again used the crime genre in order to analyze Italy's past and present alike. Thanks also to the loosening of censorship, it was easier to portray the country, its recent history and its problems without clashing with the commission's requests. Films like Lizzani's *The Hunchback of Rome* (*Il gobbo*, 1960), Duilio Coletti's *Black City* (*Il re di Poggioreale*, 1961, co-scripted by John Fante) and Florestano Vancini's *La banda Casaroli* (1962) examined well-known real-life episodes and characters, the most successful of the lot being *La banda Casaroli*, one of the best Italian films of the decade. Paolo Casaroli and his acolytes, a gang of improvised bandits in immediate post-war Italy, were emblematic figures of the period. Vancini's winning move was to cast Renato Salvatori against type as the titular lead. He was an actor more used to playing the love interest in comedies such as *Poor But Handsome* (*Poveri ma belli*, 1957) and Mario Monicelli's wonderful *Big Deal on Madonna Street* (*I soliti ignoti*, 1958).

La banda Casaroli can be seen as a rejection of the unpretentious, often politically unchallenging cinema made in the previous decade — a tendency driven and heightened by the suffocating censorship on the part of the country's leading party Democrazia Cristiana, as censorship boards would examine the scripts beforehand and had the power to influence the economic credit given to the producers by the state. The historical context is portrayed with elegance and extreme precision: old Fascist mottos painted on decaying tenements, rural strikes, empty streets with the occasional vehicle driving by — a symbol of wealth that everyone desires. Casaroli and his gang use cars in order to make easy escapes after their robberies, but in the end, ironically, it's an automobile that becomes a death trap for them when it's revealed that Casaroli can't drive.

Vancini does not absolve the characters, but he understands their reasons: the post-war confusion, the anti-bourgeois grievances, the mirage of an easy life. He portrays a generation of misfits in search of strong emotions, who are unable to submit to the logic of sacrifice and work that are needed to rebuild the country. Stylistically, *La banda Casaroli* is an extremely accomplished work, built around an elaborate flashback structure and featuring several outstanding sequences, such as the long central chase in the streets of Bologna. Interestingly, the last half-hour focuses on one of Casaroli's men, played by a young Tomas Milian, who desperately wanders around town after his boss has been arrested, and finally ends up in a cinema where he commits suicide while a newsreel announces the re-election of Democratic Christian premier Alcide De Gasperi — a further hint at Vanzini's political discourse.

The '60s, however, were a colored, chaotic decade for Italian cinema. Screens were flooded with erotic documentaries, Gothic flicks, earli *gialli*, Spaghetti Westerns, James Bond rip-offs. Most crime entries followed the latter thread, yet the connection between the fast-paced, multicolored spy yarns and the crime films of the following decade are vague at best. Even though filmmakers such as Sergio Sollima and Umberto Lenzi served their apprenticeship in the spy genre, these films' light-hearted, escapist tone was still a product of the euphoria raised by the economic boom of the early

Robert Hoffmann as Luciano Lutring, "the machine-gun soloist," in *Wake Up and Kill* (1966).

1960s, and their overall optimism was in stark contrast with the film industry's growing economic difficulties (which the explosion of Spaghetti Western could only partially hide). Moreover, despite the James Bond look-alikes' nonchalant recourse to weapons, violence was always hyperbolic, innocuous, comic book-like.

Meanwhile, the Italian underworld was changing. Carlo Lizzani examined two exemplary figures within a new generation of criminals spawned by the decade's delusions of wealth and well-being. *Wake Up and Kill* (*Svegliati e uccidi*, 1966) and *Bandits in Milan* a.k.a. *The Violent Four* (*Banditi a Milano*, 1968) were basically action movies with a strong sociological component, where the minute attention to the sociological prevailed over the spectacular hyperbole. Lizzani described an urban crime environment characterized by an individual and consumerist revenge, sometimes hidden under an ostensible social rebellion — and he did so with remarkable results. *Bandits in Milan*, released in such a crucial year as 1968, is in every way the landmark that would pave the way for 1970 crime films, and serves as an ideal starting point for this book.

Abbreviations

The following abbreviations are used in the credits list for each entry.

Crew

AArtD Assistant art director /Set designer / Set decorator
AC Assistant camera
ACO Costume assistant
AsE Associate editor
AcSc Acrobatic scenes
AD Assistant director
AE Assistant editor
AMU Assistant makeup
APD Production design assistant
AR Architect
ArtD Art director / Set designer Set decorator
ASDr Assistant set dresser
AW Assistant seamstress
B Boom man
C Camera
ChEl Chief electrician
ChG Chief grip
ChMU Chief makeup
CHOR Choreographer
CO Costumes
COA Assistant costumes / Costume assistant
CON Continuity
COper Camera operator
D Directed by
DC Dialogue coach
DCons Dialogue consultant
DD Dialogue director
DIA Dialogue
DIARev Dialogue revision
DM Dressmaker
DOP Director of photography
DubD Dubbing director
E Editing / Editor
Elec Electrician
1st AD 1st assistant director
G Grip / Head grip
GA Gaffer
Hair Hair stylist
KG Key grip
LD Lighting director
LT Lighting technician
M Music
MA Master of arms
MC Musical coordination
Mix Sound mixer
MU Makeup
PA Press attaché
PD Production designer
PDir Director(s) of photography
PrM Property master
PO Press office
S Story
SA Scenic artist
SC Screenplay
SC Screenplay collaboration
ScE Scenic effects
ScrA Script assistant
SD Set decoration
SDr Set dresser
2nd AD 2nd assistant director
2nd UD 2nd unit director
SE Special effects
SEE Special effects editor
SetD Set director / Set direction
SetP Set photographer
SetT Set Technician
SM Sound(s) Mixer
SO Sound
SOA Sound assistant
SOE Sound effects / Sound effects editor
SOEd Sound editor
SOEng Sound engineer
Songs Songs
SP Still photographer
SR Sound recordist / Sound recording
SS Script supervisor / Script girl
ST Stunts
STC Stunt coordinator / Stunt director
STD Stunt double
STDr Stunt driver
STDrC Stunt driving coordinator
STS Stunt supervisor
TAI Tailoring
TC Transportation / Transportation captain
UP Unit publicist
W Seamstress / Wardrobe
WD Wardrobe designer

Production

ADM Administrator
AP Associate producer
APM Assistant production manager
BMgr Business manager
CASH Cashier
DColl Direction collaborator
EP Executive producer
FD Financial director
GM General manager
GO General organization
PA Production assistant
PAcct Production accountant
PC Production coordinator
PI Production inspector
PM Production manager
PP Post-production
PROD Produced by
PSe Production secretary
PSeA Production secretary assistant
PSu Production supervisor
2nd PA Second production assistant
UM Unit manager
UPM Unit production manager(s)

Italian Crime Films, 1968–1980

Films are listed alphabetically within each year.

1968

Bandits in Milan, a.k.a. *The Violent Four (Banditi a Milano)*

D: Carlo Lizzani; *S:* Carlo Lizzani; *SC:* Massimo De Rita, Dino Maiuri, Carlo Lizzani; *DOP:* Giuseppe Ruzzolini (35mm, Technicolor, Techniscope); *M:* Riz Ortolani; *E:* Franco Fraticelli; *Production design, CO:* Enrico Tovaglieri; *AD:* Giorgio Gentili; *C:* Otello Spila; *AC:* Luigi Bernardini; *AE:* Adriana Benedetti; *APD:* Franco Gambarana, Sebastiano Soldati; *ArtD:* Mimmo Scavia, Renato Ricci; *SOE:* Aurelio Pennacchia; *Mix:* Mario Amari, Mario Morigi; *SE:* Andrea Cappelli; *SP:* Alfonso Avicola; *SS:* Lina D'Amico. *Cast:* Gian Maria Volonté (Pietro Cavallero), Tomas Milian (commissioner Basevi), Margaret Lee (Sorry, the prostitute), Don Backy (Sante Notarnicola), Ray Lovelock (Donato "Tuccio" Lopez), Ezio Sancrotti (Adriano Rovoletto "Bartolini"), Laura Solari (Tuccio's mother), Piero Mazzarella (Piva), Carla Gravina (Anna, the lady from Lugano), Peter Martell [Pietro Martellanza] (The pimp), Luigi Rossetti (elderly robber), Maria Rosa Sclauzero (Cavallero's secretary), Ida Meda (Sandro's wife), Totò Ruta (Arcade owner), Emy Rossi Scotti (Cavallero's wife), Enzo Fisichella (brigadeer), Gianni Bortolotti (Chief commissioner), Agostina Belli (Hostage), Pupo De Luca (Man in Fiat 1100), Ugo Bologna (Police Official), Nino Crisman (Police official), Carlo Lizzani (Police official), Carla Mancini (Assisting Girl at Razzia), Vittorio Pinelli (Andrea), Parvin Tabrizi (Police director), Giorgio Osfuri, Gianni Pulone, Aldo Vigorelli. *PROD:* Dino De Laurentiis for Dino De Laurentiis Cin.ca; *GM:* Nino E. Krisman; *PSu:* Sergio Mazzantini, Marcello Lizzani; *PSe:* Armando Zappi. *Country:* Italy. Filmed on location, in and around Milan and Turin. *Running time:* 102'; Visa n: 51114 (03.27.1968); *Rating:* not rated; *Release date:* 03.30.1968; *Distribution:* Paramount; *Domestic gross:* 1.768.051,000 lire. *Also known as: The Violent Four*; *Bandits à Milan* (France: 07.12.68 —100'); *Die Banditen von Mailand* (West Germany: 09.13.68 — 99'). *Home video:* none. OST: 7' Ariete AR 8004 (*Strange World / La giostra della vita*) sung by Katyna Ranieri

Milan, September 25, 1967. After a bank robbery gone wrong and a car chase across the streets of Milan, a gang of robbers is vanquished. Commissioner Basevi illustrates to a film crew how vice and crime thrive and flourish in a huge city with a high technological potential and a widespread economic well-being. Then the film reconstructs the stories of the four bandits and follows the preparation and execution of the robbery. The quartet was led by Piero Cavallero, a former partisan, smart and presumptuous, who posed as a businessman and led a double life, while one of his men was a seventeen-year-old kid. Cavallero eludes capture with his lieutenant Sandro Giannantonio, while the other two accomplices are captured. After a manhunt in the countryside which goes on for eight days, Cavallero and Giannantonio are surrounded and eventually surrender to the cops.

Coming after the political western *Requiescant* (1967), starring Lou Castel, *Bandits in Milan* was Carlo Lizzani's return to present-day Italy as well as one of his most ambitious films to date. As with *Wake Up and Kill*, the director chose to adapt a notorious true crime story in order to show the first examples of modern gangsterism in Italy, such as the prostitution and gambling racket, the escalation of robberies and a growing, more violent underworld. If Luciano Lutring — the "machine-gun soloist" in *Wake Up and Kill*— was moved by the logic of need, the titular *Bandits in Milan* are moved by a logic of profit. As Lizzani stated, "Earlier on there had been episodes of classical banditism, in a rural environment [...] or else because of World War II, with war veterans becoming bandits and so on. Whereas nowadays it was simply gangsterism, a phenomenon which belonged to affluent societies, such as North America in the '20s or Italy in the '60s [...] My ambition was not to simply make an action movie [...] but a film which reflected the Italian social context, with a very definite realistic and sociological setting."[1]

Bandits in Milan was based on a bank robbery gone wrong that took place on September 25, 1967, in Milan. The bandits were led by Pietro Cavallero, played in the film by Gian Maria Volonté. The four gangsters (Cavallero, his lieutenant Sante Notarnicola, Adriano Rovoletto and underage Donato Lopez) robbed many banks using the same technique over and over: three hold-ups in the same day, a short distance from each other. The greater the risks, the more the chances to get away without getting caught, given the confusion and police forces having to disperse on several fronts. Between robberies, Cavallero and his men led a normal bourgeois life. Nobody suspected them.

The Milan robbery was Cavallero's seventeenth hit. Rovoletto, the driver, waited for his accomplices in a Fiat 1100 which he stole from a nearby parking lot, but a shop owner noticed suspicious moves and called the police. A long, wild chase followed all over Milan, ending with four dead and 22 injured. Eventually the bandits' car was rammed and crashed into a tree. Rovoletto — an arm broken by a police bullet — tried to hide among the crowd, but was recognized and almost got lynched. His accomplices escaped, but their days were numbered. Donato Lopez, the younger of the trio, was arrested the following day in his own home, under his mother's eyes. Cavallero and Notarnicola fled to the countryside: a dragnet ensued, which ended eight days later, on October 3, 1967, in an abandoned signalman's box about 100 kms from Milan. *Bandits in Milan* came out in spring 1968, simultaneously at the first instance of the Assize Court of Milan, which sentenced Cavallero, Notarnicola and Rovoletto to life imprisonment, while Lopez was sentenced to 12 years and 7 months.

As with his previous crime films of the '50s and '60s (such as *The Hunchback of Rome* and *Wake Up and Kill*), Lizzani's method takes inspiration from the Neorealist lesson, "moving back from the chronicle of a single event to the social canvas that produced those social outcasts."[2] Here, however, the director opts for a more thought-provoking approach. The film begins with a semi-documentary prologue which recalls a television report: shots among the crowd, an ample use of zoom and handheld camera convey an impression of immediacy and perspective. Then the tone changes brusquely. A Commissioner (Tomas Milian)—who looks rather self-important, and was probably modeled on a then very popular real-life police Commissioner, Luigi Calabresi—guides a film crew through a series of sketches which recreate everyday episodes of criminal life: a nightclub owner refuses to pay the racket and his place is destroyed, a prostitute (Margaret Lee) is burnt alive by her pimps and so on. Lizzani's thesis is evident: in one scene the film crew interviews an elderly robber (Luigi Rossetti) who synthesizes the differences between old and new criminality with the phrase "We used to be more gentlemen."

However, the pseudo-objective approach is contradicted by the stylized set pieces (as in the nightclub scene, with balloons replacing the sight of the thugs breaking up the place) and the often incongruous details (such as the R&B song *La pelle nera* by Nino Ferrer accompanying the beating and subsequent death of a prostitute). What's more, Lizzani opts for an unrealistic, comic-book style with grotesque touches: the story of the dead prostitute is told as if it was a *fotoromanzo*, with abundance of clichés, while a scene involving a phone call between the commissioner and a nymphomaniac (played by Carla Gravina, then Volonté's lover) is outright hilarious. It's an uneasy, daring choice, which somehow puts the viewer off-guard, and bewildered many critics at the time of the film's release.[3]

It's only after such an extended and misleading build-up, that *Bandits in Milan*'s main character is introduced. Much like Luciano Lutring, Pietro Cavallero (played by an extraordinary Gian Maria Volonté) is a son of his times. He is a former partisan and

English language poster for *Bandits in Milan*, a.k.a. *The Violent Four* (1968).

left-wing militant who abandoned both his party and political struggle (because "They're all pretty good at talking nonsense in there, but I want to eat right now, and I'm going to fight my war by myself!") and reinvented himself as an entrepreneur of crime, putting into use his knowledge of guerrilla warfare. This kind of metropolitan banditism is characterized by "an individual and consumistic sense of compensation, even though it's dressed up with the colors of social rebellion,"[4] unlike the rural banditism of Lizzani's following film *The Tough and the Mighty* (*Barbagia*, 1969).

Unlike Lutring, though, Cavallero and his gang learned the rules of the game and hid their criminal activity behind the respectable cover of a ghostly agency, complete with a long-legged secretary. Lizzani achieves memorable results in depicting a cultured bandit who reads Camus and uses a language similar to that of a Communist politician, a "left-wing lexicon which is no longer shared."[5] Cavallero takes an obvious delight in his conceitedness and presumption, and after the arrest he keeps bragging to journalists about his exploits. But behind his delusions of grandeur, what is left is the nondescript nature of his activity. Compared to the ruthless and ever-spreading organized crime, Cavallero and his accomplices are willing amateurs at best.

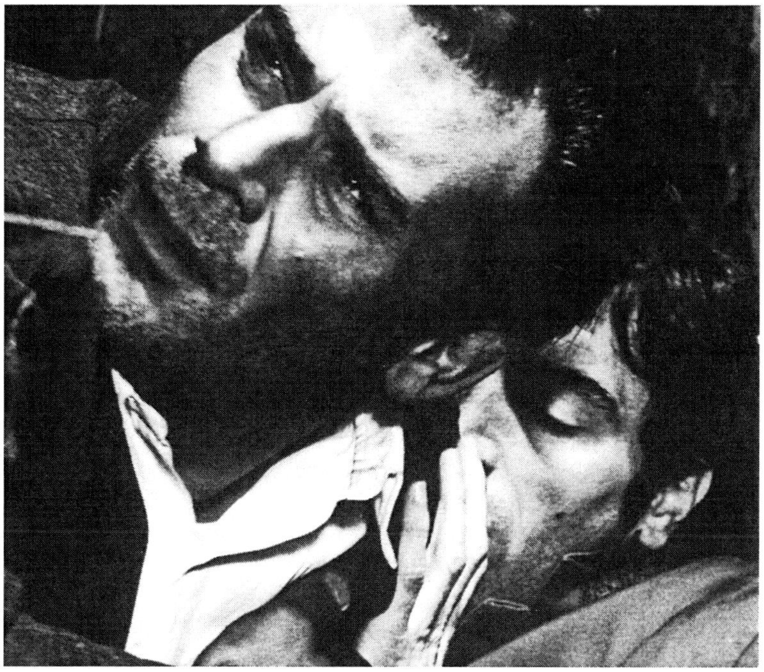

Gian Maria Volonté, left, and Don Backy in Carlo Lizzani's *Bandits in Milan* (1968).

Lizzani is particularly good at showing the petty, prosaic and petit bourgeois nature of these Padanian gangsters: the morning before their last hit, Cavallero and his men wake up early, travel from Turin to Milan and have breakfast at a bar, just like ordinary commuters. Near the end, while they're hiding from the police, Cavallero and his sidekick Notarnicola trace a balance sheet of their criminal activity as if they were normal businessmen. "Five years work, that makes 17 hits, 75 million liras. 14 million liras a year divided by three, it's about 4 million liras each ... let's say 300,000 lire a month." "Then there are expenses, the office, cars, motorway tickets, dinners ... my friend, being a bandit is an expensive job!"

At the time of its release, the fact that it had been shot on the heels of real events[6] was viewed as *Bandits in Milan*'s biggest limit: critics called it "a dynamic and lively picture which nevertheless lacks any real depth."[7] Over forty years later, this seems the real strength of Lizzani's film. The sociological analysis in real time reveals an electrical climate, and a subterranean tension which is about to explode, as shown by the impressive scenes of the crowd in revolt, trying to lynch Cavallero's accomplice, which arrived on screens during the 1968 riots in Italy's biggest cities.

Compared to *Wake Up and Kill*, *Bandits in Milan* has a more complex and multi-layered narrative construction, with a series of flashbacks that punctuate the interrogation of Rovoletto. The bank robbery scene and the frantic, extremely well-shot car chase that follows (something of a novelty in an Italian film, which contributed enormously to the pic's success) display a dynamism and sheer visual force which are still relevant nowadays, and the director makes first-rate use of on-location shooting in central Milan. The acting is also excellent: besides Volonté's powerhouse performance and the always reliable Milian in a supporting role, Lizzani assembled a strong supporting cast which included a very young Ray Lovelock, who would become one of the genre's most popular faces, and singer-turned actor Don Backy (real name Aldo Caponi) who would work again with Lizzani the following year on the rural bandit drama *The Tough and the Mighty* before moving on to ribald period comedies. Backy delivered another strong performance in Mario Bava's *Rabid Dogs* (*Cani arrabbiati*, 1974) as a psychotic bank robber. Lizzani himself has a cameo as a police official, while a very young Agostina Belli is the girl Cavallero and his men take as a hostage after the robbery.

Watching *Bandits in Milan* one has the feeling that the times were ripe for the birth of an Italian crime genre with its own original and believable traits: Lizzani's film is closely related to the chronicle of its time, it takes place in appropriate urban contexts and, more importantly, it conveys an expressive power that has nothing to begrudge the foreign models.

Notes

1. Franca Faldini and Goffredo Fofi, *L'avventurosa storia del cinema italiano raccontata dai suoi protagonisti 1960–1969* (Milan: Feltrinelli, 1984), p. 207.
2. Gian Piero Brunetta, *Storia del cinema italiano—Dal miracolo economico agli anni Novanta* (Rome: Editori Riuniti, 2001), p. 412.
3. As noted critic Guglielmo Biraghi wrote, "the film has only one flaw: a false start. Before the chronicle of that bloody day in Milan and the depiction of its prelude in a series of flashbacks, Lizzani spends more than ten minutes showing us the many aspects of crime in the rising Lombard-Piemontese metropolis, in a succession of exemplified vignettes." Biraghi, *Il Messaggero*, 3.31.1968.
4. Gualtiero De Santi, *Carlo Lizzani* (Rome: Gremese, 2001), p. 55.
5. *Ibid.*, p. 56.
6. Volonté himself had perplexities about the film: "*Bandits in Milan* was shot immediately after the events—just a couple of months later—so it lacked even a modicum of historical perspective [...] Lizzani leapt at the subject matter when it was still white hot, and even though he thoroughly explored it, he did it with the elements he could reckon with at that moment, which were not sufficient to

give him an in-depth knowledge of the facts." Faldini and Fofi, *L'avventurosa storia del cinema italiano*, p. 208.

7. De Santi, *Carlo Lizzani*, p. 56.

Bandits in Rome *(Roma come Chicago [Banditi a Roma])*

D: Alberto De Martino; *S:* Giacinto Ciaccio, Massimo D'Avack, Carlo Romano; *SC:* Giacinto Ciaccio, Massimo D'Avack, Carlo Romano, Dino Maiuri, Massimo De Rita, Alberto De Martino, Fabio Carpi, Lianella Carell, Piero Tellini; *DOP:* Aldo Tonti (35mm, Technicolor); *M:* Ennio Morricone, Bruno Nicolai, conducted by Bruno Nicolai; *E:* Otello Colangeli; *PD:* Nedo Azzini; *CO:* Piero Gherardi, Elio Micheli; *AD:* Giorgio Ubaldi, Umberto Campagna; *C:* Luciano Tonti; *AC:* Gianni Maddaleni; *AE:* Maria Napoleone; *MU:* Franco Di Girolamo; *SO:* Eraldo Giordani; *B:* Domenico Dubbini. *Cast:* John Cassavetes (Mario Corda), Gabriele Ferzetti (The commissioner), Nikos Kourkoulos (Erico), Anita Sanders (Lea Vallini), Riccardo Cucciolla (Pascutti), Luigi Pistilli (Colangeli), Osvaldo Ruggieri (Inspector Sernesi), Guido Lollobrigida (Angelo Scotese), Marisa Traversi (Blonde prostitute), Piero Morgia (Carlo Taddei), Marc Fiorini (Luciano Tarquini), Luigi Casellato (vice commissioner Angeletti), Fausto Pollicino (Luigino), Eugene Giolitti, Clara Bindi (Lady in the jewelry), Fajda Nicol (Brunette prostitute), Viviana Vanni, Ugo Adinolfi, Rossella Bergamonti, Aldo Bonamano, Pier Paolo Capponi (Director of supermarket), Emilia Della Rocca, Gianni Di Benedetto, Marcello Di Martire, Orso Maria Guerrini (lo Cascio), Giancarlo Prete, Giuliano Raffaelli (Jewelry carrier), Gaetano Santaniello, Barbara Herrera, Fabrizio Jovine, Sergio Mioni, Corrado Olmi, Giuseppe Valdembrini, Ferruccio Viotti, Ivan Giovanni Scratuglia (blind man). *PROD:* Dino De Laurentiis; *EP:* Carmine Bologna; *GM:* Domenico Bologna; *PSu:* Fernando Cinquini. *Country:* Italy. Filmed at De Laurentiis studios and on location in Rome. *Running time:* 104'; Visa n: 52656 (11.02.1968); *Release date:* 11.20.1968; *Distribution:* Paramount—De Laurentiis; *Domestic gross:* 320,840,000 lire. *Also known as: Rome contre Chicago* (France: 04.69 —104'); *Mord auf der Via Veneto* (West Germany: 09.05.69 —104'). *Home video:* none.

Rome. Mario Corda and his accomplice Erico rob a huge sum of money from the post office transit at the Termini train station. Corda then joins his unsuspecting partner Lea and their son Luigino at the circus. However, the police are on Corda's tracks: he escapes, leaving his house and family, and plans another heist—robbing a supermarket's takings—with Erico before retiring. But the hold-up goes wrong when the gun-happy Erico kills the supermarket owner and a police officer. Corda is captured and imprisoned. Erico attempts another robbery with three accomplices, which ends in bloodshed. He plans to take refuge in Greece with Eva, but his behavior becomes increasingly violent and unpredictable. Eventually a stubborn police commissioner identifies Erico's accomplices and apprehends them. Corda escapes from jail, only to find that his vicious accomplice has raped and killed

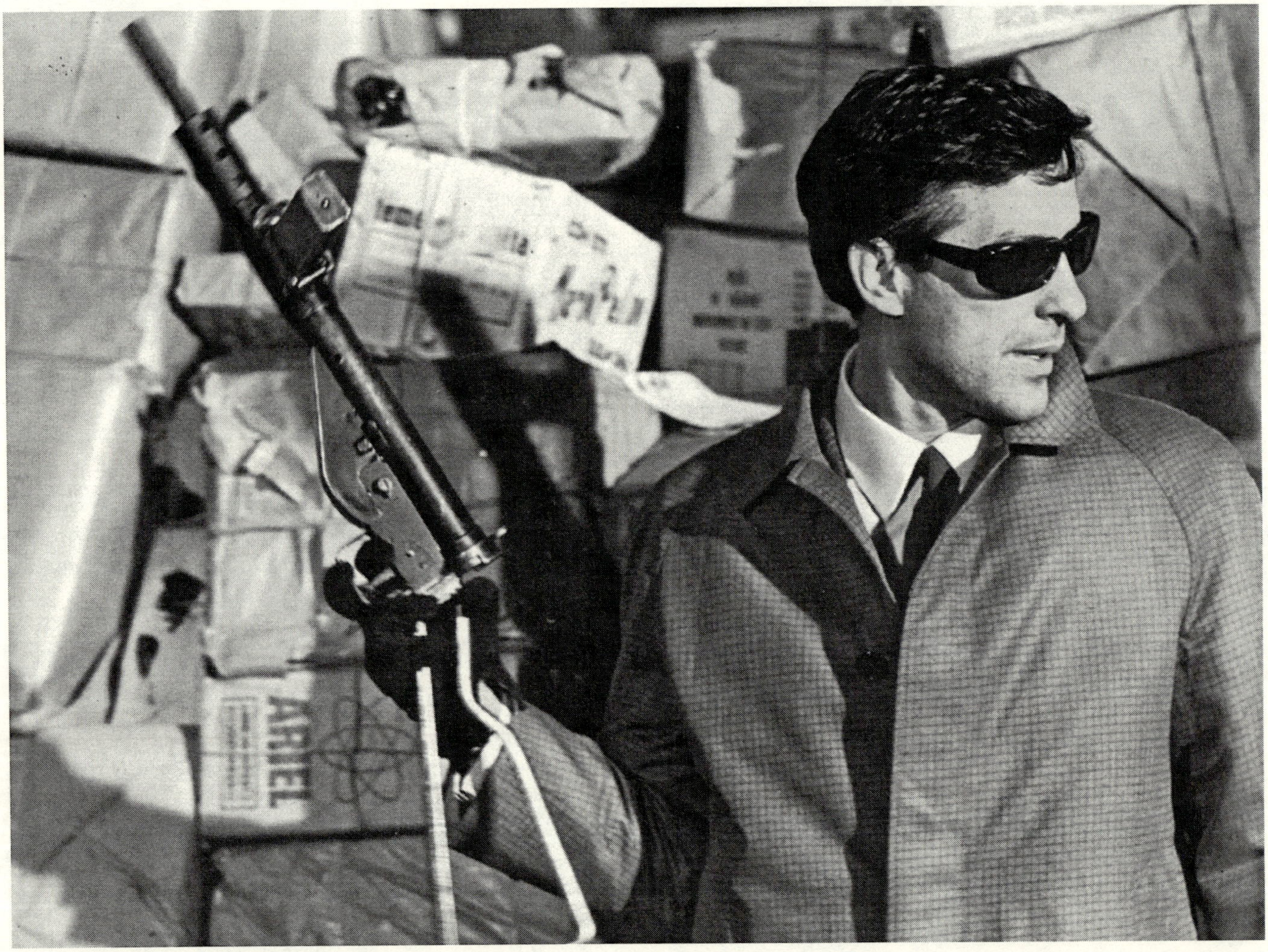

John Cassavetes in ***Bandits in Rome*** (1968).

Lea. He reaches Erico, who was about to leave on a plane, and kills him before being arrested once more.

Obviously conceived after the success of *Bandits in Milan*—as proven by the English language title—Alberto De Martino's film nonetheless leaves aside the Marxist analysis and sociological implications of Lizzani's work and concentrates on action. The Italian title, which translates to *Rome as Chicago*, gives away its makers' intentions: to create a gangster movie shaped like an American one. In other words, instead of focusing on the peculiarities and sociological traits of the Roman underworld, the script describes a fictitious Italy which looks more like an exotic version of an American city. *Bandits in Rome* is very much a product shaped for exportation, and De Martino's "Americanized Rome," in the director's own words, is a rather phony scenario to a story which sounds precious little "Italian."

Produced by Dino De Laurentiis, *Bandits in Rome* is technically first-rate: the cinematography is by Aldo Tonti (Fellini's *Nights of Cabiria*, Rossellini's *Europe '51* and *India* among others), while Ennio Morricone and Bruno Nicolai's score—itself a reworking of Morricone's music for the 1967 TV show *Musica da sera*[1]—gives the proceedings a classy touch, and De Martino's direction is efficient even though not particularly impressive, displaying an undeniable skill in filming action scenes. As for the cast, John Cassavetes was presumably enjoying a well-paid European vacation so as to finance his own directorial projects: as a matter of fact, despite being first-billed, his presence on screen is volatile. After the initial sequences, he has very little screen time, leaving the scene to Greek idol Kourkoulos, in search of an international notoriety that never came. Recalling his relationship with Cassavetes, De Martino said: "He is the most difficult actor I have ever worked with. When we first met, his wife Gena Rowlands came too. He introduced me to her as "the most intelligent director in Europe." She looked at me and said "Give him time!" (laughs). After the first week of shooting John and I started having arguments, and from then on we kept bickering and making peace, all the time. [...] However, when we finished the film he told me "Alberto, it's nice to work with you!," so at least we parted on good terms ... which didn't happen between him and Giuliano Montaldo [with whom Cassavetes did *Machine Gun McCain*, Authors' note]."[2]

As an expert gangster who leads a dual life as a middle-class bourgeois, Cassavetes' Mario Corda looks like a cleaner, more palatable version of *Bandits in Milan*'s Pietro Cavallero (he even pretends to run an import-export agency). However, Corda never really comes alive as a character. He just doesn't look and sound real, unlike Volonté's Cavallero, as the script depicts him as an old-time gangster from some '40s Hollywood movie: he repeatedly boasts of never having killed anyone, and says he is respected and revered in the underworld. Yet it's never quite clear how he ended up teaming with such an obnoxious, gun-crazy and mentally unstable partner as Erico: perhaps that can be explained by looking at the credits and counting a total of nine (!) scriptwriters, which somehow also gives away the film's uneasiness in dealing with the gangster genre and its over-reliance on clichés (take, for instance, Corda's clumsily explained escape from jail, or the rather unconvincing description of police procedural activities). That's also true for the subplot regarding Corda's love story with Lea, told in a few jarringly dull flashbacks.

However, despite the film's shortcomings (and Kourkoulos' hammy portrayal of Corda's antagonist), the character of Erico is *Bandits in Rome*'s most interesting and significant trait. A proletarian outsider who loves flamboyant dresses and fast motorbikes, and whose furious sexual appetite is complementary to his unsatiable thirst for violence, Erico is a dangerous, unpredictable and utterly vicious walking time-bomb of a madman, with absolutely no redeeming value whatsoever. A deranged, antisocial product of the Roman outskirts, a renegade who dons a platinum blond wig for a robbery not so much for camouflaging as for a deviated sense of mockery, Erico is a surprising anticipation of the following decade's most impressive villains such as Tomas Milian's Giulio Sacchi (*Almost Human*) or the hunchback Vincenzo Moretto (*Brutal Justice*). On the other hand, Ferzetti's unnamed middle-aged Commissioner is still an old-style good cop who despises violence, has a smoking habit, dresses impeccably and always follows his instinct. Of course, he never ever touches a gun. Within a few years, his '70s counterparts would drop good manners and grab the gun. However, he too has at least one line of dialogue which, even though inadvertently, predates a *leitmotif* of Italian crime films to come. To a journalist who asks him, "But what are we going to write in the newspapers?," he replies sarcastically: "Write what you always have: the police grope in the dark!"

Notes

1. Several music pieces included in the soundtrack were later released as part of the soundtrack record for Phil Karlson's *Hornets' Nest* (released in Italy as *I lupi attaccano in branco*).
2. Manlio Gomarasca, *Il cinema è quello che ci fa* [Interview with Alberto De Martino], in Aa. Vv., "Fatti di cinema. Controcorrente 3," *Nocturno Dossier* #51 (October 2006), p. 16.

The Bastard, a.k.a. *The Cats (I bastardi)*

D: Duccio Tessari; *S:* Mario Di Nardo; *SC:* Mario Di Nardo, Ennio De Concini, Duccio Tessari; *DOP:* Carlo Carlini (35mm, Eastmancolor, S.P.E.S.); *M:* Michel Magne; *Love and Money* (by Magne / Dassin) sung by Nicole Croisille; *E:* Mario Morra; *PD:* Luigi Scaccianoce; *CO:* Danda Ortona; *C:* Gastone Di Giovanni; *AC:* Ruggero Radicchi, Marcello Carlini; *AE:* Minni Marani; *APD:* Dante Ferretti; Set decorator: Bruno Cesari; *AD:* Nino [Antonio] Segurini; *MU:* Nilo Jacoponi; *Hair:* Amalia Paoletti; *SO:* Claudio Maielli; *Mix:* Alberto Bartolomei; *SP:* Giovan Battista Poletto; *SS:* Rita Agostini. *Cast:* Giuliano Gemma (Jason), Klaus Kinski (Adam), Rita Hayworth (Marta), Claudine Auger (Barbara), Margaret Lee (Karin), Serge Marquand (Jimmy), Umberto Raho (the doctor), Karl Cik (policeman), Paola Natale (dancing girl), Hans Thorner (policeman), Mirella Pompili (dancing girl), Detlef Uhle (TV announcer). *Uncredited:* Dan van Husen (Adam's mustached henchman), Luis Barboo, Antonio Mayans, Lorenzo Robledo (Adam's henchman). *PROD:* Turi Vasile for Ultra Film (Rome), P.E.C.F. (Paris), Rhein Main (Munich); Associate producer: Franz Huttl; *GM:* Danilo Marciani; *PM:* Michele Marsala, Philippe Modave; *PSu:* Franz Huttl; *ADM:* Arcangelo Picchi. *Country:* Italy / France / West Germany. Filmed in Madrid, Arizona, Nevada, New Mexico. *Running time:* 102'; Visa n: 52564 (10.26.1968); *Rating:* v.m.18; *Release date:* 10.30.1968; *Distribution:* Warner Bros; *Domestic gross:* 702,781,000 lire. *Also known as: Le batard* (05.25.69—100'); *Der Bastard* (West Germany, 06.06.69), *Kelvottomat* (Finland). *Home video:* Warner Archive Collection (DVD, USA—as *The Cats*).

Angel-face Jason and his stepbrother Adam are small-time gangsters in New Mexico, both very close to their alcoholic mother Marta. After robbing a jewelry and dispatching a rival gang, Jason tries to cut Adam out of his share, but he is betrayed by his girlfriend Karin, who is also his stepbrother's lover. Adam gets his gang to mangle Jason's gun hand. Jason is rescued and nursed back to health by the wealthy Barbara, who falls for him—yet his only thought is for revenge. After Marta inadvertedly reveals Adam and Karin's whereabouts in Queimado, New Mexico, Jason goes to avenge himself, but he is once again betrayed by Karin, with whom he is still desperately in love. Adam and Karin plan to get rid of Jason, but a tremendous earthquake upsets everybody's schemes...

Giuliano Gemma in *The Bastard* (1968) (courtesy Carlos Aguilar).

If *Bandits in Milan* and *Bandits in Rome* firmly located the gangster genre in contemporary Italy and opted for realistic—and in the case of Lizzani's film even semi-documentaristic—tones, Duccio Tessari's first gangster film *The Bastard* opts for a totally different approach. Starting from the casting of Giuliano Gemma and Klaus Kinski as stepbrothers on the wrong side of the law, to the plot's many twists and turns, up to the offbeat (and somehow off-putting) ending, it's obvious that Tessari's film is not meant to be the least bit realistic. Take the brothers' relationship with their alcoholic mother, played by Rita Hayworth: the woman is well aware of her sons' illegal activities, yet her only concern is having a bottle of whiskey at hand ("I haven't had a drink since this morning ... that's probably why I'm blue"), and even asking Jason for a crate of the juice as her birthday gift, while the scene where the happy dysfunctional family is reunited plays like a sort of demented sitcom minus offscreen laughs.

By emphasizing the subtle stream of hatred between Adam and his younger, almost child-like brother, Tessari and his official co-writers Mario Di Nardo and Ennio De Concini explicitly update one of Italian Western's favorite themes, the destructive conflicts that destroy a family from the inside. Furthermore, the director's stylish use of ample open spaces and long shots gives the film quite a different shape and rhythm compared to contemporary Italian gangster films. Indeed, *The Bastard* is a wild fantasy which openly plays like a modern-day variation on typical Spaghetti Western themes. While the latter genre is slowly moving adrift towards the kind of parodic exaggerations exemplified by 1970's *They Call Me Trinity*, *The Bastard* retains Italian Western's tendency towards violent excesses, as represented by the film's centerpiece. After ambushing his stepbrother and his fiancée Karin (the ravishing Margaret Lee, in an impressive performance as an unscrupulous, duplicitous *femme fatale*) during an intimate moment on a river-bed, Adam has Jason reveal the location of some hidden jewels by threatening to rape Karin in front of him, before it turns out she's actually Adam's lover as well. Then Klaus Kinski—wearing a bizarre pair of metal sunglasses—has one of his men (a seedy-looking doctor played by ubiquitous character actor Umberto Raho) cut off Gemma's right hand's tendons, so that he won't be able to use a gun. "You've always been such a good shot. When we were kids shooting at cans, it didn't matter ... but now ... I can't take that chance," he explains.

It's a scene that wouldn't have been out of place in Lucio Fulci's *Massacre Time* (*Le colt cantarono la morte e fu ... tempo di massacro*, 1966), which shares a peculiar Oedipal subtext with Tessari's film. The fact that *Massacre Time* was written by Fernando di Leo, Tessari's close friend and collaborator on a number of Westerns (including uncredited work on Leone's *A Fistful of Dollars*) must not be overlooked. When asked about his involvement on *The Bastard*, Di Leo used to skip the subject, but it's likely he actually had a hand in the script. For once, the scene where Gemma practices shooting with his left by trying to hit a harp's strings is another over-the-top moment in pure Di Leo style, not to mention the final earthquake, an unexpected *deus ex machina* which comes out of the blue just when one is expecting a typical climactic showdown between the brothers. The English language version, however, omits the real ending as devised by Tessari: it ends with Jason helping Adam get out of his house's ruins, only to shoot him immediately afterwards. "Don't thank me... We've got accounts to settle, and no one else is gonna get in between—not even God!" Jason spits out between shots. In the original edit, though, Jason is in turn killed by his mother, who just showed up after hearing of the earthquake on TV. Said ending eventually

Giuliano Gemma, Klaus Kinski and Rita Hayworth in *The Bastard* (1968) (courtesy Carlos Aguilar).

turned out in the American DVD release (as *The Cats*, which was the original working title).[1]

For all its merits, *The Bastard* only partially succeeds. Plot faults are all over the place, from the confusing early scene in a nightclub where Jason gets rid of rival gangsters to the lame romantic interlude between Gemma and former Bond-girl Claudine Auger (which even includes the presence of singing cowboys in a scene, as another stab at the Western genre), while a subplot about a heist job Jason performs with an associate played by Serge Marquand is just half-baked. However, Tessari gets good performances from his leading men, with Kinski voraciously stealing every scene he is in as the hypochondriac, vicious Adam and Gemma getting no less than four love scenes with his two ladies. Despite credits stating that it was an Italian / French / German co-production, actor Dan van Husen adamantly claims the film was actually an Italian / Spanish co-production, with the working title being *Los Gatos*, which would explain why it was mostly shot in Spain, outside of Madrid, while only the opening sequence was filmed in the U.S.[2]

If it proves the *fil rouge* between the Western and crime genre, on the other hand *The Bastard* predates the use that 1970's Italian crime films would make of Hollywood has-beens in its casting of Rita Hayworth (after Joan Crawford backed off) in a self-deprecating, even humiliating role. The woman who once was Gilda looks as if she's acting in a perennial drunken numbness: always with a glass in hand, she even ventures into a philosophical dissertation on the similitude between humans and liquors ("People are like whiskey, you always have to choose the best ... like you did this time") that's actually a shameless plug for J&B, whose bottles and crates feature prominently within the film, and which would become the beverage *par excellence* in Italian cinema over the years.

Notes

1. The U.S. Warner Archive Collection DVD has Italian language credits on a print with English language soundtrack. There is no audio at all for the ending, proving that the sequence never circulated in the English market before.
2. E-mail interview, May 2012.

Comandamenti per un gangster (Commandments for a Gangster)

D: Alfio Caltabiano; *S* and *SC*: Alfio Caltabiano, Dario Argento; *DOP:* Mile [Milorad] Markovic (35mm, Telecolor, Kodakolor); *M:* Ennio Morricone, orchestrated and conducted by Bruno Nicolai (Ed. C.A.M.);

Solo nostalgia (Ennio Morricone / Audrey Nohra) sung by Jane Relly; *E:* Eugenio Alabiso; *AE:* Ada Grimaldi; *PD:* Ivkov [Dragoljub Ivkov], Luciana Marinucci; *CO:* Luciana Marinucci; *C:* Emilio Varriano; Underwater Camera: Tommaso Manunza; *AD:* Nicola Balini; *MU:* Eligio Trani; *SO:* Carlo Diotallevi; *SS:* Donatella Todini; *SP:* Salvatore Consolazione; *Titles:* Gioacchino Libratti. *Cast:* Lee Tadic [Ljuba Tadic] (Northon), Al Northon [Alfio Caltabiano] ("5 Cents"), Dan May [Dante Maggio] (Old man), Rade Markon [Rade Markovic] (Albert Torio "The Saint"), Nick Ballantine, John Janick [Jovan Janicijevic], Sir John, Gene Maras [Giancarlo Marras], Joe Rast [Giusi Raspani Dandolo], Arion Lavrick, Jvan [Giovanni Ivan] Scratuglia (2nd man murdered on seafront), Gaetano Gabadi, Licio Carrara, Olivera [Olivera Vukotic] (Regina Westling). *Uncredited:* Bogdan Jakus [Dusan Janicijevic], Sergio Mioni. *PROD:* Salvatore Argento for Triumph Film 67 / Prodi Cinematografica (Rome), Avala Film (Belgrade); *PM:* Salvatore Vizzini Bisaccia. *Country:* Italy / Yugoslavia. Filmed on location in Yugoslavia. *Running time:* 96': Visa n: 51254 (04.04.68); *Rating:* v.m.14; *Release date:* 05.22.1968; *Distribution:* D.C.I.; *Domestic gross:* 106,073,000 lire. *Also known as: Poslednji obracun* (Yugoslavia, 1968); *L'enfer avant la mort* (France, 01.07.70—90'); *Hölle vor dem Tod* (12.20.68—92'). *Home video:* none. *OST:* CD C.A.M. CSE 052

Canada. Northon, a gangster who retired from business, wants to avenge the death of his sister Helen. She was married to Frank Cline, who disappeared while transporting 2000 kgs of ingots, two million dollars' worth—which belong to the Organization—by sea, leaving three dead bodies behind him. An old friend tells him about Regina Westling, a nightclub singer who has been Cline's lover and so might help him. Regina mentions a Mexican gangster, nicknamed "5 cents," whom Northon traces and eventually allies with. "5 cents" tells Norton that he's planning to get the ingots from the sunken ship, but he needs him to open the safety room where the gold is. However, Northon and "5 cents" must face a rival gangster, Albert Torio "the Saint," who works for the Organization. Northon is kidnapped and tortured by the Nazi, one of the Saint's men, but "5 cents" saves him. Northon discovers Cline's dead body inside the ship, but the gold is missing. Northon finds his old friend dead as well, and Regina is also killed by the same assassin, after revealing the gold's true hideout. Eventually, Northon and "5 cents" get the ingots, but the Saint and his men catch up with them. A confrontation at sea is about to erupt, when a member of the Organization arrives to claim the loot. It turns out that Cline and Helen were killed by the Nazi, who double-crossed the Organization at Torio's orders. A duel ensues, where Northon kills Torio. Satisfied with his revenge, he leaves all the gold to "5 cents." However, the gangsters don't know that the Police have been spying on them all along...

Alfio Caltabiano's second film as a director after the Western *Ballad for a Gunman* (*Ballata per un pistolero*, 1967), *Comandamenti per un gangster* is in many ways a significant work, despite having received modest success upon its release and still being rather obscure nowadays. First of all, it is quite simply, a Western in disguise (or, as critic Pietro Bianchi more articulately put it, "a skillful attempt at applying the Western formula to the Gangster movie trappings"[1]), that illustrates the natural transition—which would become incresingly evident several years later—between the two genres. The story—written by a young film critic with a brilliant future before him, named Dario Argento—puts together a number of Western film characters and clichés in a contemporary setting (a bogus Canada, recreated in Yugoslavia).

A number of elements recall Sergio Leone's films—including *Once Upon a time in the West* (*C'era una volta il West*, 1968): and one wonders whether Argento recycled several elements from that film's script. Examples are the theme of vengeance (a scene even has Northon contemplate a fold-up hand mirror with a picture of him and his sister, which recalls Lee Van Cleef's watch in *For a Few Dollars More*) and over-the-top villains. The Saint (Rade Markovic) is a religious maniac, "an exalted mystic who believes in the redemption of souls through the suffering of bodies" who plays a church organ and tells his victims to make the sign of the cross so that they won't go to hell after they die. A truly impressive villain, indeed, slightly let down by Markovic's mediocre screen presence. On the other hand, Caltabiano's "5 cents" is an athletic, charismatic type who dresses in black leather outfits and wears a lethal glove with iron spikes, while his dumb brother and sidekick "Mitraglia" is a flawless machine-gun specialist. Argento also displays an ear for witty dialogue which will be sorely missed in many of his later films: "5 cents" claims he is "a guy with his own ten commandments, and each one ends with the word 'money'" (hence the title), while Northon tells Mitraglia, "They should have called you Giotto" after the latter has drawn a perfect circle with a hail of gunfire.

But *Comandamenti per un gangster* is also a whodunit of sorts, and as such it shows several traits that would later become very important in Argento's *oeuvre* as a director. The unseen murderer wears black leather gloves (which are often shown in glaring close-ups), leaves coins near his victims as a calling-card and is identified by a physical detail—a scar on his wrist. Besides the fetishistic attention to gloves and weapons (Northon has an artisan build him a customized set of tools to open a safety room), there are a number of subjective shots from the murderer's point of view; also, the script was obviously conceived as a showreel for the young writer, as evidenced by its care for visual tricks, which Caltabiano wisely follows: the camera pans to reveal characters as reflected in mirrors, and there's a surprising number of sight gags, such as a point of view shot of a man who's about to be hanged and sees his opponent through the noose that he is about to wear around his neck. Obviously Argento was trying to get noticed, and he definitely succeeds, aided by Caltabiano's svelte direction. Also featured is Argento's penchant for pseudo-scientific mumbo-jumbo ("We extracted the bullets without an autopsy via an electromagnet" a coroner explains). One could go so far as to perceive the scene that takes place in a sunken ship as a blueprint for the celebrated underwater set-piece near the beginning of *Inferno* (1980), while a vital clue to the solution is provided by a talking parrot—a bird...

That's not to say *Comandamenti per un gangster* is without its faults. Besides the poor setting, car chases are definitely not Caltabiano's specialty, as shown by a so-so sequence halfway through; what's more, Tadic is as wooden as it gets as the unsympathetic hero (a fact which allows Caltabiano to chew every scene he's in). Yet it's an extremely enjoyable little film, with Ennio Morricone's groovy score—itself partly a reworking of his Western themes—being a definite asset. Last but not least, it's funny to see how Caltabiano and Argento chose to end the film on a mockingly moralistic note — something decidedly not to be found in westerns of the period. Ultimately, the film's playful approach to the genre is also its most evident shortcoming: Italian crime films to come would definitely be much bleaker, realistic affairs, which traced their roots well into Italian society.

Note

1. Pietro Bianchi, *Il Giorno*, 5.23.1968.

The Day of the Owl, a.k.a. *Mafia (Il giorno della civetta)*

D: Damiano Damiani; *S:* based on Leonardo Sciascia's novel; *SC:* Ugo Pirro, Damiano Damiani; *DOP:* Tonino Delli Colli (35mm, Technicolor); *M:* Giovanni Fusco, conducted by Bruno Nicolai; *E:* Nino Baragli; *PD:* Sergio Canevari; *C:* Franco Di Giacomo; *AC:* Giuseppe Lanci, Roberto Forges Davanzati; *AE:* Rossana Maiuri; *APD:* Carlo Ferri; *CO:* Marilù Carteny; *AD:* Guglielmo [Mino] Giarda; *2nd AD:* Gianluigi Calderone; *MU:* Oretta Melaranci; *Hair:* Elvio Dottori; *W:* Rosa Calabria; *SO:* Carlo Palmieri; *SP:* Mario Mazzoni; *KG:* Augusto Diamanti; *ChEl:* Alberto Ridolfi; *SS:* Gianni Siragusa. *Cast:* Franco Nero (Captain Bellodi), Claudia Cardinale (Rosa Nicolosi), Lee J. Cobb (Don Mariano Arena), Gaetano [Tano] Cimarosa (Machica, also known as "Zecchinetta"), Serge Reggiani (Parrineddu), Nehemiah Persoff (Pizzuco), Ennio Balbo (first mafioso at banquet), Ugo D'Alessio (second mafioso at banquet), Fred Coplan (brigadeer), Giovanni Pallavicino (marshal of Carabinieri), Laura De Marchi (Mariano's daughter), Brizio Montinaro (marshal's son), Lino Coletta (young man with mustaches at Arena's house), Giuseppe Lauricella, Vincenzo Norvese, Vincenzo Falanga. *Uncredited:* Giuseppe Namio. *PROD:* Ermanno Donati and Luigi Carpentieri for Panda Cinematografica (Rome), Les Films Corona (Paris); *GM:* Piero Donati; *PM:* Alfonso Donati, Lucio Trentini; *PSu:* Franco Cuccu; *PSe:* Federico Staracci; *ADM:* Adalberto Spadoni. *Country:* Italy / France. Filmed at Incir — De Paolis (Rome) and on location in Partinico, Sicily. *Running time:* 108'; Visa n: 50887 (02.16.1968); Rating: v.m.18 (revoked on 02.24.1968); *Release date:* 17.02.1968; *Distribution:* Euro International Film; *Domestic gross:* 1,335,244,000 lire. *Also known as: La mafia fait la loi* (France, 1969 — 100'); *Der Tag der Eule* (West Germany, 02.14.75 — 95') , *El día de la lechuza* (Spain — Home video). *Home video:* Wild East (DVD, USA — as *Mafia*, double feature w/ *I Am the Law*), Medusa (DVD, Italy), Suevia Films (DVD, Spain).

Sicily. One of the Colasberna brothers, a property developer, is shot to death in his truck near the house of Rosa Nicolosi and her husband. The case is assigned to Captain Bellodi, a man of the North. Bellodi receives an anonymous letter which informs him that the motive behind the killing is a tendering for a new motorway which is being constructed in the zone. Meanwhile, Rosa's husband disappears and the widow asks help to local mafia boss Don Mariano. Rumours spread that Nicolosi killed Colasberna because he was Rosa's lover, but Bellodi — who has a local confidant named Parrineddu — doesn't believe it. He finally has Rosa reveal the murderer's name: a man called Zecchinetta. The murder was commissioned by Pizzuco, who attempts to blow up Bellodi's car, but is stopped by Don Mariano. Bellodi arrests Pizzuco and, even though he has no proof, Don Mariano as well. But the mafia boss, who's got powerful political connections, is released and Bellodi is transferred as punishment. As Don Mariano celebrates his triumph, Parrineddu's body is found beneath the newly inaugurated motorway. The Mafia has triumphed again.

During the 1960s, Italian cinema rediscovered the tendency to reflect on the evolution, mood and problems of civil society — a debate which had been seemingly interrupted by the decline of Neorealism and in later years sporadically reprised. The initiator and reference point of this newly-revived tendency was Francesco Rosi, with such films as *Salvatore Giuliano* (1961) and *Hands Over the City* (*Le mani sulla città*, 1963). Rosi's films followed an idea of cinema with distinct expressive and stylistic qualities, that would analyze the country's recent history through filmic inquiries which took inspiration from true events, such as the 1947 massacre of communist peasants at Portella della Ginestra for *Salvatore Giuliano*.

If the '60s "Commedia All'Italiana" portrayed the ideological dissolution of the decade in a comedic — although far from absolving — way, the so-called "political-civil cinema" gave voice to the citizen's progressive loss of trust towards the institutions, as seen through the dramatization and aggrandizement of political actuality. It was, as one critic put it, "a partial compensation of that ruinous detachment from reality which [...] characterized post–Neorealist Italian cinema,"[1] and reflected a real state of crisis and civil uneasiness.

Such works left a profound political mark and expressed a neat opposition to dominating ideology. They treated such themes as justice, the inefficiency of the prison system, political corruption, Mafia. Yet — an unresolved contradiction which attracted a lot of harsh comments from left-wing critics — they were financed by the same system they were openly and, at times, radically criticizing. These political films had a powerful visual quality and "were strongly oriented towards maintaining strong links with the audience: they didn't disdain spectacle and were often inscribed within — or at the margins of — genre cinema."[2] Especially, it has to be added, the crime genre.

Sometimes, this proximity was just a pretext inside an analysis which was closer to comedy (such as in Ettore Scola's *Il commissario Pepe*, 1969) whereas in some cases it would pave the way for an allegory or a pamphlet (as is the case with Elio Petri's *Investigation of a Citizen Above Suspicion*, 1970).[3] In Damiano Damiani's films, civil and political commitment are closely linked to formal solutions and narrative themes which are deeply rooted in the crime genre. One of the director's favorite themes is the relationship between the judicial authority and police, as shown in one of his best films, *Confessions of a Police Captain* (1971), and the way our idea of righteousness has to cope with *raisons d'Etat* and the keeping of a deeply antidemocratic political system, led by men whose political and human behavior is identical to those that characterize the Mafia.

The encounter between the crime genre and committed "civil" cinema gave birth to a number of films which were intended as a strong spectacular alternative to American models, whose slavish imitation was still the recurring trait in most low budget flicks. The main literary reference point were the works of Leonardo Sciascia, such as *The Day of the Owl* (*Il giorno della civetta*, 1961) and *To Each His Own* (*A ciascuno il suo*, 1966), which denounced the spreading of the Mafia within crime narratives. Both were adapted for the screen: in 1967 Elio Petri directed *We Still Kill the Old Way* (*A ciascuno il suo*, 1967), co-scripted with Ugo Pirro and starring Gian Maria Volonté, which was a box office hit. The success of Petri's film persuaded producers Ermanno Donati and Luigi Carpentieri — who had already bought the rights to

Sciascia's book and commissioned Gianni Grimaldi for a script—to green light the project. *The Day of the Owl* was adapted by Pirro and Damiano Damiani, who radically altered and rewrote the novel for the screen. "When I write a script based on a novel, I usually don't respect the book's structure," Pirro explained. "To me, the book is a hint: I must try and preserve its message by using a different language. [...] Sciascia was very polemic and disheartened towards us scriptwriters; but you know, writers always behave like that."[4]

As another Sicilian writer, Giuseppe Fava, put it, Sciascia was convinced that the essence of the Mafia was a subtle mind game, and *The Day of the Owl* tells the story of an ethical and intellectual conflict between a captain of the *carabinieri*, Bellodi (Franco Nero) and a Mafia boss, Don Mariano (Lee J. Cobb). Damiani and Pirro retained the book's most famous lines, where Don Mariano says that he divides humanity in five categories:

"I," went on Don Mariano, "have a certain experience of the world; and what we call humanity—all hot air, that word—I divide into five categories: men, half-men, pigmies, arse-crawlers—if you'll excuse the expression—and quackers. Men are very few indeed; half-men few, and I'd be content if humanity finished with them... But no, it sinks even lower, to the pigmies who're like children trying to be grown-ups, monkeys going through the motions of their elders... Then down even lower we go, to the arse-crawlers who're legion... And, finally, to the quackers; they ought to just exist, like ducks in a pond: their lives have no more point or meaning..."

The Mafia had made its entrance in the realm of Italian cinema in an openly unrealistic guise, in Pietro Germi's *In the Name of the Law* (*In nome della legge*, 1949), a barely disguised Western set in Sicily and visually inspired by John Ford's films, where Mafia men were "men of honor" who acted according to a rigid, unwritten code of rules. To the Northern Germi, Sicily was an idealized land, almost mythical: a source of impressive poetic images, but decidedly far from reality. How could Germi's Mafia men, who quote Aristotle and preach loyalty, be compatible with those who just a couple of years earlier sent Salvatore Giuliano to shoot a crowd in cold blood at Portella della Ginestra?

Following the example of Rosi's *Salvatore Giuliano*, Damiani sweeps away the laughable distinction between "old" and "new" Mafia—with the former seen as a depositary of law and order—and depicts the progressive Americanization of *Cosa Nostra*, which becomes a replica of its overseas counterpart after the passage from the dominion of the country to that of the cities—here exemplified by the ambitious motorway which is being built with bad cement and bribes to politicians. Damiani visualizes the confrontation between the official authorities and their illegal counterparts through a striking visual idea (absent in the book), showing the two balconies on opposite sides of a square, where Nero and Cobb stay like two generals over a battlefield—or a chessboard, for that matter. From his observation post, each moves his own pawns: young widow Rosa (Claudia Cardinale), petty

Italian poster for *The Day of the Owl* (1968).

sneak Parrineddu (Serge Reggiani), hired killer Zecchinetta (Tano Cimarosa). Damiani's direction is very precise, and shows a keen eye for frame composition: the director, a former painter, used to draw storyboards for every scene on set, and his preference for long sequence shots (such as in the scene where Nero visits Rosa's house at night) gives the film a refined, classy look, aided by Tonino Delli Colli's expert cinematography.

According to assistant director Mino Giarda, the production received anonymous threatening letters while shooting in Sicily, and one day someone fired at the truck carrying the dailies (which were sent to Rome, printed and sent back to Partinico where Damiani shot most of the film). It's no wonder: compared to the abstract, deterministic tone of Sciascia's book — which was preserved in Petri's *We Still Kill the Old Way*, sometimes at the film's detriment — Damiani thrusts *The Day of the Owl* within Italy's contemporary reality of electoral frauds and political connivance: "We always voted the way you wanted us to" says Rosa to Don Mariano. The scene — Damiani's own idea — where Lee J. Cobb enters the local Democrazia Cristiana office, making an explicit reference to the complicity between Italy's largest political party and the Mafia, raised a fuss during the film's making. "They wanted to block the shooting" Giarda explains. "The police commissioner said "We can't do that. I'm sorry but I have to ask for instructions from Palermo." [...] Damiani replied that if he wasn't allowed to shoot, he would hold a press conference on the very next day and denounce the situation. We had everyone against us — not only the Mafia, but the authorities as well."[5]

The Day of the Owl was initially forbidden to minors by the Board of Censors: an absurd, arbitrary decision — officially motivated by the frequent use of foul language (mostly Sicilian dialectic expressions), its "harsh and corrosive criticism of institutions" and the lack of a happy ending — which was soon revoked in appeal after a couple of minimal dubbing alterations: Don Mariano's "arse-crawlers" (*pigliainculo* in Italian, with a more explicit sexual innuendo) became "ruffians."

Besides Damiani's powerful direction, one of the film's main assets was its casting. Franco Nero, who in a couple of years had become a western movie star thanks to the success of *Django* (1966) and found international stardom with John Huston's *The Bible* (1966) and Joshua Logan's *Camelot* (1967), was persuaded to accept the role by his lover Vanessa Redgrave, who was familiar with Sciascia's work: he injects a natural empathy in the role of Bellodi — inspired by the young Carlo Alberto Dalla Chiesa, who would be murdered by the Mafia in 1982 — making him a more likeable character compared to the novel. He and Damiani got on very well and would work again on a number of films in the following years. The same could not be said about Lee J. Cobb, whose acting affectations often irritated Damiani. As Nero recalls, during the final scene, where Cobb delivers the film's most famous monologue about humanity, "after each line he handled his cigar, and took a long pause. And I saw Damiano behind the camera, clenching his huge boxer fists and whispering 'Are you going to finish this damn dialogue or not?'"[6] The film's real revelation came from a colorful supporting actor discovered by Damiani's assistant Mino Giarda. As Zecchinetta, the mustached, squat and diminitive Cimarosa — a postal clerk who had worked as an extra in a number of Franco and Ciccio films — brought an air of spontaneity to the film, ad-libbing many lines and portraying a down-to-earth, colorful hired killer (note the opening scene where the unseen hitman is waiting for his target, eating cheese and drinking wine behind a bush).

The Day of the Owl grossed over one billion and three hundred million lire, becoming one of the season's biggest successes in Italy. Damiani's film paved the way for a subgenre about the Mafia — something which so many people back then pretended not to exist.

Notes

1. Lino Micciché, *Cinema italiano degli anni '70* (Venice: Marsilio, 1989), p. 132.
2. *Ibid.*
3. Other examples are *L'interrogatorio* (1970, by Vittorio De Sisti), *Siamo tutti in libertà provvisoria* (1971, directed by journalist Manlio Scarpelli) and *Imputazione di omicidio per uno studente* (1972, by Mauro Bolognini). All of the aforementioned films are only marginally related to the crime genre.
4. Alberto Pezzotta, *Regia Damiano Damiani* (Udine: C.E.C.— Cinemazero, 2004), p. 206.
5. *Ibid.*, p. 207.
6. *Ibid.*

Frame Up, a.k.a. *The Falling Man (Quella carogna dell'ispettore Sterling)*

D: Hal Brady [Emilio P. Miraglia]; *S:* Max Hatired [Massimo De Rita]; *SC:* Max Hatired [Massimo De Rita], Dean Maurey [Dino Maiuri] [*The Falling Man*: Henry Stanley]; *DOP:* Eric [Erico] Menczer (35mm, Technicolor, Techniscope); *M:* Robby Poitevin; *E:* Sergius Hillman [Sergio Montanari]; *PD:* Lucky Pulling [Luigi Scaccianoce]; *CO:* Will Jory; *C:* Phil Holster [Silvio Fraschetti]; *AD:* Jeffrey Darcey, Louis Glidston; *MU:* Mark Denove; *SO:* Romano Pampaloni, Armando Tarzia; *SS:* Ruth Melton. *Cast:* Henry Silva (Inspector Sterling), Beba Loncar (Janet), Charles Palmer [Carlo Palmucci] (Gary), Keenan Wynn (Commissioner Donald), Paul Carey [Pier Paolo Capponi] (O'Neil), Edward G. Ross [Luciano Rossi] (Joseph Randolph), Larry Dolgin (Kelly), Charlene Polite (Anne), Bob Molden (Rocky). *Uncredited:* Lella Cattaneo (Woman at hotel), Bill Vanders (Hotel detective). *PROD:* Felice Testa Gay for Cinegai, Jolly Film; Associate producer: Alvin Shapiro; *PM:* Gray Fredericson; *PA:* Alvin Shapiro; Charles Meredith. *Country:* Italy. Filmed at Cinecittà (Rome) and on location in San Francisco. *Running time:* Italian version (*Frame Up*): 93' / Alternate version (*The Falling Man*): 85'; Visa n: 51116 (03.22.1968); *Rating:* v.m.14; *Release date:* 04.13.1968; *Distribution:* Unidis; *Domestic gross:* 397,425,000 lire. *Also known as: Mannen, lagen och våldet* (Sweden) *Ce salaud d'Inspecteur Sterling* (France, Belgium), *Cronica negra de un policia* (Spain). *Home video:* IFS — Iver Film Services (VHS, UK, pre-cert as *Falling Man*, 84'50"), Palace Video (VHS, Greece). *OST:* CD GDM 4018.

San Francisco. Unjustly accused of the killing of an informant, Inspector Sterling is expelled from the police by his superior, Commissioner Donald. Determined to find out who framed him, Sterling becomes obsessed with his mission, even more so after his own son has been murdered so as to make him stop his investigations. He tracks down one of the two men who accused him through false testimony, Joseph Randolph, in a seedy hotel, but Randolph is killed when he's about to confess. Sterling then tails a model, Janet, hoping that she leads him to the mysterious Charlie, who seems to be the mastermind behind all the murders. The other false witness, Rock, is also killed before he can talk, and the body supposedly of Charlie is found dead in the bay. Sterling is not convinced, though, and rightly so. After surviving another attempt at killing him, he catches up with Janet again and through her he eventually discovers Charlie's real identity: Gary, Donald's son.

Emilio Miraglia's *Frame Up* is exemplary of the situation of Italian *film noir* in the mid-sixties as opposed to the growing realistic urgency and urban hysteria of films like Lizzani's *Bandits in Milan.* Titles like Miraglia's film or Franco Prosperi's *The Professional Killer* (*Tecnica di un omicidio*, 1966) and *Every Man Is My Enemy* (*Qualcuno ha tradito*, 1967) were hard-boiled flicks destined to foreign markets, starring American actors and heavily influenced by the new wave of American gangster films, darker and more violent, such as Sam Fuller's *Underworld U.S.A.* (1961), William Asher's *Johnny Cool* (1962), Don Siegel's *The Killers* (1964). However, the rip-off was limited to absorbing the genre's renewed iconography and stylistic traits, leaving untouched the more urgent themes (the breakdown of institutions, the collapse of urban structures, the rise of the underworld) that those films implied and underlined. As customary with Italian genre cinema, they also integrated elements from the whodunit and Hitchcockian thriller as well. As Brit critic Matt Blake noted, these films "seem to exist in an altogether different environment to the urban hysteria that populates productions throughout the '70s."[1]

Shot in San Francisco with a partly American cast, *Frame Up* is no exception. The hero's pilgrimage through seedy hotels, topless bars, discos, skyline roofs and of course the obligatory climbs and descents of San Francisco streets and the iconic Golden Gate, is a parade of clichés as seen through the greedy, enthusiastic eyes of someone who comes from the periphery of the empire, and Miraglia's direction overflows with wide-angle shots, nervous cuts, convoluted flashbacks. The only hint at irony is a scene where Beba Loncar exterminates a bunch of guys with a shot gun, which is revealed to be the shooting of a tv commercial for Levi's.

As with the previous year's *Assassination*, Miraglia cast Henry Silva in the lead, and the actor's impassive, stone-like face and square jaw perfectly epitomizes the idea of a world-weary, hard-boiled cop. As one Italian critic wrote, "When Henry Silva smiles, it's like a wound opens on his face,"[2] so it's not hard for him to portray a man who's obsessed with vengeance and is alienated from his family even before his kid son is shot to death before his wife's very eyes. "Everyone says you're a skunk" his better half says, and we better believe her. Inspector Sterling predates '70s tough cops in several ways: he's a loner, is cross with his superiors, has his own debatable working methods (extorting a confession at gun point, for instance) as he feels his hands are tied by police procedures. "You reporters need your garbage, don't you? You need headlines, policemen as killer, murders in cold blood..." he complains to a journalist played by Pier Paolo Capponi. "If crime goes up you say it's the cop's fault, he's too soft ... but if for once a policeman gets a confession, you're against it. There's always someone to be sorry for in your articles, the criminal!"

What's really interesting about Miraglia's film is that it circulated in two drastically different releases. The European edit (*Frame Up*) follows Sterling's quest to find out who murdered

Italian poster for *Frame Up* (1968).

his son and framed him for shooting an informant, and is characterized by a series of flashbacks showing the events that led up to the murders. About a hour in the film Sterling is shot on his door step but survives and eventually finds out who the killer is: the happy ending has him regaining his boss' (Wynn) respect.

The U.S. edit, distributed through Heritage Enterprises in 1971 and known as *The Falling Man*, runs eight minutes shorter, has the footage of Sterling being shot placed near the start of the film, and a plot which unfolds in quite a different way: after spotting a heist in progress, Sterling suffers the thugs' wrath, as his son is killed and he is himself shot while walking back home. The whole film is structured as one long flashback, punctuated by footage of Silva falling down in slow motion (hence the title) to his death — somehow similar to Romolo Guerrieri's *The Double* (1971). What's more, the story has been arbitrarily altered so that it looks like Sterling has been killed by his own boss — all of which makes precious little sense. Other differences concern the dubbing (Keenan Wynn's voice is re-dubbed in a New York accent in *The Falling Man*, while in the Euro version the actor dubbed himself) and Robby Poitevin's beat-psychedelic score, replaced on *The Falling Man* by Marcel Lawler's much inferior electronic music.

Far from being a memorable film, *Frame Up* is worth seeing mainly because of Silva's performance. After establishing himself as a reliable character actor in a number of films, plus the title villain in *Johnny Cool*, Silva moved to Italy with his family, accepting an Italian producer's offer. During his Italian experience, the Brooklyn-born actor would become one of the "poliziottesco"'s emblematic faces, playing indifferently ruthless hitmen or violent cops in such films as Fernando di Leo's *The Italian Connection* and Umberto Lenzi's *Almost Human*. And never, ever, smiling.

Notes

1. Matt Blake, *The Falling Man*, www.europeanfilmreview.co.uk/eurocrime/falling_man.html.
2. Vice, *Il Giorno*, 06.01.1968. The writer also noted: "It's one of those films where one would have to take his hat off every ten minutes or so: to salute the borrowings, the echoes, the plagiarisms."

Gangsters '70 (Gangsters '70)

D: Mino Guerrini; *S* and *SC:* Adriano Baracco, Fernando di Leo, Mino Guerrini; *DOP:* Franco Delli Colli (35mm, Technicolor, Techniscope); *M:* Egisto Macchi (ed. Rete); *E:* Enzo Micarelli; *PD:* Gianfrancesco Ramacci; *Set decorator:* Andrea Fantacci; *CO:* Heinz Riva; *COA:* Francesca Romana Cofano; *AD:* Fabrizio Gianni, Renzo Genta; *C:* Roberto Brega; *AC:* Gianni Canfarelli Modica; *MU:* Lamberto Marini; *AMU:* Giuseppe Ferrante; *Hair:* Vittoria Silvi; *W:* Vera Ceffarelli; *SO:* Piero Ortolani; *SS:* Beatrice Banfi. *Cast:* Joseph Cotten (Destil "Mezzo Miliardo"), Franca Polesello (Franca), Giampiero Albertini (Sempresì), Giulio Brogi (Rudy), Bruno Corazzari (Affatato), Dennis Patrick Hilbane (The Biochemist), Jean Louis, Franco Ressel (The Passenger), Linda Sini, Salvo Basile (Affatato's henchman), Giancarlo Badessi (Banker), Claudio Biava (Escort policeman), Giovanni Pallavicino (Affatato's henchman), Ivan Giovanni Scratuglia, Roberto Simmi (Carnera), Vivien Stapleton (Anna), Milly Vitale (Affatato's sister), Cesare Miceli Picardi (Cavallo). *Uncredited:* Eugene Walter (Card player), Mino Guerrini (Drug dealer in the park). *PROD:* Benito Pertaccini for Bema Film; *PM:* Lucio Orlandini; *PSu:* Fabrizio Mosca, Salvatore Scarfone. *Country:* Italy. *Running time:* 110': Visa n: 51333 (04.12.1968); *Rating:* v.m.18; *Release date:* 04.30.1968; *Distribution:* I.N.D.I.E.F.; *Domestic gross:* 83,977,000 lire. *Also known as:* *Gangster sterben zweimal* (West Germany, 06.13.69 — 95'), *Days of Fire*. *Home video:* UVI (VHS, Canada — Italian language)

Elderly gangster Destil, just released from prison, plans one last job: robbing a case full of diamonds from a courier. He gathers a small gang, which includes a former shooting champion and an actress who attempted suicide. Destil's friend, a cheat named Sempresì, promises he will get the money which is necessary to finance the job by playing cards, but he ends up in the hands of a rival gang whose leader Affatato loans him money in exchange for information on the hit. Destil's plan seems to go smoothly: the plane on which the traveler is carrying the jewels lands at the Fiumicino airport on account of a fake bomb alarm, and the gangsters, dressed up as cops, take the case. When they return to their hideout, however, they find Affatato's gang waiting for them. A shoot-out ensues, and only the actress and the shooting champion are left alive. They make a desperate escape attempt by car, but near the Yugoslavian border the man abandons his companion.

Besides the sociological approach of Lizzani's *Bandits in Milan* and the "American way" of Tessari's *The Bastard* or Giuliano Montaldo's *Machine Gun McCain* (1969), there is a third route to Italian crime cinema. That's the case with Mino Guerrini's *Gangsters '70*. Guerrini was a former journalist who debuted behind the camera with an interesting modern-day Gothic starring Franco Nero, *The Third Eye* (*Il terzo occhio* (1966), later remade by Aristide Massaccesi / Joe D'Amato as *Beyond the Darkness* (*Buio Omega*, 1979). Guerrini's following films were both scripted by Fernando di Leo: *Date for a Murder* (*Omicidio per appuntamento*, 1967), based on the novel *Tempo di massacro* (Massacre Time) by the prolific Sicilian writer Franco Enna,[1] was a sardonic, at times almost experimental *film noir*, graced with a racy pop imagery and plenty of dark humor, starring Giorgio Ardisson, Italy's answer to James Bond in Sergio Sollima's *Agent 3S3* films.

The following year's *Gangsters '70* was a much more serious affair. If *Date for a Murder* was colorful and crackling, *Gangsters '70* is desperate and painful — a far cry from the overall euphoria of 1960s Italian genre cinema. Guerrini and di Leo look at the French *polar* mythology of romantic failure, but also at the implacable narrative mechanism of John Huston's *The Asphalt Jungle* (1950) and Stanley Kubrick's *The Killing* (1956). Originally titled *Elegia in un cimitero d'asfalto o Il sole nero* (*Elegy in an Asphalt Cemetery or Black Sun*), and written by di Leo for an American producer, *Gangsters '70* puts together idiosyncratic gang of losers: an elderly gangster (Joseph Cotten) who is released from prison and plans one more hit, not realizing that times have changed and younger gangsters do not respect him anymore; a middle-aged card cheat (the great character actor Giampiero Albertini) who deludes himself about still being a poker ace; a drug-addicted shooting champion (Giulio Brogi) who even gives away his Olympic gold medal in exchange for a heroin dose; and a faded starlet who just attempted suicide (Franca Polesello) and who takes part of the heist, impersonating a hostess and luring a diamond courier into a trap, because it's the only role she has been offered in a while.

For all of them, the hit means a whole life's redemption. It's not just a matter of money, but a way to show to themselves they are still alive, and not to be forsaken by life and a world which goes much too fast: the title itself alludes to the following decade and to the rapidly changing underworld which is crushing and sweeping away old-style gangsters such as Destil. Di Leo and Guerrini insist on important themes: defeat, betrayal, dignity, the respect for oneself. Yet *Gangsters '70* conveys a pessimism which leaves no room for hope. The film's nameless protagonists—they know each other by their often grotesque nicknames: "Mezzo Miliardo" (Half-a-billion), "Sempresì" (Always-yes), "Il Viaggiatore" (The Passenger)—aren't too far from Gu in Melville's *Le Deuxième souffle* or Jansen in *Le Cercle rouge. Gangsters '70* offers half a dozen memorable characters, including a cruel boss with voyeuristic and incestuous tendences (Bruno Corazzari) who looks like a blueprint for Di Leo's subsequent villains.

The style is much more controlled, although Guerrini doesn't give up his favorite stylistic traits: nervous cuts, sequence shots, slow-motion bits and an inventive use of hand-held camera are put to best use, accompanied by Egisto Macchi's remarkable experimental score: an impressive example of Guerrini's technique has Albertini being trapped against a translucent metal wall and savagely beaten up in slow-motion to Macchi's distorted piece of electronic music and assorted percussions. The first half has an erratic structure, with many detours from the main plot, such as Brogi's meeting at the park with a drug dealer (played by Guerrini himself) who poses as a considerate father by carrying someone else's little boy so as not to arouse suspicion, Brogi's night wanderings while he's in a cold turkey, or Cotten's brief yet touching encounter with an old flame (Vivien Stapleton). The tighter second half is dominated by the lengthy, suspenseful hold-up at the airport and the subsequent showdown with the rival gang in a basement: the latter is a powerful, unpleasant and bloody sequence which features the kind of gory details—such as the blood-spattered features of a man who's just been shot in the face—that had been introduced by Arthur Penn's *Bonnie and Clyde* (1967), and marks a neat departure from the kind of over-the-top yet gleefully sneering violence that characterized the Italian Western. *Gangsters '70* does not end with the massacre, though: Di Leo and Guerrini revive the plot by following Brogi and Polesello's desperate escape to the border, through foggy roads and desolate winter landscapes, as if in some sort of road movie. It's an unexpected, poignant coda which gives the story more depth and pathos, while stressing the makers' original approach to the genre.

However, *Gangsters '70* went unnoticed before critics and audiences alike. 1968 was the year of erotic thrillers with diabolical lovers and exponentially increasing naked skin. Guerrini's film was soon forgotten and rediscovered much too late, towards the end of the '90s. Yet it's a fundamental work in the context of the Italian crime genre, not least because it paves the way for Fernando di Leo's later work.

Note

1. Enna—real name Franco Cannarozzo—was an ecletic figure in the Italian literary world. A poet, novelist, playwright, in a forty-year career he wrote hundreds of works, signing them with an amazing number of pseudonyms.

1969

Bootleggers (Cinque figli di cane)

D: Alfio Caltabiano. *S* and *SC:* Ferdinando Baldi, Alfio Caltabiano, José Gutiérrez Maesso, Leonardo Martín; *DOP:* Francisco Fraile (35mm, Eastmancolor, Colorscope); *M:* Riz Ortolani, conducted by the author (ed. Curci); *E:* Eugenio Alabiso; *PD:* Francisco Canet; *CO:* Maria De Matteis; *ArtD:* Gastone Carsetti; *C:* Mario Sbrenna; *AC:* Fernando Gallandi, Giuseppe Buonaurio; *MU:* Marcello Ceccarelli; *Hair:* Fausto De Lisio; *SO:* Dino Fronzetti; *SS:* Wanda Tuzi. *Cast:* George Eastman [Luigi Montefiori] (McGowan "The Irish"), Wayde Preston (Grimm Doyle), Graziella Granata (Letizia), Tano Cimarosa (Moncio), Archie Savage (Jeremiah), José Suárez (Engineer), Giovanni [Nello] Pazzafini (Gangster at brothel), Antonella Murgia (Mary), Gianni Lorenzon [Gianni Solaro] (Inspector), Sandro Dori (Mary's husband, the cuckold peasant), Mirella Pompili, Porfiria Sanchíz, Tito García (Prison warden Charlie), Goyo Lebrero (barber), Gia Sandri (Brothel Madam), Alan Collins [Luciano Pigozzi] (The boss), Paul Muller (Pythagoras), Eduardo Fajardo (Sir Louis Baymont). *Uncredited:* Ennio Antonelli (Baymont's right hand), Artemio Antonini (Gangster at brothel), Luis Barboo (Mechanic), Alfio Caltabiano (Card player), Mimmo Poli (Man at brothel), Romano Puppo (Boss' bodyguard). *PROD:* Manolo Bolognini for B.R.C. Produzione Film (Rome), Tecisa Film (Madrid); *AP:* José Gutiérrez Maesso; *GM:* Paolo Frascà; *PM* (Spain): Francisco Ocaña; *PSu:* Carlo Giovagnorio; *PSu* (Spain): Julio Parra. *Country:* Italy / Spain. Filmed at Elios Film (Rome) and on location in Spain and Amalfi. *Running time:* 98'; Visa no.: 53228 (03.04.1969) (v.m.14); *Release date:* 03.06.1969; *Distribution:* Cineriz; *Domestic gross:* 239,258,000 lire. *Also known as: América rugiente* (Spain, 06.08.1970); *Cinq fils de chien* (France, 02.04.1970—90'); *Fünf Hundesöhne* (West Germany, 05.22.1969—96'), *5 tolle Hunde* (Germany—Home video). *Home video:* none. OST: LP Ariete ARLP 2004.

Bootlegger Grimm Doyle escapes from prison with four other convicts and recruits them in a mission to destroy a rival organization held by the self-appointed "Sir" Louis Baymont and based in an impregnable convent in Mexico. The quintet team up with a prostitute, Letizia, who gets inside the convent disguised as a nurse. Baymont, however, has been informed about the mission by a spy, and Grimm and his men have to face many dangers. In the end, the fort is blown up, but only Grimm, Letizia and one of the convicts, an Irishman called McGowan, survive. It turns out Grimm is actually an undercover FBI agent whose assignment is to terminate bootlegger gangs in America.

As with a few other Italian period gangster flicks of the period, Alfio Caltabiano's second gangster film in a row after *Comandamenti per un gangster* bears the influence of Arthur Penn's *Bonnie and Clyde*, up to the point where, as one Italian critic noted, the director stages a scene where the police surround the gangsters' villa which is actually lifted almost shot-by-shot from Penn's film.[1] Yet, even though the script shamelessly recycles the plot of Robert Aldrich's *The Dirty Dozen* (plus a little bit of *Where Eagles Dare* as well) in a 1920s prohibitionist scenario, *Bootleggers* is obviously a Western in disguise. Similarities abound, both in character depiction and filmic style.

Producer Manolo Bolognini recalled: "It was set in the U.S. but the budget was low and we had to shoot it partly in Spain, while the scenes set by the sea were shot in Amalfi. I feel a bit guilty because I couldn't give the film the setting it badly needed."[2] What's more, in an attempt to capitalize on the shoestring budget (which also shows in jarring goofs such as a poorly drawn U.S. map with Oklahoma misspelled as "Oklaoma"), several scenes feature recycled sets from some other low-budget Italian Western, as with the opening prison segment and another set in a colorful brothel, where the director even goes for an unexpected sequence shot among customers and gorgeous ladies in their underwear. Later on, a wild fistfight played for laughs—where Caltabiano displays his skills as stunt director—wouldn't be out of place in the *They Call Me Trinity* series, whereas the opening shot even recalls a similar moment in Sam Peckinpah's *The Wild Bunch*—a pure coincidence, since the latter was released after Caltabiano's film—as a scorpion surrounded by fire punctures itself to death with its deadly sting. "Suicide is the only way to get out of here" sneers a slimy prison ward to the newly convicted Grimm Doyle (Wayde Preston).

However, Caltabiano never pushes the pedal of violence and unpleasantness. There is always a drop of humor in the proceedings, as shown by Luciano Pigozzi's bootlegger posing as undertaker (a cliché in itself ever since Billy Wilder's *Some Like It Hot*) and the inclusion of bizarre characters such as Tano Cimarosa (who became one of Caltabiano's best friends and co-starred in the director's subsequent films) as the Sicilian-born Moncio, a former lion tamer and circus illusionist who becomes part of Preston's five-man army assembled with ex-convicts, plus a number of humorous scenes as the aforementioned brothel fight. On the other hand, as McGowan, the Irishman who spits racist venom throughout the film, only to give up his convictions in the end, the gigantic Luigi Montefiori (later on a screenwriter and actor in such trashy Joe D'Amato epics as *The Grim Reaper*, 1980) delivers a number of cringeworthy lines: "I never worked with someone whose skin is different from mine!" he growls at Jeremiah (Archie Savage). The African American Savage—a former dancer and creator of the Afro / Cuban dance form—had moved to Italy in the '60s after a career which included a number of classics such as *Vera Cruz* (1954) and *South Pacific* (1958), and besides a small but memorable role in *La Dolce Vita*, where he danced with Anita Ekberg, he appeared in genre flicks as diverse as Antonio Margheriti's sci-fi debut *Space Men* (1960) and Giulio Petroni's western *Death Rides a Horse* (1967). This, at 55, was his last film role; Savage is systematically (and rather clumsily) replaced by a double in his fight scenes. He died in 2003.

Caltabiano directed four more films before retiring in the early 1970s: the amusing Medieval adventure/mystery yarn *Una spada per Brando* (A Sword for Brando, 1970) starring Karin Schubert, the comic Westerns *Man Called Amen* (*Così sia*, 1972) and its sequel *They Still Called Me Amen* (*Oremus, Alleluja e Così sia*, 1973), both starring Luc Merenda, and the Mafia spoof Italian Graffiti (*Tutti figli di Mammasantissima*, 1973), featuring a very young Ornella Muti.

Notes

1. Pietro Bianchi, *Il Giorno*, 03.23.1969. In his review, Bianchi mistakes Caltabiano for a Spanish director, once again proving the scarce attention Italian genre cinema benefited from critics of the time.
2. Luigia Miniucchi, *Alfio Caltabiano* (Rome: Gremese, 2009), p. 68.

C'era una volta un gangster (*Gangsters Jungle*) (There Once Was a Gangster)

D: Marco Masi. *S* and *SC:* Marco Masi; *DOP:* Giovanni Raffaldi (35mm, Eastmancolor, Staco Film); *M:* Marcello Gigante (ed. Tank); *E:* Romeo Ciatti; *PD:* Giovanni Fratalocchi; *C:* Lorenzo Sorrentino; *AE:* Renato Venturini; *AD:* Lucia Porfiri; *MU:* Angelo Roncaioli; *SO:* Carlo Diotallevi; *SE:* Celeste Battistelli; *SP:* Gaetano Piovani; *MA:* Bruno Arié; *W:* Antonietta Piredda. *Cast:* Richard Harrison (Larry Alfieri), Ingrid Schöeller (Paula), Barth Warren (Walter), Bruna Beani (Petroni's widow), Vittoria Solinas (Simona), Attilio Dottesio (Commissioner Mazzano), Anna Maria Panaro (Rosy), Gianni Pulone, Consalvo Dell'Arti (Commissioner in Chief), Ovidio Taito, Armando Cariani, Mario Darnell, Bruno Chiappafreddo, Franco Ukmar, Aldo Boron, Sandro Tassi. *PROD:* Rex Film Company; *GM:* Mario Dardanelli; *PSu:* Fernando Martorana, Salvatore Miglio; *PSe:* Romeo Corpetti. *Country:* Italy. Filmed at SCO Ostia Antica (Rome) and on location in Rome. *Running time:* 77'; Visa no.: 53871 (05.14.1969); *Rating:* not rated; *Release date:* 06.08.1969; *Distribution:* Regional; *Domestic gross:* 68,821,000 lire. *Home video:* Hobby & Work (DVD, Italy).

Together with two associates, gangster Larry Alfieri steals the loot from a robbery performed by Joe Petroni (who died in the act) and his gang, which was hidden inside a cushion in Petroni's coffin. Larry then kills his accomplices and hides the money, but is betrayed by his lover Paula, who's in cahoots with rival gangster Walter. Larry is saved by Petroni's widow, who wants her money back, and goes on Walter's trail. His informer is killed by Walter's right hand man, Mike, who pins the murder on Larry. Commissioner Mazzano, a friend of Alfieri's father (who was a cop, killed in action during a robbery) vainly tries to redeem the gangster, and resigns rather than have to arrest him. Paula, who's still in love with Larry, saves his life and goes back to him, but he rejects her. Larry takes refuge in the house of a friend, Simona. While Walter and Mike are getting ready to leave, after killing Paula, Simona—who loves Larry and wants to save him—begs Mazzano to help her stop Larry. But it's too late: in his final duel with Walter and Mike, Larry kills them both, but perishes in turn.

An obscure Z-grade crime film starring former spy movie star Richard Harrison, Marco Masi's *C'era una volta un gangster* didactically displays the transition from Spaghetti Western to contemporary crime dramas in its final scenes, set for no apparent reason in a Western village *milieu* just outside Rome. The film's hero, Larry Alfieri, catches up with his rivals as they are about to flee with the proceeds of a robbery and a shoot-out takes place inside a saloon: what follows, as the mortally wounded Larry has visions of the commissioner (Attilio Dottesio) appearing to warn him, is shown through solarized point of view shots, with somewhat psychedelic results. Unfortunately that's the only thing worth noting in Masi's film, besides Marcello Gigante's jazzy Farfisa score.

The budget is practically non-existent, and the byzantine plot twists and turns really don't go anywhere, while unintentionally ridiculous moments abound—starting from the fact that, even though the action occurs in the outskirts of Rome, all gangsters have foreign names (a hint that the original script actually had a Western setting, perhaps?). What's more, the preachy and moralistic tone is really hard to stomach.

Violence is bland and comic-book style, but Masi—a terrible filmmaker whose scant filmography includes the little-seen erotic dramas *Il seme di Caino* (1972) and *Il demonio nel cervello* (1976) plus the mysterious *L'autuomo* (1984)—manages to include a few mildly erotic moments (one featuring a laughable moment where the camera zooms from a lovemaking couple to a pair of colored soft toys on a shelf) and a gratuitous nude shower scene.

The Italian print carries the English language subtitle *Gangsters Jungle* [sic], but there is no trace of any foreign language version whatsoever.

Cry Chicago (*¡Viva América! / La vera storia di Frank Mannata)*

D: Saverio [Javier] Setó. *S:* Luigi Mondello; *SC:* Javier Setó; *DOP:* Emilio Foriscot (35mm, Eastmancolor, Tecnostampa); *M:* Gianfranco Reverberi, conducted by Gianpiero Reverberi; *Wait and Dream* (P. Cassia. G.F. Reverberi, G.P. Reverberi) sung by Anna Maria Pierangeli; *E:* Antonio Jimeno; *PD:* José Luis Galicia; *SD:* Jaime Pérez Cubero; *CO:* Esteban Gutiérrez; *MU:* Vincente Vásquez; *C:* Fernando Espiga; *AD:* Paulino González. *Cast:* Jeffrey Hunter (Francesco "Frank" Mannata), Margaret Lee (Lucia Barrett), William Bogart [Guglielmo Spoletini] (Salvatore Mannata), Gogó Rojo (Rossella Mannata), Miguel Del Castillo (O'Brien), Eduardo Fajardo (Dick O'Connor), Victor Israel (McDonald), Anna Maria Pierangeli (Bambi), Luis Induni (Buchanan, Chief of Police), Barta Barri, Beni Deus. *PROD:* Luigi Mondello for Nike Cinematografica (Rome); *AP:* Eduardo Manzanos Brochero for Coop. Copercines (Madrid); *GM:* Luigi Mondello; *PSu:* Augusto Dolfi; *PSe:* Rinaldo Scorcelletti. *Country:* Spain / Italy. *Running time:* 95'; Visa no.: 54532 (09.22.1969); *Rating:* v.m.14; *Release date:* 09.22.1969; *Distribution:* Nike (Regional); *Domestic gross:* unknown. *Also known as: Le clan des frères Mannata* (France), *Frank Mannata igaz története* (Hungary), *Wahre Geschichte des Frank Mannata* (West Germany), *Wahrheit über Frank Mannata* (East Germany). *Home video:* none.

Chicago, 1929. A young Sicilian, Frank Mannata, reaches his siblings Salvatore and Rossella: the former is the head of an affluent liquor smuggling business, and the latter runs a beauty parlor, which in fact is a hostel to illicit loves, among whom are the wives and daughters of politicians and powerful authorities. By documenting these clandestine affairs and using them for purposes of blackmail, Rossella and Salvatore obtain the complicity of those who could crush their trafficking. Determined to expand their business, Frank begins to impose upon keepers and traders his so-called "protection"; then, to acquire the monopoly of all the illegal alcohol trafficking, he gets rid of the powerful rival boss Al Messina. Frank avoids expulsion from the United States by marrying an American woman, Lucy Barrett, the daughter of a judge blackmailed by his brother. Mannata becomes so powerful as to arouse the rivalry of another gangster, Dick O'Connor, who, to force a coming to terms with him, kills Salvatore and Rossella. Pretending to yield to his demands, Frank draws O'-Connor in a death trap but his triumph is short-lived: he will soon perish with Lucy in the explosion of his car, perpetrated by one of Dick's henchmen.

The second of two Spanish-Italian period gangster flicks filmed in a row and financed by producer Luigi Mondello's Nike Cinematografica and Eduardo Brochero's Copercine, the other being *They Paid with Bullets*, Javier Setó's *Cry Chicago* benefited from a prestigious name, even though faded since his glory days, such as Jeffrey Hunter, who had wound up in Europe after his Hollywood career went downhill in the mid-sixties. However, the shooting was plagued by the budget problems so common with genre productions, and Hunter (who suffered face lacerations and powder burns on the set in the scene depicting the shoot-out between two cars) left production in Spain when the producers ran out of money for the cast and crew. He returned to the United States, where he died unexpectedly, at just 42. The film was later finished without him. Another has-been on sight is the ravishing Anna Maria Pierangeli, who is sadly reduced to a brief and far from memorable guest appearance as the singer in Mannata's nightclub. She was also destined to an untimely death, just a couple of years later, at 39.

Setó's film features the same sets and many actors in common with Julio Diamante's *They Paid with Bullets*, not to mention a script that is more or less a lackluster variation on the same storyline, which has poor Italian immigrant Francesco Mannata (Hunter) and his rise-and-fall arc in 1920s Prohibitionist Chicago. "What I just can't stand about Italians, is that they come to America as tramps and immediately want to be the bosses" one character says. Although ultimately just a pretext for the usual array of car chases, machine-gun shoot-outs and ragtime music (this time by Gianfranco Reverberi and his brother Giampiero), the theme of immigration was common to a number of Italian period gangster films — most notably Pino Mercanti's *The Underground* (1970).

Unlike Diamante's film, *Cry Chicago* does not rely on nudity and sleaze. However, despite such oddities as one scene set in a Western village which appears to be the storage site for smuggled whisky — no doubt a trick to cut corners on budget — Setó's film ends up slightly more enjoyable than its twin brother. That's mainly because of the director's amusing comic book–style direction, with lots of tracking shots, wide-angle hand-held camerawork, and at least one memorable scene when Mannata ties a victim's (Miguel Del Castillo) hands and feet behind his back with a rope which also passes around his neck so that the victim will inevitably come to strangle himself (a Sicilian Mafia method called *incaprettamento*). Setó — who had directed one of the most interesting Spanish fantastic films of the sixties, *The Sweet Sound of Death* (*La llamada*, 1965) — has his name Italianized in the credits (as would happen with Diamante on *They Paid with Bullets*). This was to be his last film as well, as the director passed away that very same year.

Detective Belli, a.k.a. *Ring of Death (Un Detective — Macchie Di Belletto)*

D: Romolo Guerrieri. *S:* based on the novel *Macchie di belletto* by Ludovico Dentice; *SC:* Franco Verucci, Alberto Silvestri, Massimo D'Avack; *DOP:* Roberto Gerardi (35mm, Technicolor); *M:* Fred Bongusto, conducted by Robby Poitevin; *The World of the Blues* is sung by Shirley Harmer; *E:* Marcello Malvestito; *PD:* Giantito Burchiellaro; *AD:* Renzo Genta; *C:* Gastone Di Giovanni; *AC:* Franco Bruni; *APD:* Francesca Saitto; *CO:* Luca Sabatelli; *COA:* Mario Della Torre; *MU:* Franco Corridoni; *Hair:* Rosa Luciani; *SO:* Guido Ortensi; *Mix:* Mario Morigi; *SS:* Serena Canevari. *Cast:* Franco Nero (Commissioner Stefano Belli), Florinda Bolkan (Vera Fontana), Adolfo Celi (Fontana), Delia Boccardo (Sandy Bronson), Susanna Martinková (Emanuelle), Maurizio Bonuglia (Mino Fontana), Roberto Bisacco (Claudio Valeri), Renzo Palmer (commissioner Baldo). *Uncredited:* Laura Antonelli (Franca), Geoffrey Copleston (Chief of Police), Silvia Dionisio (Gabriella), Marino Masé (Romanis), Vittorio Ripamonti (police agent), John Stacy (Porter) *PROD:* Mario Cecchi Gori for Fair Film; *PM:* Luciano Luna; *UPM:* Camillo Teti, Renato Fiè; *ADM:* Bruno Altissimi. *Country:* Italy. Filmed at Dear Film Studios (Rome). *Running time:* 104'; Visa no.: 54308

(08.21.1969); *Rating:* v.m.14; *Release date:* 09.06.1969; *Distribution:* Interfilm; *Domestic gross:* 616,630,000 lire. *Also known as: Exécutions* (France, 12.02.70—90'), *Die Klette* (05.29.70—101'). *Home video:* Cecchi Gori (DVD, Italy). Soundtrack: CD Avanz Records SP/CR 20006.

Franco Nero and Delia Boccardo in *Detective Belli* (1969).

Commissioner Belli, a police officer at the Foreign Office in Rome, is bribed by renowned lawyer Fontana, who will give him a few million lira if Belli has an English model—Fontana's son's lover—expelled from the country; what's more, the lawyer asks Belli to make a private investigation on a record company's owner whom Fontana's wife Vera is willing to finance. Belli discovers that the man has been assassinated. The picture of a naked woman (whose face has been cut off) which he finds in the victim's house leads Belli to suspect that the murder has been committed by either the model—whom he hasn't expelled from the country—a pop singer or even Vera Fontana. More murders follow, as Fontana's friend and his own son are found dead. The police suspects Belli, but in the end he saves his reputation by framing the real murderer, Vera Fontana. However, Belli has to renounce to Fontana's million lira in order to avoid jail.

Gangsters '70 wasn't the only attempt at grafting *film noir* themes on an Italian setting. If Mino Guerrini's film hinted at both French polar and U.S. heist classics by Huston and Kubrick, Romolo Guerrieri's *Detective Belli*—the film adaptation of a novel by Ludovico Dentice—is a more convoluted hybrid. Guerrieri's work mixes the sexy thriller subgenre, which the director had just tried his hand at with *The Sweet Body of Deborah* (*Il dolce corpo di Deborah*, 1968), with a whodunit plot whose characters and atmosphere definitely recall French noir.

The tone is cynical rather than elegiac. Franco Nero's character dresses like someone who stepped out of a Chandler novel, but he's got nothing of Philip Marlowe's romantic idealism. He's a corrupt cop, a mercenary, a son of a bitch who's a bully with the weak and slavish with the wealthy and powerful. He's opportunistic, greedy and unscrupulous, and juggles between legality and illegality always with a smile on his face. Throughout the whole film, Belli only acts for his own profit: after he is illegally hired by a wealthy lawyer (Adolfo Celi, in one of those roles he could act in his sleep) and soon finds himself tangled up in a bad story of illicit affairs and murders, Belli just tries to cut out his share, beating up people and blackmailing them in turn whenever he's got the chance. He thinks he's much smarter than anyone else, but he ends up with two bullets in his belly, and has to burn the checks he fought so much for so as not to be incriminated by his honest colleague Baldo (Renzo Palmer).

Guerrieri amply shows that he's an accomplished filmmaker in his own right. Critic Giovanni Buttafava praised the ending on the Fiumicino dock, "nocturnal, stylized, *à la* Jean-Pierre Melville, with the cold yet emotionally charged confrontation between the half-rotten–half-clean cop Franco Nero and Florinda Bolkan, with stylistic traits of *film noir* mythologizing which were rare in Italy, and rather remarkable as well."[1]

Detective Belli was rereleased in the 1970s, during the "poliziotteschi" boom, as *Tracce di rossetto e di droga per un detective* (*Traces of lipstick and drug for a detective*). If the film undoubtedly predates in part the following decade's crime genre, it's rather ironic that Nero's character is named Belli, just like the hero in Enzo G. Castellari's *High Crime* (1973), even though the two characters are poles apart.

Note

1. Giovanni Buttafava, "Procedure sveltite" in Aa. Vv. *Il Patalogo Due. Annuario 1980 dello spettacolo, Volume secondo, Cinema e televisione* (Milan: Ubulibri/Electa, 1980), p. 107.

The Electric Chair (Sedia elettrica)

D: Miles Deem [Demofilo Fidani]. *S:* Miles Deem; *SC:* Miles Deem, Mila Vitelli [Maria Rosa Valenza]; *Dia:* Alfredo Medori; *DOP:* Sergio D'Offizi (35mm, Eastmancolor, Panoramic); *M:* Marcello Gigante, conducted by Carlo Esposito; *E:* Piera Bruni; *PD/CO:* Mila Vitelli Valenza; *C:* Giuseppe Gatti; *AC:* Enrico Lucidi; *AE:* Gianfranco Simoncelli; *COA:* Giuliana Serano; *AD:* Fabrizio Diotallevi; 2nd ADs: Adriana Del Carlo, Antonino Antonucci Ferrara; *ArtD:* Pasquale Mancino; *MU:* Corrado Blengini; *Hair:* Riccardo Pratella, Francesco Pratella; *SO:* Giuseppe Mangione; *DM:* Miriam Fabricotti; *KG:* Fernando Rocco Fusco; *ChEl:* Marcello Valesani; *SS:* Rita Agostini. *Cast:* Big I. Verdi [Reza Beyk Imanverdi] (Fred Boston), Sheyla Rosin [Spela Rozin] (Fanny), Dean Stratford [Dino Strano] (Johnny Bello), Silvio Noto (Doc), Simone Blondell [Simonetta Vitelli] (Margie), Franco Ricci (Gardenia), Dennis Colt [Benito Pacifico], Frank Fargas [Paolo Figlia], Mariella Palmich, Lino Coletta, Luciano Conti, Amir Jeffry, Franca Licastro, Piero Del Papa (Tiger). *PROD:* Maria Rosa Valenza for Tarquinia Film; *PM:* Oscar Santaniello; *PSe:* Diego Spataro. *Country:* Italy. Filmed at Tirrenia Studios (Rome). *Running time:* 87'; Visa no.: 54292 (08.13.1969); *Rating:* not rated; *Release date:* 08.23.1969; *Distribution:* Tarquinia; *Domestic gross:*

32,000,000 lire. *Also known as: Hot Chair* (Sweden — Home video). *Home video:* NMP (VHS, Sweden). OST: 7" CAM AMP 69 (*Hot Chair:* includes *Gangsters a New York / Gardenia*)

Santa Monica, 1930s. Crime kingpin Johnny Bello annihilates Jack Boston's rival gang in an ambush at the docks. The only survivor, although badly wounded, is Jack's brother, Fred "the loner." Afraid of Fred's revenge, Johnny entrusts one of his men to find him and kill him. Fred escapes, and becomes friends with Bello's girlfriend Fanny, from whom he learns the details of an impending heist upon a bank truck. At the place designated for the assault on the van, Fred exterminates Johnny's whole gang, but some guards die in the crossfire, and so does Fanny. Captured and sentenced to the electric chair, Fred recounts his whole life while waiting for the execution. When he was still a child, he witnessed the murder of his parents, a trauma that would lead him along with his brother Jack on the road to banditry.

A change of pace for the director after a number of picturesquely titled (and shot) westerns, *The Electric Chair* nevertheless bears the stigmata of Demofilo Fidani's work in every single frame. A former production designer, Fidani helmed at least 20 films between 1967 and 1976 before giving up direction altogether and following his passion for the occult. He would become a notorious mystic and medium, even loosely inspiring a film, Silvio Amadio's yawn-a-thon *Il medium* (1978). *The Electric Chair*, as ever with the director, is a family effort: Fidani teams up with his wife, costume designer Maria Rosa Valenza, who also acts as producer and co-scripter, while his stepdaughter Simonetta Vitelli pops up in a small role as the hero's love interest (being even given a gratuitous and silly skating scene in a park). Fidani's regular Dean Stratford (real name Dino Strano) plays slimy villain Johnny Bello, while — in a typically unfathomable Fidani move — Iranian actor-director Reza Imanverdi was cast in the leading role, in a performance which could best be described as amateurish.

Patently shot on a shoestring, *The Electric Chair* was a half-hearted attempt at cashing in on the period gangster trend, which spawned a number of low-budget Italian flicks within a couple of years after the success of Arthur Penn's *Bonnie and Clyde*. Period details are kept to a minim*um:* a few 1920s cars, machine guns and pinstripe suits, that's that. Anachronisms abound, from interior furniture and props (the glass desk in the doctor's office is a case in point) to a nightclub scene set in a very '60s disco. Besides, Fidani's depopulated Santa Monica is actually the Roman countryside, laughably recreated with a few very un-American looking villas and little else. Dialogue is uniformly bad ("I don't have time. I got better things to do" says Bello, rejecting his lover's advances), but even worse are the awkward, heavy-handed attempts at psychological introspection such as Fred's pompous voice-over monologues, or the faucet drops that awaken his childhood trauma (which is eventually displayed in the final stylized flashback). Action scenes are pure Fidani: like in his westerns — such as *Shadow of Sartana ... Shadow of Your Death* (*Passa Sartana ... è l'ombra della tua morte*, 1969) or *Dead Men Don't Make Shadows* (*Inginocchiati Straniero ... i cadaveri non fanno ombra!*, 1970), when someone is shot he doesn't simply fall dead, but he writhes, wriggles and rolls around like a possessed soul before exhaling his last breath. And the motorbike chase through the hills near Rome must be seen to be believed.

Since the film proved to be a box office flop, Fidani quickly returned to his favorite genre. However, many scenes were later recycled by the director for his second and last stab at the genre, 1973's *Mafia Killer*.

Gangsters' Law (*La legge dei gangsters*)

D: Siro Marcellini. *S:* Siro Marcellini; *SC:* Dean Craig [Piero Regnoli], Siro Marcellini; *DOP:* Silvio Fraschetti-Pistola (35mm, Technicolor, Techniscope); *M:* Piero Umiliani; *Che mai sarà* (Tilesi / Umiliani) sung by Ira, *I Won't Shed a Tear* sung by Franco Morselli; *E:* Vincenzo Vanni; *PD:* Mimmo Scavia; *PP:* Giuseppe Fieno; *CO:* Vanda Perna; *C:* Alvaro Lanzoni, Renato Mascagni; *AC:* Marcello Carlini, Giuliano Grasselli; *AE:* Gisella Nuccitelli; *AD:* Mario Bianchi; *2nd AD:* Franco Brocani; *MU:* Marisa Tilli; *SO:* Luciano Welish; *SP:* Ermanno Consolazione; *KG:* Roberto Petani; *ChEl:* Rodolfo Filibotto; *SS:* Anna Maria Bifarini. *Cast:* Klaus Kinski (Regnier), Maurice Poli (Rino Quintero), Franco Citti (Bruno Esposito), Samy Pavel (Franco), Susy Andersen (Mayde), Hélène Chanel (Countess Elena Villani), Micaela Pignatelli (Renato's lover), Giovanni [Nello] Pazzafini (driver), Aurora Bautista (Rosi, Bruno's lover), Aldo Cecconi (Fulvio Rigani), Giancarlo Sisti (Nando, the pimp), Donatella Turri (Regnier's lover), Sergio Mioni, Luciano Mancini, Gino Bardellini, Max Delys (Renato), Lina Franchi. *PROD:* Roberto Loyola for Roberto Loyola Cinematografica; *PM:* Armando Bertuccioli; *PSu:* Antonio Palumbo; *PSe:* Silvano Zignani. *Country:* Italy. Filmed on location in Genoa. *Running time:* 95': Visa no.: 53937 (06.18.1969); *Rating:* v.m.18; *Release date:* 08.08.1969; *Distribution:* Regional; *Domestic gross:* 140,995,000 lire. *Also known as: La loi des gangsters* (France), *O fonias* (Greece — video title), *Quintero — Das As der Unterwelt* (West Germany). *Home video:* None. OST: CD Right Tempo ET 914 CD

As soon as he is released from prison, gangster Rino Quintero plans another heist with the help of fence Fulvio Rigani: a 500 million lire job at a Genoese bank. Rino's accomplices are two young jewelry thieves, Franco and Renato, and the unemployed Bruno Esposito; the robbery is financed by a Frenchman, Regnier, who will get a 30 percent of the booty. After the heist, a shoot-out with the police ensues, where Rigani is shot dead. When they are about to share the loot, Rino and the others are betrayed by Regnier, who forces them to give him half of the money. Rino swears revenge, but his adversary starts eliminating his accomplices one by one. Regnier murders Franco and tries to do the same with Bruno, but Rino shows up unexpectedly and kills him. When he is about to escape on a motorboat with Rigani's widow Mayde, though, Quintero is surrounded by the police and killed in the ensuing shoot-out.

Halfway between *Bandits in Rome*'s spectacular genre mechanism and Lizzani's documentary-like approach, a year later came *Gangsters' Law*, directed by Siro Marcellini and produced by Roberto Loyola. Marcellini's film sports an elaborate flashback structure in its first part, in order to tell the story of a bank robbery (at the National Agriculture Bank in Genoa) through the different points of view of each gang member. The plot echoes the French *polar*, and culminates in a *rififi* between gang leader Maurice Poli and his mean rival Klaus Kinski; but the opening sequence, which centers on a shoot-out between the gangsters and the police which is filmed in long shot and with nervous, choppy cuts, openly refers to *Bandits in Milan*. Another important trait is the use of Genoa, which would become the capital of Italian crime movies in the following decade: here its filmic impact is immensely aided by Piero Umiliani's guitar-driven score. One particular piece of music, the romantic *Crepuscolo sul mare*, would become one of the composer's best known tracks, and it would be reused years later in Steven Soderbergh's *Ocean's Twelve* (2004).

Whenever it tries to be more than a competent genre pic, though, *Gangsters' Law* falters. Marcellini and his co-writer Piero Regnoli even venture into clumsy sociological interpretations: one of the gangsters, Bruno (played by Pier Paolo Pasolini's friend Franco Citti, himself a subproletarian turned actor with *Accattone*, 1961), is a poor chap from the South who moved to the North to find a job because in his native town he was starving, while two of his accomplices come from wealthy families but pose as protesters. The way youth culture is portrayed betrays a certain paternalism, though, with such lines as: "Each time we get together to have fun, it's so easy for us to shout, "Death to conventional morals!" We want to destroy past taboos, but the time of responsibilities will come." Marcellini, a former assistant of Augusto Genina (*Cielo sulla palude* a.k.a. *Heaven Over the Marshes*, 1949) had become a filmmaker himself in the '50s, directing popular dramas (*Don Vesuvio*, 1958), period swashbucklers (*The Devil's Cavaliers*, 1959), sword-and-sandals (*Goliath*, 1963) and even a Western (*Lola Colt*, 1967), with mediocre results. *Gangsters' Law* was his penultimate directorial effort, followed by a war movie shot in Greece and co-directed by Vasilis Georgiadis, *Hell in the Aegean* (*Quei dannati giorni dell'odio e dell'inferno*, 1970).

Machine Gun McCain (*Gli intoccabili*)

D: Giuliano Montaldo. *S:* Mino Roli, freely [sic] based on the novel *Candyleg* by Vovid Demaris; *SC:* Mino Roli, Giuliano Montaldo; *DIA:* Israel Horowitz, directed by Lewis A. Ciannelli; *DOP:* Erico Menczer (35mm, Technicolor, Techniscope); *M:* Ennio Morricone, conducted by Bruno Nicolai (ed. General music); *The Ballad of Hank McCain* (E. Morricone / Audrey Nohra) sung by Jackie Lynton; *E:* Franco Fraticelli; *ArtD:* Flavio Mogherini; *ArtD:* Roberto Veloccia; *SD:* Ennio Michettoni, Emilio Baldelli; *CO:* Enrico Sabbatini; *AD:* Fabrizio Gianni; *AEs:* Adriana Benedetti, Pierluigi Leonardi; *C:* Silvio Fraschetti; *AC:* Renato Mascagno; *MU:* Michele Trimarchi; *Hair:* Giancarlo De Leonardis; *W:* Marcella Moretti, Nadia Vitali; *SO:* Luciano Welisch, Mario Amari, Renato Pampaloni; *Boom:* Giovanni Fratarcangeli; *Mix:* Renato Cadueri; *KG:* Orlando Dolci; *LT:* Rodolfo Fibotti; *SS:* Vittoria Vigorelli. *Cast:* John Cassavetes (Hank McCain), Britt Ekland (Irene Tucker), Peter Falk (Charlie Adamo), Gabriele Ferzetti (Don Francesco De Marco), Salvo Randone (Don Salvatore De Marco), Pierluigi Aprà (Jack McCain), Luigi Pistilli (Duke Mazzanga), Florinda Bolkan (Joni Adamo), Tony Kendall [Luciano Stella] (Pete Zacari), Gena Rowlands (Rosemary Scott), Margherita Guzzinati (Margaret De Marco), Claudio Biava (Barclay), Steffen Zacharias (Abe Stilberman), James Morrison (Joby Cuda), Bill Vanders (Steve, Rosemary's assistant), Annabella Andreoli (Assunta Esposito), Val Avery (Chuck Regan), Jack Ackerman (Britten), Ermanno Consolazione (Gennarino Esposito), Carol Doda, Billy Lee (Pepe), Dennis Sallas (Fred Tecosky), Maria Mizar, Mirella Panfili, Euplio Moscusu, Roberto Triggi, Gaetano Imbrò, Silvano Bacci, Franco Riti. *PROD:* Marco Vicario and Bino Cicogna for Euroatlantica; *PM:* Romano Cardarelli; *APM:* Agostino Pane; *PSe:* Enrico Melonari. *Country:* Italy. Filmed at Incir–De Paolis, Dear Studios (Rome) and on location in Las Vegas, San Francisco, Los Angeles. *Running time:* 116' (U.S. version: 96'): Visa no.: 53481 (03.22.69) (v.m.14); *Release date:* 04.01.1969; *Distribution:* Euro International Film; *Domestic gross:* 803,751,000 lire. *Also known as: Les intouchables* (France, 1969—114'); *Die Unschlagbaren* (West Germany, 04.30.71—119'). *Home video:* Blue Underground (Blu-ray/DVD, USA, 96'), Raro (DVD, Italy: 91'), M6 Vidéo (DVD, France, '92, as *Les intouchables*). OST: CD Dagored Red 126-2.

Small-time mafioso Charlie Adamo is planning to rob the Royal Casino in Las Vegas. To do the job, he has bankrobber Hank McCain released from prison, where the criminal was serving a life sentence. When Adamo discovers that the Casino actually belongs to his own Mafia bosses, Salvatore and Francesco De Marco, he tries to stop McCain at all costs, killing the latter's son Jack in the process. McCain and his newlywed wife, a former prostitute named Irene, carry on with the hit regardless and steal two million dollars. Soon, though, McCain finds out that the Mafia is on his track: he seeks help from his former lover Rosemary, who arranges him and Irene to escape by sea. Adamo is assassinated by the Mafia, and Rosemary is captured by De Marco's henchman Pete Zacari, but commits suicide rather than talk. However, Zacari captures Irene just when she's about to reach McCain on a boat to safety, and kills her in cold blood in front of McCain. The latter desperately offers resistance, but is killed too.

The fact that Italian distributors didn't believe in gangster stories set in their country partially explains why producers Marco Vicario and Bino Cicogna and director Giuliano Montaldo fled overseas to shoot *Machine Gun McCain* (1968), with English-speaking leads. As with *Bandits in Rome*, the cast is led by John Cassavetes—much more convincing here as the eponymous bandit than in De Martino's film—which for this occasion is reunited with his friend and favorite actor Peter Falk and his own wife Gena Rowlands. Supporting roles are played by experienced Italian actors such as Gabriele Ferzetti, Luigi Pistilli and Salvo Randone (each on screen for just a handful of minutes), while Ennio Morricone's score, which features a theme song dedicated to antihero Hank "Machine Gun" McCain, predates the baroque musical delights of Leone's *A Fistful of Dynamite* and Montaldo's own *Sacco and Vanzetti* (both 1971).[1] *Machine Gun McCain* was the Genoese director's second—and last—excursion in the genre after the enjoyable heist movie *Grand Slam* (*Ad ogni costo*, 1967), starring Edward G. Robinson, Janet Leigh and Klaus Kinski, which showed his refined technical skills. Since his debut *Tiro al piccione* (Pigeon Shooting, 1961), set in the days of the Republic of Salò, Montaldo showed he was a committed filmmaker; in his 1965 film *The Reckless* (*Una bella grinta*) he depicted one of the most interesting analyses of Italian post–World War II economy: here, he leaves commitment aside and tries his hand at a Carthusian imitation of U.S. *film noir*. Cassavetes' Hank McCain—an ex-convict released from jail by order of mafioso Charlie Adamo (Peter Falk), who wants him to rob a Las Vegas casino which, unknown to Adamo, belongs to the "family"—looks, walks and talks as if he just stepped out of a Jim Thompson novel. Which is exactly what the script by Montaldo and Mino Roli (loosely based on Vovid Demaris' 1961 novel *Candyleg*) hints at: echoes of *The Getaway* are evident throughout, especially when it comes to McCain's desperate attempt to escape the Mafia with his bride Irene (Britt Ekland) after the hit, and all characters are essentially negative and mean, with no redeeming qualities at all—take the relationship between the power-hungry yet cowardly Adamo, his boss Frank De Marco (Ferzetti) and Adamo's wife Joni (Florinda Bolkan) who is also De Marco's lover.

Machine Gun McCain was quite profitable at the Italian box office, grossing over 800 million lire (about a third of that year's No. 1 hit, Luigi Magni's *Nell'anno del signore*, still definitely a good result). The film's style patently recalls American gangster films — take for instance McCain's first encounter with Irene, or the tight robbery scenes (where Montaldo manages to at least partially hide the implausibilities in the antihero's plan). Yet the inquisitive way Montaldo shoots on location in Las Vegas and San Francisco somehow betrays the director's foreign status, as does Erico Menczer's lighting, with the predominance of yellow lights in interiors (as in the scenes in Gena Rowlands' flat) giving them an unreal quality. What's more, the way Montaldo depicts the Mafia's omnipotence is unmistakably Italian: the scenes with Randone and Ferzetti predate Fernando di Leo's portrayals of ruthless Mafia bosses in *The Italian Connection* (1972) and *The Boss* (1973), while the downbeat ending shows the director's pessimism which would come to the fore in his following films, namely *Sacco and Vanzetti* (1971) and *Giordano Bruno* (1973).

It's a pity the script sometimes drags — at least in the 96' export version, the only one available for review.[2] The relationship between McCain and his son Jack (Pierluigi Aprà) is scarcely believable and never deepened, as is the one between Hank and Irene: they meet, they make love, they marry in Las Vegas — that's all. Even a much more gifted actress than the breathtaking Britt Ekland would have been at pains trying to give depth to such a vacant character.

U.S. poster for *Machine Gun McCain* (1969).

Machine Gun McCain detaches itself from routine only when Gena Rowlands enters the picture. As Rosemary, McCain's old flame and accomplice, to whom the running man asks for help in his desperate attempt at escape by sea, she and Cassavetes share a powerful screen chemistry that is absent in the scenes between Cassavetes and Ekland. Rowland's character is a loser who already contains the seeds of the memorable one portrayed by the actress in Cassavetes' *Gloria* (1980), and allows her a memorable solo: about to be tortured by the ruthless Pete Zacari (Tony Kendall a.k.a. Luciano Stella), Rosemary kills herself rather than giving away McCain's hideout, and does so with the same contemptuous disregard as she would lighting a cigarette. The predictable nihilistic ending, on the other hand, falls somewhat flat, not to mention the rather hasty way it's shot. That had something to do with Cassavetes' refusal to shoot his death scene in the Los Angeles dock, which forced Montaldo to use a double and film it in long shots. "Cassavetes and I started in the worst possible way" he recalled. "I thought I was going to meet "the" man of New American Cinema, the director who shot 16mm low-budget b/w films, whereas I found someone who acted like a movie star when he was not behind the camera. He literally became another person. It was quite hard in the beginning, because I had a totally different idea of Cassavetes."[3] However, the two eventually got on well together, at least according to Montaldo. Cassavetes liked the way Italians worked, which was so much similar to his own approach to filmmaking: a car chase through San Francisco was shot in just a couple of days with two vehicles rented at the local Hertz office. Montaldo also recalls Cassavetes' amusement at his crew's motto, which was typical of Italian filmmaking, with its blend of improvisation, craftsmanship and detached, ironic indifference: "Se po' ffà" (Roman dialect for "It can be done").

Notes

1. Mike Patton gives an original rendition of *The Ballad of Hank McCain* in John Zorn's fifteenth anniversary edition of his Ennio Morricone tribute "The Big Gundown," released in 2000. The discordant theme that plays over the titles is available on a two-CD Ennio Morricone compilation album, "Crime and Dissonance," released in 2005 by Patton's co-owned label Ipecac.
2. A longer, more "meditative" cut of the film is believed to exist, yet all available prints are of the short U.S. version. This would explain the underdeveloped love story between Hank and Irene, for instance.
3. Faldini and Fofi, *L'avventurosa storia del cinema italiano*, p. 208.

Naked Violence (I ragazzi del massacro)

D: Fernando di Leo. *S:* based on the novel *I ragazzi del massacro* by Giorgio Scerbanenco; *SC:* Fernando di Leo, Nino Latino, Andrea Maggiore; *DOP:* Franco Villa (35mm, Eastmancolor, Telecolor); *M:* Silvano Spadaccino, conducted by Iller Pataccini (ed. RCA); *Ballerina, Ballerina* sung by Patty Pravo; *E:* Amedeo Giomini; *PD:* Franco Bottari; *ArtD:* Teresa Ferrone; *AD:* Franco Lo Cascio; *C:* Claudio Morabito; *AC:* Giovanni Abballe; *AE:* Ornella Chistolini; *APD:* Antonella Ibba; *CO:* Loredana Longo; *MU:* Carlo Sindici; *SO:* Goffredo Salvatori; *CON:* Silvana Ziviani; *UP:* Marino Onorati. *Cast:* Pier Paolo Capponi (Commissioner Luca Lamberti), Susan Scott [Nieves Navarro] (Livia Ussaro), Marzio Margine (Carolino Marassi), Renato Lupi (Mascaranti), Enzo Liberti (Luigi Carrua, Chief of Police), Giuliano Manetti (Fiorello Grassi), Danika [Danika La Loggia] (Beatrice Romani), Anna Maria La Rovere (School caretaker), Flora Carosello (Benito's aunt), Michel Bardinet (Stelvio Sampero), Jean Rougeul (Federico's father), Ettore Geri (School caretaker's husband), Priscilla Benson [Ada Pometti] (Florist, Verino's sister), Federico Mecca (Federico Dell'Angeletto), Gabriella D'Olive (Nadia Novack), Sergio Serafini (Bespectacled policeman), René Contreras (Verino Verini), Salvatore Aricò (Ettore Ellusic), Gianfranco Pellegrini (Paolino Bovato), Luciano Ferraro (Benito Verdi), Dario Sulis (Silvano Marcelli), Giovanni Imparato (Ettore Dominici), Mario Tipi (Michele Castello), Maurizio Passi, Gianni Turi, Antonio Jodice. *Uncredited:* Bruno Bertocci (policeman at school), Franco Lo Cascio (policeman Lo Cascio), Fernando di Leo, Nello Palladino (police official). *PROD:* Tiziano Longo for Daunia Film / Belfagor Cinematografica; *PM:* Armando Novelli; *PSu:* Alberto Longo; *PSe:* Vincenzo Salviani. *Country:* Italy. Filmed at Elios Film (Rome). *Running time:* 99'; Visa no.: 54998 (11.08.1969); *Rating:* v.m.18; *Release date:* 12.26.1969; *Distribution:* Italian International Film;. *Domestic gross:* 251,512,000 lire. *Also known as: The Boys Who Slaughter* (U.K.), *La jeunesse du massacre* (France), *Note 7—Die Jungen der Gewalt* (West Germany). *Home video:* Raro (DVD, Italy).

Milan. A young teacher at a night school is raped and murdered in her classroom. Her students—already known to the police and boasting criminal records—are arrested and brought to the police station. Their excessive behavior was caused by a spiked drink, and Commissioner Luca Lamberti tries to find out who gave the boys that beverage. All the other boys accuse one of them, Fiorello, who's impotent: during the interrogation he mentions a mysterious woman. Despite bureaucratic obstacles on the part of his superiors, Lamberti investigates in the prostitution and contraband milieu. When he's about to discover the truth, Fiorello kills himself. Lamberti's last effort is to take one of the boys, Carolino, home with him, hoping that a better environment might induce him to confess. But Carolino betrays the Commissioner's trust, and meets the leader of the gang, who tries to kill him. The boy finally reveals to Lamberti the name of the dispatcher, a former smuggler and police confidant who's also a transvestite.

A key year for Italian crime literature was 1966—the year when, on the occasion of *Série noire*'s issue no. 1000, Gilles Deleuze decreed the death of the detective novel—when *Venere privata* (Private Venus) was released. The first in the so-called "Milano nera" (Black Milan) cycle, it was the work of a peculiar novelist whose Italianized name was Giorgio Scerbanenco.

Born in Kiev in 1911 from an Ukraine father and a Roman mother, self-taught, "a former illustrated mag reporter with a Stan Laurel face and the soul of a Padanian-born Chandler,"[1] Scerbanenco (real name Vladimir Scerbanenko) had written all kinds of genre novels—whodunits, romance, spy stories—hiding behind a plethora of pseudonyms.[2] He was a renowned, experienced journalist, as the editor of such popular women's mags as "Novella" and "Bella," and was able to "absorb like a sponge the moods, the passional weavings, the love misfortunes and small-time dramas of the confused post–World War II Italy."[3] In a body of work which numbers more than eighty novels and over a thousand short stories, Scerbanenco's Milanese crime quadrilogy (*Venere Privata, Traditori di tutti, I ragazzi del massacro, I milanesi ammazzano al sabato*) which convey the same tones and atmospheres as the short story anthology *Milano calibro 9*, stands out for its power, complexity and stylistic accomplishment. Like no other before him, Scerbanenco succeeded in exploring and portraying the dark side of Italy after the economical "Boom," although he used to say about his books: "I simply sum up reality, that's all."

Venere privata was Italy's first hard-boiled novel. It burned bridges with the intimistic tradition of the Italian crime novel and finally turned it into an adult genre. What's more, Scerbanenco gave life to an unforgettable character: Duca Lamberti, a former doctor who has been radiated and imprisoned after he performed euthanasia on a patient, and who becomes an investigator out of mercy and not to make a living. In the following novels, Lamberti is enlisted in the police by commissioner Carrua: but readers expecting the usual crime-cop routine are in for lots of surprises. As one critic wrote: "Nothing is less "giallo" than Scerbanenco's novels. And nothing is more distant from the typical detective stories. In Scerbanenco's world there are no police or justice or established order. There are no laws either. Social order is some kind of dream, perhaps a nightmare. [...] There is no plot, even though Scerbanenco supplies one. But they are poor plots. It's obvious that Scerbanenco is more inspired by crime news in the afternoon papers than what is found in the *Roman policier* rulebook."[4]

Duca Lamberti's quadrilogy swept away the travesties and clumsy false Americanizations of authors, characters and stories which were common in Italian crime literature of the time, and it finally faced the reality of contemporary Italy, with all the social, political and territorial problems that lurked within it. The setting was Milan, the biggest city in Northern Italy: a misty, damp and crepuscular metropolis with a dirty soul, which was in continuous transformation, and seething with contradictions caused by immigration and population growth. "There is still somebody who hasn't realized that Milan is a big city" Scerbanenco has Lamberti say in *Traditori di tutti* ("Traitors of All"), "they didn't understand the leap of dimensions [...]. If one mentions Marseille, Chicago, Paris, yes, those are metropolises, packed full with delinquents, but not Milan, some stupid doesn't feel it's a big city yet." Scerbanenco here is speaking to his colleagues and readers as well: in Milan people shoot, rob and kill each other just as much as in those far away foreign cities. In a memorable excerpt from *I milanesi ammazzano al sabato* ("The Milanese kill on Saturday"), Scerbanenco synthesizes the new face of the underworld which took off in the industrial capital of the North. "With mass civilization comes mass criminality. Nowadays the police can not find a single criminal, investigate a single case, today's roundups are made with the trawls of various groups of police [...], you go fishing in this sea of crime and filth and repelled fish, big and small, come to the surface."[5]

Crime, in Scerbanenco's books, is nothing more than a form of commercial transaction involving the buying and selling of goods and humans alike: everything, everyone has a price. The horror of crime is its own obtuseness: men become slabs of meat, goods that aren't even that valuable. "Criminals are never smart" Scerbanenco writes in *I milanesi ammazzano al sabato*, "because delinquency is a form of sordid and dangerous idiocy."[6] Lamberti is painfully aware of this; that's why the triumph of good — if such an expression can be used — is exacerbated. Happy endings, to Scerbanenco, are a price that have to be paid to appease genre rules: but to the writer, there is no such thing as a proper "order of things," if not as a mere illusion that has got no connection whatsoever with the real world.

A world which is black and still, where the only possible movement is the slow emergence in front of the protagonists' eyes of the "horrible black reality" which will remain as it is "long after the theatre of good has closed its curtains. The citizens of such a desperate world, who have no inclination to suicide, have only two ways out: complete distraction or addiction. Life is a drug, either you fight it with other drugs, or you take it to the limit."[7]

Scerbanenco's disillusioned moralism already contains the ethical dilemmas which will come to the fore in the forthcoming crime films of the 1970s. In *I milanesi ammazzano al sabato* he writes: "They were right, but they didn't understand, they had to follow the law, and the law sometimes is so strange, it favors criminals and ties the hands of the righteous."[8] However, the movies based on his novels favor the whodunit elements, and are rather peculiar hybrids, halfway between murder mystery and crime story, in a period where the former is metamorphosing into the "*giallo*" *à la* Dario Argento, while the latter is splitting into gangster stories and committed political parables.

Naked Violence, based on *I ragazzi del massacro* ("The boys of the massacre," published in 1968), marked the encounter between Scerbanenco and Fernando di Leo, a combination which would be extremely important within the Italian crime genre. Di Leo avoided following the novel closely: instead, he took what he needed and basically cut to the chase: it would be useless to look for the book's carefully described social background in the film. "Scerbanenco's novel provided the inspiration, the idea, and nothing more" the director stressed. "In my film there wasn't Scerbanenco's Milan, because I wanted to express more: here's our boys, all our boys, here's what they are becoming, who we have in front of us [...] our crisis has become their crisis."[9]

As with his other Scerbanenco adaptations, di Leo drastically altered characters and psychologies. As played by one of di Leo's favorite actors, Pier Paolo Capponi, Duca Lamberti (renamed *Luca* Lamberti in the film), deprived of the burden of guilt he carries along in the novels, becomes a vigorous Commissioner who predates the protagonists of 1970s crime flicks, yet differs from them in the use of verbal violence instead of a physical one. Even more puzzling to Scerbanenco's readers is the choice of Spanish bombshell Nieves Navarro a.k.a. Susan Scott as Lamberti's love interest Livia Ussaro, a sadly underdeveloped character compared to the book.

The plot is also pruned down to a minimum. Because of its structure and narrative progress, *Naked Violence* looks almost like a *kammerspiel*: the first half — tense, minimalistic, abstract — takes place entirely within the four walls of Lamberti's office, where the commissioner questions the eleven students of a night school who gang raped and tortured to death their female teacher. The rest of the film only sporadically moves away from stark interiors, which we only glimpse behind the characters, as if they were staged scenes. Di Leo's minimalistic *mise-en-scène* is enhanced by Silvano Spadaccino's score, which introduces and accompanies each character with musical counterpoints.

The "boys of the massacre" have a distinct antiaesthetic unpleasantness. They are visibly older than the age requested by their role, and are shot through deforming wide-angle shots which only emphasize their physiognomies. They are poles apart from both Pasolini's non-actors, so true-looking and spontaneous, and the prefabricated clean-cut rebels of contemporary popular cinema. "Di Leo's "ragazzi di vita" — atrociously grotesque to look at, with their unreal-looking wigs and a camera which is almost glued to them — seem to carry on their faces the signs of an ancestral guilt; they are the abortions of a crazed society which doesn't even dare looking at the mirror anymore."[10]

Where *Naked Violence* falters, it's in plot development. In Scerbanenco's novel the eleven murderers were manipulated by a middle-aged prostitute, who wanted to avenge her husband (the man had died in jail after the teacher had denounced him). Di Leo reinvents the character, turning the prostitute into a transvestite who has a relationship with some of the boys, and acts out of jealousy. It's a ballsy choice: to go even further, and bring to the surface something untold (and unspeakable) at that time. An idea in line with the director's previous works, *Brucia ragazzo, brucia* (1968) and *Amarsi male* (1969). Unfortunately the results on screen leave a lot to be desired: the final plot twist not just weakens the story and undermines its believability, but it's also prepared and revealed quite clumsily.

On the other hand, the opening rape scene is simply astonishing. Shot through with an obsessive use of wide-angle, handheld camera, it follows the bodies and hands of the boys as they surround, graze, undress the victim, without actually showing any direct physical contact. It's a show-stopping sequence, which di Leo reprises and expands towards the end, perfectly synthesizing the disordered, irrational hysteria of murder as described by Scerbanenco.

The Raro DVD is especially noteworthy as it presents the full uncut Italian version, which was included in the special Fernando di Leo retrospective at the 2004 Venice Film Festival.

Notes

1. Francesco Specchia, *Giorgio Scerbanenco il Chandler della Bovisa, Gazzetta di Parma*, 10.27.1999.
2. Among Scerbanenco's earlier works there were a handful of crime novels starring inspector Jelling, a shy archivist from the Boston police department, which were published in the '40s in the "Giallo Mondadori" series.
3. Specchia, *Giorgio Scerbanenco il Chandler della Bovisa.*
4. Luca Doninelli, *Prefazione*, in Giorgio Scerbanenco, *Venere privata* (Milan: Garzanti, 1998), p. I.
5. Giorgio Scerbanenco, *I milanesi ammazzano al sabato* (Milan: Garzanti, 1994), p. 7.
6. *Ibid.*, p. 153.
7. Doninelli, *Prefazione*, p. III.
8. Scerbanenco, *I milanesi ammazzano al sabato*, p.154.
9. Davide Pulici, *Fernando di Leo* (Milan: Nocturno libri, 2001), p. 307.
10. Andrea Bruni, "I ragazzi del massacro," in Aa. Vv., "Calibro 9. Il cinema di Fernando di Leo," *Nocturno Dossier* #14 (September 2003) p. 25.

They Paid with Bullets — Chicago 1929 (*Tiempos de Chicago a.k.a. Tempo di Charleston — Chicago 1929*)

D: Giulio [Julio] Diamante; *S:* Eduardo Manzanos Brochero; *SC:* Eduardo Manzanos Brochero, Odoardo Fiory, Sergio Garrone; *DOP:* Emilio Foriscot (35mm, Eastmancolor); *M:* Enrico Simonetti; *Al buio con te* (Leo Chiosso) sung by Ingrid Schoeller; *E:* Antonio Jimeno; *PD:* Jaime Pérez Cubero; *SD:* José Luis Galicia; *CO:* Esteban Gutiérrez; *MU:* Vincente Vásquez; *C:* Fernando Espiga; *AD:* José Ulloa. *Cast:* Peter Lee Lawrence [Karl Hirenbach], (Erik), William Bogart [Guglielmo Spoletini] (Francesco "Frank" Lo Faro), Ingrid Schoeller (Lucie), Eduardo Fajardo (Captain Harper), Luis Induni (Mike), Fernando Sánchez Polack (Rico), Miguel Del Castillo (Senator), José Truchado, Luis De Tejada, Luis Barboo (The Irish), José Jaspe (Truck driver), Philippe Hersent (Big John), Ingrid Andre, Tito García (Turi). *PROD:* Luigi Mondello for Nike Cinematografica (Rome); *AP:* Eduardo Manzanos Brochero for Coop. Copercines (Madrid); *GM:* Luigi Mondello; *PSu:* Augusto Dolfi; *PSe:* Rinaldo Scorcelletti. *Country:* Spain / Italy. *Running time:* 88'; Visa no.: 53054 (01.03.1969); *Rating:* v.m.14; *Release date:* 01.04.1969; *Distribution:* Nike (Regional); *Domestic gross:* 129,328,000 lire. *Also known as: Die Heisse Masche Chicago 1929* (Germany). *Home video:* Polar Film (DVD, Germany — English language).

1929. In a deserted street in the Chicago countryside, homeless Italian immigrant Francesco Lo Faro watches unseen the aggression of a truckload of smuggled whiskey by a rival gang. Francesco helps the injured truck driver and brings the load to its destination, a nightclub in Chicago, home of the gang led by Erik the Swede. Under the name Frank he enters the Chicago underworld and takes part in the gang war that is going on for the domination of the city. One day, however, Chicago's leading crime boss Big John, summons all the other mobsters to avoid unnecessary bloodshed and police interventions, but Erik does not accept the deal he is offered. Thereafter all Erik's activities are boycotted to the point that he decides to acquiesce to the conditions of Big John. It's Frank then who rebels, gathering his own gang and attacking the heart of Big John's business. Later Erik, whose wife Lucky has become Frank's lover, agrees with Big John to dispatch Frank. Erik kills Frank and Lucky: but he in turn is killed by a police inspector. It was all set up by Big John, in order to get rid of two annoying competitors.

Opening with sepia and b/w stills from the Prohibitionist era, including Al Jolson in his famous blackface makeup from *The Jazz Singer*, Julio Diamante's Italian/Spanish co-production *They Paid with Bullets* is a typical entry in the transient "Roaring Twenties" subgenre that had its brief moment in Italy between 1968 and 1969. The juxtaposition of real-life and movie stills depicting gangsters, mounted with the sound of machine-gun is indicative of the film's second-hand retelling of the Roaring Twenties as something filtered through American cinema — as had already happened with the Spaghetti Western, yet quite different from the urban Italian crime films of the next decade. Unlike the Western, though, the period gangster thread wouldn't reach an identity strong enough to survive, not least because the setting didn't allow for as many permutations as the Western did, and mostly because box office results were simply not up to the effort.

The illusion of watching an American flick is broken as soon as the *repertoire* footage gives way to the opening scene, with an old truck driving down a road in the countryside, *Grapes of Wrath*–style, in what looks like a definitely un-American landscape. What follows is a by-the-numbers imitation of the usual "rise to power" routine, with laughable insertions of girls dancing the Charleston to the sound of Enrico Simonetti's Scott Joplin–

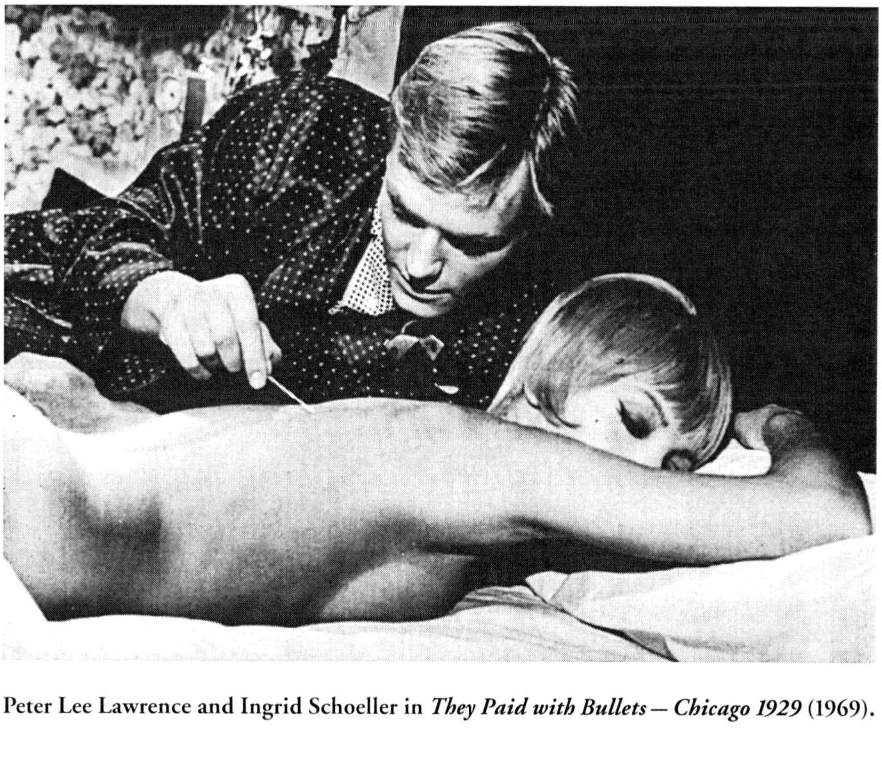

Peter Lee Lawrence and Ingrid Schoeller in ***They Paid with Bullets — Chicago 1929*** (1969).

like tunes, so as to justify the title. As one reviewer summed it up, "Didn't the Italian western pay off? Then, why not try to "Italianize" the roaring Chicago of the 1920s? It might have been a good idea, but it led to disastrous results," adding that "the whole story is told as if it was a masked ball with a *Bonnie and Clyde* theme, while the comical exterior scenes, set in the beautiful Ciociaria countryside, cannot be mistaken for the Chicago surroundings. As for these gangsters from the Testaccio district and Andalusia, they have decidedly unintentional comic effect."[1]

Besides the fact that all the battling gangsters are immigrants, respectively from Italy (protagonist Francesco Lo Faro, played by boxer-nosed Guglielmo Spoletini, here hiding under the pompous pseudonym William Bogart), Sweden (nightclub owner Erik—Peter Lee Lawrence) or Ireland ("the Irish," as played by Jess Franco regular Luis Barboo), the script hints at a half-baked political significance by relying on the clichéd collusion between the underworld and politicians ("It was 1929. Things have changed a lot since then—or have they?" a voice-over ominously comments over the final shot). Yet the film's main points of interest rely on the way Eduardo Brochero's script injects bits of sex and sleaze into the story: Lawrence is fairly amusing as the sadistic gangster whose bedroom is decorated with dolls and who enhances his libido by scratching his lover's body with pins. The gorgeous Schoeller has her share of nude scenes, while shootouts end with bodies riddled with bullets and covered with blood—one characteristic of Penn's film that the Italians enthusiastically embraced.

Note

1. Vice, *Il Giorno*, 8.18.1969.

The Tough and the Mighty (*Barbagia—La società del malessere*)

D: Carlo Lizzani. *S:* Dino Maiuri and Massimo De Rita, loosely adapted from the novel *La società del malessere* by Giuseppe Fiori; *SC:* Dino Maiuri, Massimo De Rita, Augusto Caminito, Antonio Troisio, Carlo Lizzani; *DCon:* Giuseppe Fiori; *DOP:* Michele Cristiani (35mm, Technicolor, Techniscope); *M:* Don Backy, arranged and conducted by Detto Mariano (Ed. Din); *Ballata per un balente* (Backy / Mariano) sung by Don Backy, *Applausi* (Beretta / Cavallaro) sung by I Camaleonti); *E:* Franco Fraticelli; *ArtD:* Franco Fontana; *SDr:* Massimo Tavazzi; *CO:* Carlo Gentili; *C:* Giuseppe Bernardini, Silvano Mancini, Alberto Marrama; *AC:* Daniele Nannuzzi, Gianni Maddaleni, Adolfo Troiani, Sergio Melaranci, Marcello Anconitani; *AD:* Giorgio Gentili; *2nd AD:* Armando Zappi; *AE:* Alessandro Gabriele; *MU:* Massimo Giustini, Luciano Giustini; *SO:* Domenico Dubbini; *Boom:* Giancarlo Pacella; *Mix:* Mario Amari; *SOE:* Ezio Marcorin; *SE:* Giovanni Diodato; *SP:* Alfonso Avincola; *SS:* Evelina D'Amico. *Cast:* Terence Hill [Mario Girotti] (Graziano Cassitta), Don Backy [Aldo Caponi] (Miguel Lopez), Frank Wolff (Spina, the lawyer), Rossana Krisman (Peppino's wife), Hélène Ronée (Anania), Gabriele Tinti (Nanni Ripari), Clelia Matania (Graziano's mother), Rosalba Neri (Girl at the party), Franco Silva (Arecu, a lawyer), Tano Cimarosa (Cartana), Ezio Sancrotti (Peppino Bedetto), Attilio Dottesio (Peppino's father), Marco Sancrotti, Peter Martell [Pietro Martellanza] (Antonio Masala), Remo De Angelis (Giovanni Cassitta), Alfredo Fedele, Luigi Barbini, Saro Liotta, Giuliano Quaglia, Orso Maria Guerrini, Adalberto Rossetti. *Uncredited:* Empedocle Buzzanca (Graziano's father), Costantino Carrozza (interviewed medical assistant), Gianni Di Benedetto (Chief of Police), Carlo Lizzani (a journalist), Giuliano Maielli (Graziano as a boy), Alba Maiolini, Enrico Marciani (Alfredo), Franco Megna (Gioacchino Cinna), Benito Pacifico (Coffin bearer). *PROD:* Dino De Laurentiis for Dino De Laurentiis Cinematografica; *GM:* Nino Krisman; *PM:* Giorgio Adriani; *PA:* Giuseppe Vezzani; *PSe:* Marcello Lizzani. *Country:* Italy. Filmed at Dino De Laurentiis Cinematografica Studios (Rome) and on location in Sardinia. *Running time:* 101'; Visa no.: 54591 (09.16.1969); *Rating:* v.m.14; *Release date:* 09.23.1969; *Distribution:* Paramount; *Domestic gross:* 683,611,000 lire. *Also known as: Der Blauäugige Bandit* (West Germany, 02.01.74—83'). *Home video:* None. OST: 7" >Amico DB 005 A/DB 005 B (*Ballata per un balente* / *Barbagia*)

Graziano Cassitta, a young shepherd in the wild Sardinian region of Barbagia, was educated, according to the custom of his people, to consider honor more important than life. After avenging the death of one of his brothers by killing the murderers, he is jailed, but manages to escape from the prison of Sassari in the company of a Spaniard, Miguel Tienza, with whom he takes refuge on the Supramonte, the rugged, wooded mountain range in the heart of Barbagia. Backed by Spina, a dishonest lawyer, Graziano and his gang begin a fruitful kidnapping business. While the police and special unit troops chase him to no avail, Graziano—who justifies their deeds with the purpose of taking money from the rich, thus repairing centuries-old injustices suffered by the shepherds—becomes extremely popular, and even dreams of becoming the head of a separatist movement. Frightened by his megalomania, Spina and others decide to get rid of Graziano by causing him to commit an error: the seizure of Nino Bedetto, an honest man who's anything but rich. The gesture arouses indignation throughout the island, and the population joins the police to capture the bandit, while discontent arises among the men of his own gang, no longer willing to blindly obey. During one last attack, Miguel—the only one who has remained faithful to Graziano—is killed. Graziano is able once again to avoid being captured, but not for long.

Lizzani's next project after *Bandits in Milan* was a similar effort: to tell the true story of the Sardinian bandit Graziano Mesina (here renamed Cassitta, while his sidekick becomes Miguel)—who, after escaping from prison with a Spaniard accomplice, formed a gang and became one the region's most feared kidnappers—and his personal war against the Italian armed forces.

After Luciano Lutring (*Wake Up and Kill*) and Pietro Cavallero (*Bandits in Milan*), Mesina was another exemplary character: as Lizzani explained, "several '68 movements kind of supported him, as they wanted to make him a champion of the Sardinian independence. They tried to turn him into a popular hero, that's why I was interested in making that film."[1] Working on the basis of Giuseppe Fiori's novel *La società del malessere* (The Society of Malaise, an ironic wordplay on the "Society of well-being" as promised by the consumerist economical "Boom"), the director's approach on *The Tough and the Mighty* is the same as in the previous film, mixing pseudo-documentary bits and a more traditional storytelling. The opening scenes, showing the arrival of armed troops in the savage region of Barbagia (hence the title) where Graziano hid in the mountains with his gang, are shot with the same newsreel immediacy that was one of *Bandits in Milan*'s assets, and Lizzani himself pops up as a reporter. Yet something doesn't click, and overall *The Tough and the Mighty* is a disappointing film.

Perhaps Lizzani was not as involved in the issues of Sardinia to come up with a satisfactory, effective rendition of the region's centuries-old history of fiercely sought independence. Sardinia is a civilization with barbaric aspects, which has rejected colonization, but despite the director's attempts, the portrayal of the region and its inhabitants is often one-dimensional and stereotyped. It doesn't help that the leading character is played by a miscast Terence Hill, who doesn't really give Graziano the depth he badly needed. As his friend Miguel Lopez (a.k.a. Miguel Atienza in real life), singer Don Backy — who also wrote the score and sang the end song *Ballata per un balente*— is not as convincing as he was in *Bandits in Milan*, possibly because his character is rather hastily written.

Social commentary is also not particularly enlightening. "They discovered that stealing a man is easier than stealing a sheep" a soldier comments on the phenomenon of kidnapping, which was very frequent in Sardinia and spread to the rest of Italy in the following years. It's a sharp observation, but it does not coalesce with the overtly simplistic voice-over which tells the story of young Graziano.

Lizzani's use of the zoom lens goes for immediacy but often feels like a lazy shortcut, especially during the action climax set in the mountains of Supramonte. As with *Bandits in Milan*, the Roman filmmaker is mostly interested in the economical reasons and mechanisms behind Mesina's kidnappings: in a monologue, the bandit complains that despite the huge ransoms that his victims' families pay him, he is forced to live on very little. It's a moment that recalls Cavallero and Notarnicola's bitter exchange in the previous film, but here is devoid of any punch, and gets somewhat lost in the way. The character of the seedy lawyer (Frank Wolff) who acts as Graziano's intermediary and above-suspicion accomplice (and who eventually provokes Cassitta's fall from grace) is another debatably sketched character.

Compared to another film which tells exactly the same story, Piero Livi's *Pelle di bandito* (1969), *The Tough and the Mighty*— despite the much bigger budget, the famous leads and an experienced and accomplished director — fails to achieve its goal, possibly because Livi, a Sardinian, was able to better understand and comment about his own people, despite his personal directorial and economical shortcomings. Take the scene where Graziano and Manuel escape from prison, a feat accomplished by Mesina with remarkable constancy: the bandit trained for months in prison in order to be in perfect physical form and eventually climbed over the wall with his bare hands. In Livi's film it's a central moment in order to understand the protagonist's utter perseverance, to Lizzani it's just a passing episode that must be told in order to move on to bigger things. In doing so, despite his attempts at a documentaristic feel, Lizzani loses touch with his main character and only follows his own ideological view of him. In *Bandits in Milan* this couldn't happen, as Cavallero was so obviously a product of the society that Lizzani knew and portrayed so well. Here, it turns a potentially outstanding sociological portrayal into a merely engrossing crime tale which desperately tries to be much more.

Note

1. Vito Zagarrio, *Tre volte nella polvere, tre volte … intervista a Carlo Lizzani*, in Vito Zagarrio, ed., *Carlo Lizzani: Un lungo viaggio nel cinema* (Venice: Marsilio, 2010), p. 40.

1970

Bocche cucite (Nailed Lips)

D: Pino Tosini. *S:* Pino Tosini; *SC:* Pino Tosini, Walter Alberti, Catherine Varlin; *DIA:* Giancarlo Fusco; *DOP:* Lamberto Caimi (35mm, Eastmancolor, Tecnostampa); *M:* Teo Usuelli, conducted by the author (ed. Tank); *Bocche cucite* (D'Agata/Vantellini) sung by Paola Pitti; *E:* Otello Colangeli; *ArtD:* Leonida Flores; *AD:* Michel Benoist; *C:* Roberto Seveso; *SO:* Umberto Picistrelli; *SOEds:* Sandro Occhetti, Fausto Achilli; *MU:* Aureliano Renzetti; *W:* Nuccia Aimetti; *ChEl:* Ferruccio Verzellotti; *KG:* Walter Bonetti; *G:* Onofrio Coppola; *SS:* Maria Miceli. *Cast:* Lou Castel (Carmelo La Manna "Mustafà"), Carla Romanelli (Consolata), Roland Carey (Commissioner), Jean Valmont (Salvatore Torchiello), Pier Paolo Capponi (Francesco La Manna), Lidiya Jurakic, Michel Boulé, Giancarlo Prete (Rocco Torchiello), Rosalina Neri (Moira), Pierluigi Piro, Mirella Pamphili, Bruno Boschetti (Mafia man from Zurich), Elsa Boni, Licia Lombardi, Paola Penni (Nightclub singer), Ezio Sancrotti (Mario Angelini "Tigre"), Lisa Lucchetti. *PROD:* Antonio Addobbati for United Pictures (Rome) / Lepidi Films (Reggio Emilia), Sofracima (Paris); *GM:* Nino Masini; *PM:* Marcello Papaleo; *PSu:* Leonardo Venturi. *Country:* Italy / France. Filmed at Icet–De Paolis (Milan) and on location in Cologno Monzese. *Running time:* 84'; Visa no.: 55474 (02.12.1970); *Rating:* v.m.18; *Release date:* 02.19.1970; *Distribution:* Regional; *Domestic gross:* 113,669,000 lire. *Home video:* None.

A dead body is found at the outskirts of Milan. It's that of Totonno La Manna, a Sicilian immigrant who operates in the underworld with his brothers Carmelo and Francesco and brothers-in-law Rocco and Salvatore Torchiello. Totonno was killed by a hitman from Zurich, paid by his own family to punish him: he seduced his youngest brother Carmelo's wife, Consolata, and tried to make her a prostitute, while the oblivious Carmelo was in jail. A young commissioner investigates with the help of a social worker: he arrests Rocco after a shoot-out which involves the La Manna brothers, but the criminal is released. Meanwhile Consolata — who is considered a "dishonored" woman by the La Manna family — has been forced to become Carmelo's brother's lover. She confesses everything to Carmelo. During a transfer to another prison, Carmelo escapes and kills Salvatore, then he commits suicide.

Shot in 1968 yet only released a couple of years later, Pino Tosini's film debut *Bocche cucite* is a jarring mixture of prison drama and crime film, told as a poor man's soap opera. The convoluted story drags on until the unlikely, melodramatic ending amidst dreary flashbacks, risqué interludes involving Romanelli (which allowed the film's photonovel to be published in the notorious "Cinesex" series) and abysmal scenes set in prison, packed full with clichés and laughable dialogue. In one sequence, for instance, a group of convicts are assembling sockets for an electrical company at an assembly line, while a number of effeminate homosexual prisoners are knitting baby clothes. Top-billed Lou Castel is on screen for not more than fifteen minutes, and looks improbable to say the least as a Sicilian mafioso, while the film's *de facto* protagonists are square-jawed Pier Paolo Capponi and former stuntman Giancarlo Prete, in one of his first significant screen roles.

Attempts at social commitment are clumsy to say the least: the climate of silence and fear which surrounds the underworld and the submissive role of women in a pathriarcal, male chauvinist society, are portrayed exploitatively, while the tone is often patronizing. In one scene the sympathetic social worker says to the commissioner: "These people are different from us; they carry a legacy of archaic habits and are slaves to absurd rules. But we have a duty to assist and educate them, to put them in a civil context...." In a couple of scenes, however, the nameless cigarette-holder smoking policeman (played with catatonic aplomb by Carey) shows a temper which makes him a progenitor of the violent cops who would flood the screens within a few years. He warns Rocco Torchiello (Giancarlo Prete) that he is willing to fabricate evidence in order to frame him "if only for a principle of justice"—which he does, indeed. Yet, as Rocco's trail ends with a mild sentence, after many witnesses (including the local parish priest) have portrayed him as an honest, hard-working citizen, he exclaims: "Three months of suspension—I'd rather shoot him!" something which his colleagues will definitely do.

Death Occurred Last Night (La morte risale a ieri sera [I milanesi ammazzano al sabato])

D: Duccio Tessari. *S:* based on the novel *I milanesi ammazzano al sabato* by Giorgio Scerbanenco; *SC:* Biagio Proietti, Duccio Tessari; *DOP:* Lamberto Caimi (35mm, Eastmancolor, Technostampa); *M:* Gianni Ferrio, conducted by the author (Ed. Bixio-Sam) (the songs *I giorni che ci appartengono* and *Incompatibile* by Ferrio / Tessari are sung by Mina); *E:* Mario Morra; *PD:* Enrico Tovaglieri; *ArtD:* Franco Gambarana; *C:* Roberto Seveso; *AC:* Carlo Petriccioli; *AE:* Adele Cruciani; *AD:* Lorella De Luca; *MU:* Franco Palombi; *SO:* Domenico Pasquadibisceglie; *Mix:* Alberto Bartolomei, Danilo Moroni; *G:* Onofrio Coppola; *SS:* Maria Gloria Eminente. *Cast:* Raf Vallone (Amanzio Berzaghi), Frank Wolff (Duca Lamberti), Gabriele Tinti (Mascaranti), Gillian Bray (Donatella Berzaghi), Beryl Cunningham (Herrero), Eva Renzi (Lamberti's wife), Gigi Rizzi (Salvatore), Checco Rissone (Ing. Salvarsanti), Wilma Casagrande (Concetta), Marco Mariani (Franco Baronia), Riccardo De Stefanis, Nicky Zuccola, Helga Machaty [Marlo], Maria Grazia Bettini, Elsa Boni, Marisa Cassetta, Giorgio Dolfin, Jack La Cayenne [Alberto Longoni] (the other Franco Baronia), Stefano Oppedisano (Salvatore's colleague), Renato Tovaglieri, Heidrun Hankammer. *PROD:* Giuseppe Tortorella and Artur Brauner for Lombard Film, Slogan Film (Milan), Filmes Cinematografica (Rome), Filmkunst (Berlin); *GM:* Pompeo Grassi; *PSu:* Andromedo Grassi; *PSe:* Jeanine Gaf. *Country:* Italy / West Germany. Filmed at ICET–De Paolis (Milan) and on location in Milan. *Running time:* 102'; Visa no.: 56704 (09.03.1970); *Rating:* v.m.14; *Release date:* 09.05.1970; *Distribution:* Titanus; *Domestic gross:* 568,294,000 lire. *Also known as: Gemordet wird nur Samstags* (West Germany, 07.16.1971—93'); *La mort rémonte à hier soir* (Paris, 03.08.1973); *Death Took Place Last Night* (1970—95'). *Home video:* Dynit (DVD, Italy). OST: CD Digitmovies CDDM039.

Milan. A 25-year-old mentally handicapped woman, Donatella Berzaghi, disappears. Duca Lamberti, the police commissioner who investigates the case, suspects the young woman has been kidnapped and forced into prostitution. His investigations confirm Lamberti's suspicions: yet there's no trace of Donatella until one day her corpse is found in the country-side nearby, disfigured by fire. A prostitute, to whom Duca gave hospitality in his own house so as to make her talk, gives him a hint where to find Donatella's kidnappers. Meanwhile, Donatella's father has been investigating on his own and found out who the culprits are. When Duca shows up to arrest them, he finds them dead. Berzaghi has done justice by himself.

Giorgio Scerbanenco, the father of the Italian hard-boiled novel.

I milanesi ammazzano al sabato was Giorgio Scerbanenco's last novel: it was published in 1969, a few months before the novelist's untimely death, and proved to be his darkest and most desperate work. The story of elderly widower Amanzio Berzaghi and his "baby girl," the huge, subnormal and nymphomaniac 25-year-old daughter whom Berzaghi kept locked inside his house to protect her from the outside world, is Scerbanenco's zenith; it's also a moral testament, presenting a view of the world which oozes apathy and distrust and which at times becomes almost unbearable.

It took just a few months for the film adaptation to hit the screens. Duccio Tessari's *Death Occurred Last Night* was co-produced by CCC's Artur Brauner, who was probably looking for a new fertile terrain after the waning of the Edgar Wallace–inspired Krimis that were so popular in early sixties (note how in the same period Brauner also participated in Dario Argento's debut *The Bird with the Crystal Plumage*, 1970). Adapting the novel with Biagio Proietti (Brauner's presence as scriptwriter, even though he's listed in the credits, was probably only nominal), Tessari brought a number of important variations to the book (such as a long sequence where a police ambush outside the San Siro soccer stadium goes awry) which however don't strengthen such a thin plot. What's more, Tessari dulls the desperation of Scerbanenco's pages: he practically reinvents the character of Duca Lamberti (played by Frank Wolff), gives ample room to his young assistant Mascaranti (Gabriele Tinti) who becomes a sort of comic relief (a recurring sketch has Lamberti ask his long-haired subject: "Cut your hair") and inserts a few debatably "light" sequences such as Lamberti and Mascaranti paying visits to the city's brothel. Last but not least, the character of Livia Ussaro, Lamberti's lover, becomes peripheral and nondescript.

However, not all of Scerbanenco's world is lost. Many lines of dialogue and even gestures are preserved exactly as in the book: what really matters are the mood, the settings, the characters. Some characterizations really stand out: as Donatella, who continually listens to a song by Mina, Gillian Bray looks like she's literally stepped out of the book's pages. On the other hand, despite his scarce verisimilitude with the original, Frank Wolff is a Lamberti who is finally (almost) in peace with himself: he's got a beautiful lover, a cozy house, and after dinner he relaxes by playing the guitar. Yet Lamberti's humanity makes him suffer, by way of empathy, with all the poor souls whose human miseries he happens to uncover. The film's most memorable character, however, is Raf Vallone's Amanzio Berzaghi: his lame walk and clenched-teeth speech, his dignity in dressing and behaving, all carry a tragic weight which eventually makes him much more than a champion in self-justice, as sometimes he's been hastily labeled. The scene where Berzaghi strangles the laundress who kidnapped and killed his daughter, while endlessly repeating, as a harrowing litany, "You could give her back to me, and I would take her back...," is truly unforgettable — as is the sight of the woman disappearing under a pile of newly-washed clothes, which also functions as a striking moral metaphor.

Gianni Ferrio's lively score — featuring two songs sung by the wonderful Italian singer Mina — is, to quote Kristopher Spencer, "a thoroughly engaging experience."[1]

Note

1. Kristopher Spencer, *Film and Television Scores, 1950–1979: A Critical Survey by Genre* (Jefferson, NC: McFarland, 2008), p. 260.

Defeat of the Mafia (Scacco alla mafia [Droga, mondo senza pietà])

D: Lorenzo Sabatini [Warren Kiefer]. *S* and *SC:* Alvaro Alfredo Tassani, Marian Doebbeling [actually Warren Kiefer]; *DOP* Amerigo Gengarelli (Eastmancolor, Telecolor); *M:* Stefano Torossi; Editor: Piera Gabutti; *PD:* Luigi Lodigiani; *CO:* Simone Marras; *C:* Lorenzo Sabatini; *AC:* Pier Luigi Santi; *AEs* Adelchi Marinangeli, Ernesto Triunveri; *AD:* Oddo Bracci; *SO:* Franco Borni; *Mix:* Sandro Ochetti, Fausto Achilli; *MU:* Paola Pitino; *Hair:* Vittoria Silvi; *W:* Anna Rasetti. *Cast:* Victor Spinetti (Charles Agostino), Maria Pia Conte (Jenny Ryan), Pier Paolo Capponi (Scott Luce), Alan Collins [Luciano Pigozzi] (Frankie Agostino), Néstor Garay (Jon Dahlia), Micaela Pignatelli (Marjorie Mills), Carmen Scarpitta (Countess Torreguardia), Paolo Giusti (Kiki Velour), Margherita Puratich (Susan Palmer), Luigi Bonos (Giulio), Enzo Fiermonte (Count Torreguardia), Mariella Palmich (Nun), Franco Borelli (Leone), Angela Goodwin (Vice Consul), Aldo Berti (Caccia), Lino Coletta (Taglia), Mario Guizzardi (Colonel Ruggiero), Conrad Andersen (Junkie), Lella Cattaneo (Woman at art exhibit), Mario Guizzardi (Ruggiero), Peter Bondi (Coffin Salesman), Jessica Dublin (Prostitute). *PROD:* Warren Kiefer for Afilm; *PM:* Alberto Marras; *PSe:* Felice Santosuoso. *Country:* Italy. *Running time:* 90'; Visa no. 54522 (09/22/1969); *Rating:* v.m.14; Release dates: Italy: 11/20/1970; *Distribution:* Regional; *Domestic gross:* 21,773,000 lire. *Also known as: Echec à la Maffia* (France, 11/12/74 — 92'); *Schach der Mafia* (West Germany, 08/12/72) *Home video:* AVO Film / Fletcher (VHS, U.K. — pre-cert)

Rome. A batch of heroin disappears before getting to its recipient, crippled mafia boss Frankie Agostino. The courier, drug addict Susan Turner, delivers the stuff to her accomplice instead, and later on she's found dead. A member of the Agostino family, Charles, arrives in Rome, posing as Susan's cousin, to find out what happened. During his stay in Rome, he meets a number of seedy and ambiguous characters, including gay sculptor John Dahlia, and is helped by a friend of the victim, Jenny Ryan. The ruthless Agostino eventually unwraps the mystery, leaving more dead bodies behind him, but narcotics agent Scott Luce is on his trail....

Warren Kiefer was one of Italian cinema's most amazing mysteries. He wrote seven novels, directed at least three films and scripted "perhaps twenty more, some forgettable and most forgotten," to quote his own words. Donald Sutherland, who was one of his best friends and even named his son Kiefer after him, pictured him as "a lovely cigar-smoking whiskey-drinking mystery-writing rogue of a man." Yet many sources still refer to him as a pseudonym of an Italian director named Lorenzo Sabatini, someone who didn't even exist in the first place.

Warren D. Kiefer was born in New Jersey in 1929. He was educated at the University of New Mexico, and the University of Maryland, got married and started what looked like a promising career as a novelist in 1958, with the hard-boiled novel *Pax*, co-written with Harry Middleton and published under the alias Middleton Kiefer. Then, in the late '50s, something happened. Kiefer left his home, country, family and newborn son Alden, and moved to Italy. He relocated in Rome, where he carved a niche for himself in the boiling cauldron that in those days was Cinecittà. Due to production facilities and costs, the so-called "Hollywood on the Tiber" became a powerful magnet for big-budgeted productions and small ones alike, paving the way for a U.S.-based community that savored the delights of "La Dolce Vita" and tried to make some money in the process.

Nineteen sixty-three was the year Kiefer made the big jump and directed his feature film debut. It was quite a lucky combination of events, in which a big part was played by 30-year-old New York–born Paul Maslansky. With the latter acting as producer, Kiefer wrote and directed *Castle of the Living Dead* (released in 1964), a low-budget horror movie starring Christopher Lee and Philippe Leroy and featuring the on-screen debut of Donald Sutherland (in a dual role, one of them in drag as an old witch). The picture was signed by Kiefer with the pseudonym Lorenzo Sabatini, which paid homage to the Italian Mannerist painter of the same name (1530–1576). It was economically convenient for Kiefer to pass off as an Italian, and for the film to receive law subsidies according to Italian cinema laws. "Angelo Rizzoli's Cineriz came up with the main financing, and qualified the film as an official Italo-French co-production. This complicated my credit because to receive state subsidies, an Italian director was required," Kiefer explained. "Thus, the Italian version of the film carried me only as scriptwriter and story originator, listing 'Herbert Wise' as the director. 'Wise' was an American-sounding pseudonym registered in Italy by my first A.D., Luciano Ricci. In my Cineriz contract, however, my name had to appear full card, last credit, as sole director on ALL other versions."[1]

Kiefer spent the rest of the decade in Italy, writing scripts (often uncredited[2]) and trying to put up directing projects for himself. His official output as a director includes only two more titles, *Defeat of the Mafia* (*Scacco alla mafia*, shot in late 1968 but released only in late 1970) and *Juliette De Sade* (*Mademoiselle De Sade e i suoi vizi*, shot in 1969 but released in Italy in late 1971), a spurious adaptation of De Sade's work. Both efforts were nowhere near as successful as *Castle of the Living Dead.* Indeed, they remain virtually unavailable even now.[3]

Produced by Kiefer for his own company Afilm (funded with Alvaro Alfredo Tassani on March 2, 1965, it apparently produced only this movie), the director's second film had the shooting title *Sulle tracce di Susan Palmer* (*On the Trail of Susan Palmer*) and then *Morte improvvisa* (*Sudden Death*) but it was eventually released as *Defeat of the Mafia.* Curiously, it was initially conceived as an Italian-Argentinian co-production — which is interesting, considering that Argentina is the country where Kiefer would move a few years later. It gets even more interesting when one considers that the Argentinian production company which was to finance the pic was called "Alden Film S.A.C.I.M." — Alden was the name of Kiefer's first son.[4]

Furthermore, the film's official credits are nothing short of puzzling. On the legal papers for *Defeat of the Mafia* deposited at the Ministry of Spectacle in Rome, "Lorenzo Sabatini" is credited as both director and editor, while the screenplay is credited to Tassani and Marian Doebbeling. Yet it's likely that these were only fronts and Kiefer wrote the script by himself, given the pic's offbeat tone, including the use of hard-boiled first person narration. The name Lorenzo Sabatini pops up in the end credits as well, this time credited as cameraman, while editing is credited to Piera Gabutti. What's more, the English language copy is "a Warren Kiefer — Norton L. Bloom production," whereas Bloom is nowhere to be found neither on legal papers nor anywhere else.

Despite its title, *Defeat of the Mafia* is not actually a mafia movie but a sardonic *film noir* which is quite different from other crime flicks released in Italy during the same period. For one thing, the fact that its main character, ruthless Mafia man Charles Agostino, is played with icy aplomb by Welsh comedian Victor Spinetti (*A Hard Day's Night*), showcases Kiefer's idiosyncratic view of the genre. Spinetti's is not the only odd choice in the cast, which features stage actress Carmen Scarpitta as a countess and Angela Goodwin as a U.S. vice consul, flanked by Italian B-movie *habituées* such as Luciano Pigozzi (playing a crippled mafia boss), Aldo Berti and Enzo Fiermonte.

The director's peculiar approach is also evident in the film's style and editing, which is definitely weird when compared to Italian crime films of the period. Rhythm is fragmented, direction at times haphazard. The opening sequence jarringly mixes flashes from Susan Turner's happy past — photographs, the sight of a spinning wheel at a fairground — with the present, as simplified by a close-up of a needle, while many scenes are shot with a nervous, hand-held camera, as a means of cutting down on both budget and schedule — quicker set-ups, no dolly or tracking shots etc., — and a stylistic trait to suggest a wild, unpredictable world.

Defeat of the Mafia opens with Susan's voice-over, who soon turns up to be a voice from beyond the grave, *Sunset Blvd.*-style. "All of a sudden, I had the most interesting body in Rome" she quips. The off-putting use of voice-over continues throughout the film, as the dead Susan comments, contradicts, mocks what other characters say. It's a rather intrusive trick — totally absent from the Italian language print[5] — yet it's not gratuitous at all. First, it shows how in his heart Kiefer was more a novelist than a filmmaker, constructing scripts as if they were books, with an elaborate domino structure ("Push one and they all fall down. But I didn't know anything about that at the time" Susan mutters, and the image of a falling domino chain appears under the title) and labyrinthine plot. Secondly, it displays the director's bizarre — and at times rather self-defeating — sense of humor.

Defeat of the Mafia often borders on the grotesque. In one scene Spinetti and Maria Pia Conte visit a funeral home to choose a coffin for poor Susan to be brought back in to the States, and Kiefer displays the kind of macabre jokes as seen in the coffin exhibition sequence in Dario Argento's *4 Flies on Grey Velvet* (*4 mosche di velluto grigio*, 1971). Another scene displaying an exhibit of sculptor John Dahlia (Néstor Garay) looks like something out of a Mario Bava film: Dahlia's sculptures consist of manikins arranged in macabre poses, handling knives or looking like dead bodies (and Kiefer plays on the analogy by showing a victim arranged just like one of the artist's "masterpieces"), with arms and legs protruding everywhere. The disgusting, obese gay sculptor who turns out to be a drug dealer is easily the film's most impressive creation, especially in the scene where he strangles his partner in cold blood.

The way Kiefer portrays the art exhibition is even more interesting as it somehow gives us the director's view on Roman high life. If the subjective high-angle shots of Dahlia meeting a parade of grotesque ladies and gentlemen look like an outtake from Federico Fellini's *Toby Dammit* (1968), Kiefer generally depicts Rome in a rather idiosyncratic way. Aside from the obligatory scene at the Leonardo Da Vinci airport in Fiumicino (which since its inauguration in 1960 became a common sight in Italian films, giving them an international flair), *Defeat of the Mafia*'s Rome is a far cry from the tourist-friendly one shown by many U.S. filmmakers, and rather showcases a disenchanted approach to the Eternal City. A meeting between Luce and his informer takes place in a seedy corner near the Colosseum, between pools of piss and wild cats, while the ending is set in a catacomb, in a surprising, neat Gothic touch.

For all its faults, *Defeat of the Mafia* is a weird little curio which deserves a niche in the genre's history. However, Kiefer's work in the movie business was soon to be a thing of the past, while his career as a novelist took off. Nineteen seventy-two saw the release of his second novel, *The Lingala Code*, published by Random House and dedicated to Don [Donald] Sutherland, which won the prestigious 1973 Edgar Award for Best Mystery Novel, awarded by the Mystery Writers of America. Kiefer followed it up with *The Pontius Pilate Papers* (1976, Harper), a fast-paced adventure yarn with theological undertones which somehow predated Dan Brown by a few decades. His fourth novel *The Kidnappers*, published in 1977, was set in Argentina, the country to where he had relocated after his Italian experience. He would spent the rest of his days in Buenos Aires, where he wrote three more novels, before passing away in 1995 after a massive heart attack, in Buenos Aires, as mysteriously as he had lived. It's quite a fitting end, after all: like a character from his novels, Warren D. Kiefer just disappeared, leaving behind a maze of red herrings and quite a lot of people believing he was someone else. He would have loved it.

Notes

1. Warren Kiefer, letter to Steve Johnson, July 24, 1989, by kind concession of Mr. Johnson.
2. "All this work was done in Italy and various Italian directors got the credit (because under Italian subsidy laws the producer could only collect if the film was signed by an Italian) while I got the paychecks," *Ibid.*
3. *Defeat of the Mafia* was released on home video in the United Kingdom in the '80s and was shown on Italian TV in the early 2000s.
4. Alden Films' administrator was Armando Petruccelli. According to legal papers, the agreement between the two companies involved the production of two films: *Defeat of the Mafia*, with a major Italian quota, and *El asado*, with a capital Argentinian share. The budget for Kiefer's film was 65 million lire (45,500,000 came from the coffers of the Italian company), with a five-week shooting schedule.
5. The Italian TV print is also heavily edited. A long fight scene between Capponi and Agostino's sidekicks is missing, as well as a rape/sex scene between Paolo Giusti and Micaela Pignatelli and another where Néstor Garay is in bed with two men.

Investigation of a Citizen Above Suspicion (Indagine su un cittadino al di sopra di ogni sospetto)

D: Elio Petri. *S* and *SC:* Elio Petri, Ugo Pirro; *DOP:* Luigi Kuveiller (35mm, Technicolor); *M:* Ennio Morricone, conducted by Bruno Nicolai; *E:* Ruggero Mastroianni; *ArtD* Carlo Egidi; *CO:* Angela Sammaciccia; *C:* Ubaldo Terzano; *AC:* Nino Annunziata; *ADs:* Antonio Gabbrielli, Lorenzo Magnolia; *AArtD:* Egidio Spugnini; *AE:* Adriana Olasio; *MU:* Franco Corridoni; *Hair:* Rosa Luciani; *SO:* Mario Bramonti; *Mix:* Mario Amari; Head *C:* Sergio Emidi; *SP:* Mario Tursi; *KG:* Sergio Emidi; *ChEl:* Sergio Coletta; *CON:* Armenia Balducci; *PO:* Lucherini, Rossetti, Spinola. *Cast:* Gian Maria Volonté ("Il Dottore," former head of homicide squad), Florinda Bolkan (Augusta Terzi), Gianni Santuccio (Chief of Police), Salvo Randone (Plumber), Orazio Orlando (Brigadeer Biglia), Sergio Tramonti (Antonio Pace), Arturo Dominici (Mangani), Massimo Foschi (Mr. Terzi, Augusta's husband), Vittorio Duse (Canes), Aldo Rendine (Nicola Panunzio), Aleka Paizy (Maid), Pino Patti (Head of wire-tapping office), Giuseppe Licastro, Filippo De Gara (police official), Fulvio Grimaldi (Patanè, the journalist), Ugo Adinolfi (policeman), Gino Usai (Arrested man), Franco Marletta, Giacomo Bellini, Giuseppe Terranova, Roberto Bonanni (Proietti), Vincenzo Falanga (Pallottella). *Uncredited:* Gianfranco Barra (policeman questioning Augusta's husband), Ettore Geri (Officer attending the final confession), Franco Magno (Officer attending the final confession), Enrico Marciani (Officer attending the final confession), Enzo Mondino (Officer attending the final confession), Mario Silvestri (Officer attending the final confession), Elio Petri (Sleeping policeman). *PROD:* Daniele Senatore and Marina Cicogna for Vera Film; *PM:* Romano Cardarelli; *PSu:* Hermes Gallippi, Alfredo Petr; *PSe:* Roberto Onorati; *FD:* Antonio Mastronardi. *Country:* Italy. Filmed at Incir–De Paolis (Rome). *Running time:* 115': Visa no.: 55475 (02.06.1970); *Rating:* v.m.14; *Release date:* 02.09.1970; *Distribution:* Euro International Film; *Domestic gross:* 1,928,248,000 lire. *Also known as: Enquête sur un citoyen au-dessus de tout soupçon* (France, 1970—95'); *Ermittlungen gegen einen über jeden Verdacht erhabenen Bürger* (West Germany, 11.13.70—115'), *Investigación sobre un ciudadano libre de toda sospecha* (Spain), *Inquérito a Um Cidadão Acima de Qualquer Suspeita* (Portugal), *Epäilyksen yläpuolella* (Finland), *Sledztwo w sprawie obywatela poza wszelkim podejrzeniem* (Poland), *Undersökning av en medborgare höjd över alla misstankar* (Sweden), *Undersøgelse af en borger hævet over enhver mistanke* (Denmark), *Vizsgálat egy minden gyanú felett álló polgár ügyében* (Hungary), *Yoerano pasis ypopsias* (Greece), *Her Türlü Kuskunun Ötesinde Bir Vatandas Üstüne Sorusturma* (Turkey), *Investigação Sobre um Cidadão Acima de Qualquer Suspeita* (Brazil), *Investigación de un ciudadano libre de toda sospecha* (Argentina). *Home video:* Lucky Red (DVD, Italy). OST: CD Cinevox CD MDF 311.

A large, unidentified Italian city. The head of the homicide squad of a big city is being promoted for his merits in the leadership of the Political police. On the very day of the promotion, the man—who, under the apparent safety and confidence, hides an abnormal psychology—kills Augusta Terzi, his mistress. Instead of worrying about not leaving any traces of the crime, the murderer—certain to be above all suspicion by virtue of occupying a position of power—is committed to increase the clues on his own. Following the explosion of a bomb in the police station, protesters are arrested: among them there is a student, Antonio Pace, who recognizes the commissioner as the murderer. After self-denouncing to his superiors, the man retires in his own apartment, waiting to be arrested. There, he fantasizes that his superiors, more fearful of a scandal than eager to serve justice, scrap the evidence, because he, as a policeman, is above suspicion.

The seventies, in Italy, started twenty days ahead of time. Milan, December 12, 1969: a bomb blasted inside the Bank of Agriculture in Piazza Fontana, causing 16 dead and 88 injured. It was the bloodiest in a series of terrorist acts that took place in the previous months. On April 25 (the day where Italy celebrates its liberation from Nazi domination by Allied troops) another bomb blasted at the Milan fair, while in August seven more bombs exploded on trains. All of these were immediately labeled as anarchic acts, and however germinated within the far left. It was a political sidetracking, endorsed by most newspapers, which justified in advance a possible authoritarian turn, after the socio-political turbulence that characterized 1968 and 1969, from student protests to factory workers' strikes in 1969's "hot autumn."

To many, the Piazza Fontana bombing—the most infamous of the 140 bombings that took place in the country between 1968 and 1974—signed the beginning of the so-called "strategy of tension."[1] The President of the Republic, Giuseppe Saragat, announced he would declare the state of emergency in the country, while the Ministry of Interior Franco Restivo claimed that investigations would be conducted "in all directions." The night after the bombing, the police arrested 84 suspects, among whom there was an anarchist named Giuseppe Pinelli. The suspects were released as soon as their alibis were verified. Three days later, on December 15—in spite of the norm that established that police custody should last not more than two days—Pinelli was in the building of the police station, interrogated by Antonio Allegra and Commissioner Luigi Calabresi, as well as three non-commissioned officers of the police under the Political Bureau, an agent, and an officer of police. That night, Pinelli fell to his death from the window of the office on the fourth floor where the interrogation was taking place.

The first version given by the Chief of Police was of suicide, due to the fact that Pinelli's alibi was proved to be false (according to some early rumors, Pinelli shouted: "It's the end of anarchy" before jumping down the window). This version was retracted when the dead man's alibi turned out to be credible: eventually the (highly debatable, and debated still today) "official" version would then be that Pinelli was the victim of an "active illness" due to stress, cold and insufficient nutrition, and fell accidentally. To many, though, the Anarchic trail was just a camouflage to cover the bombing's true nature: a fascist attack that was meant to weaken the resistance to an authoritarian right-winged government.

February 1970. Two months after the bomb blast, *Investigation of a Citizen Above Suspicion* was released. Although the film took shape before the latest dramatic events, Elio Petri and co-writer Ugo Pirro conveyed the mood of the period with an almost shocking precision within a crime story *sui generis*. The film was a commercial triumph: almost two billion lire grossed at the Italian box office (quite a remarkable feat for a committed film, in a season dominated by *They Called Me Trinity*, with over three billion lire), the Special Jury Prize at the Cannes Film Festival and the 1971 Academy Award as Best Foreign Language Film.

To renowned Italian film historian Gian Piero Brunetta, the film's enormous success depended on its ability to unify the audience, inventing "a system of communication that puts in motion emotional and conscious functions which are shared by fathers ad sons. It's a film that responds to Italy's middle class' need to move left."[2] *Investigation of a Citizen Above Suspicion*, in other words, speaks to everyone, young and old alike, and does it by way of the sarcastic and the grotesque.

Dialogue is sharp as a scalpel. Lines such as "Repression is our vaccine. Repression is civilization!" and "Behind each subversive there might be a criminal" are perfectly clear to everyone. These are the same words that are spent in the rooms of power, in police stations, on newspapers, after the rise of the students' movement and workers' protests to get new and fair contract laws. Even though the shooting took place before Piazza Fontana, the scene where Volonté questions a student, beating and slapping him, is inevitably charged with grim implications.

If *La Dolce Vta* challenged sexual taboos, *Investigation of a Citizen Above Suspicion* violated one even more delicate — a political one. As critic Giovanni Grazzini wrote in Italy's biggest newspaper, "Il Corriere della Sera," "like it or not, it's the first time that Italian cinema throws itself headlong into a portrayal of police environment without displeasing the censors [...] it's hard to deny that Petri's film is an important step forward to a more adult society, so sure of itself and its democracy that it allows a filmmaker to criticize an institution which once was considered no less than sacred, without having to hide behind the medieval screen represented by the crime of defamation."[3]

Investigation of a Citizen Above Suspicion would be a powerful influence on the forthcoming poliziotteschi, even though Petri's film is mainly a sarcastic fable on Power told in the form of what in crime fiction is called "inverted story": we know from the outset that Gian Maria Volonté's character is the murderer, and follow the story from his point of view. The police become the Kafka-esque secular arm of an authoritarian Power: the Kafka reference does not just apply to the end quote from *The Trial* ("Whatever we may think of him, he is a servant of the Law, and therefore belongs to the Law, and that places him beyond human judgment"), or to the way Volonté disseminates clues that prove his own culpability, in a self-destructive impulse which goes hand in hand with the awareness of his own status as untouchable. What's more, Petri's film conveys "the elusiveness, the indefinability, the indisputable arbitrariness of the lord in Kafka's *The Castle* or the judge in *The Trial*: that is, power seen as inaccessible or unimpeachable."[4]

Curiously enough, one of the films that most influenced the poliziotteschi is in may ways its dark half. Gian Maria Volonté's nameless Commissioner is a hateful caricature, brilliant in its childish pettiness. A sex addict who's sexually ridiculed by his mistress, a sadist with the weak and bullying with his subordinates, yet unctuous with the powerful, Volonté's character is definitely one step aside from the stereotype of cinema detectives as "stoic embodiments of the conscience of the world, the "right ones" as opposed to the decay of morals and the disintegration of moral codes."[5] As if to get rid of *Investigation of a Citizen Above Suspicion*'s uncomfortable shadow, the new centurions of Italian crime films would adopt a frugal lifestyle: no love affairs, indifference — if not contempt — for money and career. Such a reversal of perspective would also involve the relationship with authorities: in Petri's film these are scheming and subservient, whereas in 1970s poliziotteschi they become hostile and unattainable. What remains is the distrust of power, which in Petri has a clear ideological matrix, whereas in the poliziotteschi it is the expression of a centuries-old popular suspicion.

Notes

1. There were four more terrorist attacks on that day. A second unexploded bomb was found in another bank in Piazza della Scala, while a third exploded in Rome just a few minutes later than the one in Piazza Fontana, injuring 13 people. Two more bombs blasted off in Rome between 5:20 and 5:30 P.M., causing four more injured.
2. Brunetta, *Storia del cinema italiano*, p. 272.
3. Giovanni Grazzini, *Corriere della Sera*, 13.2.1970.
4. Micciché, *Cinema Italiano anni '70*, p. 56–57.
5. Mino Argentieri, *I "grotteschi" di Elio Petri*, in Lino Micciché, ed., *Il cinema del riflusso: Film e cineasti italiani degli anni '70* (Venice: Venezia, 1997, p. 174). *Ibid.*: "The policeman is doubly unsafe in his official role, and also in sexual activity, though still the pathological aspect of his behavior is never divorced from the connections with the social structure. Indeed, the pathological status of the character betrays tendencies latent in the so-called normality."

Mafia Connection, a.k.a. *Black Lemons (E venne il giorno dei limoni neri)*

D: Camillo Bazzoni. *S:* Giovanni Addessi; *SC:* Franco Barbaresi, Nicola Manzari, Yvette Louis, Camillo Bazzoni, Giovanni Addessi; *DOP:* Sandro Mancori (35mm, Eastmancolor, Colorscope); *M:* Carlo Rustichelli, conducted by the author (ed. Nazional Music); *E:* Nella Nannuzzi; *PD:* Camillo Del Signore, Carlo Ferri; *APD:* Luciano Leoncini;

CO: Mariolina Bono; *COA:* Silvano Giusti; *C:* Roberto Brega; *AC:* Renato Palmieri; *AD:* Claudio Failoni; *AE:* Pina La Rosa; Makeups: Maria Luisa Tilli, Franco Corridoni; *Hair:* Angelo Malantrucco, Maria Teresa Corridoni; *W:* Antonietta Maggi; *SO:* Carlo Spagnardi; *Mix:* Fausto Ancillai; *SE:* Cataldo Galliano; *SP:* Mauro Paravano; *MA:* Pino [Giuseppe] Mattei; *SS:* Rosanna Seregni. *Cast:* Antonio Sabàto (Rosario Inzulia), Peter Carsten (Orlando Lo Presti), Silvano Tranquilli (Commissioner Modica), Pier Paolo Capponi (Francesco Macaluso), Didi Perego (Concettina), Don Backy [Aldo Caponi] (Carmelo Rizzo), Florinda Bolkan (Rossana Sciortino), Lee Burton [Guido Lollobrigida] (Michele), Maria Luisa Sala (Assunta, Rosario's sister), Raf [Raffaele] Sparanero (Antonio), Frank Latimore (The American), Massimo Farinelli (Gian Carlo Lo Presti), Stefano Satta Flores (Hitman), Loris Bazzocchi (Pasquale Sciortino), Sergio Scarchilli (Bandit), Cesare D'Arpa (Vincenzo), Bruno Boschetti (Capoccia). *PROD:* Giovanni Addessi for Produzione D.C. 7 (Bari), Mega Film (Rome); *GM:* Franco Caruso; *PM:* Luigi Manini; *PSu:* Ennio Di Meo; *PSe:* Giampaolo Galluzzi; *PA:* Furio Addessi; *CASH:* Silvestro De Rossi. *Country:* Italy. Filmed at Elios Film (Rome). *Running time:* 99'; Visa no.: 55982 (04.16.1970) (v.m.14); *Release date:* 04.23.1970; *Distribution:* Panta; *Domestic gross:* 564,414,000 lire. *Also known as: C'est la loi des siciliens (Et vint le jour des citrons noirs)* (France, 04.73 — 90'), *Llegará el día de los limones negros* (Spain — Madrid, 02.04.1974), *... Y llegó el día de la vendetta* (Spain — Home video). *Home video:* Mya (DVD, USA).

Rosario Inzulia, a former affiliate to the Mafia, returns to Sicily after serving an eight-year prison sentence in the United States, paying also for crimes he didn't actually commit. Rosario tries to lead a normal, honest life, but he soon realizes he can't escape his past: his old "friends" killed his wife while he was in jail in a staged car accident, and try to do the same with him as well. Rosario doesn't go to the police, though: to get his revenge, he kidnaps Gian Carlo, the son of constructionist Orlando Lo Presti, who's in cahoots with the Mafia. Inzulia finds an unexpected help in the solitary, psychotic Carmelo Rizzo, who in turn has sworn revenge against Lo Presti. Rosario tries to have Lo Presti confess to the police, but the constructionist is murdered before he can accomplish that. In the end, Rosario realizes he can't fight the Mafia on his own: he writes a memorial with everything he knows, but before he gives it to the cops he is assassinated as well.

Born from what film historian Gian Piero Brunetta labeled as "a fixed-term contract between production market choices and directors' will,"[1] halfway through high ambitions and commercial predispositions, the so-called "civil commitment" streak soon flaked off. Besides extreme examples such as Giuseppe Ferrara's *Il sasso in bocca* (1970), where the alternating between documentary footage and restaged scenes is even more radical than in Rosi's films, other filmmakers ended up in a grey zone, helming pictures which veered uneasily between commitment and genre. Their *auteur* ambitions and approaches granted for a greater attention to form and film language, yet the results would inevitably bear the marks of compromises with market logics, and would therefore not be taken seriously by critics.

Such was the case with Camillo Bazzoni's ventures into the crime genre. Born in Salsomaggiore Terme, near Parma, in 1934, Bazzoni was the younger brother of Luigi, director of such obscure cult items as the stylish crime drama *The Possessed* (*La donna del lago*, 1965) and *Man, Pride and Vengeance* (*L'uomo, l'orgoglio, la vendetta*, 1968) an idiosyncratic Spaghetti Western take on Bizet's *Carmen* starring Franco Nero and Klaus Kinski. Camillo started as a Camera and became a renowned cinematographer; according to his director friend Francesco Barilli he actually taught a lot to Vittorio Storaro on the set of Bernardo Bertolucci's early masterpiece *Before the Revolution* (*Prima della rivoluzione*, 1964),[2] while his hand-held camera skills highlighted some of the best sequences in Mino Guerrini's *Date for a Murder*.

Bazzoni debuted behind the camera in the mid–60s with a handful of astonishing shorts which blended surrealism and science fiction, but his subsequent feature films — the western *A Long Ride from Hell* (*Vivo per la tua morte*, 1968) starring Steve Reeves[3] and the war flick *Suicide Commandos* (*Commando suicida*, 1968), with Aldo Ray — were unpretentious if competent genre efforts. *Mafia Connection* was Bazzoni's first crime film, followed two years later by *Shadows Unseen*. These two titles are exemplary of the progressive gap between politically committed cinema and its gradual drift towards what will become the so-called poliziotteschi. On *Mafia Connection*, the denunciation of Mafia abuses and power in Sicily — which culminates in the obligatory unhappy ending — becomes a secondary element in the story, which develops as a sort of Sicilian Western, with the story of one man's revenge against all.

Mafia Connection's compromised nature is best demonstrated by its prologue, where a man (played by Stefano Satta Flores) is introduced to the Mafia's inner circle (represented by a round table of men donning black shades sitting in the dark, their faces partially unseen) with a complicated occult ritual which involves slashing the man's arm so that his blood falls over a card of the Virgin Mary and then burning the icon, while the newbie member recites: "I swear on my honor to be faithful to the Mafia as the Mafia is faithful to me. This blessed picture burns together with a few drops of my blood to show that I will give my whole life to the Mafia until flesh and bone return to their natural state." It's an impressive, didactic yet overtly dramatized moment which portrays a much more romanticized image of the Mafia than as seen in Damiani's films, therefore less connected to Italian reality of the time. This fact becomes clear in another key scene, when Sabàto returns to the place where his wife was killed and questions a number of peasants to no avail: here, the close-ups of sunburned, silent faces, shot from a low-angle, provide an idea of *omertà* which recalls Pietro Germi's *In the Name of the Law*, showing that Bazzoni mostly relied on other movies (and clichés) to convey an idea of the Mafia rather than trying to have his own way with it.

The director was obviously more interested in single scenes than in the plot as a whole, as shown by the sequence where Don Backy savagely beats a prostitute (Didi Perego) on the beach, by the light of the moon. The presence of Backy is one of *Mafia Connection*'s most distinctive traits. The singer-turned-actor, who became a rather profitable name at the box office after his roles in Lizzani's *Bandits in Milan* and *The Tough and the Mighty*, delivers a wild, no-holds-barred performance as the manic Rizzo, which is even weirder in the original Italian version, considering that he is dubbed by Oreste Lionello (a popular comedian, best known for providing Woody Allen's Italian voice), and effectively counterpoints Sabàto's rather wooden turn as the film's antihero.

All in all, *Mafia Connection* is more the work of an accomplished cinematographer than that of a director, lacking inner thematic coherence but showing a stylistic flair which puts it above other genre efforts of the period (the same can be said for Bazzoni's following film, *Shadows Unseen*). Unfortunately, the film's visual qualities are sadly diminished in the U.S. DVD, which presents a below-average, washed-out fullscreen print.

Notes

1. Brunetta, *Storia del cinema italiano*, p. 631.
2. "Bazzoni used to do everything [on *Before the Revolution*]. He taught Storaro everything he knew. Camillo was a genius, in my opinion. He made Storaro what he is today." Roberto Curti and Stefano Lecchini, "Francesco Barilli: Io sono un atipico," *Buioinsala* #1 (Summer 2004).
3. Barilli on *A Long Ride from Hell*: "I even wrote a script about it, but I don't know if I'll ever make a movie out of it. It's the story of how I got to Rome and ended up on the set of *A Long Ride from Hell* as assistant director. Steve Reeves, who had spent his Italian career making sword 'n' sandal epics, invested his own money on the project: since it was going to be his last movie, he wanted it to be a great Western, a genre he always loved. To him, it was like a revenge against all people who had laughed at him as an actor. So he came back from the U.S. with all the money he collected and gave it ... to the wrong producer! Believe me, he got involved with real scoundrels. [...] The dream of his life was becoming a nightmare, since that Western was one of the most comical movies ever made. It was like being on the set of Blake Edwards' *The Party*, believe me! I saw things I thought could not happen when you are making movies. And I made a script out of that experience, a vitriolic comedy about a young cinephile coming from the countryside who's got all these fantasies about moviemaking, and eventually ends up making a terrible Western with a faded American star. Anyway, Reeves just couldn't act. But I had lots of fun, for sure! [laughs]." Barilli was Bazzoni's assistant on his second film as well: "Aldo Ray was in it, and he was constantly dead drunk. I don't remember much about *Suicidal Commandos*, frankly. Anyway, Camillo didn't have the stuff to be a director [...]. He had the skills to be a good one, but not the guts. He was always afraid of what producers would say, and that's not the way to make films. However, I learnt a lot from him. When you are on the set, working with people who really love cinema and, most of all, have something good to teach you, it's like having the best tutors in the world." *Ibid.*

The Most Beautiful Wife (La moglie più bella)

D: Damiano Damiani. *S:* Damiano Damiani; *SC:* Damiano Damiani, Sofia Scandurra, Enrico Ribulsi (law consultant: Ludovico Corrao); *DOP:* Franco Di Giacomo (35mm, Technicolor, Techniscope); *M:* Ennio Morricone, conducted by Bruno Nicolai; *E:* Antonio Siciliano; *PD, SD, CO:* Umberto Turco; *ADs* Mino Giarda, Enrique Bergier (uncredited); *C:* Giuseppe Lanci; *AC:* Gianfranco Transunto; *AE:* Giuliano Corso; *MU:* Carlo Renzini, Raffaele Cristini; *Hair:* Adriana Cassini; *SO:* Franco Groppioni; *Boom:* Corrado Volpicelli; *Mix:* Nino Renda; *W:* Lucia Costantini; *KG:* Giancarlo Serravalli; *ChEl:* Alberto Silvestri; *SP:* Bruno Oliviero. *Cast:* Ornella Muti (Francesca Cimarosa), Alessio Orano (Vito Juvara), Gaetano [Tano] Cimarosa (Gaetano Cimarosa), Joe Sentieri ("Poidomani"), Enzo Andronico (Lawyer), Pier Luigi Aprà (Lieutenant of Carabinieri), Amerigo Tot (Antonino Stella), Salvatore Vaccato, Sandro Arlotta, Diego Morreale, Mariella Palmich, Giuseppe Lauricella, Joceline Múnchenbach, Fortunato Arena, Prassede Nogara, Salvatore Moscardini, Gaetano Di Leo, Francesco Tranchina, Franco Marletta. *Uncredited:* Enrico Bergier (Priest). *PROD:* Produzioni Atlas Cinematografica, Explorer Film '58; *GO:* Bruno Turchetto; *PM:* Pasquale Petricca; *PSe:* Vito Di Bari; *PO:* Nino Vendetti, Anna Savelli. *Country:* Italy. Filmed on location in Gibellina, Santa Ninfa, Partinico, Cinisi (Sicily). *Running time:* 108'; Visa no.: 55693 (03.11.1970); *Rating:* not rated; *Release date:* 03.12.1970; *Distribution:* P.A.C.; *Domestic gross:* 633,422,000 lire. *Also known as: Seule contre la mafia* (France), *Sola frente a la violencia* (Spain). *Home video:* SPO Entertainment (DVD—Japan). OST: CD Cinevox CD MDF 326.

Don Antonino Stella, head of the Mafia in a Sicilian town, surrenders to the police as he is sure to be acquitted at trial. In his absence, Juvara Vito, his favorite, takes his place and takes on all of Don Antonino's attitudes. He puts his eyes on Francesca Cimarosa, the 16-year-old and beautiful daughter of a poor peasant, and becomes engaged to her. But the girl hides a fiery temper beneath her subdued appearance: when she realizes that Vito considers her a mere object and not a human being, she breaks off the engagement. Ashamed of this, Vito kidnaps and rapes Francesca so that she will be obliged to marry him. But things don't go as expected: Francesca denounces Vito, but the law cannot proceed because the underage girl's complaint was not signed by the parents, whom Vito threatened with the destruction of their barn. But it's Francesca who eventually sets fire to the barn, thus removing any possibility of revenge on the part of Vito. In the end Vito and his acolytes are arrested.

Made by Damiano Damiani between two very successful "Sicilian" films such as *The Day of the Owl* and *Confessions of a Police Captain*, *The Most Beautiful Wife* is usually overlooked when compared to the other two titles, just as if its main merit was the film debut of a 15-year-old, ravishing Ornella Muti. Yet *The Most Beautiful Wife* is a remarkably lucid work, which today looks even more important than upon its release, when many critics greeted it as a sort of Sicilian Western, undervaluing the Mafia theme as an accessory element to the plot. On the contrary, Damiani draws a portrait of a Mafia-infested Sicily from within, renouncing to all intermediaries between the audience and the region's situation (as was Franco Nero's character in *The Day of the Owl*). There are no "heroes" in the film, which is closer to a rural drama than to Damiani's other Mafia movies. The plot takes inspiration from the true story of Franca Viola, who in 1966 denounced the man who had raped her, refusing a repairing marriage: a situation which inverted the one described with vitriolic humor by Pietro Germi in *Seduced and Abandoned* (*Sedotta e abbandonata*, 1964). Whereas in Germi's film the plot was part of a grotesque, deforming take on cinematic language—most scenes featured exasperated wide-angle shots and over the top acting—to Damiani, the story of Francesca becomes the starting point for an in-depth analysis of the Mafia's deepest roots, in a society where *omertà*, fear and violence are the pillars of family itself.

Sicily as seen in *The Most Beautiful Wife* is a world where to submit oneself is the rule, be it to stand with bowed head the offences of the wealthy and powerful, or to accept to marry one's rapist. The rebellion of a girl who claims her right to choose and not to endure is seen as an act of arrogance or even lust: "Marriage redeems the sin" says the parish priest to Francesca, and later on he adds "We don't live for happiness" (a chilling line if ever there was one). Sicily as seen in *The Most Beautiful Wife* is an archaic, timeless land which nonetheless displays the recent scars of the devastating 1968 earthquake: a scenery that ideally connects to Damiani's 1979 *A Man on His Knees*, a film which has a lot in common with *The Most Beautiful Wife* in the way it depicts the power of the Mafia in an indirect, but no less impressive, way.

Safety Catch (Il caso "Venere privata" a.k.a. Cran d'arret)

D: Yves Boisset. *S:* based on the novel *Venere privata* by Giorgio Scerbanenco; *SC:* Antoine Blondin, Yves Boisset, Francis Cosne; *DIA:* Antoine Blondin; *DOP:* Jean-Marc Ripert (35mm, Eastmancolor, Tecnostampa); *M:* Michel Magne; *E:* Paul Cayatte; *CO:* John De Vernant; *C:*

Daniel Gaudry; *AC:* Elvidio Burattini; *AE:* Béatrice Bellest; *ADs:* Fabrizio Diotallevi, Claude Othenin-Girard; *Hair:* I. Vergottini; *SO:* Bernard Aubouy; *Mix:* Jean Nény; *SS:* Claudine Taulère; *UP:* Lucherini-Rossetti-Spinola. *Cast:* Bruno Cremer (Duca Lamberti), Renaud Verley (Davide Auseri), Marianne Comtell (Livia Ussaro), Raffaella Carrà (Alberta Radelli), Mario Adorf (Photographer), Jean Martin (Butler), Rufus [Jacques Narcy] (Photographer's assistant), Claudio Gora (Carrua), Marina Berti (Alberta's sister), Jean Mermet, Claudine Berg, Roger Lumont, Agostina Belli (Mara), Vanna Brosio (Marilina). *PROD:* Francis Cosne for FranCos Films (Paris), San Marco (Rome); *GM:* Jean-Philippe Mérand; *PM:* Enzo Boetani. *Country:* France / Italy. Filmed at Icet–De Paolis (Milan) and on location in Milan and Lake Como. *Running time:* 91'; Visa no.: 56569 (09.11.1970); *Rating:* v.m.14; *Release date:* 01.14.1970 (France); 08.27.1970 (Italy); *Distribution:* Euro; *Domestic gross:* 275,959,000 lire. *Also known as: Privado de amar* (Spain), *A hora da verdade* (Portugal), *La Traba* (Argentina), *Painajainen* (Finland). *Home video:* Hobby & Work (DVD, Italy).

Milan. Davide, a young upper-class Milanese, has a brief love affair with a young girl named Alberta, who just posed for a nude photoshoot. Despite Alberta begging him to take her with him, as she feels in danger, Davide leaves. The next day, Alberta is found dead: apparently she committed suicide. Davide, distraught, starts drinking. He is cured by a doctor, Duca Lamberti, who's also an investigator. To release Davide from his guilt, Duca investigates Alberta's death. He finds out about the girl's photoshoot, and with the help of Alberta's friend Livia, whom he uses as a bait, Lamberti identifies the maniac photographer. He saves Livia's life at the very last minute. The maniac escapes, but Davide pursues and kills him.

The second novel by Giorgio Scerbanenco to be adapted for the screen was *Venere privata*, the first in his "Duca Lamberti tetralogy." The film was released in 1970, one year after Scerbanenco's death, in a period where finally the writer's name was achieving the fame (especially critical) it deserved. It's no coincidence, given Scerbanenco's popularity in France, that *Safety Catch* was a French-Italian co-production, directed by a French filmmaker and with a largely francophone cast. Duca Lamberti had the sharp, asymmetrical features of the often overlooked Bruno Cremer, while his co-star was Renaud Verley (who had gained a certain notoriety as Telemacus in Franco Rossi's made-for-TV *Odissea* and later starred in the Spanish cult horror film *A Bell from Hell* by Claudio Guerin Hill). The cast also featured one of Italy's most popular showgirls, Raffaella Carrà, sporting an orange miniskirt and a black wig as the victim of a maniac photographer who specialized in porn and S&M shoots, played by an incongruously (and rather ridiculously) blonde-haired Mario Adorf.

Safety Catch was Boisset's second feature film after the remarkable spy story *Coplan Saves His Skin* (*Coplan sauve sa peau*, 1968).[1] The French director followed the novel rather faithfully, both in setting and characters (even marginal ones such as the scornful butler played by Jean Martin) yet eventually betrayed its spirit, at least in part. In Scerbanenco's book, Lamberti and Davide's investigations were caused by the characters' spleen, and represented a desperate attempt at giving a sense to their own life as well as that of the deceased victim, whereas Boisset's film is simply about detection. The most considerable and painful changes, however, concern the character of Livia Ussaro, Lamberti's lover: at the end of *Safety Catch* Livia leaves happy and safe in Lamberti's car with Duca and Davide, while in the book she's horribly scarred by the maniac with a scalpel. The film's clumsy, badly conceived happy ending is in jarring contrast with the novel's powerful, downbeat conclusion, where Duca pays visit to the disfigured Livia in the hospital. Considering that Fernando di Leo's *Naked Violence* also radically changed Livia's character (possibly out of the director's commercial preoccupations), it's sad to note how such a complex, beautiful female figure — so distant from the usual motifs of genre literature and so important to Lamberti and Scerbanenco as well — has been betrayed or forgotten on screen. To Scerbanenco, Livia was not so much a character as a personification, "the writer's own tenderness, his mood."[2]

Notes

1. Before his feature film debut, Boisset had directed *Le parfum de la dame en noir* (1966), an episode of the TV series *Rouiletabille*, inspired by Gaston Leroux's character. As an assistant director, he worked with Sergio Leone on *The Colossus of Rhodes*, with Jean-Pierre Melville on *The Jackal* (*L'aîné des Ferchaux*, 1962) and with Riccardo Freda on *Roger La Honte* (1966).
2. Doninelli, *Prefazione*, p. III.

The Syndicate — A Death in the Family (*Colpo rovente*)

D: Piero Zuffi. *S* and *SC:* Piero Zuffi; *SCcoll:* Ennio Flaiano; *M:* Piero Piccioni; *DOP:* Pasqualino De Santis (35mm, Technicolor); *E:* Franco Arcalli; *ArtD*, *PD:* Piero Zuffi; *AR:* Claudio Giambianco; *ArtD:* Francesco Cuppini; *C:* Mario Cimini; *AE:* Franca Pedrini; *APD:* Alessandro Cicchetti; *ADs:* Tony [Antonio] Brandt, Joe [Giuseppe] Pollini, Carmelo Bianco; *MU:* Massimo De Rossi; *SO:* Pietro Fondi; *G:* Mauro Pezzotti; *SOE:* Luciano Anzellotti; *SOE:* Roberto Arcangeli; *SE:* Aldo Frollini, Silvio Braconi; *SS:* Rosalba Scavia. *Cast:* Michael Reardon (Frank Berin), Barbara Bouchet (Monica Brown), Carmelo Bene (Billy Desco), Susanna Martinková (Fanny), Isa Miranda (Brothel manager), Eduardo Ciannelli (Parker), David Groh (Don Carbo), Victor Duncan [Vittorio Duse] (Mac Brown), Ugo Fangareggi (Hippie), Nello Pazzafini (policeman), John Mc Douglas [Giuseppe Addobbati], John Frederick, Benny Stevens, John Mazzadra, Tony Brandt, Vladimiro Tuicovich, Richard Stenta, Ben Sanders, Victoria Zinny, Frank Gonzales, Helen Mirren, Ileana Rigano (Milly), Emilio Delle Piane. *PROD:* Roberto Loyola for Roberto Loyola Cinematografica; *GO:* Alfred J. Piccolo; *PM:* Angelo Jacono, Valerio De Paolis, Armando Bertuccioli, Rodolfo Frattaioli. *Country:* Italy. Filmed at Cinecittà (Rome) and Electric Circus (New York). *Running time:* 104': Visa no.: 55788 (03.25.1970); *Rating:* v.m.18; *Release date:* 03.31.1970; *Distribution:* Loyola (Regional); *Domestic gross:* 483,376,000 lire. *Also known as: Red Hot Shot. Home video:* Hobby & Work (DVD, Italy — 80'). OST: CD Right Tempo / Easy Tempo ET 925 CD.

Mac Brown, a wealthy industrialist involved in shady dealings, is mysteriously killed on a New York street. Given the relationship of the victim with a powerful organization involved in drug trafficking, the investigation is entrusted to Captain Frank Berin of the Narcotics Bureau. With the help of some informants, Berin manages to intrude in areas of drug addicts and go back to regular drug dealers. After escaping a number of murder attempts, Berin identifies the people who are at the head of the mysterious organization. The murder of Mac Brown, however, remains unsolved even after the conclusion of Berin's investigation. In fact, it turns out that the crime had been engineered by Berin himself, who, to rehabilitate from an earlier defeat, was thus able to take up investigations on the drug ring.

The first and only film directed by the painter and art director Piero Zuffi, whose illustrious background included stage collaborations with Giorgio Strehler and Giorgio Albertazzi as well as a few but prestigious film credits (Zuffi was production designer on Roberto Rossellini's *Il generale Della Rovere*, Michelangelo Antonioni's *La notte*, Federico Fellini's episode *Le tentazioni del dottor Antonio* from *Boccaccio '70*), *The Syndicate—A Death in the Family* (known in Italy as *Colpo rovente*, literally *Red Hot Shot*) is definitely a weird, one-of-a-kind film. The mastermind behind the whole project was producer Roberto Loyola (who had just financed another crime film, *Gangsters' Law*), who gathered for the occasion—with financial means, it must be added, of uncertain origin—some of the best-known names in Italian culture and cinema. The story was penned by the renowned Ennio Flaiano, one of Fellini's closest collaborators and a respected writer in his own right with such novels as *Un marziano a Roma*; the director of photography was Pasqualino De Santis (De Sica's *The Lovers*, Visconti's *The Damned*), while the film was edited by Franco "Kim" Arcalli; last but not least, Loyola managed to assure the special participation of Italy's greatest—and most scandalous—stage director and actor, the brilliant Carmelo Bene, who just experienced a *succès de scandal* with his feature film début, the astonishing, experimental *Our Lady of the Turks* (*Nostra signora dei Turchi*, 1968), as the sociopathic hitman Billy Rizzo. However, *The Syndicate—A Death in the Family* was not the expected success, grossing under 500 million lire at the box office and leading Loyola to far less ambitious productions, such as John Shadow's decamerotic *Tales of Canterbury* (1973) and Mario Bava's *Rabid Dogs* (1974) which would be Loyola's final film as producer as he went bankrupt during post-production, leading Bava's film to over twenty years of oblivion.

The Syndicate—A Death in the Family could superficially be described as a hard-boiled story. The elements are all there: a ruthless cop (Michael Reardon) investigating the murder of a rich and ambiguous financier, a drug ring, a beautiful kidnapped heiress (Barbara Bouchet), assorted murders. Yet Flaiano and Zuffi's take on the genre is definitely idiosyncratic—an approach stressed to its limits by Arcalli's extraordinary editing work, which practically redesigned the whole film. The story is sabotaged, smashed, frayed and deconstructed to the point of becoming almost incomprehensible: what really matters are the lush, colorful set pieces, the psychedelic lighting and camera angles which pay homage to comics, the full frontal nudes and sex scenes, and perhaps most of all Piero Piccioni's irresistible music score—all piled and cluttered with omnivorous gluttony. A number of sequences stand out—autonomous, self-conclusive in themselves as if each was a short film on its own: the opening scene, where an unknown hand cuts a niche into a polystyrene block and puts a pistol in it, packs everything with gift paper and uses the concealed weapon to kill a passerby in a crowded street, without anyone noticing; another murder which takes place on stage during an underground play, among actors wrapped in candid sheets and lit by red-blood jelly lights; Carmelo Bene wandering through the streets of New York, accompanied by the character's voice-over (which in the Italian language belongs not to Bene but to dubber Ferruccio Amendola—quite an oddity in itself, since Bene's most distinctive trait was the way he used his powerful voice).

What's more, Zuffi's film reeks with anti–American spite, which echoes the common feeling among Italian intellectuals of the time. Rather than a true political rewriting of modern *film noir*, *The Syndicate—A Death in the Family* is a sardonic, mocking peek into the contradictions of imperialist "Amerika": Off-Off-Broadway productions, S&M gay bars (one decade ahead of *Cruising*), protests, free love and drugs, biker gangs wearing Nazi helmets, and so on. The result is a mad and experimental *divertissement*, as off-putting as it is ramshackle, which assembles and mixes genre cinema material and reinvents it "starting from one of those circular flash-back structures which [...] also seem to reveal the awareness that every material can be backdated, that it can depend on another one and vice versa," as Italian critic Sergio Grmek Germani wrote.[1] A structure which once again displays the skills and intuitions that made Arcalli one of Italy's greatest editors ever, and looks even more provocative (and insane) that the one attempted by Giulio Questi with his weird giallo *Death Laid an Egg* (*La morte ha fatto l'uovo*, 1968), another film characterized by Arcalli's contribution.

The Syndicate—A Death in the Family looks almost like it was assembled in post-production, with an absolute disdain for a linear narrative: many dialogue lines have been visibly added in the dubbing process. What's more, the final plot twist, which reveals the hero to be the faceless murderer of the opening scene, confirms the suspect that Zuffi and his acolytes were making a satirical film after all. In the end, Reardon walks away unpunished among the crowd ("of all the unpunished crimes in this country, mine is the one for which nobody will ever have the courage to seek the culprit," his voice-over comments) and the movie ends in the disco which we had seen in one of the early sequences, where a chaotic slideshow is being projected: images of Manson, Mao and the Black Panthers alternate with those of the film's cast, while a crowd of young people dance to the sound of Piccioni's contagious, rousing lounge-beat. The final result is not too far from the shameless exploitation of those fake documentaries of the period, such as Giuseppe Scotese's *Acid-delirio dei sensi* (1968) and Sergio Martino's *Naked and Violent* (1970), with which *The Syndicate—A Death in the Family* has in common, after all, the fact of being an authorless film: in his typical joking mood, Carmelo Bene would later call Loyola "Italy's greatest film director." A paradox which, as Germani notes, gives shape to the untold dream of a large part of Italian cinema: a film as the sum of art direction plus cinematography, without the burden of *mise en scène*.[2]

For many years, circulating copies of Zuffi's film were badly cut, clocking at a mere 80' compared to the 104' theatrical version, and missing not just nude and violent scenes, but also expository sequences which were vital to a full comprehension of the story. The full uncut version was shown in 2004 at the Venice Film Festival, during the retrospective "Italian Kings of B."

Notes

1. Sergio Grmek Germani, *Uccidete il maiale e montatelo*, in Enrico Ghezzi and Marco Giusti, eds., *Kim Arcalli: Montare il cinema* (Venice: Marsilio, 1980), p. 59.
2. *Ibid.*, p. 60.

The Underground — Il clandestino (The Underground)

D: Henry Folkner [Pino Mercanti]. *S:* Nino Lillo, Pino Mercanti; *SC:* Nino Lillo, Pino Mercanti, José Luís Jerez Aloza; *DL:* Nino Lillo; *DOP:* Julio Ortas (35mm, Eastmancolor, Kodakolor); *M:* Roberto Pregadio (Ed. Tank), *Un addio detto così*, *La ballata di Johnny e Peggy* (Lepore / Oliviero) sung by Ada Mori; *E:* Jolanda Benvenuti; *PD:* Simone Mercanti; *CO:* Giulia Rotolo; *C:* Francesco Paolo Raitano, Marcello Palmisano, Felix Miroun, Maurizio Massa; *AD:* Pietro Nuccorini; *ChMU:* Adele Sisti; *MU:* M. Antonietta Rotolo; *AMU:* Gilberto Pisciotta; *SO:* Goffredo Salvatori, Pasquale Rotolo; *W:* M. Ferroni; *SS:* M. Concetta Calafiore. *Cast:* Dan Harrison [Bruno Piergentili] (Giovanni "Johnny" Manzella), Conny Carol [Conny Caracciolo] (Peggy), Ada Mori (Nightclub singer), Ángel Aranda (Sam Baxter), Tony Rings [Antonio Anelli] (Baxter's lawyer), Antonio Pica (Aldrich), Franco Megna, Sergio Parrinello, Nino Musco, Bruno Boschetti (Ship captain), Andrea Aureli (Politician), Claudio Massa, Anna Silena, Giovanni Querel, Carla Mancini, Franco Mauroni, Pepe [José] Calvo (The Sheriff), Maria Pia Conte (Angela). *Uncredited:* Simón Cabido, Fabián Conde, Rafael Hernández, José Truchado, Jimmy Il Fenomeno [Luigi Origene Soffrano] (Scared bank client), Goffredo Unger [Goffredo Ungaro] (Baxter's thug). *PROD:* Zephyria Film (Rome), Coperfilm (Madrid); *GM:* Paolo Prestano; *EP:* José Luís Jerez Aloza; *PSu:* Domenico Luigi Rotolo; *PSe:* Anselmo Parrinello. *Country:* Italy / Spain. Filmed at Incir–De Paolis (Rome). *Running time:* 99'; Visa no.: 56329 (07.03.1970); *Rating:* not rated; *Release date:* 12.07.1970; *Distribution:* Regional; *Domestic gross:* 29,241,000 lire. *Also known as: Matar es el mi destino* (Spain). *Home video:* None.

1927. Arriving in America as a clandestine immigrant (and losing his younger brother during the trip), Johnny Manzella works for unscrupulous industrialist Sam Baxter, who employs underpaid foreign workers in his factories. After he's fired, Johnny robs Baxter's offices and distributes the money to his former co-workers. Acclaimed as some sort of Robin Hood by a newspaper called "The People" (that Baxter manages to close down), he falls for Baxter's fiancée Peggy de Saint Cyr, who is going to marry the industrialist for his money. Johnny and Peggy become a gangster couple, making a living out of robberies and fleeing Baxter's men, while the latter pins on Manzella the murder of a rival industrialist whom he dispatched in order to get at his fortune. Eventually Johnny is surrounded and killed by the police: however, before he dies he makes it look as though Peggy was his hostage, and the woman — who is pregnant with Johnny's child — agrees to marry Baxter so as to give him a bastard son in retaliation.

An oddity if there ever was one, Pino Mercanti's *The Underground (Il clandestino)* is one of the more obscure — and, to be frank, deservedly so — fruits of the short-lived period gangster subgenre that spawned after Arthur Penn's *Bonnie and Clyde*. A shoestring Italian-Spanish co-production, the film adds to its trite story — a retelling of the classic "lovers on the run" narrative — a would-be socio-political angle. Main character Giovanni Manzella becomes a sort of 1920s Robin Hood, robbing the rich and giving to the poor. The Robin Hood analogy is underlined by the presence of a corrupt (and dumb) sheriff— Spanish character actor Pepe Calvo — and what's more the script not only emphasizes the theme of immigration, but also features a subplot about a young trade unionist who's fighting for his co-workers rights. Given that the film was made during a crucial period of workers' protests in Italy — that in May 1970 culminated in a new law, the *Statuto dei Lavoratori* ("Workers' Statute"), which gave a new set of rules that protected workers from their employers, including new regulations on discharge etc. — it's easy to see how Mercanti's idea was to use a genre plot to say something about the present, with dialogue such as "With trade unions, you know where you start but not where you end."

However, whatever ambitions the film might have had, they are buried underneath amateurish filmmaking at its worst. The scant budget is so tight that the same newspaper page is shown again and again, with different titles stitched beneath the very same photo. And were it not enough that the Roman countryside has to stand for the United States, one has to suffer some truly atrocious acting from Piergentili (a former sword-and-sandal and Western beau) and Caracciolo, ill-fated comic relief courtesy of Calvo, a phony dream sequence in slow motion and tons of bad dialogue: "You know, sinners have hell, whereas to pay for their sins, even when they don't have any, poor people have bad employers." Amen.

Violent City, a.k.a. *The Family (Città violenta)*

D: Sergio Sollima. *S:* Dino Maiuri, Massimo De Rita; *SC:* Sauro Scavolini, Gianfranco Calligarich, Lina Wertmüller, Sergio Sollima; *DOP:* Aldo Tonti (35mm, Techniscope — Technicolor); *M:* Ennio Morricone, conducted by Bruno Nicolai and the author (ed. R.C.A.); *E:* Nino Baragli; *PD:* Francesco Bronzi; *ArtD:* Franco Fumagalli; *APD:* Giuseppe Aldrovandi, Giacomo Calò Carducci; *CO:* Giulio Coltellacci (for Jill Ireland); *C:* Luciano Tonti; *AD:* Fabrizio Gianni; *MU:* Mario Van Riel; *Hair:* Jolanda Conti; *SO:* Aldo De Martini; *SOA:* Gaetano Testa; *STS:* Rémy Julienne; *SE:* Carlo Rambaldi; *SS:* Bona Magrini. *Cast:* Charles Bronson (Jeff Heston), Telly Savalas (Al Weber), Jill Ireland (Vanessa Shelton), Michel Constantin (Killain), Umberto Orsini (Steve), Ray Sanders [Saunders] (Black convict), Benjamin Lev (Jeff's cell mate), Peter Dane (TV host), George Savalas (Shapiro), Beryl Salvatore (Debutante), Goffredo Unger [Goffredo Ungaro] (Thug in car). *PROD:* Arrigo Colombo and Giorgio Papi for Unidis, Fono Roma, Jolly Film (Rome), Universal France (Paris); *PM:* Alfredo Di Santo. *Country:* Italy / France. Filmed at Cinecittà (Rome) and on location in New Orleans, Miami and St. Thomas (Virgin Islands). *Running time:* 104' (U.S. version: 96'); Visa no.: 56756 (09.15.1970); *Rating:* v.m.14; *Release date:* 09.17.1970; *Distribution:* Universal; *Domestic gross:* 950,652,000 lire. *Also known as: La cité de la violence* (Paris, 10.16.1970) — *Brutale Stadt* (West Germany, 11.26.1970 — 108'). *Home video:* Anchor Bay / Blue Underground (DVD, USA), Ripley's (DVD/Blu-ray, Italy). OST: CD GDM CD Club 7029.

Jeff Heston, a highly skilled professional killer, survives an ambush set up by Jerry Coogan, a man for whom he worked. Jeff finds out that his lover, Vanessa, was double crossing him. After two years in jail, Jeff eliminates Coogan, but he does not kill Vanessa, who has since become the wife of Al Weber, a powerful New Orleans crime boss. Weber, who's in possession of photographic evidence of Coogan's assassination, blackmails Jeff, forcing him to join his organization. Persuading Jeff that she loves him again, Vanessa — who is actually in cahoots with Weber's lawyer Steve — makes Heston kill Weber and then denounces him to the police. Jeff escapes, and returns in New Orleans to kill both Vanessa — the heir of Weber's financial empire — and Steve on the day of their acquisition of Weber's company. Once he's accomplished his revenge, however, Heston is killed by a cop.

After three memorable westerns, *The Big Gundown* (*La resa dei conti*, 1966), *Face to Face* (*Faccia a faccia*, 1967) and *Run, Man, Run!* (*Corri uomo corri*, 1968), Sergio Sollima returned to the contemporary action genre, which he had engaged in with his first two films as director, the spy movie diptych *Agent 3S3: Passport to Hell* (*Agente 3S3 passaporto per l'inferno*, 1965) and *Agent 3S3: Massacre in the Sun* (*Agente 3S3 massacro al sole*, 1966) As the director recalled, he wasn't too enthusiastic about the treatment he was provided with. "The story was rather bad and rhetorical: a love story, a hitman who falls in love, nothing extraordinary. But we had the chance to shoot in the U.S., and I would do whatever it took to do that."[1] He rewrote the original story with Lina Wertmüller, the future director of *Swept Away* (*Travolti da un insolito destino nell'azzurro mare d'agosto*, 1974) and *Seven Beauties* (*Pasqualino Settebellezze*, 1975), deconstructing the original framework and adding flashbacks, so as to turn the stereotyped plot into something less predictable. "I knew American *film noir* and novels very well: I wasn't influenced by one in particular, but rather from all of them."

As for the cast, Charles Bronson was not the original choice. Among those considered for the roles of Jeff and Vanessa were Jon Voight and Sharon Tate, then Sollima and producer Arrigo Colombo settled on Tony Musante and Florinda Bolkan. When Colombo and distributor Euro International didn't reach a proper agreement, Sollima eventually managed to cast Bronson, to whom he'd sent the script. The American actor accepted on just one condition: having his wife Jill Ireland as his co-star.

The bare-bones story reworks a classical *film noir* plot, that of Jacques Tourneur's *Out of the Past* (1947). Characters and plot twists are mannered (yet on the other hand Bronson would later play a very similar disillusioned killer in Michael Winner's *The Mechanic*, 1972) and the style heavily displays the influence of recent American hard-boiled exploits, especially John Boorman's *Point Blank* (1967) in the way Sollima plays with chronology and allows the tale to dilate and digress — although the way Bronson's flashbacks develop recalls the tendency to abstraction of Italian Western (take for instance Harmonica's flashbacks in Sergio Leone's *Once Upon a Time in the West*). However, Sollima comes up with a number of extraordinary scenes. The opening car chase through the narrow pathways (and staircases!) of St. Thomas in the Virgin Islands, completely devoid of dialogue, is spectacularly executed by stunt coordinator Rémy Julienne, impeccably paced and excitingly directed: Sollima claims he wasn't ripping off *Bullitt* (1968) but just recycling a similar sequence from his second film *Agent 3S3: Massacre in the Sun*. Another set-piece is Jeff's final revenge, when the hitman shoots Vanessa and her lover/accomplice, lawyer Steve (Umberto Orsini), while they are in a panoramic lift which rises to the upper floor of a skyscraper, where the victims are waiting to take over Telly Savalas' financial empire. Here, Sollima's use of slow-motion and lack of sound (we only hear the tiny silencer shots that break the glass walls and hit the victims, caught in their ascending coffin — the instrument of social climbing becomes a deadly cage) expands and amplifies suspended time with truly remarkable results.[2]

Between the lines, *Violent City* is quite a political film, and thus it's closer to Sollima's earlier westerns. The script is closer to post–1968 cinema than to *film noir* in its depiction of capitalism and organized crime as two sides of the same coin, and the most gruesomely violent acts take place in the ultramodern offices of contemporary finance sharks. Sollima also drops clever little bits of social commentary here and there: in a scene Michel Constantin helps a blind old man cross a street, then explains to a puzzled Bronson that the old man is a drug dealer, and that the apparent civilized act was merely a cover to acquire heroin doses.

Violent City was released in the U.S. by International Co-Productions, and later in a wider rerelease by United Artists, as *The Family*, in 1973, to cash in on the success of *The Godfather*. English language versions ran eight minutes shorter, while the film was restored to its full length for the U.S. DVD edition.

Notes

1. Franca Faldini and Goffredo Fofi, *Il cinema italiano d'oggi 1970–1984 raccontato dai suoi protagonisti* (Milan: Mondadori, 1984), p. 450.
2. Sollima explained that the scene was actually made using three different locations: the building from where Bronson fired the shots was in New Orleans, the panoramic lift with Ireland and Orsini was in San Francisco, while the interiors of the cabin were filmed in Cinecittà.

1971

Cold Eyes of Fear, a.k.a. *Desperate Moments (Gli occhi freddi della paura)*

D: Enzo G. Castellari [Enzo Girolami]. *S:* Tito Carpi, Enzo G. Castellari; *SC:* Tito Carpi, Leo Anchóriz, Enzo G. Castellari; *DOP:* Antonio López Ballesteros (35mm, Techniscope, Technicolor); *M:* Ennio Morricone, directed by Bruno Nicolai (ed. General Music), played by Gruppo d'Improvvisazione Nuova Consonanza (Bruno Battisti D'Amario, Walter Branchi, Ennio Morricone, Bruno Nicolai, Vincenzo Restuccia); *E:* Vincenzo Tomassi; *PD:* Román Calatayud Alegre; *CO:* Enrico Sabbatini; *C:* Pasquale Rachini; *AC:* Giulio Battiferri, Giorgio Urbinelli, Giuliano Grasselli; *AE:* Gianfranco Amicucci; *AD:* Luís Ligero Poza; *MU:* Otello Sisi; *Hair:* Giancarlo De Leonardis; *SO:* Carlo Palmieri; *Boom:* Alvaro Orsini; *Mix:* Mario Morigi; *W:* Maria Meconi; *SS:* Maria Luisa Merci; *DIAD* (English version): Gene Luotto. *Cast:* Giovanna Ralli (Anna), Frank Wolff (Arthur Welt), Fernando Rey (Judge Horatio Bidell), Julián Mateos (Quill), Karin Schubert (Nightclub actress), Gianni Garko (Peter Bidell), Leon Lenoir [Leonardo Scavino] (Hawkins, the butler), Franco Marletta (policeman). *PROD:* José Frade for Cinemar (Rome), Atlántida Films (Madrid); *PMs* Pietro Grifi, Vittorio Noia; *PSu:* Julio Parra. *Country:* Italy / Spain. Filmed at Cinecittà (Rome) and on location in London. *Running time:* 95'; Visa no.: 57980 (03.30.1971); *Rating:* v.m.18; *Release date:* 04.06.1971; *Distribution:* Cineraid; *Domestic gross:* 197,089,000 lire. *Also known as: Los fríos ojos del miedo* (Madrid, 02.21.1972). *Home video:* Redemption (DVD, USA), Salvation (DVD, U.K.). OST: CD Dagored Red 119.

Peter Bidell, the nephew of an elderly magistrate, picks up Anna at a nightclub and takes her to his uncle's house. Here, he finds out that two thugs have infiltrated the villa after killing the waiter. The older of the two criminals, sentenced to fifteen years of prison by Peter's uncle, plans to kill the judge by blowing up his office with an explosive device. Peter and Anna try in every way to make contact with the outside world, but to no avail. Desperate, the young man causes a short circuit that leaves the house in complete darkness. The ensuing fight that breaks out ends with Peter as the only survivor.

While the newborn crime film Italian-style was moving its first baby steps on screen, Enzo G. Castellari was in Spain, shooting Westerns. That's probably the main reason why *Cold Eyes of Fear*, his first genre effort, looks so detached from Italian products of the period. Castellari stated that the script he co-wrote with Tito Carpi[1] germinated from the idea of setting almost the whole film in an apartment, suggested by Terence Young's *Wait Until Dark* (1967), which also provided the idea for the climax which takes place in total darkness, and, less obviously, by William Friedkin's *The Boys in the Band* (1970), another picture which had positively impressed the director. However, Castellari's film openly refers to William Wyler's *The Desperate Hours* (1955), as the plot (and the alternate English title as well) is virtually the same, at least superficially: a wealthy judge's family is taken hostage by a psychopathic criminal, and the ensuing suspense grows side by side with other subterranean tensions — social and erotic alike.

"We started shooting ... and on that occasion, for the only time in my life, I had the chance to shoot all the film in sequence from the first shot to the last — less a couple of exterior shots, perhaps," Castellari stated. "That's because I designed in detail the villa where the story takes place, while Tito and I were working on the script, so we conceived all the events on the villa's blueprint which we would later build in the studio."[2]

Cold Eyes of Fear relies heavily on Frank Wolff's intense performance as the fake cop who penetrates into Fernando Rey's house and progressively becomes more and more menacing and out of control, but the film's story is deeply tangled with the actor's personal drama. Since *Cold Eyes of Fear* was marketed mainly at foreign audiences (another hint at the fact that the genre was not considered palatable enough for a domestic audience), Castellari and Carpi had the script translated into English by Wolff's beloved wife, Alice, who dumped him during the shooting. Since the film was shot in sequence, Wolff's performance and the actor's depression became inextricable, on and outside the set. "Frank lived his own contorted sentimental drama while we were making the movie; his character was changing together with the actor," Castellari added. "That was the more dramatic thing: the character's psychological evolution went hand in hand with Wolff's interior transformation. [...] Frank was a force of nature, but watching him collapse after his woman left him was tremendous."[3] The actor committed suicide a few months later, in December 1971, in his hotel room in Rome.

Comparing Castellari's film with Argento's thrillers, as some do, even though just to point out the differences, is partially misleading. As mentioned earlier, the realistic setting and plot owe a lot more to crime dramas and Wolff's psycho is closer to Bogart's Glenn Griffin in *The Desperate Hours*— or, just to name a couple more examples, Duke Mantee played by Bogey in *The Petrified Forest* (1936, Archie Mayo), or Edward G. Robinson's Johnny Rocco in John Huston's *Key Largo* (1948), two crime films based on stage plays and featuring similar plots. On the other hand, what characterizes *Cold Eyes of Fear* is Castellari's tendency towards abstraction, both in style and narration. The opening sequence is a case in point: a woman (Karin Schubert) is menaced by an aggressor (Castellari's regular Rocco Lerro) who insinuates himself in her apartment, threatens her with a knife, cuts up her lingerie and forces her to have sex, but the woman eventually stabs him as they're making love. In this exact moment, however, a round of applause coming from a previously unseen audience reveals it to be all part of an erotic show in a nightclub — all shot with aggressive zooms and close-ups, sharp cuts and out-of-focus/focus passages. It's not just a moment that would have made Jess Franco proud, but also a clever echo of what would happen next, and a reflection on the "staged," theatrical nature of the film.

With her thick Italian accent and beautiful yet somehow plebeian looks, Giovanna Ralli stands out as Wolff's true opponent, a "whore on temporary export," as she labels herself, who finds herself involved in a drama she has no part in, is insulted and humiliated by everyone around, and eventually becomes a scapegoat, an innocent victim who pays for someone else's sins. On the other hand, Fernando Rey almost looks as if he belongs to another film: his inflexible, scornful judge is in a way an anticipation of the justice-crazed magistrate portrayed by the Spaniard in Jorge Grau's political giallo *Violent Blood Bath* (*Pena de muerte*, 1973). Yet, for all his filmmaking skills, Castellari is not very interested in a meditation on the fallacy of human laws and justice, which definitely puts *Cold Eyes of Fear* apart from committed crime films of the period. Once the plot is set in motion Castellari never abandons his main characters (with the exception of one flawed action scene, a brawl between biker gangs, shot in a fake-looking alley, which momentarily bogs down the proceedings) and keeps suspense high for the whole pic. He's at his best when taking claustrophobic tension to the very limit with the sheer force of the med*ium:* the final fifteen minutes contain no dialogue at all, as the antagonists hide and seek each other in the dark apartment. The whole climax is a show-stopping *piece de résistance*, dominated by the outstanding experimental score by Ennio Morricone and his *ensemble* Gruppo Nuova Consonanza.

Notes

1. Although he is credited as co-writer, Leo Anchóriz of Spain didn't have anything to do with the script, and his name appears solely for the usual co-production laws which were required to obtain a dual nationality.
2. Davide Pulici, "Il muscolo intelligente, Intervista a Enzo G. Castellari," in Aa. Vv., "Il punto G. guida al cinema di Enzo G. Castellari," *Nocturno Dossier* #66 (January 2008), p. 17.
3. *Ibid.*

Confessions of a Police Captain (*Confessione di un commissario di polizia al Procuratore della Repubblica*)

D: Damiano Damiani. *S:* Damiano Damiani, Fulvio Gicca Palli; *SC:* Damiano Damiani, Salvatore Laurani; *DOP:* Claudio Ragona (35mm, Techniscope — Technicolor); *M:* Riz Ortolani, conducted by the author; *E:* Antonio Siciliano; *PD, DO:* Umberto Turco; *C:* Giuseppe Di Biase; *AC:* Corrado Testa; *AE:* Lucia Melis; *ADs:* Stefano Rolla, Arrigo Montanari; *MU:* Raoul Ranieri; *W:* Lucia Costantini; *SO:* Francesco Groppioni; *Boom:* Corrado Volpicelli; *ChEl:* Alberto Silvestri; *KG:* Giancarlo Serravalli; *SP:* Umberto Spagna; *UP:* Luigi Biamonte. *Cast:* Franco Nero (Deputy D.A. Traini), Martin Balsam (Commissioner Giacomo Bonavia), Marilù Tolo (Serena Li Puma), Claudio Gora (District Attorney Malta), Arturo Dominici (Lawyer Canistraro), Luciano Lorcas [Luciano Catenacci] (Ferdinando Lomunno), Giancarlo Prete (Giampaolo Rizzo), Michele Gammino (Agent Gammino), Adolfo Lastretti (Michele Li Puma), Nello Pazzafini (Convict), Calisto Calisti (Callisto, a hitman), Wanda Vismara (Traini's maid), Adele Modica (Linda Paladino), Dante Cleri (Usher), Roy Bosier (Giuseppe Lascatelli), Giancarlo Badessi (Grisì, the politician), Filippo De Gara (Nicola, the mayor),

Giuseppe Alotta (Convict), Paolo Cavallina (TV speaker), Giovanni Palladino, Gualtiero Rispoli (Chief of Police), Sergio Serafini (Prison guard), Pina Lo Prato, Ugo Savona, Luigi Ursi, Rosario Rosone, Bruno Boschetti (policeman), Vincenzo Norvese, Franco Tranchina, Giancarlo Palermo. *PROD:* Euro International Film, Explorer Film '58; *PM:* Tommaso Sagone; *PSe*: Vito Di Bari, Arrigo Biasini. *Country:* Italy. Filmed at Incir–De Paolis (Rome) and on location in Sicily and Grand Hotel Villa Egea (Palermo). *Running time:* 103'; Visa no.: 57969 (03.26.1971); *Rating:* not rated; *Release date:* 03.26.1971; *Distribution:* Euro International Film; *Domestic gross:* 2,011,046,000 lire. *Also known as: Confession d'un commissaire de police au Procureur de la République* (Paris, 01.26.1972)—*Der Clan, der seine Feinde lebendig einmauert* (West Germany, 10.06.1972 —107'), *Confesiones de un comisario* (Spain—Home video). *Home video:* Wild East (Wild East (DVD, USA—Euro Crime double feature w/ *Summertime Killer*), Pop Flix (DVD, USA—as part of their *Crime Boss collection* 2DVD set), Brentwood (DVD, Canada). OST: CD Rca Records OST 114.

Palermo, Sicily. Police commissioner Giacomo Bonavia has killer Michele Li Puma released from the asylum. Dressed as a cop, Li Puma breaks into Mafia boss Lomunno's headquarters to kill him and avenge his sister Serena's honor, just as Bonavia hoped: yet Li Puma dies in the shoot-out. Public prosecutor Traini investigates the massacre: even though he suspects Lomunno of being connected with influential politicians, Traini doesn't have any evidence. When Traini finds out about Bonavia's plan, the two men's ideas of justice clash. Determined at all costs to punish Lomunno for the murder of an entrepreneur and a shepherd boy who had witnessed the first murder, Bonavia is convinced of the impossibility of fighting organized crime according to normal procedures, while the young and idealistic Traini still believes in the law as an inflexible instrument against crime. The prosecutor eventually suspends Bonavia. Serena Li Puma, who was about to testify against Lomunno, is killed by his men, and Bonavia avenges her, killing the boss in turn. The former commissioner is then stabbed to death in prison. Traini realizes that he's virtually alone and has inadequate means to strike a criminal organization whose chiefs are powerful and unsuspected personalities, probably including some of his own bosses.

Released to Italian theaters approximately one year after *Investigation of a Citizen Above Suspicion*, Damiano Damiani's *Confessions of a Police Captain* is at once the antithesis of Petri's film and a good starting point for tracking the coordinates of the Italian crime genre in the '70s. If *Investigation of a Citizen Above Suspicion* played with metaphors, Damiani sticks to the surface of things, to facts and characters. Which doesn't imply superficiality, but merely a reliance on the typical means of genre cinema.

However, *Confessions of a Police Captain* marks a turn of the screw to the classical conflict between good and evil, as the film is built on the dialectical juxtaposition of two characters who are on the same side: a disillusioned commissioner, Bonavia (an excellent Martin Balsam), who's tired of fighting the Mafia with the ineffectual weapons of the law and a young magistrate, Traini (Franco Nero), who's still convinced that law codes offer all the solutions to every single criminal case. In his private war against the powerful Lomunno (Luciano Catenacci), Bonavia releases from the asylum one of the mafioso's enemies, hoping that the latter tries to get his revenge against the boss. Which obviously happens, even though things don't go as Bonavia hoped. Lomunno escapes death, and instills in the upright Traini the doubt that the commissioner is bribed by a rival Mafia clan. The two men keep fighting (and hindering) each other, tapping each other's phone and hiding information, until eventually Traini suspends Bonavia, who decides to attain justice his own way.

However, this dialectic juxtaposition doesn't result in any catharsis. Franco Nero's character finally becomes aware of the complicity between Mafia and politics, but at the same time he discovers that he is impotent towards his superior, district attorney Malta (Claudio Gora), a character based on the district attorney of Palermo Pietro Scaglione, who was killed by the Mafia a couple of months after the film's release. As co-writer Fulvio Gicca Palli explained, "the script was nothing if not the narrative transcription of the first report of the Anti-Mafia Commission. There were rumors that Scaglione granted Mafia boss Liggio a very dubious bail, and there was talk of a complicity between them, which was somehow confirmed by Scaglione's murder by the Mafia for reasons that were never cleared. [...] At that time it was dangerous, revolutionary even, to talk about these things. Probably the film was made because of the precedent of Petri's *Investigation of a Citizen Above Suspicion*."[1]

Besides its look at the "microphysics of power,"[2] which nowadays appears much more problematic and stratified than upon its release,[3] *Confessions of a Police Captain* works remarkably as a genre film. Damiani doesn't utilize conventions and clichés in an instrumental, picky way, but he does it with conviction and consummate storyteller skills. Editing is tight, almost breathtaking at times, and the film's most memorable moments are those where the message emerges via the images, without a single line of dialogue. A case in point is the opening killing, which ends with the dying hitman taking refuge in an orange plantation, incongruously surrounded by the towering buildings which are the fruit of the wretched housing plan orchestrated by the authorities and Lomunno. Another example is the chilling scene when Marilù Tolo is murdered, her body covered with cement and buried in the foundation of a building under construction—the umpteenth monument to the victory of the Mafia over the territory and a grave for everyone who dared to oppose the "honorable society's" misdeeds. Damiani's predilection for long takes is evidenced by the crucial central dialogue between Nero and Balsam, while the many action scenes requested ample use of hand-held camera to convey their immediacy.

After his effective performance on *The Day of the Owl*, Franco Nero was an obvious choice for the role of the idealistic Traini, whereas casting his opponent Bonavia was much more laborious. Damiani's first choice was Anthony Quinn, but the actor's insistence on radically altering his character made Damiani change his mind. The same happened with Ben Gazzara, who flew back to the United States after shooting had already started. As Franco Nero states, "with Damiani you don't have to discuss: when you accept a role, you accept it. Plain and simple."[4] It was through Gazzara's agent Jay Julian that Martin Balsam was eventually cast, arriving one afternoon, making his costume test in a shop and showing up on set the very next morning.

With *Confessions of a Police Captain*, Damiani helmed a remarkable example of a cinema of both action and ideas, halfway between *auteur* discourse and exploitation. What's more, Damiani's film was also important as it managed to recount "over twenty years of Mafia activity in Sicily, from its rural origins, with the murders of Girolamo Li Causi and Placido Rizzotto (both evoked by the character of syndicalist Rizzo) to the more modern forms [...] with the inextricable web of interests between delinquency, banks, local and national politicians."[5] The director originally shot two very different endings, one in which the Mafia wins and the other where Nero arrests his superior, but with the intervention of editor Antonio Siciliano the final result was much more ambiguous—and striking. In the end, Malta asks Traini with studied indifference "Is there anything wrong?": as Damiani pointed out, "The whole Mafia culture and way of thinking is enclosed in that line, which is like a spit in the face."[6] Whereas Bonavia's act of self-justice (he kills Lomunno with his own hands) is not a retaliatory gesture but rather the acceptance of a human and professional defeat. Bonavia surrenders to the chain of violence he'd been fighting so far. Humiliated and deprived of his dignity, he'll let himself be killed in prison, in a desperate, moving sequence which somehow predates Damiani's following film, the robust, downbeat prison drama *The Case Is Closed, Forget It* (*L'istruttoria è chiusa: dimentichi*, 1972).[7]

Notes

1. Pezzotta, *Regia Damiano Damiani*, p. 226.
2. Stefano Della Casa, *Damiano Damiani, la civiltà e la regia*, in Maurizio Matrone and Massimo Moretti, eds., *4° police Film Festival* (Bologna: I Quaderni del Lumiére n° 27, 1998), p. 10.
3. Commenting on the critical fortunes of the film upon its release, Damiani explained: "Whenever our films criticize democracy too strongly, we risk to play into the hands of the right. So my film was well received by reactionaries, as they were too happy to see in it the denunciation of democracy. That's aberrant, because Italian democracy is a fake democracy." Nöel Simsolo, *Cinema 72* #164 (March 1972).
4. Pezzotta, *Regia Damiano Damiani*, p. 226.
5. *Ibid.*, p. 23.
6. *Ibid.*, p. 83.
7. Damiani shot two versions of the scene: the second, in which Balsam is just wounded, was discarded in the editing room.

Eye of the Spider (L'occhio del ragno)

D: Roberto Bianchi Montero. *S:* Roberto Bianchi Montero; *SC:* Luigi Angelo, Fabio De Agostini, Aldo Crudo; *DOP:* Fausto Rossi (35mm, Eastmancolor, Telecolor); *M:* Carlo Savina, conducted by the author (ed. Nazionalmusic); *E:* Rolando Salvatori; *PD, SD:* Mimmo Scavia; *CO:* Luciano Vincenti; *AC:* Carlo Grassilli; *AD:* Mario Bianchi; *SE:* A. Ricci; *SS:* Marisa Agostini. *Cast:* Antonio Sabàto (Paul Valéry / Franz Vogel), Klaus Kinski (Hans Fisher, "The Polish"), Lucrezia Love (Gloria), Van Johnson (prof. Orson Krüger), Teodoro Corrà (Mark Danon, "Oily face"), Fredy Unger [Goffredo Ungaro] (Mandel, Fisher's henchman), Franco Marletta (François, Mark's henchman), Peri Han (Mara, Fisher's secretary), Brigitte Brandt (Maria Innocenza), Claudio Biava ("Droga," the photographer), W. E. Arnold. *Uncredited:* Raoul Retzer (Viennese police chief at phone), Maria Tedeschi (Party guest), Paola Senatore ("Droga"'s girlfriend at the nightclub). *PROD:* Luigi Mondello for Luis Film; *PM:* Roberto Capitani; *PSu:* Augusto Dolfi; *PSe:* Rinaldo Scorcelletti. *Country:* Italy. Filmed at Cinecittà (Rome) and on location in Vienna and Marseille. *Running time:* 92'; Visa no.: 58970 (10.04.1971); *Rating:* v.m.14; *Release date:* 11.01.1971; *Distribution:* Florida (Regional); *Domestic gross:* 133,333,000 lire. *Also known as:* *L'oeil de l'araignée* (France, 1976—90')—*Das Auge der Spinne* (West Germany, 03.10. 1972—90'). *Home video:* Gb (VHS, Italy).

Vienna. Betrayed by his accomplices and badly wounded after a bank robbery, Paul Valery is sentenced to twenty years in prison. He escapes with the help of Gloria and professor Krüger, the mastermind behind the heist who now wants the loot back. After undergoing plastic surgery, Paul emerges with a new face and identity: under the name Franz Vogel, following Krüger's advices, he moves to Marseille where he traces one of his old acolytes, shady art dealer Mark Danon, gets the latter's share and kills him. Paul's other ex-accomplice, wealthy businessman Hans Fisher, finds out about his new identity, and sets up a trap to kill him. Paul survives and kills Fisher, recovering the rest of the loot, but when he returns to Krüger's place, his boss reveals his plan to dispatch him and take all the money for himself. Gloria, who's in love with Paul, shoots Krüger but is killed by the dying man. The police show up, and Paul dies in the ensuing shoot-out.

With some sixty films as director in a career spanning over 40 years, Roberto Bianchi Montero (1907–1986) is an emblematic figure in Italian popular cinema. The son of a property developer, he started his career very young as an actor, with amateur stage companies. Montero joined Ettore Petrolini's stage company in 1930 and founded his own troupe four years later; in 1936 he finally started working in the movies. His acting career—18 films between 1936 and 1942, all secondary roles in not particularly interesting films—wasn't exactly noteworthy, but Montero's dream was to become a movie director, which he did in 1943 with *Gli assi della risata* (co-directed by Guido Brignone), while his first solo effort was *L'amante del male*, in 1946. His subsequent works were all genre films, mostly destined to Southern Italy audiences or to marginal theater circuits. That's also the case with his 1971 crime film *Eye of the Spider*.

Despite its misleading title, which makes it sound as if it's a *giallo à la* Dario Argento (the Italian poster perpetrates the deceit), *Eye of the Spider* is actually a rather typical *film noir* about a thug's revenge against his old accomplices. The script hints at French *polar*, and—as with other similar films of the period—Montero opts for Austrian and French settings instead of Italian ones, in order to give the proceedings an international feel; yet its meager budget and lackluster direction sink *Eye of the Spider* from the very first scenes. The opening sequences feature a poorly shot bank robbery (which will be reprised in flashback throughout the film), a stylized trial scene with laughable expressionistic weird angles and shadows, and eventually introduce Antonio Sabàto in a truly obnoxious makeup: the actor wears an embarrassing blond wig and a clumsy fake nose, and only after his character undergoes plastic surgery, he emerges with his real face and customary black hair. Actually, *Eye of the Spider* is mainly notable for the variety of wigs worn by its stars—or rather, their stand-ins, as Kinski is obviously replaced by someone else, standing with his back to the camera, in most of the big fight scene with Sabàto. If Kinski looks bored, Van Johnson's acting is even more indifferent: it's no wonder, since his character, who refers to himself as "an artist, a genius if you like," has to deliver lines such as "If one morning all of a sudden my W.C. gets obstructed, what do you think I'm going to do, lift up my sleeves and try to fix it by myself? No way, I'm going to call a plumber, the best there is, and tell him, plumber, fix my W.C.!" Other scenes don't fare better, with dialogue such as one heard in the Marseille art gallery scene: "Where's the toilet?" "Over there, by the Titian painting."

Compared to other crime flicks of the period, Montero doesn't stint on nude scenes, something which would become much more palpable in his subsequent *oeuvre*, from the grim giallo *So Sweet, So Dead* a.k.a. *The Slasher … Is the Sex Maniac* (*Rivelazioni di un maniaco sessuale al capo della squadra mobile*, 1972, starring Farley Granger and released in the United States also in a version with hardcore inserts aptly entitled *Penetration*) to his late career incursions in out-and-out pornography. Viewers may spot a very young and very, very beautiful Paola Senatore in a wordless, brief (and chaste) role as Droga's (Claudio Biava) girlfriend in the nightclub scene. Another thing that's featured prominently, albeit gratuitously, in the film are J&B bottles.

As expected, *Eye of the Spider* made only a marginal theatrical run at its initial release. However, given Sabàto's growing popularity in the mid-seventies as well as the commercial success of the poliziotteschi, Montero's film was rereleased in Italy in 1977 as *Caso Scorpio: sterminate quelli della calibro 38*—an even more misleading title, with its fraudulent reference to Massimo Dallamano's *Colt 38 Special Squad* (*Quelli della calibro 38*, 1976) and Giuseppe Vari's *Return of the .38 Gang* (*Ritornano quelli della calibro 38*, 1977), the latter also starring Sabàto.

1972

Black Turin (*Torino nera*)

D: Carlo Lizzani. *S* and *SC:* Nicola Badalucco, Luciano Vincenzoni; *DOP:* Pasqualino De Santis (35mm, Eastmancolor, Technicolor); *M:* Gianfranco Reverberi, Giampiero Reverberi, Nicola Di Bari (ed. Radiofilmusica); *E:* Franco Fraticelli; *PD, ArtD*: Amedeo Fago; *CO:* Maria Laura Zampacavallo; *COA:* Osanna Guardini; *C:* Mario Cimini; *AC:* Giovanni Fiore, Gioacchino Tedeschi; *AE:* Alessandro Gabriele, Luigi Zita; *AD:* Giorgio Gentili; *2nd AD:* Dominique Antoine; *MU:* Piera Icardi; *SO:* Domenico Dubbini; *Boom:* Giovanni Zampagni; *Mix:* Mario Amari; *SOE:* Renato Marinelli; *SP:* Alfonso Avincola; *GA:* Antonio Donato Rosito; *KG:* Aldo Colanzi; *ChEl:* Luciano Leoni; *MA:* Remo De Angeli; *SS:* Evelina D'Amico. *Cast:* Nicola Di Bari (Avv. Stefano Mancuso), Bud Spencer [Carlo Pedersoli] (Rosario Rao), Andrea Balestri (Raffaele "Lello" Rao), Domenico Santoro (Mino Rao), Françoise Fabian (Mrs. Rao), Marcel Bozzuffi (Mariano Fridda), Guido Leontini (Marshall Coppo), Maria Baxa (Nascarella), Saro Urzì (Jaco, Cigarette smuggler), Gigi Ballista (Marinotti, the lawyer), Teodoro Corrà (Ravazza), Vittorio Duse (Camarata), Mario Pilar (Vanni Mascara), Elio Zamuto (Scarcella), Giovanni Milito (Santoro), Giovanni De Martire (Perrera), Giuliana Rivera (Puma's wife), Natalia Dezmann, Maria Cristina Deorsola (Rita), Giovanni Palmucci, Carla Mancini, Giovanni Pallavicino (Puma), Franco Balestri, Enrico Longo Doria, Pier Luigi Corrado, Giorgio Gentili, Renzo Ozzano (policeman). *PROD:* Dino De Laurentiis International Manufacturing Company (Rome), Trianon Productions (Paris); *PM:* Giuseppe Vezzani; *PSu:* Marcello Lizzani, Alfredo Petri; *PSe:* Rosario Rapicavoli; *PSeA:* Renato Di Giovanni. *Country:* Italy / France. Filmed on location in Turin and San Remo. *Running time:* 105'; Visa no.: 61026 (09.25.1972); *Rating:* not rated; *Release date:* 09.28.1972; *Distribution:* M.G.M.; *Domestic gross:* 858,820,000 lire. *Also known as: La vengeance du sicilien* (France—Paris, 11.28.1973—110'), *Der Sizilianer* (West Germany, 05.25.1973—89'). *Home video:* Stormovie (DVD, Italy).

Turin. During a football match, property developer Tommaso Fridda kills with his own hands a man named Santoro, who had previously served as his bodyguard. Fridda also plans to get rid of Rosario Rao, a factory worker who's a defender of the exploited working class, married with two children, Mino and Lello: he frames him for Santoro's murder and has him arrested. However, there exists a photo which proves Rao's innocence which photographer Cammarata gave to his cousin Ferrera, a pimp. When the witnesses are killed in fake suicides or accidents, young lawyer Mancuso starts looking for the photo, aided by Rao's children Mino and Lello, but Fridda and his men try to stop him at all costs. When Mino is seriously wounded by one of Fridda's henchmen, Rao escapes from jail and takes his revenge, killing Fridda, before giving himself up to the cops.

With *Black Turin*, described by a critic as "a semi-rustic drama set in a metropolitan environment, with an ending which recalls Matarazzo's films,"[1] Carlo Lizzani attempted to approach the themes of immigration and urbanization within a genre structure. Turin, Piedmont—the largest industrial pole in Northern Italy—gave work and home to many Southern-born families and workers who had left their hometowns to move North for a job at car manufacturer colossus Fiat. The city had just been the subject of an interesting documentary by Ettore Scola, *Trevico-Torino, viaggio nel Fiat-Nam*, and the events of the so-called "Hot Autumn" of 1969, when workers demanded better pay and working conditions during a series of strikes and protests, were still fresh.

Lizzani's film features a bizarrely assembled cast to say the least: child actors Andrea Balestri and Domenico Santoro came from the enormously successful TV version of *Pinocchio* directed by Luigi Comencini, comedy Western icon Bud Spencer was cast in an unusually dramatic role as a factory worker while, following in the trail of Lizzani's habit of casting singers such as Domenico Modugno and Don Backy in dramatic acting roles, Nicola Di Bari played the small-time lawyer who tries to find enough evidence to release him. It's casting against type, as the thin, bespectacled singer doesn't even have the *physique du rôle* to play the hero.

Lizzani's attempt at a sociological discourse on the contradictions of a complex and often degraded urban environment partially fails, though, mainly because of a rather roughly conceived script. The view on Mafia and emigration is superficial (Fulvio Marcolin's *Gli amici degli amici hanno saputo*, 1973, sounded more sincere in comparison) and saddled with squeaking melodramatic and populist excesses, while the climax is not far removed from the much more effective vigilante subgenre. However, with its car chases (where good guys drive small Fiat 500 while villains are on sedans, in a pointed social commentary) and the use of character actors such as Guido Leontini, Elio Zamuto, Marcel Bozzuffi, not to mention its title, *Black Turin* already speaks the language of the burgeoning poliziotteschi. Lizzani's film was a moderate box office success, mainly due to the presence of Spencer in the lead, but critics' reception was cold to say the least. As Lino Micciché put it, "Lizzani has several irons in the fire, or rather, not enough fire for so many irons."[2]

Notes

1. De Santi, *Carlo Lizzani*, p. 61.
2. Micciché, *Cinema italiano degli anni '70*, p. 137.

Blood Story (*Blood Story (Storia di sangue)*)

D: Amasi Damiani. *S:* Amasi Damiani; *SC:* Alberto Damiani; *DOP:* Gino Santini (35mm, Eastmancolor, Telestampa); *M:* Gianfranco Di Stefano; *E:* Amasi Damiani; *PD:* Attilio Glorioso; *CO:* Francesca Romana Cofano; *C:* Remo Grisanti; *AD:* Massimo Spiller; *SP:* Studio Galfano; *SS:* Graziella Marsetti. *Cast:* Tony Kendall [Luciano Stella] (Abraham French), Femi Benussi (Dorothy), Philip McNamara (Black), Piero Mazzinghi (Smog), Fortunato Arena (Sam), Angelo Boscariol (Dregs), Guido Benvenuti (Paul), Gualtiero Rispoli (Louis), Amedeo Timpani (Sing Sing), Ada Pometti (Prostitute), Nando Di Lena. *PROD:* Expertise United Film; *PM:* Remigio Soldini; *PSu:* Dante Lustrissimi. *Country:* Italy. Filmed at Incir–De Paolis (Rome) and at Centro Cinematografico di Mazzano Romano. *Running time:* 86'; Visa no.: 59993 (03.17.1972); *Rating:* not rated; *Release date:* 05.10.1972; *Distribution:* Cine Seven Pictures; *Domestic gross:* 31,602,000 lire. *Home video:* Dolly Video (VHS, Italy).

USA, 1930s. After an attempted robbery, Sam's gang takes refuge in an abandoned village, where another gang led by Louis is waiting for their boss, hitherto unknown. After some minor clashes the rivals eventually join forces. When reverend French and his wife Dorothy arrive in the village, looking for a treasure hidden in the cemetery, Louis believes him to be his mysterious boss, and French's ambiguous behavior seems to endorse his supposition. French is captured by the police, while the village is surrounded. The gangsters take refuge in the countryside, but are killed in a shoot-out with the cops. Dorothy escapes in the desert with Black, the only survivor, whom she's fallen for, but French—who turns out to be Louis' mysterious boss—reaches them and kills the man. He and Dorothy head back through the desert, but they have no water left....

Amasi Damiani is truly one of Italian cinema's most bizarre figures. Born in Livorno in 1937, he states to have directed 27 films between 1963 and 2000, but only a handful of them reached the theaters, usually with minimal distribution and poor grossings, and in more than one case the final results were heavily manipulated with the addition of hardcore scenes, as is the case with 1983's *Corpi nudi.* The vast majority—including titles like *La facocera* (1968) starring Karin Schubert, or *La regia è finita* (1977) with Susanna Martinková and Marina Frajese—remains unseen to this day. One of three films the filmmaker shot between 1971 and 1972, *Blood Story* is one of Damiani's less obscure efforts, having also been released on VHS in the eighties. According to the director, "since I knew many stuntmen, I decided to make a film using them as actors. [...] It was easy, because they had wonderful faces. For the three main roles I cast professional actors, such as Femi Benussi, Tony Kendall and an English, Philip McNamara, who was very good."[1]

Despite the director's enthusiasm, *Blood Story* is, quite simply, a terrible film. Shot on a shoestring, mostly at Salvatore Siciliano's Centro Cinematografico in Mazzano Romano (Italy's poorest Western village, a recurring location in many low budget Westerns of the period),[2] it's a sort of period gangster film where nothing actually happens for much of the plot, as the two rival gangs are barricaded in two opposite buildings and spend the time shooting at each other, playing cards and talking. Damiani seems totally uninterested in genre mechanics (what's more, the period gangster subgenre was long gone), while the abandoned village setting had been used in a much more impressive manner in Cesare Canevari's superb western *Matalo!* (1970). In the final massacre, the director makes ample use of slow-motion à la Penn / Peckinpah, as the gangsters meet their end in a shoot-out in the fields, with embarrassing results (the budget doesn't even allow for blood squibs, so all we have are the actors' contorting and grimacing to comical effect).

For Louis' wait for his mysterious boss to elicit comparisons with Samuel Beckett's *Waiting for Godot* would be out of place, though: on the other hand, the plot recalls in a way Damiani's previous film *I peccati di Roma,* which also featured a priest as the main character, as well as his 1972 Western *I fantasmi di Omah-ri,* also set in an abandoned village and shot at Mazzano Romano: however, these similarities only exist according to the director's own assertion, since both films are unreleased to this day—and, perhaps, it's better this way.

Notes

1. Davide Pulici and Manlio Gomarasca, "Regia Amasi Damiani," in Aa. Vv., "Misteri d'Italia. Guida ai film rari e scomparsi," *Nocturno Dossier* #47 (June 2006), p. 18.
2. The opening scene appears to have been shot in another well-known location, the old slaughterhouse in the Roman district Testaccio, which appeared in such different films as Fernando di Leo's *Rulers of the City* (1976), Bruno Mattei's erotic Nazi epic *S.S. Extermination Love Camp* (*K. Z. 9 Lager di Sterminio*, 1977) and Aristide Massaccesi's post-atomic flick *Endgame* (*Endgame—Bronx lotta finale*, 1983).

Bloody Friday (*Blutiger Freitag / Violenza contro violenza*)

D: Rolf Olsen [Rudolf Knoblich]. *S* and *SC:* Valeria Bonanno, Rolf Olsen [and Fernando di Leo, uncredited]; *DOP:* Franz X. Lederle (35mm, Eastmancolor, Telecolor); *M:* Francesco De Masi (ed. Nazionalmusic); *E:* Eva Zeyn, Amedeo Giomini; *PD:* Heinz Eickmeyer; *CO:* Siegbert Kammerer; *C:* Ernst Stritzinger; *AD:* Robert Furch; *MU:* Fritz Seyfried, Eva Uhl; *SO:* Peter Beil. *Cast:* Gianni Macchia (Luigi), Raimund Harmstorf (Heinz Klett), Amadeus August (Christian), Christine Bohm (Heidi), Ernst H. Hilbich, Walter Buschoff, Renate Roland, Horst Neumann, E.O. Fuhrmann, Ursula Erber, Ottone Mignone, Gila von Weitershausen, Daniela Giordano (Dagmar Neuss). *PROD:* Lisa Film (München), Cineproduzioni Daunia 70 (Rome); *PMs:* Armando Novelli, Günter Eulau; *PSu:* F. K. Grund, Otto Retzer. *Country:* West Germany / Italy. *Running time:* 94'; Visa no.: 61434 (11.22.1972); *Rating:* v.m.14; *Release date:* 02.06.1973; *Distribution:* Alpherat; *Domestic gross:* 135,195,000 lire. *Also known as: Violent Offender* (U.S.—Home video), *Kanli Cuma* (Turkey), *Blodig Fredag* (Norway). *Home video:* New Pentax (VHS, Italy—86'42", cut), Mercury Video (VHS, U.K.—pre-cert, 92'28"), EVC (VHS, Holland—German language), Scorpion Action Video (VHS, USA—as *Violent Offender*, cut, 84'), Video International (VHS, Norway), UIG Entertainment, MCP Sound & Media, m2 Verlag (DVD, Germany—German audio option only).

Munich. During a session in courtroom, the dangerous criminal Heinz Klett escapes with the help of his accomplices, the Italians Luigi and Stivo, and Stivo gets caught. Heinz is planning a great robbery at a bank, posing as terrorists, with Luigi, who works at a car repair garage and idolizes Heinz. Luigi's lover Heidi also gets involved in the heist, together with her brother Christian. After robbing weapons from a nearby U.S. military base, Heinz, Luigi and Christian break into the bank, killing a cop in the process. The bank is surrounded by the police, and Heinz asks for four million as ransom. One of the hostages, Marion, is the daughter of a wealthy industrialist, who agrees to pay half the sum. Stivo is released, but when he reaches Heinz' hideout he is accidentally shot by Heidi. Inside the bank,

Christian befriends the rich Marion, and tension rises among the group. After getting the four million, Heinz and his accomplices leave to meet Heidi with a pair of hostages. Luigi is attacked by a police dog and badly injured. After Heinz has raped and killed Dagmar, one of the hostages, a fight erupts. Christian hits him in the head and runs with Marion, while Luigi is accidentally shot by Heidi. Eventually the cops surround the criminals' hideout in the woods: Heidi, Christian and Heinz are all shot to death in the ensuing shoot-out.

A primarily West German / Italian production, filmed on location with a largely German-speaking cast, *Bloody Friday* is worthy of inclusion because of the involvement of Fernando di Leo's company Cineproduzioni Daunia 70. Di Leo himself revised the scenario, albeit uncredited. His touch can perhaps be detected in the way the script hints at the poor working condition of Italian immigrants (Luigi is constantly bullied and insulted by his boss), comparing them to the alienating working environment of his girlfriend Heidi, who works as a secretary in a huge firm, and in the relationship between the idealistic Luigi and the violent Heinz, whom the former idolizes.

Bloody Friday's central part predates Sidney Lumet's *Dog Day Afternoon* (1974), as the three gangsters are seized inside the bank with their hostages, and their leader (Raimund Harmstorf) passes them off as terrorists (with a cursory reference to the Baader-Meinhof gang). The script even possibly pays tribute to Billy Wilder's masterful *Ace in the Hole* (1951), as the bank siege becomes a spectacle for the outside crowd: a vendor pops up on his hot dog truck to feed the bystanders. But despite the overall pretentiousness, the results are poor, the suspense mishandled, and the dialogue often irritating, either preachy ("Crime is not the cause, but the consequence of a society!") or just plain clichéd. Harmstorf's over-the-top performance and imposing physical presence does make for an impressive, if rather hammy villain, predating such evil champions of Italian crime film as Tomas Milian (*Almost Human*) and Helmut Berger (*Beast with a Gun*).

What really drives *Bloody Friday* is, as the Italian title makes it clear, violence — brutal, unpleasant, overall nasty and disturbing. Olsen does not stint on the red paint: when Harmstorf smashes one unlucky guard's face against a wall, it looks like both the face and the wall have been redecorated with tomato ketchup aplenty; a gunshot to the belly has similar grisly effects; a cyclist is run over by the robber's car; and, in the film's most gruesome bit, a cop tries to take a grenade off an oblivious boy's hands only to suffer the explosion's aftermath himself, his intestines spilling out of his belly. The climax is a triumph of slow-motion gunshots and blood squibs, with Harmstorf meeting his end with a geyser of blood spraying from his neck onto the robbery's loot.

As the Italian immigrant Luigi, Gianni Macchia — one of di Leo's regular actors, having previously starred in the director's *Brucia ragazzo, brucia* (1969) and *Amarsi male* a.k.a. *Brucia amore brucia* (1969), and later to be featured in *Madness* (1980) — has little to do in view of an underdeveloped character, while Daniela Giordano, the other Italian presence in the cast, is the victim of a gratuitous rape scene which looks as if extraneous to the rest of the film. Several versions of the film, including the German DVD, feature quasi-subliminal next-to-hardcore shots during said scene, depicting Heinz's visions and fantasies during the rape (including slaughterhouse footage as well). As often with German co-productions, the editing is also sensibly different in the Italian and German versions, with several scenes in different order.

The Viennese-born Olsen (real name Rudolf Knoblich, 1919–1998) had been an undistinguished actor since the late forties. His filmmaking career comprised of 34 titles, including the infamous "Mondo" *Shocking Asia* (1976, signed as "Emerson Fox") and *Shocking Asia II: The Last Taboos* (1986).

Caliber 9 *(Milano calibro 9)*

D: Fernando di Leo. *S:* based on the short story *Stazione Centrale ammazzare subito* by Giorgio Scerbanenco; *SC:* Fernando di Leo; *DOP:* Franco Villa (Eastmancolor, Telecolor); *M:* Luis Enriquez Bacalov, directed by the author, played by the bands Osanna and New Trolls; *E:* Amedeo Giomini; *PD, CO:* Francesco Cuppini; *MU:* Antonio Mura; *AD:* Franco Lo Cascio; *SO:* Goffredo Salvatori; *C:* Claudio Morabito; *AC:* Enrico Biribicchi; *W:* Marcella Moretti; *CON:* Vivalda Vigorelli. *Cast:* Gastone Moschin (Ugo Piazza), Barbara Bouchet (Nelly Bordon), Mario Adorf (Rocco Musco), Frank Wolff (police Commissioner), Luigi Pistilli (Commissioner Mercuri), Ivo Garrani (Don Vincenzo), Philippe Leroy (Chino), Lionel Stander ("The American"), Mario Novelli (Pasquale Tallarico), Giuseppe Castellano (Nicola), Salvatore Arico (Luca), Fernando Cerulli (Hotel porter), Giulio Baraghini (Brigadeer), Franco Beltramme (The American's Henchman), Rossella Bergamonti (Street Woman), Bruno Bertocci (François Doremat, first courier), Empedocle Buzzanca (elderly man, second courier), Fortunato Cecilia (Vincenzo Affatato), Ernesto Colli (Alfredo Bertolon), Alberto Fogliani (American's Henchman), Ettore Geri (Barman), Imelde Marani (Blonde woman, third courier), Sergio Serafini (police officer), Alessandro Tedeschi (German courier), Giorgio Trestini (Franceschino), Diomira Vidotto (Street Woman). *Uncredited:* Artemio Antonini (The American's Henchman), Salvatore Billa (Gum-Chewing Henchman in Office), Angelo Boscariol (policeman), Marina Brengola (Street Woman), Sisto Brunetti (policeman), Omero Capanna (American's Henchman), Fernando di Leo (Man at Phone Booth), Cesare Di Vito (police official), Gilberto Galimberti (American's Henchman), Luigi Antonio Guerra (Hitman), Giuseppe Leone (American Henchman), Domenico Maggio (American Henchman), Marco Mariani (police official), Gianni Milito (American Henchman), Gastone Pescucci (police officer), Mauro Vestri (police officer). *PROD:* Armando Novelli for Cineproduzioni Daunia '70; *PM:* Lanfranco Ceccarelli; *PSu:* Vincenzo Salviani; *PSe:* Luciano Appignani. *Country:* Italy. Filmed on location in Milan. *Running time:* 101'; Visa no.: 59724 (02.08.1972); *Rating:* v.m.14; *Release date:* 02.15. 1972; *Distribution:* Lia Film; *Domestic gross:* 754,443,000 lire. *Home video:* Raro Video (Blu-Ray / DVD, USA). OST: CD Warner Fonit 8573 82332-2.

Small-time gangster Ugo Piazza is released from jail where he has been serving a three-year sentence for robbery, just to find that his former boss, the American, has sent his men to pick him up. The American's right-hand man, Rocco Musco, accuses Piazza of having stolen $300,000 from the boss and gives him a beating. However Ugo insists that he didn't steal the money, and refuses to meet the American. Rocco and his men track down Ugo again in a seedy hotel, threatening him once more. Piazza does not react, feigning indifference even when Rocco destroys his room. He is forced to turn to his good friend Chino, asking him for money to pay for the damage. Chino lives with old mafia boss Don Vincenzo, who's almost blind and in very poor health, and takes care of him. Chino gives Ugo the money, but doesn't want to get involved with his problems, even though he chases Rocco when he pops up again to bully Piazza. Ugo pays a *visit to his former girlfriend, beautiful nightclub dancer Nelly. The woman is worried about what might happen to Piazza, but he reassures her: now he's working for the boss, he'll be able to find out who committed the theft. Another courier is also killed over stolen money. Rocco is convinced that Don Vincenzo and Chino are behind it and prepares a fatal ambush. It's up to Piazza to do the killing, but Ugo refuses to shoot his friend; nonetheless, Don Vincenzo is killed. Because the mission was a failure, Piazza is beaten up by the American's henchmen, but he swears all the time that he never stole the money. Chino swears to avenge his old friend: he pops up at the American's villa, while a party is taking place, and kills the boss. A big shoot-out ensues and Piazza sides with Chino, taking out the American's henchmen, but Chino too gets killed. Piazza gets in the car and heads towards a farmhouse where, three years earlier, he had hidden the money he did, in fact, steal from the boss. Heading to meet Nelly and run away together forever, Piazza is stopped by the police, but denies any involvement in the shooting: he is quickly released and heads straight to Nelly's. What he doesn't know, though, is that the woman has another young lover, Luca, who had been following Piazza all along. Luca shoots Ugo in the back. Rocco, who was the only survivor after the shooting and had followed Ugo's moves, pops up at Nelly's place and kills Luca with his bare hands, thus avenging Piazza.*

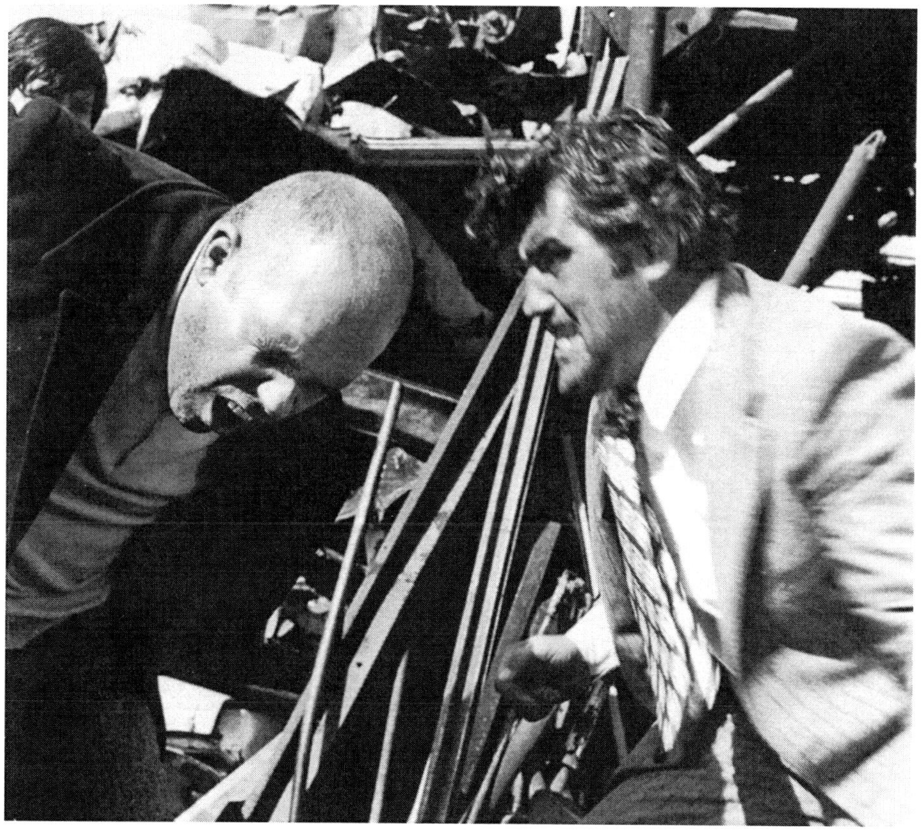

Ugo Piazza (Gastone Moschin, left) is badly beaten up by Rocco Musco (Mario Adorf, right) in *Caliber 9* (1972).

Coming after the minor *giallo Slaughter Hotel* (*La bestia uccide a sangue freddo*, 1971) which nevertheless gained much more visibility than his better works, *Caliber 9* is the heart of Fernando di Leo's cinema, a movie where everything — actors, dialogue, pacing, the marvelous score by Luis Enriquez Bacalov[1]—fits in magically, as if the director worked in a state of grace. The story of Ugo Piazza (Gastone Moschin), a small-time crook who is released from jail, only to find that old acolytes waiting for him because they suspect he stole $300,000 from them, shows the director's love of classic American and French *film noir*: John Huston, Nicholas Ray, and Jean-Pierre Melville. First of all, there is the sense of an imminent, inescapable, mocking Fate: a feeling which was originally emphasized by the inclusion of dates and timelines superimposed on screen, like a countdown (the working title was *Da lunedì a lunedì*, "From Monday to Monday"). The police are just a marginal presence, and the scenes at the police station where two commissioners — a left-winged and a reactionary one, played respectively by Luigi Pistilli and Frank Wolff— argue all the time, are perhaps the film's only real flaw, breaking the film's smooth flow and mood.[2]

Even more impressive is how di Leo adapts on screen one of Giorgio Scerbanenco's short stories, distilling the writer's universe and making it his own. "When I read Scerbanenco's books, I realized that we shared the same vision of the world. He was a realist who wrote about petty crooks and small-time criminals,"[3] he stated. Much more so than di Leo's previous Scerbanenco adaptation, *Naked Violence*, *Caliber 9* preserves the spirit rather than the letter of Scerbanenco's pages: the film's celebrated centerpiece — the sequence set in the heart of Milan, piazza Duomo, which follows two couriers exchanging mysterious packets and ending with two simultaneous, unexpected bomb blasts — comes from the short story *Stazione Centrale ammazzare subito* ("Central Station Kill Immediately") from the omnibus *Milano by Calibre 9*: the rest is all di Leo's.

Milan, the so called "black Milan" as described in Scerbanenco's books, has never been so impressive: foggy canals, decaying condos, sleazy nightclubs, empty parking lots. Di Leo doesn't go for sociological notations, but he films Italy's biggest Northern city with a realism unknown to genre cinema. The stark contrast between ultramodern, stylish apartments and squalid hotel rooms echoes the hiatus between the luxurious headquarters of the big boss, the "American" (Lionel Stander) and the poor, minuscule apartment where the elderly blind Mafia godfather Don Vincenzo (Ivo Garrani) lives with his sidekick, Chino (Philippe Leroy). This way, Di Leo effectively synthesizes the escalation of a new form of criminality replacing the old one. As Don Vincenzo says, "They call it the Mafia, but they're just

Ugo Piazza (Gastone Moschin) and Nelly (Barbara Bouchet) in *Caliber 9* (1972).

gangs. Gangs fighting each other. The real Mafia does not exist anymore. When drug dealers want to invest their earnings, they build apartment blocks. So the construction gangs kill them. Where's the Mafia in that? The real mafia is gone."

The difference between old and new criminality is a matter of methods and mentality: something which has been understood very well by the American, whose motto is "Do unto others as they would do to you ... before they do it!"—an aberration to those who still follow old concepts such as honor, respect, "rules" (at one point Chino says: "I'll do whatever you want, but don't ask me to break the rules!") which actually no one follows anymore. On the other hand, there are many loose dogs raising their heads, claiming their share with violence or craftiness: violence generates only violence, in a chain reaction that will end with no winners.

Rocco Musco (Mario Adorf) kills Luca (Salvatore Arico, right), avenging Ugo Piazza in the final scene from *Caliber 9* (1972).

Scerbanenco's characters are taciturn, and Ugo Piazza is no exception. He's a monolith of a man: cold, imperturbable, with undecipherable icy eyes. It was a brave move to choose for this role an actor such as Gastone Moschin, often seen in comedies such as Pietro Germi's wonderful *The Birds, the Bees and the Italians* (*Signore & signori*, 1966) where he usually played simpletons or awkward types. Di Leo reinvents Moschin's screen persona, turning him into a sort of Milanese version of Lino Ventura in Melville's films: his hands in the pockets of his Marine jacket, his eyes fixed on the ground to avoid other people's stare, walking fast along the canals of Milan, Piazza is a memorably doomed and solitary antihero. Mario Adorf, who plays the obtuse, bovine Rocco Musco, the Americano's right hand, is precisely the opposite: vulgarly elegant, with greasy hair and an Errol Flynn mustache, he is a subtly caricatured presence (just as the other gangsters, whose features and movements are deformed with twitches and scares) yet a vital one in the film's economy. It's Rocco whom Piazza meets first, when he gets out of jail, and the very first scene between Adorf and Moschin in Rocco's car is a small masterpiece in its own, with Rocco alternating enticements and allusive treats while Ugo stays silent. "Friends, Nicò, Pasquà, this is Ugo, Ugo Piazza, he used to work with us and he liked it. You guys like it too, right? Didn't you like it, Ugo? You liked it, you liked it! He liked it! But he wanted more.... Right, Ugo?" says Rocco with a jovial yet sinister smile.

Di Leo plays on the contrast between the imperturbable Moschin and Adorf's hammy overacting. Rocco loves to make a scene in front of his men, showing off his power: on the contrary, Ugo just keeps a low profile, waiting for his chance. A chance that comes when the gang war between Chino and the American ends with no survivors. With a masterful directorial stroke, Di Leo shows Ugo's steps—first hesitating, then running in an irresistible euphoria—in the beginning of a long, speechless sequence which follows Piazza to the abandoned house in the country where he has hidden the $300,000 that he had stolen, after all. Ugo looks like a winner: after the jail, the beatings, the fear of being killed that accompanied each and every move he made, he can finally think about the future. Too bad he has not got one.

As the mythology of *film noir* demands, the man is always in love with the wrong woman. *Milano calibro 9's femme fatale* has the angelic features of Nelly (Barbara Bouchet), Ugo's lover, introduced in a truly show-stopping scene in a nightclub, where the blonde actress is dancing atop a cube, wearing only a gold bikini, filmed by di Leo with plenty of low-angle shots that exude a hypnotic fascination. Unbeknownst to Ugo, Nelly has paired up with a much younger man, Luca, whom Ugo treated like a boy ("Have you seen how much he's grown up?" somebody tells Ugo at one point). And together they set a trap on Ugo to get the money: the Machiavellian Piazza literally becomes a fool for love, the only emotion that he is not capable of dominating beneath his armor of stolidness.

The bitter irony of *Caliber 9* is in the string of coincidences, all of them conspiring for an ending which was written into the characters' DNA. As events unfold, the game of appearances which the film—and life itself—is built upon, just collapses. Smartness becomes foolishness, love turns into treason, hostility is replaced by respect. That's why the film ends with an unexpected *deus ex machina*: Rocco, whose hatred towards Piazza has turned into admiration, becomes Ugo's avenger, killing Luca with his own bare hands while shouting: "You can't backstab a man like Ugo Piazza! You'd better not even touch someone like Ugo Piazza! Don't even go near someone like Ugo Piazza! When you see someone like Ugo Piazza, you'd better tip your hat!" Rocco's final act of revenge is caused by a sort of instinctive and primitive sense of submission—Piazza was the strongest of them all, and Rocco respects it for that, like a wild wolf would do with the leader of the pack.

Everything's lost. Ugo's been killed like a dog: the only thing that's left of him is honor. A key value of a long-lost code, which is desperately reaffirmed by someone who has just realized that it's gone forever. The very last shot is that of a cigarette slowly consuming away, on the edge of a table: a brilliant image which synthesizes a vision of the world, life, and cinema.

Notes

1. The soundtrack album includes totally re-arranged versions of the film's main music pieces. *Caliber 9* also features the "album version" of Bacalov's *Adagio (Shadows)*, played by New Trolls and originally included in their 1971 *Concerto Grosso* album. The arrangement is different from the version first heard in Maurizio Lucidi's *The Designated Victim* (*La vittima designata*, 1971).
2. Di Leo himself admitted, years later: "In my opinion—not Fernando di Leo the director but Fernando di Leo the critic—those scenes had to be cut. The movie would have become more compact." Davide Pulici, "Secondo movimento: il tempo del nero," in Aa. Vv., "Calibro 9. Il cinema di Fernando di Leo," *Nocturno Dossier* #14 (September 2003), p. 20.
3. *Ibid.*, p. 22.

Crime Boss, a.k.a. *The New Mafia Boss (I familiari delle vittime non saranno avvertiti)*

D: Alberto De Martino. *S:* Lucio Manlio Battistrada, Luigi Mordini; *SC:* Lucio Manlio Battistrada, Alberto De Martino; *DOP:* Aristide Massaccesi (35mm, Eastmancolor—S.P.E.S.); *M:* Francesco De Masi, conducted by the author (ed. Nazionalmusic); *E:* Otello Colangeli; *PD:* Antonio Visone; *CO:* Adriana Spadaro Osanna Guardini; *C:* Remo Grisanti, Mauro Lommi; *AE:* Anna Moretti; *AD:* Giorgio Ubaldi; *MU:* Franco Di Girolamo; *Hair:* Rosetta Luciani; *SO:* Pietro Ortolani; *Mix:* Bruno Moreal; *SP:* Sandro Borni; *SS:* Ivetta Blais. *Cast:* Antonio Sabàto (Antonio Mancuso), Telly Savalas (Don Vincenzo), Paola Tedesco (Monica), Giuliano Persico (Nicola Mancuso), Nino Dal Fabbro (Don Nino Faina), Sergio Rossi (Don Turi Petralia), Giorgio Piazza (Torre, the journalist), Guido Lollobrigida (Peppino Lo Surdo), Sergio Tramonti (Carmelo), Teodoro Agrimi-Corrà (Antonio, the Marselleise), Carlo Gaddi (Vanni, Don Vincenzo's henchman), Rosita Torosh (Peppino's mistress), Franco Fragalà (Don Vincenzo's mustached henchman), Orazio Stracuzzi (Sicilian), Francesco D'Adda Salvaterra (Marseillese), Graziella Cabras; Piero Morgia (Don Vincenzo's henchman), Gianfranco De Angelis (Monica's friend), Maria Valente (Mara, Nicola's wife). *Uncredited:* Salvatore Billa (Mafia boss), Alberto De Martino (Airplane passenger), Lina Franchi (Mamma Rosaria), Sofia Lusy (Nun), Annibale Papetti (Loreto Abbondanza), Franca Scagnetti (Don Faina's maid), Franco Ukmar (Marseillese's man). *PROD:* Gino Mordini for Claudia Cinematografica (Rome); *GM:* Ottavio Oppo; *PM:* Giovanni Antonio Giurgola; *PSu:* Sergio Bollino; *PSe:* Giuseppe Bruno Bossio. *Country:* Italy. Filmed at Incir–De Paolis (Rome) and on location in Milan, Palermo, Rome, Hamburg. *Running time:* 103'; Visa no.: 60095 (04.12.1972); *Rating:* not rated; *Release date:* 08.08.1972; *Distribution:* P.A.C.; *Domestic gross:* 498,812,000 lire. *Also known as: Le nouveau boss de la mafia* (Paris, 03.76—100'), *El jefe de la mafia* (Spain). *Home video:* Hobby & Work (DVD, Italy), Ds (DVD, USA), PopFlix (DVD, USA—as part of *Mafia Boss Colection* box)

Antonio Mancuso is sent from Sicily to Milan to kill Loreto Abbondanza, a Mafia traitor. Antonio (whose father Vito was killed by Abbondanza) realizes that his bosses want to frame him, so after the murder he takes refuge in Hamburg, to where his brother Nicola has emigrated, earning his living as a pimp. With an elaborate ploy, Antonio wins the trust of Don Vincenzo, a powerful Mafia boss. He and Nicola become part of Don Vincenzo's "family." Antonio falls for his boss' niece Monica, who despises Don Vincenzo, and becomes more and more rebellious towards the boss, especially after Don Vincenzo has murdered a journalist, Torre, who was investigating the connections between Mafia and politics. A Mafia war among bosses ensues, with Don Vincenzo eliminating all his rivals. Thanks to Monica, Antonio tracks down the boss to the Swiss clinic where he's hiding and kills him. He will be the new Mafia boss.

As with poliziotteschi, early '70s Mafia flicks directly derived from the committed civil cinema of the previous decade, with effects that are no less contradictory. After the enormous success of Elio Petri's *We Still Kill the Old Way* and Damiano Damiani's *The Day of the Owl*, the thread proved to be profitable, and in 1972 out-and-out crime films were still an embryonic phenomenon. The subgenre's main theme was the spreading of the Mafia in the big cities of Northern Italy (and Europe), and the results oscillated between classic *film noir* templates—that's the case with Fernando di Leo's films, Umberto Lenzi's *Gang War in Milan* and Duccio Tessari's *Big Guns*—and weird hybrids between genre and auteur cinema such as Carlo Lizzani's *Black Turin*. All of these, however, portrayed a reality that was perceived as radically different from the Sicilian one.

In 1972 Mafia was a winning word at the box office, thanks to such films as Francis Ford Coppola's *The Godfather* and Terence Young's *The Valachi Papers*, which offered a more traditional view of "Cosa Nostra." However, the Mafia subgenre would soon make room for out-and-out urban crime flicks, mainly because it was not able to create serial heroes. Nor did it allow for all the variations on the theme that the urban topographies of Milan, Rome, Genoa and Naples would offer — each a microcosm with its own reality, environment, characters and originality.

Last but not least, Mafia flicks were less astute than poliziotteschi in absorbing the remains of civil cinema. A case in point is Alberto De Martino's *Crime Boss*, which starts as a realistic portrait of Mafia laborers: the opening titles feature a typical Sicilian folk song which is soon replaced by Francesco De Masi's brass-and-guitar-driven score, as the hairy Antonio Mancuso (Antonio Sabàto) rides on his bike through Palermo streets and outskirts. "You were born here, and should have died here," he is told by Mafia boss Don Nino. "Die starving like so many, or killed with a shotgun?" he promptly replies.

Martino aptly shows Mancuso's disorientation when he flies from Sicily to Milan, to kill a Mafia traitor: the opening scenes are not dissimilar to those in Fulvio Marcolin's *Gli amici degli amici hanno saputo* (1973) where Gino Milli and Simonetta Stefanelli arrive in Turin with the illusion of a better life. De Martino even allows himself a funny cameo as the airplane passenger who watches in contempt as Antonio, who's never taken a plane in his life, can't even fasten his seat belt: if in the 1960s flying on Alitalia planes meant that Italy had finally become an International country (most genre films opened showing a plane taking off or landing at Fiumicino airport), here it represents Sicily's isolation. Yet this apparently racist statement is soon contradicted: the North may be industrialized and wealthy, but the Mafia has spread over there as well. The airport glass door that opens automatically in front of Antonio is not, as in Argento's *Suspiria* (1977), a horrific omen, but the sign that the world is just waiting for him. Sabàto's physical transformation from rough peasant to elegant Mafia boss — he trims his mustache and hair, leaves the typical Sicilian basque and velvet jacket for full suits and ties — is a metaphor for the Mafia's change of skin in Northern Italy.

The rest of the film, however, doesn't live up to its impressive opening. After Mancuso has moved to Hamburg and then to Switzerland, Lucio Battistrada's screenplay becomes cliché-ridden, as the young man first becomes friends with a powerful boss (Telly Savalas), then takes over his empire. The concept of the Mafia as a tangled labyrinth of never-ending betrayals, double-crossings and revenges somehow recalls Fernando di Leo's *The Boss*: everybody is a traitor of sorts, and the relationship between Antonio and Monica is not based on love, but on ambition ("We have the same blood, you and me!" he says as they make love). Yet De Martino is more interested in action than in the anthropological essence of *Cosa Nostra*. For all his thirst of power, Sabàto is an avenger after all, and the denunciation of the Mafia's ties with politicians and misdeeds (the character of journalist Torre, who is first used and then killed by the boss, is loosely inspired by Mauro De Mauro, assassinated by the Mafia in 1970) seems devoid of the social urgency which moved "political-civil cinema": rather, it's played only for its spectacular quality. History is less an inspiration than a pretext.

If *Crime Boss* doesn't live up to its claims ("It was the story of Caesar and Brutus, essentially [...] a bit like Shakespeare, so to speak," the director joked[1]), De Martino does display his proficient technical skills, helped by Aristide Massaccesi's efficient camerawork, as proven by the elaborate, effectively paced Hamburg hotel scam and subsequent car chase, or the shoot-out with the Marseille gang. Elsewhere the attempts at cruelty border on unintentional parody, as when one of Don Vincenzo's Marseille rivals is killed, put in a cauldron and eventually transformed into bars of soap which are mailed to his boss (Teodoro Corrà) as a threat.

Sabàto is wooden as usual as the rough but clever social climber, while Savalas' towering presence and sardonic affectations as the gardening-loving boss — who becomes a father figure for Antonio, only to be the victim of an Oedipal patricide — add a little bit of interest to a rather flatly written character, with predictable lines such as "I am the family. It's mine, I created it and I can destroy it!" Lucio Fulci fans will be pleased to hear Francesco De Masi's *Fay* on the soundtrack, which would later be prominently featured in *The New York Ripper* (1982).

Note

1. Gomarasca, "Il cinema è quello che ci fa," p. 15.

Execution Squad (La polizia ringrazia)

D: Stefano Vanzina. *S* and *SC:* Lucio De Caro, Steno [Stefano Vanzina]; *DOP:* Riccardo Pallottini (35mm, Techniscope — Technicolor); *M:* Stelvio Cipriani, arranged and conducted by the author; *E:* Roberto Perpignani, Jutta Brandstaedter; *PD, SD:* Nicola Tamburro; *C:* Luigi Filippo Carta; *AC:* Dante Di Palma; *AE* Piera Gabutti, Maria Piera Mari; *AD:* Mario Forges Davanzati; *MU:* Lamberto Marini; *Hair:* Ilda Gilde De Guilmi; *SO:* Pietro Ortolani; *Mix:* Franco Bassi; *SE:* Luciano Anzellotti; *SEE* Roberto Arcangeli; *SP: UPs:* Lucherini, Rossetti, Spinola. *Cast:* Enrico Maria Salerno (Commissioner Bertone), Mariangela Melato (Sandra), Mario Adorf (District Attorney Ricciuti), Franco Fabrizi (Bettarini), Cyril Cusack (Stolfi), Laura Belli (Anna Maria Sprovieri), Jürgen Drews (Michele Settecamini), Corrado Gaipa (Lawyer Armani), Giorgio Piazza, Ezio Sancrotti (Commissioner Santalamenti), Pietro [Piero] Tiberi, Diego Reggente, Ada Pometti (Hooker), Sergio Serafini (Journalist), Fortunato Cecilia, Ferdinado Murolo (Head of the Execution squad), Gianfranco Barra (Agent Esposito), Romualdo Buzzanca, Giovanna Di Vita, Rosemarie Lindt, Riccardo Mangano, Franco Meroni, Corrado Solari, Gianni Solaro, Franz von Treuberg (Journalist), Valentino Macchi (policeman), Luciano Bonanni (Radio operator). *PROD:* Roberto Infascelli and Peter Geissler for Primex Italiana (Rome), Dieter Geissler Filmproduktion (Münich); *GM:* Marcello D'Amico. *Country:* Italy / West Germany. Filmed at Centro Incom (Rome) and on location in Rome. *Running time:* 99'; Visa no.: 59835 (02.24.1972); *Rating:* v.m.14; *Release date:* 02.25.1972; *Distribution:* P.A.C.; *Domestic gross:* 1,696,360,000 lire. *Also known as: Das Syndikat* (West Germany, 11.17.1972). *Home video:* Subkultur (DVD, Germany), Shendene (DVD, Italy), King Records (DVD, Japan). OST: CD Digitmovies CDDM150

Rome. Two young men, Michele and Mario, attempt a robbery from a jewelry store. Michele kills the owner and a passerby who was trying to stop him. Commissioner Bertone is entrusted with the case, but he has to face many difficulties. At one point, after his men have beaten a suspect, Bertone is even placed under investigation by deputy prosecutor Ricciuti. Michele is located and killed by a vigilante execution squad, the self-dubbed "Anonymous Anticrime," which assassinates other criminals as well, so as to manipulate the public opinion and pave the way for a forthcoming fascist dictatorship. Bertone finds out that the squad is actually maneuvered by the authorities. When he goes to arrest the unsuspecting head of the "Anonymous Anticrime," former Chief of Police Stolfi, the Commissioner is murdered. Ricciuti claims he will do his best to prosecute those responsible for the killing, among whom there is also Bertone's assistant.

Many critics label *Execution Squad* as the founding stone of the awkward label poliziotteschi: the initiator of a genre, and for some, one of its few worthy examples before a progressive deterioration. Actually, Stefano Vanzina's film is just a logical continuation of the metamorphosis of political cinema which started with Damiano Damiani's *Confessions of a Police Captain*: a fact underlined by its working title, *Ipotesi del capo della Squadra Omicidi* ("Assumption of the head of the Homicide Squad"), which refers explicitly to the trend of civic commitment,[1] and by the plot: commissioner Bertone (Enrico Maria Salerno), unloved by the press because of his expeditious methods and scarce deference to power, discovers that the mysterious anti-crime team that eliminates people from the underworld hides a subversive right-wing organization in cahoots with the institutions.

For the first time in his career (still not the only one, as proven by his following film *Anastasia mio fratello* starring Alberto Sordi), Stefano Vanzina (1915–1988) abandoned his usual pseudonym Steno, which he had used since his film debut in 1949 for his previous forty-six films as director — a fact that further proves the continuity between *Execution Squad* and the "committed" socio-political thread of the late '60s. The script, co-written by Vanzina and Lucio De Caro, was initially meant to be directed by someone else, but according to Vanzina, "back then my colleagues were afraid to speak ill of the police (a fact which made me laugh, as they were all left-wing directors!). Eventually, I directed the film myself."[2] To the filmmaker, it was a radical change of pace from his favorite genre — comedy: the result featured the elements which would become obligatory in the forthcoming poliziotteschi, still in an embryonic, unresolved form.

Vanzina claimed he and De Caro took inspiration for the script by the death squads in Brazil, yet the most immediate influence seems to be Leonardo Sciascia's novel *Il contesto*,[3] which came out in 1971 and was made into a film by Francesco Rosi in 1976 (*Illustrious Corpses*). The script seems to rely on it for the character of Bertone, who recalls *Il contesto*'s protagonist, commissioner Rogas ("He had principles, in a country where no one else did," as Sciascia wrote), as well as for the political plot that his investigation uncovers. Which is yet another continuity point with the past, not a disruption.

As with *Confessions of a Police Captain*, in *Execution Squad* Vanzina adopts the point of view of a policeman and shows his sense of impotence due to the impossibility of performing his job adequately. Unlike Damiani's film, though, what hinders Bertone are not Mafia connivances but the lack of men, means, laws. Furthermore, the press is always ready to target police forces. In the film's most didactic sequence, Bertone leads a group of journalists in a night journey through Rome, showing them how criminals have their way thanks to the reforms of the code of criminal procedure and police regulations. It's a moment which recalls *Bandits in Milan*'s early sequences, where Tomas Milian illustrated the many faces of the Milanese underworld. " Our hands are tied: delinquents make fun of us and journalist hinder our work," Bertone says. "It's all over unless one reacts [...] we'd all be hostages in the hands of the underworld!" Such catchphrases will become a recurring event in forthcoming crime films.

However, the apparent reactionary approach of *Execution Squad*'s first part turns into its exact opposite in the second half, which describes the birth and diffusion of neo-fascist mentality and practices at all levels. That's the case with the mysterious execution squad which kills all those criminals who escaped the net of justice or were released because of procedural system faults. The idea of an organic subversive plan is a typical conspiracy movie element, which would later return in subsequent poliziotteschi such as Sergio Martino's *Silent Action* (1975). The mastermind behind this neo-fascist resurgence is a man above suspicion: elderly former Chief of Police Stolfi (Cyril Cusack, once again an icon of fascist repression after Truffaut's *Fahrenheit 451*) pulls the strings from the Fidelitas circle (an aptly named headquarter which hints at the Democrazia Cristiana party, whose motto was another Latin word, Libertas). If Stolfi represents a distorted view of law and order, Bertone is one of the last in a species on the verge of extinction, "the right man on the wrong side," as he's called. The Commissioner is equidistant from left and right, progressives and reactionaries; his intellectual limit is that he can't conceive (he does it too late) a political overview: the moment he does, he dies.

Execution Squad is still a film where narration carries a message — fascism finds fertile ground in the errors of democracy, especially in the field of law — which is stressed by Bertone's words in defense of the rule of law. Secondary characters, too, come from the political cinema: upright magistrate Ricciuti (Mario Adorf), who claims "I can't just think ... I need evidence!," is a clone of Franco Nero's character in *Confessions of a Police Captain*. But unlike Damiani's film, Vanzina's instills a doubt: is Ricciuti's zeal the product of an obtuse reading of the penal code or is it a clue of his connivance with the neo-fascist plot? Vanzina himself is not sure — or perhaps he doesn't want to end the film on such a downbeat note. In the end, Ricciuti seems to wake up from the laxity he has shown so far. But Adorf's final monologue is a half-baked, unconvincing rebellion, which leaves a sense of impotence: whereas in political films the only way to endure the "survival of the fittest" game was to lower one's stare and resignedly accept injustice, as Franco Nero does in Damiano Damiani's prison drama *The Case Is Closed, Forget It* and Marcello Aliprandi's *Smiling Maniacs* (1975), the poliziotteschi would reach a different conclusion — that is, where law is useless, weapons will do.

Such a resolution doesn't even cross Bertone's mind. He is a cultured, reflexive man, who doesn't use weapons ("I take care of crimes, not punishments"), "more inclined to solve, perhaps, the problems of Pi Greek rather than those of P38," as one film critic put it, "a kind of detective who's quite hard to find in the many provinces of the Italian crime genre: closer to Maigret than to Sartana."[4] That's also because of the lead, the then 46-year-old Enrico Maria Salerno: an actor whose voice, conduct and sober elegance recalls father figures like commissioner Ingravallo in Pietro Germi's *The Facts of Murder* (*Un maledetto imbroglio*, 1960) or commissioner Fioresi in Damiani's *Lipstick* (*Il rossetto*, 1960), both played by Pietro Germi, but certainly does not carry any resemblance to contemporary American models such as Harry Callahan or "Popeye" Doyle. Mature, good-looking, capable to move nonchalantly from *cinéma d'auteur* (Roberto Rossellini's *Escape by Night*, 1960; Antonio Pietrangeli's *I Knew Her Well*, 1965) to popular genres (Vittorio Cottafavi's *Hercules and the Captive Women*, 1961; Massimo Dallamano's *Bandidos*, 1968) Salerno was probably chosen because of his role as the police commissioner in Dario Argento's debut *The Bird with the Crystal Plumage* (*L'uccello dalle piume di cristallo*, 1970), which was a surprise smash hit in Italy. Curiously, though, Vanzina had initially offered the role to Lando Buzzanca, then one of Italy's most famous comedians. One wonders what the film would have been like with him in the lead.

However, the differences between *Execution Squad* and the forthcoming poliziotteschi are patent. For one, Bertone stills questions himself about his role, whereas the "iron commissioners" to come will place bullets before brains. Where Vanzina's film still stutters, however, it's in action scenes. The sequence where a robber, who's carrying a hostage on his bike, is chased by police cars, is poorly — if not clumsily — conceived and executed.

If the label of initiator doesn't really become it, *Execution Squad* was nevertheless an unexpected box office hit (1,700 billion lire, while Francesco Rosi's *Il caso Mattei* grossed 1,300 billion lire) and its effective, sarcastic Italian title (literally: "From the police, with Thanks") immediately caught the public fancy. Vanzina's film started what would become the decade's most popular and commercially fruitful thread, "a popular genre which was closed, structured around recurring figures, organized in an authentic productive series."[5]

However, the genre's putative father would abandon his offspring. Despite the commercial success of *Execution Squad*, Steno would change course, only tangentially returning to the genre — this time via his usual pseudonym — with *Flatfoot* (*Piedone lo sbirro*, 1973), where he managed to bastardize crime and comedy, creating a cop who slaps and beats instead of shooting, and who's got the big bearded face and huge hands and body of Bud Spencer, the hero of comedy Westerns. On *Policewoman* (*La poliziotta*, 1974), Steno would return to out-and-out comedy, with a paradoxical story depicting a portrayal of corruption and embezzlement which is not too dissimilar from that of many "serious" crime flicks.

Italian poster for *Execution Squad* (1972).

Note

1. Meanwhile, the wave of torrential titles persisted, sometimes with misleading results: Giuseppe Vari's *Who Killed the Prosecutor and Why?* (*Terza ipotesi su un caso di perfetta strategia criminale*, 1973), despite opening with the murder of a magistrate, is just a mediocre *giallo*, spiced with erotic scenes.
2. Faldini and Fofi, *Il cinema italiano d'oggi*, p. 451.
3. *Il contesto. Una parodia* was a vitriolic parable which caused controversy among political parties. The Communist Party (PCI) was enraged by Sciascia's thesis: in the "context" of omnipotent criminal powers which rule the country, even the biggest left-wing opposition party eventually decides that the *raison d'état* coincides with the party's own interests.
4. Davide Pulici, "Cinici, infami e violenti: il poliziesco all'italiana (parte I, 1971–1973)," *Nocturno Cinema* #1 (October-November 1994), p. 42.
5. Buttafava, "Procedure sveltite," p. 101.

Gang War in Naples (*Camorra*)

D: Pasquale Squitieri. *S* and *SC:* Pasquale Squitieri; *DOP:* Giulio Albonico (35mm, Eastmancolor); *M:* Manuel De Sica, conducted by the author (ed. R.C.A.); *Reginella* (Bovio/Lama) and *Chiove* (Bovio/Nardella) sung by Roberto Murolo; *E:* Daniele Alabiso; *AEs:* Rita Triunveri, Adelchi Marinangeli; *ArtD:* Fabrizio Frisardi; *PD:* Nicola Losito; *CO:* Rosalba Menichelli; *AD:* Gerardo D'Andrea; *C:* Sebastiano Celeste; *AC:* Maurizio La Monica; *MU:* Raoul Ranieri; *Hair:* Maria Luisa Laganga; *SO:* Angelo Amatulli; *SOE:* Renato Marinelli; *SE:* Gino Vagniluca; *SP:* Baldi Schwarze [Giorgio Garibaldi Schwarze]; *SS:* Adolfo Dragone. *Cast:* Fabio Testi (Tonino Russo), Jean Seberg (Luisa), Raymond Pellegrin (Mario Capece), Charles Vanel (Don Mimì De Ritis), Germana Carnacina (Anna), Enzo Cannavale (Nicola Cafiero), Ugo D'Alessio (Pietro Russo, Tonino's father), Lilla Brignone (Tonino's mother), Salvatore Puntillo (Commissioner Capezzuto), Marcello Filotico (Don Ciccillo Cotrufo), Benito Artesi (Valerio), Paul Muller (Politician), Giovanni Guerrieri, Mirella Mereu (Donna Carmela), Enzo Turco (Silverio), Anna Zinnemann (Nunziatina), Alberto Farnese (Croupier), Francesco D'Adda (Commissioner's assistant), Renato Chiantoni (Capece's accountant), Leopoldo Mastelloni (Cardillo, a convict), Nino Vingelli (Inmate), Sergio Serafini (Man playing billiard with Tonino), Orazio Stracuzzi. *Uncredited:* Ennio Antonelli (Gangster), Giulio Baraghini (Worker at gambling house), Gennaro Beneduce (Man at gambling house), Salvatore Billa (Slaughterhouse owner), Nestore Cavaricci (Prison guard), Vincenzo Falanga (Pietravalle's cammorist partner), Guido Lollobrigida (Cammorist), Enrico Maisto (Capece's henchman), Edoardo Mascia (Cammorist), Nazzareno Natale (Capece's henchman), Simone Santo (Man carrying holy oil). *PROD:* Sergio Bonotti for Mondial Te. Fi.—Televisione Film (Rome), Europa Film (Paris) / Parafrance (Paris); *GM:* Giancarlo Marchetti; *UM:* Maurizio Pastrovich; *PSu:* Vittorio Biferale, Francesco Manco; *ADM and CASH:* Giancarlo Ciotti. *Country:* Italy / France. Filmed at Incir—De Paolis (Rome) and on location in Naples. *Running time:* 113'; Visa no.: 60809 (08.08.1972); *Rating:* not rated; *Release date:* 08.24.1972; *Distribution:* Titanus; *Domestic gross:* 1,345,608,000 lire. *Also known as: Les tueurs à gages* (France, 08.30.1972 —100'); *Omertà—Reden heißt Sterben* (West Germany, 06.14.1973 — 88'), *Camorra* (Spain). *Home video:* Video Mercury / Filmax (DVD, Spain). OST: CD Rca Records OST 125-2

Tonino Russo, the son of a poor but honest shoemaker, emerges out of prison after serving two years for assault; soon after he is challenged to a duel by another man. The knife fight, which ends with Tonino as a winner, is seen by Camorra Don Mario Capece. Impressed by the young man's courage, Capece offers him a place in his clan. From then on, driven by an insatiable thirst for power, Tonino does his best to climb higher within the organization. As a reward for his services, Capece gives him the control of two casinos; what's more, Tonino seduces the boss' woman and then attempts to take Capece's place in a speculation business. When he discovers his betrayal, Don Mario kills his ex-lover and tries to frame Tonino, asking him to kill an untouchable leader of the Camorra. The gambit fails and Capece, knowing that Russo is going to kill him, kidnaps Tonino's little brother. However, Tonino eventually dispatches the boss and then, convinced by his father not to shoot at the police that have come onto the scene, or else he'd become a hero in the eyes of his brother, he surrenders to the cops.

With over a billion and 300 hundred million lire at the box office, Pasquale Squitieri's *Gang War in Naples* was to the Camorra what *The Godfather* was to the films on the Sicilian Mafia: a blueprint, and a commercial reference point for a new subgenre. *Gang War in Naples* also represented the impressive calling card of a new committed *auteur*: Neapolitan Pasquale Squitieri, formerly Francesco Rosi's assistant, at his fourth film as a director after the little-seen debut *Io e Dio* (1969) and a couple of Spaghetti Westerns signed as "William Redford," *Django Against Sartana* (*Django sfida Sartana*, 1970) and *Death's Dealer* a.k.a. *The Vengeance Trail* (*La vendetta è un piatto che si serve freddo*, 1971).

However, the story of Tonino Russo's rise to the top of Naples' underworld is closer to classical Neapolitan sceneggiata than to the political film. Squitieri is more interested in the knife fights, beatings and murders, underscored by popular Neapolitan songs such as *Reginella*. Naples and Neapolitan people act as a Greek chorus: an anonymous shapeless mass, with no will or personality, assisting or applauding the hero (as when Tonino gives usurer Don Ciccillo a lesson) but never showing a life of its own. Squitieri's vision is fatalistic ("Nothing ever changed here, nothing will ever change," one character says) and absolving at the same time: "Those like you are not heroes, they're only unfortunate," Testi's father tells his son in the ending, which some critics compared to Michael Curtiz's *Angels with Dirty Faces* (1938). Speaking of the finale, the director explained: "In no other Italian film could you have a scene like the one where the villain is lying on the ground, wounded, pleading with the hero to spare him, and Fabio Testi shoots him right in his gaping mouth. Then, pragmatically, I tried to cover myself from the censors. That's why I shot the ending where the father redeems his son. As a result, the film was not rated, even though it had scenes of incredible violence, never seen before! (laughs) The Board of Censors even told me that a movie like *Gang War in Naples* had to be shown in schools (laughs)."[1]

One of *Gang War in Naples*' assets is Fabio Testi's performance as Tonino Russo. "I saw Testi in a film starring Jean Gabin, *Killer* (*Le Tueur*, 1972) and I went to Paris to meet him" Squitieri recalls. "Goffredo Lombardo, the distributor, wanted me to cast Massimo Ranieri and Martin Balsam, whereas I wanted Raymond Pellegrin to play the boss. I didn't have anything against those actors, but I needed someone who would scare the audience when he came on the screen, and Fabio Testi, with his imposing physique, was just perfect."[2]

Camorra was the first chapter in an ideal trilogy—which also included another box office hit, *Blood Brothers* (*I guappi*, 1974) and a flop, *The Climber* (*L'ambizioso*, 1975)—where genre elements are tangled with a civil urge that differentiates itself from the models (namely Francesco Rosi's films) for its tendency to privilege passion over a rational discourse. "Squitieri's is an example of a "shouting" cinema, which ignores shades and semitones and does not repress its protest charge" as film historian Gian Piero Brunetta wrote; "Squitieri still believes his movies can somehow influence reality."[3] Others were very critical towards the director's ideology, which would convey "a myth of order more radical and treacherous than the one expressed by the Girolamis, both father and son."[4]

The director's technical ability is proficient from the opening scene. As film critic Domenico Monetti noted, "watching a Squitieri film does not only mean watching an Italian story as told by a filmmaker who is also an obstinate historian, but also witnessing true cinema lessons that echo the work of Luchino Visconti, Pietro Germi, Ettore Giannini, Vittorio De Sica." *Gang War in Naples*' impressive opening is a case in point. "Hands are passing a small blade inside a prison. No noise, no sound, while the opening credits roll. Without even introducing the characters, Squitieri manages to create suspense. In these few minutes the audience doesn't know anything ... only details exist: hands, sheets, faces. Yet one can perceive a suspended, rare atmosphere, as an ominous accident is expected."[5]

Notes

1. Domenico Monetti, *Pasquale Squitieri: Un autore di cinema ... e non solo* (Naples: Guida, 2009), p. 59.
2. *Ibid.*, p. 50. On the rest of the cast, Squitieri adds: "Pellegrin was my idol, he starred in a movie I adore, André Cayatte's *Are We All Murderers?* [*Nous sommes tous des assassins*, 1952]. And there was another idol of mine, Charles Vanel [...]. Jean Seberg was easy to cast, as she was Fabio's girlfriend at that time."
3. Brunetta, *Storia del cinema italiano — Dal miracolo economico agli anni Novanta*, p. 458.
4. Buttafava, "Procedure sveltite," p. 114.
5. Monetti, *Pasquale Squitieri*, p. 13.

The Godfather's Friend, a.k.a. *Hand of the Godfather*, a.k.a. *Revenge of the Godfather (L'amico del Padrino)*

D: Frank [Farouk] Agrama. *S* and *SC:* Frank Agrama, Fabio Piccioni; *DOP:* Franco Villa (35mm, Eastmancolor, Telecolor); *M:* Fred Bongusto, arranged and conducted by José Mascolo (ed. I.N.C.); *E:* Piera Bruni, Gianfranco Simoncelli; *PD:* Sam Weiss; *AC:* Enrico Biribicchi; *AE:* Gianfranco Simoncelli; *AD:* Lucia Porfiri; *MU:* Genéviève Hall; *SO:* Jules Klein; Unit *P:* Franco Brel; *SP:* Antony Alda; *SS:* Gigi Marx. *Cast:* Richard Harrison (Richard Maddock), Erika Blanc (Jenny), Krista Nell (Layla Siri), Ian Flynn [Ayhan Işık] (Antonio D'Amati [English version: Atef Damati]), Vincent Poselli, Olga Janowski, Stan Navarra, Calogero Corsini, Abe Rubicoff, John Graham, Olga Janowski, Daniella Leopardi, Paulette Simon, Tina Braun, James Walker, Alvin Lee. *PROD:* Frank Agrama for Graffiti Italiana (Rome), Shakir Sozen (Istanbul); *PM:* Freddy Alatan; *PSu:* John Puglia. *Country:* Italy / Turkey. Filmed on location in Turkey. *Running time:* 90'; Visa no.: 61599 (12.23.1972); Rating v.m.18; *Release date:* 12.24.1972; *Distribution:* Far International Film; *Domestic gross:* unknown. *Also known as: Babanin Arkadasi* (Turkey), *Godfather's lejemorder* (Denmark), *The Godfather's Friend* (U.K., 03.26. 1974, 89' 35," certified X with cuts, distributed by Chilton Films, Ltd). *Home video:* Apollon (VHS, Greece — English language w/Greek subtitles, non–U.S. version), Video Bio (VHS, Denmark — English language, non–U.S. version), Mastro (VHS, Canada — NTSC, Italian language version), Saturn (VHS, USA — U.S. version, as *Revenge of the Godfather*)

Richard Maddock, who as a child had witnessed the slaughter of his family, has become a hired killer at the service of the Godfather. After receiving a communication from an island near Istanbul, Richard moves to Naples, where he murders a man named Poselli. While he is returning home with his old flame Jenny, Richard is summoned by the Godfather himself, who orders him to dispatch Corsini, a bigwig and unfair competitor of the "Family." Afterwards, Richard will be free to leave the underworld and change his life for good. But a blood feud ensues after Richard's friend and colleague Antonio D'Amati, who works for Corsini, kills Rubicoff, the Godfather's lieutenant. Maddock eventually eliminates Corsini, but just as he is sailing away with Jenny, his boat explodes. Antonio D'Amati is the new Godfather's friend.

After about one minute into *The Godfather's Friend*, Richard Harrison beds a woman while her husband is sleeping in the nearby room. After sex, he sneaks into the man's bedroom and poisons him with the gas from his cigarette lighter. Then the returns to his hometown near Istanbul. Opening titles. When it comes to delivering the goods, director Frank (real name Farouk) Agrama gets down to business. That's (s)exploitation, after all. An Italian-Turkish co-production, *The Godfather's Friend* only refers nominally to Francis Ford Coppola's masterpiece: as a matter of fact it's a *film noir* of sorts set between Istanbul and Naples, with plenty of tourist footage as they used to do in the sixties. Harrison and Blanc are survivors of the 1960s golden age of Italian spy flicks, and one has the feeling that Agrama and Piccioni's script was a remnant from that era — take Harrison's poisoning lighter, a gadget worthy of a James Bond rip-off— spiced with liberal doses of naked female skin. The other prominent cast members are the beautiful Krista Nell and Turkish action star Ayhan Işık, who went on to co-star with Klaus Kinski on a couple of Gothic horror films by Sergio Garrone, *The Monster's Lovers* (*Le amanti del mostro*) and *Evil Face* (*La mano che nutre la morte*), both released in 1974. The other credits are unfathomable, as most actors — most likely Turkish — are credited with their characters' names.

As mentioned earlier, references to *The Godfather* are kept to a minim*um:* a Mafia boss speaks about making another boss "an offer he can't refuse," whereas the Godfather himself is an unseen, unnamed presence that's closer to the spy film's undisclosed archvillains than to Marlon Brando's Don Vito Corleone. On the other hand, Harrison's recurring flashback childhood trauma — the massacre of his family while he was a boy — derives directly from Spaghetti Westerns. Production values are pedestrian, with an over-reliance on tourist footage of Turkey — one wonders what the opening credits mean when they credit notorious Italian photographer Franco Brel as "public relations."

The result is pretty terrible, and on a par with Egyptian born Agrama's other films that reached Western audiences, an obnoxious King Kong parody (*Queen Kong*, 1976) and 1981's abysmal horror film *Dawn of the Mummy*. If the lack of sturdy direction weren't enough, one has to cope with dialogue like the following: "Is it true that for the whole month of Rhamadam these people don't drink anything at all?" "As far as that goes, they don't even screw."

As often with such co-productions, the U.S., Turkish and Italian versions are different. The Turkish cut is missing Ayhan Işık's sex scene with Krista Nell, plus another sequence where sniper Ayhan shoots a victim while water skiing.[1] This was probably because Ayhan was a very popular actor throughout the '50s and

'60s, and seeing him in such a mean role would upset Turkish audiences. The U.S. version, *Revenge of the Godfather*, has an annoying score replacing Fred Bongusto's original music, and the sex scenes are missing too.

The film was available on VHS in Greece (a fully uncut, widescreen International English language version) and in Denmark (a slightly cut edition, missing bits such as one scene where a goat is tied up in an Istanbul bazaar and has its throat cut before a crowd), while an Italian photo-novel was published in the magazine "Cinestop." However, Italian grossings were so minimal they cannot be traced in any reference book or documentation.

Farouk Agrama would embark on a fruitful business in Italy. Together with Fabrizio Alfieri, he founded Graffiti Cinematografica, which distributed a number of films in the country, including David Cronenberg's *Shivers*, Howard Ziehm's *Flesh Gordon*, Piero Vivarelli's *Nella misura in cui* ... and of course Agrama's own *Queen Kong*.

While pretty forgettable as a filmmaker, Agrama's name popped up in the news in recent years because of his association with Italy's media mogul and former Prime Minister Silvio Berlusconi, for alleged tax frauds, embezzlements and false accountings on the sale of film rights on behalf of Berlusconi's private broadcaster Mediaset which resulted in a trial that resulted with Berlusconi found guilty in first instance. According to the sentence, Agrama, Berlusconi and others fraudulently inflated the price of television rights originally purchased by Agrama so that millions of dollars in kickbacks could be paid to executives of Berlusconi's media empire. It seems that Agrama, after all these years, is still delivering the goods....

Note

1. The latter scene is placed before the opening credits in the Italian version, right after Maddock's first murder, thus showing the two hitmen — Richard and his friend Atef — at work. In the Danish tape this scene is rather haphazardly edited into the middle of the film.

The Italian Connection, a.k.a. *Manhunt (La mala ordina)*

D: Fernando di Leo. *S:* Fernando di Leo; *SC:* Fernando di Leo, Augusto Finocchi, Ingo Hermes; *DIA:* Fernando di Leo; *DOP:* Franco Villa (35mm, Eastmancolor, Telecolor); *M:* Armando Trovajoli, conducted by the author (ed. Nazionalmusic); *E:* Amedeo Giomini; *PD, CO:* Francesco Cuppini; *C:* Claudio Morabito; *AC:* Enrico Biribicchi; *AE:* Ornella Chistolini; *AD:* Franco Lo Cascio; *MU:* Antonio Mura; *SO:* Goffredo Salvatori; *W* (for Luciana Paluzzi): Alain Reynaud; *SE:* Basilio Patrizi; *MA:* Gilberto Galimberti; *ST:* Gruppo Acrobatico S.A.C.I.; *SS:* Vivalda Vigorelli. *Cast:* Mario Adorf (Luca Canali), Henry Silva (David Catania), Woody Strode (Frank Webster), Adolfo Celi (Don Vito Tressoldi), Luciana Paluzzi (Eva Lalli), Franco Fabrizi (Enrico Moroni), Femi Benussi (Nana), Gianni Macchia (Nicola), Peter Berling (Damiano), Francesca Romana Coluzzi (Trini), Cyril Cusack (Corso), Sylva Koscina (Lucia Canali), Jessica Dublin (Miss Kenneth), Omero Capanna (Don Vito's henchman), Giuseppe Castellano (Garagaz), Giulio Baraghini (Gustovino), Andrea Scotti (Garo), Imelde Marani (Cloakroom attendant), Gilberto Galimberti (Don Vito's henchman), Franca Sciutto (Dancer), Ulrich [Ulli] Lommel (Dancer), Vittorio Fanfoni (Don Vito's henchman), Giuliano Petrelli (Don Vito's henchman), Pietro Ceccarelli (Don Vito's henchman), Pasquale Fasciano (Don Vito's henchman), Alberto Fogliani (Don Vito's henchman). *Uncredited:* Empedocle Buzzanca (Don Vito's henchman), Enrico Chiappafreddo (Don Vito's henchman), Domenico Cianfriglia (Milkman), Giovanni Cianfriglia (Peppiniello), Guerrino Crivello (Bartender), Fernando di Leo (Passerby in blue shirt), Lina Franchi (Prostitute in the park), Ettore Geri (Disco Barman), Lara Wendel (Rita Canali), Renato Zero (Friend of Trini's). *PROD:* Armando Novelli for Cineproduzioni Daunia 70 (Rome), Hermes Synchron (Berlin); *GM:* Armando Novelli; *PM:* Lanfranco [Pietro] Ceccarelli; *UM:* Vincenzo Salviani, Luciano Appignani; *PA:* Augusto Petrone. *Country:* Italy / West Germany. Filmed at Dear Studios (Rome) and on location in Milan. *Running time:* 97'; Visa no.: 60885 (09.01.1972); *Rating:* v.m.18; *Release date:* 09.02.1972; *Distribution:* Alpherat; *Domestic gross:* 852,404,000 lire. *Also known as: Der Mafia-Boss — Sie töten wie Schakale* (West Germany, 12.01.1972); *Der Mafiaboss — Der Eisenfresser, Der Tod des Pate* (West Germany — alternate titles), *The Italian Connection* (USA, 1973 — 87'); *Hired to Kill, Black Kingpin, Hitmen, Hit Men,* (USA — Home video), *Ajojahti* (Finland), *De dræber som sjakaler* (Denmark), *L'empire du crime, Passeport pour 2 tueurs* (France), *Nuestro hombre en Milán* (Spain), *Maffian ger order* (Sweden). *Home video:* Raro (DVD / Blu-Ray, USA), Raro (DVD, Italy), Trinity Home Ent. (DVD — as *Hired to Kill*).

A powerful American Mafia boss decrees the death of Sicilian pimp Luca Canali, who is rumored to have stolen a shipment of heroin. Actually, Luca is only a scapegoat, and his death will be a message for all the underworld. Two hitmen, Frank Webster and David Catania, arrive in Milan to kill Luca, who's separated from his wife Anna. The killers get in touch with local Mafia boss Don Vito Tressoldi, who's actually responsible for the heroin theft: a huge manhunt ensues, as Don Vito wants to kill Canali before Webster and Catania find out the truth. However, poor Luca turns out to be a much tougher nut to crack than everyone expects. After his wife and his beloved daughter are brutally killed by one of Vito's men, Luca turns against his tormentors. He destroys Don Vito's whole gang and eventually kills the boss. In the end he faces Webster and Catania in a junkyard, and in the final showdown he dispatches them both.

Three men in a room. A Mafia boss is instructing two hitmen on their mission. "The man to be killed is a certain Luca Canali, a pimp. He worked for Don Vito Tressoldi's family but was worthless," he explains coldly. "Now he's tried a big job. You have to kill him without hiding it, so that the whole of Milan will talk about it. The whole of Italy must talk about it. Everyone must know you came from New York to hunt down Luca Canali and squash him like a louse. I want it to be spectacular!" He also teaches his men how to behave in a foreign country. "The Italians have a strange type of gangster in mind, they see him being exactly like you, and you have to dress and act like gangsters. Drink, leave big tips, put your feet on tables, they hate that in Italy. You have to act the part so that everyone knows who you are."

The opening scene of Fernando di Leo's *The Italian Connection* is not easily forgotten. First of all, it features the razor-sharp dialogue and precise camera set-ups that makes Quentin Tarantino's prologues so engrossing and striking. It's also the most interesting example of a conscious reflection on the vampire-like approach of Italian crime films against the American *film noir*, and a clever, witty criticism at the relationship of subordination between the genre and its overseas model.

Compared to the Jean-Pierre Melville references and disillusioned poetry of defeat that characterized *Caliber 9*, Fernando di Leo's previous film, *The Italian Connection* offers a more crude,

Woody Strode as Frank Webster, the hitman, in *The Italian Connection* (1972).

mordant approach, which perhaps made it the director's most commercially successful effort within the crime genre. Once again, di Leo took inspiration from Giorgio Scerbanenco's *oeuvre*: although the Milanese novelist is not mentioned in the credits, the idea of the two hitmen who come from the States to kill a small-time pimp comes from the short story *Milan by Calibro 9* ("they smiled gently at everything, with their enormous alligator teeth," Scerbanenco describes them), and from the same source come also the scene of their arrival at the hotel and the character of the hostess (played by Luciana Paluzzi) who acts as their guide, who's the focus of Scerbanenco's story. But di Leo's other main inspiration must have been Ernest Hemingway's famous short story *The Killers* and its cinematic transpositions (especially Don Siegel's 1964 version starring Lee Marvin and Clu Gulager) for the overcoming sense of fatality that accompanies the manhunt. However, unlike Hemingway's story, the prey doesn't wait for his death with resignation. Not at all.

Di Leo's original title for the film was *Ordini da un altro mondo* ("Orders from Another World"), so as to suggest a hierarchic view of crime, where the "other world" is the upper edge powerful American-based Mafia, which still subjugates the Italian one. Yet, on the other hand, from the point of view of a small-time crook such as Luca Canali (Mario Adorf) and all those like him, small fish in the swamp of Milan's underworld, the "other world" is represented by the local boss Don Vito Tressoldi (Adolfo Celi), whose wishes are orders, and who rules over the whole town with just a snap of his fingers from his palace / fortress. Luca Canali—a pimp, a "brothel's man" who's despised and laughed at by other Mafia men because "he doesn't even have a real man's job"—has not just the guts to rebel and reject his scapegoat role: he also breaks the absurd rules and power games that have labeled him as an expendable pawn who'd have to sheepishly accept his destiny.

In di Leo's world, power is measured with fear, as shown by the chilling sequence in the sawmill, where the two American killers and Don Vito challenge each other's power. "Your guys have been marked by you and by Luca Canali, but those marks fade. And when the marks fade, so does fear, but fear must never go away!" says Henry Silva before shooting two of Don Vito's henchmen in the legs. To reaffirm his pre-eminence to the "other world," Tressoldi has no other choice but to kill the two injured henchmen in cold blood. "My intentions are more serious than yours" he claims.

Less solid and refined than *Caliber 9*, *The Italian Connection* is much more impetuous and savage when it comes to action and violence. The first half follows Henry Silva and Woody Strode as they wander amidst nightclubs and prostitutes' hangouts, while the second opens with an extended, show-stopping car chase that's almost unrivalled in '70s Italian crime films, as Canali pursues the truck that ran over his wife and little daughter throughout the city to a deserted amusement park. The ending is equally outstanding, as Canali and the two killers finally have their showdown in a junkyard—a scene which has been interpreted as "an ironic take on the mirage of the Italian economic "miracle," as represented by the FIAT empire."[1]

Luca Canali (Mario Adorf) in a dramatic scene from *The Italian Connection* (1972).

On *The Italian Connection* di Leo also allows more room for sensuality, which probably caused its v.m.18 (forbidden to minors) rating. The camera lingers on Nana's (Femi Benussi) nude body, while another scene depicts a bunch of young and stoned protesters as they slowly awake after an orgy — a moment the director would reprise in *Rulers of the City* (*I padroni della città*, 1976). Even more than the director's previous work, *The Italian Connection* is an epitome of sorts of di Leo's universe. Characters, places and situations will return in his subsequent work: the lame mechanic played by Franco Fabrizi predates the character of Roberto Reale in *Blood and Diamonds* (*Diamanti sporchi di sangue*, 1978), the protesters — barely sketched here — will have a central role in *To Be Twenty* (*Avere vent'anni*, 1978), while Canali's ascent to the palace of power and the murder in the amusement park will be recycled, with lesser impact, in 1975's *Kidnap Syndicate* (*La città sconvolta: caccia spietata ai rapitori*). Last but not least, di Leo would use several times in the future the two American actors who play the killers: the taciturn, frugal Woody Strode (in *Loaded Guns*, 1975) and the impudent, lustful Henry Silva (in 1973's *The Boss* and 1983's *Killer vs. Killers*).[2]

For all its merits, *The Italian Connection*'s true strength is Mario Adorf's performance as Luca Canali. Physically, Canali is a clone of *Caliber 9's* Rocco Musco: hair slicked back, flashy suits, strong Sicilian accent. Luca starts as a caricature of sorts, a character who looks like a Metropolitan version of Tomas Milian's Mexican peasant Cuchillo as seen in Sollima's *The Big Gundown* and *Run, Man, Run*: unlike Guido Piazza in *Caliber 9*, Luca is an innocent man who has to fight for his life against the whole world. He's a hard-headed fool (literally: Luca knocks out his adversaries with head-butts, breaks a phone and even a truck's windshield with the same method) who soon gains a tragic vein and a dignity that the other characters (Don Vito, his colleagues, his wife, his prostitute mistress Nana, who persuades him to let her satisfy her customers in their bed) obstinately deny him.

Notes

1. Rubén Paniceres, *Retrato de Republica en rojo*, in Jesús Palacios and Rubén Paniceres, eds., *Cara a Cara: Una mirada al cine de género italiano, años 60/70* (Gijon: Semana Negra, Colección Hermosos y Malditos n°2, 2004), p. 167.
2. Among the cast, a minor presence is that of future director Ulli Lommel (*The Tenderness of Wolves, Mirror*) as a dancer.

Long Arm of the Godfather (*La mano lunga del padrino*)

D: Nardo [Leonardo] Bonomi. *S:* Nardo Bonomi; *SC:* Giulio Berruti, Nardo Bonomi; *DOP:* Silvio Fraschetti, Mario Capriotti (35mm, Eastmancolor, Cinescope); *M:* Silvano D'Auria; *E:* Giulio Berruti; *PD, CO:* Mimmo [Bartolomeo] Scavia; *C:* Maurizio Gennaro, Sebastiano Celeste; *AC:* Carlo Milani; *AD:* Giulio Berruti; *MU:* Gianfranco Mecacci; *AMU:* Enrico Maido; *Hair:* Ada Morandi; *SO:* Alessandro Di Carlo; *SS:* Emanuele Bruno. *Cast:* Peter Lee Lawrence [Karl Hirenbach] (Vincenzo "Raffica"), Adolfo Celi (Don Carmelo, mafia boss), Erika Blanc (Sabina), Kim Dimon, Henriette Kok, Riccardo Petrazzi, Claudio Ruffini (Tom), Piera Moretti, Attilio Pelegatti (Airplane passenger), Pietro Torrisi (Gallo), Bruno Boschetti. *Uncredited:* Eolo Capritti (Man on the bed), Goffredo Unger [Goffredo Ungaro] (Vincenzo's co-driver). *PROD:* Film Settanta; *PM:* Carlo Chamblant; *PI:* Eolo Capritti, Massimo Alberini; *PSe:* Franco Bartoli. *Country:* Italy. *Running time:* 86'; Visa no.: 60306 (06.10.1972); *Rating:* v.m.18; *Release date:* 08.11.1972; *Distribution:* M.G.M; *Domestic gross:* 199,340,000 lire. *Also known as: Der lange Arm des Paten* (West Germany — Home video), *Le parrain a le bras long* (France). *Home video:* Hobby&Work (DVD, Italy).

A young thug, Vincenzo nicknamed "Raffica," robs his boss Don Carmelo of a load of guns which he plans to sell and get 200 million dollars for. Pending the deal, Vincenzo hides in a small hotel, but a woman betrays him and Don Carmelo's men find him. Vincenzo gets rid of them and teams up with his friend Tom, a mechanic, to sell the weapons to an Arab sheik. As Vincenzo and his girlfriend Sabina go to the place where the rifles must be delivered, Don Carmelo breaks into Tom's workshop and replaces the guns with useless scrap metal. The boss' plan is to have Vincenzo killed by the buyer, once the latter discovers the deception. The trap does not work, though. Don Carmelo tries to get his money back, but he dies at the end of a furious car chase. Vincenzo sails away on a motorboat with the money and Sabina, who's seriously injured. But the boat, riddled by Don Carmelo's machine gun bullets, sinks.

The release of Francis Ford Coppola's *The Godfather* deeply marked the 1970s, not least for its marketing strategy, being the first example of saturation selling by a huge American studio. However, the film which signed the beginning of a new era for U.S. film industry, being "the tip of the iceberg of a 'new' Hollywood which is transforming and preparing, once recycled, to regain its lost predominance,"[1] did not represent to Italian film industry a commercial prototype as strong as Don Siegel's *Dirty Harry* (1970) would prove to be.

Most Italian *Godfather* sagas were more or less equally divided between serious rip-offs and laugh-out-loud parodies — such as Franco Prosperi's *L'altra faccia del padrino* (1973), starring popular imitator Alighiero Noschese, or Riccardo Garrone's *La Mafia mi fa un baffo* (1975) — and kept a low commercial profile. What they borrowed from Coppola's film were the most controversial aspects, which caused Italian critics to slant it almost unanimously: strongly stereotyped characters, folklore touches and iconography (which actually came from Mario Puzo's best selling novel), plus the image of the Mafia as a mythological, relentless entity and, most of all, the exaltation of a moral and behavioral code which was alternative and superior to the institutional one. A code in which violence and honor, revenge and respect coexist, forming an anti–Manichean ensemble where good and evil correlate. But whereas Coppola maintained a moral ambiguity and a suspension of judgment, its clones played a schizoid hide-and-seek moral game, which failed to express the same civil disdain as the poliziotteschi.

However, there's almost nothing that connects *Long Arm of the Godfather* with *The Godfather*— with the exception of its title, that is. Originally titled *La terza gobba del cammello* ("The Camel's Third Hump"), Nardo Bonomi's film was camouflaged as a *Godfather* rip-off at the very last minute (it was released in Italy just a month and a half after Coppola's film), whereas it's actually a decidedly mediocre *film noir* set in an exotic Middle Eastern country and spiced with nude scenes, courtesy of redheaded Erika Blanc, while Adolfo Celi plays a character named Don Carmelo, who's not a Mafia boss however but just an arms dealer, and leads not a "family" but a handful of thugs. The most curious thing about *Long Arm of the Godfather* is that two completely different endings exist. The version released on VHS in Italy in the 1990s on AVO Film ends with a blue-toned stop-frame showing Peter Lee Lawrence with a dead Erika Blanc in his arms, in the middle of the ocean. An older VHS release (on the CVR label) retained the film's original ending, as conceived by Bonomi and co-writer Giulio Berruti: Lawrence and Blanc (who's not dead but just injured) reach a shore, but when she finds out that the suitcase with Don Carmelo's money which they robbed is lost at the bottom of the ocean, the woman leaves her companion.

Bonomi's only other film as a director is a lost one: *Sortilegio* (l.t. *Spell*, 1970), a strange, unclassifiable film partially inspired by the work of Aleister Crowley about a woman driven to suicide by her husband with the help of a mysterious cult, co-scripted by Fellini's collaborator Brunello Rondi and starring Erna Schurer and director Marco Ferreri in a rare effort before the camera.

Note

1. Vito Zagarrio, *Francis Ford Coppola* (Milan: Il Castoro Cinema, 1995), p. 61.

The Master Touch (Un uomo da rispettare)

D: Michele Lupo. *S:* Franco Bucceri, Roberto Leoni; *SC:* Mino Roli, Nico Ducci, Michele Lupo; *DOP:* Tonino Delli Colli (35mm, Technicolor—Techniscope); *M:* Ennio Morricone, conducted by Nicola Samale (ed. Panamusic); *E:* Tony [Antonietta] Zita; *PD:* Francesco Bronzi; *CO:* Enrico Sabbatini; *SDr:* Andrea Fantacci; *ScE:* Dario Micheli; *C:* Giovanni Ciarlo; *AC:* Carlo Tafani; *AEs:* Anna Maria Roca, Angela Bordi; *AD:* Gianni Arduini; *MU:* Nilo Jacoponi, Walter Cossu; *Hair:* Maria Angelini; *SO:* Dino Fronzetti; *Boom:* Gianni Zampagni; *Mix:* Franco Bassi; *SP:* Mimmo Cattarinich; *W:* Maria Castrignano; *KG:* Augusto Diamanti; *ChEl:* Alberto Ridolfi; *MA:* Neno [Nazzareno] Zamperla; *SS:* Serena Merlini; *UPs:* Lucherini, Rossetti, Spinola. *Cast:* Kirk Douglas (Steve Wallace), Florinda Bolkan (Anna), Giuliano Gemma (Marco), René [Reinhardt] Kolldehoff (Inspector Hoffmann), Romano Puppo (Müller's henchman), Wolfgang Preiss (Müller), Bruno Corazzari (Eric), Janos [John] Bartha (Pawnbroker watchman), Vittorio Fanfoni, Luigi Antonio Guerra, Allen Stanley. *PROD:* Marina Cicogna for Verona Produzione (Rome), Paramount Orion Filmproduktion (Münich); *EP:* Manolo Bolognini; *PM:* Roberto Cocco; *PSu:* Luciano Balducci, Carlo Giovagnorio. *Country:* Italy / West Germany. Filmed at Incir–De Paolis (Rome) and on location in Hamburg. *Running time:* 112'; Visa no.: 61294 (10.28.1972); *Rating:* not rated; *Release date:* 11.21.1972; *Distribution:* Cinema International Corporation; *Domestic gross:* 1,088,366,000 lire. *Also known as: Ein Achtbarer Mann* (West Germany, 12.08.1972) *Un homme à respecter* (France, 09.27.1973—110'). *Home video:* Elstree Hill (DVD, U.K.), Alpha Video (DVD, USA), Golem (DVD, Italy). OST: CD Hexacord HCD 14.

Hamburg. Just released after two years in jail, master safecracker Steve Wallace is summoned by his wealthy ex-associate Müller, who wants him to perform a formidable theft at the Hamburg Insurance Company, where a state-of-the-art alarm system (called "Big Ben") protects a safe with over two million in it. Steve refuses, but only because he's planning to do the score by himself, the last one before retiring with his lover Anna. He teams up with a young Italian acrobat, Marco, who will provide Steve an alibi, thus protecting him from Müller's revenge once the hit has been performed. While Steve will be doing the job at the insurance company, Marco will open the safe of a pawnbroker in another part of town, using Steve's technique, and later Wallace will have himself captured by the police and serve a small time in jail for the theft he didn't actually perform to shake off Müller's suspicions. After a meticulous preparation, Steve and Marco perform the score, but something goes wrong: when Wallace takes Marco's place at the pawnbroker, he finds out Marco killed the watchman. Badly injured by the police, Wallace faces the young man, and just as Anna is leaving without them, he kills Marco and surrenders to the cops.

Crushed between the Argento-style *gialli* and the first examples of poliziotteschi, the few Italian crime films openly influenced by the French *polar* were few and far between. Even though they performed rather well at the box office, these represented just sparse oddities at the margin of a production system that was gradually converging towards a crucial commercially viable genre, either hybrids or vehicles for faded American stars. That's the case with Michele Lupo's *The Master Touch*, which teams up a big U.S. star such as Kirk Douglas and an Italian one like Giuliano Gemma, who was trying to find new ways to regain the peak of Italian box office while the Western was starting its decline. Gemma would never become a true poliziotteschi star, turning towards more committed roles in the mid-seventies: here he stands rather well in an ingenuous part that has him essentially play the same role as in Tonino Valerii's *Day of Anger* (*I giorni dell'ira*, 1967)—that is, the young naive apprentice who is taught and given a lesson in life by a fatherly figure who'll eventually become a mortal enemy. It's no wonder that Valerii himself was initially attached to the project before Lupo was called on to direct it.

However, here the point of view is reversed compared to Valerii's film. While recounting the father / son relationship, *The Master Touch* openly takes sides with the elderly, more experienced Wallace, while Gemma's open smile and angelic features serve a character that in the end brusquely shows its darker side, that of an opportunistic traitor. The confrontation between Wallace and Marco therefore becomes a symbol of the clash between "old school" criminals who follow the rules (Wallace never has any weapon on him) and "new school" ones who don't mind breaking such them.

The Oedipal aspect of the plot is enhanced by the figure of Anna (Florinda Bolkan), Wallace's lover, who becomes unwillingly attracted to the Italian acrobat. The relationship between Bolkan and Gemma is only partially hinted at, with the woman at first rejecting the younger man's tentative seduction, then presumably becoming his lover, but—as she confesses to Wallace at the end—mainly to get away from an erratic life she's become tired of. It's a decidedly interesting character, and one quite different from the usual *femme fatale* stereotypes, and even though the script doesn't leave her much room to develop it, Bolkan is impressive as ever in the role.

The film's most interesting feature, however, is the way Lupo—who was a specialist of heist films in the 1960s, with titles like *Your Turn to Die* (*Troppo per vivere ... poco per morire*, 1967) and the amusing *7 Times 7* (*7 volte 7*, 1968)—drains the plot of any playfulness, using it as an elaborate set-up to tell the crepuscular story of Wallace's failure. The long, antiseptic sequence in the ultra-modern insurance building, as opposed to the chaotic pawnbroker, is filled with little tricks and suspense bits, and is so expertly handed it makes one forget (or forgive) the script's shortcomings, such as a few details that remain partially unexplained and characters left forgotten—take Müller, played by Wolfgang Preiss (Dr. Mabuse in the 1960s German series) and his sidekick (Romano Puppo), who disappear halfway through. Ennio Morricone's flicorno-driven, mournful score is the perfect counterpart to the film's disillusioned morale, and the story moves on with assured pacing towards the impressive, bleak climax.

Shadows Unseen (*Abuso di potere*)

D: Camillo Bazzoni. *S* and *SC:* Massimo Felisatti, Fabio Pittorru (and Enzo D'Ambrosio, uncredited); *DOP:* Claudio Ragona (35mm, Eastmancolor, Technochrome — Scope); *M:* Riz Ortolani, conducted by the author (ed. Beat); *E:* Roberto Perpignani; *PD, ArtD:* Gastone Carsetti; *CO:* Fiorella Gaetano; *C:* Giuseppe Di Biase; *AC:* Roberto Forges Davanzati; *AEs:* Giancarlo Venarucci Cadueri, Romano Giomini, Jutta Brandstaetter; *ArtD:* Luigi Urbani; *ADs:* Claudio Biondi, Gabriele Polverosi; *ADs* (2nd unit): Rémy Julienne, Inge Hiesserich; *AcSc:* Rémy Julienne; *MU:* Lolli Melaranci; *AMU:* Sarah Ventura; *Hair:* Carla Indoni; *SO:* Carlo Tarchi; *SP:* Angelo Pennoni; *W:* Teresa Miccinelli; *PrM:* Emilio Zamprioli; *KG:* Giacomo Tomaselli; *ChEl:* Otello Diodato; *SS:* Patrizia Zulini. *Cast:* Frederick Stafford (Commissioner Luca Miceli), Marilù Tolo (Simona), Franco Fabrizi (Commissioner Resta), René [Reinhard] Kolldehoff (Chief of Police), Corrado Gaipa (Mauro D'Amico, a.k.a. Günther Rosenthal), Claudio Gora (District Attorney), Ninetto Davoli (Jo Jo), Raymond Pellegrin (Dr. Nicola Dalò), Umberto Orsini (Enrico Gagliardi), Judy Winter (Rosaria Cruciani), Elio Zamuto (Sgt. Francesco Mortesi), Guido Leontini (Turi De Loco), Mavì [Mavie Bardanzellu] (Luca's wife), Renato Romano (Interpol agent), Quinto Parmeggiani (Gagliardi's editor-in-chief), Michel Bardinet (Newspaper's administrator), Rosita Torosh, Piero [Pier Giovanni] Anchisi (Ballistic expert), Gianfranco Barra (Fish seller), Giorgio Paoletti, Bruna Cealti, Gaetano Scala, Luigi Antonio Guerra, Franco Angrisano (Usher), Wolf Fischer, Alida Piccoli. *Uncredited:* Bruno Alias (Man in gambling room), Gian Piero Bona, Francesco D'Adda (Marine official at dock), Lina Franchi (Woman in gambling room), Gisella Longo, Giuseppe Marrocco (Man playing roulette), Romano Targa (mustached man smoking in gambling house). *PROD:* Enzo D'Ambrosio and Oscar Di Martino for Milvia Cinematografica / Spider Film (Rome), Comacico (Paris), Dieter Geissler Filmproduktion (Munich); *PM:* Fernando Franchi; *PSu:* Claudio Murzilli, Marcel Cadaze; *PSe:* Gino Santarelli, Gudrun Gundelach; *ADM:* Aureliano Lalli Persiani; *CASH:* Margherita Cesolini. *Country:* Italy / France / West Germany. Filmed at Incir — De Paolis Studios (Rome) and on location in Palermo. *Running time:* 102': Visa no.: 59968 (03.18.72); *Rating:* v.m.14; *Release date:* 03.24.72; *Distribution:* Jumbo Cinematografica; *Domestic gross:* 364,435,000 lire. *Also known as: Abus de pouvoir* (France), *Abuso de poder* (Spain), *Näkymättömiä varjoja* (Finland). *Home video:* Cinekult (DVD, Italy).

Palermo, Sicily. Luca Miceli, a commissioner known for his unorthodox (and often violent) methods, is called in to investigate the murder of journalist Enrico Gagliardi. A mysterious phone call leads him to the presumed culprit, Turi De Loco, who's still in possession of the murder weapon and soon confesses his crime. Yet Miceli is not convinced at all, and keeps on with his inquiry. He finds out that a prostitute, Rosaria Cruciani, was with Gagliardi the night he was murdered, but Rosaria has also been killed with a lethal drug overdose. After his car has been blown up as a warning, Miceli meets the fascinating Simona, who brings him to an exclusive gambling house where Luca wins a large sum of money. Miceli pretends to accept the bribe, but thanks to Simona he eventually discovers the true reason behind Gagliardi's murder: the journalist had identified a powerful drug trafficker, Mauro D'Amico, who was posing as a German usurer. Miceli arrests D'Amico, but the man is immediately released by way of his connivance with politicians, including Miceli's superiors. Luca survives another ambush and decides to leave Italy, but D'Amico — who has already gotten rid of Simona — has him murdered.

Even more than Camillo Bazzoni's previous film *Mafia Connection*, *Shadows Unseen* is characterized by a remarkable care for visual details. Under the opening credits, a succession of colored globes dancing in the dark turn out to be car lights approaching, in an out-of-focus / focus transition that wouldn't have been out of place in Mario Bava's *Bay of Blood* (1971). The opening sequence depicting Gagliardi's arrival in the hotel lobby where he's got an appointment with a usurer named Rosenthal (Corrado Gaipa) is quite impressive too: the camera advances in the room, from the journalist's point of view, meeting the eyes of a blonde woman leaning on a piano; as the woman turns around, the camera also makes a surprising 180° turn, showing Gagliardi as he reaches the bar. Stafford's slow-motion death scene in a phone booth — perhaps inspired by the elevator scene in Sergio Sollima's *Violent City*— is also among the most striking moments in Italian crime cinema, and the sight of a phone slowly dangling as an operator's voice announces the flight times of a plane Miceli will never take also bears an unsettling — yet most likely coincidental — resemblance with the final image of Bava's *Blood and Black Lace* (*Sei donne per l'assassino*, 1964).

Even though the script by Massimo Felisatti and Fabio Pittorru draws its inspiration from actual events (the character of journalist Enrico Gagliardi, played by Umberto Orsini, somehow recalls Mauro De Mauro of the newspaper *L'Ora*, who disappeared in September 1970), unlike Florestano Vancini's *Sicilian Checkmate* (also written by Felisatti and Pittorru and made that same year), *Shadows Unseen* can already be considered a fully formed poliziotteschi.

The script chooses to leave most details unexplained: are district attorney Dalò (Raymond Pellegrin) and the chief of police in cahoots with the Mafia? It's a shortcut that definitely makes the film closer to genre clichés than to political crime dramas such as Vancini's work — a turn confirmed by the film's climax, with a dramatic car chase, directed and choreographed by Rémy Julienne. However, for all its merits, *Shadows Unseen* suffers from a half-baked plot. The revelation that Gagliardi was investigating a drug ring and had uncovered the secret identity of a powerful drug trafficker comes off rather flat and implausible, and — for a film about a drug ring in Sicily —*Shadows Unseen* is singularly reticent about its subject matter, never really mentioning the Mafia.

If Marilù Tolo plays a "girl who knows too much," a role that has a direct affiliation to the one she played in Damiani's *Confessions of a Police Captain*, the film's hero has already transformed into something different compared to Enrico Maria Salerno's old-style commissioner in *Execution Squad*. As the tough, impulsive, violent commissioner Luca Miceli, Frederick Stafford — a survivor from the golden age of Italian spy flicks — comes up with a rather wooden performance, yet his physical resemblance to real-life commissioner Luigi Calabresi immensely helps the film. Calabresi, a controversial figure in Italian chronicles of the time, especially after the mysterious death of Giuseppe Pinelli, was killed in an ambush just a couple of months after Bazzoni's film, making *Shadows Unseen*'s powerful bleak ending even more remarkable and ominous.

Commissioner Luca Miceli is a lonely and tormented man, still desperately in love with his estranged wife, who is divorcing him. Bazzoni introduces him memorably: Miceli is sitting alone in a semi-crowded beach, the only person in sight wearing shirt and tie amidst young men and women in swimming suits, a sight that immediately points out the character's loneliness and his being out of place. Frederick Stafford delivers many lines which are emblematic of the kind of heroes film audiences will soon become familiar with. "I may have slapped someone, but who doesn't?" he admits; later on we see Miceli savagely beating a suspect (Guido Leontini as a loathsome slimy villain) during an interrogation, and threatening another (Pasolini's fetish actor Ninetto Davoli in a throwaway cameo as a pimp) by means of a cigarette which Miceli dangerously approaches to Davoli's chest and a black glove which the commissioner menacingly puts on, commenting "This won't leave any sign on your face...." To Miceli, the law is an obstacle rather than a tool — hence his tendency to bypass procedures and the original Italian title (which translates to "Abuse of Power," exactly what the suspiciously cautious D.A. accuses him of).

Another characteristic which would become prominent in poliziotteschi is the hero's predisposition to self-pity, as is the case with Miceli's delusional ruminations on how hard it is to be a cop. "My job is most unfortunate, you keep making enemies and risk your life everyday for a lousy pay," he complains — yet all attempts at corrupting him (either a brand new car or a suspiciously conspicuous win at *chemin de fer* in a gambling house) are unsuccessful. It's obvious that Miceli blames his job not for the lack of money, but for the harm it did to him as a human being, alienating him from others ("This damn job takes away your trust in yourself and others too" he admits) and most of all from his beloved ones. "I make a void all around me ... I couldn't even keep a family." Yet, for all his lamentations, being a cop is obviously his only reason to live — and to die. His honesty makes him a Don Quixote, who fights against windmills all his life ("I thought we were all at the service of justice and freedom, because we're all thirsty for truth here ... yet all are ready to close one eye as soon as the truth becomes uncomfortable," he says) and is eventually dispatched by the high powers he vainly tried to expose, when he's about to leave his country ("a country where everybody's friends" he bitterly quips) for good. Live like a cop, die like a man — that's all one can hope for, that's all one's got in the end.

Sicilian Checkmate *(La violenza: quinto potere)*

D: Florestano Vancini. *S:* based on the play *La violenza* by Giuseppe Fava; *SC:* Massimo Felisatti, Fabio Pittorru, Florestano Vancini, with the collaboration of Dino Maiuri, Massimo De Rita; *DOP:* Toni Secchi (35mm, Eastmancolor, Technicolor — Techniscope); *M:* Ennio Morricone, conducted by Bruno Nicolai; *E:* Tatiana Casini Morigi; *PD:* Luciano Puccini; *CO:* Silvana Pantani; *ArtD:* Giorgio Postiglione; *C:* Giorgo Regis; *AC:* Roberto Locci; *AE:* Cesarina Casini; *AD:* Camillo Fusaro; *2nd AD:* Amanzio Todini; *MU:* Lamberto Marini; *Hair:* Bianca Casella; *SO:* Mario Celentano; *Boom:* Tonino Testa; *Mix:* Mario Morigi, Gianni D'Amico; *SetP:* Enrico Santelli; *SS:* Benedetta Viganò; *ScrA:* Rosetta Sestili. *Cast:* Enrico Maria Salerno (Prosecutor), Gastone Moschin (Colonnesi, defense attorney), Riccardo Cucciolla (Professor Luciano Salemi), Mario Adorf (Amedeo Barresi), Ciccio Ingrassia (Ferdinando Giacalone), Aldo Giuffré (Mayor Giuseppe Salemi), Michele Abruzzo (Zaccaria), Ferruccio De Ceresa (Senator), Turi Ferro (Judge Nicola Altopascio), Mariangela Melato (Rosalìa Alicata), Guido Leontini (Rosario Vacirca), Elio Zamuto (Luciano Verzì), Mico Cundari (Defense lawyer), Julien Guiomar (Commissioner Golino), Georges Wilson (Crupi), Silvia Dionisio (Giacalone's daughter), Liana Trouché (Carmela Scibili a), Alessandro Sperli (Giovanni Savoca), Consalvo Dell'Arti (Judge), Michele Gammino (Michele Alicata), Guido Celano, Alessandro Perrella (Giovanni Savoca), Marcello Di Martire (Mafia defendant), Franco Fantasia, Gianni Pulone. *Uncredited:* Antonio Anelli (White-haired defense lawyer), Franco Balducci (Gaetano, the killer), Ulla Johansen (Blonde woman with Barresi), Benito Pacifico, Vezio Natili (Bald defense lawyer), Filippo Perego (Judge), Alba Maiolini (Woman at Altopascio's funeral), Calogero Azzaretto (Vincenzo Cuomo), Romano Milani (Thick-eyebrowed defense lawyer), Romano Targa (Man at Altopascio's funeral). *PROD:* Produzioni De Laurentiis — International Manufacturing Company (Rome); *EP:* Bruno Todini; *PM:* Giorgio Morra; *PSu:* Alfredo De Laurentiis. *Country:* Italy. Shot at Dino De Laurentiis Cinematografica S.p.A. (Rome). *Running time:* 101'; Visa no.: 59719 (02.02.1972); *Rating:* v.m.14; *Release date:* 02.03.1972; *Distribution:* cinema International Corporation; *Domestic gross:* 428,867,000 lire. *Also known as: Gewalt— die fünfte Macht im Staat* (West Germany, 07.05.1973 — 90'), *Jaque mate siciliano* (Spain), *Les maffiosi* (France), *Mafian kosto* (Finland). *Home video:* Ricordi (VHS, Italy). OST: CD Avanz Records SP/CR-20040.

In a Sicilian courtroom a trial against a large group of members of two rival Mafia gangs is taking place. The background to the struggle between the two factions is the construction of a dam, advocated by Amedeo Barresi, a powerful manufacturer, and opposed by engineer Crupi, a rich landowner, who would lose his citrus groves following the implementation of the project. This led to a series of crimes, including Mafia members, politicians (such as newly elected small-town mayor Salemi, who opposes the Mafia) as well as other innocent witnesses such as Michele Alicata. The ability of defense lawyers easily dismantle the charges, poorly supported by fragile evidence and timid witnesses. Only two defendants agree to confess, and are obviously used as scapegoats by the Mafia bosses: the first, Ferdinando Giacalone, is forced to kill himself in prison, while the other, Rosario Vacirca, will be the only one sentenced to thirty years, while other defendants are all acquitted, including Barresi. Another blood feud soon ensues.

Florestano Vancini's *Sicilian Checkmate* is another example of the mingling between political and genre film which during this period was practiced also by Damiano Damiani. Opening with a series of cruel Mafia murders — victims are blown up in their car, shot and burned in furnaces — the movie soon assumes another direction: most of it takes place in a courtroom, where a trial against sixteen defendants is underway, and courtroom scenes are intertwined with flashbacks showing the various events that led to the trial. Such an approach derives from the film's source, as Vancini and his collaborators adapted the 1970 stage play *La violenza*, written by journalist and playwright Giuseppe Fava.

One of the most active and charismatic Sicilian intellectuals, Fava denounced the Mafia throughout his life, both in his plays and in the pages of newspapers ("Il Giornale del Sud") and magazines ("I Siciliani"), and was killed by the Santapaola clan in 1984. *Sicilian Checkmate* somehow retains the play's abstraction and strong symbolic motifs: the courtroom set piece is dominated by a huge opaque window behind which the rain falls ceaselessly — a symbol of the will to purify the country which moves the vehement prosecutor played by Enrico Maria Salerno. "Violence is the fifth power in our country: it reunites and maneuvers the others, submits and corrupts them" he says, in a speech that explains the film's Italian title (which translates to "Violence: Fifth Power").

The prosecutor, who denounces Mafia crimes and political connivances, is powerless before a legal system which is rotten to the core: those who agree to act as scapegoats and confess other people's crimes are condemned, while the real culprits are acquitted. Salerno's character is a variation on the theme of the Don Quixote–like magistrate as seen in Damiani's films: he is able to discover the truth, but has his hands tied by the inadequacy of the penal code and inner complicities at all levels. "This is not a trial, it's a sleight of hand!" retorts the defense attorney sarcastically when it turns out that one piece of crucial evidence (a gun) has been replaced with a rusty bolt. The Mafia not only kills, Vancini implies: it sneers at its victims.

Yet the character's powerlessness mirrors that of the filmmakers. Vancini is eventually incapable of solving the inner contradiction between the film's political essence and spectacular needs, or at least he doesn't reach Damiani's perfect synthesis. The open, angry juxtaposition between real facts shown in flashback and official truth as asserted in the courtroom displays an impetus which eventually favors easy dramatic effects and emotional shortcuts to sociological analysis, unlike in the director's earlier masterpiece *La banda Casaroli* (1962) and the historical drama *Bronte* (1971). That's because many characters are simply narrative functions incarnated by *Sicilian Checkmate*'s stellar cast. That's the case with Salerno himself, Gastone Moschin's bullying defense attorney and Mario Adorf's hammy mafioso: Fava's play and Vancini's film put in their mouths dialogue culled from the speeches of political and religious authorities. Moschin amply quotes Cardinal Ruffini, former Archbishop of Palermo, who in the notorious 1964 pastoral epistle *The true face of Sicily* denounced a fiendish media conspiracy to slander the island; it was a conspiracy with three prongs. Besides celebrated figures such as "Sicilian Gandhi" Danilo Dolci and novelist Giuseppe Tomasi di Lampedusa, author of *The Leopard* (1958),[1] the third prong of the media offensive against Sicily was the Mafia, which, Ruffini asserted, was "nothing more serious than the same kind of crime that could be found elsewhere in Italy and around the world."[2]

Sicilian Checkmate's most successful characters are the two scapegoats. Guido Leontini — a slimy looking, balding actor with an unmistakable carry-over who was a recurring presence in crime films, often playing despicable, untrustworthy characters — is remarkable as the small-time epileptic crook who'll be the only one condemned at the end of the trial. And in his first dramatic role, one year before Federico Fellini's *Amarcord*, Ciccio Ingrassia delivers an unforgettable, truly moving performance as the illiterate proletarian who is convinced to confess a murder in exchange for an apartment with running water for his family, and then is practically driven to suicide. "Everyone can kick me, everyone can spit in my face, and I always have to keep my mouth shut" he cries, a desperate, resigned statement which mirrors the one uttered by Riccardo Cucciolla, the brother of an honest mayor killed by the Mafia. "My brother's death was useless. Everything is useless in Sicily."

Notes

1. Known as the "Sicilian Gandhi," Dolci's non-violent campaigning drew attention to the hardships endured by the fishing and peasant communities of western Sicily. Tomasi di Lampedusa's enormously successful novel, brought to the screen by Luchino Visconti in 1963, was a disconsolate, pessimistic portrayal of the island's history.

2. John Dickie, *Cosa Nostra: A History of the Sicilian Mafia* (New York: Palgrave Macmillan), p. 229.

The Sicilian Connection (*Afyon — Oppio [Quello strano fiore chiamato papavero]*)

D: Ferdinando Baldi. *S:* Duilio Coletti; *SC:* Duilio Coletti, Ferdinando Baldi; *DOP:* Aiace Parolin (35mm, Technicolor, Techniscope); *M:* Guido and Maurizio De Angelis, conducted by Gianfranco Plenizio (ed. Bixio); *Afyon* (S. Duncan Smith, G. & M. De Angelis) sung by Oliver Onions; *E:* Eugenio Alabiso; *PD:* Gastone Carsetti; *CO:* Marisa Crimi; *AD:* Remo De Angelis; *C:* Gaetano Valle, Arcangelo Lannutti; *AC:* Luigi Bernardini; *MU:* Vittorio Biseo; *SO:* Dino Fronzetti; *SS:* Gloria Maria Eminente. *Cast:* Ben Gazzara (Joseph Coppola), Silvia Monti (Claude), Fausto Tozzi (Don Vincenzo Vascello), Steffen Zacharias (Selby), Luciano Catenacci (Tony Nicolodi), Mario Pilar (Ibrahim), José Greci (Lucia), Malisa Longo (Rosalia), Teodoro Corrà (Ciro Terranova), Luciano Rossi (Dr. Hans), Bruno Corazzari (Larry), Corrado Gaipa (Don Calogero), Carlo Gaddi (Albertini, the man from Marseille), Giuseppe Castellano (Mike, Narcotics agent), Jess Hahn (Sacha), Robert Fiz [Roberto Fizz] (Narcotics agent), Gianni Di Benedetto, Ezio Sancrotti (Restaurant owner), Pipino Desiderio, John Bartha (police inspector), Guy Mairesse (Don Vincenzo's man), Luciano Telli (Antoine, drug dealer), Antonio Spaccatini, Antonio Luigi Guerra, Irio Fantini. *Uncredited:* Calogero Azzaretto (Don Vincenzo's man), Omero Capanna (Don Vincenzo's henchman), Enrico Chiappafreddo, Guerrino Crivello (Gravedigger), Pino Derio (Carabinieri Marshall in prologue), Silvio Klein (New York policeman), Roberto Messina (Selby's assistant), Benito Pacifico (Albertini's man at restaurant), Romano Puppo (Selby's henchman), Sergio Testori (Albertini's man at restaurant), Sandra Wolff (Drug consignment buyer), Luciano Zanussi (Drug consignment buyer). *PROD:* Manolo Bolognini for P.A.C. (Rome), Société Cinématographique Lyre (Paris); *PM:* Luciano Catenacci; *PSu:* Carlo Giovagnorio, Anacleto Amadio. *Country:* Italy. Filmed on location in Rome, Palermo, Istanbul and New York. *Running time:* 100'; Visa no.: 61585 (12.19.1972); *Rating:* not rated; *Release date:* 12.22.1972; *Distribution:* P.A.C..; *Domestic gross:* 473,640,000 lire. *Also known as: Action héroïne* (France, 01.02.78 — 100'); *The Opium Connection* (West Germany — 97'), *La ruta del opio* (Spain). *Home video:* VideoForm (VHS, U.K. — pre-cert), Durium (VHS, Italy), Top Video (VHS, Canada). OST: Chris' Soundtrack Corner CSC 003.

Afyon, Turkey. Italian-American gangster Joseph Coppola gets in touch with a local drug trafficker and convinces him to sell 50 Kilos of morphine. The shipment will be sent to Sicily, where morphine is turned into heroin: once there, Coppola is examined by Don Vincenzo Russo, a Mafia boss who's a member of the powerful Don Calogero family. Joseph passes the test but is almost killed by a rival Marseille boss' hitmen, and only Don Calogero's intervention saves him. Coppola makes a deal with Don Calogero and leaves for the States, where the heroin is shipped in containers hidden under a merchant ship's keel. Once in the States, though, Coppola keeps all the heroin for himself and sells the drug to a U.S. trafficker, Selby — becoming a target for the Sicilian boss' revenge. However, Coppola is actually a Narcotics agent whose aim is to arrest Selby and destroy his gang — which he does. Coppola then fakes his own death so as to escape the Mafia, but just as he thinks he's safe he is shot in the middle of the street by a sniper.

"What's all that water? The sea?" casually asks the Mafia boss Don Vincenzo (Fausto Tozzi) to the undertaker. The latter is busy burying a coffin which not only contains a dead body but also the still alive, nosy Carabinieri marshal who dared to investigate what looked like a normal funeral, but wasn't—the deceased man's stomach contained packets of crude morphine, an ingenious way of smuggling drugs from Istanbul to Sicily. "The sea? Where's the sea? I don't see anything—I don't know anything," the undertaker replies, under Don Vincenzo's attentive and sardonic smile. Behind them, the vast Sicilian sea fills the horizon.

The prologue for *The Sicilian Connection* is as ferocious as it is darkly humorous, in tune with the rest of the film, a fast-paced actioner set in Turkey, Sicily and the States, halfway between Terence Young's *The Poppy Is Also a Flower* (1966)—see the semi-documentary sequences showing the harvesting and refinement of opium—and *The French Connection* (1971), and starring a convincing Ben Gazzara as an undercover police inspector on the trail of an international drug ring.

Despite its theme, however, Duilio Coletti's script is less interested in political denunciations than in entertainment. *The Sicilian Connection* features a larger than life view of the Mafia, with characterizations that somehow recall Pietro Germi's grotesque comedies, such as sweating Mafiosi with basque and mustache and women who wear mourning during the day and join visitors in their bed at night. In one scene, Gazzara is at the centre of two women's attention at Don Calogero's table, and a game of seduction takes place over lunch between a coffee and an ice-cream cup: Baldi edits a series of close-ups of Malisa Longo and José Greci's mouths as they savor spoonfuls of cream, in a humorous variation on the famous seduction scene in Tony Richardson's *Tom Jones* (1963).

What's more, Coletti and Baldi throw in a few amusing ideas, such as a heroin lab hidden underneath a ruined monastery (the chemist is genre regular Luciano Rossi), or a well-paced shoot-out in a darkened restaurant. The idea of heroin being smuggled inside corpses will be featured in other Italian crime films, namely Luigi Vanzi's *Peter, Pearl and the Pole* (*Piazza pulita*, 1973) and Andrea Bianchi's abysmal *Cry of a Prostitute* (*Quelli che contano*, 1974). On the other hand, the ending, in which Gazzara is shot in the middle of a crowded street by an unseen sniper on a rainy day in New York, just before the end credits, is not an anticipation of poliziotteschi's bleak pessimism, but rather an arbitrary, mocking note which further underlines the film's cynical approach.

The cast is top-notch: besides a compelling Ben Gazzara in the lead, Baldi gathers a number of experienced character actors who would become recurring presences in crime films of the era, such as Fausto Tozzi, Luciano Catenacci and Corrado Gaipa, the latter doing a memorable Mafia boss who in a scene draws schemes on a dashboard to explain to Gazzara what his share will be, just as if he were a math teacher.

Summertime Killer *(Ricatto alla mala* a.k.a. *Un verano para matar)*

D: Antonio Isasi-Isasmendi. *S:* Sam X. Abarbanel; *SC:* Reid Buckley, Brian Degas, Sam X. Abarbanel [and Jorge Illa, Antonio Isasi, uncredited]; *DOP:* Juan Gelpí (70mm, Eastmancolor); *M:* Luis Enriquez Bacalov; *Songs: Run and Run* (by Bacalov / S. Bardotti), *Like a Play* (Bacalov / Nelson); *E:* Ramón Quadreny, Emilio Rodríguez; *PD:* Juan Alberto Soler; *AD:* J. L. Ruiz Marcos; *SO:* A. J. Willis; *STC:* Rémy Julienne. *Cast:* Karl Malden (Captain John Kiley), Olivia Hussey (Tania Scarlatti), Christopher Mitchum (Ray Castor), Raf Vallone (Alfred Lazaro), Claudine Auger (Michèle), Gérard Barray (Tania's teacher), Gérard Tichy (Alex), Ricardo Valle (Bespectacled Mafia man), José Nieto (Elderly Mafia man), Gustavo Re (Guido, the barman), Lorenzo Larjos, Umberto Raho (Luis), Víctor Israel (Mechanic), James Cooley, Salvatore Carrara. *PROD:* Antonio Isasi and José Vicuña for Isasi Isasmendi Producciónes (Barcelona), Films 16/35, (Paris), Tritone Filmindustria (Rome); *PSu:* Antonio Irles; *PM:* Miguel Grau; *PSu:* Mario Alabiso. *Country:* Spain / France / Italy. Filmed at Isasi Studios (Barcelona) and on location in Cuenca, Tarragona, Madrid, New York, Rome, Aix-en-Provence and Portugal. *Running time:* 112' (Spanish version), 101' (Italian version); Visa no.: 66420 (04.21.1975); *Rating:* v.m.14; *Release date:* 04.24.1975; *Distribution:* Central Film; *Domestic gross:* 254,841,050 lire. *Also known as: Summertime-Killer* (West Germany, 04.20.1973—103')—*Meurtres au soleil* (France, 07.03.1974)—*The Summertime Killer* (U.K., 1974), *Target Removed* (U.K.—Home video), Blodig sommer (Denmark), *Hämnd på maffian* (Sweden), *Killer Driver* (West Germany). *Home video:* Wild East (DVD, USA—Euro Crime double feature w/ *Confessions of a Police Captain*), General (DVD, Italy). OST: CD Point Records PRCD 115.

Having witnessed the killing of his father by mobsters, Ray Castor has sworn revenge. In New York City he guns down three Mafiosi before jetting off to Rome and assassinating another gangland heavyweight with a sniper rifle. Unable to trace the mystery assassin, the New York mob offers a veteran cop, Captain Kiley, $10,000 to find out who he is and locate him. Kiley takes the job, following a hunch to Portugal and the ranch of Alfred Lazaro, whom he believes could be the killer's next target. He arrives just in time to witness Alfred being shot (although not fatally) from a long distance by Ray. A posse of Alfred's thugs try to chase Ray down on horseback but he manages to escape on his motorbike. With Kiley still on his trail, Ray kidnaps Tania, the mobster's secret 19-year-old daughter, and takes her to an isolated boathouse out in the middle of a Spanish lake. Ray and Tania start falling for each other. Ray gives Lazaro an appointment at a bullfight but again he fails to kill him, and barely escapes Lazaro's men. Kiley eventually traces Castor and the girl, but when he finds out that Ray has given up his plan for vengeance he lets the young couple go, paying for his gesture with his life.

A Spanish / Italian co-production with an International cast, Antonio Isasi-Isasmendi's *Summertime Killer* acquired a certain cult in the U.S. and even found a niche among the cauldron of homages that was Tarantino's *Kill Bill: Vol. 2*, thanks to Luis Enriquez Bacalov's theme song which pops up in the scene where Uma Thurman first enters Bill's hacienda. Another thing in common with Tarantino's film is the revenge plot: Christopher Mitchum is a silent young man ("Another victim of incommunicability?" ironically asks Olivia Hussey) who's sworn vengeance over the four mobsters who killed his father before his eyes as a child—an impressive opening set in a public swimming pool, where the man is drowned to death by the four killers.

Summertime Killer benefits from a strong beginning, as Mitchum moves from New York to Rome and eventually Portugal to dispatch his targets, executing his plan with the cold blood of an automaton, where the actor's lack of expressiveness actually helps. The director definitely has an eye for location: the floating house in the middle of the lake where Ray keeps Tania prisoner is quite impressive (the location is the Entrepeñas lake, near Guadalajara), and a scene takes place in Torres Blancas, the modern circular Madrid skyscraper later used by Jim Jarmusch in his 2009 film *The Limits of Control*. The film also benefits from the many spectacular motorbike stunts performed by Rémy Julienne's team: the scene where Ray acrobatically courts his enemy's secretary (Claudine Auger) atop a speeding motorbike surprisingly predates the Tom Cruise / Thandie Newton one in John Woo's *Mission: Impossible 2* (2000).

However, after Ray kidnaps the secret daughter (Hussey) of the fourth culprit (Raf Vallone), *Summertime Killer* stagnates in a predictable sentimental idyll—which justifies the casting of Hussey, who had gained notoriety after her role in Franco Zeffirelli's *Romeo and Juliet* (1968), which this film somehow updates—periodically interrupted by the scenes involving Karl Malden as a corrupt (yet ultimately golden-hearted) cop on the hero's tracks. However, the film is expertly directed by Spanish-born José Antonio Isasi-Isasmendi, a former film editor and scriptwriter who became a director in the '50s. During his career, Isasi helmed a number of competent adventure, action and spy films conceived for foreign markets and displaying prestigious stars, such as *That Man in Istanbul* (1965, starring Horst Bucholz, Sylva Koscina and Klaus Kinski) and *They Came to Rob Las Vegas* (1968, starring Gary Lockwood, Lee J. Cobb and Jack Palance), thanks to which he became one of Spain's most internationally respected directors during General Franco's dictatorship. Isasi eventually retired in the late '70s after his 1976 political thriller *El Perro* (*A Dog Named ... Vengeance*, starring Jason Miller) when he turned to producing and distributing. He made one more film in the late '80s, *El aire de un crimen* (Scent of a Crime, 1987, starring Francisco Rabal).

In his autobiography *Memorias tras la cámara*, Isasi talks of the film with affection, recalling the guerrilla-style shooting in New York in the days when Francis Ford Coppola was making *The Godfather*: "Coppola's crew, fifty or sixty individuals, was utterly blocking New York streets when shooting, and wherever you'd go there were people talking about the film. While this army was performing its offensive throughout the big city, Juan Gelpí and I, the camera and tripod on our shoulders, sweating hard, were running to and fro, with no money, trying to shoot our film. The Brooklyn bridge never seemed so long as when, loaded as donkeys, we had to walk from one end to the other, looking for the best shot to take."[1] Isasi also reveals that among the actors who were considered for Mitchum's role there was also a very young Keith Carradine, who was "too tall and ungainly," in Isasi's words, to form a believable onscreen couple with Hussey.

Summertime Killer was released on DVD in the U.S. as part of a double bill with Damiani's *Confessions of a Police Captain*. Italian prints credit Palmira Miglietta as co-writer. The Spanish version (which was released in 1972, while the film came out in Italy only three years later) runs sensibly longer than the Italian one.

Note

1. Antonio Isasi-Isasmendi,. *Memorias tras la cámara* (Madrid: Ocho y Medio, 2004), p. 278.

Tough Guy, a.k.a. *Murder in the Ring*, a.k.a. *The Boxer* (*Un uomo dalla pelle dura*)

D: Franco Prosperi. *S:* Armando Crispino, Lucio Battistrada; *SC:* Armando Crispino, Lucio Battistrada, Don Carlos Dunaway, Adriano Bolzoni; *DOP:* Gábor Pogány (35mm, Eastmancolor, Technocrome); *M:* Carlo Pes (ed. Pegaso); *E:* Alberto Gallitti, Fima Noveck; *PD:* Luigi Scaccianoce, Francesco Calabrese; *CO:* Osanna Guardini; *C:* Idelmo Simonelli; *AD:* Giuseppe Pollini; Casting (New Mexico): Jeanne Swain; *MU:* Lamberto Marini; *SO:* Umberto Picistrelli; *ChEl:* Luciano Marrocchi; *KG:* Mario Valentini; *SS:* Elvira D'Amico. *Cast:* Robert Blake (Teddy "Cherokee" Wilcox), Catherine Spaak (Tony's daughter), Ernest Borgnine (Captain Perkins), Tomas Milian (Hippy), Gabriele Ferzetti (Tony La Monica), Orazio Orlando (Mike Durrel), Emilio Messina (Cinc, bookmaker), Felicita Fanni (Mike's girlfriend), Joe [Giuseppe] Pollini, Fortunato Arena (Paul Levinsky), Gianni Di Segni (Alan), Aldo Cecconi, Joe Louis Murphy (Himself). *Uncredited:* Camille Keaton (Teddy's girlfriend in flashbacks), Renzo Ozzano (Klaus), Phil Mead, Quinn Hurley, Neffie Quintana, Luther Elmore, Gary Kanin, John Van Keuren. *PROD:* Felice Testa Gay for Cinegay; *GM:* Ottavio Oppo; *PSu:* Alfredo Chetta; *PSe:* Giuseppe Bruno Bossio. *Country:* Italy. Filmed at Dear Film (Rome) and on location in New Mexico. *Running time:* 89'; Visa no.: 59608 (01.12.1972); *Rating:* v.m.14; *Release date:* 02.02.1972; *Distribution:* Titanus; *Domestic gross:* 368,690,000 lire. *Also known as: Champ Cherokee*, *Fäuste aus Stein* (West Germany), *Le coriace* (Canada). *Home video:* Synergy (DVD, USA—as *The Boxer*), Rai Cinema—01 (DVD, Italy). OST: CD GDM Music 4013.

Small-time Cherokee-blooded boxer Teddy Wilcox dumps his dishonest manager and leaves for New Mexico, where—with the help of journalist friend Mike Durrel and under the guidance of old-school manager/trainer Tony La Monica—he starts a successful string of winning matches. However, unbeknownst to Teddy, La Monica is in cahoots with a betting racket and agrees to have Teddy lose his next match. The events don't go as planned, though, and Teddy wins. Soon after the match Tony is murdered by an unknown assailant, and Wilcox is the prime suspect. He teams up with Tony's daughter to find out the real culprit. Meanwhile, the murderer gets rid of all possible witnesses....

Franco Prosperi's return to hard-boiled *film noir*, a few years after his mid-sixties diptych *The Professional Killer* (*Tecnica di un omicidio*, 1966) and *Every Man Is My Enemy* (*Qualcuno ha tradito*, 1967), was another attempt at trying his hand with U.S. models. If anything, the script (credited among others to Armando Crispino, director of such effective *gialli* as *The Etruscan Kills Again* and *Autopsy*) shows once again Italian cinema's tendency to mix genres.

Shot on location in New Mexico, *Tough Guy* (also known as *The Boxer* and *Murder in the Ring*) starts as a typical boxing crime drama. Yet halfway through, after the obligatory rigged match which half-blooded Native American Teddy Wilcox (Robert Blake) is supposed to lose, his manager (Gabriele Ferzetti) is punched to death by a black-gloved figure shown through POV shots as in a Dario Argento *giallo*, and the film becomes a whodunit of sorts, as the unknown murderer gets rid of all those who know too much and investigations disclose revelatory film footage with the solution to the mystery.

However, the whodunit angle is quite flat and predictable up to the final twist, as are most characters: Spaak, as the love interest, is wasted, while Borgnine pops up as the obligatory tough cop in a throwaway cameo. Prosperi's direction is competent, with a few unexpected finesses (a homage to the tennis scene in Hitchcock's *Strangers on a Train* as Tomas Milian's character is standing silent and alert among the yelling crowd at the boxing match). Blake's Teddy is a definitely unlikable antihero (a violent, rough-mannered ex-convict and Vietnam veteran), so that the film's main point of interest is Tomas Milian's "guest appearance" as the long-haired hippie hitman, who wears a hairband and a denim shirt: a character who not just predates the sadistic Chaco in Fulci's *Four of the Apocalypse*, but is also an embryonic incarnation of what will become Milian's most popular character, Monnezza.

1973

Gli amici degli amici hanno saputo (The Friends of Our Friends Have Known)

D: Fulvio Marcolin. *S:* Rodolfo Sonego; *SC:* Fulvio Marcolin, Giamberto Marcolin; *DOP:* Mario Vulpiani (35mm, Eastmancolor); *M:* Egisto Macchi (Ed. Rete); *Sui muri di Parigi* and *Just Hold My Hand* sung by Katja Hollander; *E:* Carla Simoncelli; *AE:* Caterina Sobrini; *PD:* Francesco Vanorio; *C:* Pasquale Rachini; *AC:* Mario Bagnato, Michele Picciaredda, Alberto Lauriello; *AD:* Massimo Manuelli; *MU:* Marisa Tilli; *SS:* Clelia Bousquet. *Cast:* Simonetta Stefanelli (Annunziata), Gino Milli (Vincenzino Cipolla), Pino Caruso (Salvatore Camarro), Pascale Petit (Renata), Hélène Chanel (Suzette), Patrizia Di Giovanni, Pierluigi D'Orazio, Gennaro Fragasso, Rosario Di Giacomo, Giovanni Tarricone, Lia Dezman [Natalia Dezmann], Carlo Camilla, Elso Barboni. *Uncredited:* Calogero Azzaretto (Man on the train). *PROD:* Giorgio Patara for Nexus Film; *GM:* Giamberto Marcolin; *PSu:* Venanzio Di Venanzio. *Country:* Italy. Filmed on location in Turin and Sicily. *Running time:* 105'; Visa no.: 61734 (01.16.1973); *Rating:* v.m.18; *Release date:* 02.08.1973; *Distribution:* I.N.C.; *Domestic gross:* 177,043,000 lire. *Home video:* None.

Hired by Salvatore Camarro, a member of a Mafia "family" led by the renowned lawyer Paternò, young Vincenzino Cipolla moves to Turin with his sister Annunziata, with whom he's bound by a morbid affection. The girl finds a job in a factory, while Vincenzino becomes Salvatore's right hand, earning on his behalf a "bounty" from unskilled workers from the South who are abusively employed in Paternò's construction sites. After a double Mafia murder that he's witnessed, Vincenzo has to temporarily hide in France. Back in Turin, he finds out that Annunziata has left the factory and works as a stripper in nightclubs. Vincenzo—whose relationship with his sister has become openly incestuous—witnesses Salvatore's violent death, as the man is murdered in a tavern by one of the victims of his racketeering. Paternò summons Vincenzo and offers him a job in his organization, but pretends that Annunziata become his lover in return. Vincenzo steals 50 million from Paternò and escapes with Annunziata (who's pregnant with his baby) to Sicily, where they meet their end.

In its depiction of the life of Southern immigrants in Turin and the infiltration of the Mafia in Northern Italy's economy through the exploitation of workers, Tullio Marcolin's *Gli amici degli amici hanno saputo* explores a similar territory to Carlo Lizzani's *Black Turin*. The script, from a story by the renowned Rodolfo Sonego—one of the great screenwriters in Italian cinema, who wrote many of Alberto Sordi's best films—blends social commentary and genre, and focuses on the misadventures of a pair of naive siblings (Gino Milli and the gorgeous Simonetta Stefanelli, who played Michael Corleone's wife in Coppola's *The Godfather* one year earlier).

The narration proceeds as one long flashback, starting with the discovery of the two siblings' dead bodies—lying on a bed, hand in hand, in a house in a lost small town in Sicily—and moving back to the time when they were lured to the North by a small-time Mafioso (Pino Caruso, a well-known Italian comedian, here in a serious role). Marcolin describes the procedures of enrollment of inexperienced and gullible men and women with a sharp, bitterly detached tone, and Marcolin shows an eye for detail in scenes such as the one where Vincenzo and Annunziata move to a "hotel" which they believed was a luxurious place and turns out to be a squalid dormitory. There are a number of keen observations on the quality of life of Southern immigrants in the North, who lived in huge popular houses that looked like hives (in a humorous bit, a family even keep their hens in the bathroom) and their exploitation on behalf of the Mafia, and the feel of the period—strikes, anti-fascist protest marches, etc.—is impressively sketched.

Yet as the film goes on the characterizations do not feel strong enough to sustain Marcolin's ambitions, the digressions (such as Vincenzo's weird meeting with a transvestite and his experience in a gay nightclub) go on far too long, and the plot falters. Eventually *Gli amici degli amici hanno saputo* makes a quick and ill-fated turn toward crime melodrama in the last third, but genre elements—besides a violent killing in a central Turin bar, Vincenzo and Annunziata's final desperate attempt at escape back to their hometown and the final murder / suicide—are only superficially explored.

Battle of the Godfathers *(I re della mala,* a.k.a. *Zinksärge für die Goldjungen)*

D: Jürgen Roland. *S* and *SC:* Werner Jörg Lüddecke, August Rieger (Italian version: Tatiana Pavoni [and Luigi Cozzi, uncredited]); *Italian DIA:* Vinicio Marinucci [and Luigi Cozzi, uncredited]; *DOP:* Klaus Werner (35mm, Technicolor); *M:* Lallo [Coriolano] Gori; *E:* Licia Ludovici (Italian version), Herbert Taschner (German version); *AD:* Fredy Hünger [Goffredo Unger]; *ST:* Ralph Deny (motorboat scenes). *Cast:* Herbert Fleischmann (Otto Westermann / Italian version: Hans Werner), Henry Silva (Luca Messina / Italian version: Luc Mesina), Patrizia Gori (Silvia), Horst Janson (Erik), Véronique Vendell (Kate), Raf Baldassarre (Sergio), Ermelinda De Felice (Luca's mother), Sonja Jeannine (Tilly Mautz), Uwe Carstens, Dan van Husen (O'Brian), Wolfgang Kuhlman, Peter Lehmbrock, Victor Oto, Jack Paxton, Denes Törzs, Horst Hesslein, Heinz Sonntag, Bruno Jorneleit, Johanna König, Karl-Heinz Gerdesmann. *PROD:* Wolf C. Hartwig and Carlo Infascelli for Rapid Film (Münich), Studio Hamburg (Hamburg), Roma Film (Rome); *PM:* Felix Hock. *Country:* West Germany / Italy. Filmed in Hamburg. *Running time:* 87'; Visa no.: 64892 (07.17.1974); *Rating:* v.m.14; *Release date:* 07.26.1974; *Distribution:* Roma Film; *Domestic gross:* 410,328,000 lire.

Also known as: Salopards en enfer (Paris, 10.26.1977 — 90'), *Ilman jarruja helvettiin* (Finland), *Los ángeles de oro* (Spain). *Home video:* Media Target Distribution GmbH (2 DVD, Germany — Italian and German versions).

Otto Westermann, boss of the Hamburg underworld, completes a violent operation that allows him to seize the racing and gambling dens of prostitution in the city. When the Italian-American boss Luca Messina, expelled as undesirable from the U.S., comes to Hamburg, willing to take over Westermann's empire, the two bosses engage in a battle with no holds barred. After Westermann's son Karl, a promising boxer, is killed by Luca's men, both Messina and Westermann try to bring the war to the opponent's headquarters. Meanwhile, though, Messina's daughter Silvia and Westermann's younger son Eric fall in love. After Messina has dispatched his right-hand man Sergio and his unfaithful mistress Kate, Westermann kidnaps Silvia, but Luca does the same with Eric. The two lovers manage to escape together, while their fathers engage in a final battle throughout town which ends with Messina's death after a deadly motorboat chase. However, Westermann won't survive his opponent for long.

"This city is going to be mine!" proclaims Luca Messina (Henry Silva) when he arrives by boat at the Hamburg dock. The plot for Jürgen Roland's *Battle of the Godfathers*— a mainly German/Italian co-production, whose great original title translates to "Zinc Coffins for the Golden Boys"— can be pretty much summarized with this line and the consequences it brings.

Compared to Italian crime movies of the period, *Battle of the Godfathers* is definitely more on the comic book side. There's not the slightest attempt at social commentary, and the story is told in a perfunctory manner, with bare-bones characters and primitive cause / effect plot complications. What matters, in typical B-movie tradition, is action — shoot-outs, car chases, explosions, even a couple of Oriental martial arts experts popping up in one scene. The paper-thin script by Werner Jörg Lüddecke and August Rieger (with the latter being replaced in the Italian credits by Tatiana Pavoni) is a non-stop series of violent clashes, ambushes and shoot-outs between the two rival mob bosses — Silva's opponent is played by Herbert Fleischmann, a regular on German television — which are spiced up by the syrupy Romeo-and-Juliet subplot between the bosses' respective kids (Patrizia Gori and Horst Janson, the latter soon to star in Hammer's *Captain Kronos— Vampire Hunter*, 1974). As the Italian-American bad guy, Silva has a few cool lines ("My name is Luca Messina, but you can call me boss," he presumptively tells the rival gangsters on their first meeting) but besides his imposing screen presence the character is hardly memorable, while the wild-eyed, sideburned Fleischmann comes off as the more impressive of the rival duo.

The final over-the-top motorboat pursuit in the Hamburg canals is particularly enjoyable, even though it follows an extended car chase throughout town — with Silva hounding the two lovers (who are traveling in a car with a time bomb on it) and being followed by Fleischmann in turn — that dangerously comes close to a Keystone Kops reel. Roland, a veteran of German Edgar Wallace *Krimis*, keeps the pacing up at the expense of any finesse whatsoever, with the occasional sleazy touch (a nightclub show with two naked girls enjoying a bubble bath is interrupted by Fleischmann's men throwing a Molotov cocktail on stage; Sonja Jeannine's character is nude all the time). Supporting cast features such familiar faces as Dan van Husen and the Italian Raf Baldassarre in their usual thug routine.

Most interesting, however, are the differences between the German and Italian versions. The latter — which is shorter and more violent, sacrificing the plot — has characters' names slightly changed (Silva's Italian origins are somewhat diminished), while adding a preachy voice-over at the beginning and a score by Lallo Gori, while the German version features library music from other films such as *The Secret of Dr. Mabuse* (*Die Todesstrahlen des Dr. Mabuse*, 1964, Hugo Fregonese), *Death and Diamonds* (*Dynamit in grüner Seide*, 1968, Harald Reinl) and *Jungfrauen-Report* (1972, Jess Franco). Also, a number of scenes — such as the junk yard shoot-out, or the bit where the car which Erik and Silvia were driving away in explodes — are played out in slow motion for no apparent reason, to ridiculous effect.

The dialogue for the Italian version is credited to Vinicio Marinucci, a journalist and film critic who directed a couple of *Mondo di notte*–style documentaries in 1962/1963, namely *Le dolci notti* and *I piaceri nel mondo*. Marinucci also directed many music videos for the Cinebox / Scopitone circuit. However, director Luigi Cozzi (*The Killer Must Strike Again, Star Crash, Contamination*) recently stated that the Italian co-producer Carlo Infascelli hired him to do uncredited polishing work on the script (Cozzi had previously worked on the Infascelli-produced *The Black Hand*). "I invented the Italian title, *Il re della mala* (The King of the Underworld) and told him that the German script was too slow and weak" Cozzi explained. "Infascelli told me that he wanted to cast Henry Silva in the lead, but Silva refused the film because he didn't like the script either. So Infascelli asked me to meet Silva and, since I spoke a good English, arrange with him the changes to be made so that he would accept the role. If I succeeded, he'd have me rewrite the whole script. I met Silva at the Parco dei Principi Hotel in Rome and after a couple of hours' talk he changed his mind. Silva liked the changes I planned to make to the story and his character as well, and eventually took the role."[1] Cozzi also claimed that he helped casting the Italian actors in the film. Infascelli later helped produce and offered to distribute Cozzi's giallo *The Killer Must Strike Again*, whose idea was very loosely inspired by Giorgio Scerbanenco's novel *Al mare con la ragazza*, yet eventually took his name off the credits since — as Cozzi himself admits — he hated the final result, and got out of the production before the film was released.[2]

Notes

1. Luigi Cozzi, *L'inizio degli anni Settanta: la stagione d'oro del thriller all'italiana*, in Antonio Bruschini, Antonio Tentori. *Guida al cinema giallo e thrilling made in Italy*. Rome: Profondo Rosso, 2010, pp. 210–211.
2. *Ibid.*, p. 217.

The Big Family (*L'onorata famiglia — Uccidere è cosa nostra*)

D: Tonino Ricci. *S* and *SC:* Nino Scolaro, Arpad De Riso, Tonino Ricci; *DOP:* Gianni Bergamini (35mm, Eastmancolor, Technospes); *M:* Bruno Nicolai, conducted by the author (ed. Gemelli); *E:* Antonietta Zita; *PD and CO:* Giorgio Bertolini; *COA:* Wanda Pruni; *C:* Gianni Bonivento;

AE: Luciana Scandroglio; *AD:* Earl Rosen; *MU:* Franco Di Girolamo; *SO:* Guido Ortensi; *Mix:* Bruno Moreal; *SOE:* Renato Marinelli; *SE:* Gino Vagniluca, Giuseppe Carrozza; *SS:* Maria Rosaria Cilento. *Cast:* Raymond Pellegrin (Don Peppino Scalise), Simonetta Stefanelli (Rossana Vitale), Giancarlo Prete (Commissioner Ettore La Manna), Richard Conte (Antonio Marchesi), Maria Fiore (Nunziata Federici), Edmund Purdom (Giovanni Loharo), Aldo Barberito (Orlando Federici), Pino Ferrara (Fiorito), Sal Borgese (Turi Nannisco), Stelio Candelli (Johnny De Salvo), Umberto Spadaro (Marshall of Carabinieri), Franco Fantasia (Chief of Police), Empedocle Buzzanca (Alfio Sorge), Saro Anastasi, Luigi Antonio Guerra (Journalist), Antonia Micalizzi, Francesco Sineri, Giuseppe Bruno Bossio. *Uncredited:* Ignazio Pappalardo (Marchesi's henchman), Pietro Torrisi (Saro, Marchesi's henchman). *PROD:* National Cinematografica, Flora Film; *PM:* Sergio Borelli; *PSu:* T. David Pash. *Country:* Italy. Filmed at Incir — De Paolis (Rome) and on location in Palermo. *Running time:* 90'; Visa no.: 61997 (03.03.1973); *Rating:* v.m.14; *Release date:* 03.08.1973; *Distribution:* Variety Film; *Domestic gross:* 286,531,000 lire. *Home video:* CVR (VHS, Italy). OST: CD Edipan PAN CD 2504.

Two rival Mafia bosses, Antonio Marchesi and Peppino Scalise, contend the property development business in Palermo. Scalise eventually has his adversary assassinated by two killers, Johnny De Salvo and Turi Nannisco. Marchesi's master builder, Orlando Federici, who witnessed the murder, is soon eliminated as well in an ambush. Commissioner La Manna, who's in charge of the case, tries to persuade Federici's widow to testify against Scalise. The woman agrees, after Scalise's killers have unsuccessfully attempted to murder her, slaying her son in the process. However, the trial ends with Scalise and the assassins acquitted. La Manna doesn't give up, though, and he keeps investigating on his own: he gets in touch with Alfio Sorge, an ex-convict who wants to exact revenge upon Scalise. The man promises to give the commissioner important information, but is bumped off before he can talk. La Manna survives a murder attempt and dispatches Johnny and Turi, then he eventually finds compromising documents in Marchesi's safety box that allow him to arrest Scalise. However, just as he is being taken to prison, the boss is murdered by an unseen sniper.

A decidedly minor entry in the Mafia subgenre, Tonino Ricci's *The Big Family* exemplifies the changes that accompanied the amalgamation of political motifs within genre cinema. Ricci's film more or less recycles the plot of Damiani's *Confessions of a Police Captain*: honest commissioner La Manna (Giancarlo Prete) will try anything to arrest Mafia boss Peppino Scalise (Raymond Pellegrin), who's untouchable because of his connivances with politicians and the Church, and Scalise's business is in property development — including the reconstruction of those villages that were destroyed in the 1968 Belice earthquake. However, the more openly didactic moments seem nothing more than tinsel, a price to pay in order to deliver the conspicuously violent and grim sequences — such as the many bloody killings, or La Manna's fiancée (Simonetta Stefanelli) being raped by Sal Borgese — which are obviously the ones that the audience eagerly awaits.

Characters are pure stereotypes, starting with Pellegrin's suavely cruel Mafia boss, and the typical theme of *omertà*, an obligatory element in Mafia movies ("I'd like to know one man in Sicily who doesn't mind his own business!" La Manna comments while questioning a reticent witness), is summed up with similar rudeness in one of the film's most memorably trashy lines, as an elderly peasant tells the hero: "Even if I am being ass-fucked, the ass is still mine!" Ricci's attempts at stylistic flourishes are forgettable to say the least: in the scene of Pellegrin's stylized trial, the lawyers, judges and witnesses are shown only through their silhouettes on a wall, as if they were Chinese shadows, with almost zany results.

Big Guns (Tony Arzenta — Big Guns)

D: Duccio Tessari. *S:* Franco Verucci; *SC:* Ugo Liberatore, Franco Verucci, Roberto Gandus; *DOP:* Silvano Ippoliti (35mm, Eastmancolor, Technospes); *M:* Gianni Ferrio, conducted by the author (ed. Star); *E:* Mario Morra; *PD, ArtD:* Lorenzo Baraldi; *ArtD:* Giancarlo Pucci; *CO:* Danda Ortona; *C:* Enrico Sasso; *AC:* Renato Doria; *AEs:* Roberto Sterbini, Francesco Reitano; *AD:* Giovanni Manganelli; *MU:* Mario Van Riel; *Hair:* Iolanda Conti; *SO:* Bruno Zanoli; *Mix:* Alberto Bartolomei, Danilo Moroni; *SOE:* Renato Marinelli, Ezio Marcorin, Aurelio Pennacchia; *SP:* Francesco Narducci; *MA:* Nazzareno Zamperla; *SS:* Vittoria Vigorelli. *Cast:* Alain Delon (Tony Arzenta), Richard Conte (Nick Gusto), Carla Gravina (Sandra), Marc Porel (Domenico Maggio), Roger Hanin (Carré), Nicoletta Machiavelli (Anna, Tony's wife), Guido Alberti (Don Mariano), Lino Troisi (Rocco Cutitta), Silvano Tranquilli (Montani), Corrado Gaipa (Tony's father), Erika Blanc (Italian prostitute in Copenhagen), Rosalba Neri (Mrs. Cutitta), Giancarlo Sbragia (Luca Dennino), Umberto Orsini (Isnello), Carla Calò (Nunziata, Tony's mother), Ettore Manni (Gesmundo, sauna owner), Francesco Bonetti, Loredana Nusciak (Gesmundo's lover), Luís Suarez, Alberto Farnese (Man who meets Carré in night-club). *Uncredited:* Stella Carnacina (DJ girl in Carré's nightclub), Maria Pia Conte (Carré's secretary in nightclub), Anton Diffring (Hans Grünwald), Vittorio Pinelli (Thug in car who tries to kill Tony), Claudio Ruffini (Carré's bodyguard on train), Pietro Torrisi (Gesmundo's man), Nazzareno Zamperla (Cutitta's man). *PROD:* Luciano Martino for Mondial Te.Fi. (Rome), Alain Delon and Raymond Danon for Adel Productions (Paris), Lira Films (Paris); *GM:* Vittorio Galiano; *PM:* Averroé Stefani; *PSu:* Maurizio Pastrovich. *Country:* Italy / France. Filmed at Dear Studios (Rome) and on location in Milan, Turin, Copenhagen, Paris, Noto, Siracuse. *Running time:* 113'; Visa no.: 62913 (08.08.1973); *Rating:* v.m.18; *Release date:* 09.07.1973; *Distribution:* Titanus; *Domestic gross:* 1,945,982,000 lire. *Also known as:* *Big Guns — Les grands fusils* (Paris, 08.23.1973 — 90') — *Tödlicher Hass* (12.07.1973 — 95'). *Home video:* Titanus (DVD, Italy). OST: CD Easy Tempo 917.

Milan. Tony Arzenta is a hitman at the service of a powerful Mafia family which operates all over Europe. Tired of his job and wanting to spend more time with his family, Tony decides to quit. Yet he knows too much, so his bosses — the Parisian Carré, the German-born Grünwald, the Milanese Rocco Cutitta and the Italian-American Nick Gusto — attempt to get rid of him by putting a bomb in his car. The explosion kills Tony's wife and child, and Arzenta vows vengeance. He survives a murder attempt just after his beloved ones' funeral, chases the killers and murders them with the help of his friend Domenico Maggio; then Tony sets out to kill the head of the French branch of the organization, Carré — whom he reaches through the boss' girlfriend, Sandra — and dispatches him on a train. Afterwards Arzenta kills Grünwald, but is badly wounded in the shoot-out, and is aided towards recovery by an Italian friend in Copenhagen, Luca Dennino. Back in Milan, Domenico is tortured and murdered after revealing Tony's hideout. Arzenta survives the umpteenth ambush, though, and kills Cutitta. Then he leaves for Sicily with Sandra, to pay visit to his parents. Nick Gusto, the only living boss left, pretends to make peace and invites Tony to his daughter's wedding. Tony accepts, but after the ceremony Dennino shoots him just outside the church.

Duccio Tessari's Mafia epic is the most explicit — and successful — example of contamination between Italian-style and French *film noir*. Although the premise and (partly) the setting refer to typical Mafia movies, *Big Guns* is rather a mimetic, philological rewriting of French *polar*, and a cinematic hinge between the two genres. References to *polar* are many, starting with the presence — both as star and co-producer — of Alain Delon as a hitman who vows revenge against his bosses after his wife and son have been blown up in his car before his very eyes, up to Gianni Ferrio's music, which bears more than a passing resemblance to Claude Boiling's scores. At the time of its release, *Big Guns* was a huge hit, thanks to Delon's star appeal at the box office, but critics were rather tepid, merely judging the film at its surface level and taking note of the supposedly worn clichés.[1] Yet Tessari's inventive take on *film noir* stereotypes is shown by such moments as the elliptical closure after the long car chase in the fields, with the discovery of the dead bodies in a small church lost in the fog, or Roger Hanin's murder on the train, whose display of sheer technique almost makes it look like a scene from a Dario Argento film.

Tessari (and Delon) manage to shape one of Italian crime films' most impressive antiheroes. Tony Arzenta is a lonely, melancholy character who "is forced to follow his destiny up till the end, without any chance of redemption, and is well aware that he will eventually succumb against preponderant forces."[2] But there's much more than that. *Big Guns* displays a stylistic opulence never seen before and after in an Italian *film noir*. The attention to *décor* is emphasized by Silvano Ippoliti's gorgeous cinematography, which magnifies a chromatic palette of flaming reds and blinding whites in the interior scenes, and memorably captures the icy and foggy Milanese surroundings. Action scenes are uniformly outstanding, with Delon doing his own stunts in car chases, and violence is as unpredictable as it is striking, so much so that it assured the film a "v.m.18" rating in Italy.

Yet *Big Guns* is not simply an exercise in style. The story moves at a brisk pace, structured in an episodic manner like a Cornell Woolrich novel: each murder is a small film in itself, and each character, even those on-screen for just a line or two, leave their mark. The script (with the possible uncredited collaboration of Fernando di Leo) is complex and rich with nuances — such as the opening scenes that show Arzenta as a nice, quiet family man, who at a certain point leaves his son's birthday party to perform a hit, or the relationship between Tony and his old father Corrado Gaipa — and as the film goes along, it conveys an overwhelming sense of weariness, melancholy and futility. Between one murder and the next, Tony spends time in the empty house, listening to his son's voice on tape and surrounded by memories of his past. "You can stay here if you want" he tells Sandra (Carla Gravina), who seeks refuge in his apartment after helping him reach and kill the sadistic Carré (Roger Hanin), "just don't make me feel your presence too much."

In such a violent and grim world, women are just expendable pawns. They are murdered, beaten, humiliated and abused, like Carré's his long-suffering lover Sandra, who is savagely beaten by Cutitta's men to the sound of classical music in another extremely violent scene, or the unnamed prostitute played by Erika Blanc, who's used as a bait to lure Arzenta in an ambush in Copenhagen.

Alain Delon as Mafia hitman Tony Arzenta in *Big Guns* (1973).

In the end, Tony dies because he's still adherent to the rules everyone else steps upon: he rejects the offer of Interpol agent Montani to betray his bosses and get protection, and accepts Nick Gusto's (Richard Conte) invitation to the boss' daughter's wedding as an act of loyalty and respect which will prove fatal. Gusto promised no one of his "family" would kill either Arzenta or his family, and in fact Tony is dispatched by an outsider, his friend Dennino, who previously saved his life in Copenhagen and who used to boast about his independence. A final act that puts the last piece on the whole canvas, and "gives the sense of a world that's founded on betrayal."[3]

Notes

1. Two examples: "Tessari narrated the story without worrying about the script's naiveties, which coincide with the protagonist's, whose hand is much quicker than his brain. Nevertheless, the budget is significant and the director employs it without any naivety. The violent scenes reel off with the due crescendo

of spectacular effects, among various interior and exterior set-pieces. Not to mention that Alain Delon, with a gun in his hand, still works, and here he's surrounded by a dense array of actors," Guglielmo Biraghi, *Il Messaggero*, 9.15.1973. "It's basically a plotless flick, with characters who act only as a consequence of the film's initial factual situation. There is no plot development, and the moments of tension are few and far between. *Big Guns* could have been a good movie, had Tessari renounced to those spectacular events that nowadays are all too familiar, and devoted himself to the analysis of the film's central character, a nomad who carries both a gun and the romantic-existential halo of a wrong life, looking for an identity which gives him a reason to live," Maurizio Porro, *Il Giorno*, 9.16.1973.

2. Vittorio Albano, *La mafia nel cinema siciliano*, (Manduria TA: Barbieri, 2003), p. 51.

3. Paolo Mereghetti, *Il Mereghetti—dizionario dei film 2011* (Milan: B.C. Dalai, 2010), p. 3400.

The Black Hand (The Birth of the Mafia) (La Mano Nera [Prima della Mafia, più della Mafia])

D: Antonio Racioppi. *S:* Carlo Infascelli; *SC:* Vinicio Marinucci, Aldo Marcovecchio, Ugo Moretti, Luigi Cozzi, Antonio Racioppi; *SCcoll:* Gino Capone, Alessandro Fallai, Gastone Ramazzotti; *DIARev:* Ercole Patti; *English DIA:* Charles Howerthon; *DOP:* Riccardo Pallottini (35mm, Eastmancolor, Staco Film); *M:* Carlo Rustichelli (Ed. Nazionalmusic); *E:* Cleofe Conversi; *PD, CO:* Elio Balletti; *ArtD:* Bonaventura Fraulo; *C:* Dante Di Palma; *AC:* Luigi Conversi; *AD:* Ignazio Dolce; *SO:* Benedetto Conversi; *MU:* Giulio Natalucci, Dante Trani; *Hair:* Walter Giangrasso, Adriana Cassini; *W:* Bertilla Silvestrin; *DubD* (English version): John Gayford. *Cast:* Lionel Stander (Lieutenant Giuseppe Petrosino), Rosanna Fratello (Angela Musumeci), Mike [Michele] Placido (Antonio Turrisi), Luigi Pistilli (Don Nunzio Pantaleo), Philippe Leroy (The Professor), Roger Browne (State Attorney), Corrado Gaipa (Lawyer), Nino Vingelli (Don Gaetano), Annie Carol Edel (Mary, the prostitute), Mario Frera (Don Salvatore, the Pizzeria owner), Gilberto Galimberti (Tano Massara), Gianni Manera (Berto, Venetian worker in the mine), Giacomo Rizzo (Nicola Gerace), Sergio Ammirata (Nick Martorano, the Professor's henchman), Salvatore Billa (Johnny Biondo's sidekick), Luigi Antonio Guerra, Domenico Maggio (Johnny Biondo, Black Hand member), Guy Mairesse, Carla Mancini, Rosa Pisano. *Uncredited:* Antonio Anelli (Jury member), Angelo Boscariol (Factory worker), Omero Capanna (Newspaper vendor), Giuseppe Castellano (Irish worker in the mine), Nestore Cavaricci (Man standing in the background at the billiard saloon), Geoffrey Copleston (O'Connor), Manlio Dalla Pria, Veriano Giresi (Don Gaetano's man), Enrico Marciani (Turrisi's lawyer), Giuseppe Marrocco (Man in court), Marcello Bonini Olas (Corrupt jailer), Filippo Perego (Italian consul), Franca Scagnetti (Woman near the dumpster at the film's beginning), Luciano Zanussi (Foreman). *PROD:* Carlo Infascelli for In.Ci.S Film; *PMs:* Elio Di Pietro, Raniero Di Giovanbattista. *Country:* Italy. Filmed at INCIR-De Paolis, Elios (Rome). *Running time:* 90'; Visa no.: 62082 (03.15.1973); *Rating:* v.m.14; *Release date:* 03.16.1973; *Distribution:* Roma Film; *Domestic gross:* 230,363,000 lire. *Also known as: Auch Killer müssen sterben* (Germany), *Den Sorte Hånd. Home video:* Cinehollywood (VHS, Italy), Magnum (VHS, USA), Cinehollywood (Greece—English language), PMA (VHS, UK), Cinehollywood / Walthers Video (Denmark—as *Den Sorte Hånd*), Power Station GmbH (DVD, Germany—German audio)

Early 1900. Antonio Turrisi, a young Sicilian who emigrated to the United States, kills in self defense Massara, a killer affiliated with the "Black Hand," a powerful criminal organization. One of his bosses, the "Professor," keeps Antonio under his protection and saves him from death when Antonio, going against orders, saves Angela Musumeci, a young girl just arrived from Sicily, from becoming a prostitute. Antonio becomes a member of the Black Hand, and marries Angela. The secret organization is supporting the Governor of New York in exchange for illicit favors, and Antonio has to suppress the opposing candidate. Antonio and other members of the Black Hand are arrested but eventually acquitted following the trial. He is then sent back to Sicily to kill policeman Joe Petrosino, the organization's biggest enemy. Antonio refuses to carry out the killing, but this costs him his life.

Produced and supervised by Carlo Infascelli, *The Black Hand (The Birth of the Mafia)* is a patent attempt at exploiting the enormous popularity of the TV movie *Joe Petrosino* (1972) by Daniele D'Anza, starring Adolfo Celi. The result is a mixed bag, shot on a shoestring on recycled sets and backlots, and conveying an overwhelming sense of improvisation, as if it was made up as it went along. Which was actually the case, as co-scriptwriter Luigi Cozzi recounted: "I met Carlo Infascelli after he started working on *The Black Hand*: he wanted to change the script according to what actors asked. Philippe Leroy didn't like the script, but Infascelli wanted him in the movie. So Carlo asked him what he had to change, and Leroy told him what kind of scenes he wanted. Carlo phoned me and gave me 24 hours to add the requested scene! Another example: one evening Carlo phoned me from the set, telling me there was a problem. They just shot a scene in which the cops get into the hero's house, where a man has just been killed, but they don't notice anything and don't arrest the hero. Yet the script didn't explain why they didn't notice the dead body! Carlo told me "Luigi, write something quick and explain why the victim has disappeared!" So I came up with the idea that there was a manhole under a table, and a river underneath, so the hero just throws the body in the river, then he lets the police in! That's how my job on *The Black Hand* was like. They phoned me, and I had to find a solution. A new scene, different dialogue, all of this while they were shooting. It was crazy, but it still makes me laugh a lot when I think about it!"[1]

Cozzi was one of *nine* scriptwriters who are credited on the film, including such important names as novelist Ercole Patti as dialogue adviser. The theme is undoubtedly interesting: the rise of the Mafia in the U.S. in early 1900 amidst Italian immigrants was a topic barely touched by Hollywood movies—one example being Richard Thorpe's mediocre *The Black Hand* (1950) starring Gene Kelly—while Francis Ford Coppola would portray a similar scenario in a much more striking way in *The Godfather Part II* (1974). Besides recounting the Black Hand's clandestine rituals (such as the blood oath which bonds Antonio and the Professor), Racioppi's film stresses the political angle, hinting at the responsibility on part of the Italian politicians for the expansion of the Mafia in the American territory. However, the historical and sociological ambitions uneasily rub shoulders with a predilection for *grand-guignol* (severed heads, blood spurting from slashed arteries, tongues cut off), while the over-reliance on melodrama makes Racioppi's film a cousin of coeval period *feuilletons* such as Aldo Lado's *Sepolta Viva* (1973), Mario Lanfranchi's *The Kiss* (*Il bacio*, 1974) or Infascelli's own *Kiss of a Dead Woman* (*Il bacio di una morta*, 1974).

The cast is full of well-known faces such as Luigi Pistilli, Philippe Leroy, Lionel Stander, plus the umpteenth survivor of '60s spy flicks, Roger Browne. However, the real protagonists are singer Rosanna Fratello (who debuted as Riccardo Cucciolla's wife in Giuliano Montaldo's *Sacco and Vanzetti*) and a very young Michele Placido, who went on to become one of Italy's most famous actors and directors, here making ample use of mannerisms. However, unlike other contemporary Mafia epics, there's no trace of the condescending, hypocritical attitude that displays mobsters as romantic old timers with a rigid code of honor: as in Fernando di Leo's *The Boss* (1973), friends becomes enemies within the blink of an eye, and the over-romanticized view of Italy on part of the immigrants becomes an excuse for prevarication over the weakest. As a whole, *The Black Hand* conveys a grim, pessimistic view of Mafia as a product of greed, violence and *omertà* that is seemingly invincible.

Note

1. Gordiano Lupi, *Cozzi Stellari—Il cinema di Lews Coates* (Rome: Profondo Rosso, 2009), p. 285.

Blood in the Streets (*Revolver*)

D: Sergio Sollima. *S* and *SC:* Arduino Maiuri, Massimo De Rita, Sergio Sollima; *DOP:* Aldo Scavarda (35mm, Eastmancolor, L.V.-Luciano Vittori); *M:* Ennio Morricone, conducted by Bruno Nicolai (ed. General Music); *Un ami* (Bevilacqua / Desage / Morricone) sung by Daniel Beretta; *E:* Sergio Montanari; *AEs:* Giuliano Mattioli, Roberto Puglisi; *ArtD, WD, SetD:* Carlo Simi; *AArtD:* Sergio Palmieri; *SDr:* Guy Maugin; *C:* Enrico Cortese; *AC:* Oddone Bernardini; *ADs:* Fabrizio Castellani, André de la Croix; *German AD:* Jobst Neuschaeffer; *MU:* Amato Garbini; *AMU:* Massimo De Rossi, Alvaro Rossi; *Hair:* Luisa Vanda Piovesan; *SO:* René Longuet, Amedeo Casati; *Boom:* Domenico Pasquadibisceglie; *Mix:* Franco Bassi; *SOE:* Renato Marinelli; *SE:* Gianni D'Andrea; *W:* Anna Maria Tucci; *TAI:* Valeria Sponsali; *SP:* Divo Cavicchioli; *G:* Onofrio Coppola; *DD:* Felicity Mason (German version: Horst Sommer); *SS:* Bona Magrini; *UP:* Enrico Lucherini. *Cast:* Oliver Reed (Vito Cipriani), Fabio Testi (Milo Ruiz), Paola Pitagora (Carlotta), Agostina Belli (Anna Cipriani), Frédéric De Pasquale (Michel Granier), Marc Mazza (Bald police inspector), René Kolldehoff (Parisian lawyer), Bernard Giraudeau, Peter Berling (Grappa), Gunnar Warner, Daniel Beretta (Al Niko), Calisto Calisti (Marshall Fantuzzi), Steffen Zacharias (Joe Lacour), Michel Bardinet, Sal Borgese (Suicidal Convict), Giuseppe Pallavicino (Granier's hitman), Giacomo De Michelis, Amato Garbini, Carla Mancini, Orazio Stracuzzi, Marco Mariani (Milo's cellmate), Jean Degrave, Franco Moraldi, Ottavio Fanfani, Gianni Bortolotto. *Uncredited:* Vittorio Pinelli (Man at the railway station), Ilona Staller (naked hooker with Grappa), Jacques Herlin, Bernd Stephan. *PROD:* Ugo Santalucia for Mega Film (Rome), Societé Nouvelle de Cinematographie (Paris), Dieter Gessler Film Produktion (Münich); *PM:* Livio Maffei, Hans Brockman; *UM:* Enzo [Vincenzo] Mazzucchi, Alain Darbon; *PAs:* Gino Soldi, Jacques Schaffer, Albino Morandini; *PSe:* Carmine Del Monaco, Georgette Darbon; *BMgr:* Angelo Saragò. *Country:* Italy / France / West Germany. Filmed at Icet–De Paolis (Milan) and on location in Milan and Paris. *Running time:* 115'; Visa no.: 63118 (09.21.1973); *Rating:* v.m.14; *Release date:* 09.27.1973; *Distribution:* Panta; *Domestic gross:* 477,374,000 lire. *Also known as: La poursuite implacable* (Paris, 10.02.1974—105') *Blood the Streets* (USA 1975—111'). *Home video:* Blue Underground (DVD, USA), Pop Flix (DVD, USA—as part of their *Crime Boss collection* 2-DVD set). OST: CD Gdm CD Club 7035.

Small-time thief Milo Ruiz escapes from prison with a friend, who's badly wounded and dies soon after. Meanwhile, in Paris, a politician is killed by a man who's riding a motorbike that belongs to pop star Al Niko. Milo is arrested and put in jail again, but the prison governor, tough ex-cop Vito Cipriani, gets involved in an elaborate scheme to get him out: Cipriani's beautiful wife Anna is kidnapped and to have her back he must arrange for Milo to escape from prison. Cipriani does so, only to grab the thief so he can make a forced exchange for his wife. The pair avoid the cops and make their way across the border to Paris, when they question Milo's pop star friend Al, who has connections to the underworld. It turns out that Milo wasn't rescued from prison to do a job, but to have him silenced because he happens to know too much: his dead friend was pinned for the politician's murder—which was actually part of a political plot—and Ruiz is the only one who knows that can't be true. Cipriani goes to the police to denounce the plot, but he finds out that the authorities have shelved the case. To have his wife back, Vito has no other choice than to kill Milo himself.

Compared to Sergio Sollima's previous crime entry *Violent City*, *Blood in the Streets* is a more explicitly political film, that owes much to the films of Jacques Deray and especially José Giovanni in its openly nihilistic portrayal of the penal system. Sollima and his co-scriptwriters Dino Maiuri and Massimo De Rita (the latter two were a recurring working team in the credits of '70s poliziotteschi, even though according to some sources Maiuri's work was practically non-existent) develop an interesting story about two lonely men who are on different sides of the law but find themselves persecuted by occult powers. This becomes apparent when prison vice-director Vito Cipriani (Oliver Reed)—who has been forced to make convict Milo Ruiz (Fabio Testi) escape abroad, or else his wife (Agostina Belli) will be killed—eventually finds out that Ruiz is only a target that has to be eliminated because he knows too much about a political murder. When he goes to a Paris police station to tell the whole story, he finds that there is already an "official" version at hand to cover the uncomfortable truth, in a plot twist worthy of a Damiani or Petri film.

The most original thing about *Blood in the Streets* is the odd alliance between the two leads, as the film turns into a road movie, following Cipriani and Ruiz's run from Milan to Paris. Although there are a number of expertly executed action scenes—especially noteworthy is the shoot-out at the Parisian crossroads—Sollima looks more interested in the psychological development of the two main characters. Therefore, their evolution is told through a dialectic scheme which recalls that of the director's best westerns, namely *The Big Gundown* (1966) and *Face to Face* (1967).

However, if those Westerns were deeply soaked with a 1968 feel, *Blood in the Streets* ends on a grim, pessimistic note. After the initial difference and heavy clashes, a strong bond eventually grows between the two protagonists: but if on one hand Ruiz becomes progressively more aware of his social conscience, on the other the upright Cipriani is forced to abdicate to his moral principles, and eventually turns into a remissive instrument of a tentacular power, in a surprisingly harsh—and not the least bit conciliatory—ending.

Blessed by Ennio Morricone's truly memorable score, which alternates lyrical moments—such as the opening titles theme, which accompanies the beautiful scene where Ruiz buries his dead companion in a river's bed, a piece that was used to similarly wonderful effect in Quentin Tarantino's *Inglourious Basterds* (2009)—and rhythmic staccatos, *Blood in the Streets* makes good use of its unlikely leading duo. Although not the most gifted of actors, Testi brings a much needed physicalness to the role of the desperate escaped convict, while Reed is much more convincing here than in his other foray into the genre that same year, Dino Risi's *Dirty Weekend*. Testi was not kind when it came to recalling his experience with the legendary Brit imbiber. "The whole crew wanted to beat him after shooting ended. Reed quarreled with everybody; he was a drunk, a lunatic. He tried to bicker with me two or three times, but I was like a rubber wall. [...] He used to call us "the white negros" because we used to work nineteen hours a day instead of eight. [...] Eventually Sergio Sollima sent me to tell him that we'd finish shooting three days earlier than scheduled, just to avoid that the crew gave him a lesson. [...] It was the last film he did in Italy, I think: everyone hated him, he was impossible to work with."[1] Testi later softened his memories: in the extra interview on the 2004 U.S. DVD of the film, even though he recalls the stormy relationship between Reed and the crew, he goes so far as saying "We liked each other from the beginning, even if Oliver liked to drink.... When he came on the set drunk, he had the tendency to became violent. I was the only one able to restrain his violence because I was always humoring him." Sollima as well is rather accommodating, saying that "Oliver was a lovely person ... until two or three in the afternoon, after the 25th or 26th bottle of wine." Italian film devotees will recognize a very young (and stunning) Ilona Staller, later known as the porn star Cicciolina, who pops up uncredited as the naked girl at Peter Berling's place.

Sollima's film was released theatrically in the U.S. with a ludicrously aggressive tagline ("Makes *Death Wish* look like wishful thinking").

Note

1. Davide Pulici and Manlio Gomarasca, "Fabio Testi," *Nocturno Cinema* #2 (December 1996), p. 34.

The Bloody Hands of the Law (*La mano spietata della legge*)

D: Mario Gariazzo. *S* and *SC:* Mario Gariazzo; *DOP:* Enrico Cortese (35mm, Eastmancolor); *M:* Stelvio Cipriani; *E:* Alberto Gallitti; *PD:* Antonio Visone; *CO:* Lorenzo Baraldi; *C:* Maurizio Lucci; *AC:* Giorgio Regis, Enzo Tosi; *AEs:* Anna Muccinelli, Stefano Testa; *AD:* Fabio Traversa; *MU:* Euclide Santoli; *AMU:* Cesare Paciotti; *Hair:* Anna Graziosi; *SO:* Manlio Magara; *Mix:* Franco Bassi; *SE:* Roberto Arcangeli, Paolo Ricci; *DubD:* Massimo Turci; *SS:* Bona Magrini. *Cast:* Philippe Leroy (Commissioner Gianni De Carmine), Silvia Monti (Linda De Carmine), Tony Norton [Antonio Monselesan] (Commissioner D'Amico), Klaus Kinski (Vito Quattroni), Cyril Cusack (Judge), Sergio Fantoni (Musante), Fausto Tozzi (Niccolò Patrovita), Guido Alberti (Professor Palmieri), Pia Giancaro (Lilly Antonelli), Lincoln Tate (Joe Gambino), Rosario Borelli (Salvatore Perrone), Marino Masé (Giuseppe di Leo), Tom Felleghy (Marshal), Valentino Macchi (Genovesi, the garagist), Lorenzo Fineschi (Patrovita's man), Denise O'Hara (Elsa Lutzer), Luciano Rossi (Quattroni's man), Lorenzo Magnolia, Stelio Candelli (Agent Venturi), Giuseppe Mattei, Giulio Baraghini (Fake Carabiniere), Cosimo Cinieri (Brigadeer), Ignazio Bevilacqua, Cesare Di Vito (Patrovita's butler), Fausto Di Bella, Lino [Pasquale] Murolo (Don Beppe), Attilio Severini (Patrovita's man), Sergio Serafini. *Uncredited:* Renzo Giovanni Pevarello (Patrovita's man), Artemio Antonini (Patrovita's man), Fabio Traversa (Young man in the garage). *PROD:* Giuseppe Rispoli for Difnei Cinematografica; *PM:* Giuseppe Rispoli; *PI:* Rosario Rapicavoli; *ADM:* Marisa Schiaffino. *Country:* Italy. *Running time:* 100'; Visa no.: 63028 (09.07.1973); *Rating:* v.m.18; *Release date:* 11.03.1973; *Distribution:* Medusa; *Domestic gross:* 372,964,000 lire. *Also known as:* *La fureur d'un flic* (Paris, 05.05.76 — 88'). *Home video:* Alfa Digital (DVD, U.S.A), Cinema Network (DVD, Italy). OST: CD Digitmovies CDDM100.

Despite being guarded in the hospital where he's been taken in after the arrest, a Mafia man named Frank Esposito is assassinated by a killer arrived from New York. Commissioner Gianni De Carmine and his superiors believe that the murder was commissioned by Esposito's bosses. All witnesses are dispatched one by one, including Giuseppe De Leo, who's been arrested, and agent Venturi, who's killed in prison. De Carmine, who is disliked by his superiors because of his violent methods, finds out that some of his colleagues are bribed by the Mafia and give away vital information. Despite being severely beaten, De Carmine doesn't give up: he exposes his colleague D'Amico and identifies other above-suspicion members of the gang, namely Niccolò Petrovita and Professor Palmieri. But De Carmine has aimed too high: he is punished by the Mafia with the assassination of his wife Linda, and is transferred to Milan.

The fact that in 1973 the crime film thread was becoming commercially profitable was proven by the release of low-budget efforts such as Mario Gariazzo's *The Bloody Hands of the Law*— one of the first examples of the transferal of filmmakers, scriptwriters and actors from the waning Italian Western to the poliziotteschi. Director Mario Gariazzo debuted behind the camera in 1962 with the metaphysical *film noir Passport for a Corpse* (*Lasciapassare per il morto*) starring Alberto Lupo as a robber who tries to pass the border into a coffin and finds himself trapped inside a mortuary; his following films — *God Will Forgive My Pistol* (*Dio perdoni la mia pistola*, 1969), *An Eye for an Eye* (*Il giorno del giudizio*, 1971) and *Holy Water Joe* (*Acquasanta Joe*, 1971) — were all Westerns shot on a shoestring budget. On the other hand, Klaus Kinski — who does not utter a single word and unexpectedly disappears at the three-quarter mark of the film — reprises his usual sadistic killer role from such films as Sergio Corbucci's *The Great Silence* (*Il grande silenzio*, 1968) and Mario Costa's *The Beast* (*La belva*, 1970).

Gariazzo's film was originally to be called *Imperativo categorico: contro il crimine con rabbia* (Categorical Imperative: Against Crime with Rage), aping the torrential, verbose titles of contemporary politically committed dramas. Yet, compared to its predecessors, there's still room for a discourse on guaranteeism, but the ambitions of political denunciation have been replaced by an individualistic regression. Commissioner De Carmine (Philippe Leroy) is a violent man, who always ends up beating the guy he is questioning, and whose psychic equilibrium is on the verge of a breakdown. "Every day people read about murders, robberies, atrocities. They're tired, nauseated, angry" he complains in one of the film's monologues. "They want to react against criminals, but they can only look at their mugs on newspapers. I'm continually face to face with violence, and I feel like I'm everybody's rage. And I think that the only way to let it out is to beat ... and I hit! Hit! Hit like a savage!" This is a dangerous guy, and someone very different from the clean-cut face of self-justice as represented by Franco Nero (*High Crime*) and Luc Merenda (*The Violent Professionals*). De Carmine's only hold on sanity in the world of violence that surrounds and intoxicates him day by day is his wife Linda (the gorgeous Silvia Monti), to whom he confesses: "I hated violence and intolerance, yet I'm getting more violent and intolerant every day!" When Linda is assassinated by the Mafia so as to make De Carmine more reasonable, the effect is explosive.

The will to make its hero someone dangerously close to a madman is what makes Gariazzo's film interesting despite its patent shortcomings. As for the scant budget he had to work with, the director explained: "*The Bloody Hands of the Law* cost just 120 million, which is a ridiculous sum for an action film. [...] On the last two days of shooting I had to shoot a crucial scene where Rosario Borelli is killed by a sniper just as he's coming out of the police station ... and we didn't even have the money to buy a bottle of water. So I got really pissed off [...]. I found a terrace near where we were shooting, personally located a gun shop, asked the owner to play the sniper and went with him to film the scene myself. Since we couldn't afford to shoot outside a real police station I asked the production designer [...] to paint a sign with "police Station" on it. We stuck it by a doorway and did the scene."[1]

The Bloody Hands of the Law is also noteworthy for the way it embraces extreme violence, with an emphasis that was unknown to its U.S. models. Gariazzo's is perhaps the first Italian crime film where the depiction of violence—"livid, realistic yet at the same time almost metaphysical"[2]—takes over the narration. The scene where Klaus Kinski tortures a man (Luciano Rossi) with a blowtorch to the genitals even caused it a v.m.18 (forbidden to minors) rating. As Gariazzo explained, "initially the scene was even more violent. When the producer saw it he had me shorten it a bit. Also the scene when Leroy questions Stelio Candelli was snipped before submitting the film to censors."

Gariazzo's film got a decent DVD release in Italy in the early 2000s, while the English dubbed U.S. Alfa Digital disc (whose cover, depicting Kinski and Henry Silva, was lifted from the Italian artwork for Jürgen Roland's *Battle of the Godfathers*) is a somewhat rougher transfer.

Notes

1. Manlio Gomarasca and Davide Pulici. "A colloquio con Mario Gariazzo," interview published in the booklet of the Italian VHS release (Shendene and Moizzi).
2. *Ibid.*

The Boss, a.k.a. *Wipeout! (Il boss)*

D: Fernando di Leo. *S:* based on the novel *Il mafioso* by Peter McCurtin; *SC:* Fernando di Leo; *M:* Luis Enriquez Bacalov (ed. Nazionalmusic); *DOP:* Franco Villa (35mm, Eastmancolor, Telecolor); *E:* Amedeo Giomini; *PD:* Francesco Cuppini; *CO:* Elisabetta Lo Cascio; *C:* Claudio Morabito; *AC:* Enrico Biribicchi; *AE:* Ornella Chistolini; *APD:* Cristiano Tessari; *AD:* Franco Lo Cascio; *MU:* Antonio Mura; *W:* Anna Cirilli; *SO:* Alberto Salvatori; *SOE:* Fernando Caso; *SE:* Angelo Patrizi; *CON:* Silvia Petroni. *Cast:* Henry Silva (Nick Lanzetta), Richard Conte (Don Carrasco), Vittorio Caprioli (Chief of Police), Gianni Garko (Commissioner Torri), Pier Paolo Capponi (Cocchi), Antonia Santili (Rina D'Aniello), Corrado Gaipa (Rizzo, the lawyer), Marino Masé (Pignataro), Howard Ross [Renato Rossini] (Melende), Claudio Nicastro (Don Giuseppe D'Aniello), Gianni Musy (Carlo Attardi), Mario Pisu (Gabrielli), Pietro Ceccarelli (Maione), Andrea Aureli (Don Antonino Attardi), Giulio Baraghini (Carrasco's henchman), Salvatore Billa (Sacco, theater guard), Sergio Ammirata (Gangster), Andrea Scotti (Gangster), Giorgio Dolfin (policeman), Luigi Antonio Guerra. *Uncredited:* Artemio Antonini (Lanzetta's henchman), Bruno Bertocci (Male nurse), Empedocle Buzzanca (Marshall), Omero Capanna (First murder victim), Fernando Cerulli (Projectionist), Fernando di Leo (Gangster with sunglasses), Fulvio Mingozzi (policeman), Pietro Torrisi (Hitman), Bruno Ukmar (Attardi's man in cinema), Franco Ukmar (Attardi's man in cinema). *PROD:* Armando Novelli for Cineproduzioni Daunia 70; *GO:* Armando Novelli; *PM:* Lanfranco [Pietro] Ceccarelli; *PSe:* Vincenzo Salviani. *Country:* Italy. Filmed on location in Sicily. *Running time:* 111'; Visa no.: 61807 (01.30.1973); *Rating:* v.m.18; *Release date:* 02.01.1973; *Distribution:* Alpherat; *Domestic gross:* 573,172,000 lire. *Also known as:* *Le Boss* (Paris, 05.22.1974—85'); *Der Teufel führt Regie* (West Germany, 12.06.1974). *Home video:* Raro (DVD, Italy; DVD—Blu-Ray, USA)

Palermo. Nick Lanzetta, Mafia boss Carrasco's favorite hitman, kills rival boss Antonino Attardi and some of his men in a private screening room as they're watching a porn movie. Attardi's right-hand man Cocchi reorganizes the gang and kidnaps Daniela D'Aniello, the nymphomaniac and drug-addicted daughter of Carrasco's counselor, asking for a ransom of 500 million lire. On Carrasco's orders, Lanzetta kills Daniela's father and uncle, then breaks into Cocchi's hideout and releases the girl. After a bloody raid in one of D'Aniello's construction sites, Cocchi is killed by Commissioner Torri, who's on Carrasco's payroll. Lanzetta kills Cocchi, and Daniela is fatally wounded during the ensuing shootout. Despite the bloody gang war that's going on, the authorities do not intervene. Eventually, a truce is declared, with the approval of politicians who are linked to the Mafia. Carrasco attempts to have the now inconvenient Lanzetta dispatched, but the hitman survives to an uncertain destiny.

After his diptych on the Milanese underworld—*Caliber 9* and *The Italian Connection*—Fernando di Leo turned his gaze at the Sicilian Mafia. Although *The Boss* was loosely based on a 1970 novel by Peter McCurtin, published in Italy the following year,[1] di Leo basically reinvented the whole story and set it in a nocturnal, indefinite, depopulated Palermo. As Italian critic Davide Pulici wrote: "*The Boss* [...] relies on a denial of the city: since the very beginning Palermo is drowned in darkness, in indifferentiated blacks, in the absence of color. The rare scenes in daylight (not more than three or four in the whole film) are bathed by an ash-like light, under a low sky which looks like iron."[2]

The bloody war between the rival gangs led by Carrasco (Richard Conte) and the Calabrese Cocchi (Pier Paolo Capponi) is quite different from those seen in other Mafia films of the period. Di Leo's vision of the "honored family" is corrosive and demystifying, as the complicated web of pacts of honor and alliances on which the "family" leans is first postulated, then denied and even ridiculed by the incessant reversals of fronts: everybody betrays everybody else, in a series of double and triple crosses that leave no room for dignity and honor.

In a sense, *The Boss* is a sort of deformed, perverse twin to Duccio Tessari's *Big Guns*: in the latter, a moral point of view was still present in the character of Tony Arzenta (Alain Delon), the only one to stay faithful to a code of ethics in a world where traditional values—represented by Arzenta's old father (Corrado Gaipa), who lives in an isolated house in the Sicilian countryside—are being eradicated one by one, while di Leo's film follows the moves of Lanzetta (Henry Silva), a ruthless and robotic executioner of Carrasco's orders. Whereas Tessari's film aimed at tragedy, di Leo's focuses on derision. Richard Conte's final act of betrayal in *Big Guns*— having Tony killed in front of the church where the boss' daughter's wedding has just been celebrated — is tragic and inevitable; in *The Boss*, when Conte proclaims "I only have one word" before the umpteenth about-turn, sarcasm is palpable.

The Boss doesn't have a real climax: the showdown between Lanzetta and Cocchi occurs over a quarter of hour before the end, and is filmed in a sudden, hasty manner instead of the operatic way the audience is expecting. Then more killings follow and the film ends with the word "continues." There's no catharsis, the Mafia is a monotonous business: kill and be killed. Nothing more.

In the Mafia universe as depicted in *The Boss*—a Sicily where, as a character sarcastically quips, "the only authentic thing is orange juice"— there is no room for feelings. As Carrasco objects to the desperate D'Aniello, after the latter's daughter Rina (Antonia Santilli) has been kidnapped by the rivals: "Nothing is yours, Don Giuseppe; not even your daughter. Not when she endangers the "family" and the organization." "Family" comes first. Lanzetta doesn't have the slightest hesitation when it comes to killing D'Aniello, who had raised him like a father ("You made me what I am today" Lanzetta acknowledges). Di Leo films the scene in an abrupt manner, taking the audience off-guard: not to put emphasis on surprise, but rather to show the character's emotional void.

The violence is conspicuous and raw, starting from the opening scene in which Silva infiltrates the projection booth of a private screening room where rival gangsters are watching a porn movie, and slaughters them with a grenade-launcher. However, once again as in his previous gangster films, it's di Leo's use of language to convey the ruthlessness and squalor of the Mafia *milieu* that stands out: orders of death are hidden behind vague and allusive formulas, where corpses become "complications" or "difficulties," and what is left unsaid is more important than what is actually being pronounced, in a secret code of sorts that's known only to affiliates — who, di Leo insists, are obtuse, illiterate, even childish.

Among such brutes and savages, the character of Rina is somewhat explosive, and far from clichéd. As in his erotic films (and later in *Loaded Guns* as well as the feminist apologue *To Be Twenty*), Di Leo develops an uninhibited female character, a free girl who enjoys sex and drugs and looks like an alien in such a primitive, repressed microcosm. In a memorable scene, Rita stands over a table, wearing only a green bra and underpants, and is questioned and insulted by her kidnappers. Much to their chagrin, though, the young girl demonstrates to be far from the modest virgin they thought her to be: she's not afraid of them, and rebukes their insolence by asking for drugs and sex.

Free from the ethical tethers of committed political cinema, di Leo pulls out all the stops in portraying the various institutions, in "an open vilification which is most useful in its commercial insolence, much more than TV inquiries and 'serious' reports."[3] So in *The Boss* we have Antimafia Commission members who pretend not to see how mobsters do whatever they want, a Commissioner (Gianni Garko) who's bribed by the clan and who talks and thinks like a *picciotto*, and a Chief of Police (the great Vittorio Caprioli) who vents his anger for such corruption and violence through sarcasm ("We're all being Vietnamized!").

Fernando di Leo, center, directs Gianni Garko, left, and Henry Silva, right, in *The Boss* (1973).

If institutions are ridiculous, di Leo has no qualms about pointing out the connivance between Mafia bosses and political parties: the former control and channel votes, providing MPs to the nation's major party, Democrazia Cristiana. Just as Damiano Damiani had done in *The Day of the Owl*, di Leo made an explicit reference to this connection. "The place where the final meeting takes place, when Marino Masé pays visit to Corrado Gaipa, was the exterior of Democrazia Cristiana's official building in Palermo: I had Masé's car stop right in front of it!"[4] he recalled. Eventually, di Leo even benefited from free advertising when the then Minister of Relations with Parliament Giovanni Gioia of Democrazia Cristiana sued him for slander because his name was mentioned in one scene together with Mafia boss Tommaso Buscetta and controversial politician Salvo Lima, who was killed by the Mafia in 1992. Gioia later withdrew the lawsuit. "I mentioned Lima, in 1972–73, while Andreotti at the end of the '90s said he didn't even know Lima was connected to the Mafia; and yet, Lima's name was in the acts of the Antimafia report, when I mentioned it," di Leo explained. "In Palermo the film became quite a sensation [...]. Whereas in the rest of Italy it didn't, because people didn't know about the facts."[5]

Once the gang war has ended, the new boss has the task of "re-establishing order" in the political alliance. "Order" is the film's keyword. Don Carrasco is a "man of order," because he controls the votes of seven municipalities, and order is the subject of an illuminating dialogue between the corrupt Torri and the Chief of Police ("It's just that there's no discipline, sir — the whole region could explode. We need the old order back, even if it's Mafia order!"). This order is handy to Democrazia Cristiana and the Church alike: the Cardinal who accommodates Carrasco and coaxes him is a reference to the then Archbishop of Palermo, Cardinal Ruffini, who stated that Communists maliciously associated the Mafia with Democrazia Cristiana and declared that the Mafia was just "common delinquency" instead of a criminal association whose power spread all across the region — up to Rome itself.

Notes

1. Peter McCurtin, *Il mafioso*, "I Gialli Longanesi" no. 21(Milan: Longanesi., October 6, 1971). The novel takes place in New York and bears a few basic differences with the film. For instance, at the end of McCurtin's novel Lanzetta becomes the new boss, while Di Leo's ending is more ambiguous and uncertain. As for the characters, the black Coakley becomes the Calabrese Cocchi.
2. Davide Pulici, *Il boss*, in Aa. Vv., "Calibro 9 — Il cinema di Fernando di Leo," *Nocturno Dossier* #14 (September 2003), p. 30.
3. Buttafava, "Procedure sveltite," p. 106.
4. Davide Pulici, *Fernando di Leo* (Milan: Nocturno libri, 2001), p. 322.
5. Davide Pulici, *Secondo movimento: il tempo del nero*, in *Nocturno Dossier* #14, p. 23.

Counselor at Crime (*Il Consigliori*)

D: Alberto De Martino. *S* and *SC:* Adriano Bolzoni, Vincenzo Flamini, Leonardo Martín, Alberto De Martino; *DOP:* Aristide Massaccesi (35mm, Techniscope — Eastmancolor, Telecolor); *M:* Riz Ortolani, conducted by the author (ed. Prima); *Solo harmonica:* Franco De Gemini; *E:* Otello Colangeli; *PD:* Emilio Ruiz Del Rio; *ArtD:* Antonio Visone; *CO:* Carlo Leva; *C:* Guglielmo Vincioni; *AC:* Adolfo Troiani; *AE:* Fernanda Materni; *AD:* Giuseppe Pollini; *MU:* Franco Di Girolamo; *AMU:* Maurizio Trani; *SO:* Antonio Cardenas; *SOE:* Edgardo Papucci; *SE:* Joe Lombardi, G. Stacchini; *STC:* Sergio Mioni; *SS:* Marion Mertes. *Cast:* Tomas Milian (Thomas Accardo), Martin Balsam (Don Antonio Macaluso), Francisco Rabal (Vincent Garofalo), Dagmar Lassander (Laura Murchison), Carlo Tamberlani (Don Michele Villabate), Eduardo Fajardo (Don Calogero Vezza), Manuel Zarzo (Vezza's sidekick), John Anderson (Don Vito Albanese), Giovanni [Nello] Pazzafini (Garofalo's man in Sicily), Franco Angrisano (Dorillo), Giovanni Carbone, Fortunato Arena (Garofalo's man in Sicily), Carla Mancini, Lorenzo Piani, Carlo Gaddi (Carlo, Garofalo's driver in Sicily). *Uncredited:* Omero Capanna (Garofalo's man), Perla Cristal (Dorothy), Lina Franchi (Waitress), Ray C. Goman (Sgt. Dieterle), Bill Hicks (Killer), Debbie Letteau (Mobster's girlfriend), Sacheen Littlefeather [Marie Louise Cruz] (Maggie), Giovanni Pallavicino (Gaspare), Sergio Mioni (Garofalo's man), Renzo Pevarello (Killer in warehouse), Bárbara Rey, Luis Rico, George Rigaud (Priest), Les Waggoner. *PROD:* Edmondo Amati for Capitolina Produzioni Cinematografiche (Rome), Star Film S/A (Madrid); *GM:* Maurizio Amati; *PM:* Manuel Pérez; *PSu:* Fabrizio De Angelis; *PSe:* Guglielmo Smeraldi. *Country:* Italy / Spain. Filmed at Cinecittà (Rome), Estudios Cinematograficos (Madrid) and on location in San Francisco, Albuquerque, Palermo and Sicily. *Running time:* 100'; Visa no.: 62993 (08.25.1973); *Rating:* v.m.14; *Release date:* 08.30.1973; *Distribution:* Fida Cinematografica; *Domestic gross:* 685,486,000 lire. *Also known as: El consejero* (Madrid, 02.11.1974)—*Le conseiller* (Paris, 08.14.1974 —103')—*Im Dutzend zur Hölle* (West Germany, 07.12.1974 — 101'). *Home video:* Legocart (DVD, Italy). OST: CD Chris' Soundtrack Corner CSC009.

San Francisco. Mafia boss Don Antonio Macaluso puts a contract on the head of Torrese, a gang member who's talking too much. When Torrese is arrested, it's up to Macaluso's right hand Garofalo to dispatch him. Torrese is killed in jail by a corrupt cop but Macaluso is unsatisfied. Meanwhile, Don Antonio's godson, the young lawyer Thomas Accardo, is released from prison after a two-year sentence. Thomas, who's in love with Laura, wants to retire from the "family" and lead a honest life — something that's against the rules of the underworld. Jealous of Don Antonio's affection for Thomas, Garofalo starts a war against his own boss. Don Antonio escapes death while his lieutenants are killed. After Garofalo has attempted to kill him and Laura, Thomas returns to San Francisco to help Macaluso and fight back Garofalo. With the help of Antonio's elderly associate Don Michele Villabate, Macaluso and Accardo survive an ambush, then move to Sicily to seek help from local boss Don Calogero Vezza. Garofalo pursues them, but his men are exterminated by Macaluso's and Vezza's men. Thomas kills Garofalo but is mortally wounded in the shootout.

Compared to the director's previous *Crime Boss*, Alberto De Martino's *Counselor at Crime* is more patently in the vein of Coppola's *The Godfather*. Thanks to the U.S. setting (Albuquerque, passing for San Francisco), a good cast and well-made action sequences, *Counselor at Crime* often looks like a solid American B-movie. Tomas Milian (in one of his last shaven-face performances before beard and wigs would become an integral part of his look) is good as always in a role which was initially intended for Antonio Sabàto (De Martino and Milian would work again together in the second entry of the comedy western series featuring Milian as Charlie Chaplin look-alike Provvidenza, *Here We Go Again, Eh Providence?*, 1973). Besides the acting, Aristide Massaccesi's cinematography is especially noteworthy: "Aristide didn't talk nonsense, he knew how to do his job, and he was quick. It took him a couple of seconds to understand how to light a scene. And whenever he was in trouble with the lighting, he would take the camera in his own hands," as De Martino explained. "I'll always remember a scene in *Counselor at Crime*, the one before the reunion in the bar. I told Aristide: "Damn, I'd need a dolly on this one!," and he replied: "Don't worry, I'll do it...." "How are you gonna do that? It's a long scene!" "Just don't worry..." and he did it — and on the screen it looked just like a dolly."[1]

Yet *Counselor at Crime*'s major assets cannot overcome its overall blandness. De Martino admittedly had a few problems during the scriptwriting process. "I wrote the script with my collaborators, then we hired Leonardo Martín to write the other part. We gave the script to [producer Edmondo] Amati, who said it was fine, but he wanted to have the dialogue revised by a friend of his. This friend was Michael Gazzo, the author of the stage play *A Hatful of Rain*. [...] A month later Gazzo sent me the script, and in the first scene there was Martin Balsam in a car, talking to a coat hanger! At first I thought I didn't understand, so I called my American assistant to translate it for me ... and yes, he was really talking to a coat hanger! It turned out Gazzo had completely rewritten the script [...]. In the end we fired him and that was that. However, he got a lot of money, I think Amati paid him 5,000 dollars, so every now and then Edmondo asked me 'Couldn't we just use a line at least?' (laughs)."[2]

Perhaps only the Sicilian scenes (set in the town of Polizzi Generosa, where a notorious Mafia feud took place; as the director says, "I wanted it to look like a fortress") and the final showdown during a religious procession in Palermo stand out. The closing scene in the car is also impressive, as Milian pretends to be just fine while he's dying from a gunshot-wound in the stomach, and Balsam doesn't even notice it as he's too busy planning his comeback as San Francisco's main boss.

On the other hand, the story inevitably drags whenever Milian's love interest Dagmar Lassander, looking quite overweight, is on screen. "I should have fired Dagmar Lassander!" De Martino complained. "I cast her in Rome a couple of months before shooting started. She'd just had a baby and I told her she had to lose weight. She said "Of course, one month's a long time!" Then Dagmar came to Albuquerque and she hadn't lost an ounce. If we had been in Rome, I would have fired her, but in Albuquerque I just couldn't find a replacement."[3]

Notes

1. Gomarasca, *Il cinema è quello che ci fa*, p. 14.
2. *Ibid.*
3. *Ibid.*, p. 11. Also worthy of note is the cameo of Native American activist Sacheen Littlefeather, who presented a speech on behalf of Marlon Brando at the 1973 Academy Awards ceremony, boycotted by the actor, in protest of the treatment of Native Americans by the film industry. Brando had won an Oscar for his performance in Coppola's *The Godfather*.

Dagli archivi della polizia criminale (From the Archives of the Criminal police)

D: Paolo Lombardo. *S* and *SC:* Paolo Lombardo; *DOP:* Mario Mancini (35mm, Telecolor); *M:* Elvio Monti (ed. Astra); *Mister Powder Man* sung by Luigi Ottavo; *E:* Mario Gargiulo; *PD:* Dino Bartolomei; *C:* Ettore Corsi; *AD:* Stefano Guglielmetti; *MU:* Gennaro Visconti; *W:* Stella Battista; *SS:* Laura Toscano. *Cast:* Edmund Purdom (Teddy Webbs), Cleofe Del Cile (Margot), Alan Steel [Sergio Ciani] (Larry Brenton), Miriam Alex (Jane Colman), Enzo Fiermonte (Inspector Vernon), Andrea Montchal (Larsen), Giulio Donnini (Ibrahim), Ettore Ribotta (Bashir), Valeria Mongardini (Amina), Veronica Sava (Miss Denis / Lilian), Lino [Pasquale] Murolo (Maltese Joe), Gordon Mitchell (Peter Wilcox), Ignazio Bevilacqua (Maltese's henchman), Adriano Fraticelli (Astruan), Antonio Casale (Beduin), Emilio Messina, Roberto Messina, Sergio Testori, Raf Baldassarre (Astruan's henchman), Zula (Dancer). *PROD:* Canadian Films; *PM:* Silvano Marabotti; *PSu:* Domenico Battista. *Country:* Italy. *Running time:* 85'; Visa no.: 61864 (02.08.1973); *Rating:* v.m.14; *Release date:* 12.18.1973; *Distribution:* Alexia Cinematografica; *Domestic gross:* unknown. *Home video:* Alan Young (DVD, Italy)

London. Larsen, a corrupt cop, steals a microfilm from the Interpol secret archives. The microfilm contains the documentation of Cosa Nostra's drug ring, headed by the Sicilian "Maltese Joe." Larsen escapes to Tunis, where he plans to sell the film to Joe's rival Astruan, but he's pursued by Joe and his men. However, secret agents Teddy Webbs and Larry Brenton are on his trail. Larsen, who has found refuge at prostitute Amina's home, gives Teddy the film and is ready to surrender, but his car is blown up by Joe. Meanwhile, Teddy and his lover Jane are captured by Astruan's men. The Maltese's gang assaults Astruan's villa, eliminates his accomplices and gets hold of the microfilm. In the end, though, it turns out Teddy has kept the real microfilm himself.

One of the most obscure crime films of the decade, and perhaps the very worst, Paolo Lombardo's *Dagli archivi della polizia criminale* is an amazing example of the unfathomable ways of Z-grade Italian cinema. The film itself is actually a patchwork job *à la* Ed Wood, haphazardly put together in order to exploit the renewing interest in the crime genre. Lombardo shot new scenes featuring Purdom, Enzo Fiermonte as an Interpol inspector and Lino Murolo as Maltese Joe and spliced them together with footage from some unfinished spy flick at least five years older, starring ex–sword-and-sandal stars Alan Steel and Gordon Mitchell (who's dispatched after a couple of scenes), as well as the climactic fight scenes (shot outside Rome's Villa Miani). The results are appalling: the two different sets of actors never meet, the photography doesn't match, the sets are almost non-existent, ditto continuity, and the film features perhaps the worst day-for-night scenes ever put on the screen—on a par, perhaps, with those in Lombardo's other film as a director, the abysmal Gothic *Lucifera: Demonlover* (*L'amante del demonio*, 1972). Given that the latter was actually directed for the most part by actor Robert Woods, due to Lombardo's ill health, one wonders what did actually happen on the set of *Dagli archivi della polizia criminale*, as it looks like the cast members were left to their own devices. To please every audience, a nude dance scene by African dancer Zula is included, while a "comic" scene has Montchal in drag, chased by a drunken U.S. sailor.

Bloopers abound: supposedly English cars have wheels on the left; Roman exteriors are unconvincingly passed for British or Tunisian; Singer Valeria Mongardini tries to pass as Tunisian, but wears brown-skin makeup only on her face; Steel's shirt changes from scene to scene; Fiermonte's office features a London map which actually depicts Rome. The overall amateurishness is best summed up by the opening credits, where Purdom is misspelled "Purdon."

Dirty Weekend (*Mordi e fuggi*)

D: Dino Risi. *S* and *SC:* Ruggero Maccari, Dino Risi, Bernardino Zapponi; *DOP:* Luciano Tovoli (35mm, Eastmancolor, Boschi); *M:* Carlo Rustichelli, conducted by Gianfranco Plenizio; *E:* Alberto Gallitti; *PD:* Luciano Ricceri; *APD:* Emanuele Taglietti; *CO:* Danda Ortona; *C:* Romano Albani; *AC:* Franco Frazzi, Michele Picciaredda; *AE:* Anna Maria Roca; *AD:* Renato Rizzuto; *MU:* Otello Sisi; *AMU:* Alfredo Marazzi; *Hair:* Giancarlo De Leonardis; *SO:* Primiano Muratori; *Boom:* Maurizio Merli; *SM:* Luciano Ancillai; *SOE:* Luciano Marinelli; *SS:* Marisa Agostini. *Cast:* Marcello Mastroianni (Giulio Borsi), Oliver Reed (Fabrizio Lehner), Carole André (Daniela Marcellini "Danda"), Nicoletta Machiavelli (Silvia), Lionel Stander (General Attilio Bernasconi), Bruno Cirino (Raoul Melis), Marcello Mandò (Commissioner Spallone), Gianni Agus (Sergio), Renzo Marignano (Franco), Gianfranco Barra (Barra, first policeman), Jacques Herlin (TV newsreader), Giancarlo Fusco (TV executive), Vincenzo Loglisci (Second policeman), Claudio Nicastro (Politician), Aldo Rendine (Nicotera), Gino Rocchetti (policeman), Jean Rougeul (police official), Luigi Zerbinati (Giulio's father-in-law), Barbara Pilavin (Norma), Regina Bissio (Elsa), Filippo De Gara (Waiter), Antonino Faà Di Bruno (Conte Attilio Marlotti), Giulio Baraghini (First sniper), Ettore Venturini (Second sniper), Liz Alvorsen (Silvana), Firmino Palmieri (First camera team member), Alvaro Vitali (Second camera team member), Luca Bonicalzi (Third camera team member), Giuseppe Bruno Bossio (Fourth camera team member), Enzo Liberti (Barbieri, TV anchorman), Lino Murolo (Armando Colizzi), Piero Mazzinghi (Minister), Peter Berling (German tourist), Valerio Ruggeri (Editor in chief), Alexa Paizi (Norma's mother), Gianfranco Cardinali (Simonini), Franca Scagnetti (Tourist at Autogrill). *PROD:* Carlo Ponti for Compagnia Cinematografica Champion (Rome), Les Films Concordia (Paris); *EP:* Alessandro Von Normann; *PM:* Ennio Onorati; *ADM:* Maurizio Anticoli. *Country:* Italy / France. *Running time:* 113'; Visa no.: 61988 (03.01.1973); *Rating:* not rated; *Release date:* 03.08.1973; *Distribution:* Cineriz; *Domestic gross:* 303,187,000 lire. *Also known as: Rapt à l'italienne* (Paris, 10.02.1974—100'), *Ein Scheiss-Wochenende* (West Germany, 05.10.1974—98'). *Home video:* None.

Three anarchists, Fabrizio, Raoul and Silvia, rob a bank and kill an agent in the process. During their escape they take two hostages: pharmaceutical industrial Giulio Borsi and his young lover Daniela, who were away on a clandestine weekend together. The robbers' car is followed not only by the police, but also by the media, as the escape has become a nationally broadcast event. Fabrizio asks for 100 million lire as ransom and a plane to leave Italy for good, but Giulio's family is not willing to pay. The robbers leave the police behind and take refuge in an old villa which belongs to an elderly fascist general and his sister. Daniela, disgusted by Giulio's pusillanimity, goes to bed with Fabrizio. Eventually the police inform the robbers that the money has been assembled and a plane is ready to take off. Fabrizio and his accomplices set Daniela free and reach a small Tuscan airport with Giulio. There they fall victims to an ambush by the law enforcement and die in the shoot-out, but Giulio is mortally wounded as well by the ruthless police force.

Eleven years after his masterpiece *The Easy Life* (*Il sorpasso*, 1962) Dino Risi once again chose the form of the road movie plot to portray contemporary Italy in a blend of sarcastic comedy and harsh drama. If the earlier film was a precise depiction of the so-called economic Boom, *Dirty Weekend* deals with terrorism and violence, as seen through the perspective of bourgeois industrialist Giulio Borsi (Marcello Mastroianni), who leaves for a clandestine weekend of sex and fish-eating with his young lover (Carole André) only to be taken hostage by a trio of anarchists (led by Oliver Reed) who just robbed a bank to finance their armed struggle.

While not being a crime film in the strictest sense, *Dirty Weekend* depicts with Risi's typical black humor (aided by the contribution of his co-scripters Ruggero Maccari and especially Bernardino Zapponi, who collaborated with Fellini and would later co-write Dario Argento's best giallo *Deep Red*) Italy's violent turmoils of the time. The nightmare of urban violence becomes a recurring theme in everyday small talk, and Mastroianni's character is a perfect incarnation of bourgeois indifference towards social issues. "Today we had our daily dose of robbery again. Even if they catch them what do you think would happen, they always get away with it" he complains. "I'd rather put them to the wall and shoot, as they do in certain countries." Ironically, Borsi himself will later fall victim to the indiscriminate use of violence on behalf of the police that he earlier wished for, in one of Risi's typical bleak endings.

The story, which follows the robbers' attempt at escape by car from Rome to Tuscany, bears a passing resemblance to Mario Bava's later *Rabid Dogs* (1974), yet the director is obviously more interested in social notations and satire than in suspense. The obligatory car chase, for instance, is played for laughs, with almost slapstick results. What's more, the depiction of the media's assault—with the robbers' car chased by a convoy of TV cameramen and reporters for coverage of what has become a media event—pointedly refers to Billy Wilder's *Ace in the Hole* (1951), while the invasion of privacy on behalf of Television—see the scene where Reed's estranged wife and mother are interviewed—predates Sidney Lumet's *Dog Day Afternoon* (1975). Risi's favorite themes are also evident in the film's protagonist. Mastroianni gives a right-on-target performance as one of the filmmaker's typically puerile, sex-addicted, servile and pusillanimous middle-aged antiheroes, who desperately try to appear younger than they are (see Mastroianni's ridiculous pin-striped suit) yet simply can't cope with a world that's changing too fast for them to understand it. On the other hand, *Dirty Weekend*'s main flaw is represented by the portrayal of the three anarchists: Reed gives a physically imposing performance, but doesn't look convincing as the Marxist professor-turned-bank robber, while his two accomplices are unconvincingly sketched ciphers.

Especially noteworthy, however, is the way Risi depicts law enforcement. The character of Commissioner Spallone (Marcello Mandò) is patently modeled on the controversial real-life Calabresi, from the physical resemblance to the way he dresses (a jacket and a turtleneck sweater, which would soon become a sort of uniform for poliziotteschi heroes). In the end, Risi has Spallone handle a machine gun and dispatch the anarchists in cold blood just as they are about to take off on a plane. It's a gesture that iconically puts him on a par with analogous characters in crime flicks. Yet there's no doubt Spallone is a bad guy, the product (and servant) of a thinly disguised fascist regime which doesn't mind sacrificing innocent lives to restore order: "Two casualties are nothing when the alternative is chaos" a politician comments. With all its imperfections (a somewhat slapdash *mise en scène*, a tendency towards caricature) *Dirty Weekend* is as significant a depiction of an era as are more "serious" films as Francesco Rosi's *Illustrious Corpses*. And just as crime movies were invading the screens, depicting heroic policemen, Risi had a character deliver a cynical yet profoundly significant epitaph to the genre: "Italians hate living commissioners, not dead ones."

Flatfoot (*Piedone lo sbirro*)

D: Steno [Stefano Vanzina]. *S:* Luciano Vincenzoni, Nicola Badalucco; *SC:* Lucio de Caro; *DOP:* Silvano Ippoliti (35mm, Eastmancolor, Technospes); *M:* Guido and Maurizio De Angelis (ed. Bixio—Sam); *E:* Daniele Alabiso; *PD:* Carlo Leva; *APD:* Nicola Losito; *CO:* Luciano Sagoni; *C:* Enrico Sasso; *AC:* Enrico Doria, Maurizio Santi; *AEs:* Rita Triunveri, Brigida Mastrolillo; *AD:* Guglielmo Giarda; Makeups: Luciano Giustini, Marcello Meniconi; *Hair:* Fausto De Lisio; *SO:* Angelo Amatulli; *SOE:* Luciano Marinelli; *Mix:* Danilo Moroni; *SE:* Eros Bacciucchi; *SP:* Giorgio Garibaldi Schwarze; *STCs:* Rodolfo Valadier [Biagio Gambini], Sergio Mioni; *MA:* Giorgio Ubaldi; *SS:* Adolfo Dragone. *Cast:* Bud Spencer [Carlo Pedersoli] (Commissioner "Flatfoot" Rizzo), Adalberto Maria Merli (Commissioner Tabassi), Raymond Pellegrin (Lawyer De Ribbis), Angelo Infanti (Ferdinando Scarano, "O Barone"), Juliette Mayniel (Maria), Mario Pilar (Antonio Percuoco "Manomozza"), Enzo Cannavale (Deputy Inspector Capuano), Jho Jenkins (Jho, American sailor), Enzo Maggio (Gennarino), Salvatore Morra, Franco Angrisano (Commissioner), Carla Mancini (Restaurant guest), Alessandro Perrella, Luciano Tacconi, Dominic Barto (Tom Ferramenti), Nino Vingelli (Old man of camorra), Vittorio Duse (police Chief with U.S. Officer), Alfonso Cavotti (Chief concierge). *Uncredited:* Artemio Antonini, Giancarlo Bastianoni (Manomozza's thug), Omero Capanna (Scarano's thug), Nestore Cavaricci (Mafioso), Giovanni Cianfriglia (Ship thug), Dante Cleri (Disco owner), Roberto Dell'Acqua (Jho's slim pal), Augusto Funari, Ulla Johanssen (Blonde woman in bar), Giulio Maculani, Emilio Messina, Roberto Messina, Franco Moruzzi (Getaway driver), Nello Pazzafini, Osiride Pevarello (Bearded thug), Mimmo Poli, Aldo Rendine (School caretaker), Claudio Ruffini (Jho's fat pal), Sergio Smacchi, Pietro Torrisi (Thug), Franco Ukmar (Manomozza's thug), Marcello Verziera (Pusher — Ship thug). *PROD:* Sergio Bonotti for Mondial Te.Fi. (Rome), C.A.P.A.C. (Paris); *PMs:* Bruno Altissimi, Alfredo Melidoni; *PIs:* Vittorio Biferale, Francesco Manco. *Country:* Italy / France. Filmed at Elios Film, Incir — De Paolis (Rome) and on location in Naples. *Running time:* 110'; Visa no.: 63402 (10.24.1973); *Rating:* not rated; *Release date:* 10.25.1973; *Distribution:* Titanus; *Domestic gross:* 2,972,527,000 lire. *Also known as: Un flic hors-la-loi* (Paris, 07.23.1975 — 90') — *Sie nannten ihn Plattfuss* (West Germany, 02.14.1974 — 107'). *Home video:* Paradiso (DVD, Holland, as part of the "Bud Spencer Collection").

Naples. Commissioner Rizzo, nicknamed "Flatfoot," is feared and respected because of his good temper and his tendency to prevent crime instead of punish it. What's more, Rizzo doesn't carry a gun, but uses only his bare hands to fight criminals. The arrival of a new superior, Tabassi, who disapproves of Rizzo's unorthodox approach, and the rising of a gang of Marseilles drug traffickers cause "Flatfoot" lots of trouble. After using his methods on a suspect, Rizzo is suspended by Tabassi. He then seeks the help of the Neapolitan underworld and eventually destroys the drug ring.

Since they were so closely tangled with everyday news, the so-called poliziotteschi immediately found a niche in the collective imagination, yet they were not immune from a continuous, endemic mutation. With almost 3 billions lire grossed at the box office, Steno's *Flatfoot* was the first and most commercially successful attempt at mixing the crime genre with comedy. It's emblematic, in a way, that the same filmmaker who is often indicated as the father of poliziotteschi also directed the initiator of such a crossover, which somehow diluted the genre's harsh impact on viewers and, while protracting its commercial effectiveness, planted the seed for its self-destruction.

As Vanzina himself pointed out, though, "For better or worse, *Flatfoot* was a crime flick, and I think that hadn't I directed *Execution Squad*, producers wouldn't have allowed me to do it." The script was once again by Vanzina and Lucio De Caro, "and it had an ideology as well, only this time it was more action-oriented."[1] Steno and De Caro have fun in recounting all the newborn genre's stereotypes — the tough cop with unorthodox methods, the conflict with his superiors, the lack of trust in the law — only to overturn them. "The film's main idea was a cop who wouldn't use his gun, and who was opposed by his colleagues because of that!"[2] As played by *They Call Me Trinity*'s Bud Spencer, Commissioner Rizzo would rather use his fists: in the opening sequence he faces a stoned sailor who's shooting in the crowd from the top of a building, and proclaims: "There ain't no trouble you can't solve with your hands." However, despite the leading star's reassuring, towering presence, the film's sorties into slapstick — such as the choreographed fistfight on the ship with frozen fish used as weapons — never take over the plot, which focuses on the juxtaposition between "men of honor" and the "cardboard *guappi*" — that is, the old Camorra, which is still obedient to rigid moral codes, at least in the authors' vision, and the new underworld as represented by Marseilles "invaders," who want to sell drugs in Naples. It's as schematic, puerile and mystifying a social discourse as it gets, yet it will be a recurring trait in the so-called sceneggiata, with which *Flatfoot* shares the picturesque Neapolitan setting.

At the time of its release, though, some critics favorably compared *Flatfoot* to a classic crime drama such as Francesco Rosi's *La sfida* (1958), pointing out that Bud Spencer's presence "actually mortifies the film's ambitions. Never like in this case is a film so conditioned by its leading actor."[3] This was perhaps taking *Flatfoot* too seriously — unlike Steno's subsequent *policewoman* (*La poliziotta*, 1974), where the social satire hid a much more effective and pointed socio-political discourse — and as the film's three follow-ups showed, the *Flatfoot* saga would soon focus on out-and-out comedy, in a mere variation of Spencer's Westerns and adventure flicks co-starring Terence Hill. In *Flatfoot in Hong Kong* (1975), *Flatfoot in Africa* (1978) and *Flatfoot on the Nile* (1980) the crime plot would be just a pretext for the actor's elaborate fistfights, conceived and shot like stand-alone set-pieces much the same way Busby Berkeley would devise his dance numbers.

What's more, many of *Flatfoot*'s comedy and folklore elements were to become prominent in the future: a patent example is the presence of Neapolitan comedy actor Enzo Cannavale, who would reprise a similar role in a serious poliziotteschi (Michele Massimo Tarantini's *A Man Called Magnum*, 1977), and would also become a recurring presence in the series starring Tomas Milian as Marshall Nico Giraldi. In the following years, the crime genre would be a source of inspiration for a number of out-and-out comedies, either parodies — Franco Franchi's vehicles such as *Piedino il questurino* (1974, Franco Lo Cascio) and *Il giustiziere di mezzogiorno* (1975, Mario Amendola) — or the bawdy erotic farces starring Edwige Fenech, such as *Confessions of a Lady Cop* (*La poliziotta fa carriera*, 1976), *A Policewoman on the Porno Squad* (*La poliziotta della squadra del buoncostume*, 1979) and *A Policewoman in New York* (*La poliziotta a New York*, 1981). Fenech's series as the "poliziotta" (only nominally based on Vanzina's 1974 film), directed by a filmmaker who also tried his hand at "real" crime films such as Michele Massimo Tarantini, followed the ascent and decline of the so-called "sexy comedy," equivalent and running parallel to those of the crime genre.

Notes

1. Faldini and Fofi, *Il cinema italiano d'oggi*, p. 435.
2. *Ibid.*
3. Pietro Bianchi, *Il Giorno*, 10.27.1973.

Gang War in Milan *(Milano rovente)*

D: Umberto Lenzi. *S:* Ombretta Lanza; *SC:* Franco Enna, Umberto Lenzi; *DOP:* Lamberto Caimi (35mm, Techniscope, Technicolor); *M:* Carlo Rustichelli (Ed. '71 Roma); *E:* Iolanda Benvenuti; *ArtD:* Sergio

Palmieri; *CO:* Silvio Laurenzi; Cameras: Sergio Martinelli, Roberto Seveso; *AE:* Elisa Nardelli; *AD:* Franco Fantasia; *MU:* Sergio Angeloni; *Hair:* Wanda Belini; *W:* Adriana Manici (Antonio Sabato's wardrobe: Aldo Di Consiglio; Marisa Mell's wardrobe: Alain Reynaud); *SO:* Dino [Domenico] Pasquadibisceglie; *SOE:* Renato Marinelli; *SE:* Celeste Battistelli; *SP:* Taddeo Bontempelli; *SS:* Lucia Grazzi; *DD* (English version): Christopher Cruise. *Cast:* Antonio Sabàto (Salvatore "Totò" Cangemi), Philippe Leroy (Roger Daverti "Le Capitain"), Antonio Casagrande (Lino Caruso), Carla Romanelli (Virginia), Alessandro Sperlì (Billy Barone), Franco Fantasia (Chief Inspector Contalvi), Tano Cimarosa (Nino Balsamo), Marisa Mell (Jasmina Sanders), Piero Corbetta (Takis), Vittorio Pinelli (Orso), Domenico [Tony] Raccosta (Lupo), Claudio Sforzini (Ricciolino), Gabriella Lepori (Vanessa), Carla Mancini, Luigi Antonio Guerra (policeman), Vittorio Sancisi (Daverti's man), Vittorio Joderi (Giorgio), Naiba Pedersoli (Carmela, Salvatore's housekeeper), Lucio Como (Martin), Riccardo De Stefanis (Daverti's man), Ottavio Fanfani (Samperi, the lawyer), Idris Josuf (Daverti's man), Marta Fabiani (Vicky), Elsa Boni (Francesca), Giancarlo Busi, Ugo Bologna (Judge), Filippo La Neve (Gangster), Elena Pantano (Salvatore's mother). *Uncredited:* Ugo Bombognini (Giulio), Achille Grioni (police lieutenant), Annibale Papetti (Giorgino). *PROD:* Lombard Film (Milan); *EP:* Giuseppe Tortorella; *PM:* Gino Soldi; *PSe:* Carmine Del Monaco. *Country:* Italy. Filmed at Icet — De Paolis Studios (Milan) and on location in Milan. *Running time:* 101'; Visa no.: 61898 (02.17.1973); *Rating:* v.m.18; *Release date:* 02.21.1973; *Distribution:* Variety Film; *Domestic gross:* 631,702,000 lire. *Also known as: La guerre des gangs* (Paris, 09.26.1979 — 90'), *Burning City. Home video:* Dagored (DVD, Italy). OST: CD Beat Records CDCR 85.

Milan. Sicilian vegetable wholesaler Salvatore "Totò" Cangemi is actually kingpin of the city's largest and most lucrative prostitution ring. Everything seems to be running smoothly until one day Salvatore finds one of his girls murdered. The killing has been commissioned by a French drug lord, Roger Daverti, who had showed up and tried to convince Cangemi to join forces. The Frenchman wants to use Totò's girls to sell drugs, but Cangemi rejects the offer at first, and asks Italo-American mafioso Billy Barone for help and protection. However Salvatore, persuaded by his lover Jasmine, keeps part of the profits for himself. When Jasmine betrays him and he finds Daverti dead, Cangemi realizes that Billy exploited his rivalry with the Frenchman to frame him for the murder and take the power over his ring. In the end Cangemi dies in a shoot-out with the cops.

Even though Umberto Lenzi had directed a number of spy and action flicks in the '60s, *Gang War in Milan* is the director's first entry in the urban crime genre. Produced by Lombard Film, the same company which had financed Duccio Tessari's *Death Occurred Last Night*, the film was entirely produced and shot in Milan: in a 2000 interview Lenzi stated that "both the story and script were by Franco Enna, a popular *giallo* novelist who lived in Switzerland, whereas Ombretta Lanza [who figures as the author of the story in the opening credits] was just the daughter of one of the producers, so they just made her sign the story,"[2] although later he claimed to have completely rewritten the script because it was closer to 1930s crime flicks than to *film noir*.[3]

However, compared to Lenzi's following entries in the genre, such as *Almost Human* (1974) and *Manhunt in the City* (1975), the tone is quite different. "It's a *film noir* of sorts, a bit like Fernando di Leo's works," Lenzi explained. "The cop, who's played by Franco Fantasia — a second-rate actor [Fantasia was primarily a master of arms, Author's Note]— appears in just a couple of scenes and gets a load of detergent in the face without reacting. He almost doesn't exist as a character; the film is set completely within the underworld, it's the story of a war between two rival gangs."[4]

Rather than contemporary Mafia movies inspired by Coppola's *The Godfather*, the story is closer to an Italian classic such as Luchino Visconti's *Rocco and His Brothers* (*Rocco e i suoi fratelli*, 1960). "Antonio Sabàto and Antonio Casagrande [Cangemi's right hand in the film, Ed.] are closely related to Renato Salvatori in Visconti's film. That is, they are *terroni* [Italian pejorative term for Southerners, which is also how Jasmine calls her lover Cangemi throughout the film, Author's Note] who move North to escape a destiny of poverty and emargination. [...] There is a strong sentimental undertone, in the memories of the little village the criminals emigrated from. What I think comes out rather well from *Gang War in Milan* is that detaching from Sicily was to them a detachment from life in all senses, just like in *Rocco and His Brothers*."[5]

Philippe Leroy, left (in light jacket), and director Umberto Lenzi, right, on the set of *Gang War in Milan* (1973).

One of the central motifs is the betrayal of friendship, yet the film displays a notable lack of romanticism, which pertains to female characters as well: there's more than a hint of misogyny in the portrayal of Marisa Mell's Jasmine, who never comes off as a true *femme fatale*, but just as a distant, cold character. All other women in the film are prostitutes, with the sole exception of Cangemi's mother, an old lady in a hospice who still dreams about her native country, and Billy Barone's niece, a passive and silent figure who's a servant in her own house.

Furthermore, Lenzi and Enna avoid any mythologizing stylization in the depiction of the Milanese underworld. Protagonist Antonio Sabàto, a Sicilian immigrant who made a fortune with the prostitution racket, boasts about his irresistible social ascent: yet he's just a pimp, smart enough to make his way in a city that's seen as a land of conquest for organized crime yet too stupid to preserve his small empire against the assault of big-time gangsters. The gang war between Sabàto's and Frenchman Philippe Leroy looks like a game of chess between two clumsy players who cannot prevent the adversary's next move. However, the lack of sympathy towards the lead somehow works against the film, as Lenzi admitted. "In *Gang War in Milan* there's a basic error on behalf of the producers [...]. We shouldn't have made the protagonist a pimp. You can have a pickpocket, a drug dealer or a killer, but not a pimp, because the viewer doesn't sympathize with him. He's a dirty scoundrel with whom you can't identify" the director elaborated. "This kind of character should have been played by someone like Tomas Milian, who would have made him a slimy, repulsive character just like the hunchback [on *Brutal Justice*, Author's Note], whereas Sabàto..."[6]

Gang War in Milan was inspired by news reports (the quick rise to power of Southern bosses in Milan, the feud between king of the gambling racket Francis Turatello and Albert Bergamelli's Marseille gang), but the sociological approach combines with an urgency that's typical of Lizzani's *instant movies*. Lenzi's film has a number of inspired touches in the portrayal of minor characters, such as small-time procurer Balsamo (Tano Cimarosa) and his "cousin" (Carla Romanelli) who's just arrived from the country to become a prostitute, and who stares puzzled at the lace lingerie she has to wear for her clients. On the other hand, the episodic yet gruesome bursts of violence — the discovery of two dead prostitutes who have been horribly tortured, Sabato's sidekick being electrocuted to the genitals — predates Lenzi's following work. The film's best sequence — Cimarosa's murder in the restaurant's toilet as in the nearby room Sabàto and his acolytes are singing a popular Sicilian song — associates music with violence in a way that recalls a famous moment in Leone's *The Good, The Bad and the Ugly* (1966), and perfectly sums up Lenzi's approach to the subject matter.

Gang War in Milan depicts a remarkably well portrayed Milan, "nocturnal and secret,"[7] "a little Chicago" as Billy Barone puts it, divided between degraded outskirts, fruit markets, shady night-clubs and the gangsters' luxurious lofts decorated with colored velvets and modern art objects: an exhibition of wealth in bad taste which is also an unwitting caricature of upper-class lifestyle.

Notes

1. Manlio Gomarasca, *Umberto Lenzi* (Milan: Nocturno libri, 2000), p. 215.
2. *Ibid.*
3. Author's interview, December 2010.
4. Gomarasca. *Umberto Lenzi*, p. 215.
5. *Ibid.*, p. 215.
6. *Ibid.*, p. 216.
7. Pietro Bianchi, *Il Giorno*, 06.10.1973.

The Great Kidnapping (La polizia sta a guardare)

D: Roberto Infascelli. *S:* Marcello D'Amico; *SC:* Augusto Caminito, Roberto Infascelli; *DOP:* Riccardo Pallottini (35mm, Techniscope — Eastmancolor, Technospes); *M:* Stelvio Cipriani, conducted by the author (ed. Bixio — Sam); *E:* Roberto Perpignani; *ArtD:* Franco Bottari; *ArtD:* Mauro Passi; *C:* Carlo Tafani; *AC:* Maurizio Lucchini; *AD:* Mimmola [Maria Teresa] Girosi; *SE:* Luciano Anzellotti, Massimo Anzellotti; *SP:* Walter Civirani; *SS:* Wanda Tuzi; *PA:* Lucherini, Rossetti, Spinola. *Cast:* Enrico Maria Salerno (Cardone, Chief of Police), Lee J. Cobb (Jovine), Jean Sorel (Aloisi), Luciana Paluzzi (Renata Boletti), Claudio Gora (Samperi), Laura Belli (Laura Ponti), Gianni Bonagura (Dr. Zenoni), Ezio Sancrotti (Catalano), Ignazio Leone (policeman), Ennio Balbo (Prefect), Franco Angrisano (Journalist), Tino Bianchi (Coroner), Enzo Consoli, Remo D'Angelo, Francesco Ferrini, Luigi Antonio Guerra (Journalist), Gioacchino Maniscalco, Franco Moraldi, Giovan Battista Salerno (Massimo Cardone), Sergio Serafini (Journalist). *Uncredited:* John Bartha (policeman), Philippe Hersent (Alvise Riccardi), Enrico Osterman (Alvaro Verganò), Clara Zovianoff. *PROD:* Roberto Infascelli for Primex Italiana; *GM:* Marcello D'Amico; *PM:* Paolo Infascelli. *Country:* Italy. Filmed at Dear Studios (Rome) and on location in Brescia. *Running time:* 95'; Visa no.: 63432 (11.06.1973); *Rating:* not rated; *Release date:* 11.16.1973; *Distribution:* Euro International Films; *Domestic gross:* 1,448,633,000 lire. *Also known as: Ransom! Police Are Watching, Den Stora Kidnappingen* (Sweden). *Home video:* Alan Young (DVD, Italy), Thorn-EMI (VHS, UK). OST: CD Chris Soundtrack Corner CSC002.

Dr. Cardone arrives in a town in Northern Italy to replace the former Chief of Police Jovine, who decided to resign because of the impossibility of fighting the rising wave of criminality. Cardone, on the other hand, is willing to use an iron fist and not to have his hands tied by legalistic scruples. To capture a gang of bank robbers, he risks the lives of their hostages, then he prevents the kidnapping of a wealthy industrialist's son thanks to the use of illicit phone tappings. The criminals retaliate by kidnapping his own son, Maurizio. At first Cardone is willing to give up, but after speaking to Maurizio he makes up his mind and decides not to change his methods of fighting crime. He eventually finds out that the unsuspecting chief of the kidnapping ring is Jovine, who plans to use the ransom money for a coup d'état. Cardone arrests his predecessor and assaults the house where his son has been taken prisoner. The kidnappers escape, but after a long chase — during which a boy is killed and Maurizio suffers grave injuries after being thrown out of the kidnappers' car — the police trap and kill them.

The Great Kidnapping represents Roberto Infascelli's attempt to top the commercial success of Stefano Vanzina's *Execution Squad*, which he produced, casting Enrico Maria Salerno in the lead — here with thin mustache and wig — as Chief Commissioner Cardone and taking over the direction himself. The opening is very promising, and perfectly renders the mood of the sleepy provincial Northern town where the story is set: a sequence shot in a police car that leaves the station and drives through the town's almost deserted streets to pick up the protagonist at the train station, while the cops aboard are listening to a football match, to the sound of Stelvio Cipriani's memorable score (which Quentin Tarantino would aptly recycle in *Death Proof*, 2007[1]). However, the rest of the film looks like it was written and shot in haste. To begin with, the setting — the Lombard province — is original but just barely sketched ("It's a place like anywhere else" Cardone's assistant explains, "factories, workers, turmoils, strikes…"), secondary characters are uninteresting, and the action is relegated to the final fifteen minutes. The script — by Infascelli and Augusto Caminito — is punctuated with references to present events, such as bombs "like the one in Milan, or those that make trains derail"; and the crucial plot twist — Cardone discovers that the ransom money is used to finance subversive plots and that former Chief of Police Jovine (Lee J. Cobb) is the mastermind behind it all — recycles that of *Execution Squad* (as is the case with large chunks of Cipriani's score) without much verve.

What's more, the aforementioned twist paves the way for a pedantic scene packed full with allusions to the "strategy of tension," proving once again the filmmakers' awkward attempts at creating an interesting background to the story. An enlightening dialogue exchange goes like this: "You know better than me the new laws that were enacted to guarantee the citizens' well-being, especially with regards to the arrest, not to mention police custody. 99% of the offenders are better protected than metalworkers … and good people are not shielded from criminals." Yet Cardone himself is a half-baked hero: despite his angry proclamations ("If we keep letting others put bombs under our ass from left and right alike, without ever opposing or reacting, I believe this state of things is never going to change!") he is devoid of the typical action hero trappings, and what's more he never solicits the audience's empathy, despite Salerno's expert screen presence. Even the relationship between the hero and his own son (played by Salerno's real-life son Giovan Battista) sounds clichéd. And just one year after *Execution Squad*, critics who had looked benevolently at the newborn thread were already changing their minds. Tullio Kezich wrote about Salerno's cop in Infascelli's film: "the least a guy like him deserves is to end up under investigation; whereas the filmmakers try to make him likeable, letting us know that he acts outside the law with good intentions."[2]

Despite *The Great Kidnapping*'s success at the box office, Salerno would soon make room for younger, more energetic stars such as Franco Nero, Luc Merenda and Maurizio Merli. In the following years, he would again play commissioners in idiosyncratic films such as *City Under Siege* (*Un uomo, una città*, 1974) and *Savage Three* (*Fango bollente*, 1975), whereas he would either play the antagonist in more stereotypical genre offerings such as Sergio Martino's *Gambling City* (*La città gioca d'azzardo*, 1975), where he's the crippled elderly boss of a gambling ring in Milan, or briefly show up in "guest star" roles, as in *The Left Hand of the Law* (*La polizia interviene: ordine di uccidere*, 1975).

Notes

1. Cipriani would later recycle and rearrange the film's main theme on the score for Ovidio Assonitis' *Tentacles* (1977).
2. Tullio Kezich, *Il Millefilm. Dieci anni al cinema 1967–1977* (Milan: Mondadori, 1983), p. 487.

High Crime (La polizia incrimina la legge assolve)

D: Enzo G. Castellari [Enzo Girolami]. *S:* Leonardo Martín, from an idea by Edmondo Amati; *SC:* Tito Carpi, Gianfranco Clerici, Vincenzo Mannino, Enzo G. Castellari, Leonardo Martín; *DOP:* Alejandro Ulloa (35mm, Eastmancolor); *M:* Guido and Maurizio De Angelis; *E:* Vincenzo Tomassi; *PD:* Walter Patriarca; *SetD:* Emilio Ruiz Del Rio, Carlo Ferri; *C:* Giovanni Bergamini; *AE:* Gianfranco Amicucci, Pietro Tomassi; *AD:* Giorgio Ubaldi; *MU:* Michele Trimarchi; *SO:* Luciano Welisch, Alvaro Orsini; *StDrC:* Rémy Julienne; *StDr:* Donatella Gambini; *SS:* Maria Luisa Merci. *Cast:* Franco Nero (Commissioner Belli), James Whitmore (Chief Commissioner Scabino), Delia Boccardo (Mirella), Fernando Rey (Cafiero), Duilio Del Prete (Umberto Griva), Silvano Tranquilli (Franco Griva), Ely Galleani (Chicca), Daniel Martín (Rico), Paul Costello (Cammarano), Luigi Diberti (Coffi, Belli's assistant), Mario Erpichini (Rivalta), Stefania G. Castellari [Stefania Girolami] (Anita Belli), Bruno Corazzari (Scabino's killer), Joaquín Solis (Tony, Cafiero's servant), Edy [Edgardo] Biagetti (Griva's friend), Massimo Vanni (Truck driving thug), Zoe Incrocci (Scabino's wife), Paolo Giusti (Chicca's friend), Enzo G. Castellari (Reporter), Victor Israel (Scorfano), Carla Mancini (Girl watching TV), Lorenzo Piani. *Uncredited:* Enzo G. Castellari (Reporter at party), Paul Costello (Griva's lawyer), Mickey Knox (Newsman at party), Nello Pazzafini (Griva's murderer), Riccardo Petrazzi (Hitman), Natasha Richardson (Luisa, the girl playing hopscotch), Leonardo Scabino (Coroner). *PROD:* Edmondo Amati for Fida Cinematografica, Capitolina Produzioni Cinematografiche (Rome), Star Films (Madrid), Suevia Films (Madrid); *EP:* Maurizio Amati; *PMs:* Antonio Mazza, Manuel Perez; *PSu:* Julio Parra, Paolo Gargano; *PSe:* Pasquale Vannini. *Country:* Italy/Spain. Filmed at Incir–De Paolis (Rome) and on location in Genoa, Ligurian coast, Marseille. *Running time:* 105'; Visa no.: 62911 (08.10.1973); *Rating:* v.m.14; *Release date:* 08.12.1973; *Distribution:* Fida Cinematografica; *Domestic gross:* 1,625,825,000 lire. *Also known as: La policía detiene, la ley juzga* (Madrid, 03.07.1974), *Le témoin à abattre* (Paris, 07.09.1975 —103'), *Tote Zeugen singen nicht* (West Germany, 08.09.1974 —102'). *Home video:* King Records (DVD, Japan); Hobby & Work (DVD, Italy). OST: CD Beat Records CDCR 65.

Commissioner Belli investigates a huge drug ring between Genoa and Marseille, which involves two rival gangs. He arrests a man, "the Lebanese," who may give him precious information, but the thug is killed while he's being transferred between police stations. Suspecting that a powerful industrialist above suspicion named Griva is involved in the drug trafficking, Belli convinces his older and more cautious colleague, Chief Commissioner Scabino, to handle him a compromising dossier the latter has been compiling. However, Scabino is murdered before he can help Belli. The criminals try to silence the commissioner by killing his wife and daughter, but eventually Belli destroys the gang with the help of an elderly crime boss.

August 1973. Within ten days two films were released which reshaped and rejuvenated the prototype of the crime film hero: Enzo G. Castellari's *High Crime* and Sergio Martino's *The Violent Professionals*. *High Crime*, in particular, is the film that aggregates and encodes the canons of what critics would call poliziotteschi, which were only partially — and disorderly — outlined in Stefano Vanzina's *Execution Squad*.

"After watching *Bullitt* I had a great desire to try my hand at the crime genre, with a strong and brave hero, ready to embark on crazy car chases, breathtaking shootings, intricate investigations," Castellari explained. The director also openly acknowledges the film's reference to Italian news reports of the time. "I told producer Edmondo Amati about my idea and as always he replied "Bring me the story." I discussed it with Tito Carpi and Amati's son Maurizio. We put together a treatment based on the murder of commissioner Calabresi. I didn't want to have Amati read it, though. I asked him to let me tell him the story myself, because I'm a very good storyteller [...] that's how *High Crime* was born."[1] Despite Castellari's assertions, however, the most evident screen model is rather William Friedkin's *The French Connection*, from Fernando Rey's presence as an elderly smuggling boss who still believes in a code of honor to the opening scenes set between Marseille and Genoa.

As with Romolo Guerrieri's *La polizia è al servizio del cittadino?*, the Ligurian city becomes a fundamental presence in the film. Firstly, Genoa is Italy's most American city: a crossroad of commerce and traffic, legal and illegal alike, and a spectacular looking setting for chase scenes with its narrow alleys (*caruggi*). What's more, Genoa conveys the mutations of the urban texture in an immediate, iconographically unmistakable way: its architectural, urbanistic lacerations (such as the "Sopraelevata" motorway, "an imposing grey line which separates the historic city centre from the sea and the city from its own story as well"[2]) are open-sore wounds, badly saturated with asphalt and cement, that left an indelible mark on the overexpanding Italy of the period. Genoa was also one of the centers of the Resistance and later of the workers' struggle, an emblem of rage, courage and revolt. And in the 1970s, it was the theatre of several resounding crime episodes: the Gradolla kidnapping, one of the first that took place outside Sardinia; the murder of CIT Alessandro Floris, whose images captured by an amateur photographer would become famous even outside Italy; and the kidnapping and murder of Milena Sutter.

On *High Crime*, Castellari displays a dynamic filmmaking style which was heavily influenced by American directors such as Peckinpah, Yates and Friedkin; however, Castellari also pays reference to Kurosawa's *The Seven Samurai* for its use of slow motion. The camera moves effortlessly, pursuing the characters; the action scenes, coordinated by Rémy Julienne and shot with four or five cameras, feature nervous cuts and ample use of hand-held shots, and are conceived, shot and edited in a strict symbiosis with the brothers De Angelis' score, which abandons the martial orchestrations of Cipriani's *Execution Squad* (another inheritance of politically committed dramas) for decidedly more dynamic sounds. The rousing *Il libanese* which accompanies the first chase scene, first on

Italian poster for *High Crime* (1973).

foot and then by car, between Commissioner Belli (Franco Nero) and the Libanese, is the first example of the interaction between music and images which will be prominent within the best examples of the genre. The film's themes, most notably the funky-jazz tinted *Gangster Story* (which also hints at Miles Davis' electric period) would be later reprised in many other poliziotteschi such as *Violent Rome*, *Weapons of Death* and others, and popped up in recent years in Quentin Tarantino's *Death Proof.*

Other stylistic traits show how Castellari was perfectly at ease with the genre and its thematic and visual *ganglia*. Such are the transition with no cuts from the night scene where chief commissioner Scabino (James Whitmore) is in bed, uncertain whether to handle his secret dossier or not, and the one where the following morning he phones his superiors; the use of depth-of-field, with effects that are either theatrical (Ely Galleani and Duilio Del Prete's murder scene, with the shadows of the killers appearing behind a glass door, which is shattered by the bullets) or reminiscent of classical *film noir*. Besides, Castellari nerves the story with brief flashes which predate or repeat future or past events, with a virtuoso use of editing that the director already experimented with on *Cold Eyes of Fear*. "There is no division between editing and directing, they're one and the same. You can't decide how to film a scene if you don't know about editing. My way of directing is based on editing that's already planned and programmed. I don't shoot a single shot without a reason. The slightest detail is designed according to the editing. Close-ups, long shots, traveling shots, they all have a precise sense, in accordance with the preordained editing plan."[3]

Despite a lurid Italian title (literally, "The Police Incriminate, the Law Discharges") and dialogue such as "We risk our lives for 100,000 lire a month!" about cops' precarious economical conditions, in *High Crime* the inheritance of political committed cinema has already been fully metabolized within genre storytelling. The long shot that accompanies the tense confrontation between Belli and Scabino over a hill that dominates the city is almost literally lifted from Damiani's *Confessions of a Police Captain*, yet Scabino's secret dossier is little more than a McGuffin, a narrative trick that gets lost halfway through the film. Also, if James Whitmore's death scene is a replica of Calabresi's killing, the spectacle of the scene itself and the disruptive impact of violence as dissected in slow-motion by Castellari have the upper hand.

The film's hero too is a step apart from previous models. Belli's torrential fits of anger are just part of the protagonist's genetic kit, they are a propulsive element of the story, devoid of any socio-political ambition. Belli is young, handsome, impulsive — that's about all we have to know. "You get pissed off all the time, take your gun and handcuffs and split the world in two. The good on one side, the bad on the other" he's reproached. On *Execution Squad*, Bertone put investigation before action; whereas Belli is not one to be caged by the articles and paragraphs of the Procedure Code. He gets excited, slaps, runs, shoots: he is the archetype of the "iron commissioners" to come. Even the ending, where Belli foresees his own death in a quick flash — a scene that would be ripped off by Castellari's father Marino Girolami in *Violent Rome*— looks like a memento that will accompany the whole crime genre. All things considered, it matters little that Franco Nero, with blonde hair and elegant blue shirts, looks more uneasy than in Damiani's films, and that Belli is a monolithic character, just barely sketched and characterized through the other characters' words. Even his lover (Delia Boccardo) calls him by his surname, and the commissioner looks more in trouble with personal relationships than in his struggle against drug traffickers.

High Crime's least interesting moments are the intimate scenes between Belli, his lover and his little daughter (Stefania Castellari, the director's own daughter, who would become a recurring presence in her father's films), where Castellari's predilection for slow motion, Alejandro Ulloa's *flou* lighting and the syrupy score bring the mood close to tearjerking dramas. Also debatable are the references to present issues, where Castellari and his scriptwriters seem uncertain on how to make their hero cope with society. Belli's tie and silk shirt immediately betray him as an enemy when he shows up at the docks, occupied by workers on strike, looking for a hitman (Bruno Corazzari) who's hiding among the dockers. He is met with anger and derision and called a fascist, and the sight of Franco Nero making his way amidst the strikers recalls that of a white soldier in an Indian camp. Castellari, Tito Carpi and Gianfranco Clerici give the hero a line ("He's got nothing to do with you!," he says about the killer) which sounds as a way to prevent critics' ideological objections, and to give Belli a political virginity that the real Calabresi surely did not have. No wonder because in 1968 Castellari was in Spain shooting Westerns.

High Crime was a huge box office hit, gaining over one billion and 600 million lire and paving the way for a number of imitators, among whom a new star would be born within a couple of years.

Notes

1. Igor Grimaldi and Davide Pulici, *Enzo G. Castellari* (Milan: Nocturno Libri, 2000), p. 34.
2. Renato Venturelli, *Genova o la lacerazione del paesaggio urbano*, in Aa. Vv., *Noir in Festival 1997* (Rome: Fahrenheit 451, 1997), p. 53.
3. Grimaldi and Pulici, *Enzo G. Castellari*, p. 4.

I Kiss the Hand, a.k.a. *Family Killer (Baciamo le mani)*

D: Vittorio Schiraldi. *S* and *SC:* Vittorio Schiraldi, based on his own novel; *DOP:* Marcello Gatti (35mm, Technicolor); *M:* Enrico Simonetti, conducted by the author (ed. Bixio Sam); *E:* Franco Fraticelli; *AE:* Alessandro Gabriele; *PD, CO:* Enrico Sabbatini; *C:* Otello Spila; *AC:* Ivo Spila, Roberto Locci; *AD:* Franco Cirino; *MU:* Euclide Santoli, Giuseppe Ferranti; *Hair:* Maura Turchi; *SO:* Claudio Maielli; *SE:* Basilio Patrizi; *SP:* Mimmo Cattarinich; *MA:* Ferdinando Poggi; *SS:* M. Serena Caruffo; *UP:* Studio Longardi. *Cast:* Arthur Kennedy (Don Angelino Ferrante), John Saxon (Gaspare Ardizzone), Agostina Belli (Mariuccia Ferrante), Pino Colizzi (Masino D'Amico), Spiros Focás (Luca Ferrante), Paolo Turco (Massimo Ferrante), Marino Masé (Luciano Ferrante), Corrado Gaipa (Don Emilio Grisanti), Giuseppe Addobbati (Nicola D'Amico), Daniele Vargas (Don Santino Billeci), Accursio Di Leo (Pietro Corazza), Jane Avril [Maria Pia Luzi] (Prostitute), Franco Cirino, Giorgio Dolfin, Massimo Sarchielli (Totò Grisanti), Gianni Loffredo [Joshua Sinclair] (Stefano Ferrante), Gay Quarta [Gaetano Quartararo], Tino Bianchi (Pietrino Gambara), Giovanni Pallavicino (Piero Nicolosi), Lisa Leonardi, Isabelle Marchand. *Uncredited:* Giuseppe Lauricella, Anna

Orso (Mrs. Ardizzone). *PROD:* Danilo Marciani and Mario Di Nardo for Aquila Cinematografica (Rome); *EP:* Arcangelo Picchi; *PM:* Giorgio Russo; *PSe:* Giuseppe Bruno Bossio; *CASH:* Luigi Mongini. *Country:* Italy. Filmed at Incir—De Paolis Studios (Rome). *Running time:* 112': Visa no.: 61963 (02.23.1973); *Rating:* v.m.14; *Release date:* 02.23.1973; *Distribution:* P.A.C.; *Domestic gross:* 691,086,000 lire. *Also known as: Der Todeskuß des Paten* (West Germany). *Home video:* Ritka Video (DVD, Czech Republic—Italian audio, as *Ve spárech mafie*), P.A.C. / Lineafilm (VHS, Italy), Columbia (VHS, Japan).

Stefano, the son of Mafia boss Angelino Ferrante, is murdered in an ambush by Gaspare Ardizzone, to whom he had refused to sell a piece of land. Through his son Luciano, old Ferrante summons from the United States elderly boss Don Santino Billeci to get his revenge, but Ardizzone kills Billeci too, and becomes the leader of the local Mafia gang, which he rules over with an iron fist. Masino, the son of Angelino Ferrante's counselor, falls in love with Stefano's widow Mariuccia, who becomes pregnant with his baby. Masino has convinced Mariuccia to sell the disputed land, and therefore is convinced by his own father to commit suicide, after Mariuccia has been dispatched by Ardizzone. Angelino Ferrante is sent to internal exile after Ardizzone has denounced him: this persuades Stefano's cousin Luca to settle the score. He gets rid of Ardizzone's men and faces the cruel boss: Ardizzone dies in the shoot-out but Luca is wounded too. Since he broke the rules, Luca must die as well. Old Ferrante returns clandestinely from exile and visits the piece of land which is now a construction site: he is killed among indifferent workers, and a scraper buries his body under the soil.

Writer and journalist Vittorio Schiraldi's film debut, based on his own novel, blends commitment and genre trappings. The depiction of the Mafia's activities in property development comes in the guise of a turgid, verbose and violent melodrama in the vein of *The Godfather*—the wedding scene and elderly boss Daniele Vargas' cold blooded execution are shameless rip-offs of Coppola's film—while the character of the old Angelino Ferrante played by Arthur Kennedy is almost an epitome of all typical Mafioso clichés on screen.

The juxtaposition between the old and new Mafia, with the latter represented by the ruthless Gaspare Ardizzone (John Saxon), is accompanied by such lines as: "These are strange times, young men have no respect any longer, it's up to the old ones to fix things up." Schiraldi's film overflows with such heavy-handed dialogue, as Kennedy praises old times, complains about America's bad influence ("America's like clap: it infects immediately") and evokes a long forgotten code of honor and respect. Every line is uttered as if it was a Shakespearean quote (which unfortunately it is not), the acting is uniformly theatrical, the moral is strident, as in the scene where Don Angelino's youngest son (Paolo Turco) objects to his father: "Whoever decides to live outside the laws of the State is just an outlaw. Don't tell me the story of good and bad Mafia—you're all the same!"

Schiraldi's tendency towards bad melodrama shows in the scenes where Agostina Belli and Pino Colizzi run in the fields accompanied by Enrico Simonetti's syrupy score. The film's only memorable asset is John Saxon's over-the-top performance as the greasy-haired, foul-mouthed, machine gun–wielding Ardizzone, who literally chews every line as if he was jumping at someone's jugular, and whose scenes of domestic abuse of his long-suffering wife (Anna Orso) are accompanied by classical music.

Lady Dynamite (La padrina)

D: Al Pisani [Giuseppe Vari]. *S* and *SC:* Aldo Crudo, Gastone Ramazzotti, Giuseppe Vari; *DOP:* Carlo Cerchio (35mm, Eastmancolor, Telecolor); *M:* Mario Bertolazzi (Ed. 71); *E:* Manlio Camastro; *PD, ArtD:* Danilo Zanetti; *CO:* Lilly Zanetti; *COA:* Osanna Guardini; *AC:* Riccardo Orsini; *MU:* Fabrizio Sforza; *Hair:* Lucia Costanzi; *SO:* Gastone Fedeli, Leopoldo Rosi; *SS:* Alberto Vari. *Cast:* Lydia [Lidia] Alfonsi (Costanza Cavallo), Venantino Venantini (Tommaso Russo), Anthony Steffen [Antonio De Teffè] (Nico Barresi), Mario Danieli, Carlo Gaddi (Tommaso's man), Maurice Poli (Tony Cavallo), Luigi Antonio Guerra, Manfred Freyberger (Rosaro Spina), Giangiacomo Elia, Amedeo Mangiù, Orchidea De Sanctis (Marisa, the prostitute), Renzo Rinaldi (Salvatore Catanese), Umberto Raho (Vito Spezzino). *Uncredited:* Don Mey, Pietro Torrisi (Spina's man), Claudio Undari (Tall mobster). *PROD:* Cine Domus 2000; *GM:* Otello Cocchi; *PM:* Luigi Alessi; *PSu:* Anacleto Amadio; *PSe:* Bruno Bagella. *Country:* Italy. Filmed at Elios Film (Rome) and on location in Syracuse. *Running time:* 100'; Visa no.: 62078 (03.17.1973); *Rating:* v.m.14; *Release date:* 03.23.1973; *Distribution:* Regional; *Domestic gross:* 111,362,000 lire. *Home video:* Sundowner home Video (VHS, Australia), Video Alsen (VHS, Greece). OST: CD Beat Records CDCR 54.

Brooklyn mob boss Genco Cavallo is killed in front of his wife Costanza; prior to dying, he denounces Palermo's boss Saro Giarrattana as the man behind the deed. As Cavallo's family gropes in the dark, Costanza takes the first plane to Sicily to avenge her husband. There, she reveals her intentions to a friend, Tommaso Russo, who sends a couple of his henchmen to investigate Giarrattana. Russo's men are killed, and Costanza survives an attempted murder when her car is sabotaged. Meanwhile, journalist Nico Barresi probes into Giarrattana's powerful political connivances, namely prosecutor Vito Spezzino, who is dispatched by his "friends" before he can talk. Russo is murdered, and Barresi—who had once been Costanza's lover—saves her and hides the woman; after Barresi has been killed as well, Costanza is forced to accept Giarrattana's offer that their gangs join forces to smuggle arms in the Middle East, which was the reason behind Cavallo's murder. Costanza finds out that the hit was carried out by one of her own men, Frank; she has him killed as soon as he gets to Sicily to meet her, and eventually has her revenge on Giarrattana.

A little seen film, Giuseppe Vari's *Lady Dynamite* is at least a curious example of the kind of rip-offs that were produced in the vein of *The Godfather*. The Italian title, *La padrina* ("The Godmother"), almost sounds like a parody of sorts, as was Franco Prosperi's *L'altra faccia del padrino* ("The Other Face of the Godfather," 1973)—which poked fun at one of *The Godfather*'s most distinctive traits, Marlon Brando's performance, aped by imitator Alighiero Noschese. Whereas *Lady Dynamite* takes itself quite seriously, with plenty of violence and assorted killings. In trying to top the violence in Coppola's film, Vari often borders on the grotesque, with such examples as the final murder through rocket launcher or a Sicilian *cassata* cake stuffed with a severed hand delivered to the heroine as a warning. The story has a vaguely feminist flair, as the lead character is a woman who takes over her dead husband's mob empire. "Beware, she's dangerous!" a mobster says to her adversary, and the other sneeringly replies: "She's a female...."

However, script and direction are very poor indeed: due to a shoestring budget the American scenes take place in a hotel room (and misspelled titles on American newspapers give away the film's overall hastiness), Mafia bosses are always shown having dinner at the same table, and equally terrible are the flashbacks of Costanza and Barresi's love story, with the two lovers running across a field in a long shot with sappy music and jelly lenses.

Beside Alfonsi's tepid central performance, the rest of the cast looks rather uninvolved. Freyberger, who plays a ferocious boss, would later gain posthumous notoriety after his last film role, Pope John Paul II in Renzo Arbore's mad comedy *Il Pap'occhio* (1980).

Law Firm for a Robbery (Studio legale per una rapina)

D: Amerigo Anton [Tanio Boccia]. *S* and *SC:* Mario Moroni; *DOP:* Remo Grisanti (35mm, Eastmancolor, Telecolor); *M:* Mario Bertolazzi; *E:* Tanio Boccia; *PD:* Saverio D'Eugenio; *CO:* Sibilla Geiger; *AD:* Mario Moroni. *Cast:* Kay Fischer, George Wang, Brigitte Skay, Paul Müller, Angela Bo, Gisella Pardi, Omero Gargano, Ivano Staccioli, Gianni Solaro, Emilio Vale, Bob [Nestore] Cavaricci. *PROD:* R.G. International Films. *Country:* Italy. Shot on location in Milan. *Running time:* 88'; Visa no.: 62336 (04.18.1973); *Rating:* v.m.18; *Release date:* 06.27.1973; *Distribution:* Regional; *Domestic gross:* 96,672,000 lire.

A disbarred lawyer, arrested and put in jail, Maurice Poitier takes advantage of doctor garments to gather confidence from a dying prisoner about the plot for a multi-million robbery. Once released, Poitier searches for accomplices to prepare and perform the heist. However, the plot fails because of the unlikely jumble of little women and criminals put together as specialists by the would-be mastermind.

Tanio Boccia (1912–1982) — better known as Amerigo Anton, the elegant pseudonym under which he signed all his films — was a quite modestly gifted filmmaker, who moved his first steps in the showbiz in the '30s and '40s as a dancer and choreographer, before moving on to act in regional, dialectal stage plays. Boccia, who debuted behind the camera in 1952 and subsequently directed twenty films, was mostly known for his goofy sword-and-sandal flicks such as *Atlas Against the Czar* (1964), as well as a few Westerns: *Kill the Wicked!* (*Dio non paga il sabato*, 1967) was actually the blueprint for Sergio Canevari's inventive *Matalo!* (1970), which basically re-used the very same script. In the nineties, long after his death, Boccia was nicknamed "the Italian Ed Wood" by some critics: a largely unmotivated label, since his works, albeit rather poor, were not at all the kind of cinematic disasters signed by the Poughkeepsie-born filmmaker. Quite simply, Boccia was one of those unknown soldiers who formed the tissue of Italian genre cinema in the '50s and '60s, helming unpretentious flicks destined to unpretentious audiences. In the early '70s his output dramatically faded: *Law Firm for a Robbery* was Boccia's second-to-last effort, his final film as a director being the obscure *La guerra sul fronte Est* (War on the East Front, 1981). Written by Boccia's frequent acolyte Mario Moroni (himself a Z-grade director with such titles as the western *Mallory Must Not Die*, 1971, and the inept giallo *Ciak si muore*, 1974), *Law Firm for a Robbery* was clearly devised to compete with the crime genre then in vogue, a task it failed to accomplish: shot on a shoestring with a rather forgettable cast comprising of character actors and modest has-beens, the film sank without a trace at the box office. The Catholic Cinematografic Centre slanted it in its review, stating that "The Milanese setting, boasted by the advertising campaign, is a mere frame but not a contest. The only clear thing in this patched-up film are the recurring and far from edifying purposes: sex, violence and the torbid portrayal of the underworld." *Law Firm for a Robbery* remains largely unseen to this day, even though an English-language version exists (but is apparently untrackable) at Rome's C.S.C.

Long Lasting Days (Una vita lunga un giorno)

D: Sam Livingstone [Ferdinando Baldi]. *S* and *SC:* Sam Livingstone; *DOP:* Aiace Parolin (35mm, Eastmancolor, Technospes); *M:* Franco and Mino Reitano; *Una vita lunga un giorno* (Minniti / F. & M. Reitano) sung by Mino Reitano; orchestra conducted by Pinuccio Pirazzoli (ed. Fremus); *E:* Eugenio Alabiso; *PD:* Claudio Cinini; *CO:* Lucia Diolosa; *C:* Gaetano Valle; *AC:* Luigi Bernardini; *MU:* Vittorio Biseo; *Hair:* Giancarlo Marin; *SO:* Dino Fronzetti; *SP:* Ermanno Consolazione; *KG:* Rocco Fernando Fusco; *ChEl:* Bruno Pasqualini; *SS:* Vanda Tuzi. *Cast:* Mino Reitano (Andrea Rispoli), Ewa Aulin (Anna Andersen), Eva Czemerys (Frieda), Philippe Leroy (Philippe), Luciano Catenacci (Spyros), Franco Ressel (The Doctor), Franco Fantasia (Manolo), Dante Maggio ("Uncle" Giovanni), Giancarlo Del Duca (Philippe's right hand), Leo Brandi, Anna Maria Pescatori, Nello Pazzafini (Nello), Irio Fantini, Giuseppe Barcella, Luigi Antonio Guerra. *Uncredited:* Bruno Alias (Philippe's party guest), Artemio Antonini (Thug), Angelo Boscariol (Boarding house thug). *PROD:* Manolo Bolognini for Bobo Produzione Film (Rome); *PM:* Luciano Catenacci; *PSu:* Carlo Giovagnorio. *Country:* Italy. Filmed at Incir–De Paolis (Rome) and on location in Savona, Imperia and San Remo. *Running time:* 90'; Visa no.: 62944 (08.10.1973); *Rating:* v.m.14; *Release date:* 08.14.1973; *Distribution:* Alpherat; *Domestic gross:* 45,148,000 lire. *Also known as: Fünf Rätsel zum Tod* (West Germany). *Home video:* New Pentax (VHS, Italy).

Back in San Remo after a long period at sea, sailor Andrea Rispoli learns that the owner of the boarding house he's staying at, Mrs. Andersen, had died. Her niece Anna arrives from Sweden to take over the business, and Andrea falls in love with her. Fleeing from an attempted rape, Anna ends up in a hospital: there, a doctor tells Andrea that the young woman has a heart disease and needs urgent but very expensive surgery. Out of desperation, Andrea accepts a bored rich man's proposal: he will be the human prey of a manhunt that will take place throughout the city during the course of one night. If he will survive five murder attempts, Andrea will get $30,000. The young sailor survives the night and receives the money, only to discover that Anna is actually the rich man's lover. Embittered and disillusioned, Andrea is about to sail on a boat when he is run over by a truck.

Among the most peculiar fruits of 1970s *noir*, Ferdinando Baldi's *Long Lasting Days* is an offbeat variation on *The Most Dangerous Game*, set in the Ligurian city of San Remo. Baldi's script opposes proletarian sailor Mino Reitano to a bunch of bored, obnoxiously rich perverts, led by Philippe Leroy, whose favorite pastime appears to recruit desperate human beings to act as preys in manhunts, and conveys a feel of class struggle beyond the usual genre trappings. "I'm always above the law, sometimes even more than God," Leroy says at one point. The image of debauched rich men indulging in sex and drug-consuming is surprisingly similar to the central theme of Jess Franco's *La Comtesse perverse*, made the same year, but Baldi doesn't go for nudity and violence as much as one would expect.

Unfortunately, the script is so full of holes that *Long Lasting Days* simply doesn't work as a thriller. When the final twist unfolds, and we learn that the gorgeous Anna (Ewa Aulin) is actually Leroy's accomplice and lover, the previous attempted rape she barely escaped just makes no sense (the would-be rapist, played by the ubiquitous Nello Pazzafini, is also one of Leroy's henchmen). The direction is also not on a par with Baldi's previous *The Sicilian Connection*, and only an inventive fight in a disco—where Reitano is punched by two men while Leroy and his friends have fun on the dance floor—stands out among the rather tepid action scenes.

Long Lasting Days was conceived as a Mino Reitano vehicle. Reitano, who also wrote the interesting rock-driven score with his brother Franco, was a very popular singer in late '60s and early '70s, and tried his hand at acting, with decidedly forgettable results, starting with his film début *Tara Pokì* (1971, Amasi Damiani), a jaw-droppingly inept mixture of Mafia melodrama and Western set between Calabria and the Wild West. His obvious limits as an actor sabotage whatever attempt at *film noir* poetry Baldi hoped for, and at times Reitano's impassivity provokes unintended laughs—yet the film and its subtext cannot be fully understood without considering Reitano's image and personal background. Coming from a poor Calabrian family, Reitano moved to Germany (where he even claimed to have opened a show for The Beatles in Hamburg) before returning to Italy and becoming successful. In his songs he often focused on the theme of immigration, and his screen roles somehow connected to his public image: in his following film, Pier Carpi's overly ambitious *Povero Cristo* (1975), Reitano would play a private eye who's entrusted with a mission to find Jesus in contemporary society, only to discover that he himself is Christ. In Baldi's film, even the setting—San Remo, home of the Italian song festival, Italy's most popular music event since the '50s—has a distinctive symbolic feel, and the arbitrary, punitive ending—rather than a mere genre gimmick as it was in *The Sicilian Connection*—sounds at least congenial to the hero's will to abandon his roots. Aside from the clumsy *film noir* stuff, *Long Lasting Days* is a popular melodrama, centered on a desperate love, the mirage of a better future and the dream of a new life that vanishes at dawn.

Mafia Killer, a.k.a. *The Godfather's Advisor (La legge della camorra)*

D: Nedo De Fida [Demofilo Fidani]. *S:* Demofilo Fidani; *SC:* Demofilo Fidani, Maria Rosa Valenza [Mila Vitelli Valenza]; *DOP:* Claudio Morabito (35mm, Eastmancolor—widescreen); *M:* Lallo [Coriolano] Gori (Ed. Nazionalmusic); *E:* Giancarlo Venarucci Cadueri; *PD, CO:* Maria Rosa Valenza; *C:* Carlo De Biase; *AC:* Enrico Biribicchi; *AD:* Massimo Bernardi; *MU:* Luciana Blengini; *W:* Lucia Sepi; *SO:* Renato Cadueri; *SetT:* Augusto Possanza; *SP:* Alfio Quattrini; *KG:* Elio Bosi; *ChEl:* Fernando Massaccesi; *PrM:* Franco Zippo; *SS:* Paola Tiezzi. *Cast:* Dean Stratford [Dino Strano] (Don Gaetano Liguoro / Tony Liguoro), Mariangela Matania [Simonetta Vitelli] (Donna Carolina), Marco Guglielmi (Don Calogero Miceli), Raffaele Di Mario (Don Salvatore Caruso), Robert Macaluso [Reza Beyk Imanverdi] (Lucky De Simone), Anthony G. Stanton [Franco Ricci] (Angelo), Silvio Noto (Alfonso Caruso), Jeff Cameron (Mike Artusi), Jerry Ross, Santo Simone (Mobster), Amerigo Castrighella (Vincenzo), Enzo Pulcrano, Pietro Torrisi (Don Gaetano's man), Giorgio Dolfin, Stefano Oppedisano, Marco Mariani (Doctor), Isabella Spataro, Cesarina Zara, Angelo Casadei, Renato Fratini, Mario Castaldi, Fabio Ceroni, Giulio Di Stefano, Corrado Blengini. *Uncredited:* Lino Coletta (Louis), Paolo Figlia, Benito Pacifico (Mobster), Spela Rozin. *PROD:* Franco Clementi for Tarquinia Internazionale Cinematografica, Cinematografica Nazionale; *GM:* Demofilo Fidani; *PM:* Diego Spataro; *PSeA:* Elisabetta Bonfanti, Giulia Saccucci, Claudio Lucaferri. *Country:* Italy. *Running time:* 90'; Visa no.: 62135 (04.30.1973); *Rating:* v.m.18; *Release date:* 07.18.1973; *Distribution:* Regional; *Domestic gross:* 88,667,000 lire. *Home video:* Cecchi Gori (DVD, Italy)

Don Gaetano Liguoro, an elderly Mafia boss, is shot in front of his New York home. From his hospital bed, he asks his acolytes to track down who armed the killer's hand. Don Salvatore, a lawyer, pays visit to Donna Carolina Miceli to find out the reasons of the feud between the families Liguoro and Miceli. Carolina tells him the story of Lucky De Simone, a lonely killer who became her bodyguard out of gratitude for her father, Mafia boss Don Calogero Miceli. After her cousin Carmine has been killed by Liguoro's men, Donna Carolina summons Mike Artusi from New York. Carolina explains him that the hostility between Liguoro and Miceli was born because of the drug ring Gaetano and his brother Tony were setting up, and to which Miceli was strongly opposed. Carolina was sent to Italy by her father, while a Mafia war ensued. Donna Carolina hopes that the feud finally comes to an end, but after Don Gaetano's death Mike starts a new series of bloody retaliations.

In the early 1970s, after a number of Westerns, Demofilo Fidani decided to jump again on the crime frenzy bandwagon, by recycling ample footage from his own 1969 film *The Electric Chair* and adding a contemporary framing story. Despite the Italian title, which openly refers to Pasquale Squitieri's hit *Camorra*, the film is actually about the Mafia, as it tells the story of the rivalry between two "families" from the 1930s to contemporary times.

The scenes from *The Electric Chair* are redubbed and put in a different order and context: for instance, the delirious flashback depicting Reza Beyk Imanverdi's childhood trauma which characterized the first film's climax, here comes after about fifteen minutes into the film. Most new scenes feature Fidani's stepdaughter Simonetta Vitelli (here with the pseudonym Mariangela Matania instead of her usual *nom de plume* Simone Blondell) under a slapdash ageing make-up, recounting the story of the feud between her family and that of the cruel Don Gaetano (Fidani's regular Dino Strano) to Don Salvatore (Raffaele Di Mario), while others involve Marco Guglielmi and Strano himself (who ends up playing both Liguoro brothers: Tony is his old self from *The Electric Chair*).

The director also throws in a bit of ultra-violence, such as in the scene where Pietro Torrisi savagely beats a man, cuts his ears off Tarantino-style and puts them into a chocolate box that's delivered to Donna Carolina. Dialogue is also in typical Fidani fashion: "He paid with his death for a wrong life, the victim of a gear he found himself in, as many another, in spite of his will," Carolina says about her father. Lallo Gori's score, which at a point even rips off Narciso Yepes' famous *Jeux interdits*, is in tone with the rest of the film.

Mean Frank and Crazy Tony (*Il suo nome faceva tremare … Interpol in allarme* a.k.a. *Dio, sei proprio un padreterno!*)

D: Michele Lupo. *S* and *SC:* Luciano Vincenzoni, Sergio Donati, Nicola Badalucco; *PDir:* Aldo Tonti, Aristide Massaccesi (35mm, Technicolor); *M:* Riz Ortolani; *E:* Antonietta Zita; *PD:* Amedeo Fago; *ArtD:* Andrea Fantacci; *CO:* Elio Micheli; *C:* Remo Grisanti; *AE:* Anna Maria Roca; *AD:* Gianni Arduini; *SS:* Serena Canevari. *Cast:* Lee Van Cleef (Frankie Diomede), Tony Lo Bianco (Tony Frera), Edwige Fenech (Orchidea, Tony's lover), Jean Rochefort (Louis Annunziata), Fausto Tozzi (Massara), Mario Erpichini (Joe Sciti), Jess Hahn (Jeannot), Claudio Gora (Director of "Casa del Giovane"), Silvano Tranquilli (Sylvester, Frankie's brother), Nello Pazzafini (Convict), Robert Hundar [Claudio Undari] (Killer), Adolfo Lastretti (Al), Ugo Fangareggi (Man in café), Romano Puppo (Assassin), Carlo Hintermann (Manca), Teodoro Corrà (Gay prisoner), Renzo Marignano (Receiver), Marcello Di Martire, Bruno Boschetti, Luigi Antonio Guerra. *Uncredited:* Francesco Annibali (Man at poolroom), Artemio Antonini (Annunziata's henchman), Ettore Arena (Cop at French customs), Fortunato Arena (Prison warden), John Bartha (District attorney), Angelo Boscariol (Cop), Stefania Careddu (Lady in Piccapietra), Giovanni Cianfriglia (Annunziata's henchman), Vici De Roll (Journalist), Arnaldo Dell'Acqua (Prisoner), Bruno Di Luia (Annunziata's henchman), Tom Felleghy (police commander), Gilberto Galimberti (Truck driver), Riccardo Mangano (Driver), Giuseppe Marrocco, Fulvio Mingozzi (Official), Riccardo Petrazzi (Worker in fish factory), Osiride Pevarello (Thug in prison), Ottorino Polentini (Prisoner), Claudio Ruffini (Truck driver), Sergio Smacchi (Annunziata's henchman), Goffredo Unger (Annunziata's henchman), Steffen Zacharias (Tony's lawyer). *PROD:* Dino De Laurentiis for Giada International Company / Produzioni Cinematografiche Inter.Ma.Co. (Rome), Les Films Marceau (Paris) / Filmsonor (Paris); *EP:* Franco Cancellieri; *PM:* Roberto Cocco. *Country:* Italy / France. Filmed on location in Genoa and Marseille. *Running time:* 100'; Visa no.: 63444 (11.02.1973); *Rating:* v.m.14; *Release date:* 11.23.1973; *Distribution:* Ceiad; *Domestic gross:* 353,735,000 lire. *Also known as: L'homme aux nerfs d'acier* (Paris, 05.07.1975)—*La Pistola—The Gun* (West Germany, 05.10.1974—97'), *Escape from Death Row. Home video:* First Look (DVD, USA—included in *The Grindhouse Experience* box set, as *Frank and Tony*), BCI/Eclipse (DVD, USA—as *Escape from Death Row*, 76')

Italo-American mobster Frankie Diomede, known as "Dio," returns to Genoa after 25 years, to take care of his organization, which is being decimated by his rival Louis Annunziata. Since Frank's lieutenant is in cahoots with Louis, "Dio" ends up arrested, but comes out of prison with the help of a guard and kills the traitor. Annunziata reacts by alerting the police and even have them indict Frank for murder, then he kills his brother, to whom Frank had entrusted a secret dossier. "Dio" receives unexpected help from a petty Neapolitan thug, Big "Tony," who always dreamt of becoming his sidekick. Frank escapes from jail with Tony's assistance and goes to Marseille where once a month Annunziata sends heroin to the United States. Eventually, Frank eliminates Luis and his gang, then leaves for Tunisia, though not before advising Tony to change his ways.

Written by a remarkable trio of scriptwriters, Michele Lupo's *Mean Frank and Crazy Tony* is an odd mixture of serious and facetious, and displays a keen eye for characters. Lee Van Cleef's Frank Diomede is virtually the same character the actor played in Sergio Leone's *For a Few Dollars More* (1965), including the pipe-smoking habit—not surprisingly, since Donati and Vincenzoni co-scripted Leone's Western—transposed to modern-day Genoa, definitely one of the most eligible scenarios for urban action-crime films. Rather than a godfather, Frankie is a God in the underworld, as his nickname "Dio" ("God") implies (as does the—admittedly horrible—alternate Italian title, *Dio sei proprio un padreterno!*), whereas his co-star Tony Lo Bianco is a small-time hood who dresses like a Damon Runyon character and venerates Diomede, to the point that he ends up in jail with him and eventually helps Frankie in his revenge against the rival (played by the great Jean Rochefort) who killed Dio's brother.

If the relationship between Dio and Tony somehow recalls that between Henry Fonda and Terence Hill in Tonino Valerii's *My Name Is Nobody* (*Il mio nome è Nessuno*, 1973) the script also borrows liberally from Donati's own novel *Mr. Sharkey torna a casa*, which also dealt with a hard-boiled character in a typically Italian scenario. Lupo approaches the story with an ironic wit that recalls his previous films such as *7 Times 7* (1968) and *The Weekend Murders* (*Concerto per pistola solista*, 1970), pairing Van Cleef's deadpan mask with Lo Bianco's jaunty, at times clownish, presence. However, the picaresque comedy antics, frenetic Keystone Kops–style chases and slapstick gags uneasily rub shoulders with Grand Guignol excesses and brutal violence: for instance, Robert Hundar's character, a killer whose favorite weapon is a drill, wouldn't have been out of place in a De Palma film. The results are schizophrenic and not always convincing: all things considered, the film's best moments are those where Lupo plays out straight, as in the final showdown in the frozen fish plant.

The technical cast is first-rate, with cinematography by Aldo Tonti and Aristide Massaccesi and a funny score by Riz Ortolani. Edwige Fenech, as Lo Bianco's girlfriend, displays her gorgeous talents but hers is essentially a decorative presence. The film is also available in the U.S. in a heavily cut form, under the title *Escape from Death Row*.

No. Il caso è felicemente risolto (No. The Case Is Happily Resolved)

D: Vittorio Salerno. *S:* Augusto Finocchi; *SC:* Augusto Finocchi, Vittorio Salerno; *DOP:* Marcello Masciocchi (35mm, Eastmancolor, Telecolor); *M:* Riz Ortolani, conducted by the author (ed. Italia 71); the song *Mamma giustizia* by J. Fiastri/R. Ortolani is sung by I Nomadi; *E:* Luciano Anconetani; *PD, CO:* Emilio Baldelli; *C:* Roberto Brega, Antonio Schiavolena; *AC:* Mauro Masciocchi; *AE:* Gabriella Vitale; *AD:* Paolo Finocchi; *2nd AD:* Bruno Bossio; *MU:* Carlo Sindici; *Hair:* Ida Alicino; *SS:* Graziella Marsetti; *PA:* Tonino Pinto. *Cast:* Enzo Cerusico (Fabio Santamaria), Riccardo Cucciolla (Prof. Eduardo Ranieri), Junie Vetusto (The Concierge's daughter), Martine Brochard (Cinzia Santamaria), Enrico Maria Salerno (Giuseppe Ferdinando Giannoli "Don Peppino," the journalist), Claudio Nicastro (Dr. Rocchi, Chief of Police), Luigi Casellato (police inspector), Loredana Martinez (Olga Poddu, the victim), Enzo Garinei ("Gazzetta Sera"'s editor in chief), Umberto Raho (Don Giulio), Eleonora Mauro ("Grissino," the photographer), Gualtiero Rispoli (Marshall Basile), Roberto Santi, Franco Mazzieri (Lawyer, Ranieri's friend), Giangiacomo Elia [John Ely] (Fabio's colleague), Antonella Dogan (Prostitute), Ornella Ghezzi (Fabio's next door neighbor), Luigi Antonio Guerra, Sandra Locci, Elio Marconato, Riccardo Mangano, Giovanna Mainardi (Nannarella, prostitute talking with Giannoli), Enrico Marciani (Commissioner Pace), Piero Mazzinghi (Aldo, the barber), Nazzareno Natale (Augusto), Riziero Pauselli. *Uncredited:* Calogero Azzaretto (Mug shot), Luciano Bonanni (Stationmaster), Dolores Calò (Juror), Fernando Cerulli (TV speaker), Franz Colangeli (Lawyer), Marco Mariani (Fabio's colleague), Vezio Natili (Judge). *PROD:* Angelo Iacono for Iama Cinematografica; *EP:* Lillo Capoano;

PM: Giuseppe Mangogna; *PSu:* Vittorio Noia, Carlo Cucchi; *PSe:* Ermida Aichino, Adriano Vulpiani. *Country:* Italy. Shot on location in Bracciano and Rome. *Running time:* 98'; Visa no.: 62880 (08.07.1973); *Rating:* v.m.14; *Release date:* 08.15.1973; *Distribution:* Jumbo Cinematografica; *Domestic gross:* 190,447,000 lire. *Home video:* CDE (DVD, Italy), Orion (VHS, Switzerland — Italian language). OST: LP EMI 3C 006 17927.

While he's out fishing at the Bracciano lake outside Rome, Fabio Santamaria witnesses a brutal murder and finds himself face to face with the maniac. At first he is about to go to the police, then he changes his mind, afraid of the hassle that he might encounter. Meanwhile, the murderer, the unsuspecting high school teacher Eduardo Ranieri, goes to the police himself pretending to be the eyewitness, and describing the culprit as a man with Fabio's features. When Fabio sees his identikit on newspapers, at first he tries to change his looks — he trims his mustache, wears shades — and has his car repainted. By chance, one day he notices Ranieri and follows him to his home. Eventually Fabio decides to tell the truth to the police, but he is incriminated in turn, and is sentenced to 24 years imprisonment. However, a journalist named Giannoli, who suspected Ranieri all along, investigates on his own, but he can't find evidence of guilt. Only with the murderer's confession and suicide, Fabio will eventually be released.

For his solo film debut as a director after co-helming Ernesto Gastaldi's Gothic mystery *Libido* (1965), Enrico Maria Salerno's brother Vittorio chose a theme that has lots in common with "committed" Italian cinema. The story — young and naive Fabio (Enzo Cerusico) witnesses a brutal murder and instead of denouncing it goes through all the wrong moves while the real murderer (Riccardo Cucciolla) does his best to frame him, until he's eventually incarcerated and condemned for a crime he has not committed — was written by Augusto Finocchi, a 60-year-old retired railwayman with a passion for the movies who had previously written a number of interesting Spaghetti Westerns.[1]

Enzo Cerusico, left, Riccardo Cucciolla, center, and director Vittorio Salerno on the set of *No. Il caso è felicemente risolto* (1973) (courtesy Vittorio Salerno).

As Vittorio Salerno recalls, "I was handed a twenty page story, and the producer asked me to give it to Enrico, whom he wanted for the part of the bad guy[...]. However, Enrico didn't like it, and after a week he gave me the script back. I had an appointment with a RAI executive at noon, and I was half an hour early, so I sat on a bench in Piazza Mazzini, and started reading the story, which was called Il colpevole ["The Guilty"], just to kill time. And at the end I thought: this is great, it would be perfect for me! I would make that film! It was the first crime story in my career, I "felt" its message, its social criticism, the drama and the psychology."[2]

The plot has a number of things in common with the depictions of Italy's prison and justice system such as Nanni Loy's *Detenuto in attesa di giudizio* (l.t.: *In Prison Awaiting Trial*, 1971) starring Alberto Sordi. However, *No. Il caso è felicemente risolto* reworks the basic story of the innocent crushed by unfavorable circumstances as a thriller. The opening murder is a shocking moment which ignites a cat-and-mouse game between the killer and the eyewitness that at times recalls a perversely victimized take on the subgenre centering on private citizens taking justice into their own hands. Salerno wasn't too satisfied with the sequence: "It was badly shot, because everything had to be more hidden, the audience had only to catch a glimpse of what was happening ... hear the girl's screams but not watch her being hit too many times ... but I didn't manage to. There was simply not enough time to prepare the canes before the camera, so I had to shoot it like that ... it happens when you have to stay in schedule."[3] However, Salerno did stage an impressive sequence when the police find the dead prostitute in a corn field at night, with the victim's body intermittently illuminated by camera flashes.

The confrontation between the wily *petit bourgeois* Fabio and the cultured sex maniac also conveys a hint of social commentary. When Fabio finally finds himself face to face with the murderer, he is as servile as the typical "commedia all'italiana" characters are before their bosses, becoming "willing victims" as Pier Paolo Pasolini would brilliantly synthesize in his final film *Salò, or the 120 Days of Sodom* (*Salò o le 120 giornate di Sodoma*, 1975). As in similar political pamphlets, law enforcement are portrayed as both a distant and menacing entity from Fabio's point of view, conveying a distrust in law and order that's also typical in Italian cinema. If the authorities are irremediably obtuse, the film's *deus ex machina*— in a curious inversion of clichés — is a smart elderly journalist (played by Enrico Maria Salerno).

However, despite its ambitions, Salerno's film works as a gripping and masochistic hard-boiled allegory, which benefits a lot from its brilliant casting: Cerusico, a naturally likeable actor with boyish looks who found international notoriety thanks to the role of Tony Novello in the NBC show *The Danny Thomas Hour* (1967–1968) and the subsequent *My Friend Tony* (1969), brings a much needed empathy to a thankless role. "First

I got in touch with Enzo, whom I had appreciated in *My Friend Tony*," Salerno explained. "To me, he was the only young actor who could play the difficult character of the naïve petit bourgeois who witnesses the murder but doesn't have the guts to do his duty, [...] and just because of his lack of trust in law and his lack of a civic sense, gets framed in turn by the real murderer [...]. Enzo was so enthusiastic about the script that he immediately found a producer, Angelo Jacono, with whom he used to play poker. Two months later we were shooting in the cane thicket near lake Bracciano."[4]

As Fabio, Cerusico manages to be believable in a part that often pushes the viewer's suspension of disbelief to the limit, while Cucciolla — an actor who made a career essaying victims of society, such as in Giuliano Montaldo's *Sacco and Vanzetti*— is intelligently cast against type, a move Mario Bava would repeat in his marvelous *Rabid Dogs*.

Nevertheless, *No. Il caso è felicemente risolto* suffers from a number of incongruities and loose ends, which become evident in the rather hasty third act, not to mention a happy ending which was tacked on as a last-minute afterthought: in Salerno's original cut, Fabio is sentenced to 24 years, and even though Don Peppino, the journalist, suspects that the professor is the real culprit, he just doesn't have any evidence. As Salerno recalled, "it wasn't Angelo Jacono who wanted to change the ending ... the distributors did: the distribution company, Jumbo, was formed by regional distributors. Each provided in advance, with bills of exchange payable in four, six or twelve months, the profit he thought the film would make in his own theaters. And they thought people wouldn't like an ending where an innocent is condemned, especially one with Cerusico's friendly face. So Angelo Jacono politely 'suggested' we put a 'patch' in the end, otherwise the distributors wouldn't pay the bills and he'd end up in trouble. I accepted, even if unwillingly, and Enzo was very comprehensive, since he knew the rules of the game." Salerno shot the bit where Fabio is about to be released from his cell after Ranieri's confession and suicide. Cucciolla wasn't as accommodating, though: "He phoned me, and very politely, but firmly, expressed his dissatisfaction. He agreed to play that negative character because we were doing a committed film, otherwise he'd never do it."[5]

Vittorio Salerno, left, and his brother Enrico Maria Salerno on the set of *No. Il caso è felicemente risolto* (1973) (courtesy Vittorio Salerno).

Notes

1. Most notably Giorgio Ferroni's *Die Now, Pay Later* (1966), *Wanted* (1966), and *Two Pistols and a Coward* (Il pistolero segnato da Dio, 1968), Maurizio Lucidi's *Halleluja for Django* (*La più grande rapina del West*, 1967), Gianfranco Baldanello's *Black Jack* (1968) and Enzo Castellari's *I Came, I Saw, I Shot* (*I tre che sconvolsero il West*, 1968). Finocchi would also write Paolo Cavara's *Deaf Smith & Johnny Ears* (*Los amigos*, 1973) while his name appears on the credits merely for tax reasons on Jess Franco's *Count Dracula* (1970).
2. Davide Comotti and Vittorio Salerno, *Professione regista* (Rome: Lulu.com, 2012), p. 42. That same year Cerusico would play a police inspector in Dario Argento's offbeat TV movie *Il Tram* and a baker-turned-revolutionary in Argento's underrated period drama *The Five Days of Milan*.
3. *Ibid.*, p. 48.
4. *Ibid.*, p. 42.
5. *Ibid.*, p. 43.

Pete, Pearl and the Pole, a.k.a. *1931: Once Upon a Time in New York (Piazza pulita)*

D: Vance Lewis [Luigi Vanzi]. *S:* Tony Anthony; *SC:* Norman Thaddeus Vane; *DOP:* Riccardo Pallottini (35mm, Cinescope — Eastmancolor, Technospes); *M:* Louis Armstrong; *E:* Roberto Perpignani; *C:* Dante Di Palma; *AD:* Mimmola Girosi; *Mix:* Venanzio Biraschi; *MA:* Gaetano Scala. *Cast:* Tony Anthony (Pete Di Benedetto), Adolfo Celi (Polese), Lucretia Love (Pearl), Corrado Gaipa (Mafia boss), Richard Conte (Bruno), Lionel Stander (Pete's old gangster friend), Irene Papas (Donna Mimma, the widow). *Uncredited:* Bruno Arié (Polese's man), Raf Baldassarre (Raf, Polese's man), Loris Bazzocchi (Polese's man), David Dreyer. *PROD:* ABKCO films; *PSu:* Roger Petitto. *Country:* U.S.A. / Italy. Filmed at De Paolis Studios (Rome) and on location in West Virginia. *Running time:* 90'; Visa no.: 61969 (03.03.1973); *Rating:* v.m.18; *Release date:* 03.031973; *Distribution:* P.A.C.; *Domestic gross:* unknown. *Home video:* Blue Underground (DVD, USA — as *1931: Once Upon a Time in New York*); Perseo (DVD, Italy)

Farmington — West Virginia, 1931. Ambitious but down-on-his-luck New York City gangster Pete Di Benedetto, a former Al Capone associate, is hired by the mob to escort a deceased boss' body to New York and then to Sicily. Pete follows rival boss Polese to a distillery, where the Don dispatches another gangster, Bruno. Knowing that the family has hidden $500,000 inside the dead man's body, Pete offers Polese half if he'll help him hold up the funeral. They succeed, but when Pete demands his cut, Polese humiliates him and keeps the loot. After unsuccessfully asking an old friend's aid, Pete takes his revenge by kidnapping Polese's lover Pearl, and asking for the loot as ransom. Polese captures Pete and punishes him ferociously, leaving him for dead: when Pearl *gets back to bury him, she finds Di Benedetto is still alive and saves him. On Christmas night, Pete breaks into Polese's hideout and wipes out the whole gang, but he too is mortally wounded. As he is dying, Pete vainly asks Pearl to help him: the woman leaves with the money.*

A late entry in the period gangster thread, Luigi Vanzi's *Pete, Pearl and the Pole* is a weird little film. Shot mainly on location (despite the title, it's entirely set in West Virginia) with American money and mainly aimed at the U.S. market, it features a handful of name actors (Richard Conte, Irene Papas, Lionel Stander) who are actually on screen for a few minutes each. The project originated from a story written by star Tony Anthony, with whom Vanzi had shot a bizarre Western triptych (*A Stranger in Town*, 1967; *A Man, a Horse, a Gun*, 1967; and *The Silent Stranger*, 1968). It would be the director's last film. Besides sparse but clever period notations, such as the gramophone Anthony keeps in his car, which plays Louis Armstrong songs all the time, *Pete, Pearl and the Pole* veers wildly between a picaresque, sarcastic tone and unexpected, disturbing brutality. Characters are uniformly unpleasant, including Anthony as the self-important yet rather whiny antihero who boasts of his apprenticeship with Al Capone, and Celi as a vulgar, spaghetti-munching, cigar-chomping, razor-wielding mob boss. What's more, Vanzi delivers a number of extremely violent scenes. The idea of a corpse stuffed with money recalls the heroin-padded cadaver in Ferdinando Baldi's *The Sicilian Connection* (and the scene where Corrado Gaipa is shut up inside the coffin with the corpse while he's still alive and kicking is virtually identical to Pino Derio's demise in Baldi's film), but also worth noting are Adolfo Celi's slicing of Tony Anthony's foot with a razor and the final Christmas shotgun massacre, which takes place under the intermittent red light of a Christmas tree, and almost looks like something out of a *giallo*.

U.S. poster for Luigi Vanzi's *Pete, Pearl & the Pole* (1973).

The final showdown aside, Vanzi keeps a tight pace throughout, and puts to best use the film's sloppy set-pieces in the coal-processing plant scene, when Anthony barely escapes death. Most impressive, however, is the cynical and bleak ending, which sheds new light on what at first looked like a one-dimensional character, Lucretia Love's Pearl. "I need the money for someone who doesn't slap me and call me a whore," she says as she leaves, letting Pete bleed to death, before delivering the film's grim moral: "Do you remember what you told me? *fatti furba, fotti e fregatenn'* [get smart, screw and stop caring]."

La polizia è al servizio del cittadino? (Are the Police at the Service of the Citizen?)

D: Romolo Guerrieri [Romolo Girolami]. *S:* Goffredo Sebasti, Marcello Serralonga, Mario Cecchi Gori; *SC:* Massimo De Rita, Dino Maiuri; *DOP:* Carlo Carlini (35mm, Technicolor); *M:* Luis Enriquez Bacalov, conducted by the author; *E:* Antonio Siciliano; *PD:* Franco Cuppini; *CO:* Francesca Saitto; *COA:* Giorgio Gamma; *C:* Sergio Martinelli; *AC:* Massimo Carlini; *AE:* Rosalba Giacobbe; *AD:* Giorgio Scotton; *MU:* Sergio Angeloni; *Hair:* Marcella Favella; *W:* Nadia Panci; *SO:* Domenico Dubbini; *Boom:* Benito Alchimede; *Mix:* Giulio Barbieri; *SP:* Firmino Palmieri; *SS:* Marisa Agostini. *Cast:* Enrico Maria Salerno (Commissioner Nicola Sironi), Giuseppe Pambieri (Martino), John Steiner ("Lambro"), Venantino Venantini (Pino Mancinelli), Daniel Gélin (Pier Paolo Brera), Alessandro Momo (Michele Sironi), Memmo Carotenuto ("The Baron"), Gabriella Giorgelli ("Eros," a prostitute), Claudio Nicastro (Chief of Flying Squad), Marie-Sophie Persson (Cristina), Enzo Liberti (Greengrocer), Cinzia Bruno (Cinzia, the greengrocer's daughter), Stella Carnacina (Cristina's friend), Ubaldo Granata (Antonio Scalise), André Mazzeau, Tino Bianchi (Chief of Police), Francesco D'Adda (policeman), Giuseppe Bruno Bossio, Raoul Martinez (Silvio Merkel), Bruno Alias (Journalist). *PROD:* Mario Cecchi Gori for Capital Film (Rome), P.E.C.F. (Paris); *GO:* Luciano Luna; *PM:* Vincenzo Mazzucchi; *PSu:* Renato Fiè; *PSe:* Giandomenico Stellitano; *ADM:* Mario Lupi. *Country:* Italy. Filmed on location in Genoa.

Running time: 98'; Visa no.: 63004 (08.25.1973); *Rating:* v.m.14; *Release date:* 09.06.1973; *Distribution:* P.I.C.; *Domestic gross:* 1,033,918,000 lire. *Also known as: Auf verlorenem Posten* (West Germany), *Der letzte Beweis* (West Germany — TV), *Defendiendo a los ciudadanos* (Spain), *La police au service du citoyen* (France), *Mafioso!* (Sweden), *Politiet til tjeneste* (Norway). *Home video:* Hobby & Work (DVD, Italy). OST: CD Point Records PRCD 115.

Genoa. After the brutal killing of a dock worker, who's been found hanging from a crane, commissioner Nicola Sironi — a lonely embittered man, separated from his wife and alienated from his own son — investigates a racket which rules over the city's wholesale markets. Sironi uses a pimp named Mancinelli as bait to uncover the racket bosses, but the man is murdered and so are a local boss, Scalise, and a brave greengrocer who rose up to the racket. Sironi devises a trap, pretending the greengrocer has survived the murder attempt and setting up an ambush for the killers in a private clinic. Yet he only finds out, much to his chagrin, that his friend and assistant Martino is being bribed by the racket as well. Sironi's stubborness leads him to the powerful engineer Brera, the man who pulls the strings behind the whole racket. The repented Martino tries to get vital evidence to help Sironi, but he's brutally killed by Brera's men, and a tape containing evidence of Brera's culpability is erased. Sironi is removed from the case, and decides to take justice into his own hands: he kidnaps Brera and has him killed in a staged car accident.

After his starring role in *Execution Squad*, Enrico Maria Salerno became the first true star of the newborn poliziotteschi. The following year he was the lead in a couple of commercially successful crime films, Roberto Infascelli's *The Great Kidnapping* and Romolo Guerrieri's *La polizia è al servizio del cittadino?* Guerrieri's film takes its provocative title from a catch-phrase ("In the Democratic State, the Police are at the Citizens' Service") which appeared on posters on the walls of every police station at that time, as part of a campaign to make the law enforcement more popular and citizen-friendly, in quite a difficult time of social indignation and turbulence. In one scene, a police agent asks Commissioner Sironi the permit to hang the poster on his office's wall, meeting with the hero's sarcastic response: "Put it where you like, but not here in my office ... a policeman has the duty to be civil with everybody, but not a servant!"

As with Castellari's *High Crime*, the setting is Genoa, whose urban landscape is the story's true glue: the docks, the junctions, the "Sopraelevata," the skyscrapers recall similar images of Marseille and San Francisco, yet at the same time they convey what has been called "the city's duplicitous nature, both an industrial scenario and the promise of an exotic Mediterranean dimension."[1] Guerrieri is astute when it comes to emphasizing the story's spectacular potential: the opening sequence, showing the beating and killing of a docker who is then hung on a crane's hook, to make for a macabre warning to the other workers, accompanied only by Luis Bacalov's score, is a powerful introduction, as is the one where Salerno tails a man through the city traffic. Guerrieri doesn't shy away from violence: the scene where Mancinelli the pimp (Venantino Venantini) falls to his death from a skyscraper comes complete with a gory close-up of the scene's aftermath, shootouts feature blood aplenty, and in a harrowing scene Giuseppe Pambieri is run over by a car which crushes his hands and torso.

Besides its powerful action scenes, *La polizia è al servizio del cittadino?* is noteworthy for its bitter tone, starting from the question mark which slashes the title. Compared to *Execution Squad*, Salerno's commissioner here is devoid of his predecessor's political obtuseness: it doesn't take long before Sironi realizes that his friend and colleague Martino (Giuseppe Pambieri) is on the racket's paybook. Sironi is a disillusioned man indeed. His professional failures sum up with those in his private life: not only does he fail to protect his eyewitnesses, he practically delivers Mancinelli to his killers by using him as bait. What's more, his wife hangs the phone up on him, and his militant son (Alessandro Momo) accuses him: "I'm not ashamed of you as a cop, I'm ashamed of you as a father!" However, Sironi's lines are already an epitome of commissioners' vocabulary in the crime genre, as shown by such world-weary comments as his rants against the press ("You write that the police is brutal because sometimes we defend ourselves") and his views on what it means to be a cop: "The only way I know is to take chances, you don't get anywhere by sitting behind a desk!"

The obstinacy that Sironi shows in his personal struggle to incriminate engineer Brera (Daniel Gélin), the powerful head of the criminal organization, almost seems a way for the commissioner to vent his personal frustrations. His revenge hides perhaps a personal grudge against the world. "If you only knew how fascinating it is to fight against the giants," he tells Martino. The latter — young, handsome, womanizer — predates one of Italian crime films' most important and subversive characters, commissioner Malacarne (Luc Merenda) in Fernando di Leo's *Shoot First, Die Later* (*Il poliziotto è marcio*, 1974), and is at least an attempt at avoiding schematic characterizations — a danger which is already perceptible. Massimo De Rita and Dino Maiuri's script allows Martino a last-minute redemption, in the memorable sequence of the ambush at the yacht club, where day-for-night shooting and open spaces allow for a satisfyingly tense result.

In *La polizia è al servizio del cittadino?* the generational and methodical turnover within the underworld is depicted as complete. "These people kill. They're newcomers, they're organized, they're determined to rule the market," Sironi observes. The "old" underworld survives only in the person of the elderly burglar (Memmo Carotenuto) who cares for his family and helps the police. "My organization works because all there is around it is rotten," Brera comments. The incarnation of such a ruthless criminality is John Steiner's sneering, sadistic killer — a character the British actor would reprise often in his career.

To fight on equal terms, Sironi has to jump the thin and fleeting line between legality and illegality. "Justice is equal for all, but on the other hand it brandishes a sword," he says. He sneaks into Brera's headquarters and burgles his safe, uses all sorts of tricks to get evidence, and in the end — after he's been removed from the case — he takes justice into his own hands. It's the point of no return for the Italian crime film: a man of justice killing his adversary in cold blood — and what a way to kill him! The scene of Brera's murder is one of the most intense in the whole genre, and conveys a hint of sadism which predates what would come next. Brera wakes up in his car, realizes he is on the tracks and a train is approaching, but finds out he can't get out (Sironi took the handles off) nor start the engine. The commissioner watches impassively Brera's desperate attempts at escaping until the final clash.

The film's political references are patent. A dialogue scene has Enrico Maria Salerno paraphrasing almost to the letter a famous poem by Pier Paolo Pasolini, *Il PCI ai giovani!!* where the poet expressed his contempt towards young wealthy students and offered solidarity to the working class cops ("Tell your friends that before insulting a cop they take a good look at his face. And you, too, look at them. Cops are sons of peasants, they come from poor families, their parents couldn't afford to pay for their education, nor did they have the chance to gather in the street and express your ideas as you do"). Through the relationship between Sironi and his estranged son, Guerrieri's film depicts in a hasty yet rather effective manner the generational gap and the ongoing crisis of the traditional patriarchal family.

Note

1. Venturelli, *Genova o la lacerazione del paesaggio urbano*, p.52.

Redneck (Senza ragione a.k.a. *Squadra volante uccideteli ... senza ragione)*

D: Silvio Narizzano. *S:* Rafael Sánchez Campoy; *SC:* Win Wells, Masolino D'Amico; *DOP:* Giorgio Tonti (35mm, Eastmancolor, L.V.-Luciano Vittori); *M:* Maurizio Catalano; *Main title theme: Memphis* by John Cacavas; *E:* Thom Noble; *AE:* Alessandro Lucidi, Peppita Fairfax; *PD:* Arrigo Equini; *2nd UD:* Terry Knight, Bob Fiz [Roberto Fizz]; *C:* Luciano Tonti; *ADs:* Gus Agosti, Gianni Cozzo; *MU:* Giuseppe Capogrosso; *Hair: W:* Teresa Miccinelli; *SO:* Piero Fondi, John Bateman; *Mix:* Bill Rowe; *SOEd:* Terry Poulton; *SS:* Suzanne Ilig. *Cast:* Franco Nero (Dino Bianco "Mosquito"), Telly Savalas (Memphis "The American"), Mark Lester (Lennox Duncan), Ely Galleani (Maria), Duilio Del Prete (Captain Lenzi), Maria Michi (Princess), Aldo De Carellis (Riccardo), Bruno Boschetti (police officer), Beatrice Clary (Margaret Duncan), Tom Duggan (Anthony Duncan), Pino [Giuseppe] Mattei (Jeweler), Marion Montgomery (American woman in hotel), Antonio Paris (Shepherd boy), Wanda Pallini (First prostitute), Liliana Fioramonti (Second prostitute), Jean-Pierre Clarain (German father), Britta Barnes (German mother), Michel Barnes (German boy), Daniela Barnes (German girl). *Uncredited:* Aristide Caporale (Man at street market), Valentino Simeoni (Gas station clerk). *PROD:* Michael Lester and Silvio Narizzano for Sterle (London), Compagnia Internazionale Alessandra Cinematografica (Rome); *GM:* Mario Del Papa. *Country:* U.K. / Italy. *Running time:* 90'; Visa no.: 61798 (01.25.1973); *Rating:* v.m.14; *Release date:* 01.26.1973; *Distribution:* Euro International Films; *Domestic gross:* 137,846,000 lire. *Also known as: Redneck* (UK, 1976), *Le salopard* (Paris, 02.01.1978 — 90'), *O crocodico* (Lisboa, 02.12.1974 — 90') *Home video:* GMVS (DVD, UK)

Rome. Two bandits, Mosquito and Memphis, rob a jewelry store, but the heist ends in bloodshed as Memphis guns down the shop owner. During their escape to the French border with Mosquito's girlfriend Maria, they destroy their vehicle and steal a car, thus inadvertently kidnapping a 13-year-old boy, Lennox Duncan, the son of the British consul who was hiding in the back seat. Besides finding out that the loot actually consists of silver cutlery instead of jewels, Memphis proves to be a demented, sadistic madman: he rapes and kills Maria, then forces his companions to let a whole family of German tourists drown inside their camper. Meanwhile, Lennox is morbidly fascinated by the two criminals and their deeds. Memphis — who is badly wounded — and his two companions reach the border, but they've got the police on their trail. In the end, the two men meet a tragic death.

A British / Italian co-production, *Redneck* is one of the most unpleasant thrillers of the 1970s. The leading characters eschew any identification on behalf of the audience: the pimp/gigolo "Mosquito" (Franco Nero) is an annoying, tragicomic simpleton, whereas his accomplice, the whiny psychopath Memphis (Telly Savalas), is a bloodbrother of the "rabid dogs" that would populate Italian crime cinema in the '70s, starting with *Almost Human*'s Giulio Sacchi. Drug addicted, impotent, morbidly jealous of his partner in crime, Memphis kills women, children and animals with glee, then cries crocodile tears during the bandits' escape to the French border after a robbery ended in violence.

Savalas hams it up with wild abandon: he hums, prays, shouts, puts on a pout, in a display of acting mannerisms — including a deeply affected Southern drawl — that borders on the unbearable. The same can be said about the film itself, though: the script by Win Wells and Masolino D'Amico (a renowned film critic, journalist and translator) works on a basic road movie plot — with curious similarities to Mario Bava's *Rabid Dogs* and Dino Risi's *Dirty Weekend*— and mixes typical action movie fare (the scenes involving Duilio Del Prete as a captain aptly named Lenzi) with picaresque and even openly humorous interludes and bouts of violence, with unsettling results — even more so given the frequent grotesque touches, such as the initial escape by car, when the robbers' vehicle wreaks havoc at a funeral, or the episode set in an isolated villa in the mountains, where Moschino seduces a crazy princess (Maria Michi).

If the humor is grim and the emphasis on sexuality is — as in many Italian films of the period — decidedly politically incorrect, *Redneck* doesn't stint on sheer violence and brutality either, such as in the killing of a family of campers, which predates a similar sequence in Guerrieri's *Young, Violent, Dangerous.* Yet the film's most unpleasant moments pertain to the homoerotic implications of the weird relationship between Moschino, Memphis and their 13-year-old hostage Lennox (played by former *Oliver!* star Mark Lester), who's transfixed by his kidnappers' amorality and seems naturally inclined to evil. It's rather typical casting for Lester, who basically plays a darker variation on previous similar roles in John Hough's *Eyewitness* (1970), Curtis Harrington's *Who Slew Auntie Roo?* (1971) and James Kelley's *What the Peeper Saw* (1972). Here, as the spoilt child whose mother is more concerned about her stolen fur coat and who develops a morbid attachment to Mosquito, Lester is given an especially uncomfortable scene with a fully naked Nero in a bedroom, where the seeming surrogate father / son bond becomes something darker when, after Nero has left the room, the boy slowly undresses himself before a mirror as he mimics him. Speaking of minors, an 8-year-old Lara Wendel (still credited under her real name Daniela Barnes) briefly pops up as the German campers' daughter, along with her mother and brother.

The Canadian-born Narizzano had directed a number of interesting works such as the Hammer thriller *Die! Die! My Darling* (1965), *Georgy Girl* (1966) and the offbeat Western *Blue* (1968) starring Terence Stamp, where he had proven himself as a capable filmmaker. On *Redneck*, however, he seems totally detached from, if not scornful of, the characters and story alike. Besides Savalas' shameless overacting, Nero's performance — in a role that challenges the actor's habitual heroic turns yet is somehow coherent with his other acting roles of the period such as the clumsy vigilante in Enzo Castellari's *Street Law* (*Il cittadino si ribella*, 1974) — borders on the masochistic: he starts the film in his underwear, after he failed to sexually satisfy a woman that paid for his services, and ends it wearing a woman's fur.

Narizzano's film was later re-released in Italy as *Squadra volante uccideteli ... senza ragione* ("Flying Squad Kill Them ... For No Reason"), in an attempt at jumping on the poliziotteschi frenzy.

Ricco the Mean Machine (*Ajuste de cuentas / Un tipo con una faccia strana ti cerca per ucciderti*)

D: Tulio Demicheli. *S* and *SC:* Santiago Moncada, José Gutiérrez Maesso, Mario Di Nardo; *DOP:* Francisco Fraile (35mm, Eastmancolor, Telecolor); *M:* Nando De Luca; *E:* Ángel Serrano; *ArtD:* Lidia Soprani; *ArtD:* Rafael Ferri; *2nd C:* Ramón Sempere; *AC:* Salvador Gomez; *AE:* Felisa Rueda; *AD:* Félix Férnandez; *MU:* Maria de Elena y García; *AMU:* Tomasa Benito; *Hair:* Nuria Paradel; *W:* Carmen Ochoa; *SO:* Jesús Peña; *SR:* Tonino Paolilli; *SE:* Baquero — Molina; *SP:* José Salvador; *SS:* Olga Moller. *Cast:* Christopher Mitchum (Rico Aversi), Barbara Bouchet (Scilla), Malisa Longo (Rosa), Eduardo Fajardo (Cyrano), Manuel Zarzo (Tony), José María Caffarel (The Marseillese), Ángel Álvarez (Giuseppe Calogero), Arthur Kennedy (Don Vito), Paola Senatore (Concetta Aversi), Luis Induni (Don Gaspare Aversi, Rico's father), Tomás Blanco (Commissioner), Victor Israel (Cicala, the nightclub owner), José Canalejas (Don Vito's man), Luigi Antonio Guerra (Concetta's husband), Rina Franchetti (Rico's mother), Goyo Lebrero (Vittorio, the supermarket truck driver), Antonio Mayans (Nightclub bartender), Lorenzo Robledo (Pepe, Don Vito's henchman), Domenico Maggio (Don Vito's man) Andrea Scotti (policeman), Carla Mancini (Girl at the bar). *Uncredited:* Augustín Bescos, Sergio Testori (Don Vito's assassin). *PROD:* José Gutiérrez Maesso for Tecisa (Madrid), B.R.C. Produzione (Rome); *PM:* Faustino Ocaña; *PA:* Eduardo Esquide; *2nd PA:* Germán Quejido. *Country:* Spain / Italy. Filmed at Incir — De Paolis (Rome) and on location in Turin. Soap factory scenes filmed at Wella laboratories in Torrejon de Ardoz (Madrid). *Running time:* 89'; Visa no.: 63001 (08.22.1973); *Rating:* v.m.18; *Release date:* 08.23.1973; *Distribution:* Alpherat; *Domestic gross:* 229,985,000 lire. *Also known as: The Cauldron of Death, Der Clan der Killer* (Germany), *The Dirty Mob. Home video:* Dark Sky Films (DVD, Us)

Turin. After elderly boss Don Gaspare Aversi is killed in an ambush, Don Vito takes over his organization. Gaspare's son Rico, emerging from jail after a two year sentence, finds out that his girlfriend Rosa has become Don Vito's lover and is persuaded by his mother to take revenge against the boss. Rico is helped by Rosa's father, counterfeiter Giuseppe Calogero, and the latter's niece Scilla, who falls for him. Together with Gaspare's friend Cyrano, Rico sets up a scam to rob Don Vito 500 million lire plus the diamonds that Vito is going to buy from a Marseillaise gangster, to whom Rico and Cyrano give counterfeit money instead. However, Cyrano tries to get rid of Rico and take the money and diamonds for himself, but is killed by the Marseillaise, who discovers the scam. Rico is about to meet the same end, but he's saved by Scilla. Meanwhile, Rosa seduces Don Vito's right hand man Tony, but the crimelord catches the two lovers in bed and kills both. He then proceeds to exact revenge upon Rico's family by killing his pregnant sister and mother. Rico goes to Vito's soap factory for the final showdown, where both men lose their lives.

Another attempt at making Robert Mitchum's wooden son Chris a European exploitation star, Tulio Demicheli's *Ricco the Mean Machine* is less accomplished than Antonio Isasi's *Summertime Killer*, but is definitely gorier. Distributed in the United States by Edward L. Montoro through Film Ventures International, Demicheli's film gained something of a cult reputation because of a handful of over-the-top scenes, the most notorious being the on-screen castration of Arthur Kennedy's right hand man (played by Manuel Zarzo), who has his severed penis stuck in his mouth and is then thrown into a cauldron of sizzling soda (hence the alternate title *The Cauldron of Death*, as the film was marketed in the U.S. as a horror).

Ricco the Mean Machine's insistence on explicit violence, crudely shown in nasty close-ups — other notable moments are the opening murder of the hero's father (Luis Induni), who gets shot in the head, and a Marseille-born gangster (José María Caffarel) who has his teeth mashed in by a rifle butt — puts the film in the same vein as other Mafia movies of the period, such as Andrea Bianchi's *Cry of a Prostitute* (which even beats Demicheli's film in sheer splattery excesses), and makes for a dull, very badly written revenge story populated by barely sketched characters and riddled with plot holes.

The other main selling point of Demicheli's film is the Argentinian director's leering appetite for the bodies of his female cast: Barbara Bouchet, Malisa Longo and Paola Senatore are as gorgeous a trio as were ever seen in Italian films, and all have extended nude scenes. Senatore's character is particularly pretextual, as the woman is almost always shown in bed with her husband, from her screen introduction to her death scene. On the other hand, Bouchet's appearance, peddling counterfeit notes in the streets of Turin in red adherent trousers and a blue denim jacket that barely covers her voluptuous cleavage ("Hello, golden ass," Rico greets her the second time he sees her) is one of the film's most memorable moments. Not the same can be said, despite the actress' shining display of beauty, about Bouchet's striptease in the middle of a street at night amidst a very artificial-looking fog in front of a couple of thugs' car, which borders on the ridiculous. Longo has a great scene where she seduces Manuel Zarzo by showing up in see-through lingerie while the man is trying to build a house of cards.

Perhaps the best way to appreciate the film is on a camp level. Mitchum's laughable macho poses, deadpan delivery and absolute lack of acting skills are on a pair with Arthur Kennedy's characterization and make-up, including a black wig which desperately tries to make him look 20 years younger than he is. The icing on the cake comes after the infamous castration scene, which is followed by a shot of Bouchet licking an ice cream.

Last but not least, the U.S. title is actually a misreading of the protagonist's name — which is Rico, not Ricco, which just doesn't exist in Italy (the word means "rich" instead).

7 Hours of Violence (*Sette ore di violenza per una soluzione imprevista*)

D: Michele Massimo Tarantini. *S:* Giorgio Capitani, Lucio Chiavarelli, Paolo Levi; *SC:* Sauro Scavolini; *DOP:* Federico Zanni (35mm,

Cinescope — Eastmancolor, L.V.-Luciano Vittori); *M:* Alessandro Alessandroni (ed. Sermi Film); *E:* Antonietta Zita; *PD:* Giacomo Calò Carducci; *CO:* Dafne Ciarrocchi; *COper:* Giampiero Servo; *AD:* Angelo Vicari; *MU:* Pietro Tenoglio; *Hair:* Jole Angelucci; *SO:* Armando Bondani, Vittorio Massi; *SOE:* Sergio Basili, Aldo Ciorba; *Mix:* Bruno Moreal; *SP:* Roberto Carnevali, Antonio Benetti; *SS:* Almuth Brandes Pizzo. *Cast:* George Hilton (George Anderson), Rosemarie Dexter (Helena Karlatos), Giampiero Albertini (Inspector Athanasiadis), Steffen Zacharias (Sam Fastiropoulos), Claudio Nicastro (Kavafris), Gianni Musy (Mchael Papadopoulos), Iwao Yoshioka (Chinese thug), Ernesto Colli (Tomassian), Carlo Gaddi (Athanasiadis's assistant), Greta Vayan (Greta Papadopoulos), Renata Zamengo (Melina), George Wang (Chinese thug): uncredited: Antonio Casale. *PROD:* Vittorio Galliano and Marcello Romeo for Galassia Film, Dania Film; *AP:* Luciano Martino; *PM:* Lamberto Palmieri; *UM:* Furio Rocchi; *PSe:* Giuseppe Bruno Bossio. *Country:* Italy. Filmed at Elios Film — Dear Film Studios (Rome) and on location in Athens, Greece. *Running time:* 93'; Visa no.: 63465 (11.09.1973); *Rating:* v.m.18; *Release date:* 15.11.1973; *Distribution:* Medusa; *Domestic gross:* 256,949,000 lire. *Also known as: Un homme appelé Karaté* (Paris, 12.31.1975 — 93'). *Home video:* Bestl (VHS, Holland, English language), Rex (VHS, Greece, English language), (VHS, Denmark, English language), GVR (VHS, Italy)

Blackmailed by his own lawyer Sam Fastiropoulos, who's in possession of film negatives that depict him committing a murder, contract killer George Anderson accepts a mission in Greece, where he's got to kill Mike Papadopoulos, site foreman for the powerful shipowner Kavafris. Anderson fails to carry out the hit, but Papadopulous is mistakenly killed by his wife, who frames George for the murder. Chased by the police, George takes refuge by a young woman, Elena Karlatos, who falls for him. Meanwhile Kavafris — who turns out to be the mysterious blackmailer who hired George through Fastiropoulos in the first place, so as to get rid of his employee — puts three Chinese thugs on his trail. The trio eliminates all those who could help George escape, including Fastiropoulos, but Anderson eventually turns the tables on his persecutor: he questions Papadopoulos' wife and finds out the truth. Anderson then faces Kavafris, who has kidnapped Elena and is taking her prisoner on a wreck boat, and kills him, but he cannot save the woman.

A former editor and assistant director, Michele Massimo Tarantini became a specialist of erotic comedies in the late 1970s and early 1980s, with such titles as *Confessions of a Lady Cop* (*La poliziotta fa carriera*, 1976), *L'insegnante al mare con tutta la classe* (1979) and *La dottoressa ci sta col colonnello* (1980). Tarantini also directed two proper poliziotteschi, *Crimebusters* (*Poliziotti violenti*, 1976) and *A Man Called Magnum* (*Napoli si ribella*, 1977). *7 Hours of Violence*, his directorial debut, can also be ascribed to the genre, even though it's more of a *film noir* / action hybrid than an urban crime story.

Besides the usual references to classic *film noir*, with Hilton as the obligatory lonesome hitman, *7 Hours of Violence* is worth noting because of the laughable kung fu fighting scenes, in homage to the then-current chop-socky fashion, which in France gained it the title *Un homme appelé Karaté* ("A Man Called Karate") but virtually destroy any atmosphere the film might have had, with their appalling slow-motion shots, awkward accelerations and sound effects that belong to a Shaw Brothers film. Only Alessandro Alessandroni's pleasantly driving score rises above mediocrity.

Sgarro alla camorra (Offence to the Camorra)

D: Ettore Maria Fizzarotti. *S:* Ettore M. Fizzarotti; *SC:* Vincenzo Grano, Alfredo Melidoni, Ettore M. Fizzarotti; *DOP:* Alberto Spagnoli (35mm, Eastmancolor, L.V. Luciano Vittori); *M:* Antonio Esposito, arranged and conducted by the author (ed. A.B.C. — Rondinella); *Songs: Cielo e mare* (G. Esposito / F. Genta), *'A Camorra* (V. Annona / A. Esposito), *Giuramento* (G. Russo / A. Vian), *'O meglio amico* (L. Bovio / F. Albano), *Curtiello cu curtiello* (A. Fiorini / V. Di Domenico) sung by Mario Merola; *E:* Raimondo Crociani; *PD, CO:* Nicola Losito; *ArtD:* Antonio Angiuoni; *C:* Emilio Loffredo; *AC:* Giorgio Urbinelli; *2nd AC:* Sandro Rubeo; *AE:* Pina Triunveri, Mario D'Ambrosio; *AD:* Luigi Ferraro; *MU:* Liliana Dulac; *Hair:* Flavio Pavone; *SO:* Goffredo Salvatori; *Mix:* Romano Pampaloni; *SP:* Stefano Colombai; *ChEl:* Emilio Rubeo; *KG:* Amerigo Casagrande; *PrM:* Roberto Pace; *MA:* Rinaldo Zamperla; *DColl, PP:* Adolfo Dragone. *Cast:* Mario Merola (Andrea Staiano), Franco Acampora (Pietro Morra), Dada Gallotti (Angela), Enzo Cannavale (Vincenzo "Papela"), Pietro De Vico (Gnassa), Dolores Palumbo (Donna Carmela), Aldo Bufi Landi (Scicco), Giuseppe Anatrelli (Don Enrico Cecere), Silvia Dionisio (Gisella Gargiulo), Saro Urzì ("Great Uncle"), Vittorio La Rosa, Alessandro Perrella (Prison guard), Domenico Messina (Cecere's man), Lorenzo Piani, Vincenzo Falanga (Totò), Rinaldo Zamperla (Basettone), Pasquale Fiorante Malleo (Uncle Pasquale), Renzo Giovanni Pevarello (Don Alfonso), Vincenzo Ceparano, Sergio Testori, Alberto Amato, Giuseppe Ferrara, Armando Rossi, Crescenzo Napoleone, Gennaro Beneduce (The Fool of the village), Agostino Pieri, Ettore Annunziata, Michele Gargiulo. *PROD:* CI.PA. Cinematografica Partenopea (Naples); *GM:* Alfredo Melidoni; *PM:* Alfredo Mirabile; *PSu:* Francesco Manco; *PSe:* Guglielmo Carbonaro; *CASH:* Raffaele Esposito. *Country:* Italy. Shot on location in Cetara (Naples). *Running time:* 100; Visa no.: 62027 (03.08.1973); *Rating:* not rated; *Release date:* 03.09.1973; *Distribution:* Titanus; *Domestic gross:* 393,263,000 lire. *Home video:* Creazioni Home Video (VHS, Italy) Master (DVD, Italy)

Andrea Staiano is framed for a murder committed by Neapolitan cammorist Enrico Cecere. After serving seven years in prison, he returns to his village on the Amalfi Coast. With the help of his good friend Pietro, he restores his family boat and resumes his fishing business. One day, though, Angela — Cecere's lover, and the cause of Staiano's imprisonment— tells Andrea that he has been released through the intervention of Camorra kingpins who want to use him in their trafficking. When Andrea refuses, Angela seduces Pietro. Cecere orders Andrea to use his boat to smuggle drugs at sea, on Christmas night. Angela reveals Pietro it's all a trick set up by Cecere to trap Staiano and kill him. Pietro takes Andrea's boat and is killed in his place. Andrea then faces Cecere in a knife duel and kills him.

Although largely overlooked at the time of its release, *Sgarro alla camorra* marked the prototype of a new crime subgenre which would fully develop by the end of the decade, while the police/crime trend was gradually waning, caught in the deeper crisis that was submerging the Italian cinema industry as a whole.

The roots of the new hybrid (which could be roughly dubbed as guapparia movie, in reference to a popular Neapolitan expression which indicates the old Camorra code of honor) lied in the so-called sceneggiata, a form of play that belongs to the Parthenopean tradition and is characterized by a strong melodramatic component as well as a tragic fatalism: both lead to a final, emotionally powerful catharsis. Songs are an integral and binding part of sceneggiata, and constellate the narration in its various parts, while the social environment in which the stories take place is that of the Neapolitan underworld. The hero is the *guappo* (a word deriving from the Spanish *guapo*), a gangster with strong moral values (family, loyalty and honor) while the villain (*'o malamente*—literally "he who [acts] badly") is a grim, unfair adversary who tries to seduce the protagonist's woman or to soil his reputation. That of sceneggiata is an enclosed universe, where love and hate seem to be part of a natural order not unlike life and death: always absolute, complete, desperate.

Mario Merola was the king of the sceneggiata on stage. Of humble origins, a former cook and dock worker, Merola became a stage actor after recording a song, *Malu figlio*, which inspired a sceneggiata. Merola himself was the protagonist. He soon became the most successful actor within the genre, and was very popular among Italian immigrants in Canada and the United States. *Sgarro alla camorra* was Merola's first film. Director Ettore Maria Fizzarotti, a specialist in the so-called "musicarelli" (song-and-dance flicks starring Italian pop singers which were very popular in late '50s and '60s) diligently brought the rules of the "sceneggiata" to the silver screen, leaving ample room for Merola's songs—such as *Cielo e mare*, *A Camorra*, *Giuramento*, *O meglio amico*—which interrupt the action like in a musical. Here, however, Merola is not a real guappo yet, but an honest man who's been used by cammorists: "Always walk on the clean road, and you won't be afraid of falling into the dirt" he tells his young friend Pietro. But in the end he too embraces the law of violence.

Lurid Italian poster for *Sgarro alla camorra* (1973), Mario Merola's first sceneggiata.

The result is still unripe and uncertain, permeated by an antimodern tension which is evident throughout the film. It shows in the characters and their relationships, such as old guard Sicilian Mafia boss Saro Urzì, Andrea's friendship with Pietro, and not least the comedy relief provided by Enzo Cannavale and Pietro De Vico as two hungry morons. It's evident in the places (the village of Cetara on the Amalfi coast, seen as a timeless Eden: "It's been seven years since I left, and it seems just like yesterday") and in the way traditions are portrayed, such as the Christmas mass in the final sequences. And it's also patent in the way the story develops, such as the subplot about the chaste love story between Pietro (Franco Acampora) and Gisella (Silvia Dionisio) which is threatened by the "*malafemmena*" ("bad woman," the Neapolitan version of film *noir's femme fatale*) Angela—who by the way is not Neapolitan but French—who gets punished in the end.

Sgarro alla camorra ends in typical sceneggiata style: the final knife duel between Merola and "*'o malamente*" (Giuseppe Anatrelli), to the sound of the song *Curtiello cu curtiello* (Knife vs. Knife), is a moment of pure popular old-style cinema aimed at audiences that were not used to urban violence as shown by Vanzina and Castellari. However, character actor Giuseppe Anatrelli adds a hint of irony to his role as the evil Enrico Cecere, who boasts about his old days in the seminary ("I should have been a priest!") and wears a sacred tunic as if it was a dressing gown; on the other hand, Basettone's (Rinaldo Zamperla) savage beating and the sequence where Merola assaults a thug at the fish market hint at the formula's permeability, and suggest a possible deepening of the action component. These elements would be improved upon in future examples of the Neapolitan-based crime film which would generate a proper subgenre within a few years.

Special Killers (La ragazza di via Condotti)

D: Germán Lorente. *S* and *SC:* Adriano Asti, Germán Lorente, Miguel de Echarri; *DOP:* Mario Capriotti (35mm, Eastmancolor, Staco Film); *DOP—2nd unit:* Frederick Antoine Compin; *M:* Enrico Simonetti, arranged and conducted by the author (ed. Bixio Sam); *Una ragazza come tante* (Canterini / Simonetti) is sung by Augusto Daolio; *E:* Giancarlo Cappelli, Henri Rust; *PD:* Dino Leonetti; *ArtD:* Santiago Ontañón; *ArtD:* Camillo Del Signore; *CO:* Mario Giorsi; *C:* Giuseppe De Biase, Gaetano Valle; *AC:* Guido Tosi; *AD:* Massimo Carocci; *SO:* Pietro Spadoni; *Mix:* Alberto Tinebra; *Boom:* Vincenzo Onali; *MU:* Lamberto Marini, Franco Schioppa; *Hair:* Vitaliana Patacca; *SP:* Massimo Zeri; *STC:* Remo De Angelis; *SS:* Laura Curreli. *Cast:* Frederick Stafford (Franco Mattei), Femi Benussi (Laura Damiani), Alberto De Mendoza (Giorgio Russo), Claude Jade (Tiffany), Michel Constantin (Inspector Palma), Patty Shepard (Simone Mattei), Giacomo Furia (Bartender), Simón Andreu (Mario Ceccacci), Manuel de Blas (Franco Bertoni), Pupo De Luca (Cabbie), Giuseppe Castellano (Broccole), Dada Gallotti (Gina Necioni), Arturo Dominici (District attorney), Antonio Basile (Killer), Nino Musco (police sergeant), Antonio Gradoli (Doctor), Raimondo Toscano (2nd police sergeant), Carla Mancini (Shop assistant), Alessandro Perrella, Christine Tambay, Geneviève Menet, Edith Genella, Eva Maria Gabriel. *Uncredited:* Bruno Alias (Man at nightclub), Nestore Cavaricci (policeman), Enrico Cesaretti (Laura's friend), Nando Sarlo (Man watching strip show), Alessandro Tedeschi (Engineer), Pietro Torrisi (Killer). *PROD:* Rodolfo Sabbatini and Jean-Charles Carlus for Zafes (Rome), Midega Film (Madrid), Mandala Film (Paris); *GM:* Salvatore Gerbino; *PM:* Valentin Panero; *UM:* Miguel Ángel Bermejo; *PSu:* Augusto Dolfi, Jean-Charles Carlus; *PSe:* Ileana De Paolis. *Country:* Italy / Spain / France. Filmed at Incir—De Paolis Studios (Rome). *Running time:* 100'; Visa no.: 62904 (08.08.1973); *Rating:* v.m.18; *Release date:* 08.11.1973; *Distribution:* C.I.A. (Cinematografie Regionali Associate); *Domestic gross:* 473,896,000 lire. *Also known as: La chica de via Condotti* (Madrid, 10.14.1974), *Meurtres à Rome* (Paris, 12.07.1977—90'), *Un flic obstiné. Home video:* Film Video and Cable Sales Inc. (VHS, Denmark—as *Lejemordere*).

Simone, the alcoholic and nymphomaniac wife of private eye Sandro Mattei, is strangled by a lover while having sex. Sandro investigates on his own, and finds out the murder has been commissioned by a blackmailing ring. The murderer, Mario, is the brother of a stripper, Laura, who's the lover of a powerful and wealthy lawyer, Giorgio Russo. Mattei survives a number of attempts on his life, and falls for Laura. He eventually discovers that Russo is the mastermind behind the ring, but the lawyer frames him for murder and has the man arrested by police inspector Palma, who believes in Sandro's innocence but is powerless to help. From his cell, Mattei learns that Laura is about to marry Russo, even though she doesn't love him.

Despite an opening *giallo*-style murder scene, where guest star Patty Shepard is dispatched right before the credits, *Special Killers* is actually a bleak metropolitan *film noir* centered on a private eye whose investigation on the death of his estranged, drug-addicted and unfaithful wife uncovers a blackmailing ring. Stafford, as the disillusioned hero with an ulcer, is a walking stereotype, and dialogue doesn't help, with such lines as "This coffee's hot!" "Not as much as your situation."

Courtesy of stunt coordinator Remo De Angelis, there's room for a car chase scene that wouldn't have been out of place in a Stelvio Massi film and a fistfight in a junkyard, but Lorente seems more interested in having Shepard and the gorgeous Femi Benussi take their clothes off in front of the camera than in the rather predictable plot twists. The film almost comes alive in the downbeat ending, which somehow recalls the provocative epilogues of politically committed cinema and shows an attempt at social commentary which justifies the Italian title—literally, *The Girl of Via Condotti*: this is one of Rome's most prestigious commercial streets, with its *haute couture* houses and luxury shops, representing Laura's dream of a wealthy life which she will obtain at the expense of true love.

The song over the opening credits is sung by Augusto Daolio of I Nomadi, one of Italy's most popular and durable pop bands.

Stateline Motel (L'ultima chance)

D: Maurizio Lucidi. *S:* Giovanni Fago, Francesco Giorgi, Vittoria Vigorelli, based on the novel *L'ultima chance* by Franco Enna; *SC:* Giovanni Fago, Francesco Giorgi, Vittoria Vigorelli, Maurizio Lucidi, Fulvio Gicca Palli; *SC revision and adaptation:* Fulvio Gicca Palli; *DOP:* Gábor Pogány (35mm, Eastmancolor, Telecolor); *M:* Luis Enriquez Bacalov, conducted by the author; *La chance* and *Let Me Be* (Collin /Bacalov) sung by Roberta Flack; *E:* Renzo Lucidi; *PD:* Giulia Mafai; Assistant *PD:* Antonino Occhiuto; *COper:* Idelmo Simonelli; *AC:* Cristiano Pogany; *AD:* Francesco Cinieri; *MU:* Massimo De Rossi; *MU* (Ursula Andress): John O'Gorman; *Hair:* Adalgisa Favella; *W:* Sara Santarelli; *SO:* Pietro Spadoni; *Boom:* Angelo Spadoni; *Mix:* Venanzio Biraschi, Ultimo Lippi; *SOE:* Tonino Caciuottolo; *SP:* Mario Mazzoni; *KG:* Romeo Governatori; *ChEl:* Nunzio Colucci; *PrM:* Antonio Ferri; *G:* Vittorio Munalli, Giancarlo Farina Governatori, Quirino Fantauzzi; *Elec:* Mario Schiavone, Luciano Marrocchi, Giuseppe Scansalegna; *SS:* Paolo Lucidi; Dubbing director: Nick Alexander. *Cast:* Fabio Testi (Floyd Gambino), Ursula Andress (Michelle Norton), Eli Wallach (Joe Malcomb), Massimo Girotti (Fred Norton), Howard Ross [Renato Rossini] (Jacques, the mechanic), Barbara Bach (Emily Norton), Carlo De Mejo (Albert), Céline Lomez (Waitress), Susanna Onofri (Myriam), Luigi Antonio Guerra. *PROD:* Nicholas Demetroules for Fral Cinematografica; *GM:* Francesco Giorgi; *PM:* Luciano Appignani; *PSu:* Vincenzo Salviani; *PSe:* Vittorio Carta; *PSeA:* Paolo Fantini. *Country:* Italy. Filmed at Dear Film (Rome) and on location in Canada. *Running time:* 105': Visa no.: 63051 (09.12.1973); *Rating:* v.m.14; *Release date:* 09.14.1973; *Distribution:* Alpherat; *Domestic gross:* 230,000,000 lire. *Also known as: La dernière chance* (Paris, 08.10.1977—110'), *La ultima oportunidad (L'ultima chance)* (Spain, 1975), *Motel of Fear* (UK), *Last Chance. Home video:* Miracle (DVD, USA, 2002), Telavista (DVD, USA, 2006), EastWest (DVD, USA, 2008—with Vittorio De Sica's *Two Women*!).

On the same day that he is released from a Canadian prison after serving a six-month sentence, Floyd Gambino stages a jewel heist with his partner Joe, but during the robbery the latter kills a man. Floyd and Joe take their separate ways, intending to meet in a small U.S. town near the border and split the loot. His car breaks down, and Floyd—who's carrying the jewels—is forced to spend some days in a motel run by Fred Knowlton and his wife Michelle. The woman discovers Floyd's real identity and seduces him. When the jewels disappear, Floyd suspects the woman. Meanwhile, Michelle's lover Jacques, the mechanic, who had devised a plan to kill Floyd, dies in a freak accident. Michelle tells Floyd that she's got the loot and convinces him to run away together. Joe arrives at the motel to take his cut. He chases Michelle, who has left on a bus, and kills her, but he's fatally wounded by the woman. Floyd arrives too late to save her: he shoots Joe, but finds out that the jewels (which were stuffed into a rag doll) have been replaced with gravel by Michelle's niece Emily and her boyfriend....

Very loosely based on a Franco Enna's novel, *Stateline Motel* tries hard to be an American *film noir*. The prologue, where Testi is released from prison, recalls anything from *The Getaway* (1972,

Sam Peckinpah) to *The Hot Rock* (1972, Peter Yates) and the Canadian locations give the film an international look. What's more, director Lucidi puts together an appealing cast for foreign markets and stages a rousing car chase in the film's first ten minutes. Unfortunately, no matter how hard it tries, the script falls flat and never recovers, as soon as Testi arrives at the stateline motel owned by Massimo Girotti and Ursula Andress, in what starts like a half-baked retelling of James M. Cain's classic novel *The Postman Always Rings Twice* (interestingly, a young Girotti had played the opposite role in Luchino Visconti's 1942 masterpiece *Obsession*, loosely inspired by Cain's book) and accumulates almost every possible *film noir* cliché as it goes along, from the tiresome double and triple crossings to the idea of the loot stuffed into a rag doll (as in Charles Laughton's *Night of the Hunter*), and even a pointless nod to H. G. Clouzot's *Wages of Fear* (*Le Salaire de la peur*, 1953) as Testi foolishly wrecks his car after the robbery, while zigzagging on a snowy motorway. Andress is truly gorgeous, but she is just not convincing as a woman who's wasting her best years and beauty in a God-forsaken place and spending her days watching old cartoons on TV, while Girotti is wasted in a thankless role, and Wallach hams it up to the point of no return as Testi's sadistic, mean accomplice. Testi — not the greatest actor himself— fares slightly better as the naive handsome thief.

Lucidi, a former editor, had directed a couple of very interesting movies such as the sneering Western *Hallelujah for Django* (*La più grande rapina del West*, 1967) and the excellent giallo *The Designated Victim* (*La vittima designata*, 1971), itself an inspired retelling of Patricia Highsmith's *Strangers on a Train*, blessed by Venetian locations and powerful performances by Tomas Milian and Pierre Clementi. Here, besides the usual over-reliance on zooms — in and out — his direction is anonymous and uninspired, and fails to inject any tension into the proceedings, not to mention make the characters interesting (although Testi and Andress' mutual physical attraction is evident on screen, as the two were then a couple). The day-for-night scenes are also rather poorly done, further exposing the film's slapdash *mise en scène*. The best asset here emerges to be Luis Bacalov's score.

Superbitch, a.k.a. *Mafia Junction (Si può essere più astardi dell'ispettore Cliff?)*

D: Massimo Dallamano. *S:* based on a story by George P. Breakston; *SC:* Massimo Dallamano, Ross Mackenzie; *DOP:* Jack Hildyard (35mm, Eastmancolor, Technospes); *M:* Riz Ortolani, conducted by the author (ed. C.A.M.); *E:* Antonio Siciliano; *PD:* Elena Ricci; *CO:* Gabrielle Falk; *AE:* Giuliano Corso; *AD:* David Tringham; *C:* Dudley Lovell; *MU:* Richard Mills; *SO:* Robin Gregory Marshall; *SS:* Vivalda Vigorelli. *Cast:* Ivan Rassimov (Inspector Cliff Hoyst), Stephanie Beacham (Joann), Patricia Hayes (Mamma the Turk), Red Carter [Ettore Manni] (Morrel), Luciano Catenacci (Gamble), Verna Harvey (Eva), Giacomo Rossi-Stuart (Marco), Cec Linder (American Ambassador), Leon Vitali (Morrel's gay assistant), Ben Carrà, Giancarlo Prati, Jackie Gambino, Tutte Lemkow, James Bate, George Murcell, Morris Perry, Mario Novelli (Man on Citroen), Orazio Stracuzzi. *Uncredited:* Abdel Majid Majzaub, Michael Sheard (Williamson), Gareth Thomas (Trench-coated detective), Massimo Dallamano (Man at airport), Nello Pazzafini, Camille Keaton (Girl playing card at Escort International Service), Pietro Torrisi (Morrell's man). *PROD:* Fulvio Lucisano and Leonardo Pescarolo for Clodio Cinematografica S.p.A. (Rome), Italian International Film s.r.l. (Rome), Monymusk Productions Ltd. (London); *GM:* Alfredo Nicolai; *PM:* Basil Keys; *PSu:* Michele Germano; *PSe:* Roberta Revetria. *Country:* Italy / UK. Filmed at Safa Palatino (Rome) and on location in London, Beirut and Baalbek. *Running time:* 97'; Visa no.: 61972 (03.03.1973); *Rating:* v.m.18; *Release date:* 03.05.1973; *Distribution:* Medusa; *Domestic gross:* 353,341,000 lire. *Also known as: Blue Movie Blackmail* (UK, 1973 — 97')—*Piège pour un tuer* (Paris, 08.09.1978 — 90'), *Mamma La Turca* (Spain). *Home video:* Apprehensive Films (DVD, USA), Iif Home Video (DVD, Italy). OST: CD Beat Records CDCR 85.

Inspector Cliff Hoyst of the Narcotics Bureau works undercover for a drug trafficker, Morrel, who disguises his activity under an escort agency in London, which he only uses to gather compromising material and blackmail politicians. Sent to Lebanon to stop Morrel's rival "Momma the Turk" from buying a huge shipment of drugs, Cliff starts a war between the factions. Momma sends to London one of her men, Gamble, to force Morrel to do business with her. Without his superiors knowing, Cliff kills Gamble and his men and conceals the bodies. Morrel is about to send the drugs to New York to his associate Marco, but Momma and her gang arrive in London. They kidnap Joann, Morell's wife and Cliff's lover, but Cliff rescues the woman and manages to get 1,000,000 dollars from Momma to give her the drugs which he's going to ship to Detroit instead of New York. It's all part of an elaborate trap set up by Cliff, though: Momma's gang is surrounded by the police in a Detroit warehouse and killed in a shoot-out. Believing she's been betrayed by Morrel, Momma kills him but is in turn dispatched by the corrupt inspector. Cliff is about to leave with Joann and the million Momma gave him, but the girl, disgusted by his cynicism, kills him.

Were it not for such familiar faces to Italian film devotées as Ivan Rassimov, Ettore Manni and Giacomo Rossi-Stuart, Massimo Dallamano's *Superbitch* could well pass for a Brit B-grade crime flick. Released in Italy as *Si può essere più bastardi dell'ispettor Cliff?* ("Can Anyone Be More Bastard Than Inspector Cliff?"), as with a number of the director's films it was an Italian-British coproduction, and circulated abroad in an English language version which gave less emphasis to the thriller plot than to Stephanie Beacham's copious nude scenes.

The opening credits reserve a number of surprises, such as the names of Academy Award–winning cinematographer Jack Hildyard (*The Bridge on the River Kwai*) as director of photography and a pre-*Barry Lyndon* Leon Vitali as Manni's flamboyant gay assistant. An uncredited Camille Keaton — a recurring presence in many Italian B-films of the period before her main stab at celebrity, Meir Zarchi's notorious *I Spit On Your Grave* (1978)— pops up as well as one of the girls of Manni's escort agency.

The results are quite peculiar indeed. Rassimov's trademark photonovel sneer serves an amoral, repellent character which is far from the tough-mannered but heroic cops of the co-existing poliziotteschi. Cliff is closer to such unscrupulous adventurers of contemporary British thrillers such as Michael Caine's Carter in Mike Hodges' *Get Carter* (1971), or Oliver Reed's Harry Lomart in Douglas Hickox's *Sitting Target* (1972).

The plot — credited, in another odd occurrence, to George P. Breakston, a former child actor who became a director with such weird results as *The Manster* (1962) and *The Boy Who Cried Murder* (1966) — is quite hazy, and Dallamano is obviously more interested in Beacham's statuesque nudes than in the inevitable tourist footage in Baalbek and London. However, as in his subsequent crime films, the Italian director does not stint on violence, which always comes complete with black humor, as shown by Luciano Catenacci's slow motion death by machine gun as well as the scene where Cliff kills his own superior to cover his personal illicit undercover affairs — a sequence that Dallamano ends with a gory sight gag, as the newspaper the victim is reading on a bench gets splattered with blood when the man is shot in the head from behind.

Other grotesque touches are quite enjoyable — take the character of Momma the Turk (Patricia Hayes), a contemporary answer of sorts to Roger Corman's Ma Barker, an elderly termagant who rules with an iron fist a gang of semi-retarded thugs, or the extravagant sequences in Morrel's International Escort Agency, whose customers have the most laughably bizarre sex fetishes.

A former director of photography, Dallamano stood aside other genre filmmakers because of his refined technical skills. Some of the director's stylistic traits are present — although they are less prominent than in the rest of his filmography. The use of handheld camera and wide-angle shots, for instance, can be found in a couple of action sequences, while the risqué Super 8 films that Manni's crew shoots to use them for blackmail purposes upon the agency's wealthy customers recall Dallamano's controversial *Venus in Furs* (*Venere in pelliccia*, 1969) starring Laura Antonelli. Another asset is Riz Ortolani's score, which would be recycled in Alberto Negrin's giallo *Red Rings of Fear* (*Enigma rosso*, 1978).

As Cliff, Rassimov gives a convincing performance, even though the actor was not perfectly suited to the character. "Dallamano imposed me on *Superbitch*. Massimo had his own production company and a distribution one as well ... and he really believed in me. Maybe I wasn't the ideal choice for the role, though — I'm saying this now, watching the film again after many years — maybe Massimo should have cast another actor, someone like Fabio Testi; I was slim, I weighed just 69 kilos [152 pounds, Author's Note] and I had these tiny shoulders ... still, Massimo liked me a lot and was quite happy. However, when we did our second film together, *Colt 38 Special Squad*, I was much more in character as the nasty bomber...."[1]

Note

1. Manlio Gomarasca and Davide Pulici, "Ivan il terribile," *Nocturno Cinema* #5 (February 1998), p. 77.

The Violent Professionals (*Milano trema: la polizia vuole giustizia*)

D: Sergio Martino. *S* and *SC:* Ernesto Gastaldi; *DOP:* Giancarlo Ferrando (35mm, Eastmancolor, Cinescope); *M:* Guido and Maurizio De Angelis, conducted by Gianfranco Plenizio; *E:* Eugenio Alabiso; *PD:* Giantito Burchiellaro; *CO:* Rosalba Menichelli; *C:* Giancarlo Ferrando, Claudio Morabito; *AC:* Bruno Pellegrini; *APD:* Luigi Urbani; *AD:* Fernando Popoli; *MU:* Raffaele Cristini; *Hair:* Marcella Favella; *SO:* Bruno Zanoli; *SE:* Cataldo Galliano; *SP:* Francesco Narducci; *ST:* Donatella Gambini, Rodolfo Valadier; *SS:* Mirella Roy Malatesta. *Cast:* Luc Merenda (Commissioner Giorgio Caneparo), Richard Conte (Padulo a.k.a. Salassolio), Silvano Tranquilli (Gianni Viviani), Carlo Alighiero (Commissioner Nicastro), Martine Brochard (Maria), Luciano Bartoli (Giacomo), Lia Tanzi (Prostitute), Steffen Zacharias (Monsomerda), Bruno Corazzari (Padulo's man), Chris Avram (Vice-commissioner Del Buono), Cirylle Spiga, Rosario Borelli (Pepi Cartiglia), Anthony Vernon [Antonio Casale] (Casardi, prisoner on train), Bruno Boschetti (Padulo's henchman), Sergio Serafini (Padulo's man), Luciano Rossi (Cruciani, prisoner on train), Carla Mancini, Valeria Sabel (Del Buono's wife), Anna Eugeni (Viviani's wife), Ezio Sancrotti (Giuliani, cop on train), Enrico Marciani (Commentator), Claudio Ruffini (Caneparo's tail), Sergio Smacchi (Caneparo's tail), Susanna Melandri (Kidnapped little girl). *Uncredited:* Nestore Cavaricci (policeman), Enrico Chiappafreddo (policeman shot on train), Domenico Cianfriglia (Pool hall thug), Ennio Colaianni (Storekeeper), Franz Colangeli (policeman), Tom Felleghy (Doctor), Franco Moruzzi (Pool hall thug), Francesco Narducci (Father in car), Abramo Orlandini (policeman), Filippo Perego (police official), Riccardo Petrazzi (Robber with grenade). *PROD:* Carlo Ponti for Compagnia Cinematografica Champion, Luciano Martino for Dania Film; *PM:* Maurizio Pastrovich; *PSu:* Francesco Fantacci; *PSe:* Marcello Spingi. *Country:* Italy. Filmed at Icet–De Paolis and on location in Milan. *Running time:* 104'; Visa no.: 62938 (08.18.1973); *Rating:* v.m.18; *Release date:* 08.22.1973; *Distribution:* Interfilm; *Domestic gross:* 1,162,424,000 lire. *Also known as: polices parallèles, Rue de la violence* (France), *Milán, tiembla, la policía pide justicia* (Spain). *Home video:* Wild East (DVD, USA), Alpha Home Entertainment (DVD, USA — "Grindhouse Double Feature" with *Deadly Drifter*), No Shame (DVD, Italy), Dania Film (DVD, Italy). OST: CD Digitmovies CDDM078.

Commissioner Giorgio Caneparo is suspended from service for having shot two escaped convicts in cold blood. When his colleague Del Buono — who was investigating a gang of bank robbers — is killed, Caneparo sets out to avenge him on his own. He goes undercover in the Milan underworld and takes part as driver in a bloody bank robbery organized by a mysterious man nicknamed "Padulo." Caneparo finds out that the gang was acting as part of a subversive plan, paving the way for the advent of a fascist regime, and he discovers that Padulo is a wealthy publisher from Bergamo, who in turn follows the instructions of a mysterious boss. Caneparo discovers that the boss is one of his own superiors: he refuses to be embroiled in the subversive plot and kills him.

Produced by Carlo Ponti and Luciano Martino's Dania Film and written by the reliable Ernesto Gastaldi, Sergio Martino's *The Violent Professionals*— released in mid–August 1973, just ten days after Castellari's *High Crime*— was another box office hit in Italy. Martino's film launched one of the genre's icons, Luc Merenda: as commissioner Caneparo, the handsome Merenda looks like a macho, musclebound version of Luigi Calabresi — someone who, according to a line of dialogue, "would have punched half humanity in the face and kicked the other half in the ass." Gastaldi provides him with a childhood trauma that marked his existence, the killing of his father — a policeman, too — by some thugs against whom he had hesitated to shoot. Caneparo doesn't have such qualms. "Time's up" he sneers in one of the opening scenes before killing in cold blood two convicts who just surrendered to him after a bloody escape attempt from the train that was transporting them to another prison. The sequence is purposefully left ambiguous: Martino inserts a close-up of a convict's gun which seems about to rise, suggesting that after all Caneparo was simply the quicker to draw, just like in a Western movie duel.

Caneparo is the prototype of a new generation of crime film heroes, a younger and more athletic version of Franco Nero's character in *High Crime* and the predecessor of many undercover cops and special agents such as Franco Gasparri in Stelvio Massi's

Mark the Cop series and Ray Lovelock and Marc Porel in Ruggero Deodato's *Live Like a Cop, Die Like a Man* (*Uomini si nasce poliziotti si muore*, 1976). Martino's film centers on Caneparo's transformation when he goes undercover in the Milan underworld to get vital evidence: he just lets his hair grow a little, wears casual clothes instead of suit and tie and talks (at least in Italian language prints) an exhilarating mixture of Italian and Milanese dialect. As critic Giovanni Buttafava noted, "small time hoods and small time cops have the same faces. The typology offered by the genre is absolutely interchangeable."[1]

As Castellari did in *High Crime*, *The Violent Professionals* emphasizes another key element of the genre: car chases. When Richard Conte asks Luc Merenda to show him his ability as a driver, Martino's film puts in line an apparently endless series of driftings, U-turns and other assorted acrobatics. It's literally a show-stopping moment: diegetic time dilates as the director allows its audience a taste of exciting spectacular bits that would soon become a vital ingredient in crime films to come — even literally, in the case of the long chase scene between Merenda's BMW and the police, a segment which would be recycled and reedited in countless other films. What's most impressive, however, is the competitive enthusiasm on display, as if to show that Italian crime flicks could even top their U.S. counterparts — something similar to what happened earlier with Westerns and to what would later happen with horror films.

As with a number of its predecessors, *The Violent Professionals* deals with the expected political nuances. The plot revolves around the unsuspectable "Padulo" (Richard Conte) who organizes bank robberies with the purpose of spreading chaos and destabilizing the institutions, by using small crooks and young protesters — and who turns out to be a publisher, just like Franco Freda, the extreme right-wing terrorist who was involved in the bombing at Piazza Fontana. After shooting a pregnant woman with his machine gun, a thug (Bruno Corazzari) tells his accomplice: "You know we don't just want the money. We also have to frighten people, and convince them that things must change!" Later on, Conte adds: "People are tired of this democracy, and of the void of power that surrounds it." The funniest thing about Martino's film — and not a casual paradox, if one considers Gastaldi's skills as a scriptwriter — is that after the progressivist commissioner played by Chris Avram has been assassinated, it's up to Merenda's fascist gun-crazy cop to become the savior of democracy — in his own peculiar way, of course — whereas the young protesters who occupy villas, talk about free love and quote Mao Tse-tung ultimately prove to be impractical and even gullible to opposite political purposes.

The Violent Professionals also benefits from a lively, rock-oriented score by the De Angelis brothers. As the ambiguous Padulo, Richard Conte makes for a suitable villain, despite being obviously replaced by a double during the fight scenes. In the following couple of years, until his death in 1975, he would become one of the recurring faces in Italian poliziotteschi.

Note

1. Buttafava, "Procedure sveltite," p. 110.

Your Honor (*Servo suo*)

D: Romano Scavolini. *S* and *SC:* Romano Scavolini; *DOP:* Romano Scavolini (35mm, Eastmancolor, Telecolor); *M:* Carlo Esposito, conducted by the author (ed. Mizar); *E:* Valeria Altobelli; *PD:* Emiliano Tolve; *C:* Romano Scavolini; *AC:* Roberto Nappa; *AE:* Adalberto Ceccarelli; *AD:* Michele Brancato; *SO:* Alessandro Sarandrea; *Mix:* Bruno Moreal; *W:* Pippo Ferina; *KG:* Giulio Diamanti; *ChEl:* Otello Magalotti; *SS:* Valeria Viscione. *Cast:* Chris Avram (Prof. Martin), Lea Lander (Mafia agent), Paola Senatore (Nightclub dancer), Francesca Sebastiani (Prostitute), Alberto Bertoli, Edoardo Bartolotta, Gioacchino Maniscalco, Mirella Sapio Lombardi, Pietro Tornello, Bruno Boschetti, Antonio D'Amico, Andrea Maratea, Carla Mancini, Benedetto Ranelli, Pupella Mario. *Uncredited:* Jacques Stany (Stany). *PROD:* Armando Bertuccioli and Romano Scavolini for Lido Cinematografica, Hermann Film; *GM:* Armando Bertuccioli. *Country:* Italy. Filmed on location in Palermo and Amsterdam. *Running time:* 95'; Visa no.: 62215 (04.18.1973); *Rating:* v.m.14; *Release date:* 09.11.1973; *Distribution:* Regional; *Domestic gross:* 40,709,000 lire. *Home video:* Olympia (VHS, Switzerland), Shendene & Moizzi (VHS, Italy).

Professor Martin, who leads a miserable life in Palermo where he teaches English to the wheelchair-bound son of Mafia boss Don Calogero, is blackmailed by the gangster and accepts to become a killer for the mob. After a period of training, he turns into an experienced hitman. Martin moves to Amsterdam, where Don Calogero's adversary Don Pizzuto is hiding. Following his boss' orders, Martin kills all those who get in his way and eventually catches up with his quarry. But when he finds out that Pizzuto's own son is in a wheelchair, he hesitates, and the boy shoots him.

Mafia and godfathers are just a narrative pretext in *Your Honor*, an existential parable loosely inspired by Camus' *The Stranger*, which was written, photographed and directed by such a definitely anomalous *auteur* as Romano Scavolini. The filmmaker debuted in the '60s with a couple of allegorical, heavily experimental films, *The Blind Fly* (*A mosca cieca*, 1966), which was forbidden by the Italian board of censors due to its supposedly obscene content, and *The Dress Rehearsal* (*La prova generale*, 1968) and later spent some time in Vietnam as a war photo-journalist. His subsequent films were more on the commercial side, even though in a slightly offbeat way, as was the case with *Spirits of Death* (*Un bianco vestito per Marialè*, 1972), a weird Gothic *giallo* with Surrealist touches. On *Your Honor*, Scavolini reprises the theme of violence as an inescapable human condition, in the form of a tale about the Mafia which is colored with the director's typical weird touches and idiosyncratic style.

Scavolini looks back at the '60s dreams of "peace & love" as seen through the eyes of a loser. The protagonist, played with aplomb by Cristea Avram (a regular face in 1970s Italian genre cinema), has seen the illusions and hopes washed away in front of his eyes, and now has to undergo any kind of compromise and humiliation to earn a living. Miserably living in a shack among old *gialli* novels and spending all his money on prostitutes, he is co-opted by a Mafia boss who wants to avenge his young son (who's become a cripple after a failed murder attempt), and trained to become a lethal assassin. Rather than an elegy to the defeated in pure *film noir* style, however, *Your Honor* adopts a jarring approach and tone.

Avram's disillusioned professor finds out he's got a killer inside him, and the training sequences, based on brainwashing techniques—with nods to Stanley Kubrick's *A Clockwork Orange* (1971)—give away the film's ambitions, and definitely detach it from any realistic portrayal of the Sicilian Mafia. The ubiquitous security cameras which spy on the protagonist (often from impossible points-of-view) turn *Your Honor* into some sort of Orwellian thriller and convey the idea of a subterranean, omnipotent counter-society which controls and rules over everyday life. But the central metaphor (and original title, which means "Your *Servant*") refers to class struggle: the wealthy and powerful have the right of life and death over the poor, and manipulate them at their will like puppeteers.

However, Scavolini's ambitions clash against the film's inadequate script and *mise en scène*. The minimal budget shows in the perennial use of hand-held shots (Scavolini acted also as cameraman), the plot is too obscure and vague for its own good, becoming almost abstract during the last act, where the director's use of film *noir* stereotypes becomes openly provocative and pretextual. And the film's circular ending—where the Mafioso's son whom the protagonist has to kill is revealed to be wheelchair-bound like the son of Avram's boss himself—falls flat.

Your Honor was briefly released four years after its making, then sank without trace for almost twenty years. Only through marginal Home video releases—such as a Swiss cassette and a 2000 Italian VHS, where Paola Senatore's brief role as a nightclub stripper became the film's main selling point—it eventually surfaced to a wider audience. *Your Honor* was to be Scavolini's last Italian film: in 1976 he moved to the United States, where he shot such controversial works as *Savage Hunt* (1980) and the cult psycho-thriller flick *Nightmares in a Damaged Brain* (1981).

1974

A pugni nudi ... per una triste esperienza in un carcere minorile (Naked Fists ... After a Sad Experience in a Juvenile Detention House)

D: Marcello Zeani. *S:* Enzo Pulcrano, Luciano Brega; *SC:* Alessandro Schirò, Marcello Zeani; *DOP:* Tonino [Antonio] Modica (35mm, Eastmancolor, Telecolor); *M:* Franco Bixio, conducted by Vince Tempera (Ed. Bixio Sam, Cinevox Record); *Quando ti accadrà, L'aeroplano* (Longo / D'Alessandro) sung by D'Alessandro (Cinevox Records) *E:* Enzo Albiso; *PD:* Francesco Roselli; *C:* Luigi Ciccarese; *AC:* Carlo Acquari; *AE:* Iva Caldarini; *AD:* Giovanni Siragusa; *MU:* Giancarlo Del Brocco; *Hair:* Maria Luisa Garbini; *SO:* Raul Montesanti; *SP:* Nicola Galfano; *ST:* Gilberto Galimberti, Omero Capanna; *Wigs:* Rocchetti; *SS:* Adriana Rosi Siragusa; *UP:* Vitaliano Elia. *Cast:* Enzo Pulcrano (Paolo Vita), Femi Benussi (Anna), Vassili Karis [Karamenisis] (Marco), Rita De Angelis (Silvana, Paolo's sister), Luciano Doria (Franz), Laila Shed, Marisa Merlini (Maria, Paolo's mother), Bruno Di Luia (Bruno Di Luia "The Chinese"), Ettore Bevilacqua (Paolo's boxing trainer), Vittorio Fanfoni (Pedophile warden in prison), Alberico Donadeo, Sergio Serafini, Claudio Lattes, Alessandro Perrella. *Uncredited:* Attilio Dottesio (Professor), Gilberto Galimberti (Franz's man at the cemetery, with red jacket), Omero Capanna (Franz's man at the cemetery), Luciano Zanussi (Man at wedding). *PROD:* Franco Nardelli for Lattes Cinematografica; *GM:* Felice Lattes; *PM:* Elido Sorrentino; *PSu:* Felice Lattes; *PSe:* Marcello Lattes. *Country:* Italy. Filmed at Film Cave Studio (Rome) and on location in Rome. *Running time:* 95' (91'36"); Visa no.: 64562 (05.10.1974); *Rating:* v.m.14; *Distribution:* F.G.R..; *Release date:* 07.26.1974; *Domestic gross:* 81,662,000 lire. *Home video:* None.

As a young boy, Paolo Vita ends up in a juvenile detention house for a small theft. There, he befriends another boy, an orphan named Marco. When he gets out, Paolo tries to start his life anew as a car mechanic and walk the line. He finds a girlfriend, Anna, and starts boxing by chance. Soon he becomes one of the most promising prizefighters in town, winning 28 matches in a row. However, Paolo gets involved with a seedy boss of the Roman underworld, Franz, who asks him to lose his next match on purpose against one of his men, the "Chinese," who's also a boxer. Paolo refuses and wins the match. However, later on he is forced to go back to Franz and ask him 10 million lire so that Marco can undergo a delicate surgery. Paolo becomes Franz's henchman, and gets involved in the prostitution ring and extortion racket. His decision is reproached by family and friends, who cut all bridges with him. Paolo asks Franz to let him go so that he can get back on the ring, but the boss demands one more favor: Paolo has to rob a jewel courier. However, that's part of Franz's scheme to have Paolo arrested. While he's in prison, his mother becomes very ill. When Marco meets Franz to avenge Paolo, he is murdered by the Chinese. Eventually Paolo gets out of prison and takes his revenge. He kills the Chinese and Franz, taking his place as the new boss. One day Anna pays him visit, and tells Paolo that his mother is dying. Paolo promises the old woman to get back on the ring and wins the middle-weight championship, but soon afterwards he suffers a heart attack and dies.

An extremely obscure film, *A pugni nudi ... per una triste esperienza in un carcere minorile* is a clumsy attempt at mixing social commentary and tearjerking melodrama within a hard-boiled urban tale set in the boxing world. The partially autobiographical story is the brainchild of the film's lead and co-scenarist Enzo Pulcrano, a former middleweight champion-turned-actor who met a brief and marginal popularity in Italian cinema in the seventies. However, despite Pulcrano's heartfelt dedication, the results are decidedly poor.

The story follows all the expected clichés, as the ex-convict with a heart of gold and a fist of iron finds out he just can't lead a decent, honest life as he wanted to. The opening scenes in the juvenile detention house are a poor man's version of De Sica's *Sciuscià* (1946), replete with the expected self-pitying, while the domestic scenes at Paolo's house, with their squalid sets and poor dialogue, look like they belong to a bad sceneggiata. The crime film elements come to the fore with the character of a slimy underworld boss and his gang (including stuntman Bruno Di Luia, one of the most familiar faces in Eurocrime, here playing ... Bruno Di Luia[1]) and culminate in a four minutes long car chase which fails to liven up the proceedings. As for the cast, Femi Benussi (in one of those rare roles that didn't request her to take off her clothes) is only a decorative presence, while Federico Fellini's friend and personal trainer, Ettore Bevilacqua, plays Paolo's boxing trainer (which he was also in real life) and Greek Vassili Karis (a very minor Western film star in the early 1970s with his *Spirito Santo* movies) is the hero's unfortunate friend. However, *A pugni nudi* badly needs a charismatic character, which unfortunately the hopelessly wooden Enzo Pulcrano isn't.

After his film debut in Demofilo Fidani's *A Fistful of Death* (*Giù la testa ... hombre*, 1971), Pulcrano appeared in a number of films, mostly low-budget Westerns and comedies. With the rising of the crime genre, he was a recurring presence in poliziotteschi, including a couple of Fernando di Leo's films (his most memorable role was the illiterate thug in 1976's *Rulers of the City*), while Mario Bianchi's *La banda Vallanzasca* (1977) was one of his rare stints as the lead. In the '80s, after his popularity declined, Pulcrano even appeared in a couple of hardcore flicks (Lorenzo Onorati's *Cameriera senza ... malizia*, 1980, and *Corri, seguimi, vienimi dietro*, 1981), even though he did not perform explicit sex scenes himself. Pulcrano died in 1992: according to his friend Mario Bianchi, who directed him in *La banda Vallanzasca*, he had developed a serious drug addiction. Like the one told in the film, Enzo Pulcrano's story didn't have a happy ending either.

Note

1. As Di Luia explained, "[The film's story] is also very similar to mine. From childhood I've been familiar with prison and reform school. I went to prison at fifteen for defacing posters inviting people to vote with blank ballot forms in 1958," Fabio Melelli, *Eroi a Cinecittà* (Perugia: Mercurio, 1998), p. 56.

Almost Human *(Milano odia: la polizia non può sparare)*

D: Umberto Lenzi. *S* and *SC:* Ernesto Gastaldi; *DOP:* Federico Zanni (35mm, Eastmancolor, L.V.-Luciano Vittori); *M:* Ennio Morricone, conducted by Bruno Nicolai (ed. R.C.A.); *E:* Eugenio Alabiso; *PD:* Giorgio Bertolini; *ArtD:* Antonio Visone; *CO:* Renato Ventura; *C:* Elio Polacchi; *AC:* Mario Pastorini; *AE:* Amedeo Moriani; *APD:* Luchino Oltrona Visconti; *AD:* Alessandro Metz; *MU:* Franco Di Girolamo; *AMU:* Maurizio Trani; *Hair:* Fausto De Lisio; *SO:* Roberto Petrozzi; *Boom:* Corrado Volpicelli; *Mix:* Bruno Moreal; *SE:* Giuseppe Carozza; *SP:* Giorgio Garibaldi Schwarze; *CON:* Mirella Malatesta. *Cast:* Tomas Milian (Giulio Sacchi), Henry Silva (Commissioner Walter Grandi), Laura Belli (Marilù Porrino), Gino Santercole (Vittorio), Mario Piave (Grandi's assistant), Ray Lovelock (Carmine), Anita Strindberg (Jone Tucci), Luciano Catenacci (Ugo Majone), Pippo Starnazza (Papà), Guido Alberti (Porrino, Marilù's father), Tom Felleghy (Judge Rossi), Lorenzo Piani (Gianni), Rosita Torosh (Marta), Muzio Joris (Giulio's lawyer), Franco Ferrari (Brambilla), Francesco D'Adda (Romano), Annie Edel (Marta's friend at the villa), Elsa Boni (Papa's wife), Giuseppe Castellano (police inspector with glasses), Vittorio Pinelli (Majone's thug), Vittorio Sancisi (Majone's thug), Tony Raccosta (Majone's thug). *Uncredited:* Gianni Bortolotti (Chief of Police), Giancarlo Busi (Cop killed by Sacchi), Nestore Cavaricci (policeman), Vittorio Joderi (Majone's man), Mariano Laurenti (Sacchi's lawyer), Giuseppe Marrocco (policeman at the villa), Nello Pazzafini (Majone's thug), Claudio Sforzini (Giulio's friend at the bar), Romano Targa (policeman holding a flashlight). English version — voices: Frank von Kuegelgen (Giulio Sacchi), Robert Sommer (Ugo Majone), Ted Rusoff (Grandi's assistant). *PROD:* Luciano Martino for Dania Film; *PMs:* Gianfranco Couyoumdjian, Elio Di Pietro; *PSu:* Biagio Angelini; *PSe:* Beniamino Sterpetti; *ADM, CASH:* Angelo Sarago. *Country:* Italy. Filmed on location in Milan. *Running time:* 100'; Visa no.: 64875 (07.10.1974); *Rating:* v.m.18; *Release date:* 08.08.1974; *Distribution:* Interfilm; *Domestic gross:* 1,168,745,000 lire. *Also known as: The Death Dealer* (U.K.), *Milán tiembla, la policia pide justicia* (Spain), *La Rançon de la peur* (France — Home video), *Der Berserker* (West Germany). *Home video:* No Shame (DVD, USA), Shameless Screen Entertainment (DVD, U.K.), Neo Publishing (DVD, France), Alan Young (DVD, Italy)

Milan. Giulio Sacchi, a gun-crazy young criminal with no job, family or morals, leaves his gang and plans the kidnapping of a young woman, Marilù, the daughter of the wealthy Mr. Porrino. He finds two accomplices, Vittorio and the young, inexperienced Carmine. The gang performs the kidnapping, leaving a trail of blood behind. Commissioner Walter Grassi is convinced that Marilù's kidnapper is a crazy maniac and advises Porrino not to pay the ransom — half a billion lire — because he is sure that Marilù would be killed immediately afterwards. Meanwhile Giulio commits more killings: among his victims there is also his lover, Jone, who knows too much. Porrino pays the ransom, but Sacchi murders Marilù and his two accomplices as well. Giulio is arrested, but according to the magistrate there is not enough evidence to keep him in prison, so he is released. Grassi, who in the meantime has resigned from the police, locates Sacchi and kills him.

Giulio Sacchi is a loser. A coward. A wastrel who needs booze and pills to take courage, and who's only good at showing off with friends at the local bar. Wait a minute — what friends? Giulio Sacchi's got no friends, not even in the underworld. Everyone despises and avoids him like the plague. Because Giulio Sacchi is the kind of man who boasts about making millions, but ends up killing a cop for a dime. Giulio Sacchi is so full of hatred that if you puncture him, there won't be blood coming out, but bile.

It's Tomas Milian outrageous, unforgettable performance that indelibly marks Umberto Lenzi's *Almost Human*. On paper, Giulio Sacchi — long hair, shades, assorted tics — is a cross between *Dirty Harry*'s Scorpio (Andrew Robinson) and *The Incident*'s Joe Ferrone (Tony Musante), two of the creepier villains to ever hit the screens in the years preceding Lenzi's film. Yet as played by the extraordinary Cuban actor, Sacchi becomes much more than that: the embodiment of an ancestral, absolute fury, a destabilizing outsider who steps over the rules of a civil society. That's why Giulio Sacchi is as scary as he is obnoxious: not only does he kill young and old, women and children alike, but he even mocks his victims after death, as if the insult was the finishing stroke.

Like many other "rabid dogs," Sacchi is determined to take by force the wealth and ease he is excluded from. Yet even his class rage has a desecrating component: Sacchi lusts for the symbols of wealth just so that he can profane them: "When I get your daddy's money, you know what I'm gonna do with it?" he tells his kidnapping victim Marilù (Laura Belli), "I'm gonna wash my hot dog in champagne every single morning!" Sacchi's class hatred has a sexual component as well, as when he and his accomplices break into a country house and torture several rich bourgeois people, in a scene that predates Ruggero Deodato's *The House on the Edge of the Park* (1980). "I'm for sexual equality," Giulio sneers before forcing the landlord to perform a fellatio on him. However, there is a latent homosexuality in the character, as shown by his relationship with his young, angelic lieutenant Carmine (Ray Lovelock).

Interestingly, it was through his good friend Ray Lovelock that Milian got to play the main role. "When I was cast Tomas hadn't been chosen yet for Giulio Sacchi's role" Lovelock explained. "He was already a very popular actor at the time, and we heard he would do just a special participation. I was going to play one of the three gang members, and I still didn't know which one, either the naive young guy, the main villain or the third. I discussed the film with Tomas and told him "I heard you're doing a bit part" and he replied, "Yeah, maybe I'll play the commissioner"; "But why don't you play the bad guy, while I'm gonna play the young kidnapper who falls for the hostage? Your presence in that role would add much more weight to the film." He thought about it and finally accepted to play the main role. The producers were jumping for joy."[1]

As often in 1970s Italian cinema, the depiction of violence in *Almost Human* is insisted, repeated, protracted through the use of music and the dilatation of time on screen, according to Sergio Leone's lesson. However, Lenzi also makes an intelligent use of ellipsis to describe Sacchi's most hideous deeds. In the infamous villa scene, Sacchi and his accomplices have hung their hostages to a chandelier which they turn around in a macabre parody of a roulette. Suddenly, Giulio hears a noise from a room upstairs: with no hesitation, he opens fire against the door with his machine gun. The door opens, and a teddy bear rolls down the stairs. The effect of Sacchi's child murder is much more striking than a scene in Silvio Narizzano's *Redneck* where Telly Savalas shoots a little shepherd boy from a distance.

At the time of its release, *Almost Human* was unanimously condemned by Italian critics, who labeled the film as fascist and even booed Milian's performance, with a shortsightedness plagued by ideological prejudices. "The series of Italian crime films that openly flirt with reactionary right-wing ideology and the silent majority's tastes continues. [...] Besides the methodical falsification of facts and the exploitation of the ugliest prejudices that this film has in common with others of the same thread, the discourse is conducted with the more visceral ways of the depicting of violence, as well as with an impudent indifference towards logic and verisimilitude. All this is at the service of Tomas Milian, whose hamming knows no boundaries. There are two categories of bad actors: the negligent and the malicious ones. Milian belongs to the second" wrote the influent Morando Morandini.[2]

However, *Almost Human* is a solid genre effort, competently written and directed by the reliable Lenzi and featuring an impressive score by Ennio Morricone.[3] The film's most important trait is the capacity of filtering the feel of the time through an engrossing movie story so as to create unforgettable characters, starting with Giulio Sacchi. With this performance, Tomas Milian would give way to a number of memorable screen villains in Italian crime film, often directed by Lenzi — the "Hunchback" in *Brutal Justice* and *Brothers Till We Die* and the "Chinaman" in *The Cynic, the Rat and the Fist*— before jumping the barricade and becoming one of the genre's most beloved heroes with the character of Monnezza and inspector Nico Giraldi. But Ernesto Gastaldi's script offers other interesting characters, sometimes just sketched in a few shots: the old broker who procures Giulio's weapons, and who lives in a magazine near Milano's Naviglio canal with a senile dumb prostitute, the barflies that are Sacchi's favorite audience, his remissive lover Jone (Swedish sex bomb Anita Strindberg, in an odd casting against type).

Compared to the director's previous entry in the genre, *Gang War in Milan*, Lenzi here adopts a harsher tone, without any crepuscular tone. The elements in common with out and out poliziotteschi, however, are marginal. The opening car chase recalls Luc Merenda's raids in *The Violent Professionals*, also produced by Luciano Martino's Dania Film, then Gastaldi's script takes a different route, and gets close to U.S. grindhouse flicks such as *The Last House on the Left* in the torture scenes, while the police commissioner — an icy Henry Silva — is a marginal character, who doesn't have the dynamic, emphatic screen presence of screen icons such as Franco Nero or Maurizio Merli.

Almost Human can be described as a metropolitan hard-boiled story, which updates the typical "mad dog" character in a believable and strongly characterized urban context. That's why the crude, uncompromising depiction of violence demands an adequate retaliation in the end. In Raoul Walsh's masterpiece *White Heat* (1949), James Cagney got to the "top of the world" before dying: here, Giulio Sacchi is killed like a rabid dog, upon a pile of trash. So much for symbols.

Almost Human was initially released on home video in the U.S. in the early '80s, launched as if it was a horror flick, given Lenzi's fame as a director of such infamous cannibal movies such as *Eaten Alive!* and *Make Them Die Slowly* (a.k.a. *Cannibal Ferox*).

Notes

1. Manlio Gomarasca, "Ray faccia d'angelo," *Nocturno Cinema* #11 (July–September 1999), p. 76.
2. Morando Morandini, *Il Giorno*, 09.07.1974.
3. The score also features the music piece *Samba do desprezo*, sung by the band La Brasiliana, a song which originally appeared in Giuliano Montaldo's *Grand Slam* (1967).

City Under Siege (Un uomo, una città)

D: Romolo Guerrieri [Romolo Girolami]. *S:* loosely based on the novel *Il commissario di Torino* by Riccardo Marcato and Ugo Novelli; *SC:* Mino Roli, Nico Ducci; *DOP:* Aldo Giordani (35mm, Eastmancolor, Telecolor); *M:* Carlo Rustichelli, conducted by Gianfranco Plenizio (ed. Rizzoli Film); *E:* Antonio Siciliano; *PD:* Eugenio Liverani; *CO:* Andrea Zani; *C:* Sergio Bergamini; *AC:* Aldo Bergamini; *AE:* Lina Caterini; *AD:* Renato Rizzuto; *MU:* Raffaele Cristini; *Hair:* Marcella Favella; *SO:* Ettore Cappa; *Mix:* Gianni D'Amico; *SP:* Enzo Falessi; *ST:* Rodolfo Valadier, Donatella Gambini; *SS:* Marisa Agostini. *Cast:* Enrico Maria Salerno (Commissioner Michele Parrino), Françoise Fabian (Cristina Cournier), Luciano Salce (Paolo Ferrero), Paola Quattrini (Anna), Francesco Ferracini (Agent Balestrieri), Monica Monet (Luisa Crammi), Raffaele Curi (Franco), Carlo Puri (Vittorio Garotti), Bruno Zanin (Maria's sixteen-year-old lover), Gipo Farassino (Marshall Olinto Polito), Tino Scotti ("Cavalier" Fidelio Battista), Loris Bazzocchi (Lo Curcio), Iginio Bonazzi (Editor-in-chief), Maria Grazia Bosco, Pio Buscaglione, Gianni Cagnazzo, Anna Campori (Maria's lover's mother), Antonio Cardullo, Maria D'Incoronato (Maria), Attilio Dottesio (Coroner), Vittorio Duse (Agent Ragusa), Dino Emanuelli ("Flash," the photographer), Antonino Faà di Bruno (Col. Peretti), Eligio Irato, Carla Mancini (Girl in rotary press room), Gianni Mantesi, Bob Marchese (Informer), Paolo Percaus (Parking man at Café), Cinzia Romanazzi (Sorbona), Angelo Sacco, Gino Sovilla, Orazio Stracuzzi (Agostino), Giuseppe Tammaro. *Uncredited:* Ilona Staller (Blonde prostitute). *PROD:* Luigi Rovere for Goriz Film; *PM:* Antonio Girasante; *PSu:* Renato Panetuzzi, Elio Ottaviani; *PSe:* Pietro Salerno; *ADM:* Fernanda Ventimiglia. *Country:* Italy. Filmed at Icet–De Paolis (Milan) and on location in Turin. *Running time:* 115': Visa no.: 65430 (10.23.1974); *Rating:* v.m.18; *Release date:* 10.25.1974; *Distribution:* Cineriz; *Domestic gross:* 1,309,698,000 lire. *Also known as: Vicio en la ciudad* (Spain). *Home video:* Medusa (DVD, Italy).

Turin. Commissioner Michele Parrino, head of the flying squad, is an earnest, democratic cop who has to cope with the everyday criminal life of the city: sex crimes, thefts, armed robberies, suicides. Encouraged by his fiancée Anna and by his loyal journalist friend Paolo Ferrero, Parrino investigates the murder of a sixteen-year-old student, Grazia Aliprandi, and the disappearance of the wealthy young Giorgio Cournier. Parrino befriends Giorgio's mother, and his investigations bring the commissioner to uncover a drug and prostitution ring which involves members of powerful upper-class families. However, after Parrino's superiors remove him from the case and Ferrero sees his article rejected, both men conceive a bitter revenge.

Romolo Guerrieri's next crime film after the remarkable *La polizia è al servizio del cittadino?* was a rather offbeat affair. Starring Enrico Maria Salerno (who's excellent despite a clumsy copper-colored wig) as a world-weary police commissioner, *City Under Siege* has a rhapsodic structure, and is definitely closer to social commentary than to a proper genre actioner. The debts to Pietro Germi's *The Birds, the Bees and the Italians* (*Signore & Signori*, 1966) and Ettore Scola's *Il Commissario Pepe* (1969) are patent in the film's depiction of a city's decadent, corrupt upper class with a mixture of drama and irony. The script was based on a novel written by Riccardo Marcato and journalist Diego Novelli (the latter would become the Mayor of Turin in 1975 and remained in charge until 1985), *Il Commissario di Torino* ("The Commissioner of Turin"), itself inspired by a true life character, the head of the Flying Squad Montesano, a very popular figure back then. Montesano would also inspire another memorable character, Commissioner Santamaria in Carlo Fruttero and Franco Lucentini's best selling novels *The Sunday Woman* (*La donna della domenica*, 1974) and *A che punto è la notte* (At Which Point Is the Night, 1979). Marcato and Novelli would reprise the characters of Marcato and his sidekick, the hard-drinking journalist Paolo, in one more novel, *Dossier Pautasso* (1975).

However, the literary source is liberally manipulated by scriptwriters Nico Ducci and Mino Roli, who plunge the knife in the flaws of upper-class Turin with a more incisive tone than the film adaptation of *The Sunday Woman* directed by Luigi Comencini the following year, starring Marcello Mastroianni as Santamaria. *City Under Siege* is quite a singular work, starting with the casting: the folksinger (and future politician for the controversial Lega Nord, Italy's Northern racist party) Gipo Farassino, dubbed with a Neapolitan accent, is the Commissioner's assistant Salerno; the popular comedian Tino Scotti (Federico Fellini's *The Clowns*, 1970) is an old and senile FIAT worker who worships Gianni Agnelli (the historical president of FIAT cars) as some sort of a god; Bruno Zanin (who had just starred as Titta in Fellini's masterpiece *Amarcord*) makes a quick appearance in the opening sequence. On the other hand, a very young Ilona Staller makes a blink-and-you'll-miss-it nude appearance as a prostitute shooting a porn film.

Aided by a stronger budget than usual, courtesy of producer Luigi Rovere, who guaranteed the director the luxury of shooting the film in eleven weeks, Guerrieri mixes drama, irony, crude realism (the scene where a rape/murder victim is discovered is a case in point) and police detection with confidence, even though he occasionally relies on caricature, and keeps the film moving at a brisk pace, continually intersecting the various subplots and touching such different themes as immigration, the mechanization of factories and workers' protests, the generational gap and the corruption of morals; however, he manages to build a sharp and never absolutory portrayal of the faults and contradictions of a big city.

Such ambiguities do not spare the film's hero: Commissioner Parrino, a Sicilian who got perfectly integrated in a Northern town (in the original Italian version he speaks a perfect Italian, devoid of any accent, and knows how to move and act in high society) is one of the more complex and memorable characters in Italian crime film. Parrino is a lover of the good life, he goes at stage premieres, he is surprisingly comfortable in a tuxedo and knows how to court an upper class lady (Françoise Fabian) without the clumsiness one would expect from a man of action. Nevertheless, Parrino didn't forget his origins. Guerrieri stages a deeply moving scene where, in the poor kitchen of a grey, huge popular condo inhabited by Southern immigrants, the Commissioner starts speaking in a strict Sicilian dialect to console a poor father whose son committed suicide because he just couldn't integrate into the big city ("He didn't want to get out at night," the poor man says, "there was too much light in the streets; in our village it was always dark").

Parrino is accompanied throughout his investigations and daily adventures by a heavy drinking reporter, Paolo Ferrero (the great director/actor Luciano Salce, who's got some truly amusing lines), who at times looks like a drunken Virgil, leading Parrino through a humdrum, disenchanted vision of urban hell. For once, the Commissioner and the reporter are not rivals, but friends and ultimately accomplices, reversing the genre's usual stereotypes: in one scene, Ferrero even jokes with the Commissioner about a title his editor-in-chief has conceived: "The police sleep, the underworld kills," which sounds just like the title of a poliziotteschi.

Both men are cynical enough to swallow the corruption that surrounds them, still they hang on to a romantic idealism that makes them such beautiful losers. In the end, Parrino discovers a drug and prostitution ring that involves the sons and daughters of high-bred families, but his superiors shelve the results of his investigations, and the Commissioner is transferred to the Taxation police department; Ferrero, on the other hand, has his article on the case censored by the newspaper's editor-in-chief. The two men take their revenge by distributing the compromising dossiers at the Royal Theatre, during a glamorous opera night attended by Turin's wealthier and more powerful citizens, in a playful and cruel hoax; yet in the end Guerrieri brusquely denies any hint at a happy ending, as Parrino is overwhelmed by a sense of spleen and impotence against all the evil he must face every day.

The polyphonic scheme of Guerrieri's film was partially recycled in the slightly similar *Commissariato di notturna* (police Station by Night, 1974) by Guido Leoni, a comedy/drama centered on a Commissioner's (Gastone Moschin) first night at a police station: an attempt at recreating the social commentary of the Alberto Sordi classic *A Day in Court* (*Un giorno in pretura*, 1953, by Steno) updated to the 1970s, but without the melancholy yet biting vein of Guerrieri's film.

Crazy Joe (Crazy Joe)

D: Carlo Lizzani. *S:* Dino Maiuri, Massimo De Rita, based on a story by Nicholas Gage; *SC:* Dino Maiuri, Massimo De Rita, Carlo Lizzani (U.S. version: Lewis John Carlino); *DOP:* Aldo Tonti (35mm, Technicolor); *M:* Giancarlo Chiaramello (ed. Radiofilmusica); *E:* uncredited; *PD:* Marina Bruni (U.S. version: Robert Gundlach); *CO:* Marina Bruni (U.S. version: Ann Roth); *COA:* Robert Pusilo; *SD:* George DeTitta; *SDr:* Robert Klatt; *C:* Howard Block, Peter Garbarini; *AC:* James Contner; *AE:* Vanio Amici (U.S. version: Alison Berkley, Maurice Schell); *AsE:* Robert Lovett; *AD:* Rospo Pallenberg (U.S. version: *1st AD:* John Nicolella; *2nd AD:* John Neukum, Walter Skotchdopole; Rospo Pallenberg is credited as "creative consultant"); *SA:* Sante Fiore; *MU:* Giannetto De Rossi; *AMU:* Enzo De Alto; *Hair:* Mirella Sforza (U.S. version: Phyllis Sagnelli); *SR:* Tony Alloy; *SOEd:* David Hawkins, Maurice Schell; *Boom:* Vito Ilardo; *SOE:* Roberto Arcangeli; *Mix:* Fausto Ancillai (U.S. version: Dennis Maitland); *SE:* Joseph Lombardi; *SP:* Charles Moore; *LD:* Sol Negrin; *STC:* Jerry Brutsche; *ChG:* James Finnerty; *ChEl:* Richard Quinlan; *PrM:* Thomas Saccio; *TC:* Harry J. Leavey; *DC:* John Alarimo; *SS:* Renata Stoia; *P:* Howard Newman. *Cast:* Peter Boyle (Joe Gallo), Fred Williamson (Willie), Charles Cioffi (Vincent Coletti), Fausto Tozzi (Frank), Guido Leontini (Angelo), Rip Torn (Richie), Mario Erpichini (Danny), Paula Prentiss (Anne, Joe's girlfriend), Eli Wallach (Don Vittorio Santoni), Louis Guss (Giovanni Melfi), Franco Lantieri (Nunzio), Gabriele Torrei (Cheech), Adolfo Cosi, Dina Nella (Mrs. Falco), Franco Arena, Luther Adler (Don Ettore Falco), Vittorio Polacco, Carmine Caridi (Jelly), Tony Chiaromonte, Adam Wade (J.D.), Bruno Boschetti, Stefano Oppedisano; uncredited (Italian version): Henry Winkler (Manny), Sam Coppola (Chick), Michael V. Gazzo (Joe's uncle), Hervé Villechaize (Samson), Peter Savage (Don Marco), Cornelia Sharpe, Henry Ferrentino, Joe Anile, Nino Ruggeri, Frank Adonis (Franco family soldier gate guard), John C. Becher, Jill Elikann (Girl in sequin gown), Timothy Holley (Lou), Alexander Orfaly (Doctor), F. William Parker, Jay Rasumny (Clyde Barrow), Dan Resin (FBI agent), Robert Riesel (FBI agent), David Rosario (Boy saved in fire), Steve Vignari (Falco family soldier), Ralph Wilcox (Sam). *PROD:* Dino De Laurentiis for Produzioni De Laurentiis Inter.ma.co. (Rome), Bright-Persky Associate Features (New York); *EP:* Nino E. Krisman [Crisman]; *AP:* Peter Zinner; *UM:* Jim Gealis; *PSu:* Dick Stenta; *PSe:* Carolyn Schoenberg. *Country:* Italy / U.S. *Running time:* 100'; Visa no.: 63943 (02.02.1974); *Rating:* v.m.14; *Release date:* 02.08.1974; *Distribution:* Cineriz; *Domestic gross:* 628,266,000 lire. *Also known as: Jo le fou* (Paris, 01.14.1976—100')—*Testament in Blei* (West Germany, 1974—100')—*Crazy Joe* (U.K., 1974—99'), *Joe, el loco* (Spain), *O Mafioso rebelde* (Portugal). *Home video:* Domovideo (VHS, Italy). OST: LP International IS/20142.

Tired of his eternal position of poorly paid subordinate, Joe—a member of the Falco Mafia family—attempts, backed by his brother Richie, to take a slice of his boss' "business." However, he is defeated and ends up in jail. While Joe is serving his prison sentence, Falco instructs Joe's former friend, Vincent Coletti, to kill the most cunning and powerful Mafia boss, Don Vittorio Santoni. Vincent joins Santoni's ranks instead, and the boss rewards him by giving him Falco's "feud." Richie, tired and very ill, commits suicide. Joe is released, determined more than ever to make his way among the bosses: he makes a pact with the Afro American Willie, formerly a fellow prisoner. When Coletti, relying on their alleged marginalization, organizes a protest of the Italian-American minority which Santoni judges to be harmful for the "family," Don Vittorio has him killed. Joe is accused of the crime without any evidence: having become notorious for this, he decides to take this opportunity to challenge Don Vittorio's power. Both he and Willie will pay such an attempt with their lives.

Producer Dino De Laurentiis, who had just had a big hit in Italy with Terence Young's *The Valachi Papers* (1972), at first sight Carlo Lizzani's *Crazy Joe* seems like an attempt at repeating the commercial success of Young's film. Whereas *The Valachi Papers* recounted 50 years of and the subterranean power struggle between Mafia bosses Luciano, Costello, Anastasia and Genovese, *Crazy Joe* is—in typical Lizzani style—an instant movie inspired by the real-life figure of Joe Gallo, a small-time Cosa Nostra affiliate who ended up on the first pages with his quick rise to power, which ended on April 7th 1972 when Gallo was assassinated in the alley behind a restaurant in Little Italy.

However, Lizzani's view on the film (based on a story by Nicholas Gage) is quite different. "Why did we choose that story? To make a film on the American underworld? No, we did it because it was the mirrored image of a character typical of the '68 movements. Gallo was a young Mafioso who gathered the young against the old, just as it happened in China in the name of Mao and in the rest of the world as well. What's more—a sacrilegious thing in the Mafia—he made a pact with the Black Panthers, an interracial alliance! I could choose ten other different stories, I could do whatever I wanted and I had the money to do it, but for these reasons I chose to do *Crazy Joe*. It was a parable that symbolized a season of our contemporary society."[1]

On paper, Lizzani seemed just the right filmmaker to bring on screen in real time the war between New York Mafia factions. However, to speak as some critics did of "an application on American territory of *Bandits in Milan*'s winning formula" and of an "internationalization of Lizzani's approach to the gangster genre"[2] seems excessive. First of all, more than in the director's other films of the period, here Lizzani seemed to partially bend his style to the needs of a commercial project, and the character's complexities are left somewhat unexplored if compared to the director's ambitions, which only sporadically come to the fore—the sequence where Gallo discusses existentialism and becomes the main attraction of a high society party is a case in point. All in all, *Crazy Joe* as a whole looks like a lost occasion for such an acute social observer as Lizzani is.

Rather than *The Godfather*, *Crazy Joe* is closer to Scorsese's *Mean Streets* (1973) in its depiction of a certain Italian-American folklore—see Lizzani's music choices, as with the Opera airs that Joe and his acolytes sing in their car while driving to a rendezvous, or the use of popular songs like *Quando Quando Quando* and *Magic Moments* in the violent scenes—and in its cinephile touches: in the opening scene Peter Boyle is in a movie theater, watching Henry Hathaway's *Kiss of Death* (1947) and making a Richard Widmark impression. Curiously, Martin Scorsese was initially to be Lizzani's assistant, while the director's original choice for the role of Joe Gallo was a young and still unknown Robert De Niro, whom the director had noticed in Roger Corman's *Bloody Mama* (1970), whereas U.S. distributor Paramount imposed the talented yet commercially not very suitable Peter Boyle. This was probably one of the reasons for the film's commercial failure in Italy: just over 620 million lire, even less than mediocre genre products such as *Kidnap*, despite a sturdy cast that also included Eli Wallach, Paula Prentiss, "Blaxploitation" star Fred Williamson and Henry Winkler, soon to become Arthur "Fonzie" Fonzarelli in the TV series *Happy Days*, in his film debut. Winkler is uncredited in the Italian version, whose credits are largely incomplete (no editor is credited) and largely differ from the U.S. version, which credits Lewis John Carlino as the sole screenwriter.

Notes

1. Zagarrio, *Tre volte nella polvere, tre volte*, p. 40.
2. De Santi, *Carlo Lizzani*, 2001, p. 61.

Cry of a Prostitute (Quelli che contano)

D: Andrea Bianchi. *S:* Sergio Simonetti; *SC:* Piero Regnoli; *DOP:* Carlo Carlini (35mm, Eastmancolor, Telecolor); *M:* Sante Maria Romitelli (ed. Rolex Curci); *E:* Otello Colangeli; *PD, ArtD*: Giovanni Fratalocchi; *CO:* Alberta Santilli; *C:* Luigi Filippo Carta; *1st AC:* Massimo Carlini; *2nd AC:* Marcello Anconetani; *AE:* Antonio Cucca; *AD:* Ferdinando Merighi; *2nd AD:* Nicolangelo De Bellis; *MU:* Renzo Francioni; *AMU:* Vincenzo Napoli; *Hair:* Nicla Pertosa Palombi; *SO:* Carlo Tarchi; *Boom:* Alessandro Amoruso [Amoruto]; *Mix:* Sandro Occhetti, Mario Lupi; *SE:* Gino Vagniluca; *SP:* Roberto Marconi; *W:* Adalgisa Mosca; Tapestry: Alfredo D'Angelo; *MA:* Gianfranco Pasquetto; *PrM:* Valter Saettella; *SS:* Marina Grimaldi; *UP:* Lucia Lo Russo. *Cast:* Henry Silva (Tony Aniante), Barbara Bouchet (Margie), Fausto Tozzi (Don Ricuzzo Cantimo), Vittorio Sanipoli (Don Cascemi), Mario Landi (Don Turi Scannapieco), Mauro Righi, Dada Gallotti (Santa Scannapieco), Patrizia Gori (Carmela), Piero Maria Rossi (Paolo), Alfredo Pea (Zino), Pietro Torrisi (Alfio Scannapieco), Armando Bottin, Giancarlo Del Duca (Don Ricuzzo's henchman), Carla Mancini (Margie's maid), Orazio Stracuzzi, Enrico Marciani (Commissioner), Gennarino Pappagalli (Boss of bosses), Giuseppe Namio, Romano Milani (Mafia boss), Enrico Miotti, Bruno Salvi, Remo Pizzaroni. *Uncredited:* Fortunato Arena (Don Ricuzzo's henchman), Bruno Arié (Man in bar), Franco Beltramme (Don Turi's henchman), Omero Capanna (Don Ricuzzo's man), Tony Casale (One of Don Ricuzzo's men), Roberto Messina (Henchman in pink), Attilio Pelegatti (Morgue worker), Sergio Testori (Don Turi's henchman). *PROD:* Mauro Righi for Alexandra Cinematografica Internazionale; *PM:* Sergio Simonetti; *PSu:* Antonio Scarfone, Nicola Princigalli; *PSe:* Bruno Salvi. *Country:* Italy. Filmed at Incir–De Paolis (Rome) and on location in Savona, Ventimiglia and Sicily. *Running time:* 97'; Visa no.: 63053 (12.12.1973); *Rating:* v.m.18; *Release date:* 01.11.1974; *Distribution:* Jumbo; *Domestic gross:* 444,963,000 lire. *Also known as: Cry of a Prostitute: Love Kills* (U.S.—Home video), *Guns of the Big Shots* (U.K.), *Die Rache des Paten* (West Germany). *Home video:* Televista (DVD, USA—cut, 86'), Flamingo Video (DVD, Italy—uncut, 93'12")

Don Cascemi holds a meeting with other members of the Mob about the despicable use of dead children for the distribution and transportation of drugs through customs. One of the Mafiosi states that Don Ricuzzo Càntimo of Colle Pietra, an Italian American mobster deported from Brooklyn, is the suspected culprit. Cantimo took over the area from Don Turi Scannapieco. As a result, the two families of Cantimo and Scannapieco are at war with one another over the Colle Pietra province. Don Cascemi brings in Tony Aniante, a powerful mobster from America, to cause turmoil between the two families and find out who is using the young corpses for illegal purposes. But Aniante has a secret agenda that may bring down both families, leaving a gruesome trail of death and destruction. Pretending to act in the interest of Don Ricuzzo, Tony—who often intervenes in the cruel battles among the two gangs—absolves his duty, and both families end up destroyed. Then Aniante confronts Don Coscemi and kills him. Since the beginning he had a secret agenda prepared by "those who count." In the end, Tony replaces Cascemi, thus becoming one of the godfathers.

A late entry in the Mafia subgenre, Andrea Bianchi's *Cry of a Prostitute* (the original title, *Quelli che contano*, translates to the more apt "Those Who Count") is certainly no good, yet it is somehow typical of a couple of tendencies in Italian genre cinema. The first is the art of recycling: the plot—Mafia killer Tony Aniante (Henry Silva, redoing himself from *The Boss*) is sent to his Sicilian hometown to put two families against each other—is a barely disguised replica of Sergio Leone's *A Fistful of Dollars*, a move that scriptwriter Piero Regnoli would repeat even more openly in Stelvio Massi's *The Last Round* (1976). Bianchi's film is in many ways a Western in disguise, as the torrid Sicilian setting (which has Silva sweat profusely in every scene he's in) somehow resembles the typical South of the border environments of Italian Westerns, to the point that Càntimo's white walled country villa, where the final standoff takes place, recalls the haciendas seen in many Spaghetti flicks. Even Silva's ominous whistle is a nod to Leone's use of music (take Charles Bronson's harmonica in *Once Upon a Time in the West*, for instance).

The second noticeable tendency is the emphasis on nasty, explicit violence, which would become a rule in Italian genre cinema of the late '70s. In *Cry of a Prostitute*, Bianchi serves up a plethora of gory details that would be equaled only six years later by none other than Lucio Fulci in his gritty Neapolitan crime drama *The Smuggler* (*Luca il contrabbandiere*, 1980): a severed head rolls on the asphalt after a car accident; a child's dead body is used to conceal heroin (an idea already seen in *Pete, Pearl and the Pole* and *Afyon Oppio*, talk of recycling...); people receive gunshots to the head; Silva runs over a body with a steamroller; a head is bisected with a circular saw as in Aristide Massaccesi's *Absurd* (*Rosso sangue*, 1981). On the other hand, Sergio Simonetti's story exhibits a repellent misogyny, which is usually directed towards the character played by Barbara Bouchet. As Margie, the boss' mistress, she's nothing but a plaything, a sex manikin in nightgown and platinum hair who is used and abused throughout the film by her male owners: "You are my toy, you've got to let me have fun!" the boss whispers to her ear, in bed. The scene where Margie is sodomized by Aniante while leaning against a pig's carcass is not just reminiscent of an infamous scene in Armando Bo's *Carne* (1968), but also predates the excesses of Italian sexploitation to come, without the surreal inventiveness of Alberto Cavallone's *Man, Woman and Beast* (*Spell, dolce mattatoio*, 1977). Even worse, later on Silva savagely beats the woman with his belt before raping her.

Cry of a Prostitute was Andrea Bianchi's first proper directorial effort, even though he had been formerly credited as director or co-director for tax reasons in Italian versions of John Hough's *Treasure Island* (1972) and James Kelley's *What the Peeper Saw* (1972); he would go on to direct among others such trashy cult flicks as the giallo *Strip Nude for Your Killer* (*Nude per l'assassino*, 1975) starring Edwige Fenech, the sex/horror hybrid *Malabimba* (1979) and the zombie movie *Burial Ground* (*Le notti del terrore*,

1980) before moving on to hardcore. It is worth noting the presence of another controversial filmmaker, Mario Landi, in his one and only effort in front of the camera as Don Turi Scannapieco: a former TV director, Landi would helm a number of nasty little genre flicks such as *Giallo a Venezia* (1979) and *Patrick Lives Again* (*Patrick vive ancora*, 1980).

Cry of a Prostitute was released to DVD in the United States in a heavily cut, fullscreen version which besides the sex and gore is also missing an early sequence that's vital to the plot.

Emergency Squad (Squadra volante)

D: Stelvio Massi. *S:* Dardano Sacchetti; *SC:* Dardano Sacchetti, Adriano Bolzoni, Franco Barberi, Stelvio Massi; *DOP:* Sergio Rubini (35mm, Technicolor, Technospes); *M:* Stelvio Cipriani (ed. c.a.m.); *E:* Mauro Bonanni; *PD:* Carlo Leva; *C:* Michele Pensato; *AC:* Aldo Bergamini; *AD:* Dardano Sacchetti; *MU:* Franco Di Girolamo; *AMU:* Elisabetta Rossi; *Hair:* Jole Angelucci; *SO:* Domenico Pasquadibisceglie; *Mix:* Luciano Anzellotti; *SOE:* Mario Anzellotti; *SE:* Sergio Chiusi; *SP:* Angelo Pennoni; *KG:* Nello Adami; *ChEl:* Roberto Belli; *SS:* Evi Farinelli. *Cast:* Tomas Milian (Inspector Tomas Ravelli of the Interpol), Gastone Moschin (Marseillaise), Stefania Casini (Marta Hayworth), Guido Leontini (Mario Berlotti "Cranio"), Ilaria Guerrini (Fede, Tomas' sister-in-law), Mario Carotenuto (Brigadeer Lavagni), Ray Lovelock (Rino Micheli "The Philosopher"), Giuseppe Castellano (Beppe), Marcello Venditti ("Serbia"), Gabriella Cotignoli, Fabrizio Mazzotti, Nino Curatolo [Nino D'Errico] (Leonardi), Giorgio Basso, Antonio La Raina (Commissioner Calò), Enzo Andronico (Alberto), Luca Sportelli (Gigi, the postman), Leda Celani (Mother hostage), Carla Mancini, Orazio Stracuzzi. *Uncredited:* Annibale Papetti (Notary waving at Gigi). Note: although credited, Carla Mancini and Orazio Stracuzzi do not appear in the film. *PROD:* C.B.A. Produttori e Distributori Associati; *EP:* Amleto Adami; *PM:* Antonio Girasante; *PSu:* Andrea Petricca, Salvatore Scalzone; *PSe:* Luciano Como; *ADM:* Gian Carlo Ciotti. *Country:* Italy. Filmed on location in Pavia. *Running time:* 90'; Visa no.: 64268 (03.30.1974); *Rating:* v.m.14; *Release date:* 04.24.1974; *Distribution:* Jumbo Cinematografica; *Domestic gross:* 895,581,000 lire. *Also known as: Der Einzelkämpfer* (West Germany), *Brigade volante* (France). *Home video:* NoShame Films (DVD, USA), Cinekult (DVD, Italy), VZ-Handelsgesellschaft (DVD, Germany). Sountrack: CD Digitmovies CDDM150.

Pavia. The "Marseillaise" and his gang successfully carry out a robbery, and kill a policeman in the process. Despite the hostility towards him on the part of Commissioner Calò, who does not approve of his drastic methods, Inspector Tomas Ravelli takes on the investigation. The tough cop has been waiting five years to be able to avenge his wife's death, which occurred only a year after his marriage, in Marseille, during a similar hold-up at a bank. With the help of the faithful sergeant Lavagni, whom Calò put at his heels to control him, soon Tomas is on the Marseillaise's tracks. When the hassles begin to surface, the gang crumbles and the Marsellaise loses several men. Following the trail of dead bodies and weapons, Ravelli forces his enemy to escape to the river Po, where Mizar, a Tunisian, is waiting for him to escape by boat. Eventually Ravelli catches up with his adversary, and to better consummate his revenge, he throws away his badge before shooting him.

Stelvio Massi's first crime film brings on the transformation of poliziotteschi's central character, which gradually detaches from real-life models and passes through a process of hyperrealist deformation. At first it's not even clear which side the film's hero stands: his casual clothes and the tendency to stay and act by himself make Inspector Tomas Ravelli (Tomas Milian, who dubs himself in the Italian version, with a somehow weird effect given the actor's South American accent) a rain dog, a foreign body inside the police force. Not even his colleagues seem to consider him one of their own.

Unlike other tough cops in Italian crime films, Tomas Ravelli doesn't even care about the law: to him, being a police Inspector matters only a way to follow the tracks of his private enemy, the Marseillaise (Gastone Moschin), who killed Ravelli's wife five years earlier. In the end, when the two come face to face, first Ravelli throws away his badge, then shoots the criminal in cold blood. However, neither his past trauma, nor the pleonastic presence of a son and a sister-in-law make Ravelli a more human character: he stays distant, icy, ghostlike for the duration of the film. Massi and his co-scripters even have him flanked by a comedic sidekick (Mario Carotenuto) so as to elicit the audience's sympathies.

Ravelli is obviously a Spaghetti Western character in disguise, the illicit son of Clint Eastwood's Man With No Name, Charles Bronson's Harmonica and Anthony Steffen's Django (the ghastly titular character in Sergio Garrone's *Django the Bastard*, 1969, rather than Franco Nero's original). The film's iconography testifies to such a pedigree. In the opening sequence, where Ravelli gets dressed, Tomas Milian looks like someone who just stepped out of a Sergio Leone film, given the fetishist attention to the smallest details (the basque, the gun, a cigar between the teeth); what's more, the recurring flashback where Ravelli's wife is murdered underlines the protagonist's obsession just like the one in *Once Upon a Time in the West*. As Charles Bronson in Leone's film, Ravelli is a walking dead, a *revenant* who appears out of nowhere on the crime scene and maintains the same imperturbable expression throughout the film.

As with Westerns, crime films portray a Manichaean morale, inviting the audience to take sides. And the public response is another element that certifies the genetic affinities between the commissioners and the gunslingers, responding to crime film heroes' on-screen deeds with the same enthusiasm they reserved to Westerns a few years earlier ... even though sometimes the side taken by the audience was not the one expected by the filmmakers. As Stelvio Massi recalled, "I was ashamed like a thief at *Emergency Squad*'s première in Rome, when the audience erupted into a spontaneous applause during the scene when a police car explodes after the bandits shoot at it with machine guns. We looked at each other and said, 'These people must be crazy!'"[1]

Massi, a former cameraman and director of photography, was to become one of the genre's specialists. His second feature, *Macrò— Giuda uccide il venerdì* (1974), a retelling of the encounter between Christ and Mary Magdalene set in modern-day subproletarian Rome, had been shelved after the bankruptcy of distributor Flora Film, and *Emergency Squad*, his first crime film, was his last chance: towards the end of shooting, when the budget ran short of 15 million lire, Massi anticipated the sum himself just to finish the film. He lost the money, but won his battle: *Emergency Squad* was a surprising commercial hit and persuaded producers and distributors that Massi was the ideal choice for the action genre.

Emergency Squad already displays some of the filmmaker's stylistic traits: a tendency to avoid the usual shot/countershot routine, by including the faces of two characters in the same shot through reflecting surfaces such as a rearview mirror (take for instance the scene where the Marseillaise kills "Cranio," played by genre regular Guido Leontini); the non-trivial use of zoom lenses and long takes; the sharp, effective action scenes, as shown by the car/helicopter chase along the foggy roads of the Lombard plain — a sequence which predates a similar moment in the director's own *Convoy Busters* (1978).

The script, however, is not faultless, despite a few interesting traits such as the setting in the Northern provincial town of Pavia. The story straddles between mild political references (the Socialist bandit played by Ray Lovelock) and social commentary (Ravelli breaks into an apartment full of stoned youths) with a few second-hand borrowings (Moschin and his acolytes escape after a bank robbery dressed as monks, like in the cult '60s heist flick *Seven Golden Men*, 1966) and the characters are stereotypes. The Marseillaise is, as the banal name suggests, a mere cypher, an antagonist who becomes watchable only for Moschin's on screen personality: in the scene where he reaches his lover (Stefania Casini) with whom he's planning to escape by boat, he even manages to evokes a reminiscence of *Caliber 9's* unforgettable Ugo Piazza. The other characters — with the partial exception of Leontini's "Cranio," a faint-hearted bandit who's always got a porn mag in his hands — are forgettable if not irritating, as in the case of Casini's dumb platinum blonde, who makes for a very bad Marilyn Monroe clone.

Note

1. Matteo Norcini and Stefano Ippoliti, "Intervista a Stelvio Massi," *Amarcord* #6 (January / February 1997), p. 71.

Hold-Up (*"Hold-Up," istantanea di una rapina*, a.k.a. *Atraco en la Costa Azul*)

D: Germán Lorente. *S* and *SC:* Adriano Asti, Germán Lorente (Spanish version: and Miguel de Echarri); *DOP:* Mario Capriotti (35mm, Eastmancolor, Technospes); *M:* Franco Micalizzi; *E:* Carlo Reali; *PD:* Santiago Ontañón Fernandez; *SD:* Camillo Del Signore; *CO:* Augusta Monelli; *C:* Giuseppe Di Biase, José García Galisteo, Jean-Claude Hugon; *AC:* Guido Tosi, Manuel Mateos Valverde; *AE:* Anna D'Angelo; *AD:* Massimo Carocci (Spanish version: Rodolfo Medina); *MU:* Emilio Trani, Eric Muller; *Hair:* Vitaliana Patacca, Dolores Merlo; *W:* Anna Maria Infanti [Ana María Infante]; *SOEng:* Pietro Spadoni; *B:* Angelo Spadoni, José Antonio Arijita; *SP:* Giuseppe Botteghi, Octavio Fernández Roces; *STC:* Rémy Julienne; *SS:* Liana Ferri; *DubD* (English version): Nick Alexander. *Cast:* Frederick Stafford (Robert Cunningham), Nathalie Delon (Judy), Marcel Bozzuffi (Steve Duggins), Alberto De Mendoza (Ashley), Enrico Maria Salerno (Mark Gavin), Calisto Calisti (policeman), Manuel de Blas, Miguel Del Castillo, Santiago Ontañón, José Luis Chinchilla, Raquel Núñez. *Uncredited:* Alessandro Perrella. *PROD:* Rodolfo Sabbatini for Flaminia Produzioni Cinematografiche (Catania), Midega Film (Madrid), Paris Interproductions (PIP); *EP:* Salvatore Gerbino (Spanish version: Miguel de Echarri); *PC:* Aldo Quinzi; *PMs:* Francisco Lara Polop, Joël Lifschutz (Spanish version: Miguel Ángel Bermejo); *UM:* Augusto Dolfi, Antonio Pittalis, Jesús Narro Sancho; *ADM:* Miguel J. Echarri. *Country:* Italy / Spain / France. Filmed on location in Cannes, Marbella, Monte Carlo, Nice, San Remo, Torremolinos. *Running time:* 95'; Visa no.: 64971 (07.30.1974); *Rating:* v.m.14; *Release date:* 08.02.1974; *Distribution:* Azi; *Domestic gross:* 204,892,000 lire. *Also known as: Hold-Up, instantánea de una corrupción. Home video:* VCL (VHS, U.K.— pre-cert), VCL (VHS, Denmark). OST: CD Fin De Siècle Media FDS21.

Robert Cunningham, an ex-cop who's been removed from his job after losing his memory in the aftermath of a car accident, lives in San Remo with his lover Judith, juggling his time between bars and gambling houses. One day, Robert notices a man who turns out to be Steve Duncan, one of the thugs who carried out a robbery from an armored truck. Duncan is convinced that Robert is only pretending to be amnesiac: after the heist, the cop tracked Duncan down, killed his accomplices and took the money away with him, before being involved in the car accident. Robert and Judith move to Cannes, when Cunningham loses a huge amount of money because of his gambling habits. He is forced by a man called Ashley to become involved in a hold-up at the local casino: however, this is all part of an elaborate plan that involves Duncan, Judith (who's actually Duncan's lover) and a mysterious man whose face is never seen. After the robbery, Ashley and Cunningham split, but the former is killed by Duncan, who tracks Robert down. In the final showdown Judith kills Duncan, but soon after she and Robert are arrested by Cunningham's colleague and best friend, Inspector Mark Gavin. It's then that Robert recovers his memory, and finds out too late that Gavin is the criminal mastermind behind it all.

A sort of companion piece to *Special Killers*— same producer, director, star —*Hold-Up* is a rather bland *film noir* which doesn't do much with its intriguing idea and flashback-ridden plot, barely reminiscent of Cornell Woolrich's classic novel *The Black Curtain*. As the self-destructive amnesiac hero, who struggles to put together the pieces of his memory, Stafford is as wooden as ever, and the script doesn't make him a really interesting character: Cunningham's desperate attempts at understanding if he really was a corrupt cop who had hidden the money from a bank robbery, which result in a gambling habit and a heavy drinking problem, soon become monotonous, and the plot has its share of holes. As in Lorente's other crime film, the best part is the ending, which serves an amoral sting in the tail that is not unexpected yet is still rather biting. But it's too little, too late: besides the opening (and rather clumsily shot) heist scene, the film's showpiece is a 6-minute car chase choreographed by Rémy Julienne.

Compared to *Special Killers, Hold-Up* is also much more restrained in the exploitation area, with nudity kept to a minimum. Lorente displays unusual bits of American-inspired trickery, as in the slow motion death scenes *à la* Peckinpah and in a curious if misguided attempt at the multiple split-screen technique in a scene where Stafford reminisces about his past trauma — yet he devotes an excessive amount of footage to Stafford and Delon's walks through the streets of San Remo and Cannes. The film's best asset is Gianfranco Micalizzi's score, with its seductive female vocals and lounge mood.

Kidnap (*Fatevi vivi: la polizia non interverrà*)

D: Giovanni Fago. *S:* Adriano Bolzoni; *SC:* Adriano Bolzoni, Giovanni Fago; *DOP:* Roberto Gerardi (35mm, Eastmancolor, Technicolor); *M:* Piero Piccioni, conducted by the author (ed. United Artists — CBS — Sugar); *E:* Alberto Gallitti; *AE:* Anna Napoli; Art director: Amedeo

Fago; *ASDr:* Gianni Giovagnoni; *CO:* Annalisa Nasalli Rocca; *Casting:* Paola Rolli; *C:* Roberto Forges Davanzati; *AC:* Maurizio La Monica; *AD:* Franco Cirino; *MU:* Marisa Marconi; *Hair:* Rosetta Luciani; *SOEng:* Fiorenzo Magli; *Boom:* Manlio Urbani; *Mix:* Gianni D'Amico; *SOE:* Roberto Arcangeli; *Construction:* Mario Valentini; *PrM:* Antonio Tomaino; *SP:* Ermanno Consolazione; *G:* Alfredo Dioguardi; *GA:* Luigi Pasqualini; *T:* Nedo Angeletti; *CON:* Francesca Roberti; *DubD:* Renato Izzo. *Cast:* Henry Silva (Commissioner Caprile), Rada Rassimov (Marta, first kidnapper), Philippe Leroy ("The Professor"), Lia Tanzi (Marisa Callari), Gabriele Ferzetti (Don Francesco "Frank" Salvatore), Fausta Avelli (Luisa Bonsanti), Armando Brancia (Lawyer), Luciano Bartoli (Rosolino Federici, second kidnapper), Renato Pinciroli (Old mafioso), Paul Muller (Jimmy), Rosita Torosh (Bonsanti's wife), Alessandro Perrella (Coroner), Marco Bonetti (Pino, third kidnapper), Bruno Boschetti (Attorney), Loris Bazzocchi (Mafioso), Omero Antonutti (Engineer Bonsanti), Pino Ferrara (Mercuri, Caprile's assistant), Franco Diogene (Nino, Don Francesco's henchman), Calisto Calisti (Mafioso), Margherita Horowitz (Don Francesco's housemaid), Gianfranco Barra (Barman), Antonio Formicola. *Uncredited:* Filippo Perego (Man in Bonsanti's factory). *PROD:* Produzioni Associate Delphos; *EP:* Ottavio Oppo; *PM:* Bruno Frascà; *UM:* Bruno Perria; *PA:* Michele Capozzi; *ADM:* Aurelio Lalli. *Country:* Italy. Filmed at Palatino Studios (Rome) and on location in Como and Tremezzo. *Running time:* 100'; Visa no.: 64902 (07.13.1974); *Rating:* v.m.14; *Release date:* 08.13.1974; *Distribution:* United Artists Europe; *Domestic gross:* 658,151,000 lire. *Also known as: In der Gewalt des Kindermörders* (Germany). *Home video:* None. OST: 7" United Artists UA 35757 / CD Digitmovies CDDM170.

Lake Como. Luisa, daughter of the wealthy engineer Bonsanti, is kidnapped by two masked men and a woman, who escape on a motorboat. Among the witnesses to the kidnapping there is Marisa, a prostitute. Bonsanti, gets in touch with police Commissioner Caprile, while the kidnappers argue with their boss, whom they call "The Professor," about the ransom they are going to demand from the little girl's parents. While the engineer and his family are anxiously waiting for a telephone call from the kidnappers, Marisa is interrogated to identify the culprits in some way. However, the young woman insists she has not seen anything. Commissioner Caprile also suspects Don Francesco, a powerful Mafia boss. The police grope in the dark, but Don Francesco investigates on his own to clear his name: through Marisa, he identifies and reaches the "Professor," who in the meantime has dispatched his accomplices and has escaped. A motorboat chase on Lake Como ensues and the kidnapper is shot to death. Don Francesco and his men later inform the police about the location of Luisa's hideout.

Despite its lurid Italian title (translating to "Show Up: The Police Won't Intervene"), much more verbose than the laconic English one — which nonetheless granted the film to be picked up by United Artists in the hope of speculating over the Patty Hearst case — Giovanni Fago's film is a rather idiosyncratic entry in the then-florid kidnapping subgenre, which spawned Tonino Valerii's *Go Gorilla Go* (*Vai gorilla*, 1975) and Fernando di Leo's *Kidnap Syndicate* (1975), to mention a few. More of a talky crime drama than a full-out action flick, what makes *Kidnap* stand out from its contemporaries is the curious dichotomy between the two main characters, a spiteful Commissioner (Henry Silva) and an elderly Mafia don (Gabriele Ferzetti) who both investigate the kidnapping of a rich young girl. As film critic Guglielmo Biraghi noticed, "the film has sensibly higher ambitions than usual, if only because it tries to blend two different themes: the tale of a kidnapping on the one hand, and an investigation into the relationship between the Law and the Mafia on the other."[1] If Commissioner Caprile is powerless and gropes in the dark, it's Don Francesco who solves the case on his own, so as to clear his name and — in typical *M* fashion — shake off police suspicion. As a result, unlike his fellow colleagues in Italian crime flicks, Silva doesn't have to do much except get angry and lose his temper in his office.

Fago's film benefits from its unusual setting on the Lake Como, with the beautiful villa La Quiete in Tremezzo posing as engineer Bonsanti's (Omero Antonutti) house. Yet after the impressive opening kidnapping the story falters a bit, not least because the script (by Adriano Bolzoni and Fago, who's also the art director) doesn't bother to develop its characters: the head of the kidnappers, nicknamed "The Professor," played by Philippe Leroy, is a shallow figure, noticeable only for Leroy's aging makeup and thick glasses, one of his acolytes plays harmonica Spaghetti Western–style, another (Rada Rassimov) is a drug addict. That's it.

If its ambitions fall short, from a purely exploitation point of view *Kidnap* is anemic to put it mildly. Suspenseful moments are very few and far between until the very end, when Fago sets up a tepid speedboat chase on the lake: the sight of foggy waters in the early morning is remarkably atmospheric, but the ensuing sequence is marred by an obvious use of filters and fogs to mask a very sunny day. The film benefits from Piero Piccioni's lush score, which is rather different from the typical sounds of the genre, and alternates sensual lounge (the main theme *Kidnap*, which was released in Italy on a 7") with more rhythmic funky-soul tracks, as well as experimental parts that border on Oriental atmospheres.

Note

1. Bir (Guglielmo Biraghi), Il Messaggero, 09.14.1974.

The Killers Are Our Guests (*Gli assassini sono nostri ospiti*)

D: Vincenzo Rigo. *S* and *SC:* Bruno Fontana, Renato Romano [and Umberto Simonetta, uncredited]; *DOP:* Vincenzo Rigo (35mm, Technicolor); *M:* Roberto Rizzo, conducted by Nando De Luca; *E:* Vincenzo Rigo; *PD:* Claudio Riccardi; *C:* Roberto Seveso; *AC:* Walter Vitali, Emilio Bestetti; *AE:* Jolanda Adamo; *AD:* Giovanni Brusatori [Brusadori]. *Cast:* Anthony Steffen [Antonio De Teffé] (Dr. Guido Malerba), Margaret Lee (Eliana), Luigi Pistilli (Commissioner Di Stefano), Gianni Dei (Franco), Livia Cerini (Mara Malerba), Giuseppe Castellano (Mario), Sandro Pizzocchero (Eddie), Giovanni Brusatori [Brusadori] (Vice Commissioner), Marino Campanaro, Ferdinando Borgonovo, Giancarlo Busi (Cop), Fernanda Minelli, Teodoro Visentin, Gianni Gereghini, Gabriele Fontanesi, Ermanno Pasquini, Luigi Antonio Guerra. *PROD:* Alberto Rigo for Lombarda Film, Produzione Palumbo; *EP:* Gaspare Palumbo; *GM:* Alberto Rigo; *UM:* Alessandro Calosci. *Country:* Italy. Shot on location in Milan. *Running time:* 90'; Visa no.: 64605 (05.27.1974); *Rating:* v.m.18; *Release date:* 07.12.1974; *Distribution:* I.n.d.i.e.f.; *Domestic gross:* 258,410,000 lire. *Also known as: Killer sind unsere Gäste* (Germany), *Kamp for livet* (Norway), *Listes sto krevati mou* (Greece). *Home video:* Alfa Digital (DVD, US).

Two men and a woman — Mario, Franco and Eliana — rob a jewelry store in Milan while their leader Eddie is waiting outside the store. During the heist, the jeweler's son and a customer are killed, while Franco is seriously wounded. With him on board, and without

Eddie, the bandits fled in the car and reach the outskirts of the city. Eliana leads them to the home of Dr. Guido Malerba. The doctor is forced to operate on Franco, and the bandits stay in his house waiting for Eddie to join them. Even though they still live together, Guido and his wife Mara hate each other: they take advantage of this to flirt with Eliana and Mario. Finally, Eddie arrives, and the bandits (who just avoided being caught by the police but had to stifle Franco so as his laments wouldn't be heard by the cops) set out to leave. However, they're in for a surprise: Guido and Eliana are lovers, and the woman led her accomplices to the doctor's house on purpose to trap them and get the loot. Guido extracts a gun and kills Eddie, Mario and his wife Mara as well. Then they set out to leave for America, thinking they got away with their plan. But the police, through the testimony of a transvestite to whom Eliana had stolen the car prior to the heist, are waiting for them at the airport.

While the poliziotteschi was quickly becoming Italy's best grossing genre at the box office, another thread emerged. It was more bastardized with eroticism (the main common denominator of Italian cinema since the mid–'60s) and was focused on a group of people — preferably bourgeois and with a notable percentage of females — held prisoner by a handful of thugs — proletarian, ferocious, badly dressed — in a secluded place. The forced cohabitation would make tensions emerge in the group and awaken concealed sexual impulses. It's debatable whether the subgenre — anticipated by Enzo G. Castellari's *Cold Eyes of Fear*— had much in common with out-and-out action crime films, apart from the reference to the current climate of urban violence. However, Vincenzo Rigo's *The Killers Are Our Guests* smartly jumps on the poliziotteschi bandwagon by opening with a heist sequence and featuring Luigi Pistilli as a picturesque, foul-mouthed Commissioner who at times seems a caricature of the genre's hard-boiled cops, with lines such as "They shoot, shoot, bang, bang ... why don't they bang their meat instead?"

A Northern Italy production, *The Killers Are Our Guests* was Rigo's first film as a director: he is also the director of photography and editor. It's not badly shot — especially the opening hold-up, which concentrates on the gang member waiting outside the jewelry and doesn't show the shoot-out — and even offers a few stylistic felicities plus a deliciously cruel sting in the tail. Yet the plot is too conceited for its own good: Rigo himself labeled the script (by character actor Renato Romano) as "horrible, a fraud! Even the title sucked, it was something like *Grande rapina di tre miliardi a Milano* ("Three Billion Robbery in Milan"). And then the dialogue sucked, it was full of incongruities ... the story was the same [...]. Only, it was rough and childishly written, the lines sounded as if they came straight from a bad comic book. [...] They told me "We gotta do a commercial flick. This film is going to play in the provinces, it's a C-movie. Don't worry, we'll make a good movie afterwards."[1] Rigo didn't give up, though, and tried to make the best he could with the script. In came another writer, Bruno Fontana, "an incompetent. I came to Rome to revise the script with him and [...] we spent the night with him handwriting and his wife typewriting and correcting his papers. I got back to Milan at dawn."[2] Eventually the casting of stage actress Livia Cerini brought in the renowned novelist and playwright Umberto Simonetta (Cerini's husband, and the author of a number of novels that were turned into films, from *Il giovane normale* to *I viaggiatori della sera*), who did some badly needed uncredited work, polished the dialogue and came up with the definitive title.

The cast is weirdly assembled to say the least: Steffen is as wooden as ever and quite unbelievable as the frustrated doctor, a role that would have been perfect for Enrico Maria Salerno. As for the erotic scenes, the obligatory lesbian seduction between Margaret Lee and Livia Cerini — which Rigo states was slightly cut by the censors — looks as if it's been shot in a dual version, whereas the interlude between Cerini and her lover (Gianni Dei) — who engages in masturbation while staying outside the door just when one of the bandits is hiding inside — is more ironic than morbid. Most circulating copies were missing the prologue, where Margaret Lee struggles with a transvestite and steals his car, thus justifying an ending which otherwise comes out of the blue, as the Commissioner is waiting for the two lovers at the airport.

Note

1. Davide Pulici, "Il cinema è come una messa," in Aa. Vv., "Fatti di cinema. Controcorrente 3," *Nocturno Dossier* #51 (October 2006), p. 60.
2. *Ibid.*

The Last Desperate Hours (*Milano: il clan dei calabresi*)

D: Giorgio Stegani. *S* and *SC:* Giovanni Addessi, Camillo Bazzoni, Franco Barbaresi; *DOP:* Aldo De Robertis, Sandro Mancori (35mm, Eastmancolor, L.V.-Luciano Vittori); *M:* Gianni Marchetti (Ed. R.C.A.); *E:* Otello Colangeli; *PD:* Luciano Puccini; *ArtD:* Camillo Del Signore; *COA:* Dafne Ciarrocchi; *C:* Giuseppe Di Biase; *AC:* Augusto Bicorni; *AD:* Bruno Cortini; *MU:* Maria Luisa Tilli; *AMU:* Angelo Malantrucco; *SO:* Raul Montesanti; *Boom:* Angelo Amatulli; *Mix:* Sandro Occhetti, Mario Lupi; *SE:* Cataldo Galliano; *SP:* Mauro Paravano; *W:* Elide Candidi; *SS:* Flavia Sante Vanin. *Cast:* Antonio Sabàto (Paolo Mancuso), Silvia Monti (Laura Monachesi), Pier Paolo Capponi (police Commissioner), Nicoletta Rizzi (Lidia Mancuso), Fred Williams (Dario Lippi), Mario Donen [Mario Papotti] (Gino), Peter Carsten (Maraschi), Melù Valente (School teacher), Toni Ucci (Ugo Merenda "Bellyache"), Giulio Baraghini (The Inspector's assistant), Bruno Di Luia (Pino), Nando Marineo (Doctor), Mirella Rossi (Prostitute), Nicola D'Eramo (Transvestite informer), Elena De Merick [Demerik] (Liliana Lamanna). *Uncredited:* Antonio Anelli (Investigator at crime scene), Calogero Azzaretto (Thug), Dolores Calò (Woman stoning Mancuso), Lella Cattaneo (Woman in gambling hall), Nestore Cavaricci (Cleaner at gambling saloon), Francesco D'Adda (Agent Scalise), Pasquale Fasciano (Man at police station), Lina Franchi (Arguing prostitute), Silvio Klein (Man in casino), Alba Maiolini (Prostitute / Woman in the crowd stoning Mancuso), Nando Sarlo (Man in gambling saloon), Romano Targa (Dario's man), Luciano Zanussi (Man in gambling saloon). *PROD:* Giovanni Addessi for Cristiana Cinematografica; *GM:* Franco Caruso; *PM:* Nino Di Giovanbattista; *PI:* Alfredo Di Santo. *Country:* Italy. Filmed at Incir — De Paolis (Rome) and on location in Milan. *Running time:* 94'; Visa no.: 65630 (11.29.1974); *Rating:* v.m.18; *Release date:* 11.29.1974; *Distribution:* Overseas Film Company; *Domestic gross:* 560,728,000 lire. *Home video:* Surf/Cecchi Gori (DVD, Italy). OST: CD Beat Records DDJ002.

Milan. Paolo Mancuso, a Calabrian who emigrated to the North in search of fortune, has become a big shot in the underworld, controlling the drugs and prostitution ring. After paying a visit to his lover Laura, an ex-prostitute whom he has entrusted with a couple of shops, Mancuso is ambushed by a bunch of motorbike killers. He takes refuge in a biological lab where he is bitten by a guinea pig that carries a deadly virus. Mancuso decides to find out who wants him dead: his opponents are Dario Lippi, the owner of a clandestine gambling house, and the powerful Maraschi. Meanwhile the police Commissioner on the case has less than 20 hours to track down Mancuso, before the infection spreads. A manhunt ensues, and Mancuso is abandoned by his men: his right-hand Gino even offers Lippi and Maraschi to set up a trap for him with the aid of a doctor who should provide Mancuso an antidote. Hunted like a wild beast by the police and his former associates, Mancuso takes refuge at his lover's place, but he finds out that Laura as well is betraying him, and strangles the woman. Eventually Paolo seeks help from his estranged wife Lidia. While she desperately tries to find the antidote to cure him, Mancuso faces his acolytes in a junkyard, then settles the score with Lippi and Maraschi. Chased by the cops, he takes a bus full of schoolkids as hostage. Eventually Mancuso takes refuge in a slum, where he is stoned to death by a horde of angry slum dwellers.

A social environment that's very similar to Umberto Lenzi's *Gang War in Milan* emerges from Giorgio Stegani's *The Last Desperate Hours*, where Antonio Sabàto reprises the character of a ruthless and ambitious Southern boss that he already portrayed in Lenzi's film, coming off rather more lively than usual. The script abundantly preys American *film noir*: the film's basic idea (Sabàto's character is bitten by a guinea pig that infects him with a deadly virus and becomes the target of a massive manhunt to avoid his spreading the infection) is stolen from Elia Kazan's classic *Panic in the Streets* (1950), while the protagonist's race against time to exact revenge on those who betrayed him before he dies recall Rudolph Maté's *D.O.A.* (1950). Stegani's film owes much to Fernando di Leo's Milan-based stories as well, to the point that a showdown is set in a junkyard like in *The Italian Connection*, and the film makes fairly good use of its dilapidated suburban locations. However, the sociological ambitions end up in excruciating banalities, such as the confrontation between Mancuso and his poor but honest wife (Nicoletta Rizzi), or the ending set in a slum where the dying man takes refuge, only to be stoned to death by the derelicts inhabiting it.

Stegani has a few tricks up his sleeve, as in the junkyard shootout, but his direction is haphazard at times (take Mancuso's car accident near the beginning, which obviously suffered from a lack of budget). For the rest, he does what's expected, by adding a dose of nastiness and misogyny to the proceedings: *The Last Desperate Hours* opens with a gang rape and features a scene where a prostitute (Mirella Rossi, seen in a few Renato Polselli films) has a blade accosted to her private parts by a thug (the menacing Bruno Di Luia), while later on another woman is burned alive in her bed.

Gianni Marchetti's dynamic score, which was partly re-used in Aristide Massaccesi's *Emanuelle's Revenge / Blood Vengeance* (*Emanuelle e Françoise, "le sorelline,"* 1975) and Bruno Mattei's *SS Girls* (*Casa privata per le SS*, 1977) is definitely worth noting, not least because, at one point, an early motorcycle/car chase—a scene later recycled in Roberto Girometti's *The Iron Hand of the Mafia* (*Mafia: una legge che non perdona*, 1980)—samples Quincy Jones' *Ironside* theme.

Order to Kill (*El clan de los inmorales* a.k.a. *La testa del serpente*)

D: José Gutierrez Maesso. *S* and *SC:* Massimo De Rita, Arduino Maiuri, Santiago Moncada, Eugenio Martín, José Gutierrez Maesso; *DOP:* Aiace Parolin (35mm, Eastmancolor, Telecolor); *M:* Adolfo Waitzman (Ed. S.A.A.R.); *E:* Ángel Serrano; *PD:* Rafael Ferri; *ArtD:* Lidia Soprani; *CO:* Lucia Diolosa; *C:* Gaetano Valle; *AC:* Luis Berraquero; *ADs:* Remo De Angelis, Félix Fernández; *MU:* Fabrizio Sforza, María Elena García; *Hair:* Luciano Vito; *SO:* Antonio Cardenas; *SP:* Antonio De Benito; *SS:* Olga Moller. *Cast:* Helmut Berger (Clyde Hart [Klaus Hertz]), Sydne Rome (Anne Holden), José Ferrer (Inspector Reed), Howard Ross [Renato Rossini] (Juan), Juan Luis Galliardo (Richard Francis), Manuel Zarzo (Hugo), Álvaro De Luna (Daniel), Frank Braña (Peter Gastel), Romano Puppo (Albert Webster), José María Caffarel (Commissioner), Kevin McCarthy (Ed McLean), Elena Berrito (Rosa), Claudio Chea (Tom Sayon), Luigi Antonio Guerra, Lorenzo Piani. *Uncredited:* César Olmos. *PROD:* José Gutierrez Maesso for Tecisa, Madrid (Spagna), B.R.C.—Produzione Film (Rome), FRAL (Rome); *AP:* Productora Filmica Dominicana, Santo Domingo (Dominican Republic); *PMs:* Luciano Appignani, Faustino Ocaña; *PSu:* Carlo Giovagnorio, Luis Ocaña. *Country:* Spain / Italy / Dominican Republic. Filmed in Santo Domingo. *Running time:* 95'; Visa no.: 65080 (08.30.1974); *Rating:* v.m.14; *Release date:* 08.31.1974; *Distribution:* Alpherat; *Domestic gross:* 360,601,000 lire. *Also known as: Orden de matar* (Spain—alternate title), *Ordre de tuer* (France—Paris, 23.07.75—95'), *Mörder—Roulette* (West Germany, 01.08.75—95'), *Order to Kill* (UK 1976—95'). *Home video:* New Pentax (VHS, Italy).

After having his opponents eliminated by hired assassins, crime boss McLean reigns over the island of Santo Domingo from his fortress along a coast. Despite being close to retirement and knowing about the protections held in Washington by the gangster, U.S. Inspector Reed decides to do justice by himself. He puts together a brigade composed of three local policemen of dubious morality, led by Clyde Hart, a hitman who worked for McLean in the past. Clyde finds the task difficult not only for the training of the reluctant police officers, but also because his lover Ann has fallen into the hands of one of McLean's henchmen, her ex-lover Richard. Nevertheless, while Reed is treacherously murdered by Richard, Clyde and his men break into McLean's fortress and kill him and his whole gang. Richard and Clyde are the only survivors, but they both die in the final showdown: Ann is left helpless, chained at a car's wheel, on a lonely beach.

A forgettable Spanish-Italian coproduction, José Maesso's *Order to Kill* is a tiresome variation on the classic theme of a lonely man's vengeance, notable mainly for a script that in the second part predates Enzo G. Castellari's powerful *The Big Racket* (*Il grande racket*, 1976). The Santo Domingo setting and local extras make the film closer to Aristide Massaccesi's Caribbean porn cycle of the late seventies than to Sollima's *Violent City*, while Helmut Berger is given little to do with the clichéd character of the white-suited, world-weary hitman who's heading towards self-destruction. The script wavers between unresolved *film noir* fodder—the confrontation between Berger and his friend (Frank Braña) in a gambling house, the love story between the antihero and *femme fatale* Ann (Sydne Rome)—and a "revanchist" second half, where Berger trains a trio of cops (Howard Ross, Manuel Zarzo, Álvaro De Luna) so that elderly inspector José Ferrer can carry out his revenge against big time boss Kevin McCarthy.

Besides a ridiculously miscalculated opening on a train where a hitman (played by Enzo Castellari regular Romano Puppo) shoots a target who's traveling on another train coming from an opposite direction through an ersatz-looking electronic timing device, the script offers few thrills, and culminates in a badly conceived "big" action scene where Berger and co. assault McCarthy's headquarters plus the final confrontation between Berger and his arch-enemy (and rival in love) played by Juan Luis Galliardo, which leads to the expectedly downbeat ending.

If Berger looks at least like he's in the role of the poor man's Alain Delon, Ferrer is almost comatose as the police Inspector with a private agenda: while Berger and his men carry out their plan, Maesso has nothing better to do than show Ferrer playing a game of solitaire or biting a sandwich while waiting for a phone call from his death squad. Apart from a few nude scenes, *Order to Kill* has little to offer for exploitation fans: unlike the Maesso-produced *Ricco the Mean Machine*, violence is reduced to a few almost bloodless shoot-outs, and the low budget is displayed by such clumsy details as a car phone whose wire is obviously unattached to the vehicle it supposedly belongs to.

Renowned Spanish genre director Eugenio Martín (*Horror Express*, *A Candle for the Devil*), who is credited among the scriptwriters, minimized his contribution as well as that of Santiago Moncada. "It was Maesso's project, and Moncada and I were to write it. However, there was no way we could come up with a good plot, so we soon called ourselves out. Maesso did not give up, though, and he called an Italian scriptwriter to do the job [Massimo De Rita, also signing his associate Dino Maiuri, Author's Note]. When the film was released, Maesso credited both Moncada and I, because it suited him to have our names as well to level the co-production, yet I doubt he took advantage of any of our work."[1] As for the producer-director, Martín added: "It's a curious case, that of Maesso. A man who loves movies, and knows about movies, yet has been too often involved in hassles and unredeemable projects, cheating and surviving as best he could."[2]

Notes

1. Carlos Aguilar and Anita Haas, *Eugenio Martín: Un autor para todos los géneros* (Granada: Retroback y Séptimo vicio, 2008), p. 110.
2. *Ibid.*, p. 111.

Rabid Dogs, a.k.a. *Kidnapped (Cani arrabbiati)*

D: Mario Bava. *S:* loosely based on the short story *Man and Boy* by Michael J. Carroll; *SC:* Alessandro Parenzo [and Cesare Frugoni, uncredited]; *DOP:* Emilio Varriano [and Mario Bava, uncredited] (35mm, Eastmancolor, Telecolor); *M:* Stelvio Cipriani; *E:* Carlo Reali; *C:* Emilio Varriano; *AC:* Gianni Modica [Giovanni Canfarelli Modica]; *AD:* Lamberto Bava; *MU:* Angelo Roncaioli; *W:* Wayne Finkelman; *W:* Maura Zuccherofino; *SO:* Roberto Alberghini; *Boom:* Giuseppe Muratori; *SE:* Sergio Chiusi; *Machinists:* Cosimo Barbera, Vittorio Monterosso, Quinto Proietti; *Elec:* Toto Rinaldi, Massimo Rinaldi, Flaminio Tabbarini; *KG:* Franco Tocci; *SP:* Giuliana De Rossi; *SS:* Antonella Ballasio. *Cast:* Riccardo Cucciolla (Riccardo), Aldo Caponi ("Bisturi" / "Blade"), George Eastman [Luigi Montefiori] ("Trentadue" / "Thirty-two"), Maurice Poli ("Dottore" / "Doctor"), Lea Lander (Maria), Marisa Fabbri (Maria Sbravati), Erika Dario (Marisa Altoveti), Luigi Antonio Guerra (Employee), Francesco Ferrini [actually Gustavo De Nardo] (Gas station attendant), Emilio Bonucci (Taxi driver), Pino Manzari (Toll Collector), Ettore Manni (Bank president). *Uncredited:* Mario Bava (Man in parking lot). *PROD:* Roberto Loyola for Roberto Loyola Cinematografica (Rome); *PM:* Lucio Orlandini; *PSe:* Naldo Nibbi, Cesare Caramandi; *PAcct:* Carlo Fabris. *Additional credits* (1995 restoration): *PP:* Lea Lander; *DubD:* Renato Cecchetto; *Title designer:* Ivan Cerio. *Additional cast:* Nina Gueltzow (Woman behind the window). *Additional credits* (1997 DVD): *PROD / D* (main titles only): Peter Blumenstock; *AP:* Dieter Bosch; *DOP* (main titles only): Jürgen Haller; *E / Digital PP:* Peter Blumenstock, Michael Frense. *Additional credits* (*Kidnapped* version): Completed with the collaboration of Lamberto Bava, Mauro Bonanni, Roy Bava and Walter Diotallevi; *PROD:* International Media Corporation, Kismet Entertainment Group; *Producer:* Alfred Leone; *Executive producers:* David Allen, Harmon Kaslow; *2nd AD:* Mario Garriba; *AC:* Giuseppe Alberti; *E:* Lamberto Bava, Mauro Bonanni [uncredited]; *Hair:* Marisa Marconi; *SS:* Vanda Tucci; *KG:* Vittorio Biseo; *SO:* Mario Bramonti; *UPM:* Ugo Valenti. *Additional cast:* Fabrizia Sacchi (Mother). *Country:* Italy. Filmed on location along the Roma — Civitavecchia motorway from August 20, 1973, to September 12, 1973. *Running time:* 96'; *Release date:* 02.24.1998 (DVD premiere). *Also known as: a.k.a. Semaforo rosso* (Italy — alternative title), *Kidnapped* (USA — DVD title), *Les Chiens enragées* (France), *Wild Dogs* (Germany — DVD title). *Home video:* Lucertola Media (DVD, Germany — 96'), Marketing/Astro Record (DVD, Germany — 92'25"), Dcult (DVD, Italy), Starz/Anchor Bay (DVD, USA — as *Kidnapped*: "Kidnapped" version 95'12", "Rabid Dogs" 96'15"). OST: CD Digitmovies CDDM046.

Four bandits hold up a small drug company for the week's wages, killing several people in the process. During their escape, the cops kill the driver and shoot a hole in the gas tank. The three criminals — Doc, Thirty-two and Blade — take over a car and secure an innocent bystander, Maria, as hostage. Then they exchange vehicles at a red traffic light: the car is driven by a middle-aged man, Riccardo, transporting a sick young boy to a hospital. Maria attempts to escape but is recaptured and humiliated by the thugs, who force her to urinate in front of them. The trip then continues without disturbance. However, when Thirty-two becomes intoxicated, his actions begin to draw attention to the car. Doc and Blade attempt to restrain him, but he gets more and more out of control, finally attempting to rape Maria. Rather than risk attracting the attention of the police, Doc shoots Thirty-two, wounding him fatally. At a gas station, a hitchhiker pressures Doc into giving her a lift. The presence of the hitchhiker is clearly annoying to the other passengers. When she notices Thirty-two's deadly wound she is stabbed in the throat by Blade, and the two bodies are disposed of. The group finally reaches their destination: a ruined villa where Doc has stashed a back-up car, and the appropriate papers which will enable him and Blade to flee the country. In order to secure their safety, Doc and Blade are fully prepared to kill not only the two adults, but the comatose child as well. However, Riccardo is able to withdraw a gun, concealed in the child's blanket, and catch his would-be assassins off-guard. He shoots Doc and Blade to death, though the latter is able to kill Maria before he expires. Riccardo then moves the boy to Doc's car and promptly steals the bag full of money. Pulling over at a gas station, Riccardo puts through a call to a woman who is sobbing with grief. He assures her that he son is all right … but that if she ever wants to see him again, it will cost her three billion lire.

In the early seventies Mario Bava's career as a director was on a dead end. The disaster of *Lisa and the Devil* (1972), where producer Alfred Leone had given him *carte blanche* but which was shelved after being met with booings at the Cannes Marché,[1] had left him embittered and at his odds' ends. Gothic horror movies no longer seemed to be a profitable genre, as audiences demanded more strong and violent products (something which Bava gave them with his 1971 slasher film *Bay of Blood*, which, even though disappointing at the box office, would prove to be one of the strongest efforts in his whole career). Bava had begun working on a new project which was completely different from everything the director had ever done before. The basic idea for the film, which was tentatively titled *L'uomo e il bambino* (*The Man and the Boy*), came from a short story Bava found as an appendix on a "Giallo Mondadori" issue, in the so-called "Rivista di Ellery Queen": *Man and Boy* by Michael J. Carroll (and not Ellery Queen, as many wrote).[2]

The producer was Roberto Loyola, the man behind *The Syndicate—A Death in the Family*. Principal photography started in August 1973[3]—Bava decided to shoot the film in chronological sequence—and soon turned out to be nothing short of an ordeal. The whole film takes place on the road, along the Roma-Civitavecchia motorway, and most of it inside an old FIAT car with six people in it: a man, who's taking a sick boy (apparently his own son) to the hospital, a woman, and the three bandits who have taken them as hostages after a robbery. The constant presence of at least five people raised the temperature inside the vehicle—thanks also to the powerful spotlights and considering that the windows were closed for filmic needs—at almost 120F. Outside, at 98F, it seemed almost breezy in comparison. Then there was the trouble with the protagonist, Al Lettieri, who came on set at 9 A.M. already drunk. After just three days of shooting Bava replaced him with Riccardo Cucciolla, who on the other hand couldn't speak nor understand English, and according to his co-star Maurice Poli had to read his lines in English from the script, which was stuck to the windshield or the rearview mirror of the car, in front of him.[4] But the biggest problem, which would eventually determine the film's fate, was Loyola. Money came in fits and starts: "Our producer, Loyola, had so many money problems that, after the first week of the shoot, the crew stopped cold because their checks had not been dated," as Lamberto Bava recalled. "Everybody stopped cold for a couple of days, and then Loyola came and settled his accounts for the previous week, whereupon the technicians resumed working. But after a few more days, they stopped again because their dated checks started *bouncing*!"[5] However, Bava managed to complete shooting in the scheduled three weeks—an amazingly short amount of time, compared to the six to nine weeks' period which was commonplace at that time. Soon after principal shooting ended—what remained to be shot were a number of cutaway shots of helicopters and police cars, plus a pre-credit sequence—Loyola went bankrupt, and the film—whose title became *Ore 9 Semaforo rosso (9 A.M.—Red Light)* and eventually *Cani arrabbiati*—was shelved while still in post-production. Bava and his son Lamberto vainly tried to regain possession of it from the court, but to no avail. The unfinished film was eventually acquired by Lea Lander, and resurfaced over 20 years later, at first in semi-underground form, then in DVD: a weird destiny for such a find, an example of a kind of cinema which did not exist any longer, and yet was still extraordinarily topical, both in conception and accomplishment.

Compared to Bava's output in the realm of the fantastique, *Rabid Dogs* doesn't even look like the work of the same filmmaker. Gone are the garish colors, otherworldly atmosphere, outlandish shots and tricks: the whole film smells of sweat and gasoline, and it's firmly rooted in 1970s Italy. However, that does not mean Bava slavishly conformed to the then in vogue crime/action thread. In this sense, *Rabid Dogs* is an absolute anomaly, despite being apparently similar to the poliziotteschi: the starting point (the robbery at a courier payroll, somehow haphazardly shot) nods to crime reporting material, but Bava is not interested in sociological insights. His villains are just villains, with Western movie nicknames and minimal psychologies: Maurice Poli, "The Doctor" is the calm and rational one, Luigi Montefiori is the sex maniac "Thirty-two," singer-cum-actor Aldo Caponi (here credited under his real name and not the usual "Don Backy" pseudonym) is the psychotic "Blade." There are no police in sight, not just for the financial reasons that plagued the shooting; the lack of a moral counterpole balancing the trio's brutality significantly detaches *Rabid Dogs* from urban crime stories such as Enzo Castellari's *Street Law*, where law enforcement representatives make their appearance, even only to be accused of immobility and inefficiency. The closest reference point are contemporary vigilante flicks: good citizens Riccardo Cucciolla and Lea Lander (a little-known actress who according to Alfred Leone got involved in the film thanks to her elderly rich boyfriend invest in the picture[6]) are subjected to all sorts of harassments by the three bandits, in a sort of on-the-road variation of a standard *Desperate Hours* plot, which predates Pasquale Festa Campanile's *Hitch-Hike* (*Autostop rosso sangue*, 1977). What's more, the scene where Montefiori and Caponi chase Lander in a corn field and force her to urinate in front of them is reminiscent of a similar moment in Wes Craven's *The Last House on the Left* (1972).

Italian critic Alberto Pezzotta underlined the "determination of Bava's staging of violence. Not only the plot is lacking any moralistic retribution, but the camera's eye never looks away or steps backs. Violence always lasts too long, touches delicate topics and shows a deep awareness which is unknown to contemporary crime films."[7] Even the odd visual invention, such as the spinning top beside a dead woman who's had her throat cut, has little in common with crime genre's showy shortcuts: these moments rather recall Bava's typical *leitmotifs* such as the swinging telephone in *Blood and Black Lace*, or the wheelchair's spinning wheel in *Bay of Blood*'s opening sequence. However, transported into the real world, Bava's sardonic cynicism loses all its playful charm, and punches the viewer right below the belt. Whereas crime films traced sharp boundaries between good and evil, even though they showed the alarming spreading of violence in the process, Bava's discourse is much more ambiguous. "On one side there is us, who want the money ... and on the other side, there is all of you, who are trying to keep us from having it. It's really simple, don't you think so?" the Doctor points out. Actually, things aren't quite as simple as he thinks.

If the three criminals are obviously depicted as the bad guys since the very first sequence, Bava has a few tricks up his sleeve. What caught his attention since the beginning was the short story's unexpected final twist — an overturning that contradicted everything that had been said and done and zeroed any apology of private self-vengeance. The faint-hearted bourgeois middle-aged man, who managed to get the upper hand on his kidnappers, is actually a kidnapper himself, and the comatose boy is not his son but his victim. Not only does he get the hundred million lire loot, but he phones a desperate mother and asks a three billion lire ransom for her little boy. In the last shot we see him closing the trunk where the little boy lies, now presumably dead, and leaving the service area. It's a chilling ending which destroys any expectation at respecting genre rules: Giulio Sacchi would never have gotten away unpunished at the end of *Almost Human*. But Bava never cared about conventions anyway.

The succession of obstacles and accidents shows how Bava was interested in deepening the mechanisms of suspense rather than setting up a Manichean confrontation between the helpless hostage and the "rabid dogs." But there's more than meets the eye: take the apathy displayed by the gas station attendant in one of the film's most unnerving scenes, or the way Cucciolla's character is cruelly mocked in the service area scene (which somewhat recalls Dino Risi's *Dirty Weekend*), where first he is mistaken for a homosexual by a janitor, then he casually meets a working colleague, an encounter which throws him into a panic and provokes his kidnapper's teasings. The janitor who pops up now and then, mop in hand, throwing glances of disapproval at the strange couple formed by Riccardo Cucciolla and Luigi Montefiori, and the provoking buxom blonde who revels in front of Thirty-two's muscles and craving looks are two new entries in Bava's gallery of weird human portrayals, and worthy of *Bay of Blood* for that.

The aforementioned scene is not the only grotesque intrusion: the improvident blonde woman whose car has had a breakdown and who joins the company for a short while is such a brainless stupid, unable to keep silent even just for a second, that the viewer ends up hoping that the bandits — who are already having a hard time because of the heat and the tension — shut her mouth once and for good. Which actually happens: and the sight of the dead woman — a distorted wide angle shot of her face, her mouth semi-open and lifeless eyes — carelessly thrown off a cliff like one of *Lisa and the Devil*'s manikins, shows once again how Bava never endured fools, neither alive nor dead. On the other hand, Lea Lander's Maria and the sick child are the film's true victims: during the course of the film the former is taken hostage, humiliated, tormented, sexually harassed, eventually shot to death, while the latter is simply left to die in a trunk. A woman and a child, an image of Christian mercifulness — Maria is mockingly associated to the Christian Madonna by Thirty-Two — which is brutally contradicted and defeated by the real world's mercilessness: it's about as pessimistic and nihilistic as any genre gets.

To see *Rabid Dogs*' ending as a mocking footnote of the good/bad rulebook of coeval *film noir* would be simplistic. The moral look of Bava's previous thrillers such as *Five Dolls for an August Moon* (*5 bambole per la luna d'agosto*, 1970) and *Bay of Blood* returns: and *Rabid Dogs* can best be seen as the third part of an ideal trilogy on human sordidness and greed — Bava's own "Trilogy of Death," in a curious analogy with Pasolini's own attempted "Trilogy of Death" which started with *Salò*. That's the deepest distinctive feature of Bava's cinema, that's where his world view emerges in a clear and precise way, without any alibi or stylistic finesse to sugar the pill: after *Five Dolls for an August Moon*' dead bodies seen as quarters of beef, and *Bay of Blood*'s equation of men and insects, here human beings are seen for what they are, without any mask nor camouflage. And it's a terribly dark and grim, almost unbearable view.

After over twenty tears of limbo, *Rabid Dogs* was screened at Milan's Mifed in winter 1995 with the title *Semaforo rosso* ("Red Traffic Light"). This version, put together by Lea Lander's Spera Cinematografica with financial help from German film journalist Peter Blumenstock, without any assistance on the part of Lamberto Bava (who claimed it was completed against his wishes) was completed on the basis of a rough cut assembled by editor Carlo Reali during principal shooting, with the addition of a few shot-on-video inserts depicting joint footage, plus the sound of a police siren in the final scene, which closes on a freeze-frame of Cucciolla's face just after his phone call to the kidnapped boy's parents. Since the existing elements were without sound, the soundtrack had to be done from scratch, including dubbing (with only Cucciolla voicing his own performance) and scoring, using Stelvio Cipriani's demonstration recordings. This version premiered at the 14th Brussels International Film Festival in 1996.

The first DVD release, a limited edition of 2,000 discs on Blumenstock's own Lucertola Media label in 1998, was devoid of Spera's inserts and maintained the original ending (Cucciolla opens the trunk to check whether the boy's still alive) but added a newly shot prologue (a zoom-out shot of a woman crying behind a transparent window curtain) following Bava's script indications. A subsequent 2001 DVD release on the German label Astro (as *Wild Dogs*) and the Spanish Vella disc are devoid of the prologue and feature a longer take of the ending, with Cucciolla's car leaving the parking lot. A fourth version assembled by Alfred Leone, and intended as a rough draft, adds video footage of the missing cutaway shots and two new scenes (shot on video) in the end, one of which shows the mother on the phone with the kidnapper. This version ends with a zoom-in and a freeze-frame of the mother's face.

Then Leone and Lamberto Bava put together a *fifth* version, using stock footage of 1970s police cars taken from some P.A.C.-produced films, a newly created credit sequence and a couple of scenes shot on 35mm film by Lamberto and Roy Bava in April and May 2001 (the boy's mother, played by Fabrizia Sacchi, talks with a police commissioner and on the phone with the kidnapper), while the "crying woman" prologue is missing. Together with a new dubbing, a new music score was commissioned to Stelvio Cipriani (with, it must be added, quite debatable results), and Lamberto Bava re-edited a few scenes with the help of Mauro Bonanni, cutting bits he thought his father would have left out of the film.

All in all, the Astro version is the best of the lot, while the Leone/Lamberto Bava hybrid — which was released to DVD in the U.S. on Anchor Bay under the title *Kidnapped* (the disc also features the "Lucertola" cut of the film)—is nothing short of a mess, albeit a well-intentioned one: to quote Tim Lucas, "the new material [...] causes the film to tip its hand too early—and the closing scene of Roberto's call from the telephone booth is weakened by the insertion of Sacchi's emotings."[8]

Notes

1. In an attempt to cash in on the success of *The Exorcist*, Leone would re-edit the film with new possession scenes featuring Elke Sommer and Robert Alda, shot by an understandably disillusioned and disinterested Bava, and rereleased it in 1975 as *House of Exorcism*.
2. The story originally appeared in *Ellery Queen's Mystery Magazine*, April 1971. It was published in Italy in *Giallo Mondadori no.* 1162, 05.09.1971.
3. In Tim Lucas' mammoth biography *Mario Bava: All the Colors of the Dark* (Cincinnati OH: Video Watchdog, 2007), Lucas wrongly places the film's shooting one year later, in August 1974 (there is also quite a bit of confusion regarding Al Lettieri's death in October 1975, which, according to the book, took place "within three months" after the shooting).
4. Lucas, *Mario Bava*, p. 947. According to Poli, "even with the script, sometimes he [Cucciolla] was only able to say his lines in Italian." Yet this fact perhaps actually helped Cucciolla's performance, which is excellent in its downplay of emotions throughout the film.
5. Manlio Gomarasca and Davide Pulici, "Il talento di Mr. Bava," in Aa. Vv., "Genealogia del delitto: Guida al cinema di Mario & Lamberto Bava," *Nocturno Dossier* #24 (July 2004), p. 17.
6. Lucas, *Mario Bava*, p. 948.
7. Alberto Pezzotta, "Cani arrabbiati: Nero in tempo reale, senza lieto fine," *Segnocinema* #78 (March/April 1996), p. 9.
8. Lucas, *Mario Bava*, p. 954.

Shoot First, Die Later (Il poliziotto è marcio)

D: Fernando di Leo. *S:* Sergio Donati; *SC:* Fernando di Leo; *DOP:* Franco Villa (35mm, Eastmancolor, Telecolor); *M:* Luis Enriquez Bacalov (ed. Roch Records—Usignolo); *E:* Amedeo Giomini; *PD:* Francesco Cuppini; *APD:* Sandro Bellomia; *CO:* Giorgio Gamma; *C:* Gaetano Valle; *AE:* Ornella Chistolini; *AD:* Franco Lo Cascio; *MU:* Antonio Mura; *SO:* Goffredo Salvatori; *STC:* Rémy Julienne; *MA:* Gilberto Galimberti; *SS:* Renata Franceschi. *Cast:* Luc Merenda (Commissioner Domenico Malacarne), Richard Conte (Mazzanti), Delia Boccardo (Sandra), Raymond Pellegrin (Pascal), Gianni Santuccio (Chief of Police), Vittorio Caprioli (Serafino Esposito), Salvo Randone (Malacarne's father), Rosario Borelli (Garrito), Monica Monet (Barbara, Journalist), Elio Zamuto (Rio), Gino Milli (Gian Maria), Sergio Ammirata (Vice Commissioner Curcetti),Massimo Sarchielli (Rabal), Loris Bazoki [Bazzocchi] (Pascal's thug), Salvatore Billa (policeman), Marcello Di Falco (Pascal's thug), Attilio Duse (Aniello), Luigi Antonio Guerra, Mario Garriba, Marisa Traversi (Countess Nevio). *Uncredited:* Calogero Azzaretto (Man in front of jewelry), Empedocle Buzzanca (Postman), Bruno Bertocci (Journalist at press conference), Omero Capanna (Robber at the jewelry), Enrico Chiappafreddo (Man killed in the warehouse), Massimo Ciprari, Fernando di Leo (Cashier at the bar), Gilberto Galimberti (Robber at the jewelry), Nando Sarlo (Journalist), Aldo Valletti. *PROD:* Galliano Juso and Ettore Rosboch for Cinemaster, Mount Street Film (Rome), Mara Film (Paris); *PM:* Alberto Marras. *Country:* Italy. Filmed on location in Milan. *Running time:* 95'; Visa no.: 64039 (02.25.1974); *Rating:* v.m.18; *Release date:* 03.22.1974; *Distribution:* Titanus; *Domestic gross:* 675,994,000 lire. *Also known as: Salut les pourris* (France, 04.78). *Home video:* Raro (DVD, Italy).

Milan. The son of an upright police Sergeant, the young and ambitious Commissioner Domenico Malacarne receives lavish bribes from crime bosses Mazzari and Pascal in order to turn a blind eye to their illicit trade in the cigarette and coffee smuggling ring. This way Malacarne, who's helped by his subordinate Garrito, has put aside 60 million lire and maintains his lover Sandra, whom he has provided with a valuable art gallery. Having discovered that the bosses have expanded their interests in arms trafficking and drugs, Malacarne warns them, but Mazzari and Pascal ask him to do away with a complaint registered by a Neapolitan named Serafino Esposito that might lead the police to solve a murder case they are embroiled in. Cornered, Malacarne obeys. When he eventually decides to react against his masters, his lover Sandra, his father and Esposito are all brutally killed. Malacarne kills Pascal, but in doing so he favors Mazzari's rise to power in the underworld. In the end, Mazzari has the Commissioner killed by Garrito, who will take his place.

1974 was a tough year for Italy. It was the year of the bomb in Piazza della Loggia in Brescia, and the one on the Italicus train. It was the year the Brigate Rosse kidnapped the Genoan magistrate Mario Sossi and kept him prisoner for over a month. It was the year of the popular referendum on the divorce (which had been instituted by law for the first time in Italian history just four years earlier, in 1970), promoted by the Democrazia Cristiana party: the referendum was defeated on a 60 percent / 40 percent percentage, allowing divorce laws to remain in force.

Two years after *Execution Squad*, the Italian poliziotteschi was already a well-developed and profitable thread, which metabolized its influences and reached a definite form. The release of Fernando di Leo's *Shoot First, Die Later* came as a timely and forward-looking addition, which showed the filmmaker's destabilizing and subversive approach to the genre right from its defiant Italian title (*Il poliziotto è marcio*: literally, "The Cop is Rotten"). "That was definitely an insulting title: cops took the posters off the walls, they even phoned me: "You have to stop!" they warned me. [...] For a country like Italy, which was born from the hasty fusion of two huge blocks of regions, both bureaucratic and authoritarian—the reign of Piedmont and that of the Two Sicilies, states with ferocious police forces—plus over twenty years of Fascism (a party which was founded on police brutality), the title itself was an insult ... and so was the plot."[1]

Despite the apparent thematical affinities, *Shoot First, Die Later* is not as much an atypical example of the crime film as it is its critical and provocative antithesis. Di Leo picks up and emphasizes poliziotteschi's ambiguities and contradictions with the same polemical impetuousness that he showed in *The Boss*, where the obtuse Commissioner Torri (Gianni Garko) was a corrupt puppet in the hands of the Mafia. On the other hand, the director never got along with the heroic image of cops as displayed in the crime genre, as shown by *Caliber 9*, where two Commissioners, a left-wing (Luigi Pistilli) and a reactionary one (Frank Wolff) carry on a harsh confrontation in long and explicitly political dialogue exchanges. However, *Caliber 9* did not just pay a price to the typical urgency of politically committed cinema (Pistilli: "But tell me, when have we ever clubbed anyone who was well-off ... or is it that the wealthy are always right, and the blame forever rests with the workers, the students and the Southerners?"). Di Leo's idiosyncrasy towards the ambiguity and mental backwardness that characterized the way the Law was put into practice were reflected in the character of the left-wing policeman who is going to be transferred because of his liberal, unorthodox ideas (Wolff: "Me with my backward mentality, I get to stay here. But you who are modern, my fine friend, you go herd your sheep in Basilicata").

On *Shoot First, Die Later*, the director apparently followed the rules, only to get rid of them halfway through. In the film's first half-hour di Leo seems to give the audience a new hero to celebrate, in a spectacular crescendo which culminates in a sequence — the attempted bank robbery and the ensuing breathtaking car chase — which is among the most exciting ever seen in an Italian crime action film. Then, di Leo pulls the rug from under our feet, revealing that the fearless Commissioner, who's revered by his superiors and colleagues, is on the payroll of a hateful crime boss: thus, he undermines the very identification mechanisms he first set in motion.

Fernando di Leo, left, Luc Merenda, center, and Salvo Randone on the set of *Shoot First, Die Later* (1974).

What's more, the "rotten cop" Malacarne (a name that literally means "bad meat"), the Robin Hood in reverse who arrests small fish and protects the big ones because he can't stand to be "just a shitty starving cop" has the Apollonian features of Luc Merenda, the incorruptible Caneparo in Sergio Martino's *The Violent Professionals*. In the parade of honest and heroic Commissioners that populated Italian poliziotteschi, Malacarne is the only real negative antihero, a black sheep in a world of idealists that see their job as a mission. Malacarne doesn't care what's wrong or right: he just worries about the monthly payment he receives from cigarette smugglers.

Bad apples inside police forces are a recurring element within the genre. But they are usually balanced and counterpointed by the good and honest cops. In *Execution Squad*, Enrico Maria Salerno's death in front of his corrupt assistant is a turn of the screw that's balanced by the awareness reached by the magistrate played by Mario Adorf; in *La polizia è al servizio del cittadino?* Giuseppe Pambieri redeems and immolates, facing an atrocious death which represents the adequate punishment for betraying his colleagues and friends. In *Shoot First, Die Later* the dialectic between guilt and redemption is only apparent: in the end Malacarne is shot by his right-hand man (Rosario Borelli), who presumably is going to take his place. Nothing has changed, nothing will ever change. Di Leo doesn't allow his antihero any cathartic path: Malacarne takes bribes without any sense of guilt, and when he is forced to reveal the truth to his father (Salvo Randone), an elderly police official, he doesn't make excuses. On the contrary, he verbally attacks his old man with a monologue that's as violent as anything di Leo has filmed, for its sheer virulence: "Who are you to make morals? I've seen you lick other people's shoes all your life, just to become a fucking marshal! How many times did you beat up poor guys with your superiors' blessing? How many times did you fabricate evidence to frame someone guilty? How many abuses, how many tricks to get your *panettone* at Christmas? Even this is corruption. A stupid man's corruption, indeed!"

Di Leo was a radical pessimist. That's why his movies represented perhaps the only possible stab at civil cinema in mid-seventies Italy, after the long wave of civil commitment had faded. *Shoot First, Die Later* is an example of a cinema that's not afraid to get deep down in the mud, leaves metaphors behind (unlike Elio Petri did, with debatable results, in *La proprietà non è più un furto* [Propriety Is No Longer a Theft, 1973]) and is not suffocated by ideology. Italy, as Vittorio Caprioli says in a dialogue exchange, is the elective country of microbes from the whole universe: why sugar the pill, then?

However, di Leo was too smart and disenchanted to choose the way of plain and simple indignation. He preferred sarcasm. In *Shoot First, Die Later* the filmmaker liquidates law and order with a couple of show-stopping vitriolic lines ("Arrest and put into custody 100 to 200 people, mostly long-haired ones"; "God bless the return of police custody, after thirty years of tied hands!") uttered by a prig, idiotic Chief of Police, the second bitterly reversing the typical tirades of the genre's heroes. And he depicts with open disgust a "respectable" white collar criminality with uneasy layers and connections: Raymond Pellegrin plays a crime boss whose ferociousness is paired with a bovine obtuseness; Richard Conte is a mellifluous businessman, whose import-export agency is the liaison between the rotten cop and the underworld; Gino Milli is a creepy transvestite hitman (a reference to *Naked Violence*, perhaps?) who has one of the film's most chilling scenes, when Malacarne finds him slow dancing with his hitman lover in a dark room, proving again di Leo's ability in treating the theme of sexual ambiguity without slipping into ridiculous clichés.

To top it all, violence is never cathartic nor liberating: it is unexpected, cruel, disturbing. Take the opening sequence's knee-cappings, the brutal executions (Vittorio Caprioli is smothered with a plastic bag, Salvo Randone is drowned, Delia Boccardo is strangled with a telephone cord) or the downbeat ending in the tannery.

Even though it was a work-for-hire, the first di Leo helmed for producer Galliano Juso on a story by Sergio Donati, and despite a flawed script, *Shoot First, Die Later* contained some of di Leo's best work, and ideally ended a cycle. Not just in the director's filmography (di Leo would try his hand at a different approach with his next film, *Loaded Guns*), but in the realm of Italian poliziotteschi, in a season that saw the genre's definitive commercial exploit after the success of Castellari's and Martino's films and the decline of the Mafia movie.

Note

1. Davide Pulici and Manlio Gomarasca, "Il Boss. Intervista a Fernando di Leo," *Nocturno Cinema* #3 (June 1997), p. 26.

Il siculo (The Sicilian)

D: Francesco Arminio. *S* and *SC:* Domenico Raccosta, Francesco Arminio; *DOP:* Jano [Floriano] Zamboni; *C:* Silvestro Scarfì; *M:* Franco Chiaravalle (Ed. Lord); *E:* Lucio Tomaz; *AD:* Daniela Nardi; *2nd ADs:* Amedeo Formillo, Puccy Andreozzi. *Cast:* Tony [Domenico] Raccosta (Domenico Amato, "Il Siculo"), Barbara Barni (Doll), Riki Maiocchi (Ciro "Fulmine"), Nino Carillo ("Cervello"), Piero Sampieri ("Campana"), Nino La Rosa, Andrea Raccosta, Nino Giuffré, Gianni Anna, Alvise Moreno, Anita, Gigi Fiore. *PROD:* Guido Petteruti. *Country:* Italy. *Running time:* 74'; Visa: none; *Rating:* not rated; *Distribution:* never released theatrically.

Four gangsters—Fulmine, his lover Doll, Cervello and Campana—are traveling by car from Switzerland to Sicily with a huge load of drugs hidden inside their vehicle. In Milan they meet a fifth man, a Sicilian member of the Mafia, who is supposed to protect them during the trip. The Sicilian first persuades his accomplices to bury their weapons so as not to raise suspicion. Soon resentments start growing amidst the group, partly because of the Sicilian's commanding attitude towards his companions. After the Sicilian tries to rape the woman, he and Fulmine have a brawl, which ends with the latter's death. Cervello realizes that the Sicilian has been hired by a Mafia boss—the Advocate—to dispatch them one by one during the journey, which the hitman does with cold-blooded efficiency. Cervello tries to escape but is mistaken for a thief and lynched by an angry mob. Approaching his homeland, the Sicilian shoots Campana in the head, then strangles Doll—who was in cahoots with him all along—on a beach. After finishing his job, however, he too is eliminated by a pair of hitmen, as he knew too much for his own good....

Written by and starring Tony (real name Domenico) Raccosta, completed but never released theatrically, *Il siculo* is perhaps the most obscure entry in this book. As Raccosta explained, "It was about 1974, I think. I had the inspiration to write a story and put it down in script form, which was originally called *Non-stop*. It was the story of a journey from Switzerland to Montelepre, in the heart of Sicily, throughout Italy. To collect enough money, I got in touch with a certain Guido Petteruti, a guy from Messina who owned a heating firm. He didn't have anything to do with the movie industry, but was willing to put some money into the film. However, I put together all the rest: I cast the actors, hired the director and crew, got in touch with the processing and printing plants and so on."[1]

Il siculo was shot in three weeks with a 16mm camera, on the road. Near the end, after a car accident that involved the director of photography Floriano Zamboni, the film was completed by a local photographer. However, the distributor changed his mind and Raccosta bought the film back from the producer for a small sum. With the help of Cesare Canevari's Cineluce company, *Il siculo* was sold to Southern broadcasting networks, finding its way in television programmings. Raccosta and Canevari even envisioned a sequel, *California addio*, which was never made.

The story bears a passing resemblance to Mario Bava's *Rabid Dogs*, and the same can be said of the idea of having the protagonists characterized by their nicknames: the driver is called "Fulmine" (lightning), the accountant is "Cervello" (brain), the mad buffoon is "Campana" (literally, "bell," but meaning "nuts" in Italian lingo) and the woman is obviously "Doll." But that's where the similarities end. The opening sequence, showing the hero's arrival in Milan, his physical transformation and moves (he replaces his elegant suit-and-tie dress for a more casual look, cuts his hair, then pays a prostitute to spend the night at her place as he's got no documents to sleep in a hotel) is promising, and the bleak, foggy Milanese surroundings are impressive, but the film as a whole cannot overcome its many limits.

Besides the tragically low budget, exceedingly talky script and so-so acting—except for the impressive, icy-eyed Raccosta, the others are virtually unknown: Donald Sutherland look-alike Riki Maiocchi, the alcoholic driver, was the former singer of 1960s beat band I Camaleonti—much of the blame must be placed on the director's shoulders. "Franco Arminio was a friend of mine, he passed away a while ago," Raccosta recalled. "He'd never done anything in the movies, and was totally inexperienced. I helped him. He was a good guy, but a bit lazy: when it was time to edit the film, he never showed up in the editing room."[2]

Simply put, Arminio doesn't seem to know the basics of filmmaking. Sporadically this *naïveté* results in moments of primitive effectiveness, such as Cervello's escape through the alleys of a village, entirely shot with a hand-held camera. Elsewhere, it's just plain unbearable. Take the scene where the Sicilian bludgeons Fulmine to death, marred by terrible editing and amateurish post-production (the sound of the blows is not even in synch). Another such example is the moment where Raccosta strangles the girl on the beach: badly acted—his murderous act is telegraphed and clumsily executed—and horribly filmed in lazy long shots. What's more, the last act drags painfully, and the story loses whatever steam it had accumulated, also due to the alternating editing which follows both the final leg of the trip and the character of the Mafia boss (the so-called Advocate) who's waiting for the drug to be delivered. The ending as well, which is supposed to be biting, is completely ruined by the director's casual approach.

Raccosta's script scatters some hints at political significance here and there ("Roma caput Mafia" one character says, aping the Latin motto *Roma caput Mundi*) with simplistic results, while Franco Chiaravalle's ridiculous score is often out of place (Chiaravalle later worked on Nino D'Angelo films). The only existing print is the TV master copy, but according to Raccosta the director shot a rather explicit lovemaking scene which was cut so as to allow broadcasting. "The scene started with me behind the wheel. While driving, I took the rearview mirror and moved it so as to watch Barbara Barni's legs, as she was sitting in the back. She opened her legs, I kept watching her, watching, watching ... and I fantasized about us making love. I wanted to shoot the scene in a deserted isle near Tindari, with a long shot of me and her on the beach, all alone, then getting closer ... but the director screwed it up, so we shot it in a bedroom, with another girl, because Barbara Barni had already gone back to her hometown, L'Aquila. It was quite a long scene, indeed. Franco Arminio shot it personally with his hand-held 16mm camera. It wasn't bad, but it was almost porn ... so we took it out."

Notes

1. Davide Pulici, *Il siculo*, www.nocturno.it, 06/30/2010. All of Raccosta's quotes come from this article.
2. Curiously, the credits bear the line "direction: Francesco Arminio; produced and directed by Guido Petteruti." Given Petteruti's absolute lack of experience in the field of filmmaking, one wonders what this was supposed to mean.

Silence the Witness (*Il testimone deve tacere*)

D: Giuseppe Rosati. *S:* Giuseppe Rosati, Vito Bruschini; *SC:* Giuseppe Rosati, Giuseppe Pulieri; *DOP:* Franco Villa (35mm, Eastmancolor, Telecolor); *M:* Francesco De Masi, conducted by the author (Ed. Nazionalmusic); *E:* Amedeo Giomini; *AE:* Ornella Chistolini; *PD:* Francesco Cuppini; *C:* Gaetano Valle; *AC:* Enrico Biribicchi; *AD:* Giuseppe Pulieri; *MU:* Antonio Mura; *Hair:* Galileo Mandini; *SO:* Goffredo Salvatori; *SS:* Maria Luisa Rosen; *Color technician:* Gianni Schiavoni; *UP:* Tonino Pinto. *Cast:* Bekim Fehmiu (Dr. Giorgio Sironi), Rosanna Schiaffino (Luisa Sironi), Aldo Giuffré (Commissioner Mario Santi), Guido Leontini (Mancuso), Elio Zamuto (Judge Belli), Luigi Pistilli (Commissioner De Luca), Claudio Nicastro (Commander), Guido Alberti (Chief of Police), Romolo Valli (Excellency), Corrado Annicelli (Sironi's elderly professor), Barbara Betti (Adriana Favero), Rosario Borelli (Marshal Giulio Nardoni), Franco Ressel (Aldo Marchetti), Liana Trouché (Santi's wife), Daniele Vargas (Senator Torrisi), Franco Beltramme (Killer), Anna Molino, Andrea Scotti (Sgt. Carnevale), Luciano Rossi (Antonio, first thug), Gianrico Tondinelli (Alberto, second thug), Giulio Baraghini (Nardoni's fellow police official), Stefano Braschi, Antonio Orlando (Baker's boy), Luigi Antonio Guerra, Mario Garriba. *Uncredited:* Bruno Bertocci (INAIL official), Pietro Ceccarelli (Mancuso's man), Gilberto Galimberti (Mancuso's man), Enzo Maggio (Clerk in Belli's office), Susanna Melandri (Cristina Sironi), Romano Milani (Piscicelli), Filippo Perego (Corrupt politician), Franca Scagnetti (Woman in Sironi's ambulatory), Luciano Zanussi (Man on couch in politician's house, smoking Marlboro). *PROD:* Cineproduzioni Daunia 70; *AP:* Rodolfo Putignani; *GM:* Armando Novelli; *PM:* Lanfranco [Pietro] Ceccarelli; *PSu:* Vincenzo Salviani. *Country:* Italy. Filmed on location in Naples. *Running time:* 100'; Visa no.: 64519 (04.30.1974); *Rating:* v.m.14; *Release date:* 05.16.1974; *Distribution:* Alpherat; *Domestic gross:* 225,109,000 lire. *Home video:* Cinehollywood (VHS, Italy), Kineo (VHS, Italy), Cinehollywood (VHS, UK, pre-cert).

Naples. Engineer Aldo Marchetti, member of the European Urban Commission, secretly meets Commissioner De Luca. Marchetti wants De Luca to cover up an investigation which would disclose his real estate speculation. De Luca does not yield, and is dispatched in cold blood by a sniper that accompanies the engineer. The two men escape, but are involved in a car accident. Doctor Giorgio Sironi comes to their aid, only to find that just Marchetti has survived. Yet, when he calls for a police squad to join him on site, the car the two men were traveling on has disappeared. Sironi files a complaint to Commissioner Santi and Judge Belli. Then, watching a television broadcast from New York, Sironi recognizes Marchetti as the wounded man inside the car. He insists on his version of events, but a circle of intimidation is set in motion against him, led by Senator Torrisi and other big shots: his landlady threatens him with eviction, his insurance refunds are suspended, his wife is raped before his very eyes. Meanwhile, Commissioner Santi is promoted and transferred elsewhere, while Judge Belli is removed from the case. Finally Sironi listens to the advice of his former Professor, who "teaches" him how to live, and gives up the fight.

Produced by Ermanno Curti's Daunia 70—the company behind Fernando di Leo's most important films—Giuseppe Rosati's *Silence the Witness* is noteworthy as an example of the degeneration of the tales of civil commitment typified by Damiano Damiani. The script—by Rosati and Giuseppe Pulieri, based on a story by the director and Vito Bruschini—is so concerned to provoke outrage and indignation that it amasses an odyssey of abuse and humiliation over the shoulders of its unfortunate protagonist, an ordinary citizen who tries to rebel but is crushed under the very bureaucratic machine that is supposed to help him. "That's the difference between me and you," says the upright judge (Elio Zamuto, in a rather unusual positive role) to the suspicious commissioner (Aldo Giuffré). "To me, all citizens are innocent unless their guilt is proven, to you each man who enters a police station is guilty unless he proves his innocence," adding that "we must take away from citizens the ancestral fear of uniforms."

Yet, for all its vehement zeal, Rosati's film ends up transmitting exactly the opposite message. The web of intimidation that surrounds Sironi is depicted in typical conspiracy movie style, as everyone near the good doctor eventually turns his back on him, while the only people who could help him—such as the honest Commissioner Santi, who has the obligatory monologue on how his hands are tied by the law—are silenced or removed. The result is the sort of populist, self-pitying drama that solicits the audience's diffidence towards the institutions, without even the sharp class insights of Vittorio Salerno's *No. Il caso è felicemente risolto*. It doesn't help that the plot is rather far-fetched, and bathed in stereotypes, such as the lesson on Neapolitan *omertà* given to the protagonist by his elderly professor, or the final moralistic epigraph.

Co-scriptwriter and assistant director Giuseppe Pulieri was rather harsh towards the film: "I would never have done it, it wasn't a commercial film ... I never understood why they made it [...]. I never cared much about *Silence the Witness*, as the story was written by a certain Vito Bruschini and even though I rewrote it somehow, there was nothing to do about it. It was hopeless. [...] And Bekim Fehmiu wasn't even an actor in my opinion."[1] Yugoslavian-born Fehmiu (very popular in Italy after 1968's *The Adventures of Ulysses*) leads a very good cast full of familiar faces, such as Aldo Giuffré, Romolo Valli, Luigi Pistilli (who pops up in an all-too-brief cameo at the beginning) and the usually slimy Guido Leontini, who's got the film's most memorable sequence: a long traveling shot inside the police archive building, where his character unctuously shakes hands and tells jokes to everyone in sight while wearing a sanctimonious smile, the same smile he displays while facing Commissioner Santi with threats barely disguised as pleasantries. The beautiful Rosanna Schiaffino, one of Italy's most ravishing Italian film icons of the 1960s, whose declining career led to B-movie material (that same year she was in Giuseppe Bennati's intriguing Gothic-giallo *The Killer Reserved Nine Seats*) looks wasted in one of her last film roles. She would give up acting altogether within a couple of years. Pulieri recalls how Schiaffino was surrounded by red roses whenever she showed up on the set, as the director treated her like a diva.

Rosati spices up the proceedings with a bit of sleaze, such as the drugged *ménage-à-trois* during which an "easy" girl (Barbara Betti) is killed by a couple of thugs (Luciano Rossi and Gianrico Tondinelli), and climaxes the film with an unpleasant — even though off-screen — rape scene. Subliminal publicity can be spotted throughout the film, with a number of gratuitous shots of strategically placed Marlboro packets — a usual occurrence in those days. As for the director, Giuseppe Rosati was a curious character to say the least: a nobleman, he became a popular name (asNinì Rosati) well before turning into a filmmaker, as he had been one of the protagonists of Rome's "Dolce Vita" and a race car driver in Formula 3. He directed his first film — a spy yarn called *The Last Chance* (*Scacco internazionale*) — in 1968, and five other more in the following decade — his last effort being the whodunit *The Perfect Crime* (*Indagine su un delitto perfetto*. 1978), which Pulieri finished after the production had run out of money: the film was signed with the a.k.a. Aaron Leviathan.

Note

1. Franco Grattarola, "È arrivato il risolutore. Intervista a Giuseppe Pulieri," *Cine 70 e dintorni* #7 (June 2005), p. 21–22.

Street Law (Il cittadino si ribella)

D: Enzo G. Castellari [Enzo Girolami]. *S* and *SC:* Massimo De Rita, Dino Maiuri; *DOP:* Carlo Carlini (35mm, Technospes); *M:* Guido and Maurizio De Angelis, arranged and conducted by the authors; *Dune Buggy* (by G. & M. De Angelis / S. Duncan Smith / M. Fondato) sung by Oliver Onions [G. & M. De Angelis]; *Goodbye My Friend* (by G. & M. De Angelis / S. Duncan Smith) sung by Susy & Guy; *Drivin' All Around* by G. & M. De Angelis / S. Duncan Smith) sung by Guy (ed. R.C.A., Slalom Rizzoli); *E:* Gianfranco Amicucci; *ArtD:* Umberto Turco; *AArtD:* Ely Peyrot; *CO:* Franco Antonelli; *C:* Sergio Martinelli; *AC:* Marcello Carlini, Marcello Anconetani; *AE:* Roberto Amicucci; *2nd AsE:* Piero Bozza; *AD:* Marcello Crescenzi; *MU:* Mario Van Riel; *Hair:* Giuseppina Bovino; *SO:* Domenico Dubbini; *Boom:* Benito Alchimede; *Mix:* Antonio D'Amato; *ST:* Rocco Lerro, Alessandro Novelli; *STD:* Donatella Gambini: *STDr:* Rodolfo Valadier; *MA:* Nazzareno Zamperla; *CON:* Maria Luisa Merci. *Cast:* Franco Nero (Carlo Antonelli), Barbara Bach (Barbara Antonelli), Renzo Palmer (police Commissioner), Giancarlo Prete (Tommy), Nazzareno Zamperla (1st bankrobber), Romano Puppo (2nd bankrobber), Massimo Vanni (3rd bankrobber), Renata Zamengo (Mrs. Cavallo), Franco Borelli (Assistant Commissioner Borelli), Adriana Facchetti (Woman on the street), Mauro Vestri (Barman), François Flangé, Luigi Antonio Guerra (Gianni Rubei). *Uncredited:* Calogero Azzaretto (Casino player), Enzo G. Castellari (Man at the dock), Massimo Ciprari (Man in gambling club), Silvio Klein (policeman), Mickey Knox (Gambino), Rocco Lerro (Getaway driver), Dino Mattielli (Hitman), Romano Milani (Player at gambling club), Riccardo Petrazzi (Bar Thug), Renzo Pevarello (Man at Post office), Leonardo Scavino (Leone), Steffen Zacharias (Lawyer). *PROD:* Mario Cecchi Gori for Capital Film; *GO:* Luciano Luna; *PM:* Vincenzo Mazzucchi; *PSu:* Giandomenico Stellitano; *PSe:* Tommaso Pantano; *ADM:* Mario Lupi. *Country:* Italy. Filmed at Incir–De Paolis (Rome) and on location in Genoa. *Running time:* 100'; Visa no.: 65083 (09.04.1974); *Rating:* v.m.14; *Release date:* 09.17.1974; *Distribution:* Cineriz; *Domestic gross:* 1,723,405,000 lire. *Also known as: The Citizen Rebels* (USA — alternate), *The Anonymous Avenger* (USA — alternate), *Vigilante II* (U.K.), *Ein Mann schlägt zurück* (West Germany, 05.27.1975 — 97'), *Ein Bürger setzt sich zur Wehr* (Germany — Home video), *Dehset sehri* (Turkey). *Home video:* Blue Underground (DVD, USA), Pop Flix (DVD, USA — as part of the "Crime Boss collection" 2DVD set). OST: CD Gdm CD Club 7007.

Genoa. During a bank robbery, engineer Carlo Antonelli is taken hostage by three bandits, beaten up and left behind. Since the police are not very willing to help him, Antonelli vows to track down the criminals himself and get revenge. Armed with a camera, he collects evidence on a young robber, Tommy, and blackmails him, forcing him to get him weapons and introduce him to the underworld on the pretext of a heist. Antonelli locates the three robbers and their hideout and calls the police, but the thugs flee before the cops arrive. Without giving up and with Tommy by his side, Antonelli pretends to have been kidnapped to force the police to intervene. However, the three bandits discover Antonelli's own hideout and attempt to kill the engineer. In the final showdown, which takes place in a deserted shed, the engineer dispatches the criminals, but Tommy dies in the shooting.

Year after year, as Italy was facing a seemingly unending series of political attacks, attempted *coups d'état*, murders, robberies, as part of a devastating violent escalation, a number of films openly portrayed an ideology that postulates the necessity of fighting violence with violence. As film historian Gian Piero Brunetta wrote, "A bit like in the American models, the only possible and practicable way seems to go back to the law of the jungle, where the citizen is authorized to do justice by himself."[1]

The commercial success of Enzo G. Castellari's *Street Law* (over a billion and eight hundred million lire grossed in the 1974–75 season) paved the way for poliziotteschi's most critically panned subgenre, that of the vigilante, which tickled the audience's emotions with an arrogance that was equal only to tearjerking melodramas, and used the same tricks to provoke not pathos but indignation. The change of perspective was patent since the very titles: *Il cittadino si ribella* ("The Citizen Rebels"), *L'uomo della strada fa giustizia* ("The Ordinary Man Does Justice") placed at the centre of attention not the police but the average guy. That is, the petty bourgeois who gained a solid economic position ever since the "Boom" of the 1960s.

With the skyrocketing of urban crime, the need to defend one's property became a primary necessity. Besides the obvious yet somehow misleading nod to *Death Wish*— it is worth noting that *Street Law* was released in Italy *before* Michael Winner's film — the vigilante subgenre also recalled such prototypes as Sam Peckinpah's *Straw Dogs* (minus the disquieting anthropological notations) and Wes Craven's *The Last House on the Left* (but in a urban setting and minus the emphasis on extreme gore), both hybridized with the remnants of post–1968 political cinema, which was turned upside down and deprived of its inner meaning.

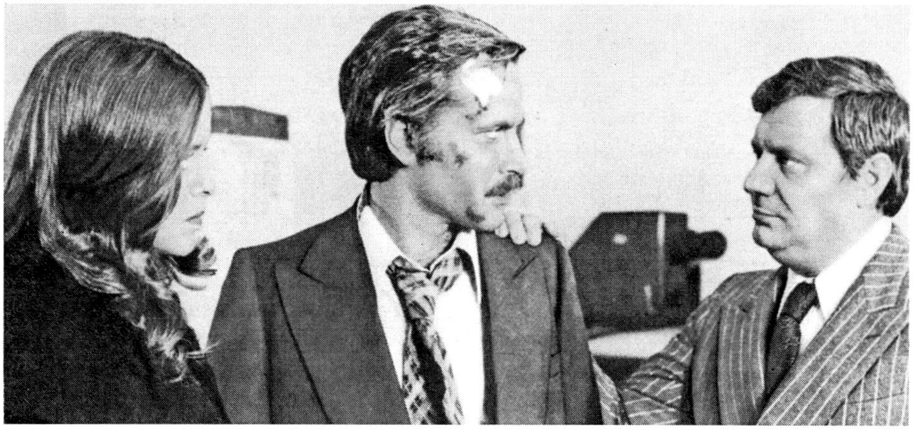

Barbara Bach, Franco Nero (center) and Renzo Palmer in *Street Law* (1973).

The civil appeal of Petri, Damiani and Vancini's films was therefore replaced by a pitying and mildly populist vision: the contradictions between the preaching ardor inherited by the prototypes (which became a mere spectacular hook) and the violent, right-winged conclusions — an inevitable consequence of a narrative development which was strictly dependent on commercial exigencies. In mid–1970s Italian cinema this meant sex and violence, as shown by the proliferation of the "rape and revenge" subgenre with films like Aldo Lado's notorious *Night Train Murders* (*L'ultimo treno della notte*, 1975), which had got as much in common with *The Last House on the Left* as with the vigilante thread.

These films were usually accused of being fascist, and not without reason. Yet the critics were usually making the mistake of judging such commercial products through an ideological point of view, applying a scheme of meanings and purposes to a kind of cinema where ideology was an oscillating, unpredictable variable. That's why the vigilante subgenre is much more faceted than it appears at face value.

Enzo Castellari's *Street Law* opens with a parade of flashes, small vignettes that exemplify the film's thesis. "Cecchi Gori didn't want me to shoot the opening sequence the way I wanted, because of the budget" Castellari revealed. "I said: "We are telling what is happening right now, and we must show right from the start all of today's facts, what newspapers are talking about, that's why the citizen rebels … everyday violence just outside our door!" […] Then, in agreement with the stuntmen and Rocco Lerro, we shot all these scenes one bit at a time, every day. They did that for free.… All of those are "stolen" bits, day by day during shooting. I wasn't given the permit to shoot them, but I just didn't care."[2]

Another key ambiguous factor is the film's protagonist. Engineer Antonelli (Franco Nero) is definitely not an infallible rectifier of wrongs as were sword-and-sandal heroes like Hercules and Maciste. On the contrary, he's rather an embryonic, unresolved incarnation of Alberto Sordi's petty bourgeois in Mario Monicelli's masterpiece *An Average Little Man* (*Un borghese piccolo piccolo*, 1977). He experiences on his own skin and in his wallet the civil chaos of the period, and ironically finds an answer in the leaflet printed during Fascism era by his anti-fascist father, which he keeps framed in his living room and states "Italiani ribellatevi" (Italians, rebel!). Antonelli *does* rebel, yet his obsessive quest for the three men who have beaten and humiliated him is not the result of a social-political awareness of any kind, nor does it bloom from the excision of his beloved ones (as was the case with Charles Bronson's character in *Death Wish*). Quite the opposite, it comes from the man's offended pride and the violation of his own property — that is, it's urged by personal, egotistical motives.

As a vigilante, Antonelli leaves a lot to be desired. He is strong with the weak and pathetically weak with the strong. He complains with the police, launches into bombastic proclamations ("If you don't take up your own defense, nobody will"), even slaps his fiancée (Barbara Bach) in true macho man style. But then he is beaten and ridiculed by almost everyone else. His quest for information in the seedy parts of Genoa costs him teasings and mockeries (he is repeatedly called "bulicchio," a dialectal word for "fag"), several punches in the face and many dents on his car. Eventually, in order to move safely in the Genoan underworld he has to blackmail a petty criminal (Giancarlo Prete). The fact that the latter is much more sympathetic than Nero's character means that something's wrong in the script by genre regulars Massimo De Rita and Dino Maiuri: there is a patent detachment between the hero ("*the* citizen," according to the Italian title) and the audience whom the movie is aimed at. After all, this is popular cinema, and viewers naturally sympathize with the proletarian bully with a heart of gold, who earns his living with small thefts and robberies but dreams of opening a car repair business, rather than the wealthy hero. What's more, most characters come out as barely sketched: Nero's three enemies — played by Castellari regulars, stuntmen Romano Puppo, Nazzareno Zamperla and Massimo Vanni — are characterized just by their different geographical origin.

All things considered, *Street Law* is much more interesting because of its flaws and imperfections rather than for its blubbering "message," and for the unresolved ambiguity of the stop-frame ending, with Franco Nero's eyes glimmering like Travis Bickle's in Martin Scorsese's *Taxi Driver* (1976). Most of all, the film is a showcase for Enzo Castellari's style as an action filmmaker. The director shoots such sequences like no other in Italy did at that time, as shown by the opening scene of the bandits' escape by car in the streets of Genoa, the climax in the abandoned warehouse (which predates Castellari's masterpiece *The Big Racket*) and especially Franco Nero's desperate run as he's chased by a thug in a cave, where Castellari dilates screen time with an exasperating use of slow-motion. The results are as powerful as they are elegant, and stand the test of time, wonderfully accompanied by one of the De Angelis brothers' best scores.[3]

Notes

1. Brunetta, Storia del cinema italiano, p. 414.
2. Pulici, "Il muscolo intelligente, Intervista a Enzo G. Castellari," p. 22–23.
3. The infectiously catchy Dune Buggy was also used that same year in the Bud Spencer–Terence Hill blockbuster comedy hit Watch Out, We're Mad! (Altrimenti ci arrabbiamo, directed by Marcello Fondato).

Three Tough Guys (Uomini duri)

D: Duccio Tessari. *S* and *SC:* Luciano Vincenzoni, Nicola Badalucco; *DIA* (French version): Georges Dutter; *DOP:* Aldo Tonti (35mm, Eastmancolor, Technicolor); *M:* Isaac Hayes, played by The Isaac Hayes Movement (Stax Records, Incense Music); orchestral arrangements by Johnny Allen; *MC:* Lester Snell; *E:* Mario Morra; *AE:* Giancarlo Tiburzi; *PD:* Francesco Bronzi; *ArtD:* Franco Fumagalli; *CO:* Marina De Tullio; *C:* Luciano Tonti; *AD:* Gianni Cozzo; *MU:* Giannetto De Rossi; *Hair:* Mirella Sforza; *W:* Elise Servet; *SO:* Roy Mangano, Paul Oddo, Jack Fitzstephens; *MA:* Neno [Nazzareno] Zamperla; *SP:* Alfonso Avincola; *SS:* Lucia Nolano; *UP:* Tom Miller. *Cast:* Lino Ventura (Father Charlie), Isaac Hayes (Lee Stevens), Fred Williamson (Joe Snake), Vittorio Sanipoli (Mike Petralia), Paula Kelly (Fay Collins), William Berger (Captain Ryan), Lorella De Luca (Anne Lombardo), Jacques Herlin (Barfly "Tequila"), Guido Leontini (Sgt. Sam), Mario Erpichini (Gene Lombardo), Bruno Boschetti, Giorgio Dolfin, Jess Hahn (Bartender), Luciano Salce (Bishop). *Uncredited:* Thurman E. Scott (Tony Red), Ira Rogers (Lou), Nazzareno Zamperla (Snake's henchman), Romano Puppo (Petralia's Hood), Claudio Ruffini (Roy, Snake's henchman), Joel Cory (Truck driver), Dutchell Smith (Hitch-hiker), Margot Novick (Prostitute), Tommy Brubaker (Hood), Buddy Stein (Driver), Max Klevin (Large Thug), Walt Scott (Petralia's man), Frank Grimaldi (Blinky), Emanuele Spatafora (Joe Bell), Hans Jungbluth (Mechanic), Nathaniel Reed (police officer), Bob Minor (Hood), Pemon Rami. *PROD:* Dino De Laurentiis for Produzioni Cinematografiche Inter. Ma. Co. (Rome), Columbia Film (Paris); *PM:* Carlo Bartolini; *PSu:* Emanuele Spatafora, Giuseppe Della Pria. *Country:* Italy / France. Filmed at Vasca Navale (Rome) and on location in Chicago. *Running time:* 92'; Visa no.: 64625 (05.16.1974); *Rating:* not rated; *Release date:* 08.13.1974; *Distribution:* Titanus; *Domestic gross:* 761,271,000 lire. *Also known as: Les durs* (05.29.1974 — 2517 m), *Zwei Fäuste des Himmels* (West Germany, 08.30.1974 — 92'), *Zwei unschlagbare Draufgänger* (West Germany — alternate), *El policía, el gángster y el violento* (Spain), *Hårdingarna* (Sweden), *Kaksi kovanaamaa* (Finland), *O Preço da Ousadia* (Brazil) *Home video:* Domovideo (VHS, Italy). OST: LP Enterprise ENS-7504 / CD Stax SCD24 7504.

Chicago. In a seedy bar, the Red Rooster, Insurance Investigator Gene Lombardo traces a gangster called Tony Red, who has robbed a bank and carried off one million dollars, but both he and the gangster get shot. Cops suspect that Lombardo wanted to take the loot for himself. Father Charlie, a tough-mannered priest who was a good buddy of Lombardo, investigates on his own to clear his friend's reputation. At the Red Rooster, Charlie learns about Tony Red's girlfriend, a woman named Fay Collins, but gets caught up in a deadly situation. He is saved by Lee Stevens, an ex-cop whose buddy was murdered in the bank robbery, and who was expelled from the police because of his negligent conduct. Together, Charlie and Lee set out to find Fay Collins, only to discover that she was Stevens' former lover, and Red's accomplice in the robbery. The duo then goes on the trail of Joe Bell, Red's other accomplice in the robbery, who's disappeared since then. They trace Bell, but he gets killed before they can talk to him. Joe Bell's killer is found dead too, and Fay — who had taken off with the money — hides in a deserted house by the docks. She calls Lee for help, but is murdered by Joe Snake, her lover, who is the man behind all the killings. Joe frames Lee for the murder, but Charlie lets him go before being arrested: together, they break into Snake's hideout and find the loot.

In the string of crime films produced by Dino De Laurentiis in the early 1970s, if Sidney Lumet's *Serpico* (1973) was the right film at the right time, depicting an unorthodox cop as a hero/ martyr in a country still shocked by the Watergate case, Duccio Tessari's *Three Tough Guys* — where the "W" word is mentioned as well in a scene — is a much lighter affair. When the film was released in Italy (where it was a moderate but not outstanding success, grossing less than half as much as Castellari's *Street Law*) not many people fully understood its affinities with "Blaxploitation," a thread which didn't quite emerge in De Laurentiis' native country. The producer was obviously aiming at the U.S. market, and his ace in the hole was Academy Award–winning songwriter Isaac Hayes, who wrote the score and co-starred alongside Lino Ventura in his acting debut. Hayes' lack of acting skills are compensated for by his imposing screen presence: in the same year he would also star in Jonathan Kaplan's *Truck Turner*, and embark on a varied film career, from John Carpenter's *Escape from New York* (1981) to Craig Brewer's *Hustle and Flow* (2005).

However, the unlikely teaming of the leads and Hayes' admittedly striking score — the main theme would later pop up in Quentin Tarantino's *Kill Bill: Vol. 2* (2004) in the Bride vs. Pai Mei fight scene — are perhaps the best Tessari's film has to offer. The script, by the expert Luciano Vincenzoni and Nicola Badalucco, waters down the violence and sleaze of contemporary U.S. black urban action films such as Larry Cohen's *Black Caesar* (1973) and injects a misfired attempt at comedy in the figure of the dynamic priest played by Ventura. The Italian-French actor doesn't look too amused with a role that feels like it belongs to a Bud Spencer film. As the dynamic Father Charlie, he rides his bike in the Chicago streets, plays basketball, bends a coin with his bare hands and slaps and punches his adversaries like a well-trained fighter, but is given little else to do in a plot that's so uninvolving it actually gives away its twist in the first scenes, when villain Fred Williamson is introduced. As for the "third tough guy," he has little screen time, and is mostly noticeable for his cool pimp-style costume — flat cowboy hat, red leather pants and a jacket he wears on his bare chest.

Tessari's direction is surprisingly bland, compared to the director's previous *Big Guns*, and apart from a couple of funny bits — Hayes cooking a raw egg on an iron, Ventura approached by a prostitute who promises to show him "Sodom and Gomorrah," Luciano Salce's amusing cameo as the bishop of Chicago — the result is quite forgettable.

What Have They Done to Your Daughters? (La polizia chiede aiuto)

D: Massimo Dallamano. *S:* Ettore Sanzò; *SC:* Ettore Sanzò, Massimo Dallamano; *DOP:* Franco Delli Colli (35mm, Eastmancolor, Technospes); *M:* Stelvio Cipriani, conducted by the author (ed. Bixio); *E:* Antonio Siciliano; *PD:* Franco Bottari; *C:* Giovanni Ciarlo; *AC:* Giancarlo Giannesi; *AE:* Loredana Cruciani; *AD:* Mimmola [Maria Teresa] Girosi; *Mix:* Romano Checcacci; *SP:* Walter Civirani; *CON:*

Vanda Tuzzi; *UPs:* Lucherini, Rossetti, Spinola. *Cast:* Giovanna Ralli (Deputy Attorney Vittoria Stori), Claudio Cassinelli (Commissioner Silvestri), Mario Adorf (Commissioner Valentini), Franco Fabrizi (Bruno Paglia), Farley Granger (Mr. Polvesi), Marina Berti (Mrs. Polvesi), Paolo Turco (Marcello Tosti), Corrado Gaipa (District Attorney), Micaela Pignatelli (Rosa, Talenti's secretary), Ferdinando Murolo (Agent Giardina), Roberta Paladini (Patrizia Valentini), Salvatore Puntillo ("Napoli"), Renata Moar (Laura Bollero), Eleonora Morana (Polvesi's housekeeper), Adriana Falco (Giuliana Bigi), Cheryl Lee [Sherry] Buchanan (Silvia Polvesi), Clara Zovianoff (Mrs. Talenti), Leonardo Severini (Agent Russo), Luigi Antonio Guerra (Journalist), Lorenzo Piani (Journalist). *Uncredited:* Bruno Alias (Journalist / policeman), Antonio Anelli (Journalist), Giancarlo Badessi (Bruno Paglia's lawyer), Francesco D'Adda (Doctor), Attilio Dottesio (Coroner), Anna Manduchi (Nurse), Giuseppe Marrocco (policeman at documentary's projection), Romano Milani (policeman at documentary's projection), Steffen Zacharias (Prof. Beltrame), Luciano Zanussi (policeman). *PROD:* Paolo Infascelli for Primex Italiana; *PM:* Roberto Infascelli; *PSu:* Egidio Valentini. *Country:* Italy. Filmed at Dear Studios (Rome). *Running time:* 90'; Visa no.: 65029 (08.09.1974); *Rating:* v.m.14; *Release date:* 08.10.1974; *Distribution:* P.A.C.; *Domestic gross:* 1,344,301,000 lire. *Also known as: The Coed Murders* (U.S.—rerelease), *La lame infernale* (Paris, 09.10.1980—90')—*Der Tod trägt schwarzes Leder* (West Germany, 06.03.1977—91'). *Home video:* Shameless (DVD, UK), Surf Video / Alan Young (DVD, Italy). OST: CD Chris' Soundtrack Corner CSC002.

A fourteen-year-old girl, Silvia Polvesi, is found hanged in an attic after an anonymous phone call by a man who is later identified as Paglia, a photographer. The police officials on the case are Commissioner Silvestri and his colleague Valentini, under the direction of the Deputy Attorney Vittoria Stori. The interrogations of suspects and witnesses, and the discovery of a tape where several sexual encounters are recorded, lead the police to an underage prostitution ring: the girls are all young students from the same school, and one of them is Patrizia Valentini, the Commissioner's own daughter. The depositions of the girls involved all point to the psychologist Beltrame as their "recruiter," but the investigation also leads to a number of wealthy customers. Meanwhile, the killer strikes again....

The tendency to explore every possible combination among different genres brought Italian producers and scriptwriters to stitch together two of the most commercially viable threads of the early 1970s: poliziotteschi and violent whodunit thrillers (or *gialli*) *à la* Dario Argento. It was a short-lived experiment, though, and rather schizophrenic in itself: blending a thread so closely tied to Italian everyday life to another rooted in nightmarish abstraction would prove to be quite difficult indeed. The reasons are evident: the *giallo* is about who, and why: detection is a private affair, and viewers' identification is not demanded through the soliciting of their civic spirit, but through the extrapolation of their deepest fantasies. The everyday prosaicness of poliziotteschi is difficult to combine with the "*giallo*"'s fantastic abstraction. Despite the heavily characterized urban and provincial settings—yet Argento's cities are actually urbanistic puzzles, made of single architectural elements stolen from their original context and assembled together in an ideal nightmarish environment, as in *Deep Red*, 1975—and themes of violence and abuse, the *gialli*'s main attraction point is rooted elsewhere.

Whether they acted out of madness, revenge or reckoning, the black-gloved killers spawned on Italian screens after *The Bird with the Crystal Plumage* (*L'uccello dalle piume di cristallo*, 1970) privileged knives to guns and practiced murder as if one of the fine arts; their victims were almost invariably women, young, beautiful and preferably nude; on the contrary, gangsters, drug dealers, thugs and Mafia bosses slaughtered indiscriminately father and sons, policemen and children, with machine guns and explosives. What's more, in *gialli* the police are not even necessary—on the contrary, it's an obstruction to the investigation, where the acumen and powers of observation of a solitary improvised detective are sufficient to unmask the murderer: that is to say, *esprit de finesse* is juxtaposed to the pachydermic procedural mechanism. In typical "giallo" fashion, cops were usually groping in the dark, especially so in Argento's films, where they often came close to caricature (take *Deep Red*'s Calcabrini, played by Eros Pagni). Epigones stuck to the detection rulebook, with a variety of Commissioner types: tough bastards (Luigi Pistilli, in Riccardo Freda's *The Iguana with the Tongue of Fire*, 1971, caused a terrorist to throw himself out of a window during a particularly violent interrogation—a nod to the real-life Calabresi), shy and homely bureaucrats (Giancarlo Giannini in Paolo Cavara's *The Black Belly of the Tarantula*, 1971), young and left-winged Southern officials (Michele Placido in Cavara's *Plot of Fear*, 1976, where a recurring gag has him throwing his superior's right-winged newspaper in the trashcan). There were even extreme cases such as Farley Granger's character in Roberto Bianchi Montero's *The Slasher ... Is the Sex Maniac* (1972) who allows the homicidal maniac to kill his own unfaithful wife before dispatching him.

The aforementioned hybrids were concentrated between 1974 and 1975, when the commercial success of the *gialli* was waning, while the poliziotteschi was imposing itself as the most popular genre at the box office, even if it hadn't yet reached its peak as well as a fully developed identity—that would happen with the appearance of its biggest star, Maurizio Merli. The results—which also included two co-productions mainly of Spanish investment, *A Dragonfly for Each Corpse* (*Una libelula para cada muerto*, 1974, León Klimovsky) and *The Killer with a Thousands Eyes* (*Los mil ojos del asesino*, 1974, Juan Bosch)—were definitely a mixed bag.[1]

Produced by Roberto Infascelli's Primex, the same company as *Execution Squad* and *The Great Kidnapping*, Massimo Dallamano's *What Have They Done to Your Daughters?* was the most successful of the lot, grossing over one billion and three hundred million at the box office. It centers on an underage prostitution ring, as did Dallamano's excellent giallo *What Have They Done to Solange?* (*Cosa avete fatto a Solange?*, 1972) as well as other films of the period, such as Rino Di Silvestro's *Prostitution* (*Prostituzione*, 1974), Carlo Lizzani's powerful *The Teenage Prostitution Racket* (*Storie di vita e malavita*, 1975) and two more *gialli*/crime hybrids, Sergio Martino's *Suspected Death of a Minor* (*Morte sospetta di una minorenne*, 1975) and Mario Caiano's *Calling All Police Cars* (*...a tutte le auto della polizia...*, 1975)—and frames the story between two moralistic tirades that refer to current real-life events.

The Italian title (which translates to "The Police Ask for Help") is in pure poliziotteschi style, and the script—by Dallamano and

Ettore Sanzò — contains an attempt at social insight and generational gaps: a distraught mother (Marina Berti) is shocked to discover contraceptive pills among her fourteen-year-old daughter's personal belongings. However, the story (which has lots of similarities with Caiano's film, as if Sanzò took inspiration from the same novel by Massimo Felisatti and Fabio Pittorru that *Calling All Police Cars* was based upon) is developed as a whodunit, and features a black-gloved, meat cleaver–wielding killer whose features are concealed behind a crash helmet — a powerful figure that was an obvious source of inspiration for both Andrea Bianchi's trashy giallo *Strip Nude for Your Killer* (1975) and Ken Hughes' *Night School* (1981). What's more, *What Have They Done to Your Daughters?* doesn't stint on blood and gore either: a particularly shocking, grisly moment has the killer sever a cop's hand with his choice of murder weapon.

Besides his habitual indulgence on morbid details, Dallamano's direction is well above average: the scene where Giovanna Ralli is attacked in a garage is a case in point, and the Argento-style sequence inside the clinic, characterized by a virtuoso use of hand-held, wide-angled camera — one of Dallamano's most recognizable stylistic traits — is absolutely remarkable. The somehow uneasy blending between the two genres is best exemplified by the sequence that immediately follows, a long chase in which the motorbike killer is pursued by police cars. The effect is heterogeneous, and kind of detracts from the earlier set-piece, despite Dallamano's technical prowess.

On the other hand, the main characters are typical crime film figures, yet they are depicted with more care than expected: the lead is not a Commissioner but a beautiful woman attorney (Giovanna Ralli), helped by a pair of police officials (Claudio Cassinelli and Mario Adorf) who are more believable and human than usual, while the always reliable Franco Fabrizi is typecast in the role of a slimy voyeur. However, individual sequences are more impressive than the film as a whole. Stelvio Cipriani's score, even though it was mostly recycled from *Execution Squad* and *The Great Kidnapping*, fills in the requirements of the action.

Note

1. Set in Milan, *A Dragonfly for Each Corpse* is a typical Argento-style "*giallo*" about a black-gloved murderer who kills junkies and prostitutes, leaving upon their bodies a dragonfly, in homage to an ancient Caldaean rite. It's worth noting for its lead character, played by Spanish horror movie icon Paul Naschy (real name Jacinto Molina): a macho, mustachioed, tough-mannered police commissioner who has a lot in common with those seen in coeval poliziotteschi — up to the point where he delivers lines like "All the victims were directly linked to the underworld. He's cleaning up the city!" *The Killer with a Thousand Eyes* is a much more tepid whodunit set in Lisbon, with Anthony Steffen as the tough cop investigating the murder of his friend and colleague. Steffen even has a scene where he busts into a drug bar that was obviously stolen from *The French Connection*, but the film's only memorable moment is when he clumsily tries to prepare for himself a fried egg. Speaking of obscure hybrids, Gianni Manera's *Ordine firmato in bianco* (Order Signed in White, 1974) deserves a footnote for its unparalleled trashiness: opening with a laughable "long-lost note from the archives of the Criminalpol" that describes the Mafia as a sort of omnipotent, unearthly entity, Manera's film is a hallucinatory mixture of Mafia movie, social commentary and "*giallo*" elements, stitched together with breathtaking incompetence. The director also helmed an equally obscure — and amateurish — Mafia movie, *Fear in the City* (*Cappotto di legno*, shot in the middle/late seventies but released only in 1981), starring his own ubiquitous self and featuring cameos by Michel Constantin, Haydée Politoff and Fred Williamson.

1975

Blood, Sweat and Fear *(Mark il poliziotto)*

D: Stelvio Massi. *S:* Dardano Sacchetti; *SC:* Adriano Bolzoni, Raniero Di Giovanbattista, Stelvio Massi, Dardano Sacchetti; *DOP:* Marcello Gatti (35mm, Technospes); *M:* Stelvio Cipriani, conducted by the author (ed. Grandi Firme della Canzone); *E:* Mauro Bonanni; *AE:* Walter Diotallevi; *PD:* Sergio Palmieri; *ArtD:* Giovanni Fratalocchi; *CO:* Rosa Falcone; *C:* Otello Spila; *AC:* Roberto Locci, Michele Pensato, Emilio Bestetti; *ADs:* Daniele Sangiorgi, Domenico D'Alessandria, Renato Ferraro; *MU:* Franco Corcione; *Hair:* Romana Piolanti; *W:* Valeria Mariani, Irene Parlagreco; *SO:* Pier Giuseppe Ghezzi; *Boom:* Antonino Pantano; *ChEl:* Aldo Carocci; *KG:* Alberto Anzellotti; *SP:* Luciano Cavalieri; *DubD:* Massimo Turci; *SS:* Grazia Conti. *Cast:* Franco Gasparri (Commissioner Marco "Mark" Terzi), Lee J. Cobb (Benzi), Sara Sperati (Irene), Giampiero Albertini (Brigadeer Bonetti), Carlo [Carlos] Duran (Grüber), Giorgio Albertazzi (Chief of Police), Andrea Aureli (Benzi's Vice), Luciano Comolli [Lucio Como] (Corrupt policeman), Francesco D'Adda (Investigating judge), Cesare De Vito [Di Vito] (Franco, the doctor), Dada Gallotti (Irene's mother), Danilo Massi (Ferri), Dino Mattielli (Zardi), Vittorio Pinelli (Gay man at Grüber's hotel), Flora Saccese [Saggese] (Franca). *Uncredited:* Ugo Bombognini (Luca), Teodoro Corrà (Benzi's secretary), Riccardo De Stefanis (policeman). *PROD:* P.A.C. (Produzioni Atlas Consorziate) (Milan); *GM:* Raniero Di Giovanbattista; *PMs:* Teodoro Agrimi [Teodoro Corrà], Gino Soldi (for Milan exteriors); *PSu:* Teodoro Agrimi [Teodoro Corrà]; *PSe:* Giuseppe Gerola, Simonetta Pierannunzi; *CASH:* Nestore Baratella. *Country:* Italy. Filmed at Icet–De Paolis (Milan) and on location in Milan and Lombardy. *Running time:* 91'; Visa no.: 66944 (08.01.1975); *Rating:* not rated; *Release date:* 08.01.1975; *Distribution:* P.A.C.; *Domestic gross:* 1,667,090,170 lire. *Also known as: Mark of the Cop* (USA — alternate title), *Mark the Narc* (Europe — alternate title), *Un flic voit rouge* (France). *Home video:* Cecchi Gori (DVD, Italy, 87'53"). OST: CD Cinevox MDF 354.

Milan. Young commissioner Mark Terzi of the Narcotics Squad is investigating a drug trafficking ring. He and his colleague Bonetti are convinced that the powerful lawyer Benzi, a renowned member of Milan's upper class, is actually the mastermind behind the ring. However, he doesn't have any evidence. Mark takes a young drug addict named Irene to his apartment in an attempt to detox her. Meanwhile a killer named Grüber, who's just been released from prison, kills a former accomplice who's become a member of Benzi's organization. Benzi's right-hand man takes pictures of the crime, and uses them to blackmail Grüber. By tailing one of Benzi's men, an ex-convict named Zardi, Mark and Bonetti find out that Benzi is smuggling the drugs inside dolls depicting Swiss guards, sent away as Holy Year souvenirs, but when he raids one of Benzi's trucks he come up with anything. Mark casually witnesses a robbery and spectacularly thwarts it by shooting at the robbers' car: one of the thugs turns out to be Zardi, who's been released from prison. Irene tells him that Zardi was her connection, and a trail leads Mark to Grüber, who has killed Zardi on Benzi's orders: Terzi confronts and kills him. But Benzi seems too powerful: Irene is lured out of Mark's house and given a lethal overdose, while Bonetti is murdered in an ambush and Mark is suspended from duty. He doesn't give up, though: he locates Benzi's secret drug lab and finally arrests him.

Nineteen seventy-five was a crucial year for poliziotteschi. The genre definitely matured and became standardized, thanks to a couple of huge commercial hits that were released in theaters within a few summer days. On August 1 Stelvio Massi's *Blood,*

Sweat and Fear came out, while August 4 saw the release of Marino Girolami's *Violent Rome*, starring the man who would become the genre's biggest star, Maurizio Merli.

Blood, Sweat and Fear was a smart commercial move on the part of Massi and producer/distributor P.A.C., which revolved around the huge popularity of its protagonist, Franco Gasparri, who at the time was Italy's most famous photonovel star. As Stelvio Massi explained, "Gasparri was cast because of his extraordinary popularity thanks to the "Lancio" photonovels he starred in. These photonovels sold five million copies a month, and a survey at the time revealed that over fifteen million people read them. With P.A.C., we made a calculation: it's impossible that all those fifteen million people go see the movie, otherwise we'd become all millionaires with just one film, and not even five million, or half of them ... let's say we have a potential audience that's approximately half of that half. And they actually came see the film!"[1]

As a matter of fact, Gasparri was a rather inexperienced actor, so much so that Massi later admitted he had to leave out a lot of close-ups from the film in order to make up for his lead's shortcomings. However, *Blood, Sweat and Tears* was not as much about plot and characters as it was about a star. And such was Gasparri, and he looked every bit like one in every single frame he appeared in.

Franco Gasparri as Commissioner Mark Terzi in ***Blood, Sweat and Fear*** (1975).

Marco Terzi is a different kind of cop, at least compared to those we usually meet in Italian flicks. Good looking, athletic, casually dressed, happily single (yet a natural womanizer), inseparable from his .44 Magnum and a Saint Bernard dog called Whisky, he's been nicknamed "Mark" after a specialization period in the United States. "There's only one like you in the whole police force" his superior admits begrudgingly. A young hero for young people, and a catchy name that was also a title and a logo to display on posters (the Italian title is *Mark il poliziotto*, "Mark the Cop"). With *Blood, Sweat and Fear*, the "tough cop" character was rejuvenated and Americanized: apparently, Massi's film owes a lot to Sidney Lumet's *Serpico* (1973), yet according to screenwriter Dardano Sacchetti the script was written in 1971. However, that was also a way to release the genre from the heavy cloak of lead that burdened over those films made during the same period which leaned on actuality. *Blood, Sweat and Fear* returns to the genre's essence of disengaged entertainment, where even the hero's catchphrases and one-liners ("Looking for trouble?" "*I* am trouble!") recall the boasts and bravados of the many Sartanas and Allelujas.

The feeble plot puts Mark against a drug traffic ring led by the wealthy Benzi (Lee J. Cobb), and not a single cliché is spared, from the upper class girl who's a heroin addict (Sara Sperati) to the sympathetic chocolate-eating cop (Giampiero Albertini) who's got a bad ending written in his DNA since he first appears on screen. Even though *Blood, Sweat and Fear* starts in a shooting range where Mark displays his unerring aim, violence is actually rather restrained (the film wasn't even given a v.m.14 rating), and the most interesting villain — the killer suffering from migraine, played by former middleweight boxing champion Carlos Duran, who has "a criminal record as long as the Great Wall of China" and takes aspirin and a glass of water in the kitchen of the man he is about to murder, with a chilling detachment that recalls Lee Van Cleef's introductory bean-eating scene in *The Good, the Bad and the Ugly*— hastily leaves the stage long before the ending. On the other hand, Lee J. Cobb has little to do as the powerful drug lord Benzi, a character that lacks the charisma to be a strong opponent. This leads to another key difference from coeval Eurocrime flicks: Mark doesn't do justice by himself, but he simply arrests Benzi in the end.

Even the expected reproaches by the Chief of Police (Giorgio Albertazzi) are much more good-natured and fatherly than those suffered by Belli (*High Crime*) and Caneparo (*The Violent Professionals*), just to name a couple. As a matter of fact these reproaches can be mainly due to the generational gap — a recurring gag has the Chief of Police complaining about Mark's long hair, a joke that could be found as early as 1953 in Franco Rossi's *I falsari*. In one scene Mark recalls his days at the University, where he ended up being beaten by the police: "How did you become a cop?" his colleague asks. "The doctor ordered me. Since in '68, at the University, I kept being banged in the head, he said: enroll in the police, and you won't get beaten up anymore!" And, yet, the references to the student movement looks more like a way to endearing the audience than a political commentary on the Italian experience of '68. There's more: despite being Italian cinema's first Commissioner that was on the other side of the barricade during those stormy days, Mark Terzi is an integrated middle-class member: he's got a degree, his taste in clothes is evident in his matching shirt and jacket, his flat is nice and clean, and littered with pop-art posters. Mark is the total opposite of Tomas Milian's Nico Giraldi, with the latter being a real working-class hero in the way he talks, dresses and, most of all, thinks.

Technically, Massi (whose son Danilo, who would later become a director in his own right, plays a young cop named Ferri, who's featured in a couple of scenes) shows he's got full control of the action scenes: the most spectacular bit has Mark stop a robbers' car that's coming at him at full speed by standing in the middle of the street and shooting at the windshield, causing the vehicle to somersault, then he simply steps aside as the wreck slides just inches by him — a truly breathtaking stunt which is even more impressive since it was shot in a central Milan street. The film also displays a number of stylish camera movements and visual tricks, such as in the opening scene at the shooting range, where the camera first shows four guns in line shooting in rapid succession through a quick change of focus, then pans right while zooming back so as to move from a lateral to a frontal view of the cops. Massi's use of the zoom lens is very interesting, as he often uses it to frame faces and bodies as reflected in rearview mirrors or other shiny objects, or pairs it with a tracking shot, as in the aforementioned opening. Another significant stylistic trait is hand-held camerawork, which is especially proficient in interior scenes. Stelvio Cipriani's score, complete with a thumping rhythm section, wah-wah guitar and saxophone and driven by a killer harmonica line, is also memorable.

Blood, Sweat and Tears cost 208 million lire; within a month of its release it had grossed over one billion and a half. Just four months later Mark's second adventure (*Mark Shoots First*) came out: the Italian crime genre had just discovered serials.

Note

1. Matteo Norcini, *Intervista a Stelvio Massi*, Amarcord no. 6, (January/February 1997), p. 69.

Calling All Police Cars, *...a tutte le auto della polizia...*

D: Mario Caiano. *S* and *SC:* Fabio Pittorru and Massimo Felisatti from their short story *A scopo di libidine*; *DOP:* Pier Luigi Santi (35mm, Eastmancolor, Staco Film); *M:* Lallo [Coriolano] Gori (Ed. Nationalmusic); *E:* Romeo Ciatti; *PD:* Renato Postiglione; *CO:* Orietta Nasalli Rocca; *AD:* Edoardo Salerno; *C:* Michele Picciaredda; *AC:* Giuseppe Venditti, Salvatore Bella, Bernardo Valli; *AE:* Margherita Santangelo; *MU:* Alberto Travaglini; *Hair:* Sergio Gennari, Carla Indoni; *SO:* Primiano Muratori; *Boom:* Maurizio Merli; *Mix:* Romano Pampaloni; *SP:* Mauro Chiari; *SS:* Gianni Ricci. *Cast:* Antonio Sabàto (Commissioner Fernando Solmi), Luciana Paluzzi (Inspector Giovanna Nunziante), Gabriele Ferzetti (professor Andrea Icardi), Enrico Maria Salerno (Carraro, Head of the Flying Squad), Elio Zamuto (Prof. Giacometti), Ettore Manni (Enrico Tumuli "Momolo"), Andrea Lala (Marshall Attardi), Marino Masè (Franz Hekker "Francesco Pagano"), Bedy Moratti (Emilia Icardi), Adriana Fiore (Stripper), Gloria Piedimonte (Carla), Franco Ressel (Gynaecologist), Andrea Scotti (Head of scientific team), Margherita Horowitz (Antonietta, Icardi's maid), Tino Bianchi (Chief of Police), Benedetto Benedetti, Mario Erpichini (Counselor Mordini), Adriano Migliano [Adriano Amidei Migliano] (police dogs instructor), Attilio Dottesio (Coroner), Leila Ducci [Durante] (Nurse), Ida Di Benedetto (House Madam), Valentino Macchi (Gas station attendant), Fernando Cerulli (Morgue watchman), Fulvio Mingozzi (police official). *Uncredited:* Salvatore Billa (Man at the villa), Nestore Cavaricci (policeman), Adriana Falco (Fiorella Icardi), Ilona Staller (Prostitute at the villa). *PROD:* Renato Angiolini for Capitol International / Jarama Film; *PM:* Ennio Onorati; Unit production managers: Francesco Guerrieri, Mario Olivieri; *PSe:* Gianni Pantano; *CASH:* Francesco Maia. *Country:* Italy. Filmed at RPA — Elios Film (Rome) and on location in and around Rome and Albano. *Running time:* 100'; Visa no.: 67019 (08.27.1975); *Rating:* v.m.18; *Release date:* 08.28.1975; *Distribution:* Capitol International; *Domestic gross:* 955,187,450 lire. *Also known as: Without Trace* (USA — DVD title), *The Maniac Responsible* (USA — Home video). *Home video:* Alan Young Pictures; Mondo Home Entertainment / Dania Film (DVD, Italy), Mya (DVD, USA — as *Without Trace*).

Fiorella Icardi, the 16-year-old daughter of a renowned surgeon, disappears under mysterious circumstances. She's later found dead, with a bullet in the back of her head, at the bottom of lake Albano, near Rome. The police suspects an innkeeper, Enrico Tummoli called "Momolo," who's a notorious peeping tom. However, by tailing Fiorella's schoolmate Carla, the police discover an underage prostitution ring that involves many upper-class girls and is led by a certain Franz Hekker, otherwise known as Francesco Pagano. Also involved is a respected politician, Counselor Mordini, a former Minister as well as a very good friend of the Icardis. The Chief of Police, however, insists that Tummoli is the murderer so that the case can be closed quickly, without raising a scandal. But Tummoli is murdered, and soon other vicious killings ensue: the victims are a gynecologist and Pagano. It becomes apparent that somebody is dispatching all those who know too much. Eventually, tire tread marks on the murder site lead Commissioner Carraro to discover the murderer's identity: Dr. Giacometti, a colleague and personal friend of Icardi's, who was Fiorella's lover, and killed the girl when she told him she was pregnant and wanted him to leave his wife for her.

Calling All Police Cars germinated on the wake of a popular TV series that was broadcast on RAI-TV between May and June 1973, *Qui squadra mobile* (Flying Squad Here), directed by Anton Giulio Majano and written by a duo of popular crime novelists, Massimo Felisatti and Fabio Pittorru, who in those years often lent their talents to the big screen as well. *Qui squadra mobile* consisted of six self-conclusive episodes that revolved around the investigating core of Rome's mobile squad: the obvious inspiration was Ed McBain's 87th Precinct novels, with a number of recurring characters that Felisatti and Pittorru would revive on paper, in a number of successful and critically acclaimed novels (*Violenza a Roma*, *La morte dalle ali bianche*, *La madama*). The cast included popular stage and film actors such as Giancarlo Sbragia (as Carraro, the head of the Flying Squad), Orazio Orlando (as Commissioner Solmi) and Elio Zamuto, while the only prominent female character, Inspector Giovanna Nunziante, was played by Stefanella Giovannini. In 1976 a second series of *Qui squadra mobile* was broadcast, with a slightly different cast led by the talented Luigi Vannucchi (Roberto Rossellini's *Anno Uno*). Like coeval poliziotteschi, *Qui squadra mobile* often took inspiration from real-life events, yet violence was inevitably toned down given the series' TV context. The protagonists were far from the gun-happy types that populated the big screen; they followed the law scrupulously and didn't let their feelings interfere with their work, What's more, they worked as a team, unlike anarchic rain dogs such as their cinematic counterparts.

Mario Caiano's film, however, was quite a different affair. The same characters from the TV series returned, played by different actors: Sbragia and Orlando make way to two stars of the poliziotteschi, respectively Enrico Maria Salerno and Antonio Sabàto, while Luciana Paluzzi pops up as Inspector Nunziante, with Zamuto turning up in a totally different, negative role. The realistic approach to police procedure that characterized *Qui squadra mobile* was preserved as well, with scenes depicting cataloguing of evidence, tire tread mark and ballistic tests etc. Nevertheless, *Calling All Police Cars* dives headlong into exploitation territory, with ample female nudity—among the young prostitutes one can briefly spot an uncredited Ilona Staller, soon to become Cicciolina, Italy's most famous porn star—and a third act that substantially moves away from the original plot and turns into a *giallo*, Dario Argento–style, as the unknown assassin dispatches a number of witnesses. The murders, shot with extensive use of POV shots, are outrageously over-the-top: a peeping tom (Ettore Manni) gets strangled, a doctor who performs abortions (Franco Ressel) has his throat slashed with a scalpel, a young girl is butchered in her bathtub. The end result is a rather inconclusive hybrid, that looks like it was assembled in order to appeal to a different audience than *Qui squadra mobile*—and somehow functions as an example of the never-ending race to excess that characterized Italian cinema of the period.

However, in adapting their story *A scopo di libidine* (included in the volume *Violenza a Roma*, published in 1974), Felisatti and Pittorru kept its palpable spite towards the social environment where the story takes place: an upper-class Rome as represented through villas with pools where middle-aged men sip their cocktails and ogle at underage girls, and exclusive brothels where bored rich teens make extra money by giving themselves to wealthy customers.

It's a world of privileged and untouchables, ruled in a strictly hierarchic way: head physician Gabriele Ferzetti, who owns a private clinic not too dissimilar from the one depicted by Luigi Zampa in the angry drama *Secrets of a Nurse* (*Bisturi la mafia bianca*, 1973), just has to make a phone call to have the whole police force at his disposal. And while the former Chief Commissioner Carraro is allowed to sit and have a coffee in upper-class homes, his bad-tempered undergraduate Solmi—whose intolerance towards the rich betrays his working-class origins—has to perform much of the dirty work.

The same stratification characterizes the sex market as depicted in the film. Powerful men meet nymphets in a villa outside Rome with the connivance of the Vice Squad, while the innkeeper played by Manni pays his customers to be able to spy on them as they make love on a lake shore, and even the murderer kills to preserve his place in this pyramidic structure.

As with Dallamano's *What Have They Done to Your Daughters?*, the film is concerned with the generation gap: a mother (Bedy Moratti) cannot even remember how her daughter was dressed like the last time she saw her, while the father (Gabriele Ferzetti) pretends to have an idyllic relationship with his "little girl" that exists only in his imagination.

The Climber (L'ambizioso)

D: Pasquale Squitieri. *S:* Pasquale Squitieri, Carlo Rivolta; *SC:* Pasquale Squitieri; *DOP:* Eugenio Bentivoglio (35mm, Eastmancolor, LV-Luciano Vittori); *M:* Franco Campanino, conducted by Gianfranco Lombardi; *The Climber* (F. Campanino) is sung by Jessy King; *E:* Mauro Bonanni; *AE:* Walter Diotallevi; *ArtD:* Francesco Calabrese; *AArtDs:* Gianfranco Pucci, Vincenzo Testa; *CO:* Roberto Ranucci; *SDr:* Carlo Gentili; *C:* Giuseppe Berardini; *AC:* Renato Ranieri, *2nd AC:* Sandro Battaglia; *AD:* Roberto Pariante; *2nd AD:* Mario Zonta; *MU:* Giovanna Manca; *SO:* Alvaro Orsini; *Boom:* Manlio Urbani; *Mix:* Danilo Moroni; *SOE:* Roberto Arcangeli; *SP:* Gianfranco Salis; *SS:* Serena Merlini Canevari. *Cast:* Joe Dallesandro (Aldo), Stefania Casini (Luciana), Raymond Pellegrin (Don Enrico, the boss), Benito Artesi (Ciriaco), Mario De Luca, Ferdinando Murolo (Carlo), Tony Askin [Antonio Aschini] (Man on train), Leopoldo Buondonno, Giovanni Cianfriglia (Gianni), Angelo Corrieri, Paolo De Lucia, Bruno Di Luia (Don Enrico's henchman), Ugo Donadio, Bernard Faber, Antonietta Fasano, Ranieri Ferrara, Marcello Filotico (Nightclub owner), Gregorio Gandolfo, Guido Giuseppone, Maria Greco, Giuseppe Leone, Enrico Maisto, Carla Mancini, Amedeo Messori, Edmondo Mascia (Don Enrico's friend), Lorenzo Piani (Bernard), Carmelo Reale (Don Enrico's henchman), Francesco Spilabotte, Francesco Torrisi, Pietro Torrisi (Boxer), Salvatore Torrisi. *Uncredited:* Angelo Boscariol (Don Enrico's man), Phillip Dallas (Boss), Franco Marino (Russo, nightclub owner), Claudio Ruffini (Don Enrico's henchman). *PROD:* Laser Film; *GM, PM*: Michele Marsala; *UPM*: Claudio Vinale; *Pse:* Carla Crovato, Guglielmo Carbonaro. *Country:* Italy. Filmed at Dear Studios (Rome) and on location in Naples and Rome. *Running time:* 110'; Visa no.: 66023 (02.07.75); *Rating:* v.m.18; *Distribution:* Titanus; *Release date:* 02.18.75; *Domestic gross:* 638,368,060 lire. *Also known as: Harley Riders—Sie kannten kein Erbarmen* (West Germany: 02.02.79—99'), *El ambicioso* (Spain). *Home video:* Creazioni Home Video (VHS, Italy). OST: LP CAM AMP 150.

Unhappy with his role as a small-time smuggler, the young Aldo does an affront to Don Enrico, chief of the Neapolitan underworld: beaten and humiliated as a result, he is forced to take refuge in Rome. There, he is rescued by a young shop assistant, Luciana, who becomes his lover. After getting involved in the theft of a bag of heroin, which costs his friend Carlo his life, Aldo gets caught by Don Enrico's men but is saved by Luciana. Aldo gradually makes his way to the top and organize his own gang. When he feels strong enough to stand up to Don Enrico, Aldo returns to Naples, faces his opponent and forces him to come to terms: to yield, that is, half of the "business." The agreement, however, does not last long, since Don Enrico has not given up on getting rid of his rival. The consequences befall upon Luciana, who—after the boss makes her believe that Aldo has repudiated her—commits suicide. Aldo reacts by eliminating Don Enrico, but soon after he falls himself, in a deadly trap set up by other leaders of the underworld.

After the phenomenal commercial success of the historical drama *Blood Brothers* (*I guappi*, 1974) Pasquale Squitieri returned to present times with his next film, yet another crime story set between Naples and Rome. As Squitieri explained, "in 1975 the Neapolitan Camorra had lost its great leaders and was subject to the Sicilian Mafia, and we mustn't forget that drug trafficking was increasing in a frightening way. In such a context, Rome represented a good basis for Naples — the Roman underworld was quite poorly organized ... as shown 40 years later by Michele Placido in *Crime Novel*."[1]

Originally, Squitieri thought of Fabio Testi in the lead as the ambitious smuggler Aldo, who dreams of becoming an underworld boss, and eventually succeeds, yet at a tremendous price. However, the director soon changed his mind, and opted for a casting choice that's easily the film's most interesting trait. "In that period I used to watch Andy Warhol and Paul Morrissey's films at the Filmstudio in Rome. To me Joe Dallesandro was a myth, and I was sure I wouldn't be able to have him in one of my films, because to me he was unreachable. [...] yet it was difficult for me to picture Fabio Testi playing the son of an American sailor and a Neapolitan prostitute. [...] Physically, someone like Lou Castel would have been good for *The Climber*. My main character was not a leader, but a miserable petty thief who lived day by day. [...] Eventually I got in touch with Joe through a journalist friend, and he was happy to be part of the project."[2]

In that period Dallesandro was a much requested name in Italian cinema: after Morrissey's grotesque horror diptych *Flesh for Frankenstein* (1973) and *Blood for Dracula* (1974), the apollonian Brooklynese actor continued his film career between Italy and France, returning in the States in the '80s. Stefania Casini, who was Dallesandro's lover at the time, co-starred as the film's love interest, providing *The Climber* with a melodrama angle, while Raymond Pellegrin once again turned up as the villain.

Squitieri's ambition was to make an anthropological and sociological portrayal that would bear more than a passing resemblance to Pier Paolo Pasolini's discourse on the anthropological mutation of the lower classes in contemporary society. "The film's theme [...] is the ambition of suburban young boys to get access to the city's wealth and well-being. What penetrates in the ever-growing suburban areas, in fact, is not its well-being but its advertising," the director pointed out. "Wealth stays in Eden. That is, the city. Those who stay out, are misfits. The city is still a myth, but a concrete one, as it represents wealth, money, power, both for the legal society and the deviant one. It's a cultural problem. Advertising serves consumer society in such a pounding way that it creates a state of inferiority and frustration in the suburban bands of the population, which makes even more acute the need to get to Eden."[3]

However, the director wasn't able to fully develop his propositions. As with *Gang War in Naples*, Squitieri displayed a keen eye in depicting the mechanisms of the Neapolitan underworld, as shown by the opening scene where a human chain of smugglers carry crates of cigarettes from a motorboat to the cars that leave one by one at full speed before the police arrive. Unfortunately the same cannot be said about characterizations, which are rather bland and uninteresting — Dallesandro's character included. If Aldo's fall from grace and his desperate attempts at getting back on his feet with a new gang in Rome are convincing enough, minor characters — such as the sleazy homosexual informer who makes a pass at Aldo while telling him about a hit the young man will perform for him — are often overwrought, and the film's second half soon turns into a dull series of showdowns until the predictable tragic ending, while the absence of the police from the storyline, even though intentional, mines the tale's believability.

The direction displays an over-reliance on long shots and zooms that gives the film a rough look — a deliberate move on Squitieri's part, so as to portray "a ragged reality that mirrored the protagonist's insecurity and violence."[4] Also noteworthy is the use of violence, which earned the film a v.m.18 rating: the resort to slow motion in violent and action scenes — such as in a weird disco fight — was obviously influenced by Peckinpah, with ample use of blood squibs; however, the insistent use of the title song in such scenes soon becomes tiresome and irritating, to the detriment of otherwise powerful scenes.

Squitieri's next film would be yet another period drama about the Mafia, *I Am the Law* (*Il prefetto di ferro*, 1977), one of his most memorable and successful works.

Notes

1. Monetti, *Pasquale Squitieri*, p. 57.
2. *Ibid.*
3. *Ibid.*, p. 183.
4. Francesco Savio, *Il Mondo*, 04.03.1975.

Four for All *(Dört Hergele — Can Arkadaşlar / Quei paracul ... pi di Jolando e Margherito)*

D: Jerry Mason [Giulio Giuseppe Negri] (actually Yilmaz Atadeniz). *S* and *SC:* Giulio Giuseppe Negri, Bruno Vani; *DOP:* Luigi De Maria (35mm, Eastmancolor, Augustus Color); *M:* Elsio Mancuso; *E:* Mario G. Corso; *PD:* Giovanni Fratalocchi; *C:* Antonio Maracchioni; *AD:* Paolo Antinori; *SO:* Alberto Vani; *Mix:* Renato Cadueri; *SS:* Mario Peverada. *Cast:* Olga Petrova (Olga), Tony Tiger [Irfan Atasoy] (Tony Tiger), Brad Euston [Fikret Hakan] (Brad), Richard Harrison (Ricky Holland "Jolando"), Gordon Mitchell (Gordon Matthews "Margherito"), Ferita Gandell [Feri Cansel], Cesare Nizzica, Nicola Morelli, Luciano Conti; Turkish version: Fikret Hakan, Richard Harrison, Altan Günbay, Gordon Mitchell, Yavuz Selskman, Irfan Yatasoy, Sami Tunc, Erol Tas, Eri Cansel, Attila Ergün. *PROD:* Giulio Giuseppe Negri and Bruno Vani for Fokus Film [actually Irfan Film]; *PM:* Bruno Vani. *Country:* Turkey. Filmed on location in Istanbul. *Running time:* 80'; Visa no.: 65942 (01.29.1975); *Rating:* v.m.18; Release date (Italy): 01.31.1975; *Distribution:* General; *Domestic gross:* 60,420,420 lire. *Also known as: Fighting Killer* (Germany — Home video). *Home video:* Video Search of Miami (DVD-R, USA), Antoniana (VHS, Italy), AVO Film / Fletcher (VHS, U.K. — pre-cert).

Istanbul. When challenged by the shareholders at a general meeting of the local underworld, mobster Joseph Cavis has all of his rivals killed and replaced by loyal henchmen. A few days later, a gang of thugs show up at Cavis' former associate Tony Tiger, kill his wife and son before his very eyes and set fire to the place. Saved by Olga, another former associate of Cavis', Tony seeks revenge: he appeals to his old army pals: Rick, Gordon and Brady. The quartet, followed by Olga, track down the executors of the massacre and kill them, then they break into Cavis' hideout. However, Cavis turns out to be innocent: the real dispatcher was Olga, out of jealousy for Tony. Both Olga and Tony die in yet another shoot-out.

Although the credits state it was directed by the Italian Giulio Giuseppe Negri (a.k.a. Jerry Mason), *Four For All* was actually a Turkish crime film helmed by Yilmaz Atadeniz, a vehicle for Turkish star/producer Irfan Atasoy, here billed as Tony Tiger (which incidentally is also his character's name), and featuring Gordon Mitchell and Richard Harrison. Negri bought the film for the Italian market, retitled it *Quei paracul ... pi di Jolando e Margherito*— a completely misleading title that makes it sounds like it's a comedy[1]— and put the name Jerry Mason on it to take writing and directing credit (distributor Bruno Vani also appears in the opening titles as co-writer). Negri then devised a poster to make it look like a Western.

Like in *The Godfather's Friend* and *Special Squad Shoot on Sight* (*La polizia ordina: sparate a vista!*, 1976, another Turkish crime film that Negri presumably bought for the Italian market, crediting himself as director) it is likely that the minor Italian names in the cast are actually fake pseudonyms for Turkish actors who appear in the film such as Kazim Kartal (credited as "Brad Euston," the same pseudonym used by Sicilian actor Ettore Aricò in Renato Polselli's *Oscenità* and *Mania*) and Erol Tas, that Negri made up to make the film look Italian. Similarly, the opening credits in the Italian copy states the film was shot at Gordon Mitchell's Cave Film Studio — a Western village in the Roman countryside — while it was obviously filmed in Turkey.

In an interview with William Connolly and Tom Betts, Gordon Mitchell (who broke his leg during the shooting) talks at length about the film and its director: ""Do you remember who directed the film?" "It was a Turkish director, but Richard and I, most of the time, were doing the directing. That's what happens with these films, you have no idea. [Tony Tiger] That's Irfan Atasoy. He was the producer of the film; he co-produced it. [...] Oh, and Richard had a thing to deal with him."[2]

Four For All was released on VHS in Britain on a pre-cert tape in 1982 on Avo Film (Fletcher).

Notes

1. The title refers to Giuseppe Colizzi's action comedy hit *Arrivano Joe e Margherito* (1974), starring Keith Carradine and Tom Skerritt.
2. William Connolly and Tom Betts, "His Name Is Chuck," *Spaghetti Cinema* #59 (December 1994).

Gambling City (La città gioca d'azzardo)

D: Sergio Martino. *S:* Ernesto Gastaldi; *SC:* Ernesto Gastaldi, Sergio Martino; *DOP:* Giancarlo Ferrando (35mm, Eastmancolor, L.V.-Luciano Vittori); *M:* Luciano Michelini (Ed. RCA); *E:* Eugenio Alabiso; *PD, ArtD:* Giorgio Bertolini; *CO:* Renato Ventura; *C:* Giuseppe Di Biase, Emilio Bestetti; *AC:* Antonio Minutolo; *AE:* Teresa Negozio; *AD:* Filiberto Fiaschi; *MU:* Stefano Trani; *Hair:* Ennio Cascioli; *SO:* Roberto Alberghini; *Mix:* Romano Pampaloni; *MA:* Riccardo Petrazzi; *SP:* Francesco Narducci; *SS:* Mirella Roy Malatesta. *Cast:* Luc Merenda (Luca Altieri), Dayle Haddon (Maria Luisa "Meme"), Corrado Pani (Corrado, the President's son), Enrico Maria Salerno (The "President"), Lino Troisi (Cardsharper), Giovanni [Franco] Javarone (Lisander), Salvatore Puntillo (Waiter at gambling house), Carlo Alighiero (Commissioner), Piero Palermini (Gambling house director), Carlo Gaddi (Man from Hamburg), Vittorio Fanfoni (Corrado's man), Loris Perera Lopes [Loris Pereira Lopez] (Doctor), Giuseppe Terranova, Bruno Ariè ("President"'s bodyguard), Sergio Ukmar (Carabiniere). *Uncredited:* Artemio Antonini ("President"'s bodyguard), Benito Pacifico (Gangster), Nestore Cavaricci (Cop), Enrico Chiappafreddo (Cardsharper's henchman), Raniero Dorascenzi (Croupier), Tom Felleghy (Surgeon), Giulio Massimini (Barman), Fulvio Mingozzi (Man playing poker), Filippo Perego (Man playing poker), Riccardo Petrazzi (Corrado's thug), Nando Sarlo (Man playing poker), Alessandro Tedeschi (Boss), Sergio Testori ("Gorilla" at the gambling house), Franco Ukmar (Cardsharper's henchman), Luciano Zanussi. *PROD:* Luciano Martino for Dania Film, Medusa Distribuzione; *PM:* Pietro Innocenzi; *PSu:* Rosalba Di Bartolo; *CASH:* Maria Spera. *Country:* Italy. Filmed at Dear Studios (Rome) and on location in Milan and Nice. *Running time:* 101'; Visa no.: 65913 (01.18.1975); *Rating:* v.m.14; *Release date:* 01.23.1975; *Distribution:* Medusa; *Domestic gross:* 777,334,540 lire. *Also known as: Hetzjagd ohne Gnade* (West Germany), *Le parfum du diable* (Canada), *The Cheaters. Home video:* NoShame (DVD — USA), NoShame (DVD, Italy)

Milan. Luca Altieri, a professional gambler, usually plays cards at Club 72. One evening, thanks to a bold bluff at the poker table, he gets hired by the club's owner, the wheelchair-bound President, who among other things is the undisputed boss of many Italian and foreign casinos. In the following days, Luca falls in love with Maria Luisa, the beautiful lover of Corrado, the President's son. A rivalry ensues, that ends with the savage beating of Luca and the murder of the boss at the hands of his cynical son. Luca and the girl, who's pregnant with his child, move to Nice, while Corrado proves to be an unworthy successor of his father. The new boss is still looking for revenge, however, and he eventually locates the fugitives in Nice. Despite Maria Luisa's recommendations, Altieri gets back to the green table and loses all his money, then he is drawn into a poker game that's just a trap for him. Warned by his only remaining friend in Milan, Luca escapes just in time: Corrado and his men get killed in a car accident, but Maria Luisa gives birth prematurely to her baby and they both die. Luca is left alone with his remorse.

With *Gambling City*, Sergio Martino deviated from the path of contemporary crime films. Even though there are references to events of the period — namely 1974's "austerity" measures, caused by the international oil crisis when in the opening scene a barman tells Merenda that "In Milan people work and go to sleep early, especially now that we have to save on energy" — and Milan exteriors are featured prominently, *Gambling City* is rather detached from Italian reality, and plays more like a timeless *film noir*.

At first, Ernesto Gastaldi's script (Martino's contribution was just nominal) seems to pay homage to *The Sting* (1973) by following the brilliant career of a womanizing and boastful cardsharp in Milan's clandestine gambling houses, helped by the clever casting of Luc Merenda in the lead and underlined by Luciano Michelini's contagious score. The script summarizes the hero's working-class arrogance: in his first appearance he dresses sloppily in a mocking contrast with the elegance of Milan nightclubs (he wears a sweater over a tee shirt with a carnation in his buttonhole and velvet trousers), and displays the same tendency to puns as Caneparo in *The Violent Professionals* ("The monk does not make the habit!"); later on he wears flashy pin-striped gangster clothes, like a typical upstart. The opening card game, with Merenda initially acting like a buffoon and eventually winning a huge sum against an expert cheater (the great character actor Lino Troisi, also seen in Duccio Tessari's *Big Guns*), looks like a homage to the classic opening of Robert Rossen's *The Hustler* (1961), and Martino shows his directing skills with cool close-ups of card tricks performed on camera. Gastaldi throws in some witty dialogue and a few humorous scenes: a fight between Merenda and Troisi is structured like a poker game, as Troisi calls trips when he's joined by two henchmen, while Merenda (who's accompanied by a pair of prostitutes who stand aside, screaming in terror) complains he's only got a pair of queens.

Then the script makes an abrupt turn towards darker territory, when Dayle Haddon (who had just become a star in Italy thanks to her role in Aldo Lado's erotic drama *The Cousin*, 1974) enters the scene as the love interest that pits the hero against the boss' malevolent son (Corrado Pani). Martino does not stint on the sleaze, though, as proven by the sequence where Pani has Haddon nearly raped by his ugly driver / bodyguard (played by Franco Javarone, later a regular in Tinto Brass films), while the scene where Merenda has his hands broken by Pani so that he can't cheat at cards is a riff on a classic Spaghetti Western moment, namely Franco Nero's torture in Sergio Corbucci's *Django* (1966). Another nod to Westerns is the device hidden under Merenda's sleeve to get an ace, which curiously predates Robert De Niro's automatic gun device in *Taxi Driver*. However, it's too little to save the film: there's even room for Merenda and Haddon running by the shore at sunset, before an ending that clumsily combines *film noir* and tearjerking melodrama.

As the film's sadistic villain Pani is constantly over-the-top, and one scene requires him to rehash the famous scene from *Kiss of Death* where Richard Widmark throws a wheelchair-bound woman down the stairs — this time the victim is Enrico Maria Salerno, not so convincing as the old embittered gambling boss. "I wrote the story with Enrico Maria Salerno in mind as the boss of a sharp — and not just violent — criminal organization which has a succession problem when the son shows he's not cut from the same cloth as his father. It's still an actual theme," Ernesto Gastaldi recalled. The scriptwriter, who considers it to be one of his best efforts, stresses the differences between *Gambling City* and other crime films of the period. "I believe the actors were very good on this film, improving upon a story that, although not very original, was rather different from crime films of the era. There's no happy ending, and that's quite unusual. I like abrupt endings, and I always laughed at those Hollywood movies that after showing the REAL ending, which is not happy, add a little bit where the hero recovers and kisses his wife and sons."[1]

Note

1. E-mail interview, January 2012.

Go Gorilla Go, a.k.a. *The Hired Gun (Vai gorilla)*

D: Tonino Valerii. *S* and *SC:* Massimo De Rita and Dino Maiuri; *M:* Franco Bixio, Fabio Frizzi, Vince Tempera; *DOP:* Mario Vulpiani (35mm, Technicolor, Technospes); *E:* Antonio Siciliano; *PD:* Luca Sabatelli; *C:* Pasquale Rachini; *AC:* Osvaldo Bagnato; *AEs:* Giancarlo Morelli, Luigi Gorini; *APD:* Egidio Spugnini, Giancarlo Mentil; *AD:* Franco Cirino; *MU:* Massimo De Rossi; *AMU:* Feliziano Ciriaci; *Hair:* Agnese Pavarotto; *SO:* Luigi Salvi; *Boom:* Benito Alchimede; *Mix:* Gianni D'Amico; *SE:* Paolo Ricci; *SP:* Giuseppe Botteghi; *STD:* Angelo Ragusa; *MA:* Remo De Angelis; *SS:* Vivalda Vigorelli. *Cast:* Fabio Testi (Marco Sartori), Renzo Palmer (Engineer Gaetano Sampioni), Claudia Marsani (Vera Sampioni), Saverio Marconi (Piero Sartori), Al Lettieri (Ciro Musante), Adriano Amidei Migliano (Commissioner Vannuzzi), Tony [Antonio] Marsina (Berto, the biker), Luciano Catenacci (Shooting range manager), Giuliana Calandra (Sampioni's wife), Maria D'Incoronato (Elisa Sartori), Ernesto Colli (watchman), Salvatore Billa (A "Gorilla"), Riccardo Petrazzi (Berto's mustached sidekick), Simone Santo (Old man at racing track), Sergio Testori (Berto's sidekick), Remo De Angelis (Berto's sidekick), Furio Meniconi (The "fence"), Franca Scagnetti (Fence's wife), Angelo Ragusa (Thug). *PROD:* Mario Cecchi Gori per Capital Film; *GM:* Luciano Luna; *PM:* Marcello Crescenzi; *PIs:* Mario Della Torre, Giandomenico Stellitano; *ADM:* Mario Lupi; *CASH:* Marcello Tassi. *Country:* Italy. Filmed at De Paolis Studios, Rome. *Running time:* 100'; Visa no.: 67415 (11.08.1975); *Rating:* v.m.18; *Release date:* 11.14.1975; *Distribution:* Cineriz; *Domestic gross:* 1,846,285,530 lire. *Also known as: De profesión: gorila* (Spain), *Der Gorilla* (West Germany), *Gorilla ser rødt* (Norway). *Home video:* Domovideo (VHS, Italy). OST: CD Chris' Soundtrack Corner CSC007.

In order to get hired as a bodyguard by wealthy engineer Gaetano Sampioni, former stuntman Marco Sartori stages a mock kidnapping with the help of his friend Ciro, which he then foils all by himself. Marco's plan is successful and he becomes Sampioni's "gorilla." But the two men don't get along at all because of the engineer's bad temper as well as Marco's own pride; what's more, Marco falls in love with Sampioni's daughter Vera, whom he has to watch over. The engineer is being threatened with anonymous phone calls and letters, which demand a huge amount of money, and the construction sites he's working at are sabotaged. Marco and his younger brother Piero investigate, and find out that one of the blackmailers is a biker with a precision shotgun and cowboy boots. To keep Sampioni from paying the mob, Marco kidnaps the engineer and hides him in a safe place, and sets up a trap with the police, which is a failure. Marco finds out that Ciro is involved with the racket, and persuades him to arrange a meeting with Berto, the biker, but falls into a trap in an abandoned palace, and miraculously escapes with his life. Yet he cannot save Ciro, who is mercilessly killed by his former accomplices. Berto's men attempt to kidnap Vera, but Marco saves her. Berto's men capture Piero, but Marco and the police come to his rescue. The racket is decimated, and Berto escapes on a train. After a breathtaking chase, Marco kills him in a duel.

After the box office success of Enzo Castellari's *Street Law*, which he financed, producer Mario Cecchi Gori decided to make another picture in the same vein to cash-in on the crime genre's popularity. He got in touch with Tonino Valerii, a skilled director who specialized in the western genre and had had quite a few box office hits in the past. Valerii's latest film, although not one of his best, was also his most popular to date: *My Name Is Nobody* (*Il mio nome è Nessuno*, 1973) starring Henry Fonda and Terence Hill, was an elegy on the death of the Western genre with comedic touches which somehow suffered from the imposing personality of producer Sergio Leone (who later claimed he had directed many scenes himself, much to Valerii's chagrin). As Valerii recalls, his first meetings with Cecchi Gori were pretty interlocutory: "Mario invited me to his home to play cards, or to have a cappuccino. He clearly wanted to know more about my temper and my political ideas. I openly told him that I didn't want to do a 'revanchist' film. Cecchi Gori didn't take it too well, yet I think he liked my straightforwardness."[1] Valerii and scriptwriter Massimo De Rita started developing a few ideas, and ended up with three basic outlines: the story of a police patrol on the night shift, structured like an omnibus film of sorts; another, which Valerii describes as "a revenge flick, in the vein of *Death Wish*," where a lawyer becomes a vigilante and uses his knowledge of crime law to take his revenge against a gang of thugs and not be punished — an idea which eventually got dropped even though both Valerii and Cecchi Gori loved it; and, finally, the story of a bodyguard.

As often in that period, ideas for crime movies came from newspapers' headlines. *Go Gorilla Go* germinated from the kidnapping escalation which took place in Italy in 1975, and which inspired a number of films, including Fernando di Leo *The Kidnap Syndicate*. As Valerii comments, "On Cecchi Gori's desk I saw a newspaper with a big headline about a wealthy Italian industrialist, who claimed that he was tired of living in such an anarchic and dangerous country, and that he was moving abroad for fear of being kidnapped. I though it was a situation which perfectly captured the troubled historical moment we were living in." Bodyguards, or "gorillas" as they were colloquially nicknamed, were an emblematic figure of the period, a new profession rapidly spreading out as many wealthy men used to surround themselves with armed, mean-looking "gorillas" for fear of being kidnapped.[2] What eventually convinced the reluctant producer, though, was the title. "I realized we got the movie when De Rita got up and with a theatrical gesture he raised his hand and proclaimed: "Go, Gorilla!" Cecchi Gori didn't hesitate for a second: "It's a deal! When you have the title, you have the movie!" And he immediately called his secretary to pay De Rita and I a sum in advance, without us having written even a line of the script!"[3]

For the leading role, Valerii cast 34-year-old Fabio Testi, who came from a couple of disappointing box office flops such as Gianfranco Baldanello's *Blood River* (*Dieci bianchi uccisi da un piccolo indiano*, 1974) and Aristide Massaccesi's *Red Coat* a.k.a. *Killers of the Savage North* (*Giubbe rosse*, 1975). His brother Piero was played by a young stage thespian in his screen debut, Saverio Marconi, while character actor Renzo Palmer (a familiar face in crime films) was a perfect choice as Sampioni, the rude proletarian who made a fortune, but still retains his rough manners and colorful, language. Al Lettieri, who played Steve McQueen's nemesis Rudy Butler in *The Getaway* (1972) and Virgil "The Turk" Sollozzo in Coppola's *The Godfather*, has a small yet incisive role as Testi's colleague and best friend who double-crosses him and later pays for his betrayal. That would be one of Lettieri's last screen roles, as he died of a heart attack on October 18, 1975, a month before the film's release.

Valerii's choice for the film's picturesque villain was quite curious: after a few bit roles in 1960s Westerns, Antonio Marsina gave up acting and became a professional photographer. "He showed up at our office accompanying his girlfriend, an actress whom we auditioned. She wasn't cast, but I thought Antonio had an interesting face. I asked him to do a screen test and in the end he got the role."

As with other crime films of the period, *Go Gorilla Go* is a Western in disguise. The film's plot patently pays reference to Akira Kurosawa's *Yojimbo* (1961), who nurtured and raised the Italian western like a warm placenta since Sergio Leone took inspiration from it in *A Fistful of Dollars* (1964). After getting the job as the irascible engineer Sampioni's bodyguard, Marco (Fabio Testi) finds out that the "gorillas" who should protect their employers are the ones who manage the blackmail and kidnapping racket. Near the beginning Marco even claims he is "the rider from the solitary valley," quoting the Italian title of George Stevens' *Shane* (1953), and that is literally the truth. Marco is a younger and more impetuous Shane, who falls for his boss' daughter instead of his wife, while Sampioni is a foul-mouthed version of Van Heflin's character — a self-made man who's ready to protect his family and possessions at all costs; and the villain, Berto, a mean-looking, black-dressed biker with Texan boots, looks like a contemporary variation on Jack Palance's Jack Wilson in Stevens' film.

Fabio Testi, left, and Al Lettieri in *Go Gorilla Go* (1975).

What's more, Valerii's background as a Western filmmaker is well in evidence. The film climaxes with a show-stopping assault on a train running at full speed and a gun duel which ends with Testi shooting Marsina in the eye through the latter's precision rifle's viewfinder. The scene was taken almost literally from Valerii's debut *Taste of Killing* (*Per il gusto di uccidere*, 1965), where the final shooting took place between Craig Hill and George Martin.

"The result was identical, but just a few critics noticed it," Valerii notes. "The way Testi leaps from the police car onto the train was another homage to a classic Western movie cliché, such as the scene in *Stagecoach* where John Wayne jumps onto stagecoach horses' backs to stop their run."

Set in the Roman suburbs, among construction sites, barracks and fences which look like frontier forts and outposts, *Go Gorilla Go* makes the outskirts of the Capital look like a wild and dangerous plain. Valerii captures the leaden and uneasy atmosphere of a country in full economical expansion yet on the edge of an abyss, shaken by anarchic spasms and submitted to the law of the fittest: a contemporary frontier, where family and friendship look as if they are about to collapse. Ultimately, *Go Gorilla Go* was much more successful than another modern-day Western such as Stelvio Massi's *The Last Round*, made the following year, which was yet another riff on *A Fistful of Dollars*.

Fabio Testi in *Go Gorilla Go* (1975).

The film's main theme is self-determination, which pushes Marco to show that he is up to the task, despite hating his job and having to endure teasings on behalf of Sampioni's site workers. "There's only one choice you have to do: decide what kind of man you want to be," Marco says to his brother, while later on he tells Sampioni: "Even though you are paying me, you didn't buy me. I am and want to remain a free man." In Valerii's film, though, freedom does not become the retaliatory urge of a private citizen who takes the law into his own hands: it's the possibility of choosing one's own future.

As in Valerii's best Westerns, namely *Day of Anger* (*I giorni dell'ira*, 1967) and *The Price of Power* (*Il prezzo del potere*, 1969), generational conflicts are central to the plot, and the relationship between father and son comes to a head with the former's death, seen as the culmination of a fate one can't escape. On *Go Gorilla Go* the father figure is split in two: on one side, the "father and master" Sampioni, a model but also a suffocating authority; on the other, Marco's older friend Ciro, who teaches Marco a life lesson. "I'm not here to judge you," Marco tells him when he finds out that Ciro has double-crossed him for money. "But I do want you to judge me," he replies, "because you are still young, and you can afford the luxury of being honest." It's a singularly touching moment, in a film filled with half-baked dialogue. "We must not suffer, we must rebel, we can not always say "not me"!" Testi proclaims in one scene: a line which could belong to any other crime film of the period in its generic demagoguism.

Valerii admits that the script was written in a haste, with lots of dialogue being frantically rewritten in the editing room to "rescue" a few scenes. But it's the action sequences that stand out in the memory, and make *Go Gorilla Go* one of the most technically accomplished crime films of the decade. The scene where Fabio Testi is trapped inside a lift cabin in an abandoned building, and the bad guys remove the cabin floor under his feet, leaving him dangling in the void, is breathtaking, and features a pioneering use of the blue-back in Italian cinema. "We had to improvise because it was the first time Blue-back was used in Italy. It was a very difficult scene to shoot. We had to rebuild three flights of stairs inside an abandoned palace about to be demolished near the Colosseum, and used two real lift cabins operated by hand through ropes and counterweights. The scene cost a lot of money, and Cecchi Gori was happy only when he saw the final result."

Violence is harsh and brutal, as often in crime films: a man on a bike is run over by the train at the climax, and the seedy owner of a shooting range (Luciano Catenacci) is brutally beaten by an angry Testi. But it's Al Lettieri's cruel death scene (bikers run over him, mangling his legs) and the gory duel between Testi and Marsina which stay in the mind long after the film has ended, and earned the film a v.m. 18 ("persons under 18 not admitted") rating. "When *Go Gorilla Go* was classified by the board of censors as forbidden to minors, Cecchi Gori insisted that I cut the most violent scenes as requested by the commission of revision. I didn't accept and no cuts were made." Nevertheless, *Go Gorilla Go* performed very well at the box office, grossing almost two billion lire, and relaunched Fabio Testi as one of Italy's most popular action heroes.

Notes

1. Interview with the author, 2002. Valerii's quotes are taken from the same interview.

2. Even Alberto Sordi, Italy's most popular comedian, jumped on the occasion, playing a hilarious would-be bodyguard in the episode "Il gorilla" of the omnibus *Che segno sei?* (1975).

3. Tommaso La Selva, *Tonino Valerii: mai temere il Leone* (Milan: Nocturno Libri), p. 100. According to Valerii, Dino Maiuri (who is credited as co-author

of the screenplay, and was often credited together with De Rita in a number of films of the period) did not take part in the writing process (interview with the author, 2008).

Hallucination Strip (*Roma drogata: la polizia non può intervenire*)

D: Lucio Marcaccini. *S:* Lucio Marcaccini; *SC:* Lucio Marcaccini, Vincenzo Mannino, José María Sánchez; *DOP:* Gino Santini (35mm, Eastmancolor, Technicolor); *M:* Albert Verrecchia, conducted by the author (Ed. R.C.A.); *Percussions:* Tony Esposito; *We've Got a Lord* (Evelyn Lenton) sung by Jacques Edouard Barbot; *CHOR:* Renato Greco; *E:* Giulio Berruti; *AE:* Mario Giacco; *2nd AE:* Patrizia Oppedisano; *PD, CO:* Luciano Vincenti; *AArtD:* Andrea Fantacci; *COA:* Silvana Pomanti; *C:* Edmondo Pisani, Enzo Tosi; *AC:* Bruno Pellegrini; *ADs:* Giorgio Mariuzzo, Diego Chialant; *MU:* Silvana Petri; *Hair:* Sergio Gennari; *SO:* Manlio Magara; *SP:* Franco Bellomo; *SS:* Clara Tamburini. *Cast:* Bud Cort (Massimo Monaldi), Marcel Bozzuffi (Commissioner De Stefani), Eva Czemerys (Rudy's mother), Annarita Grapputo (Cinzia Roldi), Settimio Segnatelli (Rudy), Maurizio Arena (Buscemi "The Sicilian"), Leopoldo Trieste (Killer), Guido Alberti (Chief of Police), Gianfilippo Carcano (Teacher), Ennio Balbo (Antique dealer), Umberto Raho (Giovanni, the waiter), Luigi Casellato (Patrizia's father), Mico Cundari (Roldi, Cinzia's father), Pupo De Luca (Commissioner's assistant), Tom Felleghy (Head physician), Francesco Ferracini (Cannavale), Anna Zinnemann (Cinzia's mother), Luca Bonicalzi (Dominic), Patrizia Gori (Alberta Ferri), Pino Luce, Walter Manfredi, Rossella Or (Manuscia), Graziella Scotese (Stefania). *Uncredited:* Bruno Alias (Party guest), Jacques Edouard "Sammy" Barbot (Singer), Rossana Canghiari (Party guest), Attilio Dottesio (Attorney), Lina Franchi (Nurse), Luciano Zanussi (The Sicilian's henchman). *PROD:* Diapason Cinematografica; *PM:* Silvio Siano; *PSu:* Nicola Venditti, Claudio Cuomo, Enzo Prosperini; *PSe:* Giuseppe Castagna, Roberta Revetria. *Country:* Italy. Filmed at Cinecittà studios (Rome) and on location in Rome. *Running time:* 95'; Visa no.: 67021 (09.03.1975); *Rating:* v.m.18; *Release date:* 12.18.1975; *Distribution:* Interfilm; *Domestic gross:* 376,816,160 lire. *Also known as: Hallucinating Trip* (Italian video title), *Darkness of the Brain, Flash* (International alternate titles). *Home video:* Hobby & Work (DVD, Italy). OST: CD GDM Music 4011.

To help a couple of friends leave Italy and move to the Far East, Massimo—a protesting student and occasionally a small drug dealer—and his rich girlfriend Cinzia steal a valuable tobacco box from Cinzia's father's collection. One night Massimo accidentally witnesses the moves of a powerful drug dealer, Buscemi "the Sicilian," who controls the heroin trafficking in Rome. Commissioner De Stefani notices Massimo, and finds out he and Cinzia are the responsible for the theft: he asks Massimo to testify against Buscemi, but the young man refuses. Massimo promises his upper-class friend Rudy to find a huge quantity of drugs for him for a party Rudy is giving: the Sicilian sells plenty of it to him, in exchange for the tobacco box. At the party, Massimo, Cinzia and Rudy all get stoned. Rudy has a very bad trip and jumps out a window. De Stefani investigates and finds out that Cinzia overdosed at Massimo's house. The police cover up the case because of the pressure from the victim's family. Determined to arrest Buscemi, whom he suspects has sold Massimo the drugs, De Stefani continues the investigations on his own, but he discovers that the Sicilian has been eliminated by his bosses. He realizes that Massimo is a target too because he knows too much, but arrives too late to save him: the Sicilian hired a killer to dispatch the young man, who is killed in the crowded, central Campo de' Fiori square, without anyone noticing—or caring.

Lucio Marcaccini's only film as a director is definitely a one-of-a-kind entry. Despite a title that makes it look like a violent crime-cop film (the Italian title reads: "Drugged Rome: The police Cannot Intervene"), this is actually a rather ambitious yet hopelessly didactic social drama about the spreading of drugs amidst Rome's youth, its perils and consequences, which recalls the similarly themed *Perchè si uccidono—La Merde* (1976, Mauro Macario). To prove his point, Marcaccini even includes a number of scenes depicting juvenile protests, such as when a high school assembly decides to occupy the building, or footage from a protest march where the protesters sing "Fascisti, borghesi, ancora pochi mesi!" ("Fascists, bourgeois, just a few more months"). The discourse on drugs, although simplistic, is notable for the director openly taking sides with the protesters against their upper class parents, who are depicted as selfish, obtuse and suffocating, and with such lines as "Can they live without anything?" "They have their dreams," referred to a young couple who hope of moving to India. The dialogue is often grating, such as when the protagonist's girlfriend (Annarita Grapputo) gives voice to her inner *cupio dissolvi* by begging him to crash together against a tree at full speed on their motorbike ("We are young, beautiful, we just made love to each other, we won't have such a happier moment for dying!").

Hallucination Strip likely took shape amidst Rome's intellectual *milieu*, as suggested by the presence among the cast of poetess Rossella Or and Fluxus artist Graziella Scotese (daughter of filmmaker Giuseppe Maria Scotese, who had helmed among others a documentary on psychedelic drugs *Acid-Delirio dei sensi*, 1967). Bud Cort, in his first film after a five-year acting hiatus following his big break with *Brewster McCloud* (1970, Robert Altman) and *Harold and Maude* (1971, Hal Ashby), looks lost among the Italian-speaking cast, and his acting affectations make him quite an unbelievable Roman high school student. The film's *piece de resistance* is a wearisome ten-minute psychedelic trip where the spoilt upper class kid Rudy (Settimio Segnatelli) realizes about his own Oedipal desires, dreaming of making love to his gorgeous mother (Eva Czemerys). The sequence also features women in snake tights (*Lair of the White Worm*–style), naked dancing girls whose bodies are painted in blue, yellow and red, a cannibalistic feast and a ludicrous bit where Rudy hallucinates that leaves and grass are growing on his body.

The half-baked crime subplot features a tough yet liberal Commissioner—quite a rare evidence in the genre: "Real drugs are what kills people, not weed cigarettes!" he blurts out in a scene—played by Marcel Bozzuffi, who's trying to collect evidence to arrest a slimy drug dealer (former '50s beau Maurizio Arena), and a demented killer (the great character actor and director Leopoldo Trieste) who talks with birds and hides a gun in a canary cage. Albert Verrecchia's score, which features the bands Cyan Three and Baba Yaga, percussionist Tony Esposito, vocalist Edda Dell'Orso and black French singer Jacques Edouard Barbot (who would later become a popular TV show host as Sammy Barbot), is quite impressive yet badly used.

Born in Rimini in 1929, Lucio Marcaccini—who had been Vittorio De Sica's assistant on *The Garden of the Finzi-Continis* (*Il giardino dei Finzi-Contini*, 1970), Nanni Loy's on *Detenuto in attesa di giudizio* (1971) and Brunello Rondi's on *Valeria dentro e fuori* (1973)—never made another film. In the following years he tried to set up co-productions with Canada, but to no avail. Marcaccini died in 1982.

How to Kill a Judge *(Perché si uccide un magistrato)*

D: Damiano Damiani. *S:* Damiano Damiani; *SC:* Damiano Damiani, Fulvio Gicca Palli, Enrico Ribulsi; *DOP:* Mario Vulpiani (35mm, Eastmancolor, Technospes); *M:* Riz Ortolani, conducted by the author (Es. Slalom / Rizzoli); *L'indifferenza* (Maggi) sung by Iva Zanicchi; *E:* Antonio Siciliano; *AE:* Lucia Melis; *PD:* Umberto Turco; *APD:* Ely Peyrot, Marcello Turco; *CO:* Gianfranco Carretti; *C:* Pasquale Rachini; *AC:* Maurizio Lucchini; *AD:* Mario Maffei; *MU:* Raoul Ranieri; *Hair:* Giuseppina Bovino; *SO:* Luigi Salvi; *Boom:* Benito Alchimede; *Mix:* Gianni D'Amico; *SP:* Giuseppe Botteghi; *KG:* Augusto Diamanti; *ChEl:* Ettore Trivelli; *SS:* Eleonora Molinari; *Medical consultant:* Dr. Salvatore Sinatra. *Cast:* Franco Nero (Giacomo Solaris), Françoise Fabian (Antonia Traini), Pier Luigi Aprà (Judge De Fornari), Giancarlo Badessi (Derrasi), Ennio Balbo (Investigating Judge), Luciano Catenacci (Lawyer Meloria), Eva Czemerys (Sibilla), Giorgio Cerioni (Dr. Valgardeni), Tano Cimarosa (Tano Barra, the parking attendant), Mico Cundari (Journalist), Enrico Di Marco Proietti (Bespectacled journalist), Claudio Gora (Actor playing the Judge in Solaris' film), Marco Guglielmi (Prosecutor Alberto Traini), Salvatore Moscardini (Toruzzo, Solaris' chauffeur), Claudio Nicastro (Party secretary), Renzo Palmer (Vincenzo Terrasini), Elio Zamuto (Ugo Selini), Gianni Zavota (Commissioner Zamagna), Michelangelo Di Benedetto, Giovanni Miceli, Sergio Valentini (Bellolampo in Solaris' film), Luigi Ursi, Elio Di Vincenzo (Vezzi, the old registrar), Gaetano Di Leo, Filippo Di Vincenzo, Alessandro Arlotta, Andrea Busalacchi, Vincenzo Norvese (Carmelo Bellolampo), Vincenzo Patti, Maurizio Di Liberto, Giovanni Lo Cascio (Giovannino). *Uncredited:* Damiano Damiani (Solaris' lawyer). *PROD:* Mario Cecchi Gori for Capital Film; *GM:* Luciano Luna; *PM:* Vincenzo Mazzucchi; *PSe:* Giandomenico Stellitano, Mario Della Torre; *ADM:* Mario Lupi; *CASH:* Marcello Tassi. *Country:* Italy. Filmed at Incir—De Paolis (Rome) and on location in Palermo. *Running time:* 110'; Visa no.: 65976 (01.29.1975); *Rating:* not rated; *Release date:* 02.05.1975; *Distribution:* Cineriz; *Domestic gross:* 1,273,018,910 lire. *Also known as: Warum musste Staatsanwalt Traini sterben?* (West Germany, 09.07.1977—105'), *Der Terror führt Regie* (West Germany—Home video), *¿Por qué se asesina a un magistrado?* (Spain). *Home video:* Medusa (DVD, Italy).

Palermo. Movie director Giacomo Solaris has just finished shooting a movie where he denounces a Magistrate's connivance with the Mafia. Even though he's not specifically mentioned in the film, prosecutor Alberto Traini knows he's the target of Solaris' work, yet he doesn't follow on his collaborators' suggestion to have the movie seized. On the contrary, he invites Solaris to his home, where Traini's wife Antonia attacks the filmmaker, believing he's responsible for the growing hate campaign against her husband. While Solaris is about to leave Palermo, Traini is murdered, just like in the film. Solaris, who's deeply upset by the event, stays in town to follow the investigations, barely tolerated by the head of the Flying Squad. A constructionist named Terrasini, a good man who's got connections with the Mafia, joins him. The situation in Palermo is tense, as Mafia families (one of whom is led by a politician, Selini) suspect each other of Traini's murder, and take advantage of the situation to settle the score: among the victims there's Terrasini. An orphan whom Terrasini protected, and who witnessed the murder, allows Solaris to unveil the truth: Traini's killing was commissioned by Antonia's lover, De Fornari, with the woman's complicity. Solaris has Selini exonerated, amid the disappointment of both journalists and cops.

As the renowned Italian critic Lino Micciché wrote in his 1975 review, Damiano Damiani's *How to Kill a Judge*—the director's fourth and last teaming with Franco Nero—is both a sequel and a (self-) critical rethinking of the director's *Confessions of a Police Captain,* up to the point that it turns the previous film's assumptions upside down.

As Damiani stated, the idea for *How to Kill a Judge* germinated a few years earlier: "the film was born out of the emotion I felt when I realized how sometimes the work of a mass communication author (because such is cinema) blends with reality or even predates it or gets involved with it. [...] Two months after *Confessions of a Police Captain* came out, a Magistrate was murdered."[1] Damiani refers to the murder of Pietro Scaglione, a notorious and much discussed Magistrate who was killed in Palermo, on May 5, 1971. It was the first illustrious Mafia murder of the 20th century. Even though it later turned out that the upright Scaglione was killed because of his investigations into the murders of trade unionists and on the strength of the Corleone "family," at first there were many rumors about his collusion with the Mafia. As Damiani pointed out, "My film had nothing to do with that case, yet I couldn't help feeling a certain anxiety before a fact that, even without having any relation to my work whatsoever, proved its thesis—if, of course, it was not a private murder case but had all the motivations that constituted the dramatic and ideologic fulcrum of my film. It was that 'if,' with all the ambiguity of its possible consequences, that suggested the idea for *How to Kill a Judge*."[2]

The film deals with ambiguity by depicting a similar scenario, and playing with viewers' expectations. When a shady prosecutor (whom he suspected to having connived with the Mafia in his film) is murdered, film director Giacomo Solaris (Franco Nero) immediately thinks it was a Mafia killing, and when the truth turns out to be much more prosaic—a crime of passion—he has to choose between revealing it (and exonerate a powerful Mafioso politician) or keep lying.

Most critics preferred to read the film as autobiographical, yet the metafilmic aspect is much more complex and contradictory. The scenes from Solaris' film that Traini (Marco Guglielmi) is shown watching feature Claudio Gora as the corrupt magistrate, and Traini is told that Solaris chose an actor that looked like him, while it was obviously the opposite: Gora played the same role in *Confessions of a Police Captain,* and Guglielmi somehow resembles him. Other scenes from the film-within-a-film show Gora being interrogated by the Antimafia commission or interrogating a suspect (theatrical and rather conceited-looking bits, with bullseye lighting and abstract, stylized set-pieces), a police car being blown up—a "surprise" effect that Traini (and the viewer) gleefully predicts ("I could have sworn they'd shot it in slow motion!")—and a surreal ending filmed with plentiful wide-angle shots that deform faces and perspectives. It's like the director is critically rethinking the stylistic devices and plot clichés of politically-committed films made thus far, but the point he is making is volatile to say the least.

The same contradiction invests Solaris' character. All in all, Damiani is being very clear in making Solaris a sincere yet not particularly gifted filmmaker, and most of all he's stressing that Solaris is not a stand-in for himself. He does not make the kind of films Damiani does, for one thing. Yet, at the same time Damiani is contradicting himself, not least with the very choice of re-using Claudio Gora in the film-within-a-film Solaris directed!

As the director stressed, the film displays a dilemma: "Is it possible not to be afraid of the truth because [as Antonio Gramsci said] truth is "always revolutionary"? The dilemma can also be summed up in a question: is there a difference between a man of culture and a politician? [....] In my opinion, the mistake many have made until now was to authorize such a dilemma [...]."[3] As co-scriptwriter Fulvio Gicca Palli underlined, the film's autobiographical tone, which depicted the director's psychological itinerary, "didn't work either as a mystery or as a political film."[4]

Even though *How to Kill a Judge* was a box office success, the intellectual confusion that pervades the ending disoriented critics. Tullio Kezich's negative review on *Panorama*, where the critic accused the film of being "an involuntary favor to the Mafia" resulted in a heated repartee between director and critic on the weekly magazine's pages.[5] Lino Micciché, in turn, ended his peremptory slating with a harsh remark: "What is left is only "consumption," which is—as this illuminating film confirms—the real "dominating ideology" of those "committed consumption" films which delude themselves (or delude to elude us) into fighting against Power."[6]

In a 2003 interview Damiani was very critical towards the film, admitting that he should have probably made different choices in terms of plot development and resolution: "Perhaps I should have shown immediately the lovers asking themselves "How can we get rid of him?" [...] and in the end I'd show the two lovers and culprits together, finally relieved, happy, untouchable."[7] A radical re-thinking that says a lot about Damiani's mixed feelings about the final result—a film which was born to exorcise the collision between reality and fiction and ended up uneasily replaying it.

Notes

1. Gian Luigi Rondi, *7 domande a 49 registi* (Turin: S.E.I., 1975), p. 67.
2. *Ibid.*
3. *Ibid.*
4. Pezzotta, *Regia Damiano Damiani*, p. 264.
5. *Panorama* #462, 2.27.1975; #467, 4/3/1975.
6. Micciché, *Cinema italiano degli anni '70*, p. 224.
7. Pezzotta, *Regia Damiano Damiani*, p. 92.

Kidnap Syndicate (*La città sconvolta: caccia spietata ai rapitori*)

D: Fernando di Leo. *S:* Galliano Juso; *SC:* Cesare Manzani, Fernando di Leo, Ernesto Gastaldi; *DOP:* Erico Menczer (35mm, Eastmancolor, Telecolor); *M:* Luis Enriquez Bacalov (ed. Gruppo Editoriale Leonardi); *E:* Sergio Montanari; *PD:* Francesco Cuppini; *APD:* Cristiano Tessari, Sandro Bellomia; *CO:* Maria Luisa Panaro; *ACO:* Mirella Novelli; *C:* Roberto Brega; *AC:* Francesco Gagliardini, Luigi Bernardini, Bernardo Valli; *AEs:* Roberto Gianandrea, Roberto Puglisi; *AD:* Angelo Vicari; *MU:* Cristina Rocca; *AMU:* Giovanna Manca; *Hair:* Gilda De Guilmi; *SO:* Goffredo Salvatori; *Boom:* Luigi Salvatori; *Mix:* Franco Bassi; *Foley artist:* Renato Marinelli; *SP:* Ermanno Consolazione; *STC:* Sergio Mioni; *MA:* Gilberto Galimberti; *Armorer:* Basilio Patrizi; *KG:* Maurizio Micalizzi; *ChEl:* Rodolfo Fibotto; *SS:* Marisa Agostini; *UP:* Matteo Spinola. *Cast:* Luc Merenda (Mario Colella), James Mason (Engineer Filippini), Irina Maleeva (Lina, Filippini's secretary), Marino Masé (Pardi), Daniele Dublino (Bonanni, the lawyer), Vittorio Caprioli (Commissioner Magrini), Valentina Cortese (Grazia Filippini), Marco Liofredi (Fabrizio Colella), Francesco Impeciati (Antonio Filippini), Alessio Juso (Boy), Enzo Pulcrano (Kidnapper "Labbrone"), Giulio Baraghini (Magrini's assistant), Renato Baldini (Antonio Policriti), Serena Bennato (Kidnapper's accomplice), Flora Carosello (Antonio Policriti's wife), Raoul Lo Vecchio (Pino Latrella "The Blond"), Renato Romano (Kidnapper), Giuseppe Colombini, Salvatore Billa (Pardi's man), Loris Bazzocchi (Kidnapper). *Uncredited:* Angelo Bergamaschi (Journalist), Lanfranco [Pietro] Ceccarelli (Bald hitman), Rolando De Santis (Cop), Cesare Di Vito (Journalist), Max Dorian (Barman), Tom Felleghy (Head of I.F.I.), Gilberto Galimberti (Van Driver), Sandro Scarchilli (Doorman at I.F.I.). *PROD:* Galliano Juso for Cinemaster; *PM:* Lanfranco [Pietro] Ceccarelli; *PSu:* Renato Fié; *PSe:* Maurizio Giorgi, Enzo Prosperini; *ADM:* Paolo Rampazzo; *CASH:* Salvatore Farese. *Country:* Italy. Filmed at Rizzoli Film (Rome) and on location in Rome and Milan. *Running time:* 110'; Visa no.: 67031 (08.27.1975); *Rating:* v.m.18; *Release date:* 08.27.1975; *Distribution:* Medusa; *Domestic gross:* 908,268,910 lire. *Also known as:* *Auge um Auge* (West Germany), *Colère noire* (France), *Dirty Deal* (France—Home video), *Running Guns* (West Germany—Home video). *Home video:* Raro (DVD—Italy).

Masked bandits, acting on behalf of unsuspectable Northern financiers, abduct Antonio Filippini, the son of a wealthy construction engineer, and his friend Fabrizio Colella, whose father is a humble mechanic, and who generously intervened in defense of his schoolmate. The kidnappers demand a ransom of ten billion lire for Antonio. Filippini resists, and tries to bargain with them by prolonging out the negotiations; to force the engineer to give up and pay the ransom, the criminals kill the poor Fabrizio. In the face of the police's absolute impotence, Colella sets out to avenge his son on his own. He detects and exterminates the kidnappers and takes possession of the ransom money, which he uses to exact revenge on those who ordered the killing. In the end, Colella locates the leaders of the organization and slaughters them all with a machine gun.

In a period where Italian cinema—popular and *auteurist* alike—produced a number of films on the subject of kidnapping, such as the gloomy *Snatch* (*La Orca*, 1976, Eriprando Visconti), Tonino Valerii's *Go Gorilla Go*, Giovanni Fago's *Kidnap*, Umberto Lenzi's *Syndicate Sadists* and the humorous *Come ti rapisco il pupo* (1976), Lucio De Caro's amusing adaptation of Donald Westlake's novel *Jimmy the Kid*, Fernando di Leo approached the same subgenre with mixed results. *Kidnap Syndicate* is far from the director's best work, a fact that's even suggested by the Italian title (translating as "The City Is Shaken: Ruthless Pursuit of the Kidnappers") which is verbose and lurid, far removed from the evocative power of the director's previous films. The story is credited to producer Galliano Juso, who had already financed di Leo's *Shoot First, Die Later*, while the script is signed by Ernesato Gastaldi, di Leo and Nicola Manzari. The director claimed: "The idea came from Juso, who told me how he wanted the film, and I wrote down the script. Kidnappings were a hot topic back then, so it was natural to make a film about them[...]. It was Galliano [Juso] who told me: "Let's do it this way." [...] In my small way, with Daunia Film, I was an independent, I really was. However, if Juso or someone else called me and then had to bring the story to [powerful distributor] Goffredo Lombardo[...], if the script hadn't that "edge" [...] Juso just couldn't make the film. [...] When you met a producer with your own film script, the producer took the phone and made eighteen calls, as many as the distributors who operated in Italy back then. If eight said yes and ten said no, the latter would win. They had the power of life and death over a film."[1] Gastaldi's version is quite different, however, and possibly more believable: "Despite being credited together with Cesare Manzani, I wrote the script by myself, as nearly always. Galliano Juso wanted to make a film about kidnappings, but I invented the whole story. I didn't work with di Leo, we just met one afternoon for a talk when the script was already finished. Fernando did make some observations about the script, most of them correct, and I adjusted the scenes which he thought were wrong. It's a nasty film about nasty times."[2]

Kidnap Syndicate's starting point introduced a classist variation to the subgenre: two children are kidnapped, the son of a wealthy engineer (James Mason) and that of a mechanic (Luc Merenda), and while the rich father does not want to pay the ten million lire ransom, his working-class counterpart would even sell his shirt to save his son. "It's easy for you to say: "I'm selling everything!": you don't have anything!" Mason blurts out in one scene. The engineer solicits the director's disgust, as if he was the film's real villain: he wears shades, always has a glass of whiskey in hand, and is obtusely resolute in treating his son's kidnapping as if it was just a commercial transaction. It's the engineer who indirectly causes the death of the other boy, who's killed by the kidnappers as an example. And it's to people like him that the Commissioner (Vittorio Caprioli)—the moral center of the film and the director's alter ego, as in *The Boss* and later in *Blood and Diamonds*—refers when he replies to his assistant, who invoked special laws against kidnappings: "And if in our beautiful Italy nobody went around carrying ten billion, as if they were peanuts, then there would be no kidnappings either!"

However, even though there are a number of barbed lines, the film as a whole is rather weak and overtly faithful to genre conventions—and this, for an innovator like di Leo, is not a small flaw. The first half recalls Kurosawa's *High and Low* (1963), as it focus on the parents' desperate wait and isolates the various characters in the luxurious interiors of Mason's villa, but it's let down by Valentina Cortese's hysterical overacting; the second part, which follows Merenda's revenge against the kidnappers, feels like a remake of *The Italian Connection*, minus the inspiration and power of its model: *Kidnap Syndicate* culminates in a rather unconvincing climax (Merenda gets to the heads of the organization) and a hastily shot showdown in a deserted amusement park, where the hero kills the kidnapper (Marino Masé) who murdered his child.

The critics lambasted the film: "All the worst defects of the worst Italian cinema can be found readily assembled in this minutely banal film, where Fernando di Leo proves once again he is not suited to the adventure film just as he wasn't to the erotic genre in the past,"[3] wrote Italian critic Claudio G. Fava, summarizing the biased attitude towards the poliziotteschi at that time. Another critic added: "It could have been a denunciation against the kidnapping racket as well as a society that's seemingly incapable to fight it efficiently. But the result is the umpteenth variation on the most banal adventure genre, with the aggravation—Western style—of the gunman who does justice on his own. [...] The audience is not too fussy and gets locked in the clever populist mechanism, eventually applauding the silent avenger's private massacre. An immoral and asocial film (the thread dedicated to the "silent majority" numbers a large amount of titles ever since *Straw Dogs*)."[4]

However, *Kidnap Syndicate* was a moderate box office success, with over 900 million lire grossed—actually about half as much as *Go Gorilla Go*, but still a profitable result.

Notes

1. Pulici, *Fernando di Leo*, p. 328.
2. E-mail interview, January 2012.
3. Claudio G. Fava, *Corriere Mercantile*, 9.12.1975.
4. Sandro Casazza, *La Stampa*, 9.5.1975.

Killer Cop (La polizia ha le mani legate)

D: Luciano Ercoli. *S:* Mario Bregni; *SC:* Gianfranco Galligarich; *DOP:* Marcello Gatti (35mm, Technicolor, Techniscope); *M:* Stelvio Cipriani (ed. Bixio); *E:* Angelo Curi; *AE:* Maria Pia Appetito; *2nd AE:* Bruno Sgueglia; *PD:* Giorgio Luppi; *APD:* Claudio Riccardi; *CO:* Carlo Gentili; *C:* Otello Spila; *AC:* Ivo Spila, Roberto Locci; *2nd AC:* Emilio Bestetti; *AD:* Giorgio Maulini; *2nd AD:* Mario Garriba; *MU:* Franco Corcione; *Hair:* Romana Piolanti; *W:* Valeria Mariani; *SO:* Amedeo Casati; *Mix:* Franco Bassi; *SOE:* Italo Cameracanna; *SP:* Angelo Pennoni; *ChEl:* Aldo Carocci; *KG:* Alberto Anzellotti; *SS:* Antonietta Gianesin. *Cast:* Claudio Cassinelli (Commissioner Matteo Rolandi), Arthur Kennedy (Attorney Armando Di Federico "Mentina"), Franco Fabrizi (Agent Luigi Balsamo), Sara Sperati (Papaya Girotti), Bruno Zanin (Franco Ludovisi), Francesco D'Adda (Attorney Bondi), Paolo Poiret (Rocco Mariani), Valeria D'Obici (Falena), Giuliana Rivera (Giuliana, Rolandi's optician friend), Franco Moraldi (De Marchi, Chief of Police), Adelio [Elio] Jotta (Minister), Enzo Fisichella (Colonel Francalange), Walter Valdi (Minister's secretary), Giovanni Cianfriglia (Hitman), Fausto Tommei (Dr. Regazzoni, the optician), Giuseppina Pentimalli, Livia Cerini (Maid in Di Federico's house), Guido Spadea (Di Federico's assistant), Sergio Tardioli (Francalange's man), Giancarlo Busi (Concierge), Ugo Bologna (Mancuso, policeman), Vittorio Pinelli (Borelli). *Uncredited:* Carlo Gentili (Man in the mirror); Annibale Papetti (Bernardi), Mimmo Raffa. *PROD:* Alberto Pugliese and Luciano Ercoli for P.A.C.—Produzioni Atlas consorziate (Milan); *GM:* Antonio Negri; *PM:* Alessandro Calosci; *PSu:* Domenico Di Parigi; *PSe:* Giuseppe Gerola; *ADMs:* Nestore Baratella, Simonetta Pierannunzi. *Country:* Italy. Filmed on location in Milan. *Running time:* 95'; Visa no.: 66264 (03.27.1975); *Rating:* not rated; *Release date:* 03.27.1975; *Distribution:* P.A.C.; *Domestic gross:* 854,798, 250 lire. *Also known as: Les dossiers rouges de la mondaine* (Paris, 09.26.1979—95'), *Boites à fillettes* (France), *La police a les mains liées* (France—Home video). *Home video:* Cecchi Gori (DVD, Italy, 92'58"). OST: CD Chris Soundtrack Corner CSC002.

A bomb explodes in the lobby of a hotel in Milan, causing many deaths and injuries. Commissioner Matteo Rolandi, who was watching a drug dealer inside the hotel, is one of the witnesses. A few hours later, his colleague and friend Balsamo comes across the man who planted the bomb, the young Franco Ludovisi, but is unable to arrest him. The next day, a mysterious killer eliminates the unfortunate policeman. While an honest magistrate, General Attorney Di Federico, conducts the official investigation, Rolandi attempts to track down the perpetrators and instigators of the massacre and Balsamo's assassination on his own. However, each time he discovers consistent evidence, the mysterious organization precedes him, by dispatching those who know too much. That's the case with Ludovisi's accomplices, Balsamo's murderer, Ludovisi himself and finally a girl, Papaya, who's allegedly Rolandi's confidante but actually an affiliate to the organi-

zation, that has a fifth column in Milan's police headquarters. Eventually Di Federico resigns, while Rolandi stubbornly continues his investigation, determined to do justice by himself.

The climate of disillusion, distrust and even fear that characterized the public opinion during the early 1970s is reflected in many poliziotteschi. The social structure appeared as if it was disintegrating, and there was a widespread, growing anger for the way authorities used the weapons of disinformation and side-tracking so as to hide what was really going on. As a result, a number of crime films dealt with the dynamics of paranoia and depicted conspiracy plots that involved the institutions. In *Execution Squad* the solution to the mystery could be found within the exclusive "Circolo Fidelitas," whose walls concealed the subversive plots of elderly magistrates, while in *The Great Kidnapping* the conspiracy involved the former Chief of Police played by Lee J. Cobb (who nonetheless was portrayed as a nostalgic old man with the fixed idea of "curing" the country); Sergio Martino's *The Violent Professional* offered yet another puppeteer above suspicion, played by the umpteenth American has-been, Richard Conte.

In 1973–74 the fascist bombings reached a peak. As historian Camillo Arcuri wrote, "[those were] all blood-dripping pretexts to disorient, provoke chaos and "re-establish order," thus actuating that one subversive design that germinated in 1969 and was never abandoned; on the contrary, it was [...] updated, like a mutating virus."[1] However, it all had a boomerang effect. To historian Guido Crainz, "what at the time looked like the peak of a subversive process, actually represented the visible announcement of its epilogue: this is perhaps the key to read the almost desperate succession of neo-fascist killings, from the one in Brescia in May 1974 to the bombing of the "Italicus" train in August of that year."[2] The official cover-ups on behalf of the Institutions started to fall down, and the existence of paramilitary fascist camps became of public dominion; in the country's most popular newspaper, "Il Corriere della Sera," Pier Paolo Pasolini wrote a desperate, angry tirade. "I know the names of those responsible for the slaughter.... I know the names of the powerful group.... I know the names of those who, between one mass and the next, made provision and guaranteed political protection... . I know the names of the important and serious figures who are behind the ridiculous figures.... I know the names of the important and serious figures behind the tragic kids.... I know all these names and all the acts (the slaughters, the attacks on institutions) they have been guilty of ... I know. But I don't have the proof. I don't even have clues."[3]

Scriptwriters and filmmakers didn't have a clue either, but this certainly did not stop them. The heavy, suffocating atmosphere that someone compared to that of Chile before the advent of general Pinochet, reached and impregnated genre cinema in general, and crime films in particular. The "strategy of tension" became one of the most useful accessories in poliziotteschi: it was a much welcome ingredient to support the audience's thirst for social complaint. The sign "any reference to individuals or actual events is purely coincidental" became an obligatory occurrence in the opening credits. Plots combined references to real-life events, rumors and hypotheses with an enthusiastic, mean-spirited cynicism.

One such example is Luciano Ercoli's *Killer Cop*. Ercoli, a director/producer who had already tried his hand at *gialli* (*Forbidden Photos of a Lady Above Suspicion, Death Walks in High Heels, Death Walks at Midnight*) and also directed a "*giallo*" / crime / adventure hybrid, *The Magnificent Dare Devil* (*Troppo rischio per un uomo solo*, 1973), starring Giuliano Gemma as a racing pilot framed for murder. With *Killer Cop*, Ercoli dives headlong into the poliziotteschi universe, and not just fills the film with references to actuality, but goes one step further. If the opening bomb attack in the hotel takes inspiration from the events at Piazza Fontana, the images of the funerals that can be seen at one point on television are actually footage from the very funerals of Piazza Fontana's victims.

Gianfranco Calligarich's script soon takes a turn towards conspiracy paranoia, as the perpetrators (including a short-sighted young man played by *Amarcord*'s Bruno Zanin) are revealed to be manipulated by powerful members of the *status quo*. The revelation that the bomb detonated by accident, as it was destined to a high tension trestle, is yet another patent reference to actual events: renowned book publisher and left-wing activist Giangiacomo Feltrinelli was found dead in 1972, the victim of a bomb explosion near a trestle: according to the official report he succumbed to his own exploding device while he was preparing an attack, yet the events surrounding Feltrinelli's death were never made fully clear.

Killer Cop underlines the basic premise for paranoia films: the truth is impossible to decipher, and the puppeteers can only be represented in an allusive manner, with their faces deformed by wide-angle shots or engulfed in darkness, thus virtually unrecognizable. That's perhaps the only way a simple genre film like *Killer Cop* can cope with the pure, simple and terrible reality of the period. The only way out is to admit the ultimate ignorance of the truth everyone is striving for. Just like Pasolini did, the film itself seems to imply: you know, we know, they know ... but we don't have the proof, we don't have any clue. That's where the poliziotteschi stops, to display the patent dichotomy between interiors and exteriors, above and below, shadow and light. That is to say, the streets swarming with life (and death) on one side, and the Palaces of Power on the other.

That said, Ercoli's film safely leans on the poliziotteschi dynamics, underlined by Stelvio Cipriani's score,[4] with a few notable characterizations. As agent Balsamo, the nice womanizer cop, clumsy and with a tendency to make up excuses, Franco Fabrizi has for once a positive role, somehow reminiscent of Kurosawa's *Stray Dog* (*Nora inu*, 1949) when Balsamo is robbed of his own gun by the man he's trailing; his character is perhaps dispatched too soon in the film. And although the Italian title itself, *La polizia ha le mani legate* ("The Police Have Their Hands Tied") reprises one of the genre's *leitmotifs*—the inability of police officials to do their duty because of the procedural obstacles imposed by the law—it's mildly surprising that the film's hero, played by Claudio Cassinelli, is actually a rather offbeat figure. Commissioner Matteo Rolandi reads *Moby Dick* and looks agreeably unconventional (yet he turns into a smart hound and eventually an avenger). He drives a second hand, battered Mercedes car, much to his colleagues' disbelief that he can afford such a status symbol with just his meager pay. "Why are you a cop?" his informant and part-time lover (Sara Sperati) asks him: "Why shouldn't I? Better a cop than a thief!" comes the disenchanted answer.

Notes

1. Camillo Arcuri, *Colpo di Stato* (Milan: RCS, 2004), p. 120.
2. Guido Crainz, *Il paese mancato: Dal miracolo economico agli anni ottanta* (Rome: Donzelli, 2003), p. 482.
3. Pier Paolo Pasolini, "Cos'è questo golpe? Io so," *Il Corriere della Sera*, 11.14.1974.
4. Not unsurprisingly, Cipriani's score includes cues from the composer's earlier soundtracks, namely *Execution Squad* and *The Great Kidnapping.*

The Left Hand of the Law (La polizia interviene: ordine di uccidere!)

D: Giuseppe Rosati. *S* and *SC:* Giuseppe Rosati, Giuseppe Pulieri; *DOP:* Riccardo Pallottini (35mm, Eastmancolor, Technospes); *M:* Paolo Vasile, conducted by Alessandro Blonksteiner (Ed. C.A.M.); *E:* Mario Morra; *PD:* Giorgio Postiglione; *CO:* Massimo Bolongaro; *C:* Idelmo Simonelli; *AC:* Daniele Nannuzzi, Enzo Tosi; *AE:* Adelchi Marinangeli; *2nd AE:* Roberto Sterbini; *AD:* Giuseppe Pulieri; *MU:* Giuseppe Ferranti; *Hair:* Corrado Cristofori; *SO:* Pietro Spadoni; *Boom:* Angelo Spadoni; *Mix:* Alberto Bartolomei; *SP:* Mimmo [Domenico] Cattarinich; *SS:* Maria Luisa Rosen. *Cast:* Leonard Mann [Leonardo Manzella] (Captain Mario Murri), James Mason (Senator Marco Leandri), Antonella Murgia (Laura, Murri's girlfriend), Fausto Tozzi (Marshal Giulio Costello), Ennio Balbo (Lombardi), Franco Interlenghi (Brigadeer Colombo), Raffaele Curi (Raffaele Bedanone, the seminarist), Janet Agren (Gloria), Stephen Boyd (Lanza), Enrico Maria Salerno (Minister of the Interior), Peppino Di Capri (Singer), Gianni Elsner (Agent Martini), Franco Ressel (Lombardi's lawyer), Andrea Scotti (Agent De Filippis), Artemio Antonini (Vitali), Mimmo Poli (Restaurant owner), Enrico Chiappafreddo (Thug outside restaurant), Goffredo Unger ("Marshall Celestini," 1st kidnapper posing as police official). *Uncredited:* Fortunato Arena (Marshall Giordani), Salvatore Billa (Murri's driver), Paul Costello, Tom Felleghy (Surgeon), Romano Milani, Sergio Testori (1st thug in restaurant), Pietro Torrisi (Cop with machine gun), Rinaldo Zamperla (2nd Kidnapper posing as police official). *PROD:* Laser Film; *PM:* Maurizio Pastrovich; *PSu:* Claudio Cuomo; *CASH:* Pier Luigi Tarabusi. *Country:* Italy. Filmed at Incir–De Paolis (Rome) and on location in Rome. *Running time:* 100'; Visa no.: 67063 (09.02.1975); *Rating:* not rated; *Release date:* 09.04.1975; *Distribution:* Gold Film; *Domestic gross:* 1,183,443,280 lire. *Also known as: Die linke Hand des Gesetzes* (West Germany), *Kanunun yumrugu* (Turkey), *Lain oikea käsi* (Finland), *Tireur d'élite* (France), *Enantia sti via* (Greece — video title). *Home video:* CDI (DVD, Italy). OST: LP CAM AMP 156.

Armed bandits kidnap an industrialist, Lombardi, and kill two cops who were chasing them. Convinced that both occurrences, the latest in a long string of similar occurrences, have a political motivation — nurturing the popular irritation and encouraging the advent of an fascist regime — police Captain Mario Murri investigates. He suspects that the masterminds behind the subversive plot are the financier Leandri and Senator Lanza, and is convinced that he's right when someone tries to get rid of him by fixing a bomb in his car. Lombardi is released but he refuses to describe his kidnappers. Lanza suggests to Leandri to promote Murri so that he's moved away from Rome. The embittered Murri resigns, but the Minister of the Interior persuades him to get back to his investigation: Lanza then organizes an attack against Murri, in which his girlfriend Laura is shot dead. Leaving all scruples of legality behind, Murri leaps into action: he kills Lanza and exterminates all the members of the gang, then he forces Leandri to talk. A grim surprise awaits him: among the affiliates of the terrorist organization there is also his friend and confidant, Marshal Costello. In a dramatic confrontation, Murri once again risks his life, but is saved at the very last minute by a colleague.

As with many 1970s Italian urban actioners, Giuseppe Rosati's *The Left Hand of the Law* deals with the perceived danger of a fascist reactionary resurgence. The verbose script, by Giuseppe Pulieri and the director, features a subversive plot that involves a homosexual senator (James Mason), his wealthy lover (Stephen Boyd), members of the Church and a cop (Fausto Tozzi) who's nostalgic of his own past as a Blackshirt.

As produced by Turi Vasile's Laser Film — one of the most active companies within the genre — Rosati's film introduces yet another short-lived star of the poliziotteschi: Leonard Mann. Born in Albion, New York, in 1947 as Leonardo Manzella, the Italian-American actor became a well-known Spaghetti Western star in the wake of Ferdinando Baldi's *Forgotten Pistolero* (*Il pistolero dell'Ave Maria*, 1969), Enzo Barboni's *Ciakmull* (*Ciakmull — L'uomo della vendetta*, 1970) and Pasquale Squitieri's *Vengeance Trail* (*La vendetta è un piatto che si serve freddo*, 1971). After such films as diverse as the period comedy *Primo Tango a Roma* (1973, Enzo Gicca Palli), the erotic drama *Il corpo* (1974, Luigi Scattini) and Stelvio Massi's bizarre rendition of the Gospel in the Roman suburbs (*Macrò — Giuda uccide il venerdì*), Mann found a renewed popularity as Captain Murri, the umpteenth variation of the tough incorruptible cop — a man who "is the only one that's still got a pair of balls THIS big in a world of castrated guys," as one character picturesquely puts it.

Rosati gives his hero a cool demeanor from the very opening scene at the shooting range (itself a sort of cliché in poliziotteschi). Murri sits alone, apart from the others, watching his companions shoot at targets; he wears mirrored Ray Ban shades and is fingering a rosary: the latter detail is yet another hint at Spaghetti Westerns, who often display heroes with religious nicknames or bizarre — at times even mocking — references to religion. Murri, however, is a rationalist. "First of all you have to learn to shoot well, then to think even better," he explains to his colleagues. "However, better a bad trial than a good funeral," he sums up, when it comes to decide whether to shoot first or not; "When you shoot, do it to strike, don't waste any bullet." He's also considerably less asocial than the standard poliziotteschi tough cop: he forms a strong bond with his subordinates, who would do anything for him, legal or not (such as stealing a bag full of documents from a suspect's car, for instance).

The poliziotteschi's rugged protagonists are monogamous by nature, yet Murri is some sort of exception. He enjoys clandestine sex meetings with his upper class bitchy informer (the gorgeous Janet Agren) but when he needs comfort he runs to his protective, maternal girlfriend Antonella Murgia (he even has a Freudian bit of dialogue, when before phoning her he tells Agren "I'm calling my mom"). In a sense, Rosati's film is emblematic of the way genre cinema often reduced female characters to the typical duality mother/prostitute: those who sleep with the hero for a maternal, protective instinct, and those who do it for their own advantage. It also retains a punishing attitude towards the hero: the *ménage-à-trois* ends bitterly, though, as Murgia's character is gunned down in his place in the obligatory slow motion shot, leaving Murri embittered with grief and thirsty for revenge—which he carries out regardless of innocents, as in one of the climactic scenes he breaks into the criminals' hideout armed with a machine gun and dispatching everyone in sight, including a (presumably innocent) prostitute who was in bed with one of the thugs, while flashes of his girlfriend's killing pass before of his eyes.

As co-scripter Giuseppe Pulieri recalls, the film was produced with an eye to the U.S. market, thus the presence of Mason and Boyd. "The contract stated that the film had to be shot in English. But with those Italian assholes [Pulieri refers to the rest of the Italian-speaking cast, Author's Note] it just couldn't be done.... So I had a fantastic idea. We dubbed the footage. We shot during the morning, dubbed the footage at night, and the next day [Maurice Red Silverstein, the American distributor] saw the rushes in perfect English. I don't know how much producer Turi Vasile had to pay for that, but it was lots of fun."[1]

An additional element of amusement for viewers, however, is undoubtedly the (not-so) occult advertising that, as so often with poliziotteschi, pops up here and there. This time, besides the usual J&B plugs, a whole scene is dedicated to displaying the virtues of the advertised product: Murri and his fiancèe are dining in a cozy little restaurant whose walls are littered with liquor posters, and the owner offers the Commissioner a Fernet Branca "just as you like it, strong and velvety ... this even makes the dead rise." He gladly accepts, while she opts for a coffee (Hag). Another weird detail—at least for Italian viewers—is the presence of Peppino Di Capri, a popular 1960s singer-songwriter, who has a throwaway cameo as a piano-bar crooner, singing a couple of bad songs in bad English.

After *The Left Hand of the Law* Pulieri wrote another script that ended up shelved. "It was called *Ministero interni urgente: niente prigionieri* ["Urgent from the Ministry of the Interior: Take No Prisoners"], teletype-style. It predated the Moro kidnapping. [...] It was a love story between the daughter of a politician and a Commissioner, played by Leonard Mann, who in the last scene, after a night of sex with the girl, leaves with cool music accompanying him, you know, "glad to have done his duty," after a neverending streak of killings ... whoever opened his mouth, he or his agents would shoot it closed again! [....] They told me it incited social hatred."[2]

Pulieri and Rosati's next project was another adventure of Commissioner Murri, *Fear in the City* (1976).

Notes

1. Grattarola, *È arrivato il risolutore*, p. 23. However, judging by lip movements a number of scenes were definitely shot in English.
2. *Ibid.*, p. 21–22.

Loaded Guns (Colpo in canna)

D: Fernando di Leo. *S* and *SC:* Fernando di Leo; *DOP:* Roberto Gerardi (35mm, Eastmancolor, Telecolor); *M:* Luis Enriquez Bacalov (ed. Nazionalmusic); *E:* Amedeo Giomini; *PD:* Francesco Cuppini; *CO:* Gaia Romanini; Assistant *CO:* Elisabetta Lo Cascio; *C:* Roberto Forges Davanzati; *AC:* Maurizio La Monica; *AE:* Tommaso Gramigna; *AD:* Franco Lo Cascio; *MU:* Antonio Mura; *Hair:* Maria Teresa Corridoni; *SO:* Alberto Salvatori; *STC:* Sergio Mioni; *MA:* Gilberto Galimberti; *SS:* Renata Franceschi; *UP:* Tonino Pinto. *Cast:* Ursula Andress (Nora Green), Woody Strode (Silvera), Marc Porel (Manuel), Isabella Biagini (Rosy), Lino Banfi (Commissioner Calogero / Taxi driver), Aldo Giuffré (Calò), Maurizio Arena (Father Best, the false priest), Rosario Borelli (Silvera's man), Carla Brait (Carmen), Renato Baldini (Alì, Drug dealer), Raoul Lo Vecchio (Blindman), Sergio Ammirata (Vice commissioner Ammirata), Loris Bazzocchi (Nora's henchman), Jimmy Il Fenomeno [Luigi Origene Soffrano] (Tano), Roberto Dell'Acqua (Zanzara), Gino Milli (Don Calò's henchman), Enzo Spitaleri (police agent with headphones), Domenico Maggio (Silvera's henchman), Salvatore Billa (Silvera's henchman), Pietro Ceccarelli (Silvera's henchman), Franco Beltramme (Silvera's henchman), Omero Capanna (Silvera's henchman), Roberto Blasi, Armando Bottin, Brunello Chiodetti, Franco Moruzzi, Sandro Scotti, Carla Mancini, Franco Pasquetto, Eros Palucci, Lorenzo Piani, Ettore Geri (Hotel porter), Sergio Testori (Nora's henchman). *Uncredited:* Artemio Antonini (Gang member), Rossana Canghiari, Augusto Funari (Henchman), Gilberto Galimberti (Silvera's bodyguard), Augusto Funari, Emilio Messina (Vagliaquinto, police car driver), Roberto Messina (Don Calò's henchman), Nello Pazzafini (Don Calò's henchman), Osiride Pevarello (Silvera's henchman), Renzo Pevarello (Nicola, Silvera's man), Romano Puppo (Alì's man in the tavern), Sandro Scarchilli (Park sweeper), Franco Ukmar (Antonio, Silvera's man). *PROD:* Cineproduzioni Daunia 70; *GM:* Armando Novelli; *PM:* Francesco Vitulano; *PSu:* Renato Fié. *Country:* Italy. Filmed at Dear Studios (Rome) and on location in Naples. *Running time:* 100'; Visa no.: 65731 (12.18.1974); *Rating:* v.m.18; *Release date:* 01.18.1975; *Distribution:* Alpherat; *Domestic gross:* 699,455,430 lire. *Also known as: Ursula l'antigang* (Paris, 01.19.1977—90'), *Les aventures d'une air-hôtesse (France—alternate), Ich polier Dir Deine Glatze, Asphalt Katze* (West Germany), *La espía se desnuda* (Spain), *Salatehtävä Napolissa* (Finland). *Home video:* Raro (DVD, Italy).

Naples. Hostess Nora Green pays a visit to mob boss Silvera and gives him a letter from a mysterious person wanted by the police and known in the underworld as the American. The missive is a death sentence for Silvera who, suspecting the complicity of the messenger, has her beaten up. Nora is tailed by Silvera's antagonist Calò as well as by Commissioner Calogero. She eventually meets a young circus acrobat named Manuel, who gives her shelter and protection. What no one knows, though, is that Nora herself is the leader of an all-female gang: she invented the elusive American, and with the help of her girls she unleashes a deadly struggle between the bands of Calò and Silvera. In the end Nora is the winner on all fronts: she obtains a huge consignment of drugs and a large purchasing sum, destroys the rival gangs and humiliates the police.

After his bleakest film to date, *Shoot First, Die Later*, Fernando di Leo moved on to quite a different territory. *Loaded Guns* was an attempt at blending the crime genre (not exactly poliziotteschi, since the similarities with it are few and far between, but rather an adventure yarn set in the underworld) and comedy, and germinated from the conviction that "farce is the funnel where sooner or later all genres converge,"[1] something that was well in evidence with the decline of Spaghetti Western after the commercial peak of the *Trinity* films.

Loaded Guns—"an amusement in two parts," as the opening titles state—offers a drastically different atmosphere from the earlier films, starting with the setting: the sunny, hot and populated city of Naples, full of voices, music and colors whereas

Milan (and even Palermo in *The Boss*) provided a nocturnal, cold and detached look. The director pokes fun at his own films: a character is nicknamed "The American" as was Lionel Stander in *Caliber 9*; Woody Strode shows up as a ferocious gangster; and the story itself, with the central character unleashing a war between two factions, looks like the umpteenth variation on the rustproof plot mechanism of *A Fistful of Dollars*.

Instead of going for parody, though, di Leo dissects a serious plot about a hostess who becomes involved in a gang war, inserting unrelated, conflicting elements. For instance, the character of the tough Commissioner is replaced by a caricature, played by comedian Lino Banfi, while epic confrontations between gangs turn into grotesque fistfights *Trinity*-style. Di Leo even casts a familiar face in comic films, Jimmy Il Fenomeno (real name Luigi Origene Soffrano, a slightly retarded non-actor whose cross-eyed look and demented laugh provided the source for many gags in unpretentious sex comedies).

However, *Loaded Guns*' real innovation is its central character, a heroine who behaves like a man in all respects. Di Leo's is a gynocentric film, dominated as it is by Ursula Andress' totemic body. She beats and gets beaten, kicks and runs, cheats and deceives. And last but not least, she goes to bed with whoever she likes. Originally, di Leo had written the character as a bisexual woman: the idea — which once again showed the director's attention towards unconventional female characters — was later dropped as di Leo felt it was too risky for the audience. "People didn't even have the term "bisexual" in their vocabulary at that time. […] No one knew its meaning. That's what I wanted to offer: a woman who not only slept with whoever she wanted, but who also had a female lover with whom to "recover" lost time. I changed my mind, because it would have become a different genre."[2]

That said, Dora Green, who uses her body as a weapon, turning the sex-centered male mentality to her advantage, predates the two feminist students in the director's controversial *To Be Twenty* (*Avere vent'anni*, 1978). Di Leo pokes fun at *film noir*'s machismo: all male characters in the film are either studs with plenty of muscles and little brain (what counts, as Dora and her girlfriends often repeat, is that they are good at lovemaking) or semi-retarded clowns. And all of them lose their wits whenever they see a nice pair of legs. All the worse for them.

Moreover, *Loaded Guns* is a showcase for 39-year-old Ursula Andress, who landed in Italy to make the best out of her waning popularity and eventually became a sex movie icon thanks to films like *The Secrets of a Sensuous Nurse / Nurse Anna* (*L'infermiera*, 1975). Di Leo treats his leading lady like a vamp: he has Andress wear a parade of showy costumes, complete with sequins and slits that allow her to show her beautiful legs, and makes her look ten years younger thanks to Roberto Gerardi's *flou* lighting. The Swiss actress, on the other hand, gives herself to the camera's eye with generosity, offering her statuesque mature body in a number of nude scenes.

Despite its qualities, however, *Loaded Guns* is a failed experiment. The main problem with the film is that the "amusement" is only di Leo's: most gags simply are not funny, and the plot is confused and chaotic rather than sparkling (as Luis Bacalov's lively score would make us believe). The film's *piece de resistance*, an overlong fight sequence in an amusement park which culminates in a duel between Woody Strode and Aldo Giuffré that pays homage to (or rather mocks) Sergio Leone's films, cannot compete with any Bud Spencer / Terence Hill choreographed fistfight. The film's most interesting traits are the sudden, unexpected brutalities: the combination of black humor and extreme violence would be one of the main assets of di Leo's script for Ruggero Deodato's *Live Like a Cop, Die Like a Man* (*Uomini si nasce poliziotti si muore*, 1976).

Notes

1. Davide Pulici, "Terzo movimento: il tempo del gioco," in Aa. Vv., "Calibro 9. Il cinema di Fernando di Leo." *Nocturno Dossier* #14 (September 2003), p. 36.
2. *Ibid.*

Manhunt in the City, a.k.a. *The Manhunt (L'uomo della strada fa giustizia)*

D: Umberto Lenzi. *S* and *SC:* Dardano Sacchetti, Umberto Lenzi; *DOP:* Memmo [Guglielmo] Mancori (35mm, Eastmancolor, L.V.-Luciano Vittori); *M:* Bruno Nicolai, conducted by the author (Ed. C.A.M.); *E:* Eugenio Alabiso; *PD:* Giorgio Bertolini; *CO:* Silvio Laurenzi; *C:* Mario Sbrenna; *AC:* Enzo Tosi; *AE:* Amedeo Moriani; *AD:* Alessandro Metz; *MU:* Raul Ranieri; *Hair:* Jolanda Angelucci; *SO:* Fernando Pescetelli; *Mix:* Bruno Moreal; *SOE:* Aldo Ciorba, Sergio Basile; *Synchronization:* Sonia De Dominicis; *SE:* Cataldo Galliano; *G:* Onofrio Coppola; *CON:* Marisa Calia; *Original DIA editor:* Frank von Kuegelgen. *Cast:* Henry Silva (Davide Vannucchi), Luciana Paluzzi (Vera Vannucchi), Silvano Tranquilli (Paolo Giordani), Claudio Gora (Attorney Ludovico Mieli), Susanna Melandri (Clara Vannucchi), Raymond Pellegrin (Commissioner Bertone), Alberto Tarallo (Liala, the Transvestite), Claudio Nicastro (Salvatore Mannino, the private eye), Luciano Catenacci (Lt. Pascucci), Claudio Sforzini (Sforzini, the journalist), Corrado Solari (Salesman), Rosario Borelli (Serafino Strombelli), Franco Balducci (Alberto Pirazzini), Nando [Ferdinando] Poggi, Gilberto Galimberti, Domenico Raccosta (Snatcher at market), Bruno Di Luia (Claudio Mazzesi). *Uncredited:* Gianni Bortolotti (Jeweler), Salvatore Billa (Franco Strombillo), Ugo Bologna (policeman), Nestore Cavaricci (policeman), Domenico Cianfriglia (Gianni, the purse snatcher who had his hands broken), Giovanni Di Benedetto (Right-winged journalist), Raniero Dorascenzi (policeman), Vittorio Joderi (Man who stops the beating at market), Rosemarie Lindt (Stripper), Fulvio Mingozzi (Franchi, policeman), Corrado Olmi, Annibale Papetti (Mieli's friend), Nello Pazzafini (Grimetti, arms dealer), Anna Maria Perego (Vannucchi's housemaid), Riccardo Petrazzi (Elio Di Pietra), Piergiorgio Plebani (Croupier), Domenico Ravenna (Priest at the hospital), Dardano Sacchetti (Journalist). *PROD:* Enzo Peri for Aquila Cinematografica (Rome); *PM:* Claudio Cuomo; *UM:* Elio Saroli, Claudio Trovò; *ADMs:* Giorgio Tregnaghi, Antonio Gabbanini; *PSeA:* Massimo Marciani. *Country:* Italy. Filmed at Elios Film (Rome) and on location in Milan. *Running time:* 100'; Visa no.: 66483 (05.02.1975); *Rating:* v.m.18 *Release date:* 05.08.1975; *Distribution:* Titanus; *Domestic gross:* 511,514,210 lire. *Also known as: Un flic hors la loi* (France). *Home video:* Medusa (DVD, Italy). OST: CD Digitmovies CDDM100.

Clara, the little daughter of the engineer Vannucchi, is killed during a robbery at a jewelry store. The father, exasperated by the inefficiency and sluggishness of the police, decides to avenge her by himself, relying on the last words of the dying child: "I saw the scorpion." Vannucchi is contacted by Mieli, a lawyer who founded a "Movement of civic self-defense"— that is, a fascist vigilante organization — who offers to help him find the murderers. Despite the dis-

approval of both his divorced wife Vera and Commissioner Bertone, Vannucchi investigates on his own: he gets in touch with a seedy private eye named Mannino, who is murdered. Through a transvestite named Liana, the engineer tracks down a gang of criminals whose chief wears a bracelet with a golden scorpion. But he gets into trouble: the thugs attack his house and try to kill him. Vannucchi survives, but his wife is badly beaten: he then decides to join Mieli's vigilante squad. In return, Mieli reveals to him the whereabouts of the criminals' hideout. Armed with a double-barreled shotgun, the engineer kills the whole gang. What he doesn't know, though, is that these were not his daughter's killers, who had been dispatched earlier in a shoot-out with the police: their leader had a scorpion tattoo on his arm. Bertone lets Vannucchi go unpunished, stating that he acted in self-defense.

As the lurid Italian title (literally: "The Average Man Does Justice") and the plot synopsis suggest, Umberto Lenzi's *Manhunt in the City* belongs to the so-called vigilante subgenre: a middle-class family man has his little daughter killed during a robbery and sets about avenging her. However, the script (by Dardano Sacchetti and the director) actually overturns the initial assumption. In his mad quest for revenge, engineer Vannucchi (Henry Silva) gets manipulated by a fascist lawyer (Claudio Gora) who heads a clandestine army of vigilantes, and ends up killing the wrong guys. As Lenzi stated, "In a sense I wanted to make a film against "citizens who rebel,"[1] yet I wanted to somehow justify my protagonist from a human point of view."[2] If one compares *Manhunt in the City* with that same year's *Violent Rome*, there's a striking contrast between the fascist squads of hooded thugs recruited in boxing gyms in Lenzi's film (as in Felisatti and Pittorru's novel *La madama*) and Richard Conte's vigilantes in the latter film, seen as the established order's last bastion.

The film never really overcomes this duplicity: in one scene Commissioner Bertone (Raymond Pellegrin) complains that he hasn't enough resources, but later on Vannucchi angrily stares at (and Lenzi zooms right into) a sign at the police station that says "The police are at the service of the citizen." Vannucchi accuses Bertone that his men are only apt at breaking skulls and intercepting phone calls, but in the end he himself can no longer control his own violent impulses, as the ambiguous final scene demonstrates. The script is also rather explicit in pointing out the dangers of the arbitrary resort to self-made justice as well as the public opinion's manipulation by way of reactionary forces that exploit indignation towards urban violence for their own purposes — Sacchetti and Lenzi even go so far as having a character (the left-winged journalist played by Silvano Tranquilli) didactically stating "We are all responsible, for we no longer believe in law and justice."

Curiously enough, the script has a few elements in common with the "*giallo*" thread: Silva's quest for a thug who wears a bracelet depicting a scorpion (following his child's last words) recalls the quest for missing details on behalf of the protagonists in concurrent *gialli*, especially since it leads to a final twist that's an aptly bitter sting in the tail. Also noteworthy, among a rather indistinct array of characters, is the sleazy private eye played by Claudio Nicastro, who is memorably introduced as he picks up a mouthful of food fallen on a porn magazine on his office desk, eating and ogling at naked girls at the same time.

Despite a wooden performance from the inadequate Silva, in a role that Lenzi originally envisioned for Claudio Cassinelli, *Manhunt in the City* works as a bare-bones genre film. As often with Lenzi, the *mise en scène* of violence is emphatic and sometimes self-satisfied, as in the initial killing of the little girl and in the final shotgun massacre; yet action scenes are shot with solid craftsmanship, especially the sequence where Silva and his wife (Luciana Paluzzi) are besieged in their villa by the thugs, which openly recalls Sam Peckinpah's *Straw Dogs*. As the director recalls, the car chases were shot on the streets of Milan with little or no permits at all. During the shooting of the opening robbery in via Montenapoleone (Milan's renowned street full of luxury shops), the criminals' escape by car was accompanied by real shots of a nearby shop owner, who at first thought that a real robbery was taking place. Those were the days in Italian genre cinema....

Presumably more because of its title and implications rather than its graphic violent content, *Manhunt in the City* was given a v.m.18 rating and quickly disappeared after its initial release: it was issued on DVD in Italy only in 2010, thirty-five years after its making. According to Lenzi, "censors found it very annoying that in the end the Commissioner, understanding the protagonist's motives that lead to his revenge, lets him go unpunished."[3]

Notes

1. Lenzi refers to the Italian title of Castellari's *Street Law*.
2. Gomarasca, *Umberto Lenzi*, p. 231.
3. *Ibid.*

Mark Shoots First (Mark il poliziotto spara per primo)

D: Stelvio Massi. *S:* Dardano Sacchetti; *SC:* Dardano Sacchetti, Teodoro Agrimi [Teodoro Corrà], Raniero Di Giovanbattista, Stelvio Massi; *DOP:* Federico Zanni (35mm, Technicolor, Technospes); *M:* Adriano Fabi, arranged by Gianni Mazza (ed. P.A.C.); *Mark* (Barbot / Fabi) sung by Sammy Barbot, *So Much Love* (Barbot / Fabi) sung by Cashin & Doneway; *E:* Mauro Bonanni; *PD, CO:* Carlo Leva; *ArtD:* Giovanni Fratalocchi; *C:* Michele Pensato, Edmondo Pisani; *AC:* Mario Pastorini; *AEs:* Walter Diotallevi, Bruna Abbatelli; *AD:* Cesare Landricina; *2nd AD:* Danilo Massi; *MU:* Dante Trani; *Hair:* Romana Piolanti; *SO:* Roberto Alberghini; *Boom:* Antonino Pantano; *SOE:* Fernando Caso; *Foley artist:* Alvaro Gramigna; *KG:* Giuseppe Raimondi; *ChEl:* Salvatore Gentile; *W:* Irene Parlagreco; *ST:* Sergio Mioni; *SS:* Luigina Lovari. *Cast:* Franco Gasparri (Commissioner Mark Terzi), Lee J. Cobb (Benzi), Nino Benvenuti (Ghini), Massimo Girotti (Spaini, Vice Chief of Police), Ely Galleani (Angela Frizzo), Spiros Focás (Morini), Andrea Aureli (Journalist), Ida Meda (Franca Frizzo), Roberto Caporali (Bernardi), Guido Celano (Mario Borelli), Francesco D'Adda (Ghini's accountant), Tom Felleghy (Dr. Marchi), Edoardo Florio (Andrea, the Sphinx), Archimede Muzi, Gianni Ottaviani, Leonardo Severini (Colantuoni). *Uncredited:* Renato Basso Bondini (Ghini's man), Giovanni Cianfriglia (Thug [footage from *Killer Cop*]), Claudio Cassinelli (Commissioner [footage from *Killer Cop*]), Cesare Di Vito (Tommasi), Margherita Horowitz (Maria Clerici), Sergio Mioni, Mauro Vestri (Sports club director). *PROD:* P.A.C. (Produzioni Atlas Cinematografica) (Milan); *GM:* Raniero Di Giovanbattista; *PM:* Teodoro Agrimi; *PSu:* Teodoro Agrimi, Lamberto Palmieri; *PSe:* Agostino Pasti, Giuseppe Cicconi; *ADM, CASH:* Gaetano Fuzio. *Country:* Italy. Filmed at Incir — De Paolis (Rome) and on location in Genova. *Running time:* 100'; Visa no.: 67697 (12.20.1975); *Rating:* not rated; *Release date:* 12.22.1975; *Distribution:* P.A.C.; *Domestic gross:* 1,227,006,000 lire. *Also known as: Marc la gachette* (Paris, 04.79), *Justice sans sommation* (France — Home video), *Das Ultimatum läuft ab* (West Germany), *Mark — Içimizdeki tehlike* (Turkey). *Home video:* Cecchi Gori (DVD, Italy).

Mark Terzi arrives in Genoa to solve a kidnapping case: the victim is Mark's old acquaintance Benzi, President of the city's bank consortium and a candidate to the city's administrative elections. Mark finds out that Benzi is being held prisoner inside an old cargo hold and releases him after dispatching his jailors, except for a man named Morini, who escapes after a long chase throughout the town. Operating alone, and ignoring the concerns of Spaini, the Vice Chief of Police, Mark learns from Judge Guglielmi that the ransom money has been recycled in illicit trades; the kidnapping ring involves important personalities, including a wealthy man named Ghini. Meanwhile, an unknown sniper who calls himself "The Sphinx" is killing innocent people at random, claiming that he won't stop until Benzi commits suicide. Mark tracks down the man at his girlfriend Franca's flat, but the latter escapes by killing the woman in cold blood. Franca's younger sister Angela helps Mark locate Morini, who is killed in a shoot-out in a theater. Guglielmi finds evidence of who's behind the kidnapping ring but is murdered too. Terzi discovers the hideout of Ghini's gang and finds evidence of illegal trades that involve some of the city's big shots; he also finds out that the Sphinx — who has planted bombs all over the city — is a victim of Benzi's illicit trafficking and graft. Eventually Terzi is able to arrest Benzi, who was the mastermind behind Ghini's kidnapping organization, then he resigns.

For the second "Mark the Cop" entry, Stelvio Massi and his co-scriptwriters moved the action from Milan to Genoa, the urban cradle of the poliziotteschi. A wise move, as *Mark Shoots First* relies much more on action than the first chapter, and the Ligurian city provides a natural spectacular setting that makes action scenes much more exciting to watch. The opening twenty minutes, with Mark sneaking into a half-demolished ship to release his old enemy Benzi from a gang of kidnappers, are an excellent showcase for Massi's expertise as an action director. He exploits every possible angle of the imposing set-piece and makes the best use of Gasparri's physical presence, first in a series of shootouts and stunts and then in a prolonged chase scene, first by car and then on foot, that starts at the dock and ends in Genoa's *carrugi*: it's a sequence that perfectly exemplifies Italian crime films' strong bond with the urban landscape.

That said, despite the four scriptwriters at work the plot is thin and implausible, starting with the idea that Mark's arch-enemy Benzi — who is inexplicably still at large despite *Blood, Sweat and Fear*'s ending, and is even presented as a candidate at Genoa's administrative elections — organized his own kidnapping at the beginning in order to acquire more popularity and votes, while the half-baked subplot featuring the activities of the mysterious Sphinx doesn't really manage to be as engrossing as it should.

Mark Shoots First is mostly an excuse to allow Franco Gasparri as much screen time as possible, within a structure that follows the previous film with minimal reworkings: Lee J. Cobb returns as Terzi's nemesis; Mark is given an assistant (Leonardo Severini) who also functions as a comic relief; there is a romantic subplot involving a paper-thin love interest (the lovely Ely Galleani) and an ex-prizefighter playing a villain (here it's middle weight champion Nino Benvenuti, in his second effort before the cameras after Duccio Tessari's Western *Alive or Preferably Dead*, 1969); Massimo Girotti replaces Giorgio Albertazzi as the patronizing superior who asks Mark "Do you always dress like this?" (the reply: "At least until I get a pay raise") and wonders whether he is "one of those troublemakers who want a police syndicate" (Terzi's reply: "No, I'm just a troublemaker, that's all").

However, Massi's direction is remarkable as ever: besides the spectacular stunts, there are plenty of impressive hand-held shots, such as Mark's irruption in an apartment where a killer named Morini (Spiros Focás) is hiding, with the camera preceding or following Gasparri along narrow corridors and rooms. Perhaps the film's most fruitful aspect is its self-reflexive attitude. It's a quality underlined by the main character (Mark Terzi is by all means an established comic book hero catapulted in a realistic setting, a fact helped by Gasparri's astonishing good looks and monolithic expression throughout) and also by one of the film's main set-pieces, the scene where Terzi chases Morini into a crowded theater where another "poliziotteschi" is being projected. This being a P.A.C. production, the film-within-a-film is Luciano Ercoli's *Killer Cop*, and Massi does a great job in interpolating footage from Ercoli's film (a sequence where Claudio Cassinelli is chasing a thug played by Giovanni Cianfriglia) into the scene, in an amusing rebound between what's happening on-screen and before it.

Compared to *Killer Cop* and other coeval examples of the poliziotteschi, the political angle is barely and unconvincingly sketched, as was with *Blood, Sweat and Fear*. Terzi is simply too far away from reality to be convincing when, in the end, he resigns from the police in a finale lifted almost verbatim from *Dirty Harry*— minus Scorpio's cold-blooded killing, that is. Another example is the obligatory character of a journalist, which usually serves as the source for the kind of banal guarantee that further legitimates the tough cop's deeds in the public's eye. Here, as played by Andrea Aureli, the stuttering reporter is just a comical throwaway presence, and nothing more.

Last but not least, *Mark Shoots First* displays another typical trait of Italian poliziotteschi: product placement. A sequence where Lee J. Cobb discusses his political moves with one of his associates takes place in a boutique's showroom, while mannequins wearing Dellera furs parade around and the brand is well in evidence in the background. Needless to say, J&B bottles are featured prominently as well: in Italian crime films, no one dies of thirst.

One Man Against the Organization (L'uomo che sfidò l'organizzazione)

D: Sergio Grieco. *S:* Sergio Grieco; *SC:* Rafael Romero Marchent, Sergio Grieco; *DOP:* Fernando Arribas (35mm, Eastmancolor); *M:* Luis Enriquez [Bacalov] (Ed. General Music); *E:* Mario Gargiulo; *PD:* Enzo Eusepi; *CO consultant:* Mario Chiari; *C:* Roberto Brega, Giovanni Ciarlo; *2nd unit C:* Gaetano Valle, Enzo Tosi; *AC:* Enrico Fontana, Stefano Francesco Gagliardini; *AEs:* Annalisa Forcella, Carlo Broglio; *2nd AE:* Annamaria Turci; *ADs:* Maria De Simone, Martín Sacristán; *MU:* Franco Di Girolamo; *AMU:* Antonio Maltempo; *Hair:* Luciano Vito; *W:* Anna Rasetti; *SO:* Carlo Palmieri; *Boom:* Pierlao Fondi; *ChEl:* Giulio Quaglietti; *KG:* Giacomo Tommaselli; *SP:* Mario Mazzoni; *STC:* Rémy Julienne; *SS:* Renata Franceschi. *Cast:* Howard Ross [Renato Rossini]

(Steve Barren), Karin Schubert (Margie), Stephen Boyd (Inspector McCormick), J. C. D. [Jean-Claude] Dreyfus (Lady Rebecca Rosenbaum), Nadine Perles (Florence Gayle), Alberto Dalbés (Harry), Pepe [José] Calvo (Zaccaria Rabajos), José Luis Chinchilla, Pietro Torrisi (Harry's henchman), Luciana Turina (Nun at the toilet), Gaspar "Indio" González. *PROD:* Bi.Di.A. Film (Rome), P.A.C. Production Artistique Cinematographic S.A. (Paris), José Frade Producciónes cinematográficas (Madrid); *GM:* Roberto Cocco; *PSu:* Piero Amati, Claudio Cuomo, Santiago Marugan; *PSe:* Giandomenico Stellitano, Francisco Yague. *Country:* Italy / Spain / France. *Running time:* 85'; Visa no.: 67124 (09.13.1975); *Rating:* v.m.14; *Release date:* 09.13.1975; *Distribution:* Agora; *Domestic gross:* 344, 513,620 lire. Shot on location in Rome, Barcelona, Madrid, Toledo. *Also known as: El hombre que desafió a la organización* (1976). *Home video:* None.

Steve, a worker at the Fiumicino airport, picks up a suitcase containing drugs on behalf of a criminal organization led by Lady Rebecca Rosenbaum, but replaces the contents with bicarbonate. Steve sells the drugs in Barcelona to trafficker Zaccaria Rabajos for a billion lire, then orders him to throw the heroin at sea. Soon he and his lover and accomplice Margie have to face the organization's revenge. On their way to Madrid, Margie is kidnapped by Lady Rebecca's right hand, Harry. To release her, Steve must give the money back to the organization. Posing as Inspector McCormick, Steve alerts the police, but Harry escapes with Margie as hostage. Steve teams up with the real Inspector McCormick to set Margie free and rout the whole gang. In the end, much to everyone's surprise, it turns out that Lady Rebecca is a transvestite. Steve and Margie flee by helicopter with the money.

An expert genre director, active since the early '50s, during the last years of his career Sergio Grieco (1917–1982) tried his hand at crime films, with mixed results. An Italian / Spanish / French co-production, *One Man Against the Organization* owes very little to the contemporary poliziotteschi, and is rather an update of classical '60s heist / adventure yarns, complete with poorly shot climactic car / helicopter chase (despite hiring the services of then leading stunt coordinator Rémy Julienne). For one, Grieco goes for a mixture of action and comedy, with results that vary from mediocre to dreadful — dialogue such as "Christopher Columbus, the inventor. He invented the egg" speak for themselves.

Grieco tries to injects some sleaze in the scene where Ross watches a silent Super-8 film of Schubert being drugged and gang-raped by Dalbés' men. What's more, the telegraphed final twist, with the masculine Lady Rebecca revealed to be a man *en travesti* (something even the most ingenuous viewer has sensed since "her" very first appearance, not least because of such unsubtle puns as "That woman has got balls this big!") is recycled from Grieco's earlier spy flick *Password: Kill Agent Gordon* (*Password: uccidete agente Gordon*, 1966) starring Roger Browne and Franco Ressel as the transvestite villain. Cinephiles will be amused in recognizing French character actor Jean Claude Dreyfus (seen in Walerian Borowczyk's *Immoral Women*, Jeunet and Caro's *Delicatessen*, Claude Lelouch's *La Belle Histoire* and many others) in one of his earlier roles as the aforementioned "Lady Rebecca."[1] As for the cast, Howard Ross a.k.a. Renato Rossini displays his muscles (and ass) but can't make for a memorable hero, while Schubert (with one of those short haircuts that afflicted many beauties in the period, and which here changes from shot to shot due to bad continuity) is an equally vapid presence. Boyd, on the other hand, is catatonic.

Luis Bacalov provides a suitably easy listening score, with South-American touches and even a hint of Bizet's *Carmen* (!) in the scene where Ross and Schubert escape from a caricatured trafficker played by Pepe Calvo.

Note

1. Dreyfus would often play transvestite roles, such as in Jacques Deray's *Le Marginal* (1983), Jean Claude Roy's *Éducation Anglaise* (1983) and Julius Amédé Laou's *La Vieille quimboseuse et le majordome* (1987).

Rudeness (Lo sgarbo)

D: Franco Martinelli [Marino Girolami]. *S* and *SC:* Antonio Margheriti, Luigi Russo; *DOP:* Franco Villa (35mm, Eastmancolor, Telecolor); *M:* Vasili Kojucharov (Ed. Nazionalmusic); *Someday Somewhere* (S. Vlavamos / R. Constantinos) sung by Demis Roussos; *E:* Otello Colangeli; *PD:* Giorgio Postiglione; *CO:* Luciano Sagoni; *C:* Gaetano Valle; *AC:* Enrico Biribicchi; *AE:* Fernanda Materni; *AD:* Romano Scandariato; *MU:* Renzo Francioni, Vincenzo Napoli; *SO:* Bernardino Franzetti, Armando Janota; *Mix:* Sandro Occhetti; *SS:* Maria Luisa Merci. *Cast:* Louis Vito Russo (Salvatore Mannino), Leonard Mann [Leonardo Manzella] (Vito), Karin Schubert (Marina), Hélène Chanel (Lady White), Guido Celano (Don Mimì), Arturo Dominici (Don Lipari), Samantha Elgard (Rosaria), Maria Rita De Angelis (Concetta), Edmondo Tieghi (Nino "The Messinese"), Pom Felleng [Tom Felleghy] (Mr. Greenberg), Jean Masrevery (Marseillese), Cesare Di Vito, Mario Guizzardi, Carla Mancini, Pasquale Murolo (Mafia boss in New York), Renzo Marignano (Lord Walley), Barbara Quero, Gustavo De Nardo, Luca Sportelli, Aldo Bonanno, Bruno Alias (Mr. Ravish), Orazio Stracuzzi. *Uncredited:* Fortunato Arena (Killer), Bruno Ariè (Cashier in gambling room), Giulio Baraghini (Mustached prostitute client), John Bartha (Rival Mafia man killed by Sal in Las Vegas warehouse), Angelo Boscariol (Rapist), Pietro Ceccarelli (Bald thug in warehouse), Attilio Dottesio (Man killed by Nino in gambling room), Giuseppe Marrocco (Guest in gambling room), Nello Pazzafini (Bouncer in gambling room), Anna Maria Perego (Elderly woman who greets Mr. Ravish), Renzo Giovanni Pevarello (Usher in gambling room), Romano Puppo (Marseillese's henchman), Franca Scagnetti (Woman in gambling room). *PROD:* Luigi Nannerini and Gabriele Crisanti for Starkiss Cinematografica (Rome), Nouvelles Les Films Océanic (Bordeaux); *PM:* Tommaso Sagone; *PSu:* Giancarlo Nannerini; *PSe:* Giulio Dini, Roberto Nannerini. *Country:* Italy / France. Filmed at Incir — De Paolis (Rome) and on location in Palermo and Paris. *Running time:* 105'; Visa no.: 64914 (07.19.1974); *Rating:* v.m.18; *Release date:* 05.11.1975; *Distribution:* Film Audax; *Domestic gross:* 356,462,330 lire. *Also known as: Le filleul* (05.18.1977 — 85'). *Home video:* Hobby & Work (DVD, Italy)

After causing trouble with a rival "family," Salvatore Mannino is sent to Sicily by his boss Don Lipari. In Palermo, he becomes a subordinate to wheelchair-bound boss Don Mimi, but proves to be overly ambitious. Sal soon runs into trouble when he falls for Marina, an orphan adopted by Don Mimì as a child, who became the boss' lover. Sal seduces Marina, with no respect for the Mafia's code of honor. Then, along with Vito and Nino "the Messinese" he robs a clandestine gambling room and flees to London, where he sets up a prostitution racket. Aided by his lover, the wealthy Lady White, Sal is introduced into high society and starts blackmailing officials and politicians who are being entertained by his women. Don Mimì forces Marina to reach Sal in London and eliminate him to expiate her guilt, but she takes Sal's side. After Don Lipari is killed, all the Mafia families in the United States decide that Sal must die. Betrayed by Nino, Sal kills him and goes to Don Mimi's house for the final showdown: meanwhile, to punish Marina, Don Mimì has her gang-raped by his men.

In the final shoot-out, Sal kills Mimì and his gang, but ends up badly wounded himself. His friend Vito helps them escape to an uncertain future, but Marina prefers to commit suicide, and die with Sal.

In the mid-seventies, just a few years after *The Godfather*, the Mafia movie was struggling for air. With the earlier commercial appeal gone, byproducts such as Marino Girolami's *Rudeness* relied overtly on sex. Produced by Gabriele Crisanti, like Andrea Bianchi's *Cry of a Prostitute*, Girolami's film (co-scripted by Antonio Margheriti) gives ample opportunity for the female cast to expose their bodies: within minutes from the opening credits, the film's hero Sal is joining a woman he's just met in her hotel room shower for a hot lovemaking session.

The presence of the unknown Louis Vito Russo in the lead, in what's apparently his only film role, gives away the measure of *Rudeness*' shoestring budget. Although the action takes place between Palermo, London and Paris, most of the film was shot in badly assembled sets (with suburban Italian villas posing as Anglo-Saxon homes, just like in a Demofilo Fidani film) with stock footage of streets and airports to create a semblance of realism. Not that Girolami really cares about that: the film's concerns — as evidenced by the director's abuse of abrupt zooms — are obviously others, such as Russo and Karin Schubert's lovemaking scene in a tomato field or Schubert being gang-raped by a crippled don's men at the climax, while most of the plot relies on Sal's scheme to blackmail politicians through a prostitution racket — which allows for an unforgettable trashy scene where the ubiquitous man of Italian cinema, Tom Felleghy, is fondling two naked women while wearing only his shirt, underpants and a bowler hat.

As for Margheriti's co-scripted dialogue, it's littered with such lines as "That bitch got you a hard-on ... you always had your head down there." Also noticeable is the way J&B bottles on display remain miraculously intact during shoot-outs.

Savage Three (*Fango bollente*)

D: Vittorio Salerno. *S:* Ernesto Gastaldi; *Treatment:* Ernesto Gastaldi, Vittorio Salerno; *SC:* Giovanni Balestrini, Ernesto Gastaldi, Lucille Laks, Vittorio Salerno; *DOP:* Giulio Albonico (35mm, Kodak, L.V.-Luciano Vittori); *M:* Franco Campanino, conducted by the author (ed. C.A.M.); *Santagà* (F. Campanino) and *Boiling Mud* (Savastano — Campanino) are played by Panama Red; *E:* Enzo Meniconi; *PD, ArtD:* Eugenio Liverani; *CO:* Emilio Baldelli; *C:* Sebastiano Celeste; *AC:* Marco Onorato; *AE:* Anita Cacciolati; *2nd AE:* Stefano Ardinzone; *ADs:* Mario Zonta, Claudio Bondì; *2nd ADs:* Eduardo Salerno, Giangiacomo Tabet; *MU:* Giovanni Morosi; *Hair:* Elda Magnanti; *W:* Angela Viglino; *SO:* Mario Faraoni; *Boom:* Giancarlo Laurenzi; *SE:* Germano Natali; *Mix:* Alberto Bartolomei; *SOEd:* Massimo Anzellotti; *KG:* Aldo Taloni; *ChEl:* Alberico Novelli; *SP:* Francesco Bellomo; *SS:* Serena Canevari; *DubD:* Riccardo Cucciolla; *UP:* Lucherini, Rossetti, Spinola, Scalera. *Cast:* Joe Dallesandro (Ovidio Mainardi), Gianfranco De Grassi (Giacomo Boatta), Guido De Carli (Peppe), Carmen Scarpitta (1st raped woman, the politician's wife), Martine Brochard (Alba Mainardi), Enrico Maria Salerno (Commissioner Santagà), Sal Borgese (Caretaker), Claudio Nicastro (Head physician), Luigi Casellato (Head of the Flying squad), Ada Pometti (2nd Raped woman), Umberto Ceriani (Commissioner Tamaroglio), Gualtiero Rispoli, Enzo Garinei (Head research center), Renzo Ozzano (Santagà's assistant), Enrico Marciani (policeman), Francesca Lionti (Prostitute), Gengher Gatti (Car-park attendant at the stadium), Clara Fascietto Sivillo. *Uncredited:* Omero Capanna (Supporter in stadium fight), Gilberto Galimberti (Supporter in stadium fight), Alba Maiolini (Giacomo's mother). *PROD:* Angelo Jacono for Comma 9; *GM:* Angelo Jacono; *PM:* Carlo Cucchi; *PSu:* Cesare Iacolucci. *Country:* Italy. Filmed at Pasquino Cine Teatro Posa (Rome) and on location in Turin. *Running time:* 85'; Visa no.: 67040 (09.17.1975); *Rating:* v.m.18; *Release date:* 09.20.1975; *Distribution:* Titanus; *Domestic gross:* 724,839,120 lire. *Also known as: Justicia para todos* (Spain), *Fango caliente / Furia Homicida* (Spain — Home video), *Hot Mud* (U.K. — informal). *Home video:* 01-Medusa (DVD, Italy — cut version, 78' 36").

Ovidio Mainardi, an employee in a huge electronic company, and his two colleagues Giacomo and Peppe give vent to their everyday frustrations by committing abrupt acts of violence. One day at the stadium they set up a brawl, then steal a car. The next day, after a futile argument with a truck driver, Ovidio kills the man with a screwdriver. After savagely murdering a prostitute and her pimp, the trio steal a taxi and kill the cab driver: they then pick up two women, rape and mutilate them. Since one of the victims was a politician's wife, the Commissioner on the case is convinced that the murders have a political motive. On the other hand, a senior police Inspector at rest, Santagà, who has met Ovidio during a computer course, starts suspecting that he is the man behind those unmotivated violent acts. At a hunting party, Ovidio humiliates the head physician, who has an affair with his wife. An eyewitness allows the police to build Peppe's identikit; he is arrested and subsequently hangs himself in prison; Ovidio poisons his wife and is shot dead by Santagà, while Giacomo, who's above suspicion, will continue with his violent acts with a pair of newly recruited accomplices.

"A society which produces everything couldn't also produce monsters?" asks lab technician Ovidio (a chilling Joe Dallesandro) to elderly Commissioner Santagà (Enrico Maria Salerno) in a scene from Vittorio Salerno's *Savage Three*. As with the director's previous film *No. Il caso è felicemente risolto*, a tale of urban violence becomes the pretext for a dark reflection on contemporary society. In a chaotic, traffic-ridden Turin, Ovidio and his two colleagues, Giacomo (Gianfranco De Grassi) and Peppe (Guido De Carli) give vent to their everyday neuroses — repetitive, alienating jobs; the stress of living in a huge city; unhappy personal relationships — with unmotivated violent acts. These are not young delinquents who belong to a gang and use violence as a means of a proletarian revenge: Ovidio and his friends are ordinary middle class citizens with a job, a house, a family, who channel the frustrations arising from the socio-environmental influences into brutal and heinous behavior.

The story was written by Ernesto Gastaldi, who claimed: "*Savage Three* was born with another title and partly another purpose. It was called *I primi tre cominciano a mordere* ("The First Three Start to Bite") and was focused on the excessive overpopulation in our cities. I co-wrote it with director Vittorio Salerno, the brother of popular actor Enrico Maria."[1] The curious original title referred to a scene where Ovidio and a doctor are watching in horror as lab mice, which have turned crazy from being caged too long, start devouring each other when Ovidio removes the partitions that separate them. "There is always one that starts to bite the others, it would be interesting to know which one" the doctor observes. "Can this happen to people as well?" Ovidio replies. "Well, perhaps if someone put them in a cage..." is the answer. Salerno then cuts to a crowded stadium where a soccer match is taking place. Supporters are shouting and throwing stuff at one another, ready to jump at each other's throat for the slightest reason. The parallelism is further underlined when the crazed Peppe is put in a claustrophobic jail and bites a cop before being locked in.

The sense of Gastaldi's apologue is transparent: violence and rage are a virus that spreads around, a collateral and unpredictable effect of consumerist society, and not even a computer can detect its volatile essence. When the Commissioner asks Ovidio to analyze some data that would give a winning state lottery combination, the computer's response (resulting from Ovidio's humorous custom setting of the electronic brain) is "go fuck yourself." There's a patent luddite element in the script, which is interesting considering that Gastaldi was primarily a science fiction writer: the scenes depicting Dallesandro and his colleagues in huge, alienating futuristic offices, all dressed in similar robes, has an equally transparent political undertone which perhaps comes from co-scriptwriter Nanni Balestrini (whom Gastaldi says not to have met, as scriptwriting probably went through different stages). A renowned poet, novelist and intellectual, Balestrini often dealt with themes of violence and terrorism in his books such as La *violenza illustrata* (1976). One reviewer labeled the film as a "Marcusian parable,"[2] evoking Herbert Marcuse's book *One-Dimensional Man* (1964), while another influence was Stanley Kubrick's *A Clockwork Orange* (1971), if only for the amount of ultraviolence that Ovidio and friends unleash when they go berserk. The sociological aspect is more schematic: Santagà's obtuse Northern colleague (Umberto Ceriani) argues about the increase of criminality due to immigration from the South, Pepe is a Pugliese immigrant who one day returns home to find that his huge family has moved to Turin and occupied his house, depriving him of his much-needed vital space — a grotesque sequence that is perhaps reminiscent of J. G. Ballard's short story *Billennium*.

Joe Dallesandro, left, Gianfranco De Grassi, center, and Guido De Carli as the three ordinary citizens who become bloodthirsty murderers in Vittorio Salerno's thought-provoking *Savage Three* (1975) (courtesy Vittorio Salerno).

Perhaps *Savage Three* would have worked better with a more expert director; yet, on the other hand, it's the film's contradictory and rough shape that makes it such a flawed yet morbidly fascinating viewing experience. As customary with Italian films of the period, violence is portrayed with sensationalistic glee. The grim crescendo culminates in the kidnapping, rape and murder of two wealthy bourgeois ladies: the scene where a grinning Dallesandro chases a victim (Carmen Scarpitta) aboard a forklift and transfixes the woman onto a wall is one of the most savage moments in 1970s Italian cinema — a period where the search for truculent effects was the norm.[3] The script's ambitions to portray the maladies of an advanced industrial society are not always up to the results, but the paroxistic *mise en scène*, which oscillates between sensationalism and misanthropy, hits the spot: the scene where Ovidio has his unfaithful wife (Martine Brochard) eat a cake stuffed with arsenic and mice poison — an occurrence that recalls the ending of Luigi Comencini's extraordinary black comedy *The Scopone Game* (*Lo scopone scientifico*, 1972) — has a distinct anti-bourgeois feel. However, despite its gruesome content, *Savage Three* conveys an understated yet very self-conscious irony (Dallesandro's flat, for instance, is decorated with Andy Warhol's multi-colored Marilyn Monroe portraits) that makes it closer to Jed Johnson's *Andy Warhol's Bad* (1977) than to Italian vigilante flicks of the period.

Savage Three ventures into poliziotteschi territory with the character of Santagà — an elderly limping cop who has been moved from the Flying Squad to the archives section after killing a suspect he was chasing — who stubbornly follows Dallesandro's trail and finally shoots him dead. However, unlike in the coeval poliziotteschi, the relationship between the Commissioner (a role Salerno had devised for Gabriele Ferzetti or Gastone Moschin[4]) and the criminal is mainly a dialectical skirmish: Santagà is the only one who realizes the true nature of the crimes, because he solely notices the disquieting signals that are scattered all around, whereas his colleagues and superiors lean on a political explanation, which is more comforting because it leads to a Manichaen, superficial interpretation of reality. Yet — and that's another sign of the film's thought-provoking concept — Santagà is reintegrated into the Flying Squad, thus becoming once again a "respectable" cop, through another act of legalized violence, that is the killing of Ovidio.

A curious aspect of Salerno's film is its production history. *Savage Three* was the only picture produced by Comma 9, a co-operative founded by five filmmakers — Pasquale Squitieri, Gianfranco Mingozzi (*Sardinia Kidnapped*, 1968; *Flavia the Heretic*, 1974), Francesco Massaro (*Il generale dorme in piedi*, 1974),

Salerno and Francesco Barilli (*The Perfume of the Lady In Black*, 1973)—as well as scriptwriters Massimo D'Avack, Barbara Alberti, Amedeo Pagani and Nanni Balestrini. Comma 9 was a self-managed company, open to directors and actors. According to Salerno, its goal was to keep production costs low (the company was founded after the big oil crisis of 1973). Profits would have to be reinvested in more productive activities in order to ensure a continuity of initiatives. Squitieri was elected president, as he managed to convince Goffredo Lombardo—the head of Italy's biggest distribution company Titanus, nicknamed "the King"—to distribute the first five films produced by Comma 9 with 250 million lire each. However, as Salerno recalls, Lombardo didn't like any of the scripts that were handed to him, until eventually Salerno proposed the distributor the script for *Savage Three*. Shot in eight weeks (four in Turin and four in Rome), the film cost 320 million lire instead of the planned 250, and even though it performed rather well at the Italian box office and was sold in foreign markets, was not the success the producers expected.

Comma 9 closed down in 1978, after the event of color TV and the proliferation of local commercial broadcasters. Gastaldi comments wryly: "I'm still amazed that they managed to screw Goffredo Lombardo and got the money to produce this one film!"[5]

Notes

1. E-mail interview, January 2012.
2. R. P. [Ranieri Polese], *Corriere della sera*, 09.25.1975.
3. The Italian DVD, released in late 2011, is the abridged 1993 version, when *Savage Three* was passed again by the Board of Censors and cut to obtain a v.m.14 rating for TV broadcasting. The film was shown in its uncut form on Spanish television in the late nineties.
4. Enrico Maria Salerno was imposed by the film's distributor Goffredo Lombardo, as Vittorio Salerno recalls: "Enrico in those years was doing one poliziotteschi after another [...] and when I want to the Titanus offices to discuss the cast, Lombardo told me just was I was afraid he would: 'Of course your brother is going to play the Commissioner, isn't he?' and since I knew how things went in the business, I replied: 'Of course Goffredo, who better than him?'" Comotti and Salerno, *Professione Regista*.
5. E-mail interview, January 2012. According to Salerno, however, Comma 9 did produce one more film, *Una vita venduta*, a war flick directed by Aldo Florio which was distributed by Istituto Luce.

Seasons of Assassins (Il tempo degli assassini)

D: Marcello Andrei. *S* and *SC:* Piero Regnoli, Alvaro Fabrizio, Marcello Andrei; *DOP:* Luciano Trasatti (35mm, Kodak, Telecolor); *M:* Albert Verrecchia, conducted by the author (ed. C.A.M. / La Galère); *Seasons of Assassins* sung by Sammy Barbot, *Gang Leader* sung by The Killers; *E:* Giulio Berruti; Set designer: Andrea Fantacci; *CO:* Luciana Marinucci; *C:* Giorgio Di Battista; *AC:* Carlo Milani; *AE:* Patrizia Oppedisano; *AD:* Alfredo Varelli; *2nd AD:* Orlando Pagliari; *MU:* Silvana Petri; *Hair:* Sergio Gennari; *SO:* Giancarlo Laurenzi; *Boom:* Alberto Salvatori; *Mix:* Mario Amari; *STC:* Sergio Mioni; *SS:* Lina D'Amico. *Cast:* Joe Dallesandro (Piero Giaranaldi), Martin Balsam (Commissioner Catrone), Magalì Noël (Rossana), Rossano Brazzi (Father Eugenio), Guido Leontini (Brigadeer), Cinzia Mambretti (Sandra), Gianluca Farnese (Claudio), Settimio Segnatelli (Angelo), Gian Piero Vinciguerra, Maria Rosaria Riuzzo [Riuzzi] (Marisa, Sandra's girlfriend), Sergio Tappa, Giovanna Mainardi (Sandra's mother), Piero Gerlini, Rosario Borelli (Car owner), Nando Marineo (Jeweler), Vittorio Mangano. *Uncredited:* Renato Basso Bondini (Man on motorbike), Ennio Colaianni (Porter), Giuseppe Marrocco (Doctor), Ottaviano Dell'Acqua (Guy at dodgem), Franco Garofalo (Worker at sawmill), Attilio Dottesio. *PROD:* Adelina Tattilo and Carlo Maietto for Mirage Cinematografica; *EP:* Renzo Maietto; *PM:* Silvio Siano; *UM:* Vincenzo De Leo; *PSu:* Giuseppe Castagna; *PSe:* Maurizio Giorgi; *ADM:* Roberto Ornaro. *Country:* Italy. Filmed at Incir–De Paolis (Rome) and on location in Rome. *Running time:* 100'; Visa no.: 67629 (12.20.1975); *Rating:* v.m.18; *Release date:* 12.27.1975; *Distribution:* Agora; *Domestic gross:* 354,087,000 lire. *Also known as: Die wilde Meute* (West Germany, 07.09.1976), *Days of Terror* (Holland—Home video), *Terrorgjengen* (Norway—Home video). *Home video:* Cinehollywood (VHS, Italy—84'), Playtime (VHS, Italy, 98'), Universal (VHS, Switzerland), Imperial (VHS, Germany). OST: 7" CAM AMP 175.

Rome. Piero, a young man from the suburbs, leads a gang of petty thieves. Despite being married to former prostitute Rossana and having a son, Piero aspires to be a big shot. Don Eugenio, a priest, tries to make them repent, but Piero and his friends don't listen. Their client is a fence named Poggi, who, however, is also an informer, and tells Commissioner Catrone about the gang's movements. Meanwhile Piero befriends young Sandra, gets her pregnant and eventually abandons her: the young girl commits suicide. Angelo, a shy boy who is influenced by the commissioner as well as Don Eugenio, is suspected of treason and killed by Piero's men. Finally, during an attempted robbery, the commissioner is able to trap the gang: Piero escapes the ambush, but is tracked down and shot dead by the police at Rossana's place.

With a title that quotes Arthur Rimbaud and Joe Dallesandro in the lead as Piero, a lowlife punk struggling to make his way in the Roman underworld, *Seasons for Assassins* puts on the table much more ambitions than it can bear. As with other films produced in that period by Carlo Maietto and "Playmen" publisher Adelina Tattilo, realistic and sociological ambitions rub shoulders with concessions to the audience, while Piero Regnoli's script is a potboiler of many different influences.

Seasons for Assassins starts as a lower-class riff on the Pier Paolo Pasolini–inspired *A Violent Life* (*Una vita violenta*, 1962, Brunello Rondi and Paolo Heusch), as Dallesandro and his men wreak urban havoc in their Alfa Romeo, causing car accidents and collisions, just for kicks. Andrei follows his characters' deeds as they steal, beat and gang rape at every possible occasion: one impressive and uneasy scene has Piero and his gang harass a young couple inside a dodgem and then savagely beating the boy (a very young Ottaviano Dell'Acqua) much to the crowd's indifference.

Piero Regnoli's script deviates from the usual poliziotteschi clichés with the character of the paunchy middle-aged, abusive and unscrupulous Commissioner Catrone (Martin Balsam), who doesn't mind using a shy teenage boy as bait to catch his opponent: however, the story dips profusely into turgid melodrama with the subplot about the naive Milanese girl (Cinzia Mambretti, seen in Lizzani's *The Teenage Prostitution Racket*) who is seduced and impregnated by Piero, and eventually raped by his men in a particularly unpleasant scene. All in all, given its insistence on brutality and violence, *Seasons for Assassins*—whose end credits claim to be based on actual events—predates the subgenre inspired by the real-life Circeo massacre, which would take off the following year.

As the suburban lowlife, Dallesandro essentially plays a meaner variation of his characters in Paul Morrissey's films: in one scene he even cradles his infant child like he did in *Flesh* (1968). Andrei and Regnoli have him take off his shirt whenever possible, and the film provides him with a strong Roman accent: yet the character of Piero — who dreams to be a big shot but essentially wastes his time in bars and arcades like an overgrown teenager and undergoes head down the harangues of a dynamic chain-smoking friar (a rather ridiculous-looking Rossano Brazzi) — is more interesting for the Italian-American actor's nervous screen presence rather than for Regnoli's stereotyped dialogue. Piero complains about a "world of shit" but the character's angst and proletarian malaise remain rather undeveloped and generic. What's more, Andrei's direction is helplessly inadequate, as shown not only by the poorly mounted opening scene but also by the random use of subjective shots featuring Catrone (a stylistic trait which is deprived of its function and significance, as Catrone is not a substantial enough character to convey the filmmakers' point of view) while the film's meager budget is shown up during the sequences set at the police station, where the Commissioner's office, which looks like a hastily adapted bourgeois living room. As Piero's embittered wife, Magalì Noël has precious little screen time.

Silent Action (La polizia accusa: il servizio segreto uccide)

D: Sergio Martino. *S:* Fabio Pittorru, Massimo Felisatti; *SC:* Fabio Pittorru, Massimo Felisatti, Sergio Martino, Gianfranco Couyoumdjian; *DOP:* Giancarlo Ferrando (35mm, Eastmancolor, L.V.-Luciano Vittori); *M:* Luciano Michelini, conducted by the author (ed. R.C.A.); *E:* Eugenio Alabiso; *PD:* Franco Calabrese; *APD:* Paolo Innocenzi; *CO:* Rosalba Menichelli; *C:* Claudio Morabito; *AC:* Antonio Minutolo; *AE:* Giuseppe Romano; *AD:* Claudio Bondì; *2nd AD:* Giuseppe Cino; *MU:* Stefano Trani; *Hair:* Alfonso Cioffi; *SOEd:* Roberto Petrozzi; *Boom:* Guglielmo Smeraldi; *Mix:* Romano Pampaloni; *SE:* Dino Galliano; *MA:* Riccardo Petrazzi; *SP:* Vittorio Piffani; *CON:* Mirella Malatesta. *Cast:* Luc Merenda (Commissioner Giorgio Solmi), Mel Ferrer (District Attorney Michele Mannino), Tomas Milian (Captain Mario Sperlì), Delia Boccardo (Maria), Michele Gammino (Lt. Luigi Caprara), Paola Tedesco (Giuliana Raimondi), Franco Giornelli (Frank Smith), Gianfranco Barra (Agent De Luca), Carlo Alighiero (Remo Ortolani), Claudio Gora (Martinetti), Claudio Nicastro (Prison warden), Antonio Casale (Giovanni Andreassi "Massù"), Gianni Di Benedetto (General Eugenio Stocchi), Arturo Dominici (Chief of Police), Carlo Gaddi (Andreassi's accomplice), Giancarlo Badessi (Vittorio Chiarotti), Clara Colosimo ("Baroness" Isadora Grimani), Tommaso Felleghi [Tom Felleghy] (Colonel Giulio Scanni), Cesare De Vito [Di Vito] (Investigator at crime scene). *Uncredited:* Ettore Arena (Prisoner), Fortunato Arena (Man dragging Scanni's body), Rossana Canghiari (Maid in Grimani's house), Massimo Ciprari (Man in gymnasium), Attilio Dottesio, Vittorio Frattura (The Judge's secretary), Giuseppe Marrocco (Doctor at hospital), Sergio Martino (Chopper pilot), Maurizio Mattioli (Head militiaman), Romano Milani (Servant), Loredana Nusciak (Mrs. Martinetti), Riccardo Petrazzi (Militiaman), Nando Sarlo (Martinetti's lawyer), Marisa Traversi (Mrs. Martinetti), Goffredo Unger (Driver), Luciano Zanussi (Mannino's assistant). *PROD:* Luciano Martino for Dania Film, Gianfranco Couyoumdjian for Flora Film, Medusa Distribuzione; *GM:* Pietro Innocenzi; *PM:* Elio Di Pietro; *PSu:* Biagio Di Pietro; *PSe:* Dario Armellini. *Country:* Italy. Filmed at Incir–De Paolis (Rome) and on location in Rome. *Running time:* 100'; Visa no.: 66275 (03.28.1975); *Rating:* v.m.14; *Release date:* 04.05.1975; *Distribution:* Medusa; *Domestic gross:* 1,039,004,690 lire. *Also known as: Der lautlose killer* (West Germany), *Der Killermafia* (West Germany), *Die Polizei klagt an — Der Geheimdienst tötet* (East Germany), *L'accusé* (France). *Home video:* NoShame (DVD, Italy). OST: CD Digitmovies CDDM091.

In July '74, a Major, a Colonel and a General all die in seemingly random incidents. Commissioner Solmi investigates on the subsequent murder of Vittorio Chiarotti, an alleged electrician who soon turns out to be a private eye instead. Rebuked by Judge Mannino for his methods, Solmi tracks down a possible witness — a prostitute — with the help of his journalist girlfriend Maria, but the witness is killed. Solmi then gets in touch with Captain Mario Sperlì, a secret agent who shows interest in the case and admits the existence of a failed coup d'état. The investigations, however, come to a dead end, even though the accumulation of murders and clues forces Mannino to take the Commissioner's side; however, the two men are duly preceded by a hidden force that is aware of their every move. The discovery of a map and Solmi's intuition lead them to the location of a clandestine training camp and identify the conspiracy's mastermind, who turns out to be Sperlì himself, a.k.a. the elusive lawyer Rienzi. However, Solmi is the next doomed victim, as he now knows too much....

The most significant and accomplished example of the politically committed poliziotteschi, Sergio Martino's *Silent Action* was released in Italy in April 1975, just a few months after Pier Paolo Pasolini's vibrant appeal on the first page of "Il Corriere della Sera" and the Italian title ("The Police Accuse: The Secret Service Kills") makes for an equally strong statement of sorts.

Screenwriters Massimo Felisatti and Fabio Pittorru recycle a number of plot elements from their short story *Telefoni sotto controllo* (in the volume *Violenza a Roma*), which revolved around the murder of a popular disc jockey. Such is the case for the scene where a seedy secret agent (who sneaked into a villa to acquire important audio tapes) is arrested, as well as the characters of the female journalist from "Paese Sera" (Delia Boccardo) and Commissioner Solmi (Luc Merenda), two popular characters from the TV series *Qui squadra mobile* and the crime novels published by the duo in the mid–'70s.

Martino's film is filled with transparent references to newspaper chronicles: the search for compromising tapes refers to the ones conserved by neo-fascist journalist and secret agent of the SID (Servizio Interno di Difesa, Information Defense Service) Guido Giannettini,[1] while the emphasis on the role of a deviant Secret Service in the plot is probably inspired by the discovery in 1973 of a secret organization called "Rosa dei Venti," connected to a parallel structure of the SID. The story focuses on the mysterious deaths of high-ranking military officers which lead to an elaborate plan of a *coup d'état* to establish a "government of public health," and one plot twist features the locating of a hidden military bases on the Apennines — itself another reference to real-life events: the camp at Piano di Rascino, near Rieti, was discovered soon after the bombing at Brescia's Piazza della Loggia: a shoot-out ensued between the conspirators and the police, which resulted in the death of a terrorist, Giancarlo Esposti.

Curiously, just a couple of years earlier Mario Monicelli devised a similar plot for one of his cruelest films, the grotesque political apologue *Vogliamo i colonnelli* (1973), starring Ugo Tognazzi as a fascist MP who assembles a gang of conspirators for a coup that ends in farce (but Monicelli cleverly has the Democrazia Cristiana take advantage of the plot to establish a real dictatorship). *Silent Action* manipulates its material (which at first read would rather suit a politically committed film than a poliziotteschi, as Luciano Michelini's score seems to suggest) within the boundaries of genre cinema. The result is even more interesting and peculiar, as given such premises, the poliziotteschi's allegedly right-wing ideology brusquely derails towards the left, and, as film critic Giovanni Buttafava pointed out, "all the genre's typical characters and traits, without changing in the least, are now serving a political discourse which is titanically *democratic*."[2] For instance, the characters' very physical connotation reveals their ideology: the obnoxious Martinetti (Claudio Gora) who receives a visit from the Commissioner while playing golf, is instantly perceived as a right-winged sympathizer, while Tomas Milian's guest participation as the SID officer in suit, tie and Rolex watch immediately warns the audience, as the actor is far removed from his usual endearingly proletarian, long-haired looks.

Felisatti and Pittorru draw a convincing and realistic portrayal of the Secret Service as a somehow rickety underworld, populated by small fish, who blackmail and are blackmailed. The dialogue is also sharper than usual, with populist proclamations giving way to more elaborate lines. If Solmi reflects on one of the poliziotteschi's favorite themes, that of the "tied hands" ("We all have our hands tied, the important thing is that somebody is still willing to untie the knots"), Milian quotes a Spanish liberal philosopher ("Ortega y Gasset said that claiming to be left or right-wing is just a way to confirm one's imbecility") and has a chilling Nietzschean monologue on democracy: "Your sickness is called false democracy. Your mistake is to believe that all men are equal, while reality is so much different. Believe me, it's much better that there be a few superior men who lead the weaker masses."

As a genre film, however, *Silent Action* delivers the goods. Martino doesn't mind recycling a stunt from his earlier *The Violent Professionals* in the opening scene, but the climax at the military camp, complete with a helicopter / car chase, is one of the genre's most rousing. The fact that the heroic Solmi dies in the end also underlines the different climate compared not just to that of the TV series, but also to Martino's previous effort. Whereas in *The Violent Professionals* the tough cop played by Luc Merenda claimed "I am against good manners, usually these are also the most foolish ones" and eventually became a progressive hero, here Solmi is shot to death in front of his home and before his fiancée's very eyes, in a bleak ending that virtually restages the real-life death of Commissioner Calabresi,[3] and once again demonstrates how Italian tough cops were all illegitimate sons of Luigi Calabresi, and all were born from a sense of guilt.

Notes

1. Already active in the French OAS, Giannettini (1930–2002) participated to a colloquium on "revolutionary warfare" May 3 to 5, 1965, in Rome, which was organized by the Institute Alberto-Pollio and quasi-exclusively financed by the SIFAR military intelligence agency. Giannettini presented one of the main reports. According to René Monzat, "this colloquium provided the theoretical framework for the Strategy of Tension" (René Monzat, *Enquêtes sur la droite extrême* [Paris: Le Monde-éditions, 1992], p. 91). Following this colloquium, in which about 20 students participated (among them, future terrorists Stefano Delle Chiaie and Mario Michele Merlino), Giannettini and other speakers were hired by the Italian Secret Service. In April 1968, these students participated in a trip to Greece involving 60 students from the "League of Greek Fascist Students in Italy" and 51 Italian neo-fascist students, organized by the Greek *junta*. In May 1969 Giannettini filed a report where he warned the SID that bombings in close spaces were being prepared. A few months later the Piazza Fontana bombing occurred. Afterwards, Giannettini's connection emerged with extreme right-wing terrorist Giovanni Ventura, author of many attacks (including, presumably, that at Piazza Fontana, together with Franco Freda: both were part of the Ordine Nuovo terrorist cell). Giannettini, a.k.a. Agent Zeta, escaped to France, and in January 1974 an arrest warrant against him was issued; in August 1974 Giannettini gave himself up to the Italian Consulate in Buenos Aires.
2. Buttafava, "Procedure sveltite," p. 113.
3. The investigations after Calabresi's murder oscillated between different trails, with no result whatsoever. In 1972 the Communist Party received an off-the-record claim from a presumably high-level source that Calabresi had confusedly sensed a connection between the Italian Secret Service, right-wing terrorists and the CIA. See Crainz, *Il paese mancato*, p. 395.

Smiling Maniacs (Corruzione al palazzo di giustizia)

D: Marcello Aliprandi. *S:* based on Ugo Betti's play; *SC:* Marcello Aliprandi, Gianfranco Clerici, Fernando Imbert; *DOP:* Gastone Di Giovanni (35mm, Eastmancolor, Cinecittà); *M:* Pino Donaggio, conducted by Giancarlo Gazzani (ed. Orchestralmusic); *Gioia al cabaret* (by P. Donaggio) sung by Evelyn Hanach and P. Donaggio; *E:* Gian Maria Messeri; *PD:* Giuseppe Bassan, Fernando Imbert; *CO:* Mariolina Bono; *SDr:* Renato Postiglione; *C:* Ubaldo Terzano, Roberto Brega, Giampiero Servo; *AC:* Massimo Carlini; *AE:* Antonio Proia; *AD:* Monica Felt [Monica Venturini]; *MU:* Raoul Ranieri; *AMU:* Augusta Pongetti; *Hair:* Giusy Bovino; *SO:* Massimo Jaboni; *Boom:* Gianfranco De Matthaeis; *SOE:* Renato Marinelli; *Color technician:* Giacomo Volpi; *SS:* Enrica Caruso. *Cast:* Franco Nero (Judge Dani), Fernando Rey (Judge Giulio Vanini), Umberto Orsini (Erzi), Gabriele Ferzetti (Judge Prandó), Martin Balsam (Carlo Goja), Mara Danaud (Flavia), Giovanna Benedetto (Elena Vanini), Umberto D'Orsi (Excellence), Renato Montanari, Roberto Antonelli (Rapist), Ugo Maria Morosi, Evelyn Hanack (Dancer), Margherita Sala, Bruno Rosa, Carla Mancini (Shop assistant in "Tintoria"), Lorenzo Piani (Bike driver), Adriano Amidei Migliano (Goja's man with bag), Francesco D'Adda, Renato Baldini (Man setting fire), Bruno Tocci (Thug), Roberto Pescara, Nicola Morelli (Judge), Aldo Bonamano (Judge), Valentino Dain. *Uncredited:* Bruno Bertocci, Angelo Boscariol (Agent in Palace of Justice), Nestore Cavaricci, Ennio Colaianni, Raniero Dorascenzi, Tom Felleghy (Goja's assistant), Giuseppe Marrocco (Man in church), Fulvio Mingozzi (Man in Centro Studi), Luciano Zanussi. *PROD:* Giorgio Venturini for Filmes (Rome); *GM:* Giancarlo Marchetti; *PM:* Cecilia Bigazzi; *PSu:* Viero Spadoni. *Country:* Italy. Filmed at Cinecittà. *Running time:* 110'; Visa no.: 65577 (11.30.1974); *Rating:* not rated; *Release date:* 01.16.1975; *Distribution:* Ital Noleggio Cinematografico; *Domestic gross:* 696,255,000 lire. *Also known as: Corrupción en el palacio de justicia* (Argentina), *Corrupción en el palacio de justicia italiano* (Spain), *Corruption in the Halls of Justice* (Australia). *Home video:* General Video (DVD, Italy). OST: CD Fin De Siècle Media FDS27.

For reasons of political prestige, the new Minister of Justice orders that action is taken urgently against the industrialist Carlo Goja. But the latter, who's been mysteriously warned of the impending raid, sets fire to a warehouse containing a compromising archive. Judge Erzi is entrusted with an investigation by the Superior Council of Justice: he arrives at the Palace of Justice to search for evidence that will lead to the indictment of the current President of the Courthouse Giulio Vanini, who had ambiguous connections with Goja. Young judge Dani, aspiring to take Vanini's place, takes advantage of Vanini's daughter's confidences to get hold of a compromising file on Goja. To avoid any further scandal, Vanini is removed by means of a promotion, while Dani becomes the new President. However, frightened by the reading of the dossier in which too many dignitaries would be involved in the indictment, Dani tries to get out of such a compromising position, but his resignation is not accepted. Once he obtained the presidency, he will either give way to corruption, or embark on a moralizing crusade that's far beyond his strength.

With a body of work consisting of only seven feature films, all of them only marginally successful or poorly distributed, Marcello

Aliprandi (1934–1997) is an often overlooked filmmaker, even by Italian cinema scholars. He certainly was not a genre director, which nowadays doesn't make his name much palatable to most cinephiles. On the other hand, his films were often too weird and artistically compromised to make him a critically respected *auteur*, even though Aliprandi's past as a stage director and as Luchino Visconti's assistant made him a rather respected figure. Aliprandi definitely didn't have the gift of timing. His films came out at the wrong moment and thus were underappreciated or misunderstood.

Born in Rome on January 2, 1934, in the mid-fifties Aliprandi left the study of Economics and enrolled in the Arts Academy "Silvio D'Amico," to study as a director. After graduation, he started working in the theater with Luchino Visconti, who then wanted him as his assistant while shooting *The Leopard* (1963). For most of the sixties Aliprandi worked on stage, directing dramas and operas: he finally made his feature film debut in 1970 with *La ragazza di latta* (originally *Mellonta Tauta*, a title inspired by an Edgar Allan Poe short story), a weird surreal sci-fi fable with blunt political overtones which was Sydne Rome's first film.

Even though he kept working as a scriptwriter (such as on *L'arma l'ora il movente*, an odd *giallo* directed in 1972 by Francesco Mazzei), it took four years before Aliprandi got behind the camera again, this time with an apparently very different project, which nonetheless featured similar political overtones.

Smiling Maniacs was an adaptation of Ugo Betti's stage play, with a contemporary setting. Written in 1944 but brought to the stage only in 1949, Betti's drama was a gloomy meditation on power and justice, with a decidedly Kafka-esque atmosphere. "The Palace is the mine and the well, it is the nest of malcontent and whispers. One starts spreading a slander, another one follows, and the day after there are ten, twenty more and ... it's like a cancer that spread and devours," the protagonist says in the opening scene of Betti's drama.

Aliprandi's version is rooted in the paranoid atmosphere of the period, whereas Betti's meditation was set in an abstract foreign city. The story focuses on the fight for power between two judges (Franco Nero and Gabriele Ferzetti) to take the place of the Presiding Judge Vanini (Fernando Rey). The latter is hiding a secret dossier on shady, corrupt Engineer Goja (Martin Balsam) who's got as many hidden secrets as politics on his paylist. After an attempt at a probe at Goja's secret archive has gone wrong, a ministry inspector (Umberto Orsini) pops up at the Tribunal to make an inquiry.

Aliprandi tries to shape the movie like some kind of a thriller, as all characters suspect and spy on each other, while Pino Donaggio's score openly mocks Morricone's work. Aliprandi's attempt at making something closer to Elio Petri and Francesco Rosi's political allegories based on Leonardo Sciascia's novels is shown by the odd surreal image — such as an ermine robe coming down on a rail in a laundry, or the scene where Vanini wakes up in his villa only to find his main door has been walled during the night in his sleep. But the director is not always able to keep all these elements in focus: Aliprandi even throws in a gratuitous, demented sequence where Vanini's wife (Mara Danaud) is assaulted by a grotesque pair of thugs (looking like they just got out of Kubrick's *A Clockwork Orange*) who strip her nude and torment her (which gained the film its U.S. title, in a desperate attempt to make it look like a crime-cop thriller). All in all, the result at times recalls the fanciful film-within-a-film shot by Giacomo Solaris (Franco Nero) in Damiano Damiani's *How to Kill a Judge*— which gives a measure of the decline (stylistic before than thematic) of politically committed cinema of the period.

Smiling Maniacs was to bring Aliprandi's biggest box office takings: not exactly a hit, but with almost 700 million lire, it was a solid commercial effort, thanks to its name cast and its proximity to the then in vogue crime genre. Yet, at the same time, this prevented the film from gaining the credibility it aimed for among most critics. The director's next work would be another peculiar effort, the odd ghost story *A Whisper in the Dark* (*Un sussurro nel buio*, 1976).

Suspected Death of a Minor (*Morte sospetta di una minorenne*)

D: Sergio Martino. *S:* Ernesto Gastaldi; *SC:* Ernesto Gastaldi, Luciano Martino; *DOP:* Giancarlo Ferrando (35mm, Eastmancolor, Technospes); *M:* Luciano Michelini (Ed. C.A.M.); *E:* Raimondo Cruciani; *PD, CO:* Elio Micheli: *APD:* Paolo Innocenzi; *SD:* Riccardo Domenici; *C:* Claudio Morabito, Salvatore Bella, Bernardo Valli; *AC:* Antonio Minutolo, Fabio Conversi; *AE:* Lidia Pascolini; *2nd AE:* Stefano Testa; *AD:* Michele Massimo Tarantini; *2nd AD:* Tiziana De Nora; *MU:* Mario Van Riel; *Hair:* Alfonso Gioffi; *SO:* Roberto Petrozzi; *Boom:* Massimo Mariani; *SP:* Vittorio Biffani; *SS:* Marisa Calia; *Press attache:* Lucherini, Rossetti, Spinola. *Cast:* Claudio Cassinelli (Commissioner Paolo Germi), Mel Ferrer (police superintendent), Jenny Tamburi [Luciana Tamburini] (Gloria), Massimo Girotti (Gaudenzio Pesce), Lia Tanzi (Carmela), Gianfranco Barra (Teti), Patrizia Castaldi (Marisa), Adolfo Caruso (Giannino), Carlo Alighiero (Chief of S.M.C.D.'s security), Franco Alpestre ("Il Menga"), Fiammetta Baralla (Pension Landlady), Barbara Magnolfi (Floriana), Aldo Massasso (Listri), Roberto Posse (Killer with sunglasses), Carlotta Witting (Director of S.M.C.D.). *Uncredited:* Bruno Alias, Umberto Amambrini, Ettore Arena, Franco Diogene (Pesce's lawyer), Dino Emanuelli (TV Journalist), Anita Laurenzi (Gloria's mother), Maurizio Mattioli (Pimp), Vezio Natili, Gennarino Pappagalli, Franca Scagnetti (Giannino's mother), Alessandra Vazzoler (Prostitute), Luciano Zanussi (Journalist). *PROD:* Luciano Martino for Dania Film; *PM:* Pietro Innocenzi; *PSu:* Beniamino Sterpetti, Massimo Civilotti; *PSe:* Marcello Tagliaferri; *ADM:* Valerio Ferri. *Country:* Italy. Filmed at R.P.A.— Elios Film (Rome). *Running time:* 100'; Visa no.: 66988 (08.09.1975); *Rating:* v.m.18; *Release date:* 08.12.1975; *Distribution:* Titanus; *Domestic gross:* 507,396,250 lire. *Also known as: Extraña muerte de una menor* (Spain). *Home video:* Medusa (DVD, Italy), Sazuma (DVD, Austria — English language).

Milan. After the violent murder of a teenager named Marisa, who was involved in a prostitution ring, Commissioner Paolo Germi — who prefers unorthodox investigating methods — pretends to be a small pickpocket to better infiltrate the underworld. He even hires an aide, a petty thief called Giannino. Through a prostitute, Carmela, a trail leads Germi to the S.M.C.D., an agency for domestic employees which actually conceals a teenage prostitution racket. The Commissioner eliminates a man nicknamed "Menga" who leads a kidnapping gang, and finds the two billion lire ransom paid for the abduction of a wealthy industrialist's son; however, he's dismissed from the investigations because of his violent methods. Germi resigns and continues his search on his own: he realizes that the mandator is the powerful banker Pesce, Marisa's uncle, who abused the girl and a number of her girlfriends. In the end, in the absence of adequate legal instruments, Germi confronts Pesce and kills him.

A mixed bag. Sergio Martino's *Suspected Death of a Minor*—originally to be called *Milano violenta* ("Violent Milan"), a title that was eventually dropped and used one year later for Mario Caiano's *Bloody Payroll*, also starring Cassinelli—is a rather uneasy hybrid between different genres: as with *What Have They Done to Your Daughters?* and *Calling All Police Cars*, it mixes the crime film and the "*giallo*," with a couple of sequences that ape Dario Argento's thrillers, complete with a pseudo–Goblin score by Luciano Michelini (who was expressly asked to write something in the vein of *Deep Red*, and it shows; unfortunately the soundtrack has not been issued on record so far). However, even though Martino was one of the better directors to emerge from the *gialli* fever, with such films as *The Strange Vice of Mrs. Wardh* (*Lo strano vizio della signora Wardh*, 1970) and *Torso* (*I corpi presentano tracce di violenza carnale*, 1973), here the thriller elements look definitely inappropriate and preposterous, especially since the script also incorporates mild comedy (such as the caricatured Commissioner played by Gianfranco Barra). Ernesto Gastaldi admitted: "In my opinion, it's a minor film, perhaps it proved tired from the very start since it was my own story. This time, the usually very good Martino didn't manage to give the film a decisive shot-in-the-arm. It's likely there were too many films of that kind during this time."[1]

That said, Gastaldi's script is not without its merits. It's about forty minutes into the film that we discover how the handsome, smart, funny and yet unscrupulous petty thief played by Claudio Cassinelli is actually a Commissioner in disguise, who has infiltrated Milan's underworld to track down a kidnapping/prostitution ring. Cassinelli's character is one of the most unconventional and interesting of 1970s Eurocrime: he always ends up with his glasses broken (either in a fight or in bed) like Woody Allen did in *Take the Money and Run* (1969), he's got a sharp tongue (with the same use of Milanese slang that characterized Caneparo in *The Violent Professionals*) and at times he almost seems to enjoy his illegal deeds—not to mention his sex encounters with a prostitute (Lia Tanzi) who leads him to the racketeers he's looking for.

Cassinelli's character is one of the elements that make *Suspected Death of a Minor* closer to Giorgio Scerbanenco's novels, together with its portrayal of the Milan underworld and depiction of secondary characters (such as the lodging-house's landlady who closes an eye to illicit encounters in her rooms) as well as the ending, where Cassinelli exacts justice on his own after realizing that his opponent (Massimo Girotti) is untouchable.

However, despite the film's obvious limits, Martino's direction has at least one inspired moment, in a memorable sequence where Claudio Cassinelli chases a thug into a Milanese cinema where the director's previous *giallo Your Vice Is a Locked Room and Only I Have the Key* (*Il tuo vizio è una stanza chiusa e solo io ne ho la chiave*, 1972) is being projected. What's more, *Suspected Death of a Minor* marks a hiatus of sorts. From then on, the *giallo* and thriller genres would follow different paths: the former, after Argento's landmark and definitive work *Deep Red*, would quickly wane and become more and more contaminated with eroticism, while the latter would become locked up in the repetition of a winning narrative scheme.

Note

1. E-mail interview, January 2012.

Syndicate Sadists (Il giustiziere sfida la città)

D: Umberto Lenzi. *S* and *SC:* Vincent Mann [Vincenzo Mannino]; *DOP:* Federico Zanni (35mm, Eastmancolor, LV-Luciano Vittori); *M:* Franco Micalizzi, conducted by Alessandro Blonksteiner (ed. R.C.A.); *E:* Daniele Alabiso; *PD:* Giacomo Calò Carducci; *CO:* Walter Patriarca; *C:* Elio Polacchi; *2nd C:* Alfredo Senzacqua; *AC:* Mario Pastorini, Bernardo Valli; *AE:* Amedeo Moriani; *AD:* Alessandro Metz; *MU:* Franco Di Girolamo; *Hair:* Jolanda Angelucci; *SO:* Bruno Zanoli; *Boom:* Angelo Amatulli; *SOE:* Aldo Ciorba, Sergio Basile; *Mix:* Bruno Moreal; *SE:* Cataldo Galliano; *SP:* Francesco Narducci; *STD* (for Tomas Milian): Riccardo Petrazzi (motorcycle scenes); *ST:* Gianluca Petrazzi; *G:* Onofrio Coppola; *SS:* Mirella Roy Malatesta. *Cast:* Tomas Milian (Rambo), Joseph Cotten (Paternò), Maria Fiore (Maria Scalia), Mario Piave (Pino Scalia), Luciano Catenacci (Conti), Guido Alberti (Bar owner), Femi Benussi (Flora), Silvano Tranquilli (Dr. Marco Marsili), Shirley Corrigan (Conti's lover), Antonio Casale (Philip Duval), Rosario Borelli (Paternò's henchman), Luciano Pigozzi (Conti's henchman), Mario Novelli (Franco), Bruno Di Luia (Conti's henchman), Giuseppe Castellano (Conti's henchman), Riccardo Petrazzi (Paternò's thug in billiard room), Tom Felleghy (Commander Ferrari, head of Mondialpol), Gianni Di Benedetto (Commissioner), Duilio Cruciani (Luigino Scalia), Alessandro Cocco (Giampiero Marsili), Evelyn Stewart [Ida Galli] (Marsili's wife), Adolfo Lastretti (Ciccio Paternò). *Uncredited:* Bruno Alias (Man in gambling room), Bruno Bertocci (Man in gambling room), Rossana Canghiari (Woman in gambling room), Nestore Cavaricci (Man in gambling room), Enrico Chiappafreddo (Giuseppe, Marsili's chauffeur), Franz Colangeli, Raniero Dorascenzi (Croupier), Rocco Lerro (Newsman waiting outside house), Francesco Narducci, Benito Pacifico (Paternò's thug in billiard room), Walter Patriarca (2nd newsman waiting outside house), Tony [Antonio] Raccosta (Man at autodrome), Claudio Ruffini (Conti's thug guarding Giampiero), Sergio Testori (Conti's thug), Luciano Zanussi (Journalist), Rinaldo Zamperla (Paternò's thug dressed as cop). *PROD:* Luciano Martino for Dania Film; *PM:* Vittorio Galiano; *PSu:* Davide Pash, Claudio Cuomo; *ADM:* Maria Spera. *Country:* Italy. Filmed at R.P.A. Elios (Rome) and on location in Milan. *Running time:* 95'; Visa no.: 66964 (08.04.1975); *Rating:* v.m.14; *Release date:* 08.16.1975; *Distribution:* Medusa; *Domestic gross:* 1,451,703,190 lire. *Also known as: Flash Solo* (West Germany, 05.04.1984—91'), *Der Vernichter* (West Germany, video title), *Rambo's Revenge* (USA), *One Just Man* (U.K.—Home video), *La venganza de Rambo / Desafío a la ciudad* (Spain), *Bracelet de sang* (France), *Final Payment* (U.S.—Home video). *Home video:* Medusa, NoShame (DVD, Italy), Media Blasters / Shriek Show (DVD, USA), Eyecatcher (DVD, Germany). OST: CD Digitmovies CDDM176.

Milan. A biker named Rambo, an ex-gangster-turned-vigilante, rides into town to visit an old friend, Pino Scalia, who now works for a security squad scrutinizing local Mafia activity. The Conti gang kidnaps the son of a wealthy engineer, Marsili; Scalia, who had exposed the kidnapping, is killed by one of Conti's men, Duval. Rambo intervenes to avenge his dead friend and release the kidnapped boy. First he dispatches Duval, then, by using the two billion ransom as bait, he puts old Paternò's gang against Conti's, so that the two factions almost exterminate one another. Even though he is alone against the ruthless survivors, Rambo kills the remaining bandits and sets the boy free. Old Paternò, isolated and humiliated, commits suicide, and Rambo leaves on his bike towards new adventures.

Despite the Italian title (which translates to "The Avenger Challenges the City"), Umberto Lenzi's *Syndicate Sadists* has only marginally to do with the "rebel citizen" thread best represented by Enzo G. Castellari's *Street Law*: Rambo (Tomas Milian) is not a harassed middle-class citizen — and not an ordinary one for sure. He is rather a Western movie character dropped into a contemporary urban environment, an illegitimate son of Clint Eastwood's Man With No Name — minus the latter's amorality, that is —, who rides a motorbike instead of a horse. What's more, his attire, attitude and speech look like a rehearsal for Milian's most popular character, Nico Giraldi. Rambo has a fluent beard, wears colored caps and has a knack for pungent dialogue. One of the film's most notorious lines, Milian's "monologue of the hole" ("Life's a hole: we are born from a hole, eat from a hole, shit from a hole and end up in a hole") predates the verbal fireworks of the actor's next films in the role of the foul-mouthed cop.

Allegedly, it was Milian who suggested the character's name, after reading David Morrell's book *First Blood*: the working title was *Rambo sfida la città* (Rambo Challenges the City). However, even though Lenzi cites Don Siegel's urban crime films as a major influence, Vincenzo Mannino's script liberally borrows characters, psychologies and narrative developments from the Western, thus openly endorsing the poliziotteschi's descent from the former.

Milian's Rambo is a metropolitan version of the lonely wandering rider: he arrives in town on his motorbike instead of a horse, puts two crime bosses one against the other, *A Fistful of Dollars*–style, and eventually leaves after destroying the rival gangs and releasing a kidnapped child. *Syndicate Sadists* also features the obligatory barroom brawl (Rambo knocks down a pair of thugs in a bar using a billiard cue), a boy who worships the hero like Brandon De Wilde did with Alan Ladd in *Shane* (1953, George Stevens) a good-hearted prostitute (Femi Benussi) who however, instead of leaving in the sunset with the lead, ends up beaten to death by the villains: there is no room for romance in the poliziotteschi genre. Even character actors like Luciano Pigozzi look like they just stepped out of a horse opera, while main villain Joseph Cotten is a surprise variation on Gabriele Ferzetti's poliomyelitic railroad tycoon in *Once Upon a Time in the West*, as his physical handicap (he's blind) is revealed only in the end — some may see it as an involuntary reversal of Cotten's role as the fake paralytic in Mario Bava's *Baron Blood* (*Gli orrori del castello di Norimberga*, 1972). The icing on the cake is Milian's ironic in-joke, when he tells Conti (Luciano Catenacci) "Corri, uomo, corri…" (Run, Man, Run) quoting the title of Sergio Sollima's follow-up to *The Big Gundown* in which the Cuban actor played the Mexican peasant Cuchillo.

Yet this material is deeply immersed within poliziotteschi's typical view of contemporary Italy, in a Milan where huge popular condos host Southern immigrants who try hard to build a better future for their offspring: "the world is harsh to *terroni* like Pino Scalia," Rambo's friend bitterly admits, addressing himself with the term (*terrone*, literally farmer) contemptuously used by Northern Italians to call those living in Southern regions. Mannino's script deals with the rise of kidnappings — the most recurring plot element in mid–1970s poliziotteschi — and hints at another common ingredient, the spread of private security agencies (see Tonino Valerii's *Go Gorilla Go*). Lenzi flavors the action with his typical indulgence on violence: beside the required shootouts and Benussi's death, a grim highlight has a thug (Giuseppe Castellano) being choked to death with the content of a heroin bag.

As engrossing as it is, *Syndicate Sadists* is somehow let down by the unrestrained use of speeded-up frames: Tomas Milian's (or actually, his stunt double Riccardo Petrazzi's) motorcycle acrobatics, which were essentially derivative of Steve McQueen's in *The Great Escape* (1963), are actively diminished by the "unrealistic" pacing. Besides being a huge hit in Italy with over one billion and five hundred million lira grossed at the box office, *Syndicate Sadists* was released in the United States by Sam Sherman's Independent International. The unrated U.S. DVD is missing about two minutes of footage: a scene where the mother of the kidnapped boy comes home and finds a bunch of reporters awaiting her, Paterno's goons searching for Rambo in a pub, and two reaction shots.

The Teenage Prostitution Racket (*Storie di vita e malavita — Racket della prostituzione minorile*)

D: Carlo Lizzani. *S:* Marisa Rusconi, Mino Giarda, based on a reportage by Marisa Rusconi; *SC:* Carlo Lizzani, Mino Giarda; *Collaboration to direction:* Mino Giarda; *DOP:* Lamberto Caimi (35mm, Kodak, Telecolor); *M:* Ennio Morricone, conducted by the author (ed. Interdemos); *E:* Franco Fraticelli; *PD, ArtD:* Franco Fumagalli; *AArtD:* Giuseppe Vianello; *CO:* Lia Morandini; *ArtD:* Natalia Verdelli; *C:* Roberto Seveso; *AC:* Dario Mulazzani; *AE:* Alessandro Gabriele; *2nd AE:* Francesco Reitano; *AD:* Gilberto Squizzato; *MU:* Silvana Petri; *Hair:* Luisa Piovesan; *SO:* Domenico Pasquadibisceglie; *Boom:* Giuseppina Saliano; *Mix:* Mario Amari; *SS:* Lucia Ferrante. *Cast:* Cinzia Mambretti (Rosina), Cristina Moranzoni (Gisella), Annarita Grapputo (Daniela), Anna Curti (Antonietta Barni), Danila Grassini (Albertina), Lidia Di Corato (Laura), Nicola Del Buono ("Velvet"), Lidia Costanzo, Sergio Masieri, Mario Mattia Giorgetti, Arturo Corso, Flora Saggese, Debora Toscanini, Sandro Pizzocchero (Alberto), Franco Ferri, Marina Fabbri, Rudy Dal Prà, Paola Faloja (Daniela's mother), Tony Casale, Franca Mantelli (Mistress of the brothel), Walter Valdi, Walter Villani, Nisca [Antiniska] Nemour, Giuliana Rivera (Gisella's mother), Guglielmo Mazzotti, Mario Mercalli (Antonietta's father), Nevio Maxie, Enzo Fisichella (Judge), Achille Grioni (Doctor), Mario Marchetti, Daniele Pagani, Luciano Dell'Acqua, Piergiorgio Plebani, Franca Aldrovandi (Psychologist), Licia Lombardi, Marisa Puntonieri, Guido Tasso, Guglielmo Graig (Head of agency), Elisa Pozzi, Giancarlo Sala, Salvatore Pistorino, Bianca Verdirosi (Hitch-hiker), Boris Stetka, Sauro Martini, Dina Castigliego, Pietro Vial, Fabrizio Jovine, Guido Spadea, Ivana Aretusi, Leda Celani, Annibale Papetti, Gino Mazzotta, Franco Pesante, Domenico Seren Gay (Master of the brothel). *Uncredited:* Suzy Fassetta (Hitch-hiker), Piermario Raimondo (Rosina's suitor), Tiziana Conti. *PROD:* Adelina Tattilo and Carlo Maietto for Thousand Cinematografica (Milan); *GM:* Livio Maffei; *PM:* Silvio Siano; *PSu:* Biagio Angelini, Amedeo Baratti; *PSe:* Roberta Veronesi, Alessandro De Luca. *Country:* Italy. Filmed at Icet — De Paolis (Milan) and on location in Milan and Genoa. *Running time:* 120'; Visa no. 66319 (04.03.75); *Rating:* v.m.18: *Release date:* 04.03.1975; *Distribution:* Alpherat; *Domestic gross:* 1,208,692,560 lire. *Also known as:* *Strassenmädchen-Report* (West Germany, 06.28.1977 — 97'): *The Prostitution Racket* (U.K., 1976 — 91'). *Home video:* Raro (DVD, Italy). OST: Screen Trax CDST 318.

The film follows the stories of six underage girls who become prostitutes in Milan and its surroundings: the naive Rosina, just arrived from Sardinia, is seduced, deceived and enslaved by a pimp; 15-year-old Antonietta is impregnated by her father and is forced to prostitute herself in an advanced state of pregnancy; Albertina receives her clients in department stores' dressing rooms or phone booths; Laura commits suicide after her pimps have killed the dog which was her only companion; Daniela is an upper-class girl who sells her body in an exclusive brothel as a means of revenge on her family.

After the World War II drama *Last Days of Mussolini* (*Mussolini ultimo atto*, 1974) starring Rod Steiger as the Duce, with his next film Carlo Lizzani returned to the present with one of his most controversial works. The idea for a film on the teenage prostitution racket came to Lizzani after reading a reportage written by Marisa Rusconi on the weekly magazine *L'Espresso*. Lizzani worked on a basic outline with journalists Massimo Fini and Claudio Lazzaro (whose names do not appear in the credits). Then, while he was in the States to work on the English-language version of *Last Days of Mussolini*, Lizzani asked his assistant Mino Giarda to get in touch with Rusconi. Starting from the journalist's material, Giarda developed a more detailed story about six underage prostitutes, introduced by the framing story where a middle-aged woman hitchhikes her way on a motorway outside Milan and offers the sexual services of her thirteen-year-old granddaughter to the drivers. The woman's introductory phrase ("Sir, would you fancy a little screwing?") came from an anecdote that Lizzani heard from Roberto Rossellini, who had had a similar experience while shooting *Journey to Italy* (*Viaggio in Italia*, 1954).

The episode structure allows for an ample sociological portrayal, where reality is filtered in a more or less direct way, and most of the stories come from Rusconi's reportage with minimal changes. Lizzani, who already depicted the theme of prostitution in the episode *L'amore che si paga* ("The Love That Gets Paid") in *Love in the City* (*Amore in città*, 1953), doesn't keep a step back from crude and explicit scenes: the film features plenty of full frontal nudity, lovemaking, sexual perversions, brutal scenes of violence. Lizzani's choice seemingly put *The Teenage Prostitution Racket* in the same territory as those crime films with similar themes, such as *What Have They Done to Your Daughters?* and *Calling All Police Cars*— including a violent ending, where members of the racket attack and set fire to the house of the middle-aged woman and her prostitute granddaughter as seen in the opening scene, causing the women's paroxistic reaction: one of the racketeers is caught and beaten to death with clubs and bricks and then decapitated with a shovel, in one of the most brutal scenes ever seen in an Italian film.

Italian poster for *The Teenage Prostitution Racket* (1975).

All of which explains the critical distrust that met the film, labeled as a "sociological *Decameron*," plagued by a "continuous oscillation between realist photo-*roman* to some sort of poor man's *Psychopathia Sexualis*."[1] However, Lizzani does never forsakes the lost dignity of his poor protagonists: as humiliating as their stories are, the underage prostitutes of *The Teenage Prostitution Racket* are never just bodies to get undressed for the camera, but they retain their pain and humanity. Male characters fare much worse: either obtuse or vicious clients, unpleasant in looks and manners alike; violent and abject pimps who trade women as if they are livestock; family fathers who are either absent, indifferent or libidinous, and have sex with girls who may be — and sometimes are — their own daughters. The immediate, rough dialogue, the insistence on indecent themes and situations, the resort to unknown actors display Lizzani's urgency to rediscover his own cinema, shaping it anew to better adhere to the reality of the time. All things considered, it's an updated rethinking of the

Neorealist lesson, but also the director's umpteenth artistic challenge, that led him to narrative and expressive choices which were typical of contemporary genre cinema.

Produced by "Playmen" publisher Adelina Tattilo and Carlo Maietto, *The Teenage Prostitution Racket* was a low-budget production, and featured a largely non-professional cast: the best-known face is that of Annarita Grapputo, who found an ephemeral glory in genre cinema — mostly the poliziotteschi, with such titles as Lucio Marcaccini's *Hallucination Strip* and Carlo Ausino's *Double Game* (1977). The film's harsh realistic look is enhanced by Lamberto Caimi's cinematography. Lizzani asked his director of photography (who worked with Ermanno Olmi and Alberto Lattuada) for scabrous and terse images, in order to show a marginal and degraded, cold and hostile Milan.

Given *The Teenage Prostitution Racket*'s daring theme, Lizzani and the producer expected the film to be seized at its release for obscenity, a rather common occurrence at that time. The first public showing took place in a little town near Milan, so that territorial jurisdiction would belong to the rather malleable Milan tribunal — and so it was: the film was denounced for obscenity and briefly seized before the charges were dropped and the case archived. However, the version released to foreign markets included more risqué inserts that in a couple of occasions descended into hardcore porn: these scenes were shot by Lizzani's assistant director Mino Giarda, without Lizzani knowing about them: the director had entrusted Giarda to film more explicit footage for export releases but would discover the addition of hardcore stuff only later on.

Upon its release, *The Teenage Prostitution Racket* caused a stir, but Lizzani found unexpected defenders such as the Catholic weekly magazine "Famiglia Cristiana." It was a good box office success, with over one billion and 200 million lire, a remarkable result for a film without any "name" actors (Antonioni's *The Passenger*, in comparison, grossed slightly less than Lizzani's film). Lizzani and Giarda toyed with the idea of a follow-up *sui generis*, *Azione! Assurdo reale* (Action! Absurd reality), a metafilmic reflection about a director and a scriptwriter who move to Milan to shoot a movie on a teenage prostitution racket. The project was dropped when Lizzani started work on another film for Tattilo and Maietto: *San Babila 8 P.M.*, a similarly "instant" movie bearing even stronger affinities to the crime genre.

Note

1. Kezich, *Il Millefilm*, p. 615.

2 Magnum .38 per una città di carogne (2 .38 Magnum for a City of Scoundrels)

D: Mario Pinzauti. *S* and *SC:* Mario Pinzauti; *DOP:* Giovanni Raffaldi (35mm, Eastmancolor); *M:* Bruno Nicolai, conducted by the author; *E:* Luciana Scandroglio; *AE:* Alessandro Ojetti; *2nd AsE:* Ugo Chiaromonte; *PD:* Giovanni Fratalocchi; *C:* Massimo Lupi; *AD:* Franco Di Dio; *2nd AD:* Renato Ferraro; *SO:* Alberto Vani; *MA:* Antonio Basile; *SS:* Lucia Luconi. *Cast:* Dino Strano (Franco Palermo), Richard Lloyd [Iloosh Khoshabe] (Giancarlo Proietti), Luigi Pistilli (Commissioner Perri), Gianni Musy (Piero Turchi), Anne Marie [Annamaria] Meyer (Silvia Ronchi), Guido Leontini (Sergio "Er Piattola"), Erna Schurer [Emma Costantino] (Gabry), Gordon Mitchell (Renato Proietti), Nino Curatola [Nino D'Errico], Enrico Curatola, Gianni Pesola, Stephy Ross, Gianna Russu, Enzo Spitaleri ("Er Piattola"'s laughing thug), Pino [Giuseppe] Carbone. *Uncredited:* Umberto Amambrini (Cop), Nestore Cavaricci (policeman on crime scene), Raniero Dorascenzi (police official on crime scene), Benito Pacifico, Sergio Smacchi, Orazio Stracuzzi. *PROD:* Candido Simeone and Giovanni Luchetti for M.N.C. Triangolo Cinematografica; *PM:* Giovanni Lucchetti; *PSu:* Bruno Vani; *PSe:* Salvatore Carrara. *Country:* Italy. Filmed at Film Cave Studio (Rome) and on location in Rome. *Running time:* 95'; Visa no.: 66775 (06.26.1975); *Rating:* v.m.18; *Release date:* 10.03.1975; *Distribution:* Regional; *Domestic gross:* 142,666,560 lire. *Home video:* Cvr (VHS, Italy)

Rome. Sicilian pulp novelist and former Mafia killer Franco Palermo finds out that his former secretary and mistress Silvia has become a prostitute. To bring her back, he becomes involved with the Roman underworld. Franco traces her pimp, Piero, but is shot in the leg and gets hospitalized. Meanwhile, Piero is eliminated by his own gang. Silvia goes back to Franco, but the writer is harassed by a small-time gangster, the slimy Sergio, who tries to extort money from him. He refuses, but is heavily beaten and humiliated by Sergio's men, suffering severe damage to the liver. Determined to exact revenge, Franco buys a couple of guns. He pays visit to a bisexual painter named Gabry, who appears to know more about the "business." She tells him about the violent brothers Proietti, who run the prostitution ring. Forced to collect prostitution money for the racket, Franco hires two Sicilian Mafia hoods to rob Sergio and take his money back. The gang retaliates by torturing and killing Silvia, with Gabry's complicity. Already close to death because of his internal injuries, Palermo goes on a deadly rampage, killing the unsuspecting heads of the racket before he meets his end in a car crash.

Shot on a shoestring and only marginally distributed at the time of its release, Mario Pinzauti's obscure *2 Magnum 38 per una città di carogne* is a miserable attempt at an urban hard-boiled yarn, entirely shot in seedy suburban exteriors and squalid sets (Gordon Mitchell's Cave Film Studio, the cheapest in Rome) with J&B bottles always in plain sight. Technically, it's a mess: flashback scenes are shot through a badly clouded lens, cuts between shots often don't match, and even Bruno Nicolai's score is recycled from other crime films.

If that wasn't enough, *2 Magnum 38 per una città di carogne* is also weighed down by its unlikely lead. Slightly balding, paunchy, ugly-looking, Dino Strano — featured in many Demofilo Fidani films under the pseudonym Dean Stratford, and here dubbed by the reliable Pino Colizzi — is definitely a far cry from a convincing hard-boiled hero, and even less so as an ardent womanizer, even though blonde Erna Schurer tells him: "There's something strange about you that turns women on." Strano's subsequent career would reach a nadir with the Renato Polselli/Bruno Vani hardcore porn *Teresa altri desideri* (1983) where he played a fading Western movie star.

The rest of the cast is an odd bunch to say the least: Luigi Pistilli (in the predictable "tough cop" routine) and Erna Schurer look like they showed up on the set by chance, while Pinzauti exhumes a forgotten sword-and-sandal hero (Turkish-born Iloosh Khoshabe, the star of *Vulcan, Son of Jupiter*, *Hercules, Samson & Ulysses* and *The Invincible Brothers Maciste* among others) as one of an unlikely duo of villainous brothers — the other is another *Peplum* veteran and Z-movie devotée, Gordon Mitchell — who enjoy blowing soap bubbles (!). The great character actor Guido

Leontini, typecast in his usual scoundrel role and displaying a limp, is saddled with the memorably sleazy nickname "Er piattola" ("Crab louse").

Apart from a scene where Dino Strano buys two guns from a gypsy in a slum, which somewhat predates *Taxi Driver* ("With this one, you can declare war against the sheiks or even organize a raid in Vietnam!" proudly says the vendor, who exhibits his guns on a table, beside hanging sausages and bottles of wine) the film's most interesting feature are the autobiographical touches: director Mario Pinzauti was a prolific pulp writer in the '60s, delivering trashy horror and crime novels assembly line–style for cheap paperback series such as "I racconti di Dracula," in the golden days of the Italian pulp industry. In what sounds like a bout of self-criticism, Dino Strano's character seems to critically evaluate the author's own literary output when he bitterly complains: "Crap ... everything I write is just crap!"

Violent Rome, a.k.a. *Violent City (Roma violenta)*

D: Franco Martinelli [Marino Girolami]. *S* and *SC:* Vincenzo Mannino; *DOP:* Fausto Zuccoli (35mm, Eastmancolor, Telecolor); *M:* Guido and Maurizio De Angelis (ed. Prima); *E:* Vincenzo Tomassi; *PD:* Antonio Visone; *CO:* Silvana Scandariato; *ArtD:* Luchino Oltrona Visconti; *C:* Guglielmo Vincioni; *AC:* Enzo Frattari, Enzo Tosi; *AE:* Lamberto Mancini; *2nd AE:* Sergio Altigieri; *AD:* Romano Scandariato; *MU:* Gianfranco Mecacci; *AMU:* Marcello Meniconi; *Hair:* Marcella Ginnoto; *SO:* Roberto Petrozzi; *Boom:* Guglielmo Smeraldi; *SOE:* Fernando Caso; *Foley artist:* Alvaro Gramigna; *SE:* G. Stacchini; *SP:* Vittorio Biffani; *W:* Maria Zara; *Props:* Angelo Bonfà; *Property set technician:* Gino De Rossi; *STC:* Benito Stefanelli; *SS:* Marion Mertes. *Cast:* Maurizio Merli (Commissioner Betti), Richard Conte (Advocate Sartori), Silvano Tranquilli (Chief of the Flying Squad), Ray Lovelock (Biondi), John Steiner (Franco Spadoni "Chiodo"), Daniela Giordano (Betti's lover), Attilio Duse (Antinori), Giuliano Esperati [Disperati] (De Rossi), Marcello Monti (The Chink), Consalvo Dell'Arti (Violante), Luciano Rossi (Delivery man), Pippo Pollaci (Pollaci), Marco Stefanelli (Grocery store robber), Brunello Chiodetti (Santini), Ruggero Diella (Young man killed on bus), Mario Novelli (Lazzari), Massimo Vanni (Valli), Francesco D'Adda (Pandolfi), Ezio Busso, Rina Mascetti (Hostage), Maria Rosaria Riuzzi (Sartori's daughter). *Uncredited:* Antonio Anelli (Man in restaurant during robbery), Francesco Anniballi (Passer-by), Artemio Antonini, John Bartha (Junk yard worker), Dolores Calò (Woman on bus), Omero Capanna (Robber in restaurant / Thug who beats Biondi), Nestore Cavaricci (policeman), Enrico Chiappafreddo (Burglar), Giovanni Cianfriglia (Robber in restaurant / Thug who beats Biondi), Massimo Ciprari (Man in billiard room), Raffaele Di Mario (Fence), Attilio Dottesio (Man on bus), Tom Felleghy (Doctor), Gilberto Galimberti (Burglar), Alba Maiolini (Woman with glasses on bus), Giuseppe Marrocco (Man in restaurant during robbery), Dino Mattielli (Zucchelli), Luciano Melani (Magistrate), Romano Milani (Man on bus), Benito Pacifico (Augusto, robber at the supermarket), Mimmo Palmara (Commissioner De Julis), Enrico Palombini (Man in restaurant during robbery), Teresa Rossi Passante (Woman in restaurant during robbery), Franca Scagnetti (Woman on bus), Pupita Lea Scuderoni (Woman on bus), Oscar Sciamanna (Man in bank during robbery), Sergio Smacchi (Sergio, the pimp), Benito Stefanelli (Robber at the supermarket), Pietro Torrisi (Burglar). *PROD:* Flaminia Produzioni Cinematografiche; *PM:* Fabrizio De Angelis; *PSu:* Dante Brini, Claudio Cuomo; *PSe:* Giandomenico Stellitano; *CASH:* Benito Mancini. *Country:* Italy. Filmed at Incir—De Paolis (Rome). *Running time:* 90'; Visa no.: 66956 (08.04.1975); *Rating:* v.m.14; *Release date:* 08.13.1975; *Distribution:* Fida; *Domestic gross:* 2,195,950,443 lire. *Also known as: Street Killers* (U.K.), *Verdammte, Heilige Stadt* (West Germany, 05.28.1976—89'), *Gewalt rast durch die Stadt* (West Germany—Home video), *Rottereden* (Norway—Home video). *Home video:* Federal Video (DVD, Italy). OST: CD Beat Records CDCR 69.

Commissioner Betti of the Roman police force lost his 18-year-old brother, who was shot for no reason by a thug during a robbery. When a very similar episode happens on a bus, Betti unleashes agents Biondi and De Rossi, disguised as beggars, to gather information and identify the criminals. He succeeds and arrests the culprits after mercilessly beating them up. When his excess of zeal and violent methods get him sacked from the force, Betti accepts the invitation of a lawyer named Sartori and becomes the head of a special squad of "vigilantes" who—thanks to the Commissioner's knowledge of the criminal milieu and the news that he still receives through his faithful assistant Biondi—wreak havoc in the Roman underworld. However, after Biondi is badly wounded in a vengeful aggression, which leaves him crippled for life, Betti realizes that he can't persevere on a path of violence that only leads to more of the same.

August 4, 1975. Just a few days after *Blood, Sweat and Fear*, another key film in the history of the poliziotteschi came out. Produced by Edmondo Amati and directed by Marino Girolami (under the a.k.a. Franco Martinelli), *Violent Rome* came to life as a blatant rip-off, an imitation of Enzo G. Castellari's *High Crime*. "After *High Crime* Amati offered me and Franco Nero another film in the same vein, to be shot immediately since the former had been a box office hit," Castellari revealed. "Of course we asked for a slightly higher sum, as it was customary after such a success, but eventually we didn't find an agreement—especially on Franco's side, as his agent didn't want to lower his economical claims [...]. That's how *Violent Rome* was born: Amati called on my father to direct the film and cast Maurizio Merli as a carbon copy of Franco's character."[1]

From the earlier film, *Violent Rome* reprised and amplified the spectacularization of violence, the exasperated use of the urban context and, more importantly, the figure of the avenger cop, who's traced on Castellari's Belli played by Franco Nero: even the surname—Betti—is almost the same, as well as the hero's looks. Commissioner Betti was played by 35-year-old Maurizio Merli, an actor who came to notoriety after a rather obscure apprenticeship, with small parts in such undistinguished films as Ruggero Deodato's *Phenomenal* (*Fenomenal e il tesoro di Tutankamen*, 1968), thanks to his leading role in the TV mini-series *Il giovane Garibaldi* (1974) by Franco Rossi. Merli was still finding his feet in the movies, after the flop of his previous film *Catene* (1974), a bland remake of Ruggero Matarazzo's classic 1949 melodrama, helmed by Silvio Amadio. Girolami, who had already directed him in the sleazy courtroom drama *Eros e Thanatos* (1969) and in the Decamerotic flick *Love Games In Florence* (*Decamerone proibitissimo—Boccaccio mio statte zitto...*, 1972), thought he had the perfect choice in his hands. With his square jaw, blue eyes and intense look, Merli gave his character a much needed conviction: his embodiment of the righteous cop was full-hearted, and made Betti—who would return in two more films, *Violent Naples* (*Napoli violenta*, 1976, Umberto Lenzi) and *Special Cop in Action* (*Italia a mano armata*, 1976, Marino Girolami)—the Commissioner *par excellence* of Italian crime cinema.

The Roman underworld of the period was filling news

headlines with stories of shoot-outs, robberies and assorted killings: gangsters such as the Marseillaise Bergamelli and Berenguer divided the city in zones of interest, each of which was dominated by one gang. Vincenzo Mannino's script depicts a similarly degenerate, inhuman metropolitan environment, with an insistence on grim tones and a programmed crudeness that leaves its mark. No place is safe anymore — banks, streets, restaurants, buses. Those who dare rebel are killed like dogs in front of their families. Rome has become a no man's land, a modern Wild West, and Betti is the avenger whose mission is righting the wrongs, by putting into practice the Bible's dictate: an eye for an eye, a tooth for a tooth. "When I find a criminal I give him his just desserts, and until I find it I have no peace," he states, and he's clearly not exaggerating. Betti's fury is almost Puritanical in its utter dedication to moral principles. He is a solitary hero, with neither roots nor regional accent; he has precarious and often frustrating sentimental relationships with strong and independent women; he hides deep scars and unexpressed anger in his past: in *Violent Rome* we learn that his brother was brutally murdered, whereas in *Special Cop in Action* it's his father who was killed by an underage robber. Betti is an outsider, who sees his job as a mission: "Wherever they send me, that's fine by me." Even after he's been removed from his job, he still carries his gun under the armpit.

Maurizio Merli, left, in a fight scene from *Violent Rome* (1975).

Violent Rome doesn't follow a proper outline, but rather depicts a series of vignettes whose characterizing thread is violence. Such a rhapsodic structure emphasizes a portrayal of urban aggressiveness that's past the point of no return. The film's most spectacular sequence comes halfway through: a chase over seven minutes long, which in any other movie would have been the climax, culminates with Betti shooting dead the hateful "Chiodo" (John Steiner), and preludes the film's second half, as the trigger-happy cop is thrown out of the police. *Violent Rome* then introduces one of the genre's most ambiguous and debatable characters, Sartori (Richard Conte), a wealthy lawyer who, just like Claudio Gora's character did in Lenzi's *Manhunt in the City*, has gathered a vigilante squad to defend property and order. Sartori is an ideologically repugnant character, and is played by an actor who's used to villainous roles: but the surprising thing in Girolami's film is that whatever Sartori's obscure scheme may be (if there is any, that is), Mannino's script never explores its implications, so that in the end Sartori turns out to be a positive character — even a victim, since his only daughter has been raped before his eyes (by none other than the genre's favorite sleazeball Luciano Rossi, while the thug's accomplice sneers at the distraught parent: "Don't close your eyes, look what he's doin' to her!"). Said scene highlights a tendency to pair violent and sexual excesses, which would become one of the poliziotteschi's main dishes; carnal violence is an obligatory ingredient, within a conception of genre cinema that demands to pile up excess and transgression — and the resulting v.m.18 (forbidden to those under 18 years old) rating — as a bait to lure audiences that are craving for strong emotions, no matter what.

Betti's relationship with violence is similarly debatable: the ex-commissioner does not hesitate when he is offered the chance to become the head of Sartori's vigilante squad, but in the end he eventually makes up his mind. "Fact is, you cannot do justice by yourself, even though the temptation is strong," he confides to his best and only (?) friend and former colleague Biondi (Ray Lovelock), who's been left paralyzed after being shot down during a robbery. It's a puzzling, paradoxical passage, as Betti has just been exonerated after shooting a pair of thugs in the back (thus implying that Sartori has made him untouchable by the Law). Furthermore, it anticipates an ambiguous, weirdly truncated ending: as Betti is leaving the clinic where his friend is staying, he's shot dead in an ambush. We soon realize that this is just Betti's hallucination, or perhaps an omen: the film abruptly ends with a freeze-frame shot of Betti coming out into the street, leaving the viewer uncertain about his future. It's another patent *High Crime* rip-off, as in Castellari's film Franco Nero's character had a similar vision of himself being shot in the back; but it's also a hasty way to get done with a story which has no beginning and no real ending whatsoever.[2]

Yet *Violent Rome*'s final shot is extremely significant: not only does this predate the tragic ending that awaits Betti at the end of the trilogy, but it bitterly reaffirms a distinct pessimism that hovers on the whole genre: sooner or later, the hero is going to be defeated. It's just a matter of time, as the disproportion between good and evil — an ubiquitous, ferocious underworld —

is too high. Such an outcome would apparently be refuted by Betti's subsequent filmic exploits, *Violent Naples* and *Special Cop in Action*: these are less gloomy affairs, not least because they offer more conventional villains instead of *Violent Rome*'s nameless, ubiquitous thugs. In the end, however, the first film's prophecy becomes reality, as *Special Cop in Action* ends with an abrupt, arbitrary, unexpected and unfair freeze-frame depicting Betti's death. An ending that's in Betti's DNA, as shown by an emblematic exchange between the Commissioner and his lover (Daniela Giordano): "You know, born to be a cop...." "Yeah, but often born *to die* a cop."

With its phenomenal success — over two billion lire (slightly less than Pasolini's scandalous *Salò*), *Violent Rome* made Merli a star. Yet the film is definitely not one of the genre's best. Much of the fault can be laid at the feet of Girolami's direction, which is awkward in the action scenes and marred by an inordinate use of the zoom lens, which underlines the hero's every intense line or facial expression. A comparison with Merli's next film, Umberto Lenzi's powerful *Brutal Justice* (*Roma a mano armata*, 1976) makes the difference even more evident.

Richard Conte, center, Massimo Vanni, second from right, and Maurizio Merli, right, in a scene from *Violent Rome* (1975).

With *Violent Rome* the central phase of poliziotteschi — the hero's serialization — had officially begun. From then on, most stories would be characterized by a fragmentary outline, which permitted the repetition of the same situations from film to film, and emphasized the interchangeability of characters and narrative blocks. What's more, the urban landscape became the main character. Before *Violent Rome*, Milan was the most common presence in the titles of action flicks and *film noir* yarns: according to Gian Piero Brunetta, "from 1968 onwards, the fact that Milan is at the centre of the strategy of tension, and that it becomes the capital of organized crime in the country, made it the ideal landscape for films with often opposite aims."[3] Whereas with Girolami's film the location becomes an original distinctive sign, a call for audiences who pay the ticket to find an on-screen portrayal of that very same violence that they experience in real life. By spectacularizing news headlines, these movies acted as a sounding board for resentment, anger and fears, and exorcised them through the creation of a character who, with the advent of Maurizio Merli, became as immediately recognizable as the icon of Christ on holy pictures for the average viewer.

As Italian critic Anton Giulio Mancino wrote, "Maurizio Merli certainly was the Italian Clint Eastwood, more than any other poliziotteschi star such as Enrico Maria Salerno, who nevertheless had been his precursor, or Franco Gasparri, Luc Merenda, Marcel Bozzuffi. Unlike all of these, Merli represented an institution of sorts, while his face and unorthodox methods perfectly identified with the recurring character as seen first in the films of Umberto Lenzi and then in those directed by Stelvio Massi. Although he essentially remained a taciturn idealist upset by ultraviolence and metropolitan chaos, Merli didn't look like the thugs he chased, nor did he try to merge with them, like Clint Eastwood or Gene Hackman. He couldn't even be mistaken for a culturally eclectic and alternative type such as Steve McQueen or *Serpico*'s Al Pacino. Maurizio Merli had an open smile, and his mustache gave him a mature look, that of an upright official rather than just a handsome guy; he had a soft spot for defenseless children, helped women and men of good will, proletarians and bourgeois alike, and would lock his jaw in anger before providing them with much-needed justice."[4]

Notes

1. Grimaldi and Pulici, *Enzo G. Castellari*, p. 37.
2. The brothers De Angelis' score was also recycling cues and music pieces from *High Crime*, namely the outstanding *Gangster Story* (in the car chase scene at Rome's EUR), *Casa di moda* and *Chicca*.
3. Brunetta, *Storia del cinema italiano*, p. 414.
4. Anton Giulio Mancino, "Maurizio Merli, Callaghan tricolore," in Anna Di Martino, Maurizio Matrone, Massimo Moretti, eds., *4° police Film Festival* (Bologna: I quaderni del Lumiére no. 27, 1998), p. 32.

1976

The Big Racket (Il grande racket)

D: Enzo G. Castellari. *S:* Arduino Maiuri, Massimo De Rita; *SC:* Arduino Maiuri, Massimo De Rita, Enzo G. Castellari; *DOP:* Marcello Masciocchi (35mm, Technospes, Telecolor); *M:* Guido and Maurizio De Angelis (ed. C.A.M.); *E:* Gianfranco Amicucci; *ArtD:* Francesco Vanorio; *AArtD:* Stefano Paltrinieri; *CO:* Luciano Sagoni; *COA:* Carlo Gentili; *C:* Antonio Schiavolena; *AC:* Claudio Tondi, Mauro Masciocchi, Maurizio Santi; *AE:* Cesarina Casini; *AD*, acrobatic scenes: Rocco Lerro; *MU:* Massimo De Rossi, Andreina Ambrosini; *Hair:* Agnese Panarotto; *SO:* Goffredo Salvatori; *Boom:* Luigi Salvatori; *Mix:* Gianni D'Amico; *SP:* Franco Vitale; *Set constructor:* Giovanni Corridori; *ChG:* Giacomo Tomaselli; *ChEl:* Tullio Marini; *ST:* Ottaviano Dell'Acqua; *STD* (for Fabio Testi): Angelo Ragusa; *SS:* Maria Pia Rocco. *Cast:* Fabio Testi (Inspector Nico Palmieri), Vincent Gardenia (Zio Pepe), Renzo

Palmer (Luigi Giulti, Restaurant owner), Orso Maria Guerrini (Gianni Rossetti), Glauco Onorato (Piero Mazzarelli), Marcella Michelangeli (Marcy), Romano Puppo (Doringo), Antonio Marsina (Attorney Giovanni Giuni), Salvatore Borgese (Sgt. Salvatore Velasci), Gianluigi Loffredo [Joshua Sinclair] (Rudy, the Marseillese), Daniele Dublino (Commissioner), Anna Bellini [Anna Zinnemann] (Anna Rossetti), Edy [Edgardo] Biagetti (Chief of Police), Salvatore Billa (Fabrizi), Giovanni Bonadonna (Cuomo), Franco Borelli (Oreste Saclà), Pietro Ceccarelli (Luigi Mayer), Domenico Cianfriglia (Rudy's henchman), Giovanni Cianfriglia (The Ox), Roberto Dell'Acqua (Luigino), Ruggero Diella (Piccio, Pepe's nephew), Dino Mattielli (Prison guard), Carmelo Reale (Vraspar, international fence), Angelo Ragusa (Giancarlo "The Badger"), Massimo Vanni (Vanni). *Uncredited:* Angelo Boscariol (Spectator at station), Omero Capanna (Rudy's henchman), Enzo G. Castellari (Cowardly storekeeper), Nestore Cavaricci (Spectator at station), Ottaviano Dell'Acqua, Lina Franchi (Scared woman at supermarket), Stefania Girolami (Stefania Giulti), Emilio Messina (Thug), Fulvio Mingozzi (Bar owner), Benito Pacifico (Rudy's henchman), Osiride Pevarello (Gate guard at Fabrizi's plant), Renzo Pevarello (Gunman at Fabrizi's plant), Sergio Ruggeri (Man in supermarket), Leonardo Scavino (Storekeeper), Martin Sorrentino (American tourist), Franco Ukmar (Thug at Fabrizi's plant). *PROD:* Galliano Juso for Cinemaster; *PM:* Lanfranco [Puccio] Ceccarelli; *APM:* Renato Fié; *PSe:* Giacomo Longo, Enzo Prosperini; *ADM:* Paolo Rampazzo; *Paymaster:* Salvatore Farese. *Country:* Italy. Filmed at Incir–De Paolis (Rome) and on location in Rome. *Running time:* 110'; Visa no.: 68925 (08.04.1976); *Rating:* v.m.18; *Release date:* 08.12.1976; *Distribution:* Titanus; *Domestic gross:* 1,479,567,800 lire. *Also known as: Big racket* (Paris, 08.02.1978 —105'), *Forajidos 77* (Spain), *El gran chantaje* (Argentina). *Home video:* Blue Underground (DVD, USA), Millennium Storm (DVD, Italy). OST: CD Digitmovies CDDM100.

Rome. Police Commissioner Nicola Palmieri is on the trail of a racketeering gang: his investigations, however, are hindered by the victims' fear and the hostility of his superiors who do not approve of his methods. Determined to go all the way, Palmieri enlists two petty criminals, Zio Pepe and his nephew Picchio, who provide him with information on the racketeers in exchange for some freedom of action. Zio Pepe warns the police of a robbery that's about to take place: a fierce gunfight ensues where the bandits are defeated, and on this occasion Palmieri is helped by an Olympic skeet shooting champion, engineer Gianni Rossetti. However, the criminals exact revenge on both Rossetti, raping his wife and burning her alive, and Pepe, making him kill his own nephew. Palmieri is forced to resign from the police. This, however, does not stop him: aided by Rossetti, Zio Pepe and other victims of the racket, Palmieri faces the gang in their lair, in a furious shoot-out.

Significantly, it was up to the director who gave birth to the vigilante subgenre to take it to its extreme consequences, by emphasizing its anti-realistic tendencies up to the point of a disturbing rarefaction of its *mise en scène*. With *The Big Racket*, Enzo Castellari left behind the urban realism that underlined the less convincing parts in *Street Law* in order to tell a crime story as if it was an abstract, modern-day cruel fairytale.

Even though the starting point is everyday crime reporting, as the director recalled, "I definitely liked the idea of making an instant-movie, just when the racket ring was becoming a really worrying occurrence for all the shop-owners in Rome."[1] However, everything in the story is drained and reduced to a mere narrative function. Characters are one-dimensional, their psychologies are barely sketched, in a minimalistic approach that turns daily misdeeds into myth: Castellari even throws in a character, Doringo (played by one of his fetish actors, stuntman Romano Puppo: Castellari originally wanted Lou Castel for the role[2]) who's nicknamed "the machine-gun soloist," in a nod to real-life criminal Luciano Lutring.

Italian poster for *The Big Racket* (1976).

The plot and characters are functional to the show-stopping action sequences, so savage and rousing that they outdo anything that had been done in Italy until then. Right from the slow-motion opening, that shows the racketeering gang wreaking havoc, destroying shop windows and setting fire to vehicles, Castellari pulls out all the stops.

The scene where Fabio Testi is trapped in his car while the vehicle is tumbling down a ditch still makes Castellari proud: "Now, whenever the film's projected at conventions, someone always gets up and asks me: 'How did you shoot that scene?' And directors, like that guy who made *Palermo-Milan One Way*: 'How did you shoot that scene?' 'Yeah sure, like I'm going to tell you!' When I don't feel like revealing how I shot it, I say I ordered buffers from the steelworks in Hamburg that were five meters across ... crap like that.

Well, I should tell you that I'm at my most creative when the driver comes to fetch me, and I stretch out on the back seat of the car for the half-hour it takes to get to the set. I think: 'I'm the director. Now I'll go to the set, do what I feel like, conjure up what I want.' I mean, I've got the stuff dreams are made of at my fingertips for the next half-hour. It's a magic time for me; it gives me cues and ideas. Visualizing the scene with the tumbling car, I thought: 'Right, if I stage it like that, if I do it this way....' We were shooting at the Fiorentini factory on the Tiburtina. It had been abandoned or shut down for reasons I can't recall. They made spare parts there for Caterpillar tractors. When I arrived, I had a look round and was charmed by these enormous iron rings that were about four, five meters across ... I saw six or seven and started to think. I did some sketches and called Giovanni Corridori from the special effects department: 'I've got an idea. We'll stand these wheels up like this; you weld them together as if we were making a big wheel, and then you weld the driver and passenger compartment of the car in the middle. We'll chop off the engine; chop off the trunk and just leave the car interior. Then we'll make the wheels turn by hand so the interior turns over....' We had plenty of space at the factory; there was a massive stretch of ground and all you could see beyond it was sky. We set the effect up and shot it there. So, once we'd got the car interior in place, I put one camera in front of Fabio and the other at the side to shoot him in profile. In rotation, you could see really the ground turning behind Fabio's head, and the stuff inside the car fell all over the place. It was incredibly realistic but it was really, really simple, we had a good laugh while we were doing it. I'd say to Fabio: 'Are you ready? Another spin, another run.... Great.'"[3]

However, if *The Big Racket* is a parable, it is a gloomy, funereal, hopeless one. It's populated by a wretched, miserable mankind, an obtuse flock that can be shaped at will: whoever raises the head and shows a little bit of civic sense is destined to pay a terrible price. The host (the great Renzo Palmer) who dared report the threats he underwent has his little daughter raped to death, and a similar fate awaits the wife of the engineer (Orso Maria Guerrini) who helped the Commissioner during a shoot-out. On the other hand, the villains are as sadistic and cruel as it comes, in a way that defies gender distinctions: the gang's most abject member is a woman (Marcella Michelangeli, Lou Castel's girlfriend at the time, who also played a terrorist in *Mark Strikes Again* and *Could It Happen Here?*), who nevertheless in one scene receives a kick in the groin, the sort of retaliation Castellari reserves to male villains, as if to certify her inner masculinity. And the film ends with its hero caught in the umpteenth violent act, furiously smashing his rifle onto the ground in a bout of helpless rage, while all around him there's only fire, smoke and dead bodies.

As for the final massacre — an orgy of bullets and blood clearly inspired by *The Wild Bunch*— the director, who considers it the best ending he's ever filmed, explained: "It was [an incredible *tour de force*] but as I said many times, I enjoy action, I like it, so it's a breeze for me to devise action scenes. It was a real shot in the arm for both the script girl and my assistant director, indeed. I invented everything on the spot: 'Now he dies this way, here, the other one dies that way, there ... here we make a special effect....' 'But who's shooting whom?' they asked me. And I replied: 'I don't know...' but everything that I liked, that I felt was the right thing to put in that scene, I shot it. And so, making it up as I went along, the ending was taking shape [...]: but while I was shooting, I didn't have it clear in my mind from the beginning. Yet I had a very neat idea of the effects I wanted: I filmed all of these, the deaths, the explosions, the leaps, and also the gruesome details."[4]

Violence is brutal, savage, excessive: there's no room for the elegiac and crepuscular accents of Castellari's metaphysical Western *Keoma* (1976), which germinated earlier than *The Big Racket* but was filmed immediately afterwards. The rape scenes are particularly vile, and almost become an endurance test for the audience: yet everything is pushed toward a hyperrealism that gradually and imperceptibly slips into the realm of the fantastic — as in the opening scene, where the apparition of the evil gang is lit by intermittent red lights that distort their features partially hidden under hockey masks and accompanied by the De Angelis brothers' pounding rock score, or in Stefania Castellari's rape scene, which ends with the dead girl's impossible *post mortem* point of view shot.

Several critics compared *The Big Racket* to Sam Peckinpah's work, but Castellari's approach is actually closer to Clint Eastwood's deconstructions of western mythology, namely *High Plains Drifter* (1971) and *Pale Rider* (1985), in the way it dries up and purifies the crime film's primordial elements — male bonding, revenge, spirit of the pack — and injects an eerie abstraction in the process. There's no sense talking about a "cynically reactionary ideology," as Italian critics of the time did.[5]

The Big Racket is not just Castellari's best film, but also a point of no return, both for the Italian crime genre and the director himself: even though he'd make such remarkable films as *The Heroin Busters* (1977), *The Inglorious Bastards* (1978), *Day of the Cobra* (1980) and the *Bronx Warriors* diptych, Castellari would never again reach such heights, if not sporadically, in isolated showpieces within the single works.

Notes

1. Grimaldi and Pulici. *Enzo G. Castellari*, p. 48.
2. Pulici, "*Il muscolo intelligente, Intervista a Enzo G. Castellari,*" p. 22.

3. *Ibid.*.
4. *Ibid.*, p. 11.
5. "The film grafts the violent Western thread *à la* Peckinpah and Siegel over the national urban crime movie genre: crime is not fought with law codes, but by countering violence with violence. However, this ambiguous Italian film does not demystify violence, but feeds it with a cynically reactionary ideology." G.Gs. [Giovanna Grassi], *Corriere della sera*, 9.11.1976.

Blood and Bullets, a.k.a. *Knell, Bloody Avenger (Sangue di sbirro)*

D: Al Bradley [Alfonso Brescia]. *S* and *SC:* Aldo Crudo, Alfonso Brescia; *DOP:* Silvio Fraschetti (35mm, Eastmancolor, Technospes); *M:* Alessandro Alessandroni (ed. Saar); *E:* Carlo Broglio; *PD:* Mimmo [Bartolomeo] Scavia; *CO:* Elena De Cupis; *C:* Luigi Quadrini; *AC:* Carlo Carlucci; *AD:* Franco Pasquetto; *MU:* Lia Amicucci; *Hair:* Giuliana Donati; *SP:* Maurizio Sposito; *SS:* Giuliana Gherardi. *Cast:* Jack Palance (Duke), George Eastman [Luigi Montefiori] (Dan Caputo, "Knell"), Jenny Tamburi [Luciana Tamburini] (Susan), Robert [Roberto] Giraudo (Captain Jeffrey), Ugo Bologna (Mallory), Jut Grams (Sharp), Renato Montalbano (Looney Toledo), Nicole Barthelmy (Belle), Giorgio Sciolette, Aldo Cecconi (Agent Owen), Gaetano Balestrieri (Peter Cotten). *Uncredited:* Artemio Antonini (Looney Toledo's henchman), Angelo Boscariol (Looney Toledo's henchman), Sisto Brunetti (Looney Toledo's henchman), Aldo Canti (Cop in airport), Nestore Cavaricci (Looney Toledo's henchman), Enrico Chiappafreddo (Mallory's henchman), Lina Franchi (Woman at airport), Benito Pacifico (Thug), Franco Pasquetto (Johnny), Nello Pazzafini (Belle's man). *PROD:* Hilda Film; *PM:* Luigi Alessi; *PSu:* Bruno Bagella; *PSe:* Luigi Colella. *Country:* Italy. Filmed at Incir–De Paolis (Rome). *Running time:* 95'; Visa no.: 69477 (12.02.1976); *Rating:* v.m.14; *Release date:* 12.11.1976; *Distribution:* C.I.A.; *Domestic gross:* 253,359,230 lire. *Also known as: Pour un dollar d'argent* (Paris, 09.20. 1978—90'). *Home video:* AVO (VHS, Italy), VFP (VHS, U.K.—pre-cert). OST: CD Escalation/Cinedelic ESC-CD001.

Dan Caputo, a former police sergeant who just got a degree in law, arrives in New York with the intention of shedding light on the death of his father Joe, a rough New York police officer, and avenge him. Mallory, the boss of a Mafia gang, sends a bunch of men to kill him at the airport, posing as masked terrorists: a massacre ensues, but Dan kills the thugs. Lieutenant Sharp and Captain Jeffrey bar him from using weapons and ask him to leave the city. Dan ignores their order and does not even heed the advice of his fiancée Susan, who waited patiently for him for many years. He wants to cleanse his father's memory, as rumors spread that the dead cop was in cahoots with a gangster named Looney Toledo. However, all those who could help Caputo are eliminated one after another, including Toledo and his sister Belle. Dan himself survives a series of attacks and eventually finds unexpected support in the ambiguous gangster Duke. Dan finds out that Jeffrey is his father's murderer, who acted under Mallory's orders: he exterminates Mallory's gang and submits the evidence to Sharp while Duke takes Mallory's place as the new boss.

Truly a filmmaker for all seasons, after a career counting sword-and-sandal epics (*Revolt of the Praetorians*), Westerns (*32 Caliber Killer*), war movies (*Kill Rommel!*), *gialli* (*Naked Girl Killed in the Park*), erotic flicks (*The Labyrinth of Sex*), bawdy comedies (*Hot Nights of Don Juan*), child adventure films (*Lone Hunter of the Wild North*) and countless hybrids (*Helen Yes ... Helen of Troy*, an abysmal comic/erotic take on Homer's *Odyssey*), and just before exploring science fiction, with a series of five *Star Wars*–inspired space operas in a row, Alfonso Brescia tried his hand at the crime genre.

However, *Blood and Bullets* is quite different from contemporaneous poliziotteschi. First of all, the characters and setting are American, although New York is poorly rendered through archive footage and a few on-location shots of Luigi Montefiiori inside a cab or wandering about, while most of the film was shot at Rome's De Paolis studios and displays some of the most distinctly non–American interiors since Demofilo Fidani's period Mafia films. Even though the hero's deceased father was by all accounts a tough cop (something we notice in a flashback scene that has him savagely beat his adolescent son), there's no trace of the urban *malaise* of similar poliziotteschi in the mild whodunit plot, and even though Brescia tries hard to ape classic *film noir* the result sounds much more like a rehash of some leftover Western script—starting with the main character's nickname ("Knell") and characterization. However, the end result is poor.

Violence is as conspicuous as it is ridiculous, starting with the opening scene at the airport (actually the hall of Rome's Cavalieri Hilton hotel, a familiar set in 1970s movies), where a bunch of gangsters disguised as terrorists and wearing hockey masks take a crowd of passengers as hostages in order to dispatch the lone Knell (one of the film's wildest ideas)—a sequence which climaxes in an obnoxiously paced shoot-out. Extras are dispatched at an alarmingly high rate, with the usual jumps and contortions that are a mark of Italian stuntmen in bad Italian films, and Knell has a soft spot for special exploding bullets: even a Mickey Mouse mechanical doll is turned into an explosive device, in a sequence that almost looks like an unintentional parody of a famous moment in Argento's *Deep Red* (1975). The body count becomes an additional laugh factor, as later on in the film some character shows up at Knell's place claiming "I heard shots"—not once but twice, while apparently the police didn't bother. To spice up the proceedings, Brescia even intercuts a chase scene underneath a (seemingly labyrinthine) basement with a striptease that's taking place in the nightclub above: the stripper's full frontal nudity anticipates the ensuing shoot-out, in an editing trick that pretty much sums up the attitude of Italian popular cinema of the period—i.e., delivering the goods.

The dialogue is similarly inane. When crime boss Jake (Jack Palance, as wooden as a stuffed bird) asks Knell if he found his hometown changed, the hero replies "It's not as sparkling as it was. It breathes heavily, and looks like an old whore." Jim Thompson would have blushed. The only consistent thing about the film is product placement: J&B bottles pop up in every corner.

However, Brescia's following entries within the genre would have the director find his feet, with a string of Neapolitan-based crime films starring Mario Merola which would mix action and lurid melodrama with effective results.

Bloody Payroll (Milano violenta)

D: Mario Caiano. *S* and *SC:* Mario Caiano; *DOP:* Pier Luigi Santi (35mm, Eastmancolor, Fotocinema); *M:* Pulsar Music Ltd. [Enrico Pieranunzi, Silvano Chimenti], conducted by Gianfranco Plenizio (ed. Clitumno); *E:* Renato Cinquini; *PD:* Giorgio Postiglione; *CO:* Fiamma Bedendo; *C:* Giuseppe Venditti; *AC:* Bruno Cascio; *AE:* Carlo Marino; *2nd AE:* Antonio Fusco; *ADs:* Edoardo Salerno, Massimo Civilotti; *MU:* Carlo Sindici; *Hair:* Carla Randazzo; *SO:* Primiano Muratori; *Boom:*

Luciano Muratori; *Mix:* Romano Pampaloni; *SE:* Luciano Anzellotti; *SP:* Giovanni Vino; *SS:* Gianni Ricci. *Cast:* Claudio Cassinelli (Raul Montalbani "The Cat"), Silvia Dionisio (Leila), Elio Zamuto (Commissioner Foschi), Vittorio Mezzogiorno (Walter), Biagio Pelligra (Tropea), Salvatore Puntillo (Inspector Tucci), John Steiner (Fausto), Luciana Scalise (Hostage girl), Margherita Horowitz (Secretary at Aspex), Luigi Casellato (Baudengo), Francesco D'Adda (Magistrate), Paolo Montesi, Massimo Mirani (Gavino), Bruna Righetti, Francesco Motolese, Luigi Marturano, Dada Gallotti ("Svociata"), Carlo Dorè. *Uncredited:* Franz Colangeli (police official), Ivana Monti, Vezio Natili (police official), Nando Sarlo (Cashier at Aspex), Oscar Sciamanna (police official), Sergio Testori (Motorcycle cop). *PROD:* Renato Angiolini for Jarama Film, Medusa Distribuzione; *PM:* Ennio Onorati; *UPM:* Mario Olivieri; *PSe:* Gianni Panta no; *CASH:* Ugo Iovane. *Country:* Italy. Filmed on location in Milan. *Running time:* 95'; Visa no.: 68072 (03.05.1976); *Rating:* v.m.14; *Release date:* 03.05.1976; *Distribution:* Medusa; *Domestic gross:* 1,015,886,510 lire. *Also known as: Commando Terror / Commando Terreur* (Canada — Home video), *Die letze Rechnung schreibt der Tod* (West Germany), *Terror Commando* (France). *Home video:* NoShame (DVD, Italy — 91'). OST: LP Cometa CMT2; CD Plastic Records PL 008.

A bandit named Raul Montalbani, also known as "the Cat," and his three accomplices assault a factory to rob the salaries. Alerted by a worker, the police catch the bandits in the act: two of them — Walter and Tropea — flee with the money, while Montalbani and another bandit, Fausto, escape capture by threatening to kill hostages and obtaining a getaway car from the police. When an unsuspecting traffic agent stops them, Fausto kills him in cold blood and escapes on a motorbike, but meets his end in a head-on collision against a truck. Raul sets out to track down his two ex-associates, who in the meantime are dispatching all those who know about their whereabouts: Montalbani joins them in an abandoned slaughterhouse, but Walter and Tropea have prepared a trap for him. The wounded Raul takes refuge in the home of a young prostitute, Leila, who falls for him. Having finally located Walter and Tropea's new hideout— which the police also got round to — Raul catches them by surprise and kills them. He dies too, however, under the blows of Commissioner Foschi.

Despite an Italian title (*Milano Violenta*, "Violent Milan") that makes it look like a sequel of sorts to Maurizio Merli's commercial exploit *Violent Rome*, and a rather standard first act, Mario Caiano's *Bloody Payroll* is actually more of a *film noir* in the style of Giorgio Scerbanenco's novels than an out-and-out poliziotteschi. As Raul Montalbani "il Gatto" (The Cat), a robber who's betrayed by his associates after a hit that's gone wrong and has to run from the police as well, Claudio Cassinelli incarnates a solitary gangster whose actions move from a feeling of repulsion towards everything and everyone. There is no trace of Jean-Pierre Melville's romanticized vision here, as proven by such lines as "Give him all the money in the world and he'll still say it's still not enough," and the somewhat haphazardly shot car stunts look almost out of place in a story that opts for more subdued tones. The heart of *Bloody Payroll* is its antihero's journey from the city's lower depths to Brianza's cozy suburban villas where the ending takes place: a journey that acquires a symbolical meaning as well, underlining Montanari's delusions of wealth as well as the distance that separates the proletarian bandits from the upper-class *milieu* they hate with all their guts.

Caiano depicts the Milan underworld with inspired and realistic traits — see one of the robbers buying a handful of adult comic books (which were immensely popular at the time among lower classes) at a newsstand during the opening scene — a fact emphasized by the muted, almost foggy colors in Pier Luigi Santi's cinematography. The director also manages to make believable the young prostitute's (Silvia Dionisio) infatuation towards the protagonist, after she helps the "Cat" and deludes herself that she loves him, only to be brutally rejected by the man. The final half-hour, as Montalbani settles the score with his associates conveys a dry feel — even in the depiction of violence — that's unusual for its time.

Bloody Payroll also benefits from its above-average cast. Beside the always reliable Cassinelli and Steiner, Biagio Pelligra and Vittorio Mezzogiorno — respectively, one of Italy's most underrated character actors and one of the very best leading men to emerge in Italian cinema of the 1980s — are top-notch as Montalbani's ex-accomplices, while Zamuto — a very fine actor usually confined to bad-guy roles — is cleverly cast against type as the Commissioner on the case. A major asset, especially for film soundtrack devotees, is the excellent funk-oriented score (signed under the a.k.a. Pulsar Music Ltd.) by renowned jazz pianist Enrico Pieranunzi and guitarist Silvano Chimenti.

Brutal Justice, a.k.a. *Assault with a Deadly Weapon (Roma a mano armata)*

D: Umberto Lenzi. *S:* Umberto Lenzi; *SC:* Dardano Sacchetti; *DOP:* Federico Zanni (35mm, Eastmancolor — Panavision, Technospes); *M:* Franco Micalizzi (ed. Clitumno); *Se l'averebbe saputo* (by R. Donati / F. Maglione) sung by Fiamma Maglione; *E:* Daniele Alabiso; *PD:* Giorgio Bertolini; *APD:* Francesco Bidoccu; *CO:* Franco Carretti; *C:* Elio Polacchi, Mario Sbrenna; *AC:* Mario Pastorini; *AE:* Maurizio Alabiso; *AD:* Goffredo Unger [Goffredo Ungaro]; *MU:* Massimo Giustini; *Hair:* Teodora Bruno, Marcello Longhi; *W:* Vanda Pruni, Davide Cenci (for M. R. Omaggio), Vanda Pruni; *W:* Anna Rasetti; *SO:* Umberto Picistrelli; *Boom:* Fabio Antonini; *Mix:* Bruno Moreal; *SE:* Gino Vagniluca; *KG:* Giuseppe Gabrielli; *ChEl:* Roberto Belli; *SP:* Mario Sabatelli; *SS:* Mirella Roi [Mirella Roy Malatesta]. *Cast:* Maurizio Merli (Commissioner Leonardo Tanzi), Tomas Milian (Vincenzo Moretto, the hunchback), Arthur Kennedy (Vice Chief of Police Ruini), Maria Rosaria Omaggio (Anna), Giampiero Albertini (Commissioner Francesco Caputo), Ivan Rassimov (Antonio "Tony" Parenzo), Biagio Pelligra (Savelli), Aldo Barberito (Polliana), Stefano Patrizi (Stefano), Luciano Pigozzi (Moretto's henchman), Luciano Catenacci (Ferdinando Gerace), Carlo Alighiero (Savelli's lawyer), Carlo Gaddi (Oronzo, the ambulance driver), Claudio Nicastro (Fence), Valentino Macchi (Franco, Paola's boyfriend), Sandra Cardini (Sandra Moretto), Gabriella Lepori (Marta Assante), Maria Rosaria Riuzzi (Paola, the raped girl), Corrado Solari (Albino, getaway driver), Dante Cleri (Licenses & permits officer), Mara Mariani (Assante's widow), Fulvio Mingozzi (Agent Colantoni), Ruggero Diella (One of Stefano's friends), Tom Felleghy (Judge Bennato), Riccardo Petrazzi (Savelli's henchman), Gaetano Russo (Gaetano, Stefano's friend), Ottaviano Dell'Acqua (Stefano's friend), Leris [Valerio] Colombaioni (Nicola, the purse snatcher), Filippo Degara [Giuseppe Cuccia] (police informer). *Uncredited:* Umberto Amambrini (Man in gambling room), Artemio Antonini (Thug in gambling room), Rossana Canghiari (Hostage with hat), Nestore Cavaricci (policeman), Enrico Chiappafreddo (Clerk at horse racing agency), Raniero Dorascenzi (Inspector Sarti), Quinto Gambi, Anna Manduchi (Woman in gambling room), Giuseppe Marrocco (Hostage), Vezio Natili (Croupier), Renzo Ozzano, Benito Pacifico (Robber at horse racing agency), Anna Maria Perego (Hostage in bank), Filippo Perego (Man in bank), Renzo Pevarello (Guard at gambling house), Claudio Ruffini (Robber at horse racing agency), Oscar Sciamanna (Bank clerk hostage), Sergio Testori (Purse snatcher on motorbike), Rinaldo Zamperla, Luciano Zanussi (Hostage), Zaira Zoccheddu (Screaming woman in restaurant). *PROD:* Mino Loy and Luciano Martino for Dania Film, Medusa Distribuzione, National Cinematografica; *PM:* Sergio Borelli; *PSu:* Lamberto Palmieri, Luciano Catenacci. *Country:* Italy. Filmed at R.P.A.-Elios Film (Rome) and on location in Rome. *Running time:* 95'; Visa no.: 67999 (02.20.1976); *Rating:* v.m.14; *Release date:* 02.25.1976; *Distribution:* Medusa; *Domestic gross:* 1,617,361,000 lire. *Also known as: Brigade Spéciale* (Paris, 09.24. 1980—90'), *Die Viper* (West Germany), *The Tough Ones* (Holland—Home video), *Rome Armed to the Teeth* (U.S.—Home video). *Home video:* NoShame (DVD, Italy), Neo Publishing (DVD, France), Alfa Digital (DVD, U.S.A.—as *Rome Armed to the Teeth*). OST: CD Beat Records BCM9502.

Rome. Commissioner Tanzi of the Homicide Squad believes that the police must not be limited by law codes to fight crime, nor does he endorse the empathy his girlfriend, a psychologist at the juvenile court, shows towards young delinquents. After receiving a tip-off, he and his men break into in an illegal gambling room, run by a Marseille-born criminal, Ferrender, but without finding any evidence of illegal activity. At the police station, the frustrated Tanzi beats one of Ferrender's men, Savelli, to make him talk, but to no avail. Savelli is released and the very next day he and his accomplices kill a guard during a hold-up. Tanzi locates Savelli's brother-in-law, a hunchback named Vincenzo Moretto, who works at a slaughterhouse: the Commissioner arrests Moretto and savagely beats him in order to extort him the whereabouts of Savelli's hideout. Moretto cuts his wrists in order to be released, and once he's out he informs the press about Tanzi's violent methods. The Commissioner is transferred from his unit to administrative duties. Meanwhile, Moretto plans to abduct and murder Tanzi's fiancée Anna, but the cop saves the woman at the very last minute. Heedless of orders, Tanzi keeps fighting crime with his own unorthodox methods: he vanquishes a gang of upper-class youths, then he tackles and apprehends a drug dealer who might lead him to the elusive Ferrender, but the man is killed by a hitman. After another robbery carried out by Moretto's gang, which ended in blood, Tanzi finally settles the score with the hunchback, who had killed Ferrender to take over his criminal empire.

In February 1976, just six months after the release of *Violent Rome*, another poliziotteschi starring Maurizio Merli and displaying the Eternal City in the title (at least in Italy) came out: *Brutal Justice* (originally *Roma a mano armata* [Armed Rome], a patent nod to Kubrick's *The Killing*, which was released in Italy as *Rapina a mano armata* [Armed Robbery]) didn't just recycle the same mosaic narrative as Girolami's film, but also—and more importantly—his hero, as Merli played a role who only differed from his previous one in the character's name: Tanzi instead of Betti.

The result was vastly superior to the prototype, and the merit goes to Umberto Lenzi. The Tuscan director, an accomplished filmmaker who had been active since the early '60s, tried his hand at practically every genre in Italian popular cinema: Lenzi was able to move from spy flicks (*008: Operation Exterminate*, 1965) to war movies (*Desert Commandos*, 1967), from comic book adventure yarns (*Kriminal*, 1966, from the eponymous controversial pocket comic book) to erotic thriller (the triptych formed by *Paranoia*, 1968; *So Sweet, So Perverse*, 1969; *A Quiet Place to Kill*,

Italian poster for ***Brutal Justice*** **(1976).**

1970, all starring Carroll Baker) with nonchalant ease, but it was in poliziotteschi that he found the ideal terrain for his style and approach to filmmaking.

"The producer had offered me a script called *Roma ha un segreto* ("Rome Has a Secret"), a spy story set in Trastevere [a popular Roman district, Author's note], which is saying something! The story simply made no sense, so I trashed the script" the director recalls. "In turn, I persuaded the producer to make a movie about the violence that pervaded Rome at that time. Within one week—and I mean it, one week!—we improvised the script from scratch."[1] Right from the opening sequence—a camera-car visiting various streets of Rome, and focusing on bank agencies—Lenzi shows he is at ease within the genre, conveying a robust rhythm and putting into practice the lesson of American action films with sharp editing cuts and assured pacing.

Brutal Justice's other main asset is putting Merli's character against a worthy, unforgettable antagonist—that is, the misshapen Vincenzo Moretto, nicknamed "il Gobbo" (The Hunchback), played by Tomas Milian. A character inspired, according to Lenzi, by a real-life figure, and charged with a frightening anti-bourgeois and antisocial anger, which the Cuban actor portrays via a remarkable performance. Particularly memorable is the scene where Moretto pisses his pants as a sign of contempt inside the police station's bathroom and then cuts his wrists with his watchband.

The Hunchback desecrates family, religion and authorities alike, and his cruelty reaches peaks worthy of Milian's previous villain Giulio Sacchi in Lenzi's *Almost Human*: during a chase scene, Moretto jumps aboard an ambulance that is carrying a sick woman and her husband to the hospital, and doesn't hesitate to shoot the man dead. Nevertheless, despite the character's hateful excesses, the Hunchback's political incorrectness reveals a malaise that is corroding the lower classes to which he belongs, and that Lenzi and Milian miraculously distill through the trappings of an action film. The director, who often declared himself an anarchist ("my concept of anarchy is the same as Malatesta's and Bakunin's"), often claimed his intention was to create the character of an out-and-out rebel who's against everyone and everything: "In my work there is always something that points towards this ideology of overturning and liberation. [...] In my crime films I couldn't carry these themes to the extreme, as they were ultimately made with the intention of celebrating law enforcement. There were just two films where I tried to portray this idea of total dispute: *Brutal Justice* and *Brothers Till We Die*, where I created the character of the "Hunchback": by desecrating everything, he becomes the spokesman of an anti-bourgeois discourse."[2]

Perhaps that's the reason for the Hunchback's phenomenal success as a character, which led to his return in Lenzi's *Brothers Till We Die* (1977). As a matter of fact, if Merli is the star, it's Milian who steals the show: the actors' obvious competitiveness makes for effective screen chemistry, as when Tanzi force-feeds Moretto with a bullet, and the Hunchback swears he's going to shit the bullet and kill Tanzi with it. Milian's got the film's most memorable lines—especially effective in the Italian version, where he's dubbed by Ferruccio Amendola, one of Italy's most popular voices, in a thick Roman accent—all of them filled with copious and picturesque profanity. The abundant resort to trivialities would become a distinctive sign in the actor's following characters, such as petty thief Monnezza (*Free Hand for a Tough Cop*, 1976; *Destruction Force*, 1977) and inspector Nico Giraldi (*The Cop in Blue Jeans* and other ten films from 1976 until 1984). Ivan Rassimov, elsewhere the main villain in such films as *Superbitch* and *Colt 38 Special Squad*, is rather wasted in a minor role, while Arthur Kennedy's cameo is the usual homage to Hollywood has-beens that was another common element in the genre.

On the other hand, Dardano Sacchetti's script doesn't shine with inventions, as most of the situation have a feel of *déjà-vu* (such as the robbery at the horse-racing agency, which is virtually identical to the one seen in *Violent Rome*, and would be recycled yet again in *Violent Naples*), while Franco Micalizzi's muscular score is truly a driving force, and Lenzi's direction is assured and not without finesse. Action scenes, as usual, convey an immediacy that was the consequence of circumstances, as most scenes were shot with no permits whatsoever. Recalling the aforementioned chase scene aboard the ambulance, Lenzi explained: "After hiding the camera on top of the ambulance, we drove at full speed and with sirens blaring in the urban traffic. [...] At a certain point, the ambulance was supposed to be chased by two police cars, but looking at the rearview mirror I noticed that there were actually four of them. What had happened was that cops had noticed an ambulance being chased by two police cars, and thought that a criminal act was going on, so two *real* police cars just joined our fake cars. Needless to say, this crazy chase ended up at the police station!"[3]

Customarily, violence makes room for sheer sadism, also colored with a touch of class resentment: in a harrowing scene, a band of upper-class delinquents gang-rape a girl who was making love with her boyfriend, violating her with a stick, while calling him "shitty proletarian." Widespread violence permeates all social classes, but if the director shows a hint of mercy, that's for the two young proletarian purse snatchers who end up run over by a truck after being released by a Juvenile Court judge (Maria Rosaria Omaggio) with a kind heart ("What does your father do?" she asks one of them; "The convict," is the reply). On the other hand, Lenzi's contempt is palpable towards the rich spoiled delinquent with an angel face (Stefano Patrizi), who practices ultraviolence for kicks together with his friends, all belonging to a far-right association aptly named Circolo Giovanile Ricreativo Monarchico (Juvenile Recreative Monarchic Circle). Such characters would become another disquieting presence in contemporaneous poliziotteschi, after the notorious Circeo massacre which took place that same year, spawning no less than three films on the subject.

Brutal Justice was picked up by grindhouse distribution company Aquarius owned by the Australian-born Terry Levene and re-released to Home video in the U.S. as *Assault with a Deadly Weapon*, in a cut and badly re-edited version which included a bizarre cartoonish title sequence featuring a skull-faced cop and cast names completely made up.[4] A U.S. grey market DVD release, *Rome Armed to the Teeth*, contains the original Euro edit.

Notes

1. Email interview with the author, May 2011.
2. Gomarasca, *Umberto Lenzi*, p. 166.
3. *Ibid.*, p. 228.
4. For the record, the leads are "Richard Holliday, Sandra Foley, Lamont Jackson, Rinaldo Rincon," the script is credited to "William Dyer" and direction to "Walter Gaines." Levene also replaced a few of the establishing shots with those of American locations: for an establishing shot of the Rome youth center where Tanzi meets Stefano, a shot of the Manhattan nightclub Fascination was used.

Il colpaccio (Big Pot) (Big Pot)

D: John L. Huxley [Bruno Paolinelli]. *S:* John L. Huxley; *SC:* Karl Seipelt, John L. Huxley; *DOP:* Aldo Di Marcantonio (35mm, Cinecolor); *M:* Charlie Mells; *E:* Bruno Paolinelli. *Cast:* Carole André (Nicky), Claudine Auger, Al Cliver [Pier Luigi Conti] (Mark Lemmon), Fausto Tozzi (Mackenzie), Gabriele Tinti (Michael), Antonio Dimitri, William Berger, Mariangela Giordano, Edmund Purdom. *PROD:* Saba Cinematografica, C.A.R.F. (Cooperativa Autori Realizzatori Film) (Rome), Neue Delta Film Produktion (Vienna). *Country:* Italy / Austria. Filmed on location in Amsterdam. *Running time:* 115'; Visa no.: 68441 (05.15.1976); *Rating:* not rated; *Release date:* 06.16.1976; *Distribution:* Dear International; *Domestic gross:* 116,425,800 lire.

1971. At the Amsterdam airport, a gang of robbers steal a shipment of diamonds. Only one of them, Mark Lemmon, is arrested and condemned to a life sentence. However, before he got caught, Lemmon managed to hide the loot in one of the city's sewers. Five years later, insurance agent Mackenzie, pretending to be a crime boss, sets up Lemmon's escape from prison with the help of three small-time crooks and his own daughter Nicky. Once escaped, Lemmon recovers the diamonds, but has to face the three accomplices and the astute Nicky, who steals the loot and brings it back to her father. However, things don't go as planned....

A very obscure title, which as of today has not surfaced on Home video, Bruno Paolinelli's *The Big Pot* is a lighter affair compared to contemporaneous poliziotteschi, and more in the vein of 1960s heist films, with passable action and slight comedy undertones, and is worth mentioning because of the opening sequence at the airport and Charlie Mells' funky score. Its box office results were meager, though. According to the film's star Al Cliver, who had just done Ruggero Deodato's *Wave of Lust* (1975), "I liked the story very much. So, to do this film, which turned out a flop because of its scarce budget, I had an argument with producer Galliano Juso, who wanted me to star in Deodato's next film *Live Like a Cop, Die Like a Man*, which eventually Marc Porel and Ray Lovelock did. I had to co-star in Lovelock's role, and Juso was willing to pay me three times as much as what Paolinelli was offering for *The Big Pot*."[1] Critics ravaged the film as well, blaming the way "the movie falls to pieces in a series of tourist vignettes worthy of bad advertising, lacking in compactness and interest, which make one regret the wastefulness of the Machiavellian starting point."[2]

The Big Pot was Bruno Paolinelli's last film. Born in 1923, the 53-year-old director had entered the movie business in the early forties as a cameraman, and after collaborating with Georg Wilhelm Pabst on *Voice of Silence* (*La voce del silenzio*, 1952, as first assistant director and collaborator to the direction) and *Cose da pazzi* (1953, for which he co-wrote the script), he debuted behind the camera with *I pappagalli* (1955), co-starring Alberto Sordi and Aldo Fabrizi. His nondescript career as a filmmaker counted seven titles overall, including a pair of mediocre spy flicks, *OSS 77 operazione fior di loto* (1965) and *Nazi S.S.* (*Borman*, 1966), plus a number of film scripts, including the animation feature *Putiferio va alla guerra* (1968) which he also produced. Paolinelli died in France in 1991.

Notes

1. Manlio Gomarasca, "Saprofito. Intervista ad Al Cliver," *Nocturno Cinema* #3 (June 1997), p. 62.
2. Anonymous, *Il Secolo XIX*, 8.10.1976.

Colt 38 Special Squad (Quelli della calibro '38)

D: Massimo Dallamano. *S* and *SC:* Massimo Dallamano, Franco Bottari, Marco Guglielmi, Ettore Sanzò; *DOP:* Gábor Pogany (35mm, Eastmancolor, Technospes); *M:* Stelvio Cipriani, conducted by the author; *I Still Get the Blues* and *I'll Find My Way to You* (by H. Shaper / S. Cipriani) sung by Grace Jones (Cinevox records); *E:* Antonio Siciliano; *PD:* Franco Bottari; *ArtD:* Mauro Passi; Assistant set decorator: Franco Passi; *C:* Idelmo Simonelli; *AC:* Giuseppe Tinelli; *AE:* Sergio Muzzi; *AD:* Bruno Cortini; *MU:* Franco Freda; *Hair:* Aldo Signoretti; *SO:* Giorgio Pallotta; *Mix:* Franco Bassi; *SE:* G. Stacchini; *SP:* Pina Di Cola; *STC:* Sergio Mioni; *SS:* Flavia Sante Vanin; *DubD:* Nando Gazzolo. *Cast:* Marcel Bozzuffi (Commissioner Vanni), Carole André (Sandra), Ivan Rassimov (Marseillese / Black Angel), Riccardo Salvino (Nicola Silvestri), Giancarlo Bonuglia (Commissioner Petrucci), Fabrizio Capucci (Cito), Francesco Ferracini (Special Squad Member), Daniele Gabbai (Franco Lubrano), Antonio Marsina (Guido Pugliese "The Blond"), Ezio Miani (Special Squad Member), Giancarlo Sisti (Roland), Franco Garofalo (Gilbert Delange / Giampiero Manni), Eolo Capritti (Nistri), Bernardino Emanuelli (Informer), Armando Brancia (Chief of Police). *Uncredited:* Francesco D'Adda (Technical specialist), Margherita Horowitz (Gambling woman), Grace Jones (Herself—Nightclub singer), Luigi Pezzotti (Vanni's son). *PROD:* Paolo Infascelli for European Inc., P.A.C.—Produzioni Atlas Consorziate; *EP:* Pino Buricchi; *PSu:* Egidio Valentini; *PSe:* Paolo Bistolfi. *Country:* Italy. Filmed at Cinestudi Dear (Rome) and on location in Turin. *Running time:* 105'; Visa no.: 68874 (07.24.1976); *Rating:* v.m.14; *Release date:* 07.24.1976; *Distribution:* P.A.C.; *Domestic gross:* 1,285,707,500 lire. *Also known as: Colt 38. Escuadra especial* (Spain), *Kaliber 38—Genau zwischen die Augen* (West Germany), *Crashforce* (West Germany, video title), *Section de choc* (France). *Home video:* No Shame (DVD, USA), Cecchi Gori Home Video (DVD, Italy). OST: LP Cinevox MDF 098.

Commissioner Vanni of the Turin police has an account to settle with the "Marseillaise," a criminal who retaliated against him by killing his wife. The increase of criminal enterprises in town persuades the Chief of Police to put a special team under Vanni's orders, consisting of four agents armed with .38 caliber shotguns. One of the officers, Nico, manages to hook Sandra, the girlfriend of the Marseillaise's right-hand man Guido; meanwhile, the gangster manages to get hold of 70 kg of dynamite and starts a series of bombings followed by blackmail notes to the authorities: he asks for 5 billion' lire worth in diamonds and a plane to leave the country. Guido, Sandra and Nico all lose their lives at the hands of the criminal, while the authorities decide to submit to the blackmail so as to prevent the destruction of Turin. However Vanni keeps up his task on his own, and eventually reaches the Marseillaise just as the latter is about to flee, killing him.

One of the poliziotteschi's recurring traits is the verbal sparring between the Commissioner and the magistrate (or the Chief of Police) about the "tied hands" that prevent the hero from persecuting the criminals the way he would like to and the *carte blanche* he so often invokes: the moment where he finally obtains it could be compared, as critic Giovanni Buttafava ironized, to a perfect orgasm.[1] If one of the thread's conventions has the hero being denied any reinforcements from his superiors, nevertheless a whole subgenre dealt with the creation of special squads — that is, the coronation of our tough cops' dreams: recruit a bunch of willing men (in their twenties, unmarried, long haired — serving the law is a job for the young and valiant), have them undergo a paramilitary training and send them to patrol the city aboard speeding motorbikes.

At least, that's what happens in Massimo Dallamano's *Colt 38 Special Squad*— that is, a step further to the idea of citizens embracing private justice and cops doing the same on their own. Special agents, free from the limits their superior has to deal with (and which he so often bypasses), live a dangerous life, at the margins of legality, which almost always ends with a hail of gunfire awaiting them. Through them, however, the Commissioner reproduces and multiplies: the fatherly, comradely, covertly homoerotic bond between the commander and his centaurs, replaces and outperforms normal affective relationships.

In Dallamano's film, Commissioner Vanni (Marcel Bozzuffi; note the bisyllabic character's name, a standard occurrence in poliziotteschi, where cops have often almost identical names) watches his men proudly as they perform spectacular stunts, and afterwards, to seal their bond, he entrusts his knights with the titular weapons, extremely precise guns that never get clogged — the Italian tantamount of Harry Callahan's .44 Magnum. *Colt 38 Special Squad* displays a gun fetish that's unusual in Italian crime films: similar examples can be found only in Tonino Valerii's *Go Gorilla Go* (where the killer played by Antonio Marsina uses a special rifle) and Stelvio Massi's *The Last Round*, where Luc Merenda is a trigger-happy gangster with a soft spot for arms models: however, both examples deal with villains, not policemen.

However, Dallamano's film is more centered on action than gunplay. Besides the expertly made chase scenes, the director displays his customary dynamic hand-held shots, and like in his earlier *Superbitch* and *What Have They Done to Your Daughters?* he doesn't stint on violence either: an exemplary scene has the camera wander about the aftermath of a bombing at the Turin railway station, amidst the dead bodies. It's a moment that once again proves the poliziotteschi's uncanny ability to filter and sometimes predate Italian crime reporting, as just four years later a similar bombing at the Bologna station would become one of the bloodiest and most shocking events in Italian history of the 20th century, and a peak in the "Strategy of Tension" that plagued the country for the whole decade.

The emphasis on violence is hardly surprising, given that the script was co-written by Ettore Sanzò, who penned some of the most violent thrillers of the decade, from Aldo Lado's *Night Train Murders* (1975) to Lucio Fulci's *The Smuggler* (1980). Gory details are stressed in insistent close-ups, more typical of the parallel Italian genre cinema, as in the scene where a thug (Franco Garofalo) has his fingers severed by a car's door.

Colt 38 Special Squad also displays a memorable villain: as the Marseillaise, a ferocious bomber who wreaks havoc in Turin with his remote-controlled bombs, always sporting an eerie sadistic grin, Ivan Rassimov is one of poliziotteschi's most obnoxious scumbags: in an unforgettable over-the-top scene he has a police informer blown to bits by an explosive package, a moment reminiscent of Fernando di Leo's *Caliber 9*. Even though it's a one-note performance (not surprisingly, given a character that doesn't even have a name in the first place), it's one that truly exemplifies the genre's strength on a purely emotional basis. "Heroes can't afford a family" the Marsellaise tells Vanni after killing his wife — a concept that returns from film to film. The difficulty to conciliate the private and professional life is a genetic defect of Italian crime film heroes: the explosions of violence that separate them from their beloved ones almost becomes a cure-all, a turn of the screw which is not just necessary but welcome, so that the hero can follow his path all the way through.

However, *Colt 38 Special Squad* is let down by a muddled, disjointed script, which allows too much room to badly-written characters such as Vanni's right-hand man (Riccardo Salvino), and cannot find a balance between the action segments, with spectacular yet shallow showy stunts — a case in point being Vanni's final car chase on a speeding freight train, which wouldn't have been out of place in an Evel Knievel exhibition — and the depiction of a vile and ruthless underworld that meticulously depicts an era of fear, anger and despair. In what might well be one of the poliziotteschi's weirdest moments, none other than Grace Jones shows up to sing a couple of numbers in a nightclub.

Colt 38 Special Squad's success (with an approximate grossing of over a billion and 200 million at the box office) spawned a sequel, although in name only: *Return of the .38 Gang* (*Ritornano quelli della calibro 38*, 1977) by Giuseppe Vari, while Domenico Paolella's *Stunt Squad* (*La polizia è sconfitta*, 1977) was an uncredited remake of sorts of Dallamano's film. On a sad note, *Colt 38 Special Squad* was to be Dallamano's last film, as the director died on November 4, 1976. He was 59.

Note

1. Buttafava, "Procedure sveltite," p. 113.

Come cani arrabbiati (Like Rabid Dogs)

D: Mario Imperoli. *S:* Mario Imperoli; *SC:* Piero Regnoli, Mario Imperoli; *DOP:* Romano Albani (35mm, Techniscope — Technicolor); *M:* Mario Molino, conducted by the author (ed. Bierre); *E:* Otello Colangeli; *ArtD:* Camillo Del Signore; *CO:* Claudia Schiff; *C:* Carlo Tafani; *AC:* Giancarlo Granatelli; *AE:* Giuliana Colangeli; *AD:* Claudio Bernabei; *MU:* Emilio Trani, Stefano Trani; *AMU:* Roberta Petrini; *SOE:* Edgardo Papucci; *SO:* Giorgio Pallotta; *Boom:* Manlio Urbani; *Mix:* Sandro Occhetti, Mario Lupi; *W:* Teresa Carrera; *SE:* Sergio Chiusi; *SP:* Giovanni Caramanico; *MA:* Sergio Mioni; *ChEl:* Tullio Marini; *KG:* Mario Monti; *SS:* Ornella Cataldo. *Cast:* Annarita Grapputo (Silvia), Jean-Pierre Sabagh (Commissioner Paolo Muzi), Paola Senatore (Germana), Cesare Barro (Tony Ardenghi), Luis La Torre (Rico), Gloria Piedimonte (Hostage), Mario Farese, Silvia Spinozzi (Lella, the prostitute), Mario Novelli (Righi, Ardenghi's homosexual right-hand man), Anna Curti (Victim), Pietro Quinzi, Paolo Carlini (Arrigo Ardenghi, Tony's father). *Uncredited:* Artemio Antonini (Caddy at golf club), Calogero Azzaretto (policeman killed at stadium), Massimo Ciprari (policeman), Lina Franchi (Prostitute), Romano Milani (Commissioner),

Luciano Zanussi (Party guest). *PROD:* Roma International Production, Silvia 70, Salamandra Cinematografica; *PM:* Carla Colisi Rossi; *PSu:* Antonio Pittalis; *PSe:* Simonetta Vitali. *Country:* Italy. Filmed at Dear Studios (Rome). *Running time:* 95'; Visa no.: 68776 (07.22.1976); *Rating:* v.m.18; *Release date:* 08.02.1976; *Distribution:* C.I.A.; *Domestic gross:* 540,089,000 lire. *Home video:* Enkromon (VHS, Greece — Italian language)

Tony Ardenghi, the son of an unscrupulous wealthy Roman industrialist, performs a series of violent deeds with his friends Rico and Silvia. During a robbery at a stadium they kill a cop, while another robbery ends with them taking a poor girl as hostage, whom they torture and murder. Then Tony and his friends kill a prostitute named Lella, who was the favorite of Tony's father. Commissioner Muzi, who's on the case, suspects Tony but can't raise any evidence against him. Together with his fellow cop lover Germana, Muzi sets up a trap, having the woman posing as another of Ardenghi's favorite prostitutes. The plan fails, though, and Muzi barely saves Germana from being raped. Eventually Germana catches the trio in the act: Tony and his friends break into a villa to savor a bit of ultraviolence, but Silvia is accidentally shot by Rico. Muzi arrives just in time to save Germana and kill Rico, while Tony escapes. The young man meets a horrible end, though: finding himself stuck in the midst of a protest march, he is savagely killed by the crowd.

The poliziotteschi being a genre strictly tied to contemporaneousness, the need to follow the latest crime news had scriptwriters and filmmakers rapidly change their stories' subjects from organized crime to other resounding examples of urban violence, one of which being the notorious "Circeo massacre," which spawned a mini-thread of films such as *I ragazzi della Roma violenta, Terror in Rome* and *Roma, l'altra faccia della violenza*, all released in 1976.

Mario Imperoli's *Come cani arrabbiati* ("Like Rabid Dogs") also takes inspiration from the above mentioned facts, depicting a trio of upper-class young delinquents, Tony (Cesare Barro), Rico (Luis La Torre) and Silvia (Annarita Grapputo) who rob, kill and rape with gleeful abandon. As Muzi, the tough cop on the case, the expressionless Jean-Pierre Sabagh is given not only a Don Quixote–like idealism and a good dose of stubborness, but also a lover colleague, Germana (the gorgeous Paola Senatore) who also functions as his dialectic pole. "What's the difference between what I feel as a person and as a police official?" he asks. "Did you ever think that persecuting criminals is a job and not a vengeance?" she replies. Unlike many of his celluloid colleagues, Commissioner Muzi has quite a satisfactory sexual life: not only does he date the lovely Germana (whom he even persuades to pose as a prostitute in order to lure Tony into a trap, with disappointing results) but he even ends up in bed with Tony's accomplice Silvia — who, during the seduction scene, recites lines from *Romeo and Juliet*; later on, during a threesome with Tony and Rico, Silvia and her friends exchange lines from *Othello*. If counting the Great Bard among their victims wasn't enough, Imperoli and Regnoli also usurp the songs of Italian poet/songwriter Fabrizio De André with debatable results: an anti-war song called *La ballata del Michè* is used over Paola Senatore's attempted rape scene, while De André's most famous song *La canzone di Marinella* accompanies the savage murder of the homosexual Righi (Mario Novelli) — it must be noted that De André's songs would also pop up in Imperoli's ensuing crime film *Canne mozze* (1977).

The script, by the director and Piero Regnoli, injects elements of social criticism in the plot: the leader of the gang, Tony, is the son of a wealthy industrialist (Paolo Carlini), and aims his rage at his father's associates and occasional partners (such as a pair of prostitutes whom he entertains every Friday, or his homosexual right-hand man). With dialogue such as "The ultimate goal in life as in a game is victory. See, everything else does not make sense: morality, culture, social conscience, religion, are all just good resources to use against those you want to dominate," the script tries hard to blame on the unscrupulous parent his son's deviant behavior. Yet, being this exploitation cinema at its most blatant, the sociological angle is outrageously pretextual, as Imperoli goes for Grand-Guignol, nudity and sleaze at any given opportunity — including carnal violence and rape by shotgun — with a persistence that earned the film a v.m.18 rating. As the evil Tony, Barro sports a passable resemblance to Helmut Berger but little acting skills. A popular male model at the time, he would become a famous jeweler. Grapputo and Senatore both have full frontal nude scenes.

As for the rest, Regnoli manages to cram as many clichés as he can — the opening robbery at the soccer stadium during a game looks like it was stolen from Pietro Germi's *Four Ways Out* (1951) — and ends the film on a truly offensive note, as Tony gets stuck in the middle of a protest march and is lynched by the rabid crowd before Muzi can save him. Ending with the line "Quando muore un assassino non è tempo di lacrime" (When a murderer dies, it's no time for tears), *Come cani arrabbiati* portrays a repulsive sense of justice that borders on out-and-out Fascism; even more abhorrent, though, is its contempt for the masses which emerges in its depiction of the final massacre. It's the kind of film that justifies all the superficial and half-baked criticism that was unjustly spat towards the whole genre.

The Cop in Blue Jeans (*Squadra antiscippo*)

D: Bruno Corbucci. *S* and *SC:* Mario Amendola, Bruno Corbucci; *DOP:* Nino Celeste (35mm, Technicolor, Telecolor), *2nd unit DOP:* Eugenio Bentivoglio; *M:* Guido and Maurizio de Angelis (ed. Nazionalmusic); *E:* Daniele Alabiso; *PD:* Claudio Cinini; *CO:* Silvio Laurenzi; *C:* Guglielmo Vincioni; *AC:* Ivo Spila, Fabio Conversi, Marco Onorato, Luigi Cecchini; *AE:* Brigida Mastrolillo; *AD:* Marina Mattoli; *MU:* Alberto Travaglini, Franco Di Girolamo; *Hair:* Jole Angelucci; *SO:* Roberto Alberghini, Raffaele De Luca; *Boom:* Stefano Piermarioli; *Mix:* Franco Bassi; *SP:* Antonello Assenza; *KG:* Mario Monti; *Chief elec:* Giuseppe Fabrizi; *MA:* Giorgio Chiusi; *SS:* Lisa Lari. *Cast:* Tomas Milian (Nico Giraldi), Jack Palance (Richard J. Russo / Norman Shelley), Maria Rosaria Omaggio, Guido Mannari (Achille Bertinari "Baronetto"), Jack La Cayenne [Alberto Longoni] (Dante Ramucci), Raf Luca (Gargiulo), Benito Stefanelli (Russo's man), Toni Ucci (Rossi "Grottaferrata"), Marcello Martana (Vice Commissioner Trentini), Vincenzo Crocitti (Stutter), Roberto Chiappa (Gibbo), Roberto Messina, Adriano Valentini, Anna Melita, Angelo Pellegrino ("Chiappetta"), Giovanni Attanasio (Carabinieri Brigadeer), Domenico Cianfriglia ("Chinese"), Franco Garofalo, Mimmo Poli (Gaetano Bozzetti), Vittorio Sancisi (Andrea Mangiagalli), Giuliano Sestili (Dante Ramucci), Massimo Stazzi. *Uncredited:* Rossana Canghiari (Woman robbed of her fur), Valerio Colombaioni, Mario Donatone, John P. Dulaney (Agent Ballarin), Iolanda Fortini, Lina Franchi (Passerby at outdoor market), Quinto Gambi, Alba

Maiolini (Nun), Enrico Marciani, Benito Pacifico, Sergio Testori. *PROD:* Galliano Juso for Cinemaster; *PM:* Pietro Innocenzi; *PI:* Francesco Vitulano; *PSe:* Maurizio Giorgi; *ADM:* Paolo Rampazzo; *CASH:* Salvatore Farese. *Country:* Italy. Filmed at Elios Film (Rome). *Running time:* 95'; Visa no.: 68028 (03.10.1976); *Release date:* 03.11.1976; *Distribution:* Regional; *Domestic gross:* 2,013,807,160 lire. *Also known as: Flics en jeans* (Paris, 08.03.1977 — 98')—*Die Strickmütze* (West Germany, 07.09. 1976 — 91'), *Escuadra anti-robo* (Spain). *Home video:* Raro (DVD, Italy).

Rome. Marshall Nico Giraldi is the nemesis of all the city's pickpockets, thanks to his wits and his knowledge of the underworld. One of his most coveted preys is Achille Pettinari, also known as "The Baronet," who continually escapes justice. Pettinari and his two accomplices just made the biggest hit of their career, by stealing a briefcase from an American, Norman Shelley: much to their surprise, the briefcase contains five million dollars, the ransom money from a kidnapping. Shelley tracks down Pettinari's accomplices and kills them, while the Baronet reveals everything to Nico. Having obtained Pettinari's collaboration, Giraldi sets up a trap for Shelley, only to find out that his adversary — whose real name is actually Richard Russo — is a powerful senior official of the U.S. embassy in Rome. In the end, however, Nico has Shelley expelled from Italy and put on trial in his home country.

The second major action film character played by Tomas Milian in 1976, Marshall Nico Giraldi, nicknamed "il Pirata" (The Pirate) is in many ways Monnezza's *alter ego*. Giraldi debuted in March 1976, with *The Cop in Blue Jeans*, while Monnezza made his first apparition five months later, in Lenzi's *Free Hand for a Tough Cop*. Giraldi had a longer life than Monnezza: eleven titles from 1976 to 1984. Anyway, Milian enriched the character from film to film, with features that originally belonged to Monnezza (the heavily made-up eyes, the mechanic's blue overalls): within a couple of years the metamorphosis was complete. Galliano Juso, who produced the first six film in the Nico Giraldi series, recalled the character's curious origins: "Giraldi was born in Naples, during a film Bruno Corbucci and I were shooting called *Il trafficone*. I had my purse snatched by a couple of thugs atop a Kawasaki motorbike. It was a spectacular snatch ... extraordinary, so beautifully executed it was unrepeatable! [...] So Bruno and I had the idea of a film about an "anti-snatch" squad, which didn't actually exist.... And when I got my car stolen we made *Hit Squad*."[1]

Giraldi's character, as conceived by Corbucci and Mario Amendola, is initially very similar to Rambo in Lenzi's *Syndicate Sadists*, although Milian already played a weird hippie hitman with a headband and a denim shirt in Franco Prosperi's *Tough Guy*. However, the Cuban actor goes over the top here, with a number of picturesque details (the multicolored caps, the sweaters and socks that Nico never takes off, not even in bed) and a patent nod to Sidney Lumet's *Serpico* (1973), whose posters are hung on the cop's apartment walls. Serpico is also the name of the mouse which Giraldi always carries with him as a pet. "Serpico pissed on me!" Giraldi blurts out at a certain point: the model becomes the object of a joke, as had happened with Spaghetti Westerns.

Compared to contemporaneous crime films, *The Cop in Blue Jeans* adopts a more playful attitude, as shown by the opening sequence: a series of spectacular snatches, in a tight montage that apes the view of urban degradation as shown by such films as *Street Law* and *Violent Rome*. Yet in Corbucci's film the sequence, instead of provoking indignation, openly goes for laughs: take the bit where a fat guy starts defecating on a public flowerbed in front of a group of Japanese tourists, who immediately start taking pictures of him, while the man's accomplices rob their baggage. The hyperrealistic exasperation has become parodic distortion, and the audience ends up taking sides with the thieves, who are smart and ingenious, while the victims are just plain stupid.[2]

The Roman underworld is shown with an indulgent, absolutory eye: as played by comedians like Toni Ucci and in the following films Bombolo (real name Franco Lechner), who would become a regular comical presence, the petty thieves, con men and purse snatchers who end up in Nico's clutches become comic reliefs, and are punished with a couple of slaps in the face as if they were disobedient (and a bit moronic) children, even though we can be sure we will meet them again in the next entry. The real villains are elsewhere: and there's really nothing to laugh at in the scene where Russo's (Jack Palance) men beat to death a poor purse snatcher in a pool room.

Tomas Milian, right, in a promotional still for *The Cop in Blue Jeans* (1976).

Another important innovation concerns Giraldi's background. The hero isn't plagued by any ghost from his past, nor did he vow himself to a mission of justice; on the contrary, he is a former criminal. His past as a repentant thief (just like Flambeau in G. K. Chesterton's Father

Brown stories) is not only a common point with Monnezza, but also provides the "link between the two worlds—the police and the underworld, that is the two communicating cinematic universes that feed the archetypal series of gangster movies and cop flicks, but also the real-life extreme professional ends that characterize 'poliziotteschi's audiences" as critic Giovanni Buttafava noted. "The environmental conditions of underdevelopment, that are invoked by certain committed films or discourses as the main cause of delinquency, do not justify anything to the eyes of crime-movie audiences, who know very well how those very same conditions may determine the enrollment in law enforcement."[3]

Unlike the following entries in the Giraldi series, the crime angle still is the most important thing in *The Cop in Blue Jeans*, whereas later on it would become just a pretext for Milian's antics. However, Corbucci and Amendola don't care about the verisimilitude of Giraldi's methods: atop his speeding motorbike, Nico drives around in the city as the head of an unlikely special squad that recalls, in a minor key, the one seen in Dallamano's *Colt 38 Special Squad*. As one critic put it, "that's not the first film where Tomas Milian rides a bike and turns into a sheriff on two wheels. *The Cop in Blue Jeans* is once again a barely camouflaged Western, in which [...] action counts much more than content. That's why the exaggerations and, partly, the philosophy that runs throughout the film are justified: beat harder and shoot first."[4] Furthermore, the relationship between the hero and his superiors changes: if Nico's serious predecessors were perennially criticized, obstructed and taken off their cases, Giraldi is almost always praised, in spite of his past as a thief and his casual look, his lack of respect towards colleagues and authorities alike and his offhand methods (like, for instance, letting a purse snatcher go once he's given him the information Nico wanted: Giraldi doesn't care about small fish).

The Cop in Blue Jeans grossed over two billion lire at the box office—almost as much as *Violent Naples*—turning into one of the year's most profitable results. Juso, Corbucci and Milian persisted in the same vein, with four more films in three years: *Hit Squad* (1976), *Swindle* (1977), *Little Italy* (1978) and *The Gang That Sold America* (1979), all very similar and built upon a tried and invariable scheme: a paper-thin crime/action plot, a foreign actor as the main

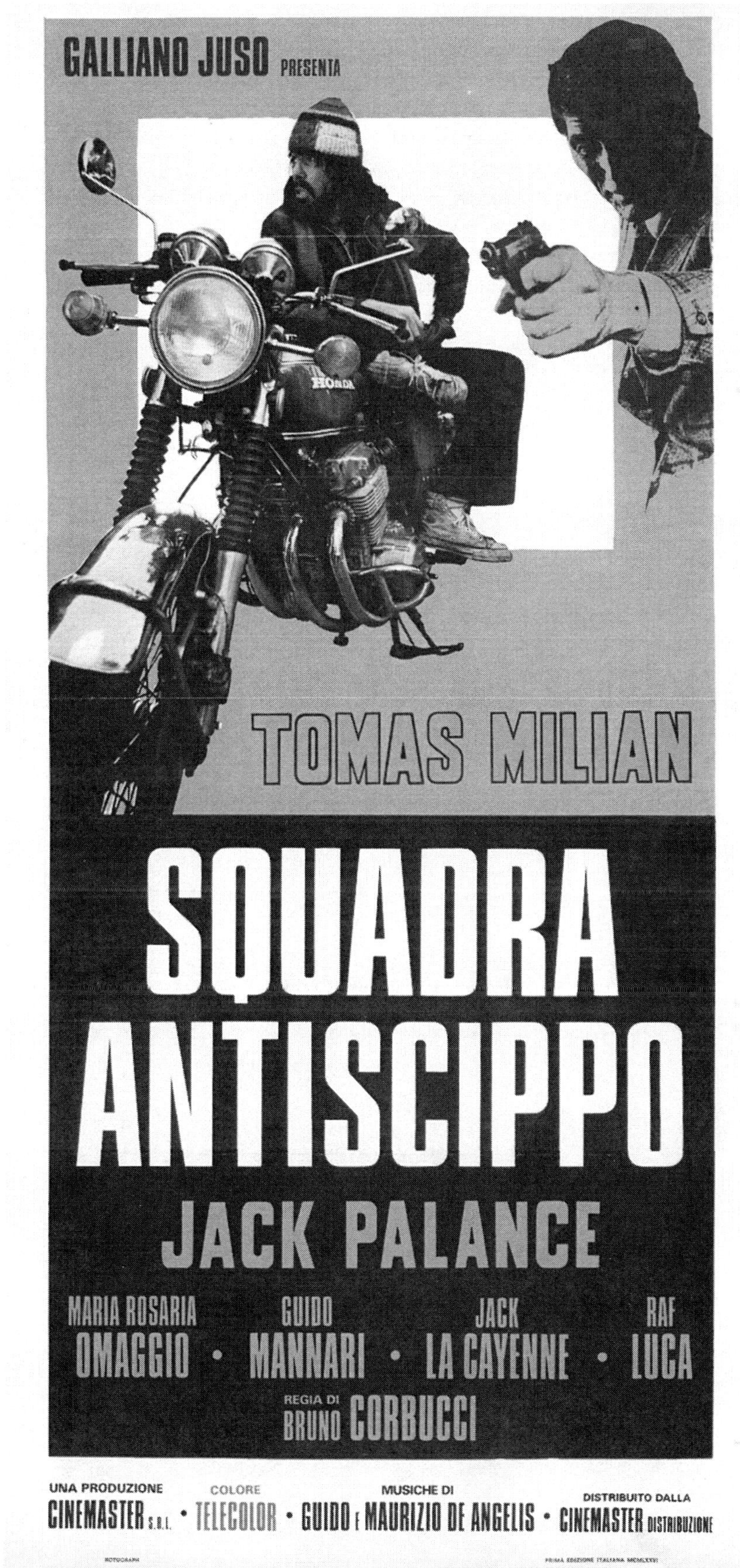

Italian poster for *The Cop in Blue Jeans* (1976).

villain (or as Milian's sidekick, as was the case with David Hemmings in *Swindle*) and an array of secondary comedy characters, from petty thief Venticello (Franco Lechner a.k.a. Bombolo) to Giraldi's assistant Gargiulo (usually played by stuntman Massimo Vanni, replacing *The Cop in Blue Jeans*' Raf Luca). The comic duets between Giraldi and Venticello (who made his first appearance in *Swindle* and gradually became one of the series' major characters, with the sole exception of *The Gang That Sold America*) are typical vaudeville stuff, while Milian's foul-mouthed dialogue, filled with rhymes and picturesquely vulgar verbal inventions, soon became part of the Roman urban slang.[5]

The following six films, also directed by Bruno Corbucci—*Assassinio sul Tevere* (1979), *Delitto a Porta Romana* (1980), *Delitto al ristorante cinese* (1981), *Delitto sull'autostrada* (1982), *Delitto in Formula 1* (1983), *Cop in Drag* (*Delitto al Blue Gay*, 1984)—, had little to do with the crime genre, and it was evident from the titles (starting with the word "Delitto," Murder, thus emphasizing the whodunit angle): the escalating comic element had inevitably modified the series' DNA. Milian's extraordinary eclecticism brought an acceleration to the genre's endemic instability, bringing much-needed box office oxygen when the economical fortunes of the poliziotteschi started to fade, yet on the other hand stressing the atrophy of a thread that was getting tiresome with the mechanical and unconvincing repetitions of the same situations and narrative schemes. In the end, Giraldi's films turned poliziotteschi into full-blown comedy, with the whodunit plots serving as glue and pretext for Milian's verbal acrobatics and the slapstick interludes featuring Bombolo and Enzo Cannavale.

Notes

1. Manlio Gomarasca, "*Quattro chiacchiere con Galliano Juso il produttore*," *Nocturno Cinema* #2, (December 1996), p. 20.
2. The film's playful tone is underlined by Guido and Maurizio De Angelis' score. The original soundtrack was never released, but a selection of music from *The Cop in Blue Jeans* as well as other Monnezza entries can be found in the CD that accompanies Pierpaolo Duranti and Erminio Mucciacito's book *Tomas Milian Il Bandito, Lo Sbirro, e Er Monnezza (Tomas Milian: The Tough Bandit, The Rough Cop and the Filthy Rat in Italian Cinema)*, published by Mediane Libri (CD Mediane/Cinedelic AMK 5017).
3. Buttafava, "Procedure sveltite," p. 109.
4. C. R. *Il Giorno*, 04.24.1976.
5. Giraldi's character became quite popular in Germany as well, where he was renamed Tony Marroni.

Crimebusters (Poliziotti violenti)

D: Michele Massimo Tarantini. S: Michele Massimo Tarantini, Adriano Belli; SC: Adriano Belli, Michele Massimo Tarantini, Franco Ferrini, Sauro Scavolini; DOP: Giancarlo Ferrando (35mm, Technicolor); M: Guido and Maurizio De Angelis; E: Attilio Vincioni; PD: Claudio Cimini; CO: Silvio Laurenzi; C: Claudio Morabito; AC: Rolando Ferrario; Assistant editors: Carlo Cofano, Emma Rolla; AD: Ettore Arena; MU: Franco Di Girolamo; Hair: Jolanda Angelucci; SO: Massimo Marini; Boom: Massimo Casseriani; Mix: Romano Pampaloni; SE: Gino Vagniluca. Cast: Henry Silva (Major Altieri), Antonio Sabàto (Commissioner Paolo Tosi), Silvia Dionisio (Anna), Ettore Manni (Vieri), Claudio Nicastro (General), Daniele Dublino (Lieutenant), Rosario Borelli (Officer in Turin), Benito Stefanelli (Thug), Thomas Rudy (Man eating chocolate), Calogero Caruana, Nicola D'Eramo, Clarisse Monaco, Rudy Reims, Franca Scagnetti (Woman in park). PROD: Giulio Scanni for Staff Professionisti Associati, Capitol International (Rome); General organization: Alessandro Altieri. Country: Italy. Filmed at R.P.A.-Elios Film (Rome). Running time: 92'; Visa no.: 68463 (05.11.1976); Rating: v.m.18; Release date: 05.11.1976; Distribution: Capitol; Domestic gross: 698,998, 550 lire. Also known as: MKS ... 118 (Paris, 06.06.1979—100'), Blutiger Schweiss—Die Ratten von Milano / Ein Profi jagt die Killer (West Germany, 05.20.1982—94'), Adistaktoi dolofonoi (Greece—Home video), Policias violentos (Spain). Home video: Alan Young (DVD, Italy), Eyecatcher (DVD, Germany—English language).

Promoted and transferred to Rome to prevent him from investigating cases of corruption in the army, Major Paolo Altieri of the Paratroopers Corps foils the kidnapping of a child, but himself is the victim of a violent assault on the part of the bandits. On that occasion he realizes that the criminals have used an experimental machine gun model that's used only in his own Corps. Altieri becomes a friend and collaborator of a police Commissioner, Tosi, and takes part in several raids on criminal activities; then, having escaped several attacks during one of which, however, his girlfriend dies and having been forced by his superior to resign from the Corps for hitting an officer, Altieri finally discovers the head of the shady "deal of the gun": an unsuspecting industrial, the lawyer Vieri, who has bribed many senior officers, all involved in a crazy subversive plan to overthrow democracy. Altieri faces Vieri and kills him, but dies in turn, killed in a tragic misunderstanding by his friend Tosi.

As it happened with the Western, the poliziotteschi eventually imploded because of an excess in brutality: a *grande bouffe* of violence which had left behind the prototypes' didactic impetus and just fed off itself. Whenever a thug fired his machine gun, there was always a poor woman passing by who ended up shot to pieces, or—even worse—run over by the robbers' car. The violent event, which at first was a brutal reminder of everyday news items, became a staple element, an ingredient to be inserted whenever the filmmakers felt like it, thus losing its effectiveness with repetition.

Michele Massimo Tarantini's *Crimebusters* is a case in point: the obligatory shoot-outs and chases are accompanied by a soundtrack of assorted yells and screams, with laughable effects. What's more, in a scene the hero, Paolo Altieri (Henry Silva) witnesses a purse snatching attempt, as a pair of thugs on motorbike assault a maid in a park. Altieri intervenes and blocks the delinquents' attempted escape. The thugs end up on the ground and are surrounded by a group of raging ladies who start hitting them with their purses. The subjective shot of the petty criminals, from below, shows the women's faces deformed by a high-angle shot, screaming and insulting towards the camera. It's a scene that recalls the one where a cop is killed and eaten in John Waters' *Pink Flamingos*, but here the paroxistic, exasperated mise en scène doesn't contemplate the grotesque as Waters did: therefore the result is unintentionally hilarious.

As for the rest, despite (or maybe just because of) its four scriptwriters, including Sauro Scavolini and future Dario Argento collaborator Franco Ferrini, *Crimebusters* is standard fare. The political angle is similarly rushed, and ends up in the usual subversive plot against democracy—another element devoid of its evocative power by the filmmaker's indifference, as seedy industrialist Ettore Manni delivers the umpteenth monologue on the "educational" necessity of social disorder: "Order has a price that must be paid. The public opinion must be oriented towards the sense we want, in order to regain trust in a strong State, which we will deliver!"

Similarly banal is the monolithic hero as played by a bored-looking Henry Silva, with Antonio Sabàto as the equally uninteresting sidekick. "You don't talk much," says love interest Anna (Silvia Dionisio) to Altieri, catching behind the hero's marble-like features a hint of humanity that gets lots to the viewer. Unfortunately for the poor girl, her beloved one doesn't follow the advice of a mean-looking thug who tells him — in what's perhaps the film's one memorable line — "If you want to stay in Rome, respect the eleventh commandment: mind your own fucking business!" Beautiful Anna gets blown away by a bomb in a cozy restaurant, before she can order a J&B or a Fernet Branca. Too bad.

Cross Shot (*La legge violenta della squadra anticrimine*)

D: Stelvio Massi. *S:* Lucio De Caro; *SC:* Lucio De Caro, Piero Poggio, Maurizio Mengoni, Dardano Sacchetti; *DOP:* Mario Vulpiani (35mm, Technicolor, Technospes); *M:* Piero Pintucci: *Amore senza mai pensare* (Pintucci / Oremus) sung by Nives; *E:* Mauro Bonanni; *PD, CO:* Carlo Leva; *COA:* Renato Moretti; *ArtD:* Giovanni Fratalocchi; *C:* Michele Pensato, Maurizio Maggi; *AC:* Mario Bagnato, Filippo Neroni; *AE:* Walter Diotallevi, Bruna Patelli; *AD:* Giorgio Maulini; *MU:* Dante Trani; *Hair:* Pasqualina Bianchini; *W:* Irene Parlagreco; *SO:* Roberto Alberghini; *Boom:* Antonio Pantano; *ChEl:* Romano Mancini; *KG:* Giuseppe Raimondi; *STC:* Sergio Mioni; *SS:* Flavia Sante Vanin. *Cast:* John Saxon (Commissioner Jacovella), Lee J. Cobb (Dante Ragusa), Renzo Palmer (Maselli), Lino Capolicchio (Antonio Blasi), Rosanna Fratello (Nadia), Antonella Lualdi (Anna Jacovella), Thomas Hunter (Agent Turrini), Giacomo Piperno (Giordani), Guido Celano (Antonio's father), Alfredo Zammi (Pasquale "Nino" Ragusa), Pasquale Basile (Nicola, Ragusa's butler), Francesco D'Adda (Radio operator), Renato Basso Bondini (Ragusa's henchman), Angelo Boscariol (Journalist), Teodoro Corrà (Charlie), Sergio Mioni (Mario). *PROD:* P.A.C.-Produzioni Atlas Consorziate (Milan); *GO:* Raniero Di Giovanbattista; *EP:* Teodoro Agrimi [Teodoro Corrà]; *UM:* Teodoro Agrimi, Vittorio Biseo; *PSe:* Agostino Pane; *APSe:* Edoardo Antonini; *CASH:* Gaetano Fuzio. *Country:* Italy. Filmed on location in Bari and Trani. *Running time:* 92'; Visa no.: 68347 (04.14.1976); *Rating:* v.m.14; *Release date:* 04.14.1976; *Distribution:* P.A.C.; *Domestic gross:* 654,940,070 lire. *Also known as: Killer der Apokalypse* (West Germany — Home video), *Kuuma ajojahti* (Finland). *Home video:* Cecchi Gori Home Video (DVD, Italy).

Bari. After killing a policeman during a robbery, young Antonio Blasi runs off aboard a car that belongs to the brother of organized crime boss Dante Ragusa. Commissioner Jacovella tracks down his two accomplices and investigates in order to locate Antonio, while Ragusa's men are also in on the hunt. Unbeknownst to Blasi, in the stolen car there is a document that could get the boss arrested. After escaping an ambush, Antonio finds shelter with his girlfriend on a vessel ship. He decides to give up and gets in touch with Maselli, a journalist who has often attacked Jacovella's methods, accusing the cop of being too violent. Antonio's decision, however, does not save him, as he's dispatched by one of Ragusa's men. However, thanks to the evidence in his possession, Jacovella can finally arrest the boss.

Besides fighting against crime, Italian cops often have to face another enemy, whose weapons are not guns but typewriters or poison-dipped pens. One of the genre's recurring images has the hero walk briskly along the police department corridors, followed by a bunch of panting journalists who pester him with provocative questions on the impotence or brutality of law enforcement. Journalists are the recipient of the tough cop's fits of rage, with tirades that border on the victimistic, as in Stelvio Massi's *Cross Shot*. "The real heroes of today are bandits!"; "Sometimes I just feel like I should give up and leave!"; "We're just here to have ourselves killed!" keeps yelling Commissioner Jacovella (John Saxon).

There's no doubt whom filmmakers like best between cops and reporters — and quite understandably so, given the poor reviews newspapers used to reserve to poliziotteschi: journalists — often played by uncredited *generici*, the same faces popping up again from film to film — offer a collection of banalities that only seem to legitimize the heroes' violent methods. The difficult relationship between the press and the police are the driving force behind Massi's film — not one of the director's best, and only modestly successful upon its release. "They'd spit on their mothers' faces if that helped them sell more copies" blurts Jacovella. If the Commissioner is abusive and fascist, his antagonist is no better than him: Maselli (Renzo Palmer), the editor-in-chief of Bari's newspaper "Gazzetta del Mezzogiorno" — the off-beat setting in the Pugliese town is one of the film's assets — is cynical and unscrupulous, divided between ideals of justice and a ribald pragmatism, who is conducting a non-stop campaign against the Commissioner through his newspaper.

The two main characters form one of the poliziotteschi's most complex double-acts. Jacovella is the kind of guy who, after capturing a robber, leaves him to his men so that they beat him to a pulp ("I want those people to know we are no longer willing to let them kill us in silence!"), Maselli — who by the way carries the name of one of Italy's most committed left-winged filmmakers — declares: "To be a good reporter, you can't let your feelings or emotions take over." In the end, Maselli's behavior is even more reproachable than Jacovella's, as he ends up hiding important information on a young delinquent (Lino Capolicchio) — who's wanted for the murder of a cop and hunted by the men of a local crime boss (Lee J. Cobb) because he's carrying compromising evidence — just to make a scoop. "I am ready anyway, either the hunt goes on or he ends up riddled with bullets. I have the headlines ready." Humphrey Bogart's Ed Hutcheson (*Deadline U.S.A.*) wouldn't have approved.

Death Rage, a.k.a. *Blood Reckoning* (*Con la rabbia agli occhi*)

D: Anthony M. Dawson [Antonio Margheriti]. *S:* Pier Luigi Andreani, Leila Bongiorno; *SC:* Guido Castaldo, Giacomo Furia; *DOP:* Sergio D'Offizi (35mm, Vistavision, Staco Film), *2nd unit DOP:* Antonio Maccoppi; *M:* Guido and Maurizio De Angelis (ed. Eurofilmusic); *E:* Mario Morra; *PD, ArtD:* Luciano Puccini; *CO:* Massimo Bolongaro; *COA:* Antonella Berardi; *C:* Enrico Lucidi; *AC:* Enrico Maggi, Aldo Bergamini; *AE:* Roberto Sterbini; *2nd unit D:* Ignazio Dolce; *MU:* Lamberto Biseo; *Hair:* Corrado Cristofori; *SO:* Pietro Spadoni; *Boom:* Angelo Spadoni; *SE:* Paolo Ricci; *SP:* Mauro Paravano; *W:* Anna Onori; Props: Luciano Tarquini; *SS:* Eva Koltaj. *Cast:* Yul Brynner (Peter Marciani), Massimo Ranieri (Angelo), Barbara Bouchet (Anny), Martin Balsam (Commissioner), Giancarlo Sbragia (Gennaro Gallo), Giacomo Furia (Cannavale), Sal [Salvatore] Borgese (Vincent, Gallo's henchman), Loris Bazzocchi (Pasquale, Gallo's henchman), Rosario Borelli (Gallo's henchman), Luigi Williams [Gigi Bonos] (Peppiniello), Renzo Marignano (Doctor). *Uncredited:* Gennaro Beneduce (Friar at police station), Paul Costello (Desk clerk), Domenico Di Costanzo (Leonardi's bodyguard), Gilberto Galimberti (Gallo's henchman), Franco Marino (Gallo's henchman), Edoardo Mascia (Gallo's henchman), Vezio Natili, Tommaso Palladino (Gallo's henchman). *PROD:* Franco Caruso and Raymond R. Homer for Giovine Cinematografica; *GM:* Franco Caruso; *PM:* Nino Di Giambattista; *UM:* Augusto Dolfi, Francesco Guerrieri; *ADM:* Ugo Iovane. *Country:* Italy. Filmed at Incir — De Paolis (Rome) and on location in Naples. *Running time:* 98'; Visa no.: 69204 (10.09.1976); *Rating:* v.m.14; *Release date:* 10.22.1976; *Distribution:* Euro International Film; *Domestic gross:* 630,234,524 lire. *Also known as: Anger in His Eyes* (U.K.), *L'ombre d'un tuer* (Paris, 08.17.1977 — 90') — *Höllenhunde bellen zum Gebet* (03.11.1977 — 98'), *Con la rabia en los ojos* (Spain). *Home video:* Pop Flix (DVD, USA — as part of their *Crime Boss collection* boxset), Cinekult (DVD, Italy — 91' 24"). OST: LP Beat Records BTF 096.

"Cosa Nostra" hitman Peter Marciani leaves New York for Naples, on a mission to kill Gennaro Gallo, who committed an offence against the "family" as his men killed a boss named Leonardi. Besides, Marciani has a personal motive to kill the boss, so as to avenge the death of his brother, who was betrayed and killed apparently by Gallo's gunman. While Gallo tries repeatedly to get rid of Peter, in vain, the killer receives unexpected help from a young man, Angelo, who lives by his wits, and a stripper, Anny. Finally, Marciani manages to surprise the boss and kill him, but he is mortally wounded too. His place in the "family" will be taken by Angelo, after the young man finds out who really ordered the murder of Peter's brother and avenges him.

Just like the poliziotteschi did, the Italian *film noir* genre fully plunged into a crepuscular phase during the decade's second half, a tendency that was anticipated by Antonio Margheriti's forays into the genre, *Death Rage* (1976) and *The Squeeze* (1978). Both starred big name foreign stars, but whereas the latter was a more American-looking production, shot in the States with an English-speaking cast, *Death Rage* benefited from a typical Italian setting — Naples.

Margheriti wisely allowed ample screen time to his charismatic American star. As the infallible hitman Peter Marciani, Yul Brynner gives his character a resonance that enhances the script's characterization. All dressed in black, impassive, ruthless and effective as the robotic gunslinger he played in *Westworld* (1973), Marciani is yet plagued by a subterranean romanticism, as can be seen in the subplot that involves Barbara Bouchet, which culminates in a scene where the woman pretends to make love with Peter to fool the cops that are staking out her place, while Marciani leaves to perform his last and fatal hit. Furthermore, the hitman is not only doomed to settle scores with his traumatic past, but also with a *cupio dissolvi* that manifests itself as a psychosomatic disease — Marciani's eyesight disturbances that Margheriti visually renders with surreal Rorschach-like red stains that pop up on the screen and carry freeze-frames of his brother's murder, echoing the blood stains Marciani leaves behind him. The pivotal murder is also shown in the obligatory slow-motion flashback that hides a revealing detail as to the identity of the mysterious mandater, thus leading to the final, predictable twist.

According to Margheriti's good friend Giacomo Furia, the character actor playing the Commissioner's assistant and also co-scripted the film, the original story came to him from another director, Silvio Siano, who told Furia it had been penned by a Spaniard. The script was written in a rush after Margheriti managed to cast Yul Brynner in the lead. The plot, which centers on the relationship between Marciani and a young Neapolitan petty crook, Angelo (Massimo Ranieri), who earns his living by falsifying horse races and quickly elects Marciani as his mentor, follows a typical genre path. Even though as often happens with Italian films, the script borrowed from various sources (one scene where Marciani inadvertently almost drops acid into his eyes comes from *Arabesque*), *Death Rage*'s main model is Michael Winner's *The Mechanic*: the script mimics the relationship between Charles Bronson and Jan-Michael Vincent, but the generational theme also echoes Italian Westerns such as Tonino Valerii's *Day of Anger* (1967), even though it doesn't fully deliver on what it promises. However, Margheriti's film is eventually less cynical than both models in its telegraphed yet effective ending, as Angelo becomes Marciani's successor ("You have to have faith that what you are doing is right, otherwise you'll never manage to justify yourself," Peter explains to his young disciple in the film's best scene, set by the sea at sundown; "Don't feel any hate: you are not killing, he was already dead when you accepted to carry the hit") and avenger.

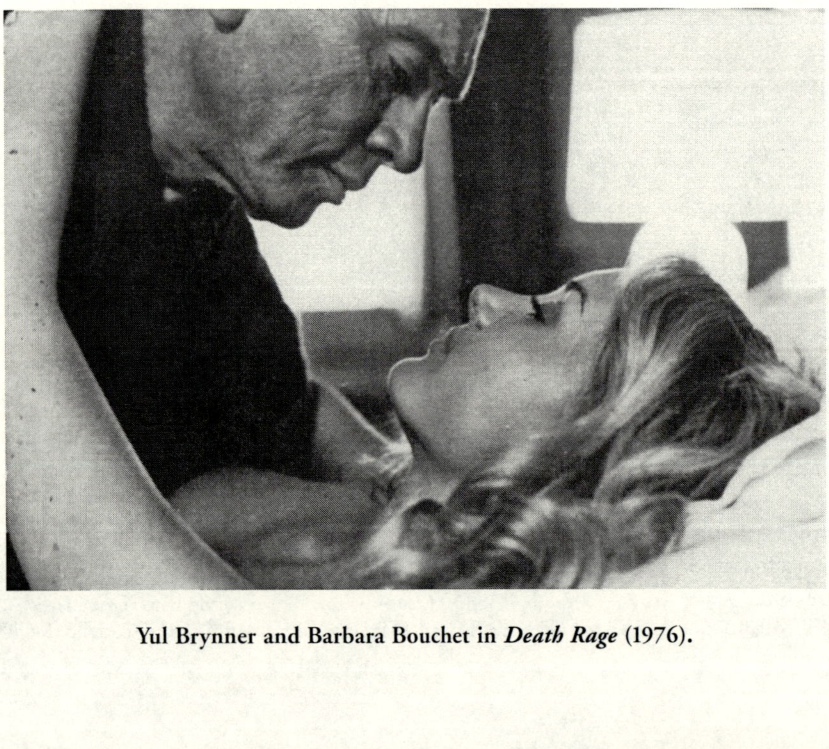

Yul Brynner and Barbara Bouchet in *Death Rage* (1976).

Margheriti's direction is assured (yet the effective action sequences — including a chase in Naples' subway — were shot by his assistant director Ignazio Dolce) and allows for plenty of local "color," but compared to poliziotteschi, the police here become a marginal, stately presence. The Commissioner played by Martin Balsam is just a spectator in the gang war that is painting the streets red with blood: he tolerates the hitman who came from overseas ("He's a public benefactor," he even quips) and tries to act as a mediator between local bosses. As the young inexperienced sidekick, Ranieri — a popular Neapolitan singer and an instinctively gifted actor who debuted in Mauro Bolognini's *Metello* (1969) — brings an endearing veracity to his role, while Bouchet — who has a memorable strip scene in a club, surrounded by mirrors that reflect her statuesque body — is as stunning as ever as the love interest. However, the two leads didn't get along at all on set. According to the actress, her co-star was quite impossible to deal with and treated the crew very rudely; Bouchet, horrified at his behavior, got back at Brynner by sending him a bouquet of carnations, a flower he was extremely phobic about being exposed to. Another asset is Guido and Maurizio De Angelis' excellent score.

The film — Brynner's last screen role before the actor fully devoted himself to the stage[1] — got a distribution overseas in the Home video circuit in the 1980s, although the American version sacrifices Margheriti's powerful opening scene, which can be seen in its complete form only on the Italian DVD. It also circulated in the States under the alternate title *Blood Reckoning*.

Note

1. Margheriti planned to make another film with Brynner, the story of two game hunters in Africa during World War I, but it never took off.

Fear in the City, a.k.a. *Hot Stuff (Paura in città)*

D: Giuseppe Rosati. *S* and *SC:* Giuseppe Rosati, Giuseppe Pulieri; *DOP:* Giuseppe Bernardini (35mm, Telecolor); *M:* Giampaolo Chiti (ed. Ping Pong); *E:* Franco Fraticelli; *PD:* Giorgio Bertolini, Osvaldo Desideri; *CO:* Maria Laura Zampacavallo; *C:* Federico Del Zoppo, Giacomo Testa; *AC:* Gianni Maddaleni, Sergio Melaranci; *AE:* Mario Cinotti; *2nd AE:* Pier Luigi Leonardi; *AD:* Giuseppe Pulieri; *MU:* Dante Trani; *Hair:* Marcello Longhi; *SO:* Alvaro Orsini; *Boom:* Alberto Moretti; *SOE:* Luciano Anzellotti; *SP:* Giuseppe Botteghi; *STC:* Sergio Mioni; *ST:* Ottaviano Dell'Acqua; *SS:* Maria Luisa Rosen. *Cast:* Maurizio Merli (Commissioner Mario Murri), James Mason (Chief of Police), Raymond Pellegrin (Lettieri), Silvia Dionisio (Laura Masoni), Fausto Tozzi (Marshall Esposito), Gianfilippo Carcano (Don Saverio), Giovanni Elsner (Agent Diotallevi), Mario Novelli (Bankrobber), Franco Ressel (Attorney Lo Cascio), Liana Trouché (Katia Fiorillo), Cyril Cusack (Giacomo Masoni), Loris Bazzocchi (Lettieri's accomplice), Tino Bianchi (Ministry of Transports), Liana Sagrillo (Prostitute), Antonio Maimone (Caputo), Franco Fantasia (Rinaldi), Claudio Nicastro (police officer), Andrea Scotti (Agent Girotti), Domenico [Mimmo] Poli (Nestore Frangipane), Artemio Antonini (Antonio Proietti, Lettieri's Henchman), Renato Basso (Lettier's henchman), Franco Beltramme (Lettieri's Henchman), Vladimiro Daddi (Lettieri's Henchman), Augusto Funari (Lettieri's Henchman), Sandro Scarchilli (Garrozzi "Calotta," Lettieri's Henchman), Sergio Testori (Lettieri's Henchman). *Uncredited:* Salvatore Billa (Victim), Salvatore Biondo (Man handcuffed at the police station), Rosario Borelli (Marshall in Nettuno), Dolores Calò (Old Woman hostage in bank robbery), Omero Capanna (Lettieri's henchman), Enrico Chiappafreddo (Angiolino, thug on bus), Domenico Cianfriglia (Thug on bus), Massimo Ciprari (Prostitute client), Ottaviano Dell'Acqua (Thug on bus), Roberto Dell'Acqua (Victim), Augusto Funari (Thug), Romano Milani, Filippo Perego (Man at airport), Anna Maria Perego (Woman at airport), Franca Scagnetti (Concierge), Valentino Simeoni (Waiter in restaurant), Marco Stefanelli (Thug on bus), Marcello Venditti (Robber), Luciano Zanussi (Man taking airplane). *PROD:* Roberto Onori for Triomphe Film; *EP:* Marcello Lizzani, Giuseppe Vezzani; *AP:* Renzo Ciabò; *PSu:* Francesco Fantacci, Lucia Nolano, Giuseppe Pulieri (uncredited); *PSe:* Antonio Jiritano; *ADM:* Sergio Rosa. *Country:* Italy. Filmed in Rome. *Running time:* 100'; Visa no.: 68981 (08.21.1976); *Rating:* v.m.14; *Release date:* 08.21.1976; *Distribution:* Indipendenti Regionali; *Domestic gross:* 1,006,693,801 lire. *Also known as: La peur règne sur la ville* (Paris, 11.02.1983 —100'). *Home video:* Alan Young, Cecchi Gori Home Video (DVD — Italy). OST: LP Beat Records CR 3 (includes music from other scores penned by Chiti).

Rome. Twelve inmates escape from the Regina Coeli penitentiary: among them are the murderer Alberto Lettieri and his gang and, forced to follow them against their will, the elderly Giacomo Masoni, a former railroad official convicted for a case of euthanasia. The Commissioner on the case is Murri, who's loved by his colleagues but opposed by the magistrates because of his violent methods. Murri either captures or kills five of the fugitives during two robberies; then, questioning Masoni's young nephew Laura, with whom he falls in love, the Commissioner discovers a trail that leads to Lettieri: in all likelihood, the bandits are going to use Masoni to take possession of a load of banknotes, tens of billions' worth, that are about to be sent by train from Milan to Rome to be destroyed. After a shoot-out with Lettieri's men, which ends with their death, Murri is likely to be suspended from service, yet the Commissioner is allowed two more days by the Chief of Police to find the criminal. In the end Murri succeeds, preventing Lettieri's hit and killing him and his accomplices.

A sequel of sorts of Giuseppe Rosati's previous poliziotteschi *The Left Hand of the Law*, from which it reprises the character of Commissioner Murri and his two assistants, *Fear in the City* was conceived as a vehicle for Maurizio Merli, then at the top of his popularity. However, the film wasn't a huge success as its makers hoped for: it came out together with *Violent Naples*, but grossed only half as much as the former. Unlike Lenzi's film, *Fear in the City* suffers from its formulaic, indifferent approach: Merli does little to enliven a character that he wears like a second skin, yet falls dangerously close to self-parody. Murri talks too much, with plenty of awkwardly overwrought dialogue: at some point he even declares he suffers from *cupio dissolvi*, a line that probably had audiences laugh out loud back then: Commissioners know about guns, not Latin. The narrative expedients, such as the violent slow-motion flashbacks where Murri recalls his wife's murder — as with Betti's background story, a number of details have been adjusted since the first film — are similarly ill-conceived.

That's not to say *Fear in the City* is completely devoid of irony. Pulieri's script starts with Murri — who's been transferred from Rome to some provincial town, a situation that would also become recurring in the future —fishing by a river, complaining that he only catches small fish, because "us cops never manage to get the big fish." As Pulieri recalls, the executive producer was Carlo Lizzani's nephew Marcello, and the production company Triomphe Film only produced another title, Lizzani's documentary *Africa nera, Africa rossa* (1978). Pulieri also reveals the expeditious way *Fear in the City* was made. "I was production supervisor on that one. Every morning, day by day, I went location scouting, and found the places where we could shoot for free [...]. There was a production manager, who was Lizzani's associate, who didn't know a thing about it [Giuseppe Vezzani, Ed.]. [...] Every day I came up with a new location. Vezzani showed up and asked "Are we paying for this?" "No, no, that's for free ... see, that lady is the concierge, give her 10,000 lire and we shoot right here."[1]

Note

1. Grattarola, *È arrivato il risolutore*, p. 23.

4 Billion in 4 Minutes (*Quelli dell'antirapina—4 minuti per 4 miliardi*)

D: Gianni Siragusa. *S* and *SC:* Italo Alfaro, Gianni Siragusa; *DOP:* Guglielmo Mancori (35mm, Technicolor—Techniscope); *M:* Franco and Mino Reitano, conducted by Detto Mariano (ed. Fremus-Fiumara, Detto Music), electronic music piece by Marco Bergamaschi; *E:* Romeo Ciatti; *ArtD:* Gabriella Bairo Puccetti; *PD:* Dario Micheli; *C:* Mario Sbrenna; *AC:* Edmondo Pisani, Aldo Bergamini; *AE:* Margherita Santangelo; *AD:* Roberto Pariante; *MU:* Giulio Mastrantonio; *SO:* Antonio Forrest; *SOE:* Luciano Anzellotti; *Mix:* Romano Pampaloni; *SE:* Basilio Patrizi; *Still photographers:* Ermanno Serto, Giancarlo Filoni; *Acrobatic scenes:* Attilio Severini; *SS:* Maria Costantina Ercoli; *UP:* Anna Maria Jensen. *Cast:* Antonio Sabàto (Raffaele), John Richardson (Francesco Vitale), Lea Lander (Peggy), Giovanni Brusatori [Brusadori] (Luca), Vassili Karis (Aldo), Attilio Severini (Sandro), Seraphen [Serafino] Profumo (Marco), Giuseppe Pollaci (Convict), Saverio Mosca (Prison director), Paul Oxon. *PROD:* Pierluigi Bairo for Bairo Cinematografica; *PM:* Armando Morandi. *Country:* Italy. Filmed at Cave Film Studio (Rome) and on location in Genoa and Rapallo. *Running time:* 101'; Visa no.: 68406 (05.04.1976); *Rating:* not rated; *Release date:* 09.11.1976; *Distribution:* Variety; *Domestic gross:* 623,180,660 lire. *Also known as: Quatre milliards en quatre minutes* (Paris, 10.11.1978—105')—*Die Mondschein-Killer* (West Germany, 1978—90'). *Home video:* AVO (VHS, Italy), Techno-Fletcher (VHS, U.K.).

From the prison cell where he is serving a sentence, criminal mastermind Francesco Vitale, also known as "the advocate," prepares a bank heist that his accomplices (who include his wife Peggy) carry out successfully, getting away with a loot comprising four billion lire. Vitale also has a plan to escape from jail, but the younger and violent Raffaele, who is serving a life sentence for murder, joins him in the attempt. The fugitives go their separate ways, and Raffaele spectacularly robs a bank, killing two cops in the chase that ensues. Later on he shows up again at Vitale's hideout, asking to join his gang. While waiting for the moment when Vitale will retrieve and share the money—which are hidden in a safe place—Raffaele discovers that Vitale's accomplices (later joined by Aldo, who's also Peggy's lover) are conspiring to dispatch the rest of the band; he also ends up in bed with Peggy, and proposes to share all the money with her. However, Vitale is smarter than his accomplices, and in the end he manages to get rid of all his companions except for Raffaele. Much to his surprise, though, the latter turns out not to be a criminal but a member of the "anti-robbery squad."

Even though its plot sounds very similar in places to *Meet Him and Die*, with a special agent gaining a convicted criminal's trust and following him in an escape from prison, Gianni Siragusa's *4 Billion in 4 Minutes* is quite a peculiar affair. The script, by Italo Alfaro and the director, is a weird variation on the classical heist movie—the opening hit, meticulously executed, wouldn't have been out of place in such films as Michele Lupo's *Your Turn to Die* (*Troppo per vivere … poco per morire*, 1967)—and in the second part the film becomes somewhat reminiscent of Cesare's Canevari *Una iena in cassaforte* (1968), as the criminals hide in an isolated villa and are constantly at each other's throats. The overall mood is detached from contemporary poliziotteschi, and is best synthesized by the film's central sequence, a spectacular bank robbery aboard a "Beetle" Volkswagen and the rocambolesque chase that follows: here, thanks also to Franco and Mino Reitano's score (unfortunately unreleased as of yet), the most patent nod to the halo of urban uneasiness that characterized the contemporaneous crime genre is almost completely devoid of its violent overtones, and becomes an openly playful recreation of a bumper car ride—as revealed by Sabàto's disarmingly amused smile.

That's why Sabàto's real identity is kept a secret until the very end, only to come out as a rather pedestrian plot twist, as quick flashbacks show us how all of Raffaele's violent deeds, bank robbery and murder included, were actually part of a Machiavellian plot in agreement with the police force. More than a simple *carabiniere*, he is a sort of a special agent in disguise, part of a non-existent "anti-robbery squad": the '70s answer to the previous decade's James Bond look-alikes, with the Mediterranean features of Antonio Sabàto replacing Anglo-Saxon predecessors such as Richard Harrison or Roger Browne. This nod to the 1960s is also obvious in the other main characters: the "advocate" John Richardson (who always dresses impeccably, wears prescription glasses and hates the sight of blood) is a typical old-fashioned villain, while the not-so-attractive Lea Lander is the obligatory bitchy dark lady.

Free Hand for a Tough Cop (*Il trucido e lo sbirro*)

D: Umberto Lenzi. *S:* Dardano Sacchetti; *SC:* Dardano Sacchetti, Umberto Lenzi; *DOP:* Luigi Kuveiller, Nino [Sebastiano] Celeste (35mm, Eastmancolor, Telecolor); *M:* Bruno Canfora (ed. Variety Film) *La ballata del trucido e lo sbirro* (G. Cascio) sung by Giorgio Cascio, *Ma come ho fatto* (B. Canfora / G. Palazio / L. Chiosso) sung by Ornella Vanoni; *E:* Eugenio Alabiso; *PD:* Giorgio Bertolini; *ArtD:* Enrico Fantacci; *CO:* Silvio Laurenzi; *AD:* Filiberto Fiaschi; *2nd AD:* Danilo Massi; *AE:* Amedeo Moriani; *2nd AE:* Marco Roselli; *C:* Elio Polacchi; *AC:* Renato Palmieri, Ivo Spila; *MU:* Franco Di Girolamo; *Hair:* Jolanda Angelucci; *SO:* Raul Montesanti; *SOE:* Roberto Arcangeli; *Mix:* Luigi Di Fiore; *SE:* Gino Vagniluca; *MA:* Riccardo Petrazzi; *ChEl:* Sergio Coletta; *KG:* Giuseppe Gabrielli; *G:* Giancarlo Mancini; *SP:* Maurizio Sposito; *SS:* Maria Luisa Merci; *Dubbing* (English version): Nick Alexander. *Cast:* Tomas Milian (Sergio Marazzi "Monnezza"), Claudio Cassinelli (Commissioner Antonio Sarti), Nicoletta Machiavelli (Mara, Brescianelli's lover), Henry Silva (Brescianelli), Robert Hundar [Claudio Undari] (Mario "The Cynic"), Biagio Pelligra (The Calabrese), Giuseppe Castellano (Vallelunga), Tano Cimarosa ("Cravatta," the fence), Dana Ghia (Clara Finzi), Renato Mori (Commissioner Franchini), Susanna Melandri (Camilla Finzi), Mario Erpichini (Paolo Finzi), Corrado Solari (Robber), Rita Forzano (Woman taken hostage at jewelry), Antonio Casale (Pasquale Tomati "Er Greve"), Massimo Bonetti (Purse snatcher), Ernesto Colli (Roscetto), Paolo Bonetti (Robber), Rosita Torosh (Drug addict at the bar), Sara Franchetti (Moretti's cleaning lady). *Uncredited:* Umberto Amambrini, Salvatore Billa (Tomati's thug), Rosario Borelli (Brescianelli's man), Angelo Boscariol (Cinema usher), Rossana Canghiari (Cinema cashier), Enrico Chiappafreddo (Hostage worker on train), Giovanni Cianfriglia (Carlini), Valerio Colombaioni (Young informer), Ottaviano Dell'Acqua (Jewelry clerk), Arturo Dominici (Chief of Police De Rita), Raniero Dorascenzi (Cop), Tom Felleghy (Jeweler), Valentino Macchi (policeman at roadblock), Fulvio Mingozzi (Federal police captain), Benito Pacifico (Tomati's henchman), Filippo Perego (Baron Picelli, the president of Petratex), Riccardo Petrazzi (Brescianelli's driver), Umberto Raho (Franco, Finzi's lawyer), Bruno Rosa (Cop in police station), Luciano Rossi (Drug dealer), Claudio Ruffini (Carlini's friend at the nightclub), Sergio Smacchi (Tomati's henchman), Sergio Testori (Brescianelli's henchman), Pietro Torrisi (Brescianelli's henchman). *PROD:* Ugo Tucci and Claudio Mancini for Variety Film, S.G.M. Film (Rome); General; *PM:* Sergio Borelli; *PSu:* Franco Coduti; *PSe:* Stefano Vicario, Maurizio Mancini; *ADM:* Walter Massi. *Country:* Italy. Filmed at R.P.A.—Elios (Rome) and on location in Rome. *Running time:* 95'; Visa no.: 69002 (08.27.1976); *Rating:* v.m.14; *Release date:* 08.27.1976; *Distribution:* Variety Film; *Domestic gross:* 1,450,688,120 lire. *Also known as: Das Schlitzohr und der Bulle* (Germany—Home video), *La mort en sursis, Le truand sort de sa planque* (France), *Le clan des pourris* (France—Home video). *Home video:* Cinekult-Cecchi Gori (DVD, Italy), AVO (DVD, Italy). OST: LP Variety Film VF 5801.

Commissioner Antonio Sarti has small-time criminal Monnezza escape from jail, as he believes the convict can help him find Brescianelli, a notorious and ruthless gangster who just kidnapped a twelve-year-old girl, Camilla Finzi. The young kidnapping victim suffers from a kidney disorder which requires regular hospital visits. If she doesn't get to the hospital in a week, then she is going to die. Sarti and Monnezza hire three other scumbags—the cynic, Calabrese and Vallelunga—whom they helped to escape the police after a robbery, as a sort of special squad outside the law. However, Sarti's job is getting risky, as he has to keep Monnezza and his acolytes in line, maintain his cover (besides Monnezza, the other three don't know he is a cop) and get to Brescianelli in time. Through a fence, Cravatta, Monnezza's acolytes gather information on one of Brescianelli's associates, a bank robber named Tomati, who provides a vital clue: they will find Sarti—who has undergone plastic surgery—by following his lover Mara. Their attempt at kidnapping the woman fails: however, another lead allows Sarti and Monnezza to locate Brescianelli's lair, only to find out that Camilla has been moved. Sarti and his men take Mara as hostage and set up a trap to lure Brescianelli at the woman's place, while Monnezza penetrates into the bandit's hideout. The final rendezvous with the gangsters ends with Monnezza and the Commissioner as the sole survivors. Camilla is safe, and Monnezza flees to freedom.

In 1976, with the advent of Maurizio Merli and the thread's subsequent reduction to an unchanging, impermeable formula, the poliziotteschi was thematically close to overt stagnation, as proven by the apparition of sub-par products such as *Crimebusters* and *Fear in the City*, where the insistence on violence and cruelty had become a tiresome cliché. In that respect, Umberto Lenzi's *Free Hand for a Tough Cop* marked the beginning of a new wave for Italian crime film. The merit was mostly owed to the film's main character: Sergio Marazzi a.k.a. "Monnezza" (literally, "Trash," in Roman slang, yet he is called "Garbage Can" in the English dub), played by Tomas Milian.

It was Milian's over-the-top characterization, in accordance to the actor's willingness to play with his screen persona and his chameleon-like ability to shape striking new characters, that turned out to be the film's winning move. A curly wig, shaggy beard, dark eyes, ragged second-hand clothes, Monnezza became the Charon that led poliziotteschi from violence into the realm of comedy. Monnezza was a sort of modern-day Rugantino, the popular character from Roman theatre, a proletarian hero whose name derives from the word "arrogance." Whereas Merli's cops are tough and taciturn, Monnezza talks in rhyme, and literally assaults the viewer with a non-stop, exuberant foul-mouthed language. He immediately identifies himself as a recognizable working class hero—even more so, he is literally a son of a bitch, as he gleefully defines himself ("My mother was a saint," he'd tell jokingly in the film's follow-up *Destruction Force*). In many ways, Monnezza is the genre's answer to so many characters played by Alberto Sordi in the most famous examples of "commedia all'italiana." Whereas Sordi was the average middle-class Italian, who got seduced and overwhelmed by the early 1960s economical escalation (the so-called "Boom"), Milian's character is a commercially palatable version of Pier Paolo Pasolini's beloved subproletarians, but without *Accattone*'s metaphysical rumination: whenever Monnezza is forced to get himself a job and raise a family (such as in *Destruction Force*), he does not lose his rebellious attitude.

Last but not least, Monnezza is also a Western character in disguise, and incarnates the genetic link between Italian Westerns and poliziotteschi. Referring to Monnezza and his alter ego Nico Giraldi, the idiosyncratic hero of *The Cop in Blue Jeans* (*Squadra antiscippo*, 1976) Milian itself stated it: "Monnezza and Nico il Pirata are close relatives of Cuchillo," that is Milian's earlier character, the Mexican peasant he played in Sergio Sollima's *The Big Gundown* (*La resa dei conti*, 1966) and *Run, Man, Run* (*Corri uomo corri*, 1968). "Nico il Pirata, on the other hand, is a modern-day rewriting of Lee Van Cleef's character in *The Big Gundown*" he added.[1]

Free Hand for a Tough Cop makes its aim very clear as from its

Henry Silva as the villain in *Free Hand for a Tough Cop* (1976).

very first sequence. Lenzi's film opens amidst the unmistakable Monument Valley landscape, as a stagecoach is chased by bandits: yet this soon turns out to be a film-within-a-film, that's being projected to a rather unusual audience, the convicts of a Roman penitentiary.[2] And it's quite an impolite audience, too: they yell at the screen, bored or mocking, sneering at the fistfight scenes in a saloon. Besides the fruitful metaphorical implications, the opening scene of Lenzi's film works not only as an assertion of the handover between the two genres, but also as a mocking, peremptory claim of hegemony. The convicts' cackles ("Who cares 'bout this bullshit?," "When is this goin' to end?," "Look at that son-of-a-bitch!" when a sheriff appears on-screen) destroy whatever power and credibility the original scenes might have had within their original context. The final stroke is up to Monnezza: "Watch my seat, would you? I got to take a shit" he says to the convict sitting next to him. The Italian Western was long dead and buried, and many had already said it, in a poetic way (Leone's *Once Upon a Time in the West*) or with a mixture of irony and melancholy (Tonino Valerii's *My Name Is Nobody*). No one, though, had been so direct and mordant.

With the advent of Monnezza, the poliziotteschi underwent a moral turn of the screw as well: the tough incorruptible cop makes room to a petty thief with a heart of gold, who collaborates with law enforcement but only for his personal interest. Once again, law and justice are ample and variable concepts, in the poliziotteschi as they were in the Spaghetti Western, and unwritten laws always get the better hand over the procedural code. The transition is apparent in Lenzi's film, where Monnezza escapes from prison with the help of Commissioner Sarti (Claudio Cassinelli), who entrusts him to find the ruthless Brescianelli (Henry Silva), the kidnapper of a sick little girl: and it doesn't take Sarti too long to persuade Monnezza: "I don't want to have a dead girl on my conscience" he says. It's much less believable, to point at one of the script's faults, that Monnezza and Sarti manage to persuade the thugs whom the former has recruited, memorably portrayed by a trio of familiar villains — Robert Hundar, Biagio Pelligra and Giuseppe Castellano — who are introduced during a train robbery scene which functions as another sneering reference to the Western. As the film makes clear, however, Monnezza is far from the average good guy, and moves in a territory of ribald amorality. As his predecessor Cuchillo, he proves to be a skilled knife thrower, and even shows more than a hint of sadism in a scene where he settles the score with a sneaker (Ernesto Colli), by forcing him to choose between two glasses of milk, one of which is poisoned. After the latter has drunk from the "safe" glass, and thinks he's safe, Monnezza shoots him in cold blood, commenting: "If it was written that you should die, it means you had to, asshole!"

Compared to Monnezza, the tough cop on the case becomes a sidekick, a best buddy who never gets the limelight for himself and even gets slapped in the end — a transition helped by Cassinelli's subtle self-mocking attitude which worked so well in *Killer Cop*. The final scene has Sarti realize that Monnezza has stolen his purse, and as he leaves the thief sneers him: "Ask 'em to pay you more!"

Free Hand for a Tough Cop also shows the poliziotteschi's progressive detachment from everyday news items. Monnezza's antics take up much of the time that was usually reserved for the villain, and the film's bad guy — played by an expressionless Silva — here becomes a mere narrative function, without even the slightest attempt at characterization, even though his name — Brescianelli — hints at the real name of a gangster who otherwise operated in the Milan area within the Marseilles clan.[3] What's more, Dardano Sacchetti's script hastily maneuvers Brescianelli's actions in a muddled, sometimes even absurd manner. The film barely juxtaposes good and bad guys, and similarly doesn't allow the present and its gloomy halo to show up if not momentarily, with curiously puzzling, even grotesque results. Such an example is the scene where Monnezza and Sarti are about to kidnap Brescianelli's girlfriend (Nicoletta Machiavelli) to get precious information from her, but their attempt fails from the very beginning because of the appearance of a terrorist commando that kills an industrialist inside a nearby car. The scene looks almost like a rip-off of the bank robbery scene in Woody Allen's *Take the Money and Run* (1969), where two different gangs show up at the same bank: yet there is no visible humorous intention in it. What's more, the terrorist commando disappears and doesn't show up again in the film, turning the scene itself into an arbitrary, gratuitous *non sequitur*. Italian film critic Giovanni Buttafava slanted the episode as "one of the most macroscopic and spiteful examples of pornographic resort to crime reporting,"[4] while this is actually something different. In its absurdity, the scene shows that the poliziotteschi has already changed its skin, and the civil commitment has been abandoned: crime films become impermeable to everyday reality, just as it's becoming bleaker, and a potentially shocking moment — the murder of a politician on the part of a terrorist squad — becomes a mere scriptwriting accident, a mechanical expedient to get the story going and add some more spice to the heroes' mission — only this, and nothing more.

Free Hand for a Tough Cop was a huge box office hit, prompting producer Galliano Juso to hastily set up another film featuring Monnezza in a haste: the result was Stelvio Massi's *Destruction Force*.

Notes

1. Franca Faldini and Goffredo Fofi, eds., *L'avventurosa storia del cinema italiano raccontata dai suoi protagonisti 1960–1969* (Milano: Feltrinelli, 1981), p. 303.
2. The Western Monnezza and the other convicts are watching is Lenzi's own *All Out*, a.k.a. *Copperface* (*Tutto per tutto*, 1968). A self-ironic in-joke, given the audience's reaction: Lenzi admittedly was not fond of his own Westerns.
3. Duranti and Mucciacito, *Tomas Milian*,, p. 56.
4. Buttafava, "Procedure sveltite," p. 116.

Hit Squad (Squadra antifurto)

D: Bruno Corbucci. *S* and *SC:* Mario Amendola, Bruno Corbucci; *DOP:* Marcello Masciocchi (35mm, Vistavision, Telecolor); *M:* Guido and Maurizio de Angelis (ed. Ariston — Nazionalmusic); *E nun ce vojo sta'* (by G. & M. De Angelis / M. Amendola / B. Corbucci) sung by Alberto Griso; *E:* Daniele Alabiso; *PD:* Claudio Cinini; *CO:* Luciano Sagoni; *COA:* Carolina Ferrara, Alessandra Cardini; *C:* Giovanni Ciarlo; *AC:* Claudio Tondi, Maurizio Santi, Mauro Masciocchi; *AE:* Brigida Mastrolillo, Alfredo Menchini; *2nd AE:* Marcello Cannone; *APD:* Adelchi Tondini; *2nd APD:* Carolina Guerrini Maraldi; *AD:* Marina Mattoli;

MU: Franco Di Girolamo, Antonio Maltempo; *Hair:* Jolanda Angelucci; *SetT:* Paolo Ricci; *SO:* Goffredo Salvatori; *Boom:* Luigi Salvatori; *Mix:* Franco Bassi; *SP:* Franco Vitale; *W:* Alessandra Pistella; *KG:* Alberto Emidi; *ChEl:* Tullio Marini; *Acrobatic scenes:* O.A.C.; *SS:* Maria Teresa Garuffo. *Cast:* Tomas Milian (Marshall Nico Giraldi), Robert Webber (Ralph Douglas), Lilli Carati [Ileana Caravati] (Vanessa), Giuseppe Pambieri (Osvaldo Proietti "Tapparella"), Giuliana Calandra (Lt. Adele Ciampini), Toni Ucci ("Filotto"), Olimpia Di Nardo (Olimpia Trippetta), Massimo Vanni (Gargiulo), Vittorio Stagni ("Er Zagaja"), Enzo Pulcrano (Salvatore Trapanese), Benito Stefanelli (Gorniani, attorney-at-law), Franco Oppini (Luigi Rapetti "Frustino"), Mimma Amendola, Giovanni Attanasio (Dumb cop), Giancarlo Badessi (Sex maniac on telephone), Nanni Bernini, Salvatore Billa (Rosario Trapanese), Anna Bonaiuto (Maidservant questioned at police station), Valerio Colombaioni (Thief in bed with maidservant), Francesco D'Adda (Owner of burgled flat), Quinto Gambi (Caciotta, thief disguised as a mover), Marcello Martana (Vice Commissioner Trentini), Roberto Messina (Commissioner Tozzi), Tony Morgan (Er Gnappetta), Franco Necker [Franco Lechner a.k.a. Bombolo] ("Er Trippa"), Mimmo Poli ("Musulmano"), Giuliano Sestili (Second thief disguised as a mover), Marco Stefanelli (Thief fighting with Giraldi on stairs). *Uncredited:* Elisa Mainardi (Teresa, Ballarin's wife), Sergio Sinceri (Man handcuffed while making love), Nazzareno Natale (Dogs' seller), Nello Pazzafini (Spanish ship commander), John P. Dulaney (Ballarin), Taylor Mead (Madman in New York street), Carmelo Reale (Officer Ascani), Mario Donatone (Pasquale Icardi). *PROD:* Galliano Juso for Cinemaster; *PM:* Fabio Diotallevi; *PSu:* Lamberto Palmieri; *PSe:* Giacomo Longo, Francesco Fantacci, Annamaria Ambrogi; *ADM:* Paolo Rampazzo; *CASH:* Salvatore Farese. *Country:* Italy. Filmed at Incir–De Paolis (Rome) and on location in Rome and New York. *Running time:* 103'; Visa no.: 69320 (10.29.1976); *Rating:* v.m.14; *Release date:* 10.29.1976; *Distribution:* Titanus; *Domestic gross:* 1,825,316,810 lire. *Also known as:* *Escuadra anti-robo* (Spain), *Hippie Nico von der Kripo* (Germany). *Home video:* 01 (DVD, Italy).

Rome. During the hot summer in the deserted city, Marshal Nico Giraldi's main occupation is arresting the many car thieves and cat burglars. After tracing back the stolen car of the beautiful hostess Vanessa, Nico finds himself in a much more complex, not to mention dangerous, case. Following a burglary at the house of a rich American, Mr. Douglas, small-time crook Tapparella and his three accomplices find a notebook in a safe, with evidence of illicit trafficking. Tapparella blackmails Douglas, but is killed by the latter's men. After one of Tapparella's accomplices is killed as well, Giraldi realizes that Mr. Douglas is willing to do anything to regain possession of the precious notebook, but he has no evidence. Nico locates Tapparella's two other accomplices, the brothers Trapanese, who have set up a deal with Douglas' men to conduct the money/notebook exchange on a train, but can't prevent them from being killed as well.

Italian poster for *Hit Squad* (1976).

Giraldi pursues Douglas from Rome to New York with Vanessa's help, and eventually secures the man to justice.

The second in the Nico Giraldi series after *The Cop in Blue Jeans, Hit Squad* had Milian definitely pin his character's look (Nico here wears a number of flamboyantly bad costumes and hats, including his customary mechanic overalls) while the plot gets thinner in order to accommodate more gags. The first part is a reworking and an expansion of *The Cop in Blue Jeans'* opening sequences, with a series of either bizarre, funny and spectacular thefts (such as Lilli Carati's character having her car stolen before her very eyes), and culminates in a scene where three cat burglars led by "Tapparella" (Giuseppe Pambieri) sneak into an apartment. Given that the thieves don't find anything of value, Tapparella asks his sidekick "Trippa" (Bombolo) to take a dump over a sofa.

The sequence has little to do with the rest of the film, but is very important for a number of reasons, besides being a pretext to introduce Tapparella and his sidekicks, who will play a vital part in the plot: first, it sets up the premise for a later gag, when Giraldi finds out who's the culprit, has his assistant scoop up the shit, locates "Trippa" and forces him to eat his own crap. Even though it plays on one of Italian cinema's recurring motifs of the period (Pasolini's *Salò*'s notorious shit-eating scenes were not the only example, another being Mauro Macario's grim drug movie *Perché si uccidono—La Merde*, which featured a disgusting excrement-eating sequence), the gag is very effective in a trivial manner, as it's constructed on the typical dualistic scheme of comedic stage routines, with the character of the fool ("*mamo*" in Italian stage lingo) being punished and humiliated for laughs. The scene works essentially because of the presence of Bombolo (real name Franco Lechner, here misspelled as Necker), a paunchy, balding, dumb-faced character actor with a strong Roman accent whose comic routine involved getting slapped and sighing like a baby when he's caught in the act. *Hit Squad* was Bombolo's first appearance in the series, which was so appreciated by audiences that the actor would become a recurring presence in the Giraldi series, and his role as Milian's favorite victim would grow bigger and bigger, at the expense of the proper crime plot.

On *Hit Squad*, it takes a full forty minutes to get to the heart of the story, which is nothing much really. The script revolves around a McGuffin of sorts: a notebook with compromising information which Tapparella and his accomplices unwillingly steal from a powerful American diplomat's safe (however, one wonders how Tapparella immediately deciphers the notes as referring to a huge foreign scandal...) which set in motion the predictable series of events. Violence is radically toned down when compared to other poliziotteschi, save for the grim scene where Tapparella is beaten to death and the spectacular segment on the train. The latter also features some first-rate stunt work, as Milian's double jumps from his motorbike atop a train, just like in a Western. For that matter, the many action scenes (with Milian obviously replaced by a stunt double) feature spectacular slow-motion bike stunts, lots of fistfights and assorted car stunts.

The sociological angle is reduced to a minimum, with the duets between Milian and his old thief pal Filotto (Toni Ucci) and a scene where Nico and his colleague show up at a combo in the suburbs, populated by petty thieves and the like. "I grew up in a street like this" Nico says. "And you gotta tell me how a poor man's not going to become a criminal here. These are not houses, they are thieves' farms!" The customary complaints about inadequate justice are limited to a couple of scenes and feel more like a due tribute than a heartfelt plea: "Here as well the law is protecting criminals!" Nico tells his cop cousin in New York (in the meantime, they are being bothered by a crazy homeless man, who is actually none other than Andy Warhol's collaborator and poet Taylor Mead!). The U.S. segment, basically an excuse to give the film an international aura, shows Italian filmmakers' typical approach to the Big Apple, shot with an almost childlike enthusiasm. Genre cinema moved well beyond its borders, bragging about a richness it didn't really have, and reflecting the renewed frenzy of a country that, despite the inflation threshold of 20 percent and the collapse of the lira against the dollar, admiringly contemplated consumerism and the brilliance of colored signs. But such enthusiasm was also the result of a craving escapist fever: away, away from the Years of Lead.

However, even though it's all been done earlier and better, *Hit Squad* is a very pleasant film to watch, mainly because of Corbucci's svelte (if far from elegant) direction, and especially thanks to Giraldi's turgidly vulgar dialogue, full of side-splittingly funny dialectal lines which inevitably get lost to a foreign audience, and benefit from great work by voice actor Ferruccio Amendola (who provides Milian' voice).

A catatonic Robert Webber plays the film's villain, while Lilli Carati, here in one of her first screen appearances, is Nico's love interest. Another actor debuting in the series is stuntman Massimo Vanni, who plays Nico's sidekick Gargiulo, while Olimpia Di Nardo—who'd eventually play Nico's girlfriend and then wife later on in the series—makes a brief appearance as well. *Hit Squad* was a box office hit indeed, grossing almost two billion, almost as much as its predecessor. The Nico Giraldi's series would resume with next year's *Swindle.*

Illustrious Corpses (*Cadaveri eccellenti*)

D: Francesco Rosi. *S:* based on the novel *Il contesto* by Leonardo Sciascia; *SC:* Francesco Rosi, Tonino Guerra, Lino Jannuzzi; *DOP:* Pasqualino De Santis (35mm, Technicolor); *M:* Piero Piccioni, conducted by the author, played by the Orchestra Unione Musicisti di Roma (ed. Eureka); *Jeanne y Paul* composed and played by Astor Piazzolla; *E:* Ruggero Mastroianni; *Casting:* Gianni Arduini; *PD:* Andrea Crisanti; *APD:* Aurelio Crugnola; *ArtD* for Casa Pattos sets: Mario Ceroli, Renato Guttuso, Mario Schifano; *SDrs:* Arrigo Breschi, Mario Dentici; *CO:* Enrico Sabbatini; *COA:* Gianni Viti; *C:* Mario Cimini; *AC:* Marcello Mastrogirolamo, Adolfo Bartoli; *AEs:* Lea Mazzocchi, Ugo De Rossi; *Supervising editor:* Enzo Ocone; *AD:* Gianni Arduini; *2nd AD:* Bruno Cortini; *MU:* Franco Freda; *Hair:* Adalgisa Favella; *SOEng:* Mario Bramonti; *Boom:* Giuseppe Muratori; *SOE:* Renato Marinelli; *Mix:* Romano Checcacci; *W:* Anda [Adriana] Masseroni; *ChEl:* Luciano Leoni; *KG:* Aldo Colanzi; *SP:* Sergio Strizzi; *SS:* Franca Santi; *P:* Nico Naldini. *Cast:* Lino Ventura (Inspector Amerigo Rogas), Tino Carraro (Chief of Police), Marcel Bozzuffi ("The Lazy," ex-convict), Paolo Bonacelli (Dr. Maxia), Max von Sydow (Riches, Supreme Court's President), Charles Vanel (Procurator Varga), Fernando Rey (Evaristo, Security Minister), Alain Cuny (Judge Rasto), Maria Carta (Madame Cres), Tina Aumont (Prostitute), Renato Salvatori (police Commissioner), Anna Proclemer (Mrs. Nocio), Alfonso

Gatto (Vilfredo Nocio), Luigi Pistilli (Cusan), Corrado Gaipa (Mafia boss), Claudio Nicastro (General), Mario Meniconi (Mechanic), Silverio Blasi (Head of Political Section), Paolo Graziosi (Galano), Carlo Tamberlani (Archbishop), Enrico Ragusa (Monk), Francesco Càllari (Judge Sanza), Accursio Di Leo (Rogas' assistant), Ernesto Colli (Detective on night duty), Renato Turi (TV anchorman), uncredited: Florestano Vancini (Interrogator), Alexandre Mnouchkine (Pattos), Felice Fulchignoni, Giorgio Zampa (Amar). *PROD:* Alberto Grimaldi for P.E.A. (Rome), Les Artistes Associés (Paris); *GM:* Alessandro Von Norman; *PI:* Franco Ballati; *PSe:* Paolo Fabbri, Lynn Kamen; *ADM:* Sergio Giussani, Anna Maria Novelli. *Country:* Italy / France. Filmed at Cinecittà (Rome). *Running time:* 120'; Visa no.: 67934 (02.06.1976); *Rating:* not rated; *Release date:* 02.12.1976; *Distribution:* United Artists Europe; *Domestic gross:* 2,028,514,451 lire. *Also known as: Cadavres exquis* (Paris, 05.26. 1976—127'); *Die Macht und ihr Preis* (05.28.1976—120'), *Excelentísimos cadáveres* (Spain), *Arvokkaita ruumiita* (Finland), *Kiváló holttestek* (Hungary), *Szacowni nieboszczycy* (Poland). *Home video:* CDE (DVD, Italy). OST: CD GDM CD Club 7013.

In a region of Southern Italy, someone kills a magistrate, then another and another. Inspector Rogas, who investigates the case, rejects the hypothesis that the killings are either a Mafia revenge or the crimes of a madman, and believes that the murderer is a pharmacist who was wrongly convicted, years before, for an alleged attempt at poisoning his wife, and has now disappeared. But when the mysterious murderer begins to kill the magistrates of the Capital, the Chief of the police requires Rogas to direct the inquiries to far-left groups, and act under the orders of a Commissioner of the political squad. Now convinced, however, that these crimes are part of a subversive plan, Rogas continues on his way, until he reaches the evidence of a political conspiracy that's going on. He notifies the secretary of the Communist Party, who has agreed to meet him in a museum, but both men are killed by a sniper. The official version given by the Chief of Police pins the murder of the Communist leader to Rogas, who is said to have been suffering a nervous breakdown. The comrades of the dead, although they know the truth, do not complain, because they judge prematurely so as to conquer power.

Leonardo Sciascia's *Il contesto* (*The Context*) was a darkly comic, paradoxical novel that made a fuss when it first appeared in 1971, as its grimly ironic story openly mimicked, although in Sciascia's exquisitely metaphorical, aerial style, the events and climate that surrounded the season of the so-called "strategy of tension."

It was somehow a puzzling move for Francesco Rosi to film it, as the director was famous for his semi-documentaristic dramas such as *Salvatore Giuliano* (1961) or the extraordinary *Il caso Mattei* (1972), whereas Sciascia's tale—set in an untold country where a series of magistrates are killed, and the murders are being used by the major political party as a pretext for an authoritarian turn of the screw—was an open metaphor of what was going on in Italy at that time. However, Rosi immediately wanted to make a film out of it, as he considered the book as a summation of all the themes he had been depicting in his films. *Illustrious Corpses* would be, according to the director, "a long journey through the monsters and monstrosities of power [...] a visual recapitulation of all aberrations and degenerations of power which I encountered in my life."[1]

With his film adaptation, Rosi took an opposite path compared to another much-discussed rendition of another Sciascia novel, Elio Petri's *Todo Modo* (1976), which adopted an openly sarcastic, outrageously grotesque tone, replete with expressionist underlinings, in its depiction of a paradoxical series of murders inside a convent where the heads of the Democrazia Cristiana have retired to reorganize their party. Rosi, on the other hand, goes for an almost metaphysical abstraction, which is patent from the very opening sequence set in Palermo's Capuchin Crypt. The title aptly referred to André Breton's famous Surrealist game *Cadavre Exquis* (in which the participants draw consecutive sections of a figure without seeing what the previous person has drawn, leading to unpredictable results) and was meant to describe the meandering nature of the film with its unpredictable foray into the world of political manipulations, as well as the "illustrious" corpses of the murdered judges.

In *Il contesto*, Sciascia theorized the assimilation of political and Mafia power, which are blurred to the point that they eventually become indistinguishable: to Rosi, it marked a return to his origins, to the forking between politically committed cinema and poliziotteschi.[2] *Illustrious Corpses* became "the result of the coexistence of different narrative registers and diverging stylistic options"[3]: compared to Sciascia's scenario, Rosi chose to put on screen an openly recognizable Italy: "I couldn't talk of corrupted powers without identifying them. I couldn't talk of an alleged *coup d'état* without saying where it took place, because in the end someone might think of a takeover in an Operetta country, which I absolutely didn't want to happen. And I couldn't mention political factions without recognizing in them some of Italy's parties."[4]

Rosi also makes use of stock footage, as in his more documentaristic films, but at the same time he overloads the material, thus giving his work a meta-historical dimension. Unlike Sciascia's book, which turns the genre into parody (albeit a darkly ferocious one), *Illustrious Corpses* follows a classic crime film narrative thread, starting with the casting of Lino Ventura in the lead. As the stubborn inspector Rogas—much less intellectual and definitely more hard-boiled than in the novel—Ventura offers an assured image of the honest yet tough cop who nevertheless has the word "defeat" written in his DNA: Rogas' frustrating quest for the literally invisible pharmacist who committed the murders (a man whose face is never seen and whose existence has seemingly been cancelled from pictures and official documents, such as in a whodunit version of Pirandello's *The Late Mattia Pascal*) at times recalls the actor's former role in José Giovanni's powerful *Last Known Address* (1970).

However, in the end, Rosi patently rejects a typical crime film ending. "The anger of not understanding completely, the fragments of the puzzle that don't fit, are an integral part of the filmmaker's morality: Rosi's is a poetry of unease" observed a critic.[5] However, the theme of reality's indecipherability—a foundation of Rosi's cinema since *Salvatore Giuliano*—laid itself open to misinterpretations and criticism. Illustrious novelist and essayist Alberto Arbasino, who literally demolished the film in an exquisitely cruel review published on "Il Corriere della Sera," wrote that "a film which mimics confused situations with a confused structure such as the "Strategy of Tension" deliberately runs the same risks as those films that mimicked the boredom of the Boom years with narrative structures that were just impeccably boring [...]. In Rosi's film, the metaphysical halo lays over all those zones where Sciascia's text, moving from the page to the image, loses its elective affinities with Borges, and with those dear conspiracies set halfway between Stevenson and Chesterton, and turns into something close to Ugo Betti,[6] dragging the same 1930s metaphysic, the symbolist anxiety, the idealistic fears, the judicial mysteries, the archival metaphors, the Pirandello-like back rooms, the characters with names like detergents [...]. Such an embarrassed interference can be noticed when the lead inspector walks with one foot in the "fanta" zone and the other in the "political" one: and just like those children's games, whenever one objects "Italy's not like that!" he jumps into the "fanta" zone with both feet [...]. Most of all, however, it's shocking to see the secretary of the Communist Party acting like those romantic international spies played by Isa Miranda, who for decades have been requiring picture galleries and amusement parks as the ideal settings for their Beautiful Shots [sic]."[7]

Upon its release, *Illustrious Corpses* caused quite a controversy, especially for the ending in which Rogas and the said secretary are killed by an unknown sniper—a double murder that's soon covered up—while the Communist Party vice-secretary who knows the truth decides not to reveal it. The film concludes with a significant dialogue exchange, as a left-wing journalist who was a friend of Rogas asks "But then the people must never know the truth?," and the politician replies: "The truth is not always revolutionary," echoing—but at the same time radically changing its content—a famous sentence by Antonio Gramsci, one of the founders of the Italian Communist Party.

The film was a box office smash in Italy, grossing over two billion lire—but not as much as Umberto Lenzi's *Violent Naples*, the year's best grossing poliziotteschi—and was shown out of competition at the Cannes Film Festival.

Notes

1. Micciché, *Cinema italiano degli anni '70*, p. 224.
2. For a comparison between the book and the film, Francesco Bolzoni, "R/S: un confronto," *Cinecritica* #3/4 (October 1986/March 1987), pp. 105–108.
3. David Brun, "'Cadaveri eccellenti' di F. Rosi. La messinscena del potere," in Aa. Vv., *Il cinema del riflusso: Film e cineasti italiani degli anni '70* (Venice: Marsilio, 1997), p. 384.
4. Giovanni Petitti, *Conversazione con Francesco Rosi: Leonardo Sciascia ispiratore*, www.frameonline.it.
5. Kezich, *Il Millefilm*, p. 98.
6. A well-known Italian playwright who wrote, among others, *Corruzione al palazzo di giustizia*, which Marcello Aliprandi turned into a film with 1975's *Smiling Maniacs*.
7. Alberto Arbasino, "Gli ermellini e l'ispettore: strategia della confusione," *Corriere della Sera* 3.4.1976.

The Last Round *(Il conto è chiuso)*

D: Stelvio Massi. *S:* Franco Mogherini; *SC:* Piero Regnoli [and Alberto Silvestri, uncredited]; *DOP:* Franco Delli Colli (35mm, Gevacolor, Staco Film); *M:* Luis Enriquez Bacalov; *E:* Mauro Bonanni; *PD:* Giuseppe Ranieri, Giovanni Fratalocchi; *C:* Michele Pensato; *AC:* Giancarlo Giannesi; *1st AE:* Evandro Postorino; *2nd AE* Angela Rosa Taccari; *AD:* Danilo Massi; *2nd AD:* Fabrizio Corallo, Vittorio Fanfoni; *MU:* Mauro Gavazzi, Marcello Di Paolo; *Hair:* Luciano Vito; *W:* Itala Giardina; *SO:* Giosuè Gudelmoni; *Boom:* Pasquale Salerno; *SE:* Cesare Battistelli; *SP:* Franco Vitale; *STC:* Sergio Sagnotti; *KG:* Giuseppe Raimondi; *GA:* Remo Dolci; *SS:* Marisa Agostini. *Cast:* Carlos Monzón (Marco Russo), Luc Merenda (Rico Manzetti), Mariangela Giordano (Lisa's mother), Giampiero Albertini (Sapienza), Gianni Dei (Beny Manzetti), Annaluisa Pesce [Luisa Maneri] (Lisa), Claudio Zucchet (Alex Manzetti), Susanna Giménez (Maristella), Leonora Fani (Nina), Mario Brega (Bobo Belmondo), Renato Basso (Presenter at "Gatto Nero"), Marcello Venditti (Rico's henchman), Franco Salamon, Nazzareno Cardinali (Rico's henchman), Attilio Severini (Rico's henchman), Elio Bonadonna, Giovanni Cianfriglia (Rico's henchman), Nello Pazzafini (Rico's henchman), Claudio Ruffini (Rico's henchman). *Uncredited:* Artemio Antonini (Attorney's escort), Fortunato Arena (Rico's henchman), Salvatore Biondo (Madonnaro), Angelo Boscariol (Man at "Gatto nero"), Ottaviano Dell'Acqua (Attorney's escort), Mimmo Poli (Garage owner), Sandro Scarchilli (Belmondo's henchman). *PROD:* Franco Calleri and Franco Monferini for F.R.A.L.; *EP:* Gabriele Crisanti; *PM:* Giuliano Simonetti; *UM:* Guglielmo Simonetti; *PC:* Giovanni Spedicati, Gianfranco Fornari, Giancarlo Nannarini. *Country:* Italy. Filmed at Incir–De Paolis (Rome) and on location in Rome. *Running time:* 100'; Visa no.: 69561 (21.12.1976); *Rating:* v.m.18; *Release date:*12.30.1976; *Distribution:* Maxi Cinematografica (Regional); World sales: So. Com. Int. (Rome); *Domestic gross:* 641,068,500 lire. *Also known as: Die letze Runde, In den Klauen der Mafia* (Germany). *Home video:* No Shame (DVD, USA), NoShame (DVD, Italy).

Young Marco Russo, a former mercenary turned drifter, sets out to avenge his mother and his sister, who were raped and killed by crime boss Rico Vanzetti. He manages to get hired by his enemy, forcing him deftly to a bloody war against a business rival, Bobo Belmondo. Then he releases Vanzetti's lover, whom the gangster kept prisoner so that he could have his way with her daughter. However, Marco is unmasked by Vanzetti and badly hurt; he takes refuge at a friend's place, who hides him and gives him time to recover. Finally, although still a little battered, Marco faces Rico and kills him.

The most eloquent example of the not-so-thin line that unites Italian Western and crime films is Stelvio Massi's *The Last Round*, an undeclared modern-day remake of Sergio Leone's *A Fistful of Dollars* starring former middleweight champion Carlos Monzón, who was trying to recycle himself as an actor with scarce results (Monzón also starred in Marcello Andrei's Western *El Macho*, 1977).[1] Scriptwriter Piero Regnoli (who had already ransacked the first film from the "Dollars trilogy" in Andrea Bianchi's *Cry of a Prostitute*) reworks and mixes the main elements of Leone's universe with a philological pique that perhaps aims at a theoretical reflection on genre stereotypes: as Rico, the sex-crazed gangster with a fetish for weapons, Luc Merenda is an updated version of Gian Maria Volonté's sadistic villains, while Monzón's lone hero—who carries a music box with the pictures of his beloved ones killed by Rico, and revives the tragedy in overexposed flashbacks accompanied by Luis Bacalov's Morricone-like score—is once again modeled on *Once Upon a Time in the West*'s Harmonica.

The overlapping of the Western repertoire and the crime genre does not exclude the references to the present: the Western village has become a big industrial city ruled by criminal gangs, where the oppressed are not the cowboys deprived of their land and cattle, but the workers who are fired with no reason and can't resort to trade unions; the "stranger" has a past as a mercenary in Africa and the South East; and falling under the baddies' fire are not the honest sheriffs but the few magistrates who don't accept to connive with the criminals. However, the vision of contemporary

Italy as a Wild West — an equation that is often explicitly mentioned in many contemporaneous poliziotteschi — is far less convincing than in, say, Valerii's *Go Gorilla Go*, not least because the setting is purposefully undetermined: the big city, obviously Rome, is never mentioned but is fixed in a fable-like dimension.

Merenda, who considers *The Last Round* one of his worst films, recalled its genesis[2]: "The producer, Rodolfo Sabatini, was a boxing fan, and wanted to launch Monzón, but to find the money they needed a "name" actor." Enter Luc Merenda, than a highly profitable name at the box office. "I couldn't care less about the film, but I liked Monzón as a boxer. Stelvio told me: "Carlos is going to co-star with you," and I thought we would play brothers or something like that, and it would be such a cool thing, even though he was totally inexperienced as an actor. [...] Then I got the script and found out I had become the villain, and this really pissed me off!" Merenda asked more money and that his scenes be rewritten and expanded by his friend Alberto Silvestri, who also wrote *Nick the Sting*. "I played a villain who's always got a smile planted on his face, while Monzon did the Merenda role — badly!"

Not surprisingly, given the genre's insistence on rape — in a period where Italian genre films pushed hard the pedal of violent sex scenes — as well as Regnoli's militancy in sexploitation, *The Last Round* features one such unpleasant moment: the victim is a blind girl, played by the enchanting Leonora Fani, one of the most abused bodies in Italian cinema of the late 1970s, from Francesco Barilli's *Pensione paura* (1978) to Mario Landi's infamous *Giallo a Venezia* (1979).

Notes

1. After his brief acting stint, Monzón's tumultuous private life went through a downward spiral: He was sentenced to jail in 1989 for murdering his wife and died in 1995 in a car crash while returning to prison.

2. Merenda's quotes are taken from Manlio Gomarasca, "Senza compromessi. Intervista a Luc Merenda.," in Aa. Vv., "Eroi and antieroi del cinema italiano," *Nocturno Dossier* #10 (April 2003).

Live Like a Cop, Die Like a Man (*Uomini si nasce poliziotti si muore*)

D: Ruggero Deodato. *S:* Fernando di Leo, Alberto Marras, Vincenzo Salviani; *SC:* Fernando di Leo; *DOP:* Guglielmo Mancori (35mm, Eastmancolor, Telecolor); *M:* Ubaldo Continiello (Ed. Nazionalmusic); *Maggie* (R. Lovelock) and *Won't Take Too Long* (Deodato / Fraser) sung by Ray Lovelock; *E:* Gianfranco Simoncelli; *PD:* Franco Bottari; *APD:* Mauro Passi; *CO:* Liliana Galli; *C:* Mario Sbrenna; *AC:* Aldo Bergamini, Renato Palmieri; *AD:* Roberto Pariante; *MU:* Alma Santoli; *Hair:* Vittoria Silvi; *SO:* Antonio Forrest; *Boom:* Renato Alfonsi; *SOE:* Marinelli; *SP:* Gianni Caramanico; *ST:* O.A.C.; *MA:* Gilberto Galimberti; *SS:* Laura Frigo. *Cast:* Marc Porel (Alfredo), Ray Lovelock (Antonio), Adolfo Celi (The Boss), Franco Citti (Ruggero Ruggerini "Rudy Ruginski"), Silvia Dionisio (Norma), Marino Masé (Guido Oddi), Renato Salvatori (Roberto Pasquini "Bibì"), Sergio Ammirata (Sergeant), Bruno Corazzari (Morandi), Daniele Dublino (Corrupt police inspector), Flavia Fabiani [Sofia Dionisio] (Lina Pasquini), Tom Felleghy (Mayor), Margherita Horowitz (Mona, a hostage), Gina Mascetti (Maricca), Marcello Monti (3rd kidnapper), Claudio Nicastro (Commissioner), Gino Pagnani (Paul, dog trainer), Enzo Pulcrano (Mario, Pasquini's henchman), Alvaro Vitali (Concierge). *Uncredited:* Angelo Boscariol, Flora Carosello (Sora Rosa), Nestore Cavaricci (Cop), Pietro Ceccarelli (Club bouncer), Enrico Chiappafreddo (Man tortured on boat), Massimo Ciprari (Sniper), Ruggero Deodato (Man walking out of bank), Bruno Di Luia (Killer), Gilberto Galimberti, Benito Pacifico (1st gunman), Sandro Scarchilli, Marcello Verziera (Pasquini's henchman on motorbike). *PROD:* Alberto Marras and Vincenzo Salviani for C.P.C. Città di Milano, T.D.L. Cinematografica; *PM:* Alberto Marras; *PSu:* Nicola Principalli; *PSe:* Peppino Salviani. *Country:* Italy. Filmed at Rizzoli Palatino (Rome) and on location in Milan. *Running time:* 100'; Visa no.: 68033 (03.10.1976); *Rating:* v.m.18; *Release date:* 03.11.1976; *Distribution:* Interfilm; *Domestic gross:* 741,142,540 lire. *Also known as:* *The Terminators* (U.K.— Home video), *Eiskalte Typen auf heißen Öfen* (West Germany), *Hombre se nace, policia se muere* (Spain), *Het recht in eigenhand* (Holland), *Iskalla typer på heta bågar* (Sweden), *Kylmät tyypit, kuumat raudat* (Finland). *Home video:* Raro (DVD, USA), Raro (DVD, Italy; 90'— no end credits!).

Alfredo and Antonio, the members of a SWAT team in Rome whose existence is known only to a few, do not arrest offenders, they kill them. The two ruthless cops devote themselves to hunting Roberto Pasquini a.k.a. "Bibi," a ferocious criminal and owner of gambling dens, who for five years has slipped their fingers with the help of a corrupt inspector. Finally, after killing four of his henchmen, Alfredo and Antonio discover "Bibi"'s secret hideout. However, they are caught by the villain and would have ended up dead if it weren't for the timely intervention of their boss.

The most important example of the "special squad" subgenre — not to mention its most unusual, unpleasant and controversial —*Live Like a Cop, Die Like a Man* is Ruggero Deodato's only foray into the poliziotteschi. Upon its release, the film disoriented not only the audience but even the most benevolent critics as well, because of the way it "pushed the pedal of extreme, uncalculated effect."[1] Deodato, who would bring graphic violence to almost insufferable excesses in his notorious *Last Cannibal World* (1977) and especially *Cannibal Holocaust* (1980), exhibits a quantity of gruesome details that's vastly superior to that of contemporaneous crime films. The film was even cut before its release when the censorship commission objected to the scene where the sadistic Bibi (the great Renato Salvatori, a former teen idol in the 1950s and one of the most underrated actors in Italian cinema) has his men gouge out the eye of a poor thug (Bruno Corazzari) and then crushes the eyeball under his heel.

Yet it's impossible to judge the film without considering the destabilizing contribution of Fernando di Leo's screenplay (originally called *Poliziotti si nasce poliziotti si muore*, Live Like a Cop Die Like a Cop, which makes for a quite different meaning), whose intent is openly critical and even parodic towards the genre. In that respect, *Live Like a Cop, Die Like a Man* is the logical prosecution of the deconstructing look at poliziotteschi's mechanics that began with *Shoot First, Die Later* and followed with the crime comedy *Loaded Guns* and the picaresque *Rulers of the City*. The effects detonate over the unsuspicious audience like a blast, in what could be described as a boomerang effect. Take the two main characters, the "angels-devils" (as di Leo defined them) played by the impossibly handsome Ray Lovelock and Marc Porel. When the latter, after the spectacular opening motorbike chase (which was actually directed by master of arms Gilberto Galimberti[2]), shoots a dying purse snatcher in cold blood, the viewer can't help but feel uneasy. These are obviously not the average tough-yet-good cops that shoot so as to exact justice.

Di Leo brings to paradoxical extremes the moral and political ambiguity that forms the basis of the poliziotteschi. What's more, he actually overthrows its premises, asking viewers — or rather, challenging them — to take sides with two "heroes" who kill with a worrying, chilling ease, without the alibi of social commitment or the spectacularization of everyday violence that's innate within most crime stories. *Live Like a Cop, Die Like a Man* is a thought-provoking dismantling of the genre and its vital mechanics: if one of poliziotteschi's vital rules was to justify the hero's resort to violence — as with the exemplary flashbacks that showed his beloved wife / brother / child being killed — here di Leo does the exact opposite. Obviously, the two leads don't care one bit about law and justice. Their boss (Adolfo Celi) tells them that they have been chosen for their tendency to violence. They just enjoy shooting, killing, destroying — always with a smile on their face, a childish yet uneasy smile that recalls that of the schoolboys in *Naked Violence*— or Alex's smile in *A Clockwork Orange*.

As Burgess and Kubrick predicted, Alfredo (Porel) and Antonio (Lovelock) are a pair of droogs who have changed sides and ended up serving the law, much to their satisfaction as well as their bosses': Power has the ironic, aristocratic features of Adolfo Celi, who orders to kill without batting an eyelid and smiles fatherly at the duo's violent excesses. High institutions just tolerate them, powerlessly, and eventually close both eyes — as in the sequence where a thug (Franco Citti) and his accomplices, who have barricaded inside a house with a hostage, are mercilessly killed by the dynamic duo.

Italian poster for *Live Like a Cop, Die Like a Man* (1976).

It's unlikely that Deodato fully understood the script's ferocious irony, which goes far beyond the occasional joke or comedian Alvaro Vitali's cameo as a concierge. The director later stated: "I felt different from my fellow filmmakers who were doing crime flicks. I wanted my film to have a more TV-like approach, I put lots of close-ups in it and took care of every detail. [...] My problem is that I always make such carefully crafted, truthful films that I then pay the price, for better or for worse."[3] Yet the contrast between di Leo's subversive approach and Deodato's professional but monolithic direction paves the way for some of the most effective moments, such as the attempted robbery that ends up before it even starts, as the robbers are shot dead on the street before they have time to act: it's the kind of preventive justice that doesn't even have the justification of a sci-fi scenario such as Steven Spielberg's *Minority Report* (2002).

If the poliziotteschi's heroes are generally lonely, with rare and unsatisfactory relationship with the opposite sex, *Live Like a Cop, Die Like a Man*'s best buddies are sexually promiscuous, taking turns in bed with any woman who falls under their spell, and their misogynist attitude suggests a subterranean homosexual complicity. The film's female presences are invariably nymphomaniacs, such as the boss' sister (Sofia Dionisio), who immediately gives up to their *avances* for a threesome[4] or the Swedish woman ("an authentic Swedish," as somebody remarks — Italians are always sticking to the myth of Scandinavian sexual freedom as in Alberto Sordi's 1960s comedies) who sunbathes in the nude on a yacht in the middle of winter. The need for gratuitous nude scenes — an obligatory occurrence in post–1968 Italian exploitation — is mercilessly exposed. On the other hand, the secretary played by Silvia Dionisio is a sharp-tongued feminist ("Masculine supremacy is bullshit! You act like Superman, you invite us to sumptuous banquet but don't get past the starters") who perhaps represents a blueprint for di Leo's subsequent sexual freedom epic *To Be Twenty* (1978).

Notes

1. Buttafava, "Procedure sveltite," p. 109. The critic also remarked: "transgression must be limited to debatable yet tolerable jokes. Violent Italy is not the last cannibal world."
2. As Ray Lovelock recalled, "I remember arriving on the set one day, and seeing Ruggero standing arms crossed by a corner of via Tomacelli in Milan. I asked him 'Ruggè, what are you doin'?' and he replied: 'What should I do, don't you see the director's already doin' everything?' And there was Galimberti over there, gesticulating and telling everybody what they had to do, regardless of Deodato (laughs). That scene was really over the top, and they just wallowed in it. We had the whole centre of Milan at our disposal.' Gomarasca, "Ray faccia d'angelo," p. 82.
3. Manlio Gomarasca and Daniele Aramu, "Il ragazzo dei Parioli: Intervista a Ruggero Deodato," *Nocturno Cinema* #1 (Summer 1996), p. 18.
4. The sex scene featuring Marc Porel and Sofia Dionisio, which starts as a rape but ends with the woman enjoying it, predates a similar sequence—and even more uneasy, since the director obviously had no satirical intention this time—in Deodato's *The House by the Edge of the Park* (1980).

Mark Strikes Again (Mark colpisce ancora)

D: Stelvio Massi. *S:* Lucio De Caro; *SC:* Dardano Sacchetti; *DOP:* Mario Vulpiani (35mm, Gevacolor, Technospes); *M:* Stelvio Cipriani, conducted by the author (ed. P.A.C.); *E:* Mauro Bonanni; *PD:* Carlo Leva; *CO:* Sergio Palmieri; *COA:* Anna Maria Rossetti; *ArtD:* Giovanni Fratalocchi; *C:* Maurizio Maggi; *AC:* Mario Bagnato, Filippo Neroni; *AE:* Walter Diotallevi; *2nd AE:* Angelo Bufalino; *AD:* Flavia Sante Vanin; *2nd AD:* Danilo Massi; *MU:* Dante Trani, Franco Corcione; *Hair:* Romana Piolanti; *SO:* Roberto Alberghini; *Boom:* Antonino Pantano; *W:* Valeria Mariani; *AW:* Franca Paoletti, Irene Parlagreco; *KG:* Giuseppe Raimondi; *ChEl:* Romano Mancini; *SetT:* Antonio Corridori, Pasquino Benassati; *SP:* Luciano Cavalieri; *Grips:* Elvio Fossali, Valtere Saettella; *ST:* Sergio Mioni; *MA:* Sergio Sagnotti; *SS:* Isabella Bruno. *Cast:* Franco Gasparri (Mark Patti), John Saxon (Inspector Altman), John Steiner (Paul Henkel), Marcella Michelangeli (Olga Kube), Andrea Aureli (Pappadato), Pasquale Basile (Terrorist), Malisa Longo (Isa), Paul Muller (Bruno Palma of the Interpol), Claudio Zucchet (Hans), Giampiero Albertini (Commissioner Mantelli); uncredited: Renato Basso Bondini (Plainclothes marshal on a train), Ugo Bombognini (Doctor), Angelo Boscariol (Man in sidewalk café), Vittorio Fanfoni (Fritz), Massimo Mirani (Karl), Anna Maria Perego (Woman in sidewalk café), Filippo Perego (Man in sidewalk café), Marcello Venditti (Marsiè). *PROD:* P.A.C. (Produzioni Atlas Consorziate) (Milan); *GM:* Raniero Di Giovanbattista; *PM:* Raniero Di Giovanbattista; *UM:* Teodoro Agrimi [Teodoro Corrà]; *PSu:* Teodoro Agrimi, Vittorio Biseo, Eolo Capritti; *PSe:* Agostino Pasti, Giovanni Fracasso; *PSeA:* Edoardo Antonini, Giuseppe Gesuele; *ADM:* Gaetano Fuzio. *Country:* Italy. Filmed at Icet—De Paolis (Milan) and on location in Rome, Milan, Vienna. *Running time:* 95'; Visa no.: 69267 (10.20.1976); *Rating:* v.m.14; *Release date:* 10.20.1976; *Distribution:* P.A.C.; *Domestic gross:* 657,027,130 lire. *Also known as: The .44 Specialist* (Nederlands, Germany—video title); *Agent très spécial 44* (France), *Brigade Anti-terroriste, Calibre 44, agent très spécial* (France—Home video). *Home video:* Cecchi Gori Home Video (DVD, Italy).

Mark Patti of the Roman police has been reassigned by his superiors as an anti-snatch agent in Trastevere, where he idly spends his time, dressed up as a hippie. His behavior induces two terrorists, Paul Henkel and Olga Kuber, to hire him as a collaborator and take him with them to Vienna. In the Austrian city, Mark offers precious information to the Interpol and the local police, but to no avail: the terrorist attacks are not prevented, and the Italian agent survives by sheer chance. Mark realizes that Interpol inspector Altman is actually endorsing the terrorists; but after Altman is killed, Patti finds out that other people among the authorities are involved as well. With the help of a Roman police official, Mark continues his undercover mission: he takes part in the hijacking of a train so as to obtain Olga's release, and with his two companions returns to Vienna, where he gets his hands on a major financier of international terrorism. In the end, though, Mark cannot identify and arrest the real leaders.

With the third entry in the "Mark the Cop" series, directed as the previous ones by Stelvio Massi, Franco Gasparri's character undergoes a few major changes: not only does Mark change his surname to Patti and leaves his .44 Magnum in the drawer, but he also becomes shabbier and working class-like, with unkempt long hair and cheap T-shirts. On *Mark Strikes Again* the hero looks like a "safe" version of Tomas Milian's Monnezza, devoid of the latter's foul-mouthed impetuosity. Only in the final scene does Mark regain the look of the first two films, while he is about to pick up a passing girl.

The film's most important turn of the screw concerns the plot: Dardano Sacchetti's script (from a story by Lucio De Caro) deals with international terrorism and has Mark move from Rome to Vienna, together with a couple of ferocious fugitives—Marcella Michelangeli, who would turn up again as a terrorist in Massimo Pirri's *Could It Happen Here?* and a hysterically over-the-top John Steiner—who turn out to be occultly maneuvered by deviated secret services.

"Terrorism must be fought with means that those who are not into this situation cannot understand," says the corrupt cop (John Saxon) who vainly tries to dispatch the hero, only to end up killed by one of his hitmen: it's the umpteenth exposition of the conspiracy theories that abound in Italian genre cinema of the era, in reference to the Strategy of Tension. However, Sacchetti's script proves to be less simplistic than usual: Mark's theory that terrorism has "a mind, a head that pulls the strings" crashes against the actual presence of an upside-down pyramidal structure. "I myself don't know whether I'm a boss or not," confesses the man who directs the terrorists' moves from the back of a carpet shop. It didn't matter knowing without having the evidence, as Pasolini wrote in his celebrated article. Truth, in the end, is unrecognizable. As one critic noted, "however, everything stays within a comic-book environment, with no precise reference to terrorism's historical and political motives, and careful not to explain who takes advantage of the politics of disorder"[1] which is certainly true.

And yet, even though sloppy at times (Stelvio Cipriani's score also reprises cues from the first film) and marred by a hasty ending, *Mark Strikes Again* nevertheless boasts the merit of developing a painful and uneasy subject matter—with terrorists spitting lines such as "People must be afraid to get out of their homes in the morning" and "The only way to overturn this system is to bring it down to lack of consensus, and no system can rely on popular consensus when it fails to notice the chaos and disorder that corrode"—within an expert action movie skin: the best sequence, where Mark narrowly survives an ambush inside an intelligence office, has Massi remaking a similar sequence in *Three Days of the Condor*, with honorable results.

However, the film was not a huge success like its predecessors, grossing just over half a million lire and leading the series to a premature end.

Note

1. Al.Fe [Alessandro Ferraù], *Paese Sera*, 1.28.1977.

Meet Him and Die (Pronto ad uccidere)

D: Franco Prosperi. *S* and *SC:* Peter Berling, Antonio Cucca, Claudio Fragasso, Alberto Marras; *DOP:* Roberto D'Ettorre Piazzoli (35mm, Vistavision, Technospes); *M:* Ubaldo Continiello, conducted by the author (ed. Bierre); *I'm Startin' Tomorrow* (by M. Fraser) sung by Ray Lovelock; *E:* Amedeo Giomini; *PD:* Dario Micheli; *C:* Franco Bruni; *AC:* Giuseppe Buonaurio; *AE:* Ornella Chistolini; *AD:* Roberto Pariante; *MU:* Giuseppe Ferranti; *Hair:* Corrado Cristofori; *SO:* Alberto Salvatori; *Boom:* Massimo Costa; *SP:* Gianni Caramanico; *MA:* Gilberto Galimberti; *Acrobatic scenes:* O.A.C.; *SS:* Marisa Calia. *Cast:* Ray Lovelock (Massimo Salvatori / Massimo Torlani), Martin Balsam (Giulianelli), Elke Sommer (Perrone's secretary), Ettore Manni (Perrone), Heinz Domez (Piero), Ernesto Colli ("Settecapelli"), Peter Berling ("Bavoso"), Riccardo Cucciolla (Commissioner Sacchi), Dante Cleri (Elderly convict), Massimo Ciprari (Robber / Marti's henchman), Francesco D'Adda (Jeweler), Philips [Phillip] Dallas (Marti), Consalvo Dell'Arti (Chief of Police in Sanremo), Gilberto Galimberti (Giulianelli's thug), Franco Galizi, Emilio Messina (Giovanni Caputo "Manolo"), Enrico Gozzo, Gino Pagnani (Marshall), Anna Taddei (Massimo's mother). *Uncredited:* Artemio Antonini ("Bavoso"'s henchman), Nestore Cavaricci (Prison guard), Cesare Di Vito. *PROD:* Alberto Marras and Vincenzo Salviani for T.D.L. Cinematografica (Rome), Hermes Synchron (Berlin); *PSu:* Goffredo Matassi; *PSe:* Inga Seryc, Pino Salviani. *Country:* Italy/West Germany. Filmed at Dear Film (Rome) and on location in Rome, Sanremo, Monte Carlo. *Running time:* 95'; Visa no.: 69080 (09.25.1976); *Rating:* v.m.14; *Release date:* 10.09.1976; *Distribution:* Overseas Film Company; *Domestic gross:* 344,182,572 lire. *Also known as: Tote pflastern seinen Weg* (West Germany, 07.28.1977), *Risking, Pronto!* (UK Home video), *Marathon Suicida* (Spain), *Flugten Fra Monte Carlo* (Denmark). *Home video:* NEW (DVD, Germany—widescreen, English language), Raro (DVD, Italy—fullscreen, Italian language), RV (VHS, UK, as *Pronto!*), Pizazz (VHS, UK—cut 8").

After a failed robbery attempt at a jeweler's store, Massimo is caught and thrown in prison. However, this is all Commissioner Sacchi's plan, as Massimo is actually an undercover cop on a mission: he has to infiltrate the gang of a powerful trafficker named Giulianelli, who's serving a prison sentence in the same penitentiary. After proving his courage in a violent fight with another convict, Massimo is asked by Giulianelli to join him in his escape from prison: the elderly boss has to settle scores with his rival "Bavoso," who betrayed him and usurped his drug business in the city. The escape succeeds, even though Giulianelli is wounded in an ambush by Bavoso's men. With Giulianelli's right-hand man Piero, Massimo moves to Monte Carlo to pick up a load of drugs on an egg truck that must be delivered to another drug boss, Perrone, whose secretary has an affair with Massimo. During the trip, however, his cover his blown and he kills Piero. Then the truck is stolen by Perrone's gang, but Massimo manages to get it back. Massimo is about to be killed by Perrone, when the latter is dispatched by his own secretary. Giulianelli is finally arrested, but the drugs are not found: Massimo discovers that Perrone's secretary was the true head of the drug ring.

In many ways, Franco Prosperi's *Meet Him and Die* marks a step forward from the subgenre dealing with police special squads (*Colt 38 Special Squad*). As Massimo, the lonely undercover cop on a mission to frame the powerful drug lord Giulianelli (a bored-looking Martin Balsam), Ray Lovelock plays a decidedly ambiguous, uneasy character, who's got more in common with the blond actor's role in Deodato's *Live Like a Cop, Die Like a Man* (also produced by Alberto Marras) than with, say, Sergio Martino's *The Violent Professionals*. If in Martino's film the undercover Caneparo (Luc Merenda) was moved by a strong sense of justice—even though his methods were decidedly far from orthodox—in Prosperi's film Massimo openly takes advantage of his mission to get his own private revenge against a pair of thugs who shot his mother during a robbery, turning her into a cripple. The bloody slow-motion flashback returns, this time openly played as a open-eyed nightmare that fuels the hero's rage: but the suspicion that Massimo is not only trying to exorcise his demons eventually reaches not only the viewer's mind but also that of his own superior, Commissioner Sacchi (Riccardo Cucciolla). "You're an irresponsible, a madman! You are using justice to kill people, it looks like you're enjoying it. You're a wild beast!"

In a perhaps unintentional deviation from a poliziotteschi stereotype, the Commissioner becomes a cautious, fatherly figure—aided by Cucciolla's thin, unimposing figure, that makes him believably pass for a lawyer when he gets to meet Massimo in prison—while the young agent turns into some sort of a gun-crazy, bloodthirsty rain dog. Massimo doesn't hesitate one second when it's time to shoot somebody: to make a thug talk, he shoots him in the shoulder, but when the other replies "You can kill me, I'm not going to talk," he does just that in cold blood. Violence is prominent as usual, with ample use of blood squibs and one nasty slow-motion bullet-to-the-head shot.

Meet Him and Die is perhaps the point of no return of the poliziotteschi's approach to violence, as it no longer even contemplates justice (albeit a debatable, violent and private one) as an aim, and not even a pretext. Unlike Deodato's *Live Like a Cop, Die Like a Man*, this is not backed by any discourse about the genre's ambiguous moral approach nor by any hint of irony—although the scene where Lovelock simply punches down a colleague that recognized him and amicably greeted him while he was walking in the street with Giulianelli's right-hand man does invite laughter in a tongue-in-cheek way.

By portraying a hero who's completely devoid of any moral imperative, *Meet Him and Die* looks somehow like a modern rendition of 1960s spy flicks, yet without their flashy exotic flair and travelogue footage. From such predecessors, however, the script—the first written by schlockmeister supreme Claudio Fragasso—updates the character of the glamorous, bitchy dark lady—here a rather ill-advisedly cast Elke Sommer, whose film career was going downhill at the time—but can't really manage to devise an interesting storyline around its chilling central character, and culminates in a disappointingly conceived ending, whose main point of interest—Marcello is deprived by his long-sought vengeance—doesn't really lead the story anywhere.

Despite a rather tight budget, Franco [real name Francesco] Prosperi—formerly Mario Bava's assistant director and a veteran of 1960s gangster films with the remarkable *Hired Killer* (1966) and *Every Man Is My Enemy* (1967), and not to be confused with

Gualtiero Jacopetti's collaborator of the same name[1]— gives the film a tight pacing, leaving ample room for acrobatic stunt scenes, such as a five-minute car chase through the streets of Rome and another elaborate pursuit that features Lovelock's stunt double climbing over a speeding truck. He also films one of the genre's crudest fight scenes, the one between Massimo and a hirsute convict (Emilio Messina) in the prison yard.

Lovelock, who as usual gets to sing one of his own songs over the credits, is adequate in the role. He would soon star in another thriller directed by Prosperi, the hyperviolent *Terror!*, as well as in another action film produced (and also directed) by Marras, the interesting *Gangbuster*.

Note

1. This occurrence was rather common, though. At the time of the film's release, one critic wrote: "Director Franco Prosperi takes advantage with remarkable craftsmanship of every occasion to make the film spectacular, exploiting his technical skills (he was Jacopetti's collaborator in all the latter's pseudo-documentaries such as *Mondo Cane* and *Africa Blood and Guts* before he moved on to crime films)." Leo [Leo Pestelli], *Il Messaggero*, 12.17.1976.

The Merciless Man (*Genova a mano armata*)

D: Mario Lanfranchi. *S* and *SC:* Mario Lanfranchi; *DOP:* Federico Zanni (35mm, Kodak-Techniscope, Staco Film); *M:* Franco Micalizzi, conducted by Alessandro Blonksteiner (ed. R.C.A.); *E:* Daniele Alabiso; *PD, CO:* Claudio Riccardi; *APD:* Marica Flandoli; *C:* Michele Pensato; *AC:* Mario Pastorini; *AE:* Maurizio Alabiso; *2nd AE:* Alessandra Olson; *AD:* Rinaldo Zamperla; *2nd AD:* Susanna Bolchi; *MU:* Giuseppe Ferrante; *AMU:* Emilia Dacò Baroni; *Hair:* Corrado Cristofori; *W:* Maria Teresa Carli; *SO:* Luciano Fiorentini; *Boom:* Gioiana Nardi; *G:* Gianni D'Andrea; *SP:* Vittorio Biffani; *SS:* Fiorella Mariani; *UP:* Tonino Pinto. *Cast:* Tony Lo Bianco (The American), Adolfo Celi (Commissioner Lo Gallo), Barbara Vittoria Calori, Howard Ross (Caleb), Maud Adams (Marta Mayer), Fiona Florence, Yanti Somer (Mayer's henchwoman), Luigi Bonos, Daniele Pagani, Ottaviano Dell'Acqua (Caleb's man), Andrea Montuschi (Vice Commissioner), Carlo Cicala Gravina, Dario Ghirardi, Angelo Villa, Andrea Giuseppe Gnecco, Giacomo Assandri, Armando Brandolino. *Uncredited:* Mario Lanfranchi (Doctor), Carmen Russo (Bar Cashier). *PROD:* Mario Lanfranchi for Intervision; *PM:* Piero Nardi; *PSu:* Goffredo Potier; *PSe:* Silvio Battistini; *PSeA:* Vittorio Carta; *ADM:* Noretta Marini. *Country:* Italy. Filmed at R.P.A.-Elios (Rome) and on location in Genoa. *Running time:* 85'; Visa no.: 69444 (11.26.1976); *Rating:* v.m.18; *Release date:* 12.04.1976; *Distribution:* Helvetia Film; *Domestic gross:* 459,086,521 lire. *Also known as: L'Homme sans pitié* (France, 85'), *At helvete med alla* (Sweden). *Home video:* Atlas Film Video (VHS, Sweden). OST: CD Digitmovies CDDM130.

A former FBI agent, expelled by Interpol and the CIA, has opened a detective agency in Genoa where he is known as the American, despite his Sicilian origins. A woman, Dr. Marta Mayer, entrusts him with the investigation on the kidnapping and murder of her father, a wealthy shipowner, and the recovery of a billion dollars which had been paid as ransom. The American must overcome a double barrier: Commissioner Lo Gallo disapproves of his illegal methods, while a gang, apparently headed by the Frenchman Caleb, attacks him many times, putting his life in danger. The American, after many adventures, ends up hospitalized in a clinic that acts as a screen to a drug trafficking ring, where he finds out that Marta Mayer, the clinic's owner, actually planned the cynical kidnapping and murder of her own father and is the head of a powerful criminal organization. The American kills the woman and her accomplice.

"So you're still a cop. Why hide it then?" "It's an old trick I use when I want to speed up procedures." The final dialogue exchange between Commissioner Lo Gallo (Adolfo Celi) and the nameless American hero (Tony Lo Bianco) says a lot about Mario Lanfranchi's *The Merciless Man* in particular and the poliziotteschi in general.

Released in Italy as *Genova a mano armata* (Armed Genoa), a clichéd title at the risk of parody if there was one, the film marked Lanfranchi's only excursion in the crime genre. Born in Parma, the husband of soprano Anna Moffo, Lanfranchi started out as a stage and opera director, before moving on to television — where he directed lots of operas, commercials etc. — and eventually landing on to genre cinema in a sparse career that included an interestingly bizarre western starring Tomas Milian as an albino (*Death Sentence*, 1968), a morbid 19th century *feuilleton* with horror elements (*The Kiss*, 1974) and a grotesque sex comedy co-written by Pupi Avati (*The Mistress Is Served*, 1976) which suffered lots of trouble with the censors.[1] *The Merciless Man*— his penultimate film before 1982's *Venezia, carnevale— Un amore* starring Rudolf Nureyev and Peter Ustinov; later on Lanfranchi moved to England, where he cultivated his true passion, owning race horses and dogs — was a weird affair.

"I wanted to do an action movie, a metropolitan Western, where the pure and uncontaminated hero pursued his very personal idea of justice, without taking into account the limits of the law," the director explained. "A man willing to sacrifice anything to achieve his goal, even at the limit of masochism, knowing that he would have to face extremely hard challenges, yet determined to pursue this kind of mission, even though the mission was not so pure because there was a money prize. He was a modern hero, who withheld a utilitarian concept of life, not a Wagnerian hero."[2]

This somewhat contradictory statement gives an idea of Lanfranchi's conflicting aims, which are reflected in the film. Lanfranchi's idea of a modern Western finds its ideal environment in Genoa, the city *par excellence* in poliziotteschi. "I had a painter friend in Genoa, whose name was Dino Baraldini, who then went to live in Japan. I often paid him a visit and I was impressed by the city's film-like quality, by its extraordinary yet varied beauty, with its variety of natural diverse sets. It was an ideal city to tell a story so grim, with solemnity, and at the same time with the turpitude of certain alleyways and suburbs" Lanfranchi added. "I was very inspired by Genoa. Initially I did not know what story I wanted to tell: I was most interested in the theatricality of Genoa, and I liked the idea of a modern Western."

The choice of Genoa was also vital for the way Lanfranchi portrayed action and violence on screen. "I wanted to keep physical violence contained as much as possible in a confined space, just like in a box. And move from open spaces to the most enclosed ones as possible. The containers had struck me very much. I visited Genoa and found several places in the harbor in the historic center which struck me. I was very impressed by the city's violent conflicts, both as a juxtaposition of diverse environments, and as a passage from the glare of the port to the semi-darkness of the alleys. It seemed to me the most important photographic theme in the film. Even the luxurious interiors, with their sophisticated furnishings and frescoed ceilings, responded to my specific criterion: contrasting environments as rich as possible with poor and degraded ones. I wanted to put this strong contrast, so typically Genoese, on film."

Much of *The Merciless Man*'s impact comes from Federico Zanni's excellent cinematography. "At first I had also talked with Ennio Guarnieri, but he didn't feel like he was open to shoot the film as quick as it was required. Zanni was a very practical, pragmatic director of photography, and willing to shoot in any light. He was willing to risk, in other words. Then there was a lot of light for the shoot, and in a film like this you had to work very quickly, as the film stock we used was not so sensitive back then. And then he did not smoke, an essential requirement as far as I was concerned! The film was shot entirely in Genoa, and anyway there's no shooting in the studio."

Yet, *The Merciless Man* is crossed by a subterranean subversive vein which becomes evident in the film's final twist, where it turns out that Lo Bianco's loner character, an apparent ex-cop who's been treated like shit by everyone, is *still* a cop on a mission. Ditto for the above-mentioned dialogue, which is so patently absurd with its reference to "procedures" that need to be sped up — the same problem each and every Commissioner complains in an Italian film while exposing the limits and frustrations of their job, and which Lo Bianco simply solves by *pretending not to be a cop* (and so be able to shoot the film's villain in cold blood!) — that it acts as an in-joke about the genre's excesses.

The way Lanfranchi's own script accumulates genre trappings betrays a subtle parodic approach, which becomes evident in the scenes between Lo Bianco and Adolfo Celi. The latter (who also appeared in the director's *Death Sentence*), with his ample belly and unathletic shape, is perhaps one of the most unlikely Commissioners in Italian poliziotteschi when compared to his contemporaries, and yet is one of the most funny and sympathetic: his continuous duets with his counterpart — with Celi's consummate underacting and ironic delivery as opposed to Lo Bianco's method performance — suggest that the director was more interested in characters than in the thin plotline, which takes off from the then-common topic of kidnappings and adds a cynical twist in the tail to it, while providing the requested amount of shootouts, beatings, car chases etc. "Actually I did not want to look back at any model, neither Italian nor American," Lanfranchi claimed. "Indeed, I tried to detach myself, although it is very difficult to do something completely new. In general, however, if anything, I was influenced by my stage work. And behind the film there was a psychological idea, closer to theatre than to the movies. Then, I tried as best I could to smuggle my idea into the scheme of action films, which obviously had some fixed canons. But what interested me was carrying the theatrical ideas over into film, and I was fascinated by a concept of a Western translated in terms of a crime flick."

As the film's unnamed hero — a patent reference to the Man with No Name in Leone's *A Fistful of Dollars*, which also extends to the character's ultimate amorality and unscrupulous behavior — Lo Bianco (whose Italian stint resulted in another oddball crime flick, Michele Lupo's *Mean Frank and Crazy Tony*) is as much over-the-top a presence as Celi is. At a certain point, some other character addresses him with a grim in-joke: "Were you a stage actor? No? Strange, you have that same sad melancholy look all ex-actors have" which can be referred as well to the many has-beens who crossed paths with the Italian crime genre. However, Lo Bianco really hams it up with gusto, either when he is eating an ice-cream like a child in the Genoa alleys, serving Celi a milkshake (which the Commissioner spits out in disgust) or doing his best Gene Hackman impression in the scene where he's kidnapped and injected with heroin by the villains (a moment lifted almost verbatim from John Frankenheimer's *French Connection II*). And his sudden bouts of ultraviolence, which granted the film a v.m.18 rating — such as shooting one guy in the bottom during a chase, kicking the bleeding gangster, shooting him in the face and then giving him a final kick before continuing the chase — are as childish as they are darkly comic.

As for the rest of the cast, Howard Ross, a.k.a. Renato Rossini, makes for an over-the-top, white-dressed villain while stunning Swedish model Maud Adams — fresh from her roles in *The Man with the Golden Gun* and *Rollerball*— is the obligatory dark lady. Genre fans will be pleased to spot short-haired Yanti Somer (who would star in Alfonso Brescia's sci-fi epics) and an uncredited, ravishing Carmen Russo as a busty bar cashier. Franco Micalizzi's accomplished score is another asset.

Notes

1. As usual, IMDb messes things up by mixing Lanfranchi's filmography with that of the character actor of the same name (who, among others, is featured in Mario Caiano's *Spies Kill Silently* and Sergio Corbucci's *Navajo Joe*) who is definitely NOT the same person.

2. This and the following quotes come from Renato Venturelli, "Eroi senza pietà: intervista a Mario Lanfranchi," in Aa. Vv., *Cinema e Generi 2010* (Genoa: Le Mani, 2010), pp. 112–122.

Nick the Sting (Gli amici di Nick Hezard)

D: Fernando di Leo. *S* and *SC:* Alberto Silvestri; *DOP:* Roberto Gerardi (35mm, Eastmancolor, Telecolor); *M:* Luis Enriquez Bacalov (the main theme *L'orologio* is played by the Roma New Orleans Jazz Band); *E:* Amedeo Giomini; *PD:* Francesco Cuppini; *CO:* Giulia Mafai; *C:* Roberto Forges Davanzati; *AE:* Ornella Chistolini; *APD:* Sandro Bellomia; *COA:* Mirella Novelli; *AD:* Angelo Vicari; *MU:* Lamberto Marini; *Hair:* Lidia Puglia; *SO:* Goffredo Salvatori; *SS:* Silvia Petroni. *Cast:* Luc Merenda (Nick Hezard), Lee J. Cobb (Robert Clark), Gabriele Ferzetti (Maurice), Luciana Paluzzi (Anna), Dagmar Lassander (Chantal), Isabella Biagini (Edy, the waitress), Fred Williams (Henry), Mario Pisu (Phil), Riccardo Salvino (Mark), William Berger (Roizman), Valentina Cortese (Regina, Nick's mother), Enzo Pulcrano, Jean-Claude Verné (René), Rosario Borelli (Ray), Eddy Fay [Eduardo Fajeta] (Rahn), Flora Carosello (Woman in gang), Sandro Scotti (Antoine), Raoul Lo Vecchio (Ribot), Sergio Ammirata (Sergio), Luigi D'Ecclesia (Duvalier, the dwarf), Fernando Cerulli (Rocchi), Giò Stajano (Jeweler Steffen), Franco Ressel (Jeweler Parker), Carmelo Reale (Rolf, Clark's henchman), Sergio Doria (Gangster), Umberto Raho (Insurance director), Fulvio Mingozzi (Claude). *Uncredited:* Spartaco Battisti (Burglar), Pietro Ceccarelli (Strauss), Fernando di Leo (film director), Dori Dorika, Tom Felleghy (Insurance director assistant), Marco Guglielmi (Will Leffern), Nello Palladino, Bruno Rosa (Parker's sideman). *PROD:* Ermanno Curti and Rodolfo Putignani for Centro Produzioni Cinematografiche Città di Milano; *EP:* Armando Novelli; *PM:* Lanfranco [Pietro] Ceccarelli; *PSu:* Renato Fiè; *PSe:* Piero Ballirano. *Country:* Italy. Filmed at Elios Film (Rome) and on location in Geneve. *Running time:* 100'; Visa no.: 68303 (04.14.1976); *Rating:* not rated; *Release date:* 04.29.1976; *Distribution:*

Interfilm; *Domestic gross:* 427,272,200 lire. *Home video:* Raro (DVD, Italy).

Geneva, Switzerland. The son of a well-known deceased fraudster, young Nick Hezard is a small time con man, totally unworthy of his "great" parent. Crime boss Robert Turner involuntarily provides Nick with the opportunity to emulate his father: after using him to defraud insurance companies by faking a jewel theft, Turner attempts to kill Nick. To exact revenge on Turner, who also killed a friend of his, Hezard conceives an elaborate con, helped by a team of expert scam artists. First he forces the boss to give him 200,000 Swiss francs for protection. This way, funded by his own victim, Nick has Turner arrested by false cops under the charge of a murder that never took place, and transferred in a mock police station, where a false magistrate eventually releases him, allowing Turner to takes refuge in Venezuela, in exchange for the four million francs paid to him by the insurance company. Turner falls headlong into the trap, and not only loses the money, but also the jewelry.

Shot after *Kidnap Syndicate*, *Nick the Sting* was — to put it bluntly — another work for hire for Fernando di Leo. What's more, the director had to work with a pre-existing screenplay, written by Alberto Silvestri and inspired (to use a gentle euphemism) by George Roy Hill's *The Sting*. According to di Leo, it was quite a good script, though, but had a couple of huge problems: it would cost too much to film as it was written, and badly needed a charismatic lead. Whereas di Leo didn't have either Robert Redford or Paul Newman, but Luc Merenda — who was quite popular in that period, but was also more of a charming face than a good actor, especially in roles that were different from his favorite "tough cop" routine.

Shooting *Nick the Sting* became an ordeal, as di Leo recalled: "Soon we started having problems. Merenda wasn't up to the task, the scenes written by Silvestri didn't come up as good as they were on paper and the other actors suffered from this situation as well. Everything became more contrived and banal. That beautiful script was falling to pieces day by day. I watched the rushes and I knew I was not going to make a good movie. I was sad and sorry, but just couldn't do anything about it. What's more, we needed lots of money to shoot the film the way Silvestri wrote it, and we were suffering because the whole production didn't have the economical dignity it so badly needed."[1]

Di Leo was pragmatic enough to know what had to be done to save the film. He made a virtue of necessity and started cutting and changing the film scene by scene as shooting went along, eliminating the best scenes (that is, the more costly and complex to shoot) and reducing Merenda's role by giving more room to the rest of the cast. He would later comment with his usual irony: "I was in the middle of a very funny situation: I had to mutilate a good film, substituting good scenes with not-so-good ones, which was rather absurd. That is to say I was rejecting caviar and asking for lumpfish eggs, claiming that the meal would be better that way."[2] However, what's left are just bare bones and scant flesh.

The cast, even though rather prestigious, is underused. As the umpteenth American boss in di Leo's filmography, who this time ends up ridiculed rather than killed, Lee J. Cobb is clearly in it for the money, and doesn't make much with a role photocopied from Robert Shaw's in George Roy Hill's film. Cobb died in February 1976, two months before the film's release. As Merenda's middle-aged sidekick Gabriele Ferzetti does his best to make up for his partner's shortcomings, while Valentina Cortese, as Nick's mother, cackles, gesticulates, rolls her eyes whenever she's on camera. And although *Nick the Sting* is quite pleasing to watch, in the end there are too many plot holes and incongruencies, especially in such a narrative mechanism, which badly needs the same precision as the "clock" from which it takes its name in order to work.[3]

Di Leo tries his utmost with the material he's given: he often resorts to split-screen — although more like smoke and mirrors to cover the budget limitations rather than because of real narrative and pacing demands — and comes up with at least one scene worthy of his reputation. That's the one where Hezard sets up a sort of film-within-a-film to frame Turner, who's being taken by a pair of fake cops to the scene of a crime for an on-the-spot investigation, and finds himself surrounded by reel cameras and paparazzi. Yet Nick's trick also deceives the crowd that's watching the scene, who are made to believe they are participating in a film shoot and instructed to act accordingly (the fake film director is di Leo himself), so that Turner's deception is complete. This way, the director plays with the boundaries between "reality" (Nick's con) and "fiction" (the fake film that is being shot is actually the "real" film, *Nick the Sting*) with pleasant metafilmic implications.

Notes

1. Pulici, *Fernando di Leo*, p. 330.
2. *Ibid.*
3. In the underworld slang, according to the film, a "clock" is a very elaborate con (which gave the film its working title *L'orologio*, The Clock).

I ragazzi della Roma violenta (The Children of Violent Rome)

D: Renato Savino. *S* and *SC:* Renato Savino; *DOP:* Aiace Parolin (35mm, Eastmancolor, Staco Film); *M:* Enrico Simonetti (Ed. Saar); *E:* Roberto Colangeli; *PD:* Massimo Galloppi; *C:* Enrico Cortese; *AC:* Maurizio Cipriani; *AE:* Fabrizio Di Blasi; *AD:* Federico Cianfarini; *MU:* Lucia La Porta; *Hair:* Ivana Bernardi; *SO:* Bernardino Fronzetti, Pietro Ortolani; *SM:* Bruno Penzo, Sandro Occhetti; *SP:* Domenico Muscara; *SS:* Paola Tiezzi; *DubD:* Rino Bolognesi. *Cast:* Gino Milli (Marco Garroni), Cristina Businari (Gianna), Emilio Locurcio (Schizzo), Sarah Crespi (Franca Faizzo), Vittorio Sgorlon, Francesco Pau (Franco), Mario Cutini (Gino), Enrico Tricarico, Gino Barzacchi (Gorilla), Alicia Bruzzo, Stefania D'Amario (Wanda), Enzo Rinaldi (Giuseppe Rossi), Adolfo Schauer, Annunziata Gregori, Paola Corazzi (Marina Boni), Marco Zuanelli (Nerone). *Uncredited:* Rino Bolognesi (Interviewer); Calogero Caruana (Cop). *PROD:* Luigi Nannerini for G.N. Cinematografica; *PM:* Santo Muré; *PSu:* Giancarlo Nannerini; *PA:* Pietro Nannerini; *ADM:* Antonino Lucidi. *Country:* Italy. Filmed at Incir–De Paolis (Rome) and on location in Rome. *Running time:* 90': Visa no.: 68155 (03.25.1976); *Rating:* v.m.18; *Release date:* 04.13.1976; *Distribution:* Maxi 14 Cinematografica; *Domestic gross:* 428,443,150 lire. *Home video:* Surf Video (DVD, Italy).

Rome. The young and wealthy Marco Garroni is the head of a gang of young Nazis from the Parioli district, while Schizzo, his friend and admirer, leads a gang of low-life thieves and rapists. Marco punishes one of his acolytes, who's guilty of loving a Communist girl, and forces the girl to have sex with another member of the gang: she will later kill herself out of shame. Marco and his friends then punish an anarchist teacher, torturing him to the genitals, then try to rob a Jewish barman. Marco then rapes and kills a girl whom he has lured in a villa at the Circeo, but he eventually falls to his death down a cliff in his car. On the other hand, Schizzo and his gang commit similar cruel deeds, that culminate in a gang-rape in a field near Cinecittà.

On September 29, 1975, two young girls—17-year-old Donatella Colasanti and her 19-year-old friend Rosaria Lopez—were lured to a villa by the sea in San Felice Circeo, a couple of hours from Rome, then systematically beaten, raped and tortured for 36 hours by a trio of upper class youths, Angelo Izzo, Gianni Guido and Andrea Ghira. Rosaria didn't survive the ordeal, while Donatella—who was first partially strangled, then repeatedly beaten in the head with an iron bar—pretended to be dead. The assassins wrapped her in a plastic bag, threw her into the trunk of Guido's Fiat 127 together with Rosaria's body, got back to Rome, parked the car just in front of Guido's house and left. Donatella's feeble screams caught a policeman's attention: a picture taken by a photographer in the moment she was finally released from the trunk shows a young girl—naked, covered in blood and bruises—with her eyes wide open in fear, and the expression of someone who has been to hell and back.

Gianni Guido was arrested immediately afterwards, while he was wandering near the car in a state of apparent mental confusion (he likely heard Donatella's screams and wanted to give her the finishing stroke). Angelo Izzo was also caught within a few hours, while Andrea Ghira fled. Soon the police found out that Gianni Guido was a member of the Neofascist Roman youth, while Izzo was out on parole after a conviction for rape. After a quick trial, Guido and Izzo were found guilty and sentenced to life imprisonment on July 29, 1976.[1]

The so-called "Circeo massacre" caused a sensation, filling newspaper headlines for months and causing a fury amidst the public opinion, mostly because those violent events overturned the bourgeois stereotypes of the good-natured, clean-cut youth as opposed to morally reproachable long-haired, low-life proletarians. How could it be that those horrible acts were the product of upper-class youngsters, the sons of well-esteemed families? What's more, the public was stricken by the arrogant, contemptuous attitude displayed by Guido and Izzo during the trial, as they claimed their "sexual, class and wealth supremacy that gave them the right to use and abuse" of their victims, as journalist Lietta Tornabuoni wrote in *Il Corriere della Sera*, labeling them the "Children of Bad Rome": "Handsome faces, fashion sweaters, beautiful cars, beautiful homes, beautiful summers: and behind all this, all the black swarm that turns a young man into a murderer. The addiction to violence that they acquired in the Fascist youth organizations they belong to [...], the violence chosen as self-affirmation and ideology. The arrogance of money and the contempt towards women, especially the poorest [...]. The void of fanciful lives, torpid, dominated by boredom, spoilt by comfort, without any hint of morality."[2]

The Circeo massacre and the following trial offered a significant portrayal of Italian society at that time. The feminist movements would take it as an example of violence towards women, the assassins' political connotation brought to the foreground the militant Anti-fascism. The Roman fascist groups, comprised of upper-class youth from the wealthy Parioli district (the so-called "Pariolini") who loved Land Rovers, martial arts and punitive expeditions against left-wing students, were similar to Milan's "Sanbabilini" (as depicted in Carlo Lizzani's *San Babila 8 P.M.*) and Turin's "Cabinotti." The Circeo massacre seemed to draw once again a line between the good and the bad, the left and the right. Just a month later, on November 2, 1975, Pier Paolo Pasolini was savagely murdered in Ostia. Those two events became two spectacular and chilling pictures of contemporary Italy, where the absorption of the middle class and the subproletarians prophesied by Pasolini fatally happened, and manifested itself through cruel rituals of extreme violence.

As Pasolini told his friend, journalist Furio Colombo, just a few hours before his death: "The Circeo killers were desperately looking for a uniform, a disguise. They would have given anything to have an order, a reason, an idea to give their massacre a sense. They didn't know, but they were already in disguise. Disguised as new assassins."[3] In his collection of essays *Lutheran Letters*, Pasolini also wrote: "It has been television which in practical terms (it is merely a means) has brought to a close the age of pity and begun the age of *hedone*. It is an age in which young people, who are at one and the same time presumptuous and frustrated, because of the stupidity and the unattainability of the models offered by school and television, in a way that cannot be checked tend to be either aggressive to the point of delinquency or passive to the point of unhappiness (which is no less a crime)."[4]

The Circeo massacre was an irresistible catalyst for Italian cinema. Those references to real-life events which popped up now and then in so many films that only marginally dealt with the problems of youth, concentrated in a number of films—*I ragazzi della Roma violenta*, *Terror in Rome*, and more marginally *Roma, l'altra faccia della violenza* and *Come cani arrabbiati*—that used the event as an exemplary parable of the state of a generation whose behavior was becoming incomprehensible for the older ones. The results were equally emblematic, mainly for the resort to excess and visual shock that characterized genre cinema.

Renato Savino's *I ragazzi della Roma violenta*—a title that blatantly emulated Marino Girolami's *Violent Rome* (*Roma Violenta*)—was released to theaters in April 1976, when the trial was still in course. The cast was filled with little-known names: the most popular of the lot, Gino Milli, had enjoyed a short-lived bout of marginal exposition a few years earlier, while the female lead Cristina Businari had been 1967's Miss Italy. Bearded, chubby character actor Marco Zuanelli was a recurring presence in Z-grade Westerns, while Gino Barzacchi was a rather popular bodybuilder.

Savino's point of view is blatant since the very beginning: *I ragazzi della Roma violenta* sports a semi-documentary prologue where a journalist interviews passers-by—all are in favor of death penalty—and ends with an on-screen line that goes as follows: "All this can really happen and involve you and your family ...

what are you doing to prevent it?." The plot juxtaposes two violent gangs, one formed by upper-class youths and the other by proletarians, in a misguided attempt at a social portrayal. Yet, despite the film's claims at depicting the period's negative feelings, *I ragazzi della Roma violenta* often falls headfirst into the grotesque — as shown by the character of the upper-class neo–Nazi who gets sexually aroused only when he plays pinball — and turns any attempt at a sociological discourse into awkwardly conceived metaphors and episodes. Marco's (Gino Milli) absent-minded parents are never shown in face, as to underline their inability to educate their son, while the latter's nebulous state of mind is exemplified in a scene at the restaurant where Marco refuses to read the list but can't decide what he wants to eat.

Savino, who usually signed his film as "Mauro Stefani," had written a handful of Westerns (including Margheriti's *Vengeance*) and directed a few little-seen sexploitation affairs such as *Grazie signore p...* (1972), *Decameron '300* (1973) and *Mamma ... li turchi!* (1973). On *I ragazzi della Roma violenta*, crude filmmaking is accompanied by a constant unpleasantness that borders on misanthropy. There is no room for love, friendship or mercy whatsoever. The anarchist professor whom the fascists mock and beat is ultimately just a caricature; Marco masturbates while reading a hard-boiled novel; the upper-class Nazi kids gather in a flat decorated by swastikas and giant Hitler portraits, where they unconsciously emulate their parents' social rituals and follow to the letter absurd sets of rules. On the other hand, the proletarian kids ape the former's violent acts, going so far as staging another gang-rape like the one perpetrated by their role models. "What I wanted to stress, yet nobody understood" Savino justified, "was the relationship between the boys of upper-class Rome and the subproletarians who emulated them, like "we can do that, too!"[5] However, the depiction of the lower-class delinquents often falls into the unintentionally hilarious, although Savino seemingly draws inspiration from Pasolini's prophecies on the anthropological mutation of the subproletarians, with the transition from an imposed-upon ideology (Fascism) to another that is passively accepted (consumerism). Everything revolves around sex, food, money. Women are commodities, to be taken and used like a motorbike or a roasted chicken. *Salò, or the 120 Days of Sodom* did not come unnoticed.

However, the film's revolting misogyny has nothing to do with Pasolini's disconsolate awareness: the sequence where the Circeo massacre is re-enacted does not spare the viewer any detail, as unpleasant as it can be (one of the victims is drowned in an aquarium while she's being raped, similarly to Rosaria Lopez), while the crude rape scenes are accompanied by the victims' interior monologues, where the women appear to enjoy the violence they are being subjected to. A Neofascist girl raped by three working-class youth even states: "It's this violence that really turns us on ... you obviously don't understand a thing about women!" The least said, the better....

Notes

1. The story of Gianni Guido and Angelo Izzo did not end with their trial. The two criminals tried to escape in 1977, taking a prison guard as hostage, but were stopped. In 1980 Guido had his imprisonment reduced to 30 years, after he "repented" and his family found an economical agreement with Rosaria Lopez' parents. He was transferred to another prison and was granted a privileged treatment. He escaped from jail on January 25, 1981. Two years later, on January 28, 1983, Guido was arrested in Buenos Aires, where he had become a car seller under a fake name. He escaped again on April 15, 1985, and was arrested in Panama in June 1994. Angelo Izzo escaped from the Alessandria prison on August 25, 1993, and was arrested in France on September 15. He obtained probation in 2004, and in 2005 his name ended again on the headlines because of a ferocious double murder: in 2007 he was sentenced to life imprisonment. Little is known about Andrea Ghira: in November 2005 the Ministry of Interior announced that he had died in 1994 of an overdose in Morocco, where he had enlisted the foreign Legion in 1976. Donatella Colasanti died, at 47, of breast cancer, on December 30, 2005. On April 11, 2008 Gianni Guido was entrusted to social services. He was released from prison on August 25, 2009, the beneficiary of a pardon.
2. Lietta Tornabuoni. "Roma male," *Il Corriere della Sera*, 10.2.1975.
3. Pier Mario Fasanotti and Valeria Gandus, *Bang Bang: Gli altri delitti degli anni di piombo* (Milan: Marco Tropea editore, 2004), p. 221.
4. Pier Paolo Pasolini, tr. Stuart Hood, *Lutheran Letters* (Manchester: Carcanet, 1987), p. 109.
5. Davide Pulici, "Renato Savino: Lo chiamavano King," *Nocturno Cinema* #13 (June-July 2000), p. 94.

Roma, l'altra faccia della violenza (Rome, the Other Face of Violence)

D: Franco Martinelli [Marino Girolami]. *S* and *SC:* Gianfranco Clerici, Vincenzo Mannino, Marie Claire Sinko Solleville; *Psychological consultant:* Laura Boggio Gilot; *DOP:* Gianni Bergamini (35mm, Eastmancolor — Vistavision, Telecolor); *M:* Franco Bixio, Fabio Frizzi, Vince [Vincenzo] Tempera (ed. Grandi Firme della Canzone); *E:* Daniele Alabiso; *PD:* Antonio Visone; *CO:* Silvana Scandariato; *C:* Sergio Bergamini; *AC:* Giovanni Bonivento; *AE:* Lamberto Mancini; *AD:* Romano Scandariato; *MU:* Alberto Travaglini [Trevaglini]; *Hair:* Adriana Quadrini; *SO:* Ludovico Scardella; *Boom:* Armando Bondani; *ChEl:* Enrico Bellacci; *KG:* Teodorico Memé; *SP:* Enzo Falessi; *CON:* Maria Teresa Caruffo; *DubD:* Ferruccio Amendola; *DIA* (French version): Maria Signorini. *Cast:* Marcel Bozzuffi (Commissioner Carli), Anthony Steffen [Antonio De Teffé] (Dr. Alessi), Enio Girolami (Commissioner Ferreri), Jean Favre (Giulio Laurenti), Roberta Paladini (Carol Alessi), Sergio Fiorentini (Nardi), Stefano Patrizi (Giorgio Alessi), Franco Citti (Berté), Enzo Andronico (Tarantini, the lawyer), Francesco Ferracini ("Blond"), Umberto Liberati (Stefano Righi), Aldo Massasso (Nardi), Valerio Merola (Andrea), Marcello Monti (Marcello Monti), Luca Raffa (Fabrizio Verdesi). *Uncredited:* Antonio Calò (Passerby), Dolores Calò (Elderly woman yelling at police car), Aristide Caporale (man in the bar), Lella Cattaneo (Party guest who gets robbed), Nestore Cavaricci (policeman), Massimo Ciprari (Man by pinball machine), Franco Diogene (Laurenti's lawyer), Attilio Dottesio (Attempted robbery victim), Tom Felleghy (Lodovici), Iolanda Fortini (Woman yelling at police car), Lina Franchi (Prostitute), Decio Gabin (Waiter at the party), Nancy Lecchini (Woman pushed down the stairs), Dino Mattielli (Gigi), Enzo Mondino (Party guest), Benito Pacifico (Robber on train at the station), Vittorio Ripamonti (Party guest), Teresa Rossi Passante (Woman at Carol's funeral), Franca Scagnetti (Woman with cart who blocks police car), Valentino Simeoni (Man in toilet), Gianni Solaro (Laurenti), Marcella Theodoly (Party guest), Goffredo Unger [Goffredo Ungaro] (Dead cop), Massimo Vanni (Vanni, cop on motorbike), Sandra Wolff (Robbery's victim), Luciano Zanussi (Man at Carol's funeral), Lydia Zanussi (Party guest who gets robbed). *PROD:* Fulvio Lucisano for Italian International Films (Rome), Fox Europa (Paris); *GM:* Raimondo Castelli; *PM:* Antonio Raffa; *PSu:* Enzo Cartuccia; *PSe:* Stefano Binaco; *ADM, CASH:* Luigi Riitano. *Country:* Italy / France. *Running time:* 92'; Visa no.: 68683 (07.10.1976); *Rating:* v.m.18; *Release date:* 07.27.1976; *Distribution:* 20th Century–Fox; *Domestic gross:* 767,418,800 lire. *Also known as: L'autre côté de la violence* (Paris, 07.06.1977)—*Die Blutigen Spiele der Reichen* (West Germany, 07.01.1977 —101'). *Home video:* Hobby & Work (DVD, Italy). OST: CD Digitmovies CDDM180.

Rome. During a robbery in a villa, four masked men kill Carol Alessi on the day of her eighteenth birthday. Stunned by the death of his daughter, Carol's father is not able to reconcile with his other son Giorgio, but decides to investigate personally so as to locate the murderers. While Commissioner Carli and his men are busy searching the city's suburbs, Alessi finds another trail on his own. Carli hears from an informer the whereabouts of a gang of robbers led by a thug named Berté: one of its members is a young orphan named Stefano, whom Carli was helping in the hope that he'd lead an honest life, and who commits suicide in jail. Meanwhile, Alessi finds out that his daughter's murderers are a trio of Rome's upper-class youth, but can't collect enough evidence to have them arrested. After being attacked and beaten by the three delinquents, Alessi takes his revenge by killing them one by one. What Alessi does not know, though, is that his own son Giorgio is a member of the gang, who in the end unwillingly kills his own father.

Released in August 1976, one year after the director's *Violent Rome*, Marino Girolami's *Roma, l'altra faccia della violenza*—signed with the filmmaker's usual *nom de plûme* Franco Martinelli — re-used the previous film's episodic structure, adding more ingredients in the process. The trio of young upper-class delinquents that rape and kill is an obvious nod to the notorious Circeo massacre as seen in *I ragazzi della Roma violenta*, while the character of the vigilante father recalls that of Lenzi's *Manhunt in the City*. What's more, if the title openly quotes Girolami's previous film, characters' actions and motivations are typical of the vigilante subgenre. However, the ideological implications of the plot are not considered, and even the scene where two girls are raped inside a hothouse looks like a useless afterthought, added later on in the proceedings as a bait to lure audiences (and probably the cause of the film's v.m.18 rating).

Compared to other films of its ilk, Girolami works on a rather consistent budget — an Italian/French co-production, the film was distributed by Italy's 20th Century–Fox — and offers many action scenes, stunts and car chases — all of them invariably featuring an abuse of slow-motion shots. An over-reliance on the same stylistic trick characterizes the violent scenes, as Steffen shoots down his victims in a blaze of blood squibs. As a film critic wrote, Girolami "apes Sam Peckinpah's slow-motion sequences in a purely decorative key, leaving room for a waste of 'neo-realistic' chronicling, where the suburban malaise that belongs to the huge popular neighborhoods gets confused with the bravado of Rome's upper-class youth."[1]

Roma, l'altra faccia della violenza is focused on the social juxtaposition between low-life and upper-class criminals. Yet this serves just as a pretext to show how violence permeates every social layer. The scene of the luxurious party, where waiters serve elaborate dishes and champagne to an array of upper-class members who are busy with superficial small-talk about their own wealth and class privileges, conveys a not-so-hidden contempt towards the rich, and the subsequent robbery, where masked thieves greedily collect the jewelry exhibited by young girl and old ladies, almost looks like a proletarian expropriation. Yet engineer Alessi (Anthony Steffen) discovers that the masked robbers who killed his daughter are not a gang of subproletarian delinquents but a group of hateful *haute bourgeois* kids, who don't "follow the rules" of the underworld, and whose leader will aptly die in a pool of mud.

The film's social discourse is most evident in the film's best sequence, where Commissioner Carli (Marcel Bozzuffi) and his men venture into a suburban, subproletarian neighborhood to catch a gang leader (Franco Citti) only to be surrounded by a raging crowd that instinctively takes sides with the robber out of a sense of aggregation and common tribal membership, whereas institutions are viewed with distrust and contempt.

As the Commissioner on the case, Bozzuffi displays a more technological attitude, supervising the spectacular opening chase from a helicopter like an accomplished film director. But he is also a father figure who helps young drifters to walk the line, a definitely warmer and more humane character than Merli's tough cops. However, despite the credits flaunting the psychological counseling of Laura Boggio Gilot, the founder of the Italian Associations of Transpersonal Psychology (AIPT), the dialogue features such ham-fisted lines as "and just like all those who come out of orphanages, he suffers from an inferiority complex"; nor does the character of Alessi's rebel son (Stefano Patrizi) show any hint of psychological depth: colluded with the killers and eventually an unintentional parricide, only to be punished by Carli with a pair of slaps in the face — the ones his father should have given him much earlier, implies the film.

The cast displays the promiscuity that characterized 1970s *auteur* and genre cinema alike when it came to human material: Patrizi, whose spoilt child face had been discovered by Luchino Visconti on *Conversation Piece* (1974), became a staple presence as the violent rich kid (see also *Brutal Justice* and *Young, Violent, Dangerous*), whereas the great Franco Citti, the subproletarian-turned-actor launched by Pasolini's masterpiece *Accattone* (1961) was typecast as the low-life criminal (see also *Live Like a Cop, Die Like a Man* and *Destruction Force*). Enio Girolami — the director's son and a rather popular star in the 1950s — has a minor role as Bozzuffi's vice.

Note

1. Anonymous, *Il Secolo XIX*, 8.14.1976. However, for all its emphasis on spectacle, Girolami's film has its share of bloopers: Massimo Vanni, who plays one of the two cops on a motorbike who get killed by Franco Citti's gang in the opening sequence, pops up alive and well halfway through the film!

Rulers of the City, a.k.a. *Mr. Scarface (I padroni della città)*

D: Fernando di Leo. *S:* Fernando di Leo; *SC:* Fernando di Leo, Peter Berling; *DOP:* Erico Menczer (35mm, Eastmancolor, Staco Film); *M:* Luis Enriquez Bacalov (ed. Nazionalmusic); *E:* Amedeo Giomini; *PD:* Francesco Cuppini; *PD:* Sandro Bellomia, Cristiano Tessari; *CO:* Giulia Mafai (models: J. Jovine); *COA:* Mirella Novelli; *C:* Roberto Brega; *AE:* Tommaso Gramigna; *AD:* Angelo Vicari; *2nd AD:* D. Schneider; *MU:* Cristina Rocca; *Hair:* Lidia Puglia; *SO:* Roberto Alberghini; *ST:* O.A.C. Group; *SS:* Silvia Petroni; *UP:* Tonino Pinto. *Cast:* Jack Palance ("Scarface" Manzari), Al Cliver [Pier Luigi Conti] (Rick), Harry Baer (Tony), Gisela Hahn (Clara), Enzo Pulcrano (Peppi), Roberto Reale (Luca), Edmund Purdom (Luigi Cherico), Vittorio Caprioli (Vincenzo Napoli), Rosario Borelli (Office manager), Pietro Ceccarelli (Luigi's Bagman), Salvatore Billa (Luigi's Bagman), Peter Berling (Valentino), Raoul Lo Vecchio (Scarface Goon), Giulio Baraghini (Scarface Goon), Enrico Palombini (Captain Beri / Actor), Spartaco Battisti (Sergeant / Actor), Fernando Cerulli (Scarface Goon), Luciano Bottin (Rick as a boy), Michele Branca (Franco), Agostino Crisafulli (Al), Bruno Di Luia (Luigi's Bagman), Gilberto Galimberti (Scarface Goon), Giovanni

[Nello] Pazzafini (Dominic), Marco Stefanelli (Maguel), Sandro La Barbera (Mario), Franco Beltramme (Trevanti). *Uncredited:* Fulvio Mingozzi (Rick's father), Mario Novelli (The Whipman). *PROD:* Armando Novelli for Cineproduzioni Daunia '70 (Rome), Seven Star Film G.M.B.H. (Münich); *PM:* Lanfranco [Pietro] Ceccarelli; *UPM:* Renato Fiè; *PAs:* Piero Ballirano, S. Albenroth; *CASH:* Vincenzo Samà. *Country:* Italy / West Germany. Filmed at Incir–De Paolis (Rome) and on location in Rome. *Running time:* 98'; Visa no.: 69368 (11.20.1976); *Rating:* v.m.14; *Release date:* 12.03.1976; *Distribution:* Overseas Film Company; *Domestic gross:* 333,059,400 lire. *Also known as: Zwei Supertypen räumen auf* (West Germany, 12.09.1977 — 88'); *Rulers of the City*; *Blood and Bullets*. *Home video:* Raro (DVD/Blu-ray, USA — as part of the Fernando di Leo Crime Collection 3DVD set); Synergy (DVD, USA); Raro (DVD, Italy).

Tony is a smooth and handsome but insignificant guy who works as a loan collector for Luigi Cherico; the number 2 mob boss in town. Wanting to make an impression on him, Tony ingeniously plunders 10 million lire from the biggest crime lord in town, the feared and relentless "Scarface" Manzari, who owed that sum to Cherico. In doing so, Tony unwillingly provokes a mafia war in Rome and finds himself amid the two camps. Luckily he receives help from Napoli, a flamboyant old school crook, and Rick, a mysterious blond shooting expert with an old personal score to settle with Manzari.

After the artistic failure of his caper comedy *Nick the Sting* (1976), Fernando di Leo returned to more familiar territories: even though it was the director's umpteenth foray into the underworld, compared to di Leo's previous *Caliber 9* and *Manhunt*, nevertheless *Rulers of the City* (also known overseas as *Mr. Scarface*) sported an ironic, picaresque vein that was closer to the filmmaker's *divertissements* such as *Loaded Guns*. That can be spotted starting from the title itself, which announces an epic scope that is actually missing from the film. The "rulers" are actually small-time crooks, suburban penniless rogues who gravitate around squalid taverns and billiard pools, and the film has a low-budget flair that perfectly suits its subject. "At this level of the underworld, people don't cut each others' throats for 300,000 dollars" di Leo noted. "It's just a matter of a few million lire, a miserable debt collecting racket and the control of a bug-infested gambling house to start a war."[1]

On *Rulers of the City*, instead of the big shots of the international organized crime, di Leo depicts a neighborhood boss with no guts (Edmund Purdom) who almost pisses his pants when a rival steps on his feet; his boastful and opportunist right-hand man (Enzo Pulcrano) who nevertheless can barely write and read; a small-time bully, Tony (Harry Baer), who drives around on a dune buggy, is more interested in women than in "business," and dreams of moving to Brazil; a taciturn thug with an unerring aim, Rick (a mustache-less Al Cliver) who is preparing for a long-awaited revenge. These are the "rulers of the city": a bunch of small fish who live hand to mouth, in a maze of double-crosses and conspiracies, bribes and kickbacks, teases and betrayals. It's a world that's about to disappear, partly because of the advent of the new organized crime, partly because of self-combustion. Such a passage is rather traumatic, and each breeds the snakes he deserves: the passive Purdom gets a bullet in the head from his assistant, in a remarkably conceived and edited sequence, while the film's main villain "Mr. Scarface" Manzari (Jack Palance), who's so full of himself he never watches his interlocutors in the eyes, realizes just before he dies that his henchman Rick is the boy whose father he had killed before his eyes, years earlier.

However, *Rulers of the City* shows di Leo in a more indulgent and benevolent mood than in his earlier films. For one thing, the director often makes room for comic interludes, because — to quote his own words — "in such a *milieu* tragedy and farce are often contiguous."[2] Such moments mostly rely on the great actor-director Vittorio Caprioli (who helmed such important films as *Parigi o cara*, 1962, and *Splendori e miserie di Madame Royale*, 1970, besides being one of Italian cinema's most reliable character actors) as the elderly, picturesque pickpocket who can perhaps be seen as the director's *alter ego*, and whose complaints about the gap between the old and new "school" sums up di Leo's view with a pleasantly ironic touch.

Rulers of the City came out one year after the tragic death of Pier Paolo Pasolini: di Leo paid homage to the great poet, novelist and filmmaker in the description of the Roman subproletarian microcosm, and in scenes such as the one where Tony shows up to collect a loan from an old man, dirty and ragged, who lives in a hut with a gorgeous young lover who's as young as his daughter, or the one where Tony and Rick wake up after a wild night with three prostitutes. There, di Leo's camera unveils and caresses the actors' naked bodies with a lyrical yet carnal abandon, that's not far from Pasolini's approach in the so-called "Trilogy of Life."

Besides its tight budget, the film is slightly let down by a pair of none-too-convincing leads: Cliver is helplessly wooden, while Baer — a German actor who worked with Fassbinder, and who was cast merely for co-production reasons[3] — is rather unbelievable as a Roman subproletarian (despite being dubbed with a strong Roman accent in the Italian version). Nevertheless, *Rulers of the City* doesn't pale in comparison with the director's masterpieces, and features some of di Leo's best-shot sequences ever. Such is the opening murder of Rick's father, where slow-motion and *flou* cinematography (courtesy of the great director of photography Erico Menczer) evoke a barbaric past that has cemented in the memory; the beautiful scene where Tony is chased on foot through the street of Rome was possibly a blueprint for the flashbacks of Steve Buscemi running away from the cops in *Reservoir Dogs* (it's no mystery that Quentin Tarantino is a great admirer of the film).[4] Last but not least, the climactic showdown in the abandoned slaughterhouse (a very common location in the Testaccio district, featured in lots of genre films from Nazi sexploitation dramas to post-apocalyptic flicks), shot with plenty of spectacular car stunts, is truly one of the great set-pieces in Italian crime cinema.

As ever with di Leo's films, action is at the service of dialogue that's fun as always (including an in-joke at the expense of his friend Duccio Tessari's *Zorro*, 1975) and never banal — this time, actually, even sinisterly ominous. Lines such as "You young guys are always in a hurry — you're in a hurry to make money, to steal, and to die…" can be read as metaphors. The dying world of those small-time gangsters somehow mirrors, perhaps unwillingly yet in an uncannily precise way, that of the Italian film industry, gasping and shaky under the offensive of the newborn commercial broadcasters and the ensuing economical hemorrhage.

On August 10, 1974, "Firenze libera" started its transmissions, breaking the monopoly of RAI-TV, the Italian state-owned public service broadcaster; with sentence no. 202 of July 28, 1976 the Constitutional Court agreeing that State monopoly over local broadcasting was unconstitutional; it stated that local broadcasting channels were legitimate, as there were no dangers of private monopolies or oligopolies, and demanded the institution of a law system in order to protect the public service and thus prevent the insurgence of such. With sentence 202/1976, the so-called "deregulation phase" started: the liberalization of public broadcasting paved the way for a competition that, in the absence of any regulatory board, would prove to be overwhelming. A couple of years later a local cable broadcasting company named Telemilano, which had been transmitting since 1975, was bought by an entrepreneur named Silvio Berlusconi, and a couple of years later it changed its name to Canale 5. In that same year Berlusconi founded Fininvest. A new "ruler of the city" was around.

"Nineteen seventy-six saw enormous amounts of money being invested in the broadcasting field," as Angelo Zaccone Teodosi wrote, "with the illusion that owning the hardware was enough to produce profit [...]. However, soon the other editorial entrepreneurs (Rusconi, Rizzoli, Mondadori) allowed the predatory Berlusconi to subject to his power the Wild West of Italian private broadcasting."[5]

By taking advantage of the lack of laws on the subject, Fininvest and other smaller companies bought as many films as they could from small distributors, often at ridiculously low prices, and offered a wide array of movies throughout the day. Compared to RAI's more timid and serious schedules, they represented a succulent alternative, but also opened a new world for average moviegoers, who used to go to the movies because of alluring titles and posters that promised excess and forbidden transgressions. Of course those titles offering sex and violence were privileged, what's more many local broadcasters offered stripteases and assorted erotic shows. Audiences soon lost interest in getting out and going to the movies (especially since going out in the evening in big cities was an occurrence faced with growing reluctance and preoccupation, given the rise of crime and violence). Why would one pay the ticket and sit on an uncomfortable wooden chair, in an awfully smelling theater, beside unknown people who would laugh and yell, fart and make noises, when whatever he or she could wish for was to be found on the small screen in their living room?

Rulers of the City was the last film produced by Daunia 70 Cinematografica, the independent company that had financed all of di Leo's previous films (with the exception of *Shoot First, Die Later* and *Kidnap Syndicate*, which were produced by Galliano Juso) starting with *Naked Violence*. From then on the director would have to face increasing economical difficulties, and his following work would inevitably suffer from the consequences — namely, shoestring budgets and difficult distribution, within a market that was becoming more and more asphyxiated — and gradually drifted towards invisibility.

Notes

1. Davide Pulici, "I padroni della città," in Aa. Vv., "Calibro 9 — Il cinema di Fernando di Leo," p. 39.
2. Pulici, *Fernando di Leo*, p. 326.
3. *Rulers of the City* was co-produced by KG Divina Film and Seven Star; besides Baer, there were two more German actors, Gisela Hahn and Peter Berling; the latter was also credited as co-scriptwriter, merely for reasons pertaining to co-production quotas, as the script was written solely by di Leo.
4. John Martin, "Tarantino Talks Trash," *Giallo Pages* #3 (1994), pp. 8–12.
5. Angelo Zaccone Teodosi, "Ipotesi di riscatto per una provincia dell'impero audiovisivo," in Enrico Magrelli, ed., *Sull'industria cinematografica Italiana* (Venice: Marsilio, 1986), p. 55.

San Babila 8 P.M. (San Babila ore 20: un delitto inutile)

D: Carlo Lizzani. *S* and *SC:* Carlo Lizzani, Mino Giarda, Ugo Pirro; *PDir:* Piergiorgio Pozzi (35mm, Eastmancolor, Telecolor); *M:* Ennio Morricone, conducted by the author; *E:* Franco Fraticelli; *PD:* Pier Giorgio Basile; *SD:* Natalia Verdelli; *CO:* Dada Saligeri, Serenilla Staccioli; *AArtD:* Renzo Maietto; *AE:* Franco Reitano; *2nd AE:* Alessandro Gabriele; *ADs:* Carlo Lazzaro, Gilberto Squizzato; *C:* Onofrio Folli; *AC:* Dario Semeraro; *MU:* Silvana Petri; *Hair:* Wanda Luisa Piovesan; *SO:* Domenico Pasquadibisceglie; *Boom:* Giuseppina Sagliano; *KG:* Carlo De Gregori; *GA:* Ettore Valsasina; *Research:* Claudio Lazzaro; *SS:* Vittoria Vigorelli. *Cast:* Daniele Asti (Franco), Giuliano Cesareo (Michele "Miki" Castiglioni), Pietro Brambilla (Fabrizio), Pietro Giannuso (Alfredo Somma), Brigitte Skay (Lalla), Gilberto Squizzato (Paolo), Grazia Beccari (Paolo's girlfriend), Mario Mattia Giorgetti (Teacher), Walter Valdi (Commissioner), Franca Mantelli (Franco's mother), Paola Faloja (Michele's mother), Sergio Tardioli, Rodolfo Dal Prà, Giovanni Colla, Franco Ferri, Achille Grioni, Wilma Casagrande, Claudio Lazzaro, Filippo Orsini, Stefano Bandini, Franco Pesante, Marisella Biancheri, Alfredo Manevari, Maddalena Galliani, Mario Mercalli, Mario Corbetta, Piera Rossi, Antonio Cascio, Carlo Gioia, Rocco Oppedisano, Vittorio Pinelli (Cop). *PROD:* Adelina Tattilo and Carlo Maietto for PTA (Produzioni Thousand Associate); *EP:* Carlo Maietto; *UPM:* Biagio Angelini, Alessandro Calosci; *PM:* Silvio Siano; *Production organizer:* Livio Maffei; *Line producer:* Vincenzo De Leo; *PSe:* Alessandro Di Luca; *PSeA:* Iolanda Lo Russo; *ADM:* Luigi Scardino; *CASH:* Roberto Ornaro. *Country:* Italy. Filmed at Icet — De Paolis (Milan) and on location in Milan. *Running time:* 105'; Visa no. 68129 (03.23.1976); *Rating:* v.m.14; *Release date:* 03.25.1976; *Distribution:* Agora; *Domestic gross:* 594,392,750 lire. *Home video:* Medusa (DVD, Italy). OST: CD Screen Trax CDST 318.

Milan. After the funeral of an old fascist hierarch, four young neo-fascists — Fabrizio, Franco and Micky, of bourgeois origin, and Alfredo, a working class southerner — perform a feat against a leftist high school. Later, after a stop in a bar in Piazza San Babila — their "den"— they pick up a girl, Lalla. Franco, who's impotent, rapes her with a truncheon. After a procession of striker passes bys, Fabrizio and his companions beat a protester who's been left behind. Then they place a bomb in a union's headquarters, but the device does not explode (Marco lacked the courage to light the fuse). Later on, the quartet indulge in a goliardic provocation outside a sex shop and end up at the police station, accused of obscene acts in public. They are immediately released and get back to San Babila. There, Fabrizio finds out about Franco's failings with Lalla and the bomb, and demands that he rehabilitate himself by killing a communist. Late in the evening, the four follow a young left-wing couple, attack them and stab the boy to death. But this time, thanks to the testimony of Lalla — to whom Fabrizio has given his knife so that she gets rid of it— the four neo-fascists are arrested.

After the controversial *The Teenage Prostitution Racket*, Lizzani's next film was another "instant movie": *San Babila 8 P.M.*, produced like the former by Adelina Tattilo (owner of the adults-only magazine "Playmen") and Carlo Maietto. The word "Sanbabilini" was quite common at that time: it was a pejorative term introduced by the press to label the extreme right-wing youngsters who used to hang out in San Babila square, in the centre of Milan. With its fascist '30s architecture and density of upper-class attendance, San Babila was an appropriate environment for the resurgence of neo-fascism in the mid–1970s, and the "Sanbabilini" quickly became a recurring presence in newspaper crime reports. One such event was the inspiration for the story Lizzani wrote with his assistant Mino Giarda (with the participation of Ugo Pirro): on May 25, 1975, a young student, Alberto Brasili, was attacked and stabbed to death by five neo-fascists in an alley near San Babila, while he was walking with his girlfriend: Brasili reportedly tore off a poster of the MSI, Italy's extreme right wing party, off a street lamp.

The four neo-fascists harassing a girl in Carlo Lizzani's controversial *San Babila 8 P.M.* (1976).

Lizzani's film follows the four young fascists during the course of one day, which climaxes with the aggression and savage killing of a man just a few steps away from one of Milan's main streets. The director's didactic intent is evident from the first scenes, and *San Babila 8 P.M.* works as a sociological treatise put on film. Of the four, Alfredo is the only one who belongs to the working class. He becomes more and more arrogant and cocky after meeting a politician who enlists young men at a shooting range and has them perform violent propaganda actions. Here Lizzani alludes to the connection between the violent youngsters who wear Celtic crosses and mirrored sunglasses as if they were an uniform, and the extra-parliamentary far right—a connection which led to many violent acts and possibly to still unsolved mass killings such as the bomb at the Bologna station on August 2, 1980, which killed 85 people and injured over 200—under the authorities' complacent eye. The director often shows the police as being Pilate-like in their passivity: cops watch the Neofascists' bravado but do not interfere because of orders coming from their superiors, and also as Fabrizio is a police informant. Only when Franco and his friends make obscene pranks to passers-by with erotic toys stolen from a nearby sex shop does the law intervene: in the ballet of appearances and political balances, only public morality and decency are considered worthy of protection by the authority.

The episode, besides underlining the political connections which allow the four protagonists to be released after just a telling-off, also stresses one of the film's most debatable aspects: Lizzani's parallelism between sexual dissatisfaction (or impotence) and acts of violence, which many critics noted (and criticized) after *San Babila 8 P.M.*'s release. Earlier on in the film, Alfredo's friends pick up a ditzy blonde (Brigitte Skay) and take her to the shop where Alfredo works as a clerk to have sex. After unsuccessfully trying to make love to her, Franco loses control and penetrates the girl with a truncheon, then he threatens to slash her if she tells his friends what happened. Later on Franco is instructed to place a charge of dynamite in a union's headquarters, but fails to light the fuse, leaving the bomb unexploded: it's yet another interrupted, "emasculated" act which serves to point out the young man's irresolution.

The heavy emphasis on awkward symbols is not the only fault of *San Babila 8 P.M.*, as Lizzani often indulges in pedantic excesses: the scene where the rich Micky has lunch with his embittered, hateful and estranged parents in their luxurious villa is a case in point. Other critics blamed Lizzani for several excessively spectacular exemplifications, such as the scene where the Neofascist "Sanbabilini" march in goose-step through the traffic-ridden square, which, despite its "dilated evocative expressionism" has been dismissed as implausible and "in stark contrast with the film's semi-documentary framework."[1]

As with *The Teenage Prostitution Racket*, Lizzani pursued a *cinéma-vérité* feel. He shot the film in the very same locations where real political struggle took place (not just San Babila square, but also the left-winged Beccaria high school and the union headquarters in Sesto where Franco fails to detonate the bomb). The political demonstrations where shot as if they were real, with the camera hidden inside a van: many people spontaneously joined actors and extras, and real scuffles followed. Piergiorgio Pozzi's hand-held camera often captures passers-by's impromptu reactions, and the scabrous cinematography observes the quartet's misdeeds with laconic detachment. Only in the final scenes, where a low tracking shot recedes from the body of the young victim, does the camera take on a moral point of view, distancing itself from the horror of what is, as the Italian original title states, "a useless murder."

As with Lizzani's previous film, the leads are virtually unknown, to achieve the desired effect. Besides Brigitte Skay, whose fame as a sex star was rapidly declining just a few years after Bruno Corbucci's *Ms. Stiletto* (1968) and Mario Bava's *Bay of Blood* (1971), the only other relatively familiar face for film buffs is that of Pietro Brambilla, who played the retarded altar boy Lidio in Pupi Avati's Gothic masterpiece *The House with the Laughing Windows* (1976). *San Babila 8 P.M.* was released just before another violent crime which involved the "Sanbabilini," the kidnapping and murder of sixteen-year-old Olga Julia Calzoni Sforza by two young neo-fascists. Yet the film performed only fairly well at the Italian box office, with a grossing of 594 million lire, nearly half as much as *The Teenage Prostitution Racket*.

Note

1. Morando Morandini, *Il Giorno*, 4.10.1976. As Morandini put it, "whoever conceived such a scene does not know Milan, nor the limits it allows its Fascists."

Sexycop (La Madama)

D: Duccio Tessari. *S:* based on the novel *La Madama* by Massimo Felisatti and Fabio Pittorru; *SC:* Massimo Felisatti, Fabio Pittorru, Franco Verucci, Duccio Tessari; *DIA:* Maurizio Costanzo; *M:* Manuel De Sica (ed. C.A.M.), conducted by Roberto Pregadio; *DOP:* Giulio Albonico (35mm, Technicolor, Techniscope); *Underwater sequences:* Enzo Bottesini; *E:* Mario Morra; *AE:* Antonio Proia; *PD:* Giuseppe Bassan; *APD:* Maurizio Garrone; *AD:* Marco Risi; *C:* Sebastiano Celeste; *AC:* Renato Doria, Marco Onorato; *CO:* Adele D'Ercole; *MU:* Raoul Ranieri; *Hair:* Nerea Rosmanit; *SO:* Massimo Iaboni, Gaetano Testa; *SOE:* Roberto Arcangeli; *SR:* Roberto Pennacchia; *Mix:* Danilo Moroni; *SE:* Cataldo Galliano; *Still photographers:* Vittorio Biffani, Carlo Alberto Cocchi; *SS:* Vittoria Vigorelli; *PA:* Lucherini, Rossetti, Spinola. *Cast:* Christian De Sica (Vito Militello "Minchiello"), Ines Pellegrini (Irma), Oreste Lionello (Commissioner Solmi), Ettore Manni (Sante Tonnaro), Gigi Ballista (The Venetian), Grazia Maria Spina (Tonnaro's wife), Nazzareno Zamperla (Valerio Merisi), Aldo Massasso (Carabinieri Captain Loffrredo), Lorella De Luca (Female doctor), Alessandra Panaro (Aunt Francesca), Francesco De Rosa (Brigadeer Squillace), Tom Skerritt (Jack), Carole André (Angela), Tiziana Pedini, Guido Savoretti, Barbara Magnolfi, Vincenzo Crocitti (Mechanic), Isabella Biardi, Franco Diogene (Greengrocer), Francesco D'Adda (policeman at Militello's house), Giorgio Di Lorenzo, Giovanni [Nello] Pazzafini (Venetian's henchman), Francesco Parisi, Dario Giacomelli, Maria Rosaria Riuzzi, Franco Zancato, Antonia Cazzola, Renato Stanisci, Luigi Curussani, Giuseppe Monteverdi, Ferdinando Tomassini. *Uncredited:* Nestore Cavaricci (Nino), Benito Pacifico, Renzo Giovanni Pevarello. *PROD:* Giorgio Venturini for Filmes Cinematografica; *PM:* Cecilia Bigazzi; *PSu:* Viero Spadoni. *Country:* Italy. Filmed at Incir–De Paolis (Rome) and on location in Rome. *Running time:* 94'; Visa no.: 67810 (01.15.1976); *Rating:* not rated; *Release date:* 01.16.1976; *Distribution:* Titanus; *Domestic gross:* 173,627,420 lire. *Also known as: La Madama l'agente Minchiello e il caso Patacchioni. Home video:* Stereophile in Video (VHS, Greece, Italian language).

Vito Militello takes a job in the Mobile Squad because he's the nephew of Francesca, the wife of Commissioner Solmi, and he saved the adulterous Solmi from being discovered by his wife. After finding a harlequin doll near the dead body of a certain Carmine Pizzuto, Vito decides to investigate on his own, with the help of young black prostitute Irma and ditzy reporter Angela (his girlfriend). Vito gets hired as a truck driver by crime boss "The Venetian" and makes arrangements with the latter's rival, Sante Tonnaro. Misunderstood and disavowed by his superiors, Vito's life would end badly if he didn't receive help from an American CIA agent. In the end, Vito discovers that "The Venetian" is operating a gold contraband ring, and that the gold is concealed in toy casings.

Published in 1974, Massimo Felisatti and Fabio Pittorru's *La Madama* ("The Madam," Rome's slang for the police, similar to "the fuzz" in the United States) was the third in the series of successful novels about Rome's Mobile Squad, which the authors wrote after the success of the TV series *Qui squadra mobile*. The book's tone was harsh and realistic, and the plot was right on target vis-à-vis the period's crime reporting, depicting a map of neo-fascist organizations that recruited volunteers through Rome's neighborhood gyms and used such squads for violent activities with the aim of overthrowing the democratic system. It was quite a surprise, then, when the film adaptation directed by Duccio Tessari came out in 1976 and turned out to be a comedy of sorts.

Devised as a vehicle for Vittorio De Sica's 25-year-old son Christian, *La Madama* reinvented (or, to many, upset) the book's plot in a humorous way with weird results. For instance, Militello is nicknamed Minchiello (a wordplay on the dialectical word "minchione," which means dumb, simpleton), Commissioner Solmi — who in another Felisatti/Pittorru adaptation, *Calling All Police Cars*, was played by Antonio Sabàto — becomes a full-blown caricature as played by Oreste Lionello (Woody Allen's Italian voice), and much of the humor draws upon the traditional rivalry between the Mobile Squad and the Carabinieri, which naturally is lost on a foreign audience. To make things even clearer, the film's alternate release title was *La Madama l'agente Minchiello e il caso Patacchioni* (The Madam, Agent Minchiello and the Patacchioni Case), accompanied by the nonsensical tagline "*'Italiani ... finalmente anche noi abbiamo il nostro Serpico!' Così lo definivano i colleghi della polizia e i cugini carabinieri*" (Italians ... finally we have our very own Serpico! That's how he was labeled by his colleagues within the police force and fellow Carabinieri).

Felisatti and Pittorru were not extraneous to the adaptation, though, as they are featured among the five scriptwriters at work (including Maurizio Costanzo, soon to become a notorious TV personality, taking care of the dialogue[1]). However, the attempt at creating a comic hero — a likeable womanizer and a smart hound, who on the other hand is incredibly superstitious — failed badly: the box office results were disappointing, and the critics ravaged the film. "Corriere della Sera"'s Renato Palazzo stated "The closest models of Duccio Tessari's film are actually the childish comic-adventure series starring Bud Spencer and Terence Hill, full of homely humor, fisticuffs and vigorous nods to slapstick comedy. The formula, however, has already been frayed for a long time, and Christian De Sica's face is not enough to freshen it up: De Sica's son is very busy throughout, hamming it up, dancing, making fun of himself, but he rarely lends depth to his character,"[2] while "Rivista del Cinematografo"'s Orio Caldiron was much harsher. "Only one thing is left to be asked: why Duccio Tessari — who, although he's never been a master filmmaker, at times managed to give his films a bullying, maliciously ironic flair — lost his way up to the point of having the dynamic duo Felisatti/Pittorru give him a lesson in style. In front of the slaughter of their own novel they might have well thought of themselves as the De Goncourt brothers [renowned 19th century French writers and critics Edmond and Jules de Goncourt, who gave name to France's most prestigious literary prize, Author's note] had they not signed the script themselves."[3]

Besides its weird cast — which among others includes Tom Skerritt, who acted in a number of films in Italy in that period, such as Giuseppe Colizzi's action comedy *Arrivano Joe e Margherito* (1974), co-starring Keith Carradine, and Paolo Cavara's excellent *giallo Plot of Fear* (1976)[4] — *La madama* is perhaps more interesting as an example of how filmmakers were quickly trying to find new ways to exploit the genre, moving away from its bleak core: a similar move happened with Sergio Corbucci's *La mazzetta*, 1978, starring Nino Manfredi, from Attilio Veraldi's book of the same name.

Notes

1. In the 1970s Costanzo worked on a number of scripts, including Pupi Avati's *The House with Laughing Windows* (*La casa dalle finestre che ridono*, 1976, although Costanzo's contribution was, by all accounts, minimal), and even directed a film, the grotesque melodrama *Melodrammore* (1978) starring Enrico Montesano. He then dedicated himself to television, surviving a huge scandal when his name was found on the list of the secret P2 association (Costanzo was the editor-in-chief of *L'Occhio*, a newspaper published by Angelo Rizzoli, another member of Licio Gelli's occult Masonic lodge).
2. R. P. [Renato Palazzo], *Corriere della Sera*, 1.28.1976.
3. Orio Caldiron, "*La Madama,*" *La Rivista del cinematografo* #5 (May 1976), p. 205.
4. On a more technical note, Dino Risi's son Marco, who would become a director in his own right, is Tessari's assistant director.

Special Cop in Action (*Italia a mano armata*)

D: Franco Martinelli [Marino Girolami]. *S:* Vincenzo Mannino; *SC:* Vincenzo Mannino, Gianfranco Clerici, Leila Buongiorno; *DOP:* Fausto Zuccoli (35mm, Gevacolor, Telecolor); *M:* Franco Micalizzi, conducted by Alessandro Blonksteiner (Ed. Prima); *E:* Vincenzo Tomassi; *PD:* Antonio Visone; *CO:* Silvana Scandariato; *C:* Guglielmo Vincioni; *AC:* Enzo Frattari; *AE:* Lamberto Mancini; *2nd AE:* Pietro Tomassi; *AD:* Romano Scandariato; *MU:* Pietro Tenoglio; *Hair:* Marcello Longhi; *W:* Stella Battista; *SO:* Gianfranco Pacella; *Boom:* Gianni Zampagni; *SOE:* Fernando Caso; *Foley artist:* Alvaro Gramigna; *SP:* Francesco Narducci; *Master of arms, ST:* Goffredo Unger [Goffredo Ungaro]; *ChEl:* Fernando Massaccesi; *KG:* Luciano Micheli; *Jeweler:* Nino Lembo; *SS:* Patrizia Zulini; *DubD:* Ferruccio Amendola. *Cast:* Maurizio Merli (Commissioner Betti), Raymond Pellegrin (Commissioner Arpino), John Saxon (Jean Albertelli), Mirella D'Angelo (Luisa), Toni Ucci (Raffaele Cacace), Daniele Dublino (Luzzi, kidnapper), Aldo Barberito (Marshall Ferrari), Sergio Fiorentini (Salvatore Mancuso, kidnapper), Franco Borelli (Bertoli), Dino Mattielli (Attardi), Rocco Oppedisano, Carlo Valli (Rocchi, kidnapper), Marcello Monti (Torri, kidnapper), Massimo Vanni (Massimo Fabbri, special agent), Fortunato Arena (Carlo Morel). *Uncredited:* Enzo Andronico (Antonio Boretti), Stelio Candelli (Forestier), Omero Capanna (Prisoner), Costantino Carrozza (Man at bank), Philip Dallas (Prison director), Cesare Di Vito (Doctor), Attilio Dottesio (Theft victim), Adolfo Lastretti (Lazzari), Antonio Maimone (Albertelli's lawyer), Rina Mascetti (Kidnapped boy's mother), Maurizio Mattioli (Prisoner), Nello Pazzafini (Prisoner), Renzo Pevarello (Prisoner), Sergio Smacchi (Bank robber), Goffredo Unger [Goffredo Ungaro] (Driver at bank robbery), Piergiorgio Plebani (policeman). *PROD:* New Film Production (Rome); *PM:* Roberto Giussani; *PSu:* Gian Maria Avetta; *PSe:* Giandomenico Stellitano; *CASH:* Benito Mancini. *Country:* Italy. Filmed at Incir–De Paolis (Rome) and on location in Turin, Milan, Genoa. *Running time:* 100'; Visa no.: 69443 (11.25.1976); *Rating:* v.m.14; *Release date:* 11.27.1976; *Distribution:* Fida; *Domestic gross:* 1,449,489,920 lire. *Also known as: Cop Hunter* (Germany), *Flic en jean, Opération Jaguar* (France), *Terror og knippelsuppe* (Denmark). *Home video:* Hokushin (VHS, U.K.— pre-cert), Danks Video Film (VHS, Denmark). OST: CD Beat Records CDCR 75.

After arresting the authors of two robberies, Commissioner Betti moves from Turin to Milan, on the trail of a gang composed of Salvatore Mancuso and three other criminals, who have hijacked a school bus with a half-dozen children. With the help of his friend Commissioner Arpino, Betti discovers the four criminals' hideout, but to have the children released he has to let Mancuso and his accomplices escape. Some time later, Mancuso is burned to death in his car, two of his accomplices are apprehended by Betti and the third crashes his car into a tree in an attempt to escape. Convinced but with no evidence that the evil boss Jean Albertelli was the mastermind behind the kidnapping, Betti tails him, until — after a short stay in prison on charges of murder which have been pinned on him — the Commissioner finally gets to see his enemy dead, albeit at the hands of another criminal. However, soon after it's Betti's turn to fall dead in an ambush....

The third and last chapter in Commissioner Betti's trilogy, released just about four months after *Violent Naples*, *Special Cop in Action* saw the return of Marino Girolami behind the camera. The Italian title literally means "Hand-armed Italy," but the film was originally conceived as *Italia Violenta*, "Violent Italy" marking a crescendo from the first two films and thus implying that violence was spreading all over the country. The script, by Francesco Mannino, Gianfranco Clerici and Leila Bongiorno, has Betti move from Turin to Milan and then to Genoa, in a voyage through Italy's violent cities of the period: "Milan's always the same, huh?" "And even more filled with criminals!" states a line of dialogue. Franco Micalizzi's score also recycled a song from *Violent Naples*' soundtrack, Bulldog's *A Man Before Your Time*, in order to stress the red thread with the previous film.

Betti's biography undergoes small changes in *Special Cop in Action*: it's his father who has been killed by an underage robber (in *Violent Rome* it was his brother). As a cop, he's as smart as in *Violent Naples*, making his antagonists kill each other; but even more than in *Violent Naples* the character's dark soul is left behind by the emphasis on action scenes. Compared to *Violent Rome*, Girolami's direction is more assured and effective, with an exciting chase through Milan's Navigli canals that rivals a similar scene Fernando di Leo filmed for *Shoot First, Die Later*. Betti's status as a pure-hearted, sunnier hero is enforced right from the opening sequence, where he gets out of his house, with his jacket casually put over his shoulder, smiles at the sight of a bunch of kids playing soccer and starts playing with them. Betti is tolerant with petty thieves (such as purse snatcher Toni Ucci), even has a couple of humorous lines, and finds himself thinking about becoming a husband and raising a family, when he falls for the beautiful Luisa (Mirella D'Angelo, whose role in this film granted her a part in Tinto Brass' *Caligula*).

That's why the film's bleak ending — where Ray Lovelock's "vision" as seen in *Violent Rome* becomes finally and tragically real, as Betti is killed in the street before Luisa's eyes — is a punch in the audience's face, as the frame freezes in a grainy black-and-white that recalls news headlines. It scarcely matters that the ending was conceived by Girolami as a spite, after "his" character had been used in a film (*Violent Naples*) directed by another filmmaker: the umpteenth recreation of Commissioner Calabresi's tragic death shows once again that in 1976 Italy, as the country was undergoing one of the most terrible and bloody periods in its history, the motto "born to be a cop, born to die a cop" as uttered in *Violent Rome* was still tragically true.

Special Squad Shoots on Sight (*La polizia ordina: sparate a vista / Gördüğün Yerde Vur*)

D: Jerry Mason [Giulio Giuseppe Negri]. *S:* based on the novel by Giulio Giuseppe Negri; *SC:* Giulio Giuseppe Negri; *DOP:* Saverio Diamanti (35mm, Eastmancolor—Augustus Color); *M:* Marcello Gigante; *Mi succede da un po'* sung by Lydia Doliwer; *E:* Luigi Batzella; *PD:* Pasquale Mancino; *SO:* Alberto Vani; *Boom:* Rodolfo Montagnani; *Mix:* Renato Cadueri; *SetT:* Pasquale Mancino; *SS:* Roberto Carnicci. *Cast:* Beba Loncar (Jane), Tony Tiger [Irfan Atasoy] (Larry Foster), Gordon Mitchell (David), Jean-Pierre Blanchard, Cesare Nizzica, Albertina Capuani, Salvatore Carrara, Michele Leite Costa; Turkish version: Figen Han (Katy), Irfan Atasoy, Gordon Mitchell, Hakkı Koşar, Süleyman Turan, Birtane Güngör (Sonia, Larry's blonde lover), Kenan Pars (Chief of Police), Altan Günbay (Davis' bald henchman), Altan Bozkurt (Fred Ferguson), Jean-Pierre Blanchard, Beba Loncar. *PROD:* Fokus Film; *PM:* Bruno Vani. *Country:* Italy / Turkey. Filmed at Cave Film Studio (Rome) and on location in Istanbul. *Running time:* 85'; Visa no.: 68161 (03.30.1976); *Rating:* v.m.18; *Release date:* 04.01.1976; *Distribution:* Regional; *Domestic gross:* 184,585,270 lire. *Home video:* Alan Young (DVD, Italy).

Davis, the head of a gang that operates in Istanbul, is trying to take possession of two valuable statues of Buddha: the first is owned by private collector Barnes, the second by the local archaeological museum. To better succeed in his goal, Davis has his lover Jane seduce journalist Larry Foster, who's able to hypnotize people, in order to use Larry's powers to his advantage. After Davis' men kill Barnes, Larry, backed by his secretary Katy, refuses to go further: Davis then kidnaps his sister Suzy and blackmails him, with the help of Larry's lover Sonia. Undercover agent Fred Ferguson, who had joined Davis' gang, is killed during the robbery at the museum, but the police intervene. Davis and the other bandits die in the resulting shoot-out, while Larry escapes with the Buddha. Meanwhile Lucy has dispatched Sonia and taken the other Buddha: she shoots Jane and is about to do the same with Larry, but is killed by the police.

Starting since the mid–'70s, Italian producers began looking at Turkey as a profitable shooting location because of economical facilitations and minimal costs. What's more, financial deals were being set up, paving the way for co-productions which would feature Turkish cast and crew. The results were invariably slapdash low-budget affairs, often pairing Italian cinema "big" names whose star was waning with local film stars in order to get good results at local box offices. However, there was also room for more obscure, impenetrable ventures. Such is *Special Squad Shoots on Sight*: a low-par subproduction shot in Turkey starring Irfan Atasoy (credited as "Tony Tiger," again his character's name in *Four For All*), a popular Turkish actor and producer who was also the lead in *Four for All*. What is puzzling is the film's real nature: the title makes it look like a poliziotteschi, even though it's actually a pulp action/heist film, and according to the credits it was based on Giulio Giuseppe Negri's novel of the same name, which is unlikely to have really existed. However, since *Four for All*—also credited to Negri under the alias Jerry Mason in Italy—was actually a Turkish film directed by Yilmaz Atadeniz, which Negri only bought, retitled and distributed in Italy with his company Fokus Film, one wonders whether this also happened with *Special Squad Shoots on Sight*.

There's little to say about this little dismal film. The needlessly convoluted plot, atrocious acting and demented fight scenes are typical of so many Turkish film of the period, while the "International" names are the declining Yugoslavian beauty Beba Loncar and stone-faced Gordon Mitchell, here in his usual typecast bad guy role. Turkish sources—besides revealing the title *Gördüğün Yerde Vur*—don't help much, as the direction is credited to "Jerry Mason" or "Jery Manson," depending on the source. Besides the Turkish exteriors, according to the credits the film was shot at Gordon Mitchell's Cave Film Studio—a staple of many Z-grade Westerns and genre films of the period (mostly Demofilo Fidani ones)—which is debatable. As Mitchell himself explained, "I built a film studio in Rome and I did things people couldn't believe that I did, because no one would think. Here's a stupid American making a film studio. To make one you need to have all kinds of stuff according to the laws of the Italian government. And you must work in Italian film cities or laboratories that are recognized by the government and you have to stand up to all the rules and regulations, and la, la, and nobody thought I could do it. Well to cut the story short, I did it. You come shoot in my studio, you will get your money from the government. I mean they give you a percentage of your loan. You work in one of the studios recognized by the government."[1]

Note

1. See http://wconnolly.blogspot.it/2009/04/gordon-mitchell-on-demofilo-fidani-and.html.

Strange Shadows in an Empty Room (*Una Magnum Special per Tony Saitta*)

D: Martin Herbert [Alberto De Martino]. *S* and *SC:* Vincent Mann [Vincenzo Mannino], Frank Clark [Gianfranco Clerici]; *M:* Armando Trovajoli, conducted by the author (ed. Prima); *DOP:* Antony Ford [Aristide Massaccesi] (35mm, Panavision); *E:* Vincent P. Thomas [Vincenzo Tomassi]; *PD:* Michael Proulux; *CO:* Louise Jobin; *C:* Jean-Jacques Gervais; *AC:* Allan Smith; *AE:* Ivan Friends [Vanio Amici]; *2nd AE:* Maryse Dufresne; *AD:* Joe Douglas; *2nd AD:* Mireille Goulet; *2nd UD* for acrobatic scenes: Rémy Julienne; *2nd unit camera:* Ivanove Wladimir; *MU:* Henry Brown; *AMU:* Luiselle Champagne; *Hair:* Pierre David; *W:* Luc Leflaquais; *SO:* Patrick Rousseau; *Boom:* Normand Mercier; *KG:* Serge Grenier; *ChEl:* Jim Gray; *PrM:* Jacques Chamberland; *Asst. prop:* Leslie-France Calder; *MA:* Tom Sutton; *SS:* Monique Maranda. *Cast:* Stuart Whitman (Tony Saitta), John Saxon (Sergeant Ned Matthews), Martin Landau (dr. George Tracer), Tisa Farrow (Julie Foster), Carole Laure (Louise Saitta), Jean LeClerc (Robert Tracer), Gayle Hunnicutt (Margie Cohn), Jean Marchand, Anthony Forrest, Andrée St. Laurent, Peter Mac Neill, Julie Wildman, James Tapp, Jérôme Tiberghien, Terence G. Ross, Dave Nichols, Jene Chandler. *PROD:* Security Investment Trust co. (Panama), Edmondo Amati for Fida Cinematografica (Rome); *Delegate producer:* Robert Ménard; *PM:* Mychèle Boudrias; *APM:* Ginette Hardy; *PSe:* Monique Maranda; *PA:* Mario Nadeau. *Country:* Italy / Panama. Filmed in Ottawa and Montreal. *Running time:* 99'; Visa no.: 68091 (03.06.1976); *Rating:* not rated; *Release date:* 03.09.1976; *Distribution:* Fida; *Domestic gross:* unknown. *Also known as: Spécial Magnum* (France, 1976—100'); *Blazing Magnum* (UK), *Big Magnum 77* (Japan), *Feuerstoß* (West Germany), *Kafta magnum* (Greece), *O batsos me to magnum* (Greece—reissue title), *Sylkevä Magnum* (Finland), *The 44 Specialist* (Philippines—English title), *Tod im College* (East Germany—TV title). *Home video:* Fortune 5 (DVD,

USA — as part of the "Grindhouse Experience" 2 boxset — fullscreen, bad quality), Lions Gate (VHS, USA — as *Strange Shadows in an Empty Room*, 97'), Columbia (VHS, Japan — as *Blazing Magnum*), Mitel (VHS, Italy). OST: CD Beat Records CDCR 78.

Captain Tony Saitta of the Montreal police discovers that his sister Louise, who died suddenly during a party, was actually poisoned. The main suspect is Dr. Tracer, who had a somewhat ambiguous relationship with the young woman. Some time later, however, a new murder occurs: the victim was a transvestite, and in his bag the police recovers a picture of Louise, who carries around her neck a valuable necklace which had been stolen months before from a woman from Toronto, Mrs. Wilkinson, who was brutally murdered. Saitta, convinced that there is a definite link between the killing of his sister and the other two crimes, must admit to Tracer's innocence: then a new murder, followed by the suicide of the apparent culprit, suggests that the case is solved. But Saitta knows that this is not true. The solution to the mystery will make him discover a bitter truth: Mrs. Wilkinson was killed by Louise — a nymphomaniac who was being cured by Tracer — along with her boyfriend. The latter, for fear of being caught, decided to get rid of any possible trace of their crime, starting by killing Louise. Saitta sets up a trap for the murderer, and eventually kills him while he's escaping on helicopter.

Shot in Canada with an English-speaking cast led by a flabby-looking Stuart Whitman, Alberto De Martino's *Strange Shadows in an Empty Room* is essentially a whodunit of sorts, with the inclusion of the odd Argento-like detail such as Gayle Hunnicutt's murder in front of her blind friend played by Mia Farrow's sister Tisa (a character patently "borrowed" from Richard Fleischer's *Blind Terror*). "I had an old story called *D come Delitto* [M for Murder] and we rearranged it a bit. We shot it in Montreal. After we finished it, the French co-producer sent us a telegram 'It's got nothing to envy in any American film,'" De Martino claimed.[1]

Nevertheless *Strange Shadows in an Empty Room* deserves an entry in this book for a number of elements that make it a rather bizarre hybrid with the crime genre. Besides the title, which hints at American counterparts such as Ted Post's *Magnum Force* (which came out in Italy as *Una 44 Magnum per l'ispettore Callaghan*, "A 44 Magnum for Inspector Callaghan"[2]), and the presence of Whitman as a hard-boiled cop with an iron fist, the script by Vincenzo Mannino and Gianfranco Clerici opens with a tightly mounted bank robbery, where Vincenzo Tomassi's skills as an editor are fully displayed, and the film's central showpiece is a show-stopping car chase (coordinated and choreographed by Rémy Julienne) which lasts for about seven minutes and a half, and pulls out all the stops. Among other things, a motorcycle plows into the requisite pile of empty boxes, but one double jump is so impressive that it's shown four times from four different camera angles. The scene culminates with both cars leaping over a moving train, getting attacked, and then the chase continues through a rock quarry. The result is outstanding.

The sequence was actually shot by the film's director of photography Aristide Massaccesi (who does an outstanding job on the film, with his hand-held camera often making up for lack of dollies). Other scenes — such as the fight between Saitta and a trio of hulking transvestites who are well-versed in karate — go wildly over-the-top in a way no U.S. mainstream flick would, as does the climactic flashback murder that unveils the film's big plot twist (and in the meantime allows the viewers to get more than a glimpse of Carole Laure's body). As far as character development goes, Saitta is unlike the average Italian cops: he's older, tougher, meaner. He doesn't have any ideals of justice (he's moved only by the need to avenge his personal loss) and is refractory to any romanticism — even though he turns out to be helpless before the realization that his beloved dead sister was a maniac and a murderer, in a grimly ironic twist. "He does all the investigations he has to, even ruins some people to get to the truth, but in the end he discovers that his sister was the one responsible...." De Martino commented on the film's final revelation.[3] Even though the filmmaker wasn't apparently aware of this, the way Laure's character dominates the whole movie, even though she's essentially on screen for a few minutes at the beginning and end, recalls a typical *film noir* technique as shown in Otto Preminger's rendition of Vera Caspary's novel *Laura*.

The final scene is equally revelatory in displaying the character's unpleasantness and utter lack of ethics, as Saitta does not hesitate to shoot at a flying helicopter, making it collapse onto the ground — an act which would result in many victims — just to see the murderer die before his eyes.

Thanks also to Armando Trovajoli's highly enjoyable score, the result — even though it's got very little to do with Italian poliziotteschi of the period — is formally impeccable and definitely engrossing: De Martino was perhaps the least "Italian" of 1960s and 1970s genre filmmakers.

Notes

1. Gomarasca, "*Il cinema è quello che ci fa*," p. 12.
2. For obscure reasons, Clint Eastwood's character Harry Callahan became Callaghan in Italian prints.
3. Gomarasca, *Il cinema è quello che ci fa*, p. 12.

Street People (Gli esecutori)

D: Maurizio Lucidi. *S:* Gianfranco Bucceri, Roberto Leoni; *SC:* Ernest Tidyman, Randall Kleiser, Gianfranco Bucceri, Roberto Leoni, Nicola Badalucco, Maurizio Lucidi; *DOP:* Aiace Parolin (35mm, Techniscope, Technospes); *M:* Luis Enriquez Bacalov, conducted by the author (ed. Nazionalmusic — General Music); *E:* Renzo Lucidi; *PD:* Gastone Carsetti; *SD:* Luigi Urbani; *CO:* Adriana Spadaro; *C:* Luigi Filippo Carta; *AC:* Maurizio Cipriani, Massimo Carta; *AEs:* Paolo Lucidi, Simonetta Vitelli; *AD:* Mario Sacripanti, Franco Fantasia; *MU:* Cristina Rocca; *SO:* Bernardino Fronzetti; *Boom:* Armando Bondani; *SOE:* Luciano Anzellotti; *SE:* Celeste Battistelli; *SP:* Bruno Calvo; *STC:* Remo De Angelis; *KG:* Fernando Fusco; *ChEl:* Bruno Pasqualini; *Property masters:* Adriano Tiberi, Silvano Natali; *W:* Vera Cefarelli; *SS:* Maria Luisa Rosen; *UP:* Tonino Pinto. *Cast:* Roger Moore (Ulysses), Stacy Keach (Charlie Hanson), Ivo Garrani (Salvatore Francesco), Fausto Tozzi (Nicoletta), Ennio Balbo (Don Giuseppe Continenza "Joe"), Loretta Persichetti (Hannah), Luigi Casellato (Pete), Pietro Martellanza (Tano), Romano Puppo (Fortunato), Rosemarie Lindt (Salvatore's girlfriend), Aldo Rendine (Mayor Rocca), Salvatore Torrisi (Salvatore's henchman), Emilio Vale, Franco Fantasia (Father Domenico), Ettore Manni (Bishop Frank Lopetri). *Uncredited:* Salvatore Billa (Mafia thug who shoots at Ulysses), Giuseppe Castellano (Mafia thug who kills Pete), John Myhers (Francis), Sven Valsecchi (Ulysses as a child), Peter Pussateri. *PROD:* Manolo Bolognini and Luigi Borghese for Aetos Produzioni Cinematografiche; *EP:* Samuel Z. Arkoff; *EP:* Guglielmo Garroni; *PM:* Armando Todaro; *UM:* Carlo Giovagnorio, Salvatore Vizzini Bisaccia. *Country:* Italy. Filmed at Incir–De Paolis (Rome) and on location in San Francisco and

Agrigento. *Running time:* 105'; Visa no.: 68162 (03.24.1976); *Rating:* v.m.18; *Release date:* 03.30.1976; *Distribution:* Agora Cinematografica; *Domestic gross:* 458,097,620 lire. *Also known as: L'exécuteur* (Paris, 05.18.1977 —100') *Abrechnung in San Franzisko* (West Germany, 08.13.1976 —102')—*Street People* (1976 — 92'). *Home video:* Koch Media (DVD, Germany — English language), Lions Gate (VHS, Us), SSV-Video (VHS, Switzerland), Vestron (VHS, UK). OST: CD Avanz Records SP/CR-00013 (included in the compilation *Fantastico Bacalov!*).

San Francisco. Three Sicilians—Tano, Fortunato and Nicoletta—steal a large amount of heroin that was hidden in a huge wooden cross sent from Sicily as a gift from San Francisco drug boss Francesco Salvatore to the Italian fishermen in the city. Salvatore entrusts his nephew Ulysses to discover the perpetrators. A trip to Sicily allows Ulysses to identify the perpetrators of the theft and, upon returning to San Francisco, he tracks them with the help of his friend Charlie Hanson. The three robbers, however, are killed by mysterious assassins: Ulysses recovers the drugs and eventually finds out that his uncle was the mastermind behind it all: he also recalls an event from his childhood, when Salvatore had killed Ulysses' father before his very eyes, in Sicily. Ulysses confronts the "boss" and kills him, then he gets rid of the drugs.

Originally titled *La croce siciliana* (The Sicilian Cross), Maurizio Lucidi's *Street People* is an accomplished Mafia-action movie that works mainly as a vehicle for Roger Moore (here rather improbably cast as a Sicilian lawyer-cum-Mafia counselor) and Stacy Keach, whose chemistry on screen emulates that of Moore and Tony Curtis (whom Keach's character, a jackass race car driver, closely resembles) in the famous TV series *The Persuaders*. The mixture of violence and humorous interludes — such as the sequence where Keach "test-drives" a car through the streets of San Francisco, literally destroying it in the process — tries hard to make up for the story's shortcomings and convoluted plot twists: a hardly surprising result given the name of six screenwriters in the credits, including Academy Award winner Ernest Tidyman (*The French Connection*) and Randall Kleiser (director of *Grease* and *The Blue Lagoon* among others). As the "Evening Independent"'s film critic Jim Moorehead wrote, "The problem is that the story line makes very little sense. Same is true with the editing. Ditto the dialog."[1] However, Lucidi manages to create a few memorable images, such as the apparition of the wooden cross, an image perhaps reminiscent of the opening of Fellini's *La Dolce Vita* where a gigantic statue of Christ is carried over Rome by helicopters.

The result is quite odd: like Alberto de Martino's American-based films, *Street People* is not "Italian" enough to be called a poliziotteschi: the San Francisco locations, Anglo-Saxon leads and bland humor help it display an "international" look, and violence is rather restrained. Yet some of the pic's main assets are typical of Italian genre cinema, such as the overuse of the zoom lens and the odd subjective point of view shot, over-the-top car chases, the familiar genre faces — Ennio Balbo is memorable as the old godfather who likes to have his feet massaged by a naked girl, while Fausto Tozzi, Romano Puppo and Pietro Martellanza are a trio of dimwitted crooks — and most of all the soft-focus recurring flashback that eventually reveals a childhood trauma, punctuated by Luis Bacalov's score, in an open nod to Sergio Leone's films.

U.S. poster for *Street People* (1976).

The film was released by American International Pictures in the U.S., in a cut 92-minute version.

Note

1. Jim Moorhead,. "Street People' A Pizza Pap," *The Evening Independent*, 12.7.1976.

Terror in Rome (I violenti di Roma bene)

D: Segri & Ferrara [Sergio Grieco, Massimo Felisatti]. *S:* Massimo Felisatti, Luigi Mordini, Giuseppe Maggi; *SC:* Massimo Felisatti, Sergio Grieco; *DOP:* Sergio Martinelli (35mm, Eastmancolor, Telecolor); *M:* Lallo Gori, conducted by the author (ed. Nazionalmusic); *E:* Giancarlo Venarucci; *ArtD:* Mario Ciccarella; *APD:* Romano Crocetti; *C:* Silvio Fraschetti, Luigi Quattrini, Marco Sperduti; *AC:* Francesco Gargiulo; *AD:* Renzo Ragazzi, Emilio Mordini; *MU:* Sergio Angeloni, Vincenzo Napoli; *SO:* Giovanni Paba; *SE:* Basilio Patrizi; *SP:* Ettore Papaleo; *SS:* Daniele De Luca. *Cast:* Antonio Sabàto (Commissioner De Gregori), Pierre Marfurt (Stefano Donini), Cesare Barro (Bruno), Franca Gonella (Marco's sister), Pupo De Luca (Marshall Turrini), Gianluca Farnese (Marco Liberatori), Giuliana Melis (Giovanna), Giacomo Rossi-Stuart (Donini, Stefano's father), Bernard Berat, Fabio Polverini, Gloria Piedimonte (Elena, rape victim), Roberto Bianchetti, Raimondo Toscano, Raffaele Di Mario (Giuseppe Liberatori, Marco's father). *Uncredited:* Gabriella De Rosa (Bianca), Claudio Ruffini (Thug). *PROD:* David Film; *GM:* Gino Mordini; *PM:* Giuseppe Gargiulo; *PSu:* Sergio Bollino, Silvano Zignani; *PSe:* Eligio Coppotelli, Mario Binaglia. *Country:* Italy. Filmed at Cave Film Studio (Rome) and on location in Rome. *Running time:* 85'; Visa no.: 68796 (07.29.1976); *Rating:* v.m.18; *Release date:* 08.12.1976; *Distribution:* C.I.A.; *Domestic gross:* 518,107,310 lire. *Also known as: Violence For Kicks* (Holland — VHS title), *Kadun soturit* (Finland), *La Nuit des excitées* (France). *Home video:* Gb Video (VHS, Italy), Eagle6 (VHS, Holland).

Rome. The city is shocked by a series of vicious crimes: a girl is kidnapped and murdered in front of the school, and her two rescuers die in the conflagration of their car, while the carrier at the city's racetracks undergoes a robbery attempt. Commissioner De Gregori and his assistant Turrini suspect Stefano Donini, the son of a well-known engineer and the leader of a gang of upper-class boys which includes Marco and Bruno. When De Gregori, basing on faulty evidence, arrests the young man, Donini's father has him immediately released: the Commissioner is then repeatedly attacked by the trio. Even the killing of the young magistrate Gualandi, guilty of having Donini's father's buildings seized as they were built illegally, does not convince the investigating judge. But De Gregori finally achieves his goal to entrap Stefano, after the latter performs a robbery at the company where Marco's father is the guardian, kills the latter and seriously injures his friend. Stefano and Bruno pick up two girls, rape and murder them: but the Commissioner stops the young criminal for good.

Even though it blatantly takes inspiration from the same events — the "Circeo massacre" that took place in September 1975 — and carries a very similar Italian title (which translates as "The Violent Ones from Upper-Class Rome"), *Terror in Rome* is a more standard poliziotteschi compared to *I ragazzi della Roma violenta. D:* filmmaker Sergio Grieco — a veteran of '60s spy movies as well as adventure flicks — and novelist/scriptwriter Massimo Felisatti under the pseudonym Segri & Ferrara, the film focuses on the conflict between angry Commissioner De Gregori (a wooden Antonio Sabàto) and wealthy delinquent Stefano Donini (Pierre Marfurt), the leader of a youth gang that practices motocross and ultraviolence.

Sabato is the usual self-pitying cop with an unhappy girlfriend ("a cop is better lost than found" he justifies when duty calls), while Stefano quotes Nietzsche's notion of will to power and talks at length about the *Übermensch*: "There are three categories of men: worms, who can only crawl and lick other people's feet; slaves, who must obey because they have neither brain nor will; and the masters, who have the power and the strength." Stefano's delirious theories on the tripartition of humanity are another nod to the Circeo massacre: Angelo Izzo loved to expose his theories on men being divided in dominating, poor and lousy to his friends at the Tortuga Bar in Rome. When he's not philosophizing, Stefano sells heroin and assaults a young couple outside town, in what stands out as one of the most repellent sequences in Italian cinema of the period: before the inevitable gang-rape, the attackers disfigure the poor girl by repeatedly grating her face against a barbed-wire fence. The scene was somehow softened in the Italian version, with the addition of bogus foliage before the camera, whereas foreign-language copies retained the original sequence.

If Marfurt plays one of Italian cinema's most obnoxious villains, the filmmakers have little sympathy for his arrogant engineer father (Giacomo Rossi-Stuart, sadly far removed from his better days): as often with the genre, it's the class struggle that characterizes the juxtaposition between the poor but honest cop and the wealthy antagonist. However, if any attempt at sociological depth is purely pretextous, the film is so badly written and directed that it is hard to believe it came from such an experienced filmmaker as Grieco and a renowned writer as Felisatti.

To reach an acceptable running time, the story is stretched beyond belief. Besides a pointless sequence where Stefano and a drug dealer play dice — the prize is the latter's lover, who had previously taken her clothes off to show the "goods" — and a semi-documentary sequence featuring real newspaper headlines (including a priceless "We gang-raped the girl, all seven, under the influence of *Deep Red*") and off-screen voices of passers-by commenting on the wave of violence, there's even room for Sabàto's monologue on a classic poliziotteschi theme — the police have their hands tied — while hitting a punching ball. Sabàto's karate skills are also prominently featured in a ridiculously speeded up fight scene.

The *pièce de résistance* is saved for the climax: after a robbery has ended in blood, Stefano and his friend take two girls (Franca Gonella and Giuliana Melis — the latter played one of the victims in Pasolini's *Salò, or the 120 Days of Sodom*) to their countryside lair, where the expected rape and double murder takes place. Even though the opening line warns that characters and events as portrayed in the film are imaginary, Grieco and Felisatti fill the scene — shot with an abuse of wide-angle shots — with references to the Circeo massacre, such as the use of syringes (here filled with heroin) and the brutal beating with an iron bar. The two victims are then burned alive — or maybe not? Franca Gonella visibly moves while she is doused in petrol, but it may well be the umpteenth goof on the part of the filmmakers. The film's slovenliness must be seen to be believed: wrong editing cuts, offsynch voices, comically speeded up car chases. One understands why Grieco and Felisatti signed the film under pseudonyms.

On top of all this, the budget is so poor that *Terror In Rome* could well pass for a Turkish movie, as shown by the squalid interiors (including a hotel room standing in for a police station) and suburban exteriors. What's more, the police are nowhere to be found due to lack of extras: the only cops in sight are Sabàto and his assistant Pupo De Luca, while the car chases don't feature the usual Alfa Romeo Giulietta cars, but just a pair of badly patched-up scraps and a Fiat 500.

The film was released in France in 1979 as *La Nuit des excitées*, with additional sex scenes. Lallo Gori's horrid theme music would turn up again in *Return of the .38 Gang*.

L'unica legge in cui credo (The One Law I Believe In)

D: Claudio Giorgi [Claudio Giorgiutti]. *S:* Claudio Giorgi; *SC:* Giustino Caporali; *DOP:* Alvaro Lanzoni (35mm, Technicolor—Techniscope, Telecolor); *M:* I Meno Uno (ed. La Voce del Padrone); *E:* Piera Bruni, Gianfranco Simoncelli; *PD, CO:* Roberto Appodia; *COA:* Angelo Nacca; *C:* Paolo D'Ottavi; *AC:* Aldo Antonelli; *AD:* Giuliano Mancini; *MU:* Vittorio Biseo; *Hair:* Gabriella Zuccherini; *SO:* Luigi Groppo; *Boom:* Vincenzo Santangelo; *SE:* Gino Vagniluca; *SP:* Giancarlo Filoni; *KG:* Matteo Giordano; *ChEl:* Italo Postorino; *W:* Luciana Pianella; *ST:* Acrobatic Team; *SS:* Anita Borgiotti. *Cast:* Raika Juri (Wanda Villani), Claudio Giorgi (Walter Villani), Michela Roc [Bianca Maria Roccatani] (Ingrid), Frank O'Neil (Gianni Villani), Gianni Medici (Valerio Fratini), Jeff Blynn (Orlando), Rosalba Grottesi (Mabel), Claudio De Renzi (Commissioner Catalano), Laura Camilleri (Olga), Katiuscia [Caterina Piretti] (Giuliana Villani). *Uncredited:* Gordon Mitchell (Geo), Nello Pazzafini (Negro), Nando Sarlo (Commissioner's assistant), Seyna Seyn (Zael), Pietro Torrisi (Hitman). *PROD:* Dante Fava for Polo Film; *GM:* Gianni Di Clemente; *PSu:* Claudio Giorgi; *PSe:* Vincenzo Cartuccia. *Country:* Italy. Filmed at Cave Film Studio (Rome). *Running time:* 85'; Visa no.: 67678 (12.30.1975); *Rating:* v.m.14; *Release date:* 01.03.1976; *Distribution:* Regional; *Domestic gross:* 397,104,881 lire. *Home video:* General (VHS, Italy).

Near a polo field, a playboy named Valerio finds the body of 20-year-old Giuliana Villani, dead from a drug overdose. Giuliana had two brothers: the wealthy Gianni, who's married to Wanda, and the tormented Walter, a former mercenary in Africa who has become a painter. Since the police grope in the dark, Walter investigates the death of his beloved sister on his own. However, Walter finds out that all the girl's friends are implied in a drug ring: he is threatened, beaten up and survives a number of assaults, while all the witnesses are dispatched one by one. In the end, after defeating a whole gang of thugs, Walter finds out that the head of the organization is his own brother, who is killed by Wanda.

Quite a weird little oddity, Claudio Giorgi's obscure *L'unica legge in cui credo* features a cast almost exclusively made up of actors specialized in Lancio's "fotoromanzi" (photonovels), including director/star Giorgi (real name Claudio Giorgiutti), his wife Raika Juri, blonde beauties Michela Roc and the young Katiuscia and, last but not least, blonde mustached Jeff Blynn, a former fashion model who gained a certain notoriety because of his behavior on the catwalk. Blynn—here in his film debut—would briefly become one of the poliziotteschi's heroes, due to his resemblance to Maurizio Merli: he co-starred in Mario Caiano's *Weapons of Death* and Alfonso Brescia's *The New Godfathers* (not to mention Mario Landi's infamous sexploitation/gory whodunit *Giallo a Venezia*, 1979).

Given these qualities, it's hardly surprising that for the most part *L'unica legge in cui credo* looks just like that—a "fotoromanzo" in motion. Characters are laughably one-dimensional, with Giorgi making for an especially unbelievable *film noir* hero—a former mercenary, penniless but driving a Porsche, who drinks J&B straight from the bottle and is desperately devoid of any talent as a painter—and the acting is similarly wooden, while the dialogue is desperately inane, with such lines as "There must be some woman you don't know" "Sure, all the ugly ones" or "I don't like being a model, but you gotta do something for a living." All in all, the whole mood is that of a sturdy melodrama, with mild violence and chaste sex plus the occasional, half-hearted nods to the crime genre: however, the plot—which mixes bad whodunit elements with feeble action bouts—is very thin, with a police Commissioner who doesn't even move from his office desk. Anyway, things do speed up near the end with a passable car chase and a shoot-out in a village, where the hero confronts a whole gang of killers (including the ubiquitous Nello Pazzafini and Pietro Torrisi).

Music is on the syrupy-romantic side, while product placement is shameless, with plenty of J&B bottles and a whole scene—a publicity shoot—centered on a bottle of Fernet Branca liquor. As with many Z-grade Italian films of the period, *L'unica legge in cui credo* was shot at Gordon Mitchell's Cave Film Studio—Mitchell himself pops up in an uncredited cameo. Giorgi would direct a few more titles, often with the a.k.a. Claudio De Molinis, including *The Exhibitionist / A Man for Sale* (*Candido erotico*, 1978), *Tranquille donne di campagna* and the ghost comedy *C'è un fantasma nel mio letto* (1981).

Violent Naples (Napoli violenta)

D: Umberto Lenzi. *S* and *SC:* Vincenzo Mannino; *DOP:* Fausto Zuccoli, Sebastiano Celeste (35mm, Cinemascope, Eastmancolor, Technostampa); *M:* Franco Micalizzi, conducted by Alessandro Blonksteiner (ed. Prima); *A Man Before Your Time* (Lenzi, Valli, Micalizzi) is played by Bulldog; *E:* Vincenzo Tomassi; *PD, SD:* Giorgio Bertolini; *CO:* Silvana Scandariato; *C:* Guglielmo Vincioni, Giacomo Testa; *AC:* Enzo Frattari, Ivo Spila; *AE:* Vanio Amici, Armando Pace; *AD:* Filiberto Fiaschi; *MU:* Dante Trani; *Hair:* Marcello Longhi; *SO:* Raoul Montesanti; *Boom:* Alfonso Montesanti; *Mix:* Bruno Moreal; *SP:* Carlo Alberto Cocchi; *MA:* Riccardo Petrazzi; *SS:* Maria Luisa Merci. *Cast:* Maurizio Merli (Commissioner Betti), John Saxon (Francesco Capuano), Barry Sullivan ("'O Generale"), Guido Alberti (Chief of Police), Elio Zamuto (Franco Casagrande), Silvano Tranquilli (Paolo Gervasi), Maria Grazia Spina (Gervasi's wife), Pino Ferrara (Don Peppino, the garage owner), Attilio Duse (Antinori), Massimo Deda (Gennaro), Carlo Gaddi (Brigadeer Silvestri), Enrico Maisto (Poli, the bodyguard), Tommaso Palladino (Head racketeer), Carlos De Carvalho (Albini), Gabriella Lepori (Mugging victim), Franco Odoardi (De Cesare), Ivana Novak (Undercover cop), Riccardo Petrazzi (Thug), Luciano Rossi (Quasimodo), Nino Vingelli (Don Antonio Polipo), Vittorio Sancisi (Kidnapper), Domenico Di Costanzo (Bankrobber), Paolo Bonetti (Thief), Giovanni Cianfriglia (Maffei, the bodyguard), Fulvio Mingozzi (police inspector Mingozzi), Pierangelo Civera (Brigadeer Battisti), Ivano Silvari, Marzio Honorato (Franchetti), Gennaro Cuomo (Victim), Domenico Messina. *Uncredited:* Nestore Cavaricci (policeman), Domenico Cianfriglia (Attacker), Mario Deda (police agent), Ottaviano Dell'Acqua (Undercover cop), Roberto Dell'Acqua (Car thief), Vincenzo Falanga

(Man at dinner table), Tom Felleghy (Inspector in Genoa), Franco Marino (Robber at Assecurancy), Edoardo Mascia (Man at dinner table), Benito Pacifico (Thug), Sergio Testori (Racketeer). *PROD:* Paneuropean Production Pictures; *GO:* Fabrizio De Angelis; *PM:* Sergio Borelli; *PI:* Lamberto Palmieri; *PSe:* Bruno Gallo, Lucia Nolano; *ADM:* Benito Mancini. *Country:* Italy. Filmed at Rizzoli-Palatino studios (Rome) and on location in Naples. *Running time:* 95'; Visa no.: 68834 (07.29.1976); *Rating:* v.m.14; *Release date:* 08.07.1976; *Distribution:* Fida Cinematografica; *Domestic gross:* 2,046,936,220 lire. *Also known as: Death Dealers* (UK), *Camorra—Ein Bulle räumt auf* (West Germany), *Opération casseurs* (Canada), *S.O.S jaguar: Opération casseurs* (France). *Home video:* Federal (DVD, Italy), PopFlix (DVD, USA—as part of the "Mafia Kingpin" 2DVD collection). OST: CD Beat Records CDCR 79.

Transferred to Naples, where the local boss of the underworld "'O Generale" rules, Commissioner Betti employs his usual unorthodox methods to fight crime, supported by a team of special agents. Despite the cowardly silence of Dr. Gervasi, Betti sheds light on the case of the rape suffered by Gervasi's wife. Then, breaking into the house of the fence "'O Polipo," the Commissioner arrests a thief. Betti sets up a trap against the racket by reopening a garage burned by the thugs and putting one of his agents as the manager. Teased by a ferocious gangster named Casagrande, Betti prevents the latter's next hit and arrests him after a spectacular chase throughout the city. However, the Commissioner fails to incriminate "'O Generale." But in the end he comes up with the usual unpredictable tactic: spying on the boss while he is about to execute a corrupt entrepreneur named Capuano, Betti kills the mobster, and frames Capuano for the murder.

The second part in Commissioner Betti's trilogy, *Violent Naples* stands out as one of the most popular and successful Italian crime films of the decade. With a gross of over two billions lire, it was the genre's best box office result in 1976—even outgrossing Francesco Rosi's *Illustrious Corpses*. Accordingly, a remarkable part of the profits (over 169 million, about twice as much as in Rome) were grossed just in Naples. As will happen with Mario Merola's films, the emphasis on the product's regional—even urban—delimitation became a lure for audiences and a way to stop the hemorrhage of audiences that was plaguing Italian cinema.

Lenzi recalls the film's phenomenal success with an anecdote: "We arrived in Naples on August 23rd for the film's premiere [...]. The city was deserted, and since it was lunchtime we went to eat with Fida's local distributor. At about three o'clock, while we were finishing eating, there was a call from the distributor's secretary who told him: "Look, there's the police here, and the Chief wants to talk to you!" The distributor got to the phone and was informed that a crowd had gathered outside the theater and was trying to get in, at all costs. It was 3:30 P.M., mid-August, hot as hell, and people were fighting in the middle of the street to see *Violent Naples*. [...] So we were immediately given another theater to get as many people as possible."[1]

Despite the harsh—and at times obtuse—criticism (one negative review culminated in the phrase "Seen one, seen all"[2]) *Violent Naples* is one of the more accomplished examples of poliziotteschi. The episodic structure is borrowed from *Violent Rome*, but Vincenzo Mannino's script aptly tightens the action around a more focused plot, while Lenzi's direction is first-rate, only occasionally falling into awkwardness—as in the speeded up motorbike chase near the beginning. The director's flair for over-the-top violence comes out in the scene where Elio Zamuto's character pushes a girl's face outside the cable railway cabin while another one is arriving, with gruesome effects, while in another scene Sullivan crushes a cop's skull with a bowling ball.

However, besides its strong spectacular qualities, *Violent Naples* is perhaps more interesting in the way it deals with its urban setting, exposing the crucial relationship between Italian crime cinema and its environment. Unlike the "*guapparia* movies" starring Mario Merola, which would become a popular subgenre within a couple of years, *Violent Naples* doesn't use the parthenopean setting as a "place where ancestral identities block the path of modernity."[3] Right from the opening credits, with Franco Micalizzi's electrically rearranged *tarantella* accompanying the image of Barry Sullivan's car driving along Naples' "Spaccanapoli" (the street that divides the city in half, separating North from South), Lenzi's Naples is in all respects a metropolis where tradition and progress coexist, in a difficult and contradictory manner, both urbanistically and culturally.

The map of the underworld is stratified as well, just like the trio of antagonists that Betti has to face. There's the old school guappo "'O Generale" (Barry Sullivan), who nevertheless is far from Mario Merola's pietistic characterizations, and represents the traditional underworld of racket extortions and "warnings" to nosy cops; there's the seedy entrepreneur Capuano (John Saxon) who walks the thin line between legality and illegality; and there's the well-dressed Franco Casagrande (Elio Zamuto) who moves and acts like American gangsters, and who's as cruel

Director Umberto Lenzi, center, and Maurizio Merli, right, on the set of *Violent Naples* (1976).

and ruthless as he is showy in his target choices and in the alibis he fabricates for himself. He is also the protagonist of the film's centerpiece, the spectacular chase on the Montesanto cable railway, which Lenzi shoots as if it was a Western, with Maurizio Merli jumping on the top of the moving cabin where Casagrande took refuge just like a cowboy would do with a quartet of galloping horses.

"To me, being a cop is a reason for living," Merli says in one of the film's most significant lines. Compared to *Violent Rome*, Betti here is a Solomonic figure who administers justice according to his own rules. As the "scugnizzo" Gennarino[4] says, "a Commissioner's job is to defend the people," no matter how. Besides chasing, shooting, fistfighting, Betti also plays cunningly, setting up Machiavellian traps for his enemies. For Betti the ends always justify the means, as shown by the final sequence on the Nisida dock, where the Commissioner becomes a hitman, killing "'O Generale" and pinning the murder on Capuano. That's the law according to poliziotteschi.

Notes

1. Gomarasca, *Umberto Lenzi*, p. 230.
2. Vice, *Il Lunedì*, 8.25.1976.
3. Giona A. Nazzaro, "Napoli, curtiello cu curtiello," in Aa. Vv., *Catalogo Noir in Festival 1997* (Rome: Fahrenheit 451, 1997), p. 57.
4. Gennarino—the little orphan who becomes like a stepson to the Commissioner—would become a recurring character in Naples-based crime films, such as Mario Caiano's *Weapons of Death*.

Young, Violent, Dangerous (Liberi armati pericolosi)

D: Romolo Girolami [Romolo Guerrieri]. *S:* Fernando di Leo, based on Giorgio Scerbanenco's short stories *Bravi ragazzi bang bang* and *In pineta si uccide meglio*; *SC:* Fernando di Leo, Nico Ducci; *DOP:* Erico Menczer (35mm, Eastmancolor, Staco Film); *M:* Gianfranco Plenizio, Enrico Pieranunzi (ed. Nazionalmusic); *E:* Antonio Siciliano; *PD:* Francesco Cuppini; *APD:* Sandro Bellomia; *CO:* Giulia Mafai; *COA:* Mirella Novelli; *C:* Roberto Brega; *AE:* Giancarlo Morelli; *AD:* Renzo Spaziani [Renzo Girolami]; *MU:* Lamberto Marini, Franco Di Girolamo; *Hair:* Jolanda Angelucci; *SO:* Alberto Salvatori, Luciano Colombo; *Mix:* Franco Bassi; *ST:* Doru Dumitrescu; *SS:* Silvia Petroni; *UP:* Lucia Lo Russo. *Cast:* Tomas Milian (Commissioner), Eleonora Giorgi (Lea), Stefano Patrizi (Mario Farra "Blond"), Max Delys (Luigi Morandi), Benjamin Lev (Giovanni Etrusco "Giò"), Venantino Venantini (Mr. Morandi), Salvatore Billa (Forger), Antonio Guidi, Diego Abatantuono (Lucio), Luciano Baraghini, Ruggero Diella (Supermarket robber), Giorgio Locuratolo (Lucio's friend), Valeria Gagliardi, Gloria Piedimonte (Lucio's friend), Tom Felleghy (Prof. Farra), Maria Rosaria Riuzzi (Lucio's friend), Carmelo Reale (Forger), Peter Berling (Oberwald), Omero Capanna (police agent), Flora Carosello (Morandi's cleaning woman), Cesare Di Vito (police agent). *PROD:* Marcello Partini and Ermanno Curti for Centro di Produzioni Città di Milano, Staco Film; *EP:* Armando Novelli; *PM:* Michele Germano; *PSu:* Francesco Vitulano; *PSe:* Piero Ballirano; *CASH:* Vincenzo Samà. *Country:* Italy. Filmed at Elios Film (Milan) and on location in Milan and Pavia. *Running time:* 100'; Visa no.: 68963 (09.02.1976); *Rating:* v.m.18; *Release date:* 09.02.1976; *Distribution:* Interfilm; *Domestic gross:* 856,779,300 lire. *Also known as: Les féroces* (Paris, 12.11.1985—95'), *Juventud armada peligrosa* (Spain). *Home video:* Raro (DVD, Italy). OST: CD Beat Records CDCR 80.

The "Blond," Giò and Luigi, three middle class Milanese youths, rob a gas station, leaving four dead behind them, including two policemen. Then they assault a bank, killing two more people. Finally, it's time for a supermarket, which they raid with a group of friends whom they dispatch after the robbery. As the police block all the exits from Milan, the Blond—who has forced Luigi's girlfriend Lea to join them—tries to obtain false passports but to no avail. The police finally manage to catch the three criminals, but an accident cuts off the chase. Leaving their stolen car behind, the Blond and his friends avoid the checkpoints by escaping through the fields, until they stumble upon two campers whom they try to rob and then kill. Meanwhile, the police have unleashed the dogs. Giò, who has been left behind by his companions, is killed by the police dogs while the Blond escapes in the car with Luigi (Lea, thanks to her boyfriend, has been released). The police are blocking the highway, and the Blond forces Luigi at gunpoint to drive at full speed towards the cops, but Luigi makes a sharp steer and drives the car down a suspended bridge.

When the father (Venantino Venantini) of one of three youngsters who left a trail of blood throughout Milan justifies his scarce attention towards his son with his working commitments ("I either look after them or provide for them"), the Commissioner (Tomas Milian) who's questioning him can't hold an outburst of anger: "Does one thing exclude the other? Do you feed kids or love them? [...] I might come across as being rhetorical, but when you choose to have children you're taking on a responsibility—not responsibilities like a car, clothes, a maid or that bullshit. I'm talking about moral responsibilities, the simplest ones like talking are often the most difficult. Talking to your children, listening to them.... When you don't talk, the problems start. The weakest ones use drugs, the more violent and disturbed ones start killing people for no reason.... If your son is a monster, it's your fault for not having given him the necessary love and support!"

Such dialogue sounds weird in the context—aren't we watching a violent crime drama about a trio of "rabid dogs" who rob gas stations, banks and supermarkets, killing with no hesitations or remorse? Of course we are, but given the names on the script and behind the camera, the result is quite different from the excessive, sleazy contemporaries such as *Terror in Rome* or *I ragazzi della Roma violenta*. First of all, even though the themes and timing render it similar to the aforementioned titles, *Young, Violent, Dangerous* actually has a prestigious literary source: Fernando di Leo's script takes inspiration from Giorgio Scerbanenco's short stories, namely *Bravi ragazzi bang bang* (the opening scene with Eleonora Giorgi at the police station and the robbery at the gas station that ends in blood) and *In pineta si uccide meglio* (the massacre of the German campers), both included in the short stories collection *Milano calibro 9*.

As shown by the dialogue between Milian and Venantini, the ideological approach is also quite different from what we've come to expect from a 1970s Italian crime film. Di Leo's ambition is to draw a sociological portrayal of youth malaise: an approach similar to Lizzani's *San Babila 8 P.M.* (although Romolo Guerrieri's direction is obviously closer to genre's trappings) which is, to di Leo, the chance to return to themes that the filmmaker already explored in *Naked Violence*.

However, on this occasion di Leo's pen is less caustic than elsewhere, and *Young, Violent, Dangerous* suffers from overtly didactic dialogue: too many things are explained and underlined, as if the filmmaker and scriptwriter were afraid that the audience wouldn't get them, while the film's best moments are those where reticence prevails. Take the relationship between the introverted Luigi (Max Delys) and the "Blond" (Stefano Patrizi): a mixture of attraction, hatred and emulation, which likely implies an untold homosexual bond, that stuns and disgusts Luigi' girlfriend (Eleonora Giorgi), who is forced to join the trio in an impossible escape through the Lombard countryside. The ensuing sexual tension somewhat predates di Leo's claustrophobic crime drama *Madness* (1980). In the film's second half— in a move that's quite bold for the genre — di Leo and Guerrieri run away from the cities and have the characters move through huge open spaces, the plains, fields and trees that were erased from urban poliziotteschi. Up to a desperate, self-destructive ending that's one of the best sequences in Italian crime cinema.

Another interesting trait is the script's self-reflective quality: one bit of dialogue has Giovanni (Benjamin Lev) put together an amazing number of lines, in-jokes, quotes and references to other crime films (something similar happened in the Italian Western with Sergio Corbucci's *Bandera Bandits*, 1972) while di Leo pays homage to his own *The Italian Connection* in the scene set in the junkyard, where the youngsters kill two thugs.

The cast is very interesting. The French Max Delys, a former model in Lancio photonovels who would die a few years later, gives the film's best performance as the tormented Luigi, while Benjamin Lev (an actor who knew a short-lived popularity by the end of the previous decade after his debut in Gianni Puccini's *I sette fratelli Cervi*) was arrested during shooting for his presumed implication in drug dealing: according to Guerrieri, most of his scenes had to be shot with a double. Tomas Milian is more restrained than usual as the humane Commissioner. "When I called Tomas to play the commissioner I struggled to convince him to play the role with his face, his hair, his looks, without any makeup" Guerrieri recalled. "That was a time when Tomas loved to disguise himself: he just played 'Monnezza' [...]. I remember we were at his place — he had a beautiful house — in a room full of mirrors. I combed his hair back and told him: 'Look how handsome you are! I really can't see why you couldn't play this character without makeup, like in all the films you have done in the past.'"[1]

Maurizio Merli, right, beating up a thug in *Violent Naples* (1976).

Young, Violent, Dangerous also marked the film debut of one of Italy's most popular actors of the following decades, Diego Abatantuono, here in a bit role as one of the trio's friends.

Note

1. Manlio Gomarasca and Davide Pulici, "Romolo Guerrieri. L'intimismo del genere," in Aa. Vv., "Controcorrente 2: Percorsi alternativi," *Nocturno Dossier* #30 (January 2005), p. 48.

1977

La banda Vallanzasca (The Vallanzasca Gang)

D: Mario Bianchi. *S* and *SC:* Vito Bruschini, Mario Bianchi; *DIA collaboration:* Claudio Fragasso; *DOP:* Maurizio Centini (35mm, Vistavision, Stacofilm); *M:* Giampaolo Chiti (Ed. Nido); *E:* Cesare Bianchini; *W:* Zaira Gibini; *STC:* Gilberto Galimberti; *ST:* Domenico Scola; *MU:* Silvana Petri; *Mix:* Alberto Tinebra. *Cast:* Enzo Pulcrano (Roberto), Stefania D'Amario (Antonella Ferreri), Antonella Dogan (Sandra), Gianni Diana (Italo), Franco Garofalo (Pino), Paolo Celli (Armando), Liliana Chiari (Caterina), Enrico Maisto (Enrico Salerno), Franco Marino (Franco Galogero). *Uncredited:* Gilberto Galimberti, Sergio Testori, Mario Bianchi (killer), Claudio Fragasso (policeman). *PROD:* Mauro Vigneti for Canadian International Films; *AP:* Vito Alescio; *PM:* Pelio Quaglia. *Country:* Italy. Filmed at Chiaramonte Quagli (Sicily). *Running time:* 100': Visa no.: 71258 (12.15.1977); *Rating:* v.m.18; *Release date:* 12.15.1977; *Distribution:* Lark Cinematografica; *Domestic gross:* 134,486,000 lire. *Home video:* Silma, GVR (VHS, Italy). *OST:* CD Digitmovies CDDM180.

Having escaped from prison so as not to be framed for a murder he did not commit, bank robber Roberto is hired by a mysterious criminal organization. By ensuring that police and press alike pin him with the murder of two Mafia bosses, the heads of the gang give him the sinister label of "Public Enemy No. 1." Then Roberto is entrusted with a kidnapping, whose victim is young Antonella Ferreri, daughter of a famous oil magnate. Unlike the other captors, Roberto behaves humanely with the girl, but when he discovers that his accomplices want to exclude him from the parting of the ransom, he decides to use Antonella as a weapon to blackmail the gang. He flees, forcing Antonella to follow him, but members of the organization — whose true aim is to exasperate the public opinion and encourage the overthrow of democracy — get to them and both are killed.

Renato Vallanzasca's deeds seemingly inspired Mario Bianchi's *La banda Vallanzasca* — or at least that's what one might think by looking at its title (literally, The Vallanzasca Gang). However, despite such an eloquent statement, the name Vallanzasca is never spelled in the film, not even once. In an attempt to avoid legal problems, the main character's name becomes Roberto, and the script liberally manipulates the bandit's true story. Unlike Vallanzasca, Roberto escapes from prison by sheer chance, and finds himself enrolled in a powerful secret organization that uses him to perform robberies and kidnappings. The film's storyline also features a love story between the criminal and one of his victims, just like the one between Vallanzasca and heiress Emanuela Trapani, at least according to tabloids. Eventually, scriptwriters Antonio Cucca and Claudio Fragasso even throw in a political subplot, perhaps inspired by Vallanzasca's allegedly true encounter with a right-wing politician who, according to the bandit, wanted him to become part of the "Strategy of Tension," as explained in the film's closing dialogue:

"We're almost like South America. Our country is detaching more and more from the rest of Europe."

"Same as Uruguay in 1973…"

"Indeed. A corrupt government, a strong Left, clandestine organizations that get more and more daring, the public opinion unsettled by murders and kidnappings such as these, the exorbitant rise of the cost of living. First came the special laws, then the army intervened in public order service, eventually the Strong Man appeared…."

However, according to the director, "Handsome René" was rather pleased with the film; even more pleased, undoubtedly, were Italian J&B wholesalers, as the film features a shameless amount of plugs for the yellow-labeled whiskey brand.

La banda Vallanzasca's only value is that of a document of its era, and especially as an example of extremely low-budget filmmaking, whose results were destined to marginal distribution and scarce box office grossings. As Bianchi recalls, "We shot the film in Chiaramonte Gulfi, a small village in Sicily. We left Rome — and may I never get up from this chair if I'm telling a lie — in an old Citroen […]. We had the back seats removed, and there were 10 or 12 of us in that car. Enzo Pulcrano followed us on his Mini with his girlfriend, who played the kidnapped girl [Stefania D'Amario, Ed.]. It looked like a hearse (laughs) and we had a cot where we lay for a couple of hours each during this trip which was seemingly never-ending."[1] The budget was so tight that Bianchi had to shoot it entirely with film leftovers: "I did *La banda Vallanzasca* with 15–30 feet long film segments…. I used to say: "We have to shoot a close-up of him"…. "Ok, then put 15 feet into the cartridge" … we spent more time trying to get something to eat than shooting stuff!"[2]

The cast, led by former prizefighter Enzo Pulcrano (seen in Marcello Zeani's *A pugni nudi*, Fernando di Leo's *Kidnap Syndicate* and *Mr. Scarface*, Ruggero Deodato's *Live Like a Cop, Die Like a Man*), who also managed to get the film made through his friendship with producer Mauro Vigneti, is similarly slapdash: Antonella Dogan was cast because she was Vigneti's wife. And the dialogue is often outrageously bad. In the opening scene in the prison's parlor, one convict urges his mother to prostitute herself in order to pay for a lawyer, while a scene between Pulcrano and his lover, after a shoot-out with the police, contains the unforgettable exchange that follows:

"What happened?"

"Nothing exceptional, something that happens every day. I killed two cops."

"You're born a winner!"

"Sure. And now I want to make love. I always get turned on, afterwards…."

Note

1. Stefano Ippoliti, Matteo Norcini and Franco Grattarola, "Mario Bianchi: 'Il mio cinema pizza e fich,'" *Cine 70 e dintorni* #5 (Summer 2004), p. 25.
2. *Ibid.*

Beast with a Gun (*La belva col mitra*)

D: Sergio Grieco. *S* and *SC:* Sergio Grieco; *DIA:* Enzo Milioni; *DOP:* Vittorio Bernini (35mm, Gevacolor, Telecolor); *M:* Umberto Smaila, conducted by Gilberto Ziglioli (Ed. National Music); *E:* Francesco Bertuccioli, Adalberto Ceccarelli; *PD:* Lucia Terzuolo; *CO:* Patricia Merluzzi; *C:* Roberto Nappa; *AC:* Antonio Tonti; *AD:* Enzo Milioni; *MU:* Carlo Sindici; *Hair:* Mauro Galati; *Mix:* Bruno Moreal; *W:* Renata Morroni; *SE:* Aldo Gasparri; *KG:* Tarcisio Diamanti; *ChEl:* Ernesto Carlesco; *PrM:* Italo Tranquilli; *MA:* Antonio Basile; *SS:* Ellen Kaufmann; *DubD:* Cesare Barbetti; Unit *P:* Edilio Kim. *Cast:* Helmut Berger (Nanni Vitali), Marisa Mell (Giuliana Carolli), Richard Harrison (Commissioner Giulio Santini), Marina Giordana (Carla Santini, Giulio's sister), Gigi Bonos (Pappalardo), Vittorio Duse (Giuliana's father), Ezio Marano (Barbareschi), Claudio Gora (Ruggero Santini, Giulio's father), Alberto Squillante (Aldo Spaccesi "Bimbo"), Maria Pascucci (Rosa Vitali, Nanni's sister), Giovanni [Nello] Pazzafini (Pietro Caporali), Antonio Basile (Mario Portesi), Sergio Smacchi (Bruno Esposito). *PROD:* Armando and Francesco Bertuccioli for Supercine; *PM:* Silvano Zignani; *PSe:* Amedeo Segatori. *Country:* Italy. Filmed at I.C.E.T. De Paolis (Milan) and on location in and around Ancona. *Running time:* 94': Visa no.: 70991 (10.25.1977); *Rating:* v.m.18; *Release date:* 10.29.1977; *Distribution:* C.I.A.; *Domestic gross:* 413,891,000 lira. *Also known as: Ultime violence* (Belgium), *Der Tollwütige, Du brutales Schweinl* (West Germany), *Der Wilde* (East Germany — TV title), *The Mad Dog Killer* (DVD title), *Street Killers, The Human Beast* (USA), *Veszett kutya* (Hungary). *Home video:* Surf Video / Hobby & Work (DVD, Italy), Starz / Anchor Bay (DVD, USA), Blue Underground (DVD, USA — as *Mad Dog Killer*).

A cruel murderer, Nanni Vitali, escapes from jail with three accomplices. Vainly chased by Commissioner Giulio Santini, who only succeeds in killing the gang's driver, Vitali retaliates by brutally murdering a police informer, then raping and abducting the latter's lover Giuliana. The woman, however, reveals to Santini that Vitali is going to use her in a robbery. The commissioner then sets a trap on Vitali but, again, only manages to capture the bandit's accomplices. After an unsuccessful attempt at killing Giuliana, Vitali kidnaps Santini's elderly father and sister with the help of a young robber: the tragic events end with the capture of Vitali and the release of the hostages.

There's a scene in Quentin Tarantino's *Jackie Brown* (1997) where the perpetually stoned crackheads Louis Gara (Robert De Niro) and Melanie (Bridget Fonda), while channel surfing in the house of arms smuggling boss Ordell Robbie (Samuel L. Jackson), get to a scene from a crime film, starring a blonde actor with a ferocious grin. "Who's that — Rutger Hauer?" Ordell asks, stopping by. "No, that's Helmut Berger," the blonde girl replies in a surprising bout of cinephile awareness. That's Berger indeed, and the film is Sergio Grieco's *Beast with a Gun*.

To understand *Beast with a Gun*, once again one has to dwell into Italy's 1970s true crime events. Renato Vallanzasca, nicknamed "il bel René" (handsome René) was an infamous bandit who monopolized newspaper headlines in the 1970s. In many respects, he was to the decade what bandit Luciano Lutring (portrayed on screen in Carlo Lizzani's *Wake Up and Kill*, 1966) was to the previous one. Blond, blue-eyed, good-looking and cocky, since he was just 20 in the late '60s Vallanzasca was already a crime boss, the head of the Comasina gang. Handsome René loved luxury and the good life, and had a lavish apartment in Milan where he lived with his girlfriend. Then, on February 28, 1972, a couple of weeks after a robbery in a supermarket, Vallanzasca was arrested. He remained in jail for four and a half years, during which he took part in many revolts, and prepared his escape. He got away from the prison's infirmary — where he was hospitalized because of hepatitis that he managed to contract all by himself through the drinking of rotten eggs and urine — on July 28, 1976, gathered his old acolytes and resumed the old habits: seventy robberies performed from late summer 1976 to February 1977.

Meanwhile Vallanzasca became a sort of movie star. Scandal tabloids put him on their covers, a lot of women wrote him love letters. And he jumped on the momentum gained through all this, by giving exclusive interviews and playing with his image of Public Enemy number one. After a failed heist at Milan's tax collection office where René's right-hand man Mario Carluccio was killed, Handsome René moved on to kidnappings: four in four months, from November '76 to January '77. The most notorious was the kidnapping of young Emanuela Trapani, whose ransom netted Vallanzasca one billion lira — and newspapers gave ample room to the alleged love story between the heiress and the gallant blue-eyed kidnapper, providing Vallanzasca with even more headlines. "If as a gangster Vallanzasca had already become a major name in the crime news section, with that kidnapping he also become a protagonist in the gossip pages, blending the myth of the ferocious gangster and that of the romantic bandit: ruthless yet a gentleman, capable of shooting as well as loving, tying his victim's wrists but feeding her oysters and champagne."[1] Vallanzasca's days were numbered, though: he was arrested in his lair on February 14, 1977 — quite fittingly, on Valentine's Day.

Released in October 1977, *Beast with a Gun* carried its patent inspiration on its sleeve. The film's poster played it unfairly: "Although the action's violent dramatic tones may recall it, any reference to the VALLANZASCA CASE [in capital letters, Authors' note] is purely casual." Sure.

Anyway, there's little of Handsome René's true story in Grieco's film — one of the most extreme and violent products of that decade's Italian crime cinema. The plot focuses on the duel between honest commissioner Santini (Richard Harrison) and an evil bandit, Nanni Vitali (Helmut Berger), Public Enemy no.1, who escapes from jail, exacts revenge on an informer who betrayed him and takes the latter's woman, Giuliana (Marisa Mell) with him. Despite Giuliana revealing Nanni's hideout, Santini proves to be helplessly inept, letting the bandit escape. Vitali retaliates by kidnapping the commissioner's father and sister, for the harrowing climax.

Besides the insistence on over-the-top violence, which culminates in the hallucinatory sequence where the informer is beaten to a bloody pulp, buried alive and covered with quicklime, *Beast with a Gun* heavily relies on its titular villain as played by the Austrian actor, whose career was rapidly going downhill in those days. After Luchino Visconti's death, Berger — who had been the director's lover for years, in an almost marriage-like relationship — became desperate not knowing what to do with his professional and personal life. This was made worse by the fact that Visconti did not make a testament during his lifetime, so Berger did not inherit anything from the director's estate and the Visconti family dropped him after the funeral.

The identification between Vallanzasca and Berger goes beyond the (debatable) physical resemblance or the bandit's deeds as portrayed (unfaithfully) on screen. In Berger's stare, "so intense that it borders on mental dissociation," as one critic defined it,[2] one can already read the inevitable decline of a whole productive system. And Berger's Dorian Gray–like face, beautiful yet already corrupted by B-movie practices, is the irresistible force that propels Grieco's camera, which lingers on those green eyes for seemingly endless periods, literally stopping the narration dead in its tracks for what the renowned Italian film critic Paolo Mereghetti described as moments of "almost zen-like suspension."[3]

It's for and through Helmut Berger that *Beast with a Gun* finds its reason to exist as a movie, in the way it sadistically soils Visconti's Ludwig, having him bare his ass and copulate on screen with his then real-life lover Marisa Mell in the film's extended rape set-piece. In Grieco's film, Berger looks like an evil king surrounded by a court of low-lifes, including such familiar faces as Nello Pazzafini and Richard Harrison. The former was perhaps Cinecittà's most famous "generico," popping up in virtually any genre film since the early 1960s, almost always as the muscular thug who gets beaten up or shot; Harrison, on the other hand, had been a regular in a number of James Bond rip-offs, and was another loser as well. After being one of the actors considered for the role that eventually went to Clint Eastwood in Sergio Leone's *A Fistful of Dollars*, in the following decade Harrison lost another ticket to celebrity. He was on the verge of becoming the poliziotteschi's most famous hero when the producers of *Violent Rome* considered him — blond, handsome, mustached, with a passing resemblance to Franco Nero — for the role of Commissioner Betti, which eventually went to Maurizio Merli. Harrison's career would spiral down to oblivion in fourth-grade co-productions made on a shoestring, between Italy and Turkey (*Four for All*) and obscure cop flicks.

On *Beast with a Gun*, in a bitterly ironic retaliation, Harrison has to play a role that was obviously written with Merli in mind, and his wild final brawl with Berger looks like a fight for survival within the dying B-movie environment. The winner, in Grieco's estimation, is Berger: the film ends on the umpteenth close-up of his face soiled with mud and blood, accompanied by Umberto Smaila's music. That's why *Beast with a Gun* truly deserves its cult reputation: for the way it settles scores with an era, dissipating the credibility of a star in disarray and bringing to an end the career of its veteran director. *Beast with a Gun* would be his last film, as Grieco would die in 1982. Tarantino's affectionate in-joke sounds like a fond requiem for a whole season in Italian cinema — ugly, dirty and mean.

Note

1. Pier Mario Fasanotti and Valeria Gandus, *Bang Bang: Gli altri delitti degli anni di piombo* (Milan: Marco Tropea editore, 2004), pp. 151–152.
2. M.G., *Il Resto del Carlino*, 10.31.1977.
3. Mereghetti, *Il Mereghetti*, p. 415.

La bravata (The Stunt)

D: Roberto Montero [Roberto Bianchi Montero]. *S:* Roberto Montero; *SC:* Odoardo Fiory, Giorgio Cristallini; *DOP:* Gino Santini (35mm, Gevacolor, Telecolor); *M:* Nino P. Tassone, Nico Fidenco, performed by Universe City and conducted by Joseph Murolo (Ed. Chroma Music); *E:* Cesare Bianchini; *PD:* Giorgio Postiglione; *ArtD:* Renato Postiglione; *CO:* Rosalba Menichelli; *C:* Felice De Maria; *AC:* Bruno Pellegrini; *AE:* Paola Pannicelli; *PDA:* Eugenio Ulissi, Giovanna Petocchi; *AD:* Marialuce Faccenna; *MU:* Marisa Marconi; *W:* Ida Cristofori; *SO:* Roberto Alberghini; *Boom:* Maurizio Merli; *KG:* Marcello Gargano; *ChEl:* Alberto Silvestri; *SP:* Claudio Cannizzaro; *SS:* Angela Rosa Taccari. *Cast:* Franca Gonella (Patrizia), Silvano Tranquilli (Dr. Milani), Ajita Wilson (Jeanette Donald), Mario Antoni [Mario Bianchi] (Piero), Domenico Bua (Fabio), Mario Garbetta (Mario Rossi), Franco Garofalo (Luca), Umberto Liberati (Giorgio), Enrico Maisto (Commissioner), Armando Marra (Ciccillo Pacchelli "Mezzapacca"), Tommaso Palladino (Mimì), Pasquale Artiano, Philip Dallas (Mario's father), Vittorio Duse (Salvatore), Tom Felleghy (Investigating Judge), Anna Maisto, Mimmo [Domenico] Maggio, Franco Marino (Workshop manager), Red Martin (Commentator), Venantino Venantini (Walter), Luciano Crovato, Vanessa Vitale (Mary), Elisabetta Macrina, Attilio Dottesio (Garage owner). *Uncredited:* Tony Askin [Antonio Aschini] (Custom official), Dirce Funari (Lesbian girl with short hair). *PROD:* Ersi Produzioni Internazionali; General manager, *PM:* Angelo Faccenna; *PSu:* Bruno Bagella; *PSe:* Ivana Della Camera. *Country:* Italy. Filmed at R.P.A. Elios (Rome) and on location in Bolsena. *Running time:* 91'; Visa no.: 70303 (05.26.1977); *Rating:* v.m.18; *Release date:* 06.11.1977; *Distribution:* Koala / Heritage; *Domestic gross:* 279,765,490 lira. *Home video:* Classica Film (DVD, Italy)

Five upper-class Roman youth — Mario, Piero, Giorgio, Luca and Fabio — steal three cars that are destined to Switzerland: hidden in one of them there are four billion lira. Mario, who's driving said car, is stopped by a police patrol and kills an agent, but is severely wounded in turn. While Walter, a man of the organization, is trying to track down the five thieves, Mario takes refuge in the house of their friend Patrizia, who entrusts him to the care of Dr. Milani, a disbarred doctor. To justify Mario's prolonged absence from home, his friends stage a phony kidnapping, which yields them a billion lira. Soon after, however, Mario disappears (his corpse is later found in a car sunk in a lake), while the police burst into Patrizia's villa just in time to kill Walter, who had finally located them, and arrest her friends. The four billion, however, have disappeared without a trace: they were stolen by Dr. Milani and his secret lover Jeanette, who also killed Mario.

Roberto Bianchi Montero was never a great filmmaker, but by the end of his career the veteran director plunged into the depths of low-grade Italian cinema. With the exception of the mildly interesting *Sewer Rats* (*Una donna per sette bastardi*, 1974), a sort of modern-day Western starring Richard Harrison,[1] and the notorious sexy giallo *So Sweet, So Dead* (1972), Montero directed a number of truly awful films in the seventies, from the erotic period farce *Caligula's Hot Nights* (*Le calde notti di Caligola*, 1977) to the jungle adventure *Savana violenza carnale* (1979), before finally diving deep into hardcore porn with his last films *Erotic Flash* (1981) and *Albergo a ore* (1981).

Even though definitely better than the aforementioned titles, *La bravata* is nothing to write home about. Once again the inspiration (Montero penned the story, while the script was by Odoardo Fiory and Giorgio Cristallini, the director of *Seagulls Fly Low*) came from the real-life deeds of upper class juvenile delinquents. The five youngsters (the actors, however, all look in their thirties) show no moral quality whatsoever; while one of them (Mario Garbetta) is in bed, badly wounded, all they care is setting up wild orgies, and eventually they take advantage of his state by setting up a fake kidnapping in order to get a ransom from their friend's rich father.

However, rather than emphasizing violence and sadism in the vein of the Circeo massacre-inspired flicks of the period, Montero's film unrolls an intricate plot which leads to a predictable but amusing final twist. The existentialist elements are laughable and so are the political ones — the protagonists steal money that's being clandestinely sent to Switzerland by powerful politicians — but at least *La bravata* is not boring, although it's cheap looking and poorly directed. There's also plenty of comic relief, thanks to the duo of dumb, sex-crazed truck drivers (played by Palladino and Marra) who get cheated, seduced and robbed, and have such bad lines as "I went blank with the black one." Last but not least, Montero doesn't lose any occasion to have his actresses take their clothes off.

The cast is one weird bunch: besides sexy starlets Franca Gonella and transsexual Ajita Wilson, there are a number of familiar character actors such as Silvano Tranquilli (with a several days-long beard just to show he's having a hard time, as the disbarred doctor), Franco Garofalo and Venantino Venantini (who steals the film as the ruthless killer Walter), while Montero's regular "Red Martin" (an elusive actor whose real name is still unknown, and who bears a passing resemblance to the late Richard Lynch) pops up in a "special participation," wearing a curly blonde wig and cuddling a poodle dog. Montero's son Mario Bianchi, in one of his rare appearances before the camera, plays one of the five youth, while stunning sex goddess Dirce Funari has an uncredited naked cameo, passionately fondling another girl's breasts. The cheap yet listenable score (the credits let us know that the recordings took place in New York City) is co-signed by Nico Fidenco, who would write the music for many Z-grade films of the period. And J&B, needless to say, abounds.

Note

1. Based on an idea by Harrison himself— who stars as a mysterious cripple whose car breaks down in the middle of nowhere, forcing him to take shelter in an abandoned mining village populated by a handful of crooks, *Sewer Rats* (a.k.a., *A Woman for 7 Bastards*) is definitely a low-budget oddity: the script looks like it was written as a period Western, and turned into a contemporary thriller in a last-minute afterthought, while the plot — with its emphasis on Harrison's physical disability — owes much to John Sturges' *Bad Day at Black Rock* (1955). Although not an out-and-out crime film, it deservers at least a footnote, if only for its cast which, apart from Dagmar Lassander's dissipated beauty, includes a parade of B-movie devotees: John Richardson, Gordon Mitchell, Ivano Staccioli, the great Andrea Checchi (*Black Sunday*) and sleazebags Luciano Rossi (as a mute hunchback who plays harmonica) and Antonio Casale.

Brothers Till We Die (La banda del gobbo)

D: Umberto Lenzi. *S* and *SC:* Umberto Lenzi; *DIA collaboration:* Tomas Milian; *DOP:* Federico Zanni (35mm, Technicolor — Techniscope); *M:* Franco Micalizzi, directed by Alessandro Blonksteiner (ed. RCA); *Roma capoccia* (A. Venditti) and *Sora Rosa* (A. Venditti—Giuliani) sung by Antonello Venditti; *E:* Eugenio Alabiso; *PD, SD:* Giuseppe Bassan; *CO:* Silvio Laurenzi; *AE:* Amedeo Moriani; *AD:* Sandro [Alessandro] Metz; *C:* Elio Polacchi; *AC:* Mario Pastorini; *MU:* Franco Di Girolamo; *Hair:* Jole Angelucci; *SO:* Raffaele De Luca; *Boom:* Stefano Piermarioli; *Mix:* Bruno Moreal; *SE:* Gino Vagniluca; *W:* Floriana Scalabrelli; *ChEl:* Roberto Belli; *KG:* Giuseppe Gabrielli; *SP:* Marcello Laurenti; *Props:* Adriano Tiberi; *SS:* Maria Luisa Merci. *Cast:* Tomas Milian (Vincenzo Marazzi "Il Gobbo" / Sergio Marazzi "Er Monnezza"), Pino Colizzi (Commissioner Sarti), Isa Danieli (Maria), Guido Leontini (Mario Di Gennaro "Sogliola"), Solvy [Solvi] Stubing (Marika Engver, embassy clerk), Luciano Catenacci (Adalberto Maria Perrone), Carlo Gaddi ("Faina," Gobbo's friend), Sandra [Alessandra] Cardini, Sal [Salvatore] Borgese (Milo Dragovic "The Albanian"), Livio Galassi ("Giggi," Gobbo's friend), Angelo Civera (Agent Romeo Esposito), Nello Pazzafini (Carmine Ciacci), Mario Piave (Commissioner Mario Valenzi), Franco Odoardi (Chief psychiatrist), Valentino Macchi (brigadier), Roberto Caporali (Man with white suit at nightclub), Rosario Borelli (Romolo, Gobbo's friend), Francesco D'Adda (Bespectacled psychiatrist), Fortunato Arena (Male nurse), Tony Morgan (Monnezza's stuttering friend), Cesare Di Vito (Psychiatrist with slit lamp), Mario Savini, Fulvio Mingozzi (Commissioner Mingozzi). *Uncredited:* Ennio Antonelli (Osvaldo Albanese), Ettore Arena (Male nurse), Salvatore Billa (Perrone's man), Massimo Bonetti (Calogero Ciacci), Angelo Boscariol (Male nurse), Rossana Canghiari (Woman at nightclub), Aristide Caporale (Maria's neighbor), Nestore Cavaricci (policeman), Enrico Cesaretti (Nightclub customer), Franz Colangeli (Nightclub porter), Bruno Di Luia (Milo's friend), Tom Felleghy (Investigating Judge), Jimmy il Fenomeno [Luigi Origene Soffrano] (mentally ill man), Alba Maiolini (Woman complaining to the police in suburbs), Giuseppe Marrocco (Nightclub barman), Taylor Mead (Mentally ill man), Nello Palladino (policeman), Riccardo Petrazzi (Perrone's chauffeur), Mimmo Poli (Salvatore), Bruno Rosa (Nightclub manager), Alberto Tarallo (Ursula, the transvestite), Valerio Colombaioni (Mechanic working with Monnezza), Luciano Zanussi (Man at nightclub). *PROD:* Luciano Martino for Dania Film / Medusa; *GM:* Pietro Innocenzi; *PSu:* Evi Farinelli; *PSe:* Alberto Paluzzi. *Country:* Italy. Filmed at R.P.A.-Elios Film (Rome) and on location in Rome. *Running time:* 98'; Visa no.: 70728 (08.10.1977); *Rating:* v.m.14; *Release date:* 08.18.1977; *Distribution:* Medusa; *Domestic gross:* 1,523,844,720 lira. *Also known as: Échec au gang* (France), *Die Kröte* (West Germany). *Home video:* Federal (DVD, Italy). OST: CD Digitmovies CDDM084.

Back in Rome after several months on the run in Corsica, Vincenzo Marazzi "The Hunchback" assaults a bank's armored car with three accomplices: Perrone, the Albanian and Sogliola. After the hit, however, the others try to get rid of him. The Hunchback survives and takes refuge at a prostitute friend's place, getting ready for revenge. Marazzi kills Sogliola by locking him in a cold storage room; he then eliminates the Albanian and causes Perrone to die of a heart attack by threatening him with a drill. In order to track down the criminal's hideout, Commissioner Sarti releases his twin brother, Sergio, a.k.a. "Monnezza," but both he and the Hunchback easily rid themselves of police surveillance. Finally, Commissioner Sarti and his men manage to surprise the Hunchback, but while his gang is forced to surrender, the criminal eludes capture by fleeing in a car. On the highway the car swerves and falls into the Tiber, disappearing underwater. But maybe the Hunchback has once again managed to pull through.

With *Brothers Till We Die*, Umberto Lenzi (who also wrote the script) and Tomas Milian brought back to life one of their most successful creations, the Hunchback, whom they had left agonizing in the last few frames of the previous year's *Brutal Justice*. This time, though, Vincenzo Moretto becomes Vincenzo Marazzi, and turns into the elder twin—he was born ten minutes earlier!—of Milian's other screen *alter ego*, Sergio Marazzi "Il Monnezza," who had appeared in *Free Hand for a Tough Cop* and *Destruction Force*. Milian's *tour-de-force* in a dual role is remarkable, however between the two main characters it's Monnezza

Italian poster for ***Brothers Till We Die*** (1977).

who gets less screen time, becoming a comic relief that's never fully in focus, at times naive and at times smart. If Milian's scenes in the asylum clearly predate the comic left-turn of the Nico Giraldi series, it's obvious that the Cuban actor was much more interested in developing the Hunchback, who becomes the film's real star.

As was Lenzi's *Almost Human*, *Brothers Till We Die* is unbalanced on the wrong side of the law, up to the point that Commissioner Sarti (Pino Colizzi) becomes a pleonastic presence, while the Hunchback turns into an almost mythical antihero, damned and loser alike — an outsider of crime who uses this as an impossible revenge on life. The character's cruelty and hatred are nourished by the awareness of his own diversity, and Marazzi's almost self-defeating cynicism is ultimately just a self-defense armor that he leaves aside just in a few brief moments of intimacy, like the ones with the pathetic, motherly prostitute (Isa Danieli) who welcomes him in her bed.

In many ways, the Hunchback is the character that's closer to Milian himself, among the many the actor played in those years, as proven by the fact that Milian himself took care of Marazzi's dialogue, filling it with his own personal obsessions. *Brothers Till We Die*'s most notorious scene has the Hunchback deliver a long monologue in a disco — a scene that deeply irritated Lenzi — which is just the most striking moment in a film filled with "a deeply anti-bourgeois resentment"[1] where even a popular song, Antonello Venditti's *Sora Rosa*, becomes a vehicle for proletarian rage and a metaphor of an angry, desperate uneasiness.[2]

Proletarian revenge is a common element in the characters created by Milian: just like Giulio Sacchi, the Hunchback is a reject, relegated to the margins of a system where the underworld is also divided into classes, in an atrocious parody of "respectable" society. With their very existence, these characters claim a diversity which is just the most evident and burning consequence of the sudden modernity that kept Italy off guard and redesigned its social map faster than expected. The will towards redemption, which was portrayed at first in gloomy tones, gradually turned to farce (as in *Delitto al ristorante cinese*, 1981, where Nico Giraldi is building an abusive villa with the complicity of his own colleagues). These two approaches can both be found in *Brothers Till We Die,* not just because of the presence of Monnezza and the Hunchback. The incredibly vulgar joke that the Hunchback tells to a rich audience is like a court jester's revenge: after letting his masters mock and humiliate him, he finally drops the mask. The claim at equality manifests itself at the lower level: bodily fluids and dejection, as the Hunchback retaliates on his audience by forcing them to drink a laxative. "I'm gonna have you shit out your bones!!!" he screams.

Feces — an ubiquitous presence in Italian cinema of the period, as shown by Marco Ferreri's *La Grande bouffe* (1973), Brunello Rondi's *Ingrid sulla strada* (1973) and of course Pier Paolo Pasolini's *Salò* (1975) — becomes once again the metaphor of how the rich and the poor belong to irreconcilable universes, as underlined by one of Monnezza's portentously vulgar lines: "You bet that the day shit turn to gold, we poor fellas will be born into this world without an asshole?!"

Notes

1. Massimo Moretti, "Il poliziotto tra ficton e realtà nel cinema italiano degli anni '70," in Maurizio Matrone and Massimo Moretti, eds., *3° police Film Festival* (Bologna: *I quaderni del Lumière* #22, 1997), p. 9.
2. On the other hand, Franco Micalizzi's score recycles for the third time the song "A Man Before Your Time," already heard in *Brutal Justice* and *Violent Naples*.

Umberto Lenzi, second from left, Riccardo Petrazzi, center, and Tomas Milian, right, with unidentified co-workers on the set of *Brothers Till We Die* (1977).

Canne mozze, a.k.a. *Il bandito dalle canne mozze* (Sawed-off Shotgun)

D: Mario Imperoli. *S:* Mario Imperoli; *SC:* Mario Imperoli, Luigi Montefiori; *DOP:* Romano Albani (35mm, Vistavision, Technospes); *M:* Manuel De Sica (Ed. Bierre); *E:* Franco Letti; *ArtD:* Enrico Fantacci; *CO:* Claudia Schiff; *C:* Massimo Di Venanzo; *AC:* Egidio Gambassi; *AD:* Claudio Bernabei; *AE:* Marisa Letti; Gloria Granati; *Hair:* Lidia Di Palma; *SO:* Massimo Mariani; *B:* Bruno Feudi; *Mix:* Romano Checcacci; *W:* Wanda Caprioli; *ChEl:* Alfredo Bramucci; *KG:* Mario Moreschini; *SP:* Letizia Cavallini; *SS:* Lucia Luconi. *Cast:* Antonio Sabàto (Giovanni Molé), John Richardson (Michele), Ritza Brown (Silvia), Jean-Pierre Sabagh, Attilio Dottesio, Roberto Panico, Claudio Cuomo, Renata Franco, Mimmo [Domenico] Bua. *Uncredited:* Calogero Azzaretto (Tony), Luciano Bonanni, Nestore Cavaricci. *PROD:* Schilton Cinematografica, Silvia Film 70; *PM:* Lucio Orlandini; *PSu:* Claudio Cuomo; *PSe:* Simonetta Vitali. *Country:* Italy. Filmed at Incir — De Paolis (Rome). *Running time:* 90': Visa no.: 70500 (08.05.1977); *Rating:* v.m.18; *Release date:* 08.05.1977; *Distribution:* C.I.A.; *Domestic gross:* 94,316,000. *Home video:* King

Video (VHS, Greece), Olympia (VHS, Germany), MVP (VHS, Canada).

A violent feud has embroiled the Sicilian Carraro and Molé families for many years. One day, having learned that his brother was killed by his rivals, Giovanni Molé escapes from prison to exact revenge. Despite the Carabinieri's stakeouts, he reaches his native area and hides in a seemingly abandoned house. His isolation is interrupted by the arrival of the rich young mistress, Silvia, accompanied by her newlywed husband Michele. He tries to react, with the result of throwing Silvia into the bandit's arms and getting himself killed by the gardener Angelino Parise, who is on the side of the Molé family. The relationship with Silvia seems to distract Molé from his violent proposal, but Carraro's killers—who meanwhile have dispatched Parise—rape Silvia and are eliminated by Giovanni. The escaped convict then reaches Carraro's slaughterhouse, where he annihilates the rival gang, losing his life in the process. Silvia, who called the police, arrives too late to save him.

Co-scripted by Luigi Montefiori (of *Antropophagus / The Grim Reaper* fame), Mario Imperoli's last film (the 46-year-old director died a few months later, on December 24, 1977) once again belongs to the realm of the crime genre, as did Imperoli's previous *Come cani arrabbiati*, but at least looks more accomplished. The lighting (by Romano Albani, who would do an outstanding job on Argento's *Inferno*, 1980) is unusually accurate, and Imperoli displays a number of curious stylistic choices, such as the use of songwriter Fabrizio De André's song *Amore che vieni, amore che vai* in the sequence where Sabàto's character is sheltered and hidden by a prostitute (Imperoli used De André's songs in *Come cani arrabbiati* as well). The central part predates Fernando di Leo's *Madness* (1980), as escaped convict Giovanni Molé (Antonio Sabàto), seeking revenge upon the Mafia boss who murdered his brother, sneaks into a villa and takes a rich couple as hostages; what follows recalls such morbid dramas as *Top Sensation* (1969, by Ottavio Alessi) and *Wave of Lust* (*Ondata di piacere*, 1975, by Ruggero Deodato), as the coward husband (a slimy John Richardson) tries to push his beautiful wife (Ritza Brown), who doesn't seems indifferent to Sabàto's macho charm, into the bandit's arms. The latter, on the other hand, spends his time looking mean and sawing off a double-barreled shotgun (hence the title). *Canne mozze* mostly lives upon its titillating moments, such as the scene where Silvia and Molé share a bed, with the woman tied to the bandit with a rough collar. The rest of the film, unfolds as the typical revenge tale, escalating in a violent massacre.

"The fact that the moral problem doesn't particularly worry the director [...] is shown by the patent sympathy with which the bandit, although the murderer of an innocent policeman, is characterized, as well as by the ambiguous demonstration of how a woman prefers a shotgun-armed bandit to a meek citizen,"[1] as one critic wrote, testifying to the usual prejudices towards the genre. Actually, *Canne mozze* works merely as an adult amoral fantasy, filled with steamy sex and ferocious violence.

Note

1. L.A. [Leonardo Autera], *Corriere della Sera*, 08.06.1977.

Could It Happen Here?, a.k.a. *Terrorism (Italia: ultimo atto?)*

D: Massimo Pirri. Story and *SC:* Morando Morandini Jr., Massimo Pirri, Federico Tofi; *PDIR:* Riccardo Pallottini (Vistavision—Kodak, Staco Film); *M:* Lallo [Coriolano] Gori; *Electronic sound landscapes:* Roberto Carapellucci; *E:* Cleofe Conversi; *PD:* Elio Micheli; *CO:* Adele D'Ercole; *AD:* Mario Jurisic; *MU:* Cristina Rocca; *PDA:* Rita De Reya, Roberta Pirri; *SO:* Roberto Alberghini; *C:* Michele Pensato; *AC:* Luigi Conversi; *AE:* Pietro Mura; *Mix:* Renato Cadueri; *ChEl:* Roberto Carapellucci; *SS:* A. M. Bifarini; *SP:* Giuliana De Rossi. *Cast:* Luc Merenda (Ferruccio), Lou Castel (Marco), Andrea Franchetti (Bruno), Marcella Michelangeli (Mara), Ines Pellegrini (au-pair girl), Luigi Casellato, Fabrizia Castagnoli, Valentino Dain, Adriana Loran, Maria Tedeschi, Nello [Giovanni] Pazzafini, Raffaele Di Maio. *PROD:* Benedetto Conversi for Una Cinecooperativa; *PM:* Raniero Di Giovanbattista. *Country:* Italy. Filmed at Icet–De Paolis (Milan). *Running time:* 90'; Visa no. 71146 (11.15.1977); *Rating:* v.m.18; *Distribution:* Sida Stella; *Release date:* 11.24.1977; *Domestic gross:* 276,482,020 lira. *Home video:* Cine International Video (VHS, Italy).

Three terrorists are preparing to kill the Minister of the Interior. Each comes from a different social milieu: Mara is a rebel girl from an upper-class family, totally devoted to the cause to the point of fanaticism; Ferruccio is a teacher at a technical institute, who despises capitalism and the alienation it produces; the third, Bruno, is an ex-convict who enjoys violence and just wants to make some money and leave the country. Concluding, however, that given the current situation of the country, the plot would only strengthen the actual government, the terrorist leaders decide to delay it. Breaching their orders, Ferruccio and his two companions carry out the job regardless. During the action, in which the Minister and his entourage are killed, Bruno also dies. The country is in chaos and repression is unleashed. Ferruccio and Mara take refuge in one of the organization's hideouts, where they end up killing each other.

A woman screams: "Murderers!" On the asphalt, chalk marks draw contours of bodies. Cartridges. Blood. Too much blood. A lifeless body has been hastily covered with newspapers. Two male nurses place the body on a stretcher and cover it with a white sheet, which soon turns red with blood. It's one of the most powerful moments of Massimo Pirri's *Could It Happen Here?*, a movie which faces one of the period's most delicate and controversial themes: left-wing terrorism.

Bombs, massacres and fascist plots are a common occurrence in Italian crime films of the period. Yet Marxist-Leninist groups such as the "Brigate Rosse" (Red Brigades) were taboo. Unlike West Germany, where renowned directors such as Rainer Werner Fassbinder (*Germany in Autumn*, 1977; *The Third Generation*, 1979), Volker Schlöndorff (*The Lost Honour of Katharina Blum*, 1975) and Margarethe von Trotta (*Marianne and Juliane*, 1981) dealt with similar phenomenons, Italian filmmakers chose not to. As Giuseppe Bertolucci stated, the reality of terrorism, "obsessively shown in its everyday tragic evolution by the media, was almost unrepresentable. To imagine a film on terrorism was like to imagine a movie on a soccer match [...]. Reality's grip was too strong, too violent."[1] With the exception of Dino Risi's harsh black comedies, such as *Dirty Weekend* (1973) whose original Italian title quoted an early Red Brigades slogan, and the even more vitriolic *Caro papà* (1979), respected auteurs didn't want to dwell on the subject. When Gillo Pontecorvo decided to make a movie on terrorism, he chose to recount ETA's murder of Spanish admiral Carrero Blanco (*Ogro*, 1979), while Carlo Lizzani went to Germany to make the disappointing *Kleinhoff Hotel* (1977), about a German terrorist who has an affair with an unsatisfied bourgeois woman (Corinne Clery).

It took Massimo Pirri to make the film nobody wanted to. Unlike many of his contemporaries, Pirri was not afraid. He was quite a peculiar *auteur*, having made his debut with the controversial erotic drama *Càlamo* (1975), and at ease with difficult, unpleasant subject matters, as shown by his third and best film *L'immoralità* (1978), the story of a child murderer on the run who falls in love with a 12-year-old girl. Unlike Stelvio Massi's *Mark Strikes Again* (1976), where terrorism was just an ingredient of a well-oiled genre plot, and terrorists were played by such familiar villains as John Steiner and behaved like common bad guys, Pirri's daring move was to tell the story from the terrorists' point of view. What's more, he cast Luc Merenda, one of the genre's most famous tough cops, as a terrorist mastermind.

The director never denied his low opinion of the crime genre: "In those years there were lots of those movies, such as *Execution Squad* ... but no one even dared touch the theme of terrorism. I was the first. Had I directed *Could It Happen Here?* five years later, that would have been a completely different pic. Whereas I did it then, at just the right time. I used to tell myself: "Look at all these hack filmmakers doing those shitty crime flicks ... now I'm going to show them what a crime film really is!" My script was originally called *Novanta minuti alle sette*... [*Ninety Minutes to Seven*], since it was supposed to be the story of the ninety minutes preceding the terrorists' attack."[2]

Pirri's emphasis is on the characters' psychology and motivations, as effectively shown in the scenes featuring Franchetti (an inexperienced actor in an idiosyncratic performance), who fantasizes of taking the first plane to South America and live a life of sex, money and fame ("My friends in the pen will die of envy," he mumbles; "I may even end up on history books"). Bruno's uninterrupted travels through city streets, accompanied by the actor's unpleasant, heavily accented, ruminant voiceover for some of the film's highlights: the scene in the public toilet, where Bruno plays with a machine gun and makes obscene drawings on the wall (he later masturbates with his gun still in hand); the clumsy approach to the Brazilian *au pair* girl (Ines Pellegrini, who gained a brief fame after her roles in Pasolini's *Arabian Nights* and *Salò*) on the bench of the gardens; the man's hysterical reaction in a crowded bar where he tried unsuccessfully to order a coffee.

Despite not being a crime film in the strictest sense, *Could It Happen Here?* makes use of the genre's recurring figures and narrative patterns. Besides an irreverent in-joke (a cab driver asks Luc Merenda "Are you in the movie biz? You got the right face, I thought I'd seen you someplace...") which somehow displays the director's lack of feeling for the genre, Pirri stages a few poorly made action scenes which patently give away the film's low budget: in one Luc Merenda is chased by a biker, then surrounded by a few thugs (one of them is the ubiquitous Nello Pazzafini), with the inevitable fistfight taking place. But even closer to the crime films of the period are a couple of more intimate scenes: Italian critic Giovanni Buttafava ironically noted that the scene where Ferruccio is home, talking to his estranged wife looks like it's almost lifted off the average crime film: "Merenda's little son and modest living room look just like the average tough cop's family and home, as well as the dialogue where the terrorist apologizes for his egocentric vocation."[3] On the other hand, the confrontation between Ferruccio and Marco, one of the leaders of the terrorist organization, played by Lou Castel, is quite similar to the typical arguments between tough cops and their superiors. Like the "iron commissioners" he used to play, even as a terrorist Merenda delivers a monologue about the necessity of violence (so as to push the masses to embrace revolution).

The latter scene is particularly significant as it actually predates the forthcoming split inside the Red Brigades between the "indomitables" (who, led by Mario Moretti, went on to kidnap and kill Italy's Prime minister Aldo Moro[4]) and the "moderate" wing. "First we were criminal bands, we were delinquents ... but now people are not afraid of us any longer, they begin to understand what we're fighting for!" Ferruccio insists, while Marco objects: "Our strategy has to be rewritten ... we must operate within a larger context, get closer to the working masses...."

Pirri does not indulge in the apology of the "armed comrades," yet he is not kind either towards the State, which is weak and ineffective. Those who have to vigilate on public order are themselves on the verge of a nervous breakdown, while a sense of unease is palpable everywhere, even in coffee bars. Italy as seen in *Could It Happen Here?* is an apparently quiet country whose dark side lurks just beneath the surface. And it's got the faces of a homeless beggar at a corner, or a staggering junkie aimlessly wandering in the middle of a street, like a zombie.

Pirri's disenchanted portrayal of the terrorist commando makes *Could It Happen Here?* somehow similar to Claude Chabrol's *Nada* (1974), based on Jean-Patrick Manchette's novel of the same name. Yet the director's rugged style, which makes effective use of hand-held camerawork following the main characters as well as newsreel footage,[5] clashes with the script's excessive—and often awkward—verbosity. In the end, Pirri does not succeed in reaching the abstraction he so obviously strives for: his approach is both mimetic (the terrorists' terminology is the same as that of real Red Brigade bulletins), but he always feels the need to explain and underline everything. An emblematic scene has Merenda looking right into the camera while an escalation of violence is taking place after the attack, and proclaiming with a satisfied grin: "That's what we wanted: chain reaction!"

Could It Happen Here? suffered from drastic re-editing, which greatly diminished its potential. The film's original edit, conceived by Pirri and Franco "Kim" Arcalli (one of Italy's most innovative editors, and a frequent collaborator of Bernardo Bertolucci), begins immediately after the attack: the surviving terrorists, Ferruccio and Mara, are on the run to their hideout, while a civil war scenery is materializing: the army imposes a curfew, rebels take guns, some people start shooting from their balcony over the bourgeoisie. At the hideout, the terrorist spend their days waiting for a phone call with their next instructions: the rest of the film is a long flashback which recounts their day up to the murder of the politician, while the epilogue hints at a future coup d'état, with the image of tanks on the streets superimposed over the last shots. None of this can be found in the "official" version, which follows the action chronologically, and hopelessly dilutes the film's impact.[6]

Could It Happen Here? was badly distributed and barely seen at the time of its release. Yet, as an instant document of the so-called "years of lead," it is simply chilling. Film critic Giovanni Grazzini wrote on Italy's most important newspaper "Il Corriere della Sera": "We should avoid at any cost that this film become a prophecy, and Massimo Pirri a Cassandra."[7] But just a few months later the kidnapping and assassination of Moro took place, similarly as to what Pirri had described in his film. Yet it fails in offering what Pirri and his co-scriptwriters Morandini Jr. and Tofi wanted: that is, a key to read Italian history of the period. The epilogue is especially jarring: despite being apocalyptic in conception, with a quote by Bertrand Russell that reads "once a generation that does not adopt violence is forged, obstacles to freedom will be abolished," it's too simplistic an ending, ineffective and inconceivable, especially in mere spectacular cinematic terms.

Notes

1. Giuseppe Bertolucci, "Diario di dieci anni," in Lino Micciché, ed., *Schermi opachi: Il cinema italiano degli anni '80* (Venice: Marsilio, 1998), p. 355.
2. Davide Pulici, "La grande promessa: Intervista esclusiva a Massimo Pirri," *Nocturno Cinema* #7 (June 1998), p. 62.
3. Buttafava, "Procedure sveltite," p. 114.
4. Moro's car was ambushed by a commando of terrorists on March 16, 1978: the politician was on his way to a session of the House of Representatives, where a discussion was supposed to take place regarding a vote of confidence in a new government led by Giulio Andreotti (of Democrazia Cristiana, Moro's Party) and with, for the first time, the support of the Communist Party. It was the first implementation of Moro's strategic vision as defined by the so-called "historic compromise." Moro's five bodyguards were all killed. The Red Brigades proposed to exchange Moro's life for the freedom of several imprisoned terrorists. Yet the government immediately took a hard line position, claiming that "the State must not bend" to terrorist demands. After 55 days of confinement, and a secret trial where he was found guilty and sentenced to death by the terrorists, Aldo Moro was executed. His body was found in the trunk of a car in the centre of Rome, on May 9, 1978.
5. In one shot, a priest gives the last blessing to a young man's body in the middle of the street: it was the body of Giannino Zibecchi, run over by a *carabinieri*'s jeep on April 17, 1975, during the violent clashes between law enforcement officers and protesters who were trying to assault the Milanese offices of extreme right-wing party MSI.
6. The original edit of Pirri's film resurfaced through an obscure Swiss VHS (on the Centauro label), whereas other home video versions retained the subsequent, chronological edit.
7. Giovanni Grazzini, *Corriere della Sera*, 05.07.1978.

The Cynic, the Rat and the Fist (*Il cinico, l'infame, il violento*)

D: Umberto Lenzi. *S:* Sauro Scavolini; *SC:* Ernesto Gastaldi, Dardano Sacchetti, Umberto Lenzi; *DOP:* Federico Zanni (35mm, Technicolor); *M:* Franco Micalizzi, conducted by Alessandro Blonksteiner (Ed. R.C.A.-Clitunno); *E:* Eugenio Alabiso; *PD:* Elio Micheli; *PDA:* Paolo Innocenzi; *CO:* Silvio Laurenzi; *C:* Elio Polacchi; *AC:* Mario Pastorini; *AE:* Amedeo Moriani; *2nd AE:* Marcello Cannone; *AD:* Filiberto Fiaschi; *MU:* Franco Di Girolamo, Pietro Tenoglio; *Hair:* Jolanda Angelucci; *SO:* Raffaele De Luca; *Boom:* Stefano Piermarioli; *Mix:* Bruno Moreal; *SE:* Gino Vagniluca; *SP:* Carlo Alberto Cocchi; *KG:* Giuseppe Gabrielli; *ChEl:* Roberto Belli; *PrM:* Umberto Innocenzi; *MA:* Riccardo Petrazzi; *SS:* Maria Luisa Merci; *UP:* Lucherini-Rossetti-Spinola-Colonna. *Cast:* Maurizio Merli (Commissioner Leonardo Tanzi), John Saxon (Frank Di Maggio), Tomas Milian (Luigi Maietto "The Chinaman"), Renzo Palmer (Commissioner Guido Astalli), Gabriella Lepori (Nadia), Robert Hundar [Claudio Undari] (Dario), Bruno Corazzari (Ettore), Marco Guglielmi (Marchetti, Di Maggio's lawyer), Gabriella Giorgelli (Maria Proietti), Guido Alberti (Tanzi's uncle), Aldo Massasso (Judge Lojacono), Brigitte [Brigida] Petronio (Hooker at Fazi's), Gianni Musy (Nicola Proietti), Gianfilippo Carcano (The "Professor"), Dante Cleri (Di Maggio's Accountant), Riccardo Garrone (Natali), Claudio Nicastro (Fazi), Massimo Bonetti ("Cappuccino"), Pietro Tiberi ("Cappuccino"'s accomplice), Franco Odoardi (Sgt. Esposito), Salvatore Billa (Salvatore), Rosario Borelli (Tony, Di Maggio's henchman), Tommaso Palladino (Di Maggio's thug), Benito Pacifico (Chinaman's henchman who tries to kill Tanzi), Franco Marino (Gigi), Fulvio Mingozzi (Inspector Pisani), Ermelinda De Felice (Landlady at "Gabriella"), Fortunato Arena (Large convict who tries to kill Di Maggio). *Uncredited:* Francesco Anniballi (Nino at the "Er Ranocchia" tavern), Ennio Antonelli (Prison barber), Antonio Basile (The traitor killed by Di Maggio), Gianni Bortolotti (Notary kept hostage by Tanzi and the Professor), Sisto Brunetti (Man who is shown Tanzi's photo on the newspaper), Omero Capanna (Thief), Costantino Carrozza (Factory worker), Nestore Cavaricci (policeman), Enrico Chiappafreddo (Cab driver), Domenico Cianfriglia (Prison guard), Raniero Dorascenzi (Bar owner), Rocco Lerro (Driver), Alba Maiolini (Woman in the crowd), Annibale Papetti (Worker who mocks Tanzi), Riccardo Petrazzi (Di Maggio's thug), Renzo Pevarello (Fazi's henchman), Claudio Ruffini (Fazi's door guard), Sergio Smacchi (Gunman at Fazi's), Sergio Testori (Blond convict who tries to kill Di Maggio), Rinaldo Zamperla (Prison guard). *PROD:* Luciano Martino for Dania Film, Medusa Distribuzione; *GM:* Pietro Innocenzi; *PSu:* Rosalba Tonti; *PSe:* Evi Farinelli. *Country:* Italy. Filmed at Elios Film (Rome) and on location in Rome, Milan and Chiasso (Switzerland). *Running time:* 100'; Visa no.: 69791 (02.03.1977); *Rating:* v.m.14; *Release date:* 02.03.1977; *Distribution:* Medusa; *Domestic gross:* 1,518,523,920 lira. *Also known as: Die Gewalt bin ich* (West Germany), *Le cynique, l'infâme, le violent* (France), *Ein Stromer ser rodt* (Denmark). *Home video:* Federal (DVD, Italy), Pop Flix (DVD, UK—English language, as part of the "Mafia Kingpin" collection), filmART (DVD, Germany—English language track). OST: CD Beat Records BCM9503.

Wounded by the accomplices of underworld boss Luigi Maietto, a.k.a. "The Chinaman," who just escaped from prison where he had been sentenced for his testimony, ex-inspector Leonardo Tanzi—who left the police in an act of protest against his superiors, who disapproved of his methods—is advised to play dead and take refuge in Switzerland. However, Tanzi acts very differently. Meanwhile the "Chinaman" has moved to Rome, following a scheme to rip off crime boss Frank Di Maggio, who runs a criminal empire in the city, and take control of all of his syndicate operations. The Chinaman and Di Maggio become unlikely allies, but Tanzi cleverly sows discord between the two gangsters, forcing them to fight each other. In the end, Tanzi eliminates both gangs.

A sequel of sorts to the director's *Brutal Justice*, Umberto Lenzi's *The Cynic, the Rat and the Fist* sees the return of Commissioner Tanzi, thus offering its star Maurizio Merli the typical role of the avenger cop. Despite one of the genre's most memorable titles, which openly riffs on Sergio Leone's *The Good, the Bad and the Ugly* (1967), the result is rather disappointing. Much of the blame must be put on the script, which turns Tanzi into a lone wolf who moves out of legality, thus depriving the character of his inner torment and turning Merli into a sort of superhero, while the plot often verges towards action/adventure territory, without having the means nor the ideas. A jaw-dropping example is the heist segment, which is a sort of extraneous body within the whole picture[1] and culminates in a scene where Merli has to move through a corridor filled with photoelectric cells (which are actually red threads, like in some Z-grade Turkish action flick). Ernesto Gastaldi, who collaborated on the film, wasn't too fond the results either: "the story wasn't mine, and I just did a supervising work on the finished script. Actually, I didn't even like the movie."[2]

The Cynic, the Rat and the Fist also suffers from badly sketched characters: the female presences are merely pretexual, like the dim-witted prostitute (Gabriella Lepori) who gets beaten by everyone and eventually disappears from the film, while the bad guys are hopelessly conventional. As the Italian-American boss who punishes a traitor (Antonio Basile) by shooting golf balls at his face before having his dogs feast on him, John Saxon hams it up but doesn't leave a memorable mark. On the other hand, as the proletarian gangster who gives around 100,000-lira banknotes with the same vulgar munificence with which he displays packets of Marlboro cigarettes for the camera in the mandatory occult advertising bits, Tomas Milian looks rather bored and uninterested in the role: a fact proven not only by the "Chinaman"'s rather approximative physiognomic characterization — an unusual occurrence for Milian — but also by the fact that he and Merli shot their footage separately, never meeting on the set and never appearing in the same scene, let alone the same shot.

From left, Franco Marino, Bruno Corazzari, Gabriella Lepori and Robert Hundar in *The Cynic, the Rat and the Fist* (1977). Note the J&B bottle in plain sight.

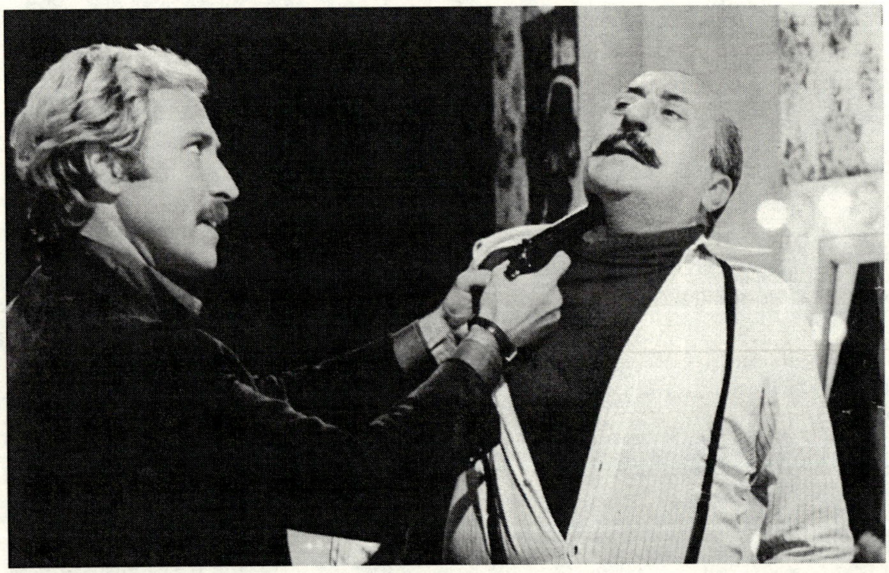

Avenger cop Maurizio Merli, left, and Claudio Nicastro in *The Cynic, the Rat and the Fist* (1977).

As a matter of fact, much of the work on the "Chinaman" is almost completely left to Milian's Italian dubber Ferruccio Amendola, and as a result the character looks less interesting than the very similar Rudy, as played by John Steiner in Mario Caiano's *La malavita attacca … la polizia risponde!*, whose plot nevertheless owes much to Lenzi's film. Paradoxically, *The Cynic, the Rat and the Fist* is less memorable for its titular characters than it is for Milian's impressive trio of henchmen, led by the gigantic, obtuse Robert Hundar (Claudio Undari, 1935–2008), one of the most recognizable faces in European popular cinema of the 1960s and '70s, from westerns (Joaquín Luis Romero Marchent's masterpiece *Seven Guns from Texas*, 1964) to sexploitation (the monstrously-endowed satyr in Alfonso Brescia's *The Beast In Space*, 1980). Another asset is the usually reliable Franco Micalizzi's energetic score.

The Cynic, the Rat and the Fist was very successful at the box office, grossing over a billion and a half lira — a result slightly surpassed a few months later by the director's own *Brothers Till We Die*. It was also Merli's best money-making performance of the year: his other cop flick *Highway Racer* did well, but Sergio Martino's grim western *A Man Called Blade* (*Mannaja*) grossed just 750 million — half as much as Lenzi's film, thus proving that outside the genre that gave him celebrity Merli was not much of a draw.

Notes

1. Not to mention that the scene in question looks awfully similar to the one in Montaldo's *Grand Slam* (1967).
2. Email interview, January 2012.

Day of Violence (*Operazione Kappa: sparate a vista*)

D: Luigi Petrini. *S* and *SC:* Luigi Petrini; *DOP:* Luigi Ciccarese (35mm, Telecolor); *M:* Franco Bixio, Fabio Frizzi, Vince Tempera (ed. Grandi Firme della Canzone); *E:* Adriano Tagliavia; *PD, ArtD:* Massimo Corevi; *AC:* Franco Sperduti; *AE:* Margherita Valboa; *AD:* Maria Pia Lepore; *MU:* Silvana Petri; *Hair:* Francesco Pratelli; *W:* Clara Fata-Citi; *CO:* Mario Russo; *SO:* Goffredo Potier; *Boom:* Franco Pirri; *SR:* Renato Cadueri; *SP:* Alfio Quattrini; *CON:* Claudio Faustini; *ChEl:* Aldo Ercoli; *KG:* Vittorio Sbrana; *Props:* Francesco Arcuri; *Painter:* Massimo Corevi; *SetT:* Augusto Possanza. *Cast:* Mario Cutini (Paolo Soprani), Marco Marati (Giovanni Arbelli), Maria Pia Conte (Anna), Patricia Pilchard (Rossana), Ely Galleani (pregnant woman in restaurant), Selvaggia Di Vasco (Barbara, Aldovrandi's lover), Daniele Dublino (blond hostage), Mario Antoni [Mario Bianchi] (Commissioner Aldobrandi), Daria Norman [Maria Francesca], Linda Sini (Isabella), Edmondo Tieghi (Hostage in restaurant), Agnès Kalpagos [Agnès Kalpagos Szabo], Pino Lorin (Rossana's boyfriend), Piero Mazzinghi (Count Camillo di Valleombrosa), Viviana Polic (Beatrice, the Count's wife), Franco D'Onofrio, Silvio Klein (police inspector's assistant), Irma Olivero, Anna Zinnemann, Alberto Mandolesi (Norman), Emilio Cecca. *PROD:* Franco Vitolo for Filmday; *PM:* Maria Francesca Pomentale; *PSu:* Francesco Vitolo; *PSe:* Laura Vitolo; Assistant production secretary: Edile Martini. Shot on location in Tirrenia. *Running time:* 100'; Visa no.: 70367 (06.08.1977); *Rating:* v.m.18; *Release date:* 06.22.1977; *Distribution:* Graffiti Italiana; *Domestic gross:* 149,994,930 lira. *Also known as: En blodig dag, Voldens dag* (Denmark), *Operation K* (France), *Ligisterna* (Sweden). *Home video:* (Finland), Olympia Video International (VHS, Germany), Cinehollywood (VHS, U.K.—cut), Video For Pleasure (VHS, Holland), Walthers (VHS, Denmark), DVS (VHS, Denmark—91'01"), Lange Video (VHS, France), ac Video (VHS, Sweden). OST: 7" Cinevox MDF 111 (*Godzilla / Escape*—as Magnetic System)[1]

An upper-class Roman youngster, Jo Arbelli, befriends a proletarian, Paolo Soprani, and confesses he couldn't make love to his girlfriend Anna. Paolo and Jo pay a visit to the young woman, rape her and accidentally kill a female neighbor. Chased by the police and penniless, they break into a restaurant and hold the clients hostage, asking for a huge ransom of one billion lira in gold ingots, a car and a plane. Commissioner Aldobrandi, who is sieging the place with his men, takes his time about it; meanwhile, he places a sniper on the building nearby. In the hours that follow, Jo's behavior becomes increasingly fierce. After the death of two hostages, Paolo is shot and dies, while Arbelli takes off by car with a woman as human shield. But he too is fatally wounded by the sniper and ends up crashing against a truck.

Luigi Petrini's *Day of Violence* is part of the subgenre that briefly bloomed between 1976 and 1977, inspired by the real-life Circeo massacre, although the director's script also derives from Sidney Lumet's *Dog Day Afternoon.* Petrini, formerly Vittorio De Sica's assistant director, was used to commercial low-budget films, even though near the end of his career he staged a theatrical production of Shakespeare's *Othello* in Rome, with some success.

"It was almost entirely set inside a restaurant in Tirrenia" Petrini recalls. "We've been shooting there for two months. I wrote the story taking inspiration from the Circeo massacre. [...] The original title should have been *Si drogavano, sparavano, uccidevano...* [They Took Drugs, Shot, Killed...], but the distributor changed it, I don't know why."[2]

Compared to other films such as Renato Savino's appalling *I ragazzi della Roma violenta*, however, *Day of Violence* seems more sincere in its portrayal of the drama of a generation in disarray, with its two antiheroes coming from opposite social environments who nevertheless form a strong male bonding relationship, as they have the same desire of overcoming a society that rejects them and does not accept any weakness, while hiding behind a hypocritical curtain of respectability, as exemplified by the varied clientele in the restaurant. "I know "respectable people" says Jo at one point to one of the hostages (Daniele Dublino), "and I can assure you they don't exist!"

However, the message is ambiguous, as is Petrini's point of view: the filmmaker wallows in the depiction of the two young criminals' brutality, and the attempts at social criticism clash against the banally sketched characterizations, throwaway dialogue and sensationalistic sequences. The budget does not allow for elaborate set-pieces, and most scenes are shot with a hand-held camera; nevertheless the film as a whole conveys a rather convincing realism. As the nervous commissioner on the case—who, as usual in the genre, complains about the bureaucratic obstacles he must deal with, and is also plagued by personal problems, so much so that he gets to meet his estranged lover (played by singer Selvaggia Di Vasco) during the siege—director Mario Bianchi has one of his few acting roles. Mario Cutini would also play the lead in Petrini's following film, *Ring* (1978), conceived by producer Vitolo as a *Rocky* rip-off. The score, by Bixio-Frizzi-Tempera, is as trashy as it gets, replete with a protest song in the credits whose lyrics translate as: "In the streets it's impossible to live / Everyday the city is trembling with fear / Among people like us, those who would never have killed / Now easily pull the trigger" and a clue liberally borrowed from Blake Edwards' *Peter Gunn.*

The film had lots of trouble with the Italian board of censors, being the one and only crime film rejected by the censorship commission, when it was first submitted with the title *Nucleo antirapina: sparate a vista.* According to the commission's official records, the film as a whole was "focused on the exaltation of violence, both physical and moral, in its crudest and most exasperated form." The producer drastically re-edited and retitled the film, cutting almost 9' from the version destined for the home market: besides the rape near the beginning, the scenes where Aldovrandi talks on the phone with his lover were eliminated, as well as the one in which Arbelli's father, who has been called by the cops to make an appeal to his son, turns on Jo instead and begrudges him the shame that has befallen his family name. These scenes can be found in the English language version.

Notes

1. Only the B-side (*Escape*) is taken from Petrini's film. The A-side is from the soundtrack of *Godzilla* (1954, Ishiro Honda), which was re-edited (badly) colorized and re-released in Italy by Luigi Cozzi at that time.
2. Alessio Di Rocco, Stefano Raffaele and Luca Rea, "Luigi Petrini. Così, Così ... più forte," in Aa. Vv., "Misteri d'Italia 3: Guida ai film rari e scomparsi," *Nocturno Dossier* # 70 (May 2008), p. 20.

Death Hunt (*No alla violenza*)

D: Tano Cimarosa [Gaetano Cisco]. *S* and *SC:* Tano Cimarosa; *DOP:* Giovanni Raffaldi (35mm, Telecolor); *M:* Alberto Baldan Bembo (ed. Saar); *E:* Giancarlo Cadueri Venarucci; *PD:* Giancarlo Nannerini; *C:* Massimo Lupi; *AC:* Carlo Neroni; *AE:* Vincenzo Di Santo; *MU:* Lucia Della Porta; *W:* Angela Vittorini; *SO:* Mario Felici; *SS:* Rosaria Cilento.

Cast: Al Cliver [Pier Luigi Conti] (Inspector Ettore Moretti), Ninetto Davoli (Mario), Martine Carell (Martine), Tano Cimarosa [Gaetano Cisco] (Tano), Rick Boyd [Federico Boido] (Duilio Brogi), Zaira Zoccheddu (Livia), Tony [Antonio] Raccosta, Nico dei Gabbiani [Nico Tirone], Guia Lauri Filzi (Rosa), Gianni Cimarosa (Pantò), Nino Lotà (Antonio Pilo), Massimo Mollica (Corsi), Uccio Golino (Marra), Paola Quattrini (Paola Corsi). *PROD:* Morgana Film (Rome); *GM, PM:* Santo Muré; *PSu:* Salvatore Carrara; *PSe:* Sonia Maggio; *ADM, CASH:* Antonino Lucidi. *Country:* Italy. Filmed on location in Messina. *Running time:* 100'; Visa no.: 70804 (09.27.1977); *Rating:* v.m.18; *Release date:* 10.21.1977; *Distribution:* Stella Film (Regional); *Domestic gross:* 205,187,700 lira. *Also known as: Kuoleman metsästäjä* (Finland). *Home video:* KM-Video/Videotime (VHS, Finland), Panorama Video (VHS, Denmark), GVC/Super GVC (Switzerland, Italian language).

Sicily. The city of Messina is at the mercy of the mob, opposed only by the young Commissioner Ettore Moretti, dutiful but not impartial to the hard way. One day, during a chase, a kidnappers' car runs over a little girl, the daughter of an unassuming gas station attendant named Tano. From that moment on the man begins his personal war against crime. Tano tracks down the kidnappers, kills them all and releases their hostage. But he is killed by a sniper, who has mistaken him for one of the criminals.

After reaching its peak between 1974 and 1976, the vigilante subgenre hosted references to real-life news items (*Roma, l'altra faccia della violenza*), got bastardized with the rape and revenge thread, then eventually expired: Mario Monicelli's masterpiece *An Average Little Man* (*Un borghese piccolo piccolo*, 1977), was the tombstone that put the last word on the season of the so-called "commedia all'italiana." By telling the story of an elderly small clerk (Alberto Sordi) who retaliates on the young delinquent who accidentally killed his son during a robbery, by kidnapping and savagely torturing him, Monicelli depicted a gangrenous social tissue, founded on clientelism and prevarication, where violence infects everyone: the choice of Sordi, the symbol of Italy's average man, was a masterful stroke, calling in for the audience's identification with what would turn out to be a ruthless murderer. Obtusely accused of being fascist — Monicelli was an outspoken Communist for his whole life —*An Average Little Man* condensed everything that the vigilante subgenre aimed at, telling it much better and more intelligently, and most of all it stressed the thread's inner ambiguity in its paradoxical parable, best summed up in the chilling ending where the protagonist — long after his revenge has been carried out — still feels the need for a violent retaliation against whoever crosses his path.

Other respected directors tried their hands at the same theme, yet with a moralistic flair that was absent in Monicelli's film. With *Sniper* (1978), Pasquale Squitieri told the story of another armed citizen who rebels, with debatable results: "an embarrassing film because of its polemical pressure which badly blends with a visible formal care" wrote Tullio Kezich.[1] With *A Dangerous Toy* (*Il giocattolo*, 1979), Giuliano Montaldo drew upon a similar theme, with a good performance by Nino Manfredi as a clerk who discovers an irresistible fascination towards fire weapons.

A late entry in the vigilante subgenre, *Death Hunt* is a long way from the aforementioned *auteurs*. In time, it became a cult movie: the prestigious film critic Giovanni Buttafava elected it in his "ideal videotheque," calling it "a *Death Wish* of sorts, halfway between the average Turkish epic and a naïve Fassbinder film."[2] Much of the film's charm comes from its star and director: the diminutive, mustached Tano Cimarosa, a Sicilian character actor discovered by Damiano Damiani in *The Day of the Owl* and a familiar face in many genre productions.

Death Hunt, Cimarosa's second film as a director (although many conjecture on the occult directorial hand of Mario Pinzauti)[3] is definitely a low-budget affair. In an interview on "Nocturno," Al Cliver (Pier Luigi Conti) recalled the film's extremely strict shooting conditions: all the "names" in the cast — Ninetto Davoli (who was also in Cimarosa's directorial debut *Reflections in Black* [*Il vizio ha le calze nere*, 1975]) Paola Quattrini, singer Nico dei Gabbiani — all appear in minuscule roles. The film also features one of Italy's pioneering porn actresses, Guia Luri Filzi, while Alberto Baldan Bembo's theme music gets repeated over and over.

As a whole, *Death Hunt* is simply disarming in its naiveness, as synthesized by the film's original title (literally, No to Violence). It starts like a particularly mean crime story, accumulating in its first half-hour a number of violent occurrences that would be enough for three films. In the opening scene a group of thugs enters a restaurant and immediately start swearing and utterly behaving antisocially. One client — a cop — asks them to leave and gets shot in the face. Then Cimarosa leaves aside the character of the tough cop played by Cliver to concentrate on himself as the film's real hero, a gas station attendant who goes on a killing spree to avenge the death of his daughter, killed by a gang of kidnappers.

If the idea of little Tano exterminating the whole gang all by himself is unlikely, the ending — where the poor man gets a bullet in the head courtesy of a police sniper who mistakenly took him for one of the kidnappers — is a show-stopping oddity, *Night of the Living Dead*-style, that drags the film down to the hell of unintentional laughs, yet certifies Cimarosa's absolute, heartfelt sincerity.

No alla violenza features the requested amount of nudity (with an emphasis on rape) and violence (Tano's favorite weapon is a huge knife and the scene where he stabs to death the gang's leader looks like Cimarosa's demented nod to *Psycho*), but the director pulls no punches when it comes to convey the film's emotional message: when Tano's daughter is run over by a car, the director cuts to a lingering shot of the little girl's blood-covered doll. Another scene, as laughable as it might be, is equally emblematic, as the hero cries before his daughter's dead body and addresses a wooden crucifix on the wall: "And you, what are you doing?"

In portraying the character's instinctive, primordial relationship with the deity, Cimarosa's film is closer to those 1950s religious black-and-white dramas that were made for uneducated country audiences than to the poliziotteschi's urban urgency. It's also closer to the Neapolitan sceneggiata starring Mario Merola that would become one of the genre's last gleamings, blending action and melodrama, violence and tears, in a turgid shameless appeal to tradition.

Notes

1. Tullio Kezich, *Panorama*, 17.10.1978.
2. Giovanni Buttafava, "Una videoteca ideale," in Aa. Vv., *Il Patalogo cinque & sei: Annuario 1983 dello spettacolo. Cinema & Televisione + Video* (Milan: Ubulibri, 1983), p. 284.
3. Cimarosa would direct his third and last film, *Uomini di parola*, in 1981.

Destruction Force (La banda del trucido)

D: Stelvio Massi. *S:* Elisa Briganti; *SC:* Dardano Sacchetti, Elisa Briganti, Stelvio Massi; *DIA collaboration:* Tomas Milian; *DOP:* Franco Delli Colli (35mm, Gevacolor, Cinescope); *M:* Bruno Canfora; *E:* Mauro Bonanni; *PD:* Carlo Leva; *CO:* Silvana Scandariato, Silvio Laurenzi; *C:* Michele Pensato; *AD:* Danilo Massi; *MU:* Maria Cristina Rocca; *SO:* Roberto Petrozzi; *Mix:* Nino Renda. *Cast:* Luc Merenda (Commissioner Ghini), Tomas Milian (Sergio Marazzi "Er Monnezza"), Elio Zamuto (Belli), Katia Christine (Carla, Ghini's girlfriend), Corrado Solari ("Chicà," Monnezza's man), Imma Piro (Agnese Rinaldi), Nicoletta Piersanti (Maria Ciacci, Monnezza's girlfriend), Alessandra Cardini (Laura), Aldo Barberito (Pieri, the journalist), Franco Citti (Antonio Lanza), Paolo Bonetti (Osvaldo Rinaldi, "Ranocchio"), Rosario Borelli (suitcase carrier), Salvatore Billa (Milone, the robber), Mario Brega (Alberti, Chief of Police), Francesco D'Adda (Murdered jeweler), Massimo Vanni (Agent Marchetti), Stefano Raspi, Giuseppe Moschini, Leonora Vivaldi, Sergio Mioni (Gianni), Franco Balducci (Nino, the fence), Domenico Di Costanzo (Romolo Tocci). *Uncredited:* Umberto Amambrini, Angelo Boscariol (Man at the restaurant), Fortunato Arena (Cab driver), Domenico Cianfriglia (Man in bar playing pinball), Roberto Dell'Acqua (Kidnapper), Jimmy Il Fenomeno [Luigi Origene Soffrano] (Passerby), Luciano Foti (Customer at restaurant), Giuseppe Marrocco (Customer at restaurant), Danilo Massi (Danilo, police agent), Benito Pacifico (Lanza's henchman), Nello Pazzafini (Lanza's henchman), Mimmo Poli (Barman), Sergio Testori (Wrangler at bar), Marcello Venditti (kidnapper), Rinaldo Zamperla (Agent escorting diamonds). *PROD:* Gianfranco Couyoumdjian for Flora Film, Variety Film; *EP:* Ugo Tucci, Claudio Mancini; *PM:* Sergio Borelli. *Country:* Italy. *Running time:* 99'; Visa no.: 70015 (03.18.1977); *Rating:* v.m.14; *Release date:* 03.18.1977; *Distribution:* Variety Film; *Domestic gross:* 1,209,066,270 lira. *Also known as: L'exécuter vous salue bien* (France, 16.07.80—105'). *Home video:* Cinekult (DVD, Italy).

After his predecessor Taddei has been killed by a bandit, the new head of the "anti-robbery" squad, Commissioner Ghini, arrests and brings to justice the murderer. Meanwhile, another dangerous criminal, the Sicilian Belli, who intends to rob two jewelry carriers, asks Sergio Marazzi "Er Monnezza"—an old-style criminal who's an expert in pickpocketing and is averse to violence—to "lend" him his young assistant Ranocchia, so as to use him as a driver in a robbery. However, the hit ends in a massacre, and afterwards Belli kills Ranocchia so as not to leave any witnesses. Ghini and Monnezza team up against the criminal: together, though acting independently, the two manage to get the better of Belli: the commissioner kills him, while Monnezza keeps the jewels.

Compared to *Free Hand for a Tough Cop*, Stelvio Massi's *Destruction Force*—the second film featuring Tomas Milian as the proletarian thief Monnezza ("Trash")—leaves a lot more room to the character. Monnezza owns a tavern, "Alla Pernacchia" ("The Raspberry"), whose customers are greeted with plenty of insults and four-letter words,[1] which serves as a cover for his illicit trafficking: a school for petty thieves, where Monnezza teaches his pupils the art of pickpocketing, *Oliver Twist*–style.

On *Destruction Force* Monnezza's presence is a sort of foreign body within the thin action plot: the sequences featuring Milian—static, centered on the actor's monologues, extraneous to the story—almost look as if they belong to another film. The reason can be found in *Destruction Force*'s peculiar genesis: after the success of *Free Hand for a Tough Cop*, producer Ugo Tucci asked Umberto Lenzi to make another crime film starring Luc Merenda; Lenzi, who was under contract with Dania Film, rejected the offer, but promised Tucci that he would convince Tomas Milian to do a special participation in the film, not knowing that the character Milian would play was Monnezza, the very

Italian poster for *Destruction Force* (1977).

same as in the previous film. Milian accepted, on the condition that he would write his own dialogue. As a result, "his scenes were sketches, *entr'actes*, sort of little films-within-the-film where Tomas Milian wrote, acted and almost "directed" his own Monnezza."[2]

The producers took advantage of the fact, making the most out of Milian's two weeks' shooting schedule and actually transforming Monnezza into the film's co-star, much to Luc Merenda's disappointment. However, as the French actor confirmed, there weren't frictions of sorts between the two stars, who had already worked together in Sergio Martino's *Silent Action*. "Milian was a very particular person, very exasperated, hysterical, talented. Many people told me to pay attention [...]. However, there was no rivalry with Tomas. The problem was that Milian entered the film at a later stage, and they had to split the two parts, mine and his." Merenda also suffered a serious accident while performing a stunt with Franco Citti, on his penultimate day on set. "Nobody asked me if I was hurt. Next day, I couldn't even move my arm. I had one more scene in the bus depot, where I had to jump from the top of a bus onto a thug. I did it and practically fell over Stelvio. I felt a terrible pain. Twenty days later, with my arm still paralyzed, I decided to hire a lawyer and sue the producer."[3]

Rushed and haphazardly assembled (Bruno Canfora's score is mostly recycled from the first film), *Destruction Force* is definitely not one of Massi's best works. The action plot especially suffers from said imbalance: as the tough cop who runs, beats and shoots as requested, Merenda's character is hatchet-developed, and the Italian dubbing (which gives the actor an unlikely Roman accent) doesn't help, although the script gives him at least one of the poliziotteschi's best lines ever about the permeability of the two worlds—law enforcement and the underworld—in a dialogue with Franco Citti, here in his usual subproletarian thug role (the film's real antagonist Elio Zamuto enters about a hour into the film). Another amusing moment is when Ghini proposes to his girlfriend to go to the movies: she promptly replies "As long as it is a funny film, and not one of those horrible Italian crime flicks!" which is Sacchetti's smart retaliation at the critics' habit of considering poliziotteschi interchangeable.

Notes

1. The scene was reprised in *Fracchia la belva umana* (1981) by Neri Parenti, starring Paolo Villaggio, where Lino Banfi plays an exhilarating tough police commissioner, in an amusing parody of the genre's clichés.
2. Manlio Gomarasca, "Il mio amico Monnezza," *Nocturno Book* #4 (Milan 2001), p. 27.
3. Manlio Gomarasca, "Senza compromessi," p. 13.

Double Game (Torino violenta)

D: Carlo Ausino. *S* and *SC:* Carlo Ausino; *DOP:* Carlo Ausino (35mm, Technicolor—Techniscope); *M:* Stelvio Cipriani (ed. C.A.M.); *E:* Eugenio Alabiso; *PD:* Sauro Roma; *CO:* Claudia Amione; *C:* Giuseppe Lino; *AC:* Tony Cannarsa; *SO:* Antonio Campa; *Mix:* Augusto Penna; *SOE:* Tonino Cacciuottolo; *KG:* Saverio Moggio; *ChEl:* Mario Stanziano; *ST:* Ernesto Sticca; *SS:* Loretta Mondino. *Cast:* George Hilton (Commissioner Ugo Moretti), Emanuel Cannarsa (Danieli), Giuseppe Alotta, Annarita Grapputo (Lucia), Franco Nebbia (Chief of Police), Laura Ferraro, Rino Moggio, Pier Giuseppe Corrado, Cinzia Arcuri, Lorenzo Gobello, Ruggero Spagnoli, Sauro Roma, Loretta Mondino, Rino Carilli, Armando Rossi, Mauro Ballesio, Tonino Campa, Nicola Saponaro, Piero Fina, Mario Castagneri, Gianfranco Boglione, Regina Fabiani, Carlo Ausino (Cigarette seller). *PROD:* Ivano Luigino Brizzi for Lark Cinematografica (Rome), Vigor Film (Turin); *PM:* Pepé Salerno; *PI:* Michele Peyretti. *Country:* Italy. Filmed at Elios Film (Rome) and on location in Turin. *Running time:* 93'; Visa no.: 70825 (10.08.1977); *Rating:* v.m.14; *Release date:* 10.13.1977; *Distribution:* Lark; *Domestic gross:* 279,355,000. *Home video:* NoShame (DVD, USA), Alan Young (DVD, Italy), Federal (DVD, Italy).

French criminals and Italian Mafiosi lure models and students, drug and rape them, then blackmail their victims with compromising photos, forcing them into prostitution. Commissioner Moretti combats the prostitution ring, helped by a mysterious "executioner" who dispatches the criminals by night, causing a bloody war between the French and the Mafia gang. Moretti and the "executioner" are actually the same person, as his colleague and friend Danieli finds out. The Commissioner attempts to eliminate the dangerous witness, but he will meet his end instead.

In the years 1975 to 1977 the poliziotteschi mania was reaching fever pitch. The Western and *gialli* days had waned, and audiences were asking for more bullets, car chases, tough cops. And as with the aforementioned genres, a number of low-budget features popped up out of nowhere, financed by improvised production companies that lasted the making of one film and practiced the old hit-and-run tactics. Given the poliziotteschi's attention to urban environment, there was also room for regional realities and filmmakers to exploit the climate. That's the case with the two crime films directed by the Turin-based Carlo Ausino, a peculiar *auteur* figure who shot all his films in his hometown, "a foreign city that hates the rest of Italy and sends its damned messengers to spread any abominable discovery" (to quote the brilliant novelists Carlo Fruttero and Franco Lucentini). After trying his hand at a post-atomic drama (*La città dell'ultima paura*, 1975), Ausino released a diptych starring his favorite (non) actor Emanuel Cannarsa: *Double Game* (1977) and *Tony l'altra faccia della Torino violenta* (1980), characterized by a noticeable disharmony between ambitions and results.

Speaking of the film, which he shot in just two weeks, Ausino explained: "*Double Game* belongs to the final era of a certain successful Italian popular cinema. It was a film I did not believe in in the least. [...] The producers told me to aim at the genre which had been commercially fruitful in the latest seasons: Italian-style crime film. 'They did *Milan, Genoa, Rome, Naples*, do *Torino violenta*... [Violent Turin, the film's Italian title].' I said: 'Ok, I'm gonna do it, but you're gonna distribute it....' So I shot the film, which was supposed to have a different title at its release, in absolute economy. It cost just 60 million liras and a distributor immediately offered double to buy it. I accepted, and it was probably the dumbest decision of my life: *Double Game* grossed one billion and three hundred million liras." Ausino was likely exaggerating, as official grossings were a mere 280 million lira, still quite a good result for such a low budget effort. The director recalled the film's crowded premiere in Turin: "We went to the Capitol theater and watched, happy and embittered at the same time, as a multitude of people assaulted the cinema, almost breaking the doors to get in."[1]

Double Game—whose original Italian title, *Torino violenta*, aped the then-popular habit of amalgamating a city's name with the adjective "violent"—is actually a late entry in the vigilante subgenre, featuring a commissioner (George Hilton) who pairs unorthodox methods and a debatable sense of justice, moonlighting as the self-appointed avenger who kills criminals by night. Commissioner Moretti's *alter ego* garners a lot of sympathy among law enforcement units, but Moretti's friend and colleague Danieli (Cannarsa) warns the other cops: "This is not the Wild West, and avengers are not fashionable anymore." Ausino's lack of skills as a filmmaker are patent in this scene, where the director feels the need to add a close-up of a police agent who nods at Danieli's words, just to make the audience understand that, indeed he is right.

Even though in the Italian version he is dubbed by Ferruccio Amendola (who provided the voice for Robert De Niro and Tomas Milian, among others) and despite the fact that he enters the film wearing a basque just like Milian in *Emergency Squad*, goes to bed with the gorgeous Lucia (Annarita Grapputo) and even shows his judo skills in a scene, red mustached Cannarsa (who was also assistant camera on set) is Italian crime film's most unlikely hero. Besides Hilton and Grapputo—who would later star in another Ausino film, the dismal Gothic *The Damned* (*La villa delle anime maledette*, 1982), other roles are played either by Ausino regulars or non professionals.

Double Game tries hard to come up with the poliziotteschi's required ingredients, with violent action—take the opening robbery at the movie theater—wild zooms and car chases filmed through the streets of Turin (Ausino explained that these scene were shot by a cameraman sitting precariously on the car's hood). But due to lack of funds Ausino was forced to steal car crashes and explosions from other films (the footage of the police car that ends down the river bed was taken from *Young, Violent, Dangerous*) and fill the film with plugs to bars, restaurants, gyms and other shops where a number of scenes take place. Also recycled is Stelvio Cipriani's score, which comes straight out of *Execution Squad* as well as other of the composer's scores.

Ausino, Hilton and Cannarsa would team up again in 2006's *Killer's Playlist—Sulla lista del killer*, a sorry mess about a young woman who enrolls in the police after being raped, in order to track down her rapist, who may be a serial killer.

Italian poster for *Double Game* (1977).

Note

1. Davide Bracco, Stefano Della Casa, Paolo Manera and Franco Prono eds., *Torino città del cinema* (Milan: Il Castoro, 2001), p. 88.

Dove volano i corvi d'argento (Where the Silver Crows Fly)

D: Piero Livi. *S:* Aldo Serio; *SC:* Aldo Serio, Piero Livi, Adriano Asti, Delia La Bruna; *DOP:* Angelo Bevilacqua (35mm, Vistavision); *M:* Claudio Tallino (Ed. Aris); *E:* Maurizio Tedesco; *AE:* Roberta Narducci; *PD, CO:* Massimo Bolongaro; *COA:* Antonella Berardi; *AD:* Antonio Altieri; *C:* Franco Frazzi; *AC:* Camillo Sabatini; *SO:* Roberto Alberghini, Maurizio Merli; *MU:* Mauro Gavazzi; *AMU:* Sergio Angeloni; *W:* Anna Onori; *SE:* Roberto Pace; *SP:* Paolo Cavicchioli; *KG:* Cosimo Barbera;

G: Saverio Martinelli, Paolo Anzelotti; *ChEl:* Ennio Di Stefano; *Electricians:* Eolo Tramontani, Massimo Bellacci; *Generator man:* Iginio De Chellis; *Props:* Vittorio Ferrero; *SS:* Maria Zola; *DubD:* Emilio Cigoli. *Cast:* Corrado Pani (Istèvene), Jenny Tamburi [Luciana Tamburini] (Giovannangela), Flavio Bucci (Simbula), Renzo Montagnani (Maineddu), Regina Bianchi (Istevene's mother), Giampiero Albertini (Istevene's father), Piero Gerlini (Carabinieri Marshall), Paolo Malco (Podda), Massimo De Rossi (Stintino), Mariangela Giordano (Basilia), Bruno Corazzari (Killer), Nino Fuscagni (Judge), Giovanni Vannini (Mayor), Gino Usai (2nd killer), Renato Guerra (Brigadeer), Cristiano Censi (Don Lussu). *PROD:* Universale Cinetelevisiva (Rome); *PM:* Ugo De Lucia; *PSu:* Fabrizio Giubilo. *Country:* Italy. Filmed at Cinecittà (Rome) and on location in Sardinia. *Running time:* 95'; Visa no.: 69628 (12.31.1976); *Rating:* none; *Release date:* 04.29.1977; *Distribution:* Ital Noleggio Cinematografico; *Domestic gross:* 83,745,610 lira. *Home video:* Video Movie (VHS, Greece).

Sardinia. One day, while he is tending sheep, the young Giacinto Fronteddu witnesses by chance a kidnapping and is killed by one of the assassins who had noticed his presence and feared he might report to the police. From Milan, where he works as a metalworker, Istèvene, the victim's elder brother, returns to his native Sardinian village for the funeral. His father and mother now expect Istèvene to avenge his dead brother, so as to carry on the ancestral tradition of revenge, and so does the whole village. But even though he feels somehow dragged back to his country's beliefs, Istèvene will make a different choice.

Piero Livi's second film returned to the themes and atmosphere of his 1969 début *Pelle di bandito,* this time with a larger budget, a professional cast and in color. The Italian title refers to a South-American legend: crows don't attack each other as they are blinded by the silver glares of their own plumage. The film's themes revolve around the conflict between tradition and modernity, primitive rural justice and the law, with a less condescending look on banditism. The point of view here is that of Istèvene (Corrado Pani), who moved away from the isle to Milan, and became civilized: when he returns, all the things that mattered to him — family, tradition, honor — look distant and useless.

According to Livi, "*Dove volano i corvi d'argento* represents the ideal sequel to *Pelle di bandito.* [...] On *Dove volano i corvi d'argento* I chose to change my point of view: violence had changed face and got organized under the control of those "masters" which at first it was opposed to. It degenerated and had no excuses whatsoever. What at first was called "crime of honor" or "feud" had mostly turned into a kidnapping business. Traditional bandits, who lived out of rustling and admitted murder only for vengeance, had become professional bandits. That's why the film's hero chooses not to kill to avenge his brother, hoping to renew that land which only taught him to believe in violence and abuse."[1]

However, unlike his debut, and despite the good use of the Sardinian landscape that at times make it look like an Italian Western of sorts, *Dove volano i corvi d'argento* is superficial, verbose and clichéd: the presence of well-known actors such as Corrado Pani, Flavio Bucci and Renzo Montagnani works against the realistic portrayal of a Sardinian village, the dialogue is sententious and the characters are just badly sketched, one-dimensional figures, each of whom works merely as a carrier of the film's message: a poor old man says "It's always the poor who kill each other, and so will it always be," the Carabinieri marshal warns the protagonist by telling him that "Without law there would be chaos," and so on.

Despite the presence of said names, *Dove volano i corvi d'argento* passed unnoticed at its release. Twenty-four years would pass before Livi would make another film, *Sos Laribiancos — I dimenticati* (2001).

Note

1. Marco Navone and Piero Mura, *Un regista indipendente: Piero Livi, i suoi film, la rassegna di Olbia* (Olbia: Argonauti, 2007).

Gangbuster (L'avvocato della mala)

D: Alberto Marras. *S:* Alberto Marras; *SC:* Claudio Fragasso, Antonio Cucca, Vittorio Vighi, Alberto Marras; *DOP:* Angelo Bevilacqua (35mm, Telecolor, Kodak); *M:* Ubaldo Continiello (Ed. Nazional Music); *E:* Amedeo Giomini; *PD:* Dario Micheli; *CO:* Laura Frigo; *AD:* Roberto Pariante; *C:* Franco Frazzi; *AC:* Camillo Sabatino; *AE:* Tommaso Gramigna; *PDA:* Augusto La Valle; *MU:* Pino Ferranti; *Hair:* Corrado Cristofori; *SO:* Goffredo Salvatori; *Boom:* Luigi Salvatori; *SP:* Gianfranco Massa, Leo Massa; *MA:* Gilberto Galimberti; *ChEl:* Ennio Di Stefano; *KG:* Antonio Tomaino; *SS:* Maria Costantina Ercoli; *DubD:* Massimo Turci. *Cast:* Ray Lovelock (lawyer Mario Gastali), Mel Ferrer (Peseti, the boss), Lilli Carati [Ileana Caravati] (Paola Carati), John Steiner (The killer), Gabriele Tinti (Tony), Umberto Orsini (Engineer Farnese), Orazio Orlando (Giorgio), Rosario Borelli (Commissioner), Romano Puppo (Peseti's henchman), Gino Pagnani (Cab driver), Salvatore Puntillo (Pandolfi), Dante Cleri (Guelfo), Alfredo Adami (Peppe), Pino Salviani, Bruno Di Luia (Farnese's henchman), Carmelo Reale (Peseti's henchman), Gilberto Galimberti (Peseti's henchman). *Uncredited:* Nestore Cavaricci (gang member), Massimo Ciprari (Peset's henchman on car), Fulvio Mingozzi (Seganti), Benito Pacifico, Pietro Zardini (priest). *PROD:* Vincenzo Salviani and Giuliano Anellucci for T.D.L. Film, Angry Film; *PM:* Paolo Tassara; *PSu:* Paolo Lucidi; *PSe:* Pino Salviani; *CASH:* Pietro Speziali. Filmed at Elios Film (Rome). *Running time:* 95'; Visa no.: 70769 (08.26.1977); *Rating:* v.m.18; *Release date:* 09.22.1977; *Distribution:* Regional; *Domestic gross:* 230,200,276 lira. *Home video:* Golden (VHS, Italy, 88'29"), Topic (VHS, Germany, 85'51" — different version with inserts from *Meet Him and Die*) Bad DVD (DVD, UK)

Mario Gastali, a young penniless lawyer, agrees to act as intermediary in a matter of stolen paintings between the "boss" Peseti, specializing in the illegal trafficking of works of art, and engineer Farnese, the unsuspected head of a kidnapping ring. Mario collects 300 million from Farnese which he has to deliver to Peseti in exchange for two valuable Gauguin paintings, but he's robbed by four thieves. Mario is actually in cahoots with the latter, but he finds out that the money cannot be spent as it comes from a kidnapping ransom, and all the banknotes are marked. Peseti hires a killer to dispatch Farnese, whom he considers the author of the fake robbery, before he discovers that Gastali is actually the responsible party. The boss abducts Mario's girlfriend Paola, forces the young lawyer to give him the keys to the safe where he has hidden the three hundred million lira and sends his killer after him. However, Mario manages to have the last laugh.

Written and produced by the same team as Lovelock's previous crime film, *Meet Him and Die, Gangbuster*— producer Alberto Marras' only film as a director — is a much more enjoyable effort than the former. Whereas *Meet Him and Die* was more of a serious affair, *Gangbuster* adopts a mildly ironic *film noir* approach. Obviously Claudio Fragasso and the other scriptwriters had in mind Robert Altman's *The Long Goodbye* when depicting

Lovelock's character Mario Gastali, a small-time lawyer (and the film's working title *L'avvocaticchio*, meant just that in Italian, and is also the term crime boss Mel Ferrer sneeringly labels Gastali with) whose main interest is his pet cat and who sometimes invites his rich girlfriend (Lilli Carati) over, not for some tenderness but because he needs a housemaid and can't pay for one.

As in *Meet Him and Die*, the hero moves on a razor's edge between legality and illegality: however Gastali's main concern is not revenge, but money — that is, so that he can pay the bills and get some food for himself and his cat. The plot, which involves Gauguin paintings, ransom money and 300 million lira, is definitely not on a par with Chandler, but moves along at a brisk pace.

For an expert in law codes, Gastali shows outstanding skills as a fighter, in a number of tongue-in-cheek fistfights that have him face some of the poliziotteschi's recurring baddies such as Gilberto Galimberti and Romano Puppo. The endearing cast — Orazio Orlando, Gabriele Tinti and Umberto Orsini also pop up in minor roles — is perhaps the film's strongest asset, and somehow makes up for Marras' haphazard direction and the shoestring budget, which is noticeable in the so-so set-pieces. The film's best moments feature a mustache-less and bald John Steiner (who presumably shot his scenes while working on Tinto Brass' *Caligula*, where he also has his head completely shaved) as a speechless "technician" who dispatches Ferrer's adversaries without saying a word. Besides Steiner's murders — all victims get a bullet in the head, with little blood spilt — the violence quota is quite light, and Lovelock doesn't fire a single shot in the whole film, while Lilli Carati never takes off her clothes. Nevertheless the film got a "v.m.18" rating in Italy.

Ubaldo Continiello's jazzy score adds to the film's overall feel, although there are a number of references to contemporary Italy, namely the many hints at the kidnapping craze, while one scene has the recurring sound of a police siren punctuating a dialogue exchange between Lovelock and Orlando.

Curiously, the German edition of the film — distributed by London's Fama Film — features distinct editing and an alternative plot, and borrows all the highlights (car chases, prison fights) from *Meet Him and Die*. The soundtrack is also different, featuring Franco Micalizzi's theme from *Merciless Man*.

Goodbye & Amen (*Goodbye & Amen — L'uomo della C.I.A.*)

D: Damiano Damiani. *S:* based on the novel *The Grosvenor Square Goodbye* by Francis Clifford; *SC:* Nicola Badalucco, Damiano Damiani; *DIA* (English version): Harry Craig; *DOP:* Luigi Kuveiller (35mm, Eastmancolor, Technospes); *M:* Guido and Maurizio De Angelis (ed. Rizzoli Film — Slalom); *E:* Antonio Siciliano; *PD:* Umberto Turco; *CO:* Franco Carretti; *ArtD:* Egidio Spugnini; *C:* Ubaldo Terzano; *AC:* Antonio Annunziata, Renato Palmieri; *AE:* Sergio Muzzi, Ugo Morelli; *AD:* Enrico Bergier; *MU:* Franco Corridoni; *Hair:* Giuseppina Bovino; *W:* Orsola Liberati; *SO:* Luigi Salvi; *Boom:* Benito Alchimede; *KG:* Sergio Emidi; *ChEl:* Sergio Coletta; *G:* Umberto Dessena; *SE:* Paolo Ricci; *SP:* Italo Tonni; *SS:* Vittoria Vigorelli. *Cast:* Tony Musante (John Dhannay), Claudia Cardinale (Aliki De Mauro), John Steiner (Douglas James Grayson), Renzo Palmer (Parenti), Fabrizio Jovine (Inspector Moreno), Wolfango Soldati (Harry Lambert), Gianrico Tondinelli (Jake), Angela Goodwin (Carson's wife), Anna Zinnemann (Renata Lambert), John Forsythe (Carson, American ambassador in Rome), Francesco Carnelutti (Agostino), Mauro Barabani, Massimiliano Baratta, Luciano Catenacci (Vincent), Nino [Antonio] Maimone (Rogers), Gino Narciso, Sergio Doria, Christian Esposito. *Uncredited:* Ruggero De Daninos (Mr. De Mauro), Gianni Di Benedetto (Minister of Foreign Affairs), Alessandro Haber (Goldie, mustached agent), Piero Palermini (Berto), Gioia Scola (Maria Soli, Lambert's lover). *PROD:* Mario Cecchi Gori for Capital Film, Rizzoli Film; *EP:* Vittorio Cecchi Gori; *GM:* Luciano Luna; *PM:* Vincenzo Mazzucchi; *PSu:* Romano Di Casimiro; *PSe:* Marcello Tassi, Tommaso Pantano; *ADM:* Mario Lupi; *CASH:* Stefano Cialoni. *Country:* Italy. Filmed at Incir–De Paolis (Rome) and on location in Rome. *Running time:* 109'; Visa no.: 71301 (12.21.1977); *Rating:* v.m.14; *Release date:* 12.23.1977; *Distribution:* Cineriz; *Domestic gross:* 1,323,645,110 lira. *Also known as: Adiós y amén* (Argentina — Home video), *Agente doble* (Spain), *Goodbye és ámen* (Hungary), *Bitmeyen gece* (Turkey), *Goodbye und Amen* (West Germany), *Hyvästi & amen* (Finland), *O Homem da CIA* (Portugal), *Zbogom i gotovo* (Croatia). *Home video:* Cinekult (DVD, Italy).

Rome. The cynical CIA agent John Dhannay is preparing a coup d'état in an African country when something unpredictable happens. At the luxurious Hilton hotel, a deranged Vietnam veteran named Grayson shoots three people and holds an actress, Aliki, and her lover Jack hostage. Due to a misunderstanding, Dhannay initially believes the man is his colleague Lambert, whom he just discovered to be a spy. Lambert is actually on vacation with his lover (while his wife is Dhannay's lover in turn). After Grayson has also abducted the American ambassador Carson, and asked for a ransom to be delivered in a suitcase, Dhannay asks Lambert to bring Grayson the suitcase on the hotel's terrace/roof and kill him with a gun Dhannay has hidden on the roof. What Lambert does not know is that Dhannay put two blanks in the cartridge: in the resulting shoot-out, Lambert and Grayson kill each other. Commissioner Moreno smells Dhannay's trick but does not intervene.

After the committed, harsh drama *I Am Afraid*, Damiano Damiani's next film looked like a *divertissement* of sorts. Adapted from a so-so action paperback by Francis Clifford, *Goodbye & Amen* has all the marks of a work for hire, and the director does not remember it fondly. "I did it because I had to. There are films when you feel that your heart is beating in a different direction, whereas others just pass along and leave you nothing. *Goodbye & Amen* did well at the box office, however. We shot it almost entirely in a hotel that had just been built on Monte Mario."[1] The film's main location, Hilton Cavalieri (now Cavalieri Waldorf Astoria), a luxurious five-star hotel which was a recurring set in many films of the period, is an impressive choice, with its modern architecture and imposing presence, and gives *Goodbye & Amen* a cold, detached feel despite its Roman setting, which was probably what the director intended to obtain, and which mirrors the main character's feelings and actions.

Clifford's novel centered on the inner contradictions between official diplomacy and the dirty underground work by special agents, with lots of subplots and characters. On his script for *Goodbye & Amen*, co-written with Nicola Badalucco, Damiani isolated one episode and inflated it to feature length. The one thing the director was interested in was the character of Tony Musante, the ruthless CIA agent who's the film's unpleasant hero, a mediocre antithesis of the many superspies built from the James Bond mold: "He was essentially the opposite of Volonté's character in *I Am Afraid*" Damiani noted. "I must say that I never shared the collective absolution that the public opinion gives to such characters. They have the alibi of working for their country, but after all they just like to kill people. Whoever enters the secret service, to me, is a despicable person."[2]

According to assistant director Enrico Bergier, "On this occasion [...] Damiani was strangely pessimistic about the movie he was making, and kept asking himself "Who's going to watch it?" He could have dared more, but usually gave up to avoid problems and concentrate on the direction. *Goodbye & Amen* could have been a wonderful film, were it not for Tony Musante. It was a linear story, but due to Musante's interferences it underwent a series of rewritings and became a film whose meaning you don't really understand. Damiani surrendered to all of Musante's requests."[3]

To flesh out the story, the script has a few tricks up its sleeve: for the first half, it plays on the real identity of the sniper played by John Steiner and even features the most inventive use for corn flakes in a thriller so far. However, even though it works rather well as a suspense thriller, and benefits from Luigi Kuveiller's excellent cinematography, *Goodbye & Amen* nevertheless lacks the filmmaker's usual touch, and its plot often sounds taut and muffled, with one too many grotesque notes — such as Tondinelli's full frontal nude scene[4] — to take its political angle seriously. And even though Damiani's direction of actors is as tight as ever, Claudia Cardinale feels wasted in a thankless role: in one debatable change from the novel, she is not the ambassador's wife but a vapid actress. Even though John Forsythe has a forgettable cameo as the ambassador, the supporting cast is strong, with such reliable presences as Renzo Palmer, Angela Goodwin and Mario Soldati's son Wolfango, who embarked on a short-lived career as an actor in the late seventies.

Just like Sam Peckinpah's *The Killer Elite* (1975), another impeccable self-sabotage mechanism, *Goodbye & Amen* plays with impalpable characters and pretextuous "committed" touches: *I Am Afraid*'s social unease makes room for an exhibited cynicism that continually threatens to destroy the film. However, Damiani's main concern is to get to the ending, an icy, beautifully conceived and mathematically shot sequence that takes place at night on the hotel roof, as Steiner and his three hostages move — all dressed alike, with black raincoats and helmets, and all doing the same movements — towards the helicopter that the war veteran has requested for his escape. It's a disquieting, chilling piece of cinema that ends with a diabolical trick in the tail: as in *I Am Afraid* a man is treacherously shot, yet this time he's been ripped off by someone smarter than him. That's the way things go.

Notes

1. Pezzotta, *Regia Damiano Damiani*, p. 96.
2. Damiani even throws in (an unusual move for such a director) a tongue-in-cheek in-joke (one of the two films Anna Zinneman is watching on TV — at the same time! — is his own *L'istruttoria è chiusa: dimentichi*, 1971).
3. Pezzotta, *Regia Damiano Damiani*, p. 96.
4. *Ibid.*, p. 281.

***The Heroin Busters** (La via della droga)*

D: Enzo G. Castellari [Enzo Girolami]. *S:* Galliano Juso, Massimo De Rita; *SC:* Massimo De Rita, Enzo G. Castellari; *DOP:* Giovanni Bergamini (35mm, Vistavision, Telecolor); *M:* Goblin (ed. Bixio Cemsa); *E:* Gianfranco Amicucci; *PD:* Corrado Ricercato; *CO:* Luciano Sagoni; *ArtD:* Gianfranco De Dominicis; *C:* Sergio Bergamini; *AC:* Giuseppe Buonaurio; *AE:* Cesarina Casini; *2nd AE:* Roberto Amicucci; *AD:* Albino Cocco; *2nd AD:* Giuseppe Giglietti; *MU:* Massimo de Rossi; *Hair:* Luisa Garbini; *SO:* Carlo Palmieri; *Boom:* Alvaro Orsini; *Mix:* Gianni D'Amico; *KG:* Guglielmo Maga; *ChEl:* Silvano Michisanti; *SetT:* Antonio Corridori; *SP:* Franco Vitale; *STC:* Rocco Lerro; *ST:* Ottaviano Dell'Acqua; *Aerial C:* Giovanni Bergamini; *SS:* Renata Franceschi. *Cast:* Fabio Testi (Fabio), David Hemmings (Mike Hamilton), Sherry Buchanan (Vera), Wolfango Soldati (Gillo), Massimo Vanni (Massimo, drug dealer), Angelo Ragusa (Dealer), Romano Puppo (Leroy's man), Sergio Ruggeri (Sergio), Johnny Loffredo [Joshua Sinclair] (Drug boss), Leon Lenoir [Leonardo Scavino] (Hashish dealer), Gianni Orlando, Salvatore Billa (policeman), Giovanni Bonadonna (Dealer), Guido Cerniglia (Colonel), Antonella Della Porta, Andrea Franchetti, Robert Hill [Roberto Dell'Acqua] (Luciano, Leroy's man), Margherita Horowitz (Drug addict's mother), Fulvio Mingozzi (Customs officer), Ettore Pigliapoco, Ferdinando Poggi, Giuliano Sestili (Fake policeman), Luigi Schiboni, Franco Ukmar (Cop), Clemente Ukmar, Patrizia Webley [Patrizia De Rossi] (Blonde lesbian). *Uncredited:* Adolfo Belletti (Old café owner), Dino Cassio (Agent at airport), Enzo G. Castellari (Undercover cop in Amsterdam), Nestore Cavaricci (Carabiniere at the Tribunal), Domenico Cianfriglia (Drug lab assistant), Giovanni Cianfriglia (Drug lab worker), Alberto Cracco (Paolo), Ottaviano Dell'Acqua (Gillo's murderer), Franco Fantasia (Jeweler), Lina Franchi (Woman at the Tribunal), Stefania Girolami (Stefania, a student), Rocco Lerro (Juan Martinez), Emilio Messina, Benito Pacifico (Assassin in Genoa), Filippo Perego (Lawyer at the Tribunal), Renzo Pevarello (Carabiniere at Tribunal), Claudio Ruffini (Man beating Gillo), Stefania Spugnini (Drug addict), Sergio Testori (Drug lab worker), Sergio Ukmar, Claudio Zucchet (Commissioner at the Tribunal). *PROD:* Galliano Juso for Cinemaster; *PM:* Maurizio Amati; *PSu:* Pasquale Vannini; *PSe:* Giandomenico Stellitano; *ADM:* Paolo Rampazzo; *Paymaster:* Salvatore Farese. *Country:* Italy. Filmed at Incir — De Paolis (Rome) and on location in Rome, Genoa, Hong Kong, Cartagena, Amsterdam, New York. *Running time:* 89'; Visa no.: 70712 (08.10.1977); *Rating:* v.m.18; *Release date:* 08.13.1977; *Distribution:* Titanus; *Domestic gross:* 1,031,183,000 lira. *Also known as: Dealer Connection — Die Strasse des Heroins* (West Germany, 03.07.1980 — 93'); *A Via da Droga / Rota proibida* (Brazil); *Action immédiate* (France); *El camino de la droga* (Spain); *Esquadrao Anti-Droga* (Portugal). *Home video:* Blue Underground (DVD, USA), King Records (DVD, Japan), Hobby & Work (DVD, Italy). OST: CD Cinevox MDF 319.

The Rome office of the International Narcotics Bureau headed by Mike Hamilton, who's convinced that the international drug traffic has its distribution center in the Italian capital, infiltrates an undercover agent, Fabio, in the ranks of the criminal organization. Fabio, who arrived in Fiumicino from Hong Kong with a shipment of drugs, manages to get himself arrested. This way, he gets in touch with Gillo and Vera, small-time drug dealers who are less criminals than victims themselves. Through them, Fabio contacts Leroy's men. Hidden behind the screen of a pharmaceuticals lab in Rome, Leroy's organization distributes the drug handled in a clandestine laboratory. Although he is followed at a distance by Mike, Fabio's task is not easy at all, because of Leroy's men's distrust of him as well as the fact that the police are unaware of his mission and thus harasses him several times. To win Leroy's confidence, Fabio is forced to act as a drug courier. Eventually unmasked by criminals and forced to fight alone, Fabio will nonetheless succeed.

Made straight after Castellari's elegiac Western masterpiece *Keoma* (1976), *The Heroin Busters* is a return to the director's favorite genre. However, unlike the previous year's *The Big Racket*, the result is a cold, technically impeccable yet overindulgent formalist exercise in style, where Castellari's dynamic visuals and adrenaline action sequences can't plug the many leaks in a comic book–style script, populated by dull characters — starting with lead Fabio Testi as an undercover cop with an unlikely look who battles a drug organization based in Rome which distributes heroin from the Third World to the United States. It's no coincidence that most supporting roles are played by Castellari's regular stunts, since what matters here are basically the action sequences.

The elaborate, thrilling opening sequence, where Mike (David Hemmings, playing an almost identical character as he did that same year in Bruno Corbucci's *Swindle*) and his men tail a drug courier to a hotel, is worthy of Brian De Palma in its complex conception and stylish execution, and ranks among Castellari's very best. Yet even the director's typically keen editing cuts — notably the dialogue exchange between Testi and Gillo (Wolfango Soldati) on the stairs, intercut with quick flashes of Sherry Buchanan and Patrizia Webley indulging in lesbian lovemaking, and Soldati's murder in the jewelry — end up looking affected within a conceited storyline that unconvincingly draws upon daily news items and is filled with glaring banalities, such as the usual ignorant view on light drugs. According to the film, whoever smokes a joint will end up shooting heroin.

Eventually, *The Heroin Busters* literally falls into pieces as a movie: the last half-hour is virtually one long, non-stop chase — on foot, by bike, car and plane (!) — between Testi and the drug dealers, which starts in the outskirts of Rome and moves on through the subway yard, the baths of Caracalla, the airport and eventually on a motorway. As one critic wrote, "seen today, *The Heroin Busters* reveals itself as the testimony of a city that in those years was continually changing [...], with Trastevere looking like a subproletarian borough filled with "Off" theatres populated by young artists, drifters and junkies; with the Tuscolana artery in the suburbs, still with Pasolinian echoes; with the cement skeletons of huge popular apartment buildings and the subway line yet to be open; the Opera stage at the baths of Caracalla invaded by tourists."[1] It's a directorial *tour-de-force*, a series of bravado showpieces that on one hand confirm Castellari's status as one of Europe's major action filmmakers of the decade and shows the director's ability in turning banally written scenes into something truly exciting — take the one where Testi shoots a drug dealer through a steel tube, or the segment set in the Rome underground. On the other hand, though, all of this just emphasizes the story's liability, which can't even stand a theoretical reading as was the case with *The Big Racket*'s narrative stylization.

Sporting Goblin's memorable (even though not on a par with the one the band just wrote for Dario Argento's *Suspiria*) score, which blends funk, psychedelia and rock with wild abandon and perfectly serves the film, *The Heroin Busters* did moderately well at the box office, although it did not perform as well as expected, due also perhaps to its "v.m.18" rating.

Note

1. Pierpaolo De Sanctis, "La via della droga," in Aa.Vv., "Il punto G. guida al cinema di Enzo G. Castellari," p. 47.

Highway Racer (Poliziotto sprint)

D: Stelvio Massi. *S* and *SC:* Gino Capone; *DOP:* Riccardo Pallottini, Franco Delli Colli (35mm, Eastmancolor, Telecolor); *M:* Stelvio Cipriani, conducted by the author (ed. C.A.M.); *E:* Mauro Bonanni; *PD:* Claudio Cinini; *C:* Michele Pensato; *AC:* Giancarlo Giannesi, Aldo Antonelli, Riccardo Dolci; *AE:* Walter Diotallevi; *2nd AE:* Maria Letti; *AD:* Danilo Massi; *MU:* Dante Trani; *Hair:* Mirella Ginnoto; *SO:* Bruno Zanoli; *Boom:* Angelo Amatulli; *SOE:* Renato Marinelli, Donato Ungaro; *Mix:* Danilo Moroni, Romano Pampaloni; *W:* Anna Cirilli; *W:* Maria Cristina Lorenzi; *ChEl:* Remo Dolci; *KG:* Giuseppe Raimondi; *PrM:* Tullio Lullo; *SP:* Bruno Bruni, Daniele Barbieri; *STC:* Rémy Julienne; *SS:* Flavia Sante Vanin; *UP:* Lucherini, Rossetti, Spinola. *Cast:* Maurizio Merli (Marco Palma), Angelo Infanti (Jean-Paul Dossena, "Nizzardo"), Giancarlo Sbragia (Marshall Tagliaferri), Lilli Carati [Ileana Caravati] (Francesca), Glauco Onorato (Pistone), Orazio Orlando (Silicato), Gaetano Balestrieri, Rosario Borelli (Marshall Bresciani), Tullio Casarino, Paolo Casella, Gabriele Domenichini, Vittorio Fanfoni (Dossena's man), Tom Felleghy (Customer in car showroom), Manfred Freyberger (Chief of Police), Claudio Giorgi [Giorgiutti], Mario Granato (Dossena's man), Michelangelo Jurlaro, Giuseppe Moschini [Ruschini], Domenico [Mimmo] Poli (Peppone, the informer). *Uncredited:* Francesco Annibali (policeman), Bruno Bertocci (Ambulance doctor), Nestore Cavaricci (policeman), Luciano Zanussi (Journalist). *PROD:* Giovanni Di Clemente for Cleminternazionale Cinematografica; *UM:* Vincenzo Santangelo; *PSu:* Vittorio Biferale, David Pash; *PSe:* Fabrizio Silvestro; *PSeA:* Vincenzo Santangelo; *ADM:* Vincenzo Lucarini, Antonio Pala. *Country:* Italy. Filmed on location in Rome. *Running time:* 105'; Visa no.: 70715 (08.09.1977); *Rating:* not rated; *Release date:* 08.10. 1977; *Distribution:* Titanus; *Domestic gross:* 1,308,550,110 lira. *Also known as: SOS jaguar, opération casse gueule* (France), *Stan's snabbaste snut!!!* (Sweden), *Venganza de un policia* (Argentina), *Highway Racer — vauhtipaholainen veressä* (Finland). *Home video:* Fortune 5 (DVD, Us, as part of the "Grindhouse Experience 2" boxset — fullscreen, bad quality), Creazioni Home Video (VHS, Italy). OST: LP CAM AMP 198.

Rome. Agent Marco Palma of the mobile squad — nicknamed "Crazy" by his colleagues, not so much for his character but because of his passion for cars and speed — launches into reckless chases through the streets of the capital whenever criminals are on the loose. The consequences are often disastrous both for himself and for those unlucky enough to sit next to him. Nevertheless, when a French criminal and ace car driver named Nizzardo ridicules the police with a series of spectacular robberies, Marco's superior Tagliaferri gives him a powerful Ferrari and entrusts him with a mission to arrest the robber. By posing as a gangster and attracting Nizzardo's attention, Marco becomes a member of the Frenchman's gang, but due to a banal mistake his true identity is uncovered. In the end, even though the young agent could arrest his enemy, Marco challenges Nizzardo to one final challenge, a spectacular car race that ends with Nizzardo's death in a fatal crash.

The first of six films starring Maurizio Merli that Stelvio Massi directed between 1977 and 1980, *Highway Racer* is something unique in the actor's career, and features a quite different atmosphere and feel from contemporaneous poliziotteschi. "It was 1976 and I was in Milan, shooting the third installment in the *Mark the Cop* series, when I met Maurizio Merli for the first time during a hiatus" Massi recalls about his encounter with the actor. "Maurizio, whom I didn't know as well as my son Danilo — who had worked with him on a few occasions — did, was shooting Marino

Girolami's *Special Cop in Action.* When I got back to Rome, I met producer Giovanni Di Clemente and asked him what would be the next film we were going to shoot, and it turned out it would be one starring that actor I just met a few days earlier, Maurizio Merli. The film was *Highway Racer*, and from then on Maurizio and I worked together as a team, making six film in four years. It was a beautiful friendship that went far beyond the professional work on set."[1]

Gino Capone's script is a patent attempt at rejuvenating both the thread and the actor's screen persona, aiming at a younger audience. Merli (mustache-less for the only time in his crime film career, and doing his own dubbing in the Italian version) is not a commissioner but a mere police agent, Marco Palma, with a flair for motors, cars and speed. Compared to Merli's previous characters, Marco's got in common a hot temper and an endearing smile, but he'd rather sit behind a wheel than fire a weapon. His obsession is not justice at all costs but being a winner, a number one — a motivation that made Palma closer to those kids in the audience who didn't really care for urban safeness as much as they craved for a brand new car. The inspiration for such a character came again from a real-life figure, brigadier Armando Spatafora, who in the 1960s had been a recurring name on newspaper headlines because of his driving skills during spectacular police operations, gaining the nickname "Poliziotto sprint," which would also become the film's Italian title.

Palma is a hero with whom younger audiences could identify with much better than *Violent Rome*'s Betti: he is closer to the proletarian universe that the film refers to, with hot rods and clandestine car races in the suburbs. His antagonist (Angelo Infanti) is equally far from the usual sadistic villains in poliziotteschi: he's an elegant, almost detached criminal, who loves horse races and during an escape by car gets himself arrested rather than running over a newborn baby in a carriage. Similarly, the final showdown is not a bloody shoot-out but a spectacular race where the two pilots try to outmatch each other.

Italian poster for *Highway Racer* (1977).

Less blood (the film didn't even get a "v.m.14" rating), more stunts: the result was a box office hit. As Massi recalled: "At the film première at the "Brancaccio" cinema in Rome there was a great deal of applause and Maurizio was quite happy. Outside the theater, youngsters were so excited by the film that they jumped into their cars and drove away at full speed, as they had just seen Maurizio do in the movie."[2] Critics were kinder than usual as well: despite remarking upon its "true reactionary ideology," most found *Highway Racer* "more amiable and astute than other films of its ilk, because it's more spectacular in its 'police and thieves on four wheels' game."[3]

Even though Merli did his share of driving for the film (such as the scenes where Palma is training in the autodrome), *Highway Racer*'s main asset are Rémy Julienne's spectacular car stunts, which recreate the atmosphere of live stunt shows and at times recall similar American films of the period. According to Massi, the French stuntman wrecked no less than 18 vehicles during shooting. One extremely well-executed scene — which Massi shot at five in the morning to avoid trouble with the authorities—has Julienne drive his car down the famous Trinità dei Monti stairway. The film's ending, with Nizzardo meeting his death during the final challenge with Palma, was practically improvised during shooting, as Julienne destroyed the car that was supposed to be driven by Infanti's character, whereas the original ending had Palma and his adversary shaking hands after their challenge had ended on a tie.

The spectacular set-pieces are amply showcased by Massi's direction, even though at times the film overrelies on crashes and slow-motion rollovers. On the other hand, the characters are often torpid, one-dimensional figures, starting with the film's insignificant and dumb love interest (Lilli Carati). Even the relationship between Marco and his superior (Giancarlo Sbragia), a former ace driver who is both a father figure and a role model to Palma, stagnates in a predictable generational confrontation.

Massi considered *Highway Racer* to be his best work, on a par with *The Rebel* (*Poliziotto solitudine e rabbia*, 1980). He would return to the theme of speed and motors in an action diptych formed by *Speed Cross* and *Speed Driver* (both released in 1980 and starring Fabio Testi, even though Massi had envisioned Merli in the lead) which, even though at times labeled as crime films, have very little to do with the genre.

Notes

1. Norcini and Ippoliti, "Stelvio Massi ricorda Maurizio Merli,," p. 12.
2. Matteo Norcini, "Vita e spettacolo di ... Maurizio Merli commissario cult," *Amarcord* #4 (September/October 1996), p. 33.
3. G. Gs. [Giovanna Grassi], *Corriere della Sera*, 09.02.1977.

I Am Afraid, a.k.a. *The Bodyguard (Io ho paura)*

D: Damiano Damiani. *S* and *SC:* Nicola Badalucco, Damiano Damiani; *DOP:* Luigi Kuveiller (35mm, Technicolor); *M:* Riz Ortolani, conducted by the author (ed. Radiofilmusica); *E:* Antonio Siciliano; *PD, SD:* Umberto Turco; *AArtD:* Egidio Spugnini; *CO:* Luciana Marinucci; Assistant *CO:* Wanda Pruni; *C:* Ubaldo Terzano; *AC:* Antonio Annunziata, Alberto Maria Pisani, Giulio Maffei; *AE:* Sergio Muzzi, Luigi Gorini; *AD:* Mario Maffei; *2nd AD:* Amanzio Todini; *Chief MU:* Franco Rufini; *MU:* Fabrizio Sforza; *Hair:* Paolo Borselli; *SO:* Rocco Roy Mangano; *Boom:* Benito Alchimede; *Mix:* Romano Checcacci; *G:* Umberto Dessena; *SP:* Giuseppe Botteghi; *SS:* Vivalda Vigorelli; *UP:* Anna Maria Tatò. *Cast:* Gian Maria Volonté (Brigadeer Lodovico Graziano), Erland Josephson (Judge Cancedda), Mario Adorf (Judge Moser), Angelica Ippolito (Gloria), Bruno Corazzari (Captain La Rosa), Paola Arduini (Irma Caterini), Giorgio Cerioni (Major Masseria), Laura De Marchi (Elsa Meroni), Aldo Farina, Giuseppe Fazio (Pastorino), Paolo Malco (Caligari), Laura Trotter (Caligari's girlfriend), Raffaele Di Mario (Colonel Ruiz), Rino Sentieri (Tognon), Aldo Valletti (Prison governor), Claudio Zucchet (Rino Lunardi). *Uncredited:* Francesco D'Adda (Man in warehouse), Vittorio Fanfoni (Fat protesting policeman), Margherita Horowitz (Cancedda's sister), Rocco Lerro (Man shooting Graziano), Luciano Rossi (Man with hidden camera), Valeria Sabel (Judge Massini's wife), Sergio Serafini (Protesting policeman in pinstripe suit), Gianrico Tondinelli (Killer in movie theater). *PROD:* Luigi and Aurelio De Laurentiis for Auro Cinematografica; *PM:* Marcello Crescenzi; *PSu:* Mario Della Torre; *PSe:* Ennio Appetecchia. *Country:* Italy. Filmed at Auro Cinematografica (Rome) and on location in Rome. *Running time:* 119'; Visa no.: 70367 (07.23.1977); *Rating:* v.m.14; *Release date:* 10.06.1977; *Distribution:* C.I.C.; *Domestic gross:* 1,708,460,918 lira. *Also known as:* *Un Juge en danger* (Paris, 05.17.1978—119'), *Ich habe Angst* (08.15.1981—120'), *Tengo miedo* (Spain). *Home video:* UVI (VHS, USA—Italian language), Nova Video (VHS, Switzerland). OST: LP CAM AMP 199.

A terrorist commando kills a magistrate as he's walking out the door. Rather than responding, brigadier Graziano hides behind a car in panic. Later on Graziano—who stays on his own while his colleagues protest because they feel abandoned by the State—is assigned as bodyguard to the meek judge Cancedda. However, Cancedda's investigations on what appears to be a banal murder reveal alarming implications: together with the judge, Graziano spies on the encounters between a fascist terrorist, Caligari, and Colonel Ruiz of the Secret Service. However, all witnesses are killed, including Cancedda. After the judge's murder, Graziano is assigned as bodyguard to judge Moser, Cancedda's substitute: with the help of seedy journalist Tognon, the brigadier finds out that Moser is in cahoots with the terrorists. After Tognon's murder, Graziano kills Ruiz in self-defense. He learns that Moser has set a trap for him, and with a smart ploy he manages to get the judge murdered in his place by the designated killer inside a movie theater. In the end, though, just when he's about to tell his superiors what he's discovered, Graziano is himself fatally shot.

After the commercially successful but artistically disappointing comedy western *A Genius, Two Partners and a Dupe*, a.k.a. *Trinity Is Back Again* (*Un genio, due compari e un pollo*, 1975), produced by Sergio Leone, Damiano Damiani returned to what he knew best. *I Am Afraid* is perhaps the most chilling document on the so-called "leaden years." The story revolves around a magistrate (Erland Josephson) who is murdered after discovering the connivance between fascist terrorists and the Secret Service, and his bodyguard Lodovico Graziano (Gian Maria Volonté), who realizes he knows too much. "It was the story of two characters who discover truths which they can't reveal, and find out they cannot get any help on the part of the Law," Damiani explained.[1]

The script, by the director and his collaborator Nicola Badalucco, is engrossing and tightly written, and it gets more and more intense as it goes along. *I Am Afraid* continually seems on the verge of abandoning its realistic path and turning into a Kafka-esque nightmare: when brigadier Graziano is entrusted to escort a magistrate (Mario Adorf) who follows the same steps as his predecessor, the story revolves on itself like a snake biting its own tail, in a mocking, symmetrical *déjà vu*. Yet Damiani, unlike Petri (*Todo Modo*) and Rosi (*Illustrious Corpses*) doesn't go for a metaphysical approach, and keeps the story stubbornly close to reality—that very same reality which in poliziotteschi is at least partially exorcised through the references to exemplary real-life stories, deformed and turned into film material by the genre's hyperrealistic approach. This includes the references to the present as well: the fugitive terrorist is modeled upon neo-fascist Franco Freda, one of the masterminds behind the Piazza Fontana bombing, while the character of Tognon (played by former singer Rino "Joe" Sentieri) represents journalist Mino Pecorelli and his controversial agency (later a weekly magazine) "OP." Just like Tognon in the film, Pecorelli would be murdered in March 1979—to many, he had found out too much about the Moro kidnapping and killing.

The choice of Gian Maria Volonté as Graziano is exemplary of Damiani's approach. Seven years after *Investigation of a Citizen Above Suspicion*, the circle is over. In Petri's film the actor played a commissioner who toyed with power, here he is a mediocre police agent, badly paid and badly dressed: the contrast between Graziano's cheap raincoats and the impeccable silk shirts worn by the commissioners played by Merenda and Merli gives an idea of *I Am Afraid*'s difference from strictly genre products, where there is always a gap between the hero and the reality that surrounds him. According to the director, "that's a character Volonté "felt" very much. I liked his sensible face, a face that had a working class feel to it, the face of someone who understands when he's being ripped off."[2]

To make the portrayal of law enforcement as closer to reality as he can, Damiani even mentions police unions and their protests—something unique in crime films, where the hero, even though badly paid (see *Killer Cop* or *Free Hand for a Tough Cop*) doesn't seem to really care about his salary. As critic Davide Pulici noted, "for the first time in an Italian film, policemen are given a class conscience, they protest and march against their superiors, claim the right to disobey orders that turn them into gun fodder, and step aside from the usual conventions [...] that portray them as either caricatures or heroes."[3]

Brigadier Lodovico Graziano doesn't have the iron armor of the contemporaneous tough cops: in fact, he's the exact opposite. "He's a simple character, a man who didn't study much; to him, being a cop is a job like any other" Damiani added.[4] Graziano's an ordinary cop, middle-aged, humble, insecure. An average man who gets involved in spite of himself in a story much bigger than him, in a plot whose meaning he does not understand; a man who is full of doubts and who makes many mistakes. A man who is understandably worried about his life. A man who *is afraid.*

Damiani's film is the most remarkable example of a cinema "with eyes wide open, in step with the times, and which doesn't try to compete with reality" as Alberto Pezzotta wrote. To the Milanese critic, *I Am Afraid* is "one of the films that, nowadays, most precisely convey the sense of threat and loss of all certainties, political and civil alike, which emerged back then for the first time."[5]

But Damiani's masterpiece is not just that. It's also a remarkably constructed thriller, which culminates in one truly extraordinary climax: a showdown in a porn movie theater where the corrupt magistrate is watching softcore flicks—a precise reference to the then frequent occurrence of magistrates seizing supposedly obscene films right after their release: the film Adorf is watching is Mario Pinzauti's *Mandinga* (1976)—and where Graziano realizes that a deadly trap has been set up for him. It all climaxes in a savage shoot-out that briefly sees Graziano triumphant. What comes next represents perhaps the most desperate ending ever featured in a 1970s Italian film, for what it shows and in the way Damiani films it. It comes unexpectedly, when the movie is almost over and Graziano has seemingly managed to get the upper hand. He's wrong, we are wrong. Graziano is killed too, but his death has a different taste than those awaiting Rogas (*Illustrious Corpses*) and Betti (*Special Cop in Action*). The latter are designated victims: in Rosi's film, the commissioner played by Lino Ventura pays for his obtuse pragmatism in fighting an ubiquitous, transcendent power, whereas Maurizio Merli's heroic cop is like a sheriff in the Wild West, wearing his badge with pride but knowing that somewhere there's a bullet awaiting him. Betti's death, shot in the back at the end of *Special Cop in Action*, makes him a truly heroic figure. That doesn't happen with Lodovico Graziano: he's just a citizen like any other, someone who happens to be a cop, a pawn in the game with no name or importance. No one will remember him, like no one remembers the many nameless victims whose blood stained the streets in Italy's darkest decade.

Notes

1. Pezzotta, *Regia Damiano Damiani*, p. 95.
2. *Ibid.*
3. Davide Pulici, "Io ho paura," in Aa. Vv., "Italia ultimo atto: Guida al cinema politico civile dalle origini a Buongiorno, notte," *Nocturno Dossier* #15 (October 2003), p. 49.
4. Pezzotta, *Regia Damiano Damiani*, p. 295.
5. *Ibid.*, p. 27.

La malavita attacca ... la polizia risponde! (Syndicate Attacks ... Police Respond)

D: Mario Caiano. *S:* Paolo Barberio; *SC:* Paolo Barberio, Mario Caiano; *DOP:* Pier Luigi Santi (35mm, Gevacolor, Telecolor); *M:* Lallo [Coriolano] Gori, conducted by the author (ed. Nationalmusic); *E:* Renato Cinquini; *PD:* Giorgio Postiglione; *CO:* Alberto Verso; *AD:* Ennio Coccia; *C:* Adolfo Bartoli; *AC:* Giuseppe Venditti; *AE:* Carlo Marino, Anna Marino; *MU:* Stefano Trani; *Hair:* Gisella Trani; *SO:* Luciano Muratori; *Boom:* Angelo Amatulli; *SOE:* Luciano Anzellotti; *Mix:* Renato Cadueri; *SP:* Mauro Chiari; *SS:* Marisa Agostini. *Cast:* Leonard Mann [Leonardo Manzella] (Commissioner Baldi), John Steiner (Rudy), Maria Rosaria Omaggio (Laura Olivieri), Chris Avram (Prof. Salviati "Il Principe"), Ettore Manni (Rampelli), Corrado Gaipa (Doctor), Liana Trouché (Irene Baldi), Lorenzo Piani (Anguilla, Rudy's henchman), Adriano Amidei Migliano (Moretto), Thomas Rudy ("Cinese," Rudy's henchman), Sergio Mioni (Vitella), Franco Ressel (Franco, jeweler), Piero Leri, Edmondo Tieghi ("Biondo"), Giuseppe Ferrara ("Padovano," Rudy's henchman), Gianni Elsner (Rudy's henchman), Massimo Mirani (Rudy's henchman), Dante Cleri ("Sor Maestro"), Paolo Figlia. *Uncredited:* Umberto Amambrini, Franco Beltramme (Mafia man killed by Salviati), Giovanni Cianfriglia (Man at funeral), Mario Granato (plainclothes cop), Emilio Messina (Barman), Roberto Messina (Man at the Alicorno), Giovanni Pallavicino (Hitman), Bruno Rosa. *PROD:* Capitol International, Jarama Film; *PM:* Ennio Onorati; *PSu:* Mario Olivieri; *PSe:* Giovanni Pantano, Alfonso Licata; *PSeA:* Giovanni Maccari; *CASH:* Francesco Maia. *Country:* Italy. Filmed at Incir–De Paolis (Rome) and on location in Rome. *Running time:* 100'; Visa no.: 70740 (08.12.1977); *Rating:* v.m.14; *Release date:* 08.24.1977; *Distribution:* Capitol Film; *Domestic gross:* 692,879,780 lira. *Also known as: La malavita si scatena* (Italy—TV version), *Kaliberi 44* (Finland), *El hampa ataca, la policia responde* (Spain). *Home video:* Hobby & Work (DVD, Italy), Filmax (DVD, Spain), Mondial (VHS, Canada), Universal (VHS, Italy), SSV (VHS, Switzerland), Magna Film (VHS, Finland).

Back from Switzerland to Rome, crime boss professor Salviati, called "The Prince," finds out that his illicit business has been partly compromised by Rudy, a presumptuous small-time bandit who dreams of becoming Rome's new underworld king. Commissioner Baldi, a young and courageous cop, takes advantage of the feud between the two, also drawing on the advice of a former colleague, Rampelli, who has become involved with the underworld. Thanks to Rampelli, who pays for his collaborationism with his life, Baldi picks up a case that remained unsolved: the killing of three bosses in a house rented by a certain Mario Olivieri, who later committed suicide. The Commissioner, having discovered that Olivieri was an employee of Salviati, gets to meet Olivieri's young paralytic daughter Laura, who is paternally maintained by Salviati. The girl finds evidence of Salviati's being the one responsible for said massacre, and Baldi saves her just in time from the Professor, who had also eliminated Rudy.

Mario Caiano's last film for the big screen, *La malavita attacca … la polizia risponde!* is an average poliziotteschi that got little exposure outside Italy (where it only enjoyed mediocre box office returns): unlike Caiano's other works, there is no trace of an English language copy so far. As with *Weapons of Death*, once again the star is curly Italo-American Leonardo Manzella a.k.a. Leonard Mann, as the umpteenth bisyllabic commissioner (Baldi), who's more casually dressed than his colleagues (forget Merli's impeccable suits and shirt) and is more convincing when it comes to pass for a drug dealer in an undercover operation. "I have *carte blanche*, I have a special squad and most of all I have no respect for anyone" he says. "I have made up my mind to clean the city." Due to the film's low-budget (displayed by Caiano's overreliance on hand-held shots) there is no special squad in sight, and the story is very similar to other crime films of the period, depicting Baldi's fight against two different gangsters — the proletarian, vulgar Rudy "The Handsome" (John Steiner) and the powerful, beyond suspicion Professor Salviati "The Prince" (Chris Avram) — with predictable results. Even though the script comes up with a few good ideas, such as the humorous initial heist carried out on an unsuspecting jeweler (Franco Ressel) by Rudy's men disguised as cops, or Baldi's agents posing as mourners at a funeral when it comes to frame Rudy during a drug deal ("Hey, that man must have been a fag! There's only men at his funeral" the gangster marvels), the similarities with Lenzi's *The Cynic, the Rat and the Fist* (which was released six months earlier) are patent.

Yet Caiano (who co-scripted the film with Paolo Barberio) does a better job than usual with the characters. "If there was an award for the greatest son of a bitch, no one would beat Rudy" one character says. As the aforementioned son-of-a-bitch (who nicknames himself "The Eight King of Rome"), Steiner does a great tongue-in-cheek impersonation: the gangster shows a debatable taste in clothes (he's changing suit from scene to scene, and is always dressed in vividly colored jackets and shirts), behaves rudely, pays everybody a drink when he enters a bar ("Put it on my bill" is his catchphrase) and boasts about his criminal empire while he's actually a small-time gangster who thinks too big for his own good.

Even though it's hard to take the Brit actor for a proletarian Roman, and the thick accent given to him by the dubbing is quite unlikely, Steiner is always fun to watch — as when he quotes Amedeo Nazzari's famous line in Alessandro Blasetti's *La cena delle beffe* (1942), "Whoever doesn't drink with me, may the plague seize him!" — and overall his character is even more memorable than the very similar one played by Tomas Milian in *The Cynic, the Rat and the Fist*. One particularly well-conceived scene has Rudy dispatch one of his henchmen who betrayed him, in a pinewood where he stopped to take a leak. "He who doesn't piss in company is either a thief or a spy" he says (a popular Italian motto), then he has his acolytes urinate over the unfortunate guy before beating him savagely and finishing him with a bullet.

On the other hand, the "Prince" (who sports a beautiful

Italian poster for *La malavita attacca … la polizia risponde!* (1977).

country villa and raises racehorses) is given a great slow-motion opening scene, where he dispatches other gangsters with a machine gun *à la* the St. Valentine's Day Massacre. The contrast between Salviati and Rudy, on which Baldi cleverly relies to get the two gangsters to fight one another, is first of all a matter of class struggle, as shown by the scene in which Rudy is invited to dinner by his rival, where Caiano underlines the former's lack of manners as opposed to Avram's impeccable behavior. The film's most interesting character, however, is ex-cop Rampelli, who plays on both sides of the law, acting as Baldi's and Rudy's informer. As played by Ettore Manni — a former teen idol in the '50s, who had also co-starred in Tony Richardson's outstanding *Mademoiselle* (1966) before falling into B-movie oblivion, due also to his physical decadence — Rampelli becomes a sort of fatherly figure to Baldi, and also an incarnation of his aspirations, as he can move beyond the law at will, like Baldi would but can't. "That's the advantage of not being a cop: no search warrants, no lawyers, no white gloves..." he quips, wallowing in an ambiguity of double and triple crosses that he abandons only in the end, when it comes to decide whether to save himself or his younger friend. In this scene — Rampelli is waiting for Rudy in a park, but the appointment is a trap set up by Rudy's men — Caiano tries hard to reach a suspended rarefaction, but unfortunately he is not Castellari.

Where *La malavita attacca ... la polizia risponde!* falls badly is when Maria Rosaria Omaggio is on-screen. As the wheelchair-bound girl whom the commissioner falls for, who plays Chopin at the piano and reads Sciascia's books, she's given a number of ear-wrenching lines ("Are you a feminist?" "No, I'm a paralytic") and her character does never even get close to being interesting. Caiano's film also loses steam towards the end: and, as proven by the scene where Baldi takes a pistol-pen out of his pocket to dispatch an enemy, which looks like something out of a 1960s Bond rip-off, he probably wasn't taking his own film seriously anymore.

A Man Called Magnum (Napoli si ribella)

D: Michele Massimo Tarantini. *S:* Dardano Sacchetti; *SC:* Dardano Sacchetti, Michele Massimo Tarantini; *DOP:* Sergio Rubini (35mm, Eastmancolor, LV-Luciano Vittori); *M:* Franco Campanino, conducted by the author and played by Panama Red Orchestra (ed. Grandi Firme della Canzone); *E:* Alberto Moriani; *PD:* Franco Calabrese; *CO:* Silvio Laurenzi; *C:* Ezio Bellani; *AC:* Alessio Gelsini; *AE:* Patrizia Malvestito; *AD:* Massimo Manasse; *MU:* Maria Cristina Rocca; *Hair:* Marcello Longhi; *SO:* Bruno Zanoli; *Boom:* Guglielmo Smeraldi; *Mix:* Bruno Moreal; *SP:* Francesco Narducci; *ST:* Roberto Alessandri; *SS:* Mirella Roy Malatesta. *Cast:* Luc Merenda (Commissioner Dario Mauri), Enzo Cannavale (Marshall Nicola Capece), Adolfo Lastretti (Pasquale Donnaregina "Dogheart"), Ferdinando Murolo (Bonino), Marianne Comtell (Carola), Mattia Machiavelli (Antonio Esposito "The Sheik"), Francesca Guadagno (Luisa), Sonia Viviani (Rosa), Giancarlo Badessi (Lawyer Cerullo), Claudio Gora (Don Domenico Laurenzi "Don Mimì"), Claudio Nicastro (Chief of Police), Enrico Maisto (Gennaro Andronico), Domenico Di Costanzo (Don Mimì's butler), Franco Marino (Ruggero, Don Mimì's chauffeur), Tommaso Palladino (Garrese), Adriana Facchetti (Luisa's governess), Salvatore Billa (Club bouncer), Fortunato Arena (Robber at the "Banco di Sconto"), Anna Cannio [Anna Walter] (Donna Concetta Quagliaruno), Geoffrey Copleston (German boss). *Uncredited:* Francesco Anniballi (Robber at the "Banco di Sconto"), Ennio Antonelli (Bonino's man at the mushroom farm), Angelo Boscariol (Arrested man), Gianni Diana (Core'e Cane's accomplice), Nello Pazzafini (Killer), Santo Simone (Cerullo's messenger to Mauri). *PROD:* Luciano Martino for Dania Film; *PM:* Franco Cuccu; *PSu:* Francesco Fantacci; *PSe:* Dario Armellini. *Country:* Italy. Filmed at Incir — De Paolis (Rome) and on location in Naples. *Running time:* 105'; Visa no.: 70621 (07.23.1977); *Rating:* v.m.14; *Release date:* 08.07.1977; *Distribution:* Titanus; *Domestic gross:* 999,562,030 lira. *Also known as: Calibre magnum pour l'inspecteur* (France), *Magnum Killer* (Grece — Home video). *Home video:* No Shame (DVD, USA), Alan Young (DVD, Italy). OST: CD Digitmovies CDDM152.

Commissioner Dario Mauri is transferred from Milan to Naples, where he is preceded by his reputation of being a tough and shrewd investigator. Meanwhile, crime boss Domenico Laurenzi, also known as Don Mimì, learns about the theft of two million dollars' worth of heroin, which make him unable to cope with his commitments to the international drug ring. Don Mimì suspects, and rightly so, that the heroin was stolen by his employee Andronico. To find out more about the latter, he orders his associate Bonino to set up a heist at the bank where Andronico keeps a safety box. After receiving an anonymous letter, Mauri and his assistant Nicola Capece vainly try to stop the heist; after a car chase, two robbers are killed by their accomplice "Dogheart." Through anonymous drawings sent by Luisa, Don Mimì's little daughter, Mauri and Capece put together the pieces of the puzzle, while Dogheart dispatches Andronico and all those involved with him. Only after a succession of killings and after risking their lives in the investigation, Mauri and Capece discover — with the help of a young prostitute named Rosa — that Don Mimì was betrayed by Bonino, who kept Andronico's stolen drugs for himself.

Despite its bombastic English title, Michele Massimo Tarantini's *A Man Called Magnum* has Commissioner Mauri (Luc Merenda) handle the titular gun only near the end, after the cop has complained about the scarce weapons he has been given by the police force. Actually, Tarantini's film is not one of the more violent examples of the genre — on the contrary, much of the film gives ample room to Merenda's assistant-cum–comic relief Nicola Capece (comedian Enzo Cannavale), and Dardano Sacchetti's story emphasizes the juxtaposition between the Northern commissioner — who at least in the beginning shows very little sense of humor, thinks only about work and looks rather annoyed by his assistant's attitude — and the Parthenopean environment. Unlike Lenzi's *Violent Naples*, here the beautiful Southern city becomes as much a setting for the usual shoot-out and car chases (not less than three, spectacularly executed by Roberto Alessandri) as it is the expression of a way of life, a sunny face of Italy as the Chief of Police boasts: "Unlike Milan's fog and smoke, we have the joy of sunshine and the finest sea in the whole world."

With its concessions to comedy and folklore — one key scene features Naples' typical "pazzariello," once played by Totò in Vittorio De Sica's *The Gold of Naples* (*L'oro di Napoli*, 1954)—*A Man Called Magnum* is perhaps the missing link between the harsh, violent climate of poliziotteschi — from which it inherits the character of the workaholic, tough commissioner, who looks like a stranger throughout — and the warmer sceneggiata. As the elderly boss don Mimì, who's betrayed by his acolytes and even by his little daughter, Claudio Gora, is an exemplary character in this sense.

Sacchetti and Tarantini's script — starting with an unusually well-devised opening scene at Naples' station — is plot-thick, and features ample opportunities for action bouts, with the sadistic killer "Core 'e cane" (Dogheart, played by the mean-looking Adolfo Lastretti) dispatching all the witnesses who could lead Mauri to a stolen batch of drugs, but the scriptwriter's touch can be detected in the drawings that Gora's daughter sends to the police to warn them of her father's activities — a cool idea that's not fully exploited as it deserved to be. Yet the director does not forget his flair for erotic comedies (in 1977 he also directed the amusing sex comedy *Taxi Girl*, starring Edwige Fenech), as shown by his reliance on shots of female bottoms walking away from camera. What's more, the more prominent female character, voluptuously statuesque Sonia Viviani, is given a couple of totally gratuitous nude scenes before being mercilessly killed out of the picture. Nevertheless, the film as a whole is a lot less bleaker than its contemporaries, mainly thanks to Cannavale's lively performance, while Merenda's — like the character he's playing — is a rather extraneous presence. What *A Man Called Magnum* does rely heavily on is product placement, with an array of J&Bs, Fernet Brancas and other assorted liquors and waters that's unrivaled in other films of the era. A gang of robbers pass each other a bottle of Pejo water in the middle of a heist ("This fresh water's just what I needed" one comments), and Merenda inevitably orders a Fernet at a bar that's riddled with plugs for said liquor.

Aided by Franco Campanino's exciting percussive score, *A Man Called Magnum* is a compelling late entry in the genre. It did quite well at the box office, with almost one billion lira. However, it was Tarantini's last entry in the genre, as the director would turn his hand again to comedy.

Onore e guapparia (Honor and "Guapparia")

D: Tiziano Longo. *S:* Tiziano Longo; *SC:* Tiziano Longo, Piero Regnoli; *DOP:* Tonino [Antonio] Maccoppi (35mm, Eastmancolor, Staco Film); *M:* Elio Maestosi, Filippo Trecca; *Nun t'aggia perdere* (A. Movedano — A. Iglio), *Onore e guapparia* (E. Schiano — T. Esposito) sung by Pino Mauro; *E:* Mario Gargiulo; *PD, CO:* Mauro Passi; *COA:* Loredana Longo; *ArtD:* Teresa Ferrone; *C:* Sandro Tamborra; *AC:* Franco Sterpa; *AE:* Maria Luciana Colangeli; *AD:* Goffredo Matassi; *MU:* Stefania Trani; *Hair:* Caterina Campana; *SO:* Giosué Gudelmoni; *Boom:* Pasquale Salerno; *SP:* Franco Campanino; *SS:* Graziella Marsetti. *Cast:* Pino Mauro (Don Gennaro Esposito), Laura Gray (Donna Concetta, Don Gennaro's wife), Mario Garbetta (Don Giggino "'O Barone"), Patrizia Pellegrino (Assunta, Don Gennaro's daughter), Giulio Lenzetti (Enrico Vinazzani), Gabriella Di Luzio (Maria, Don Gennaro's sister), Nunzia Greton (Donna Angela), Francesco Gioielli, Patrizia De Martino, Emi Salvador [Emilio Salvatore] (Pasqualino 'O Nirone), Franco Marino (Don Gennaro's henchman), Massimo Deda (Paolo, Gennaro's nephew), Vincenzo Belfiore, Francesco Maresca, Anna Molino, Giuseppe Pagano, Giuseppina Virot. *Uncredited:* Vincenzo Falanga (Don Gennaro's henchman). *PROD:* Tiziano Longo for Peg Cinematografica; *PSu:* Franco Marino; *PSe:* Stefania Bollante. *Country:* Italy. Filmed at RPA Elios (Rome) and on location in Naples. *Running time:* 95'; Visa no.: 71310 (12.22.1977); *Rating:* v.m.14; *Release date:* 12.22.1977; *Distribution:* Stella (Regional); *Domestic gross:* 391,118,355 lira. *Home video:* Domovideo, New Pentax (VHS, Italy).

Naples. The cigarette smuggling boss Don Gennaro Esposito is the undiscussed "king" in the "Sanità" quarters and is honored in all of Naples. One day, after a long stay in Milan, Don Giggino 'O Barone comes back to town: when he was younger, Don Gennaro helped him escape the police. The newcomer, who has now secured connections within the Northern underworld, offers Don Gennaro a partnership in the drug business. After Don Gennaro's disdainful rejection, Don Giggino begins a ruthless war against the boss: Don Gennaro's concealed freight is reported to the police, then it is rumored that Donna Concetta, Esposito's wife, has betrayed him with her old flame Giggino. Then 'O Barone tries to frame Don Gennaro in the smuggling of drugs by using his boats. When Giggino threatens his young daughter Assunta, Esposito is finally forced to face his opponent in the old way. After a duel with knives in a dark alley, Don Gennaro kills Giggino, then denounces his own murder, "committed for reasons of honor."

By the end of the seventies, the trend of Italian police/crime films was in decline. The huge popularity enjoyed by the genre since the beginning of the decade was gradually waning, caught in the deeper crisis that was submerging the Italian cinema industry as a whole. Nevertheless, an interesting and peculiar subgenre came to the surface, like a sort of spontaneous and geographically circumscribed excrescence of a thread which, in order to survive and perpetuate, had to branch out and bastardize.

The encounter between crime films and sceneggiata was a smart commercial move on behalf of producers; and with it we can understand the reasons for the audience's soaring addiction to the genre and consequent migration to other shores. Similar to what was happening in the same period with other hybrids (such as the films starring Tomas Milian as inspector Nico "the Pirate" Giraldi, which blended the standard cop flick with comedy and whodunnit), the so-called guapparia movie ("Guappi" being the gangsters affiliated to the Neapolitan Camorra) is also a spontaneous and uncontrolled reaction to the excesses reached by Italian crime flicks between 1975 and 1978, which mirrored the escalation of violence that plagued the country.

By circumscribing characters and stories into a precise geographical context (the city of Naples and its surroundings), these films would make a traditionalist choice: they showed a precise, decipherable reality, characterized by typologies and behaviors which could be endlessly replicated, since they were immutable. Thus, the recourse to a formula became an anchor for an audience in desperate need of a reassuring, emblematic spectacle: the dramatic excesses of the guapparia movie, no matter how heartbreaking they could be, were balanced by the expectation — which was never to be let down — of a final retaliation: baddies would be punished proportionally to their offense and, most importantly, once and for all.

Tiziano Longo's *Onore e guapparia* was the film that nourished the subgenre, coming a few years after the forerunner *Sgarro alla camorra*. It's a classic sceneggiata, complete with a climactic knife duel between Pino Mauro (a notorious, paunchy Neapolitan singer with gloriously overgrown sideburns, who would become Merola's alternative in the subgenre) and villain Mario Garbetta, with several unexpected (and clumsy) references to the present. Mauro's would-be son-in-law is a Communist activist and in one scene he lectures the bewildered protagonist on his social role, claiming that a guappo is "the natural moral institution of justice elected by people outside of authority's selfish schemes." A definition that, despite the feeble parodic purports of the script (by Longo and genre film veteran Piero Regnoli) perfectly summarizes the essence of *guapparia* in such films.

Onore e guapparia was a remarkable success in the local Neapolitan market, leading producer Ciro Ippolito to write and produce *L'ultimo guappo* (*The Last Gangster*, 1978), whose success would pave the way for a number of profitable entries, most of them starring Mario Merola.

The Perfect Killer (*Quel pomeriggio maledetto*)

D: Marlon Sirko [Mario Siciliano]. *S* and *SC:* Santiago Moncada, Mario Siciliano [additional dialogue: Mario Siciliano, Stuart Hersh—English version]; *DOP:* Alejandro Ulloa (35mm, Scopecolor, Telecolor); *M:* Stelvio Cipriani, conducted by the author; *E:* Otello Colangeli [Supervising film editor: Stuart Hersh—English version]; *W:* Karole; *C:* Edoardo Noe Burman; *AC:* Giovanni Bonivento; *AE:* Adelchi Marinangeli; *AD:* Remo De Angelis; *MU:* Miguel Sese Cortes; *SO:* Antonio Foresti; *Boom:* Armando Janota; *Mix:* Sandro Occhetti; *SP:* Ermanno Serto; *KG:* Teodorico Memé; *ChEl:* Bruno Pasqualini; *SS:* Isabel Mulà Hernandez. *Cast:* Lee Van Cleef (Harry Chapman), Tita Barker [Carmen Cervera] (Krista), John Ireland (Benny), Robert Widmark [Alberto Dell'Acqua] (Luc, the hired killer), Karin Well [Wilma Truccolo] (Liz), Al Landi [Aldo Bufi Landi] (Jack), Diana Polakov (Liv, the model), Paolo Manincor (Harry's boss), Jean-Pierre Clarain (Gert), Fabián López Tapia, Fernando Sancho (The arms dealer). *Uncredited:* Franco Caracciolo (Blond transvestite). *PROD:* Mario Siciliano for Metheus Film (Rome), Julio Pérez Tabernero P.C. (Madrid); *PM:* Paolo Mercuri. *Country:* Italy / Spain. Filmed on location in Madrid, Rome and Costa Brava. *Running time:* 105'; Visa no.: 71062 (11.09.1977); *Rating:* v.m.14; *Release date:* 11.30.1977; *Distribution:* Metheus Film (Regional); *Domestic gross:* 221,903,502 lira. *Also known as: Objetivo: matar* (Spain, 1977)—*Bye, Bye Darling* (France, 05.21.1980—91'), *Stacco* (West Germany), *Täydellinen murhaaja* (Finland), *Satanic Mechanic* (U.S.A.—Home video). *Home video:* Cine Lux (VHS, Switzerland).

After one last job—a heist at a racing track—aging hit man Harry Chapman wants to quit to rest, but his friend Jack and his mistress Krista betray him and he ends up in jail. There, Harry builds contacts, comes out early, brings a few people around to his corner, and eventually manages to get back to his old job. But the ominous "organization" for which he works sends a sadistic killer, Luc, to dispatch him. Harry travels to Costa Brava, where he meets his old friend Benny, and also Krista—who leads a boring life with Jack, and has a lover, a younger man named Gert. Harry and Krista get together again and plan to escape with Benny's help. Meanwhile, Luc has arrived in Costa Brava: he kills a young model and pins the murder on Chapman. Harry finds out that Jack and Krista want him to perform one last hit: kill Gert and get a document worth $2 million; in exchange he will have Krista for himself. Luc then kills Benny and Jack, and gets away with Krista as hostage and the money. The final confrontation between the two men ends with no apparent survivors: Krista escapes with the money. Harry awakens to find out he has been hired for yet another job: to kill Krista, which he does just as she's leaving by plane.

A low-grade Spanish/Italian co-production, *The Perfect Killer* looks little like other Italian crime efforts of the period. It's essentially a rather downbeat *film noir* starring Lee Van Cleef who, after the decline of Spaghetti Westerns, got to play his favorite "lone wolf" character in a contemporary setting. The script, by Santiago Moncada and the director, liberally draws upon other films, namely Michael Winner's *The Mechanic* (the U.S. VHS release had the amusing title *The Satanic Mechanic*) and Sergio Sollima's *Violent City*, just as much as Stelvio Cipriani's score recycles themes from the composer's previous work. The nod to Sollima's film is especially evident in the relationship between the titular antihero, Harry Chapman, and his lover who framed him and had him arrested. As played by Catalunian-born Carmen Cervera, a former Miss Spain 1961 whose love life—she married Lex Barker in 1965, then South American actor Espartaco Santoni, and in the eighties became the wife of Baron Hans Heinrich Von Thyssen, owner of one of the world's largest private art collections—is definitely much more interesting than her film career,[1] the film's *femme fatale* is helplessly vapid and lacks the acting chops and charm her role badly needs.

Despite a few cool lines ("Anybody ever tell you you look pretty?" a transvestite asks him; "My mother, when I was a baby," is the reply), Van Cleef's character is not the usual lone avenger type: Chapman at times looks like a pathetic has-been, someone who's trying to look younger than he is (which explains the outrageous-looking wig and silk scarf he sports throughout the movie). The theme of generational conflict—whom the actor had faced a few times before in his career, most memorably in Tonino Valerii's western masterpiece *Day of Anger* (1967)—here seems once again like an unintentional yet pointed self-referential meditation on genre cinema itself. "You are a killer but you'll never make a pro" Chapman tells his young opponent.

Amid has-beens (John Ireland, as Harry's barman friend who collects exotic birds), familiar genre faces (Fernando Sancho) and just plain weird characters (Paolo Manincor, as Chapman's hippie-looking, caftan-wearing boss), *The Perfect Killer* does feature a remarkable villain. Chapman's young rival killer Luc (Alberto Dell'Acqua), an arrogant, psychotic sex maniac who undergoes bouts of repellent misogynistic violence—in one scene he rapes a girl (Diana Polakov) and then savagely shoots her several times in the vagina—is a disturbing relative of the "young, violent, dangerous" upper class kids who populated contemporaneous Italian poliziotteschi. Whenever Dell'Acqua is on-screen, the film goes wild, diving deep into the period's taste for excess: another exquisitely tasteless scene, possibly lifted from Alberto De Martino's *Strange Shadows in an Empty Room*, has Luc beat up and slash a trio of razor-wielding transvestites. Such moments are much more enjoyable that the overall story, which feels needlessly contrived at times and somewhat drags in its middle section.

In Italy Siciliano's film—distributed regionally by the director's own company Metheus—went almost unnoticed at the box office (Van Cleef's star had long waned) and was, as usual, savaged by the press. As one Italian critic observed, "it looks like it was made with footage from other films, such are the editing's roughness, the script's poorness and the lack of respect towards the most elementary rules of filmmaking."[2] Yet the climax, with Chapman and Luc facing each other on a Costa Brava beach, is positively enthralling, and the misogynist ending is a nice sting in the tail.

Mario Siciliano (1925–1987) was another unknown soldier of Italian popular cinema. With Metheus Film, which he founded in 1962, he wrote, produced and directed a number of war and western flicks, often under the name Marlon Sirko, with professional yet unexceptional results — his best effort is possibly the 1970 war film *Operation Over Run*, starring Ivan Rassimov, while his supernatural *giallo Evil Eye* (*Malocchio*, 1975), featuring Jorge Rivero and Richard Conte, achieved something of a cult following over the years — before giving up to hardcore porn in the late seventies/early eighties (credited as Lee Castle).

Notes

1. After appearing in a couple of spy movies in the sixties (*Killer's Carnival*, 1966; *Die Slowly, You'll Enjoy It More*, 1967), Cervera was featured in the Paul Naschy werewolf flick *The Werewolf and the Yeti* (1975) and in the obscure Italian/U.S. coproduction *Missile X: The Neutron Bomb Incident* (1978). Her last film — and the only other one as co-star — was *El primer divorcio* (1982).
2. M.Po. [Maurizio Porro], *Corriere della Sera*, 03.28.1978.

Polizia selvaggia / Gizli kuvvet (Wild police)

D: Frank Sanders [Guido Zurli]. *S:* Frank Sanders, Elia Sasso [Türker Inanoglu] (and Fuat Uzluer, uncredited): *SC:* Frank Sanders, Marius Mattei, Elia Sasso; *DOP:* A. Serafini [Çetin Gürtop] (35mm, Eastmancolor, Telecolor); *M:* Gino Peguri (Ed. R.C.A.); *E:* Giancarlo Venarucci Cadueri; *PD:* Lamberto Giovagnoli; *AC:* Julian Henryk Czyzewsky; *AE:* Stefano Morandi; *MU:* Lucia La Porta; *W:* Giulia Stefanelli; *SO:* Alvaro Buzi; *Mix:* Renato Cadueri; *SP:* Nicola Rotella; *G:* Mario Filoni, Mario Terzigni; *SS:* Odilia Pia Coletti. *Cast:* Peter Fabian [Piero Fabiani] (Ahmet "Cimice"), Giorgio Ardisson (Captain Aziz), Tarik Akan (Lieutenant Murat), Karin Well [Wilma Truccolo] (Barbara, Gustav's wife), Colette Descombes (Neval), Edilio Kim (Gustav, the blind man), Ihsan Gedik, Nevzat Okçugil, Yonca Yücel (Lala). *PROD:* Nino Serafini for Sara Cinematografica (Rome), Erler Film (Istanbul) *EP:* Türker Inanoglu; *PM:* Santo Muré; *PSe:* Sonia Maggio. *Country:* Italy / Turkey. Filmed at Elios Film (Rome) and on location in Istanbul. *Running time:* 87'; Visa no.: 60153 (04.16.1977); *Rating:* v.m.18; *Release date:* 06.02. 1977; *Distribution:* Regional; *Domestic gross:* 74,495,600 lira. *Home video:* None.

After a failed robbery attempt at an antiques shop with two accomplices, former pimp Ahmet, nicknamed "Cimice" [Bug], makes off with a suitcase full of dollars — or so he thinks — and accidentally kills the carrier. During his escape he runs over lieutenant Murat's colleague and best friend, killing him as well. Murat sets out to catch him on his own, although the case is assigned to his colleague Aziz. Ahmet steals a car with a newborn baby in it, and takes refuge in an isolated suburban villa inhabited by a blind man, Gustav, his wife, Barbara, and the housekeeper Neval, holding them hostage. After Aziz fails to break into the house, Ahmet drowns Neval. The police besiege the villa. Aziz and Murat try another trick by giving Ahmet drugged champagne bottles, but the plan fails, and Ahmet kills Gustav. He obtains a car and flees with Barbara, whom he later dispatches. But the thug finds Murat waiting for him in his lair. The cop shows Ahmet that the money was fake and shoots him in the head.

When in 1971 he received a phone call from Turkish mogul producer Türker Inanoglu, who told him he knew his films and wanted him to come to Turkey, Guido Zurli thought someone was playing a prank on him. It was not a joke, and Zurli — whose previous filmography included a couple of Westerns, a few adventure/spy flicks and the grotesque horror comedy *The Mad Butcher* (*Lo strangolatore di Vienna*, 1971), produced by Dick Randall and starring Victor Buono — was one of those Italian filmmakers who packed their suitcase and traveled to Istanbul in the 1970s to make films with Turkish money. *Polizia selvaggia*, one of the films the Tuscan director shot by the Bosporus strait during the seventies, had a troubled story. "I took my name off the film and I signed it with an a.k.a. Frank Sanders, because I didn't agree with the title and the ending," Zurli claimed.[1] Originally titled *Faccia da ladro* [Thief Face], and then *La violenza è la mia legge* [Violence Is My Law], it was baptized *Polizia selvaggia* by the distributor "so that all students will go see it." That did not happen, as the box office results were meager (much less than 100 million).

Written — according to the director himself— by Marius Mattei, Zurli and (uncredited) Turkish scriptwriter Fuat Uzluer, and based on a true story as claimed by the credits (sure!), *Polizia selvaggia* is actually much better than the average Turkish/Italian coproductions. The linear story centers on petty thief Ahmet being chased by the police for murder, hiding in an isolated villa and taking its inhabitants as hostage, *Desperate Hours*–style, and with lots of unintentional laughs, especially in the dialogue exchanges between the blind Gustav (Edilio Kim) and the bandit. Zurli even throws in a humorous lesbian interlude when the two hostage women are forced by Ahmet to perform a Sapphic seduction before him, which is brusquely truncated before things turn too risqué, while the film's best scene has Ahmet kill the housekeeper (Colette Descombes) by drowning her in an aquarium.

As played by Piero Fabiani, the violent, psychopathic, impotent, closet homo[2] Ahmet is not only one of cinema's sleaziest and most despicable villains — he's perhaps the very dumbest, since for the whole film he fails to realize that the dollars he stole are just facsimile leaflets, publicizing (in a wonderfully inane plug) J&B whisky!

Next to Fabiani (who was supposed to distribute the film with his Manta Cinematografica company), famous Turkish star Tarik Akan plays the tough cop on Ahmet's trail. When Ardisson defines Ahmet "an interesting case study" he bluntly replies "He's not to be studied, he's to be captured," and a long sequence has Akan beat up a gang of thugs inside a ship to extract information on the man he's looking for.

The scene at the end where Akan shoots Fabiani dead, which according to the director was added in the Italian version, was the reason Zurli took his name off the film. "It's not fair that a policeman kills a murderer in cold blood, he must arrest him, otherwise he becomes a bounty killer. I didn't shoot that scene. To tell you the truth, I've never seen the film the way it was edited in Italy."[3]

Notes

1. Franco Grattarola, "Il dissacratore dei generi," *Cine 70 e dintorni* #10 (September 2005), p. 41.
2. In one amusingly homophobic scene Murat reveals that Ahmet's blonde Juno-esque lover, dancer Lala (Yonca Yücel), is a post-op transsexual. "Finally I remember! You once were a man, weren't you? You've been operated on in Casablanca!" "Lieutenant, if you reveal my secret I am finished, nobody knows it in town." "Don't worry, I respect the ladies. Ahmet is gay too, isn't he?" "Yes." "Well, you'll find another one. There are so many around!"
3. Grattarola, "Il dissacratore dei generi," p. 42. However, the director's version doesn't sound too convincing, as said ending doesn't look as if it's been stitched onto the film.

Return of the .38 Gang (Ritornano quelli della calibro 38)

D: Joseph Warren [Giuseppe Vari]. *S* and *SC:* Ettore Sanzò, Giuseppe Vari; *DOP:* Cristiano Pogány (35mm, Eastmancolor, Technospes); *M:* Lallo [Coriolano] Gori (Ed. Nazionalmusic); *E:* Giuseppe Vari; *PD, CO:* Giulia Mafai; *AArtD:* Sandro Bellomia; *C:* Renato Doria; *AC:* Marco Onorato; *AE:* Alberto Vari; *AD:* Maurice Poli; *MU:* Lamberto Marini; *Hair:* Lidia Puglia; *W:* Clara Fratarcangeli; *SO:* Angelo Spadoni; *Boom:* Claudio Romani; *SE:* Paolo Ricci; *SP:* Giuseppina Di Cola; *Set builder:* Lucio Maccarinelli; *STC:* Giorgio Ricci; *SS:* Serena Merlini Canevari. *Cast:* Antonio Sabàto (Marshall Tinto Baragli), Max Delys (Bruno), Giampiero Albertini (Folco Bordoni), Gino Milli (Toto), Luciano Rossi (Racket boss), Rick Battaglia (police commissioner), Lino [Calogero] Caruana (Thug), Gianfranco De Grassi (Antonio Rotunno), Daniele Dublino (Luca Coppola), Emilio Leoni, Piero Leri, Cesare Nizzica, Luciano Pigozzi (Romoletto), Maurice Poli (Maurice), Renzo Rinaldi (Funeral home owner), Marilda Donà (Teacher), Dagmar Lassander (Rosy). *Uncredited:* Calogero Azzaretto (Man outside school), Rolando De Santis (Severino, the waiter), Raniero Dorascenzi, Lina Franchi (Kidnapper child's mother), Gennaro Pappagalli, Franca Scagnetti, Sergio Serafini (Clothing store owner). *PROD:* Pino Buricchi for Marzia Cinematografica; *GM:* Francesco Giorgi; *PM:* Paolo Bistolfi; *ADM:* Romano Cannavacciuolo; *PSe:* Enzo Prosperini. *Country:* Italy. Filmed at Incir–De Paolis (Rome). *Running time:* 96'; Visa no.: 70055 (03.29.1977); *Rating:* v.m.18; *Release date:* 03.31.1977; *Distribution:* Capitol; *Domestic gross:* 663,884,620 lira. *Also known as: Elimination Force* (Us), *Gangsters* (USA), *Brigade Anti-racket* (France), *Killer Imperium* (Germany). *Home video:* Cinehollywood (VHS, UK—pre-cert; Greece; Italy), Mondial (VHS, Canada—Italian language), CVR (VHS, Italy), Video City (VHS, USA), Transcaribe (VHS, Portugal). OST: CD Beat Records CDCR 55.

A powerful gang, whose leader is known only to very few of its members, extorts money from retailers who do not report to the police for fear of retaliation. Finally, however, Marshal Tinto Baragli, head of the anti-racketeering squad, gets his hands on one of the gang's collectors, obtaining valuable information from him. However, the head of the racket dispatches all those who could lead the police to him. After intercepting a telephone call, Baragli manages to identify him: the bandit, unable to escape by plane, breaks into a country school, holding the teacher and pupils hostage. In response to Baragli's incautious move, the criminal kills the teacher and forces the Commissioner to accept his conditions. But one of Baragli's men, a sniper, shoots down the bandit.

A sequel in name only to Massimo Dallamano's *Colt 38 Special Squad*, Giuseppe Vari's *Return of the .38 Gang* is a weak, cheap action film that testifies to the way minor production companies approached the genre to cash in on the success of the more professional examples. As in his previous *Lady Dynamite*, Vari—a former editor (among his credits were Fellini's *Swindle* [1955]) and scriptwriter, and a veteran of Italian popular cinema since the mid–'50s—doesn't show any particular feel for the genre. The veteran filmmaker (born in 1916 and who passed away in 1993) also co-wrote the script with Ettore Sanzò, borrowing a lot from Castellari's *The Big Racket* and relying on the requested quota of action, stunts, violence and sadism: *Return of the .38 Gang* opens with a topless dancer dipping her nipples into a champagne glass whilst dancing and then getting blown up by a bomb, then a robbery in a café occurs where a child get manhandled into the street as a hostage and her protesting mother is shot point blank in the stomach. The usual plugs for J&B are featured as well (two thugs order a couple of bottles in a bar: "Hmmm, aged ten years, must be good!"), while Lallo Gori's score is all over the place. However, the film's most memorable image doesn't feature any violence nor liquor, but Dagmar Lassander wearing just a gun holster and her panties—a sign that Vari was ready to direct the erotic *Sister Emanuelle* (1977), starring Laura Gemser and Gabriele Tinti as a Vallanzasca look-alike. On the other hand, a scene bordering on the unintentionally comic has Sabàto auditioning a bunch of blind people to have them decipher a mysterious noise detected in a phone call, *Bird with the Crystal Plumage*–style.

As the leading tough cop, Sabàto is as wooden as ever; on the other hand, the manic-looking Luciano Rossi gets finally promoted to the role of Villain Number One as the elegantly dressed, hair slicked-back German racket boss in a Rolls Royce, and has the chance to overact wildly in the third act, which uneasily sits halfway between *Special Cop in Action* and Stelvio Massi's *Convoy Busters* (1978). The rest of the cast features familiar faces: the sympathetic Giampiero Albertini, former photonovel *beau* Max Delys (here as the unlikely long-haired cop who becomes the film's *deus ex machina*) and Luciano Pigozzi as an informer.

Sabato's presence in Roberto Montero's awful *Eye of the Spider* pushed distributors to re-release the film that same year as yet another sequel to Dallamano's film, under the title *Caso Scorpio: Sterminate quelli della calibro 38.*

Sahara Cross (Sahara Cross)

D: Tonino Valerii. *S:* Adriano Belli; *SC:* Ernesto Gastaldi, Adriano Belli, Tonino Valerii; *DOP:* Franco Di Giacomo (35mm, Eastmancolor, Vistavision); *M:* Riz Ortolani (Ed. Bixio-Cemsa); *E:* Mario Siciliano; *PD:* Aurelio Crugnola; *C:* Gianfranco Transunto; *AC:* Francesco Gagliardini, Luigi Conversi; *AE:* Giancarlo Morelli; *AD:* Franco Cirino; *APD:* Ivano Todeschi; *ArtD:* Gianfranco Fumagalli; *CO:* Lina [Nerli] Taviani; *MU:* Giancarlo Del Brocco; *AMU:* Alvaro Rossi; *Hair:* Gerardo Raffaelli; *SO:* Mario Bramonti; *Boom:* Giuseppe Muratori; *SP:* Mario Tursi; *KG:* Gastone Coppa; *ChEl:* Valerio Garzia; *UP:* Maria Rhule; *CON:* Elvira D'Amico; *W:* Maura Zuccherofino; *SE:* Giovanni Corridori, Pasquino Bennassati; *MA:* Nazzareno Zamperla; *Magic consultant:* Tony Binarelli. *Cast:* Franco Nero (Jean Bellard), Michel Constantin (Carl Mank), Pamela Villoresi (Nicole), Mauro Barabani (Hamid), Michael Coby [Antonio Cantafora] (Georges), Emilio Locurcio (Kemal), Luciano Bartoli (Eric), Luca Biagini (Louis), Geoffrey Copleston (Mr. Brown), Nazzareno Zamperla (Captain Zaft), Giorgio Del Bene (Grant), Antonio Ferrante, Pietro Valsecchi (terrorist). *PROD:* Donatella Senatore and Giorgio Cardelli for Cine Vera s.p.a. (Rome); *Associate co-producer:* Carthago Films, Tunisi (Tunisia); *PM:* Stefano Pegoraro; *UM:* Tarak Ben Ammar; *PSu:* Alfredo Petri, Anselmo Parrinello; *ADM:* Luigi Scardino. *Country:* Italy. Filmed at Cinecittà; Exteriors in Tunisia. *Running time:* 105'; Visa no.: 70805 (09.09.1977); *Rating:* none; *Release date:* 09.10.1977; *Distribution:* F.A.R.; *Domestic gross:* 706,960,000 lira. *Also known as: Les requins du désert* (France, 11.29.1978 —100'), *Det brutala gänget* (Sweden), *Golpe perfecto en el Sáhara* (Spain), *Nu falder hammeren, gutter* (Denmark), *Sahara Cross Duell in der Wüste* (Germany—TV). *Home video:* NEW (DVD, Germany).

Tunisia. A group of oil engineers—Jean, Carl, Georges, Louis, Hamid—meet and conceive a mysterious plan to make lots of money. A few days later, the engineers are being targeted by terrorists, and one of them, Georges, is killed in an explosion. His colleagues, led by Jean, set out to chase the terrorists and avenge him. The chase is full of pitfalls: one of the terrorists, dying and abandoned by his companions, blocks the pursuers with a grenade. Carl decides to use an old World War II trail to regain lost time, but the jeep almost goes on a mine. The engineers kill one of the terrorists and capture the other two, Kemal and Nicole, then set out for the city, but get lost in the Chott, a barren salt lake. During an overnight pause in a cave, Jean promises to release Nicole if she makes love with him, only to renege on that promise. The group arrives at another camp, where Kemal breaks free and engages in a duel with Jean aboard two excavators. The Frenchman has the upper hand again, but after the arrival of the police helicopter, Nicole grabs a gun and takes control of the situation. The two terrorists and three technicians depart by helicopter, but Jean reveals to Nicole that the weapon is not loaded, and the situation is reversed again. It is now clear that Jean and his comrades—whom the Tunisian police still consider as hostages of the terrorists—have a plan, and that they are using the terrorists as cover. Nicole and Kemal hijack a plane, demanding a ransom of three million to the IPC. The authorities cannot but accept. The terrorists release the hostages, among whom are Jean and Carl, and depart. The four engineers gather at a hotel, where their plan is revealed: Jean and his comrades used the situation to pocket the three million dollars' ransom.

After *Go Gorilla Go*'s urban violence, the African setting of Tonino Valerii's next project looks like an escape, like the one engineer Sampioni talked about in the previous film. *Sahara Cross* was born from an agreement with a Tunisian production company (one of whose members was young Tarak Ben Ammar), but the original script was very different from the finished film. "It was written by Adriano Belli and the title was *Arissa Ballerina*; it was a strange story, but very inconclusive. There was talk of a coup, with no reference to the motivations of what the characters were doing and with the aggravating circumstance of cryptic dialogue that hinted at something big that they would do, but taking care not to make this known to the audience, who then had no reason to follow the plot developments" Valerii recalls. "In short, everything was the opposite of what Hitchcock recommended, that is, that characters must ignore what the viewer knows. I told the producers I would make a film out of that script, because it just made no sense!"

Enter Valerii's old pal Ernesto Gastaldi. Together, the two rewrote the script, trying to salvage it, but their effort was only partly successful. "The attempt to overthrow the story kind of failed: since Tunisia had signed the co-production on Belli's screenplay, we had to work around it, even though it was anodyne and unstructured." The contribution of Gastaldi concerned the invention of new motivations for the characters and a few scenes like the battle between the two bulldozers, the initial setting on *gorfas*, the pre–Christian granaries."[1]

Valerii's perplexities towards the story were not unmotivated. The plot is just one unrelenting bluff, and even the less involved viewers will notice there's something wrong with the four oil engineers chasing terrorists all through the desert—apparently for the sake of vengeance, but actually for money. Behind the surface of an exotic action movie, *Sahara Cross* is just a well-camouflaged con flick in the vein of *The Sting*: paradoxically, it succeeds much more than other contemporaneous Italian imitations of George Roy Hill's film just because it keeps viewers ignorant about the characters' motives.

While speaking about the plan that his colleague Georges (Antonio Cantafora) has devised, which will make them rich "with some luck and some guts," Jean (Franco Nero) says: "It's like putting together a jigsaw puzzle—blindfolded." It's the same feeling the audience experiences, as the film's whole sense becomes clear in the very last sequence. However, Valerii slips in one very clever tongue-in-cheek joke in the scene where Franco Nero plays tricks with the cards at the bar—just as to tell us that everything is happening under our very eyes, even though we can't notice it. Take the weird lack of interest on behalf of Carl and friends when the radio broadcasts the news of them being supposedly held captive by the terrorists, or Jean's apparent carelessness which allows Nicole to get ahold of a gun and escape capture.

It's all part of the game, including the fulsome accumulation of plot twists and turns that lead Jean and his colleagues to share three million dollars paid by a powerful multinational oil company. *Sahara Cross* works best if seen as a *divertissement*, as proved by the parodic, speeded-up ending in which Franco Nero's character takes his clothes off to reveal the money he has hidden on himself.

The cast is heterogeneous to say the least: besides Nero, the other leads are Frenchman Michel Constantin and Pamela Villoresi, a stage actress who had just done Miklos Jancsó's scandalous *Vizi privati, pubbliche virtù* (1975). "Sometimes you have to make do with compromises or economical limitations," Valerii explained. "Villoresi is a very good actress, but I wouldn't cast her as a terrorist, if it weren't for a pre-signed agreement." *Sahara Cross* was shot in nine weeks, with many technical difficulties, especially in the scenes set in plain desert where it was impossible to use normal tracking shots due to the sand. To overcome these problems, Valerii used a new type of camera which had been adopted in just a few major U.S. productions: the Steadicam. It was the very first model, quite heavy (45 kilos) and without a video monitor for the director, which was added upon Valerii's request. Cameraman Gianfranco Transunto and director of photography Franco Di Giacomo were sent to a special training course in Vienna, to learn to use it." The result gives the film a smooth, refined look which is unlike many Italian films of the period. Valerii opts for long sequence shots—such as the one in the gas-station blowup scene—and builds a three-dimensional space in exteriors (the camera often revolves around the characters in 360° panoramic shots). Due to technical issues, however, Valerii had to give up on some of the most audacious ideas, such as an elaborate single ten-minute take that was supposed to open the film, *Touch of Evil*–style, shot aboard a helicopter and following a character from a hotel room throughout the town to the airport.

Despite the occasional outbursts of violence, such as Cantafora's death scene or the killing of the terrorist, Valerii doesn't push this particular pedal as he had done on *Go Gorilla Go*, but he relieves tension with picaresque diversions (the scene with Franco Nero and the mine) and old-style male bonding, as proven by the reference to ice cold beer that the friends will drink together once all is finished, a cinephile homage to J. Lee Thompson's *Ice Cold in Alex / Desert Attack* (1958). The film's most memorable showpiece is the surreal duel between the excavators, which Valerii shot backwards at 20 frames-per-second.

Sahara Cross also shows Valerii's past as a Western director: the deserts and canyons of Tunisia are filmed as if they were Almeria's, and the scenes at the arid salt lake of Chott el-Jerid are simply fascinating. Another nod to the Western is the overall cynicism. The film's five oil engineers are certainly not the usual good guys of classic adventure films: they are rather similar to Japanese *ronin*, amoral mercenaries that only think about money, nice scoundrels that nonetheless would not hesitate to kill the terrorists to avoid that the police suspect them. Just like the bounty killer Lanky Fellow in Valerii's film debut *Taste of Killing* (1966), they bet on themselves and on their own ability to survive. In the 1966 film Lanky said, "Money's never enough," here one character explains: "There are million dollars flowing through the pipelines, we just have to turn on the right tap." Surprisingly, the film's only trace of moral integrity can be found in the two terrorists — quite a bold move, considering it was 1977, the same year as Pirri's *Could It Happen Here?*—whereas the protagonists' motto (and that of the film itself, for that matter) can be synthesized in Jean's apology to Nicole after the man has persuaded her to make love, promising to release her afterwards, which of course he doesn't: "Sorry, but I have so much fun ripping people off!"

Sahara Cross did not prove the box office success the producers had envisaged, grossing just over 706 million (whereas the year's greatest hit, the Bud Spencer–Terence Hill vehicle *Crime Busters*, grossed over six billion). "We hoped for something more, sure. But inside my head I did think: "Why would people go to see a movie starring Franco Nero and Pamela Villoresi?"" Valerii commented. What's more, the distribution company Elephant Film went bankrupt, consigning *Sahara Cross* to oblivion.

Note

1. This and Valerii's following quotes are taken from an interview with the author, June 2008.

Stunt Squad (La polizia è sconfitta)

D: Domenico Paolella. *S:* Dardano Sacchetti; *SC:* Domenico Paolella, Dardano Sacchetti; *DOP:* Marcello Masciocchi (35mm, Gevacolor, Telecolor); *M:* Stelvio Cipriani, conducted by the author (Ed. P.A.C.); *E:* Amedeo Giomini; *PD:* Carlo Leva; *APD:* Daniela Casagrande; *CO:* Renato Moretti; *COA:* Tiziana Medici; *C:* Alvaro Lanzoni; *AC:* Carlo Milani, Vasco Benucci; *AE:* Tommaso Gramigna, Ornella Chistolini; *AD:* Cesare Landricina; *MU:* Stefania Trani; *Hair:* Maria Luisa Fraticelli; *W:* Franca Paoletti; *SO:* Goffredo Salvatori; *Boom:* Armando Ianota; *SE:* Paolo Ricci; *SP:* Antonio Casolini; *PrM:* Ciro Russo; *KG:* Teodorico Memé; *ChEl:* Vittorio Pescetelli; *STC:* Sergio Mioni; *SS:* Nellita Zampieri. *Cast:* Marcel Bozzuffi (Commissioner Grifi), Riccardo Salvino (Brogi), Vittorio Mezzogiorno (Valli), Claudia Giannotti (Anna), Francesco Ferracini (Platanìa), Andrea Aureli (Giovanni, bar owner), Nello Pazzafini ("Tunisian"), Alfredo Zammi (Giovanni Corsi), Pasquale Basile (Marshall Marchetti), Renato Basso Bondini (Special agent), Enzo Maggio, Sergio Mioni (Gaspar), Ivana Novak (policewoman), Simona Ogier (Rita, Valli's girlfriend), Paolo Ricci, Franco Salamon, Marina Viviani (Nurse), Claudio Zucchet (Special agent). *Uncredited:* Giancarlo Bastianoni (Drug dealer), Dolores Calò (Woman at funeral), Eolo Capritti (Bertini), Beny [Beni] Cardoso (Marchetti's widow), Raniero Dorascenzi (Journalist), Paolo Figlia (Valli's man), Tito LeDuc (Pierre), Alba Maiolini (Woman at funeral), Emilio Messina (Robber), Roberto Messina (police trainer), Romano Milani (police archivist), Vezio Natili (Man at restaurant), Benito Pacifico (Valli's henchman), Sergio Smacchi (Special agent), Goffredo Unger (Valli's henchman). *PROD:* P.A.C. (Produzioni Atlas Consorziate) (Milan); *PM:* Teodoro Agrimi [Corrà]; *PSu:* Vincenzo Cartuccia; *PSe:* Luciano Lucchi, Cesare Bastelli; *ADM:* Gaetano Fuzio. Shot on location in Bologna. *Running time:* 105'; Visa no.: 70695 (07.28.1977); *Rating:* v.m.14; *Release date:* 07.28.1977; *Distribution:* P.A.C.; *Domestic gross:* 946,317,910 lira. *Also known as: Équipe spéciale* (France), *Elimination Force* (Canada), *Sonderkommando ins Jenseits* (West Germany). *Home video:* Cecchi Gori (DVD, Italy).

Already beset by the scourge of the drug racket, Bologna is shaken by a new crime plague: some stores are being blown up by dynamite. While the public opinion reacts alarmed and shopkeepers are wavering between terror and the desire to organize their own defense, Commissioner Grifi finds out that the well-known but elusive Valli imposes his gang's costly "protection" to shop owners, and retaliates on those who refuse via the bloody bombings. Grifi obtains permission to organize a special squad: he gathers a number of brave and gifted agents, trains them in the use of weapons and techniques of defense or assault, gives them fast bikes and unleashes them at strategic points of the city, while he tries to uncover his opponents' hideout. More victims follow, until eventually Grifi tracks down Valli. The criminal flees aboard a bus. Approached by Grifi's right-hand man Brogi, Valli kills him but is then lynched by the crowd.

Released in August 1977 — a hot month, not just because of the temperatures: two left-wing terrorists were killed in a bomb blast in Turin — Domenico Paolella's *Stunt Squad* was actually an unofficial remake of Massimo Dallamano's *Colt 38 Special Squad*, with an unusual setting: Bologna, which just a few months earlier had been the theatre of violent clashes between the police and far-left protesters, that culminated in the death of Franceso Lorusso, shot by a police agent.

Dardano Sacchetti's script more or less follows the outline of Dallamano's film by putting a commissioner against a bomber, and having the former put together a special squad of biker cops to better fight the criminal. The lead was once again Marcel Bozzuffi — with Riccardo Salvino turning up again as the commissioner's right hand man — while his antagonist, Valli (a repellent creep who blows up whoever doesn't pay him money by planting bombs inside the stores' public phones) was played by Vittorio Mezzogiorno, a young and extremely talented actor who would go on to work with such directors as Francesco Rosi, Werner Herzog, Marco Bellocchio and Peter Brook before his untimely death in 1994.

Besides the requested bike/car chases, Paolella's film also features an elaborate murder sequence (the killing of a shop owner who's been hospitalized after a bomb blast) which looks like something out of a *giallo*, whereas a long scene set in a nightclub provides gratuitous nudity and juicy disco music, courtesy of Stelvio Cipriani. On the other hand, Paolella and Sacchetti even throw in an unexpected reference to Jean-Pierre Melville's *Le Samouraï* (1967) in the scene where the police break into an abandoned factory where the bomber is hidden: Valli keeps a caged canary just like Alain Delon did in Melville's film.

Paolella — a former journalist and a veteran of sword-and-sandal epics and spy flicks — doesn't seem uncomfortable with the genre: right from the very opening scenes, as the bikers ride through the deserted streets of Bologna at dawn, under Cipriani's gloomy synth score, *Stunt Squad* is a downbeat affair, where the references to contemporary news items are very precise. Paolella claimed: "I tried to make a documentary of sorts,"[1] and the dialogue mentions *agents provocateurs* and special laws, plus a number of statistics on the escalating number of bombings that commissioner Grifi (Bozzuffi) mentions, while projecting a series of slides that are taken from those years' tragic real-life events. Grifi also complains about the agents' inefficiency and lack of professionalism, pointing at the structuring of law enforcement: one agent every 230 inhabitants (compared to France's 1310 and Britain's 1480), yet almost all of them dislocated in offices, and qualitatively unfit to their task of protecting citizens. "In Italy, a cop is still a man for all seasons" observes the commissioner bitterly.

As many other tough cops in poliziotteschi, Grifi sees justice as a reason to live, yet he remains a rather insignificant character, as is his Brogi (Salvino), the requested sacrificial lamb who encounters his fate in the good sequence set on the bus, which recalls a similar one in Florestano Vancini's masterpiece *La banda Casaroli* (1962). The good guys pale before *Stunt Squad*'s ruthless villain — perhaps poliziotteschi's cruelest ever. Vittorio Mezzogiorno's Valli, who commits massacres by simply dialing a phone number, seemingly hates cops and criminals alike with the same cold, detached hatred. Valli doesn't show those devilish excesses displayed by Ivan Rassimov in *Colt 38 Special Squad*, nor does he nurture the same subproletarian grudge as Tomas Milian's hunchback. He is violent and cowardly at the same time, capable of the most gruesome cruelties and destined to be lynched in the city's main square by an angry mob, in a desperate and nihilistic ending.

Stunt Squad is also one of the most violent examples of the poliziotteschi. One particularly gross sequence has Valli's men capture and emasculate a thug named "Tunisian" (Nello Pazzafini), with "gory effects that would make Arrabal proud" as film critic Giovanni Buttafava wryly commented.[2] The same unfortunate thug had one of the genre's most memorably proverbial (and vulgar) lines: "The Law is like a dick: it gets longer and shorter, depending on the case." A crude metaphor that nonetheless explains the climate of diffidence towards justice, and is summed up by the film's Italian title, which explicitly states "The police are defeated."

Notes

1. Faldini and Fofi, Il cinema italiano d'oggi, p. 454.
2. Buttafava, "Procedure sveltite," p. 105.

Swindle (Squadra antitruffa)

D: Bruno Corbucci. *S* and *SC:* Mario Amendola, Bruno Corbucci; *DOP:* Marcello Masciocchi (35mm, Vistavision — Scopecolor); *M:* Guido and Maurizio de Angelis (ed. Nazionalmusic); *E:* Daniele Alabiso; *PD:* Claudio Cinini; *CO:* Luciano Sagoni; *C:* Giovanni Ciarlo; *AC:* Mauro Masciocchi; *AE:* Brigida Mastrolillo; *AD:* Roberto Tatti; *MU:* Franco Di Girolamo; *Hair:* Jolanda Angelucci; *SO:* Carlo Palmieri; *Boom:* Alvaro Orsini; *Mix:* Bruno Moreal; *SP:* Franco Vitale; *G:* Cosimo Barbera; *GA:* Tullio Marini; *STC:* Rocky Capella; *Acrobatics:* Roberto Alessandri; *SS:* Wanda Tuzi [Tuzzi]. *Cast:* Tomas Milian (Nico Giraldi), David Hemmings (Robert Clayton), Anna Cardini (Nico's fiancée), Alberto Farnese (Lawyer Ferrante), Massimo Vanni (Gargiulo), Leo Gullotta (Tarcisio Pollarini "Il Fibbia"), Franco Lechner (Franco Bertarelli "Venticello"), Tony [Antonio] De Leo ("Milord"), Marcello Martana (Trentini), Roberto Alessandri (Aldo Proietti "Er Picchio"), Marcello Verziera (False killer), Nazzareno Natale (Cab driver), Giancarlo Badessi (Baruffaldi), Roberto Messina (Commissioner Tozzi), Marco Tulli ("Venticello"'s accomplice), Giovanni Attanasio (Bald policeman), Omero Capanna (Armando Trani, the hitman), Andrea Aureli (Angelo Tornabuoni). *Uncredited:* Francesco Anniballi (Barman), Fortunato Arena (Porter), Bruno Arié (Card player), Mario Donatone (Swindle Victim), John P. Dulaney (Ballarin), Jimmy Il Fenomeno [Luigi Origene Soffrano] (Stand customer), Paolo Fiorino (TV interviewer), Gilberto Galimberti (Card player), Alba Maiolini (Woman), Benito Pacifico (Card player), Mimmo Poli ("Milady"), Carmelo Reale (Trani's accomplice). *PROD:* Galliano Juso for Cinemaster; *PM:* Mario De Biase; *UM:* Sandro Mattei; *PSe:* Augusto Marabelli; *PA:* Tullio Lullo; *ADM:* Paolo Rampazzo; *CASH:* Salvatore Farese, Maurizio Spinelli. *Country:* Italy. Filmed at Dear, R.P.A. Elios (Rome) and on location in Rome and San Francisco. *Running time:* 100'; Visa no.: 71112 (11.12.1977); *Rating:* not rated; *Release date:* 11.18.1977; *Distribution:* Titanus; *Domestic gross:* 1,868,917,000 lira. *Also known as: Tony Marroni — Der Superbulle schägt wieder zu* (08.14.1981 — 98'). *Home video:* 01 (DVD, Italy).

Rome. Carabinieri Marshall Nico Giraldi investigates, aided by the phlegmatic English detective Robert Clayton, a massive fraud hatched against Lloyd's of London by a mysterious insurance company

Tomas Milian as Nico Giraldi, one of his most popular screen characters.

Italian poster for *Swindle* (1977).

based in the Italian city. However, the four con men who set up the swindle are being murdered one by one despite Giraldi's efforts. Eventually, Nico finds out that the last victim only faked his own death in order to avoid being killed for real and took refuge in San Francisco. Nico and Clayton track the man down in the United States, where they pose as swindlers. Upon his arrival in Rome, handcuffed, the fourth man is killed too, but Giraldi has now enough evidence to identify the leader of the gang and arrest him.

The third entry in the Nico Giraldi series starring Tomas Milian, *Swindle* is another step away from the poliziotteschi towards comedy. The storyline is very similar to that of the first two films, but with more emphasis on the comedic angle, abetted by the film's very theme, which allows for a number of funny vignettes depicting various cons. The opening sequences, featuring Bombolo as the petty con-man Venticello ("Breeze," a nickname referring to his aerophagia...) are a case in point. Milian's makeup is also more clownish, with a huge curly wig and heavy eye make-up.

What's more important, the story written by Mario Amendola and Corbucci is a whodunit of sorts, with Nico helping an agent from Lloyd's of London (a bemused David Hemmings, playing with the typical stereotyped image of British aplomb) who's investigating a big insurance fraud, and following a trail of murders to the not-so-surprising final twist. If the plot is not irresistible, individual sequences are very entertaining, with Corbucci devising a number of pretexts for Tomas Milian's comedic routines and his duets with the imperturbable Hemmings. As expected, the humor is not very British, and decidedly politically incorrect. One such example is the scene in the gay nightclub where Milian is approached by an elderly and flamboyant homosexual (Mimmo Poli) who tries to seduce him with predictable results.

Milian is regularly replaced by his body double in the many action bits: one impressive set-piece is the long chase on the roofs after the murder at the tennis club (where Corbucci pays homage to a famous scene in Hitchcock's *Strangers on a Train*), between Nico and a hitman (Omero Capanna). The film's best invention is the homage to Cinecittà's stuntmen in the scene where Nico realizes that a murder he witnessed — a man being shot and falling off a bridge — was actually an elaborate fake, set up by a former stuntman in order to disappear, a fact that becomes apparent to him while watching a typical Spaghetti Western shooting Demofilo Fidani–style, replete with extras falling off roofs and balconies.

This in-joke is only one among a number of tongue-in-cheek cinephile moments. Besides said Hitchcock homage, there's a light-hearted discussion about cinema between Giraldi and his fiancée (Anna Cardini), a feminist student who works at a local art theater that runs boring four-hour long Polish art films: "I prefer westerns" Nico quips, when the girl mentions the name of a committed Polish director, Damianowski — a stab at Damiano Damiani's films?

As with *Hit Squad*, the plot includes a rather gratuitous sequence set in San Francisco, where Milian and Hemmings perform a series of cons in order to get in touch with the local Mafia (one such sequence is a rip-off from *Paper Moon*'s famous $10 bill scam). References to the poliziotteschi are minimal, and rather ironic, such as the talk show which Giraldi takes part in about the escalation of crime and urban violence and the peril of vigilantism. What in other films would have been a pretext to channel common fears, here it is just a way to allow Milian more room for his character's over-the-top verbal grossness, with Nico spouting a series of four-letter words on live TV, much to the crew's desperation. The brothers De Angelis score was partly assembled with music already used in *Hit Squad*.

Swindle was as profitable as the former entries, grossing almost two billion at the box office. Nico would return in the following year's *Little Italy* (*Squadra antimafia*).

Weapons of Death (Napoli spara!)

D: Mario Caiano. *S* and *SC:* Gianfranco Clerici, Vincenzo Mannino; *DOP:* Pier Luigi Santi (35mm, Telecolor); *M:* Francesco De Masi; *E:* Vincenzo Tomassi; *PD:* Antonio Visone; *CO:* Maria Luisa Panaro; *C:* Arcangelo Lannutti; *AC:* Giuseppe Venditti; *AE:* Vanio Amici, Carlo Della Corte; *AD:* Goffredo Unger [Ungaro]; *2nd AD:* Ennio Coccia; *MU:* Stefano Trani; *Hair:* Gabriella Trani; *SE:* Gino De Rossi; *SO:* Roberto Alberghini; *Boom:* Antonino Pantano; *Mix:* Bruno Moreal; *KG:* Giancarlo Lucchetti; *SP:* Giorgio Schwarze; *SS:* Margherita Reginato. *Cast:* Leonard Mann [Leonardo Manzella] (Commissioner Belli), Henry Silva (Santoro), Jeff Blynn (Guidi), Evelyn Stewart [Ida Galli] (Lucia Parise), Massimo Deda (Gennarino), Adolfo Lastretti (Pedophile), Kirsten Gille (Taxi patron), Mario Deda (Nardi, Belli's assistant), Enrico Maisto (Don Licata), Tommaso Palladino (Don Calise), Tino Bianchi (Don Alfredo), Mario Erpichini (Chief of Police), Maurizio Gueli (Serrao), Dino Mattielli (Friend of Licata and Calise), Massimo Vanni (Rosati, undercover cop), Maurizio Mattioli (Special agent who robs the gambling house), Enrico Chiappafreddo (Santoro's henchman), Benito Pacifico (Santoro's henchman), Nazzareno Cardinali (Santoro's henchman). *Uncredited:* Francesco Anniballi (Card player), Omero Capanna (Prisoner), Massimo Ciprari (Male nurse at prison), Ottaviano Dell'Acqua (Enrico 'O Luongo, Santoro's man), Luciano Foti (Cop in operations center), Mario Granato (Undercover agent), Franco Marino (Righi, Santoro's henchman), Bruno Rosa (Doctor), Valentino Simeoni (Billiard-hall customer), Claudio Zucchet (Gangster). *PROD:* Capitolina Produzioni Cinematografiche; *PM:* Roberto Giussani; *PI:* Ennio Di Meo; *PSe:* Giuseppe Auriemma. *Country:* Italy. Filmed at Incir–De Paolis (Rome) and on location in Naples. *Running time:* 99'; Visa no.: 69795 (02.17.1977); *Rating:* v.m.14; *Release date:* 02.22.1977; *Distribution:* Fida Cinematografica; *Domestic gross:* 1,049,324,370 lira. *Also known as:* *Assaut sur la ville* (France), *Die Killer-Meute* (Germany), *Väkivallan miehet* (Finland). *Home video:* Hobby & Work (DVD, Italy). OST: CD Beat Records CDCR 83.

Naples is subjected to a series of bombings by the bandit Santoro, who's operating under the protection of the Godfather Don Alfonso. Young commissioner Belli, despite the support of a special team comprised of a fake taxi driver, a motorcyclist, two tramps and street urchin Gennarino, cannot prevent the bandit from hijacking and robbing a train, attacking banks and leaving a trail of dead behind him. Belli then attempts to put a rival gang against Santoro, but the results are no better. Santoro is finally captured and put in prison, but he escapes thanks to the elderly boss' intervention, while Belli is even suspected by his superiors of being in cahoots with the boss. At this point, the only way for the Commissioner to frame the criminal is to set up a deadly trap.

Released in Italy as a sequel of sorts to Lenzi's *Violent Naples* (hence the Italian title, *Napoli spara!*, literally "Naples Shoots!"), Mario Caiano's film tried hard to give the people what they want. The obligatory "iron commissioner," as played by Leonard Mann, even had a similar name as Maurizio Merli's character in Lenzi's film (he's named Belli instead of Betti), while his co-star, former photonovel model Jeff Blynn, was chosen exactly because *he looked like* Merli.[1] Last but not least, the film inherited from *Violent Naples* the character of little "scugnizzo" Gennarino. The Italian poster played dirty, claiming: "Commissioner Belli and "Gennarino," the unforgettable *scugnizzo* seen in NAPOLI VIOLENTA, return in a great new film." The almost identical surname (Betti/Belli) and the image of Jeff Blynn (who does not play Belli, but the secondary character Guidi) at the center completed the sham. Merli-Betti is also evoked in a dialogue exchange between Leonard Mann and the kid.

As the unlikely special agent Guidi, who drives around Naples disguised as a cab driver, Blynn also exemplifies the reason why *Weapons of Death* doesn't really work, unless one considers it merely as a comic book-style, over-the-top actionfest. Even though Caiano proves that he can take advantage of the Neapolitan setting with interesting results (such as in the sequence of the tailing into the so-called Spanish Neighborhoods) and shoot convincing action sequences, the plot and characters look perfunctory, and the charismatic Henry Silva is wasted as the film's villain, suffering — at least in the Italian version — from an ill-conceived dubbing which gives him an incongruous Neapolitan accent. Compared to contemporaneous poliziotteschi, the film's moral code is also slightly different, as the film's most hateful character — a pedophile played by the sleazy Adolfo Lastretti — is punished for his crimes neither by the law (which, as always happens within the genre, is useless or insufficient) nor by the commissioner/avenger, but by the criminals themselves who consider him like a foreign body inside their world. This tendency to exclude "official" law altogether signals a progressive mutation towards the secluded moral world of the sceneggiata.

Weapons of Death is a schizophrenic poliziotteschi, where gore and Grand-Guignol galore — a cop is decapitated by a steel wire, *Toby Dammit*–style, the pedophile is eviscerated in prison — rub shoulders with embarrassing comic or melodramatic interludes. "For the occasion, scenes of the most self-satisfied brutality alternate with pathetic tear-jerking stuff, in homage to the partenopean setting," wrote one critic.[2] These scenes are centered on Gennarino, shown as an example of the Neapolitans' resources and inventiveness: the boy turns up in many scenes doing each time a different job, often bizarre ones (such as selling newspapers to couples who make love inside their car, so that they can cover the vehicle's windows and not be seen from the outside), and in one scene he even steals a new Lancia and drives it all through the city just for kicks. Gennarino even saves the commissioner's life before falling to Santoro's bullets. The film's tragic ending—which features Manni walking away with the dead child in his arms—announces the genre's merger with sceneggiata, which would take place very soon.

Notes

1. Stefano Ippoliti and Matteo Norcini, "Intervista a Mario Caiano," *Cine 70 e dintorni* #2 (Spring 2002), p. 24.

2. R. P. [Ranieri Polese], *Corriere della Sera*, 20.3.1977. The same review mocked the film's emphasis on the regional setting. "Italy's tour of violence continues, through the geographical map of the brutal and bloody 'police and thieves' flicks, Italian-style. [...] Soon it will be the turn of *Lecco violenta, Fidenza a mano armata, Torcello spara,*" he quipped (the aforementioned towns are actually provincial villages and thus unlikely titles for an urban crime flick).

1978

Blazing Flowers (Milano ... difendersi o morire)

D: Gianni [Gian Antonio] Martucci. *S:* Luca Sportelli; *SC:* Ludovica Marineo, Luca Sportelli, Gianni Martucci; *DOP:* Riccardo Grassetti (35mm, Technospes); *M:* Gianni Ferrio, conducted by the author (ed. Nido); *E:* Vincenzo Vanni; *PD:* Sergio Palmieri; *CO:* Marika Flandoli; *C:* Vittorio Dragonetti; *AC:* Massimiliano Sano; *AE:* Vincenzo Savoca; *AD:* Giacinto Bonacquisti; *MU:* Giovanni Casoli, Liliana Ponti; *Hair:* Romana Piolanti; *SO:* Domenico Pasquadibisceglie; *Boom:* Giuseppina Sagliano; *SOE:* Luciano Anzellotti; *W:* Giovanna Ravera; *MA:* Bruno Luia; Continuity: Rosaria Cilento. *Cast:* Marc Porel (Pino Scalise), Anna Maria Rizzoli (Marina "Fiorella," Pino's cousin), George Hilton (Commissioner Morani), Barbara Magnolfi (Teresa, Pino's cousin), Al Cliver [Pier Luigi Conti] (Domino), Guido Leontini (Don Ciccio), Parvin Tabriz [Tabrizi] (Virginia Mallo), Anthony Freeman [Mario Novelli] (Gazzosa), Nino Vingelli (Nicola, Pino's uncle), Amparo Pilar (Assunta), Silvia Mauri (Anna), Osvaldo Natale (Natale, Morani's assistant), Bruno Di Luia (Don Ciccio's thug). *Uncredited:* Ugo Bombognini (Flavio, head of the gambling room), Gianni Bortolotti (Alicanti), Massimo Buscemi (Pino's cellmate); Vincenzo De Toma (Prison guard), Franco Diogene (Brothel customer), Vittorio Joderi (Don Chicco's thug), Franco Moraldi (Prison warden), Riccardo Petrazzi (Thug following a prostitute), Rinaldo Zamperla. *PROD:* Giuseppe Zappulla for Ariete Cinematografica (Milan); *PM:* Solly Victor Bianco; *PSu:* Giovanni Cinus; *Accountant:* Amedeo Barati. *Country:* Italy. Filmed at Icet–De Paolis (Milan) and on location in Milan. *Running time:* 98'; Visa no.: 71210 (12.10.1977); *Rating:* v.m.18; *Release date:* 02.05.1978; *Distribution:* Lark; *Domestic gross:* 593,395,110 lira. *Also known as: Heroin* (West Germany, 07.10.1981—83'), *Blazing Bullets* (English on-screen title on Italian DVD). *Home video:* Surf (DVD, Italy).

After spending six years in prison for robbery, the Sicilian Pino Scalise moves to Milan where he stays at his uncle's place. Pino soon discovers that one of his cousins, Marina, with whom he is secretly in love, is being forced into prostitution by Don Ciccio's racket and has been deliberately strung out on heroin to be kept under control. Commissioner Morani tails Pino in the hope that sooner or later Scalise will lead him straight to the dangerous boss. When Pino gets a job as a truck driver, he's approached by Don Ciccio's thugs: if he drives a getaway vehicle for a bank heist, Marina can go free. The job is carried out but Don Ciccio goes back on the deal and forces Pino to do more "jobs" for him by threatening to kill Marina if he refuses. Things turn from bad to worse when Pino's other cousin Teresa is kidnapped by Don Ciccio's right-hand man Domino. With the slimy crime lord now demanding that Pino deliver a van load of drugs disguised as artificial flowers, the young Sicilian is once again reluctantly drawn into a life of crime. The ever more attentive Morani arrests Pino and Nicola, but Domino attacks the police car, causing an accident and killing Pino's uncle in the process. Pino survives, however, and shows up with Morani at Don Ciccio's house, ready to denounce the boss. Domino kills Don Ciccio, but is beaten to death by Pino, who releases Teresa. Instead of arresting him, Morani lets Pino go with Teresa, promising he will not incriminate him.

Within a film industry where female nudity had become an essential element and where, despite the censors' interventions, sex was getting more and more prominent, the crime genre obliged as well. In most poliziotteschi, however, there's hardly the time to glimpse a bare breast or a fugacious nude between a shootout and a bank robbery. As a matter of fact, the emphasis on sex and nudity is much more apparent in those works that are bastardized with *giallo* and thriller (*Calling All Police Cars*), in the instant movies based on real-life events (such as *I ragazzi della Roma violenta*) and in the low-budget sub-products where the amount of nudity served to balance out the lack of spectacular and filmic values.

That's the case with Gianni Martucci's *Blazing Flowers*, where the nude scenes—courtesy of the breathtaking Anna Maria Rizzoli and Barbara Magnolfi, then Porel's wife[1]—are much more exciting that the film's half-baked plot, filled with clichés worthy of a bad sceneggiata—the good guy who has to act as redeemer, the praise of family values—which sit uneasy beside the sexploitation elements. Despite an Italian title (literally: Milan ... to defend or to die) that openly apes poliziotteschi and an opening credit sequence featuring b/w shots of real-life clashes between the police and protesters in the streets and pics of young drug addicts shooting up, the tone is closer to that of a lurid comic book, as illustrated by the naive plot (see the way the drugs are smuggled inside artificial flowers) and hammy villains. Guido Leontini's despicable Don Ciccio is almost an unintentional parody of early '70s godfathers, while Al Cliver—with slick, side-parted hair and an accent similar to Peter Sellers' Inspector Clouseau—shamelessly hams it up as an unlikely French thug.

Gianni Martucci, a mediocre director, was responsible for a pair of sex comedies (*La collegiale*, 1975, and *La dottoressa sotto il lenzuolo*, 1977) and would later direct the abysmal thriller *Trhauma* (1979) and the equally bad late Gothic *The Red Monks* (1989), which was fraudulently credited to Lucio Fulci when released on video.

Note

1. Porel and Magnolfi (here playing a 16-year-old) co-starred together in Umberto Silva's period drama *Difficile morire* (1977) and in Enzo Milioni's sleazy *giallo The Sister of Ursula* (*La sorella di Ursula*, 1978).

Blood and Diamonds (Diamanti sporchi di sangue)

D: Fernando di Leo. *S* and *SC:* Fernando di Leo; *DOP:* Roberto Gerardi (35mm, Eastmancolor, Telecolor); *M:* Luis Enriquez Bacalov (Ed. Bixio—Cemsa); *E:* Amedeo Giomini; *PD:* Franco Cuppini; *APD:* Bruno Russo; *CO:* Elisabetta Lo Cascio; *C:* Franco Bruni, Enrico Sasso; *AC:* Maurizio La Monica, Fabio Conversi; *CHOR:* Umberto Pergola; *AE:* Ornella Chistolini; *AD:* Angelo Vicari; *MU:* Alfredo Marazzi; *Hair:* Lidia Puglia; *SO:* Pietro Spadoni; *Boom:* Angelo Spadoni; *Mix:* Franco Bassi; *SP:* Alfio Quattrini; *ChEl:* Luigi Pasqualini; *KG:* Alfredo Dioguardi; *SetT:* Basilio Patrizi; *PrM:* Lucio Maccarinelli; *W:* Nadia Panci; *STC:* Gilberto Galimberti; *SS:* Renata Franceschi; Unit *P:* Tonino Pinto. *Cast:* Claudio Cassinelli (Guido Mauri), Martin Balsam (Rizzo), Barbara Bouchet (Lisa), Pier Paolo Capponi (Tony), Olga Karlatos (Maria), Vittorio Caprioli (Commissioner Russo), Alberto Squillante (Enzo), Roberto [Carmelo] Reale (Marco), Riccardo Perrotti Parisio, Raoul Lo Vecchio (Weapon trader), Fernando Cerulli (Mr. Philips), Camillo Chiara, Fulvio Mingozzi (Nicola), Santo [Sandro] La Barbera, Agostino Crisafulli (Rizzo's henchman), Paul Oxon, Franco Beltramme (Tony's henchman), Erigo Palombini, Salvatore Billa (Tony's henchman), Domenico Di Costanzo (policeman), Sergio Sinceri, Paolo Manincor. *Uncredited:* Dolores Calò (Woman on the bus), Calogero Azzaretto (Man on bus/ policeman), Tom Felleghy (Doctor), Lina Franchi (Woman on the bus), Gilberto Galimberti (Rizzo's sideman). *PROD:* Umberto and Vittorio Russo for Teleuropa International Film; *GM:* Mario Pellegrino; *PM:* Franco Vitulano; *PSu:* Giuseppe Auriemma; *PSe:* Bice Paoletti; *ADM:* Mario Sampaolo. *Country:* Italy. Filmed at Elios—R.P.A. (Rome) and on location in Rome. *Running time:* 102'; Visa no.: 71547 (02.11. 1978); *Rating:* v.m.18; *Release date:* 03.17.1978; *Distribution:* Titanus; *Domestic gross:* 259,502,900 lira. *Also known as: Verta ja timantteja* (Finland). *Home video:* CG Home Video (DVD, Italy).

Assigned by his boss Rizzo to perform a heist with his friend Marco, safe-cracker Guido Mauri is arrested and sentenced to five years in prison. Convinced that he was betrayed by Rizzo, Guido decides to take revenge. Released from prison, he reacts to an attack on the bus on which he travels, believing that the bandits are killers sent to dispatch him. In the process, Guido's wife Maria is murdered; Marco, who has been lame ever since the robbery, has become a car mechanic, while Enzo, Maria's son, has turned against his stepfather. Commissioner Russo vainly attempts to redeem Mauri and stop his feud with Rizzo, while the boss' right-hand man Tony is so violent that he makes Mauri even more determined in his goal. Guido learns about Rizzo planning a diamond heist and steals the loot from Rizzo's men. Tony retaliates by murdering Marco and Guido kills him in turn. Eventually, Mauri learns from Lisa, his stepson Enzo's lover, that it was the boy who betrayed him out of jealousy, not Rizzo. Loyal to the underworld's code of honor, Guido gives the diamonds back to Rizzo and offers him the chance to punish him. The boss shoots Guido in the presence of his court of bandits, but mercifully aims at the shoulder instead of the heart.

Blood and Diamonds explicitly returns to the themes of Fernando di Leo's masterpiece, *Caliber 9*. The continuity between the two works is not casual: di Leo's original title for the film was *Roma calibro 9* (Rome Caliber 9). The affinities are many and obvious: *Blood and Diamonds* opens where *Caliber 9* ended, with a shot of an ashtray, and one last cigarette being smoked by safe-cracker Guido Mauri (Claudio Cassinelli) while waiting for a phone call that is the signal for a heist to get under way. Just like Ugo Piazza in the 1972 film, Guido gets arrested and serves a few years in prison: this time, though, when he gets out he is not a prey but an avenger, and sets out to get his own back on the boss (Martin Balsam) whom he believes has betrayed him. If Cassinelli's character—taciturn, impenetrable, lost in his own obsessions—is close to Gastone Moschin's in *Caliber 9*, Pier Paolo Capponi's Tony is a dead ringer for Mario Adorf's Rocco Musco in the former film. Even Barbara Bouchet plays a similar character, and in one scene she wears a stunning sequined two-piece that's identical to the one she wore in *Caliber 9's* disco dancing sequence. Di Leo also makes reference to *The Italian Connection*: Roberto Reale's crippled car mechanic is modeled on Franco Fabrizi's character in that film.

However, *Blood and Diamonds* is not so much a remake as it is a reversal of *Caliber 9*, and has a relationship of dialectical complementarity with it. Unlike Ugo Piazza, Guido Mauri does everything wrong: not only he is so obsessed by thoughts of revenge that he starts a private war against his own boss, but his impetus does not allow him to notice the truth that is before his very eyes all the time. In the end, Guido just ends up doing harm to the people he loves most—his wife, his best friend, his stepson.

The film's violence (which gained it a v.m.18 rating) is concentrated in the character of Tony, a "mad dog" with sadistic tendencies, impulsive and obtuse, disturbing and menacing in the way he enters the scene, in his theatrical gestures and in his way of talking: di Leo's attention to dialogue emerges here in the use of affectations and bureaucratic terms (such as Tony's catchphrase "Does it conform?") which give the idea of an uncultivated man who tries to sound well-read. Tony's bouts of violence culminate in the scene where he tortures Marco (Roberto Reale), crucifying him to a wall and then giving him the finishing stroke with a nail to the heart (the original script went even further, with the victim's face being burnt).

Overall, *Blood and Diamonds* is dominated by a sense of slackness and emptiness that engulfs the characters and their actions, perfectly captured by Luis Bacalov's score.[1] Cassinelli is a sort of automaton who walks through the film in a state of perennial impassiveness, as if he were already dead inside (di Leo claimed: "He was monotonous as an actor, but that worked fine for me as I needed just that kind of character"),[2] while the film's moral centre is once again represented by Vittorio Caprioli as the commissioner who uselessly tries to persuade Mauri to change his mind.

Di Leo has his antihero mechanically follow the underworld's code of conduct, thus stressing its inhuman laws and its ritualistic excesses, which ultimately hide a moral void. Once he learns that Rizzo did not betray him after all, Guido gives up spontaneously to the boss, not to ask for mercy but to let Rizzo kill him, as the "rules" demand. Rizzo sets up an exemplary punishment in an abattoir, having Guido walk between two lines of henchmen like an animal going for slaughter. Yet, instead of putting a bullet in his heart, Rizzo shoots Mauri in the shoulder. Di Leo closes the film on Guido's face as he gets to his feet—confused, dismayed, without a clue what to do next. There's no catharsis this time. In *Caliber 9*, Ugo Piazza's "honor" was at least rehabilitated by the violent and verbal fury of his enemy Rocco, and survived the final catastrophe. In *Blood and Diamonds*, the fact that Guido is spared by the boss doesn't change a thing: he's lost everything all the same. Honor included.

Despite being distributed by a major company—Goffredo Lombardo's Titanus—*Blood and Diamonds* came out at the wrong time. It debuted in Rome on March 17, 1978, the day after the kidnapping of Aldo Moro, in an unreal atmosphere: a deserted, frightened city with empty movie theaters. The box office takings were sorely disappointing: just 250 million in a season that saw the gradual commercial decline of poliziotteschi. The genre's best results—besides Sergio Corbucci giallo comedy *La mazzetta* (over 4,200 million), which was perceived as something radically different from the usual poliziotteschi, due to the presence of comedian Nino Manfredi, and Squitieri's *Father of the Godfathers* (2,300 million)—was Stelvio Massi's *Fearless* with just 1,146 million. All the other releases, including those starring Maurizio Merli, failed to reach the one billion mark.

Notes

1. Parts of Bacalov's score were recycled in Bruno Mattei's *Hell of the Living Dead* (*Virus—L'inferno dei morti viventi*, 1980).
2. Pulici, *Fernando di Leo*, p. 326.

Il commissario di ferro (The Iron Commissioner)

D: Stelvio Massi. *S* and *SC:* Roberto Gianviti; *DOP:* Sergio Rubini (35mm, Gevacolor, Telecolor); *M:* Lallo [Coriolano] Gori (Ed. Nazionalmusic); *E:* Mauro Bonanni; *PD:* Claudio Cinini; *CO:* Andrea Zani; *C:* Michele Pensato; *AC:* Maria Grazia Nardi; *AE:* Maria Luisa Letti; *2nd AE:* Massimo Gasperini; *AD:* Danilo Massi; *MU:* Dante Trani; *Hair:* Katia Luksza; *SO:* Luciano Muratori; *Boom:* Rinaldo Muratori; *SOE:* Luciano Anzellotti; *Mix:* Sandro Occhetti, Mario Lupi; *SP:* Angelo Pennoni; *SS:* Maria Luigia Lovari. *Cast:* Maurizio Merli (Commissioner Mauro Mariani), Janet Agren (Vera), Ettore Manni (Sergeant Ingravallo), Chris Avram (Commissioner Crivelli), Massimo Mirani (Sergio Conforti), Giampiero Becherelli (Monti), Mariangela Giordano (Mrs. Parolini), Walter Di Santo (Claudio, Mauro's son), Enzo Fiermonte (The Engineer), Franco Odoardi (policeman at the office), Franco Garofalo (Bruno "Marocchino"), Dora Calindri (Sergio's mother), Elisa Mainardi (Concierge), Mario Granato (Arduini), Fabrizio Corallo (Waiter in bar). *Uncredited:* Renato Basso Bondini (Kidnappers' accomplice), Raniero Dorascenzi (policeman at the police station), Augusto Funari (Kidnappers' accomplice), Margherita Horowitz (Sergio Conforti's neighbor), Roberto Messina (Kidnappers' accomplice), Sergio Mioni (Kidnapper), Marco Stefanelli (Sergio's friend at the bar), Marcello Venditti (Aldo, Sergio's friend at the bar), Claudio Zucchet (Maciste, Sergio's friend at the bar). *PROD:* Roberto Bessi and Renato Angiolini for Belma Cinematografica; *PM:* Ennio Onorati; *UM:* Mario Olivieri; *PSe:* Giovanni Pantano; *Accountant:* Maria Lavinia Gualino. *Country:* Italy. Filmed at RPA Elios (Rome) and on location in Rome. *Running time:* 85'; Visa no.: 72798 (12.07.1978); *Rating:* v.m.14; *Release date:* 12.07.1978; *Distribution:* Belma (Regional); *Domestic gross:* 847,768,880 lira. *Home video:* Avo (DVD, Italy). OST: CD Beat Records CDCR 55.

Commissioner Mauro Mariani is well known for his harsh methods and tendency to act on his own initiative, which caused him to be transferred from Dr. Crivelli's squad to a neighborhood police district. There, Mariani is joined by the silent and loyal sergeant Ingravallo. One day, while Mariani is with his estranged wife Vera and their son Claudio, a certain Sergio breaks into police headquarters, takes an officer hostage and demands that the Commissioner come over. Sergio wants to kill Mariani, whom he considers responsible for his father's suicide in jail: the cop arrested the man two years earlier. Vera and Claudio, who are waiting for Mariani at the precinct, end up in the hands of the madman too. Sergio then flees with the child and telephones the Commissioner, demanding that he picks him up in a location that he knows. At first, the distraught Mariani does not understand the message, then he realizes that Sergio wants to meet him in the place where he once arrested his father. Eluding Crivelli's surveillance, Mariani gets to a railway station where he confronts the madman. He is wounded in the final shoot-out, but eventually saves his son.

Released almost at the same time as *Convoy Busters* (both films came out in December 1978), *Il commissario di ferro* (The Iron Commissioner) has one of the most iconic and emblematic titles of Italian crime cinema. Yet it's a transitional and more intimate work than its title might suggest. The opening sequence, where a girl is kidnapped and commissioner Mariani (Maurizio Merli) and his colleague Ingravallo (Ettore Manni) burst into the criminals' lair and liberate the victim, is typical "poliziesco" stuff, but Roberto Gianviti's script is scattered with contradictory details.

As Mariani, Merli once again portrays an impulsive, individualist cop, who "plays with his own life as if playing a hand of cards," as his superior (Chris Avram) reproaches him. This time, however, the hero's private side is not a mere detail, but a vital part of the story: Mariani's self-denial and professional zeal is also an excuse to not stop and think about a life that's actually an empty shell. He has a ruined family behind him, an estranged wife who asked for divorce because he never spent any time with her, a son he can't even see on the day of the child's birthday. When a young thug who wants to take his revenge on Mariani kidnaps his son, the "iron commissioner" turns out to be helpless and desperate in front of a past that keeps persecuting him: his fight against crime has left a trail of hate. Merli's obligatory monologue about the impotence of the police ("otherwise let's dismiss the police, let's get out of here, and let the thieves, the murderers, the terrorists be the rulers of the city!") is not the product of a deep civic disdain, but just the consequence of the sudden nervous breakdown of a man who's tired, confused, and above all alone.

The film's structure (the action takes place in the course of one day), the choral quality of the scenes set at the police station and the characters' development seemingly pay homage to Joseph Wambaugh's books or Ed McBain's 87th Precinct series. However, although Massi shoots the action scenes with his usual stylistic flair, *Il commissario di ferro* looks rushed and slapdash at times and somehow wastes its undeniable potential. Maurizio Merli labeled it as "a movie made out of nothing,"[1] and the director was not satisfied with the results. "Of all the films Maurizio and I did together, that's the one I recall less gladly. I wasn't bad altogether, but while we were filming it there were financial problems. Halfway through the shooting the producer showed up on the set and told us: "There's no money left. Finish the film as you like." So we shot the rest of the script in a hurry, even though we had some problems shooting the exterior night scenes in the second part."[2]

Unlike Massi's other crime films of the period, *Il commissario di ferro* was not even dubbed in English for foreign markets.

Notes

1. Maurizio Merli, "Il commissario ringrazia," in Aa.Vv., *Il Patalogo Due: Annuario 1980 dello spettacolo, Volume secondo, Cinema e televisione* (Milan Ubulibri/Electa Editrice, 1980), p. 126.
2. Matteo Norcini and Stefano Ippoliti, "Stelvio Massi ricorda Maurizio Merli," *Cine 70 e dintorni* #1 (Winter 2001), p. 14.

Convoy Busters (*Un poliziotto scomodo*)

D: Stelvio Massi. *S:* Danilo Massi; *SC:* Gino Capone, Teodoro Agrimi [Teodoro Corrà], Stelvio Massi; *DOP:* Sergio Rubini (35mm, Gevacolor, Fotocinema); *M:* Stelvio Cipriani (ed. P.A.C.); *E:* Mauro Bonanni; *PD:* Franco Calabrese; *CO:* Andrea Zani; *C:* Michele Pensato; *AC:* Aldo Bergamini, Filippo Neroni; *AE:* Piero Bozza; *2nd AE:* Massimo Gasperini, Angelo Bufalini; *AD:* Danilo Massi; *MU:* Dante Trani; *Hair:* Caterina Campana; *W:* Irene Parlagreco; *SO:* Luigi Salvatori; *Boom:* Antonino Pantano; *SetT:* Pasquino Benassati; *KG:* Giuseppe Raimondi; *ChEl:* Furio Rocchi; *SS:* Flavia Sante Vanin. *Cast:* Maurizio Merli (Commissioner Francesco Olmi), Massimo Serato (Degan), Mario Feliciani (Chief of Police), Mimmo Palmara (Gorchi), Marco Gelardini (Marcello Degan), Attilio Duse (Ballarin), Olga Karlatos (Anna), Piero Gerlini (Mario, the journalist), Nello Pazzafini (Thug), Luigi Casellato (Homeless man), Maurizio Gueli (Judge Garganese), Luciano Roffi (Degan's secretary), Mirella Frumenti, Alfredo Zamarion [Alfredo Zammi] (policeman), Alice Gherardi, Alessandro Poggi, Sergio Mioni, Paola Maiolini (Waitress), Franco Salamon. *Uncredited:* Andrea Aureli (Journalist), Franco Beltramme (Thug), Enrico Chiappafreddo (Thug), Sasha D'Arc, Raniero Dorascenzi (police inspector), Alba Maiolini (Augusto's mother), Emilio Messina (Killer), Roberto Messina (Gorchi's henchman), Nello Pazzafini (Thug), Riccardo Petrazzi (Thug), Nando Sarlo (Journalist), Claudio Zucchet (Thug released by fake cops). *PROD:* P.A.C.—Produzioni Atlas Consorziate (Milan); *PM:* Teodoro Agrimi; *UM:* Mario Olivieri; *PSe:* Giuseppe Cicconi; *ADM:* Enrico Savelloni. *Country:* Italy. Filmed on location in Rome and Civitanova Marche. *Running time:* 99'; Visa no.: 72889 (12.23.1978); *Rating:* v.m.14; *Release date:* 12.23.1978; *Distribution:* P.A.C.; *Domestic gross:* 989,390,960 lira. *Also known as: Smugglar konvoj* (Sweden). *Home video:* No Shame (DVD, USA), Cecchi Gri (DVD, Italy).

Commissioner Francesco Olmi of the Rome police is a rather problematic cop because of the drastic nature of his methods and his utter incorruptibility. When he is called on to investigate on the death of two youngsters, Maria and Augusto, Olmi discovers an eyewitness, Loredana, and forces her to speak. This way, he finds out that the crimes have been commissioned by the powerful Mr. Degan, the director of Customs at Fiumicino airport, in order to cover the misdeeds of his son Marcello. Olmi also learns that Degan heads a diamond smuggling ring, but he does not have adequate evidence to prosecute him. After unsuccessfully trying to remove the commissioner, Degan escapes abroad. Transferred to a small provincial town, Olmi starts investigating on an arms trafficking ring. In a short time he tightens his grip on the gang, which is headed by a renowned publisher. By means of the local broadcasting

Italian poster for *Convoy Busters* (1978).

network, through which the traffickers exchange coded messages, Olmi sets a trap. Unfortunately, the thugs break into the school where Olmi's lover Anna teaches and take her and the children as hostages. The commissioner sneaks into the building, kills the bandits and releases the hostages.

Based on a story by the director's son Danilo, and once again starring Maurizio Merli in his fourth collaboration with the filmmaker, *Convoy Busters* is perhaps Stelvio Massi's best effort, and one of the better late Italian poliziotteschi. The film is virtually split in two: the first half is based on the genre's typical conflict between David and Goliath, as the stubborn commissioner Olmi (Maurizio Merli) uncovers the illegal traffickings of a powerful senior official (Massimo Serato), who's a diamond smuggler and the instigator of three ferocious murders. This time, however, Goliath wins: halfway through *Convoy Busters*, Degan escapes by plane after killing one of his own employees in cold blood before Olmi's eyes and in spite of genre conventions. If that wasn't enough, the film develops a central character who's at the same time the logical evolution of the avengers with a badge usually played by Merli, as well as their critical dissection. Massi uses the actor's impassive mask to create a problematic, multi-faceted figure, a fragile, uncertain person, who's becoming scared of his own violent methods — and, most shockingly, a man who is becoming part of the violent system he's fighting.

Olmi can no longer keep struggling on different fronts: the press attacks him; the investigating judge is probably in cahoots with the criminals; and one night the commissioner finds a pair of killers waiting for him in front of his home. Eventually, Olmi breaks down under the stress and accidentally kills a night watchman: it's a bold plot twist, and something unique in the history of Italian crime films.

Convoy Busters' second half radically shifts territory, atmosphere and pacing. The action moves to Civitanova Marche (Massi's hometown), a quiet village on the Adriatic sea where Olmi has been transferred. The rhythm slows down and becomes contemplative, and Massi describes his native land with a sympathetic eye, taking his time, as if he needs to detach himself from the genre's waste — just like his protagonist. In one scene, Olmi even puts his pistol in a drawer: the hero's distinctive weapon had become too heavy a burden. There's even room for a romantic idyll between the commissioner and the town's beautiful teacher (Olga Karlatos): but the dream of a new life is destined to vanish briskly, as Olmi is once again forced to become the avenger he was — only to be overwhelmed by disgust. In the end, after killing the bandits who held his lover and a class of children hostages inside the village school — a moment similar to Giuseppe Vari's *Return of the .38 Gang*, but much more skillfully executed — Olmi gets rid of the gun he hoped to leave forever in that drawer. It's a gesture that feels less like a homage to conventions (as it was in *Blood, Sweat and Fear*, whose ending just recycled almost literally that of Don Siegel's *Dirty Harry*) than it is a reflection upon a thread that's run out of its vital juices.[1]

The depiction of violence is stylized, and Massi distances himself from the character's bouts of rage — even literally, choosing an ellipsis in the sequence where Olmi beats up Degan's son (Marco Gelardini), which is filmed in a long shot while the camera concentrates on the commissioner's assistants who are watching and commenting on the scene, deploring their superior's violent excesses. *Convoy Busters* is also notable for the director's consistently stylish mise en scène. The killing of the Carabinieri in the car, only accompanied by Stelvio Cipriani's music, and the exasperated slow motion in the scene where Merli — who didn't want a double for the action sequences — shoots a thug from a helicopter (after a beautifully shot chase that somehow recalls the director's earlier *Emergency Squad*), are two eloquent examples; and so is the ground-level traveling shot that accompanies Olmi's raid on a bandits' lair. Massi also tends to avoid the usual shot/countershot routine, and films dialogue scenes by using mirrors or other reflective surfaces where both interlocutors are featured. The only disappointing element is perhaps Stelvio Cipriani's score, which recycles themes from the one Cipriani wrote for Antonio Bido's *Bloodstained Shadow* (*Solamente nero*, 1978).

Convoy Busters was unusually well-received by critics. The prestigious Vittorio Spiga praised it as Massi's best work: "Italian crime films have found in Stelvio Massi a filmmaker that has managed to renew the genre somehow: by borrowing the style of the Italian Western, its violence and characters, while taking the spectacular angle and the fast pacing from American cinema."[2] The takings, however, were not on a par with Merli's previous films: just under one billion lira. After a couple of seasons as a box office champion, the star power of Italy's best known commissioner was beginning to fade.

Notes

1. On a lighter note, the presence of a local broadcasting company as a cover for a gang of arms dealers conveys the growing discomfort towards local TV stations, whose competition was keeping audiences away from movie theaters.
2. Vittorio Spiga, "Il Resto del Carlino," 2.3.1979.

Covert Action (Sono stato un agente CIA)

D: Romolo Guerrieri [Romolo Girolami]. *S:* Vittorio Schiraldi; *SC:* Vittorio Schiraldi, Mino Roli [Emilio Pontiroli], Nico Ducci, Romolo Guerrieri [English version: John Crowther, Vittorio Schiraldi]; *DOP:* Erico Menczer (35mm, Vistavision, Staco Film); *M:* Stelvio Cipriani, conducted by the author (ed. Nazionalmusic); *E:* Antonio Siciliano; *PD, ArtD:* Eugenio Liverani; *APD* Pasquale Germano; *CO:* Massimo Bolongaro; *C:* Giuseppe Tinelli; *AC:* Maurizio La Monica; *AE:* Giancarlo Morelli, Luigi Gorini; *AD:* Renzo Spaziani [Renzo Girolami]; *MU:* Giuliano Laurenti; *Hair:* Elda Magnanti; *W:* Valeria Sponsali; *SO:* Primiano Muratori; *Boom:* Luciano Muratori; *Mix:* Romano Checcacci; *SE:* Paolo Ricci; *SP:* Giovanni Vino; *ChEl:* Rodolfo Filibotto; *KG:* Maurizio Micalizzi; *PrM:* Adriano Tiberi; *STC:* Sergio Mioni; *MA:* Remo De Angelis; *SS:* Beatrice Banfi. *Cast:* David Janssen (Lester Horton), Corinne Cléry (Anne Florio), Maurizio Merli (John Florio), Arthur Kennedy (Maxwell), Philippe Leroy (Inspector Radi Stavropoulos), Ivan Rassimov (Chiva), Giacomo Rossi-Stuart (Grant), Carla Romanelli (Aliki), Phedon Georgitsis, Dimitris Iakimidos, Tom Felleghy (Dr. Yannides), Alberto Martelli, Giorgio Scardov. *Uncredited:* Giovanni Cianfriglia (Florio's killer), Marina Haritou. *PROD:* Mihalis Lefakis for Mires Cinematografica; *EP:* Enzo Silvestri, Giuseppe Tortorella; *GO:* Franco Caruso; *PM:* Michele Germano; *UM:* Roberto Cuomo, Giuseppe Ercolani, Franco Silvestri; *Accountant:* Giorgio Oddi. *Country:* Italy. Filmed at Incir — De Paolis (Rome) and on location in Athens and Rhodes, Greece. *Running time:* 100'; Visa no.: 72190 (08.08.1978); *Rating:* v.m.14; *Release date:* 08.10.1978; *Distribution:* Capitol; *Domestic gross:*

592,232,980 lira. *Also known as: Rauschgift tötet leise* (West Germany, 11.05.1981—91'). *Home video:* Hobby & Work (DVD, Italy). OST: CD Chris' Soundtrack Corner CSC010.

When he learns that his friend John Benson was assassinated in Athens, former CIA agent-turned-novelist Lester Horton moves to Greece. He plans to search for a tape on which the deceased recorded his explosive memoirs that expose the agency's implication in military takeovers all over the world. But the CIA, represented by the unscrupulous Maxwell, is also keen to do away with Benson's memoirs. After surviving a murder attempt in Athens, Horton moves to Rhodes, where his ex-lover Anna lives. Anna is now the wife of Lester's fellow agent and friend Joe Florio. But the hounds of the CIA reach the island, eluding the efforts of an inspector on the Greek police force. Lester finds out that Joe is a drug addict and that he got hold of Benson's tape to protect himself. Joe is dispatched with a heroin overdose and Lester ends up in an asylum where he is almost lobotomized. Luckily, the Greek police Inspector saves him. After several happy days spent with Anna, Horton is located by a hitman, Chiva, who murders the woman before Lester kills him.

Shot in January and February 1978, *Covert Action* was an ambitious project for director Romolo Guerrieri and one aimed mainly at the foreign market, as shown by the casting of David Janssen (*The Fugitive*) in the lead. The story, by journalist Vittorio Schiraldi, was based on the experiences of former CIA agent Philip Agee, whose best-selling 1975 book *Inside the Company: CIA Diary*, which detailed his experiences in the agency, had sparked a controversy. Big ripples were also caused by an article in the August 1975 issue of *Playboy* magazine, which published excerpts from the book. Agee, who in 1978 co-founded *CovertAction Information Bulletin*, initiated a lawsuit with the producers over his fees and expenses.

However, Guerrieri's film has less to do with CIA politics in South America than it has with classical *film noir*, and emphasizes crepuscular tones. The unusual Greek setting — perhaps not a casual choice, since the country had just suffered a tragic dictatorship under a military junta from 1967 to 1974 — gives *Covert Action* a poignancy that sets it apart from contemporary poliziotteschi. Guerrieri stoically resists any temptation to include tourist footage, and fills the film with tired faces and losers without a future — not only the characters but the actors themselves. The scene where Janssen wakes up in an asylum bed and finds a quartet of actors that are well-known to B-movie devotees (the ubiquitous Tom Felleghy, former spy/action hero Giacomo Rossi-Stuart, Arthur Kennedy and icy-eyed villain Ivan Rassimov), perfectly summarizes the image of a movie industry populated by ghosts — an image that's close to that of the "wax figures" playing cards in Billy Wilder's *Sunset Blvd.*

Take former TV star Janssen — middle-aged, paunchy, visibly drunk in many scenes — who would die of a heart attack less than two years later; take parchment-faced Kennedy, in one of his last screen roles; and take Maurizio Merli, who had been chosen to assure the film good box office results in Italy but whose popularity was rapidly waning by the time *Covert Action* came out in August 1978. As the heroin-addicted CIA agent who's dispatched about a hour into the film, Merli tries hard to bring his usual charisma to a thankless, secondary role. "The film was not bad," he'd claim later, "but people used to tell me: "What does that mean? What's that other actor, the American, doing in it? You are supposed to be the star!"[1]

One of the reasons why *Covert Action* did not do well at the box office (just under 600 million lira) was Guerrieri's emphasis on the melancholic-romantic vein which turned out to be one of the films stronger elements. A scene where Merli is chased by car is intercut with a dialogue between Janssen and Corinne Cléry (who replaced *The Dukes of Hazzard*'s Catherine Bach as the female lead) and the film's final idyll works like a desperate love story with no future. On the other hand, the scenes set in an asylum — where Guerrieri used mostly mentally ill patients as extras — are powerfully downbeat and display Guerrieri's skills as a filmmaker. As Rassimov stated, "Guerrieri was too intelligent a filmmaker for the kind of audiences those films were aimed at; he was capable of directorial refinements that were lost on many viewers."[2] An example of this is the opening sequence, a murder shot as if it belongs to a Dario Argento thriller; or the scene where Janssen escapes Rassimov's thugs in the Rhodes market, with the introduction of Janssen's point of view shots from behind a crate of oranges that the man is carrying to hide his face from his pursuers.

Rassimov also recalls Janssen's drinking problem: "He was an effective actor but he was constantly drunk. I think I've never seen someone drink so hard. At 8 A.M. he had already finished his first bottle of wine." Janssen wasn't too satisfied with the film, as the cache of working in a foreign locale was somewhat dampened by a frustrating production experience. As customary with Italian productions, live sound was not used on set and hence non–English speaking actors spoke in their own language while playing scenes with him. According to Rassimov, one such scene featured Maurizio Merli in an Athens restaurant. "Janssen disputed Maurizio as an actor: they had this scene together which was re-shot five or six times ... even Romolo said "I can't work with this guy." However, it must be added that there's no trace of the scene in the finished film, and Merli seems to be one of the few actors who spoke English on set judging by labial movements. As for his Italian colleague, Rassimov added: "I had the impression, when I met him on the set of *Covert Action*, that Maurizio was no longer interested in those kind of films. I remember that in the movies where he played the cop, all shot in Rome, he worked just fine. Maurizio wasn't very likeable and he didn't get along very well with others on the set."

Notes

1. Merli, "Il commissario ringrazia," p. 127.
2. Gomarasca and Pulici, "Ivan il terribile," p. 77–78.

Deadly Chase (Il commissario Verrazzano)

D: Franco Prosperi. *S:* Franco Ciferri; *SC:* Franco Bottari; *DOP:* Cristiano Pogany (35mm, Telecolor, Tecnolux); *M:* Lino Corsetti (Ed. Nazionalmusic), solo trumpet: Franco Santucci; *E:* Alberto Gallitti; *PD, CO:* Giulia Mafai; *APD:* Sandro Belloma; *C:* Renato Doria; *AC:* Luigi Cecchini; *AE:* Anna Bolli; *AD:* Romano Scandariato; *MU:* Maria Cristina Rocca; *Hair:* Jole Angelucci; *W:* Sara Santarelli; *SO:* Pietro Spadoni; *SOE:* Roberto Arcangeli; *SP:* Francesco Bellomo; *KG:* Giovanni

Savini; *ChEl:* Roberto Allegretti; *PrM:* Maurizio Iacopelli; *ST:* Giorgio Ricci; *SS:* Marisa Calia. *Cast:* Luc Merenda (Commissioner Verrazzano), Giacomo Rizzo (Brigadeer Baldelli), Maria Baxa (Cora Venier), Luciana Paluzzi (Rosy), Gloria Piedimonte (Giorgia), Daniele Dublino (Commissioner Biagi), Isarco Ravaioli (Alberto Volci "The Baron"), Edmondo Tieghi (Civetta), Patrizia Gori (Giorgia), Chris Avram (Marco Verelli), Janet Agren (Giulia Medici). *Uncredited:* Artemio Antonini (Racketeer), Calogero Azzaretto (Card player), Angelo Boscariol (Verelli's butler), Omero Capanna (Robber), Attilio Dottesio (Notary Bruni), Lina Franchi (Woman at horse race), Luciano Zanussi (Customer in art gallery). *PROD:* Pino Buricchi for Holiday Cinematografica; *PM:* Francesco Giorgi; *PSu:* Paolo Bistolfi; *PSe:* Enzo Prosperini; *Accountant:* Romano Cannavacciuolo. *Country:* Italy. Filmed at Incir—De Paolis (Rome) and on location in Rome and Nice. *Running time:* 95': Visa no.: 72749 (12/07/78); *Rating:* v.m. 14; *Release date:* 12/08/1978; *Distribution:* Nucleo Star; *Domestic gross:* 443,627,250 lira. *Also known as: Flic à abatre* (Canada), *O Justiceiro de Roma* (Portugal), *Policaj, ki je ljubil zenske* (Slovenia). *Home video:* Cinehollywood, Magnum 3B (VHS, Italy).

Commissioner Verrazzano—a dynamic young cop with a gambling habit—receives a visit from the fascinating Giulia Medici, the owner of an art gallery, who begs him to reopen the case of her brother Walter's death, hastily filed a few months before as a suicide. Verrazzano, supported by Brigadier Baldelli, starts nosing around in the betting underworld. He learns from his confidant Civetta that the organization is currently headed by Alberto Volci, "The Baron," on behalf of new bosses whose identity is unknown. The case gets even more complicated when Cora, Walter's widow and now married to the wealthy Marco Verelli, in turn contacts Verrazzano. Moreover, as the cop delves deeper into the mystery, someone tries to stop him, first by killing his cat Ciro, then his lover Rosy. Removed from the case after Rosy's death, Verrazzano finds out that Giulia and Verelli are business associates, and by means of a dancer named Giorgia he obtains revealing photographs. After Cora has been dispatched as well, the Commissioner sets up a trap for Volci with the help of Civetta, who gets killed in the process. After a car chase through Rome, Verrazzano faces Volci in an amusement park and kills him. It was Volci who murdered Medici, making it look like a suicide: but the instigators were Giulia and Marco, who are lovers. Verrazzano sneaks into Verelli's house and waits for the two murderers. Verelli is about to kill Verrazzano, but Giulia shoots him, saving the Commissioner's life.

The second of the two films Franco Prosperi shot for producer Pino Buricchi in 1978 (the first being *Terror*, which came out several months earlier), *Deadly Chase* is a peculiar hybrid, that despite its aggressive Italian title (which focuses on the eponymous commissioner as if he was the umpteenth Merli clone) actually moves away from out-and-out poliziotteschi and its worn out schemes and moves closer to the melancholic, contemplative vein of *film noir*. Franco Bottari's script moves along in typical hard-boiled fashion *à la* Raymond Chandler, as the protagonist receives a visit from a beautiful woman who entrusts him with an investigation that enrolls like a (admittedly rather tiresome) whodunit—there's even a fake suicide in a locked room—complete with the hero's final explanation of the mystery's solution. Yet it provides a few good dialogue lines in the process. "It's not easy to be rich," Giulia (Janet Agren) sighs; "When you're poor, there are difficulties as well," quips Verrazzano.

The titular commissioner is a hard-boiled hero in disguise: even though he's a policeman he doesn't mind spending his spare time in illegal gambling kiosks and racetracks, only reads horse-racing bulletins and proves to be one hell of a womanizer. *Deadly Chase* provides Luc Merenda—here looking less wooden and more relaxed than in other films he did in the period—with a number of impressive female counterparts, from classy-looking Janet Agren to dancer Gloria Piedimonte (who was then enjoying an ephemeral popularity thanks to the TV show "Discoring," which even led to a starring role in the tailor-made *Baila guapa*, 1979, by Adriano Tagliavia), from the mature Luciana Paluzzi to the sensuous Maria Baxa: the latter proves to be the most striking of the lot, thanks to her memorable screen entrance, as she emerges topless from a swimming pool before the stunned Verrazzano, and to the obligatory love scene.

Compared with the justice-obsessed characters played by Merli, Verrazzano is a more pleasant presence: inattentive, elegant but rather sloppy (he forgets to shave, has his tie perennially undone), he enjoys the company of his personal harem, but seems more attached to his cat Ciro, just like Marlowe (Elliot Gould) was in Robert Altman's *The Long Goodbye* (and Ray Lovelock in *Gangbuster*)—and the opening sequence amusingly plays on viewer's expectations as we hear Verrazzano apologizing with romantic words to somebody he's awaken accidentally in the middle of the night while going out for one of his gambling bouts, only to find out he's talking to Ciro.

Prosperi's direction is professional as ever, and in one scene—the robbery in the notary's study—the filmmaker's remarkable use of high-angle hand-held shots recalls *Terror!*'s opening sequence, even though with less impressive results. Paluzzi's death scene—abrupt and unexpected in the middle of a supposedly romantic sequence, with the woman being shot in the head from a nearby car while she and Verrazzano are driving along a highway—is another highlight; while an almost surreal target practice sequence has Merenda, dressed in a white jumpsuit, walk through a shooting gallery and aim at very human-looking, pale-faced puppets which are shooting back at him (the whole thing appears to be computer-controlled, in one of those naive moments that betray the period's scarce knowledge of computers and the like).

The most patent difference with poliziotteschi comes in the sequence where Verrazzano stops a gang of robbers: what a couple of years earlier would have been the film's climax, here is dispatched in a hurry with a few slow motion shots and a so-so car crash. However, the low budget is also to blame, as Buricchi (a former accountant turned producer) was definitely a B-movie figure. Other scenes—such as the one at the police office where Verrazzano examines a bullet—also look rather patchy, while the brief sequence in Nice provides much needed tourist footage (and topless sunbathing girls) to pad the running time.

With its poor box office performance, *Deadly Chase* was evidence of Merenda's quick commercial decline as well as that of the genre itself, grossing even less than 500 million lira. It did surface abroad, however, with awful English dubbing.

Don't Shoot on Children (*Non sparate sui bambini [Squadra antisequestro]*)

D: Gianni Crea. *S:* Gianni Crea; *SC:* Manuel Vita; Dialogue, adaptation, dubbing director: Rosalba Oletta; *DOP:* Maurizio Centini (35mm, Techniscope, Stacofilm); *M:* Stelvio Cipriani; *E:* Gianfranco Amicucci; *PD:* Giorgio Marzelli; Assistant *CO:* Itala Giardina; *C:* Carlo Marotti; *AC:* Carlo Passari; *Collaboration to the direction* [sic]: Emilio Messina; *SO:* Enrico Spadoni; *SP:* Dario Cavalcanti; *SS:* Vincenzo Nobile; *Titles:* Glauco Morosini; *PP:* Fabrizio Di Blasi. *Cast:* Giancarlo Prete (Dino Settimi), Italo Gasperini (Beaumont), Marco Gelardini (Marco Settimi), Sandra Trouvé (Patrizia, Marco's girlfriend), Antonella Lualdi (Schoolmistress), Giampiero Albertini (Settimi's father), Eleonora Giorgi (Ilda). *Uncredited:* Claudio Antonacci (Motorcycle driver), Spartaco Battisti (Teacher), Roberto Messina (Beaumont's henchman). *PROD:* Cabes Cinematografica; *PM:* Benito Mercuri; *PSu:* Giovanni Spedicato. *Country:* Italy. Filmed on location in Capena and Rome. *Running time:* 95'; Visa no.: 72757 (11.28.1978); *Rating:* v.m.14; *Release date:* 12.22.1978; *Distribution:* Fida; *Domestic gross:* 107,183,960 lira. *Home video:* New Pentax (VHS, Italy), Cronos (VHS, Greece—English version).

The Settimi family has long been hounded by misfortune. Mr. Settimi, a widower in his fifties, is suffering from silicosis contracted during a long period of work in the mines. The youngest son, Marco, who is still attending school, hangs around with bad company and uses drugs. The elder, Dino, is the family's only means of financial support. One day, however, his company fires him due to the economic crisis. At the same time, Mr. Settimi's condition worsens and he is hospitalized. After looking in vain for an honest job, a desperate Dino gets in touch with Beaumont, a friend of his father's who owns a company. But this turns out to be just a screen and the young man is induced into a gang of thugs. After a hold-up attempt that ends in violence, Dino and Beaumont take refuge in a nursery school where they take the teacher Sandra and the many children hostage. The fugitives are besieged by the police, and eventually only Dino, who has made every effort to protect the teacher and children, gets away alive. He manages to see his dying father one last time before he is captured.

Despite the subtitle *Squadra antisequestro* (Anti-kidnapping Squad), Gianni Crea's *Don't Shoot on Children* doesn't have anything to do with the subgenre initiated by Massimo Dallamano's *Colt 38 Special Squad.* The story of a poor man fired from his job who falls in with a gang of criminals to pay for his father's hospital treatment looks almost like an update of 1950s tearjerking melodramas about unfortunate proletarians. "Look me in the face ... I'm not a criminal ... I'm not a criminal ... I'm not a criminal!" yells Dino (Giancarlo Prete, a former stuntman who enjoyed brief yet marginal popularity in the early '70s and often worked with Enzo Castellari, most memorably on *Street Law*) in the film's rhetorical ending. "I wanted a job, a family ... and you denied me them—all of you! Do something, otherwise other people like me will get a gun. Do something!"

The protagonist's desperate monologue somehow puts *Don't Shoot on Children* on the same league as Umberto Lenzi's *Brothers Till We Die*, which openly took sides with the working class. The upper-class world corrupts and corrodes: Dino works hard in the factory to maintain his sick father (the sympathetic Giampiero Albertini, in one of his typical "unfortunate good guy" roles) who's dying of lung cancer, while the younger son (the obnoxious Marco Gelardini, who appeared in a number of erotic comedies in those years, as well as in Massi's *Convoy Busters*) not only weighs on the family budget as he keeps studying at his brother's expenses, but he also enjoys a luxurious life with his rich friends, smoking pot and sniffing cocaine by the pool. What's more, Crea opens the film with a collection of newspaper headlines depicting the unfortunate condition of minors in Italy (underage work, abandoned children living in an asylum, parents beating their offspring to death and so on), and the dialogue mentions student protests.

However, the social urgency is not enough to make a good film, which *Don't Shoot on Children* definitely isn't. An extremely low budget production, with a recycled Stelvio Cipriani score, it suffers from poor direction and dialogue ("I love you, even though you're an intellectual," Dino says to his girlfriend, Ilda [Eleonora Giorgi]), and the overemphasis on drama—culminating in a tear-inducing ending where the whole family is reunited around the father's deathbed—doesn't gel with the slapdash crime subplot, which features the obligatory five minute car chase and in its second half resembles *Return of the .38 Gang* and Stelvio Massi's coeval *Convoy Busters*, whereas the sequence where Gelardini and friends smoke pot with hilariously exaggerated results, is worthy of *Reefer Madness.*

The film had a limited release in Italy, but an English language version exists and was released on a very rare Greek tape.

Don't Touch the Children! (*I figli non si toccano!*)

D: Nello Ferrarese [Nello Rossati]. *S* and *SC:* Roberto Gianviti, Paolo Vidali, Nello Ferrarese; *DOP:* Vittorio Bernini (35mm, Gevacolor, Telecolor); *M:* G. Ployer [Gianfranco Plenizio] (Ed. C.A.M.); *Maria* (Moxedano—Mauro—Iglio) sung by Pino Mauro; *E:* Adalberto Ceccarelli; *PD:* Toni Rossati; *AC:* Aldo Bergamini; *AD:* Paolo Vidali; *MU:* Silvana Petri, Carlo Sindici; *SO:* Umberto Montesanti; *Mix:* Sandro Occhetti; *ChEl:* Vitorio Pescetelli; *KG:* Sergio Grassi. *Cast:* Pino Mauro [Giuseppe Mauriello] (Don Raffaele Sapienza), Anna Melita (Maria), Guido Cerniglia (Mimì Fiorito), Franco Marino (Gennarino), Dario Ghirardi, Luca Priore (Alfonsino), Clarita Gatto (Gloria), Narciso Pula, Claudio Delfino, Simone Santo (Vincenzo, the dead smugglers' father), Enzo Fabbri, Carlo Sabatini, Fernando Cerulli (Car mechanic), Vittorio De Bisogno. *Uncredited:* Umberto Amambrini (Man of the Camorra), Lina Franchi (Maid), Vezio Natili (Man of the Camorra). *PROD:* Roxy International 67; *PM:* Enzo Nigro; *PSu:* Giorgio Maulini. *Country:* Italy. Filmed at Icet—De Paolis (Milan) and on location in Naples. *Running time:* 97'; Visa no.: 72290 (09.06.1978); *Rating:* not rated; *Release date:* 09.08.1978; *Distribution:* Roxy International; *Domestic gross:* 348,768,330 lira. *Home video:* Eureka (VHS, Italy), MVP (VHS, Canada—Italian language).

Don Raffaele Sapienza, the undisputed leader of the Neapolitan "guapparia," is worried: some strangers have killed two young associates who foolishly agreed to purchase smuggled goods without telling him. The unknown criminals then kidnap Alfonsino, the son of engineer Mimì Fiorito and Sapienza's ex-lover Maria, who married Fiorito while the Don was serving a prison term. After obtaining a large ransom, the kidnappers do not release the child and demand more money. Out of desperation, Maria asks Don Raffaele for help. Putting aside all resentment and ignoring the rumors spread by his jealous lover Gloria, Sapienza sets the Neapolitan underworld in motion for help. The smugglers collect the money to pay the ransom, while an identikit of the "Frenchman," the alleged head of the foreign gang, is circulated. When the man is identified, he is shadowed by street urchins. Don Raffaele and his men eventually locate the ship where the kidnapped boy is held prisoner, defy the gang and save him. Fiorito is forced to recognize his rival's loyalty and the groundlessness of the accusations against Raffaele and his wife.

Due to his northern origins, Nello Rossati — here under the name Nello Ferrarese and more popular for his erotic films such as *The Secret of a Sensuous Nurse* (1975) — was an atypical director for a sceneggiata, yet *Don't Touch the Children* is an interesting piece of work within the Neapolitan crime subgenre. The opening sequence — as two young Neapolitan smugglers at sea are killed by a rival gang from Marseille — sets the tone for the film's message. The police are virtually absent from *Don't Touch the Children*, as the whole story is seen from the point of view of the underworld.

Smuggling boss Don Raffaele (Neapolitan singing legend Pino Mauro) is the king of the city — a lonely and long-suffering sovereign, for that matter, having been abandoned by the woman he loved while he was in prison. The only other female presence — Raffaele's lover Gloria — is depicted as vapid, mean and scheming, and "only deserves to be despised" as Don Raffaele says in the end. The sceneggiata is a male world, based on bonding, honor and loyalty. "This is a disgraced business. When we stay together we protect each other. You can't be on your own" says Don Raffaele about smuggling.

Despite Mauro's far from Apollinean presence — paunchy, with bad teeth and truly unbelievable 1970s sideburns — Don Raffaele comes out as a charismatic presence. Mauro even gets to sing a song that's a paean to his lost love ("Do you remember when people forgot about eating as they listened to you singing?" he is asked by an elderly guitarist who accompanied Don Raffaele when he used to perform in restaurants to make ends meet). The script even provides him with unintentionally comic lines ("You broke my heart, indeed. But if that makes you feel better, I've been to Professor Barnard and he planted a new one in my chest" he says to his former lover Maria, in a scene that's supposed to be touching).

The way the script has the Neapolitan underworld react to the foreign intruders is emblematic: beggars, street workers, petty thieves, prostitutes and street urchins all contribute to find the French gangster who kidnapped a little boy, and the scene where the criminal walks in the alleys of the Spanish Quarter, tailed by a mob of children that, unbeknownst to him, are acting on Don Raffaele's orders (much like Sherlock Holmes' Baker Street Irregulars) provides one of the subgenre's most striking sequences, and sums up the (romantic yet debatable, to use an euphemism) idea of the Parthenopean underworld as an idyllic vital organism that exists and operates for the common good.

Father of the Godfathers (*Corleone*)

D: Pasquale Squitieri. *S:* Pasquale Squitieri, loosely based on *I complici: gli anni dell'antimafia* by Orazio Barrese; *SC:* Orazio Barrese, Massimo De Rita, Arduino Maiuri, Pasquale Squitieri; *DOP:* Eugenio Bentivoglio (35mm, Vistavision, Technospes); *M:* Ennio Morricone (ed. Slalom); *E:* Mauro Bonanni; *PD:* Umberto Turco; *APD:* Marcello Turco; *ArtD:* Egidio Spugnini; *CO:* Renato Ventura; *C:* Federico Del Zoppo; *AC:* Alessio Gelsini, Roberto Lo Re; *AE:* Walter Diotallevi, Francesco Reitano; *AD:* Roberto Pariante; *MU:* Walter Cossu, Gilberto Provenghi (for Claudia Cardinale); *AMU:* Gino Zamprioli; *Hair:* Giancarlo De Leonardis; *AHair:* Mauro Tamagnini; *SO:* Domenico Dubbini; *Boom:* Benito Alchimede; *Mix:* Romano Checcacci; *W:* Angela Vinci, Franca Lulli; *ChEl:* Giulio Quaglietti; *KG:* Giancarlo Rocchetti; *Props:* Gianni Fiumi, Vittorio Troiani; *SetT:* Gino Vagniluca; *SP:* Italo Tonni; *MA:* Nazzareno Zamperla; *SS:* Marisa Agostini. *Cast:* Giuliano Gemma (Vito Gargano), Claudia Cardinale (Rosa Accordino), Francisco Rabal (Don Giusto Provenzano), Stefano Satta Flores (Natale Calìa), Salvatore Billa (Carmelo), Remo Girone (Biagio Lo Cascio), Enrico Maisto (Matteo Agueci), Tommaso Palladino (Vincenzo Campisi), Tony Kendall [Luciano Stella] (Totò Sferlazzo), Vincent Gentile (Cosimo), Orazio Orlando (Attorney), Michele Placido (Michele Labruzzo), Dario Girardi, Giuseppe Morabito, Piero Scheggi, Emilio Delle Piane, Salvatore Moscardini, Ubaldo Lo Presti, Agatino Pellizzeri, Sebastiano Torrisi, Salvatore Torrisi, Vincenzo Norvese (Don Giusto's henchman), Salvatore Puntillo (Don Calogero), Guglielmina Jelo, Nunzia Vegna, Carlo Ferro, Paola Alabiso, Rita Mari, Bruno Di Luia. *Uncredited:* Francesco Anniballi (Rosa's bodyguard), Aristide Caporale (Storyteller), Massimo Ciprari (Traitor waiter), Dario Ghirardi (Court president), Giovanni Giancono, Mario Granato (Vito's lawyer), Giovanni Giancone, Quinto Marziali (Photographer at tribunal), Fulvio Mingozzi (Vito's lawyer), Giuseppe Sapienza (Rosa's father). *PROD:* Mario Cecchi Gori for Capital Film; *GM:* Luciano Luna; *PM:* Attilio Viti; *PSu:* Massimo Ferrero, Pietro Sassaroli; *PSe:* Tommaso Pantano; *ADM:* Mario Lupi, Giulio Cestari; *CASH:* Stefano Cialoni. *Country:* Italy. Filmed at Incir–De Paolis (Rome) and on location in Sicily. *Running time:* 120'; Visa no.: 72615 (11.04.1978); *Rating:* v.m.14; *Release date:* 11.04.1978; *Distribution:* Cineriz; *Domestic gross:* 2,304,300,190 lira. *Also known as: Corleone — Der Aufstieg des Paten* (West Germany, 01.28.1981—108'), *Corleone — Boss der Bosse* (West Germany — TV), *Der Aufstieg des Paten* (West Germany — Home video), *O ultimo padrinho* (Portugal). *Home video:* Cecchi Gori Home Video (DVD, Italy), Ecovideo (VHS, Portugal). OST: CD Dagored Red 172.

Corleone, Sicily, the 1950s. Two friends, Michele Labruzzo and Vito Gargano, live their lives in opposite ways: Michele, heading the farmers in the union's demands for land, is opposed to Baron Miceli and the Mafia boss who works for him, Don Giusto Provenzano. On the other hand, Vito becomes a Mafioso, the trusted man of Provenzano, and accepts to kill Michele and direct the Baron's estates. The unscrupulous Gargano wins the hearts of the employees, surrounds himself with trusted and armed men, cultivates political connections by having the attorney Calia elected in Parliament, and controls the economical system through his trusted bookkeeper Lo Cascio. After marrying Rosa, Michele's former girlfriend, Vito tries to take Don Giusto's place as the boss of Palermo; first he cheats him in the real estate business and then exterminates Provenzano with all his family. Respected by both the local Mafia and the American one, Vito becomes a very powerful boss — too powerful, thus causing alarm in political circles. Gargano is put on trial where he is defended by Calia, but gets away with a full acquittal due to the disappearance of compromising documents relating to his unlawful activities. Yet Gargano fails to avoid a second arrest warrant. This time, however, the police who show up to arrest him are preceded by a hired assassin, who kills Vito.

After the stark contemporary drama *Sniper*, Pasquale Squitieri returned to a more epic format with his next film, which formed a diptych of sorts with his previous historical yarn *I Am the Law* (1977). The director took inspiration from Orazio Barrese's book *I complici, Gli anni dell'antimafia*, which portrayed the story of Mafia boss Luciano Liggio. "After the success of *I Am the Law*, [producer] Mario Cecchi Gori called me to make a movie with him. I was very close to Orazio Barrese in that period and *I complici* was an important book. I was intrigued by the character of Luciano Liggio, as well as by all the connections between Mafia and politics" Squitieri recalled. "However, I don't consider *Father of the Godfathers* as one of my best works, it's definitely inferior to *I Am the Law*."[1]

For a film that wants to be both a spectacular genre yarn and a pamphlet, *Father of the Godfathers* is both turgid and banal, too worried about telling an emblematic story and, as so often is the case with Squitieri, underlining every nuance. As noted film critic Lino Micciché wrote, "*Father of the Godfathers* is harmed by the multiplicity of tones, rhythms and styles, which foul up the results in both directions it aims at, therefore the film oscillates [...] between popular ballad and turgid comic book, historical recreation and inquiry, the Western genre and committed cinema, echoing from time to time Germi and Rosi, Petri and Damiani[...]."[2] Even Ennio Morricone's bombastic score seems to suffer from the same shortcomings. Nevertheless *Father of the Godfathers* was a huge commercial success, with over two billion lira grossed at the Italian box office, and showed Michele Placido to be one of Italy's most talented young actors. He and Gemma (who won the Best Male Performer Award at the Montréal Film Festiva) would act together again the following year, in Damiano Damiani's *A Man on His Knees*.

Notes

1. Monetti, *Pasquale Squitieri*, p. 65.
2. Lino Micciché, "Corleone" di Squitieri: vivace pamphlet sulla mafia," *L'Avanti*, 11.18.1978.

Fearless (Poliziotto senza paura)

D: Stelvio Massi. *S:* Fulvio Gicca Palli; *SC:* Gino Capone, Stelvio Massi, Franz Antel; *DOP:* Riccardo Pallottini (35mm, Gevacolor, Staco Film); *M:* Stelvio Cipriani (ed. R.C.A.); *E:* Mauro Bonanni; *ArtD:* Franco Calabrese; *AArtD:* Helmut Graef; *CO:* Rosalba Menichelli; *C:* Michele Pensato, Giancarlo Giannesi; *AE:* Maria Letti; *AD:* Danilo Massi; *2nd AD:* Beatrice Banfi, Johannes Freisinger; *MU:* Dante Trani, Mirella Ginnoto; *SO:* Bruno Zanoli; *Boom:* Angelo Amatulli; *Mix:* Romano Pampaloni; *SP:* Ermanno Serto; English version by Marvel Sound, directed by Cesare Mancini. *Cast:* Maurizio Merli (Walter Spada "The Fox"), Joan Collins (Brigitte), Gastone Moschin (Karl Koper), Franco Ressel (Dr. Zimmer "Attila"), Werner Pochath (Strauss), Annarita Grapputo (Annelise von Straben), Alexander Trojan (Von Straben), Massimo Vanni (Benito), Luciana Turina (Adele), Andrea Scotti (Inspector Nardelli), Heidi Gutruf, Salvatore Billa (Strip, the pimp), Marcello Venditti (Adele's lover), Claudia Messner (Gina), Mario Frera, Mario Granato (Tancredi), Helmut Silbergasser, Jasmine Maimone (Renate). *Uncredited:* Umberto Amambrini (Strauss' henchman), Giuseppe Marrocco, Sergio Mioni (Thug beating Walter), Sandro Scarchilli (Man shitting behind a bush). *PROD:* Silvio Siano and Nicola Venditti for Promer (Rome), Franz Antel for Neue Delta Film (Vienna); *PM:* Silvio Siano; *APD:* Nicola Venditti, Christian Jungbluth, Anselmo Parrinello. *Country:* Italy / Austria. Filmed at Incir—De Paolis (Rome) and on location in Vienna. *Running time:* 100'; Visa no.: 71487 (02.02.1978); *Rating:* v.m.14; *Release date:* 02.03.1978; *Distribution:* Fida; *Domestic gross:* 1,146,557,460 lira. *Also known as: Magnum Cop* (France / Greece—Home video), *Fearless Fuzz, A Matter of Honour* (Sweden—Home video), *Die Zuhälterin* (West Germany), *Código matar* (Argentina—Home video). *Home video:* MHE (DVD, Italy), CreateSpace (DVD, USA). OST: CD Digitmovies CDDM119.

Rome. Private eye Walter Spada tries hard to make ends meet with his modest job. His agency does not offer the same up-to-date resources as his competitors and Walter doesn't even have money to pay for electricity and a telephone—not to mention a decent meal. Luckily, Spada is summoned by his friend and colleague Karl Koper, the owner of a sophisticated detective agency in Vienna, who entrusts him to find the young Annelise von Stradel, the daughter of a wealthy Austrian banker who came in Rome and joined a Buddhist community. A bunch of criminals kidnap the woman and Walter follows their tracks in Vienna. There, he finds himself involved in a mysterious and complicated story of underaged girls who were either killed or forced into prostitution. Thanks to the revelations of 14-year-old Renata, who is immediately murdered, Spada discovers that Annelise's own father is involved in the prostitution ring and that the racket is headed by Brigitte, a stripper with whom Walter has an affair. She kidnapped Annelise in order to blackmail the powerful von Stradel. Although his investigations have been successful, Spada returns to Rome as penniless as ever.

After the flawed but enjoyable *Highway Racer*, Stelvio Massi and Maurizio Merli devised another change of pace for the genre's most popular star. Co-produced by the Lancio photonovel company, with the aim of repeating the success of Massi's own *Blood, Sweat and Fear*, *Fearless* not only has Merli abandon the badge and play a private eye in a *film noir* setting, but moves the action from Italy to Austria. "*Fearless* was inspired by the character Philip Marlowe" Massi claimed. "I tried to turn Merli into a more human, less violent cop, somewhat different from those he had already successfully played. When Amati, the producer, read the script and found out that Maurizio's character was going to shoot his gun just once in the whole film, he complained: "Come on, he must be shooting like mad, or else nobody's going to watch this movie!"[1]

Deprived of poliziotteschi's main environment, however, both the story and the participants involved seem to be clueless. As the ex cop–turned–private eye Walter Spada (a name that recalls Sam Spade, and not by mere chance), Merli—who did his own dubbing in the Italian version, as he did on *Highway Racer*—plays a character who's obviously been conceived for a younger audience. For once, he dresses casually: the actor abandons his customary impeccable jackets and silk shirts for denim jumpsuit and sneakers. Secondly, he's penniless and an avid cinephile too, as the *locandinas* and lobby cards that fill the walls of his apartment show. What's more, the script (by Gino Capone and the director) leaves aside poliziotteschi's typical urban unease and opts for a more light-hearted tone: the goal is to turn Merli into a sort of photonovel hero, always with a ready wit and closer to Tomas Milian's Nico Giraldi than to the actor's previous roles.

Yet the results are schizophrenic, not to mention disharmonic: besides the duets between Merli and the always reliable Gastone Moschin (playing Merli's friend who heads an ultra-modern detective agency in Vienna which he often boasts about, trying to impress Walter), the obnoxious attempts at comedy feature a Keystone Kops–like car chase through the countryside and mild vignettes set in a restaurant and featuring stuntman/actor Massimo Vanni as Merli's sidekick. On the other hand, the film's plot about a prostitution racket—a similar topic as Massimo Dallamano's *What Have They Done to Your Daughters*, Mario Caiano's *Calling All Police Cars* and Carlo Lizzani's *The Teenage Prostitution Racket*—is decidedly unpleasant and sleazy: as the film's dark lady, Joan Collins—who enters the film after 45 minutes and almost immediately takes her clothes off—gets raped by Spada with the barrel of a gun ("I want to see the body of a woman who reached her maximum splendor only because she wasn't savagely raped at 14!" he grins).[2] Merli doesn't look too convincing most of the time, and Massi's direction doesn't fare much better either. The filmmaker's trademark showpieces—such as a fistfight shown via the opponents' shadows on a wall, or the scene where Merli is chased through the Vienna underground—rub shoulders with uninspired sequences and lengthy patches of exposition, such as when Merli and Moschin—filmed in extreme long shots—walk through a park in Vienna while their off-screen voices recite pages and pages of dialogue. Other scenes, like the slow motion opening, try hard to be iconic but to no avail.

Released in Italy in February 1978, *Fearless* was reasonably successful although its box office takings were about half as much as *Violent Naples*. Massi's two other Merli vehicles from the same year grossed notably less.

Notes

1. Norcini and Ippoliti, "Stelvio Massi ricorda Maurizio Merli," p. 14.
2. According to Massi, Collins shot almost all of her scenes in Vienna. Before accepting the part, she insisted on being sent a number of photos of Merli to see what her co-star looked like.

Little Italy (Squadra antimafia)

D: Bruno Corbucci. *S* and *SC:* Mario Amendola, Bruno Corbucci; *DOP:* Marcello Masciocchi (35mm, Vistavision—Todd Ao 35, Telecolor); *M:* Guido and Maurizio de Angelis (ed. Nazionalmusic); *E lassame perde* (by Goblin / Amendola / Corbucci) sung by Aldo Donati; *E:* Daniele Alabiso; *PD:* Claudio Cinini; *CO:* Alessandra Cardini; *ArtD:* Tullio Lullo; *C:* Giovanni Ciarlo; *AC:* Giuseppe Di Biase; *AE:* Alfredo Menchini; *2nd AE:* Mario Cinotti; *AD:* Roberto Tatti; *MU:* Franco Di Girolamo; *Hair:* Jole Cecchini; *SO:* Alvaro Orsini; *Boom:* Marco Di Biase; *Mix:* Bruno Moreal; *SP:* Franco Vitale; *W:* Alessandra Pistella; *KG:* Cosimo Barbera; *ChEl:* Vincenzo Celli; *MA:* Benito Stefanelli. *Cast:* Tomas Milian (Nico Giraldi), Enzo Cannavale (Salvatore Esposito), Eli Wallach (Gerolamo Giarra), Bombolo [Franco Lechner] (Venticello), Margherita Fumero (Maria Sole Giarra), Massimo Vanni (Gargiulo), Franco Annibaldi, Enzo Pulcrano (Masino), Roberto Messina (Commissioner Tozzi), Alfredo Rizzo (Peeping Tom). *Uncredited:* Umberto Amambrini (Man in church), Ennio Antonelli (Man at racetrack betting salon), Eros Buttaglieri (Journalist attending the execution), Azzolino Carrega (Doctor attending the execution), Raniero Dorascenzi (Pilot), John P. Dulaney (Ballarin), Tom Felleghy (W. J. Coppola, Prison warden), Iolanda Fortini (Woman on the bus), Alfonso Giganti (Man attending the execution), Quinto Marziali (Journalist attending the execution), Taylor Mead (Nico's cab customer), Tomaso Milian Jr. (Dishwasher at the restaurant), Vezio Natili (Journalist attending the execution), Benito Pacifico (False priest), Vittorio Ripamonti (Priest). *PROD:* Galliano Juso for Cinemaster; *PM:* Mario Di Biase; *PSu:* Alessandro Mattei, Augusto Marabelli; *PSe:* Vittorio Fornasiero, Maurizio Spinelli; *ADM:* Paolo Rampazzo; *CASH:* Salvatore Farese. *Country:* Italy. Filmed at Dear Film, Incir–De Paolis (Rome) and on location in Rome, New York and Las Vegas. *Running time:* 95'; Visa no.: 72397 (10.07.1978); *Rating:* v.m.14; *Release date:* 10.12.1978; *Distribution:* Titanus; *Domestic gross:* 2,112,108,180 lira. *Also known as: Tony Marroni—Elfmeter für den Superbullen* (West Germany, 06.04.1982—90'). *Home video:* 01 (DVD, Italy).

During a prison revolt, a convict named Giuseppe La Rosa—who was about to testify against mob boss Don Gerolamo Giarra—is killed by an unknown policeman. On the orders of his immediate superior, Commissioner Tozzi, Marshal Nico Giraldi fakes a robbery and is arrested by the police. Having escaped from jail with Tozzi's help, Nico moves to New York where, thanks to his friend Salvatore, he is hired as a waiter at an Italian restaurant where Don Gerolamo and his gang usually dine. At a religious ceremony in church, Nico saves Giarra's life: the boss takes him under his wing and sends him to investigate Giarra's opponent Pasquale Siragusa, a mob boss in Las Vegas. Nico is thus able to meet Marc Ferguson, the man who killed La Rosa in prison, but he is unable to arrest him as Ferguson commits suicide so as to frame Giraldi. Found guilty of murder and sentenced to death, Nico attempts to get in touch with Tozzi, and in doing so he reveals his true identity. Nevertheless, Don Jerome saves Nico in order to take revenge on the undercover cop himself. However, Nico survives with Salvatore's help and eventually returns to Rome.

The fourth entry in the Nico Giraldi series after the reasonably enjoyable *Swindle*, *Little Italy* shows how Corbucci and Amendola were quickly running out of ideas in the attempt to give the audience what they wanted. As in the previous film, the opening scenes are all for Bombolo as the petty thief Venticello, who steals all the furniture in an apartment while the owner is spying with binoculars on a beautiful girl who's taking her clothes off in the opposite house (the girl turns out to be Venticello's sister, who acts as a bait in the gang's recurring scheme). It's a typical comedy routine which shows how the scriptwriting duo were pushing the series towards straight humor, leaving the "crime" angle aside.

The plot picks up after the mandatory opening sequences showing Giraldi at work: the picturesque cop chases a racket member (Enzo Pulcrano) in an extended sequence that starts off as an amusing variation on the oft-played barber shop comic routine, where Giraldi gives the man a Mohawk cut ("Have you seen *Taxi Driver*?" he asks) before pursuing him through Rome. Even though the scene is well-paced, Corbucci's direction is patently slapdash: as will be more evident throughout the film, Milian is mostly replaced by a stunt double in all the long shots and in the many stunts. This happened in the earlier films as well, but on *Little Italy* Corbucci doesn't even bother disguising Milian's double, so we often get a glimpse of the bearded athletic man's face, which is obviously not Milian's. Whether it was just because of the film's hasty schedule or the lack of commitment of all those involved is hard to say. The result, however, is quite poor—and the same occurs in other fight scenes as well.

Then it gets worse. The storyline, which has Nico going undercover in order to uncover evidence about a murder committed in Italy by a fake cop on behalf of a powerful Mafia boss (Eli Wallach, who's patently in it for the money), is *déjà-vu* and predictable, not to mention unbelievable. Nico pretends to have crossed the line and turned corrupt, has himself arrested, escapes and ends up as an unlikely waiter in a Brooklyn pizzeria. All this is an excuse for a series of tepid comedy routines, with Cannavale acting as Milian's sidekick, and the ill-fated introduction of Margherita Fumero as Wallach's horrid daughter who immediately falls in love with Nico as the main source of jokes. Besides a couple of passable gags, including an amusing dance scene with Milian doing his best John Travolta impression (another gag has Maria Sole claiming "I've got Saturday night fever!" to Nico's response, "Then take an aspirin!"), the story drags to a miserable third act, where Nico gets arrested and sentenced to death without anybody in the Italian police apparently bothering to save him. Last but not least, the previous film's copious verbal vulgarity is decidedly toned down, in an attempt to make the result more palatable to younger audiences.

As a matter of fact, even though the Italian title (which translates as Anti-Mafia Squad) relates to typical poliziotteschi, *Little Italy* is basically a comedy in disguise. Nico Giraldi had by then become Milian's customary screen persona, as illustrated by the almost identical characters the Cuban actor played in other films that had nothing to do with the crime genre such as *Messalina Messalina*, Corbucci's stab at Tinto Brass' *Caligula*, or the broad comedy *Son of the Sheik*. Nico Giraldi would return for the fifth time in next year's *The Gang That Sold America*—which, like *Little Italy*, features a distinctly unremarkable Goblin score.

Napoli: i 5 della squadra speciale (Naples: Five Men Special Squad)

D: Mario Bianchi. *S* and *SC:* Antonio Cucca, Claudio Fragasso, Mario Bianchi; *DOP:* Luigi Ciccarese (35mm, Technicolor); *M:* Polizzy-Natili [Natala Polizzi], played by I Romans (Ed. ABR); *E:* Cesare Bianchini; *AC:* Claudio Mecchia; *AE:* Angela Rosa Taccari; *MU:* Silvana Petri; *W:* Margherita Cibeli; *SO:* Giovanni Russo; *Boom:* Giovanni Priore; *SP:* Franco Campanile; *ChEl:* Franco Cerboni; *KG:* Aldo Stella; *MA:* Gilberto Galimberti; *SS:* Graziella Marsetti; *Titles:* Alfio Menichini. *Cast:* Richard Harrison (Marcello Arcangeli), Enrico Maisto (Borri), Tommaso Palladino (Morgan), Franco Marino (Bruno Pesenti), Gianni Diana (Gianni Strinco), Lina Polito (Laura), Enzo D'Ausilio (Venanzi), Luigi Russo (Colla), Giacomo Maisto (Giovanni Privitera), Emi Salvador [Emilio Salvatore] (Barabba), Teobaldo Cerullo (Marsiani), Edmondo [Edoardo] Mascia (Eduardo Mancuso), Marcello Filotico (Lettieri), Gabriella Di Luzio (Anna). *Uncredited:* Mario Bianchi (Mario), Gilberto Galimberti. *PROD:* October 77 Films (Giugliano di Napoli); *PM:* Franco Marino. *Country:* Italy. Shot on location in Naples. *Running time:* 102'; Visa no.: 71898 (05.06.1978); *Rating:* v.m.14; *Release date:* 05.06.1978; *Distribution:* General Cinematografica; *Domestic gross:* 453,084,860 lira. *Also known as: Les 5 de la section spéciale* (France). *Home video:* SSV (VHS, Switzerland—Italian language).

Naples. The kidnapping of U.S. Ambassador Robinson leads the police to form a special team composed of ex–Commissioner Borri, who has a score to settle with the Camorra after his wife's murder, and three agents—Marcello Arcangeli, Gianni Strinco and Bruno Pesenti, who have all been removed from law enforcement for various reasons. On the advice of a senior government official, Venanzi, the squad is joined by an American hitman, Morgan. Borri realizes that Camorra boss Eduardo Mancuso is involved in the kidnapping and the simultaneous disappearance of a container of plutonium as well. What he doesn't know, however, is that Morgan is a spy and that Mancuso is in cahoots with the powerful Venanzi, who is seemingly above suspicion. Pesenti dies in a shoot-out, and when Borri and his collaborators get too close to the truth, the killer eliminates Strinco and Arcangeli as well. Determined to avenge them, Borri reaches his goal, but he does not survive the final bloodbath.

"I got a phone call from Naples, from people who took part in *La banda Vallanzasca*. They told me they'd found backers, and so I did these three films" Mario Bianchi recalled about the crime film triptych—*Napoli: i 5 della squadra speciale* (1978), *Napoli una storia d'amore e di vendetta* (1979) and *I guappi non si toccano* (1979)—which he shot back-to-back in Naples. As with the director's previous efforts, these were decidedly low budget affairs: besides lead actor Richard Harrison, *Napoli: i 5 della squadra speciale* promotes a duo of obscure Parthenopean character actors as co-stars: Enrico Maisto and Tommaso Palladino. As the title suggests, the plot recycles the typical motifs of the "special squad" subgenre, putting together a bunch of specialists: a fast driver, a karate expert, an idealist cop who knows the city very well and an angry commissioner (Maisto, for once in the good guy role) who is aiming to avenge his dead wife. The fifth member of the special squad is the mustached Palladino, as an unlikely American hitman. The rest of the story mostly consists of fistfights, shootouts and the occasional gruesomeness (such as a man who is killed and has his testicles cut off and stuck into his mouth—offscreen), at the mercy of a chaotic, incoherent mess of a script which even takes an ill-fated turn towards fantapolitics.

Napoli: i 5 della squadra speciale was intended—like other films shot in Naples at that time—for a local audience, and was scarcely distributed in the rest of the country. According to Bianchi, filming went on very smoothly, also due to the protection given by the Camorra, which seemingly had a part in the financing. "They spent so little money with my film, they couldn't help but make profits with it!" Bianchi commented. The scant budget shows in the obligatory car chase and crash, which features two old and battered Fiat 128, in a sad "I would, but I can't" moment. The overall result is squalid to say the least.

One wonders how such a trashy subproduct could be taken seriously upon release. Yet the "Corriere della Sera"'s critic labeled the script as reactionary, and added that "even though in Mario Bianchi's film the repressive institution is conniving with a power that is tainted by corruption, the hero is once again a cop who sows violence and champions self-justice," a capsule review which pretty much sums up well critics' biased approach towards the whole genre.[2]

Notes

1. Ippoliti, Norcini and Grattarola, "Mario Bianchi: 'Il mio cinema pizza e fichi,'" p. 26.
2. G. Gs. [Giovanna Grassi], *Corriere della Sera*, 5.8.1978.

Napoli ... serenata calibro 9 (Naples ... Serenade by Caliber 9)

D: Alfonso Brescia. *S:* Ciro Ippolito; screenplay: Piero Regnoli, Ciro Ippolito, Alfonso Brescia; *DOP:* Silvio Fraschetti (35mm, Gevacolor, Telecolor); *M:* Eduardo Alfieri (ed. Bideri); *Napoli calibro 9* (Mallozzi—Buonafede) sung by Mario Merola; *E:* Carlo Broglio; *PD:* Enzo Medusa; *CO:* Valeria Valenza; *C:* Antonio Minutolo; *AC:* Ugo Menegatti; *AE:* Angelarosa Taccari; *AD:* Franco Pasquetto; *MU:* Marcello Di Paolo; *W:* Maria Spigarelli; *SO:* Sandro Ochetti; *SP:* Roberto Calabrò; *SS:* Giuliana Gherardi. *Cast:* Mario Merola (Don Salvatore Savastano), Nick Jordan [Aldo Canti] (Antonio Lo Santo, "Totonno 'O Pazzo"), Ria De Simone (Marilì), Lucio Montanaro (Capezzuto), Lucio Crocetti (Esposito), Nino Vingelli (Don Raimondo "'O Prevete"), Alessandro Partexano (Paolo, Totonno's henchman), Marco Girondino (Gennarino), Letizia D'Adderio (Stellatella), Lucia Cassini (as herself), Nunzio Gallo (police Commissioner), Leopoldo Mastelloni ("The Tiger of Forcella," the transvestite),

Salvatore Puccinelli (Smuggler), Massimiliano Spinelli, Bruno Romagnoli, Gianfranca Dionisi, Giovanna Conti, Clara Bindi; uncredited cast: Sisto Brunetti (Gegè), Lina Franchi (woman at party), Giuseppe Marrocco (man at party), Vezio Natili (man at party), Luciano Zanussi (man at party). *PROD:* Ciro Ippolito for G.P.S. (Naples); *PM:* Antonio Pittalis. *Country:* Italy. Filmed at Incir–De Paolis (Rome) and on location in Naples. *Running time:* 89'; Visa no.: 72793 (12.07.1978); *Rating:* v.m.14; *Release date:* 12.08.1978; *Distribution:* Impegno Cinematografico (Carla and Angiolo Stella); *Domestic gross:* 746,195,340 lira. *Home video:* Raro (DVD, Italy). OST: Music pieces from the film can be found in the compilation CD "Italia Violenta — The Best Music of the Italian's police Movie" (CD Brioche BCHCD034).

The wife and little son of Don Salvatore Savastano, the boss of the cigarette smuggling ring in Naples, are killed in front of Savastano's very eyes by four masked robbers while the family was celebrating the boy's first Communion in a restaurant. From then on, Don Salvatore's only aim is to do justice with his own hands. Marilù, the mistress of gangster Totonno O'Pazzo — the head of the robbers who killed Savastano's family — decides to reveal the truth to Don Salvatore so as to get revenge on her unfaithful lover. One of Totonno's henchmen, however, discovers her intentions, and the gangster dispatches the woman. Thanks to Gennarino, an orphan street urchin whom Don Salvatore took under his wing, Savastano unmasks the killers, but he ends up in their hands and is about to get blown up by a bomb. Fortunately he is released just in time by Gennarino. While the four thugs are celebrating Don Salvatore's supposed death in a restaurant, he breaks into the place, gun in hand, and eliminates three of them. Totonno flees and takes Gennarino as hostage, but after a long motorboat chase Don Salvatore finally kills him. Then he surrenders to the police.

Produced by Ciro Ippolito's C.P.S. company after the commercial adventure of *L'ultimo guappo*, *Napoli ... serenata calibro 9* was one of the more successful Neapolitan crime films of the late 1970s. The plot, centered around Merola's quest for a gang of robbers who killed his wife and child, recalls out-and-out crime films like Umberto Lenzi's *Manhunt in the City* and Fernando di Leo's *Kidnap Syndicate*, while the quartet of ruthless thugs he fights are closer to the psychos portrayed by Tomas Milian and Helmut Berger, respectively in Lenzi's *Almost Human* and Sergio Grieco's *Beast with a Gun*— a fact that shows how the bonds with the crime genre were stronger in the "*guapparia* movies" released in '78–'79 than in later years.

The opening sequence — a motorboat carrying packs of Marlboro cigarettes arrives at the dock, where the smugglers' accomplices (*muschilli*, in Neapolitan dialect) hide the stuff in their car and drive away, in a perfectly synchronized operation that lasts just a handful of minutes — is an iconic moment, and defines the filmmakers' populistic strategy, which invites the audience to take sides with the smugglers, depicted as clever, inventive, courageous.

A sceneggiata wouldn't be such without at least a singing scene, and *Napoli ... serenata calibro 9* is no exception: the pretext, as usual, comes during a convivial scene, where all those present exhort Don Salvatore Savastano to sing a song. Here, the protagonist's performance turns into an ominous moment, as Brescia intercuts it with shots of the four thugs riding their bikes through the streets and finally bursting into the restaurant, interrupting the song — a blasphemous act in itself that paves the way for the opening massacre. It's only after this twelve minute prologue, which functions as a mini-film in itself, that the opening credits finally roll.

Brescia leaves ample room for tear-jerking scenes featuring a street urchin named Gennarino (little Marco Girondino was so popular that he was turned into a one-time star in the self-explanatory *Lo scugnizzo*, 1979, also directed by Brescia) and doesn't spare the comedy either, thanks to character actors Lucio Montanaro and Lucio Crocetti as a pair of dumb cops. On the other hand, the final knife duel is substituted by the hero's armed rampage, something which brings the guapparia movie closer to another popular subgenre, the *Death Wish*–style revenge flick. Both have the cult of patriarchal family and the love for sons and daughters in common, but the Neapolitan subgenre is devoid of any political subtext.

The police step aside and become a mere accessory, sometimes even laughable: *Napoli ... serenata calibro 9* features a police precinct populated by moronic cops and transvestites (among them the notorious stage actor Leopoldo Mastelloni, soon to appear in Dario Argento's *Inferno*, 1980) who improvise song-and-dance numbers. But the good gangster and the cop often share an unspoken pact of honor: *Napoli ... serenata calibro 9* ends with Merola surrendering to a police Commissioner (Nunzio Gallo), who arrests him rather unwillingly: after all, even the commissioner is convinced that Merola is the good guy.

Watching *Napoli ... serenata calibro 9*, one understands how, in the Neapolitan-based stories, the urban setting itself has mutated in comparison to contemporary crime films, where cities were portrayed as dangerous and hostile. Whereas in the guapparia movie the city of Naples becomes once again a friendly, ideal place: a maternal womb, a haven that protects and has to be protected from the evils of the outside world and the corruption of traditional values and consciences alike — here embodied by the spirited villain "Totonno 'o pazzo" played by Aldo Canti (a.k.a. Nick Jordan), a stuntman who enjoyed a short-lived popularity in the late 1960s after his role in Gianfranco Parolini's *The Three Fantastic Supermen* (1967). Canti was reportedly linked to the Italian underworld, and was found murdered in Rome's Villa Borghese park in the early '90s. Here, Canti proves his skills as a stuntman with a show-stopping somersault as he exits the restaurant from a second floor window, launching his machine gun in the air and catching it again once he's landed on the street, dozens feet below — an image that also becomes a recurring flashback that obsesses the hero, much like the "missing detail" in Dario Argento films.

On the other hand, the lesson of poliziotteschi has been learned and put to good use. And the catharsis is accompanied by a whole repertoire of effects, from slow motion to the use of music, in a dramatic crescendo which announces and amplifies the climax. *Napoli ... serenata calibro 9* culminates in a moment of glorious popular cinema at its best: the thugs are sitting around a table in their shack, listening to the titular song on the radio and have a vision of their imminent deaths, just moments before Merola breaks in, a gun in each hand as in some John Woo–directed Hong Kong action film, in an emphatic low-angle, slow motion shot. It's a scene that is exhilarating and exciting at the same time, for it's so audaciously over-the-top yet so sincere in its core that it overcomes parody and becomes almost mythical.

Brescia remade his own film in 1981 with the less successful *The Mafia Triangle* (*Napoli Palermo New York: il triangolo della camorra*, 1981), where a tough cop (Howard Ross) who can't tolerate judges and the shortcomings of the penal code is shot in the legs in front of his own house: the commissioner then has a *guappo* (Mario Merola, of course) escape from prison so that the latter can take the revenge that the law denies him.

Porci con la P. 38 (Pigs with a P. 38)

D: Gian [Gianfranco] Pagani. *S:* Gian Pagani; *SC:* Gian Pagani, Bruno Cortini; *DOP:* Gianni Raffaldi (35mm, Eastmancolor, Telecolor); *M:* Pippo Caruso, conducted by the author (ed. Grandi Firme della Canzone); *E:* Gian Pagani; *PD:* Carlo Ruo Redda; *C:* Massimo Lupi, Giuglielmo Vincioni; *AC:* Salvatore Fazio, Luigi Cecchini; *AD:* Liliana Giboni, Bruno Cortini; *MU:* Lucia La Porta; *Hair:* Vitaliana Patacca; *W:* Anna Lanfranco; *SO:* Gaetano Testa; *Mix:* Romano Checcacci; *SP:* Ermanno Serto; *KG:* Salvatore Schiavo; *ChEl:* Giovanni Bonis; *MA:* Bruno Di Luia; *SS:* Rosanna Castelletti, Teresa Puglisi. *Cast:* Marc Porel (Lt. Morris), Laura Belli (Gloria), Raymond Pellegrin (Sgt. Holden), Giancarlo Sisti (Peter), Gabriele Ferzetti (Max Astarita), Lea Lander (Mirka, Astarita's lover), Alan Collins [Luciano Pigozzi] (John Forsythe), Gigi Ventura, Walter Margara, Elena Marossero, Bill Mulasso, Franco Barbero, Paola Garbarino, Bruno Di Luia (Drug dealer). *PROD:* Dante Leonardi for Comet Film; *GM:* Enzo Boetani; *PSu:* Agostino Pasti, Salvatore Carrara; *PSe:* Francesca Arcangeli, Rosella Ferrero; *ADM:* Pier Luigi Tarabusi. *Country:* Italy. Filmed at Dear International (Rome) and in Piedmont. *Running time:* 92': Visa no.: 72191 (08.19.1978); *Rating:* v.m.18; *Release date:* 09.23.1978; *Distribution:* C.I.A. (Cinematografie Internazionali Associate); *Domestic gross:* 223,911,800 lira. *Also known as: Die Eiskalten Killer* (West Germany). *Home video:* Domovideo (VHS, Italy), Polygram (VHS, West Germany).

After an elderly crime boss retires from "business," his three lieutenants each inherit a piece of his "empire": Max Astarita is given the kidnapping ring, the prostitution racket goes to John Forsythe, while Fred Huston takes care of drug trafficking. Astarita, however, is not satisfied with his share, and after killing the old "boss" he gets rid of John and Fred as well. However, a police officer, Lieutenant Morris, finds a lighter at a murder scene which could lead to Astarita. To ward off the danger, Astarita has Morris' daughter kidnapped so he can blackmail the policeman's wife, Gloria, and force her to steal the lighter from the police station. Gloria does as she's told, but is badly wounded by Astarita's henchman. Morris discovers the truth and goes on a rampage, but he is unable to arrest Astarita, as the gangster is killed by his greedy mistress. In the final shoot-out with the woman, Morris has the upper hand and gets his daughter back.

Porci con la P. 38, Gianfranco Pagani's only film as a director, is one weird affair. Despite the title, which makes it sound like an out-and-out poliziotteschi, this late and little-seen entry is actually an ill-conceived hybrid. The storyline and characters are typical of crime genre: crime boss Astarita (Gabriele Ferzetti) attempts to become the city's kingpin by killing all his rivals, while Marc Porel plays the usual tough cop, who in one scene mercilessly beats a young drug addict to get vital information. On the other hand, the sequences where Astarita' enemies are offed one by one by a black-gloved killer wouldn't have been out of place in a *giallo*: Luciano Pigozzi is garroted like a character from Dario Argento's *Cat o' Nine Tails* (1971), while a boss' bodyguard has his eye transfixed by a spear through a door's peephole, in a scene that unwittingly predates Argento's *Opera* (1987).

However, that's not to say the film is any good. What's really jaw-dropping about *Porci con la P. 38* is the disproportion between its ambitions and means: the film is set in the U.S. but was obviously shot in some distinctly non–American-looking Northern Italian pre–Alpine region (possibly Piedmont), with exhilarating touches worthy of a Demofilo Fidani film: the Italian FIAT cars and trucks camouflaged as U.S. vehicles by means of bogus license plates and "POLICE" stickers on the sides, for example.

The direction is hopelessly crude, with obtuse zooms and badly paced scenes, with the possible exception of a barely passable car chase in the mountains and the climax (where the director apparently had a dolly at his disposal for a couple of shots) set in a factory complex where Porel faces villainess Lea Lander and kills her in cold blood — an ending reminiscent of Mario Lanfranchi's *Merciless Man*.

A former production manager, Pagani — who also wrote and edited the film — doesn't stint on the sleaze: besides a number of full frontal nudes and a scene where a few junkies are shooting heroin in a nightclub, an appalling moment of bad taste has the aforementioned killer giving a young girl an overdose, and pawing her breasts while she slips into a coma. We later find out that the poor girl has been raped by the necrophiliac murderer.

The cast feature a few good actors in small roles: a bored looking Raymond Pellegrin is Porel's assistant, while Gabriele Ferzetti fares better as the ambitious Astarita ("What a thrill power gives!" he exclaims). The film's emphasis on drug abuse would prove to be darkly ominous, as Marc Porel's career would go down the drain because of his heroin addiction. The Swiss actor died in 1983 in Casablanca, officially of meningitis, even though there are rumors he O.D.ed. He was just 34.

Provincia violenta (Violent Province)

D: Mario Bianchi. *S* and *SC:* Mario Bianchi; *DOP:* Umberto Galeassi (35mm, Eastmancolor, Telecolor); *M:* Stelvio Cipriani (Ed. C.A.M.); *E:* Maurizio Tedesco; *PD, CO:* Neno [Nazzareno] Piana; *C:* Marco Sperduti; *AC:* Roberto Benvenuti; *AD:* Francesca Montani; *MU:* Gloria Granati; *Hair:* Ultimo Peruzzi; *SO:* Candido Raini; *Boom:* Alberto Attara; *SOE:* Luciano Anzellotti; *SP:* Sergio Galasso; *KG:* Teodorico Memé; *ChEl:* Enrico Vitri; *MA:* Gilberto Galimberti; *W:* Anna Fuciarelli; *Story editor:* Lino Capoano; Continuity: Rosaria Cilento. *Cast:* Lino [Calogero] Caruana (Captain Franco Sereni), Antonella Dogan (Flavia), Alicia Leoni (Marta Ognissanti), Spartaco Battisti (Commissioner Righi), Al Cliver [Pier Luigi Conti] (Alberto Mauri), Richard Harrison (Augusto), Simona Marini (Helen), Daniela Codini (Nadia), John Benedy, Saverio Mosca (Finzi), Nicola Monteaperto, Raffaele Ponziano, Angelo Meconizzi, Sergio Testori (Augusto's henchman), Debora Gentile (Berti's daughter). *Uncredited:* Mario Bianchi (Commissioner Lozzi), Cesare Di Vito (Tony), Guia Lauri Filzi (Flavia's friend). *PROD:* Mercury Film; *PM:* Eolo Capritti; *PSu:* Marcello Meconizzi; *PSe:* Aldo Sisti; *CASH:* Fiorella Passamonti. *Country:* Italy. Filmed on location in Aversa. *Running time:* 85'; Visa no.: 71863 (01.06.1978); *Rating:* v.m.14; *Release date:* 01.06.1978; *Distribution:* Sigma E. Co.; *Domestic gross:* 173,469,670 lira. *Also known as: Provinz ohne Gesetz* (West Germany), *Kommando Siku* (West Germany — video). *Home video:* Surf (DVD, Italy). OST: LP Spark SR 857.

Augusto, the boss of the provincial Southern town of Aversa, uses a prestigious Beauty Institute directed by Flavia as a front for his illicit business: the wealthy clients are drugged and then photographed in compromising poses for blackmail. When his friend Nadia is murdered, captain Franco Sereni, on leave because of his unorthodox methods, begins to investigate. However, every bit of evidence he finds is swept away by Righi, a corrupt local inspector who is in cahoots with Augusto. Sereni's only hope are Mrs. Ognissanti, the wife of a politician, and Helen, a singer, two of the victims who are willing to talk. Helen is dispatched by Augusto's man, the sadistic Alberto Mauri, whom Sereni confronts and kills. The captain eventually gets to Flavia and Augusto: in the final confrontation, Augusto kills Flavia and takes Sereni prisoner. However, the police arrive at the eleventh hour, saving Sereni and arresting the whole gang.

"What did you do the other night?" "Nothing, I just went to the movies." "Me too." "Really?" "Yes, I went to see an Italian crime film." "Oh, I can't stand those crime films any longer!" "You're right." "They all look the same." This revealing tongue-in-cheek dialogue exchange between Antonella Dogan and Guia Lauri Filzi[1] can be read as a not-so-veiled mockery at those film critics (that is, the majority) who slated poliziotteschi by writing that they were all alike—violent, fascist and mean. And it's rather surprising that it comes from a film that is nothing but a third-grade subproduct, an imitation of an imitation, with little or no ambition at all. Self-irony? Self-sabotage? Think what you will, there's no doubt Mario Bianchi's *Provincia violenta* (literally, Violent Province: itself a title that sounds like an ill-conceived attempt at aping Merli's successes) follows the genre's clichés with slavish abandon, and in doing so it underlines the decadence of a genre that was squeezed like a lemon in all its possible combinations in just a few years. Unsurprisingly, given the shoestring budget (Stelvio Cipriani's score is mostly recycled from *Execution Squad*, and also features a piece used in Bava's *Rabid Dogs*) and technical limits, the emphasis here is on nudity and sleaze, as ample room is given to the criminal deeds of a gang of pornographers and drug dealers led by Antonella Dogan and special guest star Richard Harrison, who drug their victims (all upper class young women), strip them naked and photograph them in hardcore postures while they're still under the effect of drugs.

The need to outdo the models leads to unintentional hilariousness at times. The trigger-happy hero (not a commissioner but, more prosaically, a Carabinieri captain who doesn't mind shooting thugs in the back) is told by the Chief of Police: "This is a violent province indeed. But it's not by killing criminals that we solve our problems.... You never allow anyone to get to the trial alive!," while Al Cliver as a sadistic killer who, in the film's funniest scene, asks one of his victims: "Would you rather be drowned or strangled?"

As for *Provincia violenta*'s unlikely leading man, the balding and mustached Lino Caruana, Bianchi recalled: "He was a dear friend of mine, an acrobat from Naples who started doing small roles in Westerns [...]. He managed to put together a small budget to do this film, and was the *de facto* producer. However, the footage that had already been shot was unwatchable, so Lino called me and asked me: "Mario, gimme a hand on this one." I came over, watched the footage, which had been shot by I don't know who, and filmed some more scenes in Aversa [...] so I practically finished it."[2] However, unlike the other crime films he directed in that period, Bianchi is credited as the sole scriptwriter as well.

Notes

1. One of Italy's earlier porn actresses, here in an uncredited cameo.
2. Ippoliti, Norcini and Grattarola, "Mario Bianchi: 'Il mio cinema pizza e fichi,'" p. 26.

Quando i picciotti sgarrano (Nettuno e la mafia) (When Mafia Men Do Wrong—Neptune and the Mafia)

D: Romolo Cappadonia. *S* and *SC:* Romolo Cappadonia; *DOP:* Angelo Pocobelli (35mm, Eastmancolor, Telecolor); *M:* Francesco Auditore; *Malaspina* sung by Francesco Auditore; *E:* Romeo Ciatti; *PD, CO:* Antonino La Rosa; *APD:* Giancarlo Gobbini; *COA:* Teresa Schiavo; *C:* Ferdinando Calzavara; *AC:* Giacomo Calzavara; *AE:* Marco Paolantoni; *AD:* Giuseppe Casablanca; *MU:* Giulia Saccucci; *Hair:* Giovanna Maria Russu; *W:* Angela Vittorino; *SO:* Alberto Sapone; *Boom:* Rodolfo Montagnani; *KG:* Antonio Oliveri; *ChEl:* Antonino Di Stefano; *Props:* Arnaldo Mangolini; *SS:* Anna Maria Liguori. *Cast:* Salvatore Giuliano Jr. (Renzo), Enrica Saltutti (Tinuzza), Romolo Cappadonia (Don Mimì La Motta), Antonio La Rosa (Zu Tano), Antonia Comandé (Ledda), Giovanni Napoli (Malaspina), Sofia Amendolea (Graziella), Francesco Bartolone, Antonio Battiato, Antonino Di Stefano, Antonino Lotà (Andrea Barreca), Pasquale Raspaolo, Francesco Auditore, Paola Giordan, Rosa Mangano, Giovanni Morabito, Anna Maria Aucello, Concetta Gaffo. *PROD:* Cariddi Cinematografica (Messina); *PM:* Giuseppe Trimarchi; *PSu:* Rosetta Sestili; *PSe:* Gina Sestili. *Country:* Italy. Filmed on location in Messina. *Running time:* 94'; Visa no.: 72049 (06.21.1978); *Rating:* not rated; *Release date:* 10.31.1978; *Distribution:* Regional; *Domestic gross:* 66,231,490 lira.

Sicily. Renzo, a fisherman, works hard to repay the mortgage on his fishing boat, but has to deal with the fish market racket run by Mafia boss Don Mimì and his henchman Malaspina. Meanwhile, Renzo—who's about to marry his pregnant fiancée Ledda—falls for Tinuzza, Malaspina's former girlfriend. Don Mimì, who's got powerful protection from a politician in Rome, dispatches all those who do not bend to his orders and gets rid of a nosy journalist. Ledda discovers that Renzo is betraying her with Tinuzza, who on the other hand resumes her affair with Malaspina. Renzo finds out about it and challenges Malaspina to a knife duel, which ends with the latter mortally wounded. Before dying, Malaspina repents and accuses Don Mimì. At the trial, though, the Mafia boss gets acquitted due to his political protection and retaliates by blowing up Renzo's boat, killing him and the entire crew.

Produced by an obscure Sicilian-based company, *Quando i picciotti sgarrano* (literally: When the "boys" do wrong, Sicilian slang to signify that a *picciotto*, someone associated with the Mafia, has perpetrated an offense to his boss and deserves to die; the film's subtitle, *Nettuno e la mafia*—Neptune and the Mafia—is laughably pretentious) is a jaw-dropping, dazzling abortion of a film, so patently amateurish in all its components that it's no wonder it fell into total obscurity for over a quarter of a century after a very limited release before resurfacing on Italian TV, much to the bewilderment of crime movie fans who found themselves before an unadulterated trashy gem at its purest.

The film's opening scene—a shaky medium shot of Don Mimì

(played by director Romolo Cappadocia) in his garden with his associate Malaspina (Giovanni Napoli) and his lover — is exemplary, as the cameraman can't even keep the actors' heads in shot and cuts their top off, and the actors themselves stand waiting for an off-screen cue to deliver their lines. All scenes are filmed in medium or long shots, often with a shaky hand-held camera, and feature some of the crudest zooms ever put on screen as well as shots going abruptly out-of-focus. Furthermore, Cappadocia gleefully ignores the 180 degree rule, and often jumps the line whenever he feels like it; he even has an actor talk standing with his back to the camera, and pads the running time with endless stock footage of tuna fishing (taken from Paolo Cavara's *Virilità*, 1976) and popular festivals. The music score also liberally steals from other films, namely Ennio Morricone's cues from *Orca—The Killer Whale*, *Il Gatto* and *Hitch-Hike* and Stelvio Cipriani's *Tentacles*. The film's overall realism — no sets, no professional actors (save for the little-known Enrica Saltutti and Sofia Amendolea), characters speaking in their native dialect — has prompted someone to mention Giovanni Verga's novels and Luchino Visconti's *La terra trema* (1948), an assertion that throws 100 years of film criticism down the toilet in one sentence.

The film's amateurishness is well described by actor Tony Raccosta (who was supposed to play the lead but eventually didn't) in an interview: "I was called on to work on *Quando i picciotti sgarrano*. The producers needed a distribution deal and I introduced them to a distributor named Mulé. He told the director: 'I may be interested in the film, but I'm choosing the four lead actors, then you can do the rest of the casting.' He mentioned a few names, and I was among them. The answer was: 'Well, actually we can't, because of this, because of that....' Turns out that they were actually making actors *pay* to work on the film! The producers were the actors themselves, and they put their own money in the project! When we heard about this, we left. However, I heard that the lead used to tell people he was Salvatore Giuliano's son, so they had to give him the main role.... Cappadonia, the director, was an elderly man, about 60 years old. They used to gather in the evening, in a basement, to do the rehearsals. Once I went there myself and I couldn't help but laugh out loud: 'Hey, that's not the way rehearsals are done!' It seemed they were rehearsing a stage play: they didn't even know how to begin to make a movie."[1]

As Renzo, the film's "hero," Salvatore Giuliano Jr. (the self-proclaimed son of the famous bandit) looks like a shorter, fatter and younger version of Mario Merola, minus the latter's charisma and acting chops. Which is rather apt, for a film that openly apes Neapolitan sceneggiata, even climaxing with a knife duel (which the director films in a riotously funny slow motion). *Quando i picciotti sgarrano* also features comic relief—if such a term can be used for the scenes where a priest ogles topless sunbathing beauties on the beach!—and even attempts an ill-advised political discourse. Cappadocia has his Mafia boss endorse Sicily's separatist movements ("Hunger is the Sicilian people's most ancient companion, this damned hunger that only the independence of Sicily will defeat once and for all"), shows Mafia rituals (a death sentence for one Mafia associate is symbolized by the elderly bosses sparking off candles with their fingers) and denounces the Mafia's political connivance with a grotesque Roman politician. He even conceives a bad ending where not only the boss is acquitted on trial, but also gets revenge on the film's hero, having him and his men blown up on their boat (needless to say, the explosion is not shown but just heard, due to the shoestring budget). As inane as it may sound, *Quando i picciotti sgarrano* ends more or less like Stanley Kubrick's final masterpiece *Eyes Wide Shut* (1999), as the boss tells his lover "I want to fuck" (although Kubrick didn't have Tom Cruise pinch Nicole Kidman's bottom — Cappadocia does). Speaking of which, the film features a number of sex scenes that at times border on full-on hardcore (the TV version has obviously been excised by the most explicit shots), which wouldn't be surprising.

Note

1. Davide Pulici, *Il siculo*, www.nocturno.it, 06.30.2010.

Seagulls Fly Low (I gabbiani volano basso)

D: George Warner [Giorgio Cristallini]. *S:* Odoardo Fiory; *SC:* Odoardo Fiory, Giorgio Cristallini; *DOP:* Gino Santini (35mm, Eastmancolor, Technicolor); *M:* Roberto Pregadio, Paola and Carlo Cristallini, conducted by Roberto Pregadio (ed. C.A.M.); *E:* Carlo Reali; *PD:* Antonio Visone; *CO:* Maria Luisa Panaro; *C:* Edmondo Pisani, Alvaro Lanzoni; *AC:* Giovanni Brescini, Enrico Priori; *AE:* Anna D'Angelo; *2nd AD:* Roberto Lauretani; *AD:* Carlo Cristallini; *MU:* Dante Trani; *Hair:* Mirella Ginnoto; *SO:* Gaetano Testa; *Boom:* Antonio Testa; *SOE:* Renato Marinelli; *Mix:* Romano Checcacci; *SP:* Ermanno Serto; *W:* Angela Vinci; *ChEl:* Elgo Dentale; *KG:* Marcello Gargano; *SS:* Marialuce Faccenna; *UP:* Fraco Cauli. *Cast:* Maurizio Merli (Jeff Jacobson / Albert Morgan), Nathalie Delon (Isabelle Michereau), Mel Ferrer (Roberto Micheli), Dagmar Lassander (Amparo, the nightclub owner), Orlando Urdaneta, Andrea Esterhazy (Giorgio Calvi), Franco Garofalo (Killer), Mimmo [Domenico] Maggio, Red Martin (Spinello), Antonio Pane, Stefania Spugnini (Martini's secretary), Francesco Anniballi, Vittorio Campanella, Flora Celidano, Gianni Di Benedetto (Mauro Martini), Roberto Fusco, Silvano Gentili, Matteo Imparato, Angela Pintus, Rita Scipioni, Alvaro Tei, Isabella Zanussi, Vittorio Zarfati (Makeup man). *PROD:* Società Cooperativa Cinematografica Internazionale Zeta Film; *PM:* Francesco Vitulano; *PSu:* Pasquale Vannini; *PSe:* Enzo Prosperini, Enzo Samà; *PSeA:* Claudio Ammannati; *ADM:* Elio Di Blase; *Accountant:* Serenella Franceschi. *Country:* Italy. Filmed at Incir–De Paolis (Rome) and on location in Civitavecchia, Rome and Ponza. *Running time:* 100'; Visa no.: 71181 (11.24.1977); *Rating:* not rated; *Release date:* 01.11.1978; *Distribution:* C.I.A.; *Domestic gross:* 267,318,330 lira. *Also known as: As Gaivotas Voam Baixo* (Portugal), *Killer sterben einsam* (West Germany), *Los pajaros vuelan bajo* (Spain). *Home video:* Video Alsen (VHS, Greece — English language), Video Ciak (VHS, Italy).

Rome. Hidden behind the false name Jeff Jacobson, a former Vietnam veteran and deserter is blackmailed by Italian industrialist Roberto Micheli, who forces him to murder his business associate Mauro Martini. The American destroys the evidence that incriminates him, and gets a false passport and a lavish wage from Micheli. He's about to fly back to the United States and start a new life, but due to a misunderstanding at Fiumicino airport he blows his cover and flees, attracting the attention of the police and prompting a reaction from his two accomplices in Martini's killing. Micheli commissions a new passport to help the American (who now uses the name Albert Morgan) escape abroad, but Micheli's associate, Giorgio Calvi, takes advantage of the situation to get rid of Micheli and become sole head of the firm. Morgan, who casually witnessed the murder, flees in terror. With the help of Isabelle, the owner of a boutique in Rome with whom he falls in love, the American manages to get the new passport Micheli had commissioned before his death. At Fiumicino airport, however, Morgan discovers that Isabelle was arrested by the police. Fearing that his lover might be prosecuted, he allows Calvi's killer to get to him, and pays for his mistakes with death.

Released in January 1978, Giorgio Cristallini's *Seagulls Fly Low* represented yet another change of pace for Maurizio Merli, who, after Sergio Martino's western *A Man Called Blade* (*Mannaja*, 1977) was trying to get out of his typecast "tough cop" image. The film's *locandina* was explicit, announcing "Maurizio Merli—The Killer" under the image of a gun pointed at the viewer, and the script—by Cristallini and Odoardo Fiory—provided the actor with a romantic film noir storyline, and the role of a Vietnam deserter who is blackmailed into becoming a hitman by the unscrupulous "businessman" Micheli (Mel Ferrer) and finds himself in the middle of a deadly feud between the latter and his associate, Calvi (Andrea Esterhazy). If the film's antihero—a loner disgusted by violence yet unable to get away from it—is quite interesting, nevertheless Merli—who appears at first with a more casual look: casually dressed, with longer unkempt hair, handlebar mustache (which he trims about 30 minutes into the film) and shades—looks more at ease in the action scenes, such as a night time chase through Rome or a fistfight where for once he's the one who gets beaten up, while he seems rather embarrassed in the romantic interludes with the gorgeous Nathalie Delon.

Seagulls Fly Low's real problem may well be its director. Cristallini, a veteran filmmaker who directed his first film in 1947 and returned behind the camera in the early seventies after a fifteen-year hiatus, simply doesn't have the skills the project badly needed to save if from drowning in mediocrity. The film is indifferently shot: after a promising, dialogue-free opening sequence, where Merli follows another car to the place where he performs a surprise hit, all set to Roberto Pregadio's listless score, things go rapidly downhill. Merli's slapdash war flashbacks, set to sepia-toned, grainy stills of the Vietnam conflict and underscored by bomb blasts and machine guns, are very bad; while the romantic subplot drags the story down in the second half, with tourist trips to the isle of Ponza, would-be poignant monologues about seagulls and crêpes and a slow-motion love scene.

Seagulls Fly Low tries hard not to look Italian. The character played by Nathalie Delon is clearly inspired by Faye Dunaway's in Sydney Pollack's *Three Days of the Condor* (1975), while the only feeble link to contemporary Italy, where nevertheless the film is set, are the Brigate Rosse, mentioned by Calvi to the commissioner as a mere scapegoat to justify his fear of being the target of Merli's vengeance. The film's ending, with Merli's death in slow motion, looks like an excerpt from one of his other crime flicks. Like the desperate, nameless antihero he's playing, the actor didn't have a chance either—he couldn't escape his destiny. This was underlined once again by the film's disappointing commercial results. As with *Covert Action*, Merli's other foray into *film noir*, *Seagulls Fly Low* flopped badly at the box office, grossing just 267 million lira—about a fourth of Massi's *Fearless* which came out just one month later, and which remained the actor's only film of the year to gross over one billion: further evidence that Merli's star was beginning to fade.

Sniper (L'arma)

D: Pasquale Squitieri. *S* and *SC:* Pasquale Squitieri; *DOP:* Giulio Albonico (35mm, Eastmancolor, Technospes); *M:* Tullio De Piscopo, arranged and conduced by Nando De Luca (Ed. Curci); *E:* Pasquale Squitieri [uncredited]; *PD:* Luciana Vedovelli; *CO:* Lia Francesca Morandini; *ArtD:* Renato Ventura; *C:* Giuseppe Tinelli; *AC:* Marco Onorato; *AE:* Leda Bellini; *AD:* Gianfranco Maresca; *MU:* Alfredo Tiberi; *Hair:* Jole Cecchini; *Dressmaker:* Anna Vinci; *KG:* Giancarlo Rocchetti; *ChEl:* Giulio Quaglietti; *PrM:* Paolo Luciani; *Mix:* Gianni D'Amico; *SE:* Gino Vagniluca; *SS:* Renata Franceschi. *Cast:* Stefano Satta Flores (Luigi Compagna), Claudia Cardinale (Marta Compagna), Benedetta Fantoli (Rossana, their daughter), Clara Colosimo (Pitta Callini), Dario Ghirardi (Luigi's colleague), Pino [Giuseppe] Morabito (police commissioner), Salvatore Billa (police inspector), Viviana Polic (Maitresse) Mario Granato (Marta's lover), Paolo Bonetti (policeman Colella). *Uncredited:* Amedeo Salamon (Sardini), Bruno Bertocci (Luigi's colleague), Claudio Bigagli (Young bearded thug at the bar), Massimo Ciprari (Man in movie theater), Luciano Zanussi (sharpshooter). *PROD:* Roberto Giussani for Maratea Film; *GM:* Roberto Giussani; *PSu:* Giuseppe Ariemma. *Country:* Italy. Filmed at Rizzoli Palatino (Rome) and on location in Rome. *Running time:* 94'; Visa no.: 72262 (09.05.1978); *Rating:* v.m.14; *Release date:* 09.08.1978; *Distribution:* CIDIF; *Domestic gross:* 255,063,940 lira. *Also known as: El arma* (Venezuela), Illusion of the Gun (U.K.—Home video). *Home video:* General, Alan Young (DVD, Italy), Hillbit Ltd. (VHS, U.K.). OST: LP Carosello CLN 25080.

Luigi Compagna is a middle-class engineer who leads a banal life. His wife Marta has an affair with another man, and his daughter Rossana spends as much time as she can away from the family. One day Luigi witnesses the police arrive because three boys have broken into an apartment. He also sees an officer shoot one of the thieves, who are unarmed minors. The idea of obtaining a firearms license and buying a gun keeps growing in his mind. Luigi carries the weapon on his person wherever he goes, just as family and society are collapsing around him. After Rossana plays a mean joke on Luigi, a violent fight ensues, and his wife and daughter leave him. Luigi stops going to work, wanders aimlessly around the city and ends up in bed with a neighbor, a former opera singer who spills the beans about Marta's extramarital affair. Luigi goes to the place where Marta works and threatens the woman and her colleague with the gun, then he barricades himself in an apartment. Marta eventually manages to convince him to surrender, but a sniper—a private executioner who's more fanatical and more accurate than Luigi—kills him.

After the huge box office success of his period epic Mafia drama *I Am the Law* (*Il prefetto di ferro*, 1977), Pasquale Squitieri returned to the present with his next film. *Sniper* took a very similar path as Mario Monicelli's masterful *An Average Little Man* (1977) as well as Giuliano Montaldo's interesting yet flawed *A Dangerous Toy* (*Il giocattolo*, 1979), telling a minimal story of a man's obsession with a gun and the downward spiral towards violence that this obsession ignites.

While not a crime movie in the strictest sense, *Sniper* conveys the climate of the period as much as any Merli film. Squitieri claimed he took inspiration from Paul Morrissey's first films as well as *cinéma-vérité* "so that, regarding visual inventions, there would be nothing preplanned, as if the film had been kind of abandoned to itself, and born almost spontaneously. There was another added element that characterized filming: the civil agony that we all experienced after the abduction of Aldo Moro."[1]

Sniper exudes a sense of desperation, a gloomy, funereal feel that is rendered chromatically with an insistence on dark tones. This is especially evident in the scene where Luigi (Stefano Satta Flores) and his estranged wife Marta (Claudia Cardinale) walk at night in the deserted streets of Rome, which looks as if it has been abandoned by all other inhabitants. People are locked in their apartments, scared of going out, terrified by every small noise because it may be a thief or a maniac trying to get in.

Squitieri said that Moro's killing "had left me face to face with an authentic moral void, a muggy reality, without any outlet and even without questions. I realized that not only did we not ask ourselves what was really going on, and what had originated such a terrible drama, but we didn't even ask ourselves what part we all played in that drama."[2]

In a way, *Sniper* marks the beginning of the end of the crime genre, as it portrays a country on the verge of collapse, without any embellishment whatsoever, where any citizen is potentially a monster. "I wanted to make a movie about today's Fascism" Squitieri explained. "And it wasn't understood. Today's Fascism or Communism are called normalization. [...] It's something much more subtle, that can be operated through normalization, as television does. Television is Neofascism — or rather, Technofascism [...]. In my film I showed how a gun is stronger than a man, also because it's got a story that he doesn't have: guns have millions of books and movies about them. What's he, compared to the gun? Nothing, just a mere clerk. He buys this big gun with a huge, legendary story which he will never have, and he gets sick. Because if somebody's got a gun, as I did, in the end he must use it."[3]

"Product for use" — the same message that, say, Howard Hawks' *His Girl Friday* (1940) conveyed by means of comedy, is here expressed in a deadly serious way. As with all Squitieri's films, *Sniper* doesn't go for half measures: everything is underlined, shouted, revealed before the camera for the audience to get it, metaphors are patent, line of dialogues are didactic. A pair of scenes — one where Luigi finds out that his daughter has painted the gun with flowers, and another where he methodically reassembles the gun — superficially recall Marco Ferreri's *Dillinger Is Dead* (*Dillinger è morto*, 1969), but otherwise Squitieri's direction looks erratic. The ending itself — which should have given the apologue its paradoxical meaning — looks slapdash and unsatisfying.

The film's main asset was Stefano Satta Flores — an accomplished, underestimated actor who gives a truly great performance as a revolting character who's obsessed with pornography and violence. Tullio De Piscopo's percussive score also conveys the film's doomed atmosphere and accompanies the protagonist's descent into darkness.

Notes

1. Gian Luigi Rondi, "Sette domande a Squitieri: l'arma protagonista assoluta," *Il Tempo*, 07.13.1978.
2. *Ibid.*
3. Monetti, *Pasquale Squitieri*, pp. 60–61.

The Squeeze (*Controrapina*)

D: Anthony M. Dawson [Antonio Margheriti]. *S* and *SC:* Paul Costello, Marc Princi, Simon O'Neill [Giovanni Simonelli]; *DOP:* Sergio D'Offizi (35mm, Eastmancolor, Telecolor); *M:* Paolo Vasile, conducted by Alessandro Blonksteiner; *E:* Roberto Sterbini; *Casting:* Joe Pollini; *PD:* Francesco Bronzi; *CO:* Adriana Berselli; *C:* Enrico Lucidi; *AD:* Ignazio Dolce; *MU:* Maria Luisa Tilly; *Hair:* Giovanni Palombi; *SO:* Mario Bramonti; *SS:* Eva Koltay. *Cast:* Lee Van Cleef (Chris Gretchko / Ray Sloan), Karen Black (Clarisse Saunders), Edward Albert (Jeff Olafsen), Lionel Stander (Sam Epstein), Robert Alda (Captain Donati), Angelo Infanti (Lieutenant Williamson), Antonella Murgia (Jessica), Peter Carsten (Karl Van Stratten), Dan van Husen (Hans), Dyane Silverstein (Cashier), Steven Burch (Fred), Ron Van Clief (Duke), Bob Hevelone (Lieutenant), Roy Brocksmith (Warehouse owner), Ewald G. Spader (Electrician), Rudolf Waldemar Brem (Hens' companion henchman). *PROD:* Turi Vasile for Laser Film (Rome) / Dritte Centama Gbth (Munich); Executive producers: Raymond R. Homer, Carlo Ponti; *PM:* Ugo Valenti; *PSu:* Roberto Luvisotti, Frank Winterstein; *UM:* Peter Naguschewski; Production assistant (New York): Stephen A. Glanzrock. *Country:* Italy / West Germany. Filmed in Hamburg and on location in New York City. *Running time:* 103'; Visa no.: 73239 (03.19.1979); *Rating:* v.m.14; *Release date:* 04.01.1980; *Distribution:* United Artists Europa; *Domestic gross:* unknown. *Also known as: The Rip-Off, Die Diamantencoup / Gretchko* (West Germany), *Kuin varas yössä / Rotannaama* (Finland), *Le Grand coup / Le Renard de Brooklyn / Le Retour du parrain* (France). *Home video:* EastWest Entertainment (DVD, USA), No Shame (DVD, USA), Brentwood (DVD, USA — as part of the "Perfect Heists" box set). OST: LP Cinevox Record MDF 33.127.

Legendary safe-cracker Chris Gretchko comes out of retirement to help the son of an old friend who needs to steal some diamonds for German gangsters so he can get himself out of trouble. Gretchko has barely arrived in New York City when the crossing and double-crossing begins and the "simple job" starts spinning out of control. Chris realizes that his bosses are planning to get rid of him after the hit, and he has to take drastic counter-measures. In the end, only he and his old friend Sam will survive.

Shot in the United States but actually an Italian / West Germany co-production, Antonio Margheriti's *The Squeeze* is the director's second crime film after *Death Rage*, and once again revolves around a charismatic has-been and deals with the theme of a generational conflict between the aging hero and a younger alter ego. Lee Van Cleef, with whom Margheriti had shot a couple of humorous Westerns, *The Stranger & the Gunfighter* (1974) and *Take a Hard Ride* (1975), stars as ace safe-cracker Chris Gretchko, a lone wolf who's retired to his ranch to raise cattle, but is forced to get back on the job to help the son (Edward Albert) of a former associate. Sporting a goatee and an earring but thankfully not the unlikely wig he wore in Mario Siciliano's *The Perfect Killer* (1977), the actor looks more gruff, vulnerable and real than his usual screen persona, and Margheriti pays homage to the aging Western hero by having him appear as an out-of-time cowboy in the first scenes. The rest of the cast is top-notch, with a number of excellent American actors led by Karen Black, plus Margheriti regular Peter Carsten and Italian character actor Angelo Infanti (*Highway Racer*) as a cop.

Destined mainly for the foreign markets, *The Squeeze*— released in Italy as *Controrapina* (Counterheist), a title very similar to the filmmaker's own Gothic masterpiece *Contronatura* (1969) but much worse than the working titles *L'ultimo colpo* [The Last

Hit] and *I Tried to Live*— bears little or no resemblance to Italian poliziotteschi. The themes are classic *film noir* stuff— a betrayed friendship, the regret for times gone by, the mythology and ethical code of the "clean" criminal — the plot is pure *déjà-vu* and the score by Paolo Vasile (producer Turi's son) is one of the worst ever committed to a 1970s crime film. Yet the setting in a snowy New York is fascinating — the film was shot between early December 1977 and the end of January 1978, according to actor Dan van Husen[1]— and Margheriti's direction is as sly as ever, skillfully handling the script's many twists and turns, which culminate in an unexpected happy ending that comes as a surprising relief. Even though the films smells and looks like an American B-movie, Margheriti's touch can be glimpsed in the craftsmanship of the special effects, with the use of the director's trademark models and explosions that were so common in his science fiction and adventure films.

The Squeeze is a senile film, where the good guys are old (Van Cleef, Lionel Stander, Robert Alda), and the youths are selfish and ungrateful. It's like a 1970s film directed by a 1940s director who doesn't like the times he's aging in. In Margheriti's case, he probably was just doing his job and trying to make the best out of a genre he just didn't feel for. The results, it must be added, were very dignified and the director ranked *The Squeeze* among his best work.

Note

1. Email interview, June 2012.

Terror!, a.k.a. *The Last House on the Beach (La settima donna)*

D: Franco [Francesco] Prosperi. *S:* Ettore Sanzò; *SC:* Romano Migliorini, Giambattista Mussetto; *DOP:* Cristiano Pogány (35mm, Eastmancolor, Technicolor — Technolux); *M:* Roberto Pregadio, conducted by the author (Ed. Nazionalmusic); *Backing vocals:* Edda Dell'Orso; *E:* Franco Malvestito; *PD, CO:* Dario Micheli; *APD:* Silvio Schettino; *C:* Renato Doria; *AC:* Giancarlo Mentil; *AE:* Andrea Vari; *2nd AE:* Alberto Vari; *AD:* Flavia Sante Vanin, Francesca Roberti; *MU:* Lamberto Marini, Claudia Giustini; *Hair stylists:* Corrado Cristofori, Maria Teresa Corridoni; *SO:* Benito Alchimede; *SOE:* Luciano Anzellotti; *W:* Clara Fratarcangeli, Maria Carmela Rimini; *SP:* Walter Civirani; *ChEl:* Nunzio Colucci; *KG:* Orlando Zuccheri; *Props:* Augusto La Valle; *SS:* Giovanna Lai. *Cast:* Florinda Bolkan (Sister Cristina), Ray Lovelock (Aldo), Flavio Andreini (Walter), Sherry Buchanan (Lisa), Stefano Cedrati (Nino), Laura Tanziani, Laura Trotter, Karine Velier [Karina Verlier], Annalisa Pesce [Luisa Maneri] (Matilde). *Uncredited:* Enrico Cesaretti (Man in the bank), Giuseppe Marrocco (Man in the bank), Isabel Pisano (Maid), Luciano Zanussi (Man in the bank). *PROD:* Pino Buricchi for Magirus Film; *PM:* Francesco Giorgi; *PSu:* Paolo Bistolfi; *PSe:* Carmelo Occhipinti; Administrator, *CASH:* Romano Cannavacciuolo. *Country:* Italy. Filmed at Incir — De Paolis (Rome). *Running time:* 85'; Visa no.: 71714 (04.01.1978); *Rating:* v.m.18; *Release date:* 04.20.1978; *Distribution:* Magirus; *Domestic gross:* 25,400,000 lira. *Also known as: The Last House on the Beach* (USA), *Junge Mädchen zur Liebe gezwungen*, *Verflucht zum Töten* (West Germany), *La séptima mujer* (Spain). *Home video:* Severin (DVD, USA — as *Last House on the Beach*), Medusa (DVD, Italy), Media Suits (DVD, Japan).

Three young criminals who have just robbed a bank take refuge in a house on a hillside by the sea. There they find five teenage students who are rehearsing their year-end stage play, their governess Sister Cristina and a maid. The thugs start by killing the latter, then rape the nun and one of the girls, dispatch a postman to whom the governess had given a note for the police and, finally, murder a second girl. At this point Sister Cristina leads the girls' revenge, by eliminating one of the offenders with poison and the other with a gun. The third, Aldo, the leader of the gang and the cruelest of the lot, is savagely killed by the girls before Sister Cristina's eyes.

Blending the "thugs vs. hostages" and the "rape and revenge" subgenres, Franco Prosperi's *Terror!*— the second film he director shot for producer Pino Buricchi after *Deadly Chase*— is definitely a bastardized inclusion in this volume, mainly justified by the interesting opening sequence showing a robbery that ends in bloodshed. The sequence, which introduces the characters by showing just their feet and hands, and never showing their faces — a trick that will turn out to be vital to the plot near the end, when the same scene will be revisited, this time by showing the robbers' faces and thus explaining the role each one had in the robbery, with somewhat surprising results — is a well-executed showpiece which displays Prosperi's skills as a filmmaker.

The rest of the film belongs to the realm of sexploitation, and while it's neither the best nor the worst of the lot, *Terror!* is definitely one of the sleaziest. When the three thugs take refuge in the "last house on the beach" (to quote an alternate U.S. title that gave away the film's main inspiration) inhabited by several schoolgirls and their nun teacher Sister Cristina (Florinda Bolkan, in a nun's habit again after *Flavia the Heretic*, 1974) it's rape time, which Prosperi displays in glorious sexploitation mode. Despite Sister Cristina's attempts to protect the girls — and undergoing carnal violence herself: "Before being a nun I was a woman" she confesses, when the rapist finds out she is not a virgin) the trio has its way with the underage victims. Besides the usual product placement (J&B bottles abound), there is room for a pair of unusual details: a sequence of Giuliano Petrelli's *Eyes Behind the Wall* (*L'occhio dietro la parete*, 1977) glimpsed on a TV screen and a copy of William Faulkner's *Sanctuary* read by one of the thugs (!). The characters are roughly sketched and schematic — with the possible exception of Ray Lovelock's Aldo, where the actor's good looks are cunningly used by Prosperi to mislead viewers over the character's true nature — and the narrative progression is minimal: what is left is a succession of grim, misogynist and exploitative scenes: adolescent nudes, slow motion sodomizations, vicious wounds, assorted killings. The *pièce de resistance* is a defloration by means of a stick, so insistent and choreographed (the victim's point of view shots, high angles and slow motion, drums rolling in the soundtrack) that it makes *Night Train Murder*'s infamous flickknife rape pale in comparison. However, dubious as it may be, *Terror!* is a rather accomplished piece of filmmaking thanks to the usually reliable Prosperi. However, the film performed very poorly at the Italian box office, while it gained a marginal notoriety abroad due to its over-the-top excesses. The climax, with Lovelock being bludgeoned and kicked to death by the girls, possibly inspired the ending of Quentin Tarantino's *Death Proof* (2007).

The subgenre would definitely drift towards out-and-out sexploitation and sleaze with Raimondo Del Balzo's *Midnight Blue* (1979) and Ferdinaldo Baldi's *Terror Express* (1979), not to mention Ruggero Deodato's grim *The House on the Edge of the Park* (1980).

L'ultimo guappo (The Last "Guappo")

D: Alfonso Brescia. *S:* Ciro Ippolito; *SC:* Piero Regnoli, Ciro Ippolito; *DOP:* Silvio Fraschetti (35mm, Vistavision); *M:* Giacomo and Gianni Dell'Orto; *E:* Carlo Broglio; *PD:* Mimmo Scavia; *CO:* Adriana Bellone; *C:* Luigi Quattrini; *AC:* Ugo Menegatti; *AE:* Angela Rosa Taccari; *AD:* Gianfranco Pasquetto; *MU:* Marcello Di Paolo; *W:* Valeria Valenza; *SO:* Pietro Spadoni; *KG:* Giancarlo Serravalli; *ChEl:* Marcello Valesani; *PrM:* Mario Ciccorella; *SS:* Giuliana Gherardi. *Cast:* Mario Merola (Don Francesco "Ciccio" Aliprandi), Walter Ricciardi (Roberto Aliprandi), Luciano Catenacci (Don Pasquale Roncilio), Fabrizio Forte (Roberto as a child), Sonia Viviani (Ninfarosa), Nunzio Gallo (Giovanni). *Uncredited:* Gennaro Beneduce (Nicolino Tassi), Angelo Boscariol (Don Pasquale's henchman), Alfonso Brescia (Don Pasquale's bearded henchman), Nestore Cavaricci (Don Pasquale's henchman), Olimpia Di Maio (Rosa), Luciano Foti (Man at dancing room), Lina Franchi (Woman at dancing room), Rino Gioielli, Daniela Guzzi, Lino Mattera (Stage actor), Benito Pacifico (Drug dealer), Nello Pazzafini (Salvatore, Don Pasquale's henchman), Salvatore Puccinelli (Smuggler), Luciano Zanussi (Man at dancing room). *PROD:* Riccardo Billi and Gioele Centanni for The Hundred Years Corporation; *EP:* Ugo Valenti; *PSu:* Naldo Nibbi; *PSe:* Cesare Coromaldi. *Country:* Italy. Filmed on location in Naples. *Running time:* 95'; Visa no.: 72237 (08.10.1978); *Rating:* v.m.14; *Release date:* 08.12. 1978; *Distribution:* Heritage; *Domestic gross:* 702,082,660 lira. *Also known as: Le Dernier voyou* (France). *Home video:* RaroVideo (DVD, Italy—as part of the "Il grande cinema di Mario Merola" boxset).

Naples. After a period of absence, Don Pasquale Roncilio comes back to claim his share of the cattle market business presided over by the leader of Naples' underworld, Don Francesco Aliprandi. The latter reacts by insulting him, and Don Pasquale challenges him to a duel. Don Francesco does not show up, however, because of a vow he made to the Virgin Mary after his son Roberto had an accident. The field opens to the opponent who becomes the new boss. Several years later, Don Francesco—who is now leading a honest life as a fisherman—celebrates his son's graduation: but the young man, in love with a small-time actress named Ninfarosa, gets hired as a bookkeeper by Don Pasquale without his father knowing. What Roberto does not know is that Don Pasquale is using him to cover his illicit business. When Roberto discovers that Ninfarosa is his employer's lover, he threatens to blurt out everything he knows to the police. Don Pasquale orders his assistant Salvatore to kill Roberto at sea. Don Francesco is warned by Ninfarosa that his son is in a great danger, but he arrives too late to save him. Carrying Roberto's dead body in his arms, he shows up at the restaurant where Don Pasquale and his men are eating: in the ensuing shoot-out Francesco kills his rival and the latter's lieutenant, but is wounded in turn. Hunted by the police, he flees aboard a Greek ship.

Most of the Neapolitan-based "*guapparia* movies" can be traced back to a factory of actors, scriptwriters and technicians. One of the subgenre's masterminds was Ciro Ippolito, a young Neapolitan actor-turned-producer who in a couple of years co-scripted and produced half a dozen titles. Ippolito's usual collaborators were the prolific scriptwriter Piero Regnoli (a former journalist and film critic for the Vatican's newspaper "L'Osservatore Romano" and also a director in his own right) and Alfonso Brescia, a Roman-based director who became himself a specialist in the field with 15 films from 1978 to 1983, covering every possible variation on the theme.

Following *Onore e guapparia*'s remarkable success in the Parthenopean district, Ippolito wrote and produced *L'ultimo guappo*, starring Mario Merola and directed by Brescia, who had just finished shooting no less than five *Star Wars* rip-offs. Actually, according to Ippolito's autobiography, the treatment was written in the mid–'70s but stayed on the shelf for a couple of years for lack of financing.[1]

However, *L'ultimo guappo* became an unexpected hit: made on a shoestring (110 million lira) and destined for regional distribution in Southern Italy, it did surprisingly well even in Northern cinemas. Mario Merola—already hugely popular in Naples—became a sort of mass phenomenon, starring in seventeen films in the following five years: many of them were directed by Brescia, and all made considerable profits at the box office, though mainly in the South.

L'ultimo guappo, which pays explicit homage to the theatrical tradition of sceneggiata in the long scene where Merola watches a stage rehearsal, codified the "*guapparia*" subgenre on screen. As the imposing Don Francesco, Merola is shown from the very first scene (where he separates two quarrelling man at the market) as a tutor of law and order, fatherly and Solomonic, while his opponent, as played by Luciano Catenacci (wearing a laughable wig in the early scenes), displays his evil nature in his elegant dresses (in an attempt to look more refined than he actually is) and turns out to be slimy, scheming and duplicitous, thus embodying the typical villain of sceneggiata—*'o malamente* in Neapolitan dialect. The woman—here the junoesque Sonia Viviani—is portrayed in a patently misogynist way, as a temptress and a source of conflict and misfortune, even though in the end she repents for her sins.

The nostalgia for a mythical past of law and order emerges from the opening sequences of *L'ultimo guappo*, where Don Ciccio makes a vow to the Virgin Mary, swearing that he will humiliate himself in front of his rival if his son survives a difficult surgical operation. The religious aspect is pushed to the verge of parody, as Merola begs the statue of the Virgin, illuminated by an outlandish light, while a church organ plays in the background. Don Ciccio starts a new life in order to give his son a respectable future, but the "new" organized crime has the features of the well-dressed, cruel, icy gangsters who abandon cigarette smuggling for drug trafficking—the poison that kills youngsters and mines the delicate equilibrium on which the city's economy is funded.

"Naples' architectural and urban transformations were perceived as a symptom of an anthropological mutation of Neapolitans themselves, seen as ideal and loyal people who are continually humiliated and offended by Fate" wrote one critic. "These mutations spawned a new criminal type that wouldn't respect the old ethical code of the "camorra" and flourished on the city's moral ruins. This way, Naples becomes a sort of city/body that exhibits the stigmata of its violation through the face of Mario Merola, an unwilling avenger and a living epitome of such an equation."[2]

The attention to Neapolitan folklore denotes the film's aim at a regional audience. The Dall'Orto brothers' soundtrack blends percussion and dialectal voices with interesting results, while

Merola's songs are limited to just a couple of numbers, accompanying shots of the streets of Naples and thus injecting them with the hero's private drama. Places and rituals are also important. The family lunch is a moment of joy and warmth, while the final showdown takes place in a restaurant—with Catenacci sitting in the middle of a long table, in a perverse reversal of the Last Supper, where the bad guy is enjoying his triumph. It's the film's *piece de resistance*, introduced by Merola's point of view shot as he advances in the room and culminating in a gun duel which, like in a Sergio Leone western, is preceded by repeated close-ups of the opponents' eyes.

L'ultimo guappo moves along by means of basic, predictable plot twists: the filmmakers want the audience to know beforehand what characters will learn and go through, and therefore suffer, get angry and cry with them. By envisioning well-worn storylines that come to their inevitable conclusions, it's once again as if the filmmakers needed to exorcise the present and its unpredictability. Destiny is written all over the actors' faces, as soon as they show up on screen. And Naples—an immutable and imposing presence—becomes a character in itself: a sort of pantheistic deity, watching over the characters and their stories.

Notes

1. "I was still an actor when a book came out, *Storia della Camorra* by Vittorio Pallotti: it was an in-depth inquiry into the origins of the Camorra in the Parthenopean territory. I read the book and devised a story, *L'ultimo guappo*. I called Pallotti and asked him to write the treatment with me." Ippolito, *Un napoletano a Hollywood*, p. 37. Ippolito also recounts an amusing if unlikely encounter with Fernando di Leo, to whom the young aspiring producer wanted to give the script, while the director of *Caliber 9* mistook the casually dressed, long haired Ippolito for a terrorist with bad intentions.
2. Nazzaro, "Napoli, curtiello cu curtiello," p. 57.

1979

Big Mamma *(Il Mammasantissima)*

D: Alfonso Brescia. *S:* Ciro Ippolito; *SC:* Piero Regnoli, Ciro Ippolito; *DOP:* Silvio Fraschetti (35mm, Gevacolor); *M:* Eduardo Alfieri; *Mammasantissima* (Mallozzi/Alfieri) sung by Mario Merola; *E:* Carlo Broglio; *PD:* Romeo Costantini; *CO:* Valeria Valenza; *C:* Luigi Quattrini; *AC:* Ugo Menegatti; *AD:* Franco Pasquetto; *AE:* Angela Rosa Taccari; *MU:* Marcello Di Paolo; *W:* Maria Spigarelli; *Mix:* Romano Checcacci; *SS:* Giuliana Gherardi; *SP:* Roberto Calabrò; *PA:* Kim Gatti. *Cast:* Mario Merola (Don Vincenzo Tramontano), Malisa Longo (Assunta), Biagio Pelligra (Don Salvatore Bufalo), Elio Zamuto (The Advocate), Anna Walter (Concetta), Walter Ricciardi (Roberto), Ciro Giorgio (Antonio Esposito), Marina Viviani (Nunziatina), Lucio Montanaro (Tourist), Fabiola Toledo (Maria), Pippo Volpe, Lino Mattera (Roberto's father), Salvatore Puccinelli (Don Vincenzo's smuggler), Ruggero Pignotti (Father Stefano), Marco Girondino (Gennarino), Letizia D'Adderio, Nunzio Gallo. *Uncredited:* Angelo Boscariol, Alfonso Brescia (Doctor), Roberto Calabrò (Gypsy), Lina Franchi (Raging woman), Benito Pacifico (Don Salvatore's henchman). *PROD:* Ciro Ippolito for Orsa Maggiore Cinematografica; *PM:* Antonio Pittalis; *PSu:* Roberto Calabrò; *PSe:* Luciano Lucchi; *Accountant:* Bruno Di Bartolomei. *Country:* Italy. Filmed at Incir–De Paolis (Rome) and on location in Naples and Angri. *Running time:* 88'; Visa no.: 73095 (02.10.1979); *Rating:* not rated; *Release date:* 02.10.1979; *Distribution:* P.A.C.; *Domestic gross:* 208,000,000 lira. *Home video:* Cecchi Gori Home Video (DVD, Italy).

A good-hearted man, a loving husband and father, the Neapolitan smuggler Don Vincenzo Tramontano enjoys the power and prestige of his status. However, having discouraged a competitor from Sicily, the "Advocate," head of another organization of smugglers, and having publicly humiliated Don Salvatore Bufalo, a greedy pawnbroker, Don Vincenzo has to face two hostile enemies who are determined to get revenge on him in every way possible. First Bufalo and the Advocate attempt to rob Don Vincenzo of an important shipment of cigarettes, but to no avail; then they set a trap so as to have a pretext for legally dispatching him. Don Salvatore rapes and kills Tramontano's daughter; as expected, Don Vincenzo goes on a rampage after them. Yet he proves to be more clever than they think: he faces them both at a banquet, disguised as Pulcinella, after dispatching their "gorillas." Having accomplished his revenge, Don Vincenzo is arrested without resistance.

The third in the Neapolitan "guapparia" series directed by Alfonso Brescia and starring Mario Merola, *Big Mamma* is perhaps the best example of the hybrid between the sceneggiata and crime films, and surely the one which puts the central character of the good gangster most vividly on screen. The Italian title, *Il Mammasantissima*, refers to the status of its protagonist, a smuggling boss who's the film's hero. Here Mario Merola becomes a living monument, a symbol, a deity made of flesh and blood. The scene in which he dresses up in front of a mirror, surrounded by the women of the house, all in silent adoration, has a ritual quality which is sealed by the final sipping of a cup of coffee as if it were communion wine. The hero's almost mythical stature is celebrated with a touch of irony: the scene plays like a smart variation of a famous sequence in Francesco Rosi's first film *La sfida* (The Challenge, 1958).

Merola is Don Vincenzo Tramontano, a predestined do-gooder—"In life, we all are born with a destiny, we all have a cross to carry. And this is mine" he says—who dispenses advise and words of wisdom; a protector of the weak against the evil deeds of all the "malamente" (bad people) of this world. That is, in the universe that is Naples. *Big Mamma* is the most convincing of the lot in putting on screen a timeless, unchangeable Naples, epitomized by the parade of Pulcinellas that open the film and return in the climax: Merola dresses up as Pulcinella (Punch), the Neapolitan popular "mask" par excellence, to take his revenge on Don Salvatore (Biagio Pelligra) who raped his daughter and caused her death, and on the "Advocate" (Elio Zamuto), the rival gangster who wanted to take his place in the criminal underworld.

Compared to other Merola films of the period, *Big Mamma* wisely pairs the paunchy, imposing hero with a pair of worthy opponents, both covering different aspects of the typical "omm'e 'mmerd" (shitty man), that is, '*o malamente*, the opponent in traditional sceneggiata. As the "Advocate," Elio Zamuto embodies the elegant, well-mannered yet duplicitous rival, a character that represents the innate distrust towards the *haute bourgeoise* which he apes, trying to climb the social ladder. On the other hand, Pelligra—a great underused character actor who worked with the Taviani brothers, Marco Tullio Giordana and Giuseppe Tornatore—is the repulsive Don Salvatore, a man of the lower classes and a traitor of his own people. It's he who has the film's most emotionally upsetting scene, when Don Salvatore rapes (offscreen:

in the sceneggiata, carnal violence, nudity and sex are almost always kept away from viewers' eyes, as the stories largely play on allusions) Don Vincenzo's daughter.

As usual, the value system as expressed in the film would be debatable if not considered within the genre's traditions. The hero is a smuggler, and in a significant dialogue exchange he says "Don't they know that if the smuggling business is destroyed there will be a revolution in Naples?" "They" are not always the police, or the rival gangs: "they" are all those who don't belong to Naples, don't share the city's history nor its people's inner bonding. As film historian Gianni Rondolino wrote, "What is left is the essence of simple moralism that permeates these stories of personal offences and revenge, where justice finally triumphs. Everything happens in a city—Naples—which is perceived as a big mother, while family is the whole world. [...] The laws of blood and honor are the only accepted ones, whereas the laws of the State are seen as extraneous, even harmful if not just useless."[1]

Note

1. Gianni Rondolino, *Catalogo Bolaffi del cinema italiano 6—1978/1979* (Turin: Giulio Bolaffi Editore, 1979), p. 61.

Don't Trust the Mafia (*I guappi non si toccano*)

D: Mario Bianchi. *S* and *SC:* Antonio Cucca, Claudio Fragasso; *DOP:* Maurizio Salvatori (35mm, Staco Film); *M:* Tullio De Piscopo (ed. Curci); *E:* Cesare Bianchini; *PD:* Vincenzo Russo; *AC:* Giancarlo Granatelli; *AE:* Delia Apolloni; *AD:* Claudio Fragasso; *MU:* Marisa Marconi; *W:* Pia D'Onofrio; *SO:* Rodolfo Montagnani; *SE:* Renato Agostini; *KG:* Marcello Gargano; *ChEl:* Alberto Silvestri; *SP:* Francesco Campanile; *SS:* Graziella Marsetti. *Cast:* Gabriele Tinti (Tony Lo Bianco), Paola Senatore (Paulette Maurice), Pino Mauro (Lucien Maurice), Richard Harrison (Ferrari, Chief of Police), Marisa Laurito (Mrs. Montano), Tommaso Palladino (Monti), Enrico Maisto (Marciani), Enzo D'Ausilio (Angelo Jacomino), Emy Salvador [Emilio Salvatore] (Man at cemetery), Gianni Diana (Marco), Maddalena Russo (Girl in Tony's room). *Uncredited:* Mario Bianchi (Jacomino's henchman). *PROD:* Falco Film; *PM:* Francesco Russo; *PSu:* Carla Crovato; *PSe:* Rosetta Sestili. *Country:* Italy. Filmed at R.T.A. Elios (Rome) and on location in Aversa. *Running time:* 93'; Visa no.: 73506 (05.09.1979); *Rating:* v.m.14; *Release date:* 05.12.1979; *Distribution:* ASA Cinematografica; *Domestic gross:* 16,500,000 lira. *Also known as: Die Ungreifbaren* (West Germany). *Home video:* Meteor (VHS, Denmark—Italian language, as *Don't Trust the Maffia* [sic], 90'33"), New Pentax (VHS, Switzerland).

During excavation works in a quarry, the lifeless body of engineer Italo Montano is found. The three magistrates who investigate are convinced that the murder was part of a shady deal between the gangs of the local Jacomino and the Marseille-born Lucien Maurice. Chief of Police Ferrari entrusts Tony Lo Bianco—an Italian American and former FBI agent—with the investigation. With considerable bravery, Tony infiltrates Maurice's gang and suggests robbing a post office van; at the same time, he reveals the details of the coup to Jacomino. According to his plan, the heist turns into a massacre and only Lo Bianco and Maurice survive. However, they are then shot by Monti, a special agent who double-crossed Lo Bianco. Tony hides the wounded Maurice in a cemetery chapel and with the help of the latter's daughter Paulette, comes into possession of documents that expose the misdeeds of the corrupt prosecutors. When they submit the evidence to Ferrari, however, Tony and Paulette are fatally shot by unknown killers.

One of the three crime films Mario Bianchi filmed in Naples between 1978 and 1979 (according to the director, with money provided by people conniving with the Camorra[1]), with similar casts, *I guappi non si toccano* (literally, Don't Touch the Wiseguys) is perhaps the grimmest of the lot, and the one featuring the best cast. As a former FBI agent (who, in an amusing touch of unintentional humor, is called Tony Lo Bianco, like the actor) Gabriele Tinti takes a vacation from the string of erotic movies he was shooting in the period, while sceneggiata icon Pino Mauro—here, unlike his other films of the period, with undyed hair yet still sporting his impressive trademark sideburns—plays a (rather improbable) French boss, Maurice. The script by Antonio Cucca and Claudio Fragasso provides him with a live python named Lucifer that the Camorra boss keeps in a glass cage in the middle of his living room: "I trust him more than any other friend," he says. "He doesn't talk, doesn't ask, doesn't betray. Blind, dumb and deaf. He only knows how to kill." However, Mauro's character spends half the movie in a comatose state—an atrocious scene has him trying to communicate with his eyes—only to revive when it's time to protect his daughter (the beautiful Paola Senatore).

The story plays with the usual riff from Leone's *A Fistful of Dollars*, as Tinti pits two gangs one against the other, and as with *Napoli: i 5 della squadra speciale* the tone is dirty, cynical, gloomy to the core. If Richard Harrison, here in an extended cameo, is a ruthless Chief of Police who doesn't mind using unorthodox methods to destroy criminal gangs, Tinti's character is more of a loser than a special agent. He was thrown out of the FBI for violence and concussion, gets recruited on a dangerous mission not because of his sense of righteousness but because he's got no choice (a fact that makes him closer to the "inglorious bastards" of so many war flicks than to the heroic Commissioners played by Merli & Co.). He's beaten, betrayed, shot at and eventually killed for all his efforts.

Bianchi's direction is perfunctory as ever, and the shoestring budget shows in every shot: Tinti and Harrison secretly meet in a trailer at an amusement park, much of the film is shot in squalid hotel rooms, shabby bars and other improvised locations, car chases and stunts leave a lot to be desired, unintentionally funny scenes abound (take the planning of a robbery, where all the gangsters gather around a poorly hand-drawn road map that looks far from accurate). Palladino, as a special agent whom LoBianco nicknames "pink panther," has another hilarious scene where he teases the latter by cleaning his shoes with Lo Bianco's shirt and smearing black shoe polish on his pillow. Nevertheless, there's still room for the usual J&B plugs ("The reception was very bad, but the whiskey was great"). Bianchi shows up in one of his usual cameos as a suit-and-tie, gum-chewing guy who beats Tinti. Overall, the best thing about the film is percussionist Tullio De Piscopo's funky score. Despite an Italian language Danish video release carrying the title *Don't Trust the Mafia*, the film was probably never dubbed into English.

Note

1. Ippoliti, Norcini and Grattarola, "Mario Bianchi: 'Il mio cinema pizza e fichi,'" p. 26.

From Corleone to Brooklyn (Da Corleone a Brooklyn)

D: Umberto Lenzi. *S:* Umberto Lenzi; *SC:* Umberto Lenzi, Vincenzo Mannino; *DOP:* Guglielmo Mancori (35mm, Telecolor); *M:* Franco Micalizzi (ed. R.C.A.); *Amaramente assaiie* (P. Farrese / F. Micalizzi) sung by Vittorio Bezzi; *E:* Eugenio Alabiso; *PD:* Giuseppe Bassan; *APD:* Davide Bassan; *CO:* Carlo Gentili; *C:* Mario Sbrenna; *AC:* Alessio Gelsini; *AE:* Giuseppe Romano; *2nd AE:* Silvana Di Legge; *AD:* Stefano Rolla; *MU:* Dante Trani; *Hair:* Lidia Puglia; *SO:* Roberto Alberghini; *SP:* Franco Vitale; *KG:* Giuseppe Gabrielli; *ChEl:* Roberto Allegretti; *SS:* Maria Luisa Merci; *DubD* (English version): Nick Alexander. *Cast:* Maurizio Merli (Commissioner Giorgio Berni), Mario Merola (Michele Barresi), Van Johnson (Lt. Sturges), Biagio Pelligra (Salvatore Scalia), Venantino Venantini (Commissioner Danova), Laura Belli (Paola, Belli's ex-wife), Nando Marineo (Lo Cascio), Salvatore Billa (Giuseppe Caruso), Sonia Viviani (Liana Scalia). *Uncredited:* Tony Askin [Antonio Aschi] (Man on train), Luca Barbareschi (Brooklyn cop), Joseph Bergmann (Brooklyn cop), Ugo Bologna (Hitman), Giovanni Cianfriglia (Bogus ambulanceman), Ottaviano Dell'Acqua (Thug), Bruno Di Luia (Peppino's companion), Raniero Dorascenzi (Scientific team cop), Tom Felleghy (police official at Airport), Frank Gio (Mafioso at Esposito's restaurant), Maurizio Gueli (Doctor), Giuseppe Lauricella (Don Francesco Santoro), Rocco Lerro (Thug), Fulvio Mingozzi (Motel manager), Antonino Lotà (Scalia's accomplice), Riccardo Petrazzi (Van driver), Bruno Rosa (police official), Massimo Sarchielli (Esposito), Martin Sorrentino (Brooklyn thug), Sergio Testori (Thug), Piero Tiberi (Man at gas station). *PROD:* Sandra Infascelli for Primex Italiana; *PM:* Lucio Orlandini; *PSu:* Bruno Bagella; *PSe:* Eliana Cipri; *ADM:* Roberto Ornaro. *Country:* Italy. Filmed in Palermo, Monreale, Rome and New York. *Running time:* 95'; Visa no.: 73398 (04.13.1979); *Rating:* not rated; *Release date:* 04.13.1979; *Distribution:* Variety Film; *Domestic gross:* 398,600,000 lira. *Also known as: Von Corleone nach Brooklyn* (West Germany, 1986—90'). *Home video:* Cinekult (DVD, Italy). OST: CD Beat Records BCM9501

Italian poster for ***From Corleone to Brooklyn*** (1979).

After the murder of Salvatore Santoro in Rome, Commissioner Giorgio Berni, who is handling the case, is sent to Palermo to work with Commissioner Danova as there are good reasons to suspect that Santoro has been killed by the Mafia. Meanwhile, Lieutenant Sturges of the New York City police arrests a man who says his name is Vito Ferrando, suspected of drug trafficking and carrying no identity documents. The report that Sturges sends to Palermo states that Ferrando is actually Mafia boss Michele Barresi, who repeatedly escaped justice. Barresi is then cleared of the charges for the crime of Rome, yet in the meantime, other people close to him—his lover Liana Scala, and Francesco Santoro, Salvatore's brother—get killed as well. One of the assassins, Salvatore Scalia, a former confidant of Barresi's and Liana's brother, falls into the hands of the police. Berni obtains permission from his superiors to transfer the prisoner himself to America because Scalia's testimony may be vital to sentence Barresi.

The trip from Palermo — the Commissioner and his prisoner initially travel by car to Rome in order to muddy the waters, then take the plane — to the United States is full of pitfalls because the mobsters attempt to eliminate the dangerous witness. Berni, after hiding in his ex-wife Paola's house, gets rid of Barresi's men and gets to New York. Once there, though, he is not able to prevent Scalia's murder: the witness is killed just in front of the tribunal. However, Scalia has left a written testimony that frames Barresi.

From Corleone to Brooklyn is in many ways a symbolic work within Italian *poliziotteschi*. Umberto Lenzi's film dissolves the crepuscular melancholy of a waning genre in an "oblivious initiatic journey backwards (both of the *filone* and its symbolic hero) to its own remote origins beyond the Ocean."[1] What's more, with the symbolic teaming of its two biggest stars, *From Corleone to Brooklyn* marks the natural meeting point — both thematic and commercial — of out-and-out crime film and its Parthenopean variant, the sceneggiata. Franco Micalizzi's outstanding score even dedicates two juxtaposed themes to the "iron Commissioner" and his Mafioso opponent.

The film is structured as a *road movie*, with an eye to Clint Eastwood's *The Gauntlet*, but also with more subterranean nods to the tradition of Italian cinema and the "commedia all'italiana." It's as if *From Corleone to Brooklyn* somehow absorbed the lesson of Luciano Salce's *The Fascist* (*Il federale*, 1961) and Dino Risi's *The Easy Life* (*Il sorpasso*, 1962) — two films built on the conflict between two opposed characters on a journey through Italy that becomes a cue for a reflection on the country's history, morals, social and cultural contradictions. Lenzi takes the burden of carrying the poliziotteschi to its elephant graveyard, even though neither he nor his acolytes are aware that it's not simply a matter of a genre that's dying but of a whole production system that's about to collapse.

Merli's character maintains and amplifies the same doubts that his predecessors had in Stelvio Massi's films, while Merola reinvents himself, for once playing the bad guy, a *malamente* who undergoes periodical bouts of showy paternalism — as in the prison scene where he takes under his arm a petty Puerto Rican thief — that make him even more despicable. Another refugee from sceneggiata, Biagio Pelligra, is the film's surprising core: "he reflects his own audience in his extraordinarily tough, familiar, grim face, and when in a brief stereotyped dialogue he exposes the same socio-environmental justifications [to his belonging to the Mafia] as Giuliano Gemma did in *Father of the Godfathers*, he really touches a deep nerve, and looks like the greatest non-professional actor of Italian Neorealism."[2]

The moral tissue is gaping, and tiresomeness and discomfort prevail in an open and unconciliatory ending. It's Merola's character who has the last word: he is about to be extradited, but only "If we manage to arrive in Italy...," implying that once again Merli's character is doomed to die.

By unconsciously celebrating the death of Italian crime cinema, *From Corleone to Brooklyn* predates its further metamorphosis. In the 1980s filmmakers will move to the U.S., to shoot C-grade flicks that look like telefilms, populated by squared-jaw, suntanned cops with names like porn actors and the looks of third-grade stuntmen. Whereas Lenzi's New York is still an appendix of Italy's violent cities: American and Italian cops speak the same language, everybody understands everyone else (save for the occasional double-entendre based on foul language: a heritage of Tomas Milian's flicks, perhaps), while Brooklyn thugs have the same grins as the Roman ones who, in turn, used to ape the petty gangsters of New York's mean streets. What's more, the hotel rooms in the suburbs of the Big Apple are not that different from those on Italy's A1 Motorway, and the few portraits hanging on the walls of immigrants' houses give the illusion that the detachment from their loved ones and their home country has never really happened after all.

From Corleone to Brooklyn was one of the inspirations for Claudio Fragasso's *Palermo-Milan One Way* (*Palermo-Milano solo andata*, 1996), where a team of young cops escort a Mafioso (Giancarlo Giannini) to a trial in Milan: a rather uneasy heritage, hidden among homages to the then in vogue Hong Kong action thrillers à la John Woo and pretensions to a civil "committed" message.

Notes

1. Davide Pulici, "Faccia da sbirro: Maurizio Merli," in Aa. Vv., *4° police Film Festival* (Bologna: I quaderni del Lumiére n° 27, 1998), p. 31.
2. Buttafava, "Procedure sveltite," p. 114.

The Gang That Sold America (*Squadra antigangsters*)

D: Bruno Corbucci. *S* and *SC:* Mario Amendola, Bruno Corbucci; *DOP:* Giovanni Ciarlo (35mm, Eastmancolor, Telecolor); *M:* Goblin (ed. Bixio-Cemsa), *The Whip* and *Sound of Money* (by R. Pietsch) sung by Asha Puthli; *Welcome to the Boogie* (by W. C. Cannon / Marangolo / Pennisi / Pignatelli) sung by Charlie Cannon; *E:* Daniele Alabiso; *PD:* Claudio Cinini; *CO:* Alessandra Cardini; *C:* Giuseppe Di Biase; *AE:* Brigida Mastrolillo; *AD:* Roberto Tatti; *MU:* Franco Di Girolamo; *Hair:* Jole Cecchini; *SO:* Alvaro Orsini; *STC:* Rocco Lerro; *ST:* Massimo Pittarello. *Cast:* Tomas Milian (Nico Giraldi), Enzo Cannavale (Salvatore Esposito), Margherita Fumero (Maria Sole), Gianni Musy (Gitto Cardone), Asha Puthli (Fiona Strike), Leo Gavero (Don Vito Sarticri), Andrea Aureli (Don Mimì), Lewis Cianelli [Lewis E. Ciannelli], Angelo Ragusa (Don Vito's henchman). *Uncredited:* Bruno Alias (Barman), Francesco Anniballi (Man at funeral), Salvatore Baccaro (Rocco Dall'Orto, the usurer), Giovanni Bonadonna (Eusebio Navarro), Angelo Boscariol (Man at funeral), Lella Cattaneo (Dancer), Ombretta De Carlo (Amelia), Marcello Di Falco (Man at funeral), Cesare Di Vito (Waiter at Miami nightclub), Mario Donatone (Man at funeral), Rocco Lerro (Don Vito's hitman), Tomaso Milian Jr. (Antonio), Vezio Natili (Mafia man), Nello Pazzafini (Mafia man), Attilio Pelegatti (Mafia thug), Mimmo Poli (Arab), Simone Santo (Peppino), Pupita Lea Scuderoni (Woman in nightclub), Giuliano Sestili, Sergio Testori (Hitman at night), Franco Ukmar (Navarro's hitman), Kim Chan (Chan Chu Kai). *PROD:* Galliano Juso for Cinemaster; *PM:* Alessandro Mattei. *Country:* Italy. Filmed at Incir–De Paolis (Rome) and on location in New York and Miami. *Running time:* 90'; Visa no.: 73131 (02.22.1979); *Rating:* not rated; *Release date:* 03.01.1979; *Distribution:* Titanus; *Domestic gross:* 569,000,000 lira. *Also known as: Tony Marroni — Ein Superbulle gegen Amerika* (West Germany, 03.20.1981— 89'). *Home video:* 01 (DVD, Italy). OST: CD Cinevox MDF 324.

To help his friend Salvatore, whose Brooklyn-based restaurant is on the verge of closing down due to the excessive amount of money he must pay to the racket, Nico Giraldi agrees to court Maria Sole, the daughter of the deceased Mafia don Gerolamo Giarra, in order to have her lend him money. Nico finds out that Maria Sole's fiancé,

Gitto Cardone, is planning to take over the throne of mob boss by killing his opponents. Nico moves to Miami with Salvatore, where they pose as hired hitmen, and there he proceeds to mess up Cardone's plans with the help of a nightclub singer, Fiona Strike, who's fallen for him. Meanwhile, Nico must also be careful of Maria Fiore's suffocating stalking. Eventually Nico — who's actually an undercover Interpol agent, while Fiona turns out to be an FBI agent— succeeds.

The fifth on-screen appearance of Nico Giraldi — always with his inseparable mechanic overalls and sneakers, plus the usual array of assorted berets and scarves and a chewing gum in his mouth — is also the last to use the word "Squad" in its Italian title (which translates as Anti-gangsters Squad) — a sign that all the ties with poliziotteschi would soon be cut. From the next film on, Corbucci's films starring the Cuban actor as Italy's most picturesque and foul-mouthed cop would be structured as out-and-out comedy whodunits, with Milian sharing the spotlight with comedy sidekicks Enzo Cannavale and Bombolo (who does not appear in *The Gang That Sold America*). The titles would also underline this change of pace by emphasizing the words "Assassinio" and "Delitto" (both meaning "murder").

The story can be loosely defined as a sequel of sorts to *Little Italy*, with the characters of Salvatore Esposito (Enzo Cannavale) and Maria Sole (Margherita Fumero) returning from the previous film, but the script — penned as always by Corbucci and Mario Amendola — is singularly lazy in its tiresome concoction of the assorted gags, action scenes and feeble action plot. Milian's duets with the ugly Maria Sole are amusing only when the actor pushes the humor towards implicit vulgarity, while the crime/action framing is just a paper-thin excuse to string together a number of comic set pieces which more often than not fall flat. As Italian critic Maurizio Porro noted, "in the supposedly breakneck pacing that it tries to impose to its tiresome story, the film recalls the usual Terence Hill and Bud Spencer formula. [...] The paper-thin plot proceeds along well-worn paths, by hitching together bits of B-style comedy, crime films and Western. Whenever Corbucci leans on action [...] the pic moves ahead, even though it's all been seen and done before; on the other hand, whenever the script [...] tries to be funny, it fails badly."[1]

Besides Milian's son Tomaso (who also popped up in a cameo in 1978's *Little Italy*) in a minor role, the film is noticeable for the presence of Indian singer Asha Puthli — who gets to sing a couple of songs — as a Miami-based *femme fatale*. Decidedly less charming, but equally memorable is the appearance of the unmistakable Salvatore Baccaro (*The Beast in Heat*) as a dumb usurer who comes to collect a debt, only to find Esposito apparently dead on the kitchen table — and not noticing that the body changes position from time to time. Corbucci's direction is rather hasty overall, lacking all of the urban flair it retained in the series' first two episodes. The U.S. setting — besides some very fake-looking scenes obviously shot at a Cinecittà backdrop posing as a New York street — allow the director for a number of action stunts, including the obligatory powerboat chase in the Florida everglades. If anything, *The Gang*

Tomas Milian and Enzo Cannavale, right, in *The Gang That Sold America* (1979).

That Sold America proved that the formula was growing increasingly tiresome. Wisely, Corbucci and Amendola would choose to return to Italy for their next entry in the series, *Assassination on the Tiber* (1979).

Note

1. M. Po. [Maurizio Porro], *Corriere della Sera*, 03.23.1979.

Gardenia (*Gardenia il giustiziere della mala*)

D: Domenico Paolella. *S:* Teodoro Agrimi [Teodoro Corrà], Gino Capone, Augusto Caminito; *SC:* Augusto Caminito; *DOP:* Sergio Rubini (35mm, Eastmancolor, Technicolor); *M:* Franco Califano, conducted by Willy Brezza (ed. P.A.C.); *E:* Amedeo Giomini; *PD:* Franco Calabrese; *CO:* Andrea Zani; *C:* Michele Pensato; *AC:* Aldo Bergamini, Filippo Neroni; *AE:* Tommaso Gramigna; *2nd AE:* Angelo Bufalino; *AD:* Massimo Carocci; *MU:* Massimo Giustini; *Hair:* Caterina Campana; *W:* Irene Parlagreco; *SO:* Goffredo Salvatori; *Boom:* Antonio Pantano; *SP:* Antonio Casolini; *GA:* Agostino Gorga; *KG:* Giuseppe Raimondi; *PP:* Claudio Razzi; *SS:* Massimiliana Ferretto; *DubD:* Carlo Baccarini. *Cast:* Franco Califano ("Gardenia"), Martin Balsam (Salluzzo), Robert Webber (Tony Caruso), Eleonora Vallone (Regina Rossi), Licinia Lentini (Miriam Bella), Franco Diogene (Gardenia's friend), Maria Baxa (Gardenia's girlfriend), Venantino Venantini (Nocita), Gualtiero Rispoli ("Advocate"), Lori [Loredana] Del Santo (Laura), Lorraine De Selle (Consuelo), Renato Basso Bondini (Mustached Sicilian gangster), Roberto Della Casa (Columbian), Fabrizio Jovine (Salluzzo's partner), Melissa [Chimenti] (Singer). *Uncredited:* Calogero Azzaretto (Caruso's man), Loris Bazzocchi (Nannuzzo), Angelo Boscariol (Salluzzo's henchman), Fernando Cerulli (Barber), Sasha D'Arc (Thug), Benito Pacifico (Salluzzo's henchman), Franca Scagnetti (Cleaning lady at airport toilet), Hal Yamanouchi (Joseph Hiketomo, the drug courier). *PROD:* P.A.C.—Produzioni Atlas Consorziate (Milan), Orsa Maggiore Cinematografica (Rome); *GM:* Teodoro Agrimi; *UPM:* Enrico Savelloni; *UM:* Mario Olivieri; *PSe:* Giuseppe Cicconi, Luciano Lucchi. *Country:* Italy. Filmed at Incir–De Paolis (Rome) and on location in Rome. *Running time:* 100'; Visa no.: 73502 (05.05.1979); *Rating:* not rated; *Release date:* 05.05.1979; *Distribution:* P.A.C.; *Domestic gross:* 108,000,000 lira. *Home video:* Cecchi Gori (DVD, Italy)

Ex-gangster and gambler Gardenia (so named for his habit of wearing a gardenia in his buttonhole) is the owner of the Mayfair, a restaurant-nightclub frequented by members of Rome's upper class. Crime boss Salluzzo, with the consent of his rival Caruso, sets out to flood the city with drugs and ruthlessly eliminates other bosses who refuse to ally with him. Knowing Gardenia's privileged position, Salluzzo and Caruso try to persuade him to join them, but Gardenia, despite being a "tough guy," has his own code of honor and refuses to sell drugs. Salluzzo opts for more persuasive manners, blasting the restaurant and killing one of his friends. Gardenia, grieving since being abandoned by his girlfriend Regina, pretends to accept Salluzzo's conditions, but actually starts a war against him that gets tougher and tougher, ending with a deadly clash where Gardenia prevails: Caruso is quick to declare peace.

"If your enemy sticks it in your ass, don't move: you'd play his game." With such verbal fireworks, it's patent that Domenico Paolella's *Gardenia* draws liberally from the foul-mouthed ironic approach of Bruno Corbucci's contemporary films starring Tomas Milian as inspector Nico Giraldi. Yet *Gardenia* is in itself a somewhat endearing little tongue-in-cheek *film noir* of sorts, mostly because its unusual lead: Franco Califano, nicknamed "Il Califfo" (The Caliph), a pop singer-cum-playboy who was equally popular for his songs (often with a frankly sexual content, such as *Avventura con un travestito*) as for his love affairs and generally reckless lifestyle—which included him being busted for drug possession just before the film's release.

As the eponymous character, a womanizing gangster who always wears a gardenia flower in his buttonhole—a nod to Frank Capra's *Pocketful of Miracles* (1961)—Califano essentially plays himself, even doing his own dubbing, with a ribald self-assurance. "You have the perfumes of three different women on you; all of them rather vulgar," complains his girlfriend (Eleonora Vallone) when he gets home at dawn after a wild night. But Califano (who also wrote the score) faces the role—one of his few cinematic efforts, which is a pity given his natural screen presence—with a much-welcomed dose of self-irony. Gardenia has a number of amusingly memorable scenes, such as the one where he serves three thugs who are making a fuss in his restaurant with raw steaks and vegetables and uncooked pasta, explaining: "I don't want to either gain or lose with you, so I'm giving away this stuff at market price, but you're going to cook it at home for yourselves." Gardenia is a sort of Roman answer to Bogart, who just needs a look to make a woman fall at his feet, yet in the end he is left by the one with whom he's eventually fallen for; he managed to gain wealth and respectability by opening a classy restaurant (where he also acts as a cook and serves cheaper Chianti wine in Barolo bottles) and keep an eye over a trio of down-at-heel sidekicks, yet he suffers his new bourgeois status as if it's a prison. "He doesn't have fun anymore" one of his friends comments.

Besides the presence of Martin Balsam and Robert Webber (both playing their roles on autopilot), *Gardenia* is noteworthy for its sensuous female cast, which includes Maria Baxa (*Deadly Chase*), Licinia Lentini (soon in Castellari's *Day of the Cobra*), Lorraine De Selle (*Madness*), Melissa Chimenti (Massaccesi's *Papaya—Love Goddess of the Cannibals*), Raf Vallone's daughter Eleonora (in her film debut) and a very young Lory Del Santo (soon to become a notorious TV starlet as well as Eric Clapton's mistress). The script (by producer Augusto Caminito, who co-wrote the story with Gino Capone and Teodoro Agrimi) plays a friendly riff on well-worn *film noir* clichés, plus the odd Spaghetti Western reference (a scene between Gardenia and a fake barber rips off a similar moment in Tonino Valerii's *My Name Is Nobody*) but is notable for the "elegiac and ironically mythical tone, similar to that of a tender and jovial Roman-born Jean-Pierre Melville" as one critic defined it,[1] which hides a subtle melancholy. Even though he provides his hero with a seemingly happy ending, Paolella has Califano claim near the end: "Things are never gonna be the same," before succumbing to a bout of sadness.

Gardenia represents a further step aside from poliziotteschi and its clichés, in the way it portrays a Rome that is almost out of time, closer to 1920s prohibitionist Chicago than to the violent city where Maurizio Merli used to operate. The way Paolella deals with violence is also peculiar: compared to the grim excesses of the director's previous *Stunt Squad*, here the worst cruelties are portrayed in an unconventional, almost casual way—take the scene where Gardenia dispatches a gangster (Renato Basso Bondini) even though he's got both his arms in casts. Another good example is the scene where the restaurant's elderly chef, mortally wounded by a bomb blast, tells Gardenia before dying: "And always remember what your father used to say ... a restaurant's fortune is made by wine. Always give 'em the good wine!"

Note

1. Buttafava, "Procedure sveltite," p. 107.

Hunted City (Sbirro, la tua legge è lenta ... la mia no!)

D: Stelvio Massi. *S:* José Sánchez, Marino Girolami, Vincenzo Mannino; *SC:* José Sánchez, Stelvio Massi; *DOP:* Pier Luigi Santi (35mm, Eastmancolor, Staco); *M:* Stelvio Cipriani (ed. R.C.A.); *E:* Mauro Bonanni; *PD:* Francesco Calabrese; *AArtD:* Francesco Raffa; *CO:* Luciana Marinucci; *C:* Alessandro Ruzzolini; *AE:* Walter Diotallevi, Massimo Gasperini; *AD:* Riccardo Petrazzi; *MU:* Silvana Petri, Dante Trani; *Hair:* Jolanda Conti; *SO:* Davide Magara; *Mix:* Sandro Ochetti; *SE:* Gianni D'Andrea; *SP:* Ermanno Serto; *W:* Anna Onori; *SS:* Augusta Neumann. *Cast:* Maurizio Merli (Commissioner Paolo Ferro), Mario Merola (Raffaele Acampora), Carmen Scarpitta (Ferro's sister), Francisco Rabal (Don Alfonso), Nando Marineo (Arrigo), Massimo Dapporto (Stefano), Matilde C. Tisano (Eva Stefani), Masimo Mirani (Prof. Guidi's assassin), Lidia Costanzo (Paolo's mother), Remo Varisco, Gianni Cajafa (Paternò), Nino Carillo (Advocate Morelli), Francesco Scelsi, Anna Canzi (Luigi's wife), Franco Ferri, Sergio Masieri (Marius), Tony [Antonio] Raccosta (Spanò), Francesco Moraldi, Salvatore Puccinelli (Racketeer at Acampora's restaurant). *Uncredited:* Ottaviano Dell'Acqua, Vittorio Pinelli (Caruso), Annibale Papetti (Cardella), Francesco Salvi (policeman). *PROD:* 3C Cooperativa Cinematografica Conero; *PM:* Silvio Siano; *PSu:* Francesco Mancarella, Francesco Ortensi, Daniela Martella; *ADM:* Luigi Scardino. *Country:* Italy. Filmed at Icet–De Paolis (Milan) and on location in Milan. *Running time:* 103'; Visa no.: 74046 (09.27.1979); *Rating:* not rated; *Release date:* 09.27.1979; *Distribution:* Simba Film; *Domestic gross:* 329,000,000 lira. OST: CD Digitmovies CDDM119. *Also known as: La cité du crime* (Paris, 01.18.1984—90'), *Il poliziotto ribelle* (Italy—Home video), *Cidade a ferro e fogo* (Portugal). *Home video:* Eureka (VHS, Italy, as *Poliziotto ribelle*, prologue missing), SHV (Japan—English language), Filmitalus (VHS, Portugal)

Commissioner Paolo Ferro, an expert in the fight against the Mafia, is sent on a mission to Milan where a string of murders of financiers and lawyers took place, possibly on behalf of a Sicilian criminal organization. Ferro, however, does not hold this opinion, and an elderly mobster, Don Alfonso, who holds him in high esteem, confirms that he is right. Indeed, the mysterious killers—one of whom is Ferro's young nephew Stefano—are members of another organization of hired assassins. Ferro devises a plan to unmask the head of said organization by commissioning his own murder: he almost gets killed but is saved by one of Don Alfonso's men, sent specifically to do just that. Finally, Ferro discovers that the head of the organization is an ex–Cammorist, Raffaele Acampora, the owner of a chain of restaurants and apparently above suspicion. However, he doesn't have the necessary evidence to accuse him. It's up to Don Alfonso to do justice for him.

Produced by Salvatore Smeriglio's 3C company, *Hunted City* was the fifth collaboration between Massi and Maurizio Merli and followed the thread introduced by the director's previous films. If Mariani (*Il commissario di ferro*) was a tormented figure, persecuted by the trail of hate and vengeance provoked by his actions, *Hunted City*'s Paolo Ferro is yet again a contradictory hero. He is a cop who works in the anti–Mafia squad, yet he's a sincere and close friend to a fugitive Mafia boss, Don Alfonso (Francisco Rabal), who's portrayed as a "man of honor" in accordance with the tradition of Mafia films since Pietro Germi's *In the Name of the Law* (*In nome della legge*, 1949). Such a view is also partly affected by the cross-fertilization with sceneggiata, exemplified by the casting of Mario Merola, for the second time co-starring with Merli after Lenzi's *From Corleone to Brooklyn*. Yet *Hunted City* dismantles, piece by piece, poliziotteschi's tetragonal moral structure. Not only does the "good" Mafia boss take sides with the hero to vanquish a murderous gang whose killers are recruited among the youngsters of upper class Milan families, but he even saves Ferro's life and—in a morally ambiguous and far from conciliatory ending—does justice in his place, after the law has proven to be powerless against the head of the organization.

The Italian title (which translates as "Cop ... Your Law Is Slow, Mine Isn't!," while the working title *Città braccata* was the exact correspondent to the English language one) hints at the film's core—that is, failure. Ferro already surrendered to the logic of compromise, and without even being aware of it: he doesn't hesitate borrowing money from the Mafia to finance a police raid, and when he realizes that a war between Marseillaise and Sicilian gangs is about to start, he doesn't let the former wipe out the latter (as Betti or Tanzi would have) but he stops the massacre, because "if I have to choose, I'm choosing them [the Sicilians]—at least they are Italians!" A line which reveals the same sense of belonging to a community that pervaded the sceneggiata. After all, Ferro is once again an immigrant: he returns from abroad to his roots and his family. Yet he's too confused by the euphoria of his comeback to realize that the ideal view he has built in his mind does not coincide with reality.

Family—the expression of Ferro's aspirations at peace and tranquility—will prove to be the source of betrayal and disillusion, as embodied by Stefano (Massimo Dapporto), Ferro's beloved nephew, with whom the cop thinks he's got a privileged relationship, and who in the end turns out to be one of the killers that have been hired to kill the Commissioner.

Despite a very strong concept, the story often loses steam in a succession of barely connected sequences. Massi's direction is also perfunctory at times, with an over-reliance on the zoom lens and too many visual tricks he already employed to much more impressive effects in his earlier films. Take the scene where Ferro enters a gambling room, shot through a closed circuit monitor, which is an exact remake of a similar moment in *Mark Strikes Again*. Some of the characters are underdeveloped too: Eva (Matilde Tisano), the umpteenth traitress who's destined for a bad end without too many regrets, is sketchy to the point of misogyny, even though Merli commented that he liked the brief love story between her character and the hero.

On the other hand, one of the film's most convincing assets is the presence of Merola, here in a role which literally overturns the singer/actor's usual good-hearted Mafia bosses. "Merola was one weird character," Massi recalled. "But you end up liking him. However, he wanted to be the one and only protagonist. He and Maurizio quarreled a lot, especially when we had dinner all together, as Merola insisted on paying for all—even if there were 50 people at the table!"[1] As customary with this kind of films, during a chase scene in the streets of Milan, Massi—who was filming inside the bandits car—and his crew found themselves face to face with a real police car, with cops pointing machine gun at them, believing they were real robbers. "The producers alerted only the security guards, not the police. And, as an agent later told us, someone thought we were shooting for real. I was carrying a huge camera, which looked like a machine gun of sorts."[2]

Hunted City did not fare well at the box office, according to Massi because it was released in mid-summer (actually the film came out in late September), more likely because of bad distribution as well as the audience's growing weariness towards the genre.

Notes

1. Norcini and Ippoliti, "Stelvio Massi ricorda Maurizio Merli," p. 15.
2. *Ibid.*

Killer's Gold (*Il braccio violento della mala / Dinero maldito*)

D: Willy Regan [Sergio Garrone] / [Spanish version: José Luís Fernández Pacheco]. *S* and *SC:* Fernando Orozco, Sergio Garrone [Spanish version: Fernando Orozco, H. S. Valdes]; *DOP:* Lorenzo Cebrián (35mm, Eastmancolor, Fotofilm / LV-Luciano Vittori); *M:* Vassili Kojucharov (Ed. CAM); *E:* Gianfranco Amicucci [Spanish version: Gabi Peñalva]; *SD:* Francisco Rosella; *C:* Manuel Mateos; *AC:* Mario Martín, Agustín Rodriguez [Spanish version: J. M. Banqueri]; *AD:* José Luis Pacheco [Italian version only], Johnny Peters [Juan M. Mathias]; *AE:* Franco Capuano; *MU:* Adela Del Pino; *SP:* José Barrero; *ChEl:* Serafin Rodriguez; *MA:* Fernando Poggi; *SS:* Juan M. Mathias. *Cast:* Robert Widmark [Alberto Dell'Acqua] (Joseph), Daniela Giordano (Claudia), Dan Forrest (Jimmy), Victor Israel (Moyses), Max Boulouis [Max-Henri Boulois] (Manson), Mara Ruano, María Victoria Ruiz, Aldara Minetto, Perla Singer, Chema Tejela, Jesús San José, Gastón Ribeiro, Manuel Intiri. *PROD:* Huracan Films (Madrid), Danny Film (Rome) [Spanish version: Huracan Films only]; *EP:* Zeljko Kunkera; *Delegate P:* Jacinto Ferrer Bayarri; *PM:* Manuel Torres; *PA:* Julian Atienza; *UM:* Jesús San José, Adolfo Fernández; *ADM:* José Antonio Baca. *Country:* Spain / Italy / Mexico. Filmed in Madrid, Cuerca, Barcelona. *Running time:* 90'; Visa no.: 72675 (11.30.1978); *Rating:* v.m.18; *Release date:* 02.20.1979; *Distribution:* Regional; *Domestic gross:* 4,477,000 lira. *Also known as: Dinero maldito* (Madrid, 02.19.1979), *L'important c'est de tuer* (Paris, 06.02.1982 — 90'), *L'important c'est le fric* (France, video title). *Home video:* AVO (VHS, UK — English language), GVR (VHS, Italy, 85' 29"), Video Trans (Spain, 82' 40").

Joseph, a professional burglar and social outcast because he's a gypsy, is captured by a boss named Moyses, violently beaten by his men and repeatedly tortured to reveal the whereabouts of some hidden loot. It turns out Joseph was commissioned by Moyses to steal $4 million from a safe. Immediately after the burglary though, Moyses' men attempted to snatch the loot from him. Joseph escaped and kept the stolen goods for himself. Eventually Joseph teams up with Claudia, Moyses's lover, his right-hand man Jimmy and a black ex-prizefighter named Manson. The four kill Moyses and set out to get the loot. Soon the three men are at each other's throats, and Claudia plays a role in pitting them against each other. They are located by the men of a criminal organization and barely escape, but Claudia is mortally wounded. When the three survivors finally get to where the money is hidden, a remote mountainous region, Jimmy shoots Manson, and he and Joseph start a deadly fight. The gypsy emerges as the winner, only to find the dying Manson intent on tearing the "damned money" to pieces.

"It was a Spanish co-production, and there was also a Mexican producer whose name I can't remember. [...] It was a gangster movie which did rather well at the box office and was rather well made too,"[1] said Sergio Garrone about *Killer's Gold*. Not very much, and surely not enough to shed light on this little-known crime film, which in the Spanish version is credited to obscure Iberian filmmaker José Luís Fernández Pacheco, who appears to be just the assistant director according to the Italian copy.[2]

Killer's Gold has little or nothing to do with the poliziotteschi, being a by-the-numbers American style film noir whose main claim to originality may well be Alberto Dell'Acqua's character Joseph being a gypsy, which has him form a natural bond between outcasts with the black ex-prizefighter Manson played by singer Max-Henri Boulois (himself a director of trashy flicks like *Black Commando*, a contemporary version of *Othello* co-starring Tony Curtis as Iago). Yet *Killer's Gold* is replete with weird wide-angle shots (and looks like it was almost entirely filmed with one handheld camera), and the first half features an elaborate flashback structure via quick editing cuts — featuring psychedelic nightclub scenes, saucy lesbian interludes and Joseph's lover running in slow-motion through the fields — that is likely to make many viewers scratch their heads. Garrone and co-scripter Fernando Orozco definitely saw *Point Blank* one too many times.

As the psycho Buddhist boss Moyses, who speaks in proverbs and in one scene is seen praying before a Buddha statue to the sound of Vassili Kojucharov's Spanish-sounding score, Victor Israel has one hell of a time in one of his most extended screen roles ever. In one of the first sequences, the freaky cross-eyed Spanish character actor, wearing only his boxer shorts, even gets to fondle Daniela Giordano's breasts, with visible enjoyment, while later on he forces his lover to perform an off-screen fellatio. After Moyses' death halfway through, *Killer's Gold* moves to wide open spaces as Joseph and his accomplices move to the location of the loot's hiding place, chased by an army of gangsters — a fact somehow implied by the fact that the stolen money belonged to the mob — through the mountains and woods of a wild Spanish region. There are a number of references to Westerns, from Vassili Kojucharov's score to the harmonica played by Boulois in a nod to Leone's *Once Upon a Time in the West*, while the film culminates in a downbeat yet telegraphed twist ending *à la The Treasure of the Sierra Madre*, after what looks like one of the most exhausting fistfights ever committed to screen.

Despite Garrone's claims, *Killer's Gold* came out almost unnoticed in Italy: released in 1979, with a title (literally, The Violent Arm of the Underworld) that tried hard to make it look like a *French Connection* rip-off (Friedkin's film came out in Italy as *Il braccio violento della legge*, The Violent Arm of the Law) it raised a minimal sum at the box office. The film's working title was *I miei peggiori amici* (My Worst Friends).

Notes

1. Gianluca Castoldi, "La mano che nutriva la morte," *Nocturno Cinema* #7 (June 1998), p. 95.
2. As expected, the opening and end credits reveal many differences, with the Italian ones also featuring a number of misspellings.

A Man on His Knees (*Un uomo in ginocchio*)

D: Damiano Damiani. *S:* Damiano Damiani; *SC:* Nicola Badalucco, Damiano Damiani; *DOP:* Ennio Guarnieri (35mm, Technospes); *M:*

Franco Mannino; *E:* Enzo Meniconi; *PD:* Enzo Turco; *CO:* Mario Giorsi; Assistant *CO:* Silvano Giorsi; *C:* Renato Ranieri; *AC:* Antonio Scaramuzza; *AE:* Mario Recupito, Domenico Varone; *AD:* Enrico Bergier; *MU:* Walter Cossu, Nilo Jacoponi; *Hair:* Corrado Cristofori; *SO:* Domenico Dubbini; *Boom:* Benito Alchimede; *Mix:* Alberto Tinebra; *SP:* Giuseppe Botteghi; *KG:* Ennio Picconi; *ChEl:* Amilcare Cuccoli; *PrM:* Vittorio Troiani; *MA:* Nazzareno Zamperla; *SetT:* Celeste Battistelli; *SS:* Vittoria Vigorelli; *UP:* Lucherini, Rossetti, Spinola, Ghergo. *Cast:* Giuliano Gemma (Nino Peralta), Eleonora Giorgi (Lucia Peralta), Michele Placido (Antonio Platamone), Ettore Manni (Vincenzo Fabbricante), Tano Cimarosa (Sebastiano Colicchia), Andrea Aureli (Lamantia), Luciano Catenacci (Brigadeer Mangiapane), Fabrizio Forte (Paolo, Peralta's son), Fabrizio Jovine (Dr. Rallo), Giovanni [Nello] Pazzafini (Matranga), Nazzareno Zamperla (Agent Corleo), Francesco De Mattia (Serena), Giovanni Giancono (Tobacconist), Armando Zappi (Bar owner), Francesco Tranchina (Vinieri), Vincenzo Norvese (Ferrara), Calogera Spoto (Platamone's wife), Rodolfo Bigotti (Lamantia's son), Eolo Capritti (Allotta), Giampaolo Saccarola (Go-between). *Uncredited:* Rolando De Santis, Lina Franchi (Lamantia's wife), Alba Maiolini (Lamantia's relative). *PROD:* Mario Cecchi Gori for Rizzoli Film; *GO:* Luciano Luna; *PM:* Vincenzo Mazzucchi; *UPM:* Francesco Giorgi; *PSu:* Massimo Ferrero; *PSe:* Paolo Giorgi, Giovanni Giancomo; *ADM:* Sergio Bologna, Nestore Baratella. *Country:* Italy. Filmed at Incir De Paolis (Rome) and on location in Palermo. *Running time:* 109'; Visa no.: 73397 (04.13.1979); *Rating:* v.m.14; *Release date:* 04.13.1979; *Distribution:* Cineriz; *Domestic gross:* 388,000,000 lira. *Also known as: Ein Mann auf den Knien* (06.21.1980—110'). *Home video:* Medusa (DVD, Italy).

Former car thief Nino Peralta, now a husband and good father of two kids, is the manager of a coffee kiosk near the Cathedral of Palermo. One day, warned by his partner, Sebastiano Colicchia, Nino notices he's being stalked by a young man named Platamone, probably an assassin for hire. Before he manages to confront him directly, Nino learns he is on a list of people to be eliminated by a Mafia gang and realizes that a chain of unstoppable killing is in motion. Peralta searches in vain for those who can help him clear his name: apparently, his death sentence was decided by the fact that a cup of coffee from his kiosk had been found in the place where the wife of a big Mafia boss was being held prisoner, and the evidence would bind him to the enemy clan. Nino gets in touch with Platamone, who demands money to save his life. Nino is forced to sell the kiosk and becomes a thief once again. But, after the killing of Colicchia, Platamone's boss Don Vincenzo Fabbricante shows up and asks Nino to join his gang. To do so, he'll have to kill Platamone in turn. The young man, desperate and determined to stay away from the mob, kills Don Vincenzo instead and tries to convince Platamone to take sides with him. However, it all ends in tragedy, as Nino accidentally kills Platamone as well, after the latter attempted to denounce him.

Ten years after *The Most Beautiful Wife*, Damiano Damiani ideally latched on the archaic, crepuscular Sicily as shown in that film with *A Man on His Knees*, another crime film *sui generis* if compared to the most "straight" genre works of the decade. Here, Mafia and its dominion on the region is shown indirectly, through the deep repercussions it has on the working class. Both former car thief Nino (Giuliano Gemma)—who is now leading a honest working life, only to discover that his name has been added to a list of people that must be dispatched (the working title was *Il decimo nome*, The Tenth Name)—and his designated killer Platamone (Michele Placido) are just a pair of rain dogs, who keep biting each other instead of joining forces. They have lost their battle even before it started, they are used and abused, even humiliated: take the scene where Mafia boss Fabbricante (Romolo Valli) forces Nino to kneel down and kiss his ring, the symbol of the Don's power—a power that manifests itself with the brute force that money allows.

Like Lodovico Graziano in *I Am Afraid*, Nino Peralta is a doomed man. During the course of the film he loses whatever he's built with his own hands—a honest job, a family, respectability, freedom—and even though he survives in the end, that does not make his future look brighter—as a matter of fact, it's dubious whether he really has a future at all.

In each and every move they make, both Nino and Platamone convey a thorough desperation, because of the sense of defeat that crushes them as an ineluctable burden. According to film critic Callisto Cosulich, compared to the "mythical vision, almost 'Old frontier'-like," that emerged from the director's previous works, *A Man on His Knees* represents a "compensation towards the real world, much more complex and at the same time prosaic than the [former] mythical one: [...] the characters that Damiani singles out are not two 'men' in the Mafia meaning of the term [as defined in *The Day of the Owl*, Author's Note] and not even 'half-men' or 'pigmies,' but respectively an 'arse-crawler' and a 'quacker.'"[1]

It's a harsh, pessimistic vision and *A Man on His Knees* features one of Damiani's (and the genre's) most downbeat—and symbolical—endings: after accidentally killing Platamone, Nino literally disappears in a foggy landscape, at dusk. As assistant director Enrico Bergier puts it, "Nobody can hope to get out of this tangle that is Sicily."[2] In the 1980s—a decade starting with the murders of politician Piersanti Mattarella and magistrate Gaetano Costa, and counting among its many victims Pio La Torre, General Carlo Alberto Dalla Chiesa, Giangiacomo Ciaccio Montalto, Rocco Chinnici and Giuseppe Fava—this tangle would become more impenetrable than ever.

As Nino, Giuliano Gemma gives an impressive performance, breaking further away from his previous lighter genre roles—a wise career move that started with Valerio Zurlini's *The Desert of the Tartars* (1976) and Squitieri's *I Am the Law*. "I was chosen after a screen test. I liked the script very much, and I was really looking forward to making this film," Gemma recalled. "I got along very well with Damiani, as he's a filmmaker who knows what he wants and has a flair for framing shots, being a painter as well. He doesn't like to show you how to act, but he'd rather explain the character, why and how he must move and act in a certain way." Damiani used many long sequence shots so as to give the story a more realistic feel and filmed most of the film in Palermo, on location, immersing his actors in the Sicilian mood and people (Gemma recalls providing free coffee for passers-by between takes while standing in the coffee kiosk his character owns in the film).

Michele Placido is equally convincing as the ambiguous Platamone, a mentally unstable, whiny assassin whose relationship with Nino forms the core of the film. The scene where Platamone meets Nino for the first time, and in an oblique way tells him that he has been hired to kill him, while at the same time trying to extort money from his potential victim, is an outstanding moment of fine acting. Damiani would cast Placido in the lead of his successful 1984 TV movie *La Piovra* as Commissioner Cattani, the 1980s crime film hero *par excellence*. Damiani's old friend Tano Cimarosa, whom the filmmaker had discovered in *The Day of the Owl*, turns up as Nino's associate.

Notes

1. Callisto Cosulich, *Paese sera*, 4.15.1979.
2. Pezzotta, *Regia Damiano Damiani*, p. 287.

Napoli … la camorra sfida la città risponde (Naples … the Camorra Defies, the City Replies)

D: Alfonso Brescia. *S:* Ciro Ippolito; screenplay: Ciro Ippolito, Piero Regnoli; *DOP:* Luciano Trasatti (35mm, Gevacolor, Telecolor); *M:* Eduardo Alfieri (Ed. Bideri); *E:* Carlo Broglio; *PD:* Franco Calabrese; *CO:* Valeria Valenza; *C:* Gaetano Valle; *AC:* Renato Ranieri, Franco Fraschetti; *AE:* Angela Rosa Taccari, Sandro Broglio; *AD:* Franco Pasquetto; *MU:* Raul Ranieri; *Hair:* Nerea Rosmanit; *W:* Gabriella Morganti; *SO:* Tommaso Quattrini; *Sound mixers:* Alberto Tinebra, Romano Checcacci; *SP:* Roberto Calabrò; *SS:* Giuliana Gherardi. *Cast:* Mario Merola (Don Francesco Gargiulo), Antonio Sabàto (Vito), Jeff Blynn (Commissioner De Stefano), Walter Ricciardi (Marco Gargiulo), Liana Trouché (Elvira Gargiulo), Rik Battaglia (Dr. Rampone), Lucio Montanaro (Tony), Benito Artesi (Clothing store owner), Alessandro Partexano (Vito's associate), Sabrina Siani (Maria, Marco's girlfriend), Enzo Nandi (Tony's father), Marina Valadier [Viviani] (Clothing store owner's wife), Antonio Ciarcia, Franco Angrisano (Lawyer), Enrico Cesaretti, Ettore Venturini, Vezio Natili (Retailer), Nicola Di Gioia, Salvatore Puccinelli. *Uncredited:* Alfonso Brescia (Man at engagement party), Rossana Canghiari (Woman at party), Nestore Cavaricci (Cop), Nicola Di Gioia (Man of Camorra), Luciano Foti (Journalist), Ciro Ippolito (Perez, the journalist), Ettore Martini (Maria's father), Benito Pacifico (Vito's man), Franco Pasquetto (François), Franco Ukmar (Vito's henchman), Luciano Zanussi (Man at engagement party). *PROD:* Ciro Ippolito for G.P.S.; *PM:* Antonio Pittalis; *UM:* Naldo Nibbi, Franco Marino; *PSe:* Federica Lampronti. *Country:* Italy. Filmed at Incir–De Paolis (Rome) and on location in Naples. *Running time:* 90'; Visa no.: 74384 (11.23.1979); *Rating:* not rated; *Release date:* 11.26.1979; *Distribution:* Impegno Cinematografico (Carla and Angiolo Stella); *Domestic gross:* 229,000,000 lira. *Home video:* Raro (DVD, Italy).

Naples. A criminal organization led by Rampone imposes onerous payments on small industrialists and merchants, through a group of thugs led by Vito. Don Francesco Gargiulo, the owner of a shipyard, tries to resist but has to give in to the racket after Vito kidnaps his son Marco and rapes the latter's girlfriend Maria. Marco, looking for revenge, allows Commissioner De Stefano to frame the gang by means of some photographs he has taken while the criminals commit their deeds. The Commissioner has the victims sign a statement against the racket, but Rampone hires a killer, François, thus forcing the retailers to withdraw their complaints. De Stefano has to release Vito and his henchmen due to lack of evidence. François takes revenge on Gargiulo's son, by injecting a dose of drugs that drives him crazy. This time, however, Gargiulo decides to retaliate by himself: together with a bunch of armed citizens who have suffered similar injustice, he attacks Rampone and his gang while they are celebrating the release of Vito and the other thugs. The final showdown takes place in an underground cemetery and ends with the gang's utter defeat.

With roughly the same plot as Enzo Castellari's masterpiece *The Big Racket*, Alfonso Brescia's *Napoli … la camorra sfida, la città risponde* is much more realistic in its depiction of the city and its underworld as compared to the other Neapolitan-based crime films of the period, and is perhaps the closest to out-and-out poliziotteschi. Mario Merola is an honest businessman blackmailed by gangsters who set fire to his factory, rape his daughter-in-law and drug his son, forcing him to end up in an asylum. An important aspect in *Napoli … la camorra sfida, la città risponde*, which makes the theme even more poignant than in Castellari's *The Big Racket*, is the sacredness of one's property. Don Gargiulo is a self-made man, who in his own words started as a longshoreman and built his own fortune. "These hands have worked," he tells Vito (Antonio Sabàto).

An important difference compared to Brescia's other Neapolitan crime films is that Merola's character here is an all-round good guy, an honest person persecuted by the underworld. The proximity to the poliziotteschi is on display in many scenes, such as the rape of Sabrina Siani: her character is deflowered and gang-raped (offscreen) by Sabàto's men in front of her boyfriend, adding insult to injury, but Brescia adds an unusually hyper-realistic detail — a shot of the girl's open thighs stained with blood, something which would be out of place in a typical sceneggiata. Another common element is the character of the hard-boiled cop (Maurizio Merli look-alike Jeff Blynn, terrible as usual) who in the end lets Merola loose, implicitly legitimating his private revenge (and therefore confirming the superiority of honor's unwritten laws).

Significantly, even though he is not the main villain but just the racketeer boss's right-hand man, Sabàto's character is a "foreigner" — a Sicilian, who dresses in a flamboyantly vulgar manner and talks with the same theatrical affectation as Mario Adorf in *Caliber 9*. He's an evolution of the roles played by the actor in his crime films of early '70s such as Lenzi's *Gang War in Milan*, and at the same time a riff on the "mad bomber" character as featured in *Colt 38 Special Squad* and *Stunt Squad*.

However, the typical sceneggiata elements — such as the relationship between Don Gargiulo and his son are not forgotten either. As always, Merola gets to sing a song in the obligatory convivial scene, which is mirrored by the one featuring the triumphant bad guys drunkenly singing *Luna Rossa* (a famous Neapolitan song) in a restaurant just before the final massacre begins. As with Ciro Ippolito's other "*guapparia* movies," the film is scattered with tongue-in-cheek self-references: the silver-haired Ippolito has a secondary but important role as the righteous journalist who denounces the racket, while Brescia pops up as the bearded, cigarette-puffing guest at Merola's party, who compliments his host for the good food and wine at the beginning of a rather elaborate sequence shot.

If the plot is routine, albeit with a number of clever touches — a load of weapons hidden behind crates of vegetables and tomatoes — the Roman filmmaker has a number of fine tricks up his sleeve to spice up the proceedings: after each visit the racketeers pay to their victims, Brescia ends the sequence with a slow-motion shot of the victims pointing a gun towards the camera and shooting, thus anticipating the inevitable retaliation. Furthermore, the ominous use of Don Francesco's cigarette lighter-cum-music box is similar to that of carillons in Italian Westerns, while Brescia pulls out all the stops in the asylum scene, where

Gargiulo's son ends up in a padded cell after being drugged by the bad guys (as usual with "*guapparia* movies," drugs are the devil's work).

Napoli ... la camorra sfida, la città risponde builds up to an impressive climax: Merola picks up his guns and leads an army of honest workers against the villains, and the ending is an over-the-top shoot-out featuring bazookas, slow-motion gunblasts and blood squibs aplenty, which starts in a restaurant and ends among the catacombs of Naples' underground cemetery, Camposanto delle Fontanelle. "May God forgive me!" yells Merola after transfixing Sabàto in slow-motion with a wooden crucifix, as if he just stepped out of a vampire film. It's an eerie moment whose aural and visual Gothic overtones display the permeability of genres within the Italian movie industry. And if this sounds a bit too risky, remember Marco Antonio Andolfi's abysmal *Cross of the Seven Jewels* (1987) which put a werewolf against the Camorra (the Italian working title was, indeed, *Il lupo mannaro contro la camorra*). Nothing was impossible in Italian popular cinema, indeed.

Napoli una storia d'amore e di vendetta (Naples—A story of Love and Vengeance)

D: Mario Bianchi. *S* and *SC:* Alberto Sciotti; *DOP:* Maurizio Salvatori (35mm, Eastmancolor, Staco Film); *M:* Tony Iglio (Ed. Medium); *E:* Cesare Bianchini; *PD:* Vincenzo Russo; *AC:* Giancarlo Granatelli; *AE:* Delia Apolloni; *AD:* Graziella Marsetti; *MU:* Adele Sisti; *SO:* Rodolfo Montagnani; Giovanni Russo; *SP:* Mauro Paravano; *ChEl:* Alberto Silvestri; *KG:* Marcello Gargano; *SS:* Graziella Marsetti; *DubD:* Gianni Musy. *Cast:* Mario Da Vinci (Tony Ferrante), Sal [Salvatore] Da Vinci (Salvatore), Maria Fiore (Jolanda), Richard Harrison (Frank), Enrico Maisto (Ciro), Tommaso Palladino (Nando), Mario Deda (Michele), Gabriella Di Luzio (Maria), Alfonso Guadagni (Don Gennaro Ferrante), Maria Del Monte (Carolina), Raimondo Salvetti (Ferdinando), Francesco Ferrieri (Don Pasquale), Nunzio Gallo (Francesco), Aldo Bufi Landi (Andrea), Gianni Dei (Piero), Paola Pitagora (Lucia). *Uncredited:* Patrizio Oliva (Patrizio). *PROD:* Mario Da Vinci for M.D.V. Film (Naples); *PSu:* Giulia Saccucci; *PSe:* Marino Matteo. *Country:* Italy. Filmed at Incir—De Paolis (Rome) and on location in Naples. *Running time:* 90'; Visa no.: 74277 (10.23.1979); *Rating:* not rated; *Release date:* 10.31.1979; *Distribution:* Regional; *Domestic gross:* 103,000,000 lira.

Piero and Nando are enlisted by Frank to perform a robbery at a nightclub, posing as transvestites. During the hit, Piero, kills the owner, Don Gennaro Ferrante. Salvatore, a street urchin who works as a parking attendant at Gennaro's nightclub, witnesses the murder. Gennaro's brother Tony, an internationally famous singer who had left Naples after the breakup of his relationship with Lucia, gets back to his hometown to find the murderer, and discovers that his old flame—who, according to her parents, was too rich to marry the once poor Tony—has dedicated herself to raising orphans. Salvatore befriends Lucia and asks her to tell Tony to give up his thoughts of revenge. Through Lucia, Tony finds out that she had had a son whom she was told (by her domineering mother) had died just after birth. Lucia and Tony get together again and decide to leave Italy, adopting Salvatore. Meanwhile Piero, Nando and Frank plan to kidnap Lucia (who is Piero's stepsister) to extort money from her father, but the woman is saved by Tony. Salvatore recognizes Piero as the murderer, and in the ensuing shoot-out the thugs all die, while Tony and Lucia discover that Salvatore is their own son.

Tailor-made for its top billed star Mario Da Vinci—a Neapolitan singer, very popular in his hometown but practically unknown in the rest of Italy—and his little son Salvatore, Mario Bianchi's *Napoli una storia d'amore e di vendetta* retains the same characteristics as the director's other films of the period—a shoestring budget, slapdash direction, recurring actors—even though it lacks much of the sleaze that made *Napoli: i 5 della squadra speciale*, *Provincia violenta* and *I guappi non si toccano* such a hoot. That is not to say that *Napoli una storia d'amore e di vendetta* doesn't belong to the realm of Z-grade trash, however: as the film's hero, Mario Da Vinci—who in the film becomes sort of a world-famous Italian singer based in Las Vegas (courtesy of well-worn stock footage) is hopelessly inept. He delivers lines such as "Justice is beautiful only when you do it with your own hands!" and "I'll never get to rest until I find my brother's murderer" while trying hard to be intense, but only succeeding in making Pino Mauro look like Laurence Olivier in comparison. Little Sal Da Vinci—who gets to sing a song too—is even more grating, especially when he launches into would-be poignant monologues that set one's teeth on edge ("Tonight while I was watching the stars I asked myself why, if my parents abandoned me many years ago, why should I look for them now ... they didn't want me back then, they wouldn't want me now!"). Bianchi simply doesn't have any clue when his film goes for unintended laughs, and treats every scene with all the seriousness he can: Alfonso Brescia's contemporary films with Mario Merola are much more clever in their retelling of sceneggiata clichés.

The film's weirdest move is to have Gianni Dei and Tommaso Palladino (the latter for once without his signature mustache) wear women's clothes and act as *femminielli* (Neapolitan transvestites), with somewhat hilarious results. In addition to the feeble criminal subplot, which culminates in one of the worst climaxes ever seen in an Italian crime flick, there are plenty of sceneggiata stereotypes, which culminate in a final acknowledgment between a father and his long-lost son, while class differences are eventually overcome. For all its shortcomings, *Napoli una storia d'amore e di vendetta* shows how the guapparia movie was gradually turning into out-and-out sceneggiata, leaving aside guns and bullets and embracing more songs and tear-jerking scenes.

As for the rest of the cast, Paola Pitagora throws herself away in a heartless role, while Raimondo Salvetti provides the mandatory comic relief as a dumb fisherman. The film also features an uncredited appearance by prizefighter Patrizio Oliva, soon-to-be super lightweight champion at the 1980 Moscow Olympics.

The New Godfathers (I contrabbandieri di Santa Lucia)

D: Alfonso Brescia. *S:* Ciro Ippolito; *SC:* Ciro Ippolito, Piero Regnoli; *DOP:* Silvio Fraschetti (35mm, Technicolor—Techniscope); *M:* Eduardo Alfieri (Ed. Bideri); *Tammuriata Blu* (Mallozzi—Alfieri) sung by Mario Merola; *E:* Carlo Broglio; *PD:* Romeo Costantini; *CO:* Valeria Valenza; *C:* Luigi Quattrini; *AC:* Ugo Menegatti, Franco Fraschetti; *AE:* Angela Rosa Taccari, Sandro Broglio; *2nd AE:* Angelo Bufalino; *AD:* Franco Pasquetto; *MU:* Marcello Di Paolo; *Hair:* Teodora Bruno; *W:* Gabriella Morganti; *SO:* Pietro Spadoni; *SP:* Roberto Calabró; *SS:* Giuliana Gherardi; *UP:* Kim Gatti. *Cast:* Mario Merola (Don Francesco Autiero), Antonio Sabàto (Don Michele Vizzini), Gianni Garko (Captain Ivano Radovic), Jeff Blynn (Don Salvatore Gargiulo), Marco Girondino

(Gennarino), Lorraine De Selle (Lorraine), Marina Valadier [Marina Viviani] (Carmelina), John Karlsen (Narcotics Commission Member), Franco Diogene (Akhad), Hassan Jaber (Vito), Letizia D'Adderio (Stellatella), Mico Galdieri (Gambino), Rik Battaglia (Don Calogero Avallone), Nunzio Gallo (Commissioner Martinelli), Lucio Montanaro (Cassio Pretorio), Edmund Purdom (Head of Narcotics Commission), Debora Girondino, Sabrina Siani (Lucy Avallone), Andrea Aureli (Don Lucky), Antonio Ciarcia, Massimo Alibrandi, Giuseppe [Pino] Ferrara, Salvatore Puccinelli (Smuggler). *Uncredited:* Angelo Boscariol (Don Francesco's henchman), Alfonso Brescia (Passer-by), Massimo Ciprari, Lina Franchi (Woman in the crowd), Giuseppe Leone (Narcotics Commission Member), Rocco Lerro (Man at wedding party), Giuseppe Marrocco (Man at wedding party), Franco Ukmar (Don Francesco's henchman at docks), Luciano Zanussi (Guest at wedding party). *PROD:* Ciro Ippolito for P.A.C.—Produzioni Atlas Consorziate (Milan); *GM:* Vittorio Noia; *PM:* Antonio Pittalis; *PSu:* Aldo Nibbi; *ADM:* Enrico Savelloni; *Accountant:* Bruno Di Bartolomei. *Country:* Italy. Filmed at Incir—De Paolis (Rome) and on location in Naples. *Running time:* 90'; Visa no.: 73942 (08.23.1979); *Rating:* not rated; *Release date:* 08.25.1979; *Distribution:* P.A.C.; *Domestic gross:* 342,000,000 lira. *Also known as: Der große Kampf des Syndikats, Todesdroge Heroin* (West Germany), *Les contrebandiers de Santa Lucia* (France), *Mafian kummisedät* (Finland), *Los contrabandistas de Santa Lucia* (Spain). *Home video:* Cecchi Gori (DVD, Italy).

Following the coup in Iran, a large quantity of drugs is purchased by Mafia families in New York, who have forged an alliance for the occasion. The FBI sends Captain Radovic to Naples where the drugs, shipped from Istanbul, are likely to stop and be camouflaged before being shipped to the United States. Radovic, who's convinced that the Neapolitan smugglers are not criminals but just poor fellows who make ends meet with cigarette smuggling, gets the support of the local boss, Don Francesco Autiero. The latter introduces Radovic to another boss, Don Michele Vizzini, who, unbeknownst to both, is the intermediary in the drug trade between the East and the United States. While Autiero's men are attacked and killed at sea, Don Francesco unintentionally poisons little Stellatella, the daughter of his trusted aide Gargiulo, with a candy he took from Vizzini's candy factory. The incident reveals that the drug has been hidden in the sweets. Both Radovic and Don Francesco move to New York: during the wedding celebrations of a Mafia boss' daughter, Autiero kills Vizzini and is seriously wounded. Radovic and the FBI rush in time only to collect the corpses, arrest the bosses and confiscate the drugs.

"Smuggling in Naples is like Fiat. Only, we can't go on strike!" Mario Merola's memorable dialogue line perfectly sums up the importance of contraband in Naples' economy by comparing the business with Italy's most famous car factory in Turin, comes near the end of a sequence where the good boss shows captain Radovic (Gianni Garko) around, illustrating the rules of the smuggling business in the Parthenopean city. Possibly patterned on a similar scene in Vanzina's *Execution Squad* (where Enrico Maria Salerno showed reporters the underworld life in Rome), it's one of the best sequences in Alfonso Brescia's *The New Godfathers*, a convincing entry in the Neapolitan crime subgenre.

The film puts together a memorable string of leads: the imposing, monumental Mario Merola faces Antonio Sabàto, who—as in *Napoli ... la camorra sfida la città risponde*—embraces the villain role with gusto, while Gianni Garko plays the special cop on the case, giving much-needed strength to a role that was often sacrificed in Neapolitan-based films, and Edmund Purdom (looking as disinterested as ever) pops up in a cameo as the head of Secret Service. There's even room for Merli-look-alike Jeff Blynn, here in one of his last screen roles before he gave up acting for good.

Conceived also for foreign market consumption (unlike most other films of the subgenre), *The New Godfathers* tries hard to be cosmopolitan. According to Ciro Ippolito's autobiography, the film was born to help P.A.C.'s head Mario Bregni recover the costs of Ferdinando Baldi's *The Sicilian Connection*, which had been a flop despite its high budget.

"'Dr. Bregni, I have an idea,' I said. 'What would that be?' he replied [...]. 'To recycle this flop by making a new low-budget movie, with another story, a different title, but using the same footage as Baldi's film.' [...] So I take this film [*The Sicilian Connection*] that no one has seen to the editing room, cut all of Ben Gazzara's close-ups from the sequences shot in the U.S. and put Mario Merola's face in their place. In two weeks, I shot a story about smugglers that demanded big action scenes, performed a footage transplant and the movie was done."[1]

As unlikely as this story may be (*The New Godfathers* was made seven years after Baldi's film), it's a fact that Brescia's film—which according to Ippolito cost just 70 million lira and was indeed shot in two weeks—recycles whole segments from *The Sicilian Connection*, starting with the opening sequences that have the story move from Iran to New York and then Istanbul. The script, by Ippolito and Piero Regnoli, deals with an international drug ring just like Castellari's *The Heroin Busters*: bad guy Antonio Sabàto is in cahoots with U.S. traffickers to smuggle a shipment of drugs that are hidden inside wedding candies. Brescia even incongruously poaches a spectacular stunt—a car jumping on a train—from Massimo Dallamano's *Colt 38 Special Squad* (another P.A.C. production) in order to give the film an action movie feel.[2] However, the core of *The New Godfathers* is typical sceneggiata stuff, convincingly done: the final showdown, where Merola yells to Sabàto "Eat these candies!" and an extreme close-up of Merola's gun fills the screen before Sabàto receives a load of bullets in slow motion, is first rate.

Ippolito and Brescia even throw in a few of their usual tongue-in-cheek in-jokes: in a scene, Gianni Garko and Marco Girondino (playing his mandatory street urchin role) stop before a poster of Brescia's tear-jerking drama *Lo scugnizzo* (starring Girondino) for a gratuitous bit of not-so-occult self-promotion, before Brescia himself pops up for an amusing cameo, looking at the poster's credits and coming up with the line: "Who the f**k is this Alfonso Brescia guy?").

Note

1. Ippolito, *Un napoletano a Hollywood*, p. 102.
2. Similarly, Eduardo Alfieri's score reuses cues from *Napoli ... serenata calibro 9* and *Napoli ... la camorra sfida la città risponde*.

Target *(Bersaglio altezza uomo / Hedef)*

D: Guido Zurli. *S:* Giampaolo Spagnesi [Erdoğan Tünaş], Guido Zurli; screenplay: Giampaolo Spagnesi [Erdoğan Tünaş], Ettore Sanzò, Guido Zurli; *DOP:* Cristiano Pogany (35mm, Gevacolor, Staco Film); *M:* Stelvio Cipriani (ed. C.A.M.); *E:* Giancarlo Venarucci; *PD:* Roberto Gentile; *CO:* Silvano Minotti; *C:* Luigi Quattrini; *AC:* Giovanni Marras;

AD: Giampaolo Spagnesi; *MU:* Lamberto Marini; *SO:* Alvaro Buzi, Umberto Picistrelli; *Boom:* Silvio Spingi. *Cast:* Luc Merenda (Inspector Keaton [Turkish version: Kemal]), Gabriella Giorgelli (Jasmine [Yasemine]), Kadir Inanir (Gengis [Cengiz]), Paola Senatore (Gangster's lover), Pamela Villoresi (Gengis' wife), Joe Pidgeon [Giuseppe Colombo], Tancu Kennedy [Tanju Gürsu] (Şinasi), Attilio Severini (police informer). *Uncredited:* Reha Yurdakul, Hüseyin Baradan, Tülay Karaca, Kayhan Yıldızoğlu, Sümer Tilmaç, Kadir Kök, Muammer Gözalan, Orhan Elmas, Süheyl Eğriboz, Kudret Karadağ, İhsan Gedik, fiemsi İnkaya, Hakkı Kıvanç, Murat Erton, Tevfik Şen, Yadigar Ejder, Mehmet Yağmur, Mehmet Uğur, Osman Han, Günay Güner, Mustafa Yavuz. *PROD:* Giuseppe Colombo, Nino Serafini, Türker Inanoglu for Intercine (Rome), Sword Film (Rome), Erler Film (Istanbul); *PM:* Giuseppe Colombo; *UM:* Gianfranco Fornari. *Country:* Italy / Turkey. Filmed at Incir—De Paolis (Rome) and on location in Turkey. *Running time:* 89'; Visa no.: 73132 (02.22.1979); *Rating:* v.m.18; *Release date:* 03.09.1979; *Distribution:* Orange; *Domestic gross:* unknown. *Also known as: Deckname Skorpion* (West Germany). *Home video:* Avofilm (VHS, Italy)

On a mission in Istanbul, Inspector Keaton of Interpol disrupts the activities of a powerful drug lord and his accomplices. To get rid of Keaton, the gangsters blackmail skeet shooting champion Gengis into shooting at Keaton. First they kill his mother, then kidnap and rape his wife. In agreement with Keaton, Gengis pretends to do what the gangsters demand. Then, together with the inspector, he collaborates on the gang's final defeat.

The fact that in 1979 poliziotteschi was rapidly declining is perhaps best represented by Guido Zurli's *Target*, a cheaply made Italian/Turkish production that nonetheless features one of the genre's iconic faces—Luc Merenda. Within a couple of years the French actor had moved from being a profitable box office asset (see Massi's *Destruction Force*) to a B-movie name (Aristide Massaccesi's grim adventure film *Tough to Kill*), and as the production of crime flicks started to rapidly diminish, his career rapidly went downhill.

In Zurli's film, Merenda is not even the lead, despite being labeled as such in Italian prints: the French actor was initially on set for just three days, while the true protagonist is local star Kadir Inanir as the skeet shooting champion Gengis, who gets blackmailed by a gang of drug traffickers set in Istanbul and forced to become a hitman. The titular target is tough cop Merenda, who's survived a number of killing attempts. "Merenda actually became the co-protagonist, even though he didn't realize it while we were shooting" Zurli recalled. "He just had fun making the film, he liked Istanbul, being on the motorboat on the Bosporus and so on (laughs). Eventually, when he realized I'd made him do about half of the movie in one week's shooting, he told me "Look, if we ever meet again I'm gonna cross to the other side of the street! It's not possible to work this way!"[1] Next year, Merenda would play a caricature of sorts of his favorite character (and himself) in Tinto Brass' outstanding *Action* (1980), before virtually disappearing from sight, with the exception of a few sparse cameos (mostly in comic films, such as *Superfantozzi*, 1986, and *Missione eroica—I pompieri 2*, 1987).

As an example of the circumstances under which the film was shot, Zurli revealed that the film's executive producer, Giuseppe Colombo, was actually an actor in the film (billed as Joe Pidgeon, the literal translation of his name!). "I told Giuseppe (it was he who introduced me to the Italian producer, Spada, at a party at Isarco Ravaioli's house), 'Listen, it's useless we carry so many people, you act as executive producer!' 'But I can't do it' 'I'll teach you, don't worry.' And so we did, and later he became a famous film producer."[2]

However, *Target* has very little to recommend about it. The opening titles, which seem to come straight from some 1960s spy-action flick, are colored and naive in an endearing way, but the *mise en scène* is quite poor, with dull chases over the roofs and in the streets of Istanbul (with passers-by looking directly into the camera), lots of voice-overs stitched to long shots of actors walking around town, a Grand-Guignol murder sequence in a shower that hints at *Psycho* and one scene where the actors, sitting on a terrace by the seaside, are busier resisting the strong wind than delivering their lines. What's more, the script revolves around an unlikely, conceited premise, as the gangsters try every bad trick in the book to persuade Gengis—first they kill his mother, then they kidnap and rape his wife (Pamela Villoresi)—for a task that any skilled hitman could have reasonably performed.

The emphasis on sleaze was a characteristic of co-writer Ettore Sanzò, as in Aldo Lado's *Night Train Murders* or Franco Prosperi's *Terror!* Sanzo would recycle Pamela Villoresi's rape scene in his script for Lucio Fulci's *The Smuggler*. Zurli recalled that he chose Pamela Villoresi because she was a committed stage actress, but he thought she wouldn't accept a role in a genre film. "Actually, with Pamela I didn't want to shoot something too risqué. She was a good actress however, and never refused to do a scene ... she fell in love with director of photography Cristiano Pogany on the set, and then they got married."[3]

The female presences are rather sad-looking. The once ravishing Gabriella Giorgelli—Colombo's girlfriend at that time—looks faded and overweight, while Paola Senatore has a vacuous stare as she indifferently offers her naked body for the camera. Within a few years, due to her heroin addiction and financial problems, she was reduced to making hardcore: scenes from her only porn film, *Non stop sempre buio in sala* (1985, by Arduino Sacco) were re-used for another h/c film, *La sfida erotica* (1985, by Luigi Soldati), released while the actress was in jail.

Notes

1. Grattarola, "Il dissacratore dei generi," p. 43. Gabriele Ferzetti, who was originally cast in a small role, left the set before filming even one scene—according to Zurli, because he didn't like Turkey.
2. *Ibid.*, p. 42.
3. *Ibid.*

1980

Attenti a quei due napoletani—Sabotaggio a Napoli (Beware of Those Two Neapolitans)

D: Roy Garrett [Mario Gariazzo]. *S* and *SC:* Mario Gariazzo; *DOP:* Aldo Greci (35mm, Eastmancolor, Microstampa); *M:* Tony Iglio, conducted by the author (Ed. Piccola Vela); *E:* Vincenzo Tomassi; *PD:* Filippo Rizzelli; *CO:* Lorenzo Loreto; *C:* Roberto Romei; *AE:* Domenico Varone; *AD:* Stelio Fiorenza; *MU:* Pasquale Errico; *SO:* Giuseppe Battaglia; *Mix:* Franco Bassi; *SP:* Salvatore Caccavale; *ChEl:* Andrea

Guarino; *KG:* Giuseppe Argento; *SS:* Domenico D'Ercole. *Cast:* Pino Mauro (Pino), Billy White [Mario Garbetta] (Agent Tony Naples), Marisa Reichlin (Lisa), Franco Marino (Thug), Patrizia Albano, Gabriella Di Luzio, Enzo Berri, Roberto Garbetta (first kid at the dock), Bruno Garbetta (second kid at the dock), Alberto Amato, Alfonso Balido, Pino Battaglia, Vittorio Calandra, Ciro Cafano, Francesco Cocciola, Ferdinando Conturso, Assunta Costanzo, Ferdinando Di Lena, Vincenzo Laricchia, Luigi Mazzullo, Antonio Silvestri. *PROD:* Mario Garbetta for Cin. Ed. (Naples); *GM:* Fabio Diotallevi; *PM:* Franco Marino; *PSe:* Federico Irace. *Country:* Italy. Filmed on location in Naples. *Running time:* 85'; Visa no.: 75821 (10.31.1980); *Rating:* not rated; *Release date:* 12.04.1980; *Distribution:* Regional; *Domestic gross:* unknown. *Home video:* Azzurro (VHS, Italy)

A gang of saboteurs is trying to stop NATO's Zodiac missile project: the first launch has been sabotaged and a secret agent who collected evidence on the saboteurs has been killed. In Washington, D.C., Italian-American secret agent Tony Naples is entrusted with a mission to find the top secret documents that disclose the heads of the criminal organization. In Naples, disguised as a priest, Tony teams up with a local agent-cum-singer, Pino. Together they hatch a plan to sneak into a villa of a wealthy man, kill him and break into his safe for the documents. Their enemies find out and set a trap, but to no avail. They do manage, however, to kidnap Pino's fellow agent Lisa, but the two friends eventually release her—only to find out that Lisa is actually double-crossing them, as they discover after a second kidnapping attempt. Tony and Pino find the documents and destroy the organization, led by a pacifist scientist.

"That film was born by accident," Mario Gariazzo told *Nocturno* magazine, speaking of *Attenti a quei due napoletani*. "There was a dear friend of mine from Naples, Mario Garbetta (also known as Billy White), who sold paintings on TV. He asked me to make a movie with him. Since I was very busy, I persuaded him to take part in a project I was involved with, *Guapparia* [which eventually came out as *Onore e guapparia*, Author's note] by Tiziano Longo [...]. On that film's set I met Neapolitan singer Pino Mauro and we decided to make *Attenti a quei due napoletani*." The film's genesis gives an idea of the way lower-grade genre cinema worked those days.

The Italian title pays reference to the TV series *The Persuaders* starring Tony Curtis and Roger Moore (broadcast in Italy as *Attenti a quei due*). However, besides Mario Garbetta's passing resemblance to Tony Curtis (something that definitely can't be said of his co-star Pino Mauro, whose hair is dyed blonde for the occasion), Gariazzo's film has obviously nothing to do at all with its model, being a Z-grade comic book style spy/action flick. The budget is so miserable that we are treated with plenty of stock footage (in a desperate attempt to give the film an international feel), such as the opening sequence set in a "Missile Base in the Mediterranean Sea," as a line informs us, while most scenes are shot either in hotel rooms or in nightclubs and other sites which granted their sponsorship, in typical Italian z-movie fashion. The plot is so rickety that it gets unraveled in hasty expository dialogue between the protagonists, but Gariazzo leaves his two stars ample room to display their ego. Garbetta gets to talk about his favorite subject—paintings—and has his two sons make a "special appearance" (as proudly stated in the credits) as a pair of street urchins, while Mauro gets to sing several songs, including his piece de resistance *Guapparia* in front of an ecstatic audience.

Note

1. Manlio Gomarasca and Davide Pulici, "Il venditore di stelle: Intervista a Mario Gariazzo," *Nocturno Cinema* #3 (1995), p. 18.

The Blue Eyed Bandit (Il bandito dagli occhi azzurri)

D: Alfredo Giannetti. *S* and *SC:* Alfredo Giannetti; *DOP:* Alberto Spagnoli (35mm, Eastmancolor, Telecolor); *M:* Ennio Morricone (Ed. C.A.M.); *E:* Gianfranco Amicucci; *PD:* Giantito Burchiellaro; *CO:* Rosalba Menichelli; *APD:* Giovanni Natalucci; *C:* Giuseppe Maccari; *AC:* Enzo Frattari; *AE:* Piero Tomassi; *2nd AE:* Livia Rava; *MU:* Gianfranco Mecacci; *Hair:* Giuseppina Bovino; *SO:* Andrea Moser; *SOEng:* Sergio Marcotulli; *ASOEng:* Marco Streccioni; *SP:* Carola Saltamerenda; *SS:* Carla Giarè. *Cast:* Franco Nero (Renzo Dominici), Dalila Di Lazzaro (Stella), Carlos de Carvalho (police commissioner), Pier Francesco Poggi (Stella's lover), Luigi Montini (Brigadeer Mannella), Sergio Tabor (Palamitessa, the canteen's head), Paolo Maria Scalondro (policeman), Jole Fierro (Dominici's mother), Fabrizio Bentivoglio (Riccardo a.k.a. Rick), Giovanni Javarone [Franco Iavarone] (The Watchman), Luigi Di Gianni, Aligi Culot, Gilda Vivenzio. *Uncredited:* Mickey Knox (De Biase, Dominici's head), Ettore Martini, Carlo Gabriel Sparanero (Renzo as a child), Luciano Zanussi (worker at CI EMME I). *PROD:* Enzo Doria and Francesco Cerami for T.E.I. Film International (Rome); *PM:* Antonio Segurini; *PSu:* Vito Di Bari, *PSe:* Antonio Spoletini; *Accountant cashier:* Ernesto Poli. *Country:* Italy. Filmed on location in Genoa. *Running time:* 98'; Visa no.: 75515 (08.07.1980); *Rating:* not rated; *Release date:* 08.07.1980; *Distribution:* Martino (regional); *Domestic gross:* 407,000,000 lira. *Also known as: Den blåøyde banditten* (Norway—video title), *Der Bandit mit den blauen Augen* (West Germany), *Der Bandit mit den schwarzblauen Augen* (West Germany—video title), *Le Bandit aux yeux bleus* (France). *Home video:* Mondial Video, New Video Promotion (VHS, Switzerland—Italian language). OST: CD CAM CSE 099.

Renzo Dominici, an employee in a firm in Genoa, leads a double life: in public he is crippled, helpless and mild, and wears contact lenses to conceal his magnetic blue eyes. In a private he is an athletic criminal who's preparing the robbery of the century against the company that employs him. A fellow worker, Stella, vainly tries to seduce him, whereas Dominici usually goes to a Turkish bath populated by homosexuals, where he entices a gay attendant, Riccardo. When he finally goes into action, Renzo makes sure everyone notices his blue eyes so that no one could identify the timid employee as the bandit. He robs two and a half billion lira, and prepares to flee by boat in a few days. However, something goes wrong: during the heist, he loses a lighter which is found by Stella, who sets out to blackmail him with her lover, Palamitessa. A watchman also notices a detail, a pair of cuffs on Renzo's shirt, and realizes he's the robber. Dominici kills the watchman, then locks Palamitessa in a freezing cell. He also gets rid of Stella, but he's recognized by Riccardo, who follows him home with a pair of accomplices. The police eventually discover Dominici's secret, but it's too late. Renzo is already on a boat en route to Panama.

Despite a title that sounds like a reference to the real-life Renato Vallanzasca, *The Blue Eyed Bandit* is an escapist and definitely *rétro* affair, centered on a Clark Kent of sorts, a modest clerk who's actually a criminal mastermind worthy of Arséne Lupin or Fantômas. The fact that Alfredo Giannetti's film takes place in contemporary Genoa, amidst poliziotteschi's typical landscapes, only underlines its comic-book like qualities: the titular bandit has a poster on a wall which says "get to Hawaii," and his main goal is to leave all behind—his mediocre life, his demented hospitalized mother, his country....

As directed by Giannetti (who formerly co-scripted a number of Pietro Germi's films, including the Academy Award–winning *Divorce—Italian Style*), *The Blue Eyed Bandit* has little to do with the crime films of the past decade, and harks back to the 1960's adventurous heist flicks. Nevertheless, it maintains a curious ambiguity on his character's motivations and personality, even going so far as playing with Franco Nero's assured sex appeal—starting with the very title and the film's central image, the actor's pale blue eyes in close-up in the robbery scene—by introducing a curious homoerotic subtext (which becomes explicit in the very last scene).

As punctuated by Ennio Morricone's suitably jazzy score, the film works best as a reflection on an actor's work as a matter of illusion: Franco Nero's character Renzo Dominici is like a thesp who's rehearsing for his stage debut. He adopts two distinct personalities, practices method acting (even wearing a specially modified shoe in order to get a limp), wears elaborate make-up, camouflages his real features in a secret room which looks like a theatre dressing room, and finally disappears through a trap-door from the stage where he performed his one-man show.

Even though Giannetti's direction is perfunctory at times, and the script looks like it needed a couple more drafts, the final result has an air of playfulness that makes it endearing despite its limits. Besides Nero's amusing (and amused) performance (with lines such as "I was born with a mustache!"), the film benefits from a memorably sluttish Dalila Di Lazzaro in a lowbrow, proletarian role as Renzo's sex-hungry co-worker and a slimy, ambiguous Fabrizio Bentivoglio (soon to become one of Italy's most popular actors), whose weird relationship with Nero is the pretext for a shameless plug for a men's perfume brand.

Buitres sobre la ciudad, a.k.a. *Avvoltoi sulla città* (Vultures Over the City)

D: Gianni Siragusa. *S* and *SC:* José María Forqué, Bruno Fontana, Gianni Siragusa; *DOP:* Raul Pérez Cubero (35mm, Eastmancolor, Telecolor); *M:* Stelvio Cipriani (Ed. C.A.M.); *E:* Maruja [María Luisa] Soriano, Otello Colangeli; *PD:* Wolfgang Burman. *Cast:* Maurizio Merli (Mark Spencieri), Hugo Stiglitz (Theo), Lilli Carati (Isela), Eduardo Fajardo (Valery Bonardis), Manolo [Manuel] Zarzo (Spagliari, Trillat's associate), Fernando Sánchez Polack (Cullen), Alejandro Enciso [de Enciso] (Jacques Trillat), Francisco Braña (Haddon), José Riesgo, Mel Ferrer (Commissioner), Francisco Rabal (Bender), Nadiuska [Roswicha Bertasha Smid Honczar] (Denise Marciano), María Alvarez, José Margo, Carmen Martinez Sierra, Anastasio Campoy. *PROD:* Luís Mendez for Lotus Films (Madrid), Cooperativa Cinematografica Internazional Zeta Film (Rome); *PM:* Enrique Bellot. *Country:* Spain / Italy. Filmed on location in Madrid. *Running time:* 85'. *Home video:* Polygram (VHS, Spain).

Madrid. A sniper assassinates wealthy oil tycoon Niarchos at the inauguration of an oil plant. Convinced that this will be the most important case in his professional life, journalist Mark Spensieri begins to investigate, not listening to the fears of his girlfriend Isela. Mark is summoned by a wealthy woman, Denise Marciano, whose husband has disappeared, and is offered a huge sum to find the man. When a body is found in a river, Mark recognizes him as Mr. Marciano, but, much to his surprise, Denise denies the dead man is her husband. Convinced that the two deaths are linked, Mark keeps investigating with the help of fellow photographer Theo: he pays a visit to Marciano's associate Haddon, and soon finds himself threatened and tailed. His car is then blown up by a pair of thugs. Spensieri finds himself involved in a gang war between local Mafia and a gang from Marseille for the control of the oil business—the latter controlled by a politician, Bonardis. When Mark gets too close to the truth, he is badly beaten, while Isela is raped. Everything is against Spensieri, as even the police threaten to deport him from the country as an undesirable person, but now the case has become a personal matter for Mark, who wants revenge. He kidnaps and tortures Bender to make him confess the name of the person behind it all, but the Marseillaise gang kidnap Isela and ask Mark to swap the hostages. Mark agrees, but something goes wrong during the exchange, and a fierce shoot-out ensues during which Isela and Bender are both killed. Mark won't stop at anything to get his revenge. In the end, it turns out he is an undercover cop on a secret mission.

Merli's last crime film was a Spanish-Italian co-production (the Italian company was the same that produced *Seagulls Fly Low*), written by the veteran José María Forqué and shot in Madrid with a largely Spanish-speaking cast. Despite its rich cast, *Buitres sobre la ciudad* wasn't even released in Italy, while it was a good box office success in Mexico and South America, according to the director Gianni Siragusa. "The Italian co-producer went bankrupt, and at that point the Iberian co-producer, with my permission, prepared the Spanish language edition and distributed throughout the world but not in Italy" Siragusa explained. "The film was later bought for domestic distribution by a company that asked me to do the dubbing. The problem was that the negative was still in Spain. The Spanish producer said 'OK, but you have to give me the money that the Italian co-producer owed me...' and eventually they didn't reach an agreement. I even proposed to use the 35mm positive print, which is very good, and elaborate it electronically, but the Italian buyer disappeared. Now the rights belong to a producer, Scino Glam, who's also got a fully edited copy, as he bought all the material. There's even a scene with an explosion we did using models, which cost a lot of money and was quite well done—we shot it in Italy and it was not included in the Spanish cut. I have all the dialogue ready for dubbing: even if I'm paid just a small sum, I'll do it."[2]

The sad commercial destiny that *Buitres sobre la ciudad* met in Italy is indicative of the genre's quick commercial decline in its home country. Bungling and weighed down by Siragusa's slapdash direction, *Buitres sobre la ciudad* saddles Merli with the character of an unlikely reporter who—in a very bad final twist which comes out of nowhere in the film's last 30 seconds—is revealed to be a police captain in disguise. The final shot, with Merli leaving in the sunset while his pal Hugo Stiglitz is told the truth by the police inspector (a mortiferous Mel Ferrer, who in that same period was shooting Lenzi's *Nightmare City* in Madrid, also co-starring Stiglitz) is a needless punchline to a film that deserved better. The main ingredients of crime films Italian-style are all there: urban violence, fistfights, car chases, the hero being beaten and the girl being raped—here the two scenes are cross-edited to singularly unpleasant effect—even the customary J&B plug

("You have good taste in preferring my whisky to that of the bar down below," Frank Braña tells Merli while pouring a glass of J&B for his guest; "Wonderful" the hero agrees). Forqué's script even throws a political angle into the story, with the character of corrupt politician Eduardo Fajardo, hinting at some old-style social commitment. Yet *Buitres sobre la ciudad* never really takes off, mostly because of bad filmmaking: stunts and action scenes are clumsy (take Merli's ambush by a pair of pygmy thugs as he's coming out of a building), the editing is rough and hasty (a car chase starts in the centre of Madrid, then suddenly moves to the open countryside, just in time for a car to fall down a suitably placed cliff), and the plot is needlessly snatchy, turning in its third act into some sort of a vigilante revenge flick after the hero has his girlfriend (Lilli Carati) killed before his own eyes.

The anonymous Madrid setting does not help: the metropolitan urgency of 1970s films gets lost, while the opening scenes at the plant incongruously recall Bruno Mattei's *Hell of the Living Dead* (which was shot on the same site). Merli does his own impression, on autopilot: menacing looks, clenched jaw, and so on. He even extinguishes a cigar on Francisco Rabal's cheek to show how mean he is. But he looks tired and unconvincing throughout, and that's not a good sign. As for Lilli Carati, Siragusa claimed: "She was very good in the film, also because I had her work just two hours a day. She just couldn't make it to the set before noon. She had a drug problem...."[2] Carati's career would go downhill in the following years, culminating in a brief foray into hardcore porn, an arrest for drug possession and a pair of suicide attempts in the late 1980s, before the actress went into rehab. She recently returned on set for a film slated to be released in 2013.

Notes

1. Davide Pulici, "Il tuttofare," in Aa. Vv., "Misteri d'Italia 4," *Nocturno Cinema* #103 (March 2011), p. 79.
2. *Ibid.*

Day of the Cobra (*Il giorno del cobra*)

D: Enzo G. Castellari [Enzo Girolami]. *S:* Aldo Lado; *SC:* Fabio Carpi, Tito Carpi, Aldo Lado; *DOP:* Giovanni Bergamini (35mm, Eastmancolor, Technicolor); *M:* Paolo Vasile, conducted by Gianni Mazza (Ed. Grandi Firme della Canzone); *E:* Gianfranco Amicucci; *PD:* Stefano Maria Ortolani; *APD:* Livia Del Priore; *CO:* Carlo Carunchio; *AC:* Giancarlo Granatelli, Carlo Passari; *AE:* Roberto Amicucci, Stefania Falsetti; *AD:* Giuseppe Giglietti; *MU:* Giovanni Morosi; *Hair:* Giusy Bovino; *SO:* Giorgio Pallotta; *Boom:* Maurizio Merli; *Mix:* Gianni D'Amico; *SE:* Dino [Cataldo] Galliano; *PrM:* Vincenzo Visone; *KG:* Alberto Bertuccioli; *ChEl:* Sante Federici; *LT:* Vittorio Contino; *W:* Lucia Baldacci; *SP:* Gianfranco Salis; *Stunt sequences:* Rocco Lerro; *ST:* Claudio Pacifico, Angelo Ragusa; *MA:* Rocco Lerro; *SS:* Marisa Agostini. *Cast:* Franco Nero (Larry Stanziani "The Cobra"), Sybil Danning (Brenda), Mario Maranzana (David), Licinia Lentini (Lola Alberti / Ivan Radovic), Enio Girolami (Martino), Mickey Knox (Raul Papasian), Massimo Vanni (Beltrame), William Berger (Jack Goldsmith), Romano Puppo (Silvestri), Angelo Ragusa (Kandinsky's killer), Sasha D'Arc (Blond assassin), Carlo Gabriel Sparanero (Tim). *Uncredited:* Giovanni Bonadonna (Wardrobe guard at Nightclub), Enzo G. Castellari (Kandisky's thug at the fish market), Stefania Girolami (Papasian's secretary), Rocco Lerro (Smith), Benito Pacifico (Warehouse worker), Claudio Pacifico (Hitman), Michele Soavi (Serge Kandinsky); Franco Ukmar (Mechanic), Luciano Zanussi. *PROD:* Turi Vasile for Laser Film; *EP:* Fabrizio De Angelis; *PM:* Paolo Vasile; *PSu:* Maurizio Ciarnò; *ADM:* Roberto Luvisotti Jr. *Country:* Italy. Filmed at Incir–De Paolis (Rome) and on location in San Francisco and Genoa. *Running time:* 95': Visa no.: 75482 (08.04.1980); *Rating:* not rated; *Release date:* 08.12.1980; *Distribution:* Cinema International Corporation; *Domestic gross:* 489,000,000 lira. *Also known as: Cobra* (Paris, 03.02.1983 — 95')—*Der Tag der Kobra* (12.25.1981— 95'). *Home video:* Hobby&Work, Sony (DVD, Italy). OST: LP Cinevox MDF 33-141.

An American narcotics agent is murdered in Italy. The head of the department Jack Goldsmith hires Larry "The Cobra" Stanziani—a former cop kicked off the police force and sentenced to three years in prison for an unjust accusation of complicity with the Mafia—to carry on the investigation. Larry, who now earns his living as a seedy private investigator in San Francisco, agrees to go to Genoa to look for Serge Kandinsky, his ultimate enemy, who is suspected to have eliminated the agent, but Larry also longs to meet his little son Tim, whom he enrolled in a local boarding school after the death of his wife. In Genoa, Stanziani meets the wealthy businessman Papasian, and through his old friend David he learns that Kandinsky is the co-owner of a nightclub, the Astoria, with a certain Lola Alberti, a drug addict. From Papasian, he also learns that Kandinsky is a homosexual and has a lover, a certain Ivan Radovic. Larry ends up in bed with Brenda, a DJ at Lola's club, who tells him that Kandinsky is blackmailing Papasian, who's his secret associate, because of the latter's shady business. A severe beating from Kandinsky's men at the fish market doesn't stop Larry, who uncovers evidence that Papasian is involved in an International drug ring. Stanziani is in for a big surprise, as the curvaceous Lola turns out to be none other than Ivan Radovic in drag. Brenda kills Ivan just as he's about to dispatch Larry. After Brenda's been beaten by Papasian's right-hand man Martino, Larry confronts the businessman, but Papasian is killed before his very eyes. The solution to the mystery is in a safe in a Swiss bank where vital information on the drug ring is kept, and which must be opened with two keys: Papasian had one, but who has the other? Kandinsky's men try to kidnap Larry's son, who is accidentally run over by a truck. Mad with grief, the Cobra goes on a rampage, only to find out that Kandisky has been murdered too, and that Brenda is the one who wants him dead. After a lethal encounter with the woman, the Cobra gets back to San Francisco to settle the score with the head of the drug ring: his old pal Jack Goldsmith.

1980: the dusk of the "poliziotteschi." The seventies ended in blood with the killing of Aldo Moro, the eighties began with another bomb and 75 dead at the Bologna station, on August 2, 1980. The crime genre was on the wane, and the tone was crepuscular. In *The Rebel,* Stelvio Massi sent his lonely, raging cop away from Italy, as did Umberto Lenzi in 1979's *From Corleone to Brooklyn.* Enzo Castellari does the opposite, and returns to Genoa, the genre's virtual capital and the director's favorite location since 1973's *High Crime.* On *Day of the Cobra,* Castellari not just revisits Genoa in a *film noir* key, but he also faces his own past in the genre and draws the whole crime film season to an ideal conclusion.

"I was offered to direct the film by Turi Vasile, a renowned playwright and a very cultured man," Castellari would explain. "We got in touch because I wanted to make a movie set in the boxing world, and Vasile was interested in the idea. I found a story and wrote a script with Vasile's son [...] but the project was shelved — I don't remember why. [...] Then Vasile offered me *Day of the Cobra*, which was written by Aldo Lado, who also was initially supposed to direct it."[1]

To begin with, Castellari surrounds himself with familiar faces, also in the literal sense of the word: besides Franco Nero and the director's habitual stuntmen/villains Rocco Lerro, Massimo Vanni, Romano Puppo, he once again casts his own brother Enio and his daughter Stefania. The latter plays a young, cute secretary with a Bo Derek hairdo, allowing for a nice cinephile joke when Franco Nero flirts with her ("10 : 10 and even praise!"). Castellari himself pops up in a small role as a thug who humiliates the Cobra, having the hero literally submerged with crates of fish after he has been harshly beaten: "Cover him, it's cold," he sneers. There's even room for Castellari's trademark grim in-jokes, when Massimo Vanni is shot in the balls from below in slow motion. The effect is that of a warm, somehow nostalgic homecoming.

Yet there's no trace of the police in the city of Genoa as depicted in *Day of the Cobra*, whereas they were fighting a non-stop war against drug traffickers in *High Crime*, and proved disappointing ineffectual in 1974's *Street Law*. Times have changed, indeed. Aldo Lado's original story was set in Trieste, immediately after World War II. Depicting a city where widespread lawlessness turned into a social system during the troubled post-war period was a matter of historical observation, but choosing to move the action to present times implies a judgment on a country that's gone adrift.

"It's not San Francisco, but it looks a bit like it" says the shady Papasian: and the city seems populated almost exclusively by drug traffickers, hitmen, assorted thugs. There are chases, shootings, killings on roofs, amongst the alleys, in fish markets and fishy nightclubs, without a single cop ever popping up. Castellari's Genoa in *Day of the Cobra* looks just like the post-apocalyptic, dilapidated New York City of the director's subsequent post-atomic "Bronx diptych" (*1990: The Bronx Warriors*, 1982; *Escape from the Bronx*, 1983). The idea of a city dominated by violence is masterfully synthesized in the opening shot: the Genoan skyline, with ships attacked at the docks and cars riding on the "Sopraelevata," is suddenly obscured by the extreme close-up of the barrel of a gun which is being loaded. "I wanted to see the city from inside the barrel, and it was quite hard to do. [...] Had I shot the film a few years later, I would have used a Snorkel camera, which is as thin as a tube and can even get inside a keyhole ... then I would have started the scene *inside* the barrel, as if it was a gallery, looking at the city from there; then the camera would have slowly retreated while the bullet came in, and we'd see the character loading the gun."[2]

For Larry Stanziani a.k.a. "The Cobra" (Franco Nero) as well, returning to Genoa is nothing short of a showdown with his past. The Cobra is a refugee, who escaped from his country and his memories. Expelled from the Narcotics Bureau, he opened a shabby investigating agency in San Francisco, and earns a living by tailing unfaithful wives (one of whom turns out to be a lesbian, much to the Cobra's sardonic and self-deprecating humor: "Don't worry, there's no other man in your wife's life" he assures his client). Stanziani is an out of time antihero, a modern-day Marlowe more in the vein of *The Long Goodbye*'s Elliott Gould than Bogart.

"I wanted to shape the film as a homage to Chandler" Castellari states. "The opening scenes in Chinatown, the detective's small office ... they're all precise homages. I'd have really loved to make it a true *film noir*, but I only managed to get close: as much as I could with the sets, the way of shooting some scenes ... and of course with the main character, who was so romantic."[3] Castellari introduces him with humorous tones, such as in the scene where Stanziani receives a phone call from a woman who wants him to find her missing puppy dog (Stanziani pretends to have a non-existent secretary and writes his client's phone number on the dirty wall of his tiny kitchen-cum-office cubicle). Even Stanziani's evocative nickname seems to be an ironic counterpoint to the detective's down-on-his-luck appearance and behavior. Larry keeps a rubber ball in his pocket as an anti-stress device, consumes an incommensurate amount of chewing gum — which he unwraps, chews, spits out or sticks around in a non-stop compulsive frenzy — as a palliative for smoking, wears a rumpled coat and hat which he puts on as soon as he gets out of bed. At first, Stanziani looks like a walking cliché, an impression he manages to cancel as the story goes on.

A hitman (Sasha D'Arc) in action in *Day of the Cobra* (1980).

One of the most interesting things about *Day of the Cobra* is the idiosyncratic way Castellari deals with *film noir* stereotypes: he pays homage to them, only to subvert them when we least expect it. Take Kandinsky, the Cobra's mysterious arch-enemy: black raincoat, a club foot, an animated cane which he uses to dispatch his adversaries, he looks like a Luciferian counterpart to Stanziani. According to the rules, we expect the two to eventually meet for a last-minute showdown, so that we finally get to see Kandinsky's face (as Castellari's reticence in showing it seemingly hints at a surprise revelation). But this does not happen: Kandinsky dies when one least expects it, and his face remains unknown and unseen even post-mortem. However, film buffs will be delighted to know that the mysterious figure is played by none other than a very young Michele Soavi.

Another clever infringement to genre rules concerns the gorgeous Lola (Licinia Lentini), the long-legged, curvaceous entertainer in Kandinsky's nightclub. Introduced as a typical femme fatale, she turns out to be none other than Ivan, a Russian transvestite (!) who's also an expert in martial arts—much to the Cobra's dismay, as he is KO'd by Ivan's lethal kicks in the face. The fight scene which follows, on the nightclub's dance floor, among stroboscopic lights and punchy disco music, is deliciously tongue-in-cheek: Ivan and Stanziani exchange forbidden blows and grips which look like surreal dance steps.[4] The score by Paolo Vasile is also on target, with the amusing (and infectiously catchy) title song almost hinting at self-parody.

However, despite the many humorous interludes—the most enjoyable being the aftermath of Stanziani's awakening after the memorable fish market beating: as the private eye awakes among smelly fish, takes a cab as if nothing has happened and goes to the nearest dry cleaner's—the film's pessimistic aftertaste is palpable. The most evident example is the death of Stanziani's little son (played by Nero's own son Gabriel),[5] which Castellari shows in a series of implacable, painful black-and-white still frames. What's more, *Day of the Cobra* is, as the essence of film noir demands, a tale of betrayals, perpetrated by trusted and beloved people. Stanziani comes out as a ghost who reemerges from a past ideal world which perhaps only existed in his imagination. He is a veteran who still feeds on delusions, despite his many scars, physical and metaphorical ("Who did that to you?" the film's dark lady Brenda (Sybil Danning) asks him in bed; "A friend," is his answer). He is the last romantic in a shark-infested world, an incorruptible among the corrupted. He is a survivor. No wonder Castellari's next step would be the post-atomic genre.

Notes

1. Grimaldi and Pulici, *Enzo G. Castellari*, p. 56.
2. *Ibid.*
3. *Ibid.*
4. Amusingly, the sequence was ripped off in an episode of the *Mike Hammer* TV series starring Stacy Keach.
5. Born in 1969, the son of Franco Nero and Vanessa Redgrave, Carlo Gabriel Sparanero became a director and screenwriter on his own: he has directed three films, *Larry's Visit* (1996), *L'escluso* (1999) and *The Fever* (2004, starring Vanessa Redgrave and Sparanero's stepsister Joely Richardson). In 1985 he also recorded a 7" with his father, *Will Change the World / Cambierà*.

Franco Nero, left, in a fight scene opposite Romano Puppo, with a Spanish lobby card for *Day of the Cobra* (1980).

The Iron Hand of the Mafia (*Mafia: una legge che non perdona*)

D: Bob Ghisais [Roberto Girometti]. *S* and *SC:* Roberto Girometti, Pelio Quaglia, Pierpaolo Lubrani; *DOP:* Roberto Girometti (35mm, Telecolor); *M:* Stelvio Cipriani (ed. C.A.M.); *E:* Luciano Anconetani; *PD:* Silvana Paoletti; *C:* Marcello Anconetani; *AC:* Giovanni Brescini; *AE:* Minni Marani; *AD:* Pierpaolo Lubrani; *MU:* Massimo Camilletti; *Hair:* Anna Berardi; *W:* Nadia Fabriani; *SP:* Firmino Palmieri; *SS:* Renata Franceschi. *Cast:* Jackie Basehart (Tony), Malisa Longo (Angela), Raffaele Fortunato (Don Raffaele Nocera), Gordon Mitchell (Don Nicola), Fabrizio Marani (Michel), Raffaele Cocomero (Tony's henchman), Giovanni Cocomero (police commissioner), Tony Scarf [Antonio Scarfone] (Giovanni Capuano), Gianni Diana (Giorgio), Antonio Sorrentino (Gangster buried in pouring concrete), Annabella Schiavone (Sic-Sic's wife), Tina Trapassi (Maria), Antonella Lualdi (Denise), Margie Moreau [Margit Evelyn Newton] (Teresa), Franco Angrisano (Sic-Sic), Antonio Angrisano (Coppola's son), Nino Senatore, Antonio Panciullo, Bruno Caputi, Bruno Venturini (Bruno, the singer). *PROD:* Nino Vendetti for Cabaret Film; *AP:* Enrico Santini; *GM:* Pelio Quaglia; *PM:* Nino Di Giambattista; *PSe:* Nino Vendetti Jr. *Country:* Italy. Filmed on location in Salerno. *Running time:* 79'; Visa no.: 75839 (11.10.1980); *Rating:* v.m.14; *Release date:* 11.28.1980; *Distribution:* Samanda (Regional); *Domestic gross:* unknown. *Home video:* RCA/Columbia (VHS, Italy).

Salerno. After the death of Don Enrico, the other bosses have to decide who is going to take his place. They gather at table after the funeral, and agree that the favorite name is that of Don Raffaele Nocera, who nevertheless refuses because he wants to take care of his sick son Michel. A violent feud ensues, as all the other bosses are dispatched one by one by the power-thirsty Don Nicola. After don Enrico's nephew, Tony, survives an attack, Don Raffaele starts investigating to find out who's behind the murders; what he doesn't know is that Tony is actually the mastermind behind the killings. With the help of a local Commissioner, Don Raffaele locates the hitmen, but Tony's men kidnap his little son while the boy is with the Don's estranged wife. Nocera doesn't tell anything to the police and sets out to find the child by himself. Tony reveals to his girlfriend Angela that he's kidnapped Michel and asks her to take care of him, on a boat out at sea.

Don Raffaele is asked to pay a huge ransom in diamonds, but Tony has in mind to kill both Michel and Angela. Eventually Nocera locates the boat where the boy is being taken prisoner, while Angela kills Tony before he kills Michel.

Despite its title, there's no trace of the Mafia in Roberto Girometti's film—which should ring as a warning in itself. *The Iron Hand of the Mafia* is actually a sceneggiata, filled with all its typical elements, from cigarette smuggling to a blond boy with a poor health. Yet, as further proven by the grating comic relief (from Angrisano and Schiavone, playing a typically vocal and litigious Neapolitan couple), it's third-grade material. Even the lead Raffaele Fortunato—a stunted Merola look-alike, who according to Girometti helped the production to secure finance on location and "had a good face for the role"[1]—is a patent reminder of the film's formulaic nature: although he does not get to sing, another Neapolitan singer (Bruno Venturini) performs a couple of songs in the usual convivial context.

Compared to other Neapolitan-based flicks of the period, however, *The Iron Hand of the Mafia* has its share of nudity: besides a corny nightclub scene, the gorgeous Malisa Longo and Margit Evelyn Newton (here under a pseudonym) have ample occasions to display their bodies, but that's the film's only asset. Direction is poor, with an over-reliance on close-ups, sloppy continuity between day and night scenes and non-existent pacing: the only action sequence is a car crash which is actually recycled footage from *The Last Desperate Hours*. Violence is also mild: besides one scene where a boss is buried alive in cement, the story drags along at snail's pace, packed full of clichés, including a commissioner who says "The more criminals die, the less work we've left with" and a dialogue quoting *The Godfather*'s infamous "offer that cannot be refused."

Apart from Fortunato, the cast is clueless. Basehart, the son of the great Richard and Valentina Cortese, is a pale, uninteresting villain who's clearly more at ease in his sex scenes with the ladies than with the rest, while Mitchell—dubbed with a strong Neapolitan accent—has a cameo at the beginning as one of the Camorra bosses, then disappears for the rest of the picture.

Rather incredibly, *The Iron Hand of the Mafia* even had an English language version, although its circulation may have been very scarce. Girometti—a veteran director of photography—helmed two more films, both of them hardcore: *Le segrete esperienze di Luca e Fanny* (1980, co-starring Brigitte Lahaie and co-directed with Bernard Loubeau) and *Professione p … attrice* (1982).

Note

1. Email interview, May 2012.

Madness (Vacanze per un massacro)

D: Fernando di Leo. *S:* Mario Gariazzo; *SC:* Fernando di Leo; *DOP:* Enrico Lucidi (35mm, Eastmancolor); *M:* Luis Enriquez Bacalov; *E:* Amedeo Giomini; *PD:* Francesco Cuppini; *CO:* Carolina Ferrara; *AC:* Maurizio Lucchini; *AE:* Ornella Chistolini; *MU:* Giuseppe Ferranti, Gloria Granati; *Hair:* Placida Crapanzano, Lidia Puglia; *SO:* Goffredo Salvatori; *SP:* Mario Sabatelli; *SS:* Patrizia Amelia Zulini. *Cast:* Joe Dallesandro (Joe Brezzi), Lorraine De Selle (Paola), Patricia Bhen [Patrizia Behn] (Liliana), Gianni Macchia (Sergio). *PROD:* Armando Novelli for Midia Cinematografica; *PM:* Fabio Diotallevi; *PSu:* Vincenzo Samà. *Country:* Italy. Filmed at R.P.A. Elios Film. *Running time:* 86'; Visa no.: 74613 (01.25.1980); *Rating:* v.m.18; *Release date:* 03.07.1980; *Distribution:* Regional; *Domestic gross:* 25,300,000 lira. *Also known as: Toy* (West Germany). *Home video:* Raro (DVD, Italy).

After escaping from the Volterra prison, Joe Brezzi kills two men, steals a car and gets to the mountain cottage where he hid 300 million lira, the loot of a huge robbery, before he got arrested. However, he's interrupted by the arrival of the owners: a young couple, Sergio and Liliana, who have come to the house for a hunting weekend together with Liliana's younger sister, Paola. While waiting for the right moment to get the money, Joe spies on the three occupants and finds out about their secrets: Paola and Sergio, who pretend to hate each other in front of Liliana, are actually lovers. The next morning, while Sergio goes hunting and Liliana heads for the nearest village to buy supplies, Joe knocks Paola unconscious and sets about digging up the loot, which is buried under the fireplace. Joe and Paola have sex, but he ties her to the bed after she attempts to escape. Then it's Liliana's turn to be tied and gagged, and Sergio's to dig. Joe tells Liliana about her husband's affair with her sister. While Paola still tries to seduce him, Joe is somewhat moved by Liliana's grief, and forces the two lovers to have sex in front of him so that she realizes her husband's true nature. Paola persuades Sergio to kill Joe, get the money, and get rid of Liliana in the process. They attack Joe and Liliana while they are making love, but they both perish in the act. Joe asks Liliana to leave with him, but once he's outside the woman picks up Sergio's rifle and shoots him in the back.

After the ill-fated stab at sexual freedom (or rather, lack of) in post–1968 Italy that was *To Be Twenty* (1978), *Madness* was another work for hire as far as Fernando di Leo was concerned. It was based on a story written by Mario Gariazzo, to whom di Leo had offered script advice for *The Bloody Hands of the Law*, and whose *Holy Water Joe* (1971) and *Last Moments* (1974) were produced by di Leo's company Cineproduzioni Daunia 70. Gariazzo was also initially slated to direct. Shot in just twelve days, *Madness* was conceived as a low budget entry in a rather profitable subgenre, which included such titles as Franco Prosperi's *Terror* and Raimondo Del Balzo's *Midnight Blue* (1979). Di Leo himself was quite critical of the result: "It's a disappointing film indeed, including my toying with Lorraine De Selle's nude scenes. It's mediocre, but not because I did it wrong—I just wasn't interested in it. It often happens in a director's career that he's just a hired hand […]. You don't always have the chance to do what you want, and often you know very well you're making a bad movie, but you do it anyway." He added: "some small flicks, like *Madness*, were just bargains. The producer came and said: "I need a film, you have to do it in ten days, it must cost this much etc." and so […] I just did it."[1]

However, despite the obvious limitations—particularly evident in the opening sequence where Dallesandro escapes from prison by dangling from a rope, like in a 1930s film—the results are not as bad as one would think. Gariazzo's plotting hinges on a typical storyline à la *Desperate Hours*, which nurtured a whole subgenre in the past decade. Yet it's almost as if di Leo conceived Dallesandro's character as an answer to Terence Stamp's Visitor in Pasolini's *Teorema* (1968): an outsider whose presence brings eroticism and anarchy within an apparently solid family set up, which is actually crisscrossed by subterranean, unspeakable tensions and desires. Di Leo pushes the voyeurism and sexual ambiguity, thanks also to Dallesandro's magnetically physical screen presence: *Madness* was the last film the actor shot in Italy before returning to the States. The film's other sexual pole, Lorraine De Selle, is a memorably bitchy, animal-like dark lady, almost always naked. "A silly little snob," as her lover labels her.

Dallesandro and De Selle are the perfect counterpart for the other half of the cast. Gianni Macchia's character is a sexist pig—immediately nicknamed "asshole" by Dallasandro—who half-jokingly calls his wife and mistress "slaves," while Patricia Bhen's patent shortcomings as an actress ultimately help the film's sardonic, ant-bourgeois feel. Incidentally, Bhen—the producer's lover—appeared in just a couple more films: Mario Gariazzo's *Play Motel* (1979) and Alberto Cavallone's *La gemella erotica* (1980).

At times if feels as if the director is trying to sabotage the film, or at least to play jokes on the audiences: Dallesandro—dressed in jeans and a blue tank top and looking more like a laborer—introduces himself to an old man as an insurance salesman on the look for new clients to insure their homes against thieves. Later on Lorraine De Selle enters the film carrying a whole crate of J&B, in a shamelessly memorable plug. What's more, with posters of Marlon Brando in *Last Tango in Paris*, John Travolta and a monochrome James Dean from *Giant*, it almost looks like di Leo wanted to celebrate Dallesandro's unquestionable sex appeal. Of his experience with the former Factory superstar, di Leo recalled: "He was already cast in the lead, but I agreed because he was right for the part. He was an addict, so much so that you couldn't but feel sympathy for him. In the morning, as soon as he got on set, he drank three to five shots of cognac, then disappeared until I called him for his scenes and came back, full of dope, like a crazy horse [...]. However, he didn't miss a line. And at the end of the day he ran away, again like a crazy horse, to take some more drugs. Such a character, sweet, hearty, absolutely "out" was beloved by everyone, including myself [...]. What I remember most about *Madness* is Joe running towards me!"[2]

Despite its *film noir* appearance, *Madness* (which was released in Italy as *Vacanze per un massacro*—literally, Holidays for a Massacre, a title that originally belonged to an unfilmed Western script di Leo had penned in the 1970s) is essentially an erotic picture—that is, it's the erotic element that di Leo is more interested in. Take the scene where De Selle masturbates while Dallesandro spies on her—a patently superfluous interlude which becomes a lesson on eroticism on screen, thanks also to the use of the song *Dimenticare* by Roberto Soffici, which is playing on the radio (the use of diegetic music is a recurring trait in the film, while elsewhere, the director recycles bits from Luis Bacalov's score for *Caliber 9* and the memorable *Concerto grosso* from *The Designated Victim*)—or the rape scene, where, as usual in Italian 1970s films, the victim ends up enjoying the violence.

As a whole, *Madness* looks like a barely disguised *kammerspiel*: mostly shot in one location in the remote Abruzzi mountains, with the director making the best possible use of the shoestring budget. Although the slow-motion ending, which patently recalls Peckinpah's *Straw Dogs* in the exhibition of violence, is handled quite expertly, it remains perhaps the film's less convincing sequence, not to mention the hasty coda—too stereotyped and punitive for such a cliché-bashing director as di Leo.

Notes

1. Pulici, *Fernando di Leo*, p. 312.
2. *Ibid.*

The Rebel (*Poliziotto solitudine e rabbia*)

D: Stelvio Massi. *S:* Boschi Huber [and Massimo De Rita, uncredited]; *SC:* Boschi Huber, Art Bernd [and Massimo De Rita, Stelvio Massi, uncredited]; *DOP:* Pier Luigi Santi (35mm, Kodak, Staco Film); *M:* Stelvio Cipriani (Ed. C.A.M.); *E:* Mauro Bonanni (Italian version), Sybille Windt (German version); *PD:* Albrecht Konrad; *APD:* Francesco Raffa, Manfred Geber; *CO:* Beatrice Kothe; *C:* Maurizio Maggi, Aldo Bergamini; *AC:* Christian Karp; *AE:* Walter Diotallevi, Mario Recupito; *AD:* Frank Guarente, Riccardo Petrazzi; *MU:* Dante Trani, Caterina Campana, Susanne Schroeder; *SO:* Wolfgang Kapst, Davide Magara, Ronny Wurden; *Mix:* Sandro Occhetti; *W:* Anna Onori, Edith Pitann; *SE:* Mario Ciccarella; *ST:* Riccardo Petrazzi; *SS:* Beatrice Banfi, Maria Luisa Merci. *Cast:* Maurizio Merli (Nicola), Jutta Speidel (Vivien), Francisco Rabal (Tony), Reinhardt Kolldehoff (Hermann Stoll), Arthur Brauss (Klaus White), Benito Pacifico (Lucien), Ottaviano Dell'Acqua (Klaus' henchman), Bobby Rhodes (Mike "Jamaica"), Jako Benz, Maurizio Ferrara, Jochen Schroeder. *Uncredited:* Buddy Elias (Barman at the "Camelot"), Riccardo Petrazzi (Thug). *PROD:* Salvatore Smeriglio for Simba Film (Rome), Arthur Brauner for C.C.C. Filmkunst (Berlin); *GM:* Silvio Siano, Peter Hahne; *UM:* Anselmo Parrinello, Franco Mancarella, Luigi Scardino; *PSe:* Aldo Santalucia, Peter Wittchen, Michael Kersten; *PC:* Angelika Jendrusch. *Country:* Italy / West Germany. Filmed at CCC Filmkunst (Berlin) and on location in Formello, Venice and Berlin. *Running time:* 102'; Visa no.: 75540 (08.22.1980); *Rating:* v.m.14; *Release date:* 08.22.1980; *Distribution:* Medusa; *Domestic gross:* 508,000,000 lira. *Also known as: Il ribelle* (Italy, Home video), *Der Mann, der Venedig hiess* (West Germany, 02.20.1981—87'), *Knallharte Profis* (West Germany). *Home video:* Avo Film (VHS, Italy), Eureka (VHS, Italy—as *Il ribelle*). OST: CD Digitmovies CDDM228.

After the assassination of two prominent businessmen on a visit to Italy, Nicola, an ex-cop, is convinced by his friend Tony to assist in protecting a German banker who has arrived in Venice to forge a deal with a Murano glass factory. Nicola doesn't manage to avert the third murder, yet he does to capture one of the killer's accomplices. Nicola takes his place and sets up a phony escape, then moves to West Berlin and gets in touch with the dangerous criminal organization behind the killings. He gets hooked by a small fish in the organization, Vivien, who's been entrusted to check if he really is the escaped criminal. After surviving a murder attempt, Nicola gets hired by one of the bosses, Klaus White, but first he must kill a cop to show his skills. Nicola does as he's told, but first he manages to alert his victim. However, White still suspects him. Nicola manages to extort the information he needs from Vivien. In love with her, he reveals that he is a cop, but he can't save her from her accomplices' revenge when his cover is blown. After escaping death, Nicola manages to eliminate the organization's boss—Hermann Stoll—shooting him at the airport as he's about to leave.

The sixth and last entry in the line of crime movies directed by Stelvio Massi and starring Maurizio Merli, *The Rebel* is in many ways the gravestone on the whole season of poliziotteschi. Before attempting to go in a different direction with the action/

sport flick *Speed Cross* (1980), where he focused on spectacular motorbike stunts and moved away from the crime film formula, Massi returned to the gloomy, pessimistic atmosphere of *Il commissario di ferro* and *Convoy Busters*. The result was the director's personal favorite of his own films, together with *Highway Racer*, and Merli's personal favorite too. "We left for Germany in January 1980. It was amazing to shoot in the Berlin stadium where Hitler used to deliver his speeches to the masses, especially since it was a gloomy day, with the sky completely covered with clouds. I had shivers watching the field completely covered with white snow, and all around the black marble that the stadium was built of," Massi recalled.[1]

The original title, *Poliziotto solitudine e rabbia* (Cop, solitude and anger) indicates the film's tone, aided immensely by the wintry setting of a snow-covered Berlin. Merli's character doesn't even have a surname like his predecessors, just a name: Nicola. He is a former cop who comes out of retirement to give a friend a hand: the opening images, showing the mirage of an idyllic country life amidst nature, are an abrupt change compared to the previous films' opening scenes of urban violence. It's as if contemporary Italy had been removed, cancelled, forgotten.

As with *Fearless*, the film was an Italian/German co-production, which gives *The Rebel* a further symbolic resonance. The first part is set in Italy and climaxes in a tight action sequence in Murano, near Venice, where Massi gives Merli one of his more iconic, show-stopping scenes, as Nicola breaks through a multicolored glass window in slow motion. Then, just like in *From Corleone To Brooklyn*, the story moves abroad—to Germany, in this case—following Nicola's quest for the heads of a Northern-based criminal organization. Perhaps unintentionally, this recalls the waves of immigration to the North that brought Italian workers to Germany, Switzerland, Belgium. Nicola is, in fact, like a modern immigrant: he is alone and can only count on himself. Nobody is going to help him anyway. He is undercover: his only means of contacting the police is a phone number and can only rely on himself for survival—which means lying, behaving in a despicable manner (at one point Nicola even tortures a badly injured criminal in order to get precious information), deceiving a woman who has fallen for him, beating her, even killing. The character's devotion to his mission goes beyond obsession: Nicola even pierces his own shoulder to simulate a wound and pass for the man whose identity he's taken. But by then, he's already crossed the line between right and wrong in such a way that he can no longer turn back.

The film's main quality—loneliness—applies to Merli's performance: Francisco Rabal's character dies about fifteen minutes into the film, and unlike other poliziotteschi there is not even a well-defined antagonist as opposed to the hero (the film's tight budget is exemplified by the promotion of character actor Benito Pacifico to a more relevant role than usual), leaving Merli on screen in almost every scene in a tour de force that may well be the actor's best performance.

Halfway through, *The Rebel* is not a poliziotteschi anymore, but an out-and-out *film noir*: the occasionally clumsy dialogue, the main character's mannerisms (Merli's trademark expression: looking askance and clenching his jaw) and lamentations on the shortcomings of the law are just the remnants of a discarded skin. Besides the always compelling action scenes, Massi is clearly more interested in the intimate scenes between Merli and Jutta Speidel, the prostitute who falls for Nicola and whose death he inadvertently causes. At first Nicola's just playing the Latin lover part. "Your legs are so perfect it's a pity you don't have three," he quips, but then he becomes emotionally involved too: "I've never been with a woman I was not in love with," he confesses. Massi's camera lingers over the two lovers, their promises of love and delusions: "Do it as if you really loved me," Vivien says. Such an emphasis on bleak romanticism (unfortunately marred at times by Stelvio Cipriani's mediocre score, which even squeezes in a terrible syrupy song) is something unthinkable just a few years earlier. It's as if the director tried to squeeze one more moment of tenderness just before giving up altogether.

The ending seems like *déjà vu* from Massi's earlier *Convoy Busters*, where the hero chased his adversary to the airport but saw him take off on a plane, unable to catch him. Here, though, Nicola manages to put his last bullet to good use, by shooting (in the back) the head of the organization just as he's stepping aboard a plane: but then the camera quickly moves back, in the opposite direction to the departing hero. The feeling is that of a curtain falling, over both Merli's career (the other film he starred in that year, *Buitres sobre la ciudad*, wasn't even distributed in Italy) and the whole genre.

Note

1. Norcini and Ippoliti, "Stelvio Massi ricorda Maurizio Merli," p. 15.

The Smuggler, a.k.a. *Contraband (Luca il contrabbandiere)*

D: Lucio Fulci. *S:* Ettore Sanzó, Gianni De Chiara; *SC:* Ettore Sanzó, Gianni De Chiara, Lucio Fulci, Giorgio Mariuzzo; *DOP:* Sergio Salvati (35mm, Kodak, Staco Film); *M:* Fabio Frizzi, conducted by the author (ed. Nazionalmusic); *E:* Vincenzo Tomassi; *ArtD:* Francesco Calabrese; *AArtD:* Luciano Tarquini; *CO:* Massimo Lentini; *C:* Mario Sbrenna, Franco Bruni; *AC:* Maurizio Lucchini, Daniele Cimini, Giovanni Brescini; *C*—sea sequences: Alessio Gelsini, Massimo Pan; *AE:* Giancarlo Tiburzi; *2nd AE:* Armando Pace; *AD:* Roberto Giandalia; *MU:* Fabrizio Sforza; *AMU:* Antonio Maltempo; *Hair:* Ida Gilda De Guilmi; *W:* Berta Betti; *SO:* Ugo Celani; *Boom:* Eros Giustini; *Mix:* Gianni D'Amico; *Special makeup effects:* Franco Di Girolamo; *SE:* Germano Natali, Roberto Pace; *SP:* Francesco Bellomo; *Studio photographer:* Roberto Russo; *ST:* Giorgio Ricci, Attilio Severini, Omero Capanna, Giuseppe Mattei; *MA:* Sergio Sagnotti, Nazzareno Cardinali; *KG:* Ennio Brizzolari; *ChEl:* Alfredo Fedeli; *SS:* Daniela Tonti, Egle Guarino. *Cast:* Fabio Testi (Luca Ajello), Ivana Monti (Adele Ajello), Marcel Bozzuffi (François Jacquin "The Marsigliese"), Saverio Marconi (Luigi Perlante), Guido Alberti (Don Morrone), Daniele Dublino (Assistant prosecutor), Giordano Falzoni (Charlie, the doctor), Giulio Farnese (Alfredo Squillante), Fabrizio Jovine (Chief of Police), Ofelia Meyer (Ingrid), Ferdinando Murolo (Sciarrino), Tommaso Palladino (Capece), Venantino Venantini (Captain Tarantino), Ajita Wilson (Luisa), Luciano Rossi (Marsigliese's drug expert), Salvatore Billa (Marsigliese's henchman), Virgilio Daddi (Marsigliese's henchman), Romano Puppo (Marsigliese's assassin), Cinzia Lodetti (Ursula), Giovanni [Nello] Pazzafini (Hitman at the pits), Rita Frei (Filomena, Don Morrone's maid), Aldo Massasso (Murolo), Antonio Mellino (Driver). *Uncredited:* Angelo Boscariol (Smuggler), Omero Capanna (Marsigliese's henchman), Enzo D'Ausilio (Smuggler boss), Marcello Filotico (Old Boss Friend), Lucio Fulci (Don Morrone's assassin with machine gun), Enrico Maisto (Michele Ajello), Benito Pacifico (Thug at Perlante's), Salvatore Puccinelli (Murolo's henchman). *PROD:* Sandra Infascelli for Primex Italiana, C.M.R. Cinematografica; *PM:* Sergio Jacobis; *UM:* Nicola Venditti, Giulio Longo, Vittorio Bucci; *PSes:* Eliana Cipri, Dina Pallich, Matteo Marino; Assistant *PSe:* Luca Garzotto; *ADM:* Roberto Ornaro; *CASH:* Danilo Martelli, Romano de Francesco. *Country:* Italy. Filmed at Incir De Paolis (Rome) and on location in Naples. *Running time:* 96'; Visa no.: 75421 (08.07.1980); *Rating:* v.m.14; *Release date:* 08.08.1980; *Distribution:* Cidif; *Domestic gross:* 756,203,700 lira. *Also known as: Das Syndikat des Grauens* (05.07.1982 — 96'). *Home video:* Blue Underground (DVD, Us — English language, as *Contraband*). OST: 7" Cinevox MDF 133 (*You Are Not the Same / New York Dash*, performed by Cricket)

Naples. Luca Ajello and his brother Michele are owners of several boats and speedboats that they use to smuggle cigarettes. One day, they lose a load with a loss of two hundred million lira; what's more, they realize that a gang war is taking place to upset the balance between the contraband bosses. Initially they suspect that the mastermind is a certain Sciarrino: after the murder of Michele and other leaders, Luca confronts him directly. Sciarrino, however, pleads innocence and, in turn, meets his end at the hands of persons unknown. Luca then entrusts his wife Adele and his little son Francuccio to his father-in-law Don Morrone, and tries to get an agreement with Luigi Squillante. The situation becomes clearer when Adele is kidnapped by a Frenchman, François Jacquin, known as "The Marsigliese." Jacquin gets in touch with Luca and orders him to put his boats in the service of the drug smuggling racket, of which he is boss. Luca tries to fight back, but is almost about to succumb when the elderly Don Morrone, a retired boss, who gathers a gang of old gangsters and massacres Jacquin and his gang.

Shot in eleven weeks between the De Paolis studios in Rome and Naples, from December 3, 1979 to March 1980, with the working title *Il contrabbandiere / Violenza* ("The Smuggler / Violence"), Lucio Fulci's *Luca il contrabbandiere* was the director's only foray into the crime film. According to Giorgio Mariuzzo, who co-wrote the script with Fulci from an original story by Gianni Di Chiara and Ettore Sanzò, "the project originated with Sandra Infascelli [...] but the story just didn't work. Lucio called me to reshape it, and so I did. [...] I basically 're-structured' the story, giving it the right rhythm and pacing: first, second and third act, which at the time was something rather new. [...] I also added a number of violent scenes: Lucio loved these kind of things, even though in real life he was a good sport. Fulci got bored during the scriptwriting phase. He used to get started and put three or four ideas on paper, some of them really brilliant, but he just didn't have the patience to go on and write the script scene by scene. [...] It was a very good movie, too bad the title was awful. Very good movie, very well shot, with American-like pacing."[1]

The Smuggler apparently falls into the same subgenre as the Neapolitan-based flicks starring Mario Merola. Yet Fulci sabotages the firm solemnity of the sceneggiata, which the film apparently follows by focusing on the conflict between good cigarette runners and bad drug smugglers (obviously foreign ones: the invader from Marseille has the face of Marcel Bozzuffi, who somehow reprises his role in *The French Connection*) under the Vesuvio. Fulci pays homage to classic sceneggiata moments such as the pro-smugglers speech ("There are no less than 200,000 people in Naples who earn their living on smuggling because they just can't get any other job ... what are they gonna do now? Steal, rob, sell drugs ... if we don't change this city's social structure the economy is gonna sink!," dialogue that sounds like it was culled from *The New Godfathers*) or the fast boat chases that could belong to either *Big Mamma* or *The New Godfathers*. But Fulci's Naples is quite different from the utopian Eden as it appeared in the aforementioned films: it's rather, as one critic put it, "a labyrinthine, Piranesian maze intoxicated by violence and whose miasmas seize the city."[2]

What's ironic in all this is that *The Smuggler* was partly financed by real Neapolitan smugglers. After two weeks' shooting at the De Paolis studios, the money finished. When the crew moved to Naples, as Fulci himself recalled, they were "adopted" by the local smugglers who even gave them their motorboats and worked as extras in the sequences at sea. They took Fulci and his assistants in Naples' best restaurants and gave the crew weekly pay. What's more, these occult financers even intervened in the script, by insisting that the title *Violenza* be dropped (as they felt it wasn't fair to their image) and lines against drug trafficking be added. Among these additions, there's the scene upon a ferry boat where all the bosses are gathered, which Fulci — almost certainly ironically — considered to be the best in the film. In accordance with the director's notoriously spiteful attitude towards film producers, it's no wonder he highly praised the Neapolitan smugglers as the best — and most intelligent — producers he ever worked with. One peculiar and uncredited presence on set was Giuseppe Greco, the son of Mafia boss Michele (also known as "The Pope"), who observed the shooting and used to ask Fulci technical questions. Greco later directed a couple of flicks on his own (*Vite perdute*, 1992, and *I Grimaldi*, 1997), both shameless apologies of the Mafia world.

On *The Smuggler*, Fulci's usually explosive take on genres adopts the shape and tone of a splatter movie, in a paroxistic, hypertrophic exhibition of atrocities that ideally recalls the filmmaker's other horror films of the period. Blood and gore are over the top: throats are slashed, faces are blasted away with shotguns, people are disfigured, burned, maimed and abused. The director's own so-called "aesthetic of evagination" as applied to the body, here finds a new terrain: however, the cruelest excesses come perhaps from Sanzò, who recycles the scene where Luca's wife (Ivana Monti) is raped from Guido Zurli's *Target*, but with a surplus of misogynistic savagery ("No ... this time we have to do it right ... face down!" grins the Marseillese to his men, while Luca listens powerlessly to his wife's anal rape over the phone).

There is no pity and no innocence whatsoever, in *The Smuggler*. The eponymous hero, a sort of sub-proletarian Robin Hood, doesn't have Merola's physical corpulence but Fabio Testi's athletic physique: yet Luca is an insignificant, anodyne character with no charisma at all. Fulci is much more interested in the villains and their deeds: the spirited eyes — in trademark extreme close-up, of course — of the coke-snorting Luigi Perlante (Saverio Marconi) as he has his right-hand man get killed in an explosion, Bozzuffi disfiguring the drug carrier who tried to cheat him, the grinning hitman as played by Romano Puppo. The final massacre, with the old bosses taking their guns and "cleaning up" Naples (Bozzuffi even dies on a mound of trash, just like Tomas Milian in Lenzi's *Almost Human*) ridicules the film's models by using the weapon of hyperbole: the old gangsters (one of whom is the director himself) who incongruously pop up from behind iron grates, kiosks and phone booths to kill the French invaders summarize Fulci's anarchic and iconoclast spirit. The director's black humor is patent in the scenes depicting the elderly Camorra boss (Guido Alberti) whom we see sitting in front of his TV, watching Westerns and playing with the remote control, like an ordinary retired man, in a series of almost comedic sketches that punctuate the film, only to be revealed as the *deus ex machina* of the story in the end. It's a grim ironic punchline to a singularly dark, mean film.[3]

Notes

1. Paolo Albiero and Giacomo Cacciatore, *Il terrorista dei generi: Tutto il cinema di Lucio Fulci* (Rome: Unmondoaparte, 2004), p. 195.
2. Nazzaro, "Napoli, curtiello cu curtiello," p. 57. It must be added that some scenes were shot by Fulci's assistant director Roberto Giandalla, such as the dragnet in the alleys of the popular neighborhood. As Giandalla recalls, "I remember Lucio telling me: 'You really did a hell of a job, they look like they belong to a Rosi film!'" Albiero and Cacciatore, *Il terrorista dei generi*, p. 360.
3. The English language version, however, does not retain Don Morrone's final line to the Chief of Police ("Drugs got nothing to do with Naples' sun") which sounds even more like an ironic stab at the *guapparia* subgenre.

Tony: Another Double Game (*Tony, l'altra faccia della Torino violenta*)

D: Carlo Ausino. *S:* Carlo Ausino; *SC:* Carlo Ausino, Luciano Vincenzoni; *DOP:* Carlo Ausino (35mm, Eastmancolor, Technospes); *M:* Stelvio Cipriani (Ed. C.A.M.); *E:* Eugenio Alabiso; *CO:* Claudia Amione; *C:* Giuseppe Lino; *AC:* Tony Cannarsa; *MU:* Giusy Pennisi; *Hair:* Pietro Pennisi; *SO:* Antonio Campa; *Boom:* Mimmo Morleo; *Mix:* Augusto Penna; *SP:* Mauro Ballesio; *ChEl:* Lello Ropolo; *Elec:* Sergio Lino; *KG:* Nunzio Morales; *G:* Saverio Moggio; *SS:* Nicoletta Scarfì. *Cast:* Emanuel Cannarsa (Tony), Giuseppe Alotta (Santini), Paul Teicheid (Inspector Salvatore Gregori), Nicole Florì, Rino Moggio, Tony Campa, Cinzia Arcuri, Ruggero Spagnoli, Lorenzo Gobello, Armando Rossi, Benedetto Mocellin, Mario Pesare, Elsa, Vincenzo Cavaliere, Nicola Saponaro, Michele Terlizzi, Mario Zucca, Nunzia Carducci, Lucrezia Piana, Gianni Consoli, Salvatore Foti, Mimmo Morleo, Nino Ciccarese, Carla Samale, Sauro Roma, Gianpero Spinazzola, Antonio Messina, Luciano Rebuffello, Fabrizio Greco, Luigi Agostino, Gianni Manunta, Tullio Rossini, Giordana Serra, Attilio Cagnoni, Lino Vitale, Giuseppe Agostino, Leonardo Crasto, Gianluigi Ghione, Loredana Dal Cortivo, Gian Piero Nebbia. *PROD:* Carlo Ausino for Vigor Film; *PM:* Nunzia Ausino; *PSu:* Michele Peyretti. *Country:* Italy. Filmed on location in Turin. *Running time:* 88'; Visa no.: 75174 (05.17.1980); *Rating:* v.m.14; *Release date:* 05.22.1980; *Distribution:* Vigor Film (regional); *Domestic gross:* unknown. *Home video:* NoShame (DVD, Italy); NoShame USA (DVD, USA—bonus on the *Double Game* DVD)

Turin. A woman is kidnapped and released after her family pays a ransom of half a billion lira. Another kidnapping soon follows: this time the victim is a child from a wealthy family. A down-on-his luck loner named Tony witnesses the kidnapping and attempts to block it, but does not succeed and is wounded by a bullet fired by one of the criminals; in hospital, he risks death from the same gang. Once dismissed, Tony discovers that the boy's cousin is implicated in the kidnapping. The child is then liberated by the police. Inspector Gregori, believing that Tony is involved in the kidnappings, keeps persecuting him. Tony is forced to flee, because he is also chased by the heads of the criminal organization who want to avenge the failure of their plan. In the end Tony kills the gangsters in a shoot-out in a disco, but is in turn mortally wounded.

Although the Italian title implied that the film was a sequel of sorts to the director's *Torino violenta* a.k.a. *Double Game*, Carlo Ausino's second entry in the crime genre *Tony l'altra faccia della Torino violenta* (literally: Tony, the Other Side of Violent Turin) had no relation whatsoever with the previous film, except for the presence of Ausino's recurring actor Emanuel Cannarsa in the lead. Ausino's working title was in fact just *Tony*, and the film is much more character-driven than its predecessor, and only marginally tied to poliziotteschi. The titular hero is a young drifter, a rebel against the rules of society—before dying, his father reproaches him for not having studied—who doesn't have a regular job and lives day to day. A loner with a heart of gold, a womanizer and the monarch of a miracle court of homeless people and petty thieves, who is destined to be crushed by society. "You live your life on a razor's edge, sooner or later you'll cut yourself" he's been told.

As with *Double Game*, Ausino tries hard to make the red-headed, mustached and definitely not very handsome Cannarsa look like a believable *film noir* hero, yet he only succeeds in underlining the lead's unlikely screen presence. For instance, in his first scene, Tony leaves an occasional lover's bed, only to realize that the woman put some money in his pocket as a reward for his services: "This asshole didn't understand a thing," he mumbles, before throwing back the money over the woman's body and leaving. The beautiful girl, still half-asleep, keeps searching for him beside her, gropingly. Suspension of disbelief does not work here.

The story, which focuses on a gang of kidnappers, looks as if it had been conceived a few years earlier, when the theme was order of the day ("People are afraid for themselves, nowadays, and it's hard for them to think of others," a character observes), while the contribution to the script of the *renowned* Luciano Vincenzoni, one of the pillars of post-war Italian cinema (Mario Monicelli's *The Great War*, The Pietro Germi's *Seduced and Abandoned* and *The Birds, the Bees and the Italians*, Leone's *For a Few Dollars More* and *The Good, the Bad and the Ugly*, among others) can perhaps be sensed in the theme of generational conflicts and in the character of the hateful Inspector Gregori (played by Paul Theicheid, another member of Ausino's "Factory"), a fascist son of a bitch who has a personal grudge towards the hero, and looks like he just stepped out of a politically committed film of the early '70s. "Inspector Gregori was in the riot squad before this," recalls a journalist to another cop. "One day he was with the squad outside FIAT facing a workers' demo. Things were still calm when the students joined the workers. Suddenly we saw the inspector's face turn pale, and he hurled himself at the students.... No, at just one student.... His son. He was on the other side of the barricade. You should have seen him: he got his ass well-kicked! And he was told he'd get more of the same back home!" The same kind of incommunicability between different generations emerges in the dialogue between Tony and his elderly father, when the protagonist says: "You have to think, pop. It's the basis of everything. You only have hope if you think for yourself. You can't let others think for you, it's too dangerous." All in all, the result is at the same time more sincere than *Double Game*, but also more vulnerable, as it would have taken a much more accomplished director and cast to make the film work.

However, for all his customary weird angle shots (such as from behind a glass table) and slow motion sequences (the kidnapping scene), Ausino — who manages to come up with some moderately stylish scenes, such as a killer's night visit to the clinic where Tony is hospitalized[1] — cannot detract attention from the film's miserable budget. A grating example is a police ambush staged like something out of a Brian De Palma film, which comes out as clumsy and amateurish as it gets. Stelvio Cipriani's *déjà-vu* score was culled as usual from previous films, while plugs for the odd bar, shop or gymnasium are painfully patent.

Tony passed the censorship board in May 1980, to general indifference. "When I did *Tony*, I was told it was less spectacular but more heartfelt and intimate. But I had to wait for a year and a half to do it, and I had to do it with my own money. What's more, the producers wanted to add a more commercial subtitle, and as if that wasn't enough in that same period the private broadcasting networks were born — so everybody stayed home watching TV," Ausino complained.[2]

Virtually impossible to see for years, *Tony* was eventually released on DVD in 2005 both in Italy and United States (in Italian language with English subtitles) by NoShame Films. Keeping in spirit with the Italian title, the U.S. version was retitled *Tony: Another Double Game*. Due to print damage NoShame released the film as a bonus on their release for *Double Game*. According to the label, all the original elements for this movie no longer exist. The 35mm print used for the DVD release came from director Carlo Ausino's private collection and is believed to be the last print in existence.

Notes

1. Sadly, the scene is abruptly cut in the DVD print, missing the bit where Tony dispatches the killer from his hospital bed.
2. Email interview with the director, June 2012.

La tua vita per mio figlio (Your Life for My Son)

D: Alfonso Brescia. *S:* Monica Felt; *SC:* Piero Regnoli, Alfonso Brescia; *DOP:* Silvio Fraschetti (35mm, Eastmancolor, Telecolor); *M:* Eduardo Alfieri, conducted by the author (Ed. ABICI); *Ninna nanna Napulitana* (Mallozzi — Alfieri) sung by Mario Merola; *E:* Carlo Broglio; *PD, CO:* Valeria Valenza; Cameras: Giovanni Marras, Oddone Bernardini; *AE:* Fabrizio Di Blasi; *AD:* Gianfranco Pasquetto; *MU:* Raoul Ranieri; *Hair:* Armenio Marroni; *SO:* Ugo Celani; *Boom:* Eros Giustini; *SP:* Carlo Alberto Cocchi; *SS:* Giuliana Gherardi. *Cast:* Mario Merola (Francesco Accardo), Antonio Sabàto (Antonio Esposito), Maria Fiore (Maria Accardo), Rick Battaglia (Calogero Ermetta), Nick Jordan [Aldo Canti] (Michele Rovasino), Marco Girondino (Gennarino), Ugo Bologna (Sante Asciolla), John Benedy [Giovanni De Benedetto] (Ravasino's man), Paolo Villarosa, Emiliano Di Meo. *Uncredited:* Angelo Boscariol (Tennis player), Sisto Brunetti (Man in the bar), Nestore Cavaricci (Man in the bar), Luciano Foti (Passerby), Lina Franchi (Shoeshop customer). *PROD:* Filmes International, Italian International Film; *PM:* Cecilia Bigazzi; *PSu:* Viero Spadoni. *Country:* Italy. Filmed at Icet–De Paolis (Milan) and on location in Milan. *Running time:* 90'; Visa no.: 75193 (5.19.1980); *Rating:* not rated; *Release date:* 5.23.1980; *Distribution:* D.L.F. Distribuzione Lanciamento Film; *Domestic gross:* unknown. *Home video:* Iif Home Video (DVD, Italy).

Francesco Accardo, a former mobster who moved to Milan and started a new honest life with his wife Mary and their son Gennarino, is recruited through his old friend Antonio Esposito by Mafia boss Don Calogero Ermetta, who's determined to assert his supremacy over a rival "family" and forced to kill a certain Sante Asciolla. Accardo vainly tries to rebel, but when Gennarino is kidnapped, he reluctantly obeys. However, when he's face to face with the designated victim, Accardo is unable to pull the trigger and someone in the shadows shoots in his place, killing Asciolla. When he returns home, Francesco finds out that Gennarino was not kidnapped by Don Calogero's men. Thereafter, he learns that he'll have to pay a ransom of two hundred million lira. What really happened was that, without knowing it, Accardo became a sort of "price" for the agreement between the old mafia boss Don Calogero and the new boss Michele Rovasino. Fortunately for him, Francesco is helped by Antonio Esposito, whose life he saved twenty years earlier. By paying with his own life, Esposito saves both Accardo and Gennarino.

Of all the Brescia/Merola series, *La tua vita per mio figlio* is the closest to the *film noir* canon, and a welcome change of pace from the actor's usual Neapolitan sceneggiata routine. The script, by Brescia and veteran B-movie hack Piero Regnoli, moves Merola from the sunny and familiar streets of Naples to the foggy, inhospitable Milan, and makes his hero an immigrant, who left his Southern hometown to escape from his violent existence and lead a normal life with his family in the North, yet finds out that his past has returned to haunt him. The typical *film noir* theme is thus heightened by the contrast between Merola and the environment, which plays a complementary role to the one played by Naples in Brescia's other films. Despite his economical success, Don Accardo still feels like a fish out of water in Milan. Even though he tries to forget the past, he cannot reject his roots — nor wants to, after all.

Even though it is barely hinted at, the theme of immigration and racism towards Southerners is impossible to pass unnoticed: when his son speaks in Milanese slang, Francesco reproaches him ("Speak in Italian!"), and later on in the film he goes looking for help in a council tenement block — a scene that offers Brescia the pretext for a stunning shot that has Merola backed by a huge beehive-like condo inhabited by immigrants, perfectly epitomizing the sense of displacement and sacrifices that many families from the South underwent when moving to an illusory well-being in the North.

As for sceneggiata trappings, they are merged within a starker crime film narrative. Accardo's slow-motion flashbacks, which gradually reveal a crucial episode in his past (him saving his friend Antonio's life in an ambush) in typical Leone style, are rather effective. As with *The New Godfathers*, Brescia doesn't shy away from recycling other films' footage, in true B-movie spirit. A case in point is the opening sequence, where a pair of thugs (one is Nick Jordan a.k.a. Aldo Canti, a former stuntman and the main villain in *Napoli serenata calibro 9*) murder two men on a tennis court and escape by a car, chased by a police vehicle throughout the streets and suburbs of Milan: the car chase was entirely lifted from Marino Girolami's *Special Cop in Action.* Merola — who gets to sing only one song, a lullaby to his son, played by Marco Girondino — is as monolithic and convincing as ever, while Antonio Sabàto moves away from his customary sceneggiata villains to play a more tormented character than usual.

The Warning (L'avvertimento)

D: Damiano Damiani. *S* and *SC:* Damiano Damiani, Nicola Badalucco, Arduino Maiuri, Massimo De Rita; *DOP:* Alfio Contini (35mm, Eastmancolor); *M:* Riz Ortolani; *E:* Antonio Siciliano; *PD:* Andrea Crisanti; *CO design:* Giulia Mafai; *ArtD:* Massimo Tavazzi; *COper:* Sandro Tamborra; *AC:* Sandro Grossi, Francesco Damiani; *AD:* Enrico Bergier; *Chief makeup artist:* Walter Cossu; *Makeup artist:* Gino Zamprioli; *Hair:* Corrado Cristofori; *SO:* Luigi Salvi; *Boom:* Benito Alchimede; *Mix:* Alberto Tinebra; *SP:* Italo Tonni; *MA:* Neno [Nazzareno] Zamperla; *Technician:* Celeste Battistelli; *W:* Clara Fratarcangeli; *KG:* Giancarlo Rocchetti; *ChEl:* Antonio Leurini; *PrM:* Vittorio Troiani; *SS:* Egle Guarino. *Cast:* Giuliano Gemma (Commissioner Antonio Barresi), Martin Balsam (Chief of Police Martorana), Laura Trotter (Silvia Laganà), Giancarlo Zanetti (Brizzi), Guido Leontini (Gianfranco Puma), Marcello Mandò, Franco Odoardi (Chief Commissioner Vincenzo Laganà), Deddi Savagnone, John Karlsen (Ferdinando Violante), Julian Jenkins (Lopez), Andrea Scazzola (Sandro La Grutta), Ennio Antonelli, Geoffrey Copleston (Vesce), Giordano Falzoni (Milanesi), Giulia Fossà (Girl at police station), Vincent Gentile (Ludovico Vella), Giorgio Lucchese (Carlo Mannino), Roberto Malia, Elio Marconato, Richard McNamara, Mike Morris (Massimiliano Giorgio), Anna Maria Pescatori (Mother in the suburbs), Piero Pugnalini, Giampaolo Saccarola, Simone Santo, Andrea Scazzola (Sandro La Grutta), Edmondo Tieghi, Fabiana Udenio. *Uncredited:* Paolo Paoloni (big shot at wedding party). *PROD:* Mario Cecchi Gori for Capital Film; *GM:* Luciano Luna; *Delegate producer:* Francesco Giorgi; *PSu:* Giandomenico Stellitano; *PSe:* Paolo Giorgi, Armando Zappi; *ADM:* Mario Lupi, Giulio Cestari. *Country:* Italy. Filmed at Incir-de Paolis (Rome) and on location in Rome. *Running time:* 110'; Visa no.: 75477 (08.01.1980); *Rating:* not rated; *Release date:* 08.15.1980; *Distribution:* Cineriz; *Domestic gross:* 1,011,000,000 lira. *Also known as: Die tödliche Warnung* (West Germany). *Home video:* Cecchi Gori (DVD, Italy), Media Home Entertainment (VHS, USA — 101'). OST: LP Cinevox CIA 5063.

Vincenzo Laganà, head of the Flying Squad in Rome, is ready to ask Chief of Police Martorana for the prosecution of members of a Mafia organization that operates in the capital's banking environment. With the excuse of protecting the repentant lawyer Milanesi, who provided Laganà with crucial evidence, three strangers dressed as cops enter the police station and kill both Laganà and the lawyer. That same day, Commissioner Barresi finds an anonymous transfer of 100 million lira in his bank account. He is then appointed as Laganà's successor. Barresi suspects Martorana's moral integrity, and believes that Laganà's widow, Silvia, is in cahoots with the killers. Nevertheless, he pretends to be corruptible, and through the slimy middleman Puma he meets a mysterious Frenchman who belongs to the criminal organization. In order to frame Martorana, Barresi pretends to accept the organization's offer: but after his colleague Brizzi (who was protecting two hidden eyewitnesses on Barresi's orders) and Silvia Laganà are both killed, he finds out that Martorana is honest, and was just trying to double cross the criminals, like Barresi. They eventually join forces and arrest all the suspects at a wedding party in a luxury hotel in Via Veneto. They have very little evidence though, and Investigating Judge Vesce is puzzled ... but at least Martorana and Barresi have done their duty.

Co-scripted with Nicola Badalucco, Massimo De Rita and Dino Maiuri, *The Warning* is in many ways a summary of Damiani's *oeuvre*, as it resumes *I Am Afraid*'s paranoid, conspiratorial atmosphere while at the same time reworking *Confessions of a Police Captain*'s psychological war, transposed to the world of finance and fixers. The film's protagonist, commissioner Barresi (a convincing Giuliano Gemma) finds himself in the middle of an ambiguous, hardly decipherable situation: on the same day that his colleague, the Chief of the Flying Squad, is eliminated by a killer commando because of his investigations into the collusion between big business and the underworld, Barresi finds a huge sum on his own bank account. He pretends to be malleable and ready to cover up the case, so as to find evidence on Chief of Police Martorana (Martin Balsam), whom he believes is being bribed by the criminals. Once again, the mutual distrust between two men on the same side of the law only favors their enemies: each tries to frame the other but eventually only undermines his colleague's efforts, and subsequently both are defeated. However, this time Damiani leaves a little hope at the end: Barresi and Martorana realize their mistakes and decide to arrest the unsuspected heads of the criminal organization, even though they know they don't have enough evidence. Then they leave together, walking through the city streets, in a state of controlled euphoria: at least, this time they have won the battle, no matter what will happen next.

Although the references to real-life events are simplified and transformed in the script, *The Warning* is quite effective in conveying the climate of suspicion that hovered over Italy at that time. A few months after the release of Damiani's film, in March 1981 a crucial event in Italian history took place: the discovery of the secret list of members (including Italy's future Prime Minister Silvio Berlusconi) of Licio Gelli's Propaganda Due (P2), a pseudo–Masonic Lodge in name only but actually a subversive organization whose goal was a consolidation of the media, suppression of trade unions and the rewriting of the Italian Constitution, according to document called the "Plan for Democratic Rebirth," which the police found at Gelli's home. P2 was a subterranean power, a "State within the State," as it was labeled, which was implied in many Italian crimes and mysteries, including the collapse of the Vatican-affiliated Banco Ambrosiano and the murders of journalist Mino Pecorelli and banker Roberto Calvi. "There is, in our society, a kind of tangled skein which, if we fail to disentangle [...], is going to get even more garbled, threatening to smother us," Damiani told to film critic Gian Luigi Rondi.[1]

As Barresi, Gemma here plays a *sui generis* hero, full of doubts and forced to play his game with cunning instead of weapons, improvising one bluff after the other and trying to adapt his own image to what other people think of him. Barresi realizes that his ace in the hole is always to smile at others, like the slimy Puma (the usually great Guido Leontini) does: his, however, is not Maurizio Merli's reassuring and open smile, but the servile, opportunistic and conniving grimace of someone who realizes which way the wind blows and acts accordingly. Damiani chose Gemma, after working with him on *A Man on His Knees*, because of the actor's malleability: "No pre-established positions, fixed characters — he's always ready to start from scratch. In Hollywood he'd be one of the big shots, like James Stewart or Gary Cooper ... with a characteristic they didn't have, an interior anxiety, an uncertainty that's just marginally conceived," explained Damiani. "For my commissioner I wanted his open face, his patent cleanliness, and then a shadow which later could justify the doubt, the suspicion."[2]

Once again, *The Warning* shows Damiani's ability to build complex and articulate sequences, where architectural spaces play a leading role: the opening massacre inside the police station, where the killers penetrate the building dressed as cops, and the final sequence in the hotel where a wedding party is taking place, are among Damiani's best ever. However, as his assistant director Enrico Bergier pointed out, "by focusing on characters and dialogue, Damiani was starting to shoot his films in a way that was already similar to TV fiction. His filmmaking style hadn't changed a lot through the years, but television took a lot from there."[3] It is no coincidence that Damiani's subsequent work was a TV movie on terrorism, *Parole e sangue* (Words and Blood, 1981), which was destined to oblivion after being broadcast only once in September 1982. A totally different destiny would await *La Piovra* (The Octopus, 1984), another TV movie starring Michele Placido which showed the Mafia in step with the times: the focus was, like in *The Warning*, on its financial activities. *La Piovra* was a commercial triumph with an audience of over 15 million, and would indelibly mark the history of Italian television, as well as collective imagination and everyday language.

Notes

1. Gian Luigi Rondi, "Damiani: il clima del sospetto," *Il Tempo*, 7.20.1980.
2. *Ibid.*
3. Pezzotta, *Regia Damiano Damiani*, p. 293.

Appendix One: Italian Crime Films, 1981–2013

The eighties saw the abrupt decline of Italian crime films. It was not a mere commercial crisis, however. Besides the low box office results and tight budgets, there was obviously very little desire to confront the present. The kidnapping and killing of Aldo Moro had been a point of no return in this respect: the "attack on the heart of the Nation," as the Brigate Rosse called it, left a deep mark, unveiling a political and cultural reality in serious trouble. The movie industry — including genre filmmakers as well as *auteurs*— found itself incapable of reading and deciphering everyday life in all its complex contradictions. More or less consciously, the poliziottesco also reflected on its own *impasse*, both thematic and economic. The comic/action hybrids starring Tomas Milian, which only superficially pertained to the genre, still made money, as did — but only in Southern cities — the sceneggiate starring Mario Merola, which were reassuring in their apology of traditional values (honor, feelings, family) and were gradually turning into full-on melodramas.

Meanwhile the more politically committed figures acted out their long-due vengeance against poliziottesco: Gian Maria Volonté, who had played the lead in one of the most crucial films for the development of the genre such as Elio Petri's *Investigation of a Citizen Above Suspicion*, co-wrote and starred in the grotesque parody *Stark System* (1980), directed by his partner Armenia Balducci, in which he played Divo Stark, a former *Carabiniere* who had been beaten by workers on strike in 1970 and later turned into a crime film star. Replete with fake crime film titles such as *Lotta feroce* (Fierce Fight) and *La polizia non lo lasciò solo* (The Police Didn't Leave Him Alone), *Stark System* impressed the critics less for its qualities than for Volonté's patent acrimony towards poliziottesco and the genre film industry as well. "Gian Maria Volonté must have really hated his own character," wrote renowned critic Tullio Kezich: "he wears a wig worthy of a stage comedian, talks with an adenoidal voice, doesn't allow him a hint of common sense, and even has us take a look at him on the john and while he's masturbating."[1]

However, in 1980 aiming at the poliziottesco (which was just a pretext in Balducci's film anyway) was like shooting the Red Cross. Its sudden disappearance from the screens in the early 1980s was the inevitable consequence of the death of popular Italian cinema as a whole. Between 1980 and 1985 the number of viewers-per-year fell from 241.8 million to 123.1 million, that is almost half as much: a collapse that caused the closure of many movie theaters. Many survived by switching to hardcore porn. "The birth of the red light circuit," wrote Barbara Corsi, "was an extreme attempt at capturing the public's attention, the last chance for the theaters risking extinction to resist a bit longer, like castaways on a raft."[2]

The victims were mostly the weakest ones, the second and third-rate theaters, which hosted mainly popular low-budget films and allowed them to stay in circulation for a long time. On the other hand, the need to modernize the theaters themselves (most still had uncomfortable and creaky wooden seats, old projectors and bad sound) and the diffusion of saturation selling lead to the affirmation of the concept of film as an event. American companies regained their domineering position in the market, and the intervention of broadcasting networks acquired primary importance.

Before it was the distributor, who guaranteed a minimum amount of money beforehand to the producer (the so-called *minimo garantito*) who had the last word on which films to finance, which actors to cast and even which title to choose: now it was RAI and Fininvest who ruled. Producers became mere executors. And politicians washed their hands of it, Pontius Pilate–style. By 1990, with the notorious "Mammì law" which disciplined the radio and television system, the broadcasting networks' financial power was not only imposed on production, but on product content as well. Films were being basically thought out and shaped for TV consumption — therefore, they were deprived of any potentially offensive, transgressive or controversial element. Such a violent genre as the crime film didn't have any room left any longer — at least, not within the Italian film industry, and ditto for horror films.

The collapse of the whole production system involved many of the more representative genre filmmakers of the 1970s, such as Stelvio Massi, Umberto Lenzi, Enzo Castellari. Some did their best to adapt to the new rules, by cranking out flicks that were either aimed at less demanding markets such as South America or released directly to home video. The starting point was the same as ever: to rip off a recognizable U.S. model, which in the mid–1980s could be either the muscular action of Stallone's *First Blood* (1982), the urban grand-guignol of *Cobra* (1986), or the buddy cop movie *à la Lethal Weapon* (1987).

However, the overall approach had drastically changed, as had the market and its rules. What really mattered once was to find an Italian distributor, whereas now it was necessary to find a *foreign* one. Simply put, genre films grossed very little at the box office in Italy, whereas the producers would cover the costs by selling them to a few foreign countries. This was a tremendous limit, because to meet foreign demands genre outings were characterized by a slavish imitation of the American movie and TV imagery of the period, filled with U.S. locations, uninteresting storylines and square jaws that looked as if they came straight out of a TV series. An exemplary champion of such a tendency was producer-director Fabrizio De Angelis, with such titles as *Deadly Impact* (*Impatto mortale*, 1984), starring Bo Svenson and Fred Williamson, *The Overthrow* (*Colpo di stato*, 1987) and *The Last Match* (*L'ultima partita*, 1990), the latter filled with a who's who of *has beens* (Henry Silva, Ernest Borgnine, Martin Balsam). Alfonso Brescia left the guapparia movie behind too, and directed a *Lethal Weapon* rip-off starring Richard Roundtree and Harrison Muller (*Miami Cops*, 1989) while Michele Massimo Tarantini went to Brazil to shoot *The Hard Way* (1989) starring Henry Silva and Miles O'Keeffe.

What's more, it soon became apparent that there were no generational replacements on hand. As critic Lino Micciché put it, "when the ship of Italian cinema started sinking, with its many leaks — structural, productive and pertaining to the technology of marketable goods — what was missing was a new generation capable of picking up the flag in the middle of the storm."[3]

In other words, the filmmakers couldn't find any more inspiration by confronting themselves with the society in which they were living. Once reality was put on film in the attempt to exorcise it cathartically; now there was the self-important tendency to gaze at one's own navel. Moviegoers, on the other hand, were deserting Italian product and preferred to spend their money on foreign films. The only genre that kept resisting was comedy, which engulfed all others — including the crime films, with such titles as Carlo Verdone's *I due carabinieri* (1984) and Maurizio Ponzi's *Il tenente dei carabinieri* (1986). Once again, Italian cinema was the mirror of a society that had decided there was nothing to worry about in its own country. It was time to laugh.

Those who wanted to talk about their times, discovered it was easier to do on the small screen, which was endemically forced to examine the present. Television became the prime environment for crime films in the 1980s. TV movies produced in the decade embraced and manipulated the expressive input coming from cinema, while at the same time anesthetizing the form and diluting the pacing. Besides quality TV series like Damiano Damiani's *La Piovra*, other works were conceived for dual exploitation, both on the small screen and — in a reduced form — in theaters. Such was Giorgio Bontempi's *Notturno* (1983), an intricate spy potboiler which somewhat recalled Damiani's *Goodbye & Amen*: genre cinema, but thought out for television — nothing less, nothing more. Aided by a strong genre cast, featuring Tony Musante as a Polish nobleman who becomes a hitman, Maurizio Merli and Claudio Cassinelli redoing their typical movie characters and a great Omero Antonutti as a killer tormented by the memories of his days as a political prisoner, *Notturno* deserved a better fate than the obscurity it fell into.

TV series offered many filmmakers the opportunity to keep working. Damiani, Vancini, Lizzani, Sollima, Valerii, Tessari, being unable to bring their projects to the big screen, accepted the limitations and compromises that working for television implied. But it was a snake biting its own tail, as it was television's prevarication that prevented these filmmakers from making more films. A similar fate awaited other directors such as Sauro Scavolini, who in the 1980s directed a number of TV crime movies such as *Un foro nel parabrezza* (1984) and *Il colpo* (1988), the latter telling the story of a former cop (Fabio Testi) who robs a bank to pay for his gambling debts, and the commissioner (Marcel Bozzuffi) who's on his trail. It might have been a good-to-great film, if only it had been done ten years earlier.

Television also created new stars or relaunched faded ones. One such example was Ray Lovelock, while Bud Spencer, after the end of his team-up with Terence Hill, more or less recycled his old *Flatfoot* character in the TV series *Big Man* (1987) directed by Steno, and in Enzo Castellari's *Detective Extralarge* (1991), a buddy cop series co-starring former *Miami Vice* star Philip Michael Thomas.

La Piovra's enormous success paved the way for a brief rerun of committed, civil-themed films. One such example was Giuseppe Ferrara's *A Hundred Days in Palermo* (*Cento giorni a Palermo*, 1984), which told the story of the last few months of General Carlo Alberto Dalla Chiesa, killed by the Mafia in 1982, starring Lino Ventura. Mafia was once again a hot and lucrative topic. Producers tried to resuscitate the Mafia film, an illusion that did last a couple of years thanks to such titles as Damiani's *Pizza Connection* (1985) and Giuseppe Tornatore's debut *The Professor* (*Il camorrista*, 1986). Both were licensed in dual versions, a short theatrical cut and a longer one for the small screen, even though in the case of Tornatore's film — an over-the-top, extremely violent biography of the Camorra boss Raffaele Cutolo, played by Ben Gazzara, which patently followed the steps of the 1970s Mafia films — it was just the theatrical edit that was released in the end. Another similar venture was Pasquale Squitieri's *The Repenter* (*Il pentito*, 1985) with Tony Musante, Franco Nero and Max Von Sydow.

The rest, in that desolate void that was 1980s Italian cinema, were just isolated particles that here and there displayed a vague resemblance of sorts to the crime genre. Sergio Corbucci's *I giorni del commissario Ambrosio* (1988), starring the great Ugo Tognazzi, was a kind of *film noir* adapted from Renato Olivieri's novel. It was supposed to be the pilot for a TV series that never got made, while Gabriele Lavia's atrocious *Evil Senses* (*Sensi*, 1986), where the actor/director starred as a killer on the run who hides in a brothel, was like Mickey Spillane on acid, and Lavia's narcissism allowed him to deliver such lines as "Shoot me, and I'll meet the bullet as if it was an appointment of love." Much more interesting were Tinto Brass' deconstruction of the *noir* genre *Snack Bar Budapest* (1988) and Davide Ferrario's *La fine della notte* (The End of the Night, 1989), a chilling tale very similar to Penelope Spheeris' *The Boys Next Door* (1986) and set in the desolate Italian province.

The 1990s, if possible, were even worse. A decade of impoverished cinema, in both the images and imagery, for impoverished minds. Films talked the same flat and sloppy language as their televisive counterparts. They said and meant very little, and did it badly too. Overall, Italian cinema revealed its inadequacy to talk about reality, to explain it, not to mention reinvent it in a poetic and/or spectacular manner.

Attempts at crime films were few and far between, and more on the dramatic side. Francesco Rosi's return to Sicily, *The Palermo Connection* (*Dimenticare Palermo*, 1990) and Damiano Damiani's *The Dark Sun* (*Il sole buio*, 1990) were mediocre efforts as best. What's more, both appeared to be as far from reality as their main characters — respectively, an the Italian-American politician (James Belushi) and a Sicilian nobleman (Michael Paré) — outsiders who return to a home country they no longer understand and end up being manipulated by someone else. Much more successful was the Mafia movie *La scorta* (The Escort, 1993) by Ricky Tognazzi, the story of several young cops who are assigned to be the bodyguards of a judge (Carlo Cecchi) who's been threatened by the Mafia. Tognazzi's film hinted at the terrible recent events in Italian history (the murder of judge Falcone, blown up by the Mafia on May 23, 1992, and his colleague Borsellino, killed just a couple of months later in another bomb blast) and did it with the same strong spectacular assets as Damiani's 1970s films, aided by a splendid cast of young actors.

In the mid–1990s a few titles had some critics praise a resurrection of the genre. These films germinated from the encounter between television aesthetics and the good-hearted rhetorics of the unknown heroes as celebrated by *La scorta*. Stories and characters came from the past, dressed in new clothes and with an eye on the latest cinephile buzz. That was the case with Giulio Base's *Poliziotti* (Policemen, 1995) and especially Claudio Fragasso's *Palermo-Milan One Way* (*Palermo-Milano solo andata*, 1996). Base's film took its inspiration from a true event that happened in the 1970s and inspired a famous article by Pasolini. It told the story of a young and naive police rookie (Kim Rossi-Stuart) who is plagiarized by a Luciferian criminal (Michele Placido) whom the cop has to keep under surveillance in hospital with a colleague (Claudio Amendola). Despite its excellent cast (especially Rossi-Stuart, the son of 1960s genre star Giacomo, in an outstanding performance), *Poliziotti* suffered from Base's directorial self-indulgence (that is, shooting every scene as if it were the climax, with the result of exhausting the viewer).

Fragasso, who started as a scriptwriter in the late 1970s and put his name on some of the very worst crime films made in Italy in that period (Mario Bianchi's *La banda Vallanzasca* and *Don't Trust the Mafia*, to name a couple) before moving on to equally bad horror films (i.e. the notorious *Troll 2*) tried to regain a new respectability by following *La scorta*'s mixture of genre trappings and civil commitment with the story of a witness in a Mafia trial (Giancarlo Giannini) who must be escorted from Palermo to Milan by a group of young cops, while Mafia killers try every trick in the book to stop him. The plot was virtually the same as Umberto Lenzi's powerful *From Corleone to Brooklyn*, while the road movie structure allowed Fragasso to stage a number of tense action scenes around Italy. Yet the result was often similar to that of an average TV movie, not just because of the many faces borrowed from the small screen, but also because of the lack of a distinct directorial hand: Fragasso even aped Hong Kong action fare, with cops acrobatically shooting with two guns just like in a John Woo movie and lots of ill-conceived slow-motion shots. However, the box office results were promising enough to give Fragasso a certain commercial power, which he immediately dilapidated with the obnoxious *film noir Coppia omicida* (1998) before landing on TV with *Operazione Odissea* (1999), a barely disguised remake of *Palermo-Milan One Way* for the benefit of TV audiences. After many other mostly forgettable works for the small and silver screen, Fragasso eventually directed a passable sequel to his magnum opus in 2007: *Milano Palermo — il ritorno* (Milan — Palermo — The Return).

Another noteworthy effort was producer Claudio Bonivento's debut behind the camera, *Altri uomini* (Other Men, 1997), the story of crime bosses Francis Turatello and Angelo Epaminonda's rise to power in 1970s Milan. The fact that the characters' names were changed was perhaps a hint that Bonivento didn't really have the guts to tell the story — a violent, ruthless and shocking one — as it had to be told. *Altri uomini* took its obvious inspiration from Martin Scorsese's *Goodfellas* (1990) with its flashback structure held together by the voice-over of the film's "hero" Claudio Amendola ("Better be someone as a criminal, than a honest nobody," he quips), but didn't have neither the style nor the means to live up to its ambitions. The meager budget shows, the action scenes are either off-screen or haphazardly shot, and one has never the feel of a real in-depth look at a crucial period in Italy's history. What's more, the tone is self-absolutory: "The worse has gone, even though we believed it was the best," as Amendola's character sums up the film's morale. The result, despite Bonivento's efforts, is once again closer to a TV movie. Which would also be the director's downfall on *Squadra mobile scomparsi* (1999) and *L'attentatuni* (2001).

The 1980s and 90s also hosted a submerged genre cinema, made for regional consumption, untouched by new fashions and threads, able to survive virtually out of nothing and of course irredeemably awful. That was the case with Paolo Pecora's semi-amateurish *Faida* (1989), featuring Gordon Mitchell, or the two films directed (under the pseudonym Michele Castellani) by Giuseppe Greco, the son of Mafia boss Michele Greco. *Vite perdute* (Lost Lives, 1992) juxtaposed small-time local delinquents (the good guys) to the big time criminals, who come from outside and corrupt the *milieu*, while the abuse of Catholic iconography recalled Mario Merola's sceneggiate. *I Grimaldi* (The Grimaldis, 1997) was Greco's zero-budget answer to *The Godfather*, as hagiographic and self-absolutory as it could get. Ninì Grassia's pedestrian *Il burattinaio* (The Puppet Master, 1994), a Mafia movie shot between Naples and Miami and featuring Fabio Testi, Orso Maria Guerrini and stuntman Massimo Vanni, was eventually released to home video (on the director's own label) five years after its making.

After Quentin Tarantino's 1994 triumph at the Cannes film festival with *Pulp Fiction*, Italy discovered the term *pulp*. The effects — some of them long-term — also afflicted a few crime films made in the following years. Stefano Incerti's *Prima del tramonto* (Before Sunset, 1999) was launched as a "Mediterranean *Pulp Fiction*," because of its elaborate jigsaw structure and unity of time (the story takes place in one single day), while following three different stories in the Apulia region: a Moroccan (Said Taghmaoui) leaves his bride, the daughter of a mob boss, at the altar and escapes with a woman from his own land; two killers rob boat people of their money; two post office clerks become murderers. Incerti's aim was to use the genre palimpsest to address such topics as clandestine immigration, racial integration, and the moral drift in contemporary Southern Italy, once again seen as a modern no man's land. The main influences were Scorsese's and Abel Ferrara's films, yet the most impressive moments were the action scenes, while the characterizations and sparse grotesque touches were either schematic or didactic.

Fabio Segatori's *Terra bruciata* (1999), the story of a stuntman (Raoul Bova) who ends up in the middle of a mob war, was a blatant attempt at creating a Tarantino-style mixture, blending *film noir*, Hong Kong-style action scenes and the odd reference to Westerns with debatable results. The director's subsequent *Hollywood Flies* (2005), featuring Brad Renfro, Casper Van Dien and Vinnie Jones amongst others, was no better either.

Claudio Caligari's *L'odore della notte* (The Smell of the Night, 1998) was mistaken by many as a half-hearted stab at Tarantino's urban *noir*, yet the film — based on the true story of the so-called "Clockwork Orange gang" which terrorized Rome in the 1970s — is much more than that. Caligari borrowed a typical 1970s crime film storyline, by following the criminal deeds of Remo (Valerio Mastandrea), a cop who moonlights as a robber and sneaks into villas inhabited by Rome's upper class families with his two accomplices. Yet the film's genre structure is constantly sabotaged by the protagonist's torrential voice-over, which mixes bureaucratic pedantry and emphatical rhetoric, and constantly detaches the viewer from the story that's being told. *L'odore della notte* is a much more refined and complex film than it seems. The cinephile bouts — ranging from *The Great Train Robbery* to *Taxi Driver*— are not simply tongue-in-cheek references, but have a deep symbolic and narrative meaning that gives the characters further resonance, while the "pulp" bits rub shoulders with clever social and psychological touches. Remo's constant need for money stems from the desire to rise to a bourgeois status: his criminal life is essentially aimed at homologating.

By the end of the 1990s, the poliziottesco was being rediscovered by the younger generations, mainly as a "find" from the 1970s, a decade too conveniently elected as a mythical "golden age" (leaving of course aside any reference to terrorism, social crisis, bombings, etc.). As a result, said rediscovery was often devoid of any socio-historical quality and mainly focused on the cinephile pleasure of exhuming a kind of moviemaking and storytelling that was so different from contemporary habits. Like the erotic comedies, the Decamerotics, the Spaghetti Westerns, the trashy psychedelic horror flicks made in the same decade, suddenly poliziottesco was "in" once again.

Marco Ponti paid reference to Carlo Ausino's modest *Double Game* in the ultra-hip *A/R Andata+ritorno* (2004); most newspapers journalists learnt from Quentin Tarantino about the existence of a certain Fernando di Leo (who had died nine months earlier) during the 2004 Venice retrospective on the so-called "Secret History of Italian Cinema"; and the Vanzina brothers (sons of the same Stefano who practically launched the genre with *Execution Squad*) released *Il ritorno del Monnezza* (2005), an attempt at exhuming the kind of crime/comedy hybrids starring a foul-mouthed Tomas Milian that made million liras in the late seventies. The result was a failure on all fronts: the sloppy *mise-en-scène* betrayed a hasty shooting schedule, and the emphasis on four-letter words that made Milian's films so popular among moviegoers was drastically reduced due to political correctness. *Il ritorno del Monnezza* was so superficial to the point of confusing (whether intentionally or not isn't the point) the characters of Monnezza (the petty thief played by Milian in *Free Hand for a Tough Cop*, *Destruction Force* and *Brothers Till We Die*) and Nico il Pirata (the cop played by Milian in the series started with *The Cop in Blue Jeans*), much to the audience's indifference.

Meanwhile, at the dawn of the new millennium, a few promising young filmmakers started flirting with *film noir*, by using its dynamics to portray contemporary Italy, its lack of values and perspectives, and did it with an intelligent, at times innovative style. Although only tangentially pertinent to this study, Matteo Garrone's *The Embalmer* (*L'imbalsamatore*, 2002)— based on a true crime book by Vincenzo Cerami — was one such example, which the director would follow with the equally remarkable *First Love* (*Primo amore*, 2004) before finding international acclaim with his adaptation of Roberto Saviano's best-selling book on the Camorra *Gomorra* (2008), which won the Jury Grand Prize at the Cannes Film Festival, and *Reality* (2012). Paolo Sorrentino's stylish *The Consequences of Love* (*Le conseguenze dell'amore*, 2004) was a Mafia movie disguised as a platonic love story (or vice versa) which also served as an impressive calling card: Sorrentino's next film, *Il divo* (2008) was an outstanding biography of Italy's former P.M. Giulio Andreotti (who was eventually put on trial for his connivence with the Mafia) told in a flamboyantly spectacular way, as the director recreated the escalation of the Mafia in the 1990s with touches worthy of Scorsese at his very best. Sorrentino then went on to direct Sean Penn in the outlandish road movie *This Must Be the Place* (2011).

The ascent of many talented young novelists brought new life to the crime genre. Carlo Lucarelli's novels *Lupo Mannaro* (Werewolf) and *Almost Blue*— both centered on the cop vs. serial killer dynamics — were both put on film in 2000 (Lucarelli also collaborated to Dario Argento's *Sleepless*, 2001, and eventually debuted behind the camera in 2012 with *L'isola dell'angelo caduto*, an adaptation of his own book). Marcello Fois wrote scripts for the TV series *Distretto di polizia* and *La squadra*. Massimo Carlotto adapted his own autobiographical novel *Il fuggiasco* (2003, Andrea Manni). Carlo Sigon debuted with *La cura del Gorilla* (2006), the story of a schizophrenic bodyguard-cum-detective based on Sandrone Dazieri's novels. Even Michele Soavi returned to the big screen with *The Goodbye Kiss* (*Arrivederci amore, ciao*, 2006), based on another novel by Carlotto. Soavi's film — the story of Giorgio (Alessio Boni), a former left-wing-activist-turned-terrorist who, after fleeing to Central America to fight with a guerrilla movement, returns to Italy to lead a respectable bourgeois life, but is blackmailed by a corrupt police inspector

(Michele Placido)—was a tough, uncompromising directorial tour de force that showed how the director who once was labeled as "the future of Italian horror" hadn't lost his skills after a twelve year hiatus from the big screen (Soavi had worked exclusively on television after 1994's *Cemetery Man*). What's more, with its hero's obsessive pursuit of his dream of becoming a "respectable" citizen, which leads him down a road paved with larceny, pimping, drug-dealing, rape, heist and murder, *The Goodbye Kiss* effectively epitomized the radical transformation of a whole country and its unending moral drift.

By now the crime genre had gained a halo of respectability: *film noir* was as fashionable as ever—perhaps even too much, as filmmakers now treated it as a mere pretext to make barely disguised auteur films, instead of savoring the genre in itself—a case in point being Daniele Vicari's disappointing *The Past Is a Foreign Land* (2008), based on a novel by magistrate-cum-novelist Gianrico Carofiglio. The story of an upper-class law student (Elio Germano) with a passion for poker games, and his association with a ruthless boy of the same age (Michele Riondino) who enrolls him in a drug smuggling business, claims to be a parable about the seduction of evil, yet fails to make its irritating and empty characters convincing, and displays a superficial *film noir* attitude. On the other hand, Michele Placido's *Crime Novel* (*Romanzo criminale*, 2005) was the film that finally convinced critics and producers alike that the crime film was a very marketable genre once again. Based on the best-selling novel by yet another magistrate and novelist, Giancarlo De Cataldo, the (true) story of the Magliana gang, who ruled over Rome through the 1970s and '80s, was also a way of retelling twenty years of Italian history. Blessed with a substantial budget and a cast packed with a who's who of Italian cinema (Kim Rossi-Stuart, Stefano Accorsi, Claudio Santamaria, Pierfrancesco Favino, Jasmine Trinca), *Romanzo criminale* was nothing short of an epic (its long version stretched nearly to three hours' length). The overflowing narrative material of the novel's 600-plus pages was cleverly adapted by scriptwriters Stefano Rulli and Sandro Petraglia, who together with Placido and the author eliminated subplots and characters, while prioritizing the sad and romantic tone and the themes of lost innocence, defeat and betrayed friendships. The film was a huge box office hit, paving the way for a profitable TV series directed by Stefano Sollima, Sergio's son.

Genre fans were left somewhat puzzled, perhaps expecting an up-to-date recreation of 1970s poliziottesco *à la* Umberto Lenzi or a nod to Fernando di Leo's hard-boiled films. Watching the film, and leaving aside the hip, frantically edited opening sequences (which clumsily try to pass it as some sort of hybrid between *Goodfellas* and Guy Ritchie's *Snatch*), it becomes clear that Placido was trying to exploit the lesson of filmmakers such as Rosi and Damiani—that is, making a kind of cinema which blends spectacular values and social commitment. The epilogue, purposely written for the screen, is a homage to Rosi's *Illustrious Corpses*, while the film's very best scene—where il Freddo (Rossi-Stuart) kills a traitor friend amidst the dunes of the Ostia beach—brings to mind the desolate ending of Damiani's underrated *A Man on His Knees*, which co-starred Placido. Even though the direction is at times debatable in its *auteur*-like winks and not always impeccable—the sequence of the bombing at the Bologna station in 1980 is bogged down by the use of bad CGI—the result is flawed yet impressive nonetheless. Placido later returned to the genre with less convincing results. *Angel of Evil* (*Vallanzasca—Gli angeli del male*, 2010), a biography of the bandit Renato Vallanzasca (who inspired a few films in the late 1970s, including Mario Bianchi's horrid *La banda Vallanzasca*) had all of *Romanzo criminale*'s shortcomings and none of the former film's qualities, and was noteworthy mainly for Kim Rossi-Stuart assured performance in the lead. *The Lookout* (*Il cecchino*, 2012) is a stylish and spectacular but ultimately flawed stab at French polar, starring Daniel Auteuil and Mathieu Kassovitz.

As of today, Italian crime films are "in." They are no longer seen as inferior genre product, and are often detached from the typical urban atmosphere of 1970s poliziotteschi. Out-and-out genre efforts are relegated to a marginal market, and deservedly so in the case of Stefano Calvagna's obnoxious Fascist movies (such as *Il lupo*, 2007) and Claudio Fragasso's pedestrian *Le ultime 56 ore* (2010). More often than not, though, a *film noir* concoction is an excuse for character studies *à la* Simenon, like Andrea Molaioli's accomplished if mannered debut *The Girl by the Lake* (*La ragazza del lago*, 2007), starring Toni Servillo as a world-weary commissioner or Claudio Cupellini's *A Quiet Life* (*Una vita tranquilla*, 2010), with Servillo again as a former Camorra acolyte-turned-restaurateur in Germany, who finds out that his son in turn has become a killer for the mob. Another such case is Emiliano Corapi's *Sulla strada di casa* (2011), where the director seems afraid of directing a "simple" crime film and uselessly complicates the story by throwing in unnecessary ellipses, flashbacks and flash forwards, while Paolo Franchi's unpleasant *Fallen Heroes* (*Nessuna qualità agli eroi*, 2007) uses the genre elements—the story of an ambiguous relationship between a broker and a neurotic young man who team up to murder the latter's usurer father in an idiosyncratic way, within a more complex and thought-provoking (yet flawed) discourse about identity and an almost experimental form which at times recalls Antonioni's last works. The film caused something of a stir in Italy because of a pair of rather explicit sex scenes, one of which involved actor Elio Germano displaying his erect member (actually a fake prop) on screen, but it flopped badly at the box office.

Cop stories are more alike violent urban dramas—with all the pretensions and authorial touches associated with the commonly accepted idea of "committed" cinema—than mere genre films, a case in point being Stefano Sollima's choral and controversial *A.C.A.B.—All Cops Are Bastards* (2012), which follows the lives of four members of the special corps, but despite its attempts to shed light on the credo of violence inside the armed forces (a very controversial subject in Italy in the last few years due to the many episodes of "accidental" killings and lethal beatings) falls short of being convincing due to the many compromises the script undergoes. All cops are bastards indeed in the film, as according to the title, but each and every one of the main characters are more or less justified in their temperamental shortcomings and fits of rage by their personal experience, while the portrayal of violence (emphasized by the use of rock songs on the soundtrack such as White Stripes' *Seven Nation Army* or Pixies' *Where Is My Mind?*) is debatably ambiguous in a film that is supposed to condemn the characters' fascination for violence but ends up allowing the audience to identify with it, in a manner not too far removed from soap operas — so that in the end it not only fails to put together a coherent discourse on the topic, but also lacks the rough-edged power that its 1970s predecessors retained in their often admittedly Manichean approach to social issues. Which leads one to wonder about the effectiveness of crime film (let alone genre cinema of *any* kind) in contemporary Italy — a country so detached from itself it can no longer benefit from a collective on-screen catharsis.

Notes

1. Tullio Kezich, *Il nuovissimo Millefilm* (Milan: Mondadori, 1983), p. 370.
2. Barbara Cors, *Con qualche dollaro in meno: Storia economica del cinema italiano* (Rome: Editori Riuniti, 2001).
3. Lino Micciché, "Il lungo decennio grigio," in Aa.Vv., *Schermi opachi: Il cinema italiano degli anni '80* (Venice: Marsilio, 1998), p. 8.

Appendix Two: Italian Crime Films' Most Significant Directors

Alfonso Brescia *(Rome, 1.6.1930—5.5.2001)*

Truly a filmmaker for all seasons, with 51 titles in a 30-year career, Alfonso Brescia was one of the most prolific and versatile Italian filmmakers of the 1970s. The son of a film producer, he started his career in the movie business against his father's will. To persuade Alfonso to change his mind, Brescia Sr. had him start off as the production driver, hoping that getting up early in the morning to pick up the actors at home and drive them to the studios would turn him against working in films. The trick did not work. For a long time, young Alfonso was an assistant director and worked in the production offices. He eventually directed his first film, *Revolt of the Praetorians*, in 1964.

Brescia's output over the years can be used as a blueprint to follow the evolution of genre cinema in Italy. There were sword-and-sandal epics (*Revolt of the Praetorians*), then Westerns (*Killer Caliber 32*, 1967), war films (*Hell in Normandy*, 1968), erotic *mondo* flicks (*The Labyrinth of Sex*, 1969), *gialli* (*Naked Girl Killed in the Park*, 1972), period erotica (*Poppea: A Prostitute in Service of the Emperor*, 1972), Amazon flicks (*Battle of the Amazons*, 1973) Superhero/martial yarns (the Shaw Brothers coproduction *Super Stooges vs. the Wonder Women*, 1974), children's' adventure (*Lone Hunter of the Wild North*, 1975), contemporary erotica (*Sweet Teen*, 1976), science fiction (*War of the Robots*, 1978). Whatever genre it was—you name it, Brescia did it. Sometimes, even three or four at the same time.

With four or five films per year, often signed with the pseudonym Al Bradley, Brescia's *oeuvre* could hardly be described as refined. Brescia was indeed a hack, yet a reliable one. The huge, bearded director was well-known for his jovial attitude on set, but he knew how to deliver the goods quite well, was a fast worker and—most important of all—never lost money on a film. When *Star Wars* became a worldwide hit, he shot five science fiction films in a row, with the same cast, sets and crew, and had them released in the next three years: *The War in Space* (*Anno zero: guerra nello spazio*, 1977), *War of the Planets* (*Battaglie negli spazi stellari*, 1977), *War of the Robots* (*La guerra dei robot*, 1978) *Star Odyssey* (*Sette uomini d'oro nello spazio*, 1979) and *The Beast in Space* (*La bestia nello spazio*, 1980). To spice things up, the latter was a sci-fi porn which ripped off Walerian Borowczyk's *The Beast* and even starred the same leading lady as Boro's film, Sirpa Lane (who experienced a brief bout of popularity in Italy), alongside porn star Marina Hedman. Brescia also saved—sometimes, salvaged—a number of films, replacing the original directors or shooting additional footage for rerelease. Cases in point were Raimondo Del Balzo's tearjerker *The Last Snows of Spring* (*L'ultima neve di primavera*, 1973), which was a tremendous hit in Italy and Japan, and Enzo Castellari's *The House by the Edge of the Lake* (*Sensività*, 1979), for which Brescia shot some admittedly awful suspense scenes in order to turn Castellari's ambiguous erotic fantasy into a full-blown horror flick.

Brescia's first entry in the crime genre was 1976's less than mediocre *Blood and Bullets*, but soon he found his place in the genre working with Mario Merola in a series of Neapolitan crime films which mixed action, melodrama and songs and were aimed at Southern Italian audiences. Merola considered him the only director he truly trusted, and their collaboration lasted five years and twelve films, from 1978's *L'ultimo guappo* to 1982's *Giuramento*.

In the eighties, with the decline of genre cinema, Brescia's output drastically diminished. His last works included the post-atomic flick *Iron Warrior* (1987), the buddy-cop movie *Miami Cops* (1989) and the truly bad *giallo Omicidio a luci blu* (1991), starring Florence Guerin and David Hess. In the last years of his life, Brescia simply could not find work anymore, as the genre industry had practically disappeared. In 1995 he produced and directed one last film, *Club Vacanze*, to try to restart his career, but no distributor bought it and Brescia could not get his money back.

Brescia became ill and died in Rome in 2001. Some producers who still owed him money showed up at the funeral.

Enzo G. Castellari *(Born Enzo Girolami; Rome, 6.29.1938)*

There's one anecdote Enzo Castellari gets never tired of telling, and it's about whether a movie is good or not: you can tell it's good when, mentioning its title to somebody—somebody *from Rome*, that is, since Romans possess an instinctive, cruel sense of humor in their DNA, refined in thousands years of history—he replies "Me' cojoni!," a colorful Roman dialect expression which could be roughly translated as "Good heavens!" in the sense it implies surprise and wonder. On the other hand, if the other replies with the even more vulgar "E 'sti cazzi!" meaning that he couldn't care less, the title sucks. And so does the movie—guaranteed.[1]

That's how Enzo Castellari's cinema is. When it's good, it leaves viewers in a state of astonishment and wonder, struck and bewildered by the filmmaker's flair for over-the-top action sequences, his refined film technique, his pictorial sense of composition. When it's bad, it's simply bad and best forgotten. The director himself is no man of half measures, neither are his movies. One of Italy's best genre directors, Enzo G. Castellari grew up in a family of filmmakers. The pointed G stands for Girolami, Enzo's real surname: his father, Marino Girolami, a prizefighter-turned-director, was one of Italian cinema's unknown soldiers, with almost 80 films helmed from 1949 to 1982. Enzo's uncle Romolo Girolami (a.k.a. Romolo Guerrieri) was also a skillful filmmaker, and his brother Ennio was an actor.

Even though he got a degree in Architecture and dabbled as a prizefighter in his early days too, Castellari started his career in the movie biz when he was very young. "I was born with the movies. My biggest joy was when my father came to pick me up at school and took me with him to the editing room, where he was working on one of his pictures. To me, the really fascinating element in the movies is editing. [...] And my best holidays consisted of showing up on the set and watching my father shoot a movie. And whenever somebody asked, 'Who's bringing a chair on set?' I yelled: 'Me!'; 'Who's getting us a cup of coffee?' 'Me!' 'Who's gonna be the actor's stand-in?' 'Me!' 'Who's jumping out of that window?' 'Me!'"[2]

Stunt double, second assistant director, first assistant director, master of arms, scriptwriter, even "ghost director" on a couple of films signed by León Klimovsky, the Western *Some Dollars for Django* (*Pochi dollari per Django*, 1966) and the action movie *A Ghentar si muore facile* (1967) which he shot for the most part. Not yet thirty, Castellari was already a veteran of sorts.

Then, in 1967, he eventually got to direct his "official" debut, a Western shot in Spain and starring Guy Madison, *Blake's Marauders* (a.k.a. *Renegade Riders*). On that occasion, Castellari consciously tried to duplicate the style of a film that had made a big impression on him, Sidney J. Furie's *The Appaloosa* (1966) starring Marlon Brando. Furie's use of close-ups would be one of the major influences in his *oeuvre*, together with Kurosawa's masterpiece *The Seven Samurai*.

Of Castellari's first films — all of them Westerns — *Go Kill Everybody and Come Back Alone* (*Ammazzali tutti e torna solo*, 1968), starring Chuck Connors, definitely stands out with its unusual seaside setting and Pop culture influences. It still is one of the most original and striking Spaghetti Westerns of its era.

After the World War II movie *Battle Command* (*La battaglia d'Inghilterra*, 1969), Castellari tried his hand at a thriller with the claustrophobic, underrated *Cold Eyes of Fear* (*Gli occhi freddi della paura*, 1971). After the comedy *Ettore Lo Fusto* (Hector the mighty, 1972), a parodic retelling of Homer's *Iliad* set in modern-day suburban Rome, and the tongue-in-cheek Western *The Sting of the West* (*Tedeum*, 1972), which if anything displayed the director's scarce feeling for comedy — a characteristic underlined by his 1976 swashbuckler farce *The Loves and Times of Scaramouche* (*Le avventure e gli amori di Scaramouche*) starring Michael Sarrazin and Ursula Andress — Castellari eventually got to direct his first true poliziottesco, *High Crime* (*La polizia incrimina, la legge assolve*, 1973) starring Franco Nero. Besides being a box office hit, it was the beginning of a fruitful professional association as well as a strong friendship. Castellari and Nero made seven films together, the most recent being *Jonathan of the Bears* (*Jonathan degli orsi*, 1995). The best — and perhaps Castellari's masterpiece — was the elegiac Western *Keoma* (1976), but the mid-to-late seventies were a blessed period for the director, who helmed several outstanding films. Even debatable results such as *Street Law* (*Il cittadino si ribella*, 1974), a take on the vigilante subgenre that lead to critics accusing Castellari of being fascist — showed a director whose technical skills created some of the best action scenes ever filmed in a non-American picture, the best example being the ultra-violent *The Big Racket* (*Il grande racket*, 1976) starring Fabio Testi, who was also in the director's next crime flick, *Heroin Busters* (*La via della droga*, 1977).

A recent portrait of Enzo G. Castellari.

Another movie from the period that acquired cult status was *Inglorious Bastards* (*Quel maledetto treno blindato*, 1978), a war movie starring Bo Svenson and Fred Williamson and built around a typical "wild bunch on a deadly mission behind enemy lines" premise, whose title inspired Quentin Tarantino's *Inglourious Basterds* (2009). Although somewhat overrated, *Inglorious Bastards* was a mixture of Castellari's favorite elements and its disappointing box office results left him embittered. His next film, *The Last House Near the Lake* (*Sensività*, 1979) was a work-for-hire affair (Castellari also played a secondary role as a commissioner), nonetheless resulting in one of the director's weirdest films, an erotic–Gothic hybrid that deserves rediscovery. On the other hand, *The Shark Hunter* (1979) was a tongue-in-cheek exotic adventure that looked (and probably was) half-improvised on the spot. Curiously, in that same period Castellari rejected the offer to direct *Zombie*, which was passed on to Lucio Fulci, as he felt he wasn't the right director for an out-and-out horror film.

The eighties were a mixed bag for Castellari. After the melancholic *film noir The Day of the Cobra* (*Il giorno del cobra*, 1980), which didn't do as well as expected due to the decline of poliziottesco, Castellari directed a blatant Jaws rip-off, *The Last Shark* (*L'ultimo squalo*, 1981) which was soon withdrawn from distribution when Universal sued the production. His next film, the post-atomic science fiction/action yarn *1990: The Bronx Warriors* (*1990: I guerrieri del Bronx*, 1982), albeit far from being his best work, was a surprise hit, spawning a short-lived yet rather fruitful subgenre inspired by John Carpenter's masterful *Escape From New York* (1981), which included Castellari's sequel to his own film *Escape from the Bronx* (*Fuga dal Bronx*, 1983). However, from the mid-eighties on, Castellari's output was aimed at foreign markets, with professionally shot yet far from memorable efforts such as the crime flicks *Striker* (1987) and *Hammerhead* (1990), the misjudged sci-fi/crime hybrid *Light Blast* (*Colpi di luce*, 1985), starring Erik Estrada, and at least one abortion of a movie in *Sinbad of the Seven Seas* (1989), a totally terrible fantasy epic with Lou Ferrigno as the eponymous hero, which was completed and re-edited with uncredited work from Luigi Cozzi.

In the 1990s Castellari mostly worked on made-for-TV projects, such as the *Detective Extralarge* series featuring Bud Spencer and Philip Michael Thomas, and the ill-fated mini-series *The Return of Sandokan* (*Il ritorno di Sandokan*, 1996) with Kabir Bedi reprising the title role, and *Deserto di fuoco* (1997). Castellari claimed that in recent years he shot lots of action scenes in the U.S. for unnamed B-grade adventure and crime movies, but the body of his output is uncertain to say the least. However, the director made an unexpected directorial comeback in 2010 in total Italian style, by exploiting the success of Quentin Tarantino's *Inglourious Basterds*, whose release focused attention on Castellari as well as his own *Inglorious Bastards*.[3] Despite its title, however, *Caribbean Basterds*—note the typo which recalled the one in Tarantino's film!—was a sexploitation quickie about three upper class youngsters who play dirty tricks on their parents' friends while dressed like Alex De Large's droogs in *A Clockwork Orange*, only to end up chased by the police and the drugs ring in the Caribbeans. The movie got a theatrical release in Italy—something of an event given the state of Italian genre cinema—but performed poorly. However, at 75, Castellari is not ready for retirement yet: he's planning to return to directing with a self-penned script which mixes Western and horror.

Notes

1. The Italian "me cojoni" is much more down-to-earth—it literally means "are ya kiddin' me?" and not, as some may think, "my balls," whereas "sti cazzi" is, plain and vulgar referred to one's own member.
2. Pulici, *Il muscolo intelligente*, p. 8.
3. Castellari had a cameo (which unfortunately ended up in the cutting room floor) in Tarantino's epic, as a Fascist hierarch in the Parisian movie theater where the explosive climax takes place

Damiano Damiani (*Pasiano di Pordenone, 7.23.1922–Rome, 3.7.2013*)

The fact that—despite being a technically accomplished and thematically innovative filmmaker, a politically committed director and the helmer of at least a dozen outstanding films—Damiano Damiani never succeeded in becoming a full-fledged auteur for most critics, can be explained by Italy's biased attitude towards genres. Damiani's output was too diverse and at the same time too "commercial"—covering such genres as the action and crime film, the Western and even horror—to win the acclaim of those critics who always prioritized theme over form, message over results.

A former painter, Damiani got involved in the movie business in the late '40s as production designer and writer, working on such films as *Aphrodite, Goddess of Love* (*La Venere di Cheronea*, 1957, Fernando Cerchio, Viktor Tourjansky). He was pushing 40 when he helmed his first film as director: *Lipstick* (*Il rossetto*, 1960), a harsh, realistic crime drama co-written by Cesare Zavattini (De Sica's collaborator on a number of major works including *The Bicycle Thief*) and starring the great director Pietro Germi as a commissioner who investigates the murder of a prostitute, whose only witness, a twelve year-old girl, has a crush on the assassin (Pierre Brice). To Damiani, genre was just a pretext to develop psychologies and portray an Italy where greed and petit bourgeois hypocrisy were the ruling elements in a country torn between the appetite for modernity and the dominance of a retrograde mentality, while the style was assured and even refined, with an impressive reliance on sequence shots and frame composition.

Damiani's subsequent works crowned him as one of the major emerging filmmakers of the decade. *Il sicario* (1961) was another introspective drama in guise of a Hitchcockian crime film. Based on a true story (a man in dire straits accepts a murder assignment on part of his former boss, who wants to get rid of his associate), it offered a grim view of the economic "Boom." *L'isola di Arturo* (1962) and *La noia* (1963) were both literary adaptations of prestigious novels (by Elsa Morante and Alberto Moravia). Among Damiani's first films, however, *La rimpatriata* (1963) stood out as one of the best and most courageous works of the decade in sketching the balance of the "economic miracle" through the story of five friends in their Forties who meet again after many years.

After the mid-'60s, Damiani's output changed rather dramatically, and became at once more daring and commercial. *The Witch* (*La strega in amore*, 1966) was a flawed but fascinating adaptation of Carlos Fuentes' spellbinding novel, in the form of a one-of-a-kind contemporary Gothic yarn, while *A Bullet for the General* (*Quien sabe?*, 1966) was a political adventure story set in Mexico during the revolution (Damiani always rejected the term "Western") starring Klaus Kinski, Lou Castel and Gian Maria Volonté. It paved the way for a slew of films on the subject—the so-called Tortilla Western cycle—and established Damiani as a "popular" director thanks to its huge box office success, but it was also one of the very first films to analyze the process of decolonization, even though through the filter of a genre yarn. The director's next film, *The Day of the Owl* (*Il giorno della civetta*, 1968), would be another landmark, this time in the contemporary Mafia movie genre, forming a diptych of sorts with Elio Petri's *We Still Kill the Old Way* (*A ciascuno il suo*, 1967), also based on a novel by Leonardo Sciascia, one of Italy's major writers of the century.

After another Moravia adaptation, *A Complicated Girl* (*Una ragazza piuttosto complicata*, 1969), which had trouble with the censors for its daring subject matter (resulting in being briefly seized after release) and was not as successful as hoped, Damiani returned to Sicily and to the Mafia with *The Most Beautiful Wife* (*La moglie più bella*, 1970) and *Confessions of a Police Captain* (*Confessione di un commissario di polizia al Procuratore della Repubblica*, 1971). The latter's phenomenal success was another brick in the wall of the then-developing poliziottesco, and proved that Damiani was at his best when conjugating civil commitment with genre material. The director's subsequent output was varied both in themes and in results: a powerful prison drama (*The Case Is Closed, Forget It* / *L'istruttoria è chiusa, dimentichi*, 1971), a harrowing period drama about a real-life child murderer in the Fascist era (*The Assassin of Rome* / *Girolimoni, il mostro di Roma*, 1972), an ambitious but ultimately flawed political allegory (*The Devil Is a Woman* / *Il sorriso del grande tentatore*, 1974) and a very disappointing comic western produced by Sergio Leone (*A Genius, Two Friends, and an Idiot* / *Un genio, due compari, un pollo*, 1975), conceived as a sequel of sorts to Tonino Valerii's *My Name Is Nobody* (*Il mio nome è Nessuno*, 1973) and starring Terence Hill.

Damiani's return to more familiar territories was the much-discussed *How to Kill a Judge* (*Perché si uccide un magistrato*, 1975), which turned out to be yet another commercial success but caused a fuss among the critics, resulting in an unprecedented amount of negative reviews. On the other hand, *I Am Afraid* (*Io ho paura*, 1977) was one of his very best efforts, and proved how he was still in tune with his times — and difficult times they were. The director's subsequent output was solid yet somehow discontinuous, alternating commercial projects (such as the spy yarn *Goodbye & Amen*, 1977) and more personal works (*A Man on His Knees* / *Un uomo in ginocchio*, 1979; *The Warning* / *L'avvertimento*, 1980). Perhaps sensing the decline of Italian popular cinema, Damiani even tried his hand at a hired job across the ocean, a prequel of Stuart Rosenberg's *Amityville Horror* (*Amityville Possession*, 1982) which, at least to this writer, turned out better than the original. However, he eventually ended up working in television.

Once again, the results were both commercially successful and seminal: *La Piovra* (Octopus, 1984) was the most successful TV series of the decade, spawning a number of sequels and renewing the Mafia movie genre while adapting it to the small screen's needs and demands. Damiani's subsequent made-for-TV efforts (*Uomo di rispetto*, 1992; *Una bambina di troppo*, 1994; *Ama il tuo nemico* and its sequel, 1999–2001) suffered from the growing omologation that plagued the Italian film industry, and so did his works for the big screen. Even though they remained highly watchable, the International mafia movie *Pizza Connection* (1985) and *The Dark Sun* (*Il sole buio*, 1990) were packed full with good intentions, but suffered from half-baked plots and lazily recycled clichés, not to mention one too many concessions to TV-style filmmaking and pacing.

However, there were exceptions: *The Inquiry* (*L'inchiesta*, 1986) was an offbeat drama set just after Christ's death and conceived as a sort of mystery, as a Roman magistrate (Keith Carradine) is sent to Judea to investigate the disappearance of a local carpenter named Jesus Christ, but his investigations are hindered by the local Prefect, Pontius Pilate (Harvey Keitel). The equally intriguing *Massacre Play* (*Gioco al massacro*, 1990) was a *kammerspiel* of sorts starring Tomas Milian and Elliot Gould (both delivering amazing performances) as two filmmaker friends who play a bitter battle of wits, with dialogue lines worthy of David Mamet and a cynical metafilmic look which was much more focused than in Damiani's *How to Kill a Judge*. However, the film — one of the director's own favorites — was a box office flop.

Damiani's more recent films were unworthy of his name: *Angel of Death* (*L'angelo con la pistola*, 1992) was a goofy stab at the woman-as-hitman subgenre as started by Luc Besson's *Nikita*, while the truly awful *Alex l'ariete* (2000), starring World Ski champion Alberto Tomba as the unlikely cop hero, was ridiculed by critics and audiences alike upon release. It was a sad footnote to such a prestigious filmography. However, Damiani's final film *Killers on Holiday* (*Assassini dei giorni di festa*, 2002) was an intriguing apologue on the themes of deceit and the methodology of representation, along the vein of *Massacre Play*. Too bad it came and went almost unnoticed, in the sad landscape of early 2000s Italian cinema.

Fernando di Leo (San Ferdinando di Puglia, 1.11.1932—Rome, 12.2003)

With 17 films as a director and about 50 scripts from 1964 to 1985, when the inexorable crisis of Italian cinema pushed him into a forced retirement, Fernando di Leo is one of Italy's most interesting yet underestimated personalities of the period. Born in San Ferdinando di Puglia in 1932, the literate, open-minded, nonconformist di Leo always chose to do things his own way. To consider him as just the director of *Caliber 9* (*Milano calibro 9*, shot in 1971 but released in Italy in early 1972) would be a mistake. With his crime films based on Giorgio Scerbanenco's stories, di Leo depicted the Milanese underworld with a harsh and often brutal realism, and with memorable results. Yet one cannot underestimate di Leo's output outside the genre: with such films as *A Woman on Fire* / *Burn, Boy, Burn* (*Brucia ragazzo, brucia*, 1969), *A Wrong Way to Love* (*Amarsi male*, 1969) and *Seduction*, (*La seduzione*, 1973), the director portrayed female psychology and desire on screen with a sensibility that was quite different from Italian erotic cinema of the period. Even though he made "commercial" and genre films, di Leo was able to maintain autonomy, producing many of his works with his own production company Daunia Cineproduzioni 70, from 1969 to 1976; he also wrote almost all of his scripts. It's not an exaggeration to consider him an *auteur* with a precise and coherent artistic trajectory within Italian cinema of the 1970s. Take the dialogue, for instance: di Leo's characters talk in a peculiar, literate manner, even when they are murdering, torturing or making love, while the use of dialectal terms both as a euphonic device and as an anthropological connotation achieves extremely complex effects. This is not to say di Leo made only good films: his *oeuvre* is extremely discontinuous, with opaque and routine works rubbing

Fernando di Leo.

shoulders with overlooked gems. Yet even his failures and his minor efforts have interesting elements: the controversial, ambitious pro–Feminist parable *To Be Twenty* (*Avere vent'anni*, 1978) has a nasty sting in the tail, with an ending so abrupt, cruel and downbeat that it caused the film to be hastily re-edited, and its powerful message not just softened but completely overturned.

After a brief period at Rome's official film school (Centro Sperimentale di Cinematografia), di Leo made his debut as a director in 1963 with *Un posto in paradiso* ("A Place in Heaven"), an episode of the omnibus comedy *Gli eroi di ieri ... oggi ... e domain* ... ("Heroes of Yesterday ... Today ... and Tomorrow...") co-directed by Enzo Dell'Aquila, which had trouble with the censors due to its explicit anticlerical overtones. But his first real breakthrough was as a scriptwriter. Although his name does not appear in the credits, it is widely acknowledged that di Leo co-wrote Sergio Leone's *A Fistful of Dollars* (*Per un pugno di dollari*, 1964) and *For a Few Dollars More* (*Per qualche dollaro in più*, 1965). During those years he scripted a number of Westerns, which all number amongst the most original and interesting of the period, such as Florestano Vancini's *Days of Vengeance* (*I lunghi giorni della vendetta*, 1967, *very* loosely based on Alexandre Dumas' *The Count of Monte Cristo*) and Giorgio Capitani's *Every Man for Himself* a.k.a. *The Ruthless Four* (*Ognuno per sé*, 1968, a sort of remake of *The Treasure of the Sierra Madre* with homosexual and Oedipal subtexts).

The Western was the top-selling genre at the time, whereas few seemed to care about *film noir*. Di Leo, on the contrary, loved it: he discovered Hammett through the French writer André Gide ("At first I was really intrigued by the fact that Gide cited him as an author on a par with Hemingway or Steinbeck" he claimed) and was an avid viewer of old Warner and RKO noir flicks. He decided to try and find his own way to Italian *film noir*—one that would be different from both the sociological approach of Lizzani's films and the 'American' one. His first effort was the script for *Date for a Murder* (*Omicidio per appuntamento*, 1967), based on Franco Enna's novel *Tempo di massacro*, written in 1955: di Leo updated the setting to contemporary Rome and contaminated the hard-boiled plot (a womanizing private eye investigates his best friend's disappearance) with nods to contemporary spy movies (the hero is Giorgio Ardisson, Agent 3S3 in Sergio Sollima's spy flicks), while consistently balancing the tone between seriousness and self-parody with unexpected, grotesque and nasty gags. The director, former journalist Mino Guerrini, adopted an exhilarating, colorful pop style with unusual stylistic inventions and a remarkable use of handheld camera (by future director Camillo Bazzoni). Di Leo and Guerrini followed it up with the much bleaker *Gangsters '70* (1968). Unfortunately the film, released at a time when the market was flooded with erotic thrillers, flopped at the box office. Guerrini's career would go downhill from here, while di Leo started directing his own scripts: a war flick, *Red Roses for the Führer* (*Rose rosse per il Führer*, 1968) and a couple of erotic films: *A Woman on Fire* and *A Wrong Way to Love*. For his fourth-and-a-half film, *Naked Violence* (*I ragazzi del massacro*, 1969) he returned to *film noir* territory, adapting a novel by Giorgio Scerbanenco, whose writings would nourish the director's best works—which *Naked Violence* is not, even though it remains a key work in his filmography.

Although highly praised by genre fans, the *giallo Slaughter Hotel* (*La bestia uccide a sangue freddo*, 1971), starring Klaus Kinski, Margaret Lee and Rosalba Neri, was a throwaway work-for-hire which, despite a few clever touches—such as the ironic idea of having a women's asylum filled with weapons and torture instruments which the killer would, of course, use prominently—can be considered a decidely minor addition to di Leo's *oeuvre*, even though it nevertheless gained much more visibility than his better works.[1]

Next came *Caliber 9* (*Milano calibro 9*, 1972), di Leo's masterpiece, followed by another outstanding work, *The Italian Connection* a.k.a. *Manhunt* (*La mala ordina*, 1972), inspired like the former by Scerbanenco's writings and characterized by a cruder, more caustic look. Ending di Leo's so-called "trilogy of the *milieu*" was an incredibly violent, cynic and darkly ironic Mafia movie, *The Boss* (*Il boss*, 1973), starring Henry Silva, which ranks alongside his best work and got him into trouble with politicians and authorities because of the director's crude exposé of the connection between Mafia and Italy's major party, Democrazia Cristiana. Di Leo's anarchic temper was equally evident in *Shoot First, Die Later* (*Il poliziotto è marcio*, 1974), an apparently standard poliziottesco—and actually another work for hire from a script by Sergio Donati—about a cop played by Luc Merenda, who in one scene proudly announces: "Yes sir, I'm corrupt! I'm a scoundrel and a traitor! I got 60 million in my bank account, a high-class mistress, and whenever I raise my voice everybody stands to attention!" It's the one and only case in the whole genre, once again a proof of di Leo's subversive approach to clichés.

Fernando di Leo, center, directs Frank Wolff, left, and Luigi Pistilli on the set of *Caliber 9* (1972).

The director's subsequent films were more or less disappointments. Neither the comedy *noir Loaded Guns* (*Colpo in canna*, 1975) nor the Ernesto Gastaldi-scripted *Kidnap Syndicate* (*La città sconvolta: caccia spietata ai rapitori*, 1975) made much of an impression, the latter being di Leo's most standard entry in the genre that far. *Nick the Sting* (*Gli amici di Nick Hezard*, 1976), a mildly enjoyable rip-off of George Roy Hill's *The Sting*, didn't fare better. After a couple of interesting yet flawed scripts — Romolo Guerrieri's *Young, Violent, Dangerous* (*Liberi armati e pericolosi*, 1976) once again based on Scerbanenco, and Ruggero Deodato's hyperviolent, subtly parodic buddy cop movie *Live Like a Cop, Die Like a Man* (*Uomini si nasce poliziotti si muore*) both released in 1976[2]— his next film as a director was a return to form. *Rulers of the City* (*I padroni della città*, 1976), starring Jack Palance, was the umpteenth incursion into the underworld, but with a more palpable comic feel. It was the last film produced by di Leo's own company and his subsequent output would suffer from that.

In 1978 di Leo licensed two pics, the *film noir Blood and Diamonds* (*Diamanti sporchi di sangue*) and the erotic drama *To Be Twenty*, followed by the underrated *Madness* (*Vacanze per un massacro*, 1980). None of them were truly up to the director's standards — except perhaps *Blood and Diamonds*, a low-key return to *Caliber 9*'s storyline and atmosphere — but di Leo could not be blamed for the films' shortcomings. He was just trying to survive, like many others. After an unfortunate experience with the TV series *L'assassino ha le ore contate* (1981), six one-hour long made-for-TV movies produced by RAI Uno and scripted by Fabio Pittorru, which are still unreleased to this day, di Leo churned out a shaky war action flick, *The Violent Breed* (*Razza violenta*, 1984) before directing what was going to be his last film, *Killer vs. Killers / Death Commando* (1985).

Originally conceived as a remake of Huston's *The Asphalt Jungle* (1950), *Killer vs. Killers* was far from brilliant, yet at times even moving in its refusal to follow the path of contemporary action/crime films. Henry Silva once again played the leading role, a taciturn hitman who is part of a commando sent to steal a formula in a military base. But the heist — which is hastily performed halfway through the film — is less important than what happens next: the dealer (Edmund Purdom) orders the members of the gang to be rubbed out. What is left of the Huston connection are the names of several characters (Jaffe, Sterling), while the director's typically sardonic humor pops up here and there: a guy who's carrying a bag chained to his wrist has his hand amputated with huge garden scissors; one of Silva's associates likes to pay a couple of girls to dance naked in front of him in his living room (after the hit, the girls become four); Silva practices his aim by shooting passers-by in a park with sedative bullets. But the budget was way too tight, and it shows, especially in the action scenes. Overall, *Killer vs. Killers* looks as if di Leo got tired after a while: the final showdown in a zoo, with Silva killing enemies by the dozen with a bazooka, among escaped animals, sounds exciting on paper but is haphazardly shot. What's more, co-producer Albert [Cola] Janni — who would gain some notoriety years later with his impression of politician Massimo D'Alema in satirical TV shows — is an absymal co-protagonist. Silva often complains "You are not a professional!," and it sounds like di Leo's private revenge against such a waste. *Killer vs. Killers* quickly disappeared into oblivion: it wasn't even released theatrically in Italy, where it surfaced over 20 years later on DVD.

Starting from the mid-nineties, the Italian magazine *Nocturno Cinema* introduced Fernando di Leo's work to a new generation of fans, first with a pair of massive, groundbreaking interviews, then a number of features on his films and a whole monographic issue in September 2003, just a few months before the director's untimely death in December 2003. The following years saw the definitive critical recognition of Fernando di Leo as one of the most important Italian directors of the 1970s, and a true innovator of the crime genre.

Notes

1. *Slaughter Hotel* was also released in a version featuring hardcore inserts of female genitalia and lesbian intercourse. This version circulated in France under the title *Les insatisfée poupées érotiques du Docteur Hichcock*, in a nod to Riccardo Freda's celebrated Gothic masterpiece.
2. Di Leo often did uncredited polish work on other scripts, such as Duccio Tessari's *Big Guns* (*Tony Arzenta*, 1973) and the German co-production *Bloody Friday* (*Blutiger Freitag*, a.k.a. *Violenza contro la violenza*) directed by Rolf Olsen. Another uncredited job, this time behind the camera, was the erotic comedy *Sesso in testa* (1974), officially signed by actor Sergio Ammirata, who often appeared in di Leo's films.

Romolo Guerrieri (Born Romolo Girolami; Rome, 12.5.1931)

Growing up in a family of filmmakers is not easy, and Romolo Girolami obviously felt that his surname was uncomfortable to carry. The Girolami family was an institution of sorts at Cinecittà. Everybody was in the movies. Romolo's elderly brother, Marino, had been a director since the '50s, and his nephews Ennio and Enzo were respectively an actor and a director too. That's why Romolo decided to use his mother's surname when he started his career as a filmmaker. As was customary in those days, it had taken a long path as an assistant director — almost 40 titles, including Giuseppe De Santis' World War II epic *Attack and Retreat* (*Italiani brava gente*, 1964) — before Guerrieri was given the chance to debut behind the cameras, not counting 1961's *Beauty on the Beach* (*Bellezze sulla spiaggia*) directed by his brother Marino and assembled with bits from other films, which Romolo signed but did not direct. Predictably, he started with Westerns, as everybody was making them back in the mid '60s. *Seven Guns for Timothy* (*Sette magnifiche pistole*, 1966), shot in Spain and starring Errol Flynn's son Sean, was light-hearted and almost parodic, closer to Giraldi and Tessari than to Leone.

Guerrieri's output as a director was relatively scarce, compared not only to that of his family, but within genre cinema as well: his attention to screenplays and his care in choosing and preparing his next projects made him an outsider. His subsequent films, *Johnny Yuma* (1966, written by Fernando di Leo) and *Guns of Violence* (*10.000 dollari per un massacro*, 1967) were rather peculiar efforts compared to contemporaneous Westerns, with subtle original touches such as the presence of the sea in the latter. Yet Guerrieri moved on to different genres, preferring not to be labeled. Although not one of the director's favorite films, *The Sweet Body of Deborah* (*Il dolce corpo di Deborah*, 1968) proved to be a key title in the evolution of the Italian thriller: its enormous success spawned a subgenre of erotic gialli loosely based on Henri-Georges Clouzot's *Diabolique* (which included Umberto Lenzi's trilogy *Paranoia*, *So Sweet, So Perverse* and *A Quiet Place to Kill*) and relaunched Carroll Baker as a star in Italy. Guerrieri's next project was a *film noir*, *Detective Belli* (*Un detective*, 1969) about a corrupt cop — one of the very first in Italian cinema — played by Franco Nero, followed by *The Divorce* (*Il divorzio*, 1970), an ambitious, vitriolic comedy about a much-discussed topic (the law on divorce finally passed in December 1970) starring Vittorio Gassman, which proved that Guerrieri was not a mere genre director. His following film, *The Double* (*La controfigura*, 1971), starring Jean Sorel, Ewa Aulin and Lucia Bosé, was yet another peculiar thriller, based on a critically acclaimed novel and built around an elaborate flashback structure — perhaps too elaborate, as Guerrieri later complained.

Then came a string of crime films, as Guerrieri approached the genre at the peak of its popularity. "All these crime films we used to make — Marino, Enzo and I — we didn't talk about them between us" he explained. However, his contribution to the genre is sensibly different from that of his relatives: for one, Guerrieri's film distinctly convey a melancholic, pessimistic feel, given the fact that the commissioners in *La polizia è al servizio del cittadino?* (1973) and *City Under Siege* (*Un uomo, una città*, 1974) were played by Enrico Maria Salerno, a far cry from Maurizio Merli's athleticism.

On *La polizia è al servizio del cittadino?* Guerrieri had to deal with his star's notoriously difficult reputation, as Salerno expected to discuss each shot he was in with the director beforehand, and then decide whether he liked it or not. To make things clear, on the first day of shooting Guerrieri set up the lighting and camera positions, as soon as Salerno showed up he told the actor what was required of him, promptly establishing a hierarchy between the filmmaker and the actor from the outset. The result was a very fruitful working relationship, which continued in *City Under Siege* and in the World War II drama *Salvo d'Acquisto* (1975).

Despite *La polizia è al servizio del cittadino?*'s ending where the commissioner kills the powerful crime boss he can't arrest, Guerrieri rejected the accusations of Fascism on the part of the critics that were the norm in those days. "I personally suffered because of these accusations, because I felt and still feel absolutely anti–Fascist, and it was not my will to create violent characters who dealt out justice on their own" the director explained, underlining the different positions that characterized the view of the crime genre on part of filmmakers and critics of the time. "Those were the stories, those were the characters that people wanted to see. Movies always reflect the historical period in which they are made, and you can't do anything about it. [...] And moviegoers often found them liberating. It's like with Dario Argento's films: by being scared, one becomes somehow relieved."[1]

Young, Violent, Dangerous (*Liberi, armati, pericolosi*, 1976) and *Covert Action* (*Sono stato un agente CIA*, 1978) were further examples of the director's peculiarity compared to his contemporaries. The former, based on stories by Giorgio Scerbanenco and again written by Fernando di Leo, was only superficially close to the subgenre featuring violent youths and featured yet another humane commissioner, played by an unusually low-key Tomas Milian. *Covert Action*—an ambitious thriller conceived for foreign markets and starring David Janssen—was more crepuscular than explosive, more introspective than exciting, and turned out to be a box office flop. "After *Covert Action*, I told myself, "Either I make a big international picture, or I'll do like some of my colleagues, and accept small films, five weeks' shooting each, and make some money." Big, big mistake...."[2]

Guerrieri's subsequent works were in fact two nondescript comedies, *L'importante è non farsi notare* (1979), starring then-popular TV female impersonators Sorelle Bandiera, and *La gorilla* (1982), a mild sex farce with Lory del Santo as a bodyguard. The latter proved to be an ordeal for the director as the ravishing Del Santo simply couldn't act, forcing him to reshoot many scenes again and again. Eventually, he was so exasperated that at one point he asked his star: "I beg your pardon, but are you an actress?" Then came *The Final Executioner* (*L'ultimo guerriero*, 1983), a tepid post-atomic adventure written by Roberto Leoni and loosely inspired by *The Most Dangerous Game*.

Like many of his contemporaries, Guerrieri ended up working in TV. *Due vite, un destino* (1992) was a better-than-average crime film with a prestigious cast (Michael Nouri, Fabio Testi, Carol Alt, Rod Steiger, Burt Young, Philippe Leroy....) about the unlikely team-up between an American hitman (Nouri) and an Italian commissioner (Testi), and one of the few last worthy addictions to the genre, within the increasingly banal and uninteresting realm of TV movies. That same year Guerrieri helmed the dreadful *A tutte le volanti*, the pilot for a TV series which never took off. Produced by Mario Cecchi Gori, it was a politically correct crime film that sums up the very worst of what was about to come. It was the director's final film, as Guerrieri abandoned the movie business and became involved with volunteer associations.

Notes

1. Manlio Gomarasca and Davide Pulici. "Romolo Guerrieri. L'intimismo del genere," in Aa.Vv., "Percorsi alternativi: Controcorrente 2," *Nocturno dossier" #30* (January 2005), p. 51.
2. Ibid.

***Umberto Lenzi** (Massa Marittima, 8.6.1931)*

When he directed his first poliziottesco, *Gang War In Milan* (*Milano rovente*, 1973), the 42 year-old Umberto Lenzi was already a veteran of sorts. One of the undisputed leading figures in Italian genre cinema, Lenzi was a movie enthusiast since his early grade school years, where he founded various film fan clubs while studying Law. He then started out as a journalist for various local newspapers and magazines, such as the prestigious "Bianco e Nero," and eventually put off his Law studies to pursue the technical arts of filmmaking. Lenzi enrolled at Rome's Centro Sperimentale di Cinematografia in 1956, and for his final exam he made *I ragazzi di Trastevere*, a short film heavily inspired by Pasolini's writings. Even though the swashbuckler *Queen of the Seas* (*Le avventure di Mary Read*, 1961) is generally considered his official debut as a director, prior to that Lenzi actually directed a film in Greece in 1958 entitled *Mia Italida stin Ellada / Vacanze ad Atene*, which was never released.

The sixties were a busy decade for the Tuscan filmmaker, who got to display his eclecticism by jumping from one genre to the next, according to what the market was asking for: grim melodramas (*Duel of Fire, / Duello sulla Sila*, 1962), adventure flicks (*The Triumph of Robin Hood / Il trionfo di Robin Hood*, 1962), historical dramas (the excellent *Catherine of Russia / Caterina di Russia*, 1963), pirate films (*Sandokan the Great / Sandokan la tigre*

Umberto Lenzi behind the camera.

di Mompracem, 1963), sword-and-sandal (*Messalina vs. the Son of Hercules / L'ultimo gladiatore*, 1964), and even weird crossovers such as the cult favorite *Samson and the Slave Queen* (*Zorro contro Maciste*, 1963) which featured the titular muscleman (actually Maciste in the Italian version) as opposed to swashbuckler legend Zorro.

Lenzi's technical prowess made him the ideal director for action and spy flicks when James Bond mania exploded in Italy, with such titles as *008: Operation Exterminate* (*A 008, operazione sterminio*, 1965). He was one of the first directors to bring the so-called "fumetti neri" to the screen with *Kriminal* (1966). Blonde-haired, handsome Glenn Saxson played the ruthless titular adventurer who performed his deadly deeds donning a skeleton suit and mask, and Lenzi opted for a lighter tone in jarring contrast with the comic strip's explosive mixture of sex and violence. "I saw it recently on TV and it seemed even better than when I shot it in 1966: then I was a bit perplexed, now I appreciate the aspect of irony in it, something which comic strips didn't have because they were vulgar, horrible," he would claim.[1] Lenzi argued with the comic book's creator Max Bunker (real name Luciano Secchi) about some major changes he made to the character because "it was a bit Nazi-skin fascist. We made a fun film." However, the results were rather disappointing, lacking the comic book's tongue-in-cheek attitude and political uncorrectness, while much of the film looked more like one of those travelogue James Bond rip-offs that were flooding the screens at the time.[2]

Perhaps Lenzi was struggling to make more adult films, as certified by one of his best efforts ever, the war movie *Desert Commandos* (*Attentato ai tre grandi*, 1967), which allowed him to put to good use his passion for Twentieth century history (nowadays Lenzi is widely regarded as one of the leading authorities on the Spanish Civil War). His subsequent war film, *Legion of the Damned* (*La legione dei dannati*, 1969), benefited from a script by Dario Argento. In that same period, however, Lenzi also directed a couple of none-too-impressive Westerns, *Pistol for a Hundred Coffins* (*Una pistola per cento bare*, 1968) and *All Out* (*Tutto per tutto*, 1968), which he himself dismissed by jokingly saying that he just didn't like horses. However, Lenzi achieved impressive box office results in Italy and abroad with a triptych of erotic thrillers starring Carroll Baker that were heavily influenced by French *film noir* of the period: *Orgasmo* (1968, released in the United States as *Paranoia*, leading to a somewhat confusing situation in years to come), *So Sweet, So Perverse* (*Così dolce ... così perversa*, 1969) and *Paranoia* (a.k.a. *A Quiet Place to Kill*, 1970). The mixture of sexual innuendo, complex Machiavellian plots and upper class settings — although drawing liberally from Jacques Deray and René Clement (in interviews at that time Lenzi claimed *Swimming Pool* and *Rider on the Rain* to be among his favorite films) not to mention Henri-Georges Clouzot's masterpiece *Diabolique* (1955) — was a winning one, as it took advantage of Italy's relaxing censorship and helped put aside the more puerile genre offerings of the previous years.

With the commercial explosion of Dario Argento's *gialli*, Lenzi followed the trend, albeit in his own personal way: *Seven Blood-stained Orchids* (*Sette orchidee macchiate di rosso*, 1972) was a more plot-driven affair than other *gialli* of the period, with references to Cornell Woolrich novels, while *Knife of Ice* (*Il coltello di ghiaccio*, 1972) was a grim variation on Robert Siodmak's *The Spiral Staircase* (1945). The flawed yet underrated *Spasmo* (1974) was an attempt at merging giallo and psychological thriller, whereas the gruesome *Wide-Eyed in the Dark* a.k.a. *The Secret Killer* (*Gatti rossi in un labirinto di vetro*, 1974) was at least noteworthy for its trashy, mind-blowing twist.

In that period, Lenzi also paved the way for one of Italian cinema's most debatable genres, the cannibal film, with the violent adventure movie *The Man from Deep River* (*Il paese del sesso selvaggio*, 1972) starring Ivan Rassimov. He would return to the genre in the late 1970s with a pair of film that are perhaps among his best known to fans, although far from his most impressive work: *Eaten Alive* (*Mangiati vivi!*, 1980) and the infamous *Cannibal Ferox* a.k.a. *Make Them Die Slowly* (1981).

The mid-seventies finally saw Lenzi's encounter with the crime film. It was a match made in heaven (or hell, for that matter): the filmmaker's cynical attitude towards violence made him one of the ideal directors to explore a genre rooted in the period's turbulent reality. From 1975 to 1979 Lenzi devoted himself almost exclusively to crime films — the only exceptions were two royally cast World War II war flicks, *Battle Force* (*Il grande attacco*, 1978) and *From Hell to Victory* (*Contro 4 bandiere*, 1979) — rounding off this experience with the remarkable *From Corleone to Brooklyn* (*Da Corleone a Brooklyn*, 1979). The 1980s, with the decline of genre cinema, saw him once again move along different paths, yet this time with decidedly less remarkable results. However, the early '80s saw the release of some of Lenzi's most notorious films, such as the trashy, gory horror *Nightmare City* (*Incubo sulla città contaminata*, 1981) and the aforementioned *Cannibal Ferox*. Lenzi dabbled again with horror and thriller later in the decade, although with disappointing results, on *Ghosthouse* (*La casa 3*, 1988, signed with his Nabokov-inspired a.k.a. Humphrey Humbert), the slasher flick *Nightmare Beach* (*Nightmare Beach — La spiaggia del terrore*, 1989), credited to Harry Kirkpatrick since Lenzi refused to sign it, and more low budget fodder such as *The Hell's Gate* (*Le porte dell'inferno*, 1989) and the abysmal *Demons 3* (*Demoni 3*, 1991) which remains his worst film. In late 1980s Lenzi also directed a couple of TV horror movies for Reteitalia (*The House of Witchcraft* and *The House of Lost Souls*) before ending his career with a couple of passable yet nondescript cop flicks in the vein of American movies of the period.

With 65 films as a director, Umberto Lenzi is a sort of institution in Italian genre cinema. His legendary bad temper and irritating self-importance made him lots of enemies, yet his creative enthusiasm allowed him to survive the death of genre cinema and start anew in a different direction. Much more vital than his age would make people think, in later years Lenzi has embarked on a successful career as a novelist, with a series of successful murder mysteries set in 1930s and '40s Cinecittà, which feature real-life characters of the Italian movie industry during Fascism.

Notes

1. Andrea Giorgi, "Eating Lenzi: Umberto Lenzi interviewed," *Necronomicon* #5 (1994).

2. A sequel, *Il marchio di Kriminal* (1967), again starring Saxson, was directed by Fernando Cerchio.

Carlo Lizzani (Rome, 4.3.1922)

One of the most important filmmakers in Italian post-war cinema, Carlo Lizzani is also a renowned film critic and the author of some of the most significant books on Italian cinema (such as 1953's *Storia del cinema italiano*). His activity as a director has always been deeply entangled with his political views: a member of Italy's Communist Party, he debuted in 1946, scripting and playing a role (Don Camillo, the priest killed by the Nazis) in Aldo Vergano's *Il sole sorge ancora*, one of the first examples of Post-World War II Neorealism. Lizzani also worked on such notable films of the late 1940s as Roberto Rossellini's *Germany Year Zero*, Alberto Lattuada's *The Mill on the Po* (both 1948) and Giuseppe De Santis' *Bitter Rice* (*Riso amaro*, 1949), for which he received an Academy Award nomination for Best Original Story.

In those years Lizzani directed several documentaries which were financed by the Communist Party and addressed deeply felt social issues (such as *La lunga lotta*, about peasants' fights and strikes for their rights): all of them were either banned or heavily cut by the severe, anti–Communist board of censors presided over by future Prime Minister Giulio Andreotti. His first films as director were equally persecuted by the censors. *Attention! Bandits!* (*Achtung! Banditi!*, 1951), which evoked the Resistance against Nazi troops, was denied distribution abroad; the script for *Ai margini della metropoli* (At the Edge of the Big City, 1953), based on a real-life crime, had to be drastically changed in order to be filmed; and *Chronicle of Poor Lovers* (*Cronache di poveri amanti*, 1954), based on Vasco Pratolini's celebrated novel, was denied foreign distribution too. Nevertheless, in the '50s and '60s Lizzani established himself as one of Italy's most interesting filmmakers, with such works as *La muraglia cinese* (The Great Wall of China, 1958), a documentary on post-revolutionary China; *The Hunchback of Rome* (1960), the story of a real-life partisan-turned-bandit who operated and which featured Pier Paolo Pasolini in one of his rare acting roles; *L'oro di Roma* (The Gold of Rome, 1961), which examined events around the final deportation of the Jews of Rome and the Roman roundup of October 1943; and *Il processo di Verona* (The Verona Trial, 1962), on the trial of Fascist hierarchs after Mussolini's escape to Salò.

These works demonstrated that Lizzani's favorite themes were rooted in recent history, and they were paired with the director's innately robust filmmaking. The results retained the spectacular qualities of genre cinema while unmistakably being *auteur* films. In the mid-sixties, after a period of rather disappointing works, Lizzani tried his hand at the Western genre, which was in vogue after the huge success of Sergio Leone's *A Fistful of Dollars*: both *The Hills Run Red* (*Un fiume di dollari*, 1966) and *Requiescant* (1967) were slated by critics, despite Lizzani's political approach to the genre as well as the presence of Pasolini as a priest in the latter film. In the same period, the director embraced different themes, often taking inspiration from everyday news stories. The results were cutting edge crime films such as *Wake Up and Kill* (*Svegliati e uccidi*, 1966) and the groundbreaking *Bandits in Milan* (*Banditi a Milano*, 1968), together with less effective works—*The Tough and the Mighty* (*Barbagia*, 1969); *Black Turin* (*Torino nera*, 1972); *Crazy Joe* (1974)—which somehow diminished his reputation among the critics, who saw these films as commercial compromises. Lizzani's best film of the 1970s was the grim black comedy-drama *Roma Bene* (1971), while the mid-seventies saw him once again take inspiration from the news for the impressively downbeat *The Teenage Prostitution Racket* (*Storie di vita e malavita*, 1975) and the flawed *San Babila 8 P.M.* (*San Babila ore 20: un delitto inutile*, 1976), both covered in this book as well.

After *Kleinhoff Hotel* (1977), a pretentious erotic drama on the subject of terrorism starring Corinne Cléry which was perhaps his worst film to date, Lizzani became the director of the Venice Festival, with uniformly praised results. In the '80s his output was sparse: after the underrated kammerspiel *The House with the Yellow Carpet* (*La casa del tappeto giallo*, 1982) he directed the trashy crime crama *Mamma Ebe* (1985) and the drama *Caro Gorbaciov* (Dear Gorbachev, 1988, co-starring Harvey Keitel). In the 1990s, however, Lizzani helmed one of his best films ever, *Celluloide* (Celluloid, 1996) a heartfelt retelling of the genesis of Rossellini's masterpiece *Rome Open City* (*Roma città aperta*, 1945). Admirably lucid and active despite his age, Lizzani hasn't stopped

Peter Boyle, center, and director Carlo Lizzani on the set of *Crazy Joe* (1974).

making films, documentaries and TV movies, while also continuing his work as an essayist: his latest feature film, 2007's *Hotel Meina*, about a little-known Nazi massacre in 1943's Northern Italy, once again shows the director's urgency to explore and analyze 20th century history, so as to preserve its memory and significance for the younger generations.

Stelvio Massi *(Civitanova Marche, 3.26.1929—Velletri, 3.26.2004)*

One of the filmmakers most associated with poliziottesco throughout his career, Stelvio Massi brought a neat visual style and a melancholic vein to the crime genre, which characterized most of his collaboration with Maurizio Merli and, as a consequence, the whole series in its fading years. Born in Civitanova Marche, Massi studied Architecture at Rome's academy, but he eventually left to follow his dreams in the movie business. He started as an assistant set designer, then he found his way behind the camera, first as assistant camera, then as cameraman and eventually as director of photography.

Massi's style as a director of photography was brilliantly unorthodox, as shown by his excellent work in Giorgio Albertazzi's seminal TV movie *Jekyll* (1969), a thought-provoking modern-day reworking of Stevenson's story. Massi specialized in Westerns, bringing his refined visuals to such films as Tonino Valerii's *The Price of Power* (*Il prezzo del potere*, 1969), to which he provided some remarkable depth of field shots reminiscent of Gregg Toland's work.

Then, as many of his colleagues had before him, he got to take that big step up the career ladder. Massi's film debut as a director took place in 1973 with *Halleluja to Vera Cruz* (*Partirono preti tornarono ... curati*, 1973, signed with the a.k.a. Newman Rostel), a nondescript Western comedy starring Lionel Stander. Judging from his first films, Massi's directorial career looked as if it would be less than memorable. *Macrò—Giuda uccide il venerdì* (1974) was an overambitious attempt at retelling the passion of Christ in modern-day Rome, amidst prostitutes and drug dealers, while *Five Women for the Killer* (*5 donne per l'assassino*, 1974) was a grim, trashy *giallo* characterized by a few excessively violent murder scenes and little else (not counting an uncredited cameo by a young and ravishing Ilona Staller).

Luckily, Massi found the poliziottesco and the poliziottesco found him. Even though not on a par with his best efforts, *Emergency Squad* (*Squadra volante*, 1974), starring Tomas Milian as a revenge-obsessed cop, displayed the director's flair for the genre, but it was the *Mark the Cop* trilogy that definitely labeled Massi as an action director, due to his keen eye for shooting action scenes, excellent use of hand-held camera and a refreshing extraneousness from the standard visual trappings of genre filmmaking. After a couple of interesting but flawed poliziotteschi—*The Last Round* (*Il conto è chiuso*, 1976), an undeclared remake of Leone's *A Fistful of Dollars* starring ex prizefighter Carlos Monzón and Luc Merenda as the villain, and the Milian/Merenda vehicle *Destruction Force* (*La banda del trucido*, 1977), Massi finally met Maurizio Merli, who would not only become his favorite actor but also one of his best friends.

With six films in four years, their association marked the trajectory of the whole genre, from 1977's box office hit *Highway Racer* to 1980's crepuscular *The Rebel*. The sudden decline of poliziottesco—as well as Merli's popularity—forced Massi to part ways with the actor. Producers forced him to cast Fabio Testi instead of Merli in the action diptych *Speed Cross* and *Speed Driver* (both 1980) which somehow returned to the atmosphere of *Highway Racer*, even though drastically toning down the crime angle.

Even though it counts no less than 32 titles, Massi's body of work as a director is largely unknown even in his home country, and it suffered a lot from the crisis in the Italian movie industry. His output in the 1980s and 1990s was erratic to say the least: after a couple of "*sceneggiate*" starring Mario Merola, he licensed a nasty trio of *Mondo* movies (*Mondo cane oggi: l'incredibile*, 1986; *Mondo cane 2000*, 1988; *Droga sterco di Dio*, 1989) for producer Gabriele Crisanti, which dubiously referred to Gualtiero Jacopetti's *Mondo Cane* (1962), and *The Black Cobra* (1987), the first entry in the urban crime series starring Fred Williamson. Patently aimed at the U.S. market, these were low budget quickies that retained little of Massi's trademark style, just like the erotic thriller *Arabella, Black Angel* (*Arabella l'angelo nero*, 1989), which the director signed under the a.k.a. Max Steel. His last films, the Venezuelan-shot war flick *The 5th Day* a.k.a. *Wardogs* (*Il quinto giorno*, 1993, which spawned a sequel directed by Massi's son Danilo) and the action yarns *High Risk* (*Alto rischio*) and *Balkan Runner* (*La pista bulgara*), both shot in 1993 in Sofia, were slightly better, all decently shot but marred by bland clichéd scripts and clumsy acting. As expected, though, they had little or no circulation at all in Italy and ended up going straight to home video.

Massi died on the day of his 75th birthday, in 2004.

Appendix Three: Stars of Italian Crime Films

***Franco Gasparri** (Senigallia, 10.31.1948 — Rome, 3.31.1999)*

Well before he rose to prominence as *Mark the Cop*, Franco Gasparri's striking green eyes were already a trademark. Like many other stars of the poliziottesco, Gasparri was already famous before he made his debut in the genre. Yet, unlike all of his colleagues, he wasn't even a movie star.

The putative son of artist Rodolfo Gasparri (one of Italy's best known movie poster artists) who later designed the locandinas for all of his son's films, Franco had debuted on screen as a kid in a few Sword-and-sandal flicks, Guido Malatesta's *Goliath Against the Giants* (*Goliath contro i giganti*, 1961) and Gianfranco Parolini's *Samson* (*Sansone*, 1962) and *The Fury of Hercules* (*La furia di Ercole*, 1962).

Gasparri's career in photonovels started by sheer chance. During his service in the army Franco met a popular photonovel actor, Luis La Torre, who suggested he groped his career in show business by sending his photos to the major publishing houses. Franco took his advice and was called to star in a picture story for the photonovel magazine "Sogno," then owned by Rizzoli, entitled *Rendetemi mia figlia* (Give me back my daughter) and in which he appeared alongside Patrizia Ceccarini and Renato Stazzonelli under his real name Gianfranco Gasparri. It was 1970, the picture story was cute, but the publisher did not call Franco back. Instead he found work with a competing publisher, "Lancio." He let his hair grow and his popularity skyrocketed. In a short time Franco Gasparri — now a tall, incredibly handsome man with long dark hair and magnetic green eyes — was Italy's most popular and loved photonovel star. Rizzoli bitterly regretted their decision and offered mind-boggling sums of money to get him back, but Franco remained faithful to "Lancio."

Born in the 1950s, photonovel were a form of popular novels, similar in form to comic books due to the presence of balloons with dialogue, but with actual stills instead of artworks. The Italian photonovel industry was a very huge phenomenon, following — and sometimes launching — subgeneres. In the sixties, there were lots of horror and crime photonovels (at times adapted from actual films, yet often created from scratch and shot in the same sets as Gothicfilms were, such as the ubiquitous Balsorano castle), while in the 1970s the biggest publishing house "Lancio" concentrated on romance, adventure and dramas, aiming at a larger audience.

In 1975 over 8,600,000 photonovels a month were sold on newsstands (since January 1975 most were in color), and five million of them were published by "Lancio." New stars were born and Italian girls hung the pictures of their favorite actors on their bedroom wall. Besides Gasparri, other famous names were Jean Mary Carletto, Claudia Rivelli (Ornella Muti's sister), Nuccia Cardinali, Adriana Rame, Michela Roc and Katiuscia. Due to his spellbinding looks, and unlike most of the others, soon Gasparri became a real movie star, as popular as Italy's most famous actors. He had appeared in a few films — Jean-Piere Lefebvre's *Ultimatum* (1973), with Lee J. Cobb, and a pair of erotic dramas starring the gorgeous Zeudi Araya, *La preda* (1974, Domenico Paolella) and *La peccatrice* (1975, Pier Ludovico Pavoni) — but with *Blood, Sweat and Tears* he had all the limelight all to himself.

1975 represented the peak of Gasparri's career and personal life as well. He married Stella Macallé and they had a daughter, Stella; his second daughter, Luna, would be born in 1978. Exploiting the enormous popularity of some of its players, "Lancio" published "Lanciostory," a comic book which among others featured the serial *The Adventures of Jacques Douglas*, featuring a character named Ken Rogers who was Gasparri's dead ringer. "Lancio" also began publishing photonovels in England. Even though outside Italy the publisher thought it was more appropriate to give pseudonyms to actors (so it was that Michela Roc was renamed Maggie Rogers, Adriana Rame became Anna Rivers and Claudia Rivelli turned into Marion Martin), Franco Gasparri continued to be Franco Gasparri. He was famous enough to not have to change his name.

However, after the three *Mark the Cop* installments Gasparri returned to his more satisfactory career in photonovels (overall he featured in 429 stories, 390 times as the lead), perhaps sensing that without solid acting chops his days in the movie biz were numbered, and possibly to dedicate more time to his family. However, a tragic fate awaited him. In 1974, a fan letter appeared in the mail page of "Lancio," asking him what excited him the most. Gasparri answered: "Riding my motorbike." It was a black Kawasaki 900. It was whilst riding his bike on June 4, 1980, that Gasparri had a near-fatal accident. A fracture to the cervical vertebrae was the result of the terrible crash. Gasparri spent a month in intensive care and was then transferred to the Stoke Mandeville Hospital in England, where he remained for five months, in the hope that the world's best neurologists would restore the use of his legs, but there was nothing that could be done. Franco Gasparri remained paralyzed for the rest of his life, both legs and arms. "I was handsome, rich, famous, carefree, full of hopes and projects, happy. Suddenly all this is over," he said in an interview.

Franco Gasparri and Ely Galleani in a scene from *Mark Shoots First* (1975).

Gasparri's career was over, even though he continued working as an in-staff writer in photonovels. He died in 1999 after a sudden respiratory crisis. His wife Stella had passed away five years earlier.

Ray Lovelock (Rome, 6.19.1950)

Despite his English name and Nordic features, Raymond Ray Lovelock is as Italian as pasta. The son of an English father and Italian mother, angel-faced Raymond was born in Rome and has always lived in Italy. Even though his dream was to become a football player, he eventually ended up in Cinecittà where he took his first steps in the movies. Lovelock's first speaking role came at 17 in Giulio Questi's violent Western *Django, Kill! / If You Live, Shoot* (*Se sei vivo spara*, 1967) starring Tomas Milian, who would become Ray's best friend. Milian encouraged Lovelock's debut as a singer with his eponymous short-lived band Tomas Milian Group on the 7' *La pazzia / Il cavallo bianco*: "I used to go at Tomas' place with my guitar and we sang and played Bob Dylan songs. One day Tomas told me he signed a record deal with CGD and asked me to help him form a band."[1] Over the years, Lovelock would often write and sing songs for the movies he starred in, often in the style of pleasant if unmemorable folky ballads. In 1968 Carlo Lizzani cast the eighteen-year-old Lovelock in his seminal *Bandits in Milan* as Donato Lopez, the youngest of Gian Maria Volonté's gang members: the film's success made him a popular name and resulted in more screen roles.

In the 1970s Lovelock's long blond hair and winning smile were a feature of many genre films, where he was usually cast as the peace-loving hippie, most notably in Tonino Cervi's horror fairytale *Queens of Evil* (*Il delitto del diavolo*, 1970) and Umberto Lenzi's thriller *Oasis of Fear* (*Un posto ideale per uccidere*, 1971), where he played alongside Ornella Muti and Irene Papas. Due to his meek, naturally endearing screen presence, his roles in poliziotteschi were at first very similar: Ray would either be the naive, angelic guy who gets involved with bad company — take for instance Lenzi's hyper-violent *Almost Human* (*Milano odia: la polizia non può sparare*, 1974) — or the good cop who suffers a tragic fate (Marino Girolami's *Violent Rome / Roma violenta*, 1975). Then, Lovelock got to play more ambiguous characters, such as the disturbingly violent and possibly homosexual special agent in Deodato's *Live Like a Cop, Die Like a Man* (*Uomini si nasce poliziotti si muore*, 1976) or the vengeful undercover cop in Franco Prosperi's *Meet Him and Die* (*Pronto ad uccidere*, 1976) Prosperi also directed Lovelock in the grim *Terror!* a.k.a. *The Last House on the Beach* (*La settima donna*, 1978), where the actor plays an out-and-out villain, something which he already done in the past (see Armando Crispino's excellent giallo *Autopsy / Macchie solari*, 1975, starring Mimsy Farmer). Horror fans also recall him in Jorge Grau's zombie cult classic *Let Sleeping Corpses Lie* (*Non si deve profanare il sonno dei morti*, 1974).

During the years, Lovelock' handsome features and fluent English granted him roles in International productions such as Norman Jewison's *The Fiddler on the Roof* (1971), Antonio Calenda's *Fury* (1973), George Pan Cosmatos' *Cassandra Crossing* (1976) or Umberto Lenzi's World War II epic *Battle Force* (*Il grande attacco*, 1978), alongside Henry Fonda, John Huston and Orson Welles. While shooting *Battle Force*, Lovelock got an offer to move to the U.S., an option he refused, following Milian's advice: "Better be a mouse's head than a tiger's tail," that is, better be the lead in a small pic than do a small part in a huge one. Which is ultimately what he did.

Lovelock's versatility allowed him not to become typecast in one genre, and helped him to ride out the 1980s after his career took a dive, forcing him to appear in marginal films such as Lucio Fulci's mediocre giallo *Murder Rock* (*Murderock — Uccide a passo di danza*, 1983) and Antonio Bido's *Mak π 100* (1987), before finding renewed popularity thanks to the small screen, appearing in many TV movies, mini-series and soap operas. In 2008, at almost 60, the still handsome Lovelock debuted on stage, in an adaptation of *The Bridges of Madison County* with Paola Quattrini.

Note

1. Gomarasca, "Ray faccia d'angelo," p. 72.

Luc Merenda (Nogent-le-Roi, 9.3.1943)

"I was a rebel, and when I was 18 I realized that everything my wonderful parents taught me was wrong. Then life taught me that I was the one who was wrong"[1] quipped Luc Merenda in an interview, recalling his experience in the movie business. One of the greatest stars of Italian genre cinema in the 1970s was a Frenchman, even though of Italian descent on the part of his grandfather. Born in a village near Paris, Luc Charles Olivier Merenda lived a wild and fast life, as his passion for cars proves.

He also displayed a strong, often rebellious temper which perhaps alienated him from the producers in more than one occasion.

As a child Luc lived in Morocco, China, Japan and Africa, before returning to Paris, where he trained in French boxing (or *savate*). In order to enroll at the Columbia University, Luc eventually ended up in America, where he started a career in modeling. His handsome appearance and magnetic presence soon brought him many film offers—including an amusing encounter in a Parisian street with Marc Allegret, who offered him a role on the spot which Merenda, who was thoroughly uninterested in becoming a film actor, promptly refused.

Merenda's film debut was in 1970, in Pierre Kalfon's *OSS117 prend des vacances*. "Kalfon asked me: 'Do you speak English?' 'Yes' 'Can you fight?' 'I am a French boxing champion' 'Can you drive?' 'I do races' 'Can you act too?' 'Well, not really (laughs). But I can make up for it with all the rest...' and so I signed a contract for five films."

However, even though he was not—and would never be—a Laurence Olivier of sorts, Luc's career soon took off, as he was in *Le Mans* (1971) with Steve McQueen and in Terence Young's bizarre Western *Red Sun* (1971), playing alongside a *parterre de roi* which included Charles Bronson, Ursula Andress, Alain Delon and Toshiro Mifune. Then it was time to move to Italy: according to Merenda it was a pasta dish he ate that made him decide that Italy was his promised land. His first Italian films were a Western/comedy, *Man Called Amen* (*Così sia*, 1973) directed by stuntman Alfio Caltabiano, which was a surprise hit, and the Zeudi Araya vehicle *La ragazza fuoristrada* (1973).

Luciano Martino had Merenda sign a contract for three films, starting with *The Violent Professionals* (*Milano trema: la polizia vuole giustizia*, 1973), his first poliziottesco and the film that made him a star. Even though his most popular roles were in crime films, Merenda also took part in Sergio Martino's excellent *giallo Torso* (*I corpi presentano tracce di violenza carnale*, 1973) produced by Carlo Ponti, and in Duccio Tessari's bleak mystery *Puzzle* (*L'uomo senza memoria*, 1974). Martino was the director with whom Merenda worked most regularly, with four films in a couple of years, most notably in the political thriller *Silent Action* (*La polizia*

Italian poster for *Silent Action* (1975), one of Luc Merenda's most convincing poliziotteschi.

accusa: il servizio segreto uccide, 1975) where he reenacted the death of commissioner Calabresi, while *Gambling City* (*La città gioca d'azzardo*, 1975) was an unfortunate attempt at playing a more romantic role than usual.

Merenda also worked with Stelvio Massi on a couple of films, which are not among the actor's favorites: on the set of *Destruction Force* (*La banda del trucido*, 1977) he suffered an accident which caused him lots of bad consequences, both physically and professionally. During a fight scene with Franco Citti, Merenda—who had to perform a stunt while having his hands handcuffed to his back—fell badly and injured a couple of vertebrae. He subsequently sued the producer, Gianfranco Couyoumdjian. He won, but he subsequently found it increasingly difficult to get screen roles.

Merenda also starred in three films directed by Fernando di Leo. "I don't remember our first encounter, but I immediately liked him" Merenda recalls. "I met him in his office on Via del Corso, saw his face and appearance and thought 'This man is cool!' Fernando could have done much more, but he just didn't feel the need to. He as a very intelligent man, always with his head in the clouds, thinking about his books." Of the three pics Di Leo and Merenda made together, *Shoot First, Die Later* (*Il poliziotto è marcio*, 1974) was by far the most successful, and allowed the filmmaker to give his star an interesting, thought-provoking role as a corrupt cop who is literally the reversal of Merenda's star-making role in *The Violent Professionals*.

With the decline of poliziottesco, Merenda's star began to fade as well. He also made some unwise career moves, while trying to get rid of his typecast image. Francesco Barilli's grim World War II drama *Pensione paura* (1978), where he played a slimy, repellent gigolo was an undeserved flop, due to the distributor's bankruptcy, and Aristide Massaccesi's *Tough to Kill* (*Duri a morire*, 1979), a mercenary tale set in Africa and based on a script by Sergio Donati, was another ill-fated attempt at a change of pace. "The script was wonderful, a few years earlier it had even been offered to Delon. The director, Joe D'Amato, whom I didn't know, was not really a director, but the producer was nice. We shot it in Santo Domingo, and I realized we were not shooting the script I loved. It was like Shakespeare and Dante being read by someone who just didn't 'get' it."

In that same period, a couple of minor poliziotteschi he starred in—Franco Prosperi's *Deadly Chase* (*Il commissario Verrazzano*, 1978) and Guido Zurli's *Target* (*Bersaglio altezza uomo*, 1979)—only underlined Merenda's quick commercial decline. Massimo Pirri's terrorist drama *Could It Happen Here?* (*Italia: ultimo atto?*, 1977) was a totally different story—a script Merenda loved which in his opinion was partially ruined by Pirri's shortcomings and the producer's interference which resulted in the original cut being drastically altered.

The actor also felt unsatisfied with the kind of films he was regularly working in. Tinto Brass' *Action* (1980), which Merenda also co-produced, was a great opportunity to poke fun at his own image and do something different. The result was possibly Brass' best film to date, and allowed Merenda to do something he had scarcely done earlier—act. However, after *Action* Merenda's career stagnated. He spent his last years in Italy playing secondary roles in comedies where he spoofed his macho image (most memorably in *Superfantozzi*, 1986, when he played Adam alongside Paolo Villaggio as "Fantozzi"). Then, in the end, Luc Merenda took a radical decision, abandoning the movie business and becoming an antiquarian in Paris—a world he had only sporadically abandoned. His last role was opposite Jennifer Beals in Samuel Fuller's TV movie *Tinikling ou "La madonne et le dragon"* (1990), followed seventeen years later by a brief cameo in Eli Roth's *Hostel: Part II* (2007) where, in a tongue-in-cheek homage to his career, he plays an Italian detective. It's a decision Merenda does not regret at all, as he stays true to his own temper and creed. "There's too many people who try to rip you off, while I've always stayed sincere" he commented. "I lost so many films, so many contracts, because I just don't accept any compromise."

Note

1. All of Merenda's quotes are taken from Manlio Gomarasca, "Senza compromessi: Intervista a Luc Merenda," in Aa. Vv., "Eroi & antieroi del cinema italiano," *Nocturno Dossier* #10 (April 2003).

Maurizio Merli *(Rome, 2.8.1940—Rome, 10.3.1989)*

The obituaries reporting the news of Maurizio Merli's untimely death—he passed away at just 49, on March 10, 1989, after a heart attack while playing a tennis match—were singularly elusive about the actor's career. One such obituary, on "La Stampa," recalling the actor's best known films, mentioned *Priest of Love* (1981, Christopher Miles), which was, and still is to this date, unreleased in Italy. No mention was made of Merli's poliziotteschi, the films that made him a star in the mid-to-late seventies. It was as if five whole years of his career had been cancelled.

Born in Rome on February 8, 1940, Maurizio Merli took his first steps in the movie business after his experience as a very young model/actor in the then very popular photonovels. However, during the sixties, his film roles were mostly limited to bit parts. He was an uncredited, barely noticeable extra in Luchino Visconti's *The Leopard* (*Il Gattopardo*, 1963), played bit parts in such films as Franco Franchi and Ciccio Ingrassia's Western comedy *Two R-R-Ringos from Texas* (*Due rrringos nel Texas*, 1967) and Ruggero Deodato's masked superhero flick *Phenomenal* (*Fenomenal e il tesoro di Tutankamen*, 1968) but failed to make an impression. Meanwhile Merli kept acting on stage: one such stint was *L'Orlando Furioso*, a critically acclaimed stage rendition of Lodovico Ariosto's poem directed in 1968 by Luca Ronconi.

The 1970s would be a totally different story. After a couple of Decamerotic flicks (one of whom, *Love Games in Florence* / *Decameron proibitissimo*, was directed by *Violent Rome*'s Marino Girolami), Merli finally got his first leading role in Tonino Ricci's *White Fang to the Rescue* (*Zanna bianca alla riscossa*, 1974) co-starring Henry Silva. 1974 was the year when things started to change for the better for Merli. The event that finally helped him reach the limelight was the TV mini-series *Il giovane Garibaldi* (Young Garibaldi), where Merli played Italy's most beloved historical hero and which was a tremendous success. That same year Merli also starred in the remake of Raffaello Matarazzo's notorious melodrama *Catene*, directed by Silvio Amadio. Then, after a cou-

A poster art depicting Maurizio Merli as the tough cop.

ple more TV movies, it was finally time for him to become one of Italy's most popular faces.

Much has been written about Merli's physical resemblance to Franco Nero (who dyed his hair blond on Castellari's *High Crime*), which helped him get cast in the lead in *Violent Rome* (*Roma violenta*, 1975). The fact is, Merli was in the right place at the right time. Watching the actor who played Garibaldi, the man who "made" Italy, fight crime as the fearless commissioner Betti, was like nurturing a hope for a better country. Merli was the perfect hero — strong, gentle, handsome, courageous. Unlike Clint Eastwood's Man with No Name, he had ideals. He was a solitary soul but did not despise women — on the contrary. Most of all, his character didn't contain an ounce of the self-irony that characterized so many Spaghetti Western heroes. Merli and his characters never laughed — they smiled. And their smile made all the difference.

Another factor that helped Merli's popularity was the fact that in most films he starred in from 1975 to 1977, he did not use his voice, but was dubbed by one of Italy's most famous voice actors, Pino Locchi (who also dubbed Sean Connery, Tony Curtis and Mario Girotti/Terence Hill, among others). Merli started dubbing himself on Stelvio Massi's *Highway Racer* (*Poliziotto sprint*, 1977) and would keep using his own voice in all Massi's subsequent films. Merli's somewhat thinner voice was at first perceived as unsettling for those who had learned to love the actor's deeper tones.

Anecdotes about Merli's immense popularity abound. According to one amusing story, one day he was stopped by the traffic police for a check while he was driving his car. Believing mistakenly that the officers had immediately recognized him because of his reputation as a film actor, Merli introduced himself to them as "Commissioner Betti," his most popular movie alter ago ... and risked being sued for having provided false information. However, his success in poliziotteschi did not apply to his other film roles. Sergio Martino's crepuscular Western *A Man Called Blade* (*Mannaja*, 1977) was a box office disappointment, not the least because of the genre's waning popularity. Yet, unlike such contemporaries as Tomas Milian and Franco Nero, Merli seemed to be stuck within the crime genre. People wanted him as the intrepid commissioner, and when it didn't happen — see Romolo

Guerrieri's *Covert Action* (1978)—they just didn't buy the tickets.

After 1980, the year of Stelvio Massi's *The Rebel*, Merli's career rapidly slid into the gutter. Producers just didn't call him anymore. Massi recalled how he originally chose Merli for the lead role on *Speed Cross*, but the producers imposed Fabio Testi, who took Maurizio's place as the action hero "par excellence." Testi appealed to a younger audience, while Merli's moustache made him look more like the classic hero type. But that was obviously just an excuse. Fact was, Merli wasn't much loved in the movie business. "The producers chose Testi because they were afraid that there would be problems on set due to Maurizio's non-stop bickering with the crew in some of his previous films,"[1] Massi revealed.

Merli's behavior on set was definitely unpopular indeed. Massi himself, one of the actor's best friends together with his son Danilo, recalled: "He loved to tease crew members on set, except that the wisecracks he yelled at them were not particularly nice, such as 'You have a job because I got you a job...' or 'You gotta thank me for the food you're eatin.'" Even though he was ironic, such an attitude was very annoying at times, and those who didn't know him might have thought he was being mean. So, as soon as they could, they made him pay for that."[2] Such an attitude was confirmed by many others. Bobby Rhodes, who worked with Merli on *The Rebel*, said: "The encounter with Merli was a bit traumatic. I can't really say many good things about Maurizio, from a certain point of view. He was an egocentric person and, in my opinion, he was a bit envious of his colleagues. He used to say bad things about Franco Nero."[3] Giuseppe Pulieri, who was the assistant director on *Fear in the City* (*Paura in città*, 1976), didn't have kind words for him either, calling him stingy—a notion Massi belied, recalling Merli's generosity in his private life—and recalling that whenever he came to get his weekly pay, the actor used to blow raspberries at him.[4]

Retrospectively, Merli's bully ways were essentially a shield to hide his insecurities, as displayed by his touchy, competitive, superstitious character. According to Massi, he used to wear the same shoes he wore on *Violent Rome* on all of his films. What's more, "Maurizio was very vain and loved his own beauty. He rejected all the make up artists and hairdressers, as he wanted only Dante Trani on the set. Dante became his personal makeup artist."[5] Merli obviously took his popularity very seriously, as if he knew that once it was gone there would be no coming back. And he was right.

Yet, with his sudden fall to oblivion, Merli looks every bit like a scapegoat, whose punishment and defeat would symbolically signify the end of a whole era. It wasn't something planned, but it was obvious at that time that people wanted to turn page, move on, forget. A decade of playful disengagement and fun was about to turn the collective imaginary of a nation into a blurry mess with no room for civil commitment—a change of pace best exemplified by the very successful TV shows of Silvio Berlusconi's broadcasting network, such as "Drive-In."

In the nine years between *The Rebel* and his death, Merli made just a handful of films. He played a secondary role in *Priest of Love* co-starring Ava Gardner and Ian McKellen, a best forgotten biographical drama on the life of D. H. Lawrence, which failed to make Merli popular abroad, and didn't even surface on Italian screens. *Notturno* (1983, Giorgio Bontempi) was a made-for-TV spy movie with a prestigious cast—Tony Musante, Claudio Cassinelli, Omero Antonutti—that deserved much better than the obscurity it fell into: it was filmed in 1982 and released theatrically one year later in a truncated two-hour version, which flopped badly, while the seven-part original version was only broadcast in February 1986. That year, writer/director Alberto Bevilacqua cast Merli—who had not played in one single picture in the last four years—as commissioner Walter Mantegazza for his ambitious project *Tango Blu* (1987), a grotesque comedy-drama featuring a varied cast (including Franco Franchi in his last movie role) which Merli even helped finance. But *Tango blu* was another tremendous flop, both critically and commercially.

The actor's last appearance was in the TV series *Casa Caruzzelli* (1989), which was broadcast only after his death. To make up for the frustration and resentment towards a world that had turned its back on him, Maurizio Merli played soccer and tennis, focusing his angst on competitiveness. It was as if the tennis court was a set and his racket was a gun. Like Betti at the end of *Special Cop in Action* (*Italia a mano armata*, 1976), he died unexpectedly and unfairly. And even though it was a heart attack that got him, those obituaries were worse than a load of bullets in the back.

Notes

1. Norcini and Ippoliti, "Stelvio Massi ricorda Maurizio Merli," p. 15.
2. Ibid.
3. Manlio Gomarasca, "Furia nera," *Nocturno Cinema* #3 (June 1997), p. 70
4. Grattarola, "è arrivato il risolutore," p. 24.
5. Norcini and Ippoliti, "Stelvio Massi ricorda Maurizio Merli," p. 15.

***Tomas Milian** (Havana, Cuba, 3.3.1933)*

If Lon Chaney was Hollywood's man of a thousand faces, Tomas Milian definitely deserved a similar credit during his stay in Italy—a career which spanned 40 years and about 100 films, making him one of the most popular and beloved faces in Italian cinema.

Born in Havana in 1933 (not 1932 as a number of sources, including the IMDb, state), Tomás Quintín Rodríguez Varona y Milian was the son of Lola and Tomás—a general of Gerardo Machado's regime. Milian had a traumatic childhood. After the *coup d'état* by Fulgencio Batista, his father was arrested, and committed suicide in front of his eyes when Tomas was just twelve. Acting, to the young Tomas, was more of an escape than a passion: he was bitten by the bug in 1955, after watching James Dean in *East of Eden*.

In 1957 Milian left Cuba for good and moved to the United States, where he got the citizenship. He enrolled at the Miami Acting Studio, then moved on to New York, where his acting teacher was so impressed by his skills that he had him enroll at the prestigious Actors' Studio. After his first bit parts in Broadway plays, Tomas took part in the TV series *Decoy*, starring Beverly Garland.

However, it was written in the stars that Tomas' future would be far from the United States. The Cuban actor arrived penniless in Italy in 1959, and ended up at the renowned Spoleto festival where he played in a pantomime by Jean Cocteau, There, he was noticed by Mauro Bolognini, who immediately cast him in *The Big Night* (*La notte brava*, 1959), based on a novel by Pier Paolo Pasolini. The film launched Milian as one of the more promising young actors of Italian cinema.

Tomas' next step was one he would later regret: he signed a contract with Franco Cristaldi's Vides and for six years he played in committed art films, directed by such prestigious filmmakers as Francesco Maselli (*I delfini*, 1961), Alberto Lattuada (*L'imprevisto*, 1961), Florestano Vancini (*La banda Casaroli*, 1962), Valerio Zurlini (*Le soldatesse*, 1965), Luchino Visconti (*Boccaccio '70*'s episode *Il lavoro*) and Pier Paolo Pasolini (a bit uncredited role in *La ricotta*, in the omnibus *Ro.Go.Pa.G*, 1965)—plus Carol Reed's *The Agony and the Ecstasy* (1965) where he was cast as Michelangelo's rival painter Raffaello Sanzio. However, this working deal with Cristaldi left Milian unsatisfied: for one, his voice was always dubbed, the salary was not enough and the roles were not to his taste. With a bold move, Milian did not renegotiate the deal and took a different path, that of popular cinema.

In a period dominated by the Spaghetti Western, it was hardly surprising that Milian—due also to his strong Latin features, which made him look like a true Mexican—starred in a number of south of the border epics. In Sergio Sollima's *The Big Gundown* (*La resa dei conti*, 1966) Milian portrayed the first in a gallery of unforgettable characters, the Mexican peasant Cuchillo, framed for a rape and murder he didn't commit and chased by an expert bounty killer played by Lee Van Cleef. The audience loved Cuchillo, and loved the way such a character related to the Italian sub-proletarian classes, as the actor's extraordinary performance drove the political and populist message of Sollima's film. Cuchillo returned in *Run, Man, Run* (*Corri uomo corri*, 1968), but by this time Milian was possibly Western's number one star, after a string of roles that included the ruthless bandit in Sollima's *Face to Face* (*Faccia a faccia*, 1967), where he played opposite Gian Maria Volonté, the albino gunman in Mario Lanfranchi's *Death Sentence* (*Sentenza di morte*, 1967) and most memorably the titular revolutionary in Giulio Petroni's epic *Tepepa* (1968), featuring Orson Welles, one of Milian's own favorite films—not forgetting Giulio Questi's ultraviolent *Django, Kill! / If You Live Shoot* (1967) where Milian met one of his closest friends, Ray Lovelock. Most of the characters Milian played had strong political connotations, and reflected the way Italian Westerns approached

Italian poster for *Almost Human* (1974), one of Tomas Milian's most controversial roles.

the political turmoil of 1968. "I did my revolution in films" the actor used to say.

Carlo Lizzani's *Bandits in Milan* (1968) was a return to contemporary Italy, and featured a subtly mimic performance by Milian, who took inspiration from Commissioner Calabresi for his role as the TV-friendly cop who illustrates the rise of criminality to a television crew. In the late '60s and early '70s Milian alternated more committed roles (such as in Liliana Cavani's *The Cannibals / I cannibali*, 1970, and the Dennis Hopper drugged extravaganza *The Last Movie*, 1971) with more commercial films. He moved from playing a dirty Brazilian bandit (*O' Cangaceiro*, 1969) to a timid, bespectacled husband (in Pasquale Festa Campanile's *Where Are You Going All Naked? / Dove vai tutta nuda?*), a man framed for his wife's murder (the excellent Hitchcockian giallo *The Designated Victim / La vittima designata*, 1971) and a Renaissance man (Lucio Fulci's gritty historical dramam *Beatrice Cenci*, 1969), a hippie hitman (*Tough Guy / Un uomo dalla pelle dura*, 1972) and a newspaperman investigating on a child murderer (Fulci's *Don't Torture a Duckling / Non si sevizia un paperino*, 1972) with a remarkable versatility.

Milian's chameleon-like on screen persona betrayed the actor's psychological uncertainties, which led him to alcohol and drugs: Umberto Lenzi recalls how Milian used to drink a bottle of vodka a day and get high on amphetamine when shooting *Almost Human* (1974), a behavior he passed on to Lovelock on the film's set. In the early '70s, Milian pushed his tendency at using make-up to change his on-screen appearance even further, as shown in *Life Is Tough, Eh Providence?* (*La vita, a volte, è molto dura, vero Provvidenza?*, 1972) and its sequel *Here We Go Again, Eh Providence?* (*Ci risiamo, vero Provvidenza?* 1973)—a pair of surreal comic Westerns in which he starred as a bounty killer who was a dead ringer for Charlie Chaplin's vagabond—and Sergio Corbucci's *Shoot First ... Ask Questions Later* (*Il bianco, il giallo, il nero*, 1975, co-starring Giuliano Gemma and Eli Walllach) where he played a Japanese samurai. Both films highlighted Milian's skills as a comedian and his use of facial mimickry.

Something similar would happen in the crime films in which Milian appeared regularly, becoming one of the genre's biggest stars. The poliziottesco gave Milian ample room to push the pedal of characterization, giving life to a number of unforgettable characters, such as the chilling Giulio Sacchi in Lenzi's *Almost Human*—possibly Milian's greatest performance in the genre—or the hunchback Vincenzo Moretto (later Marazzi) as seen in *Brutal Justice* (*Roma a mano armata*, 1976) and *Brothers Till We Die* (*La banda del gobbo*, 1977). But it was the twin birth of Monnezza, in Lenzi's *Free Hand for a Tough Cop* (*Il trucido e lo sbirro*, 1976) and Nico Giraldi in Bruno Corbucci's *The Cop in Blue Jeans* (*Squadra antiscippo*, 1976) that provided Milian not only with a phenomenal success at the box office, but also with the opportunity of sticking to one character he was enamored with. Monnezza represented all the things Milian loved about Rome and its people, who adopted the actor and made him feel one of them. Milian even got to write his own dialogue, something that eventually resulted in an argument with Umberto Lenzi on the set of *Brothers Till We Die*, as the director wasn't too fond of Milian's over-reliance on four-letter words and vulgarity.

The films featuring Monnezza and later the Nico Giraldi series allowed Milian to create an on-screen persona that would return over and over—a stale mask which could be applied to whatever character he was playing, with a few notable exceptions (such as Bernardo Bertolucci's intense Oedipal drama *La luna*, 1979). Milian was getting lazy, or perhaps he wasn't strong enough to turn his back to popularity and success.

Then, eventually, Giraldi's clownish costumes and wigs turned out to be a prison, while the genre was moving on to a dead end. It was perhaps Milian's performance in Michelangelo Antonioni's *Identification of a Woman* (*Identificazione di una donna*, 1982) that lit the spark of awareness in him, and by the mid–'80s the actor decided to metaphorically kill the character that was gradually killing him. He gave up altogether on the Giraldi series, the last entry being the awful *Delitto al blue gay* in 1984, and accepted to show his real self—balding, aging, without any makeup or wig—in small, little-seen films where he had the opportunity to play different roles from those he was used to, such as Claude D'Anna's adaptation of Oscar Wilde's *Salomé* (1986), Aurelio Chiesa's interesting low-key sci-fi tale *Distant Lights* (*Luci lontane*, 1987) and Damiano Damiani's thought-provoking *Massacre Play* (1989).

Then, unexpectedly, Milian—now approaching 60—took a dramatic decision: to go back to the U.S. and start over. For the Cuban actor, who had been an Italian citizen since 1969, it was a way of putting himself to the test. Milian's new Hollywood career was disappointing: lots of small roles, even though under the direction of prestigious filmmakers—Oliver Stone's *JFK* (1991), Steven Spielberg's *Amistad* (1997), James Gray's *The Yards* (2000)—yet a far cry from his glory days. However, in 2000, Steven Soderbergh's *Traffic* provided him with one of the best parts of his career, as the Mexican drug lord General Arturo Salazar. Other projects were far less successful: the sit-com *Frannie's Turn* was cancelled after half a dozen installments, while Giuseppe Ferrara's *Roma nuda*, the film that marked Milian's return to Italy in 2011 and where the actor would play a retired police inspector, was shelved due to lack of money.

By leaving Italy and starting anew in the U.S., burning all bridges with the past, Milian made a suicidal career move—yet a fundamental one for the passionate actor he is. And it's impossible not to admire the man's will to move on, at any cost, in order to still feel alive—and not just an icon on a big screen.

Franco Nero *(born Francesco Sparanero; San Prospero, Parma, 11.23.1941)*

In a scene of Quentin Tarantino's latest film *Django Unchained* (2012), the titular hero played by Jamie Foxx has a conversation with a moustached stranger at a bar. "What's your name?" the other man asks. "Django ... the D is silent" he replies. The other man knows too well: he is Franco Nero, the *original* Django in Sergio Corbucci's now legendary 1966 western. With about 180 titles in his filmography, Francesco Sparanero is one of Italy's best known actors worldwide, one of those faces that are instantly recognized even when popping up for a blink-and-you'll-miss-it cameo, like in Tarantino's film.

Nero's transition from nobody to movie star was amazingly brief: the son of a Carabinieri Marshal, he moved from the provinces to Rome at a young age, debuting in a small role in Giuseppe Fina's *Pelle viva* (1962). Between 1965 and 1966 the handsome, blue-eyed young actor appeared in Antonio Margheriti's sci-fi flicks *The Wild Wild Planet* (*I criminali della galassia*, 1965) and *The War of the Planets* (*I diafanoidi vengono da Marte*, 1966) had a small role in Antonio Pietrangeli's masterpiece *Io la conoscevo bene* (I Knew Her Well, 1965) and starred as the necrophile nobleman in Mino Guerrini's morbid Gothic tale *The Third Eye* (1966), the blueprint for Aristide Massaccesi's gory cult item *Beyond the Darkness* (*Buio omega*, 1979). That same year he became the world's most notorious gunslinger, who memorably enters the film carrying a coffin behind him in a muddy Western town, in Corbucci's *Django*, and played Abel in John Huston's *The Bible*.

The 25-year-old Nero was to become an internationally known name by playing Lancelot in Joshua Logan's *Camelot* (1967), which also allowed him to meet the love of his life Vanessa Redgrave, who played Guinevere. Soon Nero was everywhere. He worked with such notable filmmakers as Elio Petri (*A Quiet Place in the Country* / *Un tranquillo posto di campagna*, 1968), Damiano Damiani (*The Day of the Owl*, 1968), Tinto Brass (*Drop-out*, 1970, and *La vacanza*, 1971) and Luis Buñuel (*Tristana*, 1970), but he wisely divided himself between *auteur* and genre cinema, appearing in a number of memorable Westerns (Corbucci's *The Mercenary*, 1968, and *Compañeros*, 1970) *film noir* (*Detective Belli*, 1969), *gialli* (Luigi Bazzoni's *The Fifth Cord* / *Giornata nera per l'ariete*, 1970).

Furthermore, Nero's presence characterized two of the most important and influential crime films of the decade: Damiani's *Confessions of a Police Captain* and Castellari's *High Crime*. In the latter, the actor — his hair dyed blonde for the occasion — furnished the model for the genre's most iconic character, Maurizio Merli's commissioner Betti in *Violent Rome*. Nero sporadically frequented the crime genre in the 1970s, most notably in Castellari's *Street Law* as well in Damiani's *How to Kill a Judge* and Tonino Valerii's action-packed *Sahara Cross* (1977), yet his most memorable role, however, was the title character in Castellari's extraordinary Western *Keoma* (1976), where he played a sort of Christ-like figure (curiously enough, Nero did play Jesus Christ in Giulio Paradisi's mind-boggling horror epic *The Visitor*, 1978).

In the late '70s, when his star power became to wane in Italy, Nero again turned to the foreign markets, acting in such films as Guy Hamilton's *Force 10 from Navarone* (1978), Serghei Bondarchuk's kolossal *Red Bells* (1982) as well as Rainer Werner Fassbinder's scandalous *Querelle De Brest* (1982), alongside Brad Davis. As had happened with the genre's boom, Nero was a key figure in a couple of crepuscular crime films: *The Blue Eyed Bandit* (*Il bandito dagli occhi azzurri*, 1980) and most notably Castellari's *The Day of the Cobra* (1980). In late '80s he even reprised his Django role for an official sequel — the first in twenty years after a plethora of imitations and rip-offs — Nello Rossati's disappointing *Django 2* (*Django 2: il grande ritorno*, 1987).

Nero's frantic activity led him to further increase his film appearances, in Italy and abroad, even though most of the films he acted were far from memorable. A few titles are worth mentioning: Renny Harlin's *Die Harder* (1990), where he plays opposite Bruce Willis, Pupi Avati's intimate drama *Fratelli e sorelle* (1992), Enzo Castellari's crepuscular Western *Jonathan of the Bears* (*Jonathan degli orsi*, 1994). The large majority, however, were on the level of the trashy instant movie *The Versace Murder* (1998), where he played the controversial gay stylist Gianni Versace. Recently, Nero lent his voice to Uncle Topolino in Pixar's *Cars 2* (2011). Then, one day, came a phone call from Mr. Tarantino...

Franco Nero in Enzo Castellari's *High Crime*.

Henry Silva (Brooklyn, 15.9.1928)

One of the most unlikely stars of Italian poliziottesco was an actor whose singularly shaped features allowed him to play either the hero or the bad guy, and always looking as mean and hard as a piece of roughly sculpted alabaster. As one Italian critic wrote, "When Henry Silva smiles, it's like a wound opens on his face."[1] No wonder he smiled very little in his career — and when he did, his wasn't a reassuring smile ... not at all.

The only son of Jesus and Angeline, natives of Puerto Rico, Henry Silva grew up in Harlem. He quit high school to work in a thread factory and later became a longshoreman. After that, to quote a 1971 interview article, "he made the abrupt switch to soda jerk at a Schrafft's drugstore, where he fell in with what his old pals might have considered evil companions — a bunch of

Henry Silva in *The Boss* (1973).

young actors. He got the bug, did summer stock, studied at the Actors Studio, did live TV dramas, and then received his biggest break — the role of the dope-pushing Mother in *A Hatful of Rain*, first on Broadway, then in the movie version."[2]

A honorary member of Frank Sinatra's Rat Pack due to his performance in *Ocean's Eleven* (1960), Silva's Hollywood career appeared to be that of a typical character actor: typecast as the villain, rarely allowed to do more than his routine, one rare exception being William Asher's phenomenal *Johnny Cool* (1963), the actor's favorite film. Another weird turn was John Frankenheimer's *The Manchurian Candidate* (1962), where Silva plays his usual villain routine, but this time posing as an Oriental — which says a lot about that astonishing face. But by 1970 it was clear that his future was to be either in B-movie flicks such as the western *The Animals*, which he also helped finance,[3] or on TV (*F.B.I.*, *Hawaii 5–0*), as the occasional villain.

Or maybe not.

Silva discovered Europe — or Europe discovered him, depending on one's point of view. Silva's stint in Italian cinema had the same rejuvenating effect for him that Euro Westerns had for another character actor-turned-star, Lee Van Cleef. "'Funny thing,' he said, 'over here they see me as a bad guy; in Europe they see me as a hero.'"[4] Soon Silva became a requested leading man for all seasons in Italian crime films. Besides Fernando di Leo's powerful *The Italian Connection* (where he and Woody Strode are a pair of badass killers worthy of a Don Siegel film), he played Mafia killers (*The Boss*, 1973; *Cry of a Prostitute*, 1974), Mob bosses (*Weapons of Death*, 1977), sadistic gangsters (*Free Hand for a Tough Cop*, 1976) but also commissioners (*Almost Human*, 1974; *Kidnap*, 1974), uncorruptible Army majors (*Crimebusters*, 1976), even a distraught father-turned-vigilante in Umberto Lenzi's underrated *Manhunt in the City* (1975). Yet only a capable filmmaker like Fernando di Leo was able to make the best out of his monolithic acting and turn him into a true movie icon, capable of filling the screen with his imposing presence. In *The Italian Connection* Silva is the most talkative and arrogant of the two hitmen sent to Italy to kill the small-time pimp played Mario Adorf, while in *The Boss* he is finally given a tormented and fascinating character to deal with.

The eighties were a less busy decade, yet they offered Silva a handful of memorable villain roles, especially that of Floyd Wrangler in Enzo Castellari's post-atomic adventure yarn *Escape from the Bronx* (*Fuga dal Bronx*, 1983). He also co-starred in a couple of films directed by Fernando di Leo, *The Violent Breed* (*Razza violenta*, 1984) and the director's last film *Killer vs. Killers* (1985), where he once again played a taciturn killer whose favorite weapon is a bazooka, and — in one of di Leo's typically weird touches — lives in a zoo full of wild animals whom he lets loose at the climax to dispatch the bad guys. However, both were harsh commercial disappointments (the latter was only released in Italy in 2004, directly to DVD).

In the late eighties, facing the decline of Italian genre cinema, Silva returned to the United States, where he played in such diverse films as Paul Bartel's *Lust in the Dust* (1985) and the Steven Seagal vehicle *Above the Law* (1988) — not forgetting Lewis Teague's cult gem *Alligator* (1980) and especially Warren Beatty's *Dick Tracy* (1990). Among his later performances, the most notable are Wim Wenders' *The End of Violence* (1997) and especially Jim Jarmusch' extraordinary *Ghost Dog* (1999), where he played mob boss Ray Vargo. His last screen to date role was a cameo in Steven Soderbergh's 2001 remake of *Ocean's Eleven*.

Notes

1. Vice, *Il Giorno*, 06.01.1968
2. Jack Mayor, "He's Not Just Another Pretty Face," *Providence Evening Bulletin*, 10.29.1971.
3. Silva even promoted the pic with a solo publicity tour, which says a lot. "I own a piece of the movie," he said, with a slight smile. "If he doesn't promote the film, no one will. Such is life in the new Hollywood." *Ibid.*

Fabio Testi *(Peschiera del Garda, 8.2.1941)*

With his handsome looks, square jaw and imposing physique, Fabio Testi was a natural born star — perhaps the most Hollywoodian-looking Italian actor of the 1970s, a Latin mixture of Tyrone Power and Gary Cooper. Born in Peschiera del Garda, on the lake Garda in Northern Italy, young Fabio spent his youth breathing the scent of movies, as a number of adventure and pirate films were shot on the lake, and eventually found his way to the set, as a stuntman and a double. However, to him at first cinema and TV were just a means to pay for his architecture studies, until eventually he was bitten by the bug for good.

Yet the Venetian actor's apprenticeship in the movie business was not as easy as one may think, even though his first steps were with none other than Sergio Leone. Testi was one of the many stunt doubles that were employed on the set of *The Good, the*

Bad and the Ugly (1966), and Leone gave him a small role in his subsequent production, *Once Upon a Time in the West* (1968), as one of Henry Fonda's henchmen. Eventually, though, Testi's part ended up in the cutting room floor — except for one single shot — because Leone thought he was too clean-looking for the film. In the meantime, the young actor had to make do with what his agent offered him, which weren't exactly A-grade pictures. It was art director-turned-director Demofilo Fidani who gave Testi his first on-screen role as one of the villainous henchmen in *Straniero ... fatti il segno della croce!* (Stranger, Make the Sign of the Cross, 1967). Actually, it was a first time for both the actor and the director: Fidani specialized in poverty-row style Westerns shot around Rome (and occasionally tried his hand at other genres, including crime films), while Testi would move on to bigger things ... though not before a brief but dense stint into low-grade genres, which included a third-rate Zorro movie (Rafael Romero Marchent's *E continuavano a chiamarlo figlio di...*, 1969), a very bad thriller (Harald Philipp's *Death Knocks Twice*, 1969, co-starring singer Dean Reed and Anita Ekberg), and yet more Fidani-directed Westerns (*Django Meets Sartana*, 1970, where he played Sartana opposite Fidani regular Hunt Powers a.k.a. Jack Betts).

Then came Testi's leap into stardom, which can be summed up in three words: Vittorio De Sica. Here's how Fidani recounted the picturesque story of how Testi was cast in the veteran director's Academy Award winning *The Garden of the Finzi Continis* (*Il giardino dei Finzi-Contini*, 1970) while he was about to star in Fidani's *Jungle Master* a.k.a. *Karzan, Jungle Lord* (*Karzan, il favoloso uomo della giungla*, 1972). "I cast Fabio Testi in the lead, he was my creature. One day I went location scouting at the Botanical Garden in Rome [...]. There I met Vittorio De Sica, who was doing the same thing. [...] We smoked a cigarette and he told me: 'I'm worried because I've been doing screen tests and I need a young Latin actor, but can't find anyone. You shoot lots of Westerns, do you by any chance have a Latin guy to recommend? Or are your actors all Americans?' 'Of course not, Vittorio, they're all Italians!' 'Can you recommend one?' 'Well, *maestro*, I do have one kid. He can't act to save his life, but with you as a guide ... you know, I never have enough time, I always go for the first take' 'Who's this guy?' 'You don't know him, his name is Fabio Testi. [...] I'll send you one of my rushes as if it was a screen test. You'll see, his face really comes out on film.' So I did ... and he cast Fabio. [...] I'd gladly have waited until De Sica finished shooting to continue with my own movie, but De Sica had Fabio cut his hair!"[1] As debatable as it may sound, given Fidani's notorious habit of embellishing his own career and filmography, the story paints a nice and even poetic picture of Italian cinema in those days, where a master and a hack would meet in the same location, have a smoke and even share some small talk about their job.

Anyway, after *The Garden of the Finzi Continis* Testi was finally a big box office name. As with many Italian stars of the period, he didn't get picky, and most importantly he didn't loosen up his agenda: "Vanity, in an actor, must be balanced by humility" he would comment. So, Testi kept starring in *auteur* and genre movies alike. Examples of the former were Giuseppe Patroni Griffi's *'Tis Pity She's a Whore* (*Addio fratello crudele*, 1971), an adaptation of John Ford's Elizabethan drama co-starring Charlotte Rampling, Denys de la Patellière's *Le Tueur* (1972, where he played the bad guy opposite Jean Gabin), Claude Chabrol's gritty *Nada* (1974, based on the novel by Jean-Patrick Manchette), where Testi was impressive as the leader of a arnarchist/terrorist task force, Andrzej Zulawski's *That Most Important Thing: Love* (*L'important c'est d'aimer*, 1975), Mauro Bolognini's *The Inheritance* (*L'eredità Ferramonti*, 1976) and Monte Hellman's crepuscular Western *China 9, Liberty 37* (1978). Although not the most accomplished of thesps, Testi faced every role with a determination and a commitment that won him respect. He also managed to gain a reputation as a womanizer, pairing with such screen beauties as Edwige Fenech, Charlotte Rampling, Ursula Andress and Jean Seberg, something which made Testi a rather popular name abroad as well, if never an out-and-out star. His most durable relationship was with Spanish actress Lola Navarro, whom he married in 1979 and who gave him three children before the couple separated in 1996.

Fabio Testi in a scene from *The Smuggler* (1980).

During his peak years, though, Testi mostly dabbled within genres — mostly crime films, in such diverse works as Pasquale Squitieri's *Gang War in Naples* (1972), Sergio Sollima's *Blood in the Streets* (1973), Tonino Valerii's *Go Gorilla Go* (1975), Enzo G. Castellari's *The Big Racket* (1976) and *The Heroin Busters* (1977) and Lucio Fulci's ultra-gory *The Smuggler* (1980). Yet some of his most impressive roles were in a pair of violent, morbid gialli, Massimo Dallamano's *What Have You Done to Solange?* (*Cosa avete fatto a Solange?*, 1972) and Alberto Negrin's *Red Rings of Fear* (*Enigma rosso*, 1978). Another memorable role was as the card cheat in Lucio Fulci's bleak *Four of the Apocalypse* (*I 4 dell'Apocalisse*, 1975), where he played opposite Tomas Milian, which unfortunately flopped at the box office, in a time when the genre was dying.

Even though Testi was cast in a role devised for Maurizio Merli in Stelvio Massi's *Speed Cross* and *Speed Driver*, the early '80s marked a decline in the actor's popularity, due also to a number of debatable choices on his part, such as Gianfranco Baldanello's trashy thriller *The Uranium Conspiracy* (*A chi tocca, tocca!*, 1978), Silvio Amadio's syrupy drama *A Gun for a Cop* (*Il carabiniere*, 1981) and Fabrizio Lori's terrorist drama *The Hawk and the Dove* (*Il falco e la colomba*, 1981). From the eighties onwards Testi worked mainly in television, and reunited with Enzo Castellari in the mini-series *Il ritorno di Sandokan* (1996, where he replaced Philippe Leroy as Yanez) and *Deserto di fuoco* (1997). Among his rare ventures on the big screen there were such underestimated works as Monte Hellman's *Iguana* (1988; Testi also had a bit role in Hellman's most recent film, 2010's *Road to Nowhere*), but also dreary, trashy stuff such as Ninì Grassia's awful crime film *Il burattinaio* (which Testi claimed to have de facto co-directed to help Grassia) and Flavio Mogherini's disappointing giallo *Passionate Crime* (both 1994). Testi's popularity on the small screen went beyond TV fiction, as the actor took part in a number of reality shows such as *L'isola dei famosi* (2003), the Spanish *El gran hermano* (2005) and *La talpa* (2008). In the late 2000s, he even embarked on a short-lived, disastrous political career, running for mayor in Verona. Equally brief was his career as a singer, with a little known 7' released in 1984, *Palma de Majorca / L'artista*. Nowadays, Testi's main interest is agriculture—a passion transmitted to him by the great Gabin: he owns the third largest kiwi farm in Italy.

Note

1. Marco Giusti and Stefano Della Casa, "Li chiamavano ... Spaghetti Western," *Nocturno Cinema* #11 (July–September 1999), p. 56.

Bibliography

Books and essays on crime cinema and directors

Albano, Vittorio. *La mafia nel cinema siciliano: Da In nome della legge a Placido Rizzotto*. Manduria: Barbieri, 2003.

Baldi, Alfredo. *Schermi proibiti: La censura in Italia 1947–1988*. Venice: Marsilio, 2002.

Bracco, Davide, Stefano Della Casa, Paolo Manera, and Franco Prono, eds. *Torino città del cinema*. Milan: Il Castoro, 2001.

Brown, Paul J. and Darrin Venticinque. *Castellari: Action Italian Style*. Ringstead: Midnight Media, 2007.

Brunetta, Gian Piero. "Il cinema italiano dal neorealismo alla Dolce vita," in *Storia del cinema mondiale III tomo I*. Turin: Einaudi, 2000.

_____. *The History of Italian Cinema: A Guide to Italian Film from Its Origins to the Twenty-First Century*. Princeton, NJ: Princeton University Press 2011.

_____. *Storia del cinema italiano: Il cinema del regime 1929–1945,* Rome: Editori Riuniti, 2001.

_____. *Storia del cinema italiano: Dal miracolo economico agli anni Novanta*, Rome: Editori Riuniti, 2001.

_____. *Storia del cinema italiano: Dal neorealismo al miracolo economico 1945–1959*. Rome: Editori Riuniti, 2001.

Buccheri, Vincenzo. "I generi cinematografici: lo specchio della mutazione." In Aa. Vv., *Storia del cinema italiano 1970–1976*. Venice: Marsilio — Edizioni di Bianco and Nero, 2008.

Buttafava, Giovanni. "Procedure sveltite," in Aa. Vv., *Il Patalogo Due. Annuario 1980 dello spettacolo, Volume secondo: Cinema e televisione*. Milan: Ubulibri/Electa, 1980.

Castellano, Alberto, and Vincenzo Nucci. "Facce, panze, lacrime (La nuova sceneggiata napoletana e i suoi eroi)," in *Il Patalogo 5&6: Annuario 1983 dello spettacolo*. Milan: Ubulibri, 1983.

Comotti, Davide, and Salerno Vittorio. *Professione regista*. Rome: Lulu.com., 2012.

Corsi, Barbara. *Con qualche dollaro in meno: Storia economica del cinema italiano*. Rome: Editori Riuniti, 2001.

Crovi, Luca. *Tutti i colori del giallo*. Venice: Marsilio, 2002.

Curti, Roberto. *Italia odia*. Turin: Lindau, 2006.

_____. "Le mani legate: Cinema di genere e misteri d'Italia," in Christian Uva, ed., *Schermi di piombo*. Cosenza: Rubbettino, 2011.

_____. *Il mio nome è Nessuno: Tonino Valerii*. Rome: Unmondoaparte, 2008.

Della Casa, Stefano. *Storia e storie del cinema popolare italiano*. Turin: La Stampa, 2001.

De Santi, Gualtiero. *Carlo Lizzani*. Rome: Gremese, 2001.

Di Martino, Anna, Maurizio Matrone and Massimo Moretti, eds. *4° Police Film Festival*. Bologna: Lumiére, 1998.

Duranti, Pierpaolo, and Erminio Mucciacito. *Tomas Milian Il Bandito, Lo Sbirro, e Er Monnezza / Tomas Milian: The Tough Bandit, The Rough Cop and the Filthy Rat in Italian Cinema*. Milan: Mediane Libri, 2007 (Italian / English text plus CD).

Faldini, Franca, and Goffredo Fofi. *Il cinema italiano d'oggi 1970–1984 raccontato dai suoi protagonisti*. Milan: Mondadori, 1984.

_____. *L'avventurosa storia del cinema italiano raccontata dai suoi protagonisti 1960–1969*. Milan: Feltrinelli, 1984.

Fedeli, Franco. "Indagine su un filone molto sospetto," in *Il Patalogo Due. Annuario 1980 dello spettacolo, Volume secondo: Cinema e televisione*. Milan: Ubulibri/Electa, Milano, 1980.

Gambetti, Giacomo. *Florestano Vancini*. Rome: Gremese, 2000.

Giusti, Marco. *Dizionario dei film italiani stracult*. Milan: Sperling and Kupfer, 1999.

Gomarasca, Manlio. *Umberto Lenzi*. Milan: Nocturno Libri, 2001.

Grasso, Aldo. *Enciclopedia della televisione*. Milan: Garzanti, 2002.

Grimaldi, Igor, and Davide Pulici, eds. *Enzo G. Castellari*. Milan: Nocturno Libri, 2000.

Grmek Germani, Sergio. "Uccidete il maiale e montatelo," in Enrico Ghezzi and Marco Giusti, eds., *Kim Arcalli: Montare il cinema*. Venice: Marsilio, 1980.

Ippolito, Ciro. *Un napoletano a Hollywood*. Naples: Tullio Pironti Editore, 2010.

Isasi-Isasmendi, Antonio José. *Memorias tras la cámara: cincuenta años de un cine español*. Madrid: Ocho Y Medio, Libros De Cine, 2004.

Kezich, Tullio. *Il FilmSessanta*, Milan: Il formichiere, 1979.

_____. *Il Millefilm*, Milan: Mondadori, 1983.

_____. *Il nuovissimo Millefilm*, Milan: Mondadori, 1983.

La Selva, Tommaso. *Tonino Valerii*. Milan: Nocturno Libri, 2000.

Lucas, Tim. *Mario Bava: All the Colors of the Dark*. Cincinnati, OH: Video Watchdog, 2007.

Lupi, Gordiano. *Tomas Milian, Il trucido e lo sbirro*. Rome: Profondo Rosso, 2004.

Magrelli, Enrico, ed. *Sull'industria cinematografica italiana*. Venice: Marsilio, 1986.

Matrone, Maurizio, and Massimo Moretti, ed. *3° Police Film Festival*. Bologna: Lumière, 1997.

Mereghetti, Paolo. *Il Mereghetti: Dizionario dei film 2011*. Milan: B.C. Dalai, 2010.

Micciché, Lino. *Cinema italiano degli anni '70*. Marsilio: Venezia, 1989.

_____, ed. *Il cinema del riflusso. Film e cineasti italiani degli anni '70*. Venice: Marsilio, 1997.

_____, ed. *Schermi opachi: Il cinema italiano degli anni '80*. Venice: Marsilio, 1998.

Miniucchi, Luigia. *Alfio Caltabiano*. Rome: Gremese, 2009.

_____. *Il mondo di Tano Cimarosa: 50 anni di cinema italiano*. Rome: ByBess Edizioni, 2006.

Navarro, Giorgio, and Fabio Zanello. *Tomas Milian: Er cubbano de Roma*. Florence: Igor Molino Editore, 1999.

Noir in Festival 1994. Milan: Il Castoro, 1994.

Noir in Festival 1997. Rome: Fahrenheit 451, 1997.

O'Leary, Alan. *Tragedia all'italiana: Cinema e terrorismo tra Moro e memoria*. Tissi: Angelica Editore, 2007

Paniceres, Rubén. "Retrato de Republica en rojo," in Jesús Palacios and Rubén Paniceres, eds., *Cara a Cara: Una mirada al cine de género italiano, años 60/70*. Gijon: Semana Negra, Colección Hermosos y Malditos no. 2, 2004.

Pezzotta, Alberto. *Regia Damiano Damiani*. Udine: C.E.C. Cinemazero, 2004.

Pulici, Davide. *Fernando di Leo*, Milan: Nocturno Libri, 2001.

Quintana, Ángel. *El cine italiano, 1942–1961: Del neorrealismo a la modernidad*. Barcelona: Paidós Studio, 1997.

Sesti, Mario. *Tutto il cinema di Pietro Germi*. Milan: Baldini and Castoldi, 1997.

Thompson, Tristan, and Paul J. Brown. *Blazing Magnums: Italian Crime Thrillers,* vol. 1. Ringstead: Midnight Media, 2007.

Tordini, Alessandro. *Così nuda così violenta: Enciclopedia della musica nei mondi neri del cinema italiano*. Rome: Arcana, 2012.

Uva, Christian. *Schermi di piombo: Il terrorismo nel cinema italiano*. Cosenza: Rubbettino, 2007.

_____. *Strane storie. Il cinema e i misteri d'Italia*. Cosenza: Rubbettino, 2011.

Vito Zagarrio, ed. *Carlo Lizzani: Un lungo viaggio nel cinema*. Venice: Marsilio, 2010.

Periodical articles

"Calibro 9. Il cinema di Fernando di Leo." *Nocturno Dossier* #14 (September 2003).

Castoldi, Gian Luca. "Umberto Lenzi, il realismo fantastico." *Amarcord* #4 (September-October 1996) and #5 (November-December 1996).

"Eroi ed antieroi del cinema italiano." *Nocturno Dossier* #10 (April 2003).

"Genealogia del delitto: Guida al cinema di Mario e Lamberto Bava." *Nocturno Dossier* #24 (July 2004).

Gomarasca, Manlio. "Er cubano de cinecittà." *Nocturno Cinema* #2 (December 1996).

_____. "Pace e tranquillità. Stelvio Massi: identikit di un cineasta." *Nocturno cinema* #10 (June-July 1999).

_____. "Quattro chiacchiere con Galliano Juso il produttore." *Nocturno Cinema* #2 (December 1996).

_____. "Solitudine e rabbia. La figura del poliziotto nel cinema di Stelvio Massi." *Nocturno Cinema* #8 (October 1998) and# 10 (June-July 1999).

_____, and Daniele Aramu. "Il ragazzo dei Parioli: Intervista a Ruggero Deodato." *Nocturno Cinema* #1 (Summer 1996).

Ippoliti, Stefano. "I giorni del commissario Betti." *Nocturno Cinema* #3 (June 1997).

_____, and Matteo Norcini. "Intervista a Mario Caiano." *Cine 70 e dintorni* #2 (Spring 2002).

_____, _____, and Grattarolla Franco. "Mario Bianchi: Il mio cinema pizza e fichi." *Cine 70 e dintorni* #5 (Summer 2004).

"Italia ultimo atto: Guida al cinema politico civile dalle origini a Buongiorno, notte." *Nocturno dossier* #15 (October 2003).

Martin, John. "Tarantino Talks Trash." *Giallo Pages* #3 (1994).

"Monnezza e i suoi fratelli: Guida al cinema poliziesco di Tomas Milian." *Nocturno Dossier* #39 (October 2005).

Navarro, Giorgio. "Monnezza and Giraldi ovvero ... quando 'li mortacci' scossero Cinecittà." *Amarcord* #4 (September-October 1996).

Nazzaro, Giona A., Vittore Baroni, and Daniele Brolli. "Speciale Italian Neo-Noir." *Rumore* #152 (September 2004).

Norcini, Matteo. "Vita e spettacolo di ... Maurizio Merli commissario cult." *Amarcord* #4 (September-October 1996).

_____ and Stefano Ippoliti. "Intervista a Stelvio Massi." *Amarcord* #6 (January-February 1997).

Pezzotta, Alberto. "Cani arrabbiati: Nero in tempo reale, senza lieto fine." *Segnocinema* #78 (March-April 1996).

"Il poliziesco all'italiana." *Nocturno Book* #4 (March 2001).

Pulici, Davide. "Bologna ... a mano armata." *Nocturno Cinema* #7 (June 1998).

_____. "Il giorno del cobra." *Nocturno cinema* #2 (December 1996).

_____. Gomarasca, Manlio. "Intervista a Fabio Testi." *Nocturno Cinema* #2 (December 1996).

_____. "La grande promessa: Intervista esclusiva a Massimo Pirri." *Nocturno Cinema* #7 (June 1998).

_____. "Killer contro Killers: il film perduto di Fernando di Leo." *Nocturno Cinema* #5/6 (February 1998).

_____. "Renato Savino: Lo chiamavano King." *Nocturno Cinema* #13 (June-July 2000).

_____, and Manlio Gomarasca. "Il Boss: Intervista a Fernando di Leo." *Nocturno Cinema* #3 (June 1997).

"Il punto G. Il cinema di Enzo G. Castellari." *Nocturno Dossier* #66 (January 2008).

Zanello, Fabio. "Faccia a faccia. Intervista a Sergio Sollima." *Amarcord* #12 (March-April 1998).

Historical and sociological works on post-war Italy

Arcuri, Camillo. *Colpo di Stato.* Milan: RCS, 2004.

Bocca, Giorgio. *Il terrorismo italiano, 1970–80.* Milan: Rizzoli, 1981.

Crainz Guido. *Il paese mancato: Dal miracolo economico agli anni ottanta.* Rome: Donzelli, 2003.

Di Bella, Franco. *Italia nera.* Milan: Sugar, 1960.

Fasanotti Pier Mario and Gandus Valeria. *Bang Bang: Gli altri delitti degli anni di piombo.* Milan: Tropea, 2004.

_____. *Kriminal tango: Grandi casi di cronaca nera tra 1960 e 1970.* Milan: Tropea, 2002.

_____. *Mambo italiano: Tre lustri di fatti e misfatti 1945–1960.* Milan: Tropea, 2000.

Lumley, Robert. *Dal '68 agli anni di piombo.* Florence: Giunti, 1998.

Medici, Sandro. *Vite di Poliziotti.* Turin: Einaudi, 1979.

Pasolini, Pier Paolo. *Lettere luterane.* Turin: Einaudi, 1976.

Quadrelli, Emilio. *Andare ai resti: Banditi, rapinatori, guerriglieri nell'Italia degli anni Settanta.* Rome: DeriveApprodi, 2004.

Wu Ming. *Asce di guerra.* Milan: Tropea, 2000.

On the web

The ever-growing amount of forums and blogs dedicated to Italian genre cinema in general and the poliziottesco in particular makes it difficult to map these sites accurately. However, I would like to point out at least the remarkable Lovelockandload (www.lovelockandload.net) which has a forum section entirely dedicated to Eurocrime, with plenty of precious information on home video releases and assorted trivia.

Index

Numbers in ***bold italics*** indicate pages with photographs.